Contemporary Authors®

NEW REVISION SERIES

Explore your options!
Gale databases offered in
a variety of formats

DISKETTE/MAGNETIC TAPE

Many Gale databases are available on diskette or magnetic tape, allowing systemwide access to your most-used information sources through existing computer systems. Data can be delivered on a variety of mediums (DOS-formatted diskette, 9-track tape, 8mm data tape) and in industry-standard formats (comma-delimited, tagged, fixed-field).

CD-ROM

A variety of Gale titles are available on CD-ROM, offering maximum flexibility and powerful search software.

The information in this Gale publication is also available in some or all of the formats described here. Your Gale Representative will be happy to fill you in.

ONLINE

For your convenience, many Gale databases are available through popular online services, including DIALOG, NEXIS, DataStar, ORBIT, OCLC, Thomson Financial Network's I/Plus Direct, HRIN, Prodigy, Sandpoint's HOOVER, The Library Corporation's NLightN, and Telebase Systems.

A number of Gale databases are available on an annual subscription basis through GaleNet, a new online information resource that features an easy-to-use end-user interface, the powerful search capabilities of BRS/SEARCH retrieval software and ease of access through the World-Wide Web.

For information, call

GALE
1-800-877-GALE

An ITP Information/Reference Group Company

Contemporary Authors®

A Bio-Bibliographical Guide to
Current Writers in Fiction, General Nonfiction,
Poetry, Journalism, Drama, Motion Pictures,
Television, and Other Fields

PAMELA S. DEAR
Editor

NEW REVISION SERIES
volume 50

GALE

an International Thomson Publishing company I**T**P®

STAFF

Pamela S. Dear, *Editor, New Revision Series*

John D. Jorgenson, *Pre-Manuscript Coordinator*
Thomas Wiloch, *Sketchwriting Coordinator*
Deborah A. Stanley, *Post-Manuscript Coordinator*

Jeff Chapman, Brigham Narins, Aarti Dhawan Stephens,
Kathleen Wilson, and Janet Witalec, *Contributing Editors*

Polly A. Vedder, *Associate Editor*

George H. Blair and Daniel Jones, *Assistant Editors*

Katherine Bailey, Suzanne Bezuk, Bruce Boston, Gary Corseri, Erika Dreifus, Ellen French,
Joan Goldsworthy, Conner Gorry, Lisa Harper, Anne Janette Johnson, Elizabeth Judd,
Anne Killheffer, Brett A. Lealand, Doris Maxfield, Robert Miltner, Julie Monahan, John Mort,
Ryan Reardon, Jean W. Ross, Bryan Ryan, Pamela L. Shelton, Kenneth R. Shepherd,
Denise Wiloch, Michaela Swart Wilson, and Tim Winter-Damon, *Sketchwriters*

Tracy Arnold-Chapman, Emily J. McMurray, and Pamela L. Shelton, *Copyeditors*

James P. Draper, *Managing Editor*

Victoria B. Cariappa, *Research Manager*

Barbara McNeil, *Research Specialist*

Michele P. Pica, Norma Sawaya, and Amy Terese Steel, *Research Associates*

Alicia Noel Biggers and Julia C. Daniel, *Research Assistants*

♾ ™ This book is printed on acid-free paper that meets the minimum requirements
of American National Standard for Information Sciences-
Permanence Paper for Printed Library Materials, ANSI Z39.48-1984.

Library of Congress Catalog Card Number 81-640179

ISBN 0-8103-9341-7
ISSN 0275-7176

Printed in the United States of America.

I(T)P™   Gale Research, an ITP Information/Reference Group Company.
ITP logo is a trademark under license.

10 9 8 7 6 5 4 3 2 1

Contents

Indexing note: All *Contemporary Authors New Revision Series*
entries are indexed in the *Contemporary Authors* cumulative
index, which is published separately and distributed with even-
numbered *Contemporary Authors* original volumes and odd-
numbered *Contemporary Authors New Revision Series* volumes.

**As always, the most recent *Contemporary Authors* cumulative
index continues to be the user's guide to the location of an
individual author's listing.**

Contemporary Authors
was named an
***"Outstanding
Reference Source"*** *by
the American Library
Association Reference
and Adult Services
Division after its 1962
inception.*
*In 1985 it was listed by
the same organization
as one of the
twenty-five most
distinguished reference
titles published in the
past twenty-five years.*

Preface

The *Contemporary Authors New Revision Series* (*CANR*) provides completely updated information on authors listed in earlier volumes of *Contemporary Authors* (*CA*). Entries for individual authors from *any* volume of *CA* may be included in a volume of the *New Revision Series*. *CANR* updates only those sketches requiring significant change.

Authors are included on the basis of specific criteria that indicate the need for significant revision. These criteria include bibliographical additions, changes in addresses or career, major awards, and personal information such as name changes or death dates. All listings in this volume have been revised or augmented in various ways. Some sketches have been extensively rewritten, and many include informative new sidelights. As always, a *CANR* listing entails no charge or obligation.

How to Get the Most out of *CA*: Use the Index

The key to locating an author's most recent entry is the *CA* cumulative index, which is published separately and distributed with even-numbered original volumes and odd-numbered revision volumes. It provides access to *all* entries in *CA* and *CANR*. Always consult the latest index to find an author's most recent entry.

For the convenience of users, the *CA* cumulative index also includes references to all entries in these Gale literary series: *Authors and Artists for Young Adults, Authors in the News, Bestsellers, Black Literature Criticism, Black Writers, Children's Literature Review, Concise Dictionary of American Literary Biography, Concise Dictionary of British Literary Biography, Contemporary Authors Autobiography Series, Contemporary Authors Bibliographical Series, Contemporary Literary Criticism, Dictionary of Literary Biography, DISCovering Authors, DISCovering Authors: British, Drama Criticism, Hispanic Literature Criticism, Hispanic Writers, Junior DISCovering Authors, Major Authors and Illustrators for Children and Young Adults, Major 20th-Century Writers, Native North American Literature, Poetry Criticism, Short Story Criticism, Something about the Author, Something about the Author Autobiography Series, Twentieth-Century Literary Criticism, World Literature Criticism,* and *Yesterday's Authors of Books for Children.*

A Sample Index Entry:

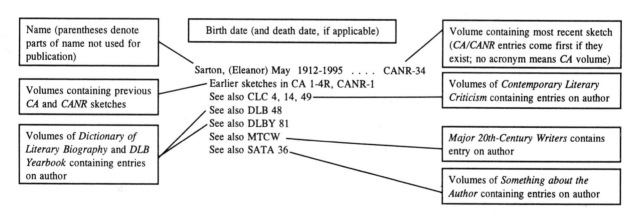

For the most recent *CA* information on Sarton, users should refer to Volume 34 of the *New Revision Series,* as designated by "CANR-34"; if that volume is unavailable, refer to CANR-1. And if CANR-1 is unavailable, refer to CA 1-4R, published in 1967, for Sarton's First Revision entry.

How Are Entries Compiled?

The editors make every effort to secure new information directly from the authors. Copies of all sketches in selected *CA* and *CANR* volumes previously published are routinely sent to listees at their last-known addresses, and returns from these authors are then assessed. For deceased writers, or those who fail to reply to requests for data, we consult other reliable biographical sources, such as those indexed in Gale's *Biography and Genealogy Master Index,* and bibliographical sources, such as *National Union Catalog, LC MARC,* and *British National Bibliography.* Further details come from published interviews, feature stories, and book reviews, and often the authors' publishers supply material.

* Indicates that a listing has been compiled from secondary sources believed to be reliable but has not been personally verified for this edition by the author sketched.

What Kinds of Information Does an Entry Provide?

Sketches in *CANR* contain the following biographical and bibliographical information:

- **Entry heading:** the most complete form of author's name, plus any pseudonyms or name variations used for writing

- **Personal information:** author's date and place of birth, family data, educational background, political and religious affiliations, and hobbies and leisure interests

- **Addresses:** author's home, office, or agent's addresses as available

- **Career summary:** name of employer, position, and dates held for each career post; resume of other vocational achievements; military service

- **Membership information:** professional, civic, and other association memberships and any official posts held

- **Awards and honors:** military and civic citations, major prizes and nominations, fellowships, grants, and honorary degrees

- **Writings:** a comprehensive, chronological list of titles, publishers, dates of original publication and revised editions, and production information for plays, television scripts, and screenplays

- **Adaptations:** a list of films, plays, and other media which have been adapted from the author's work

- **Work in progress:** current or planned projects, with dates of completion and/or publication, and expected publisher, when known

- **Sidelights:** a biographical portrait of the author's development; information about the critical reception of the author's works; revealing comments, often by the author, on personal interests, aspirations, motivations, and thoughts on writing

- **Biographical and critical sources:** a list of books and periodicals in which additional information on an author's life and/or writings appears

Related Titles in the *CA* Series

Contemporary Authors Autobiography Series complements *CA* original and revised volumes with specially commissioned autobiographical essays by important current authors, illustrated with personal photographs they provide. Common topics include their motivations for writing, the people and experiences that shaped their careers, the rewards they derive from their work, and their impressions of the current literary scene.

Contemporary Authors Bibliographical Series surveys writings by and about important American authors since World War II. Each volume concentrates on a specific genre and features approximately ten writers; entries list works written by and about the author and contain a bibliographical essay discussing the merits and deficiencies of major critical and scholarly studies in detail.

Available in Electronic Formats

CD-ROM. Full-text bio-bibliographic entries from the entire *CA* series, covering approximately 100,000 writers, are available on CD-ROM through lease and purchase plans. The disc combines entries from the *CA, CANR,* and *Contemporary Authors Permanent Series* (*CAP*) print series to provide the most recent author listing. It can be searched by name, title, subject/genre, and personal data, and by using boolean logic. The disc will be updated every six months. For more information, call 1-800-877-GALE.

Magnetic Tape. *CA* is available for licensing on magnetic tape in a fielded format. Either the complete database or a custom selection of entries may be ordered. The database is available for internal data processing and nonpublishing purposes only. For more information, call 1-800-877-GALE.

Online. The *Contemporary Authors* database is made available online to libraries and their patrons through online public access catalog (OPAC) vendors. Currently, *CA* is offered through Ameritech Library Services' Vista Online (formerly Dynix), and is expected to become available through CARL Systems. More OPAC vendor offerings will follow soon.

GaleNet. *CA* is available on a subscription basis through GaleNet, a new online information resource that features an easy-to-use end-user interface, the powerful search capabilities of the BRS/Search retrieval software, and ease of access through the World-Wide Web. For more information, call Melissa Kolehmainen at 1-800-877-GALE, ext. 1598.

Suggestions Are Welcome

The editors welcome comments and suggestions from users on any aspects of the *CA* series. If readers would like to recommend authors whose entries should appear in future volumes of the series, they are cordially invited to write: The Editors, *Contemporary Authors,* 835 Penobscot Bldg., Detroit, MI 48226-4094; call toll-free at 1-800-347-GALE; fax to 1-313-961-6599; or e-mail at conauth@gale.com.

CA Numbering System and Volume Update Chart

Occasionally questions arise about the *CA* numbering system and which volumes, if any, can be discarded. Despite numbers like "29-32R," "97-100" and "149," the entire *CA* series consists of only 126 physical volumes with the publication of *CA New Revision Series* Volume 50. The following charts note changes in the numbering system and cover design, and indicate which volumes are essential for the most complete, up-to-date coverage.

CA First Revision

- 1-4R through 41-44R (11 books)
  Cover: Brown with black and gold trim.
  There will be no further First Revision volumes because revised entries are now being handled exclusively through the more efficient *New Revision Series* mentioned below.

CA Original Volumes

- 45-48 through 97-100 (14 books)
  Cover: Brown with black and gold trim.
- 101 through 149 (49 books)
  Cover: Blue and black with orange bands.
  The same as previous *CA* original volumes but with a new, simplified numbering system and new cover design.

CA Permanent Series

- *CAP*-1 and *CAP*-2 (2 books)
  Cover: Brown with red and gold trim.
  There will be no further *Permanent Series* volumes because revised entries are now being handled exclusively through the more efficient *New Revision Series* mentioned below.

CA New Revision Series

- *CANR*-1 through *CANR*-50 (50 books)
  Cover: Blue and black with green bands.
  Includes only sketches requiring extensive changes; **sketches are taken from any previously published *CA*, *CAP*, or *CANR* volume**.

If You Have:	You May Discard:
CA First Revision Volumes 1-4R through 41-44R **and** *CA Permanent Series* Volumes 1 and 2	*CA* Original Volumes 1, 2, 3, 4 and Volumes 5-6 through 41-44
CA Original Volumes 45-48 through 97-100 **and** 101 through 149	**NONE:** These volumes will not be superseded by corresponding revised volumes. Individual entries from these and all other volumes appearing in the left column of this chart may be revised and included in the various volumes of the *New Revision Series*.
CA New Revision Series Volumes *CANR*-1 through *CANR*-50	**NONE:** The *New Revision Series* does not replace any single volume of *CA*. Instead, volumes of *CANR* include entries from many previous *CA* series volumes. All *New Revision Series* volumes must be retained for full coverage.

A Sampling of Authors and Media People
Featured in This Volume

Pat Barker

Barker is a prize-winning English novelist, whose works about working-class England and World War I have been praised for their spare, direct prose and social insight. *The Ghost Road,* the third installment in her acclaimed World War I trilogy, received the 1995 Booker Prize.

Wendell Berry

An American poet, novelist, and essayist, Berry draws on his experiences as a Kentucky farmer to address ecological issues and what he considers humanity's growing alienation from nature. Berry's works also stress the importance of community and include *The Memory of Old Jack, The Country of Marriage,* and *The Unsettling of America.*

Alice Childress

An American playwright and novelist, Childress is primarily known for her controversial young adult novel *A Hero Ain't Nothin' but a Sandwich,* which details a teenager's growing addiction to heroin. Her books and plays have been praised for their frank treatment of racial issues and compassionate characterizations.

Marguerite Duras

Hailed as one of France's most original contemporary writers, Duras frequently explores such themes as love and the existential conflicts of the individual in lyrical works that juxtapose biographical and fictitious elements. Often set in Indochina, some of her best-known works include *The Vice-Consul* and *The Lover.*

Carolyn Forche

Chiefly regarded as a political poet, Forche is best known for such works as *The Country between Us,* which documents the horrors of the Salvadoran Civil War during the late 1970s, and the *Gathering the Tribes,* which focuses on community, memory, and sexuality.

Gabriel Garcia Marquez

Winner of the 1982 Nobel Prize for Literature, Colombian novelist Garcia Marquez is credited with creating a unique connection between the real and the fantastic, which has come to be known as "magical realism." Major themes in his works, which include *One Hundred Years of Solitude,* and *Love in the Time of Cholera,* range from the political and social to love and solitude.

Winston Groom

Groom is an American novelist and nonfiction writer who was catapulted to best-seller status with the highly successful film adaptation of his novel *Forrest Gump.* Groom's works often center on the Vietnam War and politics and society in the Deep South.

Denise Levertov

Levertov is considered one of the most significant American poets since World War II. Concerned with themes of love, community, and war, her works include *The Double Image* and *The Sorrow Dance,* and often imbue commonplace objects with personal and religious significance.

David Malouf

An Australian novelist and poet, Malouf has been praised for the vivid, sensuous descriptions and evocative settings that characterize his work. His novel *Remembering Babylon,* which received the 1994 *Los Angeles Times* Book Award for Fiction and was nominated for a Booker Prize, addresses the relationships between politics, language, and identity.

Mary McCarthy

One of America's most prominent intellectuals, McCarthy was renowned for her outspoken opposition to hypocrisy. Honesty was the dominant theme in McCarthy's work, and her first novel, *The Company She Keeps,* is typical in its focus on a young woman's quest for her one true identity.

Kenzaburo Oe

Winner of the 1994 Nobel Prize for Literature, Oe is highly regarded for his imaginative and formally innovative novels that examine alienation and anxiety among members of Japan's post-World War II generation. Oe's works express deep concern with the implications of nuclear power and include the novels *The Catch* and *The Silent Cry,* and the essay collection *Hiroshima Notes.*

Vikram Seth

An Indian novelist and poet, Seth has been praised for the wit and humor of his writing and for his versatility. His works range from the verse novel *The Golden Gate* to his travelogue *From Heaven Lake.* His novel *A Suitable Boy* is considered a vivid and lavishly detailed portrait of India's diverse society and culture.

Jane Smiley

Smiley is an award-winning American novelist and short story writer whose works center on family relations. In her novel *A Thousand Acres,* which received a Pulitzer Prize in 1992, Smiley explores the ways in which greed, revenge, and jealousy can lead to a family's downfall.

Peter Taylor

An American short story writer, novelist, and playwright, Taylor was acclaimed both for his highly accomplished short stories and for his Pulitzer Prize-winning novel, *A Summons to Memphis.* Taylor's fiction centers on the changing values of Southern society and dramatizes the suffering of those unable to reconcile themselves to social change.

Contemporary Authors®

NEW REVISION SERIES

*Indicates that a listing has been compiled from secondary sources believed to be reliable but has not been personally verified for this edition by the author sketched.

ABLEY, Mark 1955-

PERSONAL: Born May 13, 1955, in Leamington, England; son of Harry (an organist) and Mary (a teacher; maiden name, Collins) Abley; married Ann Beer (a university professor), August 15, 1981; children: Kate, Megan. *Education:* University of Saskatchewan, B.A. (with high honors), 1975; Oxford University, B.A. (with first class honors), 1978, M.A., 1983. *Religion:* Anglican.

ADDRESSES: Agent—c/o Writers' Union of Canada, 24 Ryerson Avenue, Toronto, Ontario, M5T 2P3, Canada.

CAREER: Canadian Broadcasting Corp., Toronto, Ontario, researcher in television drama department, 1978-79; freelance journalist, travel writer, editor, and broadcaster, 1979-87; *Gazette,* Montreal, book-review editor, 1989-91, feature writer, 1987-89, 1991—.

MEMBER: PEN, Writers' Union of Canada, League of Canadian Poets.

AWARDS, HONORS: Rhodes scholar at St. John's College, Oxford University, 1975-78; Canada's National Magazine Foundation, Fiona Mee Prize for literary journalism, 1980; Society of Authors, London, Eric Gregory Award for poetry, 1981; Mark Harrison Prize, 1992.

WRITINGS:

(Editor) *The Parting Light: Selected Writings of Samuel Palmer,* Carcanet, 1985.
Beyond Forget: Rediscovering the Prairies (travel), Douglas & McIntyre, 1986, Sierra Books (San Francisco, CA), 1987, Chatto & Windus (Toronto), 1988.
Blue Sand, Blue Moon (poetry), Cormorant, 1988.
Heartland: Prairie Portraits and Landscapes (text to photographs by Ottmar Bierwagen), Douglas & McIntyre, 1989.
Glasburyon (poetry), Quarry, 1994.

Contributing editor, *Maclean's,* 1979-87, *Saturday Night,* 1986-92; editor of special Canadian issue of *Verse,* 1986. Regular contributor to *Times Literary Supplement,* 1980—; contributor to numerous Canadian magazines. Writer and narrator of four series for CBC-Radio's "Ideas," 1981-87.

WORK IN PROGRESS: A personal, idiosyncratic memoir, expected 1997.

SIDELIGHTS: Mark Abley told *CA:* "As a working journalist, I have all too little time to write poetry, the art for which I once lived. But I remain committed to poetry, not as a rarefied genre inaccessible to most intelligent readers, but as a medium which can touch the minds and hearts of many people who ordinarily shun the form. There is no reason why poetry cannot be intelligible and excellent at the same time. The failure of many poets to reach the public is not only the result of a debased public taste or a monopolistic system of book distribution; it's also the fault of the writers in question.

"My first book, *The Parting Light: Selected Writings of Samuel Palmer,* was a labor of love: the product of my desire to excavate the literary work of one of Britain's finest painters. Like his friend and mentor, William Blake, Samuel Palmer was blessed with an imagination that transcended any single medium. I chose as an epigraph Geoffrey Grigson's rhetorical question, 'How much literature do we hide beneath our mere invention and restriction of the term?'

"In my travel book, *Beyond Forget: Rediscovering the Prairies,* I felt free to adapt a flexible form to my own purposes. The book included descriptions of birds and wild places, encounters with Western Canadians, fragments of autobiography. The challenge was to keep all these subjects in some king of discipline.

"I have little talent for fiction. But in the future, God and circumstances permitting, I intend to return to the medium of travel. As long as I can breath and think, I will be wrestling with the quixotic angel of poetry."

* * *

ALDING, Peter
See JEFFRIES, Roderic (Graeme)

* * *

ALEXANDER, Robert
See GROSS, Michael (Robert)

* * *

ALINE, Countess of Romanones
See QUINTANILLA, (Maria) Aline (Griffith y Dexter)

* * *

ALLAN-MEYER, Kathleen 1918-

PERSONAL: Born February 25, 1918, in Dunellen, NJ; daughter of Andrew A. (a bank accountant) and Ethel (a nurse; maiden name, Creen) Allan; married Joseph V. Meyer (an insurance underwriter), February 12, 1941 (deceased); children: Jane S., Leslie A. (daughter). *Education:* New York University, B.S. (summa cum laude), 1940; graduate study at Hofstra University, 1955; San Jose State College (now University), nursery school certificate, 1971. *Religion:* Christian.

ADDRESSES: Home—32101 O'Bayley Drive, Fort Bragg, CA 95437.

CAREER: Blackett-Sample-Hummert (advertising agency), New York, NY, secretary, 1940-43; homemaker, 1943-56; Grace Church, Massapequa, NY, director of preschool, 1956-63; St. Matthew's Episcopal Day School, San Mateo, CA, director of preschool, 1963-86; teacher of creative writing, 1981-83; St. Ambrose Sea Breeze School, Foster City, CA, part-time preschool work, 1987-1995; freelance writer.

MEMBER: Society of Children's Book Writers and Illustrators, California Writers Club, Burlingame Writers Club.

WRITINGS:

JUVENILE

The Time-to-Sleep Book, Western Publishing (New York City), 1978.
Ishi: The Story of an American Indian, Dillon (Minneapolis, MN), 1980.
Gerrie the Giraffe, Ideals Publishing (Milwaukee, WI), 1981.
God Sends the Seasons, Our Sunday Visitor (Huntington, IN), 1981.
Ireland: Land of Mist and Magic, Dillon, 1983.
God's Gifts: Hearing, Abingdon (Nashville, TN), 1985.
God's Gifts: Seeing, Abingdon, 1985.
God's Gifts: Smelling, Abingdon, 1985.
God's Gifts: Tasting, Abingdon, 1985.
God's Gifts: Touching, Abingdon, 1985.
Bear, Your Manners Are Showing, Standard Publishing (Cincinnati, OH), 1987.
Little Bear's Surprise, Standard, 1989.
Little Bear's Big Adventure, Standard, 1990.
Little Bear Finds a Friend, Standard, 1991.

OTHER

Kindergarten Guide (teacher's manual), Hayes School Publishing, 1977.
Father Serra: Traveller on the Golden Chain, Our Sunday Visitor, 1990.
Tul-Tok-A-Na, the Small One, Council of Indian Affairs Education, 1992.
I Have a New Friend, Barron's Educational (Woodbury, NY), 1995.

Contributor of poems, articles, and stories to magazines, including *Accent on Youth, First Teacher, Hopscotch, Instructor, Jack and Jill, Ranger Rick,* and *Wee Wisdom.*

WORK IN PROGRESS: Another photo-essay, multicultural book for Barrow's Educational.

SIDELIGHTS: Kathleen Allan-Meyer told *CA:* "I was the youngest of five children of English-born parents. I wrote for the school newspaper in junior and senior high school, and my aim was to study journalism at New York University (NYU). Because our family never had any money to send the children to college, I was fortunate to receive a scholarship there. Besides taking journalism and advertising courses at NYU with some of the finest professors of the day, I joined the staffs of the college newspaper and yearbook. I felt very proud when I was chosen to be the first woman literary editor of the yearbook.

"A wonderful four years ended with graduation. I attempted to find work as a newspaper reporter or an advertising copy-writer, but in those days there was a great deal of prejudice against women in such fields. I had to settle for a job as a secretary with a radio advertising company, where I worked for the script editor of 'Stella Dallas,' 'John's Other Wife,' and 'Young Widder Brown.' The following year I married a young man I had met at NYU.

"When our youngest child was about two years old, I began to write stories to amuse her and her sister. I never thought to send the stories to a publisher. When both girls were out of college, I began writing in earnest and sold my first piece in 1969 to *Jack and Jill.* I haven't stopped since. I started to write books and found that the most difficult part is getting the first sentence and the first paragraph on paper. After I am satisfied with them, I can forge ahead.

"One of my favorite books to write, and one of the most successful, was *Ishi: The Story of an American Indian.* Ishi's life, with its hardships and sadness, provides a fine model of how one can cope with great difficulties. I feel that the children of today have many traumas in their lives, and they will be able to see the wisdom of adjusting to and making the best of whatever comes along, just as Ishi did. "Writing my books has been a great joy for me, and to discover that young people have found the same joy in reading them makes my life very worthwhile!"

*   *   *

ANDERSON, Judith H(elena) 1940-

PERSONAL: Born April 21, 1940, in Worcester, MA; daughter of Oscar William (a pharmacist) and Beatrice (a homemaker; maiden name, Beaudry) Anderson; married E. Talbot Donaldson, May 18, 1971 (died April 13, 1987). *Education:* Radcliffe College, B.A., 1961; Yale University, M.A., 1962, Ph.D., 1965.

ADDRESSES: Home—2525 East Eighth St., Bloomington, IN 47408. *Office*—Department of English, Indiana University—Bloomington, Bloomington, IN 47405.

CAREER: Cornell University, Ithaca, NY, instructor, 1964-66, assistant professor of English, 1966-72; Yale University, New Haven, CT, visiting lecturer in English, 1973; University of Michigan, Ann Arbor, visiting assistant professor of English, 1973-74; Indiana University—Bloomington, associate professor, 1974-79, professor of English, 1979—.

MEMBER: Modern Language Association of America, Renaissance Society of America, Shakespeare Association of America, American Association of University Professors, Spenser Society (president, 1979), Milton Society.

WRITINGS:

The Growth of a Personal Voice: "Piers Plowman" and the "Faerie Queene," Yale University Press (New Haven, CT), 1976.

Biographical Truth: The Representation of Historical Persons in Tudor-Stuart Writing, Yale University Press, 1984.

(Editor with Elizabeth D. Kirk) William Langland, *Will's Vision of Piers Plowman,* Norton (New York City), 1990.

Words That Matter: Linguistic Perception in Renaissance English, Stanford University Press (Stanford, CA), 1996.

(Editor with Donald Cheney and David A. Richardson) *Spenser's Life and the Subject of Biography,* in press.

Contributor to books, including *Essential Articles for the Study of Edmund Spenser,* edited by A. C. Hamilton, Archon Books, 1972; *Poetic Traditions of the English Renaissance,* edited by Maynard Mack and George de Forest Lord, Yale University Press, 1982; *Acts of Interpretation: The Text in Its Context,* edited by Mary J. Carruthers and Elizabeth D. Kirk, Pilgrim Books (Norman, OK), 1982; *The Passing of Arthur: New Essays in Arthurian Tradition,* edited by Christopher Baswell and William Sharpe, Garland (New York City), 1988; *Unfolded Tales: Studies in Renaissance Romance,* edited by George M. Logan and Gordon Teskey, Cornell University Press (Ithaca, NY), 1989; *The Spenser Encyclopedia,* edited by Hamilton and others, University of Toronto Press, 1990; *Approaches to Teaching Spenser's "Faerie Queene,"* edited by David Lee Miller and Alexander Dunlap, Modern Language Association of America (New York City), 1994; and *Sounding of Things Done: Essays in Honor of S. K. Heninger, Jr.,* edited by Peter E. Medine and Joseph Wittreich, University of Delaware Press (Newark, DE), in press. Also contributor to literature journals.

WORK IN PROGRESS: Translations: The Limits of Metaphor in Early Modern England.

BIOGRAPHICAL/CRITICAL SOURCES:

PERIODICALS

American Historical Review, number 90, 1985.
Renaissance Quarterly, number 37, 1984.
Speculum, April, 1978.
Times Literary Supplement, July 8, 1977; July 20, 1984.
Yearbook of English Studies, number 10, 1982.

*   *   *

ANDERSON, Rachel 1943-

PERSONAL: Born March 18, 1943, in Hampton Court, Surrey, England; daughter of Donald Clive (a writer and military historian) and Verily (a writer; maiden name, Bruce) Anderson; married David Bradby (professor of theater studies at London University), June 19, 1965; children: Hannah, Lawrence, Nguyen Than Sang (adopted son), Donald. *Education:* Attended Hastings School of Art, 1959-60. *Politics:* Socialist. *Religion:* "Church of England Christian."

ADDRESSES: Office—c/o Oxford University Press, Oxford OX2 6DP, England; c/o Henry Holt, 115 West 18th St., New York, NY 10011.

CAREER: Writer. Chatto & Windus Ltd., London, England, publicity assistant, 1963-64; worked for a brief period in editorial department of *Women's Mirror,* London, 1964. Has also worked in the news department of the British Broadcasting Corp. (BBC) and as a broadcaster for the BBC's *Woman's Hour.*

WRITINGS:

Pineapple (novel), J. Cape (London), 1965.
The Purple Heart Throbs: A Survey of Popular Romantic Fiction, 1850-1972, Hodder & Stoughton (London), 1974.
Dream Lovers, Hodder & Stoughton, 1978.
Moffatt's Road, illustrated by Pat Marriott, J. Cape, 1978.
The Poacher's Son, Oxford University Press (Oxford, England), 1982.
Little Angel Comes to Stay, illustrated by Linda Birch, Oxford University Press, 1983.
Winston's Wonderful Weekend, Lion Books, 1983.
The War Orphan, Oxford University Press, 1984.
Tim Walks, illustrated by Trevor Stubley, CIO Publishing, 1986.
Little Angel, Bonjour, illustrated by Birch, Oxford University Press, 1987.
French Lessons, Oxford University Press, 1988.
The Bus People, Oxford University Press, 1988.
The Boy Who Laughed, Macmillan (London), 1989.
Jessy Runs Away, illustrated by Shelagh McNichols, A & C Black (London), 1989.
For the Love of Sang (autobiographical), Lion Books, 1990.
Best Friends, illustrated by McNichols, A & C Black, 1991.
Paper Faces, Oxford University Press, 1991.
Happy Christmas Little Angel, illustrated by Birch, Oxford University Press, 1991.
Tough as Old Boots, illustrated by Birch, Methuen (New York City), 1991.
When Mum Went to Work, Oxford University Press, 1992.
The Working Class, Oxford University Press, 1993.
Black Water, Oxford University Press, 1994.
Jessy and the Long-Short Dress, illustrated by McNichols, A & C Black, 1994.
Princess Jazz and the Angels, Methuen, 1994.
Letters from Heaven, Heinemann (London), 1995.

The Dolls' House, Oxford University Press, 1995.

TRANSLATOR

The Cat's Tale, Oxford University Press, 1985.
(With David Bradby) *Renard the Fox,* illustrated by Bob Dewar, Oxford University Press, 1986.
Wild Goose Chase, Oxford University Press, 1986.
Little Lost Fox, Oxford University Press, 1992.

OTHER

Also author of radio play, *Tomorrow's Tomorrow,* 1970, and children's musical, *Fairy Snow and the Disability Box,* 1981. Contributor of short stories to *The Oxford Christmas Story Book, The Oxford Merry Christmas Book, Stories for Four Year Olds,* and several other anthologies. Contributor of articles to *Observer* (London), *Good Housekeeping, Homes & Gardens, Times* (London), *Weekend Telegraph, Punch, Guardian,* and other magazines and newspapers in England. Children's book page editor, *Good Housekeeping,* 1979-88.

SIDELIGHTS: Rachel Anderson told *CA:* "[I was] brought up in a literary family, i.e. my widowed mother wrote children's stories, non-stop, to support her five fatherless children. [I am] incapable of doing anything else so [I] had to be a writer." Anderson, who speaks French and Italian, also wrote that she is a "practicing Christian but find God often very annoying by the silence."

"As a result of one of our sons being mentally handicapped," Anderson continued, "I have been actively involved, both in the things I write about, and in more practical ways, with the needs and care of young people and children who are intellectually and/or socially disadvantaged.

"As I grow older, I seem to be writing more rather than less. Is time running out? Mostly I endeavour to do as my grandmother Rachel did and to be an admirer of creation and a lover of flowers and children. Amen."

In 1975 Anderson starred in *Fateful Eclipse,* a television drama by Nigerian writer Loalu Oguniyi, which was broadcast on Western Nigerian Television.

* * *

ANDREZEL, Pierre
See BLIXEN, Karen

* * *

APPIGNANESI, Lisa 1946-
(Jessica Ayre)

PERSONAL: Born January 4, 1946, in Lodz, Poland; daughter of Aron (a businessman) and Hana (Lipschyz)

Borenstein; married Richard Appignanesi (a writer), January 3, 1967 (divorced, 1982); currently living with John Forrester; children: (first marriage) Joshua; (with Forrester) Katrina Max. *Education:* McGill University, B.A., 1966, M.A., 1967; Sussex University, D.Phil., 1970. *Politics:* "Left of center."

ADDRESSES: Agent—Caradoc King, A. P. Watt, 20 John St., London NC1N 2DR, England.

CAREER: Centre for Community Research, New York, NY, staff writer, 1970-71; University of Essex, Colchester, Essex, England, lecturer in literature, 1971-73; New England College, Sussex, England, lecturer in literature, 1973-80. Writers and Readers Publishing Cooperative, founding member and editorial director, 1975-81; Institute of Contemporary Arts, London, director of seminars, 1981-86, deputy director, 1986-90. Independent television producer of programs for Channel 4 and British Broadcasting Corp., 1986—. Writer, full-time, 1990—.

WRITINGS:

(With Douglas and Monica Holmes) *Language of Trust,* Science House, 1972.
Femininity and the Creative Imagination: A Study of Henry James, Robert Musil, and Marcel Proust (criticism), Barnes & Noble (New York City), 1973.
The Cabaret (nonfiction), Studio Vista (London), 1975, Universe Books, 1976.
Simone de Beauvoir, Viking (New York City), 1988.
(With John Forrester) *Freud's Women,* Basic Books (New York City), 1992.
Memory and Desire (novel), Dutton (New York City), 1992.
Dreams of Innocence, Dutton, 1995.
A Good Woman, HarperCollins (London), 1996.

EDITOR

Brand New York, Quartet Books (London), 1982.
(With Steven Rose) *Science and Beyond,* Basil Blackwell (Oxford, England), 1986.
(With Hilary Lawson) *Dismantling Truth: Reality in the Postmodern World,* St. Martin's (New York City), 1989, Weidenfeld and Nicolson (London), 1989.
Ideas from France: The Legacy of French Theory, Free Association Books (London), 1989.
Postmodernism: I.C.A. Documents, Institute of Contemporary Arts (London), 1986, new edition, Free Association Books (London), 1989.
(With Sara Maitland) *The Rushdie File,* Fourth Estate (London), 1989, Syracuse University Press (Syracuse, NY), 1990.

OTHER

Also author of fiction under the pseudonym Jessica Ayre. Editor of "ICA Documents" series for Institute of Contemporary Arts, 1985-88. Contributor of articles and reviews to scholarly journals and to the Sunday *Times* (London). Also regular contributor to radio and television programs.

SIDELIGHTS: Lisa Appignanesi has written and edited books on a variety of subjects, including feminism, art history, and biography. She and Sara Maitland co-edited *The Rushdie File,* which was praised by *New York Times Book Review* contributor Edward Mortimer as "a very valuable sourcebook of documents" pertaining to author Salman Rushdie, who was condemned to death by the Ayatollah Khomeini after the publication of Rushdie's allegedly anti-Muslim novel *The Satanic Verses. The Rushdie File* provides a chronology of events pertaining to the book's publication and the uproar that followed; it also reprints reviews of the book, interviews with the author, samples of international reactions to Khomeini's death threat, and other related material.

Freud's Women, written in collaboration with John Forrester, examines Sigmund Freud's personal relationships with women and his theories on female psychology. Commenting in *Women's Review of Books,* Sheila Bienenfeld described *Freud's Women* as "detailed, scholarly and gracefully written." The authors address the oft-levelled charge that Freud was a misogynist who viewed women as nothing more than incomplete males. Appignanesi and Forrester argue that while some of the psychoanalyst's ideas about female sexuality may have been eccentric and old-fashioned, his relationships with women—particularly his mother, wife, daughter, and female patients and proteges—were, in Bienenfeld's words, "generally warm and long-lasting, free of the bitterness and acrimony that ended many of his friendships with men."

Appignanesi and Forrester further argue in *Freud's Women* that many of the best and brightest women of Freud's era subscribed to his theories, and that Freud routinely treated his female patients and students with all the respect he accorded their male counterparts. Bienenfeld summarized: "Wonderfully written throughout, [*Freud's Women*] is really two books in one: an intriguing collection of brief biographies of women . . .and also an intellectual history and close reading of the 'women's issue' as it has developed in psychoanalysis." Richard Wollheim, contributor to the *New York Times Book Review,* also found great merit in *Freud's Women.* He called it "a marvelously rich and engrossing work of intellectual history, deftly composed around the ambiguity in its title. Freud's women are in part the real women in his life and in part woman in the abstract, whose psychology he tried to reconstruct, never wholly to his satisfaction. The originality of this book lies in the many connections it traces between the two. . . . It is a relief to find two authors who are strong and free enough to recognize Freud's genius without falling into idolatry, and who can narrate its story in a fine cadenced prose."

Having established a solid reputation as an author of scholarly works, Appignanesi crossed into fiction with the 1992 novel *Memory and Desire.* Jennifer Selway, reviewer for the London *Observer,* called *Memory and Desire* "a thinking woman's block buster romance." Set in glamorous locations around Europe and in Manhattan, the multigenerational saga follows aristocrats and intellectuals through numerous adventures. A *Publishers Weekly* review noted Appignanesi's wide-ranging and diverse background in art, literature, and history and called *Memory and Desire* an "enjoyable if not particularly memorable read."

BIOGRAPHICAL/CRITICAL SOURCES:

PERIODICALS

Choice, February, 1993, pp. 923-31.
Kirkus Reviews, November 15, 1991, p. 1416.
Library Quarterly, October, 1991, pp. 429-43.
London Review of Books, December 3, 1992, p. 17.
New Republic, October 8, 1990, pp. 31-39.
New Statesman and Society, May 26, 1989, p. 38.
New Yorker, February 8, 1993, p. 113.
New York Times Book Review, April 28, 1985; July 22, 1990, p. 3; January 24, 1993, p. 21.
Observer (London), July 14, 1991, p. 63; December 12, 1993, pp. 22.
Publishers Weekly, January 6, 1992, p. 49.
Southern Humanities Review, fall, 1995, pp. 374-77.
Times Literary Supplement, July 19, 1991, p. 20; December 4, 1992, p. 11; December 18, 1992, p. 20.
Women's Review of Books, April, 1993, pp. 21-22.*

*   *   *

APPLEWHITE, James W(illiam) 1935-

PERSONAL: Born August 8, 1935, in Stantonsburg, NC; son of James W. (a farmer) and Jane Elizabeth (Mercer) Applewhite; married Janis Forrest (an administrative assistant), January 28, 1956; children: Lisa, Jamey, Jeff. *Education:* Duke University, A.B., 1958, M.A., 1960, Ph.D., 1969.

ADDRESSES: Home—606 November Dr., Durham, NC 27712. *Office*—Department of English, 308 Allen Building, Duke University, Durham, NC 27706.

CAREER: Poet. Duke University, Durham, NC, professor of English and former director of Institute of the Arts.

MEMBER: Poetry Society of America, Fellowship of Southern Writers.

AWARDS, HONORS: Emily Clark Balch Prize from *Virginia Quarterly Review,* 1966, for "The Journey"; National Endowment for the Arts grant, 1974; Borestone Mountain Poetry Awards, 1975, for "Roadside Notes" and 1977, for "William Blackburn, Riding Westward"; Guggenheim fellow, 1976; winner of 1979 Associated Writing Programs Contemporary Poetry Series Award; North Carolina Literary and Historical Association poetry award, 1981, 1986; recipient of prize in *International Poetry Review* 1982 competition; North Carolina Poetry Society award, 1990; American Academy and Institute of Arts and Letters, Jean Stein Award in Poetry, 1992; *Shenandoah* magazine, James Boatwright III Prize for Poetry, 1992; North Carolina Department of Cultural Resources, North Carolina Award in Literature, 1993.

WRITINGS:

POETRY

(Editor with Anne Lloyd and Fred Chappell) *Brown Bag,* [Greensboro, NC], 1971.
War Summer: Poems (chapbook), Back Door (Edmonds, WA), 1972.
Statues of the Grass, University of Georgia Press (Athens), 1975.
Following Gravity, University Press of Virginia (Charlottesville), 1980.
Forseeing the Journey, Louisiana State University Press (Baton Rouge), 1983.
Ode to the Chinaberry Tree and Other Poems, Louisiana State University Press, 1986.
River Writing: An Eno Journal, Princeton University Press (Princeton, NJ), 1988.
Lessons in Soaring, Louisiana State University Press, 1989.
A History of the River, Louisiana State University Press, 1993.

OTHER

(Editor) *Voices from Earth,* [Greensboro, NC], 1971.
Seas and Inland Journeys: Landscape and Consciousness from Wordsworth to Roethke (criticism), University of Georgia Press, 1985.

Contributor to anthologies, including *American Poetry Anthology,* 1970, and *A Modern Southern Reader,* 1986.

WORK IN PROGRESS: Another book of poems, *Inheriting the Homeplace.*

SIDELIGHTS: A native of the South, James W. Applewhite's poems are concerned with that area and with the relationship between the past and the present. For instance, in his collection *Statues of the Grass,* as Claire

Hahn observed in *Commonweal*: "What [Applewhite] is ultimately seeking for in his dedication to history are images which form . . . some way in which his inescapable inheritance can be metamorphosized into a present value."

Applewhite told *CA:* "I have been concerned for some time with the interaction of my own native southern American speech and the literary tradition of poetry in English. The long monologue from the point of view of a middle-aged southern woman in *Following Gravity* deals with this problem, this artistic opportunity. The poems of *Ode to the Chinaberry Tree* use my own speech and my own familiar landscape to reconstitute, in personal terms, traditional forms, tones, poetic modes. The title ode takes off from Wordsworth's 'Ode: Intimations of Immortality,' but uses very specific and lowly memories of my own childhood and growing up.

Yet the ode form, the rhymed stanzas, are preserved. My 'Greene Country Pastoral' provides a version of the pastoral elegy from the heart of eastern North Carolina. I suppose I am working to assimilate literary English and southern reality to one another.

"*A History of the River* dramatized cultural changes in my region, especially during the accelerated development following World War II. Essentially, I have had to confront a change of world, during my own lifetime and that of my father. In [*Inheriting the Homeplace,* (in progress)] I find myself in the changing present, father of sons and son of a failing father, as I quest for a continuity of time and times through hikes beside rivers, canoe trips, meditations on lakes, sailing jaunts into open ocean. In these poems, I enact my quest to know the heart of time by thinking and moving on water."

BIOGRAPHICAL/CRITICAL SOURCES:

BOOKS

Naipaul, V. S., *A Turn in the South,* Knopf (New York City), 1989.

PERIODICALS

American Book Review, summer, 1987.
Appalachian Journal, spring, 1976.
Choice, July/August, 1976.
Commonweal, October 22, 1976.
Hudson Review, winter, 1984.
North Carolina Literary Review, spring, 1993.
Poetry, April, 1984.
Sewanee Review, spring, 1982.
Southern Poetry Review, spring, 1976.
Southern Review, autumn, 1976; winter 1995.
Verse, winter, 1989.
Virginia Quarterly Review, autumn, 1983; winter, 1987.

ARDAGH, John 1928-

PERSONAL: Born May 28, 1928, in Blantyre, Malawi; son of Osmond Charles and Margot (Biheller) Ardagh; married Jennifer Berry, September 13, 1952; married Ludmila Patokova (a doctor of medicine), November 20, 1968; married Katharina Schmitz; children: (first marriage) Nicholas. *Education:* Worcester College, Oxford, M.A. (honors), 1951. *Politics:* Liberal Democrat. *Religion:* Church of England.

ADDRESSES: Home—Kensington, England. *Agent*—Marie Schebeko, 66 rue de Miromesil, Paris 8e, France.

CAREER: Freelance writer and journalist. Correspondent in France for *Times,* London, England, 1955-59; staff writer, *Observer,* 1961-66.

MEMBER: Society of Authors, Franco-British Council.

WRITINGS:

The New French Revolution: A Social and Economic Survey of France, 1945-1967, Secker & Warburg (London), 1968, Harper (New York City), 1969, 3rd edition published as *The New France: DeGaulle and After,* Penguin (New York City), 1977.
A Tale of Five Cities: Life in Provincial Europe Today, Secker & Warburg, 1979.
France in the 1980s, Secker & Warburg, 1982, revised edition published as *France Today,* Penguin, 1987.
The American Express Pocket Guide to the South of France: Provence and the Cote d'Azur, Simon & Schuster (New York City), 1983.
Rural France: The People, Places, and Character of the Frenchman's France, Century Publishing (London), 1983.
(Editor) *The Penguin Guide to France,* Viking (New York City), 1985, published in England as *The Collins Guide to France,* Willow Books (London), 1985.
Germany and the Germans: An Anatomy of Society Today, Harper, 1987, published in England as *Germany and the Germans,* Hamish Hamilton (London), 1987, revised edition published as *Germany and the Germans: After Reunification,* Penguin (London), 1991, new revised edition, 1995.
Writers' France: A Regional Panorama, Hamish Hamilton, 1989.
(With Colin Jones) *Cultural Atlas of France,* Facts on File (New York City), 1991.
The Shell Guide to Germany, Simon & Schuster, 1991.
Ireland and the Irish: Portrait of a Changing Society, Viking, 1995.

Contributor to *Observer, Times, Sunday Times,* and other British newspapers.

The New French Revolution has been published in French and German.

WORK IN PROGRESS: The Oxford Book of France, a critical anthology of French literature, for Oxford University Press; *France 2000,* for Penguin and Hamish Hamilton.

SIDELIGHTS: John Ardagh is a journalist who specializes in European history and culture. Among his most notable works are *France Today,* which has sold over 250,000 copies; *A Tale of Five Cities: Life in Provincial Europe Today,* based on the his own extended visits to five European cities; *Writers' France: A Regional Panorama,* in which Ardagh explored French locations that have inspired various literary works; and *Germany and the Germans: An Anatomy of Society Today, Ireland and the Irish,* and *Cultural Atlas of France,* all of which are detailed overviews of the history, customs, and artistic life of Germany, Ireland, and France.

To research *A Tale of Five Cities* Ardagh lived in Newcastle, England; Toulouse, France; Stuttgart, Germany; Bologna, Italy; and Ljubljana, Slovenia. In discussing each of these cities, he reported on their "history, local government system, town planning, civic awareness, cultural life, living standards . . ., education, industry and foreign minorities," according to Harry Ree in the *Times Educational Supplement.* Ardagh's observations of life in these towns and of the differences and similarities in terms of population are presented in what a *New Yorker* critic calls "a delightfully discursive and chromatic style." *A Tale of Five Cities,* the critic concluded, is an "unusual and original book."

Following *France in the 1980s, Rural France: The People, Places, and Character of the Frenchman's France,* and other works on France, Ardagh published *Writers' France,* which focuses on French locales which have inspired French and foreign writers. Written as a kind of travel book, with excerpts from some of the works discussed, *Writers' France* is, as Thomas Swick wrote in the *New York Times Book Review,* something "of a coffeetable book—but one as delectable to read as it is to look at."

In *Germany and the Germans* Ardagh turned his attention to France's neighbor to the east, providing, as Peter Graves reported in the *Times Literary Supplement,* "a snapshot of contemporary Germany from every conceivable angle. . . ." In this work, Laurie Taylor wrote in *Punch,* Ardagh "deals adeptly not only with the many variations of West German culture . . . but also with fundamentalist and liberal Turks, the invigorating new youth culture of the Greens, and the grey depressed world beyond the [Berlin] Wall" in Communist East Germany.

Ardagh collaborated with historian Colin Jones to write *Cultural Atlas of France,* which Anne Kelly Knowles of the *Journal of Historical Geography* noted, "celebrates the diversity of France in lavish photographs of color-drenched landscapes, master works of art, and icons of popular culture. The text . . . will entertain arm-chair travelers and students." The critic for the *Times Literary Supplement* argued that *Cultural Atlas of France* "succeeds admirably in conveying as much information as possible within its self-imposed format."

BIOGRAPHICAL/CRITICAL SOURCES:

PERIODICALS

American Reference Book Annual, Volume 24, 1993, p. 66.
Books, October, 1989, p. 34.
Journal of Historical Geography, July, 1992, pp. 347-348.
Listener, August 8, 1968.
New Statesman & Society, December 6, 1991, p. 45.
New Yorker, March 17, 1980, p. 167.
New York Times Book Review, February 9, 1969; June 10, 1990, p. 49.
Punch, April 15, 1987, p. 43.
Reference Book Review, January, 1992, p. 22.
Times Educational Supplement, January 25, 1980, p. 25.
Times Literary Supplement, May 15, 1987, p. 520; December 6, 1991, p. 28; October 30, 1992, p. 28.
Wall Street Journal, December 4, 1990.*

*   *   *

ARDEN, J. E. M.
See CONQUEST, (George) Robert (Acworth)

*   *   *

ARGYLE, Michael 1925-

PERSONAL: Born August 11, 1925, in Nottingham, England; son of George Edgar (a school teacher) and Phyllis (Hawkins-Ambler) Argyle; married Sonia Kemp (a lexicographer), June 24, 1949; children: Miranda, Nicholas, Rosalind, Ophelia. *Education:* Emmanuel College, Cambridge, M.A., 1952. *Religion:* Church of England.

ADDRESSES: Home—309 Woodstock Rd., Oxford, England. *Office*—Department of Experimental Psychology, Oxford University, South Parks Rd., Oxford, England.

CAREER: Oxford University, Oxford, England, university lecturer, 1952-69, reader in social psychology, 1969-92, emeritus reader, 1992—, acting head of department of experimental psychology, 1978-80, fellow of Wolfson College, 1965, governor of Pusey House, 1976-88.

Fellow, Center for Advanced Study in the Behavioral Sciences, Stanford, CA, 1958-59; visiting professor at numerous universities, including University of Michigan, University of Delaware, University of Kansas, University of British Columbia, University of Ghana, University of Leuven, Hebrew University of Jerusalem, University of Bologna, University of Adelaide, and Flinders University of South Australia; Rose Morgan Professor, University of Kansas; lecturer in Greece, Italy, Finland, New Zealand, Australia, Egypt, and Japan. Chairperson, organizer, or participant in conferences, 1964-87; has given lectures throughout the world. Psychologist to Civil Service Selection Board, 1963-68. Member of advisory committee, British Sports Council, 1975-78; member of Royal Society Group on Non-Verbal Communication, 1968-71, and Council for National Academic Awards, 1974-78 and 1980-84. Examiner for universities. *Military service:* Royal Air Force, navigator, 1943-47; became flying officer.

MEMBER: International Society for the Study of Social and Personal Relationships, European Association for Social Psychology, British Psychological Society (honorary fellow; chairperson of Social Psychology Section, 1964-67, 1972-74), American Society of Experimental Social Psychology (foreign member).

AWARDS, HONORS: Numerous research grants, 1958-91; Distinguished Career Contribution Award, International Society for the Study of Personal Relationships, 1990; D.Sc., Oxford University; D.Sc.Psych., University of Brussels; D.Litt., University of Adelaide.

WRITINGS:

The Scientific Study of Social Behaviour, Methuen (London), 1957.

Religious Behaviour, Free Press of Glencoe, 1959.

(With George Humphrey) *Social Psychology through Experiment,* Methuen, 1962.

(With A. T. Welford and others) *Society: Problems and Methods of Study,* Routledge & Kegan Paul (London), 1962.

(With M. Kirton and T. Smith) *Training Managers,* Acton Society Trust (London), 1962.

Psychology and Social Problems, Methuen, 1964.

The Psychology of Interpersonal Behaviour, Penguin Books (London), 1967, 5th edition, 1994.

Social Interaction, Methuen, 1969, Aldine (Hawthorne, NY), 1970.

The Social Psychology of Work, Taplinger (New York City), 1972, 2nd edition, 1989.

(Editor) *Social Encounters: Readings in Social Interaction,* Aldine, 1973.

Bodily Communication, Methuen, 1975.

(With Benjamin Beit-Hallahmi) *The Social Psychology of Religion,* Routledge & Kegan Paul, 1975.

(With Mark Cook) *Gaze and Mutual Gaze,* Cambridge University Press (Cambridge, England), 1975.

(With Peter Trower and B. Bryant) *Handbook of Social Skills,* Methuen, 1978, Volume 1: *Social Skills and Mental Health,* Volume 2: *Social Skills and Work.*

(With Trower) *Person to Person,* Harper, 1979.

(With Adrian Furnham and Jean Ann Graham) *Social Situations,* Cambridge University Press, 1981.

(With Monika Henderson) *The Anatomy of Relationships: The Rules and Skills Needed to Handle Them Successfully,* Heinemann (London), 1985.

The Psychology of Happiness, Methuen, 1987.

Also author of *Cooperation,* 1991, *The Social Psychology of Everyday Life,* 1992, *Experiments in Social Interaction,* 1993, *Psychology and Leisure,* and, with Beit-Hallahmi and L. B. Brown, *Religious Behaviour: Beliefs and Experience.* Member of editorial board of *International and Intercultural Communication Annual* and *Applied Social Psychology Annual.* Editor of "Social Psychology Monographs" series, Penguin Books, 1967-74, and "International Series in Experimental Social Psychology," Pergamon (Elmsford, NY), 1979—. Contributor to professional journals in Great Britain, Europe, and the United States. Member of editorial board or consulting editor to *International Journal for the Psychology of Religion, British Journal of Social and Clinical Psychology, Journal of Applied Social Psychology, Journal for the Theory of Social Behaviour, Journal of Human Movement Studies, Journal of Nonverbal Behavior, Basic and Applied Social Psychology, Social Indicators Research, Review of Personality and Social Psychology, Journal of Social and Personal Relationships, Behaviour Research and Therapy, Language and Communication,* and *Journal of Social and Clinical Psychology.*

Many of Argyle's books have been translated into Chinese, Japanese, Portuguese, French, Dutch, German, Italian, Spanish, and Bulgarian.

*   *   *

ARISTIDES
See EPSTEIN, Joseph

*   *   *

ASBELL, Bernard   1923-
(Nicholas Max)

PERSONAL: Born May 8, 1923, in Brooklyn, NY; son of Samuel and Minnie (Zevin) Asbell; married Mildred Sacarny, January 2, 1944 (divorced April 2, 1971); married Marjorie Baldwin, June 11, 1971 (divorced August, 1977);

married Jean Brenchley, July 21, 1990; children: (first marriage) Paul, Lawrence, Jonathan, Jody. *Education:* Attended University of Connecticut, 1943-44.

ADDRESSES: Home—237 Wooded Way, State College, PA 16803.

CAREER: Richmond Times-Dispatch, Richmond, VA, reporter, 1945-47; public relations agent in Chicago, IL, 1947-55; *Chicago* (magazine), Chicago, managing editor, 1955-56; University of Chicago, Chicago, lecturer in nonfiction writing, 1956-60; Middlebury College, Middlebury, VT, lecturer in nonfiction writing at Bread Loaf Writers' Conference, 1960-61; University of Bridgeport, Bridgeport, CT, lecturer in journalism, 1961-63; Pennsylvania State University, University Park, associate professor of English, 1984-92. Lecturer, Yale University, 1979. Founder and director, New England Writers Center, 1979-84. Consultant to Educational Facilities Laboratories, 1963, 1970, Ford Foundation, 1963, 1968-69, Secretary of Health, Education, and Welfare, 1965-68, Carnegie Corp., and International Business Machines Corp. (IBM). Justice of the Peace in Wilton, CT, 1966-67. *Military service:* U.S. Army, 1943-45.

MEMBER: American Society of Journalists and Authors (president, 1963), Authors Guild, National Press Club.

AWARDS, HONORS: Educational Writers Association, first prize for magazine coverage of education, 1956, citation, 1966; National Education Association (NEA) School Bell Award, 1965; National Council for the Advancement of Educational Writing, second place award for best educational writing in magazines, 1968; L.H.D., University of New Haven, 1978.

WRITINGS:

When F.D.R. Died, Holt (New York City), 1961.
The New Improved American, McGraw (New York City), 1965.
Careers in Urban Affairs, Peter H. Wyden (New York City), 1970.
What Lawyers Really Do, Peter H. Wyden, 1970.
(Under pseudonym Nicholas Max) *President McGovern's First Team,* Doubleday (New York City), 1973.
The F.D.R. Memoirs, Doubleday, 1973.
(With Clair F. Vough) *Productivity: A Practical Program for Improving Efficiency,* American Management Association, 1975.
The Senate Nobody Knows, Doubleday, 1978.
(With David Hartman) *White Coat, White Cane,* Playboy Press (New York City), 1978.
(Editor) *Mother and Daughter: The Letters of Eleanor and Anna Roosevelt,* Coward, McCann & Geoghegan, 1983.
(With Gerald Amster) *Transit Point Moscow,* Holt, 1985.

(With Joe Paterno) *Paterno: By the Book,* Random House (New York City), 1989.
(With Karen Wynn) *What They Know about You,* Random House, 1991.
The Pill: A Biography of the Drug that Changed the World, Random House, 1995.

*   *   *

ASHFORD, Jeffrey
   See JEFFRIES, Roderic, (Graeme)

*   *   *

ASKA, Warabe
   See MASUDA, Takeshi

*   *   *

AVRUCH, Kevin Andrew 1950-

PERSONAL: Born February 22, 1950, in Brooklyn, NY; son of Benjamin (a restaurateur) and Edith (a milliner; maiden name, Kramer) Avruch; married Sheila Kathleen Smith (a program evaluator), March 25, 1977; children: Carla Rachel, Elizabeth Sophia. *Education:* University of Chicago, A.B., 1972; University of California at San Diego, M.A., 1973, Ph.D., 1978.

ADDRESSES: Home—9122 Ashmeade Dr., Fairfax, VA 22032. *Office*—Department of Anthropology, George Mason University, 4400 University Dr., Fairfax, VA 22030.

CAREER: University of California-San Diego, La Jolla, CA, lecturer, 1978-79; University of Illinois, Chicago, assistant professor, 1979-80; George Mason University, Fairfax, VA, assistant professor, 1980-84, associate professor, 1984-93, professor of anthropology, 1993—.

MEMBER: American Anthropological Association, Association for Israel Studies, Middle East Studies Association, Society for Psychological Anthropology.

AWARDS, HONORS: Nomination for National Jewish Book Award, 1982, for *American Immigrants in Israel: Social Identities and Change.*

WRITINGS:

American Immigrants in Israel: Social Identities and Change, University of Chicago Press (Chicago), 1981.
Conflict Resolution: Cross-Cultural Perspectives, Greenwood Press (Westport, CT), 1991.

Contributor of book chapters on conflict resolution and Middle East studies. Also contributor to periodicals, including *American Ethnologist, Middle East Journal,* and *Negotiation Journal.*

WORK IN PROGRESS: Continuing research in politics and religion of the Middle East and in cross-cultural approaches to conflict analysis and conflict resolution.

*   *   *

AYRE, Jessica
    See APPIGNANESI, Lisa

B

BARKER, Pat(ricia) 1943-

PERSONAL: Born May 8, 1943, in Thornaby-on-Tees, England; married David Barker (a professor of zoology), January 29, 1978; children: John, Annabel. *Education:* London School of Economics and Political Science, London, B.Sc., 1965.

ADDRESSES: Home—3 Edlingham Rd., Newton Hall, Durham DH1 5YS, England. *Agent*—Aitken, Stone & Wylie, 29 Fernshaw Rd., London SW10 OTG, England.

CAREER: Writer. Worked as teacher in England, 1965-70.

MEMBER: Society of Authors, PEN.

AWARDS, HONORS: Named one of Britain's twenty best young writers by Book Marketing Society, 1982; Fawcett Prize from Fawcett Society, 1982, for *Union Street;* M.Litt., University of Teesside, 1993; Special Award, Northern Electric Arts Awards, 1993; Guardian Fiction Prize, 1993, for *The Eye in the Door;* Booker Prize for fiction, 1995, for *The Ghost Road.*

WRITINGS:

NOVELS

Union Street, Virago Press (London), 1982, Putnam (New York City), 1983.
Blow Your House Down, Putnam, 1984.
The Century's Daughter, Putnam, 1986.
The Man Who Wasn't There, Virago, 1989, Ballantine (New York City), 1990.
Regeneration, Viking (London), 1991, Dutton (New York City), 1993.
The Eye in the Door, Viking, 1993, Dutton, 1994.
The Ghost Road, Viking, 1995, Dutton, 1996.

ADAPTATIONS: Union Street was made into a feature film entitled *Stanley & Iris* by Metro-Goldwyn-Mayer in 1989, starring Robert De Niro and Jane Fonda.

SIDELIGHTS: Pat Barker is among the most acclaimed writers to emerge from England in the 1980s. Her novels have earned praise for both their spare, direct prose and their depictions of working-class life. Once in danger of being labeled merely a feminist writer for her stories of struggling women in industrial England, Barker has since earned praise as a voice for the human condition in general. "It has been Pat Barker's accomplishment to enlarge the scope of the contemporary English novel," noted Claudia Roth Pierpont in the *New Yorker.* Pierpont further described Barker as "an energetic writer who achieves much of her purpose through swift and easy dialogue and the bold etching of personality—effects so apparently simple and forthright that the complications of feeling which arise seem to do so unbidden."

Barker's first three published novels draw upon her memories of working-class women of her mother's and grandmother's generations. She herself grew up in Thornaby-on-Tees, an industrial town in the north of England. In an interview with *CA,* the author recalled that she turned to writing her "gritty" and "realistic" works after failing to sell a series of middle-class novels of manners. She was encouraged to explore her own background by the author Angela Carter, who read a Barker work in progress during a writer's conference. Barker told *CA:* "I think along with the desire to write about the sort of environment I'd grown up with came a desire to write, initially at least, more about women because I felt that, although the men in that environment had also been deprived of a voice, and were not being given any kind of public recognition of their experiences of life, the women had been in a way still more deprived. . . . I was writing about the most silenced section of our society."

Union Street, Barker's first novel, concerns seven neighboring women near a factory in northeast England. Life for these women is trying and unrewarding. Some of them are married to alcoholics; some of them are victims of spousal abuse; all of them seem resigned to suffering. Meredith Tax, writing in the *Village Voice,* described the novel's characters as "women who have given up on love." Tax added, however, that Barker "dramatizes the strength of her working-class people without sentimentality, for she knows the way they participate in their own victimization." Tax also added that the various women in *Union Street* experience growth and strength through their suffering, noting that the novel's "point is life, and how rich and hard it is, and the different ways people have of toughing it through the pain without being crushed."

Many critics shared enthusiasm for *Union Street.* Ivan Gold, who wrote in the *New York Times Book Review* that Barker's "pungent, raunchy . . . dialogue" alternates "with passages of fine understated wit," called *Union Street* a "first-rate first novel." Likewise, Eileen Fairweather wrote in *New Statesman* that "Barker may have written the latest, long over-due working-class masterpiece," and Elizabeth Ward wrote in the *Washington Post Book World* that "Barker achieves immediate distinction with *Union Street.*" Ward added that though "the book's vision . . . is of a life brutal and scabrous in the extreme," Barker nonetheless includes "a flicker of affirmation" for each of the main characters. Ward called *Union Street* "a singularly powerful achievement." A film version of the book, entitled *Stanley & Iris,* was produced in 1989.

Barker enjoyed further acclaim with her next novel, *Blow Your House Down.* Like *Union Street,* the second novel details events in the lives of several women in working-class, industrial England. Unlike the women in *Union Street,* though, the characters in *Blow Your House Down* are prostitutes, and their problems include not only those of the women in *Union Street*—notably abuse and financial insecurity—but one of survival in a red-light district frequented by a vicious, Jack the Ripper-style killer.

Many reviewers praised *Blow Your House Down* as a gripping account of life in a gloomy industrial town. *Encounter* critic James Lasdun noted: "Pat Barker has an impressive feel for the starkness of English working-class existence at its roughest end." Lasdun cited Barker's "perfect ear for dialogue" and called her second novel "disturbingly convincing." Similarly, Ward wrote in the *Washington Post Book World* that Barker's greatest achievement in the work "is in the way she creates, with a minimum of descriptive writing, the desolate world of the prostitutes and at the same time lets the world reflect particular states of mind." Ward deemed *Blow Your House Down* "a courageous and disturbing novel." Katha Pollitt, who wrote of Barker's second novel in the *New York Times Book Re-*

view, hailed *Blow Your House Down* as "swift, spare and utterly absorbing" and acknowledged Barker's ability "to make us see her characters from within, as they see themselves, and thereby reveal the full individuality and humanity of women who have got short shrift both in literature and in life."

The Century's Daughter, Barker's third novel, offered further insights into the hardships of being a woman in industrial England. The work's protagonist is Liza Jarrett Wright, an octogenarian who recounts her life to Steven, a homosexual social worker who befriends her while trying to move her from a doomed neighborhood. Liza tells Steven of her childhood spent in poverty and neglect. She also recalls her son, killed during World War II, and her promiscuous daughter, who's child Liza raised herself.

Comparing *The Century's Daughter* to Barker's preceding novels, reviewers found it more sentimental but equally compelling. Norman Shrapnel, writing in the *Guardian,* commended Barker's "vigour, concern, and power of observation" and declared that "we here have a good novelist getting into her stride." Anne Boston wrote in *New Society* that Barker "has a fine sense of dramatic control" and that she "extracts memorable, likeable humanity, gritty humour and a kind of redemption" from the work's "desolate landscape." Boston concluded: "Pat Barker gives an authentic voice to the lives of the poor and dispossessed as few other English contemporary novelists have managed to do."

In a 1992 *Village Voice* interview, Barker admitted that the success of her first three novels led her to fear that she was being "boxed in" by public expectations. "I had become strongly typecast as a northern, regional, working-class feminist . . . label, label, label," she commented. "You get to the point where people are reading the label instead of the book." Not one to accept such limitations, Barker extended her imaginative reach and entered the world of the male psyche. *The Man Who Wasn't There* tells the story of Colin, a fatherless teenager who concocts fantasies about himself and his absent parent in an effort to alleviate the silent grief he feels. *Times Literary Supplement* reviewer Kathleen Jamie praised the book for its authentic vision of post-war Britain. "Pat Barker's talent is for people, period and dialogue; and in Colin she perfectly creates the mind of a 1950s twelve-year-old, a latch-key kid," the critic wrote.

Even more successfully, Barker turned to the history of World War I and wrote a trilogy of novels about mentally ill soldiers and the therapist who struggles with his own moral values while treating them. *Regeneration,* published in 1992, drew a wealth of acclaim on both continents. The novel follows Royal Army hero Siegfried Sassoon through his "treatment" at Craiglockhart War Hospital in Edinburgh in 1917. Sassoon has been sent to Craiglockhart after writing a letter denouncing his country's political motives in the conflict and refusing to suffer any more agonies on behalf of an ungrateful nation. His case is taken by Dr. William Rivers, an army psychologist who soon realizes the similarities between the stresses suffered by trench soldiers and those experienced by poor women on the home front.

In her *New Yorker* review of the work, Pierpont called *Regeneration* "an inspiring book that balances conscience and the vitality of change against a collapsing world—a book about voyages out." *New York Times Book Review* correspondent Samuel Hynes wrote that *Regeneration* "is an antiwar war novel, in a tradition that is by now an established one, though it tells a part of the whole story of war that is not often told—how war may batter and break men's minds—and so makes the madness of war more than a metaphor, and more awful. . . . Ms. Barker is a writer who is content to confront a cruel reality without polemics, without even visible anger and without evident artifice."

The Eye in the Door continues the saga of Dr. Rivers and his shell-shocked patients, this time focusing on a bisexual lieutenant named Billy Prior who suffers from bouts of amnesia. "*The Eye in the Door* succeeds as both historical fiction and as sequel," wrote Jim Shepard in the *New York Times Book Review*. "Its research and speculation combine to produce a kind of educated imagination that is persuasive and illuminating about this particular place and time." Shepard further noted, "Ms. Barker memorably renders the pride and fierce shame, bewilderment, humiliation, fear and icy self-disgust of those young men who, raised to venerate a concept of honor based on self-control, nevertheless broke down under the lunatic horror of trench warfare. She has a nicely understated sense of the apt detail that conveys their vulnerability and need, even as their self-esteem demands that they resolutely deny both." The critic concluded that the novel "is an impressive work, illuminating with compassion and insight the toll the war exacted from Britain's combatants and their world."

The third novel in the World War I trilogy, entitled *The Ghost Road*, was published in 1995 and received that year's Booker Prize for fiction. Both Rivers and Prior return, with Rivers employed at a hospital in London and Prior returning to the battlefront. *Times Literary Supplement* reviewer Peter Parker noted that the final installment in this story "amply fulfills the high expectations raised by its predecessors," and concluded: "*The Ghost Road* is a startlingly good novel in its own right. With the other two volumes of the trilogy, it forms one of the richest and most rewarding works of fiction of recent times. Intricately plotted, beautifully written, skillfully assembled,

tender, horrifying and funny, it lives on in the imagination, like the war it so imaginatively and so intelligently explores."

Barker the novelist has emerged from the trenches, so to speak, with a reputation that is growing in both Britain and America. Nixon noted, "Few novelists are so unsentimentally animated by people's ability to chalk up small, shaky, but estimable victories over remorseless circumstances. Readers come away from all her novels with an altered feeling for the boundaries and capacities of human courage. . . . With the exceptions of Angela Carter and Salman Rushdie, no British writer in the past twenty years has produced three novels to equal *Union Street, Blow Your House Down,* and *Regeneration*."

BIOGRAPHICAL/CRITICAL SOURCES:

BOOKS

Contemporary Literary Criticism, Volume 32, Gale (Detroit), 1985.

PERIODICALS

Atlantic, May, 1992, p. 128.
Boston Globe, April 12, 1992, p. B44; May 8, 1994, p. B16.
Encounter, September-October, 1984.
Forbes, July 18, 1994, p. 24.
Guardian, September 26, 1986.
Harper's, November, 1983.
London Review of Books, April 20, 1989, p. 20; October 21, 1993, p. 22.
Los Angeles Times, September 6, 1984; May 27, 1994, p. E6.
Los Angeles Times Book Review, April 12, 1992, p. 6.
Ms., January, 1984.
New Society, October 3, 1986.
New Statesman, May 14, 1982; June 8, 1984.
New Statesman and Society, March 3, 1989, pp. 45-6; May 31, 1991, p. 37; September 10, 1993, p. 40.
New Yorker, August 10, 1992, pp. 74-6; September 5, 1994, p. 111.
New York Times, December 8, 1990, p. A18; April 15, 1992, p. C21.
New York Times Book Review, October 2, 1983; October 21, 1984; December 21, 1986; March 29, 1992, pp. 1, 23; December 6, 1992, p. 89; May 15, 1994, p. 9.
Observer (London), May 30, 1982.
Publishers Weekly, September 21, 1984.
Spectator, August 4, 1984.
Times Literary Supplement, July 13, 1984; April 14, 1989, p. 404; August 9, 1995, pp. 4-5.
Tribune Books (Chicago), May 22, 1994, pp. 1, 9.
Village Voice, December 6, 1983; July 14, 1992, p. 91.
Voice Literary Supplement, September, 1984.

Washington Post, October 1, 1986; April 3, 1992, p. D1; May 20, 1994, p. C2.

Washington Post Book World, September 18, 1983; September 9, 1984.

*   *   *

BARRETT, C(harles) Kingsley 1917-

PERSONAL: Born May 4, 1917, in Salford, Lancashire, England; son of Fred (a Methodist minister) and Clara (Seed) Barrett; married Margaret Heap, August 16, 1944; children: Anne Penelope, Charles Martin Richard. *Education:* Cambridge University, B.A., 1938, M.A., 1942, B.D., 1948, D.D., 1956.

ADDRESSES: Home—22 Rosemount, Durham DH1 5GA, England.

CAREER: Methodist minister. Minister in Darlington, England, 1943; University of Durham, Durham, England, lecturer in theology, 1945-58, professor of divinity, 1958-82. Hewett Lecturer in the United States, 1961; Shaffer Lecturer at Yale University, 1965; Delitzsch Lecturer in Muenster, Germany, 1967; Cato Lecturer in Australia, 1969; Tate-Wilson Lecturer in Dallas, TX, 1975; McMain Lecturer in Ottawa, Ontario, 1976; Sanderson Lecturer in Australia, 1983; West-Watson Lecturer in New Zealand, 1983; Didsbury Lecturer in Manchester, England, 1983; visiting professor, Pittsburgh Theological Seminary, 1984; Woodruff Visiting Professor, Candler School of Theology, Emory University, 1986.

MEMBER: British Academy (fellow), British and Foreign Bible Society (vice president, 1963—), Society for Old Testament Study, Society of Biblical Literature (honorary member), Studiorum Novi Testamenti Societas (president, 1973-74).

AWARDS, HONORS: Burkitt Medal for Biblical studies, 1966; D.D. from University of Hull, 1970, and University of Aberdeen, 1972; Dr. Theol. from University of Hamburg, 1981; von Humboldt Forschungspreis, 1988.

WRITINGS:

The Holy Spirit and the Gospel Tradition, Macmillan (London), 1947.

The Gospel According to St. John, Macmillan, 1955, 2nd edition, S.P.C.K. (London), 1978.

(Editor and reviser) Wilbert Francis Howard, *Fourth Gospel in Recent Criticism and Interpretation,* 4th edition, Epworth (London), 1955.

(Editor) *The New Testament Background: Selected Documents,* S.P.C.K., 1956, Macmillan, 1957, 2nd edition, S.P.C.K., 1987.

Biblical Preaching and Biblical Scholarship, Epworth, 1957.

A Commentary on the Epistle to the Romans, A. & C. Black (London), 1957, Harper (New York City), 1958.

Westcott as Commentator, Cambridge University Press (Cambridge), 1959.

Yesterday, Today, and Forever: The New Testament Problem, University of Durham Press (Durham), 1959.

Luke, the Historian, in Recent Study, Epworth, 1961.

From First Adam to Last, Scribner (New York City), 1962.

The Pastoral Epistles in the New English Bible, Clarendon Press (Oxford), 1963.

Biblical Problems and Biblical Preaching, Fortress (Philadelphia), 1964.

History and Faith: The Story of the Passion, B.B.C. Publications, 1967.

Jesus and the Gospel Tradition, S.P.C.K., 1967, Fortress, 1968.

The First Epistle to the Corinthians, Fortress, 1968.

The Signs of an Apostle, Epworth, 1970.

Das Johannes-evangelium und das Judentum, Kohlhammer, 1970, translation by D. M. Smith published as *The Gospel of John and Judaism,* Fortress, 1975.

New Testament Essays, S.P.C.K., 1972.

A Commentary on the Second Epistle to the Corinthians, Harper (New York City), 1973.

Reading through Romans, Fortress, 1977.

(Editor) *Donum Gentilicium,* Oxford University Press, 1978.

Essays on Paul, S.P.C.K., 1982.

Essays on John, S.P.C.K., 1982.

Church, Ministry, and Sacraments in the New Testament, Paternoster Press, 1985.

Freedom and Obligation: A Study of the Epistle to the Galatians, S.P.C.K., 1985.

Paul: An Introduction to His Thought, Chapman (London), 1995.

A Critical and Exegetical Commentary on the Acts of the Apostles, T. & T. Clark (Edinburgh), 1995.

Also contributor to numerous joint volumes. Contributor of articles to various periodicals.

WORK IN PROGRESS: Researching the Acts of the Apostles and early Christian history.

*   *   *

BAUER, Marion Dane 1938-

PERSONAL: Born November 20, 1938, in Oglesby, IL; daughter of Chester (a chemist) and Elsie (a kindergarten teacher; maiden name, Hempstead) Dane; married Ronald C. Bauer (an Episcopal priest), June 25, 1959 (divorced December 27, 1987); children: Peter Dane, Elisabeth Alison. *Education:* La Salle-Peru-Oglesby Junior

College, A.A., 1958; attended University of Missouri, 1958-59; University of Oklahoma, B.A., 1962. *Politics:* Democrat. *Religion:* Episcopalian. *Avocational interests:* Camping, theater, cats.

ADDRESSES: Home—8861 Basswood Rd., Eden Prairie, MN 55344-7407.

CAREER: High school English teacher in Waukesha, WI, 1962-64; Hennepin Technical Center, Minneapolis, MN, instructor in creative writing for adult education program, 1975-78; instructor at University of Minnesota Continuing Education for Women, 1978-85, Institute of Children's Literature, 1982-85, and The Loft, 1986-93; Carnival Press, Minneapolis, editor, 1982-88.

MEMBER: Authors Guild, Authors League of America, Society of Children's Book Writers and Illustrators.

AWARDS, HONORS: American Library Association, Notable Childrens Book, 1976, for *Shelter from the Wind;* Society of Children's Book Writers, Golden Kite Honor Book, 1979, for *Foster Child;* Jane Addams Children's Book Award, Jane Addams Peace Association and Women's International League for Peace and Freedom, and Teachers' Choice Award, National Council of Teachers of English, all 1984, for *Rain of Fire;* Newbery Honor Book, American Library Association, Notable Childrens Book, *School Library Journal*'s best books of 1986, *Booklist* Editors' Choice, 1987, Flicker Tale Children's Book Award, 1989, and Golden Archer Award, 1989, all for *On My Honor;* Children's Book of Distinction, *Hungry Mind Review,* 1992, for *Face to Face;* Notable Children's Book citation, American Library Association, 1992, for *What's Your Story?: A Young Person's Guide to Writing Fiction;* American Booksellers Association, Pick of the Lists, and *School Library Journal*'s Best Books of 1994 citation, for *A Question of Trust;* American Library Association, Best Book for Young Adults and Recommended Book for Young Adult Readers, Minnesota Book Award for older children, and Gay-Lesbian-Bisexual Book Award for Literature, 1995, for *Am I Blue?: Coming Out from the Silence.*

WRITINGS:

JUVENILE NOVELS: EXCEPT AS NOTED

Shelter from the Wind, Clarion Books (Boston, MA), 1976.
Foster Child, Clarion Books, 1977.
Tangled Butterfly, Clarion Books, 1980.
Rain of Fire, Clarion Books, 1983.
Like Mother, Like Daughter, Clarion Books, 1985.
On My Honor, Clarion Books, 1986.
Touch the Moon (novella), Clarion Books, 1987.
A Dream of Queens and Castles, Clarion Books, 1990.
Face to Face, Clarion Books, 1991.

What's Your Story?: A Young Person's Guide to Writing Fiction (nonfiction; first book in trilogy; also see below), Clarion Books, 1992.
Ghost Eye (novella), Scholastic (New York City), 1992.
A Taste of Smoke, Clarion Books, 1993.
A Question of Trust, Scholastic, 1994.
(Editor and contributor) *Am I Blue?: Coming Out from the Silence* (short stories), HarperCollins (New York City), 1994.
When I Go Camping with Grandma (picture book; illustrated by Allen Garns), BridgeWater Books (Mahwah, NJ), 1995.
A Writer's Story, from Life to Fiction (nonfiction; second book in trilogy), Clarion Books, 1995.

Also author of *God's Tears: A Woman's Journey,* a chancel drama performed as a one-woman show. Contributor of short stories to anthologies. Also contributor of articles and short stories to periodicals, including, *Cricket, Alan Review, Writers' Journal, School Library Journal,* and *Boys' Life.*

JUVENILE GUIDEBOOK EDITOR

Paul J. Deegan, *Nashville, Tennessee,* Crestwood House (New York City), 1989.
Deegan, *New York, New York,* Crestwood House, 1989.
Nancy J. Nielsen, *Boundary Waters Canoe Area, Minnesota,* Crestwood House, 1989.
Sallie Stephenson, *Orlando, Florida,* Crestwood House, 1989.
Mary Turck, *Chicago, Illinois,* Crestwood House, 1989.
Turck, *Washington, DC,* Crestwood House, 1989.

WORK IN PROGRESS: A collection of stories written by students with commentary, entitled *Our Stories, A Fiction Workshop for Young Authors,* for Clarion; *Alison's Wings* and *Alison's Puppy* (easy readers), for Hyperion; *If You Were Born a Kitten* (picture book), for Simon & Schuster; *Turtle Dreams* (easy reader), for Kingfisher; and a tentatively titled fantasy novel, *Beyond the Wall,* for Scholastic.

SIDELIGHTS: An award-winning author, Marion Dane Bauer writes novels focusing on problems that young people face. Her novel *On My Honor,* for example, tells of an athletic rivalry between two school friends that leads to a tragic death. *A Question of Trust* concerns a boy's reaction to his parents' break-up, and *Face to Face* deals with a boy's struggle with accepting his new stepfather. Bauer's more recent fiction has introduced fantasy elements into her stories. *Ghost Eye,* for example, tells the story of a cat who can see ghosts. Bauer has also edited the anthology *Am I Blue?: Coming Out from the Silence,* the first young adult anthology of stories about gay and lesbian teenagers.

In the Newbery Honor Book *On My Honor,* Joel challenges his friend Tony to a swimming competition. Not wanting to confess that he cannot swim very well, Tony sets out for the sandbar and drowns when he is unable to fight against the current. *On My Honor* is based on a real incident from Bauer's own childhood, she once told *CA:* "Every one of my books draws from the core of my life and experience though none of them is autobiographical. *On My Honor* is the only one which comes directly from an actual occurrence, but it is based on something which happened to a friend of mine when we were both thirteen. (He and another boy, whom I did not know, went swimming in the Vermillion River near my home in Oglesby, Illinois. The other boy didn't swim, and he suddenly hit deep water and went under. My friend dived for him, repeatedly, but was unable to save him, and he went home afraid to tell anyone what had happened.) This is all I ever knew of the actual event, and from this knowledge come the central facts of the story. And yet the deeper story, the story of questions about responsibility and guilt, comes from a place no more mysterious than my own life and my own experience as a friend, as a parent, as a teacher and editor and writer of books."

In *A Question of Trust,* Brad's parents have broken up and his mother has left the family to live on her own in an apartment. Unable to forgive his mother for leaving him and his younger brother, Brad refuses to see or call his mother. When a stray cat has kittens in the family's shed, Brad and his brother help care for the cats behind their disapproving father's back. In the process, Brad comes to a greater understanding of his mother's actions and finally forgives her. *A Question of Trust,* the critic for *Horn Book* writes, "has powerful scenes, memorable, realistic characters, vivid dialogue, and palpable emotions."

Bauer again deals with a young person accepting a parent in the novel *Face to Face.* In this story, Michael Ostrom blames himself for his parents' divorce and idolizes his father, who now lives in another state. Because Michael cannot accept his stepfather, he jumps at the chance to visit his father for a vacation. But spending time with him only brings Michael to the realization that his father is a weak and unpleasant man. Upon his return home, he finally tries to reconcile himself with his stepfather. As Maeve Visser Knoth writes in *Horn Book,* "Bauer remains true to Michael's perspective, portraying characters as the boy sees them but painstakingly revealing the flaws in his vision as well."

Am I Blue? gathers together sixteen stories about gay and lesbian teenagers, all written by authors for young adults. Bauer edited the collection because she felt that many teenagers struggle with their sexual identities, some even attempting suicide in despair. *Am I Blue?,* writes Katherine Paterson in the *Washington Post Book World,* "will help them look at themselves and others with respect, humor, hope and, yes, love. When a book that sets out to do good turns out to be as good as this one, we are all the winners."

Bauer once told *CA:* "I write for children because there is a child in me who refuses to be subjugated into all the proper forms of adulthood. I write for children because such writing allows me to deal with all my old feeling issues in a context that approximates the original experience. I write for children because I figured, when I began, that if I wrote what was acceptable for children and managed to get published, I would still be acceptable to my parents and to my own children. I write for children because there is something in the inner workings of my brain which returns, always, to origins and to the form underlying form. I write for children because I like children, especially the twelve-year-olds I return to most often. They are so beautiful in that moment, so knowing and so innocent in the same breath. I write for children because I think children are important, not only for what they will be tomorrow—which is what they are usually trumpeted for—but for what they are today."

BIOGRAPHICAL/CRITICAL SOURCES:

BOOKS

Something about the Author Autobiography Series, Volume 9, Gale (Detroit), 1990.

PERIODICALS

Booklist, September 15, 1992, p. 148; January 15, 1994, p. 924; January 1, 1995, p. 824.
Horn Book, November-December, 1991, p. 74; spring, 1993, p. 55; January-February, 1994, p. 68; July, 1994, p. 448.
Lambda Book Report, January, 1994, p. 13.
Los Angeles Times Book Review, April 22, 1990, p. 12.
Publishers Weekly, March 16, 1990, p. 70; November 16, 1992, p. 25; September 27, 1993, p. 64; February 7, 1994, p. 88; May 2, 1994, p. 310.
Quill & Quire, January, 1992, p. 34.
School Library Journal, October, 1992, p. 112; April, 1993, p. 80.
Voice of Youth Advocates, February, 1994, p. 364; April, 1994, p. 22; August, 1994, p. 141.
Washington Post Book World, May 8, 1994, p. 22.
Wilson Library Bulletin, June, 1993, p. 104; September, 1994, p. 116.

* * *

BERRY, Wendell (Erdman) 1934-

PERSONAL: Born August 5, 1934, in Henry County, KY; married Tanya Amyx, May 29, 1957; children: Mary

Dee, Pryor Clifford. *Education:* University of Kentucky, A.B., 1956, M.A., 1957.

ADDRESSES: Home—Lanes Landing Farm, Port Royal, KY 40058.

CAREER: Writer and farmer. Stanford University, Stanford, CA, Wallace Stegner Writing Fellow, 1958-59, lecturer, 1959-60, visiting professor, 1968-69; New York University, New York City, lecturer, 1962-64; University of Kentucky, Lexington, member of faculty, 1964-70, distinguished professor of English, 1971-72, professor of English, 1973-77, 1987-93.

AWARDS, HONORS: Guggenheim Foundation fellow, 1961-62; Vachel Lindsay Prize, *Poetry* magazine, 1962; Bess Hokin Prize, *Poetry* magazine, 1967, for "Six Poems"; Rockefeller Foundation grant, 1967; first-place winner, Borestone Mountain Poetry Awards, 1969, 1970, 1972; National Institute of Arts and Letters Literary award, 1971; Friends of American Writers Award, 1975, for *The Memory of Old Jack;* Jean Stein Award, American Academy of Arts & Letters, 1987; Lannan Foundation Award for nonfiction, 1989; University of Kentucky Libraries Award for intellectual excellence, 1993; Aiken-Taylor Award for Poetry, *Sewanee Review,* 1994; T. S. Eliot Award, Ingersoll Foundation, 1994; honorary doctorates from Centre College, Transylvania College, Berea College, University of Kentucky, Santa Clara University, and Eureka College.

WRITINGS:

FICTION

Nathan Coulter: A Novel, Houghton (Boston), 1960, revised edition, North Point Press (Berkeley, CA), 1985.

A Place on Earth: A Novel, Harcourt (New York City), 1967, revised edition, North Point Press, 1983.

The Memory of Old Jack, Harcourt, 1974.

The Wild Birds: Six Stories of the Port William Membership, North Point Press, 1986.

Remembering: A Novel, North Point Press, 1988.

Fidelity: Five Stories (contains "Pray without Ceasing," "A Jonquil for Mary Penn," "Making It Home," "Fidelity," and "Are You All Right?"), Pantheon (New York City), 1992.

Watch with Me: And Six Other Stories of the Yet-Remembered Ptolemy Proudfoot and His Wife, Miss Minnie, nee Quinch, Pantheon, 1994.

POETRY

November Twenty-six Nineteen Hundred Sixty-Three, Braziller (New York City), 1964.

The Broken Ground, Harcourt, 1964.

Openings: Poems, Harcourt, 1968.

Findings, Prairie Press (Iowa City, IA), 1969.

Farming: A Handbook, Harcourt, 1970.

The Country of Marriage, Harcourt, 1973.

An Eastward Look (also see below), Sand Dollar (Berkeley, CA), 1974.

Reverdure: A Poem, Press at Colorado College (Colorado Springs, CO), 1974.

Horses, Larkspur Press (Monterey, KY), 1975.

To What Listens, Best Cellar Press (Crete, NE), 1975.

Sayings and Doings (also see below), Gnomon Press (Frankfort, KY), 1975.

The Kentucky River: Two Poems, Larkspur Press, 1976.

There Is Singing Around Me, Cold Mountain Press (Austin, TX), 1976.

Clearing, Harcourt, 1977.

Three Memorial Poems, Sand Dollar Books, 1977.

The Gift of Gravity (includes "The Gift of Gravity" and "Grief "), illustrated by Timothy Engelland, Deerfield Press (Old Deerfield, MA), 1979.

A Part, North Point Press, 1980.

The Salad, North Point Press, 1980.

The Wheel, North Point Press, 1982.

Collected Poems, 1957-1982, North Point Press, 1985.

Sabbaths, North Point Press, 1987.

Sayings and Doings [and] *An Eastward Look,* Gnomon Press, 1990.

Entries: Poems, Pantheon, 1994.

The Farm, Larkspur Press, 1995.

ESSAYS

The Rise, University of Kentucky Library Press (Lexington, KY), 1968.

The Long-Legged House (includes "The Tyranny of Charity," "The Landscaping of Hell: Strip-Mine Morality in East Kentucky," "The Nature Consumers," "The Loss of the Future: A Statement against the War in Vietnam," "Some Thoughts on Citizenship and Conscience in Honor of Don Pratt," "The Long-Legged House," and "A Native Hill"), Harcourt, 1969, portions reprinted as *A Native Hill,* introduction by Raymond D. Peterson, Santa Rosa Junior College (Santa Rosa, CA), 1976.

The Hidden Wound, Houghton, 1970, reprinted with a new afterword, North Point Press, 1989.

The Unforeseen Wilderness: An Essay on Kentucky's Red River Gorge, photographs by Ralph Eugene Meatyard, University Press of Kentucky (Lexington, KY), 1971, revised and expanded edition published as *The Unforeseen Wilderness: Kentucky's Red River Gorge,* North Point Press, 1991.

A Continuous Harmony: Essays Cultural and Agricultural (contains "A Secular Pilgrimage," "Notes from an Absence and a Return," "A Homage to Dr. Williams," "The Regional Motive," "Think Little,"

"Discipline and Hope," "In Defense of Literacy," and "Mayhem in the Industrial Paradise"), Harcourt, 1972.

Civilizing the Cumberland: A Commentary (bound with *Mountain Passes of the Cumberland,* by James Lane Allen), King Library Press (Lexington, KY), 1972.

(Contributor) James Lane Allen, *The Blue Grass Region of Kentucky, and Other Kentucky Articles,* Books for Libraries, 1972.

The Unsettling of America: Culture and Agriculture, Sierra Club Books (San Francisco, CA), 1977.

Recollected Essays, 1965-80 (includes "The Rise," "The Long-Legged House," "A Native Hill," "Nick and Aunt Georgie," "Discipline and Hope," "A Country of Edges," "An Entrance to the Woods," "The Unforeseen Wilderness," "The Journey's End," "The Body and the Earth," and "The Making of a Marginal Farm"), North Point Press, 1981.

The Gift of Good Land: Further Essays, Cultural and Agricultural, North Point Press, 1981.

Standing by Words: Essays, North Point Press, 1983.

(Editor with Wes Jackson and Bruce Colman) *Meeting the Expectations of the Land: Essays in Sustainable Agriculture and Stewardship,* North Point Press, 1984.

Home Economics: Fourteen Essays, North Point Press, 1987.

What Are People For?: Essays, North Point Press, 1990.

Sex, Economy, Freedom and Community: Eight Essays, Pantheon, 1993.

Another Turn of the Crank, Counterpoint Press, 1995.

OTHER

(With Meatyard and A. Gassan) *Ralph Eugene Meatyard,* Gnomon Press, 1970.

Wendell Berry Reading His Poems (sound recording), Archive of Recorded Poetry and Literature (Washington, DC), 1980.

Cancer in Colorado: A Report of the Colorado Central Cancer Registry, Colorado Central Cancer Registry, Colorado Department of Health (Denver), 1982.

The Landscape of Harmony, Five Seasons (Madley, Hereford, England), 1987.

Traveling at Home, wood engravings by John DePol, Bucknell University (Lewisberg, PA), 1988.

Harland Hubbard: Life and Work, University Press of Kentucky, 1990.

Also author of *Standing on Earth,* 1991. Contributing editor, *New Farm Magazine* and *Organic Gardening and Farming.* Contributor to periodicals, including *Nation, New World Writing, New Directions Annual, Prairie Schooner, Contact, Chelsea Review,* and *Quarterly Review of Literature.*

SIDELIGHTS: Wendell Berry is acknowledged as a master of many literary genres, but whether he is writing poetry, prose, or essays, his message is always essentially the same: humans must learn to live in harmony with the natural rhythms of the earth or perish. His *The Unsettling of America: Culture and Agriculture,* which analyzes the many failures of modern, mechanized life, is one of the key texts of the environmental movement, but Berry, a political maverick, has criticized environmentalists as well as those involved with big business and land development. In his opinion, many environmentalists place too much emphasis on wild lands without acknowledging the importance of agriculture to our society. Berry strongly believes that small-scale farming is essential to healthy local economies, and that strong local economies are essential to the survival of the species and the well-being of the planet. In an interview with *New Perspectives Quarterly* editor Marilyn Berlin Snell, Berry explained: "Today, local economies are being destroyed by the 'pluralistic,' displaced, global economy, which has no respect for what works in a locality. The global economy is built on the principle that one place can be exploited, even destroyed, for the sake of another place."

Berry further believes that traditional values, such as marital fidelity and strong community ties, are essential for the survival of humankind. In his view, the disintegration of communities can be traced to the rise of agribusiness—large-scale farming under the control of giant corporations. Besides relying on chemical pesticides and fertilizers, promoting soil erosion, and causing depletion of ancient aquifers, agribusiness has driven countless small farms out of existence and destroyed local communities in the process. In the *New Perspectives Quarterly* interview, Berry declared that this is morally as well as environmentally unacceptable: "We must support what supports local life, which means community, family, household life—the moral capital our larger institutions have to come to rest upon. If the larger institutions undermine the local life, they destroy that moral capital just exactly as the industrial economy has destroyed the natural capital of localities—soil fertility and so on. Essential wisdom accumulates in the community much as fertility builds in the soil."

Berry's themes are reflected in his life. As a young man, he spent time in California, Europe, and New York City. Eventually, however, he returned to the Kentucky land that had been settled by his forebears in the early nineteenth century. He taught for many years at the University of Kentucky, but eventually resigned in favor of full-time farming. He uses horses to work his land and employs organic methods of fertilization and pest control; he has also worked as a contributing editor to *New Farm Magazine* and *Organic Gardening and Farming,* which have published his poetry as well as his agricultural treatises.

It was as a poet that Berry first gained literary recognition. In volumes such as *The Broken Ground, Openings: Poems, Farming: A Handbook,* and *The Country of Marriage,* he wrote of the countryside, the turning of the seasons, the routines of the farm, and the life of the family. Reviewing *Collected Poems, 1957-1982, New York Times Book Review* contributor David Ray calls Berry's style "resonant" and "authentic," and claims that Berry "can be said to have returned American poetry to a Wordsworthian clarity of purpose. . . . There are times when we might think he is returning us to the simplicities of John Clare or the crustiness of Robert Frost. . . . But, as with every major poet, passages in which style threatens to become a voice of its own suddenly give way, like the sound of chopping in a murmurous forest, to lines of power and memorable resonance. Many of Mr. Berry's short poems are as fine as any written in our time."

But it was Berry's essays that brought him to a much broader readership. In one of his most popular early collections, *The Unsettling of America: Culture and Agriculture,* Berry argues that agriculture is the foundation of our greater culture. He makes a strong case against the U.S. government's agricultural policy, which promotes practices leading to overproduction, pollution, and soil erosion. *Dictionary of Literary Biography* contributor Leon V. Driskell calls *The Unsettling of America* "an apocalyptic book that places in bold relief the ecological and environmental problems of the American nation." Another essay collection, *Recollected Essays, 1965-1980,* has been compared to Henry David Thoreau's *Walden.* Charles Hudson, writing in the *Georgia Review,* notes that "like Thoreau, one of Berry's fundamental concerns is working out a basis for living a principled life. And like Thoreau, in his quest for principles Berry has chosen to simplify his life, and much of what he writes about is what has attended this simplification, as well as a criticism of modern society from the standpoint of this simplicity." In his most recent collection, *Sex, Economy, Freedom and Community: Eight Essays,* Berry continues to berate those who carelessly exploit the natural environment and damage the underlying moral fabric of communities. David Rains Wallace declares in the *San Francisco Review of Books:* "There's no living essayist better than Wendell Berry. His prose is exemplary of the craftsmanship he advocates. It's like master cabinetry or Shaker furniture, drawing elegance from precision and grace from simplicity." Wallace allows that at times, "Berry may overestimate agriculture's ability to assure order and stability," yet he maintains that the author's "attempts to integrate ecological and agricultural thinking remain of the first importance."

Farming and community are central to Berry's fiction as well as his poetry and essays. Most of his novels and short stories are set in the fictional Kentucky town of Port William. Like his real-life home town, Port Royal, Port William is a long-established farming community situated near the confluence of the Ohio and Kentucky Rivers. In books such as *Nathan Coulter, A Place on Earth,* and *The Wild Birds: Six Stories of the Port William Membership,* Berry presents the lives of seven generations of farm families. Most of the narratives occur in the first half of the twentieth century; as *Dictionary of Literary Biography* contributor Gary Tolliver explains, "this represents the final days of America's traditional farm communities just prior to the historically critical period when they began to break apart under the influence of technological and economic forces at the end of World War II." Connecting all the stories is the theme of stewardship of the land, which Tolliver says is "often symbolized as interlocking marriages between a man and his family, his community, and the land." *Fidelity: Five Stories* brings the story of Port William up to date, as it examines the community in the early 1990s. What emerges, *Los Angeles Times Book Review* contributor Noel Perrin argues "is a wounded but still powerful culture." Berry's writing style varies greatly from one book to the next. *Nathan Coulter,* for example, is an example of the highly stylized, formal, spare prose that dominated the late 1950s, while *A Place on Earth* is described by Tolliver as "long, brooding, episodic" and "more a document of consciousness than a conventional novel." Critics generally have found favor with Berry's fiction, both for the quality of his prose and for the way he brings his concerns for farming and community to life in his narratives. As Gregory L. Morris states in *Prairie Schooner:* "Berry places his emphasis upon the *rightness* of relationships—relationships that are elemental, inherent, inviolable. . . . Berry's stories are constructed of humor, of elegy, of prose that carries within it the cadences of the hymn. The narrative voice most successful in Berry's novels . . . is the voice of the elegist, praising and mourning a way of life and the people who have traced that way in their private and very significant histories."

Considering Berry's body of work, Charles Hudson marvels at the author's versatility and praises him for his appreciation of the plain things in life. "In an age when many writers have committed themselves to their 'specialty'—even though doing so can lead to commercialism, preciousness, self-indulgence, social irresponsibility, or even nihilism—Berry has refused to specialize," Hudson writes in the *Georgia Review.* "He is a novelist, a poet, an essayist, a naturalist, *and* a small farmer. He has embraced the commonplace and has ennobled it." Pondering Berry's message of responsibility to the land, Larry Woiwode states in the *Washington Post Book Review:* "If one were to distill the thrust of his thought, it might be, All land is a gift, and all of it is good, if we only had the eyes to see that. . . ." Berry, Woiwode continues, is "speaking with calm and sanity out of the wilderness. We would do well to hear him.''

BIOGRAPHICAL/CRITICAL SOURCES:

BOOKS

Angyal, Andrew J., *Wendell Berry*, Twayne (Boston), 1995.

Contemporary Literary Criticism, Gale (Detroit), Volume 4, 1975, Volume 6, 1976, Volume 27, 1984, Volume 46, 1988.

Dictionary of Literary Biography, Gale, Volume 5: *American Poets since World War II*, 1980, Volume 6: *American Novelists since World War II*, 1980.

Merchant, Paul, editor, *Wendell Berry*, Confluence (Lewiston, ID), 1991.

PERIODICALS

American Spectator, December, 1990, pp. 51-52.

Best Sellers, December 1, 1970, pp. 374-75.

Boston University Journal, Volume 25, no. 3, 1978, pp. 69-72.

Christian Science Monitor, July 3, 1987, pp. B1, B8; March 2, 1984, p. B4.

Commonweal, June 6, 1986, pp. 345-46; October 12, 1990, p. 582-84.

Georgia Review, spring, 1982, pp. 220-23; winter, 1977-78, pp. 579-81; summer, 1982, pp. 341-47.

Hudson Review, winter, 1986, pp. 681-94; summer, 1993, pp. 395-402.

Iowa Review, winter, 1979, pp. 99-104.

Los Angeles Times Book Review, April 27, 1986, p. 6; November 6, 1988, p. 4; January 10, 1993, p. 8.

Nation, November 9, 1970, pp. 472-74; May 3, 1986, pp. 626-27.

National Review, November 14, 1967.

New Perspectives Quarterly, spring, 1992, pp. 29-34.

New York, May 3, 1986, pp. 626-27.

New York Review of Books, June 14, 1990, pp. 30-34.

New York Times Book Review, September 25, 1977; December 20, 1981; December 18, 1983, p. 8, 16; November 24, 1985, pp. 28-29; April 13, 1986, p. 22; September 27, 1987, p. 30; January 1, 1989, p. 14; November 15, 1992, p. 20; October 17, 1993.

Parabola, fall, 1993.

Parnassus: Poetry in Review, spring/summer, 1974; fall, 1981, pp. 131-54; January, 1989, pp. 317-30.

Partisan Review, Volume 44, no. 2, 1977, p. 317.

Poetry, May, 1974; October, 1985, pp. 40-42; April, 1988, pp. 37-38.

Prairie Schooner, fall, 1971, pp. 273-74; winter, 1986, pp. 102-104.

Renascence, summer, 1983, pp. 258-68.

San Francisco Review of Books, winter, 1988-89, pp. 49-50.

Sewanee Review, summer, 1974.

Shenandoah, autumn, 1969.

Southern Review, October, 1974, pp. 865-77; October, 1976, pp. 879-90; autumn, 1984, pp. 958-68.

Stand, autumn, 1993, p. 81.

Studies in Short Fiction, winter, 1994, pp. 117-18.

Times Literary Supplement, April 10, 1981, p. 416; June 26, 1987, p. 698.

Village Voice, December 23-29, 1981, p. 47.

Virginia Quarterly Review, spring, 1983, p. 62; spring, 1989, p. 56; summer, 1991, pp. 88-89.

Washington Post Book World, February 15, p. 8; January 1, 1982, p. 5; March 13, 1983, p. 10; November 24, 1993, p. C2.

*　　　*　　　*

BINCHY, Maeve 1940-

PERSONAL: Born May 28, 1940, in Dublin, Ireland; daughter of William T. (a lawyer) and Maureen (a nurse; maiden name, Blackmore) Binchy; married Gordon Thomas Snell (a writer and broadcaster), January 29, 1977. *Education:* University College, Dublin, B.A., 1960.

ADDRESSES: Home—London, England; and Dublin, Ireland. *Office*—*Irish Times*, 85 Fleet St., London EC4, England. *Agent*—Chris Green, 2 Barbon Close, Great Ormond St., London WC1 N3JX, England.

CAREER: Taught at Zion Schools, Dublin, Ireland; Pembroke School for Girls, Dublin, teacher, 1961-68; *Irish Times*, London, England, columnist, 1968—; writer.

AWARDS, HONORS: International Television Festival Golden Prague Award, Czechoslovak Television, Prague, and Jacobs Award, both 1979, for *Deeply Regretted By*.

WRITINGS:

NOVELS

Light a Penny Candle (Literary Guild dual selection), Century (London), 1982, Viking (New York City), 1983.

Echoes (Literary Guild alternate selection), Century, 1985, Viking, 1986.

Firefly Summer, Century, 1987, Delacorte (New York City), 1988.

Silver Wedding (Book-of-the-Month Club alternate selection), Century, 1988, Delacorte, 1989.

Circle of Friends (Book-of-the-Month Club main selection), Franklin Library (Franklin Center, PA), 1990.

The Glass Lake, Delacorte, 1995.

STORY COLLECTIONS

The Central Line: Stories of Big City Life (also see below), Quartet (London), 1978.

Victoria Line (also see below), Quartet, 1980.

Maeve Binchy's Dublin Four, Ward River Press (Swords, Ireland), 1982, published as *Dublin Four,* Century, 1983.

London Transports (contains *The Central Line: Stories of Big City Life* and *Victoria Line*), Century, 1983.

The Lilac Bus: Stories, Ward River Press, 1984, Delacorte, 1991.

The Copper Beech, Delacorte, and Orion (Dublin and London), 1992.

OTHER

End of Term (one-act play), produced in Dublin, Ireland, 1976.

My First Book (nonfiction), Irish Times Ltd. (Dublin), 1976.

The Half Promised Land (play), produced in Dublin, 1979, produced in Philadelphia, PA, at Society Hill Playhouse, 1980.

Deeply Regretted By (television screenplay), Radio Telefis Eireann, 1979.

Maeve's Diary (nonfiction), Irish Times Ltd., 1979.

Ireland of the Welcomes (television screenplay), Radio Telefis Eireann, 1980.

Contributor to books, including *Portrait of the Artist as a Young Girl,* edited by John Quinn, Methuen (London), 1986; and *Territories of the Voice: Contemporary Stories by Irish Women Writers,* edited by Louise DeSalvo, Kathleen Walsh D'Arcy, and Katherine Hogan, Beacon Press (Boston), 1989.

ADAPTATIONS: Echoes was made into a mini-series televised in Great Britain in 1988 and in the United States on Public Broadcasting Service in 1990.

WORK IN PROGRESS: Avoid Disappointment, a book of linked short stories.

SIDELIGHTS: Maeve Binchy is a versatile Irish writer whose best-selling novels have won her critical acclaim and an international following. Set most frequently in rural Ireland, Binchy's stories of family life and intimate friendships appeal to a predominantly female audience. A resident of both Dublin, Ireland, and London, England, Binchy—also a reporter of London daily life for the *Irish Times*—is praised as thorough in her storytelling and both astute and affectionate in her characterizations. Many of Binchy's female protagonists are women who take control of their lives in the midst of coping with such societal ills as alcoholism, adultery, and divorce. Critics note that although her writing sometimes lacks profundity, it transcends the superficiality frequently featured in popular romance novels through such subtle feminist undertones. "In 1963 we all played by the rules," commented Binchy to Cathy Edwards in the *San Francisco Review of Books.* "I want to write about people who make their own deci-

sions. Women of my generation were fooled a bit—maybe all women are."

Though best known for her novels, Binchy began her fiction writing career with short stories and plays. As she once told *CA:* "Because the kind of stories I used to write for the *Irish Times* had a fictional or almost dramatic element to them, sometimes I was approached by people in theater or television asking why didn't I try my hand at writing plays. And because I started everything in life a little bit later than everybody else (to be a cub journalist at twenty-eight was very old), I felt, OK, maybe at thirty-five, thirty-six, thirty-seven I could start to write plays as well." Dublin's Abbey Theatre encouraged new talent, and produced Binchy's *End of Term* in 1976. While one of her plays, *The Half Promised Land,* was eventually staged as far away as Philadelphia, Pennsylvania, Binchy would fare far better with her efforts at writing short fiction. Her collections *London Transports* (originally published in two volumes as *Central Line* and *Victoria Line*) and *Maeve Binchy's Dublin Four* focus on the tedium of city life and the individual plights of female protagonists. In *London Transports,* for example, the women are often dissatisfied in their relationships with men and drawn into the corruption of Binchy's seedy London. *Times Literary Supplement* contributor Helen Harris pointed out that though the themes of *London Transports* are often bleak, Binchy writes with "ease and buoyancy." Harris also declared that the author's "portrayal of the small skirmishes of day-to-day urban survival is enjoyable; her wry observation of the different layers of London life is uncomfortably acute."

Turning to a small rural town for the primary setting of her first novel, *Light a Penny Candle,* Binchy depicts the twenty-year friendship of Elizabeth White and Aisling O'Connor. The girls meet when Elizabeth, a ten-year-old Londoner, is sent by her parents to live with the O'Connor family in Ireland at the start of World War II. Together the two friends experience the joys and hardships of growing up, and their close relationship endures despite such ordeals as Elizabeth's difficulties with her uncaring parents once back in London, Aisling's love affair with a one-time boyfriend of Elizabeth's, and both women's failed marriages. As in many of Binchy's stories, the book's male characters are often presented as insensitive, noncommittal, and the source of the women's problems. "It's been a while since I've enjoyed such a loutish, incompetent, drunken, selfish collection of men in one novel," remarked Carol Sternhell in the *Village Voice.* The reviewer, on the other hand, found most of the female characters "practical, competent, and loving." Although some critics complained about what one reviewer writing in *Harper's* termed a "too heavy-handed and contrived" ending in which "one disaster after another comes crashing down too quickly," the novel received much praise. "With its barreling plot and clamorous characters, *Light a Penny Candle* is a lilting book," asserted Dennis Drabelle in the *Washington Post Book World*. Sternhell called the author's effort an "impressive first novel" and proclaimed that "Binchy's strength is in her honesty: she refuses to trim all edges to get us drunk on easy answers."

The characters' conflicts in Binchy's second novel, *Echoes,* also are not easily resolved. In the small resort town of Castlebay, Ireland, the citizens find themselves victims of poverty and a code of behavior that is both archaic and illiberal. An excerpt from the book depicting Castlebay appeared in Susan Dooley's *Washington Post* review: "People would never die of loneliness, as they might in a big English city; but attitudes could be cruel, and tolerance was low . . . families couldn't cope with what they called 'shame and disgrace.' " The protagonist of *Echoes,* Clare O'Brien, is a poor shopkeeper's daughter determined to surpass her family's inferior social status. Clare eventually attends a Dublin university and marries the son of the town doctor. Her endeavors are encouraged by Angela O'Hara, an unconventional teacher who, tied to Castlebay by an obligation to care for her ailing mother, wishes to help Clare leave the town behind. In the end Clare struggles with a bad marriage and discovers that she is not destined for a life outside of Castlebay. Carolyn See of the *Los Angeles Times* faulted *Echoes* for its somber message and stated, "Pity the women at home who read this—and believe it." See added, however, that "all of the sociological details of the town of Castlebay are right on the money."

In *Firefly Summer* Binchy, in the words of Michele Slung in the *New York Times Book Review,* "once again gives us rural Ireland, a frequently maddening yet ultimately seductive place that can render problems only in contrasting shades of old and new, past and present, strange and familiar." Patrick O'Neill, the story's main character, is an American millionaire who comes to the Irish town of Mountfern in the 1960s with the goal of converting a dilapidated manor house into a luxury hotel. His experience in a town made up of people who are either eager or reluctant to accept his business venture is the subject of the novel. Slung thought that *Firefly Summer* "is the best Binchy yet. . . . Here she does what she does best, which is to manufacture experience in which we fully share."

"With *Silver Wedding*," noted Robert Plunket in the *New York Times Book Review,* "Binchy tries something a little bit different, and as she does so you can sense a remarkably gifted writer beginning to flex her muscles." Instead of focusing on the dynamics of small-town life, in her fourth novel Binchy examines the personal conflicts of the members of one family and their friends. In the last chapter of the book, all of the characters unite for Deidre and

Desmond Doyle's twenty-fifth wedding anniversary party. The author devotes each of the previous chapters to one individual in the story, ultimately revealing the emotions, resentments, and ambitions of a cast of characters whose lives are all connected in some way. Plunket pointed out that the author's choice of "guilty secrets" as one theme of *Silver Wedding* left him "wish[ing] she'd come up with something a bit more clever," but he acknowledged that "Binchy is a wonderful student of human nature" and described the book as "an effortless pleasure to read."

The 1991 appearance of *Circle of Friends* marked the publication of another Binchy novel destined for bestsellerdom. Set in the 1950s, the book revolves around three young women with contrasting personalities who come of age and develop a close friendship while attending the University College in Dublin. Although Susan Isaacs suggested in the *New York Times Book Review* that "a cynical reader might reflect [that] this sort of fiction is so commonplace that the characters will be completely fungible," she lauded Binchy for portraying her protagonists as "modern women, each, in her own way, ambitious, intelligent, perceptive." Isaacs summed up the reason for Binchy's immense popularity when she declared that "the author doesn't daze the reader with narrative bombshells (or, for that matter, with brilliant language), but recounts ordinary events . . . with extraordinary straightforwardness and insight."

The short story collection *The Copper Beech* followed closely on the heels of *A Circle of Friends*. Published in 1992, it is a set of interlinking stories set in the small Irish village of Shancarrig, amid the triumphs and defeats, passion and perfidy of a generation of schoolchildren who grow up in the town during the 1940s and 1950s. The tree of the book's title stands in the center of the Midlands schoolyard, its bark bearing the inscribed initials of these children, and the many who came before them. The town drunk, the quiet young Catholic priest, Miriam Murphy, and the grocer's wife with the roving eye each make an appearance either center stage or in the chorus of one of the collection's stories. *The Copper Beech* "has its share of murder, adultery, alcoholism, unwanted pregnancies and lots more," Anne Tolstoi Wallach commented in the *New York Times Book Review*. "Bad things happen to good people, good things happen to bad people, but because this is the new Maeve Binchy it all comes right in the end."

The decade of the 1950s is once again the setting for *The Glass Lake,* a novel that recounts the affairs of the McMahon family. After her mother is presumed dead after her boat is found abandoned on Lough Glass and an unrecognizable body discovered several weeks later, 12-year-old Kit McMahon discovers what appears to be a suicide note. Kit burns the note unopened but is haunted by guilt.

Meanwhile, her mother has actually fled to London and the arms of a former boyfriend where she becomes a successful businesswoman. The meeting of mother and daughter a decade later lies at the crux of *The Glass Lake,* which Chris Chase, writing in *Cosmopolitan,* called "a wonderful old-fashioned melodrama, a morality tale in which we are warned that if you take up with a good-looking lounge lizard, you will live to regret it."

A resident of London for almost 15 years, Binchy now lives outside Dublin with husband and fellow writer Gordon Snell. "We have a lovely room with a long, long desk and two word processors," the novelist told *CA* when asked about living with another writer. "We get on perfectly well sitting beside each other. Just the sound of the keyboard and the printer is all we hear. If one of us doesn't like what the other has said, the rule is ten minutes of sulking time. . . . After that the sulks can be construed as being moody or difficult. . . . We're not perfect in our judgment of each other's work, but at least we're honest. And normally we're praising—but if we don't like something, we say it straight out."

Binchy told *People* magazine that the message within her novels and short stories is that once people take charge of their life, they can make things work out for the best. "And maybe that's a reassuring idea," she added. "I wouldn't like to be thought of as patting people on the head, but I wouldn't be at all offended by people who think my books are comforting."

BIOGRAPHICAL/CRITICAL SOURCES:

BOOKS

Bestsellers 90, Issue 1, Gale (Detroit), 1990, pp. 3-4.

PERIODICALS

British Book News, May 1986, p. 308.
Chicago Tribune, March 17, 1991, Sec. 6, p. 3; October 27, 1991, Sec. 14, pp. 3, 11.
Cosmopolitan, February 1995, p. 18.
Detroit Free Press, December 23, 1990.
Harper's, April 1983, pp. 75-76.
Los Angeles Times, February 6, 1986; January 14, 1991, p. E3.
New York Times Book Review, January 12, 1986, p. 20; September 18, 1988, p. 13; September 10, 1989, p. 18; December 30, 1990, p. 8; December 8, 1991, p. 22; December 29, 1992, p. 16.
People, December 14, 1992, pp. 34-35.
San Francisco Review of Books, winter 1992, pp. 6-7.
Times Educational Supplement, May 24, 1991, p. 38.
Times Literary Supplement, November 28, 1980, p. 1366; April 1, 1983, p. 324; March 30, 1984, p. 354.
Village Voice, May 17, 1983, p. 50.

Washington Post, January 17, 1986; September 11, 1989, p. D3; December 24, 1990, p. C3; November 7, 1991 p. C3.
Washington Post Book World, May 1, 1983, p. 10.*

*   *   *

BIRKS, Tony 1937-

PERSONAL: Born November 1, 1937, in Manchester, England; son of Edwyn Ainsworth (a publisher) and Nora Lilian (a writer) Birks; married Margaret Leslie Hay (an editor), July 14, 1972; children: Paul Raphael, Adam Nicholas. *Education:* University of London, D.F.A., 1958; St. Edmund Hall, Oxford, M.A., 1961; University of Grenoble, Premier Degree, 1964. *Avocational interests:* Tennis, sailing, theater.

ADDRESSES: Home and office—Marston House, Marston Magna, Yeovil, Somerset BA22 8DH, England.

CAREER: Oxford School of Art, Oxford, England, lecturer in ceramics and sculpture, 1959-63; Thames & Hudson (publisher), London, England, art editor, 1964-68; George Rainbird Ltd., London, sponsor editor, 1968-71; Alpha Books (then Alphabet & Image Ltd.), Sherborne, Dorset, managing director, 1972—. Alpha House Gallery, Sherborne, managing director, 1991-95. General editor, *Modern Ceramic Monographs,* Marston House.

MEMBER: The Arts Club (London).

AWARDS, HONORS: Slade sculpture prize, 1958; TV Westward award, 1973, for ceramics; National Book League award, 1980, for book design; Bookseller-Deloitte design prize, 1988.

WRITINGS:

The Art of the Modern Potter, Country Life Books, 1967, 2nd edition, Van Nostrand (Wokingham, England), 1977.
Building the New Universities, David & Charles (Newton Abbot, England), 1972.
The Potter's Companion, Dutton (New York City), 1974.
Meyer's Ornament, Duckworth (London), 1974.
(Contributor) Emmanuel Cooper and Eileen Lewenstein, editors, *New Ceramics,* Van Nostrand, 1974.
Outline Guide to Pottery, Blandford Press (Dorset, England), 1975.
Pottery: A Complete Guide, Pan Books (London), 1979, State Mutual Book, 1982.
Hans Coper, Harper (London), 1984.
Lucie Rie, Chilton (Radnor, PA), 1989.
The Complete Potter's Companion, Bulfinch, 1993.

WORK IN PROGRESS: A biography of William Dampier.

SIDELIGHTS: From serving as art editor of the student-run magazine *Isis* while a student at Oxford University, to his role as general editor of Modern Ceramic Monographs for Marston House publishers, author and artist Tony Birks has, throughout his writing career, been concerned with communicating the latest developments in the arts—painting, sculpture, ceramics, architecture—to a wide audience.

Birks once told *CA* that he is "interested in all forms of design of all periods, especially architecture and carpets."

BIOGRAPHICAL/CRITICAL SOURCES:

PERIODICALS

Times Literary Supplement, December 9, 1983.

*   *   *

BLASING, Randy 1943-

PERSONAL: Born July 27, 1943, in Minneapolis, MN; son of Alfred Charles (a businessman) and Mary (a bookkeeper; maiden name, Mathias) Blasing; married Mutlu Konuk (a professor), August 21, 1965; children: John Konuk. *Education:* Carleton College, B.A., 1965; University of Chicago, M.A., 1966.

ADDRESSES: Home—44 Benefit Street, Providence, RI 02904. *Office*—Copper Beach Press, English Department, P.O. Box 1852, Brown University, Providence, RI 02912.

CAREER: Randolph-Macon College, Ashland, VA, instructor in English, 1966-67; College of William and Mary, Williamsburg, VA, instructor in English, 1967-69; Community College of Rhode Island, Lincoln, instructor, 1969-72, assistant professor, 1972-80, associate professor, 1980-88, professor of English, 1988—. Lecturer at Pomona College, 1977-79.

AWARDS, HONORS: National Endowment for the Arts fellow, 1981; Ingram Merrill fellow, 1989.

WRITINGS:

Light Years: Poems, Persea (New York City), 1977.
To Continue: Poems, Persea, 1983.
The Particles: Poems, Copper Beech Press (Providence, RI), 1983.
The Double House of Life: Poems, Persea, 1989.
Graphic Scenes, Persea, 1994.

TRANSLATOR; WITH WIFE, MUTLU KONUK BLASING

Things I Didn't Know I Loved: Selected Poems of Nazim Hikmet, Persea, 1975.
Hikmet, *The Epic of Sheik Bedreddin and Other Poems,* Persea, 1977.
Hikmet, *Human Landscapes,* Persea, 1982.

Hikmet, *Rubaiyat,* Copper Beech Press, 1985.
Hikmet, *Selected Poetry,* Persea, 1986.
Poems of Nazim Hikmet, Persea, 1994.

OTHER

Contributor of poems and translations to magazines, including *American Poetry Review, Paris Review, Virginia Quarterly, The Southern Review, Michigan Quarterly Review,* and *Poetry.* Editor of Copper Beach Press, 1983—.

*   *   *

BLIXEN, Karen (Christentze Dinesen) 1885-1962 (Pierre Andrezel, Isak Dinesen, Osceola)

PERSONAL: Born Christentze Dinesen on April 17, 1885, in Rungsted, Denmark; died September 7, 1962, of emaciation in Rungsted; daughter of Wilhelm (an army officer and writer under his own name and his Indian name Boganis) and Ingeborg (Westenholz) Dinesen; married Baron Bror Blixen-Finecke (a big-game hunter and writer), January 14, 1914 (divorced, 1921). *Education:* Studied English at Oxford University, 1904; studied painting at Royal Academy in Copenhagen, in Paris, 1910, and in Rome.

ADDRESSES: Home—Rungstedlund, Rungsted Kyst, Denmark.

CAREER: Writer, 1907-62, from 1934 writing in English and translating her own work into Danish. With husband, Baron Blixen, managed a coffee plantation in British East Africa (now Nairobi, Kenya), 1913-21, assumed management herself until failing coffee prices forced relinquishing farm in 1931. Commissioned by three Scandinavian newspapers to write a series of twelve articles on wartime Berlin, Paris, and London, 1940.

MEMBER: American Academy of Arts and Letters (honorary member), National Institute of Arts and Letters (honorary member), Bayerische Akademie der Schoenen Kuenste (corresponding member), Danish Academy (founding member), Cosmopolitan Club (New York).

AWARDS, HONORS: Ingenio et Arti Medal from King Frederick IX of Denmark, 1950; The Golden Laurels, 1952; Hans Christian Andersen Prize, 1955; Danish Critics' Prize, 1957; Henri Nathansen Memorial Fund award, 1957.

WRITINGS:

ALL PUBLISHED IN DANISH UNDER NAME KAREN BLIXEN AND IN ENGLISH UNDER PSEUDONYM ISAK DINESEN

Sandhedens Haevn (play; title means "The Revenge of Truth"; produced at Royal Theatre, Copenhagen,

1936), [Tilskueren], 1926, Gyldendal (Copenhagen), 1960.

Seven Gothic Tales (Book-of-the-Month Club selection), Smith & Haas, 1934, Danish translation published as *Syv Fantastiske Fortaellinger,* Reitzels (Copenhagen), 1935.

Out of Africa (also see below; Book-of-the-Month Club selection), Putnam (London), 1937, Random House (New York City), 1938, with illustrations, Crown (New York City), 1987, as *The Illustrated Out of Africa,* Cresset Press (London), 1989, Danish translation published as *Den Afrikanske Farm,* Gyldendal, 1937.

Winter's Tales (Book-of-the-Month Club selection), Random House, 1942, Danish translation published as *Vinter-Eventyr,* Gyldendal, 1942.

Om revtskrivning 23-24 marts 1938, Gyldendal, 1949.

Farah, Wivel (Copenhagen), 1950.

Daguerreotypier (two radio talks presented January 1951), Gyldendal, 1951.

Babettes Gaestebud (first published in English as "Babette's Feast," in *Ladies' Home Journal*), Fremad (Copenhagen), 1952; with other stories as *Anecdotes of Destiny* (also see below), Random House, 1958, Danish translation published as *Skaebne-Anekdoter,* Gyldendal, 1958; as *Babette's Feast, and Other Anecdotes of Destiny,* edited by Martha Levin, Vintage (New York City), 1988.

Omkring den Nye Lov om Dyreforsoeg, Politikens Forlag (Copenhagen), 1952.

Kardinalens tredie Historie (title means "The Cardinal's Third Tale"), Gyldendal, 1952.

En Baaltale med 14 Aars Forsinkelse (title means "Bonfire Speech Fourteen Years Delayed"), Berlingske Forlag (Copenhagen), 1953.

Spoegelseshestene, Fremad, 1955.

Last Tales, Random House, 1957, Danish translation published as *Sidste Fortaellinger,* Gyldendal, 1957.

Skygger paa Graesset, Gyldendal, 1960, published as *Shadows on the Grass* (also see below; Book-of-the-Month Club selection), Random House, 1961.

(Author of introduction) Truman Capote, *Holly* (Danish translation of *Breakfast at Tiffany's*), Gyldendal, 1960.

(Author of introduction) Olive Schreiner, *The Story of an African Farm,* Limited Editions Club, 1961.

On Mottoes of My Life (originally published in *Proceedings of The American Academy of Arts and Letters and The National Institute of Arts and Letters,* Second Series, Number 10, 1960), Ministry of Foreign Affairs (Copenhagen), 1962.

(Author of introduction) Hans Christian Andersen, *Thumbelina, and Other Stories,* Macmillan (New York City), 1962.

Osceola (collection of early stories and poems), Gyldendal, 1962.

(Author of introduction) Basil Davidson, *Det Genfundne Africa,* Gyldendal, 1962.

Ehrengard (also see below), Random House, 1963, Danish translation by Clara Svendsen, Gyldendal, 1963.

Karen Blixen (memorial edition of principal works), Gyldendal, 1964.

Essays, Gyldendal, 1965, expanded edition published as *Mitlivs mottoer og andre essays,* 1978.

Efterladte Fortallinger, Gyldendal, 1975.

Carnival: Entertainments and Posthumous Tales, Danish portions translated by P. M. Mitchell and W. D. Paden, University of Chicago Press, 1977.

Breve fra Afrika, Volume I: 1914-1924, Volume II: 1925-1931, Gyldendal, 1978, published as *Letters from Africa, 1914-1931,* edited by Frans Lasson and translated by Anne Born, University of Chicago Press, 1981.

Daguerreotypes and Other Essays, Danish portions translated by P. M. Mitchell and W. D. Paden, University of Chicago Press, 1979.

'Det droemmende barn' og andre fortaellinger, Gyldendal, 1979.

Modern aegteskab og andre betragtninger, Gyldendal, 1981, published as *On Modern Marriage: And Other Observations,* St. Martin's (New York City), 1986.

Isak Dinesen's Africa: Images of the Wild Continent from the Writer's Life and Words, Sierra Books (San Francisco), 1985.

Samlede essays, Gyldendal, 1985.

Out of Africa [and] *Shadows on the Grass,* Vintage, 1985.

Anecdotes of Destiny [and] *Ehrengard,* Vintage, 1985.

Karyatiderne en ufuldendt historie, edited by Sonia Brandes, Gyldendal, 1993.

PUBLISHED UNDER PSEUDONYM PIERRE ANDREZEL

Gengaeldelsens Veje, Danish translation by Clara Svendsen, Gyldendal, 1944, published as *The Angelic Avengers* (Book-of-the-Month Club selection), Random House, 1946.

OTHER

Contributor of short stories, articles, and reviews to *Atlantic, Botteghe Oscure, Harper's Bazaar, Heretica, Ladies' Home Journal, Saturday Evening Post, Tilskueren,* and *Vogue,* sometimes under the pseudonym Osceola.

ADAPTATIONS: The Immortal Story was adapted as a motion picture directed by Orson Welles, Altura, 1969; *Out of Africa,* a film adaptation by Kurt Luedtke loosely based on *Out of Africa* and *Letters from Africa,* was filmed by director Sydney Pollack, Universal, 1985; "Babette's Feast" was filmed by director Gabriel Axel, Orion Pictures, 1987; it received the 1987 Academy Award for best foreign-language film. Dinesen herself recorded excerpts from her books for Gyldendal, and made two films, consisting of readings, for *Encyclopaedia Britannica.* Irene Worth made a sound recording of "The Old Chevalier" in 1978; several works have been recorded as books-on-tape.

SIDELIGHTS: Karen Blixen, better known by her pen name Isak Dinesen, remains one of Denmark's most widely acclaimed modern authors. A prose stylist who wrote skillfully in English as well as in her native Danish, Dinesen composed exotic and archaic tales that set her apart from the literary traditions of her day. Although initially snubbed by critics in her native country, she enjoyed both critical and commercial success in Britain and the United States and was twice nominated for the Nobel Prize. In addition to her considerable literary contributions, Dinesen is perhaps equally well known for her remarkable life, documented in such autobiographical works as *Out of Africa* and *Shadows on the Grass.* As David Lehman noted in *Newsweek:* "She likened herself to Scheherazade—and fully lived up to the name. . . . [leading] a life as wildly improbable and flamboyantly romantic as her exotic and spellbinding tales."

Born Christenze Dinesen on April 17, 1885, in Rungsted, Denmark, in a seaside house once inhabited by Johannes Ewald (1743-1781), Dinesen was widely considered Denmark's greatest lyric poet. She led a happy childhood until tragedy shattered her comfortable existence. In 1895 her father, Wilhelm, hung himself. Dinesen had always been very close to her father, and his suicide was a shock. "I was ten years old when father died. His death was for me a great sorrow, of a kind which probably only children feel," she wrote in *Daguerreotypes and Other Essays.* According to Parmenia Migel in *Titania: The Biography of Isak Dinesen,* Dinesen later reflected: "It was as if a part of oneself had also died . . . the desolate feeling that there was no one to remember the talks on Ewald's Hill . . . suddenly one was pushed into the foremost row of life, bereft of the joy and irresponsibility of childhood." Dinesen's brother Thomas, with whom she remained close as an adult, later speculated that their father had suffered from syphilis, a disease that Dinesen herself would contract years later.

Tutored at home by a series of governesses, Dinesen showed early artistic promise and as a teenager studied drawing, painting, and languages at a private school in France. In 1903, after a series of comprehensive exams, she was admitted into the Royal Academy of Fine Arts in Copenhagen. There she developed her affinity for painting, an affinity that would later be reflected in the rich descriptive style of her writing. According to Judith Thurman in *Isak Dinesen: The Life of a Storyteller,* Dinesen later wrote: "[I owe painting] . . . for revealing the nature

of reality to me. I have always had difficulty seeing how a landscape looked, if I had not first got the key to it from a great painter. I have experienced and recognized a land's particular character where a painter has interpreted it to me. Constable, Gainsborough and Turner showed me England. When I travelled to Holland as a young girl, I understood all the landscape and the cities said because the old Dutch painters did me the kind service of interpreting it." Dinesen dropped out of the Academy several years later and soon thereafter took up writing. Between 1904 and 1908 she wrote the first draft of a puppet play entitled "The Revenge of Truth," as well as a series of tales she called "Likely Stories." Mario Krohn, an art historian Dinesen had met at the Academy, read her work and encouraged Dinesen to take her writing seriously. Krohn also arranged to have some of her stories read by Valdemar Vedel, editor of one of Denmark's most distinguished literary magazines, *Tilskueren.* According to Thurman, Vedel wrote to Krohn that one of Dinesen's tales, "The Hermits," was "so original . . . and so well made that I would like to take it for *Tilskueren.*" The tale was published in 1907 under the pseudonym Osceola. Two years later Krohn himself became editor of *Tilskueren* and accepted Dinesen's story "The de Cats Family" in 1909.

During these years Dinesen spent much of her time in the company of her upper-class relatives, and soon found herself deeply but unhappily involved with her second cousin, Hans Blixen-Finecke. The failed love affair had a great impact on Dinesen. According to Thurman she later recalled: "More than anything else, a deep, unrequited love left its mark on my early youth." Extremely depressed, Dinesen left Denmark in 1910 to attend a new art school in Paris. Thurman relates that when Mario Krohn visited Dinesen in Paris and asked her about her literary ambitions she answered that she wanted "all things in life more than to be a writer—travel, dancing, living, the freedom to paint." When she returned to her family estate at Rungstedlund several months later, Dinesen turned to writing as a diversion, revising "The Revenge of Truth" and composing early versions of tales such as "Carnival" and "Peter and Rosa."

A voyage to Rome two years later did little to assuage her depression over her unrequited love, and upon her return Dinesen shocked her family and friends by announcing that she was to marry Hans's twin brother, Bror Blixen. Based on advice from relatives, the engaged couple decided to go to Africa, then thought to be a land of opportunity and excitement for young people with initiative. In 1913 Bror Blixen left for British East Africa and, with capital provided largely by Dinesen's family, purchased a six-thousand-acre coffee plantation outside of Nairobi, Kenya. The following January Dinesen joined the Baron; the two were married on the fourteenth of that month. Dinesen would not return to writing fiction for many years, but 1914 marks the beginning of her letters to her family and friends, correspondence later compiled and published as *Letters from Africa.*

The early months in Africa passed well. Dinesen enjoyed living on the plantation and accompanying her husband on safari. She was also taken with her African servants, particularly her cook, Farah, who went on to become Dinesen's friend and confidant. During her time in Africa she socialized with the upper-class Europeans living there, many of whom would become models for characters in Dinesen's tales. However, several months after her arrival in Kenya, Dinesen began to suffer from what she believed to be malaria but which later turned out to be a case of syphilis contracted from her husband. To receive treatment, she returned to Europe. Although the primary syphilis was arrested, Dinesen was to suffer the lingering effects of the disease throughout her life.

The next years were difficult ones for Dinesen, both personally and financially. The philandering Baron embarked on extended safaris, ignoring his duties to both the farm and his wife. Meanwhile, despite her family's continued financial support, the coffee farm was losing large amount of money. Forced to return to Denmark for treatment of blood poisoning, Dinesen confided her marital problems to her mother and brother Thomas. These problems, combined with the ongoing financial setbacks on the farm, caused Bror's dismissal and Dinesen's appointment as the sole manager of what became known as the Karen Coffee Company. Although her family urged divorce, Dinesen agreed only to a separation from the Baron. "I would never demand a divorce or try to push it through against Bror's will. I do not know how anyone can do that unless one is quite frenzied; and even though I have occasionally been angry with Bror or, rather, perhaps, in despair over his behavior, there is far, far too much binding us together from all the years of difficulty we have shared here, for me to be able to take the initiative in putting an end to what, if nothing else, was a most intimate relationship. . . . In any case, it is my heartfelt hope that he will be happy . . . I feel for Bror, and will until I die, the greatest friendship or the deepest tenderness that I am capable of feeling," Dinesen explained in *Letters from Africa.* In the end, however, it was the Baron who requested and received the divorce.

About this time Dinesen met Denys Finch Hatton, a handsome English pilot and hunter who was to become her companion and lover as well as the first audience for her tales. During Finch Hatton's occasional, and often unannounced, visits, Dinesen would relate to her friend tales she had thought up during his absence. Dinesen liked to think of herself as a modern Scheherazade, weaving imaginative tales to lengthen Finch Hatton's visits.

In 1923, inspired by a debate between her mother and brother concerning sexual morality, Dinesen wrote a long essay entitled "On Modern Marriage and Other Considerations," her first formal writing effort in years. The following year she resubmitted "The Revenge of Truth" to *Tilskueren.* When it was accepted for publication the following year Dinesen wrote in *Letters from Africa:* "With regard to 'The Revenge of Truth.' I don't want anything in it changed; but I imagine there is little chance of it ever being published. I don't think there is anything blasphemous in it, simply that it is written from an atheist's viewpoint. I believe it would be impossible to write if one gave consideration to who is going to read one's work,—but for that matter I don't think I will be writing anything in the near future."

During the mid- and late 1920s the Karen Coffee Company suffered enormous financial setbacks, and it soon became clear that Dinesen would be forced to sell the farm. To alleviate her anxiety, she started writing down those fantastic tales she had recounted to Hatton during his stays. She later recalled in *Daguerreotypes and Other Essays:* "During my last months in Africa, as it became clear to me that I could not keep the farm, I had started writing at night, to get my mind off the things which in the daytime it had gone over a hundred times, and on a new track. My squatters on the farm, by then, had got into the habit of coming up to my house and sitting around it for hours in silence, as if just waiting to see how things would develop. I felt their presence there more like a friendly gesture than a reproach, but all the same of sufficient weight to make it difficult for me to start any undertaking of my own. But they would go away, back to their huts, at nightfall. And I sat there, in the house, alone, or perhaps with Farah, the infallibly loyal, standing motionless in his long white Arab robe with his back to the wall, figures, voices, and colors from far away or from nowhere began to swarm around my paraffin lamp." In such a manner, Dinesen wrote two of her *Seven Gothic Tales.* By 1931 the farm had been auctioned off. While awaiting her return to Denmark, Dinesen learned that Finch Hatton had been killed when his small plane crashed in Tanganyika. She looked on Africa for the last time in May of 1931.

Once home at Rungstedlund, Dinesen began to write almost immediately, working in her father's old office. Now, however, her motives were serious. "My home is a lovely place; I might have lived on there from day to day in a kind of sweet idyll; but I could not see any kind of future before me. And I had no money; my dowry, so to say, had gone with the farm. I owed it to the people on whom I was dependent to try to make some kind of existence for myself. Those Gothic Tales began to demand to be written," she later wrote in *Daguerreotypes and Other Essays.* Two years later, at age forty-eight, Dinesen completed her first collection of stories, *Seven Gothic Tales.*

Although *Seven Gothic Tales* was written in English, Dinesen experienced some difficulty getting the book into print; few publishers were willing to bet on a debut work by an unknown Danish author. Several British publishers rejected the manuscript before it came across the desk of Dorothy Canfield Fisher, a friend of Thomas Dinesen and member of the Book-of-the-Month Club selection committee. Impressed with the collection, Fisher sent it to publisher Robert Haas, who was equally impressed and released *Seven Gothic Tales* the following year.

An aura of mystery surrounded the book's publication. When it offered *Seven Gothic Tales* as its April 1934 selection, the Book-of-the-Month Club newsletter stated simply, "No clue is available as to the pseudonymic author." Dinesen herself confused matters by preceeding her maiden name with a man's first name—Isak, Hebrew for "one who laughs." Her true identity was not revealed until over fifty thousand copies of *Seven Gothic Tales* were in print. With this collection Dinesen began a long and rewarding relationship with American readers, as five of her books became Book-of-the-Month Club selections.

In *Seven Gothic Tales* Dinesen introduced stylistic and thematic motifs that are to be found throughout much of her subsequent work. She derived these motifs largely from two nineteenth-century literary movements—the Gothic and the decadent. As in the novels written in these genres, Dinesen's tales are often characterized by an emphasis on the emotional and spiritual, a nostalgia for the glory of past ages, a predilection for exotic characters, and an overriding sense of mystery, horror, and the supernatural. Eric O. Johannesson noted in *The World of Isak Dinesen* that "The spinechilling tale of terror, with its persecuted women, its ghosts, and its mysterious convents and castles, as well as the cruel tale, with its atmosphere of perversity and artificiality, have served as sources of inspiration for Dinesen." While critics clearly recognized Dinesen's debt to these traditions, several felt that Dinesen went beyond them. Langbaum maintained in *Isak Dinesen's Art: The Gayety of Vision* that she is "an important writer because she has understood the tradition behind her and has taken the next step required by that tradition. Like the other, more massive writers of her generation—Rilke, Kafka, Mann, Joyce, Eliot, Yeats, . . .—she takes off from the sense of individuality developed in the course of the nineteenth-century to the point of morbidity, and leads that individuality where it wants to go. She leads it back to a universal principle and a connection with the external world."

Seven Gothic Tales also introduces Dinesen's preoccupation with the principle of interdependence, which she fur-

ther develops in later works. In *Seven Gothic Tales* there are interrelationships among individual stories in the volume as well as the existence of stories within stories. Comparing such constructions to "a complex kaleidoscope," Elizabeth Ely Fuller wrote in the *New Boston Review* that "Each character and each event works as a little bit of mirror reflecting another character or event, and then turning slightly to catch some other reflection. To reinforce this overall plot structure, Dinesen uses mirror images and similes repeatedly as the characters muse on their own nature and on their relation to others. To any one of them, the story makes no sense, but taken as a whole, the stories, like a piece of music or a minuet, form a complete pattern of movement." The principle of interdependence works on a thematic level in *Seven Gothic Tales* as well, as such disparate concepts such as good and evil, comedy and tragedy, and art and life, are intricately linked.

In spite of poor health and repeated hospitalizations, Dinesen continued to work on a book of memoirs entitled *Out of Africa.* Considered by many to be the greatest pastoral romance of the twentieth century, *Out of Africa* enjoyed immediate and lasting critical acclaim, particularly from British and American critics. In a *Chicago Tribune* review, Richard Stern called the work "perhaps the finest book ever written about Africa," claiming that "it casts over landscape, animals, and people the kind of transfixing spell 'Ulysses' casts over Dublin." Katherine Woods, writing in the *New York Times,* praised the book's absence of "sentimentality" and "elaboration" and avers, "Like the Ngong hills—'which are amongst the most beautiful in the world'—this writing is without redundancies, bared to its lines of strength and beauty." Even those critics who found fault with the book's structure commended Dinesen's style. "The tale of increasing tragedy which fills the latter half of the book seems not quite so successful as her earlier chapters," noted Hassoldt Davis in the *Saturday Review of Literature.* "But," he added, "her book has a solid core of beauty in it, and a style as cadenced, constrained, and graceful as we have today." Hudson Strode seemed to capture the sentiments of many critics when he wrote in *Books:* "The author casts enchantment over her landscape with the most casual phrases. . . . Backward, forward, she goes, a spark here, a flare there, until she has the landscape fairly lit up before you with all its inhabitants and customs in place. The result is a great naturalness."

Letters from Africa, the posthumously published compilation of Dinesen's correspondence with her family and friends, sheds a good deal of light on *Out of Africa.* Begun soon after her arrival to Africa in 1914, these letters provide the private, often painful story behind the romantic vision of life presented in her famous memoir. As these letters show, Dinesen endured a number of hardships during her seventeen years in Africa. Lingering bouts of illness, marital problems, increasing loneliness, and financial worries all caused her despair. But, despite their painful revelations, there were intermittent periods of happiness, even elation. This is particularly evident in Dinesen's descriptions of her growing attachment to the land of Africa and its people. "Immediately after lunch, Bror and I drove by car to our own farm. It is the most enchanting road you can imagine, like our own Deer Park, and the long blue range of Ngong Hills stretching out beyond it. There are so many flowering trees and shrubs, and a scent rather like bog myrtle, or pine trees, pervades everything. Out here it is not hot at all, the air is so soft and lovely, and one feels so light and free and happy," Dinesen wrote in one of her early entries in *Letters from Africa.*

Letters from Africa follows Dinesen's development from naive bride to able plantation manager to financially ruined-but-unembittered divorcee. Remarked Kathleen Chase in *World Literature Today:* "We see Dinesen unmasked in all her moods and emotions, prejudices and predilections, her thoughts, her periodic nostalgia for Denmark (always flying the Danish flag) and her idyllic relationship with the English safari leader Denys Finch Hatton." Indeed, many of these letters chart Dinesen's increasing romantic feelings for Finch Hatton. As she wrote to her brother Thomas in 1928, "That such a person as Denys does exist,—something I have indeed guessed at before, but hardly dared to believe,—and that I have been lucky enough to meet him in this life and been so close to him,—even though there have been long periods of missing him in between,—compensates for everything else in the world, and other things cease to have any significance." Though Dinesen later experienced difficulty in her relationship with Finch Hatton, most of her letters recall their friendship glowingly.

These letters also revealed a good deal about a more negative aspect of Dinesen's personality, notably her patrician outlook. By her own admission, she felt an affinity for the aristocracy and a general disdain for all that was bourgeois. In fact, she often called herself "God's little snob." The correspondence in *Letters from Africa* does little to change such a reputation. "Karen Blixen was a terrible snob. Critics have long waxed ingenious in defending her short stories from charges of noblesse oblige; those defenses will be harder to make on the evidence of this collection," claimed Carl Bailey in the *Village Voice.* A *New York Times Book Review* contributor admitted that *Letters from Africa* often put Dinesen in a poor light. "Her letters reveal a difficult woman: inconsistent and often cruel in her rejection of family life, emotionally demanding and given to what she herself called 'showing off.'" However, most critics have maintained that the overall portrait of Dinesen that emerges from these letters is a positive one. Wrote Victoria Glendinning in the *Washington Post Book World:* "It is her will and complete lack of self-pity that make Karen Blixen so sympathetic and save her from the alienating intensity of other solitary searches such as, for example, Simone Weil. She quotes a definition of true piety as 'loving one's destiny unconditionally.' To be able to do this without losing her resilience was part of Karen Blixen's achievement." Adds Richard Stern in the *Chicago Tribune,* "If these [letters] are not as brilliant as those in her great memoir, there is at least the material for one portrait greater than all the others, that of the great human being behind them all."

In 1940 Dinesen was commissioned by the Copenhagen daily newspaper *Politiken* to spend a month in Berlin, a month in Paris, and a month in London and to write a series of articles about each city. Although the advent of World War II caused the cancellations of the Paris and London visits, Dinesen's recollections of Hitler's Germany were later compiled in the posthumous collection *Daguerreotypes and Other Essays.* About this time Dinesen also began work on her second set of stories, although completion of the volume was delayed, however, by complications arising from tertiary syphilis. Dinesen eventually finished this second set of tales and, in 1942, *Winter's Tales,* a book that derives its title from one of Shakespeare's plays, was published in the United States, England, and Denmark.

With *Winter's Tales* Dinesen broke from the relative realism of *Out of Africa* and returned to the highly imaginative style which characterizes *Seven Gothic Tales.* Although these two collections share a number of similarities, *Winter's Tales* is simpler in style and closer in setting to modern Denmark. "Suffused with vague aspirations toward some cloudy ideal," noted Clifton Fadiman in the *New Yorker,* "with a longing for the impossible, with a brooding delight in magnificent and absurd gestures, with a quality of sleepwalking, they are as far removed from 1943 as anything can well be." Some critics, however, found fault with Dinesen's unique writing style: In a *Commonweal* review J. E. Tobin claimed, "The characters lack even the vague shape of ghosts; the atmosphere is that of stale perfume; the writing, called quaint by some, is downright awkward." The general consensus, however, was one of commendation for both the form and content of *Winter's Tales.* Struthers Brut, writing in the *Saturday Review of Literature,* summed up such a reaction when he maintained: "Often as you read the tales you wonder why you are so interested, so constantly excited, for the tales themselves, all of them symbolic, are not especially exciting in their plots, and the characters are frequently as remote as those in fairy tales, and a great deal of the time you are wandering in a fourth dimension where nothing is clear.

But the final effect is unforgettable, just as the moments of reading are unforgettable."

Winter's Tales, along with *Seven Gothic Tales* and *Out of Africa,* are generally considered to be Dinesen's masterpieces. Between their publication and the 1957 publication of *Last Tales,* there was a fifteen-year hiatus during which she published only one book—*The Angelic Avengers,* a thriller novel released in 1946 under the pseudonym of Pierre Andrezel. Dinesen was never proud of *The Angelic Avengers* and for many years refused to acknowledge herself as the book's author. Even after such acknowledgment, Dinesen criticized the book, claiming that she wrote it solely for her own amusement as a diversion from the grim realities of Nazi-occupied Denmark. In spite of her disclaimers, the book, a bestseller in Denmark and a Book-of-the-Month Club selection in America, was generally well-received.

The primary reason for Dinesen's sparse production between 1942 and 1957 was her continual poor health. Despite a series of corrective operations, she suffered lingering bouts of illness that greatly hampered her creative output, and she spent much of the 1940s convalescing and occasionally traveling. By 1950 her health had improved, and she delivered a series of broadcasts for Danish radio in which she described her African servant and friend, Farah. These broadcasts foreshadowed some of the material that would later be included in *Shadows on the Grass.* Dinesen's seventieth birthday, in 1955, was feted worldwide. In August of that same year she underwent an operation in which several spinal nerves were severed, as well as surgery on an ulcer. After the surgery she became an invalid, never again ate normally, and never weighed more than eighty-five pounds. According to Thurman she wrote at the time: "[These] past eight months have been more horrible than I can really describe to others—such continuous, insufferable pains, under which I howled like a wolf, are something one cannot fully comprehend. I feel that I have been in an Underworld. . . . The problem for me now is how I shall manage to come back into the world of human beings. It sometimes feels practically insoluable, though I believe that if I find something to look forward to, it could be possible."

In spite of her poor health and advanced age, Dinesen experienced a great renaissance during the late 1950s and early 1960s. During this period she published three works within a four-year span—*Last Tales* in 1957, *Anecdotes of Destiny* in 1958, and *Shadows on the Grass* in 1961. By now Dinesen was hailed worldwide as a major literary figure and had been nominated for the Nobel Prize several times. When Ernest Hemingway accepted his Nobel Prize in 1954 he said that the award should have been given instead to "that beautiful Danish writer Isak Dinesen."

As in her earlier volumes, the stories in *Last Tales* vary in time and place but deal with similar character types and themes, primarily exotic, often aristocratic characters in conflict or in harmony with their destinies. Destiny, more specifically one's control over it, is one of Dinesen's major themes. In her view, such a coming to terms involves an acceptance of one's fate as determined by God. "Dinesen's tales, like the stories in the *Arabian Nights,* proclaim the belief in the all but magic power of the story to provide man with a new vision and a renewed faith in life," Johannesson wrote. "Her figures are often Hamlet figures, melancholy men and women who wait for fate to lend them a helping hand, who wait for the storyteller to provide them with a destiny by placing them in a story." Although *Last Tales* was her first set of stories in over fifteen years, many critics found that Dinesen had managed to retain her artistic mastery. As a *Time* reviewer noted of *Last Tales:* "The characters are large, heroic figures and they are brought to earth with a resounding crash. Such men and women are rare in contemporary fiction; the art to make them live vitally—as Author Dinesen does—is rarer still."

A year after the release of *Last Tales, Anecdotes of Destiny* was published in both the United States and Denmark. A collection of five tales, *Anecdotes of Destiny,* with its preference for exotic locales and predominantly nineteenth-century settings, resembles her early work. The overall critical reaction to *Anecdotes of Destiny* was somewhat mixed. In his *Manchester Guardian* review of the book W. L. Webb described it as "a collection of elaborate fairy tales for elderly epicures, very cold, cultured, and romantic, with a faint *Yellow Book* flavour, and belonging to no world outside of the writer's imagination." But he adds, "One can often admire their jewelled-movement ingenuity without conceding the claims of the faithful to a Larger Significance." Some critics felt that *Anecdotes of Destiny* did not quite measure up to Dinesen's other writing. "If these stories are not quite so weird as the author's earlier ones, they are also not quite so effective. . . . And occasionally they seem to sprawl somewhat carelessly," remarked Howard Blair in the *San Francisco Chronicle.* On the other hand, critic R. H. Glauber felt that the stories in *Anecdotes of Destiny* were consistent with Dinesen's previous work. "If they lack something of the complex plotting we had in earlier stories, they have a new feature that more than makes up for it—a sense of fate that hangs over the characters and toward which they rush with dignified haste," Glauber wrote in the *New York Herald Tribune Book Review.* 'Babette's Feast,' a short story that was later filmed as a motion picture, was ranked "with the best Dinesen has ever written."

Although now in her mid-seventies and predominantly bedridden, Dinesen remained active following the publication of *Anecdotes of Destiny.* In 1961 *Shadows on the Grass,* a collection of four short essays, was released. The last of Dinesen's books published during her lifetime, it was written during a time of great suffering and was often dictated from a hospital bed a few paragraphs at a time. Like *Out of Africa* before it, *Shadows on the Grass* takes as its subject matter Dinesen's years in Africa. While it includes reminiscences about the excitement of hunting lions and the hazards of raising coffee on the equator, the book's main focus is Dinesen's recollections of her African servants. The last of Dinesen's Book-of-the-Month Club selections, *Shadows on the Grass* met with almost universal acclaim. "The four stories in 'Shadows on the Grass' are triumphantly sentimental and gently anecdotal; yet within their miniature frame they have many of the qualities of the finest story-telling," wrote William Dunlea in *Commonweal.* Critics particularly lauded Dinesen's manner in evoking memories from her past; Phoebe Adams, writing in the *Atlantic,* praised Dinesen's acuteness of perception and "ability to find an undercurrent of wonder in any situation." A *Time* reviewer concurred, claiming: "What the baroness does in this book is scarcely tangible enough to describe. She dips a branch of memory into the pool of the past until it is crystallized with insights, landscapes, literature, and animals that seem as if painted by Henri Rousseau."

Dinesen died in September of 1962, less than a year after the publication of *Shadows on the Grass.* Her legacy has been kept alive by a series of posthumously published works including *Carnival: Entertainments and Posthumous Tales* and, more recently, by a major motion picture. The 1985 film, *Out of Africa,* starring Klaus Maria Brandauer as Baron Blixen, Robert Redford as Finch Hatton and Meryl Streep as Dinesen, won a total of seven Oscars, including best picture. The film was instrumental in causing renewed interest in both Dinesen and her work; two years after its release, Vintage Books had sold over 653,000 copies of *Out of Africa,* thus making Dinesen a bestselling author almost twenty-five years after her death.

One of Dinesen's chief projects near the end of her life was the preservation of Rungstedlund, a sixteenth-century Danish inn that had been purchased by her father and in which she was born six years later. While she would leave Rungstedlund for Africa soon after the tragic death of her father, Dinesen returned and wrote her five collections of short stories here. She established the Rungsted Foundation, a private institution that purchased the house and surrounding land and entrusted with preserving the area as a bird reserve after her death. In July of 1958 Dinesen gave a radio talk on the future of Rungstedlund, asking listeners to donate one Danish crown to the Foundation; over eighty thousand listeners complied with her request.

After her death, in keeping with her wishes, Rungstedlund was preserved as a museum and bird sanctuary, which houses numerous family artifacts, and a library of over two thousand of the author's books. Dinesen herself is buried in the sanctuary, beneath a beech tree where nightingales on their way to Africa stop to roost. The coffee plantation that lies southernmost in their path, in the Ngong Hills of Kenya, has also been turned into a museum site.

Dinesen considered herself more of a storyteller than a writer. According to Donald Hannah's *'Isak Dinesen' and Karen Blixen: The Mask and the Reality,* Dinesen once wrote: "I belong to an ancient, idle, wild and useless tribe, perhaps I am even one of the last members of it, who, for many thousands of years, in all countries and parts of the world, has, now and again, stayed for a time among hardworking honest people in real life, and sometimes has thus been fortunate enough to create another sort of reality for them, which in some way or another, has satisfied them. I am a storyteller." While she did, indeed, lead a remarkable life, it is the translation of that life to the stuff of fiction that she will be best remembered. "Of a story she made an essence; of the essence she made an elixir," wrote Eudora Welty in the *New York Times,* "and of the elixir she began once more to compound the story."

BIOGRAPHICAL/CRITICAL SOURCES:

BOOKS

Aiken, Susan Hardy, *Isak Dinesen and the Engendering of Narrative,* University of Chicago Press, 1990.

Bjornvig, Thorkild, *The Pact: My Friendship with Isak Dinesen,* Louisiana State University Press, 1974.

Contemporary Literary Criticism, Gale, Volume 10, 1979, Volume 24, 1984.

Dinesen, Isak, *Out of Africa,* Putnam (London), 1937, Random House, 1938, reprinted with illustrations, Crown, 1987, Danish translation published as *Den Afrikanske Farm,* Gyldendal, 1937.

Dinesen, I., *Skygger paa Graesset,* Gyldendal, 1960, published as *Shadows on the Grass,* Random House, 1961.

Dinesen, I., *Daguerreotypes and Other Essays,* Danish portions translated by P. M. Mitchell and W. D. Paden, University of Chicago Press, 1979.

Dinesen, I., *Breve fra Africa,* Volume I: *1914-1924,* Volume II: *1925-1931,* Gyldendal, 1978, published as *Letters from Africa, 1914-1931,* edited by Frans Lasson and translated by Anne Born, University of Chicago Press, 1981.

Dinesen, Thomas, *My Sister, Isak Dinesen,* translated from the Danish by Joan Tate, M. Joseph (London), 1975.

Conelson, Linda, *Out of Isak Dinesen in Africa: The Untold Story,* Coulsong List (Iowa City, IA), 1995.

Hannah, Donald, *'Isak Dinesen' and Karen Blixen: The Mask and the Reality,* Putnam, 1971.

Henriksen, Aage, *Isak Dinesen; Karen Blixen: The Work and the Life,* translated by William Mishler, St. Martin's (New York), 1988.

Henricksen, Liselette, *Isak Dinesen: A Bibliography,* University of Chicago Press, 1977.

Johannesson, Eric O., *The World of Isak Dinesen,* University of Washington Press, 1961.

Langbaum, Robert, *The Gayety of Vision: A Study of Isak Dinesen's Art,* University of Chicago Press, 1964.

Migel, Parmenia, *Titania: The Biography of Isak Dinesen,* Random House, 1967.

Pelensky, Olga, *Isak Dinesen: The Life and Imagination of a Seducer,* Ohio University Press (Athens), 1991.

Pelensky, O., editor, *Isak Dinesen: Critical Views,* Ohio University Press, 1993.

Stambaugh, Sara, *The Witch and the Goddess in the Stories of Isak Dinesen: A Feminist Reading,* UMI Research Press (Ann Arbor, MI), 1988.

Svendsen, Clara, editor, *Isak Dinesen: A Memorial,* Random House, 1964.

Svendsen, C., editor, *The Life and Destiny of Isak Dinesen,* Random House, 1970.

Thurman, Judith, *Isak Dinesen: The Life of a Storyteller,* St. Martin's, 1982.

Trzebinski, Errol, *Silence Will Speak: A Study of the Life of Denys Finch Hatton and His Relationship with Karen Blixen,* University of Chicago Press, 1977.

Whissen, Thomas R., *Isak Dinesen's Aesthetics,* Kennikat Press (Port Washington, NY), 1973.

PERIODICALS

American Scholar, autumn 1963.

Atlantic, June 1943; January 1947; December 1957; November 1960.

Bookmark, December 1957.

Books, April 8, 1934; March 6, 1938.

Books and Bookmen, February 1968.

Books West, Volume I, number 7, 1977.

Chicago Daily Tribune, April 21, 1934.

Chicago Sunday Tribune, December 8, 1957.

Chicago Tribune, December 27, 1985, Sec. 7, p. 37; March 30, 1986, Sec. 12, p. 10; June 4, 1986, Sec. 5, pp. 1, 3; January 5, 1987, Sec. 5, p. 3.

Chicago Tribune Book World, September 23, 1979; June 7, 1981.

Christian Science Monitor, June 5, 1943; December 23, 1960; June 13, 1963; February 11, 1980; September 14, 1981; January 21, 1986, p. 38.

Commonweal, September 28, 1934; June 18, 1943; January 31, 1947; December 13, 1957.

Harper's, March 1971.

Hudson Review, winter 1964-65, pp. 517-30; spring 1978; winter 1981-82.

International Fiction Review, January 1978.

Journal of the Folklore Institute, January-April 1978, pp. 23-44.

Journal of Narrative Technique, winter 1985, pp. 82-90.

Library Journal, May 15, 1979.

Locus, January 1992, p. 56; September 1993, p. 64.

Los Angeles Times, November 25, 1985; December 8, 1986; January 5, 1987.

Manchester Guardian, December 31, 1937; November 28, 1958.

Massachusetts Review, summer 1978, pp. 389-406.

Modern Fiction Studies, winter 1978, pp. 521-32.

Nation, April 18, 1934, p. 449; November 8, 1958; November 5, 1977.

New Boston Review, spring 1978.

New Outlook, April 1934.

New Republic, June 7, 1943; January 3, 1961; October 22, 1977; March 21, 1988, pp. 26-27.

New Statesman, November 23, 1957; November 1, 1958; October 30, 1981.

New Statesman and Nation, October 20, 1934; April 17, 1943; April 19, 1947.

Newsweek, December 23, 1985.

New Yorker, May 15, 1943; November 9, 1968; December 5, 1977; November 19, 1979; September 7, 1981.

New York Herald Tribune Book Review, June 5, 1947; November 3, 1957; October 12, 1958.

New York Herald Tribune Books, June 16, 1963.

New York Herald Tribune Weekly Book Review, January 5, 1947.

New York Review of Books, May 4, 1978; July 17, 1986, p. 21.

New York Times, March 6, 1938; January 5, 1947; November 3, 1957; October 12, 1958; December 30, 1985; March 20, 1986.

New York Times Book Review, June 9, 1963; September 20, 1981; December 8, 1985; February 23, 1986, pp. 3, 37; October 16, 1987.

Observer, July 27, 1986, p. 23; January 23, 1994, p. 22.

Publishers Weekly, March 13, 1987.

San Francisco Chronicle, October 26, 1958.

Saturday Review, October 6, 1934; November 2, 1957; March 16, 1963; December 10, 1977.

Saturday Review of Literature, April 14, 1934; March 5, 1938; May 15, 1943; January 18, 1947.

Spectator, November 29, 1957; October 17, 1958.

Texas Studies in Literature and Language, winter 1978, pp. 615-32.

Time, November 4, 1957; January 6, 1961; September 27, 1968; February 9, 1987.

Times, (London), December 3, 1986.

Times Literary Supplement, March 13, 1943; January 13, 1978; July 28, 1978; April 4, 1980; September 11, 1981.

Village Voice, September 2, 1981.

Virginia Quarterly Review, autumn 1968.

Washington Post Book World, August 9, 1981.

Wilson Library Bulletin, November 1991, p. 16.

World Literature Today, spring 1979; spring 1980; spring 1981; spring 1982.

Yale Review, summer 1943.*

*   *   *

BOWLES, Paul (Frederick) 1910-

PERSONAL: Born December 30, 1910, in New York, NY; son of Claude Dietz (a dentist) and Rena (Winnewisser) Bowles; married Jane Auer (a writer), February 21, 1938 (died, 1973). *Education:* Studied music with Aaron Copland in New York and Berlin, 1930-32, and Virgil Thomson in Paris, 1933-34; also attended School of Design and Liberal Arts, New York, and University of Virginia.

ADDRESSES: Home—2117 Tanger Socco, Tangier, Morocco. *Agent*—William Morris Agency, 1350 Avenue of the Americas, New York, NY 10019.

CAREER: Writer. Composer for stage, operas, film scores, ballets, songs, and chamber music; musical works include scores for *The Glass Menagerie, Love's Old Sweet Song, My Heart's in the Highlands,* and *Sweet Bird of Youth,* and for the ballets *Pastorelas, Yankee Clipper,* and *Sentimental Colloquy.* Visiting professor, San Fernando Valley State College (now California State University, Northridge), 1968.

AWARDS, HONORS: Guggenheim fellowship, 1941; National Institute of Arts and Letters Award in Literature, 1950; Rockefeller grant, 1959; National Endowment for the Arts creative writing fellowship, 1978, and senior fellowship, 1980; American Book Award nomination, 1980, for *Collected Stories of Paul Bowles, 1939-1976.*

WRITINGS:

NOVELS

The Sheltering Sky, New Directions (New York City), 1949, Vintage Books (New York City), 1990.

Let It Come Down, Random House (New York City), 1952.

The Spider's House, Random House, 1955.

Up above the World, Simon & Schuster (New York City), 1966.

Points in Time, Ecco Press, 1982.

Too Far from Home: The Selected Writings of Paul Bowles, introduction by Joyce Carol Oates, Ecco Press, 1993.

SHORT STORIES

The Delicate Prey and Other Stories, Random House, 1950.

A Little Stone: Stories, J. Lehmann (Tyne and Wear, England), 1950.

The Hours after Noon, Heinemann (London), 1959.

A Hundred Camels in the Courtyard, City Lights (San Francisco), 1962.

The Time of Friendship, Holt (New York City), 1967.

Pages from Cold Point and Other Stories, P. Owen (London), 1968.

Three Tales, F. Hallman, 1975.

Things Gone and Things Still Here, Black Sparrow Press (Santa Barbara, CA), 1977.

Collected Stories of Paul Bowles, 1939-1976, Black Sparrow Press, 1979.

Midnight Mass, Black Sparrow Press, 1981.

A Distant Episode: The Selected Stories, Ecco Press, 1988.

Call at Corazon, P. Owen, 1988.

Unwelcome Words: Seven Stories, Tombouctou Books (Bolinas, CA), 1988.

A Thousand Days for Mokhtar, and Other Stories, P. Owen, 1989.

POETRY

Scenes, Black Sparrow Press, 1968.

The Thicket of Spring: Poems, 1926-1969, Black Sparrow Press, 1972.

Next to Nothing, Starstreams, 1976.

TRANSLATOR FROM THE MOGHREBI

Driss ben Hamed Charhadi, *A Life Full of Holes,* Grove (New York City), 1963.

Mohammed Mrabet, *Love with a Few Hairs,* P. Owen, 1967.

Mrabet, *The Lemon,* P. Owen, 1969.

Mrabet, *M'Hashish,* City Lights, 1969.

Mrabet, *The Boy Who Set the Fire and Other Stories,* Black Sparrow Press, 1974.

Mrabet, *Hadidan Aharam,* Black Sparrow Press, 1975.

Mrabet, *Harmless Poisons, Blameless Sins,* Black Sparrow Press, 1976.

Mrabet, *Look and Move On,* Black Sparrow Press, 1976.

Mrabet, *The Big Mirror,* Black Sparrow Press, 1977.

Five Eyes, Black Sparrow Press, 1979.

Mrabet, *The Beach Cafe,* Black Sparrow Press, 1980.

Mrabet, *The Chest,* Tombouctou Books, 1983.

Marriage with Papers, Tombouctou Books, 1986.

TRANSLATOR FROM THE FRENCH

Jean-Paul Sartre, *No Exit,* Samuel French (New York City), 1946.

Isabelle Eberhardt, *The Oblivion Seekers,* City Lights, 1975.

Also translator of other works from French.

TRANSLATOR FROM THE ARABIC

Mohamed Choukri, *For Bread Alone,* P. Owen, 1973.

Choukri, *Jean Genet in Tangier,* Ecco Press, 1974.

Choukri, *Tennessee Williams in Tangier,* Cadmus Editions (Santa Barbara, CA), 1979.

OTHER

(With Lucchino Visconti and Tennessee Williams) *Senso* (screenplay), Domenico Forges Davanzati, 1954.

Yallah (travel essays), McDowell, Obolensky, 1957.

Their Heads Are Green and Their Hands Are Blue (travel essays), Random House, 1963, published in England as *Their Heads Are Green,* P. Owen, 1963, Abacus/Sphere, 1990.

Paul Bowles in the Land of the Jumblies (screenplay), Gary Conklin, 1969.

Without Stopping: An Autobiography, Putnam (New York City), 1972, revised edition, Ecco Press, 1991.

(Translator from the Spanish) Rodrigo Rey Rosa, *The Beggar's Knife,* City Lights, 1985.

Two Years beside the Strait: Tangier Journal 1987-1989 (diary), P. Owen, 1990, published in the United States as *Days: Tangier Journal 1987-1989,* Ecco, 1991.

Tanger: Vues Choisies (travel pictorial), photographs by Jellel Gasteli, Editions E. Koehler (Paris), 1991.

Conversations with Paul Bowles (interviews), edited by Gena Dagel Caponi, University Press of Mississippi (Jackson, MS), 1993.

Morocco (travel pictorial), photographs by Barry Brukoff, H. N. Abrams (New York City), 1993.

In Touch: The Letters of Paul Bowles, edited by Jeffrey Miller, Farrar, Straus & Giroux (New York City), 1994.

Paul Bowles Photographs, edited by Simon Bischoff, Scalo Publishers (New York City), 1994.

Portable Paul and Jane Bowles, edited by Millicent Dillon, Viking Penguin (New York City), 1994.

Also translator of other works from Spanish and Italian.

ADAPTATIONS: Bowles recorded his short stories "The Delicate Prey" and "A Distant Episode" on an album for Spoken Arts in 1963; his novel *A Hundred Camels in the Courtyard* was recorded for Cadmus Editions in 1981; a feature film version of *The Sheltering Sky* narrated by Bowles was released by Warner Bros. in 1990.

SIDELIGHTS: Paul Bowles's fiction depicts the frailty of Western rationalism. In the essential Bowles story, American or European travellers visit a civilization that they consider vastly inferior to their own, usually in the North African desert. When they enter that more primitive world, however, their Western values quickly disintegrate. Inevitably, contact with the older culture transforms the traveller's world view; not infrequently, it destroys them. Although he remains best known for his novel *The Sheltering Sky,* Bowles has also distinguished himself as a composer, short story writer, translator, and poet.

Even as a child, Bowles wrote fiction and music; he was sixteen years old when the highly-regarded magazine *transition* published his surrealist poetry. A 1931 trip to Paris really marked the beginning of his adult writing career, however, for it was then that he met and became friends with author Gertrude Stein and her companion, Alice B. Toklas. These two women were to give Bowles important direction concerning his literary efforts. Stein was not fond of surrealism, and her criticism of Bowles's poetry was harsh. In a *Dictionary of Literary Biography* essay, Lawrence D. Stewart quotes her as saying to the young writer: "Now Bravig Imbs, for instance, he's just a very bad poet. . . . But you—you're not a poet at all!"

Stein believed that some time away from Western culture would help Bowles discover his own style. Alice Toklas, who according to Stewart "had a talent for putting people in a proper setting," suggested Morocco. In so doing, she introduced the young author to the place where he would live for most of his life, and which would serve as the setting for the greater part of his fiction. He rented a house in Tangier, sharing it with composer Aaron Copland, who was then serving as Bowles's musical mentor. Although primarily concerned with his composition at this time, Bowles did send some prose passages to Gertrude Stein from Tangier, which pleased her much more than had his poetry. Stewart quotes a letter to Bowles in which Stein wrote: "I like your story, I like your descriptions, go on with them."

It would be ten years before Bowles would seriously devote himself to writing fiction, however. In the meantime, he returned to New York City; there he was in demand as a composer of theater music, providing scores for works by such notable playwrights as Tennessee Williams and William Saroyan. One of Bowles's most unusual projects during this period was a ballet choreographed by Spanish artist Salvador Dali. The dance was complicated by costumes featuring floor-length underarm hair, bicyclists riding across the stage, and a large mechanical tortoise which sometimes charged straight for the dancers' feet. "Hisses and catcalls were more or less constant on opening night," recalls Bowles in his *Contemporary Authors Autobiography Series* (*CAAS*) essay.

It was in 1942 that Bowles again became inspired to write fiction. Watching his wife, Jane Auer, at work on her novel *Two Serious Ladies* "was the thing that detonated the . . . explosion," Stewart quotes Bowles. His stories were soon appearing in such diverse publications as *Harper's Bazaar, View, Mademoiselle,* and *Partisan Review.*

When he had collected enough to make up an entire volume, he sent them to a publisher "hoping somehow to bypass the unwritten law which makes it impossible for a writer to publish a book of short stories until after he has published a novel," notes Bowles in *CAAS.* He did not succeed in this aim, but after reading his stories, editors at Doubleday were willing to commission a novel. A vivid dream of Morocco convinced Bowles that he must return there to write. Soon he was en route to Fez, and within eight months he had completed *The Sheltering Sky,* a novel so startling that upon receiving the manuscript, Doubleday demanded the return of their advance money, declaring that what Bowles had produced was not a novel.

Subsequently published by New Directions, *The Sheltering Sky* has since been praised as a masterpiece of existential literature. Theodore Solotaroff expresses the opinion of many critics in a *New Republic* article, calling it "one of the most beautifully written novels of the past twenty years and one of the most shattering. Bowles is not the philosopher that Sartre or Camus were, but he is an existentialist to his fingertips, and beside the emotional concreteness of *The Sheltering Sky,* books like *Nausea, The Age of Reason,* or *The Stranger* seem vague, arbitrary, imaginatively barren."

According to Stewart, Bowles himself describes *The Sheltering Sky* as "an adventure story, in which the actual adventures take place on two planes simultaneously: in the actual desert, and in the inner desert of the spirit." The main characters are Port and Kit Moresby, two sophisticated American drifters whose feelings of emptiness are revealed in Port's remark to his wife: "We've never managed, either of us, to get all the way into life." Their wanderings take them to the North African desert. There, writes *Esquire* contributor Tobias Wolff, "in the silent emptiness of desert and sky, the knowledge of their absolute isolation from other people comes upon them so violently that it subverts their belief in their own reality and in the reality of their connection to each other. Doubting that connection is, of course, prelude to betraying it. And betray it they do, in every way." Port falls mortally ill; Kit abandons her dying husband for another man. Eventually, she becomes the mindlessly contented slave of an Arab named Belqassim. Subjugation brings her such peace that when Belqassim loses interest in her, she searches for another captor. When French colonial authorities finally locate Kit, she has abandoned her identity so completely that she fails even to recognize her own name.

"*The Sheltering Sky* has been called nightmarish; that description lets us off the hook too easily, because it implies a fear of the unreal," believes Wolff. "The power of this novel lies precisely in the reality of what it makes us fear—the sweetness of that voice in each of us that sings the delight of not being responsible. . . . Our failing resistance

to . . . attacks on our sense of worth as individuals is the central drama of our time. *The Sheltering Sky* records the struggle with complete fidelity, impassively noting every step in the process of surrender. Like *The Sun Also Rises* and *Under the Volcano,* Bowles's novel enacts a crucial historical moment with such clarity that it has become part of our picture of that moment."

With a critically acclaimed novel to his credit, Bowles was able to publish his collection *The Delicate Prey and Other Stories.* The stories in this volume, writes Wolff, extend "the perceptions of the novel into even more exotic and disturbing terrain." The title story, for example, delineates a hashish-maddened hunter's murder of three brothers, and the revenge of the slain brothers' tribesmen: after capturing the killer, they bury him up to his neck in sand and abandon him to the elements. In "A Distant Episode," which Tennessee Williams called in *Saturday Review of Literature* "a true masterpiece of short fiction," an American linguistics professor, betrayed by his native guide, is seized by a band of hostile nomads. Mutilated and dressed in a suit of flattened tin cans, the professor is then kept as a hideous pet by the tribesmen, who teach him to dance for their amusement. "The curiosity-seeker has himself become a curiosity, comically and ineffectually armored in the detritus of his own culture," notes Wolff. "The story is a tour de force, an ominous parable of the weakening of the individual will to survive." Solotaroff states that the stories in *The Delicate Prey,* "with their lucid, quiet evocation of mood and motive leading to revelations of scarifying depravity," are so powerful that they make "the nihilism of the early Hemingway seem like a pleasant beery melancholy. . . . These stories . . . make one feel they were written with a razor, so deftly and chillingly do they cut to the bone."

The brutal action that is prevalent in Bowles's stories is in sharp contrast to his cool, detached prose. Stylistically, "he is a classic, master craftsman; precise, incisive, knowing," writes Stephen Koch in *Washington Post Book World.* "There is always some strange mystery lurking in his stories, and there is never a shoddy or lazy line. The result combines the exemplary and the unspeakable in a way that cannot be found anywhere else." Stewart agrees that "Bowles' productions are too finely fashioned ever to be thought ugly—no matter what his subject and materials. His struggle has always been to get further into human consciousness and to explore its manifestations." And Irving Malin writes in *Ontario Review* that although Bowles's fiction frequently depicts some sort of savagery, the author cannot be considered "a sensationalist," for "he does not glory in his painstaking depiction of madness or destruction or mysticism. He believes that life is unpredictably cruel—even to cruel heroes!—and that his accurate, intense art must *contain* the cruelty. His style is thus stripped of prettiness. It is clear, direct, bold."

Bowles's subsequent fiction continued to feature the elements that made *The Sheltering Sky* and *The Delicate Prey* unique: exotic locations, existential concerns, and pristine prose. *Let It Come Down* follows a bank clerk as he flees the desolation of his life in New York City for Tangier, where he experiences a rapid disintegration. In *The Spider's House,* four expatriate Westerners are caught up in the violence of revolution in Fez. *Up above the World* tells of a jaded American couple traveling across South America, whose entanglement with a stranger leads to their brainwashing and murder. The similarities found in Bowles's works have led some critics to suggest that the author made his strongest statement in his first two books and had failed to develop artistically thereafter. While admiring the author's stylistic mastery, Bernard Bergonzi in the *New York Review of Books* finds "what he does with it very limited and ultimately monotonous. He places his characters before us and then destroys them in an unerring way: it is a remarkable performance, but one expects something more from literature." Francis King concurs in a *Spectator* article that Bowles unfortunately restricts himself to a "constant retreading of the same narrow plot, instead of the exploration of previously untrodden jungle."

Other reviewers maintain that within his self-imposed limits, Bowles demonstrates a versatility and virtuosity that places him at the forefront of American letters. "The novels and stories come at you from every direction, told from the points of view of men, women, Europeans, Arabs, priests, lunatics, murderers, merchants, beggars, animals, and spirits," points out Wolff. "His tales are at once austere, witty, violent, and sensuous. . . . His language has a purity of line, a poise and authority entirely its own, capable of instantly modulating from farce to horror without a ruffle and without giving any signal of delight in itself. In short, Bowles has proven himself, on the evidence of an extraordinary body of writing, to be one of our most serious and authentic literary artists."

Paul Bowles's writing was curtailed when his wife suffered a stroke and, afterwards, a long physical decline. "During the latter years of Jane's illness . . . it was impossible for me to write fiction," he reveals in *CAAS.* "The periods which I had to myself were of very short duration: fifteen or twenty minutes, instead of several hours. Frequent interruptions destroyed creative impetus." Discovering that "the act of translating did not suffer in any way from being stopped at short intervals," however, Bowles began what he considers to be some of his most important work—the publication of tales told by his young Arab friends. These tales, often produced when the narrators are high on *kif* (a marijuana-related substance), were tape recorded, transcribed, and translated by Bowles. They illustrate the

ways of thought that the American author has come to appreciate during his many years in North Africa.

After Jane Auer's death in 1973, Bowles once again turned to fiction. Some critics indicate that the work produced during this period may be his most distinguished. Wolff describes Bowles's 1982 publication, *Points in Time,* as "a nervy, surprising, completely original performance, so original that it can't be referred to any previous category of fiction or nonfiction." The book's structure reflects Bowles's musical training; it is divided into several sections or "movements." In this way, the author combines legends, historical anecdotes, description, and passages of popular song to create a portrait of Morocco through the years. It is accomplished with "a centered precision that at times reaches perfection and becomes so memorable, it does damage to the eye and the brain of the reader," says Ben Pleasants in the *Los Angeles Times Book Review.* Wolff agrees that *Points in Time* is "a brilliant achievement, innovative in form, composed in a language whose every word, every pause feels purposeful and right." Conrad Knickerbocker concludes in a *New York Times* article that among American writers, Bowles continues to stand "in the front rank for the substance of his ideas and for the power and conviction with which he expresses his own particular vision, which, if hellish, is totally appropriate to the times."

Points in Time was followed by several short story collections including *A Distant Episode: The Selected Stories, Unwelcome Words: Seven Stories,* and *Call at Corazon.* These collections represent over forty years of Bowles's work and reflect his long-established exploration of themes concerning the acculturation, miscegenation, and syncretism of Westerners as they explore foreign locales. During this exploration, Bowles's characters often encounter, and sometimes participate in, brutal and grotesque acts. In the story "Hugh Harper" from *Call at Corazon,* for example, Bowles's English protagonist has a penchant for drinking the blood of young Muslim boys. In his review of *Unwelcome Words* in the *Times Literary Supplement,* John Ryle concludes that "the Islamic wonder-tale converges in Bowles's work with the horror story. West and East meet in the act of violence. . . . It is hard to know if he is trying to move you to shiver or shrug or smile—or none of these things."

A Bowlesian revival of sorts came in the wake of these collections. Spearheading this revival was an unauthorized biography by Christopher Sawyer-Laucanno entitled *An Invisible Spectator: A Biography of Paul Bowles,* published in 1989. Bowles was distressed by this treatise, according to a 1988 journal entry published in *Antaeus* and quoted by Ryle: "Twice or three times a year [Sawyer-Laucanno] arrives from Boston, where he's busy writing that biography which I rejected before he started. . . . I've repeatedly told [him] I won't help him in any way. . . . I wonder if he knows how deeply I resent his flouting my wishes." Also contributing to the author's resurrection was an international reissue of *The Sheltering Sky,* a film adaptation of that work by director Bernardo Bertolucci, and a reprint of Bowles's travel essays *Their Heads Are Green,* all in 1990. That these books, first published in 1949 and 1963 respectively, should be continually reprinted attests to Bowles's recognition as one of the foremost contributors to American literature. As Michael Upchurch states in the *New York Times Book Review,* "his work exists well outside the flux of literary fashions. After a long period of obscurity, it has stood the test of time as well as any American writing of the 1940's and 50's." This renewed keen interest in Bowles's life and works was crowned in 1991 with the publication of Michelle Green's study *The Dream at the End of the World: Paul Bowles and the Literary Renegades in Tangier.*

Bowles's *Two Years beside the Strait: Tangier Journal 1987-1989* was also published during this period. In this diary, Bowles witnesses and records occurrences which often assault the senses, delivering these short tales with an eloquence and distance usually reserved for the snapshot. In one of the entries, for instance, "Bowles describes a 'typical tale of Ramadan violence' in a market," notes Millicent Dillon in the *Times Literary Supplement.* "One Moroccan merchant refuses to allow another to sit close to him. Tired, the second man sits down for a minute; the first one kills him. This story is told without further comment. No judgment is made." Some critics felt that Bowles maintained *too* much distance from his subject in *Two Years beside the Strait,* and were disappointed that the journal did not explicate the author's life—long a bone of contention among Bowles's readers. Gerald Nicosia laments in *Washington Post Book World* that "it is precisely that withdrawn and detached mode of observation that makes Bowles's journal, *Days,* such a 'humdrum' read—to use his own description in the 'Preface.' Except for a few wonderful passages of natural observation, you could never guess that this was a journal of one of the major writers of our century."

Fans and critics had hoped for more revealing insights from the author in *Conversations with Paul Bowles* and *In Touch: The Letters of Paul Bowles,* published in 1993 and 1994 respectively. Unfortunately, "he deliberately deceives the interlocutor, offering diverse, ambivalent remarks" in the interviews contained in *Conversations,* Malin comments in *Studies in Short Fiction.* Malin quotes Bowles as saying, "the man who wrote the books didn't exist. No writer exists. He exists in his books and that's all," and observes of Bowles that "by distancing the writer from biographical investigation, he privileges the text, and at the same time adds to his legend as invisible man."

More personal and insightful, *In Touch* offers readers a closer look into the author through his correspondences between 1929 and the present. The letters present glimpses of notorious artists of the time including William Burroughs, Aaron Copland, and Tennessee Williams, as well as a melancholy documentation of Bowles's wife's illness and untimely death. *In Touch* reveals something of the private life of Bowles, but the real worth of this collection is that "the descriptive passages found in the letters often rival those of his novels and stories," according to Upchurch. Jack Sullivan, reviewing *In Touch* for the *Washington Post Book World,* remarks, "These newly published letters—some 400 of them, selected from over 7,000 pages—are a major publishing event and an endless source of fascination." He continues, "these letters can be as ceremoniously formal as Bowles's public persona or as surreal and off-the-wall as his wildest fiction." For those readers still demanding personal insight into the author, Upchurch comments, "The most intimate and freewheeling interview with Mr. Bowles appears . . . at the back of . . . *Paul Bowles Photographs,* where Mr. Bowles's personal revelations ('I always was more auto-erotic') and his choice gossip about fellow Tangerines are the draw."

For readers anxious for his fiction, Bowles complied in 1993 with *Too Far from Home: The Selected Writings of Paul Bowles.* A collection of previously released work save for the title story, "the publishers describe this book as 'Paul Bowles's first novel for 25 years.' But . . . at some 15,000 words, it is no more a novel than a handkerchief is a bedsheet," asserts Francis King in the *Spectator.* Although new, the story "Too Far from Home" reverts to the theme of Americans trying to adapt to a foreign culture. Through brother and sister Tom and Anita, Bowles illuminates the prejudices and contrasts inherent in acculturation. In a letter to a friend, quoted by James Campbell in *Times Literary Supplement,* Anita writes, "I am being forced to participate in some sort of communal consciousness that I really hate. I don't know anything about these people. They're all black, but nothing like 'our' blacks back in the States." Her brother Tom is a painter and, in contrast to his sister, not at all affected by the rigors of Saharan living or Anita's inability to adjust to her new surroundings. Bowles includes horror scenes typical of his past stories and explores supernatural themes as well. Although many critics were disappointed that Bowles's extended hiatus from short stories did not result in more than *Too Far from Home,* interest in his subject matter survives. "Right or wrong, beauty and terror go wonderfully well together in his work," states Madison Smartt Bell in the *Chicago Tribune,* "and this selection should increase our awareness that Bowles is one of the most important writers of our times."

In a departure from his previous work, Bowles collaborated with photographer Barry Brukoff to produce the pictorial entitled *Morocco* in 1993. Bowles wrote the text to accompany eighty photos by Brukoff, which depict scenes from Tangier, Fez, Marrakesh, and the Sahara. In the introduction, Bowles reasserts his commitment to objectivity: "To aid the reader's imagination in its task of seizing the essence of how things were but no longer are, and of how they are now, it is important that a chronicler adhere to a scrupulous honesty in reporting. Any conscious distortion is equivalent to cheating at solitaire: the purpose of the game is nullified."

BIOGRAPHICAL/CRITICAL SOURCES:

BOOKS

Aldridge, John W., *After the Lost Generation*, Noonday, 1951.

Allen, Walter, *The Modern Novel*, Dutton (New York City), 1965.

Bainbridge, John, *Another Way of Living: A Gallery of Americans Who Choose to Live in Europe*, Holt, 1968.

Bertens, Hans, *The Fiction of Paul Bowles: The Soul Is the Weariest Part of the Body*, Humanities (Atlantic Highlands, NJ), 1979.

Bowles, Paul, *Morocco*, H. N. Abrams, 1993.

Bowles, Paul, *Without Stopping*, Putnam, 1972.

Caponi, Gena Dagel, *Paul Bowles: Romantic Savage*, Southern Illinois University Press (Carbondale, IL), 1994.

Contemporary Authors Autobiography Series, Volume 1, Gale (Detroit), 1984.

Contemporary Literary Criticism, Gale, Volume 1, 1973, Volume 2, 1974, Volume 19, 1981.

Dictionary of Literary Biography, Gale, Volume 5: *American Poets since World War II*, 1980, Volume 6: *American Novelists since World War II*, Second Series, 1980.

Green, Michelle, *The Dream at the End of the World: Paul Bowles and the Literary Renegades in Tangier*, HarperCollins (New York City), 1991.

Hibbard, Allen, *Paul Bowles: A Study of the Short Fiction*, Twayne (New York City), 1993.

Miller, Jeffrey, *Paul Bowles: A Descriptive Bibliography*, Black Sparrow Press, 1986.

Patteson, Richard F., *A World Outside: The Fiction of Paul Bowles*, University of Texas Press (Austin, TX), 1987.

Pulsifer, Gary, editor, *Paul Bowles by His Friends*, P. Owen, 1992.

Sawyer-Laucanno, Christopher, *An Invisible Spectator: A Biography of Paul Bowles*, Weidenfeld & Nicolson (New York City) and Bloomsbury (London), 1989.

Solotaroff, Theodore, *The Red Hot Vacuum and Other Pieces on the Writing of the Sixties*, Atheneum (New York City), 1970.

Steen, Mike, *A Look at Tennessee Williams*, Hawthorn (New York City), 1969.

Stewart, Lawrence D., *The Illumination of North Africa*, Southern Illinois University Press, 1974.

Stewart, *The Mystery and Detection Annual*, Donald Adams, 1973.

PERIODICALS

Books and Bookmen, June, 1968.

Boston Globe, June 25, 1989, p. A16; March 4, 1990, p. 15; January 10, 1991, p. 69; January 14, 1991, p. 29.

Chicago Tribune, August 9, 1988, section 5, p. 3; June 25, 1989, section 14, p. 6; March 4, 1993, pp. 1, 9.

Choice, April, 1994, p. 1291.

Commonweal, March 7, 1952.

Critique, Volume 3, number 1, 1959.

Esquire, May, 1985.

Film Comment, May/June, 1991, pp. 18-20, 22-23.

Gargoyle, number 24.

Harper's, October, 1959.

Hollins Critic, April, 1978.

Illustrated London News, January 28, 1967.

Life, July 21, 1967.

Listener, February 2, 1967; February 23, 1989, pp. 32-33.

London Magazine, November, 1960; February, 1967; June, 1968.

Los Angeles Times, April 9, 1981; August 13, 1991, p. E5; February 22, 1993, p. E1.

Los Angeles Times Book Review, September 16, 1984; July 17, 1988, p. 14; May 26, 1991, p. 10.

Mediterranean Review, winter, 1971.

Nation, September 4, 1967.

National Observer, July 24, 1967.

New England Review, spring, 1980.

New Republic, September 2, 1967; April 22, 1972; January 7, 1991, p. 33.

New Statesman, January 27, 1967; April 15, 1988, pp. 39-40.

New Statesman and Society, February 25, 1994, pp. 40-41; November 4, 1994, p. 40.

New York Review of Books, November 9, 1967; May 18, 1972; November 23, 1989, pp. 6-12.

New York Times, March 12, 1966; March 21, 1972; July 24, 1988, section 2, p. 27; October 17, 1989, p. C21.

New York Times Book Review, March 2, 1952; March 9, 1952; August 25, 1963; March 10, 1966; August 6, 1967; April 9, 1972; September 20, 1979; April 7, 1991, p. 7; September 15, 1991, p. 7; June 26, 1994, p. 1.

Observer (London), April 10, 1988, p. 41; February 19, 1989, p. 44. *Ontario Review*, spring-summer, 1980.

Partisan Review, winter, 1968.

Publishers Weekly, October 4, 1993, p. 63.

Punch, February 8, 1967.

Rolling Stone, May 23, 1974.

San Francisco Review of Books, summer, 1991, pp. 9-10.

Saturday Review of Literature, December 23, 1950; October 20, 1955.

Spectator, March 30, 1985; June 30, 1990, pp. 35-36; March 5, 1994, pp. 34-35.

Studies in Short Fiction, summer, 1994, pp. 531-533.

Time, August 4, 1967; August 27, 1979.

Times (London), August 20, 1981; August 11, 1985.

Times Literary Supplement, September 30, 1949; February 2, 1967; May 9, 1968; October 13, 1972; May 13, 1988, p. 526; September 15, 1989, pp. 995-996; March 9, 1990, p. 266; September 7, 1990, p. 938; March 4, 1994, p. 21.

Tribune Books (Chicago), February 13, 1994, p. 3.

USA Today, July 21, 1989, p. D4.

Voice Literary Supplement, April, 1986.

Washington Post Book World, September 9, 1979; August 2, 1981; August 14, 1988, p. 12; June 11, 1989, p. 3; August 4, 1991, p. 11; December 5, 1993, p. 17; August 14, 1994, p. 11.

World Literature Today, autumn, 1989, p. 681.

—*Sidelights by Conner C. Gorry*

* * *

BOYLE, (C.) Kevin 1943-

PERSONAL: Born May 23, 1943, in Northern Ireland; son of Louis (a cab driver) and Elizabeth (McArdle) Boyle; married Joan Smyth, August 28, 1976; children: Mark Stephen. *Education:*Queen's University of Belfast, LL.B., 1966; Cambridge University, Diploma in Criminology, 1966; graduate study at Yale University, 1972-73.

ADDRESSES: Office—Human Rights Centre, University of Essex, Colchester, CO4 3SQ, Essex, United Kingdom.

CAREER: Lecturer in law in Belfast, Northern Ireland, 1967-77; professor of law and dean of law school in Galway, Ireland, 1978-86; Article 19, London, England, director, 1986—. Human Rights Centre, University of Essex, director, 1989—. Barrister at law; consultant to New Ireland Forum.

WRITINGS:

(With Thadden P. Hillyard) *Law and State: The Case of Northern Ireland,* Martin Robertson (Oxford, England), 1975.

Ten Years on in Northern Ireland, Cobden Trust (London), 1980.

Sentencing Law and Practice in Northern Ireland, Servicing the Legal System Publications, 1983.

(With M. Allen) *Sentencing Law and Practice,* Sweet & Maxwell (London), 1985. (With Tom Hadden) *Ire-*

land: A Positive Proposal, Penguin (West Drayton, Middlesex, England and New York City), 1985.

South Africa: The Pass Laws, Amnesty International (London), 1986.

Information Freedom and Censorship, A World Report, Times Books (London), 1988.

(With Hadden) *Northern Ireland: The Choice,* Penguin, 1994.

WORK IN PROGRESS: A world report on freedom of religion or belief.

SIDELIGHTS: Kevin Boyle told *CA:* "The idea that human rights might actually be enjoyed by all the people on this earth has motivated most of my activities. After three years in London as founding director of Article 19, the International Centre against censorship, I took up a professorship of law at Essex University UK and am director of the Human Rights Centre there. Apart from my educational and research role at Essex, I have become involved in working for the human rights of Kurdish people, mainly through international human rights litigation against the countries denying their rights."

BIOGRAPHICAL/CRITICAL SOURCES:

BOOKS

Van Voris, W. H., *Violence in Ulster,* University of Massachusetts Press, 1975.

* * *

BRACKNEY, William (Henry) 1948-

PERSONAL: Born January 30, 1948, in Washington, DC; son of Samuel H. and Mildred P. Brackney; married Kathryn G. (an artist), May 23, 1970; children: Noel C., Erin A., G. Raphe. *Education:* University of Maryland, B.A. (with honors), 1970; Eastern Baptist Theological Seminary, M.A., 1972; Temple University, M.A., 1974, Ph.D., 1976.

ADDRESSES: Office—McMaster Divinity College, McMaster University, Hamilton, Ontario L85 4K1, Canada.

CAREER: Ordained Baptist and Methodist minister; pastor of United Methodist church, 1972-76; Houghton College, Houghton, NY, assistant professor, 1976-79; American Baptist Historical Society, Valley Forge, PA, executive director, 1979-86; Eastern Baptist Theological Seminary, Philadelphia, PA, professor of history of Christianity, 1985-89, vice president and dean, 1986-89; Divinity College, McMaster University, Hamilton, Ontario, principal and professor of historical theology, 1989—.

MEMBER: American Society of Church History, Society of American Archivists.

WRITINGS:

Travel Guide to Baptist Historical Sites, American Baptist Board of National Ministry, 1981.

(Editor) *Baptist Life and Thought, 1600-1980,* Judson (Valley Forge, PA), 1983.

Dispensations of Providence, American Baptist Historical Society (Rochester, NY), 1984.

The Baptists, Greenwood Press (Westport, CT), 1984.

(Editor) *Faith, Life, and Witness,* Stanford University Press (Stanford, CA), 1990.

Christian Voluntarism in Britain and North America: A Bibliography and Critical Assessment, Greenwood Press, 1995.

(Editor) *Faith, Life and Work,* Stanford University Press, 1995.

The Voluntary Spirit in Christian Tradition, Eerdmans (Grand Rapids, MI), 1996.

Editor of *American Baptist Quarterly.**

*   *   *

BRANCH, Alan E(dward) 1933-

PERSONAL: Born January 10, 1933, in London, England; son of Leslie (a cashier) and Gertrude (a secretary; maiden name, Bartlett) Branch; married Kathleen Debenham (a district nurse), March 5, 1960; children: David Alan, Anna Louise. *Education:* Attended City of London College, 1952-55. *Avocational interests:* Reading, cricket, music, walking.

ADDRESSES: Home—19 The Ridings, Emmer Green, Reading, Berkshire RYK 8XL, England.

CAREER: Sometime shipping executive with Sea Containers; consultant on shipping and export matters for British Department of Trade and Industry, 1975—, and for World Bank and other international organizations in Jordan, Tanzania, Malaysia, Thailand, and Spain. Director of International Trade Studies, Basingstoke Technical College. Visiting professor, Institute of Maritime Studies; visiting lecturer at universities in the United Kingdom and other countries.

MEMBER: Chartered Institute of Transport (fellow), Institute of Export (fellow).

WRITINGS:

The Elements of Shipping, Chapman & Hall (London), 1964, 7th edition, 1995.

A Dictionary of Shipping/International Business Trade Terms and Abbreviations, Witherby (London), 1976, 4th edition, 1995.

Elements of Export Practice, Chapman & Hall, 1979, 3rd edition published as *Export Practice and Management,* 1995.

The Economics of Shipping Practice and Management, foreword by T. Bolton, Chapman & Hall, 1982, 3rd edition published as *Maritime Economics, Management, and Marketing,* 1996.

The Elements of Export Marketing and Management, Chapman & Hall, 1984, 2nd edition, 1990.

Dictionary of Commercial Terms and Abbreviations, Witherby, 1984.

Elements of Port Operation and Management, Chapman & Hall, 1986.

(With Juma Abu-Hakmeh) *Dictionary of English-Arabic Commercial, International Trade and Shipping Terms,* Witherby, 1988.

Import/Export Documentation, Chapman & Hall, 1990.

Elements of Import Practice, Chapman & Hall, 1990.

(With Michael Hedderly, Jose Foppiano, and Chris Thorby) *Multi-Lingual Dictionary of Commercial International Trade and Shipping Terms,* Witherby, 1990.

SIDELIGHTS: Alan E. Branch told *CA:* "All my eleven books in international trade are written for both executives in the business and students of the subject, and are selling in over 200 countries."

Branch also commented, "I believe that education in shipping and international trade is very important to increasing professionalism in this area. Such professionalism is most essential to the provision of well-managed and operated services and the development of world trade and resources."

*   *   *

BRAUNSTEIN, Mark M(athew) 1951-

PERSONAL: Born August 6, 1951, in New York, NY; son of Benjamin L. (a teacher) and Clare (Pitilon) Braunstein. *Education:* State University of New York at Binghamton, B.A., 1974; Pratt Institute, M.S., 1978; also attended Carnegie-Mellon University. *Politics:* "Indifferent." *Religion:* "Judeo-Buddhist." *Avocational interests:* Painting, photography, calligraphy, studying religion and philosophy.

ADDRESSES: Home—P.O. Box 456, Quaker Hill, CT 06375. *Office*—Box 5394, Connecticut College, New London, CT 06320.

CAREER: Rosenthal Art Slides, Chicago, IL, art slide librarian, 1978-80; H. W. Wilson Co., New York City, indexer, 1980-82, assistant editor of *Art Index,* 1982-83; Rhode Island School of Design, Providence, head of Slide and Photograph Collection, 1983-87; Connecticut College, New London, CT, visual resources librarian for art history department, 1987—.

MEMBER: Art Libraries Society/North America, College Art Association of America.

WRITINGS:

Radical Vegetarianism: A Dialectic of Diet and Ethic, Panjandrum (Los Angeles, CA), 1981, revised edition, Panacea Press (Quaker Hill, CT), 1993.
(Coeditor) *Slide Guide: Slide Sources for Art and Architecture,* Libraries Unlimited (Littleton, CO), 1985.
The Sprout Garden: Indoor Grower's Guide to Gourmet Sprouts, Book Publishing Company (Summertown, TN), 1993.

Contributor to *Life in the 21st Century,* 1981. Also contributor to various periodicals, including *Vegetarian Times, Twenty-first Century Journey, East West Journal, Agada, The Trumpeter: Journal of Ecosophy,* and *Iris: Notes in the History of Art.*

SIDELIGHTS: Mark M. Braunstein told *CA:* "*Radical Vegetarianism* is a product of my work experience, ranging from the dairy farm and chicken factory to the produce market and health food store. Still an aspiring painter and poet, I set aside murals for morals and poetics for polemics. Why write? Not to be rich, nor to be read, but to be right. By changing people's diets, *Radical Vegetarianism* has changed their lives. That is more than can be claimed about my or anyone's painting or poetry.

"As a native New Yorker . . . my life's ambition is to fast for forty days and forty nights in Death Valley. I dream in color, with lots of greens."

BIOGRAPHICAL/CRITICAL SOURCES:

PERIODICALS

Vegetarian Times, February, 1982.

*   *   *

BRISCOE, D(avid) Stuart 1930-

PERSONAL: Born November 9, 1930, in Millom, Cumbria, England; son of Stanley (a sales representative) and Mary (Wardle) Briscoe; married Jill Pauline Ryder (a teacher), June 29, 1958; children: David Stanley Campbell, Judith Margaret, Peter Alan Stuart. *Religion:* Christian. *Avocational interests:* Reading, running, golf.

ADDRESSES: Home—201 Pine Terr., Oconomowoc, WI 53066.

CAREER: District Bank Ltd., Spring Gardens, Manchester, England, member of inspection staff, 1955-60; Elm-

brook Church, Brookfield, WI, pastor, 1970—; secretary of Capernwray Missionary Fellowship, and evangelist and Bible teacher in over fifty countries. *Military service:* Royal Marine Commandos, 1948-50.

WRITINGS:

The Fullness of Christ, Zondervan (Grand Rapids, MI), 1965.
Living Dangerously, Zondervan, 1968.
Where Was the Church When the Youth Exploded?, Zondervan, 1972.
Discovering God, Zondervan, 1975.
Getting into God, Zondervan, 1975.
Bound for Joy, Regal Books (Ventura, CA), 1975.
What Works When Life Doesn't, Victor Books (Wheaton, IL), 1976.
All Things Weird and Wonderful, Victor Books, 1977.
Let's Get Moving, Regal Books, 1978.
Patterns for Power, Zondervan, 1979.
Sound Sense for Successful Living, Fleming Revell (Old Tappan, NJ), 1979.
The Communicator's Commentary: Romans, Word, Inc., 1982.
When the Going Gets Tough, Regal Books, 1982.
(With wife, Jill Briscoe) *Songs from Green Pastures,* Thomas Nelson (London), 1982.
(With J. Briscoe) *Mountain Songs,* Thomas Nelson, 1982.
Spirit Life, Fleming Revell, 1983.
Songs from Deep Waters, Thomas Nelson, 1984.
A Heart for God, Thomas Nelson, 1984.
River Songs, Thomas Nelson, 1984.
Tough Truth for Today's Living, Word, Inc., 1984.
Beyond Limits, Here's Life (San Bernardino, CA), 1985.
Taking God Seriously, Word, Inc., 1985.
Playing by the Rules, Fleming Revell, 1985.
How to Be a Motivated Christian, Victor Books, 1987.
The Communicator's Commentary: Genesis, Word, Inc., 1987.

Also author of *Apostle's Creed, The Fruit of the Spirit, Happiness beyond Our Happenings, I Peter—Holy Living in a Hostile World, Living Love, Marriage Matters, The Ten Commandments,* and *Transforming the Daily Grind,* all published by Shaw; *Dry Bones, Enjoying the Good Life, Everyday Discipleship, Hearing God's Voice, Life, Liberty and the Pursuit of Holiness,* and *Pulling Together,* all published by Victor Books; *Expository Nuggets—Christians, Expository Nuggets from Gospels,* and *Fresh Air in Pulpit,* all published by Baker; *Now for Something Totally Different* and *What It Means to Be Real,* both published by Word; *Purifying the Church,* Regal; *Spiritual Stamina,* Multnomah (Portland, OR); *Expository Nuggets—Psalms and Proverbs, Expository Nuggets—Genesis and Exodus,* and *Our Favorite Verse.*

SIDELIGHTS: D. Stuart Briscoe once told *CA:* "My major objective in writing on Biblical subjects is to give the sense of the Bible to my contemporaries and explain and apply it in such a way that they will find it immensely credible, wholesome, palatable, and eminently practical."

*   *   *

BROWN, Stuart C(ampbell) 1938-

PERSONAL: Born August 16, 1938, in Edinburgh, Scotland; son of John Duncan (a chartered accountant) and Violet (Creed) Brown; married Mavis Brownlee (a social worker), March 29, 1966; children: Frances, Jonathan. *Education:* University of St. Andrews, M.A., 1960; University of London, Ph.D., 1963.

ADDRESSES: Home—45 Westoning Road, Harlington, Bedfordshire LV5 6PB, England. *Office*—Faculty of Arts, Walton Hall, Open University, Milton Keynes, Buckinghamshire MK7 6AA, England.

CAREER: University of London, Birkbeck College, London, England, lecturer in philosophy, 1965-72; Open University, Milton Keynes, Buckinghamshire, England, senior lecturer, 1972-80, reader, 1982-85, professor of philosophy, 1986—, dean, Faculty of Arts, 1990-94. Former assistant director, Royal Institute of Philosophy.

WRITINGS:

Do Religious Claims Make Sense?, Macmillan (New York City), 1969.
(Editor with Wolfe Mays) *Linguistic Analysis and Phenomenology,* Macmillan (London), 1972.
(With Clive Lawless) *Political Philosophy,* Open University Press (Stony Stratford, England), 1973.
Religious Belief, Open University Press, 1973.
(Editor) *Philosophy of Psychology,* Macmillan (London), 1974.
(Editor) *Philosophers Discuss Education,* Macmillan (London), 1975.
Language and Reality: Philosophical Investigations, Open University Press, 1976.
Realism and Logical Analysis, Open University Press, 1976.
Verification and Meaning, Open University Press, 1976.
(Editor) *Reason and Religion,* Cornell University Press (Ithaca, NY), 1977.
(With Alasdair Clayre) *Work, Morality, and Human Nature,* Open University Press, 1978.
Secular Alternatives to Religion, Open University Press, 1978.
(Editor) *Royal Institute of Philosophy Lectures,* Vol. 12: *1977-78: Philosophers of the Enlightenment,* Harvester Press (Brighton, England), 1979.

(Editor) *Philosophical Disputes in the Social Sciences,* Humanities (Atlantic Heights, NJ), 1979.
(With P. N. Furbank and Clive Emsley) *The 'Encyclopedie,'* Open University Press, 1980.
(With Furbank and John Clarke) *Adam Smith's 'Wealth of Nations,'* Open University Press, 1980.
Philosophical Problems: Proof and the Existence of God, Open University Press, 1980.
(With Alan Harris) *Mapping Inquiry,* Open University Press, 1980.
(With Christopher Wilson) *Scientific Revolutions,* Open University Press, 1981.
(Editor with John Fauvel and Ruth Finnegan) *Conceptions of Inquiry,* Methuen (London), 1981.
Objectivity in Inquiry, Open University Press, 1981.
Reason and Experience: Leibniz, Open University Press, 1983.
(Editor) *Objectivity and Cultural Divergence,* Cambridge University Press (Cambridge), 1984.
Leibniz, University of Minnesota Press (Minneapolis), 1984.
(With Godfrey Vesey, *Introduction to Philosophy,* Open University Press, 1986.
(Editor and translator, with R. Niall D. Martin) *G. W. Leibniz: Discourse on Metaphysics and Related Writings,* Manchester University Press (Manchester), 1988.
(Editor) *Nicolas Malebranche: His Philosophical Critics and Successors,* Van Gorcum (Assen, The Netherlands), 1991.
(Editor) *British Philosophy and the Enlightenment,* Routledge (London), 1995.
(Editor, with Diane Collison and Robert Wilkinson) *Biographical Dictionary of Twentieth Century Philosophers,* Routledge, 1996.

Also editor of *Hume: Essays on Miracles and Providence.*

*   *   *

BUCHAN, Kate
See ERSKINE, Barbara

*   *   *

BUGENTAL, James F(rederick) T(homas) 1915-

PERSONAL: Born December 25, 1915, in Fort Wayne, IN; son of Richard (a contractor) and Hazel (a music teacher; maiden name, Veness) Bugental; married Mary Edith Smith, February 11, 1939 (divorced, 1967); married Elizabeth C. Keber, May 23, 1968; children: James O., Jane P., Karen M. *Education:* Glendale Junior College,

A.A., 1937; West Texas State Teachers College (now West Texas State University), B.S., 1940; George Peabody College for Teachers (now George Peabody College for Teachers of Vanderbilt University), M.A., 1941; Ohio State University, Ph.D., 1948.

ADDRESSES: Home and office—24 Elegant Tern Rd., Novato, CA 94949.

CAREER: Diplomate in clinical psychology, American Board in Professional Psychology, 1953; licensed psychologist, State of California, 1958; licensed marriage, family, and child counselor, State of California, 1964. Personnel administrator, U.S. Civil Service and Tennessee State Civil Service, 1941-44; Georgia School of Technology (now Georgia Institute of Technology), Atlanta, assistant professor of psychology and assistant director of Veterans Guidance Center, 1944-46; Ohio State University, Columbus, assistant instructor in psychology, 1947-48; University of California, Los Angeles, assistant professor of psychology, 1948-54; Psychological Service Associates, Los Angeles, partner, 1953-69; Stanford Research Institute, Educational Policy Research Center, Menlo Park, CA, research consultant, 1968-71; Stanford University, Medical School, Stanford, CA, associate clinical professor, 1971-76, emeritus, clinical faculty, 1976—. Private practice of psychotherapy, 1953-88. Instructor, Fifth Annual Post-Doctoral Institute in Clinical Psychology, Arizona State University, 1963; Pope John XXIII Lecturer, University of the Pacific, 1972; visiting professor, U.S. International University, 1976, 1977, 1981; visiting scholar, University of Montana, 1988. Charlotte Buhler Memorial Lecturer, Division of Humanistic Psychology, American Psychological Association, 1974; Rockefeller Teaching Scholar, California Institute of Integral Studies, 1995—. Adjunct faculty member, Saybrook Institute, 1979-90, emeritus professor, 1990—. Clinical psychologist, Lawson Army General Hospital, 1945-46. Inter/Logue, director, 1981-87. Member of board of directors, Esalen Institute, 1964-69. Lecturer and conductor of classes and workshops for hospitals, organizations, institutions, and universities.

MEMBER: American Psychological Association (fellow), Association for Humanistic Psychology (president, 1962-63), American Ontoanalytic Association, Association for Transpersonal Psychology, California State Psychological Association (president, 1960-61), Sigma Xi, Psi Chi, Pi Gamma Mu, Phi Delta Kappa.

AWARDS, HONORS: Certificate from Division of Clinical Psychology, American Psychological Association, 1986, for "distinguished contribution to the discipline of clinical psychology"; Rollo May Award, Mentor Society, 1987, "for contributions to the literary pursuit"; Path-

finder Award, Association for Humanistic Psychology, 1991; D.H.L., Saybrook Institute, 1993.

WRITINGS:

Interviewer's Manual, Tennessee Department of Personnel, 1942.

Psychological Interviewing, privately printed, 1951, revised edition, 1966.

(Editor with P. C. Buchanan, G. Hearn, T. Kroeber, and I. Weschler) *A Report on the Western Training Laboratory in Group Development,* University of California, Los Angeles Extension (Los Angeles), 1953.

Processes of Communication, privately printed, 1962, revised edition, 1986.

The Existential Orientation in Intensive Psychotherapy, privately printed, 1963.

The Search for Authenticity: An Existential-Analytic Approach to Psychotherapy, Holt (New York City), 1965, enlarged edition, Irvington (New York City), 1981-84.

(Editor and contributor) *Challenges of Humanistic Psychology,* McGraw (New York City), 1967.

The Human Possibility, SRI International, 1971.

The Humanistic Challenge of the Seventies, Stanford Research Institute (Stanford, CA), 1971.

The Search for Existential Identity: Patient-Therapist Dialogues in Humanistic Psychotherapy, Jossey-Bass (San Francisco), 1976.

Psychotherapy and Process: The Fundamentals of an Existential-Humanistic Approach, Addison-Wesley (Reading, MA), 1978.

Talking: The Fundamentals of Humanistic Professional Communication, privately printed, 1980.

The Art of Psychotherapy: A Workbook and Readings Resource for Counselors and Psychotherapists, privately printed, 1982, enlarged edition, 1984.

The Art of the Psychotherapist, Norton (New York City), 1987.

Intimate Journeys: Stories from Life-changing Therapy, Jossey-Bass, 1990.

Also author of *Cultural Trends and Institutional Requirements in a Pluralistic Society,* 1970, *We Must Mobilize Our Concern for Human Destiny,* 1982, *Prescription for Survival,* 1983, and *Are You a Conversational Pollutor or a Conversational Pro?,* 1983.

OTHER

Contributor to books, including *The Psychological Variables in Human Cancer,* edited by J. A. Gengerelli and F. J. Kirkner, University of California Press (Berkeley), 1954; *Graduate Education in Psychology,* edited by A. Roe and others, American Psychological Association (Washington, DC), 1959; *The Profession of Psychology,* edited by W. B. Webb, Holt, 1962; *Humanistic Viewpoints in Psy-*

chology: A Book of Readings, edited by F. T. Severin, McGraw (New York City), 1965; *Documents of Dialogue,* edited by H. H. Ward, Prentice-Hall, 1966; (with G. V. Haigh) *Call to Adventure,* edited by R. J. Magee, Abingdon (Nashville, TN), 1967; *The Human Course of Life: A Study of Goals in the Humanistic Perspective,* edited by C. Buhler and F. Massarik, Springer Publishing (New York City), 1968; *The Unfinished Business of William James,* edited by R. MacLeod, American Psychological Association, 1969; *Organizational Frontiers and Human Values,* edited by W. H. Schmidt, Wadsworth (Belmont, CA), 1970; *Existential Humanistic Psychology,* edited by T. C. Greening, Brooks/Cole (Monterey, CA), 1971; *The Analytic Situation,* edited by H. M. Ruitenbeck, Aldine (Hawthorne, NY), 1973; *New Frontiers of Humanistic Psychology,* edited by D. Nevill, Gardner Press (New York City), 1977; *Interpersonal Behavior and Management,* edited by A. G. Athos, J. Gabarro, and J. Holtz, Prentice-Hall, 1978; *Psychotherapy Handbook,* edited by R. Herink, J. Aronson (New York City), 1978; *Working with the Dying and Grieving,* edited by V. Young, International Dialogue (Davis, CA), 1984; *Psychotherapist's Casebook,* edited by I. L. Kutash and A. Wolf, Jossey-Bass, 1986; *Existential-Phenomenological Perspectives in Psychology,* edited by R. Valle and S. Halling, Jossey-Bass, 1988; *What is Psychotherapy: Contemporary Perspectives,* edited by J. K. Zeig and W. M. Munion, Jossey-Bass, 1990; (with M. M. Sterling) *Modern Psychotherapies: Theory and Practice,* edited by S. Messer and A. Gurman, Guilford (New York City), 1995.

Contributor to periodicals, including *Credit Union Executive, Humanistic Psychologist, Independent Practitioner, Journal of Humanistic Psychology, Journal of Integrative and Eclectic Psychotherapy, Journal of Personality, Psychiatry, Psychology Today, Psychotherapy, Psychotherapy Patient,* and *Voices.* Author of numerous reports and professional papers. Author of regular column, "The Persons behind the Ideas," *Journal of Humanistic Psychology,* 1965-66. Associate editor, *Psychological Reports,* 1958-65; assistant editor, *Journal of Humanistic Psychology,* 1963-66, then member of editorial board, 1963—. Member of editorial board of periodicals, including *Clinician's Research Digest, Existential Psychiatry, Interpersonal Development, Journal of Applied Behavioral Science, Journal of Transpersonal Psychology, Psychological Reports,* and *Psychotherapy: Theory, Research, and Practice.*

WORK IN PROGRESS: Theory into Practice: A Resource for Therapists and Their Instructors and Supervisors.

SIDELIGHTS: James F. T. Bugental once told *CA:* "In my writing I try to challenge the boundaries between textbooks and popular literature, between factual reporting and using fiction to portray deeper truths, between the objective and the subjective, and between the personal-emotional and the shared-overly rational. That wise and much quoted authority, Anonymous, once said, 'It's not that things are illusory, but that their separateness in the fabric of reality is illusory.'

"Psychology is, or should be, the most absorbing writing in the world. It tells us, or should tell us, about ourselves. It reminds us, or should remind us, of what we most value, of what we most deeply experience, and of how we seek to give our lives meaning. Sadly, much psychological writing has seemed to be about some other species and thus it has failed the opportunities it so abundantly has.

"I think there are signs that a new generation of psychological writers is breaking free of the constraints that emasculated so much of the field's productivity, making it safe, respectable, and vapid. Still the battle is far from won, and the psychological literature continues to be too dominated by those who pattern their work and their writing on an out-moded and scientistic model.

"To all younger psychologists I want to say, give yourself free rein to tell your own truth as fully and faithfully as you can. Then call into play your own sense of proportion, your maturing intuition of the broader implications of your work, your esthetic judgment, your personal sense of responsibility and commitment. Use these to refine, tighten, and make more eloquent and honest what you have to say. Finally, take the risk and endure the struggle to submit your work again and again to editors until it is published. And if you don't find such an editor, get mad and start a journal, publish your own book, in some way *get what you have to say out where it can be read.*"

*　　*　　*

BURKE, Colin Bradley 1936-

PERSONAL: Born January 3, 1936, in San Francisco, CA; son of Thomas (a leatherworker) and Eva (Sale) Burke; married Rosita Turner, 1972; children: Lucas Scott, Colin Andrew. *Education:* San Francisco State College (now University), B.A., 1962, M.A., 1968; Washington University, St. Louis, MO, Ph.D., 1973. *Politics:* Independent/New Dealer. *Religion:* Protestant.

ADDRESSES: Office—Department of History, University of Maryland, Baltimore County, 5401 Wilkens Ave., Catonsville, MD 21228.

CAREER: San Francisco State College (now University), San Francisco, CA, lecturer in social science, 1969-72; University of Maryland, Baltimore County, Catonsville, assistant professor of history, 1972—. Worked as professional musician, 1952-72.

MEMBER: Social Science History Association.

AWARDS, HONORS: Fellow of Newberry Library, 1974, and National Endowment for the Humanities, 1976-77; Spencer Foundation grant, 1978-79.

WRITINGS:

American Collegiate Populations: A Test of the Traditional View, New York University Press (New York City), 1982.

Information and Secrecy: Vannevar Bush, Ultra, and the Other Memex, Scarecrow Press (Metuchen, NJ), 1994.

It Wasn't All Magic, NSA, 1996.

Contributor to history journals.

WORK IN PROGRESS: The American Ultra Spy, The Information Age Emerges, and *Higher Education, 1970-2000.*

SIDELIGHTS: Colin Bradley Burke once told *CA:* "My work on nineteenth-century American colleges and their students was prompted by an interest in American education and by an intuition that the standing Whig interpretations of development of American higher education were, at minimum, too simplistic. My book and the work of many others—such as that of David Allmendinger—reveal that the United States has not experienced a linear progression to an equitable educational system and that the determinants of the higher educational system were more complex, both before and after the American Civil War, than previously pictured."

*   *   *

BURKE, John (Frederick) 1922-
(Jonathan Burke, Owen Burke, Jonathan George, Joanna Jones, Robert Miall, Sara Morris, Martin Sands; Harriet Esmond, a joint pseudonym)

PERSONAL: Born March 8, 1922, in Rye, Sussex, England; son of Frederick Goode (a police officer) and Lilian Gertrude (Sands) Burke; married Joan Morris, September 13, 1941 (divorced, 1963); married Jean Williams, June 29, 1963; children: (first marriage) Bronwen, Jennifer, Sara, Jane, Joanna; (second marriage) David, Edmund. *Education:* Attended Holt School, Liverpool, England. *Politics:* Socialist. *Religion:* Agnostic. *Avocational interests:* Music.

ADDRESSES: Home and office—5 Castle Gardens, Kirkcudbright, Dumfries & Galloway DG6 4JE, Scotland. *Agent*—Harold Ober Associates, Inc., 40 East 49th St., New York, NY 10017; and David Higham Associates Ltd., 5-8 Lower John St., Golden Sq., London W1R 4HA, England.

CAREER: Writer. Museum Press Ltd., London, England, associate editor, 1953-56, production manager, 1956-57; Hamlyn Publishing Group Ltd., London, editorial manager of "Books for Pleasure" group, 1957-58; Shell International Petroleum, London, publicity media executive, 1959-63; Twentieth Century-Fox Productions, London, European story editor, 1963-65. *Military service:* Royal Air Force, Royal Electrical and Mechanical Engineers, and attachment to Royal Marines during liberation of Europe, 1942-47; became sergeant.

MEMBER: Society of Authors, Danish Club (London).

AWARDS, HONORS: Rockefeller Foundation Atlantic Award in Literature, 1947, for *Swift Summer.*

WRITINGS:

NOVELS

Swift Summer, Laurie (London), 1949.
Another Chorus, Laurie, 1949.
These Haunted Streets, Laurie, 1950.
The Outward Walls, Laurie, 1951.
Chastity House, Laurie, 1952.
The Poison Cupboard, Secker & Warburg (London), 1956.
The Suburbs of Pleasure, Dial (New York City), 1967.
Expo 80, Cassell (London), 1972.
The Black Charade: A Dr. Caspian Story, Coward, 1977.
Ladygrove: The Third Adventure of Dr. Caspian and Bronwen, Coward, 1978.
The Devil's Footsteps, Coward, 1979.

AS JONATHAN BURKE: NOVELS, UNLESS OTHERWISE NOTED

The Dark Gateway, Panther Books, 1954.
The Echoing Worlds, Panther Books, 1954.
Twilight of Reason, Panther Books, 1954.
Pattern of Shadows, Museum Press (London), 1954.
Hotel Cosmos, Panther Books, 1954.
Deep Freeze, Panther Books, 1955.
Revolt of the Humans, Panther Books, 1955.
Alien Landscapes (short stories), Museum Press, 1955.
Pursuit through Time, Ward, Lock (London), 1956.
Echo of Barbara, John Long (London), 1959.
Fear by Installments, John Long, 1960.
Deadly Downbeat, John Long, 1962.
Teach Yourself Treachery, John Long, 1962.
The Twisted Tongues, John Long, 1964, published as *Echo of Treason,* Dodd (New York City), 1966.
Only the Ruthless Can Play, John Long, 1965.
The Weekend Girls, John Long, 1966.
The Gossip Truth, Doubleday (Garden City, NY), 1967, published as *Gossip to the Grave,* John Long, 1967.
Someone Lying, Someone Dying, John Long, 1968.
Rob the Lady, John Long, 1969.
Four Stars for Danger, John Long, 1970.

NOVEL; AS OWEN BURKE

The Figurehead, Coward, 1979.

NOVELS; AS JONATHAN GEORGE

The Kill Dog, Doubleday, 1970.
Dead Letters, Macmillan (New York City), 1972.

NOVELS; AS JOANNA JONES

Nurse Is a Neighbor, M. Joseph (London), 1958.
Nurse on the District, M. Joseph, 1959.
The Artless Flat-Hunter, Pelham Books (London), 1963.
The Artless Commuter, Pelham Books, 1965.

NOVELS; AS ROBERT MIALL

UFO, Pan Books (London), 1970.
UFO 2, Pan Books, 1971.
Jason King, Pan Books, 1972.
Kill Jason King!, Pan Books, 1972.
The Protectors, Pan Books, 1973.
The Adventurer, Pan Books, 1973.

NOVEL; AS SARA MORRIS

A Widow for the Winter, Barker (London), 1961.

NOVELS; WITH WIFE, JEAN BURKE, UNDER JOINT PSEUDONYM HARRIET ESMOND

Darsham's Tower, Delacorte (New York City), 1973, published as *Darsham's Folly,* Collins (London), 1973.
The Eye Stones, Delacorte, 1975.
The Florian Signet, Fawcett (New York City), 1977.

TRAVELOGUES

(With William Luscombe) *The Happy Invaders: A Picture of Denmark in Springtime,* R. Hale (London), 1956.
Suffolk, Batsford (London), 1971.
England in Colour, Batsford, 1972.
Sussex, Batsford, 1974.
Illustrated History of England, BCA Publications, 1974, revised edition, 1985.
English Villages, Batsford, 1975.
South East England (juvenile), Faber & Faber London), 1975.
Czechoslovakia, Batsford, 1976.
Suffolk in Photographs, Batsford, 1976.
Beautiful Britain, Batsford, 1976.
Historic Britain, Batsford, 1977.
Life in the Villa in Roman Britain, Batsford, 1978.
Life in the Medieval Castle in Britain, Batsford, 1978.
Look Back on England, Orbis (London), 1980.
The English Inn, Batsford, 1981.
Musical Landscapes, Webb & Bower (Exeter, England), 1983.
Roman England, Norton (New York City), 1984.
A Traveller's History of Scotland, Murray (London), 1990.

Contributor to Reader's Digest/Automobile Association tourist publications.

FILM AND PLAY ADAPTATIONS

The Entertainer, Four Square, 1960.
Look Back in Anger, Four Square, 1960.
The Three Hundred Spartans, Signet (New York City), 1961, published as *The Lion of Sparta,* Four Square, 1961.
Flame in the Streets, Four Square, 1961.
The Angry Silence, Hodder & Stoughton (London), 1961.
The Boys, Pan Books, 1962.
Private Potter, Pan Books, 1962.
The Man Who Finally Died, Pan Books, 1963.
The World Ten Times Over, Pan Books, 1963.
Guilty Party, Elek (London), 1963.
The System, Pan Books, 1964.
A Hard Day's Night, Dell (New York City), 1964.
Dr. Terror's House of Horrors, Pan Books, 1965.
Those Magnificent Men in Their Flying Machines, Pocket Books (New York City), 1965, published as *That Magnificent Air Race,* Pocket Books (London), 1965.
The Trap, Pan Books, 1966.
The Hammer Horror Omnibus, Pan Books, 1966.
The Power Game, Pan Books, 1966.
The Second Hammer Horror Omnibus, Pan Books, 1967.
Privilege, Pan Books, 1967.
Till Death Do Us Part, Pan Books, 1967.
(As Martin Sands) *Maroc 7,* Pan Books, 1967.
(As Martin Sands) *The Jokers,* Pan Books, 1967.
The Smashing Bird I Used to Know, Pan Books, 1967.
Smashing Time, Pan Books, 1968.
The Bliss of Mrs. Blossom, Pan Books, 1968.
Chitty Chitty Bang Bang: The Story of the Film, Pan Books, 1969.
Moon Zero Two: The Story of the Film, Signet (New York City), 1969.
(As Martin Sands) *The Best House in London,* Mayflower Books (New York City), 1969.
Strange Report, Hodder & Stoughton, 1970.
All the Right Noises, Hodder & Stoughton, 1970.
Dad's Army, Hodder & Stoughton, 1971.
Luke's Kingdom, Fontana (London), 1976.
The Prince Regent, Fontana, 1979.
The Bill, Volumes 1-6, Mandarin (London), 1985-1992.
The Fourth Floor, Thames Methuen (London), 1986.
King and Castle, Thames Methuen, 1986.
London's Burning, Simon & Schuster (New York City), 1992.
London's Burning: Blue Watch Blues, Simon & Schuster, 1995.
London's Burning: Flashpoint, Simon & Schuster, 1995.

OTHER

Safe Conduct (television play), produced by Granada TV, 1965.

(Editor) *Tales of Unease* (story anthology), Pan Books, 1966.

Tales of Unease (television plays based on anthology of same title edited by Burke), produced by London Weekend TV, 1969.

(Editor) *More Tales of Unease* (story anthology), Pan Books, 1969.

(Story editor and contributor) *The Frighteners* (television plays), produced by London Weekend TV, 1972.

(Editor) *New Tales of Unease* (story anthology), Pan Books, 1976.

A Dictionary of Music, Crossroad (New York City), 1988.

Also author of radio plays produced by British Broadcasting Corp.-Radio, including *The Prodigal Pupil, The Man in the Ditch,* and *Across Miss Desmond's Desk.* Author of screenplay, *Terror for Kicks.* Translator of two books from the French; also collaborator on three translations from the Danish.

ADAPTATIONS: Echo of Barbara was filmed by Independent Artists; *Nurse Is a Neighbor* was filmed as *Nurse on Wheels,* Anglo-Amalgamated; *Terror for Kicks* was filmed as *The Sorcerers.*

WORK IN PROGRESS: An historical study of Sir John Forster, Warden of the Marches during Anglo-Scottish warfare and cattle rustling during the 16th century.

SIDELIGHTS: John Burke once told *CA* that he has "always had a strong sense of *place* and cannot write either fiction or historical/topographical works without personal knowledge of setting and background." He therefore travels widely throughout Britain to gain material for his writings. He mentioned that he relies "a great deal" on his wife, Jean, for her collaborative efforts under the joint pseudonym Harriet Esmond. Burke plays piano, harpsichord, and clarinet and knows French and Danish.

*　　*　　*

BURKE, Jonathan
　　See BURKE, John (Frederick)

*　　*　　*

BURKE, Owen
　　See BURKE, John (Frederick)

BYATT, A(ntonia) S(usan Drabble) 1936-

PERSONAL: Born August 24, 1936, in Sheffield, England; daughter of John Frederick (a judge) and Kathleen Marie (Bloor) Drabble; married Ian Charles Rayner Byatt (an economist), July 4, 1959 (divorced, 1969); married Peter John Duffy, 1969; children: (first marriage) Antonia, Charles (deceased); (second marriage) Isabel, Miranda. *Education:* Newnham College, Cambridge, B.A. (first class honors), 1957; graduate study at Bryn Mawr College, 1957-58, and Somerville College, Oxford, 1958-59.

ADDRESSES: Home—37 Rusholme Rd., London SW15 3LF, England.

CAREER: University of London, London, England, staff member in extra-mural department, 1962-71; Central School of Art and Design, London, part-time lecturer in department of liberal studies, 1965-69; University College, London, lecturer, 1972-80, senior lecturer in English, 1981-83, admissions tutor in English, 1980-83; full-time writer, 1983—. Associate of Newnham College, Cambridge, 1977—; fellow of University College, London, 1984—. British Council Lecturer in Spain, 1978, India, 1981, and in Germany, Australia, Hong Kong, China, and Korea; George Eliot Centenary Lecturer, 1980. Member of panel of judges for Booker Prize, 1973, Hawthornden Prize, and David Higham Memorial Prize; member of British Broadcasting Corp. (BBC) Social Effects of Television Advisory Group, 1974-77; member of Communications and Cultural Studies Board of the Council for National Academic Awards, 1978; member of Kingman Committee on the Teaching of English, 1987-88.

MEMBER: Society of Authors (member of committee of management, 1984-88; chairman of committee, 1986-88).

AWARDS, HONORS: English Speaking Union fellowship, 1957-58; fellow of the Royal Society of Literature, 1983; Silver Pen Award for *Still Life;* Booker Prize, 1990, and Irish Times-Aer Lingus International Fiction Prize, 1990, both for *Possession.* D.Litt. from University of Bradford, 1987, University of Durham, 1991, University of Nottingham, 1992, University of Liverpool, 1993, University of Portsmouth, 1994, and University of London, 1995.

WRITINGS:

FICTION

The Shadow of the Sun, Harcourt (London), 1964.
The Game, Chatto & Windus, 1967 (London), Scribner (New York City), 1968.
The Virgin in the Garden (first novel in tetralogy), Chatto & Windus, 1978, Knopf (New York City), 1979.
Still Life (second novel in tetralogy), Chatto & Windus, 1986, Scribner, 1987.

Sugar and Other Stories, Scribner, 1987.

Possession: A Romance, Chatto & Windus, 1990, Vintage (New York City), 1991.

Angels and Insects: Two Novellas, Chatto & Windus, 1992.

The Matisse Stories, Chatto & Windus, 1994.

The Djinn in the Nightengale's Eye, Chatto & Windus, 1995.

NONFICTION

Degrees of Freedom: The Novels of Iris Murdoch, Barnes & Noble (New York City), 1965.

(Contributor) Isobel Armstrong, editor, *The Major Victorian Poets Reconsidered,* Routledge & Kegan Paul (London), 1969.

Wordsworth and Coleridge in Their Time, Nelson, 1970, Crane, Russak (New York City), 1973, reissued as *Unruly Times,* Hogarth (London), 1989.

Iris Murdoch, Longman (London), 1976.

(Editor and author of introduction) George Eliot, *The Mill on the Floss,* Penguin (Middlesex, England), 1979.

(Contributor) Malcolm Bradbury, editor, *The Contemporary English Novel,* Edward Arnold (London), 1979.

(Editor) George Eliot, *Selected Essays, Poems and Other Writings,* Penguin, 1989.

(Editor) Robert Browning, *Dramatic Monologues,* Folio Society (London), 1990.

Passions of the Mind, Chatto & Windus, 1991.

OTHER

Author of prefaces to the following novels published by Virago (New York City) except as indicated: Elizabeth Bowen, *The House in Paris,* Penguin, 1976; Grace Paley, *Enormous Changes at the Last Minute,* 1979; Paley, *The Little Disturbances of Man,* 1980; Willa Cather, *My Antonia,* and *A Lost Lady,* 1980, and *My Mortal Enemy, Shadow on the Rock, Death Comes to the Archbishop, O Pioneers!,* and *Lucy Grayheart.* Also author of dramatized radio documentary on Leo Tolstoy, July, 1978; author of dramatized portraits of George Eliot and Samuel Taylor Coleridge for the National Portrait Gallery. Regular reviewer for the London *Times* and the *New Statesman;* contributor of reviews to *Encounter, New Review,* and *American Studies.* Member of editorial board of *Encyclopaedia,* Longman-Penguin, 1989.

SIDELIGHTS: Because of A. S. Byatt's wide experience as a critic, novelist, editor, and lecturer, she "offers in her work an intellectual kaleidoscope of our contemporary world," wrote Caryn McTighe Musil in the *Dictionary of Literary Biography.* "Her novels, like her life, are dominated by an absorbing, discriminating mind which finds intellectual passions as vibrant and consuming as emotional ones." Musil indicated that Byatt's first novel, *The Shadow of the Sun,* reflects the author's own struggle to combine the role of critic with that of novelist on the one hand, and the role of mother with that of visionary on the other. *The Game,* "a piece of technical virtuosity," according to Musil, "is also a taut novel that explores with a courage and determined honesty greater than [D. H.] Lawrence's the deepest levels of antagonism that come with intimacy. Widely reviewed, especially in Great Britain, *The Game* established Byatt's reputation as an important contemporary novelist, though the book's readership was not extensive."

Byatt's novel *The Virgin in the Garden* was described by *Times Literary Supplement* reviewer Michael Irwin as a "careful, complex novel." The book's action is set in 1953, the year of the coronation of Queen Elizabeth II, and Irwin reported that "its theme is growing up, coming of age, tasting knowledge." The book "is a highly intellectual operation," pointed out Iris Murdoch in *New Statesman.* "The characters do a great deal of thinking, and have extremely interesting thoughts which are developed at length." "The novel's central symbol," Musil related, "is Queen Elizabeth I, a monarch Byatt sees as surviving because she used her mind and thought things out, unlike her rival, Mary, Queen of Scots, who was 'very female and got it wrong.' " In Musil's opinion, the work initiated "the middle phase of [Byatt's] career as a novelist. Much denser [than her previous novels] and dependent on her readers' erudition, [*The Virgin in the Garden*] achieves a style that suits Byatt. It blends her acquisitive, intellectual bent with her imaginative compulsion to tell stories," Musil pointed out.

The 1990 publication of *Possession* brought even greater attention to Byatt. In *Possession,* Byatt tells the story of Roland Michell and Maud Bailey, two contemporary literary scholars whose paths cross during their research. Roland is an expert on the famous Victorian poet Randolph Henry Ash, while Maud's interest is Christabel LaMotte, an obscure poet. Roland and Maud discover evidence that the two Victorians were linked in a passionate relationship; their joint investigation into the lives of the two writers leads to a love affair of their own. Byatt was widely acclaimed for her skillful handling of this complex story. In a *Spectator* review, Anita Brookner called *Possession* "capacious, ambitious . . . marvelous," and noted that it is "teeming with more ideas than a year's worth of ordinary novels." Danny Karlin declared in *London Review of Books* that Byatt's romance was "spectacular both in its shortcomings and its successes; it has vaulting literary ambitions and is unafraid to crash."

Much of the plot of *Possession* is conveyed through poetry and correspondence attributed to Ash and LaMotte, and many reviewers marvelled at Byatt's sure touch in creating authentic voices for the fictional Victorians. *New York Times Book Review* contributor Jay Parini commented:

"The most dazzling aspect of *Possession* is Ms. Byatt's canny invention of letters, poems and diaries from the 19th century. She quotes whole vast poems by Ash and LaMotte, several of which . . . are highly plausible versions of [Robert] Browning and [Christina] Rossetti and are beautiful poems on their own." Parini was also enthusiastic about the manner in which the love story of Ash and LaMotte serves as "ironic counterpoint" to the modern affair between Maud and Roland. Parini concluded: "*Possession* is a tour de force that opens every narrative device of English fiction to inspection without, for a moment, ceasing to delight." The literary world's high regard for the novel is reflected in the fact that Byatt was awarded England's prestigious Booker Prize for *Possession* in 1990.

Not every critic found favor with *Possession,* however. In a *New Criterion* article, Donna Rifkind called Byatt "deplorably inept at creating imitations of important Victorian poetry" and stated that "the best that can be said of this novel is that it is a kind of intellectual cult book." In her view, "the most effective aspect of *Possession* is not its satire of contemporary academic warfare, its literary self-consciousness, or the complexity of its detective-story plot. . . . [It is] its eloquent declaration of a single simple point: that Roland and Maud, highly trained specialists in the very latest theories about sexuality and the ego, do not know the first thing about finding sexual fulfillment for themselves." Still, far more reviews echoed the sentiments expressed by Joyce Carol Oates in *Vogue.* She called *Possession* "lushly sensuous, . . . vigorously intelligent, canny," "highly idiosyncratic," and "wonderfully entertaining."

The praise continued when *Angels and Insects* was published in 1992. This volume contains two novellas set in the Victorian era. The first, "Morpho Eugenia," concerns a biologist who becomes part of a wealthy household with an ugly secret. The second, "The Conjugial Angel," revolves around the Victorian fascination with spiritualism. Marilyn Butler, a reviewer for *Times Literary Supplement,* called *Angels and Insects* "more fully assured and satisfying than *Possession*" and rated it as Byatt's "best work to date." *Belles Lettres* contributor Tess Lewis asserted that "Byatt brings vividly to life the divided Victorian soul—split between faith in the intellect and instinct, free will and determinism, and rationalism and spiritualism. . . . The sheer beauty of many scenes as well as Byatt's luxurious, evocative language remain with the reader long after the clever plots and intriguing, but occasionally too lengthy, intellectual constructs have faded. Byatt's writing is masterful."

With *The Matisse Stories,* Byatt moved into a new phase, one in which she adopted a more concrete style. The stories in the book all make some reference to the French impressionist painter Henri Matisse. "The lasting impression the reader has of Antonia Byatt's three stories in this collection is of an extravagance of color, a riot of color, venous-blue and fuchsia-red and crimson and orange henna and copper," David Plante related in the *Los Angeles Times Book Review.* "Byatt's fiction . . . is essentially informed by an intelligent, even a scholarly mind, pitched more to interpretation rather than fact in itself, to 'ideas' rather than 'things.' But it is as though in 'The Matisse Stories' Byatt were trying to break out onto another level, that of making art." London *Observer* writer Helen Dunmore agreed: "These stories show us Byatt still advancing in her technique and range. Like Matisse she is excited by the way a vase of flowers, a white book or a human being stands in the stream of everyday light, and like Matisse she knows how to set down her observations."

Byatt once told *CA:* "Perhaps the most important thing to say about my books is that they try to be about the life of the mind as well as of society and the relations between people. I admire—am excited by—intellectual curiosity of any kind (scientific, linguistic, psychological) and also by literature as a complicated, huge, interrelating pattern. I also like recording small observed facts and feelings. I see writing and thinking as a passionate activity, like any other."

BIOGRAPHICAL/CRITICAL SOURCES:

BOOKS

Contemporary Literary Criticism, Gale (Detroit), Volume 19, 1981, Volume 65, 1991.
Dictionary of Literary Biography, Volume 14: *British Novelists Since 1960,* Gale, 1983.

PERIODICALS

Belles Lettres, fall, 1993, pp. 28-29.
Books and Bookmen, January 4, 1979.
Chicago Tribune, June 13, 1993, section 14, p. 3.
Chicago Tribune Book World, January 12, 1986.
Christian Science Monitor, March 31, 1992, p. 13; May 25, 1993, p. 13.
Encounter, July, 1968.
London Review of Books, March 8, 1990, pp. 17-18.
Los Angeles Times, November 18, 1985.
Los Angeles Times Book Review, October 28, 1990, pp. 2, 13; June 13, 1993, p. 8; April 23, 1995.
Ms., June, 1979.
New Criterion, February, 1991, pp. 77-80.
New Leader, April 23, 1979.
New Republic, January 7-14, 1991, pp. 47-49.
New Statesman, November 3, 1978.

New Statesman and Society, March 16, 1990, p. 38.

New York Times Book Review, July 26, 1964; March 17, 1968; April 1, 1979; November 24, 1985; July 19, 1987; October 21, 1990, pp. 9, 11; June 27, 1993, p. 14.

Observer (London), March 11, 1990, p. 68; January 2, 1994, p. 17.

Spectator, March 3, 1990, p. 35; January 15, 1994, p. 28.

Times (London), June 6, 1981; April 9, 1987; March 1, 1990.

Times Literary Supplement, January 2, 1964; January 19, 1967; November 3, 1978; June 28, 1985; March 2, 1990, pp. 213-14; October 16, 1992, p. 22.

Vogue, November, 1990, pp. 274, 276.

Washington Post, March 16, 1979; November 22, 1985.

Washington Post Book World, March 29, 1992, p. 11; May 2, 1993, p. 1, 10.

Yale Review, October, 1993, 135-37.

—Sketch by Joan Goldsworthy

C

CAMERON, Lorna
See FRASER, Anthea

*   *   *

CAMERON, Peter 1959-

PERSONAL: Born November 29, 1959, in Pompton Plains, NJ; son of Donald O. (an economist) and Sally (a homemaker; maiden name, Shaw) Cameron. *Education:*Hamilton College, B.A., 1982.

ADDRESSES: Home—New York, NY. *Agent*—Candida Donadio & Associates, Inc., 231 West 22nd St., New York, NY 10011.

CAREER: St. Martin's Press, New York City, subsidiary rights assistant, 1982-83; Trust for Public Land, New York City, word processor, 1983—. Assistant professor at Oberlin College, Oberlin, Ohio, 1987.

MEMBER: PEN, Authors Guild.

AWARDS, HONORS: Short stories included in *Prize Stories: O. Henry Awards:* "Homework," 1985, and "Excerpts from Swanlake," 1986; National Endowment for the Arts Grant fellowship, 1987; PEN-Hemingway Award, honorable mention, 1987.

WRITINGS:

One Way or Another (short stories), Harper (New York City), 1986.
Leap Year (novel), Harper (New York City), 1990.
Far-Flung (short stories), HarperCollins (New York City), 1991.
The Weekend (novel), Farrar, Straus (New York City), 1994.

SIDELIGHTS: Peter Cameron received widespread critical attention for his first book, *One Way or Another,* a collection of what many reviewers characterized as sensitive, well-crafted short stories that focus on the crises and decisions ordinary people have to face in their everyday lives. Often compared to the works of minimalist writers Ann Beattie and Raymond Carver, Cameron's stories present such crises in a bare, blunt way, according to a number of critics. In *Boston Review,* for instance, Rosellen Brown argued that his style, like that of "[most] postsixties fiction writers," is "unabashedly impersonal" and "attempts to defy the inevitability of point-of-view" with a "concomitant reduction in emotional volume," while Victor Kantor Burg, in the *New York Times Book Review,* noted that events in Cameron's stories occasionally happen "abruptly and unpredictably."

A major theme in Cameron's work is the sense of isolation and disaffection people experience when faced with dilemmas for which they can find no solution. Divorced from the emotional support of close relationships with family or friends, the central characters in *One Way or Another* reflect what David Leavitt, as quoted by Amy Hempel in the *Los Angeles Times Book Review,* described as "an attitude of angry betrayal" born of a world where "marriages and families, rather than providing havens, are themselves the fulcrums of the most sweeping upheavals." In "Memorial Day," for example, a teenage boy is dismayed when his divorced mother quickly remarries a man only thirteen years his senior, while a young woman in "Fear of Math," taking a summer course in calculus to enter college, retreats from her parents' arguing, and thinks, when her mother begins to confide in her, "Don't tell me this, don't say any of this. I don't want to know you're unhappy." Such are the preoccupations of the author's characters; they are "young adults," according to Alice H. G. Phillips in the *Times Literary Supplement,* "wrapped up in their own problems, surprised that other people can feel pain." But in spite of the apparent self-centeredness of his characters—a condition that led Brown to charge that his stories end "one after the other, in emotional disengagement"—critics applauded Cameron for his handling of what Phillips called the "serious unhappiness and vague hopes" of his heroes, especially when he "allows himself to be swept away by [their] uncertainties [and makes] them his own."

In his novel *The Weekend,* Cameron continued to explore the lives of emotionally repressed characters. The plot unfolds in the comfortable country house of an independently wealthy couple, John and Marian. One year after John's brother Tony died in their home from complications of AIDS, Tony's lover Lyle pays a visit to John and Marian, bringing along his new companion, Robert. Grief, loneliness, and tension come to the surface, and Robert eventually leaves the house. Kevin Allman, commenting on the novel in *Washington Post Book World,* was not particularly enthusiastic. He found the characters self-absorbed and tiresome, and concluded that "while there's nothing wrong with *The Weekend,* there's nothing terribly compelling about it, either. . . . [Cameron's] triumphs here are the kind that shine in a short story but stretch thin over the course of a whole novel."

Other reviewers, such as Michael Dorris, differed sharply from Allman in their assessment of *The Weekend.* Writing in the *Los Angeles Times,* Dorris observed that "like the late British novelist Barbara Pym, Peter Cameron has the rare ability to take an ordinary event, a period of time in which almost nothing ostensibly happens, and invest it with heart and significance. . . . 'The Weekend' is a short book, but it's concise in the way of a poem or brilliant one-act play: each line, each word matters." Joyce Reiser Kornblatt also gave high marks to Cameron's work, declaring in the *New York Times Book Review* that "at its best moments, 'The Weekend' echoes Virginia Woolf, E. M. Forster, D. H. Lawrence and F. Scott Fitzgerald. . . . And if Mr. Cameron's novel does not always reach that level of artistry, it is still a pleasure to encounter the work of a contemporary American novelist who aspires to such complexity, precision, lyricism and compassion."

BIOGRAPHICAL/CRITICAL SOURCES:

BOOKS

Cameron, Peter, *One Way or Another,* Harper, 1986.
Contemporary Literary Criticism, Volume 44, Gale, 1986.

PERIODICALS

Boston Review, August, 1986.
Los Angeles Times, July 28, 1994, p. E6.
Los Angeles Times Book Review, May 11, 1986.
Newsweek, September 15, 1986.
New York Times Book Review, June 22, 1986; October 25, 1987; May 29, 1994, p. 16.

Times Literary Supplement, September 5, 1986.
Tribune Books, October 5, 1986.
Washington Post Book World, June 26, 1994, p. 4.*

*   *   *

CARPENTER, Kenneth J(ohn) 1923-

PERSONAL: Born May 17, 1923, in London, England; immigrated to United States, 1977; son of James F. (in commerce) and Dorothy (a teacher; maiden name, George) Carpenter; married Antonina Pecoraro, June 18, 1977. *Education:* Cambridge University, B.A., 1944, Ph.D., 1948, Sc.D., 1975.

ADDRESSES: Home—6201 Rockwell St., Oakland, CA 94618. *Office*—Department of Nutritional Science, University of California, Berkeley, CA 94720-3104.

CAREER: Rowett Institute, Aberdeen, Scotland, scientific officer in nutrition, 1948-56; Cambridge University, Cambridge, England, lecturer, 1956-75, reader in nutrition, 1975-77, fellow of Sidney Sussex College, 1961-77; University of California, Berkeley, professor of experimental nutrition, 1977-92, chair of department of nutritional science, 1981-83; historical editor, *Journal of Nutrition,* 1990—. Royal Society fellow, Central Food Research Institute, Mysore, India, 1960.

MEMBER: American Association for the History of Medicine, History of Science Society, British Nutrition Society.

AWARDS, HONORS: Kellogg fellow, Harvard University, 1955-56; fellow, American Institute of Nutrition, 1992; Atwater Medal, U.S. Department of Agriculture, 1993.

WRITINGS:

Pellagra, Hutchinson Ross (Stroudsburg, PA), 1981.
The History of Scurvy and Vitamin C, Cambridge University Press (Cambridge), 1986.
Protein and Energy: A Study of Changing Ideas in Nutrition, Cambridge University Press, 1994.

WORK IN PROGRESS: White Rice and Vitamin B: A Chapter in Colonial Science.

SIDELIGHTS: Kenneth J. Carpenter once told *CA:* "My interest is in the history of ideas and the diversity of cultural beliefs. I try to relate this to what I see in my professional work as a scientist in the field of nutrition."

BIOGRAPHICAL/CRITICAL SOURCES:

PERIODICALS

European Journal of Clinical Nutrition, Vol. 49, 1995, p. 307.

Nature, November 13, 1986.

New England Journal of Medicine, January 22, 1987.

Times Literary Supplement, November 7, 1986; January 13, 1995.

* * *

CASTEL, J(ean) G(abriel) 1928-

PERSONAL: Born September 17, 1928, in Nice, France; son of Charles (in business) and Simone (Ricour) Castel; children: Christopher, Maria, Marc, Matthew. *Education:* University of Aix-Marseille, B.Sc. and Phil., 1947; University of Paris, LL.B. and LL.M., 1950; University of Michigan, J.D., 1953; Harvard University, S.J.D., 1958. *Religion:* Roman Catholic. *Avocational interests:* Travel, riding, swimming, scuba diving, music, and painting.

ADDRESSES: Home—R.R. 5, Orangeville, Ontario, Canada. *Office*—Osgoode Hall Law School, York University, Toronto, Ontario, Canada.

CAREER: United Nations, Department of Economic Affairs, New York City, legal research assistant, 1952; employed with Dewey, Ballantine, Busby, Palmer, & Wood (law firm), New York City, 1953; McGill University, Montreal, Quebec, assistant professor, 1954-55, associate professor of law, 1955-59; York University, Osgoode Hall Law School, Toronto, Ontario, professor of law, 1959—; barrister and solicitor, Toronto, 1960—. Visiting professor, Laval University and University of Montreal, both 1959-68, University of Mexico, 1963, University of Lisbon, 1964, University of Nice, 1968, University of Puerto Rico, 1973, University of Montreal, 1979, University of Ottawa, 1980, McGill University, 1981, University of Aukland, 1981, University of Paris I (Sorbonne), 1982, and University of Aix-Marseille, 1983-95. President, committee on private international law, Office for the Revision of the Civil Code (Quebec). Consultant to Department of External Affairs, Canadian Government, and Canada Law Reform Commission, 1978-80. *Military service:* Served with French resistance, 1944-45.

MEMBER: International Law Association, International Academy of Comparative Law, International Faculty of Comparative Law, Academie du Var, Canadian Bar Association (council, 1957-86), Association of Canadian Law Teachers, Royal Society of Canada (fellow).

AWARDS, HONORS: Fulbright scholar, 1950; British Commonwealth fellow, 1962; Killam scholar, 1986; member of Order of Canada; Chevalier Legion d'Honneur; Confederation Medal and Jubilee Medal; Order of Ontario; distinguished research professor, Queen's Counsel; honorary doctorate, University of Aix-Marseille.

WRITINGS:

Foreign Judgments: A Comparative Study, McGill University Press (Montreal), 1956.

Private International Law, Canada Law Book, 1960.

Cases, Notes and Materials on the Conflict of Laws, Butterworths (Toronto), 1960, 6th edition published as *Conflict of Laws,* 1986.

Civil Law System of Quebec, Butterworths, 1962.

International Law, Chiefly as Interpreted and Applied in Canada, University of Toronto Press (Toronto), 1965, 6th edition, 1994.

Canadian Conflict of Laws, two volumes, Butterworths, 1975, 3rd edition, 1995.

(With S. A. Williams) *International Criminal Law,* York University (Toronto), 1975.

Introduction to Conflict of Laws, Butterworths, 1978, 2nd edition, 1986.

Droit International Prive Quebecois, Butterworths, 1980.

(With Williams) *Canadian Criminal Law: International and Transnational Aspects,* Butterworths, 1981.

(With Armand de Mestral and William C. Graham) *International Business Transactions and Economic Relations: Cases, Notes, and Materials on the Law as It Applies to Canada,* Emond Montgomery, 1986.

International Judicial Cooperation, Government of Canada, 1987.

Extraterritoriality in International Trade, Butterworths, 1988.

(With de Mestral and Graham) *The Canadian Law and Practice of International Trade,* Emond Montgomery, 1991.

Contributor to periodicals. Editor, *Canadian Bar Review,* 1957-85.

WORK IN PROGRESS: A new edition of *The Canadian Law and Practice of International Trade.*

SIDELIGHTS: J. G. Castel once told *CA:* "There are no shortcuts to scholarship."

* * *

CHADWICK, Henry 1920-

PERSONAL: Born June 23, 1920, in Bromley, Kent, England; son of John (a barrister) and Edith (Horrocks) Chadwick; married Margaret Elizabeth Brownrigg, 1945; children: Priscilla, Hilary, Juliet. *Education:* Magdalene College, Cambridge, B.A. and Mus.B., 1941. *Avocational interests:* Music.

ADDRESSES: Home and office—46 St. John Street, Oxford OX1 2LH, England.

CAREER: Ordained priest, Church of England, 1943; Wellington College, Berkshire, England, assistant master,

1945; Cambridge University, Queens' College, Cambridge, England, fellow and chaplain, 1946-58, dean, 1950-55; Oxford University, Christ Church, Oxford, Regius Professor of Divinity and canon, 1959-69, dean, 1969-79; Cambridge University, Divinity School, Regius Professor of Divinity, 1979-82; Master of Peterhouse, Cambridge, 1987-93. Visiting professor, University of Chicago, 1957; Forwood Lecturer, University of Liverpool, 1961; Hewett Lecturer, Union Theological Seminary, 1962; Gifford Lecturer, University of St. Andrews, 1962-64; Burns Lecturer, University of Otago, 1971. Delegate, Oxford University Press, 1960-79.

MEMBER: British Academy (fellow), Academie des Inscriptions et Belles Lettres (correspondent), American Academy of Arts and Sciences, American Philosophical Society, Goettingen Academy.

AWARDS, HONORS: D.D., University of Glasgow, 1957, and Yale University, 1970; D.Teol., University of Uppsala, 1967; D.H.L., University of Chicago, 1978; Humboldt Prize, 1983; Leopold Lucas Prize, Tuebingen, 1989.

WRITINGS:

(Editor and translator) Origen, *Contra Celsum,* Cambridge University Press (Cambridge, England), 1953, revised edition, 1980.

(Editor, with John E. L. Oulton) *Alexandrian Christianity,* Westminster (London), 1954.

(Editor and translator) Gotthold Lessing, *Lessing's Theological Writings,* A. & C. Black (London), 1956, Stanford University Press (Stanford, CA), 1957.

(Editor) Wilfred Lawrence Knox, *Sources of the Synoptic Gospels,* Volume 2, Cambridge University Press, 1957.

(Editor) *The Sentences of Sextus: A Contribution to the History of Early Christian Ethics,* Cambridge University Press, 1959.

(Editor) *St. Ambrose on the Sacraments,* Loyola University Press (Chicago), 1960.

The Vindication of Christianity in Westcott's Thought, Cambridge University Press, 1961.

(Contributor) M. Black and H. H. Rowley, editors, *Peake's Commentary on the Bible,* Thomas Nelson (Surrey, England), 1962.

(With Hans Von Campenhausen) *Jerusalem and Rome: The Problem of Authority in the Early Church,* Fortress (Philadelphia), 1966.

Early Christian Thought and the Classical Tradition, Oxford University Press (Oxford, England), 1966.

The Early Church, Penguin (London), 1967, published as *The Early Christian Church,* Eerdmans (Grand Rapids, MI), 1969, revised edition, 1993.

Die Kirche in der antiken Welt, de Gruyter (Germany), 1973.

Priscillian of Avila: The Occult and the Charismatic in the Early Church, Oxford University Press, 1976.

Boethius: The Consolations of Music, Logic, Theology and Philosophy, Oxford University Press, 1981.

History and Thought of the Early Church, Variorum (London), 1982.

Augustine, Oxford University Press, 1986.

(With G. R. Evans) *Atlas of the Christian Church,* Macmillan (New York City), 1987.

Heresy and Orthodoxy in the Early Church, Variorum, 1991.

Augustine's Confessions, Oxford University Press, 1991.

Tradition and Exploration, Canterbury Press (Norwich, England), 1993.

General editor, Harper's "New Testament Commentaries," 1958—; editor, *Journal of Theological Studies,* 1954-85. Contributor to professional journals.

SIDELIGHTS: Henry Chadwick's *Boethius: The Consolations of Music, Logic, Theology and Philosophy* is considered by some critics to be one of the finest works on the respected Roman philosopher. "Chadwick has given us not only the first complete intellectual portrait, and a wholly convincing one: he has also allowed its subject to emerge from his pages enhanced in stature, in interest and importance," R. A. Markus writes in the *Times Literary Supplement.*

Of his writing, Chadwick told *CA:* "The story of the Christian Church is a fascinating narrative, and I have tried to write a true account especially (but not only) of the career of this society with its faith (and sometimes its follies) in the centuries of antiquity, during which Christianity enforced the transition from Ancient to Medieval, and on to Modern. I have tried to write about the people involved in this story with human sympathy and understanding for their problems. A particular interest has been in the divisions and splits of the Christian society, and, partly as a by-product of trying to write true history, I have also written pieces in the attempt to reconcile, without fudge or smudge, bodies which live separate lives and have come to feel themselves to be rival groups. Having retired from administrative office, I now have more leisure to read and write church history."

BIOGRAPHICAL/CRITICAL SOURCES:

PERIODICALS

Times Literary Supplement, January 8, 1982; August 15, 1986.

CHESTER, Laura 1949-

PERSONAL: Born April 13, 1949, in Cambridge, MA; daughter of George Miller (a lawyer) and Margaret (Sheftall) Chester; married Geoffrey M. Young (a writer and editor), August 28, 1969; children: Clovis, Ayler. *Education:* Attended Skidmore College, 1967-69; University of New Mexico, B.S., 1972.

ADDRESSES: Home—25 Rose Hill, Alford, MA 01230.

CAREER: Stooge (magazine), Albuquerque, NM, co-editor, 1969-74; The Figures (small press), Berkeley, CA, co-editor, 1975-82.

AWARDS, HONORS: Stelhoff Poetry Prize from Skidmore College, 1969; Kappa Alpha Theta poetry award from University of New Mexico, 1970.

WRITINGS:

Tiny Talk, Roundhouse, 1972.
(With husband, Geoffrey M. Young) *The All Night Salt Lick,* Tribal Press, 1972.
Nightlatch, Tribal Press, 1974.
Primagravida, Christopher Books, 1975.
Proud and Ashamed, Christopher Books, 1977.
Chunk Off and Float, Cold Mountain, 1978.
Watermark, Figures (Great Barrington, MA), 1978.
My Pleasure, Figures, 1980.
Lupus Novice: Toward Self-Healing, Station Hill Press (Barrytown, NY), 1987.
Free Rein, Burning Deck Press (Providence, RI), 1988.
In the Zone: New and Selected Writing, Black Sparrow Press (Santa Rosa, CA), 1988.
The Stone Baby, Black Sparrow Press, 1989.
Bitches Ride Alone (stories), Black Sparrow Press, 1991.
The Story of the Lake (novel) Faber, 1995.
Kingdom Come (novel), in press.

Contributor of articles and poems to literary magazines.

EDITOR

(With Sharon Barba) *Rising Tides: Twentieth Century American Women Poets,* Simon & Schuster (New York City), 1973.
Deep Down: The New Sensual Writing by Women, Faber (Boston, MA), 1988.
Cradle and All: Women Writers on Pregnancy and Birth, Faber, 1989.
The Unmade Bed: Sensual Writing on Married Love, HarperCollins (New York City), 1992.

Also co-editor of *Best Friends.*

SIDELIGHTS: Laura Chester writes of contemporary American women who suffer from failed love relationships and personal turmoil. Her fiction, according to Francesca Lia Block in the *Los Angeles Times Book Re-* view, "looks unflinchingly at the loss and alienation in the lives of American women" but Chester nonetheless "offers hope." In addition to her stories and poems, Chester has also edited several anthologies of women's writing on sexual topics.

In the short story collection *Bitches Ride Alone,* Chester presents a group of stories narrated by an anonymous divorcee who tells of her search for a stable and fulfilling relationship with a man. She longs, as Eric Mendelsohn explains in the *American Book Review,* "for sexual companionship in a world dominated by flawed men." The stories are told in a style that is a "weaving together of narrative and desire," as Mendelsohn states. They tell of infidelity, the inability of men and women to understand each other, and the painful efforts people make to find love. "But even in the most painful situations," Block comments, "the narrators transform their experience through dreams or fantasies."

Chester has edited several anthologies of women's writing, including *Deep Down: The New Sensual Writing by Women, Cradle and All: Women Writers on Pregnancy and Birth,* and *The Unmade Bed: Sensual Writing on Married Love.* Although Lennard J. Davis of the *Nation* believes that *The Unmade Bed* "will do little to dissuade the middle-aged couple that their sex looks anything but married," Block finds that Chester's selections "reflect her appreciation of the sensual and emotional depths reached through married love."

Chester's novel *The Story of the Lake* is the chronicle of "the passions, struggles, dangerous liaisons and dark secrets in the lives of four extremely wealthy Milwaukee and Chicago families," notes Jenny McPhee in *New York Newsday.* Commenting on the popularity of the historical romance and the family saga, McPhee concludes that Cheater's "sumptuous prose . . . [and] vibrant, sprawling saga . . . fits happily right into this trend." A *Publishers Weekly* reviewer notes Chester's "sensuous period detail" and concludes that *The Story of the Lake* is a "fine novel."

Chester told *CA:* "Being a bride of the sixties, I was influenced by feminism, and yet my writing has never been one of statement. Though I've worked from an intimate perspective, where the intuitive is a formative force, I've also wanted my writing to have a life of its own, word for word's sake, beyond gender, personal history, or explanation.

"My writing often feels similar to the semi-conscious linking of the twilight reverie, what we go to sleep on, the prickling of memory, of audial and surface phenomenon, each unit moving on, yet all held together, as mixed motion in time, like the day in the life of any nurturer. A peopled poetry, an inclusive poetry, taking us beyond the isolation of 'I' familiar to poetic vision.

"I've always understood that a poem, or any piece of writing, has something of its own life, its own force, but now I see that it can also become part of a greater upward or downward spiral. I do not want to limit myself to the perpendicular of intellectualism, nor the squiggles of siren stuff, but I do want to be receptive to the unpredictable curve, letting a wholeness come through me, thought, word and feeling inseparable, inspiration firmly linked to the craft-work of shaping. Writing for me has got to be grand."

BIOGRAPHICAL/CRITICAL SOURCES:

PERIODICALS

American Book Review, November, 1988, p. 7; October-November, 1993, p. 27.
Booklist, January 1, 1992, p. 810.
Choice, September, 1979, p. 828.
Los Angeles Times Book Review, March 8, 1992, p. 8.
Nation, March 29, 1993, pp. 418-20.
Newsday (New York), July 9, 1995.
New York Times, February 15, 1974, p. 31.
Observer (London), February 12, 1989, p. 50.
Parnassus, spring, 1981, p. 284.
Publishers Weekly, November 17, 1989, p. 47; March 27, 1995.
Review of Contemporary Fiction, spring, 1993, p. 260.
Small Press, August, 1989, p. 36.
Times Educational Supplement, April 13, 1990, p. 24.

*   *   *

CHILDRESS, Alice 1920-1994

PERSONAL: Surname is pronounced "*Chil*-dress"; born October 12, 1920, in Charleston, SC; died of cancer, August 14, 1994, in Queens, NY; married second husband, Nathan Woodard (a musician), July 17, 1957; children: (first marriage) Jean (Mrs. Richard Lee). *Education:* Attended public schools in New York, NY.

ADDRESSES: Office—Beacon Press, 25 Beacon St., Boston, MA 02108-2824. *Agent*—c/o Flora Roberts Inc., 157 W. 57th St, New York, NY 10019.

CAREER: Playwright, novelist, actress, and director. Began career in theater as an actress, with her first appearance in *On Strivers Row,* 1940; actress and director with American Negro Theatre, New York City, for eleven years, featured in the plays *Natural Man,* 1941, *Anna Lucasta,* 1944, and *Florence,* which she also wrote and directed, 1949; also performed on Broadway and television. Lecturer at universities and schools; member of panel discussions and conferences on Black American theater at numerous institutions, including New School for Social Research, 1965, and Fisk University, 1966; visiting scholar at Radcliffe Institute for Independent Study (now Mary Ingraham Bunting Institute), Cambridge, MA, 1966-68. Member of governing board of Frances Delafield Hospital.

MEMBER: PEN, Dramatists Guild (member of council), American Federation of Television and Radio Artists, Writers Guild of America East (member of council), Harlem Writers Guild.

AWARDS, HONORS: Obie Award for best original Off-Broadway play, *Village Voice,* 1956, for *Trouble in Mind;* John Golden Fund for Playwrights grant, 1957; Rockefeller grant, 1967; *A Hero Ain't Nothin' but a Sandwich* was named one of the Outstanding Books of the Year by *New York Times Book Review,* 1973, and a Best Young Adult Book of 1975 by American Library Association; Woodward School Book Award, 1974, Jane Addams Children's Book Honor Award for young adult novel, 1974, National Book Award nomination, 1974, and Lewis Carroll Shelf Award, University of Wisconsin, 1975, all for *A Hero Ain't Nothin' but a Sandwich;* Sojourner Truth Award, National Association of Negro Business and Professional Women's Clubs, 1975; Virgin Islands film festival award for best screenplay, and first Paul Robeson Award for Outstanding Contributions to the Performing Arts, Black Filmmakers Hall of Fame, both 1977, both for *A Hero Ain't Nothin' but a Sandwich;* "Alice Childress Week" officially observed in Charleston and Columbia, SC, 1977, to celebrate opening of *Sea Island Song;* Paul Robeson Award, 1980; *Rainbow Jordan* was named one of the "Best Books" by *School Library Journal,* 1981, one of the Outstanding Books of the Year by *New York Times,* 1982, and a notable children's trade book in social studies by National Council for the Social Studies and Children's Book Council, 1982; honorable mention, Coretta Scott King Award, 1982, for *Rainbow Jordan;* Radcliffe Graduate Society Medal, 1984; Audelco Pioneer Award, 1986; Lifetime Achievement Award, Association for Theatre in Higher Education, 1993.

WRITINGS:

Like One of the Family: Conversations from a Domestic's Life, Independence Publishers, 1956, reprinted with an introduction by Trudier Harris, Beacon Press (Boston), 1986.
(Editor) *Black Scenes* (collection of scenes from plays written by African Americans), Doubleday (New York City), 1971.
A Hero Ain't Nothin' but a Sandwich (novel; also see below), Coward (London), 1973.
A Short Walk (novel), Coward, 1979.
Rainbow Jordan (novel), Coward, 1981.
Many Closets, Coward, 1987.

Those Other People, Putnam (New York City), 1989.

PLAYS

Florence (one-act), first produced in New York City at American Negro Theatre, 1949.

Just a Little Simple (based on Langston Hughes's short story collection *Simple Speaks His Mind*), first produced in New York City at Club Baron Theatre, September, 1950.

Gold through the Trees, first produced at Club Baron Theatre, 1952.

Trouble in Mind, first produced Off-Broadway at Greenwich Mews Theatre, November 3, 1955, revised version published in *Black Theatre: A Twentieth-Century Collection of the Work of Its Best Playwrights,* edited by Lindsay Patterson, Dodd (New York City), 1971.

Wedding Band: A Love/Hate Story in Black and White (first produced in Ann Arbor, MI, at University of Michigan, December 7, 1966; produced Off-Broadway at New York Shakespeare Festival Theatre, September 26, 1972; also see below), Samuel French (New York City), 1973.

String (one-act; based on Guy de Maupassant's story "A Piece of String"; also see below), first produced Off-Broadway at St. Mark's Playhouse, March 25, 1969.

Mojo: A Black Love Story (one-act; also see below), produced in New York City at New Heritage Theatre, November, 1970.

Mojo [and] *String,* Dramatists Play Service (New York City), 1971.

When the Rattlesnake Sounds: A Play (juvenile), illustrated by Charles Lilly, Coward, 1975.

Let's Hear It for the Queen: A Play (juvenile), Coward, 1976.

Sea Island Song, produced in Charleston, SC, 1977, produced as *Gullah* in Amherst, MA, at University of Massachusetts—Amherst, 1984.

Moms: A Praise Play for a Black Comedienne (based on the life of Jackie "Moms" Mabley), music and lyrics by Childress and her husband, Nathan Woodard, first produced by Green Plays at Art Awareness, 1986, produced Off-Broadway at Hudson Guild Theatre, February 4, 1987.

Also author of *Martin Luther King at Montgomery, Alabama,* music by Woodard, 1969; *A Man Bearing a Pitcher,* 1969; *The Freedom Drum,* music by Woodard, produced as *Young Man Martin Luther King* by Performing Arts Repertory Theatre, 1969-71; *The African Garden,* music by Woodard, 1971; and *Vashti's Magic Mirror.*

SCREENPLAYS

Wine in the Wilderness: A Comedy-Drama (first produced in Boston by WGBH-TV, March 4, 1969), Dramatists Play Service, 1969.

Wedding Band (based on her play of the same title), American Broadcasting Companies (ABC-TV), 1973.

A Hero Ain't Nothin' but a Sandwich (based on her novel of the same title), New World Pictures, 1978.

String (based on her play of the same title), Public Broadcasting Service (PBS-TV), 1979.

OTHER

Author of "Here's Mildred" column in *Baltimore Afro-American,* 1956-58. Contributor of plays, articles, and reviews to *Masses and Mainstream, Black World, Freedomways, Essence, Negro Digest, New York Times,* and other publications.

SIDELIGHTS: Alice Childress's work is noted for its frank treatment of racial issues, its compassionate yet discerning characterizations, and its universal appeal. Because her books and plays often deal with such controversial subjects as interracial relationships and teenage drug addiction, her work has been banned in certain locations. She recalled that some affiliate stations refused to carry the nationally televised broadcasts of *Wedding Band* and *Wine in the Wilderness,* and in the case of the latter play, the entire state of Alabama banned the telecast. In addition, Childress noted that as late as 1973 the novel *A Hero Ain't Nothin' but a Sandwich* "was the first book banned in a Savannah, Georgia school library since *Catcher in the Rye.*" Despite such regional resistance, Childress won praise and respect for writings that a *Variety* reviewer termed "powerful and poetic."

A talented writer and performer in several media, Childress began her career in the theater, initially as an actress and later as a director and playwright. Although "theater histories make only passing mention of her, . . . she was in the forefront of important developments in that medium," wrote *Dictionary of Literary Biography* contributor Trudier Harris. Rosemary Curb pointed out in another *Dictionary of Literary Biography* essay that Childress's 1952 drama *Gold through the Trees* was "the first play by a black woman professionally produced on the American stage." Moreover, Curb added, "As a result of successful performances of [*Just a Little Simple* and *Gold through the Trees*], Childress initiated Harlem's first all-union Off-Broadway contracts recognizing the Actors Equity Association and the Harlem Stage Hand Local."

Partly because of her pioneering efforts, Childress is considered a crusader by many. But she is also known as "a writer who resists compromise," explained Doris E. Abramson in *Negro Playwrights in the American Theatre: 1925-1959.* "She tries to write about [black] problems as honestly as she can," thus, the problems Childress addressed most often were racism and its effects. Her *Trouble in Mind,* for example, is a play within a play that focuses on the anger and frustration experienced by a troupe of black actors as they try to perform stereotyped roles in a play that has been written, produced, and directed by whites. As Sally R. Sommer explained in the *Village Voice,* "The plot is about an emerging rebellion begun as the heroine, Wiletta, refuses to enact a namby-Mammy, either in the play or for her director." In the *New York Times,* Arthur Gelb stated that Childress "has some witty and penetrating things to say about the dearth of roles for [black] actors in the contemporary theatre, the cutthroat competition for these parts and the fact that [black] actors often find themselves playing stereotyped roles in which they cannot bring themselves to believe." And of *Wedding Band,* a play about an interracial relationship that takes place in South Carolina during World War I, Clive Barnes wrote in the *New York Times,* "Childress very carefully suggests the stirrings of black consciousness, as well as the strength of white bigotry."

Both Sommer and the *New York Times*'s Richard Eder found that Childress's treatment of the themes and issues in *Trouble in Mind* and *Wedding Band* gives these plays a timeless quality. "Writing in 1955, . . . Alice Childress used the concentric circles of the play-within-the-play to examine the multiple roles blacks enact in order to survive," Sommer remarked. She found that viewing *Trouble in Mind* years later enables one to see "its double cutting edge: It predicts not only the course of social history but the course of black playwriting." Eder stated: "The question [in *Wedding Band*] is whether race is a category of humanity or a division of it. The question is old by now, and was in 1965, but it takes the freshness of new life in the marvelous characters that Miss Childress has created to ask it."

The strength and insight of Childress's characterizations have been widely commented upon; critics contend that the characters who populate her plays and novels are believable and memorable. Eder called the characterizations of *Wedding Band: A Love/Hate Story in Black and White* "rich and lively." Similarly impressed, Harold Clurman wrote in the *Nation* that "there is an honest pathos in the telling of this simple story, and some humorous and touching thumbnail sketches reveal knowledge and understanding of the people dealt with." In the novel *A Short Walk,* Childress chronicled the life of a fictitious black woman, Cora James, from her birth in 1900 to her death in the middle of the century, illustrating, as *Washington Post* critic Joseph McLellan described it, "a transitional generation in black American society." McLellan noted that the story "wanders considerably" and that "the reader is left with no firm conclusion that can be put into a neat sentence or two." What is more important, he asserted, is that "the wandering has been through some interesting scenery, and instead of a conclusion the reader has come to know a human being—complex, struggling

valiantly and totally believable." In her play *Moms,* Childress drew a portrait of real-life comic Jackie "Moms" Mabley, a popular black comedienne of the 1960s and 1970s. Dressed as a stereotypical shopping-bag lady, Moms Mabley was a television staple with her stand-up routine as a feisty woman with a sharp tongue. Childress, Mel Gussow writes in the *New York Times,* "shrewdly gives Moms center stage and lets her comic sensibility speak for itself."

In several novels aimed at a young adult audience, Childress displayed her talent for believable characterization. In the novel *A Hero Ain't Nothin' but a Sandwich,* the author creates a portrait of a teenaged heroin addict by giving us his story not only from his point of view but from several of his friends and family as well. The *Lion and the Unicorn*'s Miguel Oritz stated, "The portrait of whites is more realistic in this book, more compassionate, and at the same time, because it is believable, more scathing." In *Those Other People,* Childress tells of a group of young friends who are all outsiders: a homosexual, a wealthy black sister and brother, a teacher who has molested one of his students, and a psychiatric patient who was sexually abused as a girl. Each character tells his or her story in separate chapters. The result is a multi-faceted look at a pivotal incident at their school which calls into question matters of race and sexual preference. Kathryn Havris, writing in the *School Library Journal,* called *Those Other People* "a disturbing, disquieting novel that reflects another side to life." A *Publishers Weekly* critic concluded that the novel was "a penetrating examination of bigotry and racism."

Some criticism has been leveled at what such reviewers as Abramson and Edith Oliver believed to be Childress's tendency to speechify, especially in her plays. "A reader of the script is very much aware of the author pulling strings, putting her own words into a number of mouths," Abramson says of *Trouble in Mind.* According to Oliver in the *New Yorker,* "The first act [of *Wedding Band*] is splendid, but after that we hit a few jarring notes, when the characters seem to be speaking as much for the benefit of us eavesdroppers out front . . . as for the benefit of one another."

Others, however, have acclaimed Childress's work for its honesty, insight, and compassion. In his review of *A Hero Ain't Nothin' but a Sandwich,* Oritz wrote: "The book conveys very strongly the message that we are all human, even when we are acting in ways that we are somewhat ashamed of. The structure of the book grows out of the personalities of the characters, and the author makes us aware of how much the economic and social circumstances dictate a character's actions." Loften Mitchell concluded in *Crisis:* "Childress writes with a sharp, satiric touch. Character seems to interest her more than plot. Her characterizations are piercing, her observations devastating."

Alice Childress once told *CA:* "Books, plays, teleplays, motion picture scenarios, etc., I seem caught up in a fragmentation of writing skills. But an idea comes to me in a certain form and, if it stays with me, must be written out or put in outline form before I can move on to the next event. I sometimes wonder about writing in different forms; could it be that women are used to dealing with the bits and pieces of life and do not feel as [compelled to specialize]? The play form is the one most familiar to me and so influences all of my writing—I think in scenes.

"My young years were very old in feeling, I was shut out of so much for so long. [I] soon began to embrace the low-profile as a way of life, which helped me to develop as a writer. Quiet living is restful when one's writing is labeled 'controversial.'

"Happily, I managed to save a bit of my youth for spending in these later years. Oh yes, there are other things to be saved [besides] money. If we hang on to that part within that was once childhood, I believe we enter into a new time dimension and every day becomes another lifetime in itself. This gift of understanding is often given to those who constantly battle against the negatives of life with determination."

BIOGRAPHICAL/CRITICAL SOURCES:

BOOKS

Abramson, Doris E., *Negro Playwrights in the American Theatre, 1925-1959,* Columbia University Press (New York City), 1969.

Betsko, Kathleen, and Rachel Koenig, *Interviews with Contemporary Women Playwrights,* Beech Tree Books (Taylors, SC), 1987.

Children's Literature Review, Volume 14, Gale (Detroit), 1988.

Contemporary Literary Criticism, Gale, Volume 12, 1980, Volume 15, 1980.

Dictionary of Literary Biography, Gale, Volume 7: *Twentieth-Century American Dramatists,* 1981, Volume 38: *Afro-American Writers after 1955: Dramatists and Prose Writers,* 1985.

Donelson, Kenneth L., and Alleen Pace Nilson, *Literature for Today's Young Adults,* Scott, Foresman (Glenview, IL), 1980, 2nd edition, 1985.

Evans, Mari, editor, *Black Women Writers (1950-1980): A Critical Evaluation,* Doubleday-Anchor (New York City), 1984.

Hatch, James V., *Black Theater, U.S.A.: Forty-five Plays by Black Americans,* Free Press (New York City), 1974.

Mitchell, Loften, editor, *Voices of the Black Theatre,* James White (Clifton, NJ), 1975.

Street, Douglas, editor, *Children's Novels and the Movies,* Ungar (New York City), 1983.

PERIODICALS

Atlanta Constitution, March 27, 1986, p. 1.

Crisis, April, 1965.

Freedomways, Volume 14, number 1, 1974.

Horn Book Magazine, May-June, 1989, p. 374.

Interracial Books for Children Bulletin, Volume 12, numbers 7-8, 1981.

Lion and the Unicorn, fall, 1978.

Los Angeles Times, November 13, 1978; February 25, 1983.

Los Angeles Times Book Review, July 25, 1982.

Ms., December, 1979.

Nation, November 13, 1972.

Negro Digest, April, 1967; January, 1968.

Newsweek, August 31, 1987.

New Yorker, November 4, 1972; November 19, 1979.

New York Times, November 5, 1955; February 2, 1969; April 2, 1969; October 27, 1972; November 5, 1972; February 3, 1978; January 11, 1979; January 23, 1987; February 10, 1987, p. 16; March 6, 1987; August 18, 1987; October 22, 1987.

New York Times Book Review, November 4, 1973; November 11, 1979; April 25, 1981.

Publishers Weekly, November 25, 1988, p. 67.

School Library Journal, February, 1989, p. 99.

Show Business, April 12, 1969.

Variety, December 20, 1972.

Village Voice, January 15, 1979.

Washington Post, May 18, 1971; December 28, 1979.

Wilson Library Bulletin, September, 1989, p. 14.

OBITUARIES:

PERIODICALS

Boston Globe, August 18, 1994, p. 57.

Chicago Tribune, August 21, 1994, p. 8.

Jet, September 5, 1994, p. 18.

Los Angeles Times, August 19, 1994, p. 20.

New York Times, August 19, 1994, p. 24.

Time, August 29, 1994, p. 25.

Washington Post, August 19, 1994, p. 4.*

*　　　*　　　*

CHRISTMAS, Joyce 1939-
(Christmas Peterson, a joint pseudonym)

PERSONAL: Surname originally Smith, changed by marriage in 1970; born August 17, 1939, in Hartford, CT;

daughter of Wilfred R. (in business) and Anne (a nurse; maiden name, Plumb) Smith. *Education:* Attended Radcliffe College; Harvard University, B.A. (magna cum laude), 1961.

ADDRESSES: Home—21-19 45th Rd., Long Island City, NY 11101. *Office*—Chervenak, Keane & Co., 307 East 44th St., New York, NY 10017. *Agent*—Evan Marshall, 6 Tristam Place, Pine Brook, NJ 07058-9445.

CAREER: Writer (magazine), Boston, MA, 1963-68, began as editorial assistant, became associate editor; public relations and advertising writer and copy editor, 1968-73; *Writer,* associate editor, 1973-76; public relations and advertising writer and copy editor, 1976—. Chervenak, Keane & Co. (hotel consultants), New York City, hotel computer consultant and managing editor of *CKC Report: Hotel Technology Newsletter,* 1981—.

MEMBER: International Association of Hospitality Accountants, International Association of Crime Writers, Authors Guild, Mystery Writers of America, Sisters in Crime.

WRITINGS:

(With Jon Peterson, under joint pseudonym Christmas Peterson) *Hidden Assets,* Avon (New York City), 1981.
Blood Child, Signet (New York City), 1982.
Dark Tide, Avon, 1983.

"LADY MARGARET PRIAM MYSTERY SERIES." PUBLISHED BY FAWCETT (NEW YORK CITY)

Suddenly in Her Sorbet, 1988.
Simply to Die For, 1989.
A Fete Worse Than Death, 1990.
A Stunning Way to Die, 1991.
Friend or Faux, 1991.
It's Her Funeral, 1992.
A Perfect Day for Dying, 1994.

"BETTY TRENKE MYSTERY SERIES," PUBLISHED BY FAWCETT

This Business Is Murder, 1993.
Death at Face Value, 1995.

OTHER

Ghostwriter of numerous nonfiction books. Contributor of juvenile plays to *Plays;* contributor of short stories to *Ellery Queen's Mystery Magazine;* contributor of articles to trade publications for the hotel industry.

WORK IN PROGRESS: Another mystery series novel.

SIDELIGHTS: "I began my career as an editor," Joyce Christmas told *CA,* "and found the transition to ghosting nonfiction an easy one. It was easier still to move from

there to writing my own fiction and anything else that needed to be written."

* * *

CHURCHLAND, Patricia Smith 1943-

PERSONAL: Born July 16, 1943, in Oliver, British Columbia, Canada; immigrated to the United States, 1984; daughter of Wallace J. (a farmer) and Katie (a nurse; maiden name, James) Smith; married Paul M. Churchland (a professor), August 9, 1969; children: Mark M., Anne K. *Education:* University of British Columbia, B.A., 1961; University of Pittsburgh, M.A., 1966; Oxford University, B.Phil., 1969. *Religion:* Atheist.

ADDRESSES: Department of Philosophy, University of California, San Diego, La Jolla, CA 92093.

CAREER: University of Manitoba, Winnipeg, professor of philosophy, 1969-84; University of California, San Diego, La Jolla, professor of philosophy department, 1984—. Adjunct professor, Salk Institute, 1993—.

WRITINGS:

Neurophilosophy: Toward a Unified Science of the Mind-Brain, MIT Press (Cambridge, MA), 1986.
(With T. J. Sejnowski) *The Computational Brain,* MIT Press, 1992.

* * *

CLAY, Rosamund
See OAKLEY, Ann (Rosamund)

* * *

CLINE, C(harles) Terry, Jr. 1935-

PERSONAL: Born July 14, 1935, in Birmingham, AL; son of Charles Terry (in the Red Cross) and Mildred (Vann) Cline; married Linda Street (a writer), October 23, 1959 (divorced December, 1977); married Judith Richards (a writer), June 30, 1979; children: (first marriage) Cabeth, Blaise Meredith, Charles Terry III, Marc Andrew. *Education:* Attended Florida State University, 1957.

ADDRESSES: Home and office—115 North Ave., Fairhope, AL 36532. *Agent*—Harvey Klinger, Inc., 301 West 53rd St., New York, NY 10019.

CAREER: Writer. Worked at a variety of radio and television jobs, including announcer, disc jockey, newsman, and manager in the southeastern United States; House of Chimpions, Thomasville, GA, owner, 1960-63; Colonial Educational Exhibits, Dothan, AL, owner, 1964-69; Land Alive Foundation, Mobile, AL, executive director, 1970-72. *Military service:* U.S. Army, 1960.

WRITINGS:

Damon, Putnam (New York City), 1975.
Death Knell, Putnam, 1979.
Cross Current, Doubleday (Garden City, NY), 1981.
Missing Persons, Arbor House (New York City), 1981.
The Attorney Conspiracy, Arbor House, 1983.
Prey, New American Library (New York City), 1985.
Quarry, New American Library, 1987.
Reaper, Donald Fine (New York City), 1989.

Also author of a children's play, a musical, and several articles.

WORK IN PROGRESS: A new suspense novel.

SIDELIGHTS: C. Terry Cline Jr. once told *CA* that both his ex-wife, Linda, and his second wife, Judy, work on writing projects with him. Linda has two published works, one of which was a Disney film. Judy has several books published, including two about Terry—*Summer Lightning,* and *After the Storm.* Having worked on everything together, they divide the income between them.

More recently, Cline recalled a personal experience: "I quit smoking March 5, 1990, at 3:30 in the morning. I quit thinking March 6, 1990. I threw away a half-finished book March 7, 1990. I went mad March 8, 1990.

"Day after day I sat at the typewriter and typed. Reams piled up behind me—and it was all the same first page. My wife, Judy, walked through the office and commented, 'You're going to rust your typewriter crying on it like that. . . .'

"Recently, teaching a class on creative writing, I was asked what advice I would give an aspiring young writer. My reply: 'DO NOT QUIT SMOKING IN THE MIDDLE OF A LIFE.'"

*   *   *

CLUTTERBUCK, Richard 1917-
(Richard Jocelyn)

PERSONAL: Born November 22, 1917, in London, England; son of Lewis St. John Rawlinson (a colonel in the British Army) and Isabella (Jocelyn) Clutterbuck; married Angela Barford, May 15, 1948; children: Peter, Robin, Julian. *Education:* Cambridge University, M.A. (mechanical sciences), 1939; attended British Army Staff College, 1948, Imperial Defence College, 1965, and Uni-

versity of Singapore, 1966-68; University of London, Ph.D. (politics), 1971. *Avocational interests:* Canoeing at sea (led a canoe party of twenty-four soldiers across the English Channel to France in 1960).

ADDRESSES: Office—Department of Politics, University of Exeter, Exeter, England.

CAREER: British Army, officer, 1937-72, became Engineer-in-Chief of the Army, with rank of major general, served in more than fifteen countries around the world, including France, Belgium, Ethiopia, Egypt, Algeria, Palestine, Malaya, and the United States; University of Exeter, Exeter, England, reader in political conflict, 1972-83. Member, General Advisory Council, British Broadcasting Corp., 1975-81.

MEMBER: Institute of Civil Engineers (London; fellow).

AWARDS, HONORS: Military: Officer of Order of the British Empire, 1958, for service in Malaysia; Companion of Order of the Bath, 1972, for service as Engineer-in-Chief of the Army. Civilian: George Knight Clowes Prize, *Army Quarterly,* 1954; Toulmin Medal, Society of American Military Engineers, 1963; Bertrand Stewart Prize, Ministry of Defence.

WRITINGS:

Riot and Revolution in Singapore and Malaya, 1945-1963, Faber (London), 1963, revised and expanded version published as *Conflict and Violence in Singapore and Malaysia: 1945-1983,* Westview Press (Boulder, CO), 1985.
The Long, Long War, Praeger (New York City), 1966.
Protest and the Urban Guerilla, Cassell (London), 1973.
Living with Terrorism, Faber, 1975.
Guerrillas and Terrorists, Faber, 1977, Ohio University Press (Athens), 1980.
Kidnap and Ransom, Faber, 1978.
Britain in Agony: The Growth of Political Violence, Faber, 1978, Penguin (New York City), 1980.
The Media and Political Violence, Macmillan (London), 1981.
Industrial Conflict and Democracy: The Last Chance, Macmillan, 1984.
(Editor) *The Future of Political Violence: Destabilization, Disorder and Terrorism,* Macmillan, 1986.
Kidnap, Hijack and Extortion, St. Martin's Press (New York City), 1987.
Terrorism and Guerrilla Warfare, Routledge (London), 1990.
Terrorism, Drugs, and Crime in Europe after 1992, Routledge, 1990.
International Crisis and Conflict, St. Martin's Press, 1993.
Terrorism in an Unstable World, Routledge, 1994.

Drugs, Crime and Corruption, New York University Press (New York City), 1995.

CONTRIBUTOR

Anthony Deane-Drummond, editor, *Riot Control,* Royal United Service Institute for Defense Studies (London), 1975.

Jennifer Shaw and others, editors, *Ten Years of Terrorism,* Royal United Services Institute for Defense Studies, 1979.

Paul Wilkinson, editor, *British Perspectives on Terrorism,* Allen & Unwin (London), 1981.

David Watt, editor, *The Constitution of Northern Ireland,* Heinemann (London), 1981.

OTHER

(Under pseudonym Richard Jocelyn) *Across the River* (novel), Constable (London), 1957.

Also author of play, *A Means to an End,* broadcast by Radio Malaya, 1958. Contributor of more than one hundred articles to British and American periodicals.

WORK IN PROGRESS: Research for a new book, *Public Safety and Civil Liberties.*

SIDELIGHTS: Described by Laurie Taylor in the London *Times* as a "soldier-turned-expert in political violence turned academic," Richard Clutterbuck has written numerous books on terrorism and political violence. A thirty-five-year veteran of the British Army, he has both experienced and researched the various forms of urban unrest in modern societies, from Southeast Asia to Northern Ireland.

E. J. Kahn Jr. states in a profile of Clutterbuck in the *New Yorker,* "It was Clutterbuck's Army service—in, among other sectors of tension and upheaval, Palestine, Trieste, and Southeast Asia—that got him interested in the investigation and analysis of what he has termed 'the prevalent form of conflict for our time.'" Other critics have acknowledged this, although differing in their assessments of his work. While *New Republic* reviewer John Deedy believes that Clutterbuck's views as expressed in *Protest and the Urban Guerilla* are "strongly Union Jack . . . and occasionally arbitrary," another critic, writing for *Choice,* remarks, "Clutterbuck writes as a committed and sensible member of the liberal-democratic camp and his book is both a useful corrective to the writings of the revolutionaries and a warning to democrats everywhere."

In both *The Media and Political Violence* and *Britain in Agony: The Growth of Political Violence,* Clutterbuck explores the influence of the media, particularly television, on domestic political violence. In a *Times Literary Supplement* review of *The Media and Political Violence,* Paul Johnson writes that Clutterbuck "demonstrates, pretty convincingly I think, that certain groups in our society do have an interest in promoting hostility towards the police, and that television (though not the press) makes it easier for them to accomplish their object." "Clutterbuck's book," Johnson continues, "shows that television, and especially the BBC, is far more likely to fall for anti-police propaganda than the press." He concludes, however, that in "light of Clutterbuck's own evidence, the media are only one of the various factors which tend to stimulate or aggravate violence, trade-union extremists and fringe political groups being rather more important."

Clutterbuck's examination of violence in modern society has continued with *Kidnap, Hijack and Extortion, International Crisis and Conflict,* and *Drugs, Crime and Corruption,* a study of production, distribution, and financing in the illegal drug industry. Some of the radical alternatives that Clutterbuck proposes in *Drugs, Crime and Corruption* include suppression, government licensing, and decriminalization. He also encourages a forum for international debate on ending the corruption of society due to the widespread use of illegal drugs.

BIOGRAPHICAL/CRITICAL SOURCES:

PERIODICALS

Choice, May, 1975.
Conflict Studies, February 1991; March 1994.
European, September 21, 1990.
Listener, August 16, 1990.
New Republic, November 2, 1974.
New Yorker, June 12, 1978.
Times (London), March 1, 1980.
Times Literary Supplement, July 31, 1981, September 7, 1984, September 30, 1985, August 29, 1986.

*   *   *

COATES, Ken 1930-

PERSONAL: Born September 16, 1930, in Leek, England; son of Eric Arthur (a surveyor) and Mary (Griffiths) Coates; married Tamara Tura, August 8, 1969. *Education:* University of Nottingham, B.A. (with first class honors), 1959.

ADDRESSES: Office—8 Regent Street, Mansfield, Nottingham, NG18 1SS, England; European Parliament, 79-113 Rue Belliard, Brussels, Belgium; and Bertrand Russell Peace Foundation, Bertrand Russell House, Gamble St., Nottingham NG7 4ET, England.

CAREER: Worked in British coal mines, 1948-56; University of Nottingham, Nottingham, England, 1960—, began as assistant tutor, became tutor, senior tutor, reader in adult education, then special professor, 1989—. President, Nottingham Labour party, 1964-65; member, Bertrand Russell Peace Foundation, 1965—; joint secretary, European Nuclear Disarmament Liaison Committee, 1981-90. European Parliament, Brussels, Belgium, member, 1989—, chairperson, Sub-Committee on Human Rights, 1989-94, rapporteur, Temporary Employment Committee, 1994—.

WRITINGS:

(With Richard Silburn) *Poverty, Deprivation, and Morale in a Nottingham Community,* University of Nottingham (Nottingham, England), 1967.

(With Tony Topham) *Industrial Democracy in Great Britain,* MacGibbon & Kee (London), 1967.

(With Silburn) *Poverty: The Forgotten Englishmen,* Penguin (London), 1970.

The Crisis of British Socialism, Spokesman (Nottingham), 1971.

Essays on Industrial Democracy, Spokesman, 1971.

(With Tony Topham) *The New Unionism: The Case for Workers' Control,* P. Owen (London), 1972.

Beyond Wage Slavery, Spokesman, 1977.

Democracy in the Labour Party, Spokesman, 1977.

(With Topham) *The Shop Steward's Guide to the Bullock Report,* Spokesman, 1977.

The Case of Nikolai Bukharin, Spokesman, 1978.

(With Topham) *Trade Unions in Britain,* Spokesman, 1980.

(With Silburn) *Beyond the Bulldozer,* University of Nottingham, 1980.

Work-Ins, Sit-Ins, and Industrial Democracy, Spokesman, 1981.

Heresies, Spokesman, 1982.

An Alternative Economic Strategy, Spokesman, 1982.

The Social Democrats, Spokesman, 1983.

The Most Dangerous Decade, Spokesman, 1984.

(With Topham) *Trade Unions and Politics,* Basil Blackwell (London), 1986.

China and the Bomb, Spokesman, 1986.

(Editor) *Freedom and Fairness: Empowering People at Work,* Spokesman, 1986.

Israel's Bomb—The First Victim: The Case of Mordechai Vanunu, Spokesman, 1986.

(Editor) *Perestroika: The Global Challenge,* Spokesman, 1988.

Think Globally, Act Locally: The United Nations and the Peace Movements, Spokesman, 1988.

(With Topham) *The Making of the Transport and General Workers' Union,* Volume 1, Basil Blackwell, 1991, as *The Making of the Labour Movement,* Spokesman, 1994.

Human Rights in the World: A Report to the European Parliament, Spokesman, 1992.

(Editor, with Michael Barratt Brown) *A European Recovery Programme: Restoring Full Employment,* Spokesman, 1993.

The Right to Work: The Loss of Our First Freedom, Spokesman, 1995.

Putting Europe Back to Work, Spokesman, 1995.

Contributor to periodicals, including *International Socialist Journal, New Left Review, Tribune,* and *Week.* Editor, *European Labour Forum, Spokesman,* and bulletin of Institute for Workers' Control; member of editorial panel, *New Socialist.*

SIDELIGHTS: Ken Coates told *CA:* "The values that are reflected in all my writings are those of libertarian socialism, and the British movement for workers' education has played an evident part in shaping my thought. I have been involved in a continuous debate about industrial democracy. I helped to form the Institute for Workers' Control in 1968. This resulted in several books and a constant journalistic discussion in newspapers and magazines in many different countries. As a partisan of nuclear disarmament, I was one of the founding members of European Nuclear Disarmament, which launched the so-called 'Russell Appeal' in 1980, resulting in the development of the European Nuclear Disarmament Conventions (Brussels, 1982, Berlin, 1983, Perugia, 1984, Amsterdam, 1985, Paris, 1986, Coventry, 1987, Lund, 1988, Vitoria, 1989, and Helsinki, 1990). As a member of the Bertrand Russell Peace Foundation for more than twenty years, I have been actively engaged in many questions of human rights, problems of political prisoners, and related issues.

"The fall of Communism left a large number of human rights questions unresolved in the East, and did nothing to diminish arbitrary oppression in the first and third worlds. When I was elected to the European Parliament, I decided to concentrate my efforts on its Sub-Committee on Human Rights, of which I became the chairman.

"Continued economic difficulties resulted in permanent mass unemployment in a number of European countries, and acute levels of social crisis in many other parts of the world. The problems in Britain were so pressing that I decided to devote myself to the aim of recovering full employment, which has dominated my written, as well as my political action, in recent years."

*　　　*　　　*

COLDSMITH, Don(ald Charles) 1926-

PERSONAL: Born February 28, 1926, in Iola, KS; son of Charles I. (a Methodist minister) and Sara (Willett) Coldsmith; married Barbara A. Brown, August, 1949 (divorced, 1960); married Edna E. Howell, November 6,

1960; children: Carol, April, Glenna, Leslie, Connie. *Education:* Baker University, A.B., 1949; University of Kansas, M.D., 1958. *Politics:* Republican. *Religion:* Methodist.

ADDRESSES: Home—2800 West 30th Ave., Emporia, KS 66801.

CAREER: Young Men's Christian Association (YMCA), Topeka, KS, youth director, 1949-54; Bethany Hospital, Kansas City, KS, intern, 1958-59; private practice of medicine in Emporia, KS, 1959-88; full-time writer, 1988—. Former Congregational minister, gunsmith, taxidermist, radio disc jockey, piccolo player, and grain inspector. Adjunct professor of English and director of Tallgrass Writing Workshop, Emporia State University. Trustee, Baker University, Kansas. Member of speakers' bureau, Kansas Humanities Council. *Military service:* U.S. Army, 1944-46; served in the Philippines and Japan.

MEMBER: Western Writers of America (president, 1983-84), Appaloosa Horse Club, National Rifle Association, American Medical Association, Young Men's Christian Association, National Cattlemen's Association, Kansas Livestock Association, Kansas Medical Society, Flint Hills Medical Society.

AWARDS, HONORS: Golden Spur Award for best original paperback, Western Writers of America, 1990, for *The Changing Wind;* Distinguished Kansan of the Year, Native Sons & Daughters of Kansas, 1993; Edgar Wolfe Literary Award, 1994.

WRITINGS:

Horsin' Around (collected articles), Naylor (San Antonio, TX), 1975.
Horsin' Around Again (collected articles), Corona, 1981.
The Changing Wind, Bantam (New York City), 1990.
The Traveler, Bantam, 1991.
World of Silence, Bantam, 1992.
Runestone (novel), Bantam, 1995.

"SPANISH BIT SAGA" SERIES: HISTORICAL NOVELS

Trail of the Spanish Bit, Doubleday (New York City), 1980.
Buffalo Medicine, Doubleday, 1981.
The Elk-Dog Heritage, Doubleday, 1982.
Follow the Wind, Doubleday, 1982.
Man of the Shadows, Doubleday, 1983.
Daughter of the Eagle, Doubleday, 1984.
Moon of Thunder, Doubleday, 1984.
The Sacred Hills, Doubleday, 1985.
Pale Star, Doubleday, 1986.
River of Swans, Doubleday, 1986.
Return to the River, Doubleday, 1987.
The Medicine Knife, Doubleday, 1987.
The Flower in the Mountains, Doubleday, 1988.

Trail from Taos, Doubleday, 1989.
Song of the Rock, Doubleday, 1989.
Fort de Chastaigne, Doubleday, 1990.
Quest for the White Bull, Doubleday, 1990.
Return of the Spanish, Doubleday, 1991.
Bride of the Morning Star, Doubleday, 1991.
Walks in the Sun, Bantam, 1992.
Thunderstick, Doubleday, 1993.
Track of the Bear, Doubleday, 1994.
Child of the Dead, Doubleday, 1995.
Bearer of the Pipe, Doubleday, 1995.

OTHER

Also author of *Rivers West: The Smoky Hill,* 1989. Author of "Horsin' Around," a self-syndicated weekly newspaper column. Contributing editor, *Horse, of Course.*

Some of Coldsmith's "Spanish Bit Saga" series books have been published in German.

WORK IN PROGRESS: Kenzas, a historical novel, for Bantam.

SIDELIGHTS: Don Coldsmith told *CA* that his "Spanish Bit Saga" series has more than six million copies in print and that his weekly newspaper column, "Horsin' Around," has appeared in publications with circulations totaling more than 250,000 readers over twenty-four years. He added that he has been labelled "the most published living Kansan."

BIOGRAPHICAL/CRITICAL SOURCES:

PERIODICALS

Booklist, May 1, 1982, p. 1131; September 1, 1982, p. 27; February 1, 1985, p. 756; May 15, 1991, p. 1779.
Publishers Weekly, February 24, 1992, p. 45; May 10, 1993, p. 51.
Roundup Quarterly, summer, 1990, p. 48; winter, 1990, p. 47; spring, 1991, p. 47; summer, 1991, p. 49; fall, 1991, p. 62; summer, 1992, p. 48; fall, 1992, p. 49.

*　　　*　　　*

CONQUEST, (George) Robert (Acworth) 1917-
(J. E. M. Arden, Victor Gzay, Ted Pauker)

PERSONAL: Born July 15, 1917, in Great Malvern, England; son of Robert Folger W. and Rosamund A. (Acworth) Conquest; married Joan Watkins, 1942 (divorced, 1948); married Tatiana Mihailova, 1948 (divorced, 1962); married Caroleen Macfarlane, 1964 (divorced, 1977); married Elizabeth Neece, 1979; children: (first marriage) John Christopher Arden, Richard Charles Pleasonton. *Education:* Attended University of Grenoble, 1935-36;

Magdalen College, Oxford, B.A., 1939, M.A., 1972, D.Litt., 1974.

ADDRESSES: Home—52 Peter Coutts Cir., Stanford, CA 94305.

CAREER: Writer. H. M. Foreign Service, 1946-56, served in Sofia, Bulgaria, as press attache and as second secretary, and as first secretary of the United Kingdom delegation to the United Nations; London School of Economics and Political Science, London, England, Sydney and Beatrice Webb Research Fellow, 1956-58; University of Buffalo (now State University of New York at Buffalo), Buffalo, NY, visiting poet and lecturer in English, 1959-60; Columbia University, Russian Institute, New York, NY, senior fellow, 1964-65; Smithsonian Institution, Woodrow Wilson International Center for Scholars, Washington, DC, fellow, 1976-77; Hoover Institution, Stanford, CA, senior research fellow, 1977-79, senior research fellow and scholar-curator of the Russian and Commonwealth of Independent States collection, 1981—; Harvard University, Ukranian Research Institute, Cambridge, MA, research associate, 1983—. Distinguished visiting scholar, Heritage Foundation, 1980-81; member of advisory board, Freedom House. *Military service:* Oxfordshire and Buckinghamshire Light Infantry, 1939-46; served in the Balkans.

MEMBER: Royal Society of Literature (fellow), British Academy (fellow), Society for the Advancement of Roman Studies, British Interplanetary Society (fellow), Travellers Club.

AWARDS, HONORS: PEN Prize, 1945, for poem "For the Death of a Poet"; Festival of Britain verse prize, 1951; Officer, Order of the British Empire, 1955; *Washington Monthly* Book Award nomination, 1987, for *The Harvest of Sorrow: Soviet Collectivization and the Terror-Famine;* grants from the Ukrainian Research Institute and the Ukrainian National Association; Alexis de Tocqueville Memorial Award, 1992; D.H.L. from Adelphi University, 1994.

WRITINGS:

NONFICTION

(Under pseudonym J. E. M. Arden) *Where Do Marxists Go from Here?,* Phoenix House, 1958.
Common Sense about Russia, Macmillan (New York City), 1960.
The Soviet Deportation of Nationalities, St. Martin's (New York City), 1960, revised edition published as *The Nation Killers: The Soviet Deportation of Nationalities,* Macmillan, 1970.
Courage of Genius: The Pasternak Affair, Collins (New York City), 1961, published as *The Pasternak Affair: Courage of Genius,* Lippincott (New York City),

1962, reprinted, Octagon Books (New York City), 1979.
Power and Policy in the U.S.S.R.: The Study of Soviet Dynastics, Macmillan (London), 1961, St. Martin's, 1962, published as *Power and Policy in the U.S.S.R.: The Struggle for Stalin's Succession, 1945-60,* Harper (New York City), 1967.
The Last Empire, Ampersand Books (Princeton, NJ), 1962.
The Future of Communism, Today Publications, 1963.
Marxism Today, Ampersand Books, 1964.
Russia after Khrushchev, Praeger (New York City), 1965.
The Great Terror: Stalin's Purge of the Thirties, Macmillan, 1968, revised edition, Penguin (New York City), 1971, new edition published as *The Great Terror: A Reassessment,* Oxford University Press (Oxford), 1990.
Where Marx Went Wrong, Tom Stacey, 1970.
V. I. Lenin, Viking (New York City), 1972, published in England as *Lenin,* Fontana, 1972.
(Translator) Aleksander Isaevich Solzhenitsyn, *Prussian Nights: A Narrative Poem,* Farrar, Straus (New York City), 1977.
Kolyma: The Arctic Death Camps, Viking, 1978.
Present Danger—Towards a Foreign Policy: Guide to the Era of Soviet Aggression, Hoover Institution Press (Stanford, CA), 1979.
The Abomination of Moab (essays), M. T. Smith (England), 1979.
We and They: Civic and Despotic Cultures, M. T. Smith, 1980.
(With Jon Manchip White) *What to Do When the Russians Come,* Stein & Day (Briarcliff Manor, NY), 1984.
Inside Stalin's Secret Police: NKVD Politics, 1936-9, Macmillan, 1985.
The Harvest of Sorrow: Soviet Collectivization and the Terror-Famine, Oxford University Press, 1986.
Tyrants and Typewriters (essays), Hutchinson, 1988.
Stalin and the Kirov Murder, Oxford University Press, 1989.
Stalin: Breaker of Nations, Viking, 1991.

POETRY COLLECTIONS

Poems, St. Martin's, 1955.
Between Mars and Venus, St. Martin's, 1962.
Arias from a Love Opera and Other Poems, Macmillan, 1969.
Casualty Ward, Poem-of-the-Month Club (London), 1974.
Coming Across, Buckabest Books, 1978.
Forays, Chatto & Windus (London), 1979.
New and Collected Poems, Hutchinson (London), 1988.

Also contributor, under pseudonym Ted Pauker, to *The New Oxford Book of English Light Verse;* has also written under pseudonym Victor Gzay.

NOVELS

A World of Difference: A Modern Novel of Science and Imagination, Ward, Lock, 1955, new edition, Ballantine (New York City), 1964.
(With Kingsley Amis) *The Egyptologists,* J. Cape (London), 1965, Random House (New York), 1966.

EDITOR

(With others) *New Poems: A PEN Anthology,* Transatlantic (Albuquerque, NM), 1953.
New Lines, St. Martin's, 1956.
Back to Life: Poems from behind the Iron Curtain, St. Martin's, 1958.
New Lines 2, Macmillan, 1963.
(And author of introduction) Pyotr Yakir, *A Childhood in Prison,* Macmillan (London), 1972.
(And author of introduction) *The Robert Sheckley Omnibus,* Gollancz (London), 1973.
(And author of introduction) Tibor Szamuely, *The Russian Tradition,* McGraw (New York City), 1974.
The Last Empire, Hoover Institution (Stanford, CA), 1986.

Literary editor, *Spectator,* 1962-63; editor, *Soviet Analyst,* 1971-73.

EDITOR WITH KINGSLEY AMIS

Spectrum: A Science Fiction Anthology, Gollancz, 1961, Harcourt (New York City), 1962.
Spectrum 2, Gollancz, 1962, Harcourt, 1963.
Spectrum 3, Gollancz, 1963, published as *Spectrum: A Third Science Fiction Anthology,* Harcourt, 1964.
Spectrum 4, Gollancz, 1964, Harcourt, 1965.
Spectrum 5, Gollancz, 1966, Harcourt, 1967.

EDITOR, "SOVIET STUDIES" SERIES: PUBLISHED AS "THE CONTEMPORARY SOVIET UNION" SERIES BY PRAEGER

Industrial Workers in the U.S.S.R., Bodley Head (London), 1967, Praeger (New York City), 1968.
Soviet Nationalities Policy in Practice, Bodley Head, 1967, Praeger, 1968.
The Politics of Ideas in the U.S.S.R., Bodley Head, 1967, Praeger, 1968.
Religion in the U.S.S.R., Bodley Head, 1968, Praeger, 1969.
The Soviet Police System, Bodley Head, 1968, Praeger, 1969.
The Soviet Political System, Bodley Head, 1968, Praeger, 1969.
Justice and the Legal System in the U.S.S.R., Bodley Head, 1968, Praeger, 1969.

Agricultural Workers in the U.S.S.R., Bodley Head, 1968, Praeger, 1969.

WORK IN PROGRESS: A book on the causes of this century's disasters; a book on the nature of history; a book on the Soviet anti-Semitic purge of 1948-53; a book of poems; a book of light verse; an autobiography.

SIDELIGHTS: Robert Conquest is known for his literary endeavors as well as for his scholarly writings on recent political history and is considered one of the world's leading specialists on Russian affairs. Walter Goodman of the *New York Times* calls him "perhaps the West's preeminent chronicler of the sufferings Communist rule has brought upon the Soviet people, especially during the reign of Stalin." Arch Puddington, writing in *Commentary,* describes Conquest as "the preeminent historian of the formation of the Stalinist system." In addition to his position as an expert on the former Soviet Union, Conquest is also known as a poet and editor who played a pivotal role in the Movement, a British literary school of the 1950s. As John Press observes in the *Dictionary of Literary Biography,* "it is rare for a man to be accepted by his fellows as an imaginative writer and, at the same time, as an authority on political matters."

In 1955 Conquest first gained notice with the publication of *A World of Difference: A Modern Novel of Science and Imagination* and the collection, *Poems. A World of Difference* is a science fiction story in which Conquest plays some inside jokes, such as naming space ships after his literary friends. The book marked his first association with the science fiction genre. In the 1960s, Conquest returned to the field with longtime friend Kingsley Amis to edit the popular *Spectrum* science fiction anthologies.

Many of the pieces in *Poems* were originally published in prominent British literary magazines. As a collection, the works earned Conquest critical praise. G. S. Fraser, for example, finds in his review for the *New Statesman and Nation* that the collection reveals "the range of mind of a liberal and humane person who has travelled, loved, felt the pressure of his time, and thought seriously about poetry, war and life." A critic for the *Times Literary Supplement* describes Conquest as "a writer who has received many influences, poetic and social, and made of them something genuinely his own." Press points to the impressive range of these early poems, a quality to be found in all of Conquest's later collections as well.

Along with such figures as Donald Davie, D. J. Enright, Philip Larkin, and Kingsley Amis, Conquest formed part of a loosely defined group of 1950s British writers called the Movement. These writers issued no manifesto of beliefs and agreed to no set literary theory, but their general approach to literature shared a common perspective. Each of the Movement writers disliked the overly emotional writing of the 1950s and were determined to restore a balance and order to literature.

With his *New Lines,* an anthology of many of the Movement poets, Conquest helped establish the group as a viable presence on the British literary scene. He also presented their argument against the predominant poetry of the time. Poets, Conquest argued in his introduction to *New Lines,* have made "the mistake . . . of giving the Id, a sound player on the percussion side under a strict conductor, too much of a say in the doings of the orchestra as a whole." He called for a poetry "written by and for the whole man, intellect, emotions, sense and all." "The publication of *New Lines,*" Blake Morrison writes in *The Movement: English Poetry and Fiction of the 1950s,* "changed the status of the Movement. . . . The group now had the imprint of a reputable publisher; it was the object of much comment in literary periodicals; it had even begun to attract attention abroad." Press believes that *New Lines* "remains the most influential anthology published in England since World War II" and maintains that "on the strength of *New Lines* alone Conquest merits a place in the development of postwar English poetry."

At the same time he was establishing himself in the literary world, Conquest was also working for the British Foreign Service in Bulgaria and at the United Nations. After leaving governmental work in 1956, he took a position at the London School of Economics and Political Science. He has since been affiliated with several universities and research institutes as an expert on Russian affairs.

Conquest's writings on the former Soviet Union and communism have consistently documented the abuses of totalitarianism. Press explains that "Conquest has always displayed a firm hostility toward the USSR, but his views are neither irrational nor fanatical." The brutal reign of Soviet strongman Joseph Stalin has been the focus of several Conquest books, including *Soviet Deportation of Nationalities, The Great Terror: Stalin's Purge of the Thirties, Kolyma: The Arctic Death Camps,* and *The Harvest of Sorrow: Soviet Collectivization and the Terror-Famine.* Conquest's political works, Morrison states, uncover "Soviet injustice and brutality of various kinds."

The Great Terror was the first book to fully document the political murders of Stalin's purges, a time in the late 1930s when many Soviet leaders were arrested and executed on false charges. It is "the definitive compilation of the horrors of Stalin's purges of 1936-38, when millions of people, mainly loyal Communists, were killed or sent to their deaths in prison camps at the hands of the secret police," according to Craig R. Whitney in the *New York Times Book Review.* This period of mass murder enabled Stalin to consolidate his position as Soviet leader, eliminate his enemies and potential rivals, and terrorize the

populace into submission. Conquest consulted some two hundred published volumes on the period, official government documents, and the accounts of emigres and defectors to assemble the book. In his review for the *New Statesman,* John Gross describes *The Great Terror* as "impressive alike in its narrative sweep, its meticulous scholarship and the clarity with which Mr. Conquest has organised and presented an immense mass of highly complex material." An *Economist* critic claims it is "a masterpiece of historical detection," while Press speculates that "this massive, scholarly work may well be Conquest's most lasting achievement."

In *The Harvest of Sorrow* Conquest turns to another horrific episode in Stalin's reign, the widespread terror brought about by the collectivization of Soviet agriculture. In 1930 Stalin declared that the nation's kulaks, the wealthier class of peasants, were to be "liquidated as a class." At the same time the kulaks were being executed or shipped to prison camps, poorer peasants were forcibly removed from their family farms and made to work on state-run, collective farms. All farmland became property of the government, and all farm produce became state property as well. To insure that the peasants would not steal any food while working in the fields, armed guards were put into watchtowers in prison camp style. Resistance to collectivization was intense. Some villages were bombed by military aircraft; many peasant families were arrested and shipped to Siberian prisons. When resistance was particularly fierce in the Ukraine—the Soviet Union's primary agricultural region—Stalin ordered all food in the area to be confiscated by the army. The Ukraine's borders were then sealed off so that hungry peasants could not leave to find food, while Russians in other areas were forbidden entry. According to Conquest's estimate, nearly fifteen million people died during the famine and deportations—more than were lost by all nations in the First World War.

Because official Soviet history denied that the famine of the 1930s was caused by the communist government's policies, many of the facts concerning the period have been suppressed. For example, when the Soviet census board of 1937 reported statistics showing the drastic drop in population during the decade, Stalin had the board members arrested and executed. The Soviet press was forbidden to comment on the famine. Blame for the drop in agricultural production, a fact that could not be hidden from outside observers, was attributed to such causes as sabotage, incompetent meteorologists, and the peasants of the Ukraine. Western newsmen were prohibited from visiting the region, while well-fed model villages were prepared by the secret police for the benefit of selected foreign visitors. Most Western observers disbelieved the scattered reports of a famine, finding it unlikely that such an event could be so well hidden. As Puddington explains, the facts were "obscured in a thick fog of official Soviet lies and the indifference of the West." Over half a century later, Conquest's book was the first comprehensive presentation of the facts about the deliberately created famine. Speaking to Goodman, Conquest reveals that he wrote *The Harvest of Sorrow* to "register previously not recognized facts on Western consciousness in a form weighty enough to be irrefutable."

Because of the long suppression of the tragedy, Patricia Blake explains in *Time,* the story of the famine has reached the West "only in fragmentary fashion, as the facts filtered through decades of unrelenting Soviet denial." To write his book, Conquest gathered first-person accounts from peasant survivors and from communist functionaries who later defected, and consulted secret Soviet documents smuggled to the West. His extensive research makes *The Harvest of Sorrow* the most complete picture available of the tragic event. "Reports of the famine . . . have long been available in the West," Goodman states, "but not until now has it been rendered as fully or in such grim detail." As Eugene H. Methvin comments in the *National Review,* "Conquest has provided a fine, thoroughly documented full-dress historical study of this genocidal campaign."

Critical reaction to *The Harvest of Sorrow* ranks it as an important historical work with implications for contemporary political realities. Writing in the Toronto *Globe and Mail,* Michael R. Marrus believes that "Conquest's well-documented book provides a crushing indictment of the Soviet experience in a measured and sober fashion. . . . We are dealing with a crime of terrible proportions—a continuing blot upon the Soviet leadership that has not yet acknowledged what happened." Methvin states that the Soviet government was "ineluctably shaped by this dirty terrorist history. . . . The line of succession from Stalin to Gorbachev is unbroken. . . . Until the people in that apparatus today can openly examine their history and consider the need for constitutional safeguards, we must recognize that we are dealing with a mad machine capable of anything." Gross admits in the *New York Times* that "after *Harvest of Sorrow* there can be no excuse for ignoring what happened or playing down its enormity."

The breakup of the former Soviet Union, and the attendant release of its government's records, has brought vindication for many of Conquest's assertions. The author has also found a new audience for his work in Russia itself. "My books on the Stalin period have been published in large editions in Russia and the other East European countries with much acclaim, even before the end of the regime," he tells *CA.* "Of course, I wrote my books on

Communism without any thought that they would be so published, and vindicated: they were entirely for the English, and other non-Soviet, readership." His intended audience notwithstanding, Conquest is now recognized as "the West's No. 1 expert on Stalin's purges," to quote Robert V. Daniels in the *Los Angeles Times Book Review.* A new edition of *The Great Terror,* published in 1990, has led Daniels to comment: "Conquest has now updated and fleshed out his classic study of the purges. The extraordinary thing is how closely the new information fits with the conclusions he had to work out 20 years ago through scraps of evidence and logical conjecture." *Spectator* contributor Richard Lamb notes that events in modern Russian history have enhanced Conquest's reputation. "Today he is completely vindicated because a mass of evidence from Russia makes Conquest's charges irrefutable," Lamb concludes.

"Robert Conquest has always expressed scorn for those who cannot see the realities of life in the USSR behind the political rhetoric," writes *Spectator* correspondent Catherine Andreyev. Nevertheless, Conquest has always been careful to explain that he is not deliberately writing anti-Soviet diatribes. "I'm a historian," he tells Bevis Hillier of the *Los Angeles Times,* "and at least part of it is that I like finding out facts that are hard to find out. . . . I'm just inquisitive." This inquisitive impulse has drawn praise from critics such as *Spectator* contributor Andrei Navrozov, who calls the author "a pioneer, exploring the jealously guarded secret past of a closed society." Conquest's books have indeed earned him an outstanding reputation as a chronicler of recent political history. Gross cites *The Great Terror* and *The Harvest of Sorrow* in particular as being "indispensable reading for anyone who wants to understand the shaping—and misshaping—of the modern world." Because of Conquest's success as both a poet and an expert on the Soviet Union, Press calls him a "man of affairs who is also a man of letters."

Conquest tells *CA:* "If I had to reconcile my various output, I think I would say that imagination is helpful in examining and establishing what are, on the face of it, highly improbable facts. In Russia they very often ask me incredulously how it was that Orwell understood them and many 'experts' didn't. Science fiction in particular is a great help: for it was truer to see the Communists as Martians than as good or bad humans of a normal world.

"I don't know why one writes poetry. I still publish two or three poems a year, and have a book nearly ready. The mere act of *writing* is easier in verse, in the narrow sense that it is not so long. My handwriting is illegible and I type very badly: so I dislike the actual writing, as against the research, of prose books quite a lot."

BIOGRAPHICAL/CRITICAL SOURCES:

BOOKS

Dictionary of Literary Biography, Volume 27: *Poets of Great Britain and Ireland, 1945-1960,* Gale (Detroit), 1984.

Morrison, Blake, *The Movement: English Poetry and Fiction of the 1950s,* Methuen (New York City), 1980.

Salmon, Arthur Edward, *Poets of the Apocalypse,* Twayne (Boston), 1983.

PERIODICALS

American Political Science Review, September, 1965.
Canadian Forum, May, 1958.
Commentary, June, 1987.
Economist, October 19, 1968.
Essays in Criticism, number 8, 1958.
Globe and Mail (Toronto), December 20, 1986.
Guardian, November 17, 1961; May 11, 1962.
Hudson Review, Volume 14, number 4, 1961.
Listener, October 9, 1969.
Los Angeles Times, November 19, 1986.
Los Angeles Times Book Review, May 20, 1990, p. 1, 8.
Manchester Guardian, October 7, 1955; July 13, 1956.
Month, May 1956.
Nation, August 11, 1962; September 28, 1969.
National Review, May 4, 1971; February 27, 1987.
New Statesman, December 20, 1958; May 21, 1960; June 9, 1961; November 24, 1961; May 27, 1968; September 27, 1968; June 27, 1969; March 31, 1978.
New Statesman and Nation, October 29, 1955; July 7, 1956.
Newsweek, November 17, 1986.
New York Review of Books, August 5, 1965; June 19, 1969.
New York Times, January 1, 1956; May 26, 1978; October 7, 1986; October 15, 1986.
New York Times Book Review, April 4, 1965; October 27, 1968; June 18, 1978; October 26, 1986; January 15, 1989, p. 13.
Poetry, November, 1957; December, 1960.
Spectator, July 20, 1956; June 3, 1960; November 17, 1961; May 4, 1962; July 15, 1989, p. 30-1; September 1, 1990, p. 31; September 14, 1991, p. 29-30.
Time, December 8, 1986.
Times (London), September 4, 1986.
Times Literary Supplement, May 30, 1955; September 30, 1955; July 13, 1956; January 9, 1959; June 10, 1960; June 9, 1961; December 1, 1961; December 14, 1962; September 2, 1965; October 3, 1968; August 7, 1969; September 4, 1970; May 12, 1978; September 20, 1991, p. 5.
Yale Review, October 1962.

COOK, Michael   1931-

PERSONAL: Born July 7, 1931, in Farnborough, England; son of Garnet Henry (an author and mathematician) and Lydia Mabel (a teacher; maiden name, Ellis) Cook; married Margaret Ann O'Neill (an inspector of schools), August 5, 1955; children: Francis, Dominic, Polly, Jerome, Sophy. *Education:* Magdalen College, Oxford, B.A. (with honors), 1954. *Politics:* Labour. *Religion:* Roman Catholic.

ADDRESSES: Home—12 Grosvenor Ave., West Kirby, Wirral L48 7HA, England. *Office*—Department of Archives, University of Liverpool, Liverpool L69 3BX, England.

CAREER: Devon Record Office, Exeter, England, assistant archivist, 1955-58; City of Newcastle upon Tyne, England, city archivist, 1958-68; University of Liverpool, Liverpool, England, university archivist, 1968-94, Senior Fellow in Archival Studies, 1994—. Visiting lecturer at University of Istanbul, 1982, and University of Lisbon, 1986 and 1987. Director of National Archives of Tanzania, 1964-66; director of archival training at University of Ghana, 1975-77. Consultant to UNESCO on Africa, Southeast Asia and the Caribbean. Craighurst School, Liverpool, Chair of Governors. *Military service:* British Army, Royal Signals, 1950-51.

MEMBER: International Council on Archives, Society of Archivists, Business Archives Council.

WRITINGS:

Archives Administration, Dawson (Folkestone, Kent), 1977.

Archives and the Computer, Butterworth (Sevenoakes, Kent), 1980, 2nd edition, 1986.

Manual of Archival Description, Society of Archivists (Ipswich, England), 1986, 2nd edition, with Margaret Proctor, Gower (Aldershot, England), 1989.

The Management of Information From Archives, Gower, 1986.

Information Management and Archival Data, Library Association Publishing (London), 1993.

WORK IN PROGRESS: Research on cataloguing rules and standards for the exchange of archival information, for Society of Archivists and British Library.

SIDELIGHTS: Michael Cook once told *CA:* "I am devoted to the idea of bringing together archives, libraries, and scientific information services as part of a national information system that will get proper public recognition. I am also campaigning for a return to UNESCO membership."

BIOGRAPHICAL/CRITICAL SOURCES:

PERIODICALS

Information Development, October 1986.
Times Literary Supplement, August 1, 1986.

* * *

COOK, Ramsay 1931-

PERSONAL: Born November 28, 1931, in Alameda, Saskatchewan, Canada; son of George Russell and Lillie Ellen (Young) Cook; married Margaret Eleanor Thornhill; children: Margaret Michele, Markham Glen. *Education:* University of Manitoba, B.A., 1954; Queen's University, Kingston, Ontario, M.A, 1955; University of Toronto, Ph.D., 1960. *Avocational interests:* Theater, music, movies, birdwatching.

ADDRESSES: Office—York University, North York, Toronto, Ontario M3J 1P3, Canada.

CAREER: University of Toronto, Toronto, Ontario, professor of history, 1958-68; York University, Toronto, currently professor of history. Harvard University, Cambridge, MA, visiting professor of Canadian studies, 1968-69; Bicentennial Professor of Canadian History, Yale University, New Haven, CT, 1978-79. Also worked as a television commentator.

MEMBER: Royal Society of Canada (fellow), Canadian Historical Association (president, 1983-84), University League for Social Reform (past president).

AWARDS, HONORS: President's medal, University of Western Ontario, 1966 and 1968; Tyrrell Medal, Royal Society of Canada, 1975; Guggenheim fellow, 1980-81; Governor General's Literary Award for nonfiction, Canada Council, 1986, for *The Regenerators: Social Criticism in Late Victorian English Canada;* Order of Canada, 1986; Imperial Order of the Sacred Treasure (Japan), 1994.

WRITINGS:

(With Kenneth McNaught) *Canada and the United States,* Clarke, Irwin (Toronto), 1963.
The Politics of John W. Dafoe and the Free Press, University of Toronto Press (Toronto), 1963.
(With John T. Saywell and John C. Ricker) *Canada: A Modern Study,* Clarke, Irwin, 1963, 3rd edition, 1977.
Canada and the French-Canadian Question, Macmillan (Toronto), 1966.
Provincial Autonomy: Minority Rights and the Compact Theory, 1867-1921, Queen's Printer, 1969.
Royal Commission on Bilingualism and Biculturalism: Studies, Queen's Printer, 1969.

(Author of introduction) Eleanor Cook, editor, *The Craft of History,* Canadian Broadcasting Corp. (CBC), 1973.
(With Robert Craig Brown) *Canada, 1896-1921: A Nation Transformed,* McClelland & Stewart (Toronto), 1974.
The Maple Leaf Forever: Essays on Nationalism and Politics in Canada, Macmillan, 1977.
The Regenerators: Social Criticism in Late Victorian English Canada, University of Toronto Press, 1985.
Canada, Quebec and the Uses of Nationalism, McClelland & Stewart, 1986, 2nd revised edition, 1995.
(With Arthur Ray, Christopher Moore, Graeme Wynn, Peter Waite, and Desmond Morton) *The Illustrated History of Canada,* edited by Craig Brown, Lester & Orpen Dennys, 1987.

EDITOR

The Dafoe-Sifton Correspondence, 1919-1927, D. W. Friesen, 1966.
Politics of Discontent, University of Toronto Press, 1967.
Confederation, University of Toronto Press, 1967.
Constitutionalism and Nationalism in Lower Canada, University of Toronto Press, 1969.
French-Canadian Nationalism: An Anthology, Macmillan, 1970.
(With Michael Behiels) Andre Laurendeau, *The Essential Laurendeau* (translated from the original French by Joanne L'Heaureaux and Richard Howard), Copp (Toronto), 1976.
(With Carl Berger) *The West and the Nation: Essays in Honour of W. L. Morton,* McClelland & Stewart, 1976.
(With Wendy Mitchinson) *The Proper Sphere: Woman's Place in Canadian Society,* Oxford University Press, 1976.
The Voyages of Jacques Cartier, University of Toronto Press, 1993.

OTHER

Contributor to scholarly journals and popular magazines, including *Canadian Forum, Cite libre, Literary Review of Canada,* and *Saturday Night.* Editor, *Canadian Historical Review,* 1963-68; general editor, *Dictionary of Canadian Biography.*

BIOGRAPHICAL/CRITICAL SOURCES:

PERIODICALS

Canadian Forum, April-May, 1970.
Globe and Mail (Toronto), April 26, 1986; September 20, 1986; September 19, 1987.

CORK, Richard (Graham) 1947-

PERSONAL: Born March 25, 1947, in Eastbourne, England; son of Hubert Henry and Beatrice Hester (Smale) Cork; married Vena Jackson, March 21, 1970; children: Adam, Polly, Katy, Joe. *Education:* Trinity Hall, Cambridge, received degree (with first class honors), 1969, Ph.D., 1978.

*ADDRESSES: Home—*24 Milman Rd., London NW6 6EG, England.

CAREER: Evening Standard, London, art critic, 1969-77, 1980-83; *Studio International,* London, editor, 1975-79; *Listener,* London, art critic, 1984-90; *Times,* London, chief art critic, 1991—. Slade Professor of Fine Art, Cambridge University, 1989-90; Henry Moore Senior Fellow, Courtauld Institute, London, 1992-95. Member of art panel of Arts Council of Great Britain, 1971-74; chairperson, Visual Arts and Architecture Panel, Arts Council of England, 1995—.

AWARDS, HONORS: Llewelyn Rhys Prize, National Book League, 1977, for *Vorticism and Abstract Art in the First Machine Age;* Sir Banister Fletcher Prize, 1985, for *Art beyond the Gallery in Early Twentieth-Century England.*

WRITINGS:

Vorticism and Abstract Art in the First Machine Age, Volume I: *Origins and Development,* Volume II: *Synthesis and Decline,* University of California Press (Berkeley), 1976.
The Social Role of Art: Essays in Criticism for a Newspaper Public, Gordon Fraser Gallery (London), 1980, State Mutual Book (New York City), 1981.
Art beyond the Gallery in Early Twentieth-Century England, Yale University Press (New Haven, CT), 1985.
David Bomberg, Yale University Press, 1987.
A Bitter Truth: Avant-Garde Art and the Great War, Yale University Press, 1994.

Contributor to periodicals, including *New Statesman, Times Literary Supplement,* and art magazines in Europe and the United States.

WORK IN PROGRESS: A history of British sculpture in the 20th century.

SIDELIGHTS: As an art critic and art historian, Richard Cork's scholarly studies have been instrumental in recreating several modernist movements in England. In his two-volume *Vorticism and Abstract Art in the First Machine Age* Cork chronicles the rise and fall of the early twentieth-century English movement known as Vorticism. "Cork in about 200,000 words on nearly 600 large and very well illustrated and well documented pages has provided us with . . . a view of Vorticism as a group effort of a dozen young men and women . . . which was to provide this country with an equivalent of Italian Futurism, French Cubism and German Expressionism. . . . Cork keeps to a fairly strict chronology, and moves from one artist to another, taking us month by month through that exciting time," writes Alan Bowness in the *Times Literary Supplement.* In reviews of Cork's two-volume work, *Spectator* contributor Bryan Robertson finds that Cork "has written an elaborately detailed survey of Vorticism. He is scrupulously fair to all the protagonists." In contrast with Bowness, Robertson believes Cork has emphasized the special role Lewis played in this movement. Regarding volume one of Cork's study, *Origins and Development,* Robertson feels the book is "an important contribution to art history, and with it Cork occupies a position of honour among those younger art historians who are busily setting the record straight" concerning the evolution of art in England.

Regarding *A Bitter Truth: Avant Garde Art and the Great War,* published in 1994, Thomas Frick, writing in the *Los Angeles Times* calls the work "the first book to comprehensively treat its subject, and it does so masterfully, teaming with telling anecdote and telling detail." And reviewer David Ekserdjian agrees in the London *Times:* "[Cork] triumphantly proves what ought to be a truism, namely that it is perfectly possible to combine all the paraphernalia of serious scholarship with a prose style that responds with feeling to the greatest art."

Cork once told *CA:* "I like to perform a dual role, as art historian and art critic. Both roles are equally important to me, and I see them as complementary activities."

BIOGRAPHICAL/CRITICAL SOURCES:

PERIODICALS

Art Line, January/February 1985.
Arts Review, September 16, 1977.
Artscribe, July 1977.
Los Angeles Times, November 13, 1994, p. 6.
Observer (London), February 8, 1987.
Spectator, May 8, 1976; January 8, 1977; June 22, 1985.
Times (London), June 27, 1994, p. 35.
Times Literary Supplement, March 18, 1977; June 13, 1980; February 6, 1987.

* * *

COWAN, Peter (Walkinshaw) 1914-

PERSONAL: Born November 4, 1914, in Perth, Western Australia, Australia; son of Norman Walkinshaw and Marie (Johnson) Cowan; married Edith Howard, June 18, 1941; children: Julian Walkinshaw. *Education:* University of Western Australia, B.A., 1941, Diploma in Education, 1946. *Avocational interests:* Nature and wildlife conservation, particularly in Australia.

ADDRESSES: Home—149 Alfred Rd., Mount Claremont, Western Australia, Australia. *Office*—English Department, University of Western Australia, Nedlands, Western Australia, Australia.

CAREER: Clerk, farm laborer, and casual worker in Australia, 1930-39, and teacher, 1941-42; University of Western Australia, Nedlands, parttime teacher, 1946-50; Scotch College, Swanbourne, Western Australia, senior English master, 1950-62; University of Western Australia, senior tutor in English, 1964-79. *Military service:* Royal Australian Air Force, 1943-45.

AWARDS, HONORS: Commonwealth literary fellowship, 1963, to write *Seed;* Australian Council for the Arts fellowship, 1975 and 1980; honorary research fellow, University of Western Australia Department of English, 1982; Order of Australia, A.M., 1987; Patrick White Award, 1992; honorary D.Phil., Edith Cowan University (Perth), 1995.

WRITINGS:

SHORT STORIES

Drift, Reed & Harris, 1944.
The Unploughed Land, Angus & Robertson, 1958.
The Empty Street, Angus & Robertson, 1965.
The Tins and Other Stories, University of Queensland Press, 1973.
Mobiles, Fremantle Arts Centre Press, 1979.
A Window in Mrs. X's Place, Penguin, 1986.
Voices, Fremantle Arts Centre Press, 1988.

NOVELS

Summer, Angus & Robertson, 1964.
Seed, Angus & Robertson, 1966.
The Color of the Sky, Fremantle Arts Centre Press, 1986.
The Hills of Apollo Bay, Fremantle Arts Centre Press, 1989.
The Tenants, Fremantle Arts Centre Press, 1994.

OTHER

(Editor) *Short Story Landscape* (anthology), Longmans, Green, 1964.
(Editor, with Bruce Bennett) *Spectrum One: Narrative Short Stories,* Longman, 1970.
(Editor, with Bennett) *Spectrum Two: Modern Short Stories,* Longman, 1970.
(Editor) *Today* (short stories), Longman, 1971.
(Contributor) *This Is Australia,* Hamlyn, 1975.

(Editor) *A Faithful Picture: The Letters of Eliza and Thomas Brown at York in the Swan River Colony, 1841-1852,* Fremantle Arts Centre Press, 1977.
(Editor) *A Unique Position* (biography), University of Western Australia Press (Nedlands), 1978.
(Editor, with Bennett and Hay) *Spectrum Three: Experimental Short Stories* (anthology), Longman Cheshire, 1979.
(Contributor) Bennett, editor, *The Literature of Western Australia,* University of Western Australia Press, 1979.
(Editor, with Bennett and Hay) *Perspectives One* (short stories), Longman Cheshire, 1985.
Maitland Brown: A View of Nineteenth-Century Western Australia (biography), Fremantle Arts Centre Press, 1988.

Contributor of short stories to anthologies.

WORK IN PROGRESS: Articles on Western Australian literature.

BIOGRAPHICAL/CRITICAL SOURCES:

BOOKS

Barnes, John, *An Australian Selection,* Angus & Robertson, 1974.
Bennett, Bruce, editor, *The Literature of Western Australia,* University of Western Australia Press, 1979.
Bennett, Bruce, and Susan Miller, editors, *Peter Cowan: New Critical Essays,* University of Western Australia Press-Centre for Studies in Australian Literature, 1992.
Cowan, Peter, *A Window in Mrs. X's Place,* introduction by Bruce Bennett, Penguin, 1986.
Hewett, Dorothy, editor, *Sandgropers,* University of Western Australia Press, 1973.
Jones, Evan, editor, *Commonwealth Literary Fund Lectures,* Australian National University Press, 1961.

PERIODICALS

Meanjin Quarterly, Number 2, 1960; Number 2, 1966.
Times Literary Supplement, June 19, 1987.
Westerly, number 3, 1973.

*   *   *

CRNJANSKI, Milos 1893-1977
(Milos Tsernianski; C. R. Mill, a pseudonym)

PERSONAL: Born October 26, 1893, in Csongrad, Hungary; died November 30, 1977, in Belgrade, Yugoslavia; naturalized British citizen, 1951; son of Thomas (a notary) and Mary (Vujitsch) Crnjanski; married Vida Ruzic (a dollmaker and clothes maker), November 10, 1921. *Edu-*

cation: Studied at University of Vienna, University of Paris, and University of Berlin; University of Belgrade, B.M., 1926; University of London, Diploma in Foreign Affairs, 1951. *Religion:* Serbian Orthodox.

CAREER: Professor of history in Belgrade, Yugoslavia, 1922-27 and 1930-35; *Politika* (daily newspaper), Belgrade, staff member, 1922-24; Royal Yugoslav Legation, Berlin, Germany, cultural attache, 1928-29, press attache, 1935-38; *Vreme* (daily newspaper), Belgrade, staff member, 1930-35; Royal Yugoslav Legation, Rome, Italy, press counselor, 1938-41; Royal Yugoslav Government in War, London, England, press counselor, 1941-45. *Military service:* Austro-Hungarian Army, 1914-18.

MEMBER: PEN.

AWARDS, HONORS: Serbian Academy Prize, 1930, for *Seobe;* two literary awards, 1930, for *Knjiga o Nemackoj;* NIN award, 1971, for *Roman o Londonu.*

WRITINGS:

Maska: Poeticna komedija (title means "The Mask: A Poetic Comedy"; also see below), Nakl. Drustva hrv. Knjizevnika (Zagreb), 1918.

Lirika Itake (poetry; title means "The Lyrics of Ithaca"; also see below), Cvijanovic (Belgrade), 1919.

Price o muskom (title means "Tales of the Masculine"; also see below), Cvijanovic, 1920.

Dnevnik o Carnojevicu (novel; title means "The Diary about Carnojevic"; also see below), Sveslovenska Knjizara (Belgrade), 1921, published with *Seobe* (also see below), Minerva, 1956.

Naze Plaze na Jadranu (booklet; title means "Our Adriatic Beaches"), Izdanje Jadranske (Belgrade), 1927.

Seobe (novel; first published serially in *Srpski Knjizevni Glasnik,* 1927; also see below), Geca Kon (Belgrade), 1929, published with *Dnevnik o Carnojevicu,* Minerva, 1956, first and second books of *Seobe* published in two volumes as *Seobe i druga knjiga seoba,* Srpska Knjizevna Zadruga (Belgrade), 1962, translation of first volume by Michael Henry Heim published as *Migrations,* Harcourt (New York City), 1994.

Ljubav u Toskani (travel; title means "Love in Tuscany"; also see below), Geca Kon, 1930.

Knjiga o Nemackoj (travel; title means "A Book on Germany"), Geca Kon, 1931.

Belgrade (short history and guide), Bureau Central de Presse (Belgrade), 1936.

Konak (play; title means "Hostel"; also see below), Minerva (Belgrade), 1958.

Itaka i komentari (poetry and prose; title means "Ithaca and Commentaries"; also see below), Prosveta (Belgrade), 1959.

Lirika, proza, eseji (poetry, prose, and essays; also see below), Matica Srpska (Novi Sad), 1965.

Serbia, Seobe, Lament nad Beogradom (includes long poem "Lament nad Beogradum" [title means "Lament over Belgrade"; first published in 1962]; also see below), Matica Srpska, 1965.

Tri poeme, Prosveta, 1965.

Sabrana dela (title means "Collected Works"; includes *Ljubav u Toscani, Antologija kineske lirike, Pesme starog Japana,* and *Kod hiperborejaca*), compiled by Riksanda Njegus and Stevan Raickovic, edited by Nikola Milosevic, introduction by Milan Bogdanovic, Volumes 1-3: *Seobe,* Volume 4: *Poezija: Lirika Itake [and] Komentari [and] Antologija kineske lirike [and] Pesme starog Japana [and] Lament nad Beogradom,* Volume 5: *Proza: Dnevni o Carnojevicu [and] Price o muskom [and] Suzni krokodil,* Volume 6: *Putopisi,* Volumes 7-8: *Kod hiperborejaca,* Volume 9: *Drame: Maska [and] Konak [and] Tesla,* Volume 10: *Eseji,* Prosveta, 1966.

Izabrana dela, four volumes, Prosveta, 1967.

Lirika, Prosveta, 1968.

Kap spanske krvi (novel; title means "A Drop of Spanish Blood"; first published serially in *Vreme,* 1932), Nolit (Belgrade), 1970.

Roman o Londonu (novel; title means "A Novel of London"), two volumes, Nolit, 1971.

Price o muskom, Suzni krokodil, Maska, Beogradski izdavacko-graficki zavod (Belgrade), 1973.

Sabrane pesme, Srpska knjizevna zadruga, 1978.

Knjiga o Mikelandjelu (essays; title means "A Book about Michelangelo"), Nolit, 1981.

Sumatra i druge pjesme, Veselin Malsesa (Sarajevo), 1981.

Embahade (memoirs; title means "Embassies"), Nolit, 1983.

O Banatu i o Banacanima, Knjizevna zajednica Novog Sada (Novi Sad), 1989.

Politicki spisi, Sfairos (Belgrade), 1989.

(Editor and translator) *Antologija kineske lirike i Pesme starog Japana,* Narodna biblioteka Srbije (Belgrade), 1990.

Crnjanski o nacionalsocijalizmu, Beletra (Belgrade), 1990.

Eseji i prikazi, Knjizevna zajednica Novog Sada, 1991.

Nova Evropa, Knjizevne novine (Belgrade), 1991.

Ispunio sam svoju sudbinu, Beogradski izdavacko-graficki zavod, 1992.

Also author of booklet *Boka Kotorska* (title means "The Bay of Kotor"), 1928, novel *The Shoemakers,* 1946, and of many essays, articles, and other writings, some under pseudonym C. R. Mill. Contributor to *Serbian Poetry from the Beginnings to the Present,* Yale Center for International and Area Studies (New Haven), 1988. Contributor to *El Economista.* Editor and publisher, *Ideje* (title means "Ideas"; anti-Marxist weekly), 1933-34.

SIDELIGHTS: Milos Crnjanski, a novelist, poet, and essayist, is widely regarded as one of the best Serbian writers of the twentieth century. An ardent Serbian nationalist and a conservative, Crnjanski enjoyed modest success as an author between the two World Wars and, after spending years in exile, lived to see his work granted new appreciation in his homeland. *Dictionary of Literary Biography* contributor Nicholas Moravcevich noted that Crnjanski's large body of work "ranks among the highest accomplishments of modern Serbian literature." The critic added: "While the range and depth of both his prose and his verse place him in the forefront of twentieth-century Serbian writers, the singularity of his style gives him an even more extraordinary place."

Born in 1893 in Csongrad, Hungary, Crnjanski attended public schools and pursued his interests in art history and philosophy until the outbreak of World War I, when he was drafted into the Austro-Hungarian army and sent to the Serbian front. His actual battle experience was curtailed by illness, but he did participate in several battles during the summer of 1915. These and his encounters with wounded soldiers in hospitals imbued him with a deep antipathy for war that soon found its way into his poetry and fiction.

As early as 1917 the young Crnjanski began to publish poetry in literary journals. His first full-length volume, *Lirika Itake,* was published in Belgrade in 1919. Moravcevich noted of that work: "The book was an instant success, establishing Crnjanski as a notable contemporary author within the Belgrade literary community." After some further study at the University of Belgrade and the Sorbonne, Crnjanski settled in Yugoslavia and joined a prominent literary circle there. During the 1920s he supported himself and his wife by working as a school teacher and a journalist, principally with the newspapers *Vreme* ("Time") and *Politika* ("Politics"). He also found time to complete his best-known novel, *Seobe,* which was first published in serial form in 1927.

Seobe, translated in 1994 as *Migrations,* tells the story of a hapless soldier, Vuk Isakovic, who dreams of a true Serbian homeland while fighting in an irrelevant military campaign. The novel's action is set not in the modern era but in the mid-eighteenth century, when the Serbs were in thrall to the empress Maria Theresa of Austria. Its themes include the search for a new and better homeland, the horrors of war, and the Serbs' long history of grievances against the West. In reviewing the translation for the *New York Times Book Review,* Ken Kalfus concluded that the novel "illuminates many of the passions that drive the fighting in the former Yugoslavia, a conflict that continues to elude public understanding."

The appearance of *Seobe* "was a major literary event," according to Moravcevich. Crnjanski's fame was fleeting, however. His rightist political views and controversial book of travel pieces from Italy, *Ljubav u Toskani,* created a rift between him and some of his modernist literary friends. Crnjanski eventually founded the journal *Ideje* ("Ideas") as a platform for his political views, but in the mid-1930s he left Yugoslavia as a diplomat, posted first to Berlin and later to Rome. He was living in Rome at the outbreak of World War II.

In April of 1941 Crnjanski relocated to Lisbon, Portugal, and then moved on to London. He and his wife remained there throughout the war and—with the Communist takeover of Yugoslavia at war's end—decided not to return home. Thus began a twenty-year exile during which Crnjanski and his wife struggled to make ends meet in a series of humiliating jobs. This experience found its way into Crnjanski's fiction as *Roman o Londonu,* a two-volume novel about an emigre Russian in England. Moravcevich called this work, Crnjanski's last fiction, "a fitting conclusion to a lifelong literary career in which the idea of the rise and fall in the search for spiritual tranquility and home is a predominant and ever-present symbol."

One outcome of Crnjanski's isolation and unemployment in England was a sequel to *Seobe.* Published with its predecessor in *Seobe i druga knjiga seoba,* the story picks up with Vuk's adopted son, Pavel, who finally persuades his father's family to leave Austria for Russia. The completion of this portion of the novel in the late 1950s marked the beginning of a resurgence of interest in Crnjanski's work in Yugoslavia. The country's leading publishing houses began to reprint his work and issue new titles, and in 1965 the Yugoslavian government officially invited Crnjanski back into the country. He accepted the offer, and the following year his ten-volume *Sabrana dela* ("Collected Works") was published in Belgrade.

Crnjanski died in Belgrade in 1977, an admired elder statesman in Yugoslavian arts and letters. In addition to his novels and original poetry, he also published translations of Japanese poems, travel essays, political essays, and ruminations about his homeland. In the years since his death numerous critical studies of his work have been published in eastern Europe and abroad.

BIOGRAPHICAL/CRITICAL SOURCES:

BOOKS

Dictionary of Literary Biography, Volume 147: *South Slavic Writers before World War II,* Gale, 1994, pp. 33-39.
Dzadzic, Petar, *Prostori srece u delu Milosa Crnjanskog,* Nolit (Belgrade), 1976.

Norris, David, editor. *Milos Crnjanski and Modern Serbian Literature.* Astra Press (Nottingham, England), 1988.

Norris, *The Novels of Milos Crnjanski: An Approach through Time,* Astra Press, 1990.

PERIODICALS

Kirkus Reviews, March 1, 1994, pp. 244-45.
New York Times Book Review, July 24, 1994, p. 25.*

*   *   *

CRONYN, Hume 1911-

PERSONAL: Born July 18, 1911, in London, Ontario, Canada; immigrated to United States, 1931; son of Hume Blake (a financier and member of Canadian Parliament) and Frances Amelia (Labatt) Cronyn; married second wife, Jessica Tandy (an actress), September 27, 1942; children: Christopher Hume Tandy, Susan Cronyn Tettemer. *Education:* Attended McGill University, 1930-31; studied drama at Mozarteum, Salzburg, Austria, 1932-33; American Academy of Dramatic Arts, diploma, 1934.

ADDRESSES: Home—63-23 Carlton St., Rego Park, NY 11374. *Agent*—Sam Cohn, International Creative Management, 40 West 57th St., New York, NY 10019; and Martha Luttrell, International Creative Management, 8942 Wilshire Blvd., Los Angeles, CA 90211.

CAREER: Actor, writer, director, and producer, 1931—. Actor in stage productions, including *Up Pops the Devil,* 1931; *The Second Man, The Late Christopher Bean, He Knew Dillinger,* and *Mountain Ivy,* all 1934; *Three Men on a Horse* and *Boy Meets Girl,* both 1936; *Room Service* and *High Tor,* both 1937; *Escape This Night* and *There's Always a Breeze,* both 1938; *Off to Buffalo* and *The Three Sisters,* both 1939; *Susan and God, Ways and Means, We Were Dancing, Shadow and Substance, The Devil's Disciple, Kiss the Boys Goodbye, Family Portrait, Our Town, The White Steed, Margin for Error, Golden Boy, The Weak Link,* and *Retreat to Pleasure,* all 1940; *Mr. Big,* 1941; *It's All Yours,* 1942; *The Male Animal,* 1944; *The Survivors,* 1948; *The Little Blue Light,* 1950; *The Fourposter,* 1951; *Madam, Will You Walk,* 1953; *The Honeys* and *A Day by the Sea,* both 1955; *The Man in the Dog Suit,* 1958; *Triple Play* (includes *Portrait of a Madonna, A Pound on Demand, Bedtime Story,* and *On the Harmful Effects of Tobacco*), both 1959; *Big Fish, Little Fish,* 1961; *The Miser, The Three Sisters,* and *Death of a Salesman,* all 1963; *Hamlet* and *The Physicists,* both 1964; *I Hear America Speaking, Richard III,* and *The Cherry Orchard,* all 1965; *A Delicate Balance,* 1966; *Hadrian VII,* 1969; *The Caine Mutiny Court Martial,* 1971; *Promenade All!, Happy Days, Act without Words I,* and *Krapp's Last Tape,* all

1972; *Noel Coward in Two Keys,* 1974; *Merchant of Venice* and *A Midsummer Night's Dream,* both 1976; *The Gin Game,* 1977; *Foxfire,* 1980; *Traveler in the Dark,* 1984; and *The Petition,* 1986.

Director of stage productions, including *Portrait of a Madonna,* 1946, *Now I Lay Me Down to Sleep,* 1949, *Hilda Crane,* 1950, *Madam, Will You Walk,* 1953, *The Egghead,* 1957, and *Triple Play,* 1959.

Producer of stage productions, including *Junior Miss* and *It's All Yours,* 1942, *Slow Dance on the Killing Ground,* 1964, and *The Gin Game,* 1977.

Actor in films, including *Shadow of a Doubt* and *The Cross of Lorraine,* both 1943; *The Seventh Cross, Main Street after Dark,* and *Lifeboat,* all 1944; *A Letter for Evie* and *The Sailor Takes a Wife,* both 1945; *The Green Years, The Postman Always Rings Twice,* and *The Ziegfeld Follies,* all 1946; *Beginning of the End* and *Brute Force,* both 1947; *The Bride Goes Wild,* 1948; *Top o' the Morning,* 1949; *People Will Talk,* 1951; *Crowded Paradise,* 1956; *Sunrise at Campobello,* 1960; *Cleopatra,* 1963; *Gaily, Gaily* and *The Arrangement,* both 1968; *There Was a Crooked Man,* 1969; *Conrack* and *Parallax View,* both 1973; *Honky Tonk Freeway,* 1980; *The World according to Garp* and *Rollover,* both 1981; *Impulse,* 1983; *Brewster's Millions* and *Cocoon,* both 1984; *Batteries Not Included,* 1986; *Cocoon the Return,* 1988; and *Camilla* and *The Pelican Brief,* both 1993.

Actor in television productions, including *Her Master's Voice,* 1939; *The Marriage* (also producer), 1953-54; *Omnibus, The Ed Sullivan Show,* and *The Fourposter,* all 1955; *The Great Adventure, The Confidence Man,* and *The Big Wave,* all 1956; *The Five Dollar Bill* and *Member of the Family,* both 1957; *The Bridge of San Luis Rey,* 1958; *The Moon and Sixpence* and *A Doll's House,* both 1959; *Juno and the Paycock,* 1960; *John F. Kennedy Memorial Broadcast,* 1963; *Hamlet,* 1964; *Many Faces of Love,* 1977; *The Gin Game,* 1979; *Foxfire,* 1987; *Dayone,* 1988; *Age Old Friends,* 1989; *Broadway Bound,* 1991; *Christmas on Division Street,* 1991; and *To Dance with the White Dog,* 1993. Produced and directed *Portrait of a Madonna* for television, 1948.

MEMBER: Actors' Equity Association, Dramatists Guild, Screen Actors' Guild, Screen Writers' Guild, American Federation of Television and Radio Artists, Society of Stage Directors and Choreographers.

AWARDS, HONORS: Comoedia Matinee Club Award, 1952, for *The Fourposter;* Barter Theatre Award, 1961, for outstanding contribution to theatre; Delia Austria Medal, New York Drama League, 1961, for *Big Fish, Little Fish;* Antoinette Perry (Tony) Award, League of New York Theatres and Producers, and *Variety* New York Drama Critics Poll Award, both 1964, for *Hamlet;* award from the American Academy of Dramatic Arts, 1964, for alumni achievement; Herald Theatre Award, 1967, for *A Delicate Balance;* Los Angeles Drama Critics Circle Award for best actor, 1972, for *The Caine Mutiny Court Martial;* Straw Hat Award for direction, Council of Stock Theatres, 1972, *Promenade All!;* Obie Award, *Village Voice,* 1972, for *Krapp's Last Tape;* honorary doctor of laws, University of Western Ontario, 1974; Creative Arts Award, Brandeis University, 1978; Los Angeles Drama Critics Circle Award for best actor, 1979, for *The Gin Game;* elected to American Theatre Hall of Fame, 1979; Humanitas Prize for best television script of programs longer than one hour, Human Family Institute, 1985, for *The Dollmaker;* Christopher Award and Writers Guild Award, both 1985, both for *The Dollmaker;* Alley Theatre Award, 1987, in recognition of significant contributions to the theatre arts; National Medal of Arts, 1990, for outstanding contribution to the arts; Emmy Award and ACE Award, both 1990, both for *Age Old Friends;* Emmy Award, 1992, for *Broadway Bound;* Antoinette Perry Lifetime Achievement Award, 1994; Emmy Award, 1994, for *To Dance with the White Dog;* New York State Governor's Award, 1994, for contribution to artistic life in New York State.

WRITINGS:

Rope (film script), Warner Bros., 1948.
Under Capricorn (film script), Warner Bros., 1949.
(With Susan Cooper) *Foxfire* (two-act play; produced in Stratford, Ontario, 1980; produced on Broadway, 1982), Samuel French, 1983.
(With Cooper) *The Dollmaker* (television movie screenplay), American Broadcasting Company (ABC), 1985.

Author, with Cooper, of unproduced screenplay, "Dinner at the Homesick Restaurant." Contributor of short stories and articles to periodicals.

WORK IN PROGRESS: A documentary on Kenyan wildlife; role in *Marvin's Room.*

SIDELIGHTS: In a distinguished career spanning more than fifty years on the stage and screen, Canadian-born actor Hume Cronyn has shown himself among the most versatile of performers. His work has ranged from acclaimed character roles in Hollywood thrillers and Broadway comedies to award-winning performances in plays as diverse as William Shakespeare's *Hamlet* and Samuel Beckett's *Krapp's Last Tape.* Some of Cronyn's best-known stage appearances have been opposite his wife, Jessica Tandy, in hit two-character plays like *The Fourposter* and *The Gin Game,* which earned the couple kudos for their collaborative skill in capturing the subtle nuances of intimate relationships. Besides being an actor, Cronyn is an award-winning director, producer, and writer for stage,

screen, and television. For his contributions to the arts he was awarded the National Medal of Arts in 1990, as well as the Tony Lifetime Achievement Award in 1994.

Cronyn discovered his love for the stage while acting in college productions as a pre-law student at McGill University in Montreal. He left McGill after one year and came to the United States in 1931 to study at the American Academy of Dramatic Arts and work in stock and repertory companies in Washington, D.C., and New York City. Cronyn made his professional debut in Washington in *Up Pops the Devil,* and first appeared on Broadway at the age of twenty-three in 1934, as the janitor in Burgess Meredith's comedy *Hipper's Holiday.* The play folded after four performances, but Cronyn went on to appear in a series of highly successful Broadway comedies during the mid-1930s, including *Three Men on a Horse, Boy Meets Girl, High Tor,* and *Room Service.*

In 1940 Cronyn won his first starring role on Broadway in Allan Wood's comedy *The Weak Link.* In that production Cronyn played Peter Mason, a hapless chess genius who becomes the unwitting mastermind of a gang of bank robbers. During the succeeding war years, he produced and acted in several stage revues for military servicemen and women in the United States and Canada.

Cronyn launched his film career in 1943, acting in Alfred Hitchcock's thriller *Shadow of a Doubt. New York Times* critic Bosley Crowther dubbed Cronyn's portrayal of Herbie Hawkins "a modest comic masterpiece," and the actor went on to sign a multi-picture contract with Metro-Goldwyn-Mayer (MGM). Though his slight build and plain features disqualified him as a leading man, Cronyn had great success in supporting and character roles, winning an Academy Award nomination for his performance in the 1943 MGM drama *The Seventh Cross* and critical kudos for his portrayal of Arthur Keats in the 1946 murder drama *The Postman Always Rings Twice.*

In addition to his acting work, Cronyn wrote scripts for two Hitchcock-directed films produced by Warner Bros. in the late 1940s. He adapted the script for the 1948 suspense melodrama *Rope* from Patrick Hamilton's play *Rope's End;* Arthur Laurents wrote the screenplay for the film, which starred James Stewart and John Dall. In 1949 Cronyn adapted the script for *Under Capricorn* from Helen Simpson's novel of the same title. The picture, a melodramatic tale of love, guilt, and murder set in nineteenth-century Australia, featured a screenplay by James Bridie and performances by Ingrid Bergman and Joseph Cotten.

Even as he developed new skills as a film scriptwriter, the versatile and energetic Cronyn continued to act and direct in regional and New York theaters. He directed an Actor's Laboratory Theatre production of Tennessee Williams's

Portrait of a Madonna in Los Angeles in 1946, and in 1949 he appeared in the title role of an American National Theatre and Academy touring production of *Hamlet.* Cronyn made his Broadway directorial debut with Ludwig Bemelman's *Now I Lay Me Down to Sleep* in 1950; in 1951 he returned triumphantly to the Broadway stage as an actor in Jan de Hartog's two-character play *The Fourposter.* Cronyn's partner in this three-act comedy about the vagaries of married life was his real-life wife, Jessica Tandy, an English-born actress. The pair's stage collaboration—the first of several memorable duets Tandy and Cronyn would play—delighted critics and audiences alike, and *The Fourposter* became a smash box-office hit that ran for more than two years.

Cronyn and Tandy appeared together in two other New York stage productions in the 1950s. The first of these, which Cronyn also directed, was *Madam, Will You Walk,* a Sidney Howard comic fantasy that opened the Phoenix Theatre in 1953. They joined forces again in *Triple Play,* a group of four short theater pieces that Cronyn directed in 1959, sharing the stage in *Portrait of a Madonna* and the Sean O'Casey sketches *A Pound on Demand* and *Bedtime Story,* while Cronyn did a solo turn in Chekhov's dramatic lecture *On the Harmful Effects of Tobacco.* "Give Mr. Cronyn a wig, mustache and glasses, and he is about the best character actor in the business," exulted Brooks Atkinson about this last performance.

In 1961 Cronyn appeared with Jason Robards in *Big Fish, Little Fish,* a comedy by Hugh Wheeler directed by Sir John Gielgud. *New York Times* critic Howard Taubman credited the actor with a "superbly grumpy and humorous performance" in the character role of Jimmie Luton, a crusty, homosexual art teacher. After joining the play's London production the following year and working with the Minnesota Theatre Company in classical repertory in 1963, Cronyn took the role of Polonius in the Broadway production of *Hamlet* in April, 1964. Commenting on Richard Burton's lead performance in his review of the play, Taubman added: "worthy of being on the stage with this Hamlet is Hume Cronyn's superbly managed and richly fatuous Polonius." Cronyn's tour de force earned him the Tony Award and top ranking in the 1964 New York Drama Critics' Poll.

After this triumph, Cronyn and Tandy performed at the White House at the request of President and Mrs. Johnson in *I Hear America Speaking* in 1965. The following year they appeared together again on the Broadway stage in Edward Albee's *A Delicate Balance.* Although he lost an eye to cancer in 1969, Cronyn barely paused in his career, going on to win the Los Angeles Drama Critics Circle Award for best actor in 1971 and, in 1972, the Off-

Broadway Obie Award for his role in Beckett's *Krapp's Last Tapes.*

In 1980 Cronyn made his debut as a playwright with *Foxfire,* a two-act drama he wrote with Susan Cooper based on the Foxfire books about rural Appalachian life. The play was first produced at the Stratford, Ontario, Shakespeare Festival and then staged in Minneapolis before opening on Broadway in 1982. Tandy starred as Annie Nations, a seventy-nine-year-old mountain matriarch facing the dilemma of whether or not she should sell her old homestead to go live with her son in Florida. Her son Dillard (played by Keith Carradine) is anxious for her to sell out, make some money on the land, and help him take care of his children, but the memory of her dead husband, Hector, whose family had worked the spread for generations, counsels otherwise. As Hector Nations, Cronyn appeared in flashbacks and as a ghostly narrator, delivering pungent opinions "laced with crackerbarrel vignettes and Tevye-like biblical quotations" and flavored with "dyspeptic comic relish," wrote Frank Rich in the *New York Times.* Though appreciative of the play as a vehicle for Tandy, Rich found Cronyn's written role cliched and the overall story a predictable dramatic patchwork. The play was a popular success, however, and moved on to Los Angeles in 1985.

Cronyn collaborated again with Cooper on his first television movie screenplay, *The Dollmaker,* an adaptation of Harriette Arnow's novel that was broadcast by ABC in May, 1984. Jane Fonda starred as Gertie Nevels, a gritty and resourceful mother of five from the Kentucky mountains who struggles to keep her family's values intact after economic pressures force them to move to Detroit during the Second World War. Cronyn and Cooper won the 1984 Humanitas Prize for their script, cited as a "moving depiction of the glories, the demands and the heroism involved in being a mother" and a "lucid statement that it is loving relationships, not things, that make human beings happy."

Cronyn and Tandy illuminated another such loving relationship in *The Petition,* a play that brought the couple back to Broadway in 1986. Like *The Fourposter, The Petition* explores the joys and frustrations of marriage, in this case, that of a retired English general and his aristocratic wife of more than fifty years. Tandy and Cronyn "have interwoven a silken artistry of characterization with the homespun fabric of marriage as depicted by people who are actually married," remarked William A. Henry III in *Time.* "*The Petition* displays them at the full height of their rhetorical powers and the full depth of their painstaking domestic detail." Cronyn and Tandy both received Tony Award nominations for their performances.

BIOGRAPHICAL/CRITICAL SOURCES:

BOOKS

Ross, Lillian, and Helen Ross, *The Player: A Profile of an Art,* Simon & Schuster, 1962.

PERIODICALS

America, January 22, 1983.
Chicago Tribune, November 7, 1984.
Globe and Mail (Toronto), May 12, 1984.
Los Angeles Times, February 18, 1983; November 26, 1985.
New Leader, December 27, 1982.
Newsweek, June 24, 1985.
New Yorker, October 21, 1961; October 17, 1977.
New York Times, March 5, 1940; September 29, 1944; May 3, 1946; August 27, 1948; September 9, 1949; October 25, 1951; December 2, 1953; April 16, 1959; March 16, 1961; April 10, 1964; September 23, 1966; April 17, 1972; November 21, 1972; November 23, 1972; November 12, 1982; May 11, 1984; July 10, 1985.
People, June 2, 1986.
Time, February 27, 1984; May 12, 1986.

* * *

CROW, Donna Fletcher 1941-

PERSONAL: Born November 15, 1941, in Nampa, ID; daughter of Leonard S. (a real estate investor) and Reta (a teacher; maiden name, Book) Fletcher; married Stanley D. Crow (an attorney), December 14, 1963; children: Stanley D., Jr., Preston, John, Elizabeth Pauline. *Education:* Attended Pasadena College, 1960-62; Northwest Nazarene College, B.A. (summa cum laude), 1964. *Politics:* Republican. *Religion:* Nazarene.

ADDRESSES: Home—3776 La Fontana Way, Boise, ID 83702.

CAREER: Nampa High School, Nampa, ID, English and drama teacher, 1963-64; Lexington Christian Academy, Lexington, MA, English and drama teacher, 1965-66; Boise High School, Boise, ID, teacher of English, 1967-68; Northwest Nazarene College, Nampa, ID, member of adjunct faculty, 1988.

MEMBER: National Federation of Press Women, Romance Writers of America, Christian Writers' League of America, Writer's Information Network, Idaho Press Women.

AWARDS, HONORS: Mount Herman Christian Writer's Conference, writer of the year, 1983; Idaho Writer of the Year award, 1988; Idaho Press Women, award for out-

standing historical fiction, 1989; Mount Herman Christian Writer's Conference, Pacesetter Award, 1990; National Federation of Press Women, award for historical fiction, 1993, for *Glastonbury: The Novel of Christian England;* Northwest Nazarene College, award for professional achievement, 1994.

WRITINGS:

NOVELS

Greengold Autumn, Zondervan (Grand Rapids, MI), 1984.
The Desires of Your Heart, Zondervan, 1985.
Love Unmerited, Zondervan, 1986.
Brandley's Search ("Cambridge Collection" series), Victor Books (Wheaton, IL), 1986.
To Be Worthy ("Cambridge Collection" series), Victor Books, 1986, published as "Camberidge Chronicles" series, Crossing, 1994.
A Gentle Calling ("Cambridge Collection" series), Victor Books, 1987, published as "Cambridge Chronicles" series, Crossing, 1995.
Something of Value ("Cambridge Collection" series), Victor Books, 1987.
The Castle of Dreams, Tyndale (Wheaton, IL), 1992.
Glastonbury: The Novel of Christian England, Crossway Books (Westchester, IL), 1992.
Kathryn: Days of Struggle and Triumph ("Daughters of Courage" series), Moody Press (Chicago, IL), 1992.
Elizabeth: Days of Loss and Hope ("Daughters of Courage" series), Moody Press, 1993.
A Most Inconvenient Death ("Lord Danvers Mystery" series), Moody Press, 1993.
Stephanie: Days of Turmoil and Peace ("Daughters of Courage" series), Moody Press, 1993.
Grave Matters ("Lord Danvers Mystery" series), Moody Press, 1994.
Treasures of Her Heart ("Cambridge Chronicles" series), Crossing, 1994.
Where Love Begins ("Cambridge Chronicles" series), Crossing, 1995.
Encounter the Light ("Cambridge Chronicles" series), Crossing, 1995.
To Dust You Shall Return ("Lord Danvers Mystery" series), Moody Press, 1995.
Into All the World ("Cambridge Chronicles" series), Crossing, 1996.
The Fields of Bannockburn, Moody Press, 1996.

FOR CHILDREN

Professor Q's Mysterious Machine, David Cook (Elgin, IL), 1983.
The Evil Plot of Dr. Zarnof, David Cook, 1983.
Mr. Xanthu's Golden Scheme, David Cook, 1985.
General Kempthorne's Victory Tour, David Cook, 1987.

PLAYS

Called unto Holiness (produced in Boise, ID, 1978), Lillenas, 1982-83.

A Rumor of Resurrection (produced in Boise, 1980), Lillenas, 1983.

An Upper Room Experience (one-act; produced in Boise, 1982), Lillenas, 1983.

Puppets on Parade (produced in Nampa, ID, 1981), Lillenas, 1985.

Because You Ask Not (produced in Boise, 1982), Standard Publishing, 1985.

That Was Then, produced in Nampa, 1987.

The Case of the Mysterious Parable (juvenile), Lillenas, 1989.

Also author of play *Balance Due: A Modern Faustus;* author of screenplays *The Caravan Connection,* Nazarene Publishers, and *Wilberforce: Light to a Nation.*

OTHER

Recipes for the Protein Diet, Gold Quill, 1972.

The Frantic Mother Cookbook (autobiography), Harvest House (Eugene, OR), 1982.

Contributor to *Leading Children in Worship,* edited by Robert D. Troutman and Evelyn Beals, Aldersgate, 1980; *Mountain Tops,* edited by Jane Allen, Faith for Today, 1983; *Church Kitchen Handbook,* Concordia (St. Louis, MO), 1985; and *A Moment a Day,* Regal, 1988. Also contributor to *The Zondervan Family Cookbook.* Contributor to magazines, including *Arkenstone, Christian Writer, Family Life Today, Fiction Writer's Monthly, Living with Children, The Lookout, Modern Liturgy, Plastercraft, Preacher's Magazine, Rave Reviews, Romance Writer's Report,* and *Virtue.*

WORK IN PROGRESS: One Generation unto Another: The Story of Northern Ireland, for Moody Press, 1997.

SIDELIGHTS: Donna Crow told *CA:* "My passion is history—especially British history. It's my goal to give my readers on both sides of the Atlantic an appreciation of their heritage and the role the Christian faith has had in building our nations. I want my readers to be able to experience actual events in history through my characters.

"I spent my first five years as a professional writer writing for every opportunity that came along: children's books, plays, cookbooks—even poetry and ghostwriting. That was an important part of learning my craft. Now, besides my writing, I teach in two or three writer's conferences a year—usually on the how-to's of novel writing. Helping new writers get started is important to me, and I want to improve the literary quality of our work.

"For my own writing I now concentrate on what I love most—historical novels. 'The Cambridge Chronicles' is a six-book series on the history of the Evangelical Movement in 18th- and 19th-century England. The 'Lord Danvers Mysteries' are true-crime murder mysteries set in Victorian England and Scotland. For 'The Daughters of Courage' series I used my own family history to tell the story of Idaho pioneers—and, of course, I worked in as much good Scots history as I could. My *Glastonbury* was the first mega-novel in the religious market. It covers 1500 years of British history from the birth of Christ to the Reformation. It was named 'best historical novel of 1993' by the National Federation of Press Women.

"I have just completed *The Fields of Bannockburn,* the story of Scotland from the coming of Christianity through Independence. I am now at work on a third mega-novel, this, the story of Northern Ireland.

"One of my greatest joys has been spending five summers in Great Britain doing research. I have always been able to take some of my children with me, and I have made many wonderful friends in the British Isles. I am now planning my next trip and warning my husband that it's his turn to carry the luggage."

*   *   *

CUOMO, George (Michael) 1929-

PERSONAL: Born October 10, 1929, in New York, NY; son of John Joseph (a machinist) and Lillian (Vogt) Cuomo; married Sylvia Epstein, August 15, 1954 (divorced, 1994); children: Celia, Douglas, Gregory, Rosalind, Michael. *Education:* Tufts University, B.A., 1952; Indiana University, M.A., 1955.

ADDRESSES: Home—276 Pelham Road, Amherst, MA 01002. *Agent*—Ellen Levine Literary Agency, 15 E. 26th St., Suite 1801, New York, NY 10010.

CAREER: Taller & Cooper (manufacturers), New York City, worked in advertising and public relations, 1953-54; University of Arizona, Tucson, instructor in English, 1956-61; Victoria University, Victoria, British Columbia, Canada, associate professor of English, 1961-65; California State College at Hayward (now California State University, Hayward), professor of English, 1965-73; University of Massachusetts—Amherst, professor of English, 1973—. *Arizona Daily Star,* Tucson, copy editor, summers, 1956-61. *Military service:* U.S. Army, 1948-49.

MEMBER: Authors Guild, Authors League of America, Phi Beta Kappa.

AWARDS, HONORS: Second prize in Bantam-*Esquire* short story contest; National Endowment for the Arts award in fiction; Guggenheim fellowship.

WRITINGS:

Becoming a Better Reader (textbook), Holt (New York City), 1960.

Jack Be Nimble (novel), Doubleday (New York City), 1963.

Bright Day, Dark Runner (novel), Doubleday, 1964.

Among Thieves (novel; Literary Guild selection), Doubleday, 1968.

Sing, Choirs of Angels (short stories), Doubleday, 1970.

The Hero's Great Great Great Great Great Grandson (novel), Atheneum (New York City), 1971.

Geronimo and the Girl Next Door (poetry), Bookmark (Knightstown, IN), 1974.

Pieces from a Small Bomb (novel), Doubleday, 1976.

Becoming a Better Reader and Writer, Crowell (New York City), 1978.

Family Honor: An American Life (novel), Doubleday, 1983.

Trial by Water (novel), Random House (New York City), 1993.

A Couple of Cops (nonfiction), Random House, 1995.

Contributor of short stories, poems, and articles to journals and periodicals, including *Saturday Review, Nation, Saturday Evening Post, Story,* and *Antioch Review.*

SIDELIGHTS: George Cuomo, a retired English professor and writer who lives in Massachusetts, is author of eight novels about various aspects of modern American history. Among his best-known works are *Among Thieves,* a treatment of the prison system and *Family Honor: An American Life,* a story about the American Labor movement. *Chicago Tribune* critic Bill Mahin notes: "In addition to convincing plots and narratives, Cuomo's body of work . . . provides a stiletto-sharp view of our changing times and values. . . . Lack of communication is at the heart of Cuomo's present-day world."

About Cuomo's *Among Thieves,* W. G. Rogers of the *New York Times Book Review* observes: "The author argues with passion that almost everybody is dumb about crime; in his view, law officials don't really know how to do right, criminals don't know how to do wrong. Unfortunately, some of this significant message is overshadowed by the page-one style in which the story is told." Rogers finds Cuomo's plotting skillful, even "harrowing," but opines that "meaning has been somewhat sacrificed to pace." A *Times Literary Supplement* critic admires Cuomo's efforts in *Among Thieves,* remarking that "though lengthy the book hardly ever seems wasteful" and complimenting his prose as having a "suitable toughness" while allowing him to be "caustically funny at the expense of pompous officialdom."

Cuomo's more recent *Family Honor* has been cited for the way in which its central character, an Italian-American,

flies in the face of stereotype. Vincent Sirola, the protagonist of *Family Honor,* is depicted as an honest, realistic, and intelligent labor leader who wins contracts and negotiates settlements without caving in to the interests of either the Communists or the mob. "Cuomo seems to be suggesting that the forgotten heroes of the labor movement were self-effacing, reasonable men, unflappable but tenacious," concludes John Jay Osborn, Jr., in the *New York Times Book Review.* " 'Family Honor' is conceived as a literary memorial to these unknown soldiers." According to Judith Chettle in the *Washington Post Book World,* the novel "promises an Italian-American hero of . . . conventional achievement; someone who would be a salutary antidote to the pervasive ethnic caricature."

Trial by Water, Cuomo's 1993 novel, moves from considerations of ethnic differences to those of class distinctions in a small Massachusetts community. Centering on the trial of an upper-class youth accused of murdering a pair of lower-class teenagers by pushing their car into a lake, *Trial by Water* "has a rich sense of contemporary ambiguity," according to Mahin. The critic concludes of the work: "Although 'Trial by Water' is a mystery . . . it is far more a sad commentary on the isolation and alienation of the times."

In *A Couple of Cops,* a nonfiction work, Cuomo traces the on and off duty lives of two police officers—his cousins, John Cuomo and Al Della Penna. His cousins do most of the storytelling and according to the *New York Times Book Review*'s James W. Hall, Cuomo 'tries, most of the time successfully, to keep his novelistic skills hidden away and to let his subjects do the storytelling.' Hall finds that 'most readers will find that *A Couple of Cops* covers fresh turf, providing an honest and vivid portrait of the way the police truly work.' A *Kirkus Reviews* contributor notes that Cuomo's 'deep background knowledge of his two cousins brings insight into their differing personalities, approaches to work, and attitudes toward the job,' and concludes that the mix of police work and family background is 'masterfully blended together.'

BIOGRAPHICAL/CRITICAL SOURCES:

BOOKS

Dictionary of Literary Biography Yearbook: 1980, Gale (Detroit), 1981, pp. 178-83.

PERIODICALS

Chicago Tribune, March 15, 1993, section 5, p. 3.
Kirkus Reviews, February 1, 1995.
Library Journal, November 1, 1970.
New York Times Book Review, August 25, 1968, p. 30; November 13, 1983, p. 18; March 28, 1993, p. 23; April 23, 1995.
Times Literary Supplement, July 17, 1969, p. 783.

Washington Post Book World, August 7, 1983, p. 6.
Writer, February 1970.

*　　*　　*

CUSHMAN, Stephen B. 1956-

PERSONAL: Born December 17, 1956, in Norwalk, CT; son of Bigelow P. (a teacher) and Anne (a librarian; maiden name, Toffey) Cushman; married Sandra Bain (a massage therapist), June 19, 1982; children: Samuel Bain, Simon Bain. *Education:* Cornell University, B.A., 1978; Yale University, M.A., 1980, M.Phil., 1981, Ph.D., 1982.

ADDRESSES: Home—Route 7, Box 227, Charlottesville, VA 22901. *Office*—Department of English Language and Literature, Bryan Hall, University of Virginia, Charlottesville, VA 22903.

CAREER: University of Virginia, Charlottesville, assistant professor, 1982-88; associate professor, 1988-94; professor of English, 1994—.

MEMBER: William Carlos Williams Society.

AWARDS, HONORS: Fellow of American Council of Learned Societies, 1986-87; Fulbright lecturer in Greece, 1993; Mayo Distinguished Teaching Professor, 1994-97.

WRITINGS:

William Carlos Williams and the Meanings of Measure, Yale University Press (New Haven, CT), 1985.
Fictions of Form in American Poetry, Princeton University Press (Princeton, NJ), 1993.

WORK IN PROGRESS: Blue Pajamas, poems; *The Genre of Generals,* a research project about Civil War memoirs.

SIDELIGHTS: Stephen B. Cushman told *CA:* "Since the publication of *Fictions of Form in American Poetry,* I have been concentrating on putting together a book of my own poems, *Blue Pajamas.* Although there are many poet-critics writing in the United States today, they constitute a relatively small percentage of either poets or critics. For me the writing of poetry complements other kinds of writing, and I would feel incomplete if I had to stick to only verse or prose. Meanwhile, after two books about the formal aspects of poetry, my research has shifted to the study of narrative representations of the American Civil War, both in verse and prose, fiction and non-fiction. In particular, I am especially interested in the various kinds of memoirs that leaders on both sides felt compelled to write after the war. In the near future, I will be exploring this genre, as well as its relation to later narratives of the war."

BIOGRAPHICAL/CRITICAL SOURCES:

PERIODICALS

American Literature, May, 1986.
Choice, March, 1994.
Journal of Modern Literature, November, 1986.
Times Literary Supplement, June, 1994.
Virginia Quarterly Review, spring, 1986.

*　　*　　*

CUSSLER, Clive (Eric) 1931-

PERSONAL: Born July 15, 1931, in Aurora, IL; son of Eric E. and Amy (Hunnewell) Cussler; married Barbara Knight, August 28, 1955; children: Teri, Dirk, Dana. *Education:* Attended Pasadena City College, 1949-50, and Orange Coast College, California. *Politics:* Non-partisan. *Religion:* None. *Avocational interests:* Collecting automobiles, searching for historic shipwrecks.

ADDRESSES: Home—Telluride, CO, and Paradise Valley, AZ. *Agent*—Peter Lampack, The Lampack Agency, 551 Fifth Ave., New York, NY 10017.

CAREER: Bestgen & Cussler Advertising, Newport Beach, CA, owner, 1961-65; Darcy Advertising, Hollywood, CA, creative director, 1965-68; Mefford Advertising, Denver, CO, vice president and creative director, 1970-75; Aquatic Marine Dive Equipment, Newport Beach, CA, member of sales staff. *Military service:* U.S. Air Force, 1950-54; served as aircraft mechanic, became sergeant.

MEMBER: National Underwater & Marine Agency (founder and chairman), Classic Car Club of America, Royal Geographic Society (London; fellow), Explorers Club of New York (fellow).

AWARDS, HONORS: Ford Foundation Consumer Award, 1965-66, for best promotional campaign; first prize, Chicago Film Festival, 1966, for best thirty-second live action commercial; International Broadcasting Awards, 1964, 1965, 1966, 1972, 1973, for year's best radio and TV commercials; first place award, Venice Film Festival, 1972, for sixty-second live commercial; Clio Awards, 1972, 1973, 1974, for TV and radio commercials; Lowell Thomas Award, Explorers Club of New York, for underwater exploration; numerous honors for work in shipwreck discoveries and marine archaeology.

WRITINGS:

NOVELS

The Mediterranean Caper, Pyramid Publications (New York City), 1973.
Iceberg, Dodd, Mead (New York City), 1975.

Raise the Titanic, Viking (New York City), 1976.
Vixen 03, Viking, 1978.
Night Probe, Bantam (New York City), 1981.
Pacific Vortex!, Bantam, 1983.
Deep Six, Simon & Schuster (New York City), 1984.
Cyclops, Simon & Schuster, 1986.
Treasure, Simon & Schuster, 1988.
Dragon, Simon & Schuster, 1990.
Sahara, Simon & Schuster, 1992.
Inca Gold, Simon & Schuster, 1994.
Shock Wave, Simon & Schuster, 1996.

ADAPTATIONS: Raise the Titanic, based on Cussler's novel and starring Jason Robards and Richard Jordan as Dirk Pitt, was released by Associated Film Distribution in 1980; all of Cussler's books are available on audiotape.

SIDELIGHTS: Clive Cussler earned his living writing award-winning advertising copy until the success of his underwater adventure novels featuring his hero, Dirk Pitt, enabled him to leave the business world and pursue his writing interests full-time. Since then, his adventure tales have sold over seventy million copies in thirty-five languages and 105 countries.

Cussler almost lives the same sort of adventurous life as Dirk Pitt: tramping the Southwest deserts and mountains in search of lost gold mines and ghost towns, as well as funding and leading more than thirty expeditions in search of lost ships and aircraft. Cussler and his team of NUMA scientists and engineers (his fictional National Underwater and Marine Agency became a reality) have discovered and surveyed nearly seventy historically significant shipwrecks around the world, including the long-lost Confederate submarine *Hunley,* the German submarine *U-20* which sank the *Lusitania,* the famous Confederate raider *Florida,* the Navy dirigible *Akron* which crashed at sea during a storm in 1933, and the troop transport *Leopoldville* which was torpedoed on Christmas Eve of 1944 off the coast of Cherbourg France, killing over eight hundred American soldiers. Cussler donates all of his recovered artifacts from the archaeological sites to museums and universities.

Cussler has also built a premier collection of over eighty classic and vintage automobiles. From European classic body styles to American town cars to 1950s convertibles, they are all carefully restored by Cussler and his crew of experts to concours d'elegance condition.

Cussler's chosen genre, his avocations, and even his entry into publishing reveal his willingness to take risks. Almost thirty years ago, after his first manuscript received numerous rejections, the author created a clever ploy to promote his second work: he printed up stationery with the name of a fabricated West Coast literary agent and used it to send recommendations for his books to major New York agencies. Within a month he had a contract, and has remained with the same agent ever since.

Cussler's bestselling novels relate the adventures of Dirk Pitt, a handsome, witty, courageous, devil-may-care character who, like his creator, collects classic cars and searches for lost ships. *Armchair Detective* reviewer Ronald C. Miller offered this description: "Dirk Pitt has the archeological background of Indiana Jones and the boldness of James Bond. He is as skilled and comfortable underwater as Jacques Cousteau, and, like Chuck Yeager, he can fly anything with wings." Yet Pitt is far from superhuman, *Tribune Books* editor David E. Jones observed: "Cussler has created a caring, cared-about, flesh and blood human being" who takes wrong turns and suffers from lapses in judgment, but who "also thinks faster on his feet than most and has an uncanny ability to turn negative situations into positive ones." This combination has proved to be tremendously appealing to readers, even though reviewers have often faulted Cussler's writing style and his improbable storylines. *New York Times Book Review* critic Newgate Callendar cited Cussler as "the cliche expert nonpareil" in a review of *Raise the Titanic* and asserted that "Cussler has revived the cliche and batters his reader with choice specimens: 'the cold touch of fear'; 'a set look of determination in the deep green eyes'; 'before death swept over him'; 'narrow brush with death' " in *Inca Gold,* and *Best Sellers* contributor Ralph A. Sperry dismissed the author's prose in *Cyclops* as "the prosaic in the service of the implausible."

Cussler shrugs off negative responses to his work. "Because I was locked in for eighteen years writing the short, snappy ad copy, I could never sit down and write a Fitzgerald-Hemingway-Bellow-type Great American Novel," he once told *CA.* "But [that experience] did prepare me to write easy, understandable prose, and also to look at writing and publishing from a marketing angle."

Cussler recalled to *CA* that at the beginning of his writing career, "blood and guts adventure" was not universally accepted in the publishing field. Initially he was told that his adventures would never sell and that critical opinion was against him, but these views have softened with the growth of the author's popular appeal. When Cussler complained to his agent, Peter Lampack, about negative reviews, Lampack, Cussler said, "came back with a classic statement: 'Listen, when we start getting good literary reviews, we're in big trouble.' "

While early reviews of Cussler may have been dismissive, reviews of his latest works have generally recognized his stories as full of action, fun to read, and extremely popular, while nonetheless pointing out the incredibility of his plots. Discussing *Dragon,* the author's 1990 release, *Publishers Weekly* critic Sybil Steinberg admitted that although the storyline was "improbable," Cussler had still come up with "a page-turning romp that achieves a level of fast-paced action and derring-do that . . . practitioners of modern pulp fiction might well envy." Peter L. Robertson, in his *Tribune Books* review of *Treasure,* placed Cussler's stories "in the tradition of Ian Fleming's James Bond," and added, "Cussler has developed and patented a vibrant, rollicking narrative style that seldom shows signs of relenting." *Inca Gold,* which finds Dirk Pitt in the Amazonian jungles on a quest to thwart a group of smugglers, is "pure escapist adventure, with a wry touch of humor and a certain self-referential glee (Cussler himself makes a cameo appearance)," a *Publishers Weekly* reviewer noted, "but the entertainment value meets the gold standard." *Booklist* reviewer Joe Collins noted that the author's fans "are already familiar with his gift for hyperbole," and recommended that new readers take Cussler's "breathless approach with a grain of salt and just relax and enjoy the adventures of Pitt and company" in *Inca Gold.*

In an interview with Connie Lauerman in the *Chicago Tribune,* Cussler reflected on his work. "I look upon myself more as an entertainer than merely a writer. It's my job to entertain the reader in such a manner that he or she feels that they received their money's worth when they reach *the end* of the book." Cussler also considers the impact of his books on children. "I have quite a large following of young people," he told *CA.* "That's why I don't believe in using four-letter words, and any sex is simply alluded to, never detailed. I've had letters from kids as young as eight who enjoy Pitt and his adventures. And because I try to write my stories in a simple, forward manner, I'm especially pleased by letters from mothers and school teachers, who tell me their children and students had refused to read before they were given one of my books. Now they read everything in sight and are hooked on reading."

Cussler has found that his readers enjoy the pictures of Dirk Pitt's cars included on the backs of his book jackets. He also told *CA* that he takes great fun in his cameo appearances; he and Pitt always meet up, with Cussler often supplying his hero with vital information before sending him on his way to subdue the villains. While his stories may seem tailor-made for Hollywood, Cussler emphasized that he refuses to sell them for adaptation until he can be assured of a quality production.

Asked how he comes up with his intricate plots, the author told *CA:* "First comes the overall concept. This is, of course, the old cut-and-dried, time-tested *What-if.* What if, for example, they raise the *Titanic?* In *Night Probe,* what if Canada and the United States became one country? I also use a prologue that describes something in the past that sets up the plots in the present. Then I end with

an epilogue that sews all the corners together. My plots are pretty convoluted; I usually juggle one main plot and as many as four subplots. Then the trick is to thread the needle in the end and give the readers a satisfying conclusion."

BIOGRAPHICAL/CRITICAL SOURCES:

PERIODICALS

Armchair Detective, fall, 1994, p. 496.
Best Sellers, August, 1981; May, 1986.
Booklist, April 1, 1994, p. 1404.
Books and Bookmen, May, 1984.
Chicago Tribune, February 10, 1980; August 13, 1984.
Chicago Tribune Book World, June 21, 1992, p. 6.
Critic, summer, 1977.
Globe and Mail (Toronto), August 10, 1985.
Inside Books, November, 1988, pp. 31-34.
Los Angeles Times, June 21, 1979; September 25, 1981; March 21, 1986.
Los Angeles Times Book Review, August 5, 1984; March 20, 1988.
New York Times Book Review, December 19, 1976; September 25, 1977; October 18, 1981; February 16, 1986; May 29, 1988; June 17, 1990; May 22, 1994, p. 6.
People, July 2, 1984; September 21, 1992, p. 93.
Publishers Weekly, August 23, 1976; June 12, 1981; April 13, 1984, p. 50; January 3, 1985, p. 41; May 4, 1990, p. 51; April 13, 1992, p. 40; March 28, 1994, p. 80.
Tribune Books (Chicago), March 20, 1988; May 22, 1994, p. 6.
Washington Post, October 24, 1978; August 10, 1981; June 22, 1984; April 11, 1988.
Washington Post Book World, March 2, 1986; June 7, 1992, p. 8.

*   *   *

CUTLER, Roland
(Cary Morgan)

PERSONAL: Born in New York, NY; son of Charles (an artist and musician) and Rose (Shapiro) Cutler; married Ruth Truran (a psychologist); children: (from previous marriage) Cary (son), Morgan (daughter). *Education:* Hunter College (now of the City University of New York), B.A.; Brooklyn Law School, LL.B.

ADDRESSES: Home—Los Angeles, CA. *Agent*—Major Client's Agency, 343 North Maple Dr., Beverly Hills, CA 90210.

CAREER: Worked variously as a commercial artist, art and history teacher at public schools in New York City, filmmaker, freelance comedy and screenwriter, practicing attorney.

MEMBER: Writers Guild of America (West).

AWARDS, HONORS: Special jury award, Edinburgh Film Festival, for *The Next to Last Man;* gold medal, Atlanta Film Festival, for *The Locusts;* Porgie Award, *West Coast Review,* for *The First Born;* Edgar Allan Poe Award, Mystery Writers of America, for *The Seventh Sacrament.*

WRITINGS:

NOVELS

The First Born, Fawcett (New York City), 1978.
The Gates of Sagittarius, Dial (New York City), 1980.
Precious, Jove (New York City), 1980.
(As Cary Morgan) *The Spoils of Eden,* Signet Books (New York City), 1981.
(As Morgan) *Forests of the Night,* Signet Books, 1982.
The Medusa Syndrome, Signet Books, 1983.
The Seventh Sacrament, Dial, 1984.
To Kill a King, Berkley Publishing (New York City), 1987.

Also author of *Garden of Women,* 1995.

FILMS

The Next to Last Man, released independently, 1966.
The Locusts, Avco Embassy, 1972.

The Corner Bar, American Broadcasting Co. (ABC-TV), 1972.
Willie Dynamite, Universal, 1973.
Blood Red, Hemdale, 1988.
Article 99, Orion, 1992.

SIDELIGHTS: Roland Cutler once told *CA:* "Development as a writer is a continuous struggle to make one's work have greater meaning to all the centers of experience—heart, mind, and body. This can be accomplished no matter what the vehicle. Once the author lights the reader's imagination he has the opportunity to go where he will in exploring the totality of the human condition. But he owes his best. That is, to discover, invent, and reinvent always.

"While I don't require Balzac's famous monks' habit to keep me before the computer, the discipline required offers unique personal satisfactions. Learning the craft brings one closest to the life of a medieval guildsman. One begins as an apprentice—even if it is to oneself—rises to journeyman, then strives to fulfill his vision through the mastery of form and content. What all that means is best said by some words of Conrad: 'No I don't like work. I had rather laze about and think of all the fine things that can be done. I don't like work—no man does—but I like what is in the work—the chance to find yourself. Your own reality—for yourself, not for others—what no man can ever know.' "

D

DALY, (Arthur) Leo 1920-

PERSONAL: Born January 23, 1920, in Dublin, Ireland; son of William (a railway engineer) and Rebecca (Foreman) Daly; married Brigid Mary Murphy (a nurse), November 24, 1943; children: Rosaleen Rebecca, Kathleen Nuala, Louise Elizabeth, William Francis, Eugene Leo, John Kieran, Justine Mary, Bridiane. *Education:* Awarded second level to leaving certificate from St. Mary's College; Medio-Psychological Association, certificate in psychiatric nursing, 1943; International School of Colour Photography, diploma, 1955. *Religion:* Roman Catholic.

ADDRESSES: Home and office—10 Mary St., Mullingar, County Westmeath, Ireland.

CAREER: Mental Health Authority, Mullingar, Ireland, psychiatric nurse, 1943-66; freelance photojournalist, 1966-69; Radio-Telefis-Eireann, Dublin, Ireland, broadcaster, 1969-75; writer, photographer, and editor, 1975—. Teacher of photography in adult education classes and vocational schools.

MEMBER: National Union of Journalists, Mullingar Archaeological and Historical Society (founder).

AWARDS, HONORS: Premier Award, National Drama Festival, 1947, for one-act play *Death's Echo;* design award, Institute of Creative Advertising and Design, for *James Joyce and the Mullingar Connection.*

WRITINGS:

FICTION

The Rock Garden (novel), Lilliput Press (Westmeath, Ireland), 1984.
Island Lovers (short stories), Westmeath Examiner (Westmeath, Ireland), 1993.

NONFICTION

James Joyce and the Mullingar Connection, Dolmen Press (Laoighis, Ireland), 1975.
Oileain Arann (title means "The Aran Islands"), Albertine Kennedy Publishing, 1975.
(Editor, with Gearoid O'Brien, and contributor) *The Midlands,* Albertine Kennedy Publishing, 1979.
Titles (essays), Albertine Kennedy Publishing, 1981.
James Joyce at the Cross Keys, Bloomsday (Mullingar, Ireland), 1991.
Austin Friars, Westmeath Examiner, 1994.

PLAYS

Death's Echo (one-act play), produced in Mullingar, Ireland, 1947.
Islands and Authors (Radio-Telefis-Eireann series), edited by P. O. Connluain, Gill & Macmillan (Dublin), 1982.
Tenors in the Life of James Joyce (radio play), Radio-Telefis-Eireann (Dublin), 1982.
(With Bernard Sharc) *Only 2/6 Return* (radio play), Radio-Telefis-Eireann, 1992.

CONTRIBUTOR

Ronnie Walshe, editor, *Sunday Miscellany,* Gill & Macmillan, 1975.
Midland Moments, Athlone Press, 1976.
Thomas Kennedy, editor, *The Dublin Handbook,* Albertine Kennedy Publishing, 1978.
Breandan and Ruairi O'Leithir, editors, *An Aran Reader,* Lilliput Press, 1991.

OTHER

Work represented in anthologies, including *New Irish Writing,* Irish Press. Contributor of articles, stories, photographs, and reviews to periodicals, including *Books Ire-*

land, *Cara, Hibernia,* and *Ireland of the Welcomes,* and to national and provincial newspapers.

WORK IN PROGRESS: A play, "The Jealous Wall," in 1995 being considered for presentation at the national level.

SIDELIGHTS: Leo Daly once commented to *CA:* "Initially my literary interest was in writing for the theatre. In the early 1940s I had some success with a one-act play, but did not pursue my luck. Having become interested in photography and being freed from my hospital work because of an accident, I accepted an offer to study color photography in Kent, England. My qualification from this course led me into photojournalism, which I still practice occasionally during the infrequent lulls in my present occupation as reviewer, editor, and literary 'handyman.'

"Thanks to an understanding employer and the blessings of my wife and family, I was able to retire from my hospital work in 1966 with a reasonable pension, and this release gave me an opportunity to concentrate on my writings. I undertook a short spell of study with the British Drama League, intending to return to writing for the theatre, but returned instead to writing short stories. And I was rewarded by publications in the late sixties and early seventies in *New Irish Writing* and by Radio-Telefis-Eireann broadcasts.

"During the early 1970s I concentrated on research. Throughout this period I subsidized my precarious existence by radio and television work, magazine and newspaper features, and photographic contributions. My outstanding award was when I was given an opportunity to read my paper *James Joyce in the Cloak of St. Patrick* at the James Joyce International Symposium in Zurich in 1979. An expanded version of this paper was published as one of the essays in *Titles.*

"This schizoid literary occupation [often] diverted me from my main object, the completion of the novel *Give Me Your Hand* (later published as *The Rock Garden*), which was in the process of what might be termed perpetual revision. But as a firm believer in the maxim, 'Talent does what it can and genius what it *must,*' I am encouraged to continue. Generally speaking, what has been said about me as an author and journalist and about my work is, in my own opinion, more important than anything I might offer, and I am content to let others speak for me. My work has been generally well received even in academic circles where I know I am an intruder, but they have been generous. For this I am grateful, and I feel that my late vocation is vindicated.

"The author James Joyce has played an important part in my literary career, but has made things difficult for me because all I write is judged by commentators as being imita-

tive of Joyce's works. I am sure that Joyce would not agree. All Irish writing is said to be *aural,* and I give talks on this quality in Joyce's works. For the Joyce Centenary in 1982, I presented an entertainment of readings and songs, 'An Encounter with Music and Song in the Works of James Joyce.' "

*   *   *

DAVIS, Allen F(reeman) 1931-

PERSONAL: Born January 9, 1931, in Hardwick, VT; son of Harold Freeman (a store owner) and Bernice (Allen) Davis; married Roberta Green (a secretary), June 16, 1956 (divorced); children: Gregory, Paul. *Education:* Dartmouth College, A.B., 1953; University of Rochester, M.A., 1954; University of Wisconsin, Ph.D., 1959.

ADDRESSES: Home—2032 Waverly St., Philadelphia, PA 19146. *Office*—Department of History, Temple University, Philadelphia, PA 19122.

CAREER: Wayne State University, Detroit, MI, instructor in history, 1959-60; University of Missouri—Columbia, assistant professor, 1960-63, associate professor of history, 1963-68; Temple University, Philadelphia, PA, professor of history, 1968—. Visiting professor of American civilization, University of Texas at Austin, 1983; John Adams Chair, University of Amsterdam, Amsterdam, Netherlands, 1986-87. *Military service:* U.S. Army, 1954-56.

MEMBER: American Historical Association, Organization of American Historians, American Association of University Professors, American Civil Liberties Union, American Studies Association (executive secretary, 1972-77; president, 1989-90).

AWARDS, HONORS: Friends of Literature Award, 1970, for *Eighty Years at Hull House;* Christopher Award, 1974, for *American Heroine: The Life and Legend of Jane Addams;* fellow: American Council of Learned Societies, 1971-72, Society of American Historians, 1974, and National Endowment for the Humanities, 1975-76; senior Fulbright lecturer, 1986-87.

WRITINGS:

(With Jacob Cooke and Robert Daly) *March of American Democracy,* Volume 5, Scribner (New York City), 1965.

(Editor with Harold Woodman) *Conflict or Consensus in American History,* Heath (Lexington, MA), 1966, 2nd edition, 1967, Volume 1: *Conflict or Consensus in Early America,* Volume 2: *Conflict or Consensus in Modern America,* 4th edition, 1976, Volume 1: *Conflict and Consensus in Early American History,* Volume 2: *Conflict and Consensus in Modern American History,* 8th edition, 1992.

Spearheads for Reform: The Social Settlements and the Progressive Movement, 1890-1914, Oxford University Press (Oxford, England), 1967, 2nd edition, Rutgers University Press (New Brunswick, NJ), 1984.

(Editor with Mary Lynn McCree) *Eighty Years at Hull House,* Quadrangle, 1969.

(Author of introduction) Jane Addams, *Spirit of Youth and the City Streets,* University of Illinois Press (Champaign, IL), 1972.

American Heroine: The Life and Legend of Jane Addams, Oxford University Press, 1973.

(Editor with Mark Haller) *The Peoples of Philadelphia: A History of Ethnic Groups and Lower-Class Life, 1790-1940,* Temple University Press (Philadelphia), 1973.

(With Jim Watts) *Generations: Your Family in Modern American History,* Knopf (New York City), 1974, 3rd edition, 1983.

(Editor) *Jane Addams on Peace, War and International Understanding,* Garland Press, 1976.

(Editor) *For Better or Worse: The American Influence on the World,* Greenwood (Westport, CT), 1981.

(With Fredrick Miller and Morris Vogel) *Still Philadelphia: A Photographic History, 1890-1940,* Temple University Press, 1983.

(With Gary Nash and others) *The American People,* Harper (New York City), 1986, 3rd edition, 1994.

(With Miller and Vogel) *Philadelphia Stories: A Photographic History, 1930-1960,* Temple University Press, 1988.

(Editor with M. McCree Bryan) *One Hundred Years at Hull House,* Indiana University Press (Bloomington, IN), 1990.

Editor of "American Civilization" series, twenty-eight volumes, Temple University Press, 1978-95. Contributor to history and social studies journals, including *American Historical Review, American Quarterly, Journal of Politics, Labor History,* and *Mid-America.*

*   *   *

DAVIS, Burke 1913-

PERSONAL: Born July 24, 1913, in Durham, NC; son of Walter Burke and Harriet (Jackson) Davis; married Evangeline McLennan, August 11, 1940 (divorced, 1980); married Juliet Halliburton, February 6, 1982; children: (first marriage) Angela, Burke III. *Education:* Attended Duke University, 1931-32, 1933-34, and Guilford College, 1935-36; University of North Carolina, A.B., 1937.

ADDRESSES: Home—Rt. 1, Box 66, Meadows of Dan, VA 24120.

CAREER: Charlotte News, Charlotte, NC, sports editor and reporter, 1937-47; *Baltimore Evening Sun,* Baltimore, MD, reporter, 1947-51; *Greensboro Daily News,* Greensboro, NC, reporter and columnist, 1951-60; Colonial Williamsburg, Williamsburg, VA, writer, 1960-78.

MEMBER: Nefarian Society.

AWARDS, HONORS: Fletcher Pratt Award, Civil War Round Table of New York, 1958, for *Jeb Stuart: The Last Cavalier;* Mayflower Cup, Society of Mayflower Descendants in North Carolina, 1959, for *To Appomattox: Nine April Days, 1865;* North Carolina Award for Literature, 1973; elected to North Carolina Journalism Hall of Fame, 1984; North Caroliniana Award, University of North Carolina, 1989.

WRITINGS:

NOVELS

Whisper My Name, Rinehart (Boulder, CO), 1949.
The Ragged Ones, Rinehart, 1951.
Yorktown, Rinehart, 1952.
The Summer Land, Random House (New York City), 1965.

BIOGRAPHIES

They Called Him Stonewall, Rinehart, 1954.
Gray Fox: Robert E. Lee and the Civil War, Rinehart, 1956.
Jeb Stuart: The Last Cavalier, Rinehart, 1957.
(Editor and author of introduction) Henry Brainerd McClellan, *I Rode with Jeb Stuart,* Indiana University Press (Bloomington), 1958.
Marine: The Life of Lt. General Lewis B. (Chesty) Puller, USMC, Little, Brown (Boston), 1962.
The Billy Mitchell Affair, Random House, 1967.
A Williamsburg Galaxy, Colonial Williamsburg (Williamsburg, VA), 1968.
George Washington and the American Revolution, Random House, 1975.
Old Hickory: A Life of Andrew Jackson, Dial (New York City), 1977.
War Bird: The Life and Times of Eliott White Springs, University of North Carolina Press (Chapel Hill), 1987.

HISTORY

To Appomattox: Nine April Days, 1865, Rinehart, 1959.
Our Incredible Civil War, Holt (New York City), 1960, reprint published as *The Civil War: Strange and Fascinating Facts,* Random House, 1988.
The Cowpens-Guilford Courthouse Campaign, Lippincott (Philadelphia, PA), 1962.
(With Roy King) *The World of Currier & Ives,* Random House, 1968.

Get Yamamoto, Random House, 1969.
The Campaign That Won America: The Story of Yorktown, Dial, 1970.
Sherman's March, Random House, 1980.
The Long Surrender, Random House, 1985.
History of the Southern Railway, University of North Carolina Press, 1985.

JUVENILE

Roberta E. Lee (fiction) illustrated by John Opper, Blair (Winston-Salem, NC), 1956.
America's First Army, Colonial Williamsburg, 1962.
Appomattox: Closing Struggle of the Civil War, Harper (New York City), 1964.
(With wife, Evangeline Davis) *Rebel Raider: The Biography of Admiral Semmes,* Lippincott, 1966.
Yorktown: The Winning of American Independence, Harper, 1969.
The Billy Mitchell Story, Chilton (Radnor, PA), 1969.
Getting to Know Jamestown, Coward, 1971.
Getting to Know Thomas Jefferson's Virginia, Coward, 1971.
Heroes of the American Revolution, Random House, 1971.
Amelia Earhart, Putnam (New York City), 1972.
Biography of a Leaf, Putnam, 1972.
Three for Revolution, Harcourt (San Diego, CA), 1975.
Biography of a Kingsnake, Putnam, 1975.
Black Heroes of the American Revolution, Harcourt, 1976.
Newer and Better Organic Gardening, Putnam, 1976.
Runaway Balloon: The Last Flight of Confederate Airforce One, Coward, 1976.
Biography of a Fish Hawk, Putnam, 1977.
Mr. Lincoln's Whiskers, Coward, 1978.

BIOGRAPHICAL/CRITICAL SOURCES:

PERIODICALS

Best Sellers, June 15, 1970.
Book Week, July 2, 1967.
Book World, July 27, 1969.
Newsweek, June 19, 1967.
New York Review of Books, February 15, 1968.
New York Times, August 25, 1980.
New York Times Book Review, July 2, 1967; May 19, 1985.
Washington Post, June 19, 1980.
Washington Post Book World, April 7, 1985.

*   *   *

DAVIS, Francis   1946-

PERSONAL: Born August 30, 1946, in Philadelphia, PA; son of Dorothy (a medical clerk; maiden name, McCart-

ney) Davis. *Education:* Attended Temple University, 1964-69.

ADDRESSES: Office—The Atlantic Monthly, 745 Boylston Street, Boston, MA 02116. *Agent*—Mark Kelley, 1619 Broadway, Suite 570, New York, NY 10019.

CAREER: WHYY-FM Radio, Philadelphia, PA, producer and host of "Interval" (weekly jazz music program), 1978-83; *Philadelphia Inquirer,* Philadelphia, jazz critic, 1982—; *Musician,* jazz editor, 1982-85; *Atlantic Monthly,* music critic, 1984—; National Public Radio, jazz critic for "Fresh Air," 1987; *7 Days,* New York City, staff writer, 1988-90. University of Pennsylvania, Philadelphia, instructor in Folk and Blues, 1995—.

MEMBER: National Writers Union.

AWARDS, HONORS: Grammy nomination (with Martin Williams and Dick Katz), 1989, for liner notes to *Jazz Piano;* Guggenheim fellow, 1993; Pew fellow, 1994, for literary nonfiction; Morroe Berger-Benny Carter fellow, Institute of Jazz Studies, Rutgers University, 1994.

WRITINGS:

In the Moment: Jazz in the 1980s, Oxford University Press (New York City), 1986.
Outcats, Oxford University Press, 1990.
The History of the Blues, Hyperion Books, 1995.
Bebop and Nothingness, Schirmer (Boston), 1996.

Contributor to periodicals, including *Atlantic, Cadence, Connoisseur, Down Beat, High Fidelity, Jazz Times, Phoenix* (Boston), *Times Literary Supplement, Village Voice,* and *Washington Post Book World.* Contributing editor of *Musician,* 1982-85, *High Fidelity,* 1984—, and *Atlantic Monthly.* Columnist, *The Wire* (UK), 1990—.

WORK IN PROGRESS: A biography of saxophonist John Coltrane, to be published by Knopf.

SIDELIGHTS: Francis Davis's *In the Moment: Jazz in the 1980s* was hailed as "the jazz book of 1986" by Ken Tucker of the *Philadelphia Inquirer. In the Moment* is a collection of jazz criticism articles that Davis wrote for various periodicals. Davis's reviews and interviews concern themselves with better known jazz artists such as Sonny Rollins and Anthony Davis, but also with more obscure musicians, including the Vienna Art Orchestra's Mathias Ruegg and pianist Sumi Tonooka. As David Nicholson explained in the *Washington Post Book World,* "much of Davis' book deals with the tension between composition and improvisation" in contemporary jazz. Labeled "an incisive interviewer and rethinker" by Kevin Whitehead in *Down Beat,* Davis is also "often a wonderful writer" with "an eye for terrific images" according to Neil Tesser in the *New York Times Book Review.* "Due to the fluidity of Davis's style," declared Richard B. Kamins in

Cadence, "you can almost touch the people and hear the music that he writes about."

Davis once told *CA:* "As a music critic, I consider myself a beat reporter. My job is to report the facts, but my opinion of the performance in question becomes the chief fact it is my duty to report.

"Among jazz critics, my major influences have been Martin Williams and Nat Hentoff, the co-editors of the short-lived magazine *Jazz Review.* Between them, Williams and Hentoff revolutionized jazz criticism: Williams by applying a critical rigor more associated with judgment of literature and 'serious' music; Hentoff by emphasizing the social climate in which jazz musicians create. I try to integrate both approaches.

"However, in a way that is difficult for me to specify, the pop critic Robert Christgau and the film critics Pauline Kael and Andrew Sarris have influenced my thinking and writing to an even greater extent than Williams and Hentoff. Perhaps it is simply because of the assumptions they make, and I wish to make, that art criticism is implicit social criticism, that criticism is a kind of literature, that opinions and impressions and ideas are somehow of real value."

BIOGRAPHICAL/CRITICAL SOURCES:

PERIODICALS

Cadence, April 1987.
Down Beat, March 1987.
New York Times Book Review, January 4, 1987.
Philadelphia Inquirer, November 28, 1986.
Washington Post Book World, December 21, 1986.

*   *   *

DAVIS, Keith F. 1952-

PERSONAL: Born June 29, 1952, in Middletown, CT; son of Joel N. (an educator) and Ruth Ann C. (an educator) Davis; married Patricia Hammer (a product manager), April 18, 1981. *Education:* Attended Drew University, 1970-72; Southern Illinois University at Carbondale, B.S., 1974; University of New Mexico, M.A., 1978.

ADDRESSES: Office—Fine Art Programs #284, Hallmark Cards, Inc., Kansas City, MO 64108.

CAREER: George Eastman House, Rochester, NY, research intern at International Museum of Photography, 1978-79; Hallmark Cards, Inc., Kansas City, MO, curator of Fine Art Collections, 1979-89, chief curator, 1990-92, fine art programs director, 1992—. Trustee, Friends of Photography, San Francisco, 1988—.

MEMBER: Society for Photographic Education (member of national board of directors, 1984-87).

AWARDS, HONORS: Fellow of National Endowment for the Humanities, 1986-87.

WRITINGS:

Desire Charnay, Expeditionary Photographer, University of New Mexico Press (Albuquerque), 1981.
Todd Webb: Photographs of New York and Paris, 1945-1960, Hallmark Cards (Kansas City, MO), 1986.
Harry Callahan: New Color, Photographs 1978-1987, Hallmark Cards, 1988.
George N. Barnard: Photographer of Sherman's Campaign, Hallmark Cards, 1990.
Clarence John Laughlin: Visionary Photographer, Hallmark Cards, 1990.
The Passionate Observer: Photographs by Carl Van Vechten, Hallmark Cards, 1993.
An American Century of Photography: From Dry-Plate to Digital, the Hallmark Photographic Collection, Hallmark Cards/Abrams (New York City), 1995.

Contributor to *Photography in Nineteenth-Century America,* edited by Martha A. Sandweiss, Amon Carter Museum of Western Art (Fort Worth, TX)/Abrams, 1991.

SIDELIGHTS: Keith F. Davis told *CA:* "My approach to the history of photography is inclusive and interdisciplinary. I am interested in photography's place in the larger cultural realm and in its function as both documentation and artistic expression. My research has embraced both nineteenth- and twentieth-century photography, with an emphasis on American work.

"When I became curator at Hallmark in 1979, the corporate photographic collection contained some 650 twentieth-century prints by leading photographers such as Harry Callahan, Andre Kertesz, Edward Weston, and Imogen Cunningham. By 1995 the collection had grown to twenty-six hundred prints by four hundred photographers. Exhibitions from this holding have toured extensively in the United States, Canada, New Zealand, Australia, Great Britain, France, and Switzerland. My most recent book, *An American Century of Photography: From Dry-Plate to Digital, the Hallmark Photographic Collection,* surveys the highlights of this collection while attempting to present a concise, yet fresh, perspective on the larger history of modern American photography."

BIOGRAPHICAL/CRITICAL SOURCES:

PERIODICALS

Art and Antiques, May, 1986.
Forum, summer, 1981; March, 1982.
New Art Examiner, January, 1982.
Popular Photography, June, 1981.

Sky, June, 1982.

*   *   *

DAVIS, Ronald L(eroy) 1936-

PERSONAL: Born September 22, 1936, in Cambridge, Ohio; son of E. Leroy and Ruth (Dudley) Davis; married Marilyn Bowden, July 3, 1958 (divorced, 1965). *Education:* University of Texas, Main University (now University of Texas at Austin), B.A., 1956, M.A., 1958, Ph.D., 1961. *Politics:* Democrat.

ADDRESSES: Home—6013 East University Blvd., Dallas, TX 75206. *Office*—Department of History, Southern Methodist University, Dallas, TX 75275.

CAREER: Kansas State College (now Emporia State University), Emporia, assistant professor of history, 1961-62; Michigan State University, East Lansing, assistant professor of humanities, 1962-65; Southern Methodist University, Dallas, TX, associate professor, 1965-72, professor of history, 1972—, director of oral history project, 1973—. Director, DeGolyer Institute for American Studies, 1974—.

MEMBER: American Historical Association, Organization of American Historians, Western History Association, Southern Historical Association, Texas State Historical Association, Texas Institute of Letters, Phi Beta Kappa.

WRITINGS:

History of Opera in the American West, Prentice-Hall (Englewood Cliffs, NJ), 1965.

Opera in Chicago: A Social and Cultural History, Appleton, 1966.

The Social and Cultural History of the 1920's, Holt (New York City), 1972.

Hollywood Beauty: Linda Darnell and the American Dream, University of Oklahoma Press (Norman, OK), 1991.

The Glamour Factory: Inside Hollywood's Big Studio System, Southern Methodist University Press (Dallas, TX), 1993.

John Ford: Hollywood's Old Master, University of Oklahoma Press, 1995.

Contributor to history, art, and opera journals.

SIDELIGHTS: Most of history professor Ronald L. Davis's work has been in the area of American social and cultural history, including examinations of the role of opera in the American West. With *Hollywood Beauty: Linda Darnell and the American Dream* and *The Glamour Factory: Inside Hollywood's Big Studio System,* Davis looks at the role of Hollywood in the history of the twentieth century. In *Hollywood Beauty,* Davis views the story of Linda Darnell, a young 1930s starlet forced into the studio system by her pushy mother, as an example of the way major studios exploited their performers. "Darnell's life," writes a reviewer for *Publishers Weekly,* "illustrates the grimy side of the one-time Hollywood star system." Instead of looking at one person moving through the Hollywood system, *The Glamour Factory* surveys the entire Hollywood studio system itself. "Made up largely of sections of interviews from the SMU Oral History Program," declares Eric Smoodin for *Film Quarterly,* "the book is an organizational marvel rather than a methodological one; as Davis cuts and pastes his citations into narratives about work in the various departments of the Hollywood studios between, roughly, 1925 and 1965, he includes not only directors, producers, writers, and other high-profile professions but also makeup artists, talent scouts, and set painters." Barbara Einhorn in *Sight and Sound* differs in her enthusiasm for the book. "What Davis does not do," she states, "is add to the specialist (or even semi-specialist) reader's knowledge of what Hollywood was and how it worked." "Finally, then," Smoodin concludes, "this is a book with some wonderful insights into film history, but one that lacks a coherent historical methodology. It is still, however, a potentially valuable text because of the way that it stresses not simply labor but all manner of labor."

BIOGRAPHICAL/CRITICAL SOURCES:

PERIODICALS

Film Quarterly, summer, 1994, pp. 42-43.
Publishers Weekly, March 15, 1991, p. 51.
Sight and Sound, May, 1994, pp. 35-36.
Yale Review, spring, 1967.

*   *   *

DE JONGE, Marinus 1925-

PERSONAL: Born December 9, 1925, in Vlissingen, Netherlands. *Education:* University of Leiden, Th.D., 1953.

ADDRESSES: Home—Libellenveld 19, 2318 VE, Leiden, Netherlands.

CAREER: University of Leiden, Leiden, Netherlands, professor of New Testament and early Christian literature, 1966-90.

WRITINGS:

The Testaments of the Twelve Patriarchs: A Study of Their Text, Composition, and Origin, Assen (Netherlands), 1953, 2nd edition, 1975.

De Brieven van Johannes, Nijkerk (Netherlands), 1968, 4th edition, 1988.

Jezus, inspirator en spelbreker, Nijkerk, 1971, translation by J. E. Steely published as *Jesus, Inspiring and Disturbing Presence,* Abingdon (Nashville, TN), 1974.

(Editor and contributor) *Studies on the Testaments of the Twelve Patriarchs: Text and Interpretation,* Leiden, 1975.

Jesus: Stranger from Heaven and Son of God: Jesus Christ and the Christians in Johannine Perspective, Society of Biblical Literature Sources for Biblical Study (Missoula, MT), 1977.

(With H. M. J. van Duyne) *Taal en Teken: Ontmoetingen met Jezus in het evangelie van Johannes,* Nijkerk, 1978.

(With others) *The Testaments of the Twelve Patriarchs: A Critical Edition of the Greek Text,* Leiden, 1978.

(With van Duyne) *Van tekst tot uitleg: Luisteroefeningen in het Nieuwe Testament,* The Hague, 1982.

(With H. W. Hollander) *The Testaments of the Twelve Patriarchs: A Commentary,* Leiden, 1985.

(Editor and contributor) *Outside the Old Testament,* Cambridge University Press (Cambridge, England), 1986.

Christology in Context: The Earliest Christian Response to Jesus, Westminster (Philadelphia, PA), 1988.

Jezus als Messias: Hoe Hij zijn zending zag, Boxtel/Bruges, 1990, translation published as *Jesus, the Servant-Messiah,* Yale University Press (London and New Haven, CT), 1991.

Jewish Eschatology, Early Christian Christology and the Testaments of the Twelve Patriarchs: Collected Essays, Leiden, 1991.

Contributor of numerous essays and articles to books and periodicals.

*   *   *

DE MARINIS, Rick 1934-

PERSONAL: Born May 3, 1934, in New York, NY; son of Alphonse and Ruth (Siik) De Marinis; married Carole Joyce Bubash (an artist and writer); children: Richard Michael, Suzanne Louise, Naomi Anna. *Education:* Attended San Diego State College (now University), 1952-54; University of Montana, B.A., 1961, M.A., 1967. *Politics:* Independent.

ADDRESSES: Office—Department of English, University of Texas at El Paso, El Paso, TX 79968. *Agent*—Candida Donadio and Associates, 121 West 27th St., New York, NY 10001.

CAREER: University of Montana, Missoula, instructor in English, 1967-69; San Diego State University, San Diego,

CA, assistant professor of English, 1969-76; University of Texas at El Paso, professor of English, 1988—. Visiting writer at Arizona State University, 1980-81, and distinguished writer-in-residence at Wichita State University. *Military service:* U.S. Air Force, 1954-58.

AWARDS, HONORS: Drue Heinz Literature Prize, 1986, for *Under the Wheat;* Literature Award, American Academy of Arts and Letters, 1990.

WRITINGS:

NOVELS

A Lovely Monster: The Adventures of Claude Rains and Dr. Tellenbeck, Simon & Schuster (New York City), 1976.

Scimitar, Dutton (New York City), 1977.

Cinder, Farrar, Straus (New York City), 1978.

The Burning Women of Far Cry, Arbor House (New York City), 1986.

The Year of the Zinc Penny, Viking (New York City), 1989.

The Mortician's Apprentice, Norton (New York City), 1994.

COLLECTIONS

Jack and Jill: Two Novellas and a Short Story, Dutton, 1979.

Under the Wheat, University of Pittsburgh Press (Pittsburgh, PA), 1986.

The Coming Triumph of the Free World, Viking, 1988.

The Voice of America, Norton, 1991.

OTHER

Contributor of short stories to periodicals, including *Esquire, Harper's, Malahat Review, Colorado State Review, Paris Review, Antaeus,* and *Antioch Review.*

SIDELIGHTS: Rick De Marinis is known for his black comedies rendered in the spirit of fables and traditional tales. "De Marinis tells stories that resemble fairy tales with a modern, black humor twist," writes Marcia Froelke Coburn in the *Chicago Tribune.* "Their point of view has a bend in it, a distortion that casts everything in a new, dark light." Greg Johnson describes De Marinis's stories in the *Georgia Review* as "reminiscent of the postmodernist fictions of Barth or Barthelme in their flamboyance, playfulness, and self-conscious artifice."

In his early works De Marinis wrote modern, imaginative versions of traditional stories. His *A Lovely Monster: The Adventures of Claude Rains and Dr. Tellenbeck,* for example, is an updated rendition of the Frankenstein tale. In De Marinis's story, Dr. Tellenbeck uses the latest in medical technology—including lasers and a cell-glue compound—to build an artificial man who, like the Frankenstein original, lacks the human love he craves. The story, narrated by the monster, is "provocative, amusing, [and] ambiguous," according to a critic for the *Atlantic*. Martin Levin of the *New York Times Book Review* claims that "it is irresistible. If you can put down a novel about a synthetic man, you aren't human." Another early novel, *Cinder*, tells the story of Ulysses Cinder, who comes into possession of an ancient genie with magical powers. "What at first seems silly and merely whimsical," a *Booklist* critic remarks, "becomes an actually charming fable-like tale."

Because of their fantastic nature, these early works were often compared to the writings of Kurt Vonnegut, Vladimir Nabokov, and John Nichols. But, as John Clute notes in the *Washington Post Book World*, De Marinis's "fables of moral convulsion and comic despair . . . may have seemed too much like science fiction for some readers, too unconsolingly bleak for others." After the appearance of *Jack and Jill: Two Novellas and a Short Story*—described by a *Booklist* critic as a collection of "fablelike tales [that] portray social misfits suddenly wrenched off into exotic fantasies"—De Marinis took a seven-year break from writing.

In 1986 he returned with a collection of short stories, *Under the Wheat*, and a novel, *The Burning Women of Far Cry*, both of which received critical praise. *Under the Wheat*, winner of the 1986 Drue Heinz Literature Prize, is "a collection of powerful, irreverent short stories," Janet Shaw explains in the *New York Times Book Review*. Clute of the *Washington Post Book World* believes it to contain "stories of almost unfailing excellence." In the *Georgia Review*, Johnson notes the diversity of the stories in *Under the Wheat*, a quality he perceives as a distinctive feature of short fiction in the 1980s. "These seven stories," Johnson writes, "seem deliberately arranged . . . to illustrate the author's technical virtuosity, progressing from . . . brooding realism [to] surrealistic comedy."

Though the stories in *Under the Wheat* vary widely in approach, they share a common perspective. De Marinis, Shaw explains in the *New York Times Book Review*, "puts a bend in the world to give us a long hard look at characters who embody on a grand scale the psychological and spiritual deformities in our culture." The title story, for example, concerns a man whose job it is to inspect missile silos before the missiles are installed. The desolate farm fields of North Dakota where the silos are found, the small opening of empty sky one can see from the bottom of a silo, and the narrator's own troubled marriage combine to make a complex statement about militarism and hopelessness. In "Life between Meals," a man compensates for his unhappy life by purposely eating as much as he can, topping three hundred pounds by story's end. "The narrator's infatuation with food," *Georgia Review*'s Johnson comments, "suggests a pathological hunger for power and

control." The *Chicago Tribune*'s Coburn believes that De Marinis's "power lies in a wallop of terse language and an unrelenting vision of the grotesque as the proper metaphor for today's world." "Readers of any persuasion," Johnson maintains, "will admire the versatility and technical skill that characterize this volume as a whole."

The Burning Women of Far Cry also won critical acclaim. The novel tells the story of a young man coming of age in the 1950s. Jack's father has just killed himself; his mother has remarried and driven her second husband to madness. Jack leaves home to escape her destructive influence and drifts around the country aimlessly. After a serious accident, he returns home to visit his mother and begins to realize that he must fashion a new life for himself. The novel ends with Jack finding a job and a girlfriend, the future promising stability and a measure of happiness.

Despite the grim nature of the plot, Shaw explains that in *The Burning Women of Far Cry*, De Marinis "is writing farce" and the novel is filled with "a dark humor." Clute believes that there is an "extraordinary sense of triumph the reader takes away from the final pages" of the novel when it becomes clear that Jack has overcome his unfortunate family background. About *Under the Wheat* and *The Burning Women of Far Cry*, Clute argues that "taken together, [these] two new books are a literary event of real importance."

De Marinis writes with a spontaneous energy and comic exuberance that gives his work an invigorating power. Coburn finds "an almost electrical surge of power" in De Marinis's prose. "Like shock therapy," she continues, "his stories jolt us and change our point of view." Clute maintains that "De Marinis has the fabulist's wit [and] the grave muscle of Antaeus."

BIOGRAPHICAL/CRITICAL SOURCES:

PERIODICALS

Atlantic, February, 1976.
Booklist, September 15, 1978; December 1, 1978.
Chicago Tribune, November 4, 1986.
Chicago Tribune Book World, January 21, 1979.
Georgia Review, summer, 1987.
Harper's, September, 1978.
New York Times, May 12, 1977.
New York Times Book Review, February 1, 1976; December 14, 1986.
Washington Post Book World, October 23, 1977; January 11, 1987.

DEVON, D. G.
See GROSS, Michael (Robert)

* * *

DEXTER, Susan (Elizabeth) 1955-

PERSONAL: Born July 20, 1955, in Greenville, PA; daughter of Ward (in sales) and Donna Jean (a bookkeeper; maiden name, Orr) Dexter. *Education:* Attended vocational-technical high school in New Castle, PA. *Politics:* "Republican (by lack of any consuming interest)." *Religion:* Presbyterian. *Avocational interests:* "I enjoy: carousel horses, canaries, weaving, spinning, herbs, dark chocolate, the *Star Wars* movies, England, Sam Waterston and Harrison Ford. I have never had the pleasure of being owned by a cat, but I currently share my life with a Peruvian guinea pig, my horse, and a blue-eyed dog. Most of us live in the vintage house the book sales enabled me to buy and restore. (The horse rents.) I have a collection of silver rings, none magical that I know of, and several thousand books."

ADDRESSES: Home—1510 Delaware Ave., New Castle, PA 16105.

CAREER: Fishers Big Wheel, Inc. (discount department store chain), New Castle, PA, fashion layout artist, 1974-92; church librarian, Northminster Presbyterian Church, 1992—. Guest lecturer and author at schools and conventions; member of board, Friends of the New Castle Public Library, 1993—.

MEMBER: Richard III Society.

AWARDS, HONORS: Merit Award, 1976, Distinguished Award, 1982 and 1983, all from Lawrence County Open Art Shows.

WRITINGS:

"THE WINTER KING'S WAR" TRILOGY

The Ring of Allaire, Del Rey Books (New York City), 1981.
The Sword of Calandra, Del Rey Books, 1985.
The Mountains of Channadran, Del Rey Books, 1986.

"THE WARHORSE OF ESDRAGON" SERIES

The Prince of Ill Luck, Del Rey Books, 1994.
The Wind-Witch, Del Rey Books, 1994.
The True Knight, Del Rey Books, 1996.

OTHER

The Wizard's Shadow, Del Rey Books, 1993.

Contributor of novella *Thistledown* to *Once Upon a Time: A Treasury of Modern Fairy Tales,* edited by Lester del Rey and Risa Kessler, Del Rey Books, 1991; and to *Excalibur* (anthology), edited by Richard Gilliam, Martin H. Greenberg, and Edward E. Kramer, Warner Books (New York City), 1995. Also contributor of articles, short stories, and illustrations to periodicals, including *Ricardian Register, Horse Illustrated,* and *Magazine of Fantasy and Science Fiction.*

WORK IN PROGRESS: The Wandering Duke and *Graycloak,* both novels.

SIDELIGHTS: Susan Dexter told *CA:* "I think I was born to be a writer—it just took me a long time to figure it out, so I trained as a visual artist along the way. As a commercial artist, I deal in images, but I *think* in words—sort of like being bilingual. I never had an imaginary playmate, but I used to hold conversations in my head between two and three people, none of them being me, myself. (I was relieved to discover that these voices were *characters,* not psychoses!) I find the most bizarre, obscure facts fascinating to know. [The game] Trivial Pursuit is a snap, and research is half done before I deliberately start in on it.

"The question I am asked most frequently—after the perennial 'Where do you get your ideas?'—is 'Have you ever thought of writing anything else?' As if fantasy is somehow shameful, only a step toward becoming worthy to write something else, something real, something 'better.' I can only answer in the negative and add in amazement, 'Why would I?'

"Why fantasy? One can make the claim that it's the oldest form of literature—because it *is*—but people tend to confuse that with the oldest profession, which hardly helps the image. One can declare that *all* fiction is fantasy, that even science fiction is but a subset of it, though a huge one; that's to no avail. Say 'fantasy,' 'fairy tales,' and too often too many an ear hears 'children's' stories' with disdain, as if these are naturally lesser in craft, in content. It's hard to bear. Tales of wonder, of magic, deserve respect.

"*I* like to think of fantasy as a broad umbrella under which I can write *any* sort of tale I choose. I can't think of a single thing that wouldn't fit. Fantasy is a land without limits, its only boundaries my imagination. It's a good home for those things I love best—horses and falcons and castles, noble heroes and wise maidens, swords and capes and magic. Child's play? Not so! Serious business, because underneath the 'cool' window-dressings lie all the dark wonders of the human heart, not hidden at all, but revealed to us as we slowly train our eyes to see ancient truths once more.

"That's on a good day, a rare, fine day. But even on the more mediocre days, I can still have the fun of wearing a dashing cape, swinging a gleaming sword in a just cause, riding a steed that effortlessly outruns the wind. What can beat all that? Certainly not 'mainstream fiction' or 'reality!' "

*　　*　　*

DICKENSON, James R. 1931-

PERSONAL: Born December 31, 1931, in McDonald, KS; son of Richard Doak (a farm fuel dealer) and Anna Avis (a teacher; maiden name, Phipps) Dickenson; married Mollie Anne McCauley (a writer), March 2, 1963; children: (stepchildren) Elizabeth Anne Lerch Oxley, John Hunt Lerch. *Education:* San Diego State College (now University), A.B., 1953; University of Iowa, M.A., 1959, additional study, 1960-62. *Politics:* Democrat. *Religion:* Protestant.

ADDRESSES: Home and office—4101 Glenrose St., Kensington, MD 20795. *Agent*—Ronald Goldfarb, 918 16th St. NW, Washington, DC 20006.

CAREER: Huntington Park Daily Signal, Huntington Park, CA, reporter, 1959-60; United Press International (UPI), San Francisco, CA, reporter, 1960; *National Observer,* Silver Spring, MD, rewriter, sports writer, political reporter, and columnist, 1962-74; *Washington Star,* Washington, DC, editor, political reporter, and author of column "Politics Today" (also syndicated by *Washington Star-New York Times* News Service to about four hundred newspapers), 1974-81, national editor, 1979; *Washington Post,* Washington, DC, national politics editor, 1981-84, national political reporter and columnist, 1984-89; freelance writer and media consultant, Washington, DC, 1989—. Notable assignments include coverage of the 1964 and 1965 World Series, the 1967 Newark and Detroit urban race riots, and political campaigns, including presidential campaigns, 1964-88, and primary elections and national conventions. Host and moderator of Smithsonian Institution program "The Smithsonian Forum on the Media and Society." Former guest lecturer at American University and Catholic University; former lecturer at Syracuse University; frequent public speaker. *Military:* U.S. Marine Corps, 1954-58; became first lieutenant.

MEMBER: White House Correspondents Association, U.S. Senate Press Gallery, U.S. House Press Gallery.

WRITINGS:

Home on the Range: A Century on the High Plains, Scribner (New York City), 1995.

SIDELIGHTS: James R. Dickenson told *CA:* "My decision to make my career as a political journalist was greatly influenced by my interest in history and the fact that one of my uncles owned our hometown weekly newspaper for several years. When I decided against academia I went to Washington, DC, to report on history in the making.

"My first book, *Home on the Range,* is a combination of history and journalism. The original inspiration was the stories my maternal grandmother told me about my family's history, and I began it as a family history. Because this involved their settling the western frontier in Kansas in the 1880s, I broadened it to make it a history of the settling and development of the High Plains, the area between the Missouri River and the Rocky Mountains, from the Texas Panhandle in the south to Saskatchewan in the north. The book recounts the development of this area up to the present.

"My interest in history was greatly stirred by such historians as Samuel P. Hays, my first mentor at Iowa, Arthur M. Schlesinger, Jr., Richard Hofstadter, William E. Leuchtenburg, and others."

*　　*　　*

DINESEN, Isak
See BLIXEN, Karen

*　　*　　*

DIPPIE, Brian William 1943-

PERSONAL: Born September 5, 1943, in Edmonton, Alberta, Canada; son of Thomas Louvain (a credit manager) and Evelyn Isabel (Brander) Dippie; married Donna Ruth MacKenzie (a social worker), September 7, 1965; children: Blake Thomas, Scott Brian. *Education:* University of Alberta, B.A., 1965; University of Wyoming, M.A., 1966; University of Texas, Ph.D., 1970.

ADDRESSES: Home—4026 Hessington Pl., Victoria, British Columbia V8N 5C6, Canada. *Office*—Department of History, University of Victoria, Victoria, British Columbia V8W 3P4, Canada.

CAREER: University of Victoria, Victoria, British Columbia, assistant professor, 1970-75, associate professor, 1975-83, professor of history, 1983—.

MEMBER: Western History Association (member of council, 1994-96), Montana Historical Society, South Dakota State Historical Society.

AWARDS, HONORS: Elected member of National Cowboy Hall of Fame; Wrangler Western Heritage Award for outstanding art book, 1993, for *Charles M. Russell, Word Painter: Letters 1887-1926.*

WRITINGS:

Custer's Last Stand: The Anatomy of an American Myth, University of Montana Press, 1976, revised edition, Bison Books, 1994.

(Compiler) *Custer's Last Stand,* Viking (New York City), 1977.

The Vanishing American: White Attitudes and U.S. Indian Policy, Wesleyan University Press (Middletown, CT), 1982.

Remington and Russell: The Sid Richardson Collection, University of Texas Press (Austin), 1982, revised edition, 1994.

Looking at Russell, Amon Carter Museum of Western Art (Fort Worth, TX), 1987.

(With Chris Bruce and others) *Myth of the West,* Henry Art Gallery, University of Washington (Seattle), 1990.

Catlin and His Contemporaries: The Politics of Patronage, University of Nebraska Press (Lincoln), 1990.

(With Jules D. Prown and others) *Discovered Lands, Invented Pasts: Transforming Visions of the American West,* Yale University Press (New Haven, CT), 1992.

EDITOR

(With John M. Carroll) *Bards of the Little Big Horn,* Guidon Press, 1978.

"Paper Talk": Charlie Russell's American West, Knopf (New York City), 1979.

Nomad: George A. Custer in "Turf, Field, and Farm," University of Texas Press, 1980.

Charles M. Russell, Word Painter: Letters 1887-1926, Amon Carter Museum of Western Art/Abrams (New York City), 1993.

The Russell Reader (anthology of essays), Montana Historical Society (Helena), 1996.

OTHER

Author of introduction to books, including *Frederic Remington (1861-1909): Paintings, Drawings, and Sculpture in the Collection of the R. W. Norton Art Gallery,* R. W. Norton Art Gallery (Shreveport, LA), 1979; and *Old Neutriment: Memories of the Custers,* by G. Wagner, University of Nebraska Press, 1989. Also author of a catalog of the collection of the Frederic Remington Art Museum, Ogdensburg, NY, and of essays on the artistic interpretations of Custer's Last Stand and on Charles M. Russell's painting in his prime years. Contributor to numerous books. Contributor to periodicals, including *American Heritage, American Quarterly, Montana, Wilson Quarterly, Southwest Art,* and *Cultures.*

WORK IN PROGRESS: A catalog of the collection of the Frederic Remington Art Museum, Ogdensburg, NY; essays on the artistic interpretations of Custer's Last Stand, and on Charles M. Russell's painting in his prime years; editing an anthology of essays on Charles M. Russell for the Montana Historical Society, Helena, to be titled *The Russell Reader,* to be published in 1996.

SIDELIGHTS: Brian William Dippie once told *CA:* "My tastes as a cultural historian are eclectic, ranging from fine art to the comic book. I have always been fascinated with the idea of the Wild West and the images associated with it. Much of my work has been an attempt to trace the development of the western myth. At present, I am particularly involved in the study of the western artists—an interest that takes me back to my childhood in Alberta and family vacations in Montana: Great Falls—Charlie Russell's home town, the Historical Society at Helena—with its fine collection of Russell and other western painters. Montana was also the site of Custer's Last Stand—an early and continuing obsession of mine.

"Playing cowboys and Indians was more fun when you knew that there was at least *one* time the Indians won. The fact that a military disaster could be turned into a national myth intrigued me then and intrigues me still, particularly as the popular understanding of Custer's Last Stand changes to accommodate present concerns, and the heroic 'boy general' of yesteryear becomes, for our times, a genocidal maniac, a blunderer, a fool. Historical events do not change, but the myths they engender do. My question is, 'Why?' "

Dippie more recently told *CA:* "My interest continues to focus on Western American art, a field of scholarship that has really blossomed in the past decade. Studies of individual artists as well as thematic interpretations have enriched and enlivened the discussion. I'm proud to be part of it all. I have published essays on allegorical art and photography depicting the destiny of the American Indian (a long-term fascination of mine), and I continue to work on the visual construction of Custer's Last Stand. This and some of my other publications involve the whoppers told by putative 'sole survivors' of the Last Stand (another long-term fascination), and I still anticipate the day when I will have the time to write a book on these wonderful charlatans."

*   *   *

DIXON, Dougal 1947-

PERSONAL: Born March 1, 1947, in Dumfries, Scotland; son of Thomas Bell (an engineer) and Margaret (Hurst) Dixon; married Jean Mary Young, April 3, 1971; children: Gavin Thomas, Lindsay Kathleen. *Education:* University of St. Andrews, B.Sc. (with honors), 1970, M.Sc., 1972. *Avocational interests:* Scuba diving, film and video ("part-owner and projectionist of the local small-town independent cinema—a job done for love of the art form rather than the money!").

ADDRESSES: Home—55 Mill Lane, Wareham, Dorset BH20 4QY, England.

CAREER: Mitchell-Beazley Ltd. (publisher), London, England, book editor, 1973-78; Blandford Press, Poole, Dorset, England, book editor, 1978-80; freelance writer and editor, 1980—. Part owner and projectionist for independent cinema. Civilian instructor for Air Training Corps. Chairman of Parent Teachers Association, Sandford Middle School, 1985-87; member of board of governors, Sandford First School, 1985-89. Created dinosaur artwork for The Dino Gallery, Los Angeles.

MEMBER: Bournemouth Science Fiction and Fantasy Group (vice-chairman, 1980-81; chairman, 1981-82; secretary, 1990—).

AWARDS, HONORS: Hugo Award nomination, 1982, for *After Man: A Zoology of the Future;* Rhone Poulenc Science Book Prize nomination, 1991, for *The Big Book of Prehistoric Life;* Helen Roney Sattler Award, 1993, Distinguished Achievement Award from Educational Press Association of America, 1993, and Outstanding Science Trade Book Award from Children's Book Council, 1994, all for *Dougal Dixon's Dinosaurs.*

WRITINGS:

The Doomsday Machines, D. C. Thompson, 1980.
After Man: A Zoology of the Future, St. Martin's (New York City), 1981.
Resources of the Earth (teaching pack), Science Museum, 1982.
Geology, F. Watts (New York City), 1982.
Geography, F. Watts, 1983.
Forests (picture atlas), F. Watts, 1984.
Mountains (picture atlas), F. Watts, 1984.
Deserts and Wastelands (picture atlas), F. Watts, 1984.
Jungles, revised edition (Dixon was not associated with previous edition), Gloucester Press (New York City), 1984.
A Closer Look at Prehistoric Reptiles, revised edition (Dixon was not associated with previous edition), Gloucester Press, 1984, published in England as *Prehistoric Reptiles,* Hamish Hamilton (London), 1984.
Minerals, Rocks and Fossils: The Earth's Life History, Macdonald & Co. (London), 1984.
(With Jane Burton) *Time Exposure: A Photographic Record of the Dinosaur Age,* Beaufort Books (New York City), 1984, published in England as *The Age of Dinosaurs: A Photographic Record,* Sphere Books (London), 1984.
In Times to Come, Thomas Nelson (Nashville, TN), 1985.
Ice Age Explorer, Bantam (New York City), 1985.
Find Out about Dinosaurs and the Prehistoric World, Hamlyn (Twickenham, England), 1986.
Secrets of the Earth, Hamlyn, 1986.
Be a Dinosaur Detective, Templar, 1987.
The First Dinosaurs, Gareth Stevens, 1987.

The Jurassic Dinosaurs, Gareth Stevens, 1987.
The Last Dinosaurs, Gareth Stevens, 1987.
Hunting the Dinosaurs, Gareth Stevens, 1987.
The Illustrated Dinosaur Encyclopaedia, Golden Press (New York City), 1988.
Colourfax: Dinosaur and Fossil Activity Book, Hamlyn, 1988.
The New Dinosaurs, Salem House, 1988.
The Macmillan Illustrated Encyclopedia of Dinosaurs and Prehistoric Animals, Macmillan (New York City), 1988.
Be a Fossil Detective, Macmillan, 1988.
Dino Dots, Meadowbrook (Deephaven, MN), 1988.
Today's World: The Planet Earth, Gloucester Press, 1989.
The Big Book of Dinosaurs, Bison Books, 1989.
Wayland Library of Science and Technology, Wayland (Hove, East Sussex, England), 1990, Volume 1: *Air and Oceans,* Volume 2: *The Changing Landscape.*
Man after Man: An Anthropology of the Future, St. Martin's, 1990.
The Giant Book of Dinosaurs, Hamlyn, 1990.
The Big Book of Prehistoric Life, Hamlyn, 1990.
The Big Book of the Earth, Hamlyn, 1991.
(With Rupert Matthews) *Hamlyn Illustrated Encyclopaedia of Prehistoric Life,* Hamlyn, 1992.
Equinox Junior Animal Series: Animal Evolution, Andromeda (Maquoketa, IA), 1992.
The Practical Geologist, Quarto, 1992.
Explore the World of Prehistoric Life on Earth, Ilex Press (Fawley, Southampton, England), 1992.
Dinosaurs: Giants of the Earth (also see below), Highlights for Children (Honesdale, PA), 1992.
Dinosaurs: The Real Monsters (also see below), Highlights for Children, 1992.
Dinosaurs: All Shapes and Sizes (also see below), Highlights for Children, 1992.
Dinosaurs: A Closer Look (also see below), Highlights for Children, 1992.
Dinosaurs: The Fossil Hunters (also see below), Highlights for Children, 1992.
Geography Facts, Barnes & Noble (New York City), 1992.
Earth Facts, Apple Press (Milwaukie, OR), 1992.
Young Geographer: The Changing Earth, Wayland, 1992.
Tell Me about Dinosaurs, Kingfisher, 1993.
Spotlights: Prehistoric Life, Andromeda, 1993.
Questions and Answers about Dinosaurs, Kingfisher, 1995.
Digging up the Past: The Search for Dinosaurs, Wayland, 1995.
Dinosaurs, Ladybird Books (Loughborough, Leicester, England), 1995.
Nature Guide: The Weather, Studio Editions, in press.

EDITOR

(With Erik Abranson) *The Physical Earth*, Mitchell-Beazley (London), 1977.

N. B. Marshall, *Developments in Deep Sea Biology*, Blandford Press (Poole, Dorset, England), 1980.

B. Halstead, *Dinosaurs*, Blandford Press, 1981.

Kate Petty, *Dinosaurs*, F. Watts, 1984.

Life and Science: The Earth, Bertelsman, 1984.

Encyclopedia of the Earth, Macmillan, 1986.

CONSULTANT AND EDITOR IN PART

Martyn Bramwell, editor, *The Mitchell-Beazley Atlas of the Oceans*, Mitchell-Beazley, 1977.

Robin Baker, editor, *The Mystery of Migration*, Macdonald & Jane's (London), 1980.

David G. Smith, editor, *The Cambridge Encyclopaedia of Earth Sciences*, Cambridge University Press (Cambridge, England), 1981.

(With Jan Anderson) *The Days of the Dinosaurs*, Thomas Nelson, 1985.

(With L. Bender) *The Story of the Earth*, F. Watts, 1989, Volume 1: *Volcano*, Volume 2: *River*, Volume 3: *Mountain*, Volume 4: *Glacier*, Volume 5: *Island*, Volume 6: *Desert*.

Science Projects: Fossils, Templar, 1990.

How Nature Works, Mitchell-Beazley, 1991.

(With D. Johanson) *Journey from the Dawn*, Hutchinson (London), 1992.

I Wonder Why Triceratops Had Horns, Kingfisher, 1994.

Dinosaur Pack, Dorling Kindersley (London), 1994.

OTHER

Also author of *Dougal Dixon's Dinosaurs* (contains *Dinosaurs: Giants of the Earth*, *Dinosaurs: The Real Monsters*, *Dinosaurs: All Shapes and Sizes*, *Dinosaurs: A Closer Look*, and *Dinosaurs: The Fossil Hunters*), 1992. Also contributor to numerous books, including *Enjoying Nature with Your Family: Look, Learn, Collect, Conserve, Explore the Wildlife of Town and Country in Fascinating Projects and Experiments*, edited by Michael Chinery, Crown (New York City), 1977, published in England as *The Family Naturalist*, Macdonald & Jane's, 1977; *The International Book of the Forest*, edited by M. A. Janulewicz, Mitchell-Beazley, 1981; *The Ordnance Survey National Atlas of Great Britain*, Country Life (Twickenham, England), 1986; and *Amazing Science Facts*, Quarto, 1993.

Also illustrator of "The Unfolding River" wallchart, Quarto, 1992; also creator of alien designs for *Equinox* program, broadcast December, 1992. Also contributor to numerous encyclopedias and dictionaries, including *Everyman Encyclopaedia*, *The Encyclopaedia of Knowledge*, *The World Reference Encyclopaedia*, *20th Century Encyclopaedia*, *Encyclopaedia of Scotland*, *Encyclopaedia of Science*, *Hutchinson Pocket Encyclopaedia*, *Dictionary of Essential Knowledge*, and *Encyclopaedia Britannica*. Contributor of articles and artwork/illustrations to periodicals, including *Film Making*, *Cinemagic*, *Omni*, *World of Dinosaurs*, *Dinosaurs!*, *Focus*, and *Geology Today*. Also creator of *Dinosaurs: Fun, Fact and Fantasy* (video), Longman Video, 1982; also creator of "Dominant Species" (computer game), Dragon Strategic Systems.

ADAPTATIONS: The "*After Man* Exhibition," based on Dixon's book, toured Japan in 1984, and the United States in 1985-86; eight sculptures of *After Man* animals were placed in the Newquay Zoo, Cornwall, in 1983; *After Man* was broadcast by Nexus Television, Tokyo, October, 1990; *Dinosaur* was broadcast by Granada Television, September, 1991.

WORK IN PROGRESS: *The Illustrated Dinosaur Encyclopaedia*, for Octopus (London); *The New Dinosaurs*, for Eddison/Sadd; *A Guide to Fossil Vertebrates*, for Marshall Editions (London).

SIDELIGHTS: Dougal Dixon's *After Man: A Zoology of the Future* postulates animal forms which might evolve in fifty million years' time, after man has exterminated himself by polluting the environment and exhausting the earth's natural resources. Based on current understanding of genetic, evolutionary, and geologic concepts, *After Man* is "a brilliant idea cautiously and slowly developed via an introductory series of excellent essays on cell genetics, evolution by natural selection, animal behavior, food chains and the origins and history of life on earth," according to *Times Literary Supplement* reviewer Redmond O'Hanlon.

What makes Dixon's work different from other works of speculative fiction, comments Timothy Ferris in the *New York Times Book Review*, is the fact that "each of [the author's] creatures is presented not merely as an inmate of a fanciful zoo, but as complete with an ancestry and an ecological role about which Mr. Dixon obviously has thought long and hard." Similarly, Dan Brothwell states in *British Book News* that Dixon's earth "is no world of absurd monsters," because "the author has taken careful note of the biological factors that account for the evolution of lifeforms and has moulded his zoology of the future on the biological reality of the past and present." Nonetheless, says Ferris, the book "does not pretend to prophesy, and Mr. Dixon emphasizes that he considers it unlikely that nature will imitate his art."

Dixon once told *CA*: "My education was almost purely scientific but my interests are primarily artistic. I entered publishing as a career to combine both inclinations. The speculation about the future processes of evolution, the subject of *After Man*, began in the 1960s from a chance remark my father made about extinction. My interest was rekindled in 1979 when I saw a 'save the whale' badge; I started the book after that.

"I suppose I can trace my writing career back to my early school days when I devoted a lot of spare time to drawing and writing comic strips for my own amusement. The strips were generally on science fiction or futuristic themes, and usually contained some strange-looking animals—obviously a foretaste of *After Man.* I also contributed regularly to the school magazine. It was not until after my university education and until I had taken up a career in publishing that I appreciated the mechanics of having work published and began writing seriously.

"With *After Man* I intended to put forward and describe salient points of evolution and ecology—but in a totally novel and, I hope, attractive way. I also used the book to indulge my fantasies of weird animals and was most gratified to have it nominated for a special achievement in science fiction award in 1982. The philosophy behind the book is optimistic—it is all about survival—despite my device of dismissing man in the introductory section. Happily most reviewers realized this, but a number still think that the book is 'really' about the extinction of man. The science fiction film industry is showing a great deal of interest in *After Man* as the background for a film, and I do not think this will detract from its instructional theme in any way. The book is currently published in sixteen foreign editions.

"I work at home. When I wrote *After Man,* my study overlooked a panorama of bird-populated marsh, river plain, forest, sea inlet, and the Purbeck Hills, from which come the best British dinosaur fossils. It was pure inspiration for a book on natural history and evolution. I now live in a town house but still in the same magnificent area."

As a practical geologist, Dixon took part in the 1985 Open University/Earthwatch expedition to the Askja caldera in central Iceland. He is currently involved in excavating a dinosaur-rich site in Jurassic rocks at Durlston on the Dorset coast.

BIOGRAPHICAL/CRITICAL SOURCES:

PERIODICALS

British Book News, February, 1982.
Economist, January 9, 1982.
Los Angeles Times Book Review, December 4, 1983.
New York Times Book Review, April 4, 1982; December 25, 1983.
Science Books and Films, September, 1982.
Science Fiction and Fantasy Book Review, July, 1982.
Science Fiction Review, November, 1983.
Scientific American, December, 1981.
Times Literary Supplement, September 30, 1983.

DOANE, (R.) Michael   1952-

PERSONAL: Born August 3, 1952, in Sioux Falls, SD; son of Richard Arthur and Margaret Louise (Koehler); married Claudine Renee Ripoche; children: Guillame, Sarah. *Education:* Attended University of South Dakota, 1970-75.

ADDRESSES: Home—1710 San Leandro Lane, Montecito, CA 93108-2640. *Agent*—Molly Friedrich, 708 Third Ave., New York, NY 10017.

CAREER: Writer.

WRITINGS:

NOVELS

The Legends of Jesse Dark, Knopf (New York City), 1984.
The Surprise of Burning, Knopf, 1988.
Six Miles to Roadside Business, Knopf, 1990.
City of Light, Knopf, 1992.
Bullet Heart, Knopf, 1994.

WORK IN PROGRESS: Blind Lillian's Roses.

SIDELIGHTS: Michael Doane's first book, *The Legends of Jesse Dark,* traces the bleak and sordid life of its title character. Jesse's life unfolds in four legends, the first detailing his attempt to save himself and his sister Rose from their abusive, alcoholic father. The remaining legends revolve around Jesse's time as a drug-dealing university student, his position as an assistant manager of a pornographic book store, and his attempt to kidnap the newborn son of Rose, who has become a mental patient, before the child is given up for adoption. Although *New York Times Book Review* contributor Russell Banks faulted Doane for his use of stereotypical characters and cliched prose, he enthusiastically praised the first legend of the book. Banks declared that he was almost willing to overlook the book's faults "because of the power and honesty of the first 100 pages. The man who wrote those pages is a gifted, promising writer."

Doane's second novel, *The Surprise of Burning,* juxtaposes the lives and eras of Hunter Page and his mother, Lela Maar. Lela, a legendary jazz and blues singer who performed during the 1930s and 1940s, died giving birth to Hunter during a World War II bombing of London, England. Hunter subsequently grew up obsessed with discovering the identities of his parents. In a narrative that shifts between the lives of mother and son, Doane depicts Lela's success as a white jazz and blues singer, her drug problems, her involvement with anarchists in the 1930s, and her journey to England during World War II as well as Hunter's efforts to recover from serving as a photojournalist in the Vietnam War and his attempt to retain custody of and to come to terms with his adopted half-Vietnamese son. Doane was praised for his smooth handling of the novel's chronological changes and for his "flashes of alternately shattering and shimmering prose" by Itabari N. Njeri, writing in the *Los Angeles Times Book Review;* Njeri faulted Doane, however, for some "historical and cultural improbabilities" that surface in the novel as well as for what she considered to be contrived plot twists. *New York Times* reviewer Michiko Kakutani, though, was more enthusiastic, asserting that "Hunter Page comes alive in this novel as a believable individual *and* as a malleable symbol." Kakutani continued, "There's a fierce lyricism to Mr. Doane's descriptions; . . . they possess the ability to startle us and to make us think. This is a fine and powerful novel, a testament to this young writer's rich and maturing talents."

Doane explores further the themes of family connections and identity in his third novel, *Six Miles to Roadside Business.* Set in the small town of Roadside Business, Utah, the novel tells the story of Vance Ravel, who has just returned to Roadside Business and his family after spending three years in California. Two other story lines accompany the narrative, one of which involves Ravel's father, a career U.S. Army sergeant who is assigned to observe nuclear testing in the 1950s. The dangers of nuclear exposure are kept secret from Sergeant Ravel and his colleagues, and eventually, cancer-stricken and despondent, he kills himself by walking into a nuclear test explosion. The other story line focuses on Vance Ravel's life before he left his family for California. His early years, characterized by an obsession with the circumstances of his father's death, are spent experimenting with a variety of drugs and religions in a search for spiritual fulfillment. Eventually Ravel settles down with his wife and son in their desert home, only to be made the center of a cult that, based on his father's self-immolation, worships Ravel as their prophet. The cult disrupts the lives of Ravel and his family, forcing Ravel to escape to California. Upon his return he must deal with the last remnants of the cult as well as his estranged family. "Doane draws the reader into an exploration of the nature and origins of faith and the great and terrible responsibility that comes with human inventions, whether technical or ideological," commented Kit Reed in a *Washington Post* review. Although one critic noted that the story of Sergeant Ravel made the other story lines seem insubstantial, Reed concluded, "Tense, intelligent and provocative, *Six Miles to Roadside Business* is a delight and a marvel."

City of Light was described as a "labyrinthine thriller" by *New York Times Book Review* critic Rand Richards Cooper, who noted, "Like Mr. Doane's last novel, . . . *City of Light* focuses on a convergence of politics, technology and personal experience." The story follows Thomas Zane, an agent for a fictional amnesty organization who tracks down human-rights violators via computer. "The novel gives real life to the idea of a computer network," Cooper assessed, "transforming it in the reader's mind from a screen or wire or flow of data into a place."

Cooper had reservations about *City of Light*'s appeal to the general reader. "For computer freaks, this may be drama of the highest order," he remarked. "For the layman looking for a more traditional, human thrill, [some] passages may seem muted, garbled or even unintentionally funny." Giles Foden, however, writing in *Times Literary Supplement,* described *City of Light* as "a postmodern novel with heart, full of eloquence that warns off its own eloquence, stylish writing that doesn't consign victims to the *amnestia* of mere style."

Doane's fifth novel, *Bullet Heart,* is "a moving story of survival, of keeping family and community together after devastating loss," Craig Lesley reported in the *New York Times Book Review.* The story is of a fictional war between whites and Native Americans in 1972 South Dakota, precipitated by the disturbance of a pioneer graveyard: the remains of the pioneers are reburied with dignity, but the bones of an Indian girl found in the graveyard are shipped to the State Capitol and stored as relics. *Washington Post Book World* reviewer Gary Amdahl connected Doane's fictional story to an actual shootout in 1975 between members of the FBI and the American Indian Movement in South Dakota. Amdahl found the story "so engrossing and culturally important it ought to be told and retold as often, and by as many writers as care to take it on, as possible, at least until Leonard Peltier (who was found guilty in 1977 of the murders of two FBI agents in the wake of the actual 1975 gun battle at Pine Ridge) gets his case reviewed." A *Publishers Weekly* reviewer concluded, "Doane creates a batch of vivid, painstakingly crafted puzzle pieces that on assembly yield a persuasive impression of the truth."

BIOGRAPHICAL/CRITICAL SOURCES:

PERIODICALS

Chicago Tribune, September 21, 1990.
Los Angeles Times Book Review, January 20, 1985, p. 8; March 20, 1988, p. 3.
New Yorker, November 16, 1992, p. 143; July 24, 1994, p. 6.
New York Times, March 16, 1988.
New York Times Book Review, November 4, 1984, p. 37; April 10, 1988, p. 24; March 4, 1990, 38; December 9, 1990, p. 24; November 8, 1992, p. 11; August 21, 1994, p. 24.
Observer (London), January 15, 1989, p. 48; March 10, 1991, p. 61.
Publishers Weekly, February 12, 1988, p. 69; June 22, 1990, p. 44; September 1, 1992, p. 64; May 16, 1994, p. 50.

Times (London), March 14, 1991, p. 20.
Times Literary Supplement, January 13, 1989, p. 42; January 22, 1993, p. 20.
Tribune Books (Chicago), December 20, 1992, p. 3.
Washington Post, November 7, 1990.
Washington Post Book World, July 3, 1994, p. 9.
West Coast Review of Books, Volume 14, number 1, 1988, p. 29.

*   *   *

DOMAN, June 1930-
(Meryle Secrest)

PERSONAL: Born April 23, 1930, in Bath, England; immigrated to Canada, 1948; immigrated to United States, 1953, naturalized citizen, 1957; daughter of Albert Edward (a toolmaker) and Olive Edith May (Love) Doman; married David Waight Secrest (a journalist), September 23, 1953 (divorced, 1965); married Thomas Gattrell Beveridge (a singer and composer), November 23, 1975; children: (first marriage) Cary Doman, Martin Adams, Gillian Anne. *Education:* Attended girls' high school in Bath, England. *Avocational interests:* "European travel, foreign languages, painting, environmental problems (including air, water, and soil pollution and the acute problem of noise in twentieth-century America)."

ADDRESSES: Home—Walpole, NH. *Agent*—Murray Pollinger, 4 Garrick St., London WC2E 9BH, England.

CAREER: Hamilton News, Hamilton, Ontario, women's editor, 1949-50, *Bristol Evening Post,* Bristol, England, reporter, 1950-51; *Columbus Citizen,* Columbus, OH, food editor, 1955-57; *Washington Post,* Washington, DC, feature writer, 1961-69, cultural reporter, 1969-72, editor and art critic, 1972-75; freelance writer, 1975—. Affiliated with F&R Lazarus & Co., 1953-55.

MEMBER: British Commonwealth Society of North America, Washington Independent Writers Association.

AWARDS, HONORS: Award from Canadian Women's Press Club, 1950, for "An interview with Barbara Ann Scott"; woman of the year citation, Hamilton Press Club, 1951; Pulitzer Prize and American Book Award nominations, 1981, for *Being Bernard Berenson;* Guggenheim fellowship, 1981-82.

WRITINGS:

UNDER PSEUDONYM MERYLE SECREST

Between Me and Life: A Biography of Romaine Brooks, Doubleday (New York City), 1974.
Being Bernard Berenson, Holt (New York City), 1979.
Kenneth Clark: A Biography, Weidenfeld & Nicolson (London), 1984, Holt, 1985.
Salvador Dali, Dutton (New York City), 1986, published in England as *Salvador Dali: The Surrealist Jester,* Weidenfeld & Nicolson, 1986.
Frank Lloyd Wright, Knopf (New York City), 1992.
Leonard Bernstein: A Life, Knopf, 1994.

Contributor of articles to magazines and periodicals.

SIDELIGHTS: Under the pseudonym Meryle Secrest, June Doman has painted compelling biographical portraits of a number of prominent personalities in the world of twentieth-century arts. In books such as *Salvador Dali, Frank Lloyd Wright,* and the Pulitzer Prize-nominated *Being Bernard Berenson,* Doman has earned the praise of critics for her thorough research and engaging style.

"Biography seems to be the natural outgrowth of my journalistic experience," Doman once told *CA,* "and skills acquired as a researcher and interviewer are particularly valuable in unearthing documentary information." Because of her many years of journalistic training and experience, she attaches particular importance to interviews as a source of information about her chosen subject. "Flawed though the human memory is," she notes, "and biased as the reminiscence may be, colored by circumstance and prejudice, it is still a potentially rich source of information that can be obtained by no other means."

Her first book, *Between Me and Life: A Biography of Romaine Brooks,* was most influenced by her experience as a reporter. "I began," she recalls, "with the intention of reporting anything and everything that could be discovered about the personality and with the determination to keep my personality in the background. I completed the manuscript and realized that the biography simply didn't work. So I threw it away as a source and completely rewrote the book, taking another year to do it, and recast it in the form which seemed much more sympathetic to my own assets as a writer. I eliminated extraneous detail and concentrated on developing and illustrating my own point of view about Romaine Brooks." Although the book was only mildly successful, it was well reviewed by critics in both England and the United States, which encouraged Doman to leave journalism and devote herself to writing biography.

When tackling the wealth of information that was available on Bernard Berenson, a noted authenticator of Italian art, Doman found it necessary to eliminate detail. "A ridiculous amount of material exists, documenting almost every aspect of his life except his childhood and business dealings," she told *CA.* "So the challenge to present a coherent picture continues. I find myself unalterably opposed to the current vogue for biography which I find unreadable—and if I can't read it, why should I write it?" In the view of many critics, Doman met her challenge in *Being Bernard Berenson:* Robert Hughes noted in the *New*

York Review of Books that Doman's narrative "is the liveliest evocation of this strangely conflict-ridden man that has yet been written, a portrait with the unmistakable ring of psychological truth."

Noted art historian Kenneth Clark provided Doman with his insight and reminiscence for her biography of Berenson; she was so taken with Clark's personality that she made him the subject of her third biography. *Kenneth Clark,* which some reviewers noted was approached by its author as an act of hero-worship, was problematic for Doman when Clark, who was still alive at the time of its writing, protested about certain details and forced Doman to rewrite much of the book. The critical opinion that followed was mixed. "This is not a book that does full justice to Kenneth Clark's distinction," commented John Gross in the *New York Times,* "but neither . . . does it trivialize him. Or if it does, it is only because humanizing someone usually involves a degree of trivializing as well, and Miss Secrest does undoubtedly succeed in making Clark seem more human than he did before."

Architect Frank Lloyd Wright, surrealist painter Salvador Dali, and composer-conductor Leonard Bernstein have also been the subjects of Doman's energetic interest. Her *Frank Lloyd Wright* was the first biography of the man to be compiled with access to the complete microfiche Wright archives, and in the *New York Review of Books* Martin Filler judged it "likely to remain the most satisfactory treatment of Wright's life until a definitive multivolume study appears."

Doman's work as a biographer has been repeatedly praised by critics for its broad focus and intelligent insights into the character of her subject, characteristics of biography she believes to be important. "If I have any criticism of biography in [the United States], it's that it's too much inclined to a very objective, scholarly approach," she told John F. Baker in *Publishers Weekly.* "That way you get just a huge collection of facts, but somehow the personality of the subject seems to slip away. And there is no such thing as a definitive biography."

BIOGRAPHICAL/CRITICAL SOURCES:

PERIODICALS

Economist, January 26, 1980, p. 103.
Los Angeles Times Book Review, January 20, 1985, p. 1; December 14, 1986, p. 3.
Newsweek, November 5, 1979, p. 107.
New York Review of Books, December 20, 1979, pp. 19-29; January 13, 1994, pp. 28-33.
New York Times, January 8, 1985, p. 23; November 27, 1986, p. 23.
New York Times Book Review, November 14, 1979, p. 7; November 3, 1986, p. 9; December 19, 1993, p. 28.

Publishers Weekly, January 11, 1985, pp. 73-74.
Spectator, November 29, 2986, p. 24.
Time, October 5, 1992, p. 86.
Times (London), March 3, 1980.
Times Literary Supplement, January 18, 1980, p. 51; May 17, 1985, p. 537.
Washington Post Book World, January 4, 1987, p. 9.

       *   *   *

DONZE, Mary Terese 1911-
(Sister Mary Terese)

PERSONAL: Surname is pronounced *Dun*-zee; born December 17, 1911, in East St. Louis, IL; daughter of Leon S. and Josephine (Mueller) Donze. *Education:* St. Louis University, B.A. (magna cum laude), 1944; St. Mary College, Leavenworth, KS, M.S., 1966.

ADDRESSES: Home—4483 Lindell Blvd., Apt. 643, St. Louis, MO 63108.

CAREER: Entered Roman Catholic women's religious community, Congregation of the Adorers of the Blood of Christ (A.S.C.), 1925; became Roman Catholic nun, 1929, name in religion, Sister Mary Terese; teacher in elementary and high schools in Illinois and Missouri, 1929-74; served as principal of elementary schools; teacher of yoga in St. Louis, MO, 1976-80; full-time writer, 1974—. Director of novices in Congregation of the Adorers of the Blood of Christ, 1948-56. Inventor.

MEMBER: McKendree Writers Association.

AWARDS, HONORS: National Catholic Book Award, Catholic Press Association, 1982, for *In My Heart Room,* 1993, for *Jesus Forgives My Sins,* and 1994, for *I Can Pray about Anything.*

WRITINGS:

Teresa of Avila, Paulist Press (Ramsey, NJ), 1982.
The Kingdom Lost and Found: A Fable for Everyone, Ave Maria Press (Notre Dame, IN), 1982, Indian edition published as *The Mystery of the Unbreakable Bubbles.*
In My Heart Room (prayers for children), Liguori Publications (Liguori, MO), Book 1 with coloring book, 1982, Book 2, 1990.
Of Course You Can Write!, J. Weston Walch, 1983.
Down Gospel Byways, Liguori Publications, 1983.
Touching a Child's Heart, Ave Maria Press, 1985.
Prayer and Our Children, Ave Maria Press, 1987.
Step Up Close to Jesus, Creative Communications for the Parish, 1988.
Jesus, My Special Friend, Creative Communications for the Parish, 1991.
I Can Pray the Rosary, Liguori Publications, 1991.
I Can Pray the Mass, Liguori Publications, 1992.

I Can Pray with the Saints, Liguori Publications, 1992.
Jesus Comes to Me, Liguori Publications, 1993.
Jesus Forgives My Sins, Liguori Publications, 1993.
I Can Pray about Anything, Liguori Publications, 1994.

Contributor of articles and stories to magazines, including *Journal of Reading, Aunt Jane's Sewing Circle, Catholic Digest, Highlights for Children, Sisters Today,* and *Workbench.*

Step Up Close to Jesus was also published in Indonesia.

SIDELIGHTS: Mary Terese Donze once told *CA:* "While most of my books have a religious theme, I have articles and stories published on subjects as varied as making an inexpensive footstool, a cure for hiccups, and the first woman Jesuit. There was a time when I searched about for interesting topics on which to write. Over the years I have learned that it isn't so much the topic that matters as the writer's enthusiasm. I attribute my measure of success to my ability to sell myself on the subjects I choose to write about. I make an effort to learn as much as I can about my subject, and at a certain point in this process, the thing begins to grip me. At that point I feel the need of sharing my discovery and almost literally shouting, 'Hey! Look what I found.' After that there is still the matter of finding the right words, but the words will never come nor be convincing without the enthusiasm.

"If this sounds like a writing placebo, try writing an article on the importance of small things. Then choose the small and unpromising period (.) as your subject. Tell yourself you are going to get excited about this small dot. After a bit of real effort you will be amazed at the incredible value of this speck-of-ink-on-paper: its placement in a horizontal row of numbers, its use at the end of a sentence, its intrusion into music, the facility with which it can be used in comparisons. Its substitution for what one dares not say in print. . . ."

＊　　＊　　＊

DRAPER, Hastings
See JEFFRIES, Roderic (Graeme)

＊　　＊　　＊

DUNNE, John Gregory 1932-

PERSONAL: Born May 25, 1932, in Hartford, CT; son of Richard Edwin (a physician) and Dorothy (Burns) Dunne; married Joan Didion (a writer), January 30, 1964; children: Quintana Roo (daughter). *Education:* Princeton University, A.B., 1954.

ADDRESSES: Home—New York, NY. *Agent*—(literary) Lynn Nesbit, Janklow-Nesbit, 598 Madison Ave., New York, NY 10022; (film) ICM, 8942 Wilshire Blvd., Beverly Hills, CA 90211.

CAREER: Author.

WRITINGS:

NOVELS

Vegas: A Memoir of a Dark Season, Random House (New York, NY), 1974.
True Confessions (also see below), Dutton (New York, NY), 1977.
Dutch Shea, Jr., Simon & Schuster (New York, NY), 1982.
The Red White and Blue, Simon & Schuster, 1987.
Playland, Random House, 1994.

SCREENPLAYS; WITH WIFE, JOAN DIDION

Panic in Needle Park (based on the book of the same title by James Mills), Twentieth Century-Fox, 1971.
Play It as It Lays (based on Didion's book of the same title), Universal, 1972.
(With others) *A Star Is Born,* Warner Bros., 1976.
True Confessions (based on Dunne's novel of the same title), United Artists, 1981.
Hills Like White Elephants (from the short story of the same title by Ernest Hemingway), Home Box Office (HBO), 1990.
Broken Trust (based on the novel *Court of Honor* by William Wood), Turner Network Television (TNT), 1995.
Up Close and Personal, Disney, 1996.

OTHER

Delano: The Story of the California Grape Strike, Farrar, Straus (New York, NY), 1967, revised edition, 1971.
The Studio (nonfiction), Farrar, Straus, 1969.
Quintana and Friends (essays), Dutton, 1978.
Harp (autobiography), Simon & Schuster, 1989.
Crooning: A Collection (literary journalism), Simon & Schuster, 1990.

Author with Didion of column, "Points West," *Saturday Evening Post,* 1967-69; columnist for *New West,* 1967-69, and *Esquire,* 1976-77, 1986-87. Contributor to numerous periodicals, including *Atlantic, Esquire, Harper's, Holiday, Interview, Life, National Review, New Republic, New York Review of Books, Omni,* and *Publishers Weekly.*

SIDELIGHTS: "Crackling dialogue, gritty characters, a fierce, unblinking stare at acts of brutality—these elements mark the novels of John Gregory Dunne," wrote fellow novelist Anne Tyler in the *New York Times Book Review.* "These and one other, perhaps the most important: a fascination with the invisible web that links certain disparate people and events."

Dunne began his career as a writer at *Time* magazine and moved on to freelance work before publishing his first novel, *Vegas: A Memoir of a Dark Season,* in 1974. Since then Dunne has worked in a variety of genres producing books that explore the Irish Catholic experience in graphic language and carefully rendered detail.

Vegas presents three main characters—a lounge comic, a private detective, and a poetry-writing prostitute—who are composites of real people Dunne encountered in Las Vegas, Nevada. "The book is bitter and touching at once, utterly compulsive reading," writes Peter Straub in *New Statesman.* "The dialogue is from the bottom of the world, spoken by people who hustle by reflex and have passed caring that the hustle is all they've got." *New York Times Book Review* contributor Jonathan Yardley calls it "a fine, wry, perceptive, graceful book" and concludes that *Vegas* "does as much for the dark side of the American funhouse as Hunter Thompson's *Fear and Loathing in Las Vegas* did for the manic side." Although it was never a bestseller, *Vegas* is Dunne's favorite of his own novels—"not because I think it is my best," he explained to Digby Diehl in *Chicago Tribune Magazine,* "but because it is the book that taught me how to write." It is also the first book in which Dunne mines what he now routinely refers to as the "Mother Lode"—his Irish American heritage.

That heritage figures prominently in *True Confessions,* Dunne's first bestseller and, according to *New York Times* reviewer Christopher Lehmann-Haupt, "the book he was born to write." Loosely patterned after the 1947 Black Dahlia murder case, *True Confessions* is a murder mystery in which the solution to the murder doesn't matter at all. Instead, Dunne emphasizes the relationship between two Irish Catholic brothers who get involved in the case— Tom Spellacy, a police lieutenant, and Des Spellacy, an ambitious priest. When the victim's severed head turns up in a seedy urban parking lot, Tom launches an investigation that implicates not only the most prominent member of his brother's parish, but his brother as well.

"The book is not a suspense novel or murder mystery in the ordinary sense," noted *New York Review of Books* contributor Robert Towers. "Rather, it is concerned with tracing—interestingly and deftly—the 'ripple effect' which the case has upon the racketeers, contractors, blarneying lawyers, glad-handing undertakers, whores, and the variously tainted members of the police force and clergy who populate this crowded work." John B. Breslin wrote in the *Washington Post Book World* that "what Dunne wants to explore are the ironies that shape people's lives, sometimes tragically but just as often providentially."

Despite the book's widespread popularity (hardcover sales of more than 50,000 copies, more than a million paper-

back sales, and a film adaptation), some critics, such as *Newsweek*'s Raymond Sokolov, believe that "Dunne does not quite fulfill the potential of his material. He lets the whodunit side of his story slip too far from view during the long passages of parochial intrigue. His canvas is overcrowded with distracting vignettes of scheming priests and laymen." *Saturday Review* contributor Robert M. Strozier believes "there's just too much smart banter, too much plot, too much gratuitous weirdness, too much cuteness. . . . The book has energy and substance, but unfortunately there's just too, too, too much of everything." *Times Literary Supplement* critic Anthony Bailey regards the novel as a promise for the future: "*True Confessions* has a muscle-bound, dirty-talking strength which suggests that Mr. Dunne—stretching his wings a little and looking at the glories as well as the detritus of creation—has it in him to write a first-rate Irish American novel."

Some critics believe that Dunne fulfilled that promise with *Dutch Shea, Jr.,* which also explores the theme of corruption in an Irish Catholic milieu. Shea, a divorced lawyer who represents the kind of clients no one else will touch— pimps, muggers, arsonists—is a disillusioned man drifting through life passively. "The drift is interrupted by the death of Shea's much-loved only child, Cat, an adopted daughter who is the random victim of an IRA bomb in a London restaurant," according to Thomas M. Gannon in *America.* "As he mourns Cat's death, Shea's own life edges toward a crisis, for he, like his father before him and for similar, imprudently well-intentioned reasons, is an embezzler." The story climaxes when Shea's crime is discovered and he is forced to face the consequences of his acts.

Because Shea spends so much time among criminals and degenerates, the book is full of foul language and graphic sexual scenes. This emphasis reflects Dunne's knowledge that "he can safely float a novel on a tide of racist slurs, ethnic jokes and what, in more fastidious days, were thought to be irregular sexual connections—and that he can collect the benefits of such ornamentation at the cash register—without actually opening himself to charges of bad taste," according to *Newsweek*'s Peter S. Prescott. But Adam Mars-Jones, writing in the *Times Literary Supplement,* found the emphasis disturbing: "Even when there is no obvious occasion for revulsion, no severed nipple, no shredded baby, Dunne finds ways of letting the corruptible body know just what he thinks of it." "John Gregory Dunne isn't exposing the spiritual emptiness of modern life. . . . He is turning disgust into another cheap thrill, and fetishizing what he claims to denounce."

Other reviewers are less critical of Dunne's graphic content. *New York Times* reviewer Christopher Lehmann-Haupt, for instance, thought "the unlikely combination of gags, social satire and personal tragedy holds together even better than it did in Mr. Dunne's earlier novel *True Confessions.*" And in the *New York Times Book Review,* contributor George Stade wrote that "Dutch Shea's examinations and cross-examinations of cops and whores, of Myron Mandel, super-pimp, of Packy Considine, jailbird and fence, of Roscoe Raines, burglar . . . , of Robert Beaubois, torch, are all funny, often chastening, sometimes ghastly, and always deftly handled by Dutch Shea and Mr. Dunne." In the opinion of *National Review* contributor Jeffrey Brodrick, "Dunne presents not so much a plot that unfolds as a character that unravels. Once the bomb goes off we do little more than follow the vibrations, the shudders, through Dutch's head. Dutch doesn't blow up, he collapses inward for the remaining 352 pages of the novel. Dutch Shea, Jr. is broken from page one. He's a cooked bird and he doesn't even care."

Why does one go on reading when Shea's ultimate demise is so predictable? "Because we hope against hope that Dunne's bright, witty, sad and entirely sympathetic hero will *not* do what we dread he *might* do," according to Evan Hunter in the *Washington Post Book World;* "and because the novel is so rich in character and detail . . .we are compelled to turn the pages as rapidly as our fingers can move." Hunter concluded that "Dunne has written a fine novel that examines and dissects a unique individual whom we come to know—and indeed love and admire—as the story unfolds toward its tragic end. By so movingly bringing to life this troubled and complicated man, he has illuminated our own human condition—and that, in the long run, is what good fiction is all about."

The Red White and Blue is far broader in scope and more challenging than Dunne's previous novels, covering a span of some thirty years, from the Vietnam era to the present. Elena Brunet noted in *Los Angeles Times Book Review* that "the subject of this sweeping novel is as large and dramatic as our recent history, refashioned and transcended into fiction." According to Tyler in the *New York Times Book Review,* "what makes the history come alive are the voices, which are recorded so faithfully and so unforgivingly that the speakers, if they were real, would wince to read their own remarks."

The narrator-protagonist, Jack Broderick, is a former reporter, now Hollywood screenwriter, who recounts a wide-ranging, blackly humorous and disturbing portrait of American history, as witnessed from a jaundiced, omnipotent viewpoint reminiscent of the snappy, cynical first-person narratives of the hard-boiled detective and crime genres. Jack is the son of self-made billionaire Hugh Broderick. Hugh, Jack, Jack's older brother, Father Augustine "Bro" Broderick—a celebrity priest of the Benedictine order—and his sister, Priscilla—who not only married the president's brother but slept with the president himself—constitute the Irish-American family at the

center of the story. Leah Kaye, Jack's first wife, is a radical lawyer who specializes in defending anti-establishment types. The novel opens with the murder of Bro and Leah by gunman Richie Kane, a poor Irish-American and an embittered, hate-filled, rightwing Vietnam War veteran whom Jack had interviewed for his book during the Vietnam era.

Discussing the structure of *The Red White and Blue,* Tyler noted, "Nowhere on these pages does B follow A. . . . Time is deliberately muddled here. It's not just reversed—that would be too neat—but stirred with a stick. . . . The effect is to make us conscious of the complexity of the web—the confusion of historical events ricocheting off each other." Clancy Sigal of *Tribune Books* described the novel as "a long pageant full of twitching characters who dangle and stumble their way from the radical Sixties through Vietnam to the present."

Jonathan Yardley of *Washington Post Book World* argued that the novel loses its narrative momentum long before the end: "The first 50 or 60 pages of *The Red White and Blue* come at you in a great rush; for a while it seems John Gregory Dunne is going to take you for one hell of a ride, and the prospect is exhilarating. But then a funny thing happens: *The Red White and Blue* runs out of gas, with more than 400 pages yet to go." Yardley attributes this in part to the observation that the book "is so crammed with characters and themes that there's scarcely breathing room for anyone. . . . Dunne . . . creates so many fictional characters who are obvious representatives of well-known real people that at times the novel collapses into mere *roman a clef*—funny and penetrating *roman a clef,* to be sure, but *roman a clef* all the same."

Though Richard Eder of the *Los Angeles Times Book Review* found that the author's "writing is witty and awesomely accurate in its detail" and has "an alluring and impeccable surface," the critic concluded, "For all its skill and detail, *The Red White and Blue* is essentially inert. Dunne does not manage to do what he seems most to want to do: give us a new insight into public ills by means of private symptoms. Dunne's public world is recognizable enough not only because we have read about it in the newspapers and seen it on television. His characters illustrate it, but they do not construct it." *Village Voice* reviewer M. George Stevenson found Dunne's writing "still a bit one-sentence-paragraph happy for my taste, and he is not immune to over-detailing both his plots and his characters. . . . Still, *The Red White and Blue* is a big book about big subjects and a classy performance—qualities rare enough to set it apart." Thomas R. Edwards, in the *New York Review of Books,* declared, "*The Red White and Blue* has the intricate design of a complex motion picture, with lots of flashbacks and tricky cross cutting. Dunne, who has written screenplays, makes the method work here—the book is continuously powerful, often both funny and horrifying, and never dull."

The semi-autobiographical "*Harp* is rather like the life story of an Irish writer as you might hear it in a single long night in a bar, especially if you were Irish too, and the writer could take the corresponding liberties," wrote Jack Miles in the *Los Angeles Times Book Review*. Alan D. Williams reported in the *Village Voice* that, though it is not "a formal autobiography or even memoir," *Harp* "is instead the chronicle and atlas—motivated by a midlife medical crisis—of a feisty, tirelessly curious, and gruffly compassionate sensibility." The book's title is derogatory slang for "Irish Catholic," and the word appeals to Dunne: "I call myself a harp because I like the sound of the word—it is short, sharp and abusive," he writes. From this perspective Dunne reflects on a selection of the people, places, and things that have passed through his life so far, meanwhile awaiting a verdict from the cardiologists on his medical crisis. "*Harp* may not quite pass the test of engaging the reader who has never heard of Dunne, but there isn't a boring page in it," Williams asserts.

In *Harp* Dunne recounts his time in the army, the deaths of several family members, a trip to Ireland to research his family tree, his opinions on well-known figures including Katharine Hepburn, his move from Los Angeles to New York, his surreptitious inspections of friends' medicine cabinets, and a number of other personal events and insights. He "is not naturally introspective," however, observed R. Z. Sheppard in *Time*, "which may be bad news for the self-help set but is good news for readers who like stylish structure and snappy prose, to say nothing of snappishness." Donna Rifkind expressed a different opinion in the *Times Literary Supplement*, finding that Dunne's "observations are not uninteresting (though hardly exceptional), but *Harp* meanders so far from its premise that the project begins to seem less an act of self-analysis than an excuse to make a book." Chicago *Tribune* editor Joseph Coates, referring to such authors who write about themselves as Philip Roth, John Updike, Anthony Trollope, and Dunne, asked "Why do they do it? Such efforts seem not only self-defeating (in every sense of the term), but they also can be professionally suicidal." The reviewer added that "*Harp* never achieves the narrative intensity or density of detail of *Vegas*," and that in *Harp* Dunne "has not written a bad book, just a wasteful one that not only cannibalizes his previous fiction . . . but also seems to obviate future novels." Raymond A. Schroth presented a more favorable assessment in *Commonweal*, concluding that *Harp* shows Dunne to be "a middle-aged married man on a journey with a notebook and the courage to share the journey's humor and its pain."

With *Playland*, Dunne returns to the novel form and the territory he explored in the nonfictional *Studio—*

Hollywood and the film industry. Also returning is journalist and screenwriter Jack Broderick from *The Red White and Blue*, who sets about unraveling the story of the downfall of imaginary 1930s child star Blue Tyler. In the process readers learn of her teenage affair with gangster Jacob King, founder of Playland and a character based on real-life gangster Bugsy Siegel, creator of Las Vegas. "A cranky, take-no-prisoners cynicism is Dunne's style, honed in his books *Harp*, *Dutch Shea, Jr.*, and *The Red White and Blue*, where narrator Broderick chronicled the simultaneous shooting of his ex-wife . . . and his brother. . . . In fact, Broderick carries over not only his personal woes but also a bagful of characters from that novel to *Playland*," Chicago *Tribune* contributor Sugar Rautbord observed.

"*Playland* is Dunne's version of *The Great Gatsby*," Mark Horowitz asserted in the *Washington Post Book World*, "only this time the hero gets shotgunned to death in Vegas and Daisy's a nympho." *New York Times Book Review* critic Janet Maslin found the "most successful part of this novel is its bawdy, admiring portrait of that time and place, filled with jaundiced observations and half-familiar show-business anecdotes," and David Ehrenstein noted in the *Los Angeles Times Book Review* that "Real people are crammed cheek by jowl alongside imaginary characters." While *Spectator* reviewer Charlotte Raven believed that the "view of Hollywood which emerges could have been written by anyone with a passing knowledge of film and no great interest in originality," Ehrenstein described *Playland* as "first-rate pop fiction writing: tart, evocative, nicely observed." Horowitz, who acknowledged that Dunne "happens to be one of my favorite writers," also describes the author as "an acquired taste. He can be sour and mean-spirited, but he's smart and funny and his prose is always elegant and precise."

BIOGRAPHICAL/CRITICAL SOURCES:

BOOKS

Contemporary Literary Criticism, Volume 28, Gale, 1984.
Dictionary of Literary Biography Yearbook: 1980, Gale, 1981.
Dunne, John Gregory, *Vegas: A Memoir of a Dark Season*, Random House, 1974. Dunne, John Gregory, *Quintana and Friends*, Dutton, 1978.
Winchell, Mark Royden, *John Gregory Dunne*, Boise State University (Boise, ID), 1986.

PERIODICALS

America, January 13, 1968; July 5, 1969; July 31, 1982.
Antioch Review, fall, 1989, p. 503.
Atlanta Journal-Constitution, March 22, 1987, p. J9; October 7, 1990, p. N10.
Atlantic, February, 1978.

Boston Globe, March 19, 1987, p. 73; August 20, 1989, p. 102; October 22, 1989, p. 8; August 26, 1994, p. 56.

Chicago Tribune, August 24, 1990, section 5, p. 3; August 22, 1994, section 5, pp. 1-2.

Chicago Tribune Book World, January 21, 1979.

Chicago Tribune Magazine, May 2, 1982.

Commonweal, February 9, 1968; November 3, 1989, pp. 592, 594.

Entertainment Weekly, August 13, 1993, p. 69; August 12, 1994, p. 49.

Globe and Mail (Toronto), November 18, 1989.

Horizon, January, 1981.

Listener, March 22, 1990, p. 29.

Los Angeles Times, February 1, 1987, section 6, p. 1; January 30, 1994, p. M3.

Los Angeles Times Book Review, March 1, 1987, pp. 1, 8; July 3, 1988, p. 10; August 27, 1989, pp. 1, 11; August 19, 1990, p. 1; June 23, 1991, p. 14; April 18, 1982; August 14, 1994, pp. 1, 5.

Maclean's, April 6, 1987, p. 52.

National Observer, March 8, 1971.

National Review, December 16, 1969; August 6, 1982.

New Leader, May 26, 1969.

New Republic, December 2, 1967; May 10, 1969; March 9, 1974; August 2, 1994, pp. 35-38.

New Statesman, November 1, 1974; March 23, 1990, pp. 36-37.

Newsweek, January 21, 1974; October 10, 1977; April 19, 1982; September 18, 1989, pp. 77-78.

New Yorker, March 11, 1974; April 24, 1978; May 24, 1982; August 1, 1994, p. 24.

New York Review of Books, January 26, 1978; June 10, 1982; August 13, 1987, pp. 50-51; September 22, 1994, p. 34.

New York Times, May 7, 1969; January 10, 1974;, September 2, 1977; October 11, 1977; January 25, 1979; September 25, 1981; April 1, 1982; February 8, 1987, section 6, p. 18; February 19, 1987, pp. C21, 23; September 20, 1987, section 7, p. 32; September 11, 1989, p. C22; February 11, 1991, p. C11; August 4, 1994, p. C15; September 14, 1994, pp. C1, C8.

New York Times Book Review, November 12, 1967; February 3, 1974; October 16, 1977; January 28, 1979; March 28, 1982; June 2, 1985, p. 50; March 1, 1987, p. 3; July 17, 1988, p. 34; September 10, 1989, p. 3; August 5, 1990, section 7, p. 7; October 14, 1990, p. 56; August 28, 1994, p. 7.

Observer (London), August 9, 1987, p. 23; February 3, 1991, p. 54.

People Weekly, October 2, 1989, pp. 29-30; February 11, 1991, p. 9; September 26, 1994, p. 34.

Playboy, April, 1989, p. 26.

Publishers Weekly, August 22, 1994.

Saturday Review, October 29, 1977; February 17, 1979; April, 1982.

Spectator, April 28, 1990, p. 30, March 18, 1995, pp. 33-34.

Time, June 27, 1969; November 7, 1977; March 29, 1982; March 9, 1987, p. 75; August 28, 1989, p. 65; August 29, 1994, p. 75.

Times Literary Supplement, December 27, 1974; February 8, 1980; April 21, 1978; September 17, 1982; October 16, 1987, p. 1135; May 11, 1990, p. 488.

Tribune Books (Chicago), February 22, 1987, p. 6; August 21, 1988, p. 8; September 10, 1989, p. 3; July 7, 1991, p. 8; August 2, 1994, p. 1; August 14, 1994, pp. 3, 9.

USA Today, March 3, 1987, pp. D1, D6; August 25, 1989, p. D4; August 26, 1994, p. D6.

Village Voice, March 31, 1987, pp. 52, 54; November 14, 1989, p. 59.

Vogue, September, 1989, p. 512.

Wall Street Journal, April 14, 1987, p. 30; August 26, 1994, p. A8; October 6, 1994, p. A19.

Washington Post, January 11, 1979; April 30, 1982.

Washington Post Book World, October 23, 1977; March 28, 1982; June 30, 1985, p. 12; February 22, 1987, p. 3; July 3, 1988, p. 12; September 3, 1989, pp. 1-2; September 9, 1990, pp. 7-8; June 2, 1991, p. 12; July 31, 1994, p. 1.

West Coast Review of Books, Volume 15, number 1, 1989, p. 78.

Yale Review, summer, 1968.

*   *   *

DURANG, Christopher (Ferdinand) 1949-

PERSONAL: Born January 2, 1949, in Montclair, NJ; son of Francis Ferdinand and Patricia Elizabeth Durang. *Education:* Harvard University, B.A., 1971; Yale University, M.F.A., 1974. *Religion:* "Raised Roman Catholic."

ADDRESSES: Agent—Helen Merrill, 361 West 17th St., New York, NY 10011.

CAREER: Yale Repertory Theatre, New Haven, CT, actor, 1974; Southern Connecticut College, New Haven, teacher of drama, 1975; Yale University, New Haven, teacher of playwriting, 1975-76; playwright, 1976—. Actor in plays, including *The Idiots Karamazov* and *Das Lusitania Songspiel.*

MEMBER: Dramatists Guild, Actors Equity Association.

AWARDS, HONORS: Fellow of Columbia Broadcasting System (CBS), 1975-76; Rockefeller Foundation grant, 1976-77; Guggenheim fellow, 1978-79; Antoinette Perry Award (Tony) nomination for best book of a musical from League of New York Theatres and Producers, 1978, for

A History of the American Film; grant from Lecomte du Nouy Foundation, 1980-81; Off-Broadway Award (Obie) from *Village Voice,* 1980, for *Sister Mary Ignatius Explains It All for You;* Hull-Warriner Award, Dramatists Guild, 1985; Lila Wallace-*Reader's Digest* Fund Writer's Award, 1994.

WRITINGS:

PLAYS

The Nature and Purpose of the Universe (first produced in Northampton, MA, 1971; produced in New York City, 1975), Dramatists Play Service, 1979.

Robert, first produced in Cambridge, MA, 1971; produced as *'dentity Crisis* in New Haven, CT, 1975.

Better Dead Than Sorry, first produced in New Haven, CT, 1972; produced in New York City, 1973.

(With Albert Innaurato) *I Don't Generally Like Poetry, But Have You Read "Trees"?,* first produced in New Haven, CT, 1972; produced in New York City, 1973.

(With Innaurato) *The Life Story of Mitzi Gaynor; or, Gyp,* first produced in New Haven, CT, 1973.

The Marriage of Betty and Boo (first produced in New Haven, CT, 1973; revised version produced in New York City, 1979), Dramatists Play Service, 1985.

(With Innaurato) *The Idiots Karamazov* (first produced in New Haven at Yale Repertory Theatre, October 10, 1974), Dramatists Play Service, 1980.

Titanic (also see below; first produced in New Haven, CT, 1974; produced Off-Broadway at Van Dam Theatre, May 10, 1976), Dramatists Play Service, 1983.

Death Comes to Us All, Mary Agnes, first produced in New Haven, CT, 1975.

When Dinah Shore Ruled the Earth, first produced in New Haven, CT, 1975.

(With Sigourney Weaver) *Das Lusitania Songspiel,* first produced Off-Broadway at Van Dam Theatre, May 10, 1976.

A History of the American Film (first produced in Hartford, CT, at Eugene O'Neill Playwrights Conference, summer, 1976; produced on Broadway at American National Theatre, March 30, 1978), Avon, 1978.

The Vietnamization of New Jersey (first produced in New Haven, CT, at Yale Repertory Theatre, October 1, 1976), Dramatists Play Service, 1978.

Sister Mary Ignatius Explains It All for You (first produced in New York at Ensemble Studio Theatre, December, 1979), Dramatists Play Service, 1980.

The Nature and Purpose of the Universe, Death Comes to Us All, Mary Agnes, 'dentity Crisis: Three Short Plays, Dramatists Play Service, 1979.

Beyond Therapy (first produced Off-Broadway at Phoenix Theatre, January 5, 1981), Samuel French, 1983.

The Actor's Nightmare (first produced in New York at Playwrights Horizons, October 21, 1981), Dramatists Play Service, 1982.

Christopher Durang Explains It All for You (contains *The Nature and Purpose of the Universe, 'dentity Crisis, Titanic, The Actor's Nightmare, Sister Mary Ignatius Explains It All for You* and *Beyond Therapy*), Avon, 1982.

Baby with the Bathwater (first produced in Cambridge, MA, 1983; produced in New York City, 1983), Dramatists Play Service, 1984.

Sloth, first produced in Princeton, NJ, 1985.

Laughing Wild, first produced in New York City, 1987.

Cardinal O'Connor [and] *Woman Stand-up,* first produced as part of musical revue *Urban Blight,* New York City, 1988.

Chris Durang & Dawne (cabaret), first produced in New York City, 1990.

Naomi in the Living Room, first produced in New York City, 1991.

Media Amok, first produced in Boston, 1992.

Putting It Together, first produced in New York City, 1993.

For Whom the Southern Belle Tolls, first produced in New York City, 1994.

Durang Durang (six short plays, including *For Whom the Southern Belle Tolls* and *A Stye in the Eye*), first produced in New York City, 1994.

Also author, with Robert Altman, of screenplay *Beyond Therapy,* 1987. Writer for television series *Comedy Zone* and for *Carol Burnett Special.* Lyricist of songs for plays.

SIDELIGHTS: Early in Christopher Durang's career, a *New York Times* reviewer included him in the constellation of "new American playwrights," dramatists such as Michael Cristofer, Albert Innaurato, David Mamet, and Sam Shepard who follow in the footsteps of Tennessee Williams, Arthur Miller, and Edward Albee. Writers like Durang, the reviewer claimed, "are not one-play writers—a home run and back to the dugout—but artists with staying power and growing bodies of work."

"Christopher Durang has the wit, the high, rebellious spirits, and the rage of the born satirist," remarks the *New Yorker's* Edith Oliver. "He is also one of the funniest, most original playwrights at work." Focusing on social conventions and morality, Durang parodies American life. He mimics the most average situation and carries it to the extreme. His characters dare to say whatever they think or do whatever they feel, which often results in children snapping at their parents or maids overseeing the heads of households.

Stylistically, Durang specializes in collegiate humor. He deals in cartoons and stereotypes, employing mechanical dialogue and brand names to exploit cliches. In one play, for instance, a character feels compelled to make small talk with a pharmacist, so he asks, "What's in Tylenol?" "The characteristic of [Durang's] humor," Richard Eder explains, "is that it does not step back for comic perspective. It does not really see its target. It leaps onto it, instead, engages it totally, and burrows its head into it as if it were a mock target; much in the same way that a mother is a mock target for a not terribly naughty child."

Thus far, Durang has parodied drama, literature, movies, families, the Catholic church, show business, and society. But his lampoons are not vicious or hostile; they are controlled comedies. He "is a parodist without venom," Antonio Chemasi writes in *Horizon* magazine. "At the moment he fixes his pen on a target, he also falls in love with it. His work brims with an unlikely mix of acerbity and affection and at its best spills into a compassionate criticism of life."

Durang's first target as a professional playwright was literature. In 1974 the Yale Repertory Theatre produced *The Idiots Karamazov,* a satire of Dostoyevsky's *The Brothers Karamazov.* The play, featuring Durang in a leading role, was applauded by critics for its "moments of comic inspiration." "I was . . . impressed—with their [Durang's and his co-author Albert Innaurato's] wit as well as their scholarship," Mel Gussow states in the *New York Times.* The playwright followed *The Idiots Karamazov* with *Das Lusitania Songspiel,* a musical travesty that met with critical and popular success. "From the evidence presented [in *Das Lusitania Songspiel*]," writes Oliver, "Mr. Durang is a spirited, original fellow . . . , who brings back to the theatre a welcome impudence and irreverence."

Durang's major success of the seventies was *A History of the American Film,* for which he was nominated for a Tony Award in 1978. A tribute to movie mania, the play illustrates America's perceptions of Hollywood from 1930 to the present. *A History of the American Film* parodies some two hundred motion pictures and chronicles the evolution of movie stereotypes in American culture. There are five characters: a tough gangster typified by James Cagney, an innocent Loretta Young type, a sincere guy, a temptress, and a girl who never gets the man of her dreams. The production parodies movies such as *The Grapes of Wrath, Citizen Kane,* and *Casablanca.* Show girls dressed up like vegetables satirize the razzmatazz of big Hollywood productions by singing "We're in a Salad." And the character portraying Paul Henreid's role in *Now, Voyager* is forced to smoke two cigarettes when Bette Davis's character refuses one because she does not smoke. "In Durang's hands," writes *Time's* Gerald Clarke, "the familiar images always take an unexpected turn, however,

and he proves that there is nothing so funny as a cliche of a different color."

The play's production utilizes a number of innovative techniques. Actors sit in movie theater seats facing the audience. Sometimes they play the roles of the movies' stars; for other scenes they make up part of the audience. When *A History of the American Film* parodies older movies, the stage, sets, and props are black, white, and gray, a clever simulation of black-and-white movies. To Eder, the production is "a circus car driven by clowns, powered by soap bubbles and fitted out with bepers [sic] and exploding wheels . . . [that] wobbles and squeals through 60 years of American movies." The play, notes Chemasi, is "a chronicle so preposterous yet scholarly that the Marx Brothers and a diligent film historian might have collaborated on it."

According to Chemasi, Durang's play is "a history of ourselves and how large a role the movies have played in that history." Inspired by a 1932 Depression romance, *A Man's Castle,* starring Spencer Tracy and Loretta Young, *A History of the American Film* proved to Chemasi that Americans look at themselves when they watch movies. "I thought I would write my own hobo shantytown romance," Durang explains, "and it began to spin off into satire. I suddenly realized the character called Loretta could also be the girl in the Busby Berkeley movie who goes on when the star breaks her leg. Then I realized she could be everyone."

After the success of *A History of the American Film,* Durang wrote two satires of suburban families, *The Vietnamization of New Jersey* and *The Nature and Purpose of the Universe,* as well as a parody of the Catholic church. Called a "savage cartoon" by Mel Gussow and a "clever and deeply felt work" by Frank Rich, *Sister Mary Ignatius Explains It All for You* uses the character of an elderly nun to expose the hypocrisies of Catholicism. The nun, Gussow writes, is "a self-mocking sister [who] flips pictures of hell, purgatory and heaven as if they are stops on a religious package tour." Her list of the damned includes David Bowie, Betty Comden, and Adolph Green, and she lists hijacking planes alongside murder as a mortal sin. "Anyone can write an angry play—all it takes is an active spleen," observes Rich. "But only a writer of real talent can write an angry play that remains funny and controlled even in its most savage moments. *Sister Mary Ignatius Explains It All for You* confirms that Christopher Durang is just such a writer."

In October, 1981, the Obie-winning *Sister Mary Ignatius* was presented on the same playbill as *The Actor's Nightmare,* a satire of show business and the theater. Using the play-within-a-play technique for *The Actor's Nightmare,* Durang illustrates the comedy which ensues when an actor is forced to appear in a production he has never rehearsed. Earlier in 1981, the Phoenix Theatre produced Durang's *Beyond Therapy*, a parody in which a traditional woman, Prudence, and a bisexual man, Bruce, meet through a personal ad, only to have their relationship confounded by their psychiatrists. Hers is a lecherous, he-man Freudian; his is an absent-minded comforter. "Some of Durang's satire . . . is sidesplitting," comments a *New York* reviewer, "and there are many magisterial digs at our general mores, amores, and immores."

A writer heaped with honors early in his career may begin to feel the weight of the mantle later on. Recent criticism of Durang's work has been mixed. In a review in the *Daily News*, Douglas Watt turns a cold eye on Durang's 1983 drama, *Baby with the Bathwater:* "[Durang] continues to write like a fiendishly clever undergrad with some fresh slants but an inability to make them coalesce into a fully sustained evening of theater." Rich, writing in the *New York Times*, admits a note of irritation: "We can't ignore that Act I of *Baby with the Bathwater* is a strained variation on past Durang riffs. We're so inured by now to this writer's angry view of parental authority figures that at intermission we feel like shaking him and shouting: 'Enough already! Move on!' " Rich concludes: "The author's compulsive gag-making might also be in tighter control. . . . Some of the punchlines are indeed priceless, but not all of them are germane." John Simon sounds a similar theme in his review in *New York Magazine:* "Christopher Durang is such a funny fellow that his plays cannot help being funny; now, if they could only help being so undisciplined." Simon sums up: "Free-floating satire and rampant absurdism are all very well, but even the wildest play must let its characters grow in wildness and match up mouth with jokes." In a review in the *Nation*, Eliot Sirkin finds that Durang "is, at heart, a writer who divides humanity into the humiliators and the humiliated." Sirkin compares Durang's methods to those of Tennessee Williams: "When Williams created an overwhelming woman, he didn't create a psychopathic fiend—at least not always. . . . Durang's witches are *just* witches."

Durang's next play *The Marriage of Bette and Boo* draws from the playwright's own childhood. In his review for the *New York Post*, Clive Barnes summarizes the characters: "The father was a drunk, the mother rendered an emotional cripple largely by her tragic succession of stillborn children, the grandparents were certifiably nutty, the family background stained with the oppression of the Roman Catholic Church, and the son himself is primarily absorbed in a scholarly enquiry into the novels of Thomas Hardy. Just plain folks!" Rich, writing in the *New York Times*, finds that "*Bette and Boo* is sporadically funny and has been conceived with a structural inventiveness new to the writer's work. . . . But at the same time, Mr. Du-

rang's jokemaking is becoming more mannered and repetitive. . . . *Bette and Boo* has a strangely airless atmosphere." Simon writes in *New York Magazine:* "Christopher Durang's latest, *The Marriage of Bette and Boo*, is more recycling than writing. Here again, the quasi-autobiographical boy-hero growing up absurd."

In a 1990 *Chicago Tribune* interview with Richard Christiansen, Durang revealed that he felt "burned out on New York, and that includes its theater." For a time Durang left the theater to tour with a one-hour cabaret act, *Chris Durang & Dawne*. Durang explained his "premise" to Christiansen: "I was fed up with being a playwright and had decided to form my own lounge act with two back-up singers and go on a tour of Ramada Inns across the country." Parodying the typical lounge act, Durang's show featured a rap version of "Surrey with a Fringe on Top," a dramatic rendering of *Man of La Mancha*'s song "Aldonza," and deliberately bad adaptations of standard rock classics. The show was, ironically, a success.

In 1992 Durang returned to the theater with *Media Amok*, a lampoon of the characters and obsessions of television talk-shows. Noting its content, Durang told Kevin Kelly of the *Boston Globe* that he had become "more political." The play features an elderly couple watching television talk shows which assault them constantly with the same three topics: abortion, gay rights, and racial tension. All of the topics are handled in a flippant and inflamatory fashion.

In 1994 *Durang Durang*, a series of six sketches taking swipes at fellow playwrights Tennessee Williams, Sam Shepard and David Mamet, debuted in New York City. One section, the one-act play entitled *For Whom the Southern Belle Tolls*, is a parody of *The Glass Menagerie*, while *A Stye in the Eye* focuses on Shepard's typical cowboy characters. In a *New Yorker* review, Nancy Franklin calls the play "Beckett with a joy buzzer." She concludes: "Sitting through *Durang Durang* is a little like going on the bumper cars at an amusement park: you're so caught up in the exhilarating hysteria that it doesn't matter to you that you're not actually going anywhere except—momentarily, blissfully—outside yourself." In a *New York Times* review, Ben Brantley finds *Durang Durang* "endearing and exasperating . . . juvenile and predictable." Reviewing *Durang Durang* for the *Los Angeles Times*, Laurie Winer sees the play as an embodiment of Durang's current stature as a playwright: "There's Durang the sharp-tongued, ostensibly confused observer of his time, and Durang the very bright Harvard student who needs to move once and for all beyond college parody, perhaps beyond being the consummate outsider. He has created a play in which for a moment you can hear that voice, but not for long enough."

BIOGRAPHICAL/CRITICAL SOURCES:

BOOKS

American Theatre Annual, 1978-1979, Gale, 1980.
American Theatre Annual, 1979-1980, Gale, 1981.
Contemporary Literary Criticism, Gale, Volume
     27, 1984, Volume 38, 1986.
New York Theatre Annual, Volume 2, Gale, 1978.

PERIODICALS

Atlanta Constitution, March 18, 1994, p. P17.
Boston Globe, March 22, 1992, p. B25.
Chicago Tribune, January 21, 1990.
Daily News (New York), March 31, 1978; November 9,
     1983.
Entertainment Weekly, April 16, 1993, p. 31.
Horizon, March, 1978.
Los Angeles Times, August 11, 1989, p. 8; November 25,
     1994, p. 1.
Nation, April 15, 1978; February 18, 1984, pp. 202-204.
New Republic, April 22, 1978.
Newsweek, April 10, 1978.
New York, April 17, 1978; January 19, 1981; October 23,
     1989, p. 166; November 28, 1994, p. 76.
New Yorker, May 24, 1976; April 10, 1978; January 19,
     1981; November 28, 1994, pp. 153-155.
New York Magazine, November 21, 1983, pp. 65-68; June
     3, 1985, pp. 83-84.
New York Post, March 31, 1978; November 9, 1983; De-
     cember 12, 1983, p. 80; May 17, 1985, pp. 268-269.
New York Times, November 11, 1974; February 13, 1977;
     March 17, 1977; May 11, 1977; August 21, 1977; June
     23, 1978; December 27, 1978; February 24, 1979; De-
     cember 21, 1979; February 8, 1980; August 6, 1980;
     January 6, 1981; October 22, 1981; November 9,
     1983, p. C21; May 17, 1985, p. 3; June 27, 1994, p.
     C13; November 14, 1994, p. 11.
Saturday Review, May 27, 1978.
Time, May 23, 1977.
USA Today, May 17, 1985.
Variety, November 14, 1994, p. 54.
Washington Post, December 11, 1994, p. 4.
Women's Wear Daily, May 20, 1985.
World Literature Today, summer, 1991, p. 487.

*   *   *

DURAS, Marguerite 1914-

PERSONAL: Original name Marguerite Donnadieu; born
April 4, 1914, Giadinh, Indochina (now Vietnam); daughter of Henri (a mathematics teacher) and Marie (Legrand)
Donnadieu; divorced; children: one son. *Education:* Graduated from Lycee de Saigon; University of Paris, Sorbonne, licences in law and political science; also studied
mathematics.

ADDRESSES: Home—5 rue Saint-Benoit, Paris 75006,
France.

CAREER: Novelist, screenwriter, and playwright. Emi-
grated from Indochina to Paris at age seventeen; secretary
at French Ministry of Colonies, Paris, 1935-41.

AWARDS, HONORS: Prix Ibsen, 1970, for her play,
L'Amante anglaise; Goncourt Prize, 1984, for novel
L'Amant; Ritz Paris Hemingway Prize, 1985, for
L'Amant; Prix Jean Cocteau; Grand Prix Academie du
Cinema.

WRITINGS:

FICTION

Les Impudents, Plon (Paris), 1943.
La Vie tranquille, Gallimard (Paris), 1944.
Un Barrage contre le Pacifique, Gallimard, 1950, transla-
     tion by Herma Briffault published as *The Sea Wall,*
     Pellegrini & Cudahy (London), 1952, same transla-
     tion published with a preface by Germaine Bree, Far-
     rar, Strauss (New York City), 1967, translation by
     Antonia White published as *A Sea of Troubles,* Meth-
     uen (New York City), 1953.
Le Marin de Gibraltar, Gallimard, 1952, translation by
     Barbara Bray published as *The Sailor from Gibraltar,*
     Grove (New York City), 1966.
Les Petits Chevaux de Tarquinia, Gallimard, 1953, trans-
     lation by Peter DuBerg published as *The Little Horses
     of Tarquinia,* J. Calder (London), 1960.
Des Journees entieres dans les arbres (short stories; title
     means "Whole Days in the Trees"), Gallimard, 1954.
Le Square, Gallimard, 1955, translation by Sonia Pitt-
     Rivers and Irina Morduch published as *The Square,*
     Grove, 1959, French language edition, published
     under original French title, edited by Claude Mor-
     hange Begue, Macmillan (New York City), 1965.
Moderato cantabile, Editions de Minuit (Paris), 1958,
     translation by Richard Seaver published as *Moderato
     Cantabile,* Grove, 1960, French language edition, ed-
     ited by Thomas Bishop, Prentice-Hall (Englewood
     Cliffs, NJ), 1968, another French language edition,
     edited by W. S. Strachan, Methuen, 1968, also pub-
     lished with supplemental material as *Moderato canta-
     bile* [suivi de] *L'Univers romanesque de Marguerite
     Duras,* Plon, 1962.
Dix heures et demie du soir en ete, Gallimard, 1960, trans-
     lation by Anne Borchardt published as *Ten-thirty on
     a Summer Night,* J. Calder, 1962, Grove, 1963.
L'Apres Midi de Monsieur Andesmas, Gallimard, 1962,
     translation by Borchardt published together with
     Bray's translation of *Les Eaux et forets* (play; also see

below) as *The Afternoon of Monsieur Andesmas* [and] *The Rivers and Forests*, J. Calder, 1965.

Le Ravissement de Lol V. Stein, Gallimard, 1964, translation by Seaver published as *The Ravishing of Lol Stein*, Grove, 1966, translation by Eileen Ellenbogen published as *The Rapture of Lol V. Stein*, Hamish Hamilton (London), 1967.

Four Novels (contains *The Square, Moderato Cantabile, Ten-thirty on a Summer Night*, and *The Afternoon of Monsieur Andesmas*), translations by Pitt-Rivers and others, introduction by Bree, Grove, 1965.

Le Vice-consul, Gallimard, 1966, translation by Ellenbogen published as *The Vice-consul*, Hamish Hamilton, 1968.

L'Amante anglaise, Gallimard, 1967, translation by Bray published as *L'Amante Anglaise*, Grove, 1968.

Detruire, ditelle, Editions de Minuit, 1969, translation by Bray published as *Destroy, She Said*, Grove, 1970.

Abahn, Sabana, David, Gallimard, 1970.

L'Amour, Gallimard, 1971.

India Song: Texte-theatre-film, Gallimard, 1973, translation by Bray published as *India Song*, Grove, 1976.

(With Xaviere Gauthier) *Les Parleuses*, Editions de Minuit, 1974.

Suzanna Andler; La Musica & L'Amante anglaise, translation by Bray, J. Calder, 1975.

(With Jacques Lacan and Maurice Blanchot) *Etude sur l'oeuvre litteraire, theatrale, et cinematographique de Marguerite Duras* (nonfiction), Albatros (Paris), 1976.

Le Camion, suivi de Entretien avec Michelle Porte, Editions de Minuit, 1977.

Le Navire Night; Cesaree; Les Mains negatives; Aurelia Steiner, Mercure de France (Paris), 1979.

Vera Baxter ou Les Plages de l'Atlantique, Albatros, 1980.

L'Homme assis dans le couloir, Editions de Minuit, 1980, translation by Bray published as *The Man Sitting in the Corridor*, North Star Line, 1992.

L'Ete '80, Editions de Minuit, 1981.

Outside, Albin Michel (Paris), 1981, translation by Arthur Goldhammer published under title *Outside: Selected Writings*, Beacon Press (Boston), 1986.

L'Homme atlantique, Editions de Minuit, 1982.

La Maladie de la mort, Editions de Minuit, 1982, translation by Bray published as *The Malady of Death*, Grove, 1986.

Savannah Bay, Editions de Minuit, 1983.

L'Amant, Editions de Minuit, 1984, translation by Bray published as *The Lover*, Pantheon (New York City), 1985.

La Douleur, POL (Paris), 1985, translation by Bray published as *The War: A Memoir*, Pantheon, 1986.

La Mouette de Tchekhov, Gallimard, 1985.

Les Yeux bleus cheveux noirs, Editions de Minuit, 1986, translation by Bray published as *Blues Eyes, Black Hair*, Pantheon, 1988.

La Pute de la cote normande, Editions de Minuit, 1986.

Emily L., Editions de Minuit, 1987, translation by Bray published under same title, Pantheon, 1989.

Green Eyes, translation of the French novel *Yeux verts* by Carol Barko, Columbia University Press (New York City), 1990.

L'Amante de la Chine du Nord, Gallimard, 1991, translation by Leigh Hafrey published as *The North China Lover*, New Press (New York City), 1992.

Summer Rain, Scribner (New York City), 1992.

Yann Andrea Steiner, translation by Bray, Hodder & Stoughton (London), 1994.

PLAYS

Les Viaducs de la Seine-et-Oise (translation by Bray produced as *The Viaduct* in Guildford, England, at Yvonne Arnaud Theatre, February, 1967), Gallimard, 1960.

(With James Lord) *La Bete dans la jungle* (adaptation of *The Beast in the Jungle* by Henry James), produced, 1962.

Theatre I (contains *Les Eaux et forets, Le Square*, and *La Musica; La Musica* produced as *The Music* Off-Off-Broadway at West Side Actors Workshop and Repertory, March, 1967), Gallimard, 1965.

Three Plays, translation by Bray and Sonia Orwell (contains *The Square, Days in the Trees*, and *The Viaducts of Seine-et-Oise; Days in the Trees* produced in Paris at Theatre de France, and on BBC-Television *Wednesday Play*, 1967), Calder & Boyars, 1967.

Theatre II (contains *Suzanna Andler, Des Journees entieres dan les arbres, Yes, peut-etre, Le Shaga*, and *Un Homme est venue me voir; Suzanna Andler* first produced in Paris at Theatre Mathurins, December, 1969; translation by Bray produced on the West End at Aldwych Theatre, March 7, 1973), Gallimard, 1968.

L'Amante anglaise (based on the novel), produced in Paris at Theatre National Populaire, December, 1969, produced in French as *L'Amante Anglaise* on the West End at Royal Court Theatre, 1969, produced in French Off-Broadway at Barbizon-Plaza Theatre, April 14, 1971, translation by Bray first produced as *A Place without Doors* in New Haven, CT, at Long Wharf Theatre, November 21, 1970, produced Off-Broadway at Stairway Theatre, December 22, 1970, same translation produced as *Lovers of Viorne* on the West End at Royal Court Theatre, July 6, 1971.

La Danse de mort, produced in Paris, 1970.

Ah! Ernesto, F. Ruy-Vidal (Paris), 1971.

India Song (also see below), Gallimard, 1973, translation by Bray published under same title, Grove, 1976.

L'Eden cinema (produced in Paris, 1977), Mercure de France, 1977.

Agatha, Editions de Minuit, 1981, translation by Howard Limoli published as *Agatha* [and] *Savannah Bay: 2 Plays,* Post-Apollo Press (Sausalito, CA), 1992.

La Musica deuxieme (produced in Paris, 1985), Gallimard, 1985.

SCREENPLAYS

Hiroshima, mon amour: Scenario et dialogues (based on the novel by Alain Resnais; film produced in 1959), Gallimard, 1960, translation by Seaver published as *Hiroshima, mon amour: Text by Marguerite Duras for the Film by Alain Resnais,* Grove, 1961.

(With Gerard Jarlot) *Une Aussi longue absence* (based on the novel by Henri Colpi), Gallimard, 1961, translation by Wright published under original French title together with above translation as *Hiroshima, mon amour* [and] *Une Aussi longue absence* (movie scripts), Calder & Boyars, 1966.

Moderato cantabile (based on the novel), Royal Films International, 1964.

(With Jules Dassin) *Ten-thirty p.m. Summer* (film version of her novel, *Ten-thirty on a Summer Night*), Lopert, 1966.

Detruire, dit-elle (based on the novel), Ancinex/ Madeleine Films, 1970.

La Musica (based on the play), United Artists, 1970.

Nathalie Granger (film produced by Monelet & Co., 1972), published in *Nathalie Granger* [suive de] *La Femme du Gange,* Gallimard, 1973.

Also author of screenplays *Jaune le soleil,* 1971, *India Song,* 1975, *Baxter, Vera Baxter,* 1975, *Son Nom de Venise dans Calcutta desert,* 1976, *Des Journees entieres dans les arbres,* 1976, *Le Camion,* 1977, *Le Navire Night,* 1978, *Cesaree,* 1979, *Les Mains negatives,* 1979, *Aurelia Steiner, dite Aurelia Melbourne,* 1979, *Aurelia Steiner, dite Aurelia Vancouver,* 1979, *Agatha et les lectures illimitees,* 1981, *L'Homme atlantique,* 1981, *Dialogue de Rome,* 1981, and *Les Enfants,* 1985.

OTHER

(With Michelle Porte) *Les Lieux de Marguerite Duras* (interview), Editions de Minuit, 1977.

La Vie materielle, POL, 1987.

Practicalities: Marguerite Duras Speaks to Jerome Beaujour, Grove, 1990.

La pluie d'ete, POL, 1990.

Le Monde Exterieur, POL, 1993.

Ecrire, Gallimard, 1994.

Contributor to *Vogue.*

ADAPTATIONS: Un Barrage contre le Pacifique was filmed as *The Sea Wall* by Columbia Pictures, 1958, and was also translated and adapted by Sofka Skipworth as *A Dam against an Ocean,* for British Broadcasting Corp. (BBC), 1962; *The Sailor from Gibraltar* was filmed by Lopert, 1967; *L'Amant* was filmed as *The Lover* and released by Metro-Goldwyn-Mayer, 1992.

SIDELIGHTS: Marguerite Duras has written novels, films and plays for over four decades, often drawing upon the details of her own life to fashion her fictional narratives. "Her main raw material," writes Alan Riding in the *New York Times,* "is of course herself, an extraordinary life cut like cord into sections and variously displayed in her books as elegant bows or tight knots." Carol J. Murphy, in her article for the *Dictionary of Literary Biography,* explains that Duras "has evolved what might be called a core story of passionate love and desire undercut with death. Successive texts echo or decant the story in an increasingly fragmented, lyrical style which has come to characterize Duras's poetic prose."

Duras was born in the French colony of Indochina (now the country of Vietnam) where her parents had moved to teach school. Following the death of her father when Duras was four years old, her mother spent the family's savings on a rice plantation, hoping the venture would prove viable enough to support her and her three young children. Unfortunately, the colonial officials who sold her the plantation were dishonest, the land was virtually worthless because of recurring flooding from the sea, and Duras's mother found herself broke and trying to raise her family far from home. The family's many troubles in Indochina form the backdrop for many of Duras's novels.

In 1932 Duras left Indochina to attend school in France. During World War II she was a member of the French Resistance movement working against the Nazi occupiers. She later joined the Communist Party, only to be dismissed in 1950 along with a number of other French intellectuals for ideological differences. Her continuing involvement with leftist political causes led to trouble with American officials over a travel visa in 1969. Duras, wishing to attend a New York Film Festival showing of her *Detruire, dit-elle,* had to prove to officials her adherence to anti-communist principles. Duras was also an apologist for the student uprisings in Paris in 1968 and a supporter of French president Mitterand during the 1980s.

Although Duras first began writing during World War II, her first book to earn critical attention was 1950's *Un Barrage contre le Pacifique,* translated as *The Sea Wall.* Largely autobiographical, the novel revolves around her mother's failed efforts to save her rice plantation from destruction by building a sea wall to protect the crops from flooding. Within this framework are told the stories of

Duras's unwelcome courtship by the son of a local Chinese planter and her brother's succumbing to a life of indolence. "Straightforward, chronologically ordered, and easy to read, *The Sea Wall* fits within the conventions of the nineteenth-century novel," writes Judith Graves Miller in *Theatre Journal*. "Indeed, of Duras's . . . novels, it is the most traditional." The story first told in *The Sea Wall* was to be retold in several later Duras's works.

In *Le Marin de Gibraltar,* translated as *The Sailor from Gibraltar,* Duras first turned from realistic fiction to a more symbolic representation of experience. The sailor of the novel, searched for by the character Anna and the male narrator, undergoes a series of transformations and becomes a criminal, a lover, and a folk hero in turn. Every clue followed by Anna and the narrator results in fresh stories about the sailor's possible identity until it is clear that there is no sailor at all, only Anna in search of him and the narrator chronicling the search. In *Le Marin,* Marilyn R. Schuster writes in the *French Review,* "Duras dismantles conventional character and demonstrates that it is through its absence that the female subject's story can begin to be articulated."

Duras's novels of the 1950s experiment with some of the techniques of the French *nouveau roman,* or antinovel, school. In *Le square,* translated as *The Square,* she presents a pared-down narrative in which dialogue comprises virtually the entire book; plot is minimal, and the characters—through their conversation—come to share a sense of isolation and longing. Similarly, the 1958 novel *Moderato cantabile* is composed of a series of conversations between Anne, the wife of a wealthy businessman, and Chauvin, a man who works for her husband, in which they speculate as to the truth about the murder they have both witnessed.

In 1959 Duras was invited by film director Alain Resnais to write the screenplay *Hiroshima, mon amour.* The story of a French actress working in Tokyo whose affair with a Japanese architect calls to mind her disastrous wartime affair with a Nazi officer, *Hiroshima, mon amour* was a worldwide success. Leslie Hill, writing in *Paragraph: The Journal of the Modern Critical Theory Group,* finds that in the film "private disaster is echoed, outstripped, overwhelmed, effaced by public catastrophe. . . . Like the comparison of the bombing of Hiroshima with a casual affair . . . , the association is scandalous. But the scandal, by transgressing the limit of what is properly imaginable, bears witness: to the unimaginable catastrophe of war and of representation." As Joanne Schmidt notes in *Belles Lettres,* however, "even after [Duras] wrote the screenplay for a film that became a landmark in world cinema, her reputation remained marginal."

The screenwriting experience nonetheless shaped Duras's novels of the 1960s and later, adding cinematic techniques to her narrative. James P. Frakes describes the cinematic elements of Duras's fiction to be "not only visual (dynamic lighting effects, slow dissolves, juxtaposition of startling images, rapid cuts) but aural. The murmur of voices is brilliantly counterpoised in each novel [with sounds of the larger world to create] a masterfully orchestrated sound track."

In the Goncourt Prize-winning novel *L'Amant,* translated as *The Lover,* Duras returned to the autobiographical terrain first covered in *The Sea Wall,* this time focusing her attention on the love affair between the young woman character and the wealthy Chinese planter. Because of the thirty-year difference between publication of the two books, many of the family members Duras had fictionalized in *The Sea Wall* were dead by the time she wrote *The Lover,* allowing her to deal with some aspects of the story she had not attempted earlier. As Duras explains in the second novel: "I've written a good deal about the members of my family, but then they were still alive, my mother and my brothers. And I skirted around them, skirted around all these things without really touching them."

In *The Lover* Duras writes from the perspective of a sixty-year-old woman recalling her first sexual experience. Because of its focus on the memory of past events rather than on the events themselves, the novel sets the past into an emotional context apart from a strict chronological recounting. This technique gives the story what several critics see as a powerful intensity. Eva Hoffman, writing in the *New York Times,* finds *The Lover* to display a "compressed intensity" which combines "the seemingly irreconcilable perspectives of confession and objectivity, of lyrical poetry and nouveau roman." Similarly, Miranda Seymour in her review of the novel for *Spectator* remarks that "in a little more than a hundred pages, [Duras] creates a world more charged with passion, despair and hatred than most of us are likely to encounter in a lifetime" and further compliments the book's "hypnotically beautiful images and unswerving emotional frankness." Writing in the *New York Times Book Review,* Diane Johnson finds that *The Lover* contains "an unremitting intensity, an effect on some subliminal reserve of emotion in the reader that one might suspect or resist if the passion and sincerity of the author were for a moment in doubt."

Duras returned again to the autobiographical material covered in *The Sea Wall* and *The Lover* in the 1991 novel *L'Amant de la Chine du Nord,* translated as *The North China Lover.* This novel began as a series of notes Duras wrote while working on a screenplay version of *The Lover.* These notes, exploring ideas left untouched in the earlier novel, retell the story of a young woman and her older Chinese lover in a manner that combines cinematic techniques with the *nouveau roman.* As Elaine Romaine writes in *Belles Lettres,* the novel "contains wide spaces between short paragraphs, directions for a camera, and even chapters devoted to single line images." Although *The North China Lover* retells the story found in earlier Duras novels, its emphasis on "the sexual attraction all the characters share for one another" is its own, as David Plante writes in the *New York Times Book Review.* Ultimately, the novel "sends a strange thrill through you," Plante believes. "How Marguerite Duras manages to make that happen is amazing."

In *The War: A Memoir* Duras collects six narratives of her World War II experiences with the French Resistance. Two of these narratives are fiction; the other four are autobiography. Writing in the *New York Times Book Review,* Francine du Plessix Gray finds the book's title chapter, an account of Duras's husband being rescued from a concentration camp and nursed back to health, to be "the most powerful text I have read about that period. . . . It is equally sublime as a literary work and as an act of witness." Speaking of the same text, Maria Margaronis in the *Nation* praises how the story is "splintered into tiny, sharp sentences, pointing every which way, fixed painfully in the claustrophobic space of waiting." According to Frederick J. Harris in *America,* the story is a "very powerful and often beautiful and touching memoir."

Duras draws inspiration from a more recent period in her life in the novel *Yann Andrea Steiner,* transforming her real-life partner Yann Andrea into a fictional character. Centering on the couple's initial meeting twelve years earlier, the primary narrative is contrasted with the story of a young boy and girl whose family histories share the tragedy of French deportation of Jews during World War II. While James Woodall, writing in the *Guardian Weekly,* judges the novel to be "touching, certainly, but oblique almost to the point of opacity," Janet Barron in *New Statesman* finds more to praise. Calling *Yann Andrea Steiner* "a bleakly passionate novella and, at times, a poem in prose," she describes it as an "evocation of history that looks with horror on stories too painful to be told."

Speaking of the relationship between her fiction and her life, Duras is quoted by Riding as explaining: "Even when my books are completely invented, even when I think they have come from elsewhere, they are always personal." Speaking of how a writer should approach his work, Duras states: "You shouldn't have a subject. You have to go into the forest; you shouldn't be afraid, and it comes, all alone; stories of love, of foolishness, they come on their own, as if you were walking like a blind man before they arrived." "The trajectory of Duras's fictional enterprise," Murphy concludes, "remains firmly entrenched in desire—the desire to know how to understand and express that which continually slips away from human under-

standing." Schmidt finds that "Duras is one of the most powerful and gifted French women writers of our time, with one of the richest and most fertile intellects."

BIOGRAPHICAL/CRITICAL SOURCES:

BOOKS

Alazet, Bernard, *Le navite night de Marguerite Duras: ecrite l'effacement,* Presses Universitaires de Lille (Lille, France), 1992.

Alleins, Madeleine, *Marguerite Duras: Medium de reel,* L'Age d'homme, (Lausanne, Switzerland), 1984.

Ames, Sanford S., editor, *Remains to Be Seen: Essays on Marguerite Duras,* Peter Lang (New York City), 1988.

Bajomee, Danielle, and Ralph Heyndels, editors, *Ecrire dit-elle: Imaginaires de Marguerite Duras,* Editions de l'Universite de Bruxelles (Brussels, Belgium), 1988.

Blanchot, Maurice, *The Sirens' Song: Selected Essays,* Indiana University Press (Bloomington), 1982, pp. 199-206.

Blanchot, *La Communaute inavouable,* Editions de Minuit (Paris), 1983, pp. 51-93.

Blot-Labarrere, Christiane, *Marguerite Duras,* Seuil (Paris), 1994.

Chapsal, Madeleine, *Quinze Ecrivains,* Rene Julliard, 1963.

Cismaru, Alfred, *Marguerite Duras,* Twayne (New York City), 1971.

Cohen, Susan D., *Women and Discourse in the Fiction of Marguerite Duras: Love, Legends, Language,* University of Massachusetts Press (Amherst), 1993.

Contemporary Literary Criticism, Gale (Detroit), Volume 3, 1975, Volume 6, 1976, Volume 20, 1982, Volume 34, 1985, Volume 40, 1986, Volume 68, 1991.

Cranston, Mechthild, editor, *In Language and in Love, Marguerite Duras: The Unspeakable: Essays for Marguerite Duras,* Scripta Humanistica (Potomac, MD), 1992.

Dictionary of Literary Biography, Volume 83: *French Novelists since 1960,* Gale, 1989, pp. 71-83.

Duras, Marguerite, *Four Novels,* introduction by Germaine Bree, Grove, 1965.

Duras, Marguerite, *The Lover,* Pantheon, 1985.

Gauthier, Xaviere, *Les Parleuses,* Editions de Minuit, 1974, translation by Katharine A. Jensen published as *Woman to Woman,* University of Nebraska Press (Lincoln), 1987.

Glassman, Deborah N., *Marguerite Duras: Fascinating Vision and Narrative Cure,* Fairleigh Dickinson University Press (Rutherford, NJ), 1991.

Guers-Villate, Yvonne, *Continuite/Discontinuite de l'ouevre durassienne,* Editions de l'Universite de Bruxelles, 1985.

Hill, Leslie, *Marguerite Duras: Apocalyptic Desires,* Routledge & Kegan Paul (London), 1994.

Hofmann, Carol, *Forgetting and Marguerite Duras,* University Press of Colorado (Niwot, CO), 1991.

Kaivola, Karen, *All Contraries Confounded: The Lyrical Fiction of Virginia Woolf, Djuna Barnes, and Marguerite Duras,* University of Iowa Press (Ames), 1991.

Lamy, Suzanne, and Andre Roy, *Marguerite Duras a Montreal,* Editions Spirale (Montreal), 1981.

Marini, Marcelle, *Territoires du feminin avec Marguerite Duras,* Editions de Minuit, 1977.

Montrelay, Michele, *L'Ombre et le nom sur la feminite,* Editions de Minuit, 1977.

Moore, Harry T., *Twentieth Century French Literature since World War II,* Southern Illinois University Press (Carbondale, IL), 1966.

Murphy, Carol J., *Alienation and Absence in the Novels of Marguerite Duras,* French Forum Monographs (Lexington, KY), 1982.

Peyre, Henri, *French Novelists of Today,* Oxford University Press (Oxford, England), 1967.

Pierrot, Jean, *Marguerite Duras,* Jose Corti (Paris), 1986.

Porte, Michelle, and Marguerite Duras, *Les Lieux de Marguerite Duras,* Editions de Minuit, 1977.

Schuster, Marilyn R., *Marguerite Duras Revisited,* Twayne, 1993.

Selous, Trista, *The Other Woman: Feminism and Femininity in the Work of Marguerite Duras,* Yale University Press (New Haven, CT), 1988.

Seylaz, Jean-Luc, *Les Romans de Marguerite Duras,* Minard (Paris), 1963.

Skoller, Eleanor Honig, *The In-Between of Writing: Experience and Experiment in Drabble, Duras, and Arendt,* University of Michigan Press (Ann Arbor), 1993.

Vircondelet, Alain, *Marguerite Duras ou le temps de detruire,* Seghers (Paris), 1972.

Willis, Sharon, *Marguerite Duras: Writing on the Body,* University of Illinois Press (Urbana), 1987.

PERIODICALS

Atlantic, September, 1970.

Belles Lettres, winter, 1989, pp. 12-13; spring, 1993, p. 9.

Books Abroad, winter, 1967; spring, 1968; summer, 1969; spring, 1970.

Books and Bookmen, July, 1968.

Book World, November 10, 1968.

Cahiers de la Compaigne Madeleine Renaud-Jean-Louis Barrault, December, 1965; October, 1979; September, 1983.

Chicago Tribune, May 27, 1992.

Choice, October, 1970.

Christian Science Monitor, November 29, 1968; July 30, 1970.

College Literature, June, 1993, pp. 98-118; February, 1994, pp. 46-62.

Encounter, February, 1963.

L'Esprit Createur, spring, 1993, pp. 63-73.

Film Quarterly, summer, 1992, pp. 45-46.

French Review, October, 1984, pp. 48-57; October, 1992, pp. 77-88; December, 1993, p. 385.

Guardian Weekly, April 3, 1994, p. 29.

Harper's Bazaar, September, 1992, p. 374.

Hudson Review, autumn, 1967.

Illustrated London News, January 14, 1967; February 4, 1967.

Kenyon Review, January, 1967.

Le Monde, January 12, 1990, p. 24; June 28, 1991, p. 18.

Le Quotidien de Paris, October 13, 1987.

L'Express, March 27-April 2, 1967; March 31-April 6, 1969; June 16-22, 1969; November 23-29, 1970.

Listener, October 5, 1967.

London Magazine, May, 1967; October, 1968.

Los Angeles Times Book Review, October 16, 1987, p. 20; April 30, 1989, p. 9; January 12, 1992, p. 10; June 14, 1992, p. 6.

Mercure de France, June, 1958.

Nation, March 16, 1963; January 11, 1971; November 8, 1986, pp. 493-496.

New Leader, August 14, 1967; February 8, 1971.

New Republic, December 28, 1992, pp. 24-25.

New Statesman, January 20, 1967; April 7, 1967; September 29, 1967; May 3, 1968; July 14, 1970; July 16, 1971; January 12, 1990, p. 36; June 12, 1992, p. 40; January 28, 1994, pp. 70-71.

Newsweek, January 16, 1967; January 11, 1971.

New York, January 11, 1971; May 3, 1971.

New Yorker, November 8, 1968; July 14, 1986, p. 83.

New York Herald Tribune Book Review, February 7, 1960.

New York Times, March 15, 1953; September 14, 1969; August 23, 1970; January 3, 1971; September 7, 1972; June 10, 1985, p. C17; March 26, 1990, p. C11.

New York Times Book Review, November 8, 1959; February 19, 1967; July 2, 1967; November 17, 1968; June 23, 1985, pp. 1, 25; May 4, 1986, pp. 1, 48-49; July 13, 1986, p. 18; May 28, 1989, p. 18; May 20, 1990, p. 30; February 23, 1992, p. 12; December 27, 1992, p. 7.

New York Times Magazine, October 20, 1991, pp. 44-53.

Observer (London), February 26, 1967; September 24, 1967; May 5, 1968; October 13, 1968; September 6, 1970.

Paragraph: The Journal of the Modern Critical Theory Group, March, 1989, pp. 1-22.

Plays and Players, August, 1970; September, 1971; October, 1972.

PMLA, March, 1987, pp. 138-152.

Punch, January 11, 1967; November 6, 1968.

Revue des Sciences Humaines, April-June, 1986.

Saturday Review, November 23, 1968.

Signs: Journal of Women and Culture in Society, winter, 1975, pp. 423-434.

Spectator, January 4, 1986, p. 29.

Stage, June 17, 1971; July 15, 1971; October 21, 1971; January 27, 1972.

Theatre Arts, November, 1963.

Theatre Journal; December, 1981, pp. 431-452.

Time, July 7, 1967; November 1, 1968; December 14, 1970.

Times Literary Supplement, January 19, 1967; June 22, 1967; October 5, 1967; May 30, 1968; September 25, 1970; October 30, 1970; March 9, 1990, p. 248; June 26, 1992, p. 22; February 25, 1994, p. 24.

Variety, October 1, 1969; October 8, 1969; December 9, 1970; December 16, 1970; January 13, 1971; April 12, 1971; April 14, 1971; July 21, 1971; August 25, 1971; September 6, 1972; March 28, 1973.

Village Voice, March 16, 1967; July 15, 1986, pp. 47, 50.

Women's Review of Books, October, 1990, pp. 19-20.

World Literature Today, summer, 1988, pp. 436-437.

Yale French Studies, summer, 1959.*

E

EKINS, Paul (Whitfield) 1950-

PERSONAL: Surname is pronounced "*Ee*-kins"; born July 24, 1950, in Djakarta, Indonesia; British citizen born abroad; son of John Robert (a businessperson) and Lydia (a writer and homemaker; maiden name, Daukes) Ekins; married Susan Lofthouse (a singer), September 24, 1979; children: John Paul Whitfield. *Education:* Imperial College of Science and Technology, London, B.Sc., 1971; Birkbeck College, London, M.Sc. (Economics), 1988.

ADDRESSES: Home—42 Warriner Gardens, London SW11 48U, England. *Office*—Department of Economics, Birkbech College, 7-15 Gresse Street, London W1P 1PA, England.

CAREER: Kennington Technical College, London, teacher of mathematics, 1971-72; professional classical singer, 1973-79; Ecology party (now Green party), London, general secretary, 1979-82; Warminster Arts Centre, Wiltshire, England, director, 1982-83; Campaign for Fair Votes, London, field organizer, 1983-84; The Other Economic Summit (TOES), London, director, 1984-87; University of Bradford, Bradford, England, research fellow in peace studies and research director of Right Livelihood Award, 1987-90; Birkbech College, London, research fellow, department of economics, 1990—. Cochairperson of council of Green party, 1984-85; member of New Economics Foundation; public speaker; guest on television and radio programs.

AWARDS, HONORS: Global 500 Award, UN Environment Program, 1994, for outstanding environmental achievement.

WRITINGS:

(Editor) *The Living Economy: A New Economics in the Making,* Routledge & Kegan Paul (London), 1986.

(Editor) *Real Life Economics: Understanding Wealth Creation,* Routledge & Kegan Paul, 1992.
A New World Order, Routledge & Kegan Paul, 1992.
The Gaia Atlas of Green Economics, Anchor/Doubleday (New York City), 1992.

Author of ecology and economy pamphlets. Contributor to magazines, including *Ecological Economics, Environmental Ed., Resource Economics, Resurgence,* and *Science and Public Policy.*

WORK IN PROGRESS: Research on all aspects of the relationship between economic growth and environmental sustainability.

SIDELIGHTS: Paul Ekins once told *CA:* "It has been clear to me since 1979 that humanity is in trouble. Our international relations are in trouble as we continue to rely on war and weapons as problem-solvers in an age of mass destruction and potential apocalypse; our social relations are in trouble as greed, materialism, and consumerism relentlessly drive out other human values; our ecological relations are in trouble as industrialism and population growth destroy apace the biosphere on which humankind depends.

"My writing and other activity spring from the perception that the solutions to these dire problems are both economic and political: we need a new economics that goes beyond 'economic growth' and emphasizes ecologically-sound human growth in a stable society, and we need new political initiatives that turn the new imperative for ecological balance into workable and equitable policies that can command widespread support.

"*The Living Economy* was a step in this direction. Mark Satin of *New Options* called it 'the very best example of post-liberal, post-socialist economic thinking to have appeared in any forum or format.' I hope that my more recent work has managed to make further progress."

BIOGRAPHICAL/CRITICAL SOURCES:

PERIODICALS

Guardian (London), September 15, 1986.
Times (London), August 14, 1986.

* * *

ELLIS, Sarah 1952-

PERSONAL: Born May 19, 1952, in Vancouver, British Columbia, Canada; daughter of Joseph Walter (a clergyperson) and Ruth Elizabeth (a nurse; maiden name, Steabner) Ellis. *Education:* University of British Columbia, B.A., 1973, M.L.S., 1975; Simmons College, M.A., 1980.

ADDRESSES: Home—4432 Walden St., Vancouver, British Columbia, Canada V5V 3S3. *Office*—North Vancouver District Library, 1280 East 27th St., North Vancouver, British Columbia, Canada V7J 1S1.

CAREER: Vancouver Public Library, Vancouver, British Columbia, children's librarian, 1976-81; North Vancouver District Library, North Vancouver, British Columbia, children's librarian, 1981—. Lecturer at University of British Columbia.

MEMBER: Writers Union of Canada, Canadian Society of Children's Authors, Illustrators, and Performers, PEN, Women and Words Society.

WRITINGS:

FOR CHILDREN

The Baby Project, Groundwood Books (Vancouver), 1986.
Next-Door Neighbors, Groundwood Books, 1989.
Putting Up with Mitchell, Brighouse Press (Vancouver), 1989.
Pick-up Sticks, Groundwood Books, 1991.
Out of the Blue, Groundwood Books, 1994.

Author of "News From the North," a column on Canadian children's books in *Horn Book.*

WORK IN PROGRESS: A set of short stories for young adults.

SIDELIGHTS: Sarah Ellis once told *CA:* "As a librarian, critic, and storyteller, I had approached children's books from a variety of viewpoints before I decided to try my own hand at writing. I enjoy the challenge of trying to write simply and concretely, I like the emotional directness of children's books, and I am endlessly fascinated with the subject of the family. In *The Baby Project* I cre-

ated a slightly eccentric, happy family that has to live through a tragedy. The reader I had in mind was an eleven-year-old girl who, deaf to the admonishments of her mother to go outside in the fresh air, likes to lie on a musty-smelling camp cot at a summer cottage, read a book in one go, cry a bit, and feel great afterwards."

* * *

ELMSLIE, Kenward 1929-

PERSONAL: Born April 27, 1929, in New York, NY; son of William Gray (a speculator) and Constance (Pulitzer) Elmslie. *Education:* Harvard University, B.A., 1950. *Avocational interests:* Attending rehearsals of his work, cooking, weeding, walking, tennis, movies, reading newspapers, seeing friends.

ADDRESSES: Home—Poets Corner, Calais, VT.

CAREER: Writer. Composer/librettist panel member, National Endowment for the Arts, 1973-76. Publisher of Z Press.

MEMBER: American Society of Composers, Authors and Publishers (ASCAP).

AWARDS, HONORS: National Endowment for the Arts award, 1967, for poem "The Power Plant Sestina"; Frank O'Hara Award for poetry, 1971; librettist grant, National Endowment for the Arts, 1980.

WRITINGS:

The Orchid Stories (novel), Doubleday (New York City), 1973.
Bimbo Dirt, illustrations by Ken Tisa, Z Press (Calais, VT), 1982.
(With Tisa) *Palais Bimbo Snapshots* (postcard series), Alternative Press, 1982.
26 Bars (tales; also see below), illustrations by Donna Dennis, Z Press, 1987.

POETRY

Pavilions, Tibor de Nagy Editions, 1961.
The Baby Book, Boke Press, 1965.
Power Plant Poems, C Press, 1967.
The 1967 Gamebook Calendar, Boke Press, 1967.
The Champ, Black Sparrow Press (Santa Barbara, CA), 1968.
Album, Kulchur (New York City), 1969.
Girl Machine, Angel Hair, 1971.
Circus Nerves, Black Sparrow Press, 1971.
Motor Disturbance, Columbia University Press (New York City), 1971.
Tropicalism, Z Press, 1975.
Topiary Trek, Topia Press, 1977.
The Alphabet Work, Titanic Books, 1977.

Communications Equipment, Burning Deck (Providence, RI), 1979.

Moving Right Along, Z Press, 1980.

Sung Sex, Kulchur, 1990.

The Figures, Black Sparrow Press, 1994.

Bare Bones, Bamberger Books, 1995.

OPERA LIBRETTI

Miss Julie (music by Ned Rorem; produced by New York City Opera, 1965; also see below), Boosey & Hawkes (Oceanside, NY), 1965.

Lizzie Borden (music by Jack Beeson; produced by New York City Opera, 1965; also see below), Boosey & Hawkes, 1965.

The Sweet Bye and Bye (music by Beeson; produced by Juilliard Opera Co., 1956; also see below), Boosey & Hawkes, 1966.

The Seagull (music by Thomas Pasatieri; produced by Houston Grand Opera, 1973), Belwin-Mills, 1973.

Washington Square (music by Pasatieri; produced by Michigan Opera Theater, 1976), Belwin-Mills, 1977.

Three Sisters (also see below), music by Pasatieri, commissioned by the National Endowment for the Arts librettist program, 1980, produced by Opera Columbus, 1986.

PLAYS

The Grass Harp (musical; based on the novel by Truman Capote; produced on Broadway at the Martin Beck Theatre, 1971), Samuel French (New York City), 1972.

Lola (musical; also see below), first produced Off-Broadway by the York Theatre Company, April, 1982.

City Junket (produced Off-Broadway by the Eye and Ear Theatre, 1980), Bamberger Books, 1987.

Postcards on Parade, Bamberger Books, 1994.

RECORDINGS

Lizzie Borden (LP), Desto Records, 1967.

The Sweet Bye and Bye (LP), Desto Records, 1970.

The Grass Harp (LP), Painted Smiles, 1972.

Rare Meat (cassette), Watershed Tapes, 1979.

Highlights from 'Miss Julie' (LP), Painted Smiles, 1980.

Kenward Elmslie Visited (LP), Painted Smiles, 1982.

Palais Bimbo Lounge Show (LP), Painted Smiles, 1985.

Lola (LP), Painted Smiles, 1985.

Three Sisters (LP), Painted Smiles, 1986.

26 Bars (cassette), Z Press, 1987.

OTHER

Contributor to numerous anthologies, including *An Anthology of New York Poets,* edited by Ron Padgett and David Shapiro, Random House (New York City), 1970;

Angels of the Lyre, edited by Winston Leyland, Panjandrum (Los Angeles), 1975; *Homage to Frank O'Hara,* edited by Bill Berkson and Joe Lesueur, Creative Arts, 1980; *Epiphanies,* edited by George Myers Jr., Cumberland Press (Freeport, ME), 1987; *Out of This World: An Anthology, 1966-1991,* edited by Anne Waldman, Crown (New York), 1991; and *The Gertrude Stein Awards in Innovative American Poetry 1993-1994,* edited by Douglas Messerli, Sun & Moon (College Park, MD), 1995. Art critic, *Art News,* 1966-67. Editor, *Z Magazine.*

BIOGRAPHICAL/CRITICAL SOURCES:

BOOKS

Ashbery, John, editor, *Penguin Modern Poets 24: Kenward Elmslie, Kenneth Koch, James Schuyler* (anthology), Penguin Books (New York City), 1974.

Bamberger, William C., *Kenward Elmslie: A Bibliographical Profile,* Bamberger Books, 1993.

PERIODICALS

New York Times, April 27, 1980.

OTHER

Elmslie, Kenward, *Kenward Elmslie Visited* (LP recording), Painted Smiles, 1982.

*   *   *

EMERSON, Earl W. 1948-

PERSONAL: Born July 8, 1948, in Tacoma, WA; son of Ralph W. and June (Gadd) Emerson; married Sandra Evans, April 25, 1968; children: Sara, Brian, Jeffrey. *Education:* Attended Principia College, 1966-67, and University of Washington, Seattle, 1967-68.

ADDRESSES: Home—North Bend, WA. *Agent*—Dominick Abel, Dominick Abel Literary Agency Inc., 146 West 82nd St., Suite 1B, New York, NY 10024.

CAREER: Seattle Fire Department, Seattle, WA, lieutenant, 1978—. Guest of honor, Left Coast Crime Convention, 1992.

MEMBER: Mystery Writers of America, Private Eye Writers of America.

AWARDS, HONORS: Shamus Award, 1985, for *Poverty Bay.*

WRITINGS:

MYSTERY NOVELS

The Rainy City, Avon (New York City), 1985.

Poverty Bay, Avon, 1985.

Nervous Laughter, Avon, 1986.

Fat Tuesday, Morrow (New York City), 1987.

Black Hearts and Slow Dancing, Morrow, 1988.
Deviant Behavior, Morrow, 1988.
Help Wanted: Orphans Preferred, Morrow, 1990.
Yellow Dog Party, Morrow, 1991.
Morons and Madmen, Morrow, 1993.
The Portland Laugher, Ballantine (New York City), 1994.
The Vanishing Smile, Ballantine, 1995.*

*   *   *

EPSTEIN, Ann Wharton
See WHARTON, Annabel (Jane)

*   *   *

EPSTEIN, Joseph   1937-
(Aristides)

PERSONAL: Born January 9, 1937, in Chicago, IL; son of Maurice and Belle (Abrams) Epstein; married second wife, Barbara Maher (an editor), February 27, 1976; children: (first marriage) Mark, Burton. *Education:* University of Chicago, A.B., 1959. *Religion:* Jewish.

ADDRESSES: Office—Department of English, Northwestern University, 633 Clark St., Evanston, IL 60201; and *American Scholar,* 1811 Q St. NW, Washington, DC 20009.

CAREER: American Scholar, Washington, DC, editor, 1975—. Visiting lecturer in literature and writing at Northwestern University, 1974—. *Military service:* U.S. Army, 1958-60; served in United States.

AWARDS, HONORS: L.H.D., Adelphi University, 1988; Heartland Prize, *Chicago Tribune,* 1989, for *Partial Payments: Essays on Writers and Their Lives.*

WRITINGS:

Divorced in America: Marriage in an Age of Possibility, Dutton (New York City), 1974.
Familiar Territory: Observations on American Life (addresses, essays, lectures), Oxford University Press (Oxford, England), 1979.
Ambition: The Secret Passion, Dutton, 1980.
(Editor and author of introduction) *Masters: Portraits of Great Teachers,* Basic Books (New York City), 1981.
The Middle of My Tether: Familiar Essays, Norton (New York City), 1983.
Plausible Prejudices: Essays on American Writing, Norton, 1985.
Once More around the Block: Familiar Essays, Norton, 1987.
Partial Payments: Essays on Writers and Their Lives, Norton, 1989.

A Line out for a Walk: Familiar Essays, Norton, 1991.
The Goldin Boys: Stories, Norton, 1991.
Pertinent Players: Essays on the Literary Life, Norton, 1993.

Contributor, sometimes under the pseudonym Aristides, of numerous articles, essays, and book reviews to magazines and journals, including *American Scholar, Commentary, New Republic, Harper's, New Yorker, New York Times Magazine, New York Times Book Review, Current History, Writer, New Criterion,* and *Hudson Review.*

SIDELIGHTS: Deemed a "conglomerate man of letters" by Isa Kapp in *Washington Post Book World,* Joseph Epstein has been widely praised by critics for his learned essays on American life and letters. As editor of national honor society Phi Beta Kappa's quarterly journal, *American Scholar,* Epstein regularly contributes essays under the pseudonym Aristides. These and other Epstein essays have been collected in a series of books that span a variety of concerns, from the familiar to the erudite, including the author's conviction that language and literature in the United States are in decline. *Studies in Short Fiction* reviewer Rodney Stevens called Epstein "one of the few major critical voices of our time," applauding the author for bringing "wit, grace, and perception to the genre of critical letters."

A self-described "language snob," Epstein argued in *Commentary* that "the duty of everyone who considers himself educated is to keep language alive by using it with respect and precision," while observing that the current trend is toward a "preference for the vague over the particular." A visiting lecturer in English at Northwestern University, Epstein takes to task people who consider themselves educated, particularly the "well-scrubbed college-educated," as being those who are most guilty of misusing language. Citing several neologisms used by students and professionals alike, Epstein rails against the lapse in the standards of language use that allows clarity and correctness to be sacrificed for popular and political trends. Epstein is clear about what he feels are the effects of such inexactness: "The condition of language today is such that communication threatens to be clogged, perception clouded, the possibility for serious discourse lessened," he wrote in *Commentary.* Reality itself is threatened, asserts Epstein, by vague and abstract terms that obfuscate the meaning behind the words. In *American Scholar* he summarized the principles behind his own language use: "Take out all language that is pretentious and imprecise, under-educated and over-intellectualized. Question all language that says more than it means, that leaves the ground but doesn't really fly. Question authority only after you have first seriously consulted it; it isn't always as stupid as it looks. Never forget that today's hot new phrase becomes tomorrow's cold dead cliche."

Though Epstein rejects the idea that he is a critic, claiming that he doesn't have the "learning" to be counted in that class, he does see his self-appointed task as "trying to correct taste," according to Neil Baldwin in a *Publishers Weekly* interview. Epstein takes his job seriously because, he told Baldwin, "literature is important to me; if I read something I think falls short of the mark . . . I am going to be compelled to declare it." Epstein views much of contemporary American literature as falling "short of the mark." "We are currently in the midst of a distinctly second-rate literary era," opined Epstein in *Commentary*. Bemoaning the short supply of great writers in the United States, Epstein pointed to what he terms "gravity" as being absent in most authors' work. He defines "gravity" as the "quality that confers greatness in literature, even on comic literature; gravity has to do with high and undeflected seriousness, with recognition that literature provides the best record of the common humanity of all." Epstein admires several contemporary Soviet writers who he believes demonstrate this quality in their work: Aleksandr Solzhenitsyn, Andrei Sinyavski, and Vladimir Voinovich. He also enjoys some Western writers of another era who he claims have "gravity," including Henry James, James Joyce, Willa Cather, and Joseph Conrad. Yet Epstein feels that several contemporary American writers entirely miss the mark, many whose books frequently appear on bestseller lists: John Updike, Norman Mailer, Joan Didion, and John Irving.

Epstein cites several possible reasons to explain the declining quality of literature in the United States. Stating that since World War II writers have enjoyed greater freedom from censorship, he observed in *Commentary* that "this new freedom does not seem to have resulted directly in any master-works or marked any towering advance in human understanding of the kind that literature at its best makes possible." Epstein also points to an overabundance of indiscriminate literary criticism as contributing to literature's decline. The goal of criticism, remarked Epstein in *Commentary*, is to "distinguish between trivial and important art, between bad and good art." Yet, he noted, nearly every contemporary American writer has been the subject of at least one lengthy study, causing him to comment that criticism "is all so vastly overdone, so thoroughly out of proportion."

More than any other factor responsible for a failing American literature is writing's "nearly complete absorption by American universities," asserted Epstein in *Commentary*. Noting that prior to World War II the majority of writers stayed outside the parameters of the university, Epstein maintains that the trend has reversed itself. Rather than drawing from their experiences in the "great and very real world," the author declared that most writers are now "locked away" in universities where their "true subject is

lost to them." The result, he wrote in *Harper's,* is "two full generations of American novelists who, through their college education, have been brought up on a bitter diet of literary modernism and the tradition of alienation from their country." Added to this, noted Epstein, is an infusion of politics into literature—as evident in the works of contemporary novelists such as Joseph Heller, Donald Barthelme, and Thomas Pynchon—that "does not make for a cogent or even a very readable literature." "American writing itself," he lamented in *Commentary,* "has never seemed less important, and more lost, than it does now."

Epstein's own writing has drawn the praise of numerous critics for his clear and cogent style. In his interview for *Publishers Weekly,* Baldwin described Epstein as "an author who sounds just the way he writes: relaxed, fluent, yet precisely articulate; erudite without a trace of the off-putting highbrow; conversant, in the best sense of the term; and, yes, downright funny in a surprising, impromptu way."

In his first book, *Divorced in America: Marriage in an Age of Possibility,* Epstein writes from experience about divorce in contemporary American society. Published in 1974, the book was described in a *Newsweek* review as a "refreshingly thoughtful, exceedingly literate, personally insightful book." Epstein has divided his book into a three-part discussion of divorce that begins with an analysis of the beleaguered institution of marriage as well as the forces in today's society that threaten to undermine it. In the second section, he describes the legal proceedings of a divorce. He ends the book with a discussion about the effects of divorce on the individuals involved. Interwoven throughout all three parts is the author's account of his own divorce, which, reported Sara Sanborn in the *New York Times Book Review,* he does not view as a "creative" experience, but rather as a personal failure. "As cultural commentary," wrote Sanborn, *Divorced in America* "is generally perceptive and sometimes enlightening, dense with the experiences and observations of a comprehensive intelligence." While she asserted that the "book is far from profound" because it contains many well-known facts about the subject, the reviewer lauded Epstein's prose style, calling it "always fluent and easy, self-assured without being pretentious, frank without being embarrassing." Writing in the *Washington Post Book World,* Sonya Rudikoff held that in *Divorced in America* the author "presents situations of real feeling and immediacy" with a "poignancy" that "has all the nuance of domestic poetry about it, the poetry of making do and making the best of it with rueful dignity."

Epstein's second book-length work of nonfiction, *Ambition: The Secret Passion,* was published in 1980 and met with mixed critical reviews. In it Epstein examines the changing attitudes in America toward ambition, asserting that the pursuit of ambition is no longer held in high esteem by most Americans. The author suggests a few reasons why ambition is scorned in America, citing a tradition of literature dating from the turn of the century in which ambition is treated as a self-destructive vice. Included in his discussion are several short sketches about famous Americans who are unabashedly ambitious, including Benjamin Franklin, Henry Ford, and Edith Wharton. Hailing Epstein as a "discerning critic, whose muscular prose is both lucid and discriminating," Christopher Lehmann-Haupt, writing in the *New York Times*, nonetheless asserted that Epstein's book "progresses very circuitously," likening its arrangement to a "three-ring circus, with criticism, anecdote and biography doing their turns simultaneously." The critic added that while the biographies are "rather too familiar," they are "nevertheless extremely pointed and lively." Writing in *Time*, R. Z. Sheppard stated that while he agreed with the author's observations about success in America, "the difficulty arises when Epstein attempts to stretch a valid literary observation into a broad cultural thesis." The reviewer maintained that Epstein needed more facts to prove his "sweeping statements," while commenting that the book's organization "creates confusions and repetitions." James Wolcott concurred, writing in the *New Republic* that he preferred Epstein's "tidy" essays, and suggested that the author "might have written a succinct essay that could have carried a pugnacious smack" in contrast to the book's "padded sprawl." Yet James Sloan Allen, writing in the *Saturday Review*, praised Epstein for his "graceful, learned meditations on the cultural emblems of ambition," adding that the author has "given us the image of our own entangled wishes and fears." Pointing to Epstein's broad study of ambition that includes mention of related areas such as status-seeking, snobbery, and the fear of failure, Jack Richardson of the *New York Times Book Review* concluded: "All of this Mr. Epstein has handled with a good amount of wit and with the clear, straightforward analysis of a man with a point of view."

Epstein also edited and wrote the introduction to a collection of sixteen essays, containing portraits of exceptional teachers by their well-known students, entitled *Masters: Portraits of Great Teachers.* For the collection, noted figures from various fields, including physics, literature, anthropology, and music, wrote about the classroom presence of such luminaries as J. Robert Oppenheimer, C. S. Lewis, Ruth Benedict, and Nadia Boulanger. *New York Times* reviewer Anatole Broyard praised the idea behind the book but surmised that "half of the writers, teachers and scholars who wrote these essays did not follow Mr. Epstein's instructions." Rather than describing how the teachers conducted class, Broyard noted, most of the writers only relate what was taught. "These are resumes, not

portraits," he observed, adding, "there is no image of the man in action." Josiah Bunting III, writing in the *Washington Post*, contended that all of the teachers "resist effective reminiscence," making it "impossible for their essayists to convey to us, in terms really compelling, what it was that made their students admire them." He asserted that the "book's value is as absorbing reminiscence rather than as useful commentary."

Epstein's first collection of essays, *Familiar Territory: Observations on American Life*, was published in 1979 and is comprised of fourteen selections from *American Scholar*. His subjects center around life in the United States—the commonalities, quirks, language, and customs of contemporary America. Epstein's book, according to Kapp of the *Washington Post Book World*, is a "one-man revival of the familiar essay at its most genial and urbane," in which the author "tackles homely rather than earthshaking subjects: food, exercise and language, not nuclear war or the welfare state." The book garnered mostly favorable reviews from critics, who drew attention to Epstein's accomplished writing style and subtle wit. Writing in the *New York Times Book Review*, Benjamin DeMott declared that Epstein "has a gift for apposite quotation and allusion" and is "adept at inventing amusing new uses for old epithets." Reflecting on Epstein's self-portrayal in his essays as an ingenuous and ofttimes befuddled bystander, DeMott claimed that although "the intention is always humorous, . . . the reader hungers for a stronger note, less affected and more self-respecting." The critic maintained, however, that when Epstein drops his baffled persona, "he is a critic with real force of mind." Referring to Epstein's tone as "easygoing" and "neighborly," Charles Fenyvesi of the *New Republic* commented that the author's writings "reveal a man of exemplary sobriety, understated scholarship, and balanced judgment." Noting that Epstein's "serious thoughts" are "seldom heard here without an encouraging word of levity or a hilarious reminiscence," reviewer Kapp concluded that the essays "have to do with worldly things that affect our tastes, the palates of our minds, but they go on inevitably to an appraisal of our attitudes and the kind of people we are."

The Middle of My Tether: Familiar Essays, published in 1983, is a second selection of Epstein's essays from the *American Scholar*. "Like any good writer," reported Broyard in the *New York Times*, "Epstein looks closely at the very things most of us hardly notice." Among the topics he covers are book dedications, cliches, sending and receiving letters, and memories of his childhood in Chicago. Writing in the *Detroit News*, Bruce Cook asserted that Epstein's essays make an "eloquent and convincing . . . argument . . . for the revival of the essay form," remarking that although the author uses an informal tone, his writings "never seem thin, forced, or tricked-out." Cook praised

Epstein's autobiographical pieces, while commenting that the author is not "self-servingly confessional in the manner so popular today." Referring to the spirit of Epstein's essays, Broyard hailed the author as "a cross between a *flaneur,* or observant stroller, and a streetcorner evangelist" who "confesses, exhorts, mourns and celebrates."

In *Plausible Prejudices: Essays on American Writing* and in *Partial Payments: Essays on Writers and Their Lives,* Epstein has narrowed his focus to topics built on literary themes. Published in 1985 and 1989 respectively, the collections cover Epstein's views on the state of language and literature in the United States while revealing the authors he most particularly admires. Reviewing *Plausible Prejudices* for the *Washington Post,* critic Jonathan Yardley called Epstein a "tough and demanding critic but not a mean or spiteful one" when confronted with what he perceives to be a dearth of good American literature. "He recognizes excellence when he finds it," noted Yardley, who asserted that there is little excellence to be found in contemporary fiction. Though the critic agreed with Epstein's claim that many contemporary writers have "twisted literature to serve political ends," he took exception to the author's views on some distinctly political novels, some of which, Yardley contended, deserve more credit than they were accorded by the writer. Yet, Yardley maintained, "with devastating finality, [Epstein] strips away the veneer of political trendiness with which contemporary fiction is coated and reveals the shallowness underneath." Asserting that Epstein's "most interesting work has been his literary criticism," *Chicago Tribune* feature writer Stevenson Swanson hailed the writer's literary essays as "pieces of lasting interest." Epstein uses the publication of a book, explained the critic, to review the author's work in its entirety. He "reads an author's works, identifies the common elements and themes, leavens criticism with biography, and tries to place the writer in his time and in the larger tradition of literature," expounded Swanson. Praising Epstein for reminding him of some great, forgotten writers, as well as for deflating the "inflated reputations" of many popular contemporary authors, the reviewer reported that Epstein "takes his main jobs to be the upholding of standards and the restoration of literature to its former place of importance." Because Epstein frequently interjects lighthearted commentary into his essays, Swanson speculated that the author might be taken less seriously than he should be. Additionally, the reviewer noted, Epstein needs to clarify some of his unsupported and unexplained assertions in order for readers to evaluate the author's ideas. Yet Swanson judged Epstein to be a compelling writer who leaves the readers wanting to know "more rather than less" about the writer's views.

Partial Payments, which won the 1989 Heartland Prize from the *Chicago Tribune,* continues Epstein's ruminations about the state of the modern literary canon. In his *Washington Post Book World* review of the work, Michael Dirda noted: "Not quite a critic, yet more than a reviewer, Epstein is funny, smart, mildly boastful, fearless, politically conservative, narrow in his taste in fiction (give him that old-time realism) and a pleasure to read." Dirda also remarked, "There is nothing really new in anything he writes, beyond an engaging point of view and a fine prose style—neither to be sniffed at and both the hallmarks of the born essayist." *Chicago Tribune* contributor Karl Shapiro maintained that in *Partial Payments* Epstein "comes through as the voice of the general literate reader," concluding that the modern essay "has regained a good deal of its literary status in our time, much to the credit of Joseph Epstein."

Epstein has done more than write about other people's fiction: he has published some himself. His 1991 collection, *The Goldin Boys,* presents a series of stories set in and around Chicago, Epstein's home virtually since birth. All of the stories appeared in periodicals prior to their publication together in the book, but some critics commended the way the various tales seem linked by time, place, and theme. *Chicago Tribune* reviewer George Garrett claimed that the stories in *The Goldin Boys* "show us a wonderful storyteller at work, uninhibited by his editorial habits and losing nothing by comparison with his very best work in other forms." Garrett described the title story as "a little masterpiece that sets the tone for the whole collection, even as it proves that Joseph Epstein's gifts are true and abundant and altogether enviable." *New York Times Book Review* correspondent Daniel Stern called *The Goldin Boys* "a collection of beautifully realized short stories woven from the rich experience of families, lovers and money. It is full of Chicago street smarts and large-as-life characters who sing witty, sad songs before leaving us, entertained, touched and enriched by our encounter."

Epstein did not begin publishing fiction until he was nearly forty-five. His reputation as an essayist was solid by then and has remained substantial ever since. He has continued to pursue familiar topics in books such as *A Line out for a Walk* and *Pertinent Players: Essays on the Literary Life,* both published in the early 1990s. Remarking on the change Epstein's work has undergone in this decade, Chicago *Tribune Books* reviewer Rockwell Gray wrote: "Joseph Epstein has done much to give the familiar and literary essay renewed currency in recent years. . . . He has become less the polemical social critic and, probably to his readers' delight, more the ever curious spectator who carries his convictions lightly. The issues he now engages—the folly of dogmatic political correctness, the arrogance of literary theory, the fickle touch of fame—are woven gracefully into a larger concern with well-wrought work that honors the tradition of letters invoked in [*Perti-*

nent *Players*]." In a *Hudson Review* discussion of *Pertinent Players,* Thomas Filbin concluded: "Joseph Epstein's importance lies in having a willful affection for his subjects that doesn't rise or fall with the fashion. He eschews theories of literature in favor of the practice of literature, and aims to deliver a broader version of truth than the narrowness of specialization permits. . . . Epstein is droll and earnest company, and even if you aren't a member of his particular sect of literature, the tour of its hall of heroes is not to be missed."

BIOGRAPHICAL/CRITICAL SOURCES:

BOOKS

Winchell, Mark Royden, *Neoconservative Criticism: Norman Podhoretz, Kenneth S. Lynn, and Joseph Epstein,* Twayne (Boston), 1991.

PERIODICALS

American Scholar, summer, 1984; spring, 1985.
Chicago Tribune, November 11, 1979; February 24, 1985; January 8, 1989, p. 7; September 17, 1989, p. 7; October 13, 1991, pp. 6-7.
Commentary, August, 1976; July, 1978; June, 1980; February, 1981; March, 1982; September, 1985.
Detroit News, January 8, 1984.
Harper's, November, 1977.
Hudson Review, summer, 1992, pp. 331-38; spring, 1994, pp. 123-26.
Los Angeles Times Book Review, February 24, 1985, p. 7.
National Review, August 12, 1991, pp. 52-3.
New Republic, November 10, 1979; January 24, 1981; March 7, 1981.
Newsweek, July 1, 1974.
New York, July 26, 1993, pp. 52-3.
New York Times, December 29, 1979; January 16, 1981; April 25, 1981; October 20, 1983.
New York Times Book Review, June 16, 1974; November 4, 1979; January 18, 1981; April 5, 1981; February 24, 1985, p. 8; November 3, 1991, p. 10; September 19, 1993, p. 20.
Publishers Weekly, December 16, 1983; March 1, 1985.
Saturday Review, January, 1981.
Studies in Short Fiction, fall, 1987, pp. 472-73.
Time, January 19, 1981.
Times Literary Supplement, August 2, 1985, p. 857.
Tribune Books (Chicago), September 5, 1993, p. 6.
Wall Street Journal, April 22, 1991.
Washington Post, May 1, 1981; February 20, 1985; April 10, 1991, p. B2.
Washington Post Book World, June 30, 1974; December 16, 1979; January 29, 1989, p. 4.

ERSKINE, Barbara 1944-
(Kate Buchan)

PERSONAL: Born August 10, 1944, in Nottingham, England; daughter of Stuart Nigel Rose (a chartered surveyor) and Pamela (Anding) Erskine; married Michael Hope-Lewis (a company director); children: Adrian James, Jonathan Erskine Alexander. *Education:* University of Edinburgh, M.A. (with honors), 1967.

ADDRESSES: Agent—Blake Friedmann, 37-41 Gower St., London WC1E 6HH, England.

CAREER: Freelance editor and writer.

MEMBER: Society of Authors.

AWARDS, HONORS: Nominated for award from Romantic Novelists Association, 1987, for *Lady of Hay.*

WRITINGS:

Lady of Hay (romance novel), Dell (New York City), 1987.
Kingdom of Shadows (historical novel), Delacorte (New York City), 1989.
Encounters (short stories), HarperCollins (London), 1990.
Child of the Phoenix (historical novel), HarperCollins, 1993.
Midnight Is a Lovely Place, Signet Books (New York City), 1995.

HISTORICAL ROMANCES UNDER PSEUDONYM KATE BUCHAN

Black Fox, Mills & Boon (London), 1979.
Satan's Mountain, Mills & Boon, 1980.
The Flame Stone, Mills & Boon, 1981.
Rebecca's Lady, Mills & Boon, 1984.
Buccaneer Bride, Mills & Boon, 1986.

OTHER

Contributor of history articles and short stories to magazines, under name Barbara Erskine.

WORK IN PROGRESS: House of Echoes, a ghost story set in East Anglia, England, to be published in 1996.

SIDELIGHTS: Barbara Erskine once told *CA:* "Family stories of our descent from the ancient kings of Scotland fostered an early, if romanticized, interest in history. This developed later into a serious study of the subject, but the irresistible urge to 'fill in the gaps' of history turned me into a novelist, rather than a biographer. Other interests of mine include art, psychology, ecology, and the paranormal. (The last was encouraged by my grandfather, who left me his enormous collection of ghost books.) These interests are all reflected in my writing.

"For me, the setting of my novels, the 'spirit of place,' is of enormous importance. In *Lady of Hay,* the place came first—the lovely, wild, empty Welsh Marches, and then came the ghosts and the need to give them flesh and blood in a novel. For the next novel, I returned to the Scotland of those earliest childhood stories: a beautiful, untamed, violent land, peopled by characters from our own family tree—a circumstance which brings them somehow agonizingly close to me."

*　　*　　*

ESMOND, Harriet
  See BURKE, John (Frederick)

*　　*　　*

ESPEY, John (Jenkins) 1913-
  (Monica Highland, a joint pseudonym)

PERSONAL: Born January 15, 1913, in Shanghai, China; son of John Morton (a missionary) and Mary Lucretia (Jenkins) Espey; married Alice Martha Rideout (a library assistant), August 6, 1938 (died June 14, 1973); currently lives with Carolyn See (a writer); children: Alice Maude, Susan Mary. *Education:* Occidental College, A.B., 1935; Oxford University, B.A., 1937, B.Litt., 1939, M.A., 1941. *Politics:* Democrat.

ADDRESSES: Office—Department of English, University of California, 405 Hilgard Ave., Los Angeles, CA 90059.

CAREER: Occidental College, Los Angeles, CA, instructor, 1938-41, assistant professor, 1941-46, associate professor of English, 1946-48; University of California, Los Angeles, assistant professor, 1948-50, associate professor, 1950-56, professor of English, 1956-73, professor emeritus, 1973—.

MEMBER: Modern Language Association of America, Philological Association of the Pacific Coast, Long Christmas Dinner Society, Phi Beta Kappa.

AWARDS, HONORS: Rhodes Scholar, 1935; Guggenheim fellow; Silver Medal of Commonwealth Club of California, 1946, for *Minor Heresies;* fellow, Institute for Creative Arts, University of California, 1964-65, and Institute for Humanities, 1966-67; Proclamation from City of Los Angeles and Long Beach Literary Hall of Fame Award, both 1983, both for *Lotus Land.*

WRITINGS:

Minor Heresies, Knopf (New York City), 1945.
Tales out of School, Knopf, 1947.
The Other City, Knopf, 1950.

Ezra Pound's "Mauberley": A Study in Composition, University of California Press (Berkeley), 1955, reprinted, 1974.
(With Charles Gullans) *A Checklist of Trade Bindings Designed by Margaret Armstrong,* University Library, University of California, Los Angeles, 1958.
The Anniversaries, Harcourt (San Diego), 1963.
An Observer, Harcourt, 1965.
(With Gullans) *The Decorative Designers, 1895-1932,* University Library, University of California, Los Angeles, 1970.
(With Richard Ellmann) *Oscar Wilde: Two Approaches,* William Andrews Clark Memorial Library, 1977.
The Empty Box Haiku, Symposium Press (Los Angeles), 1980.
(With Carolyn See and Lisa See Kendall under joint pseudonym Monica Highland) *Lotus Land,* Coward, 1983.
(With See and Kendall under joint pseudonym Monica Highland) *110 Shanghai Road,* McGraw (New York City), 1986.
The Nine Lives of Algernon, illustrated by Claire Eder, Capra (Santa Barbara, CA), 1988.
(With See and Kendall under joint pseudonym Monica Highland) *Greetings from Southern California* (nonfiction), Graphic Arts Press, 1988.
Strong Drink, Strong Language, John Daniel, 1990.
(With See) *Two Schools of Thought: Some Tales of Learning and Romance,* John Daniel, 1991.
(With Gullans) *Margaret Armstrong and American Trade Bindings,* Department of Special Collections, University Research Library, University of California, Los Angeles, 1991.
Winter Return, John Daniel, 1992.
Minor Heresies, Major Departures: A China Mission Boyhood, University of California Press, 1994.

Contributor to periodicals, including *Harper's, New Yorker,* and *Arizona Quarterly.*

ADAPTATIONS: Both Monica Highland novels, *Lotus Land* and *110 Shanghai Road,* have been optioned for television mini-series.

WORK IN PROGRESS: Sweet Chariots, "reminiscent sketches of family automobiles."

SIDELIGHTS: A noted scholar and serious novelist, John Espey began a new phase of his career when he started writing epic novels with Carolyn See and Lisa See Kendall under the joint pseudonym Monica Highland. Espey and his collaborators seized upon the idea of writing an epic novel after viewing a television mini-series and deciding that they could do better. The three did not take the project too seriously at first, as Espey commented to John Baker in a *Publishers Weekly* interview: "It begins like taking a girl out on a blind date. It's a lark, a sort of joke. Then, quite unexpectedly, you fall in love." *110 Shanghai Road,* the trio's second novel, is set in China and takes much of its background from Espey's own upbringing in the Orient—"You don't really plagiarize from yourself, you cannibalize," he remarked to Peter Collier in the *Washington Post Book World.* Currently professor emeritus at the University of California, Espey and his collaborators are working on another Monica Highland novel. Monica "uses more and different adjectives than either of us might use individually," Espey told Collier, "but she has her own voice. That's the fun of it."

BIOGRAPHICAL/CRITICAL SOURCES:

PERIODICALS

Critique, winter, 1964-65; spring-summer, 1966.
History of Education Quarterly, Volume 35, number 1, 1995.
Los Angeles Times Book Review, March 20, 1983; July 13, 1986.
Michigan Quarterly Review, spring, 1995.
Publishers Weekly, February 4, 1983.
USA Today, May 13, 1994.
Washington Post Book World, March 6, 1983; July 28, 1986; August 31, 1986; August 2, 1987; March 13, 1994.

*   *   *

ESSOP, Ahmed   1931-
(Ahmed Yousuf)

PERSONAL: Born September 1, 1931, in Dabhel, Surat, India; son of Ebrahim (a shop owner) and Ayesha (Kalang) Essop; married Farida Karim (a shop assistant), April 17, 1960; children: Shehnaaz, Phiroz, Soraya, Zarina. *Education:* University of South Africa, Pretoria, B.A. (English and philosophy), 1956, M.A. (English; with honors), 1964. *Religion:* Islam.

ADDRESSES: Home—43 Lark St., Lenasia, Johannesburg, South Africa; and P.O. Box 1747, Lenasia, Johannesburg 1820, South Africa. *Office*—Ravan Press, P.O. Box 145, Randburg, Johannesburg 2125, South Africa.

CAREER: Central Indian High School, Newtown, Johannesburg, South Africa, teacher, 1958-60; Witwatersrand Indian College (now Witwatersrand Technikon), Newtown, teacher, 1961-64; Nirvana High School, Lenasia, Johannesburg, teacher, 1965-72; Transvaal College of Education, Fordsburg, Johannesburg, lecturer, 1973; Decor Decorators, Fairview, Johannesburg, assistant manager, 1978-79; Silver Oaks High School, Eldorado Park, Johannesburg, teacher, 1980-86; writer, 1986—.

MEMBER: African Writers' Association, Congress of South African Writers.

AWARDS, HONORS: Schreiner Award, English Academy of Southern Africa, 1979, for *The Hajji and Other Stories.*

WRITINGS:

(Under pseudonym Ahmed Yousuf) *The Dark Goddess* (poetry), Mitre Press (London), 1959.
The Hajji and Other Stories, Ravan Press (Johannesburg, South Africa), 1978.
The Visitation, Ravan Press, 1980.
The Emperor, Ravan Press, 1984.
Noorjehan and Other Stories, Ravan Press, 1990.

Also contributor to *Forced Landing,* edited by Mothobi Mutloatse, Ravan Press, 1980. Contributor of short stories to periodicals, including *Staffrider* and *English Academy Review.*

WORK IN PROGRESS: A collection of short stories.

SIDELIGHTS: Indian-born Ahmed Essop, a writer of short stories, novels, and verse, was educated and lives in South Africa. Recognized for his ability to create a sense of place, Essop sets several of his works, including *The Hajji and Other Stories,* in Fordsburg, the South African suburb within metropolitan Johannesburg, boasting the largest population of Indians outside the subcontinent. Essop writes of the Fordsburg of his youth, prior to 1960, when his people retained a strong sense of "Indianness." He portrays traditional Indian customs observed in South Africa, such as arranged marriages, the wearing of saris, preparing Oriental dishes, and Hindu fire-walking, and he captures the Fordsburg Indians' regional dialect of English.

In addition to his mastery of literary place and setting, Essop is noted for possessing an understanding of human nature and a reservoir of pity for even the most disagreeable characters. He delves into his characters' psyches and presents them without pretense or deceit, frequently exploring the theme of losing human dignity and suffering the subsequent humiliation. Nearly half of the stories of *The Hajji* satirize human beings unable to live up to their own expectations.

The protagonist of Essop's first novel, *The Visitation,* is Mr. Sufi, a wealthy property owner who is married but quietly keeps a mistress in each of his apartment buildings. A racketeer, Gool, eventually blackmails Sufi and appropriates his rent money and mistresses. He acts as ruthlessly as Sufi had, though where Sufi conducted himself with cultivated decorum, Gool operates vulgarly and brutally. Gool doubles as a caricature of criminality and as Sufi's mirror image, forcing Sufi to recognize his own corrupt nature. Essop's second novel, *The Emperor,* is set in Lenasia, a government-built township beyond Johannesburg's perimeter populated by less traditional Indians. In the novel Essop again defines place and addresses one of his favorite themes: the loss of human dignity. *The Emperor* is the story of the rise and fall of Mr. Dharma Ashoka, an Indian headmaster with an unquenchable thirst for power.

Noorjehan and Other Stories, writes Cherry Clayton in the foreword to the book, "moves more strongly into the politicised decades of the seventies and eighties, showing in its more extreme moods the violence that has marked these years. His [Essop's] focus is often on the young, both as victims of social and political wrongs and as those who may seek extreme solutions to them. The key stories is this collection deal with moments of politicisation and crises of conscience, though he retains a focus on the 'little man' (or woman) who has to endure the daily working of an often corrupt social system."

BIOGRAPHICAL/CRITICAL SOURCES:

BOOKS

Essop, Ahmed, *Noorjehan and Other Stories,* Ravan Press, 1990.

PERIODICALS

Commonwealth, Volume 8, 1985.
English in Africa, Volume 17, 1990.
Theoria: A Journal of Studies, May, 1988.

*   *   *

EVANS, Lee
   See FORREST, Richard (Stockton)

*   *   *

EYSENCK, Hans J(urgen)   1916-

PERSONAL: Born March 4, 1916, in Berlin, Germany; son of Eduard Anton (an actor) and Ruth (an actress; maiden name, Werner) Eysenck; married Margaret Malcom Davies, 1938; married second wife, Sybil Bianca Giuletta Rostal, 1950; children: (first marriage) Michael; (second marriage) Gary, Connie, Kevin, Darin. *Education:* Attended University of Dijon and University of Exeter; University of London, B.A., 1938, Ph.D., 1940. *Politics:* Liberal. *Religion:* Church of England. *Avocational interests:* History of science, tennis, squash, swimming, sailing, table tennis, photography, film.

ADDRESSES: Home—10 Dorchester Dr., London SE24 0DQ, England. *Office*—Institute of Psychiatry, Univer-

sity of London, Denmark Hill, London SE5 8AF, England.

CAREER: Research psychologist, Mill Hill Emergency Hospital, 1942-45; Maudsley Hospital, London, England, psychologist, beginning 1945; University of London, Institute of Psychiatry, London, reader in psychology and director of department, 1950-55, professor of psychology, 1955-83, professor emeritus, 1983—. Psychologist, Bethlem Royal Hospital. Visiting professor, University of California, Berkeley, and University of Pennsylvania.

MEMBER: International Society for the Study of Individual Differences (president), American Psychological Association (fellow), British Psychological Society.

AWARDS, HONORS: D.Sc., University of London, 1962; American Psychological Association, Distinguished Scientist Award, 1988, Presidential Citation, 1993; William James fellow, American Psychological Society, 1994.

WRITINGS:

Dimensions of Personality: A Record of Research, Routledge & Kegan Paul (London), 1947, Macmillan (New York City), 1948.
The Scientific Study of Personality, Macmillan, 1952.
The Structures of Human Personality, Methuen (London), 1952, Wiley (New York City), 1953, 3rd edition, Barnes & Noble (New York City), 1970.
Uses and Abuses of Psychology, Penguin Books (New York City), 1953.
The Psychology of Politics, Routledge & Kegan Paul, 1954, Praeger (New York City), 1955.
Psychology and the Foundations of Psychiatry, H. K. Lewis (London), 1955.
Sense and Nonsense in Psychology, Penguin Books, 1957, revised edition, 1958.
The Dynamics of Anxiety and Hysteria: An Experimental Application of Modern Learning Theory to Psychiatry, Praeger, 1957.
(With G. Granger and J. C. Brengelmann) *Perceptual Processes and Mental Illness,* Chapman & Hall (London), 1957.
Manual of the Maudsley Personality Inventory, University of London Press (London), 1959.
Know Your Own I.Q., Penguin Books, 1962.
(With wife, Sybil Bianca Eysenck) *Manual of the Eysenck Personality Inventory: Personality Questionnaire,* University of London Press, 1964.
Crime and Personality, Houghton (Boston), 1964, 3rd edition, revised and enlarged, Routledge & Kegan Paul, 1977.
(With Stanley Rachman) *The Causes and Cures of Neurosis: An Introduction to the Modern Behaviour Therapy Based on Learning Theory and the Principles of Conditioning,* Robert R. Knapp, 1965.

Fact and Fiction in Psychology, Penguin Books, 1965.

Smoking, Health and Personality, Basic Books (New York City), 1965.

Check Your Own I.Q., Penguin Books, 1966.

The Effects of Psychotherapy, International Science Press, 1966.

The Biological Basis of Personality, C. C. Thomas (Springfield, IL), 1967.

(With S. B. Eysenck) *Personality Structure and Measurement,* Robert R. Knapp, 1969.

The I.Q. Argument: Race, Intelligence and Education, Liberty Press, 1971, published in England as *Race, Intelligence and Education,* Temple Smith (Aldershot, England), 1971.

Psychology Is about People, Liberty Press, 1972.

Sex and Personality, Open Books (Wells, Somerset, England), 1972, University of Texas Press (Austin), 1976.

(With Glenn D. Wilson) *The Experimental Study of Freudian Theories,* Methuen, 1973.

Eysenck on Extraversion, Wiley, 1973.

The Inequality of Man, Temple Smith, 1973.

(With Wilson) *Know Your Own Personality,* Temple Smith, 1975, Barnes & Noble, 1976.

(With S. B. Eysenck) *Psychoticism as a Dimension of Personality,* Russak Crane, 1976.

(With C. D. Frith) *Reminiscence, Motivation, and Personality: A Case Study in Experimental Psychology,* Plenum (New York City), 1977.

You and Neurosis, Temple Smith, 1977, Sage Publications (Beverly Hills, CA), 1979.

(With D. K. B. Nias) *Sex, Violence, and the Media,* St. Martin's (New York City), 1978.

(With David W. Fulker) *The Structure and the Measurement of Intelligence,* Springer-Verlag (New York City), 1979.

(With Wilson) *The Psychology of Sex,* Dent (London), 1979.

(With L. Eaves) *The Causes and Effects of Smoking,* Temple Smith, 1980, Sage Publications, 1981.

(With son, Michael Eysenck) *Mindwatching,* M. Joseph (London), 1981, published as *Mindwatching: Why People Behave the Way They Do,* Doubleday (New York City), 1983, paperback edition published as *Mindwatching: Why We Behave the Way We Do,* Prion (London), 1995.

(With Leon Kamin) *The Intelligence Controversy,* Wiley, 1981, published in England as *The Battle for the Mind,* Macmillan, 1981.

(With Carl Sargent) *Explaining the Unexplained: Mysteries of the Paranormal,* Weidenfeld & Nicolson (London), 1982.

(With Nias) *Astrology: Science or Superstition?,* Temple Smith, 1982.

(With Sargent) *Know Your Own PSI-Q,* Multimedia, 1983.

(With Betty Nichols Kelly) *"I Do": Your Guide to a Happy Marriage,* Multimedia, 1983.

(With M. Eysenck) *Personality and Individual Differences: A Natural Science Approach,* Plenum, 1985.

Decline and Fall of the Freudian Empire, Viking (London), 1985.

Rebel with a Cause (autobiography), W. H. Allen (London), 1990.

Smoking, Personality, and Stress: Psychosocial Factors in the Prevention of Cancer and Coronary Heart Disease, Springer Verlag, 1991.

(With D. Evans) *Test Your IQ,* Thorsons/HarperCollins (London), 1994.

Genius: The Natural History of Creativity, Cambridge University Press (Cambridge, England), 1995.

EDITOR

Handbook of Abnormal Psychology: An Experimental Approach, Pitman Publishing (London), 1960, Basic Books, 1961, 2nd edition, Robert R. Knapp, 1973.

Experiments in Personality, two volumes, Routledge & Kegan Paul, 1960, Humanities (Atlantic Highlands, NJ), 1961.

Behaviour Therapy and the Neuroses: Readings in Modern Methods of Treatment Derived from Learning Theory, Macmillan, 1960.

Experiments with Drugs: Studies in the Relation between Personality, Learning Theory and Drug Action, Macmillan, 1963.

Experiments in Motivation, Macmillan, 1964.

Experiments in Behaviour Therapy: Readings in Modern Methods of Treatment of Mental Disorders Derived from Learning Theory, Macmillan, 1964.

Readings in Extraversion-Introversion, three volumes, Staples, 1970, Wiley, 1972.

Encyclopedia of Psychology, three volumes, Search Press (Tunbridge Wells, Kent, England), 1972, Seabury (New York City), 1979, 2nd edition, Continuum (New York City), 1979.

(And author of comments) *The Measurement of Intelligence,* Williams & Wilkins (London), 1973.

Case Studies in Behaviour Therapy, Routledge & Kegan Paul, 1976.

The Measure of Personality, University Park Press (Baltimore, MD), 1976.

(With Wilson) *A Textbook of Human Psychology,* University Park Press, 1976.

(With Rachman) *Advances in Behaviour Research and Therapy,* Pergamon (Elmsford, NY), Volume I, 1977, Volume II, 1979.

Die Grundlagen des Spaetmarxismus, Verlag Bonn Aktuell, 1977.

A Model for Personality, Springer-Verlag, 1981.

A Model for Intelligence, Springer-Verlag, 1982.
Personality, Genetics, and Behaviour, Praeger, 1982.
(With Jan Strelau) *Personality Dimensions and Arousal,* Plenum, 1987.
(With Irene Martin) *Theoretical Foundations of Behavior Therapy,* Plenum, 1987.
(With V. A. Gheorghiu, P. Netter, and R. Rosenthal) *Suggestion and Suggestibility,* Plenum, 1989.

OTHER

Also contributor to *The Language of the Game,* by George Wills Beadle, University of London Press, 1961; and *Hans Eysenck: Consensus and Controversy,* edited by Sohan Modgil and Celia Modgil, Falmer Press (London), 1986. Editor, "International Series of Monographs on Experimental Psychology," Pergamon, 1964—. Also founding editor of *Behaviour Research and Therapy* and *Personality and Individual Differences.* Also author of sound recordings *The Present and Future of Behavior Therapy,* Sigma Information, 1972, and *A Behavioral Theory of Neurosis,* Jeffrey Norton (Guilford, CT), 1974.

SIDELIGHTS: Hans J. Eysenck once told *CA:* "I have written three types of books. One [type] is strictly academic-scientific, such as *Reminiscence, Motivation, and Personality: A Case Study in Experimental Psychology.* 'Reminiscence' is a technical term in learning theory, and the book represents fifteen years of work on my part and that of my students, and I imagine it is almost unreadable for most nonpsychologists. I have also written a fair number of popular books, such as *Uses and Abuses of Psychology,* which has sold in the millions. In comparison, *Reminiscence, Motivation, and Personality* only sold a few hundred copies! *Uses and Abuses of Psychology,* in contrast to *Reminiscence, Motivation, and Personality,* only took a fortnight to write, suggesting that there is a strong negative correlation between sales and the time taken to write a book.

"I have also written a number of books which are technical in principle but fairly easy to read for an educated layman; my book *Crime and Personality* is an example of this, as is *Smoking, Health and Personality.* These books, as might be expected, sell better than the technical ones, but not as well as the popular ones.

"Although English is not my first language, I have a good background in English, German and French literature, and write very easily. I dictate my articles directly into a tape recorder, and they seldom need revision. It might be argued that that is exactly what is wrong with my books, but I once decided to carry out an experiment to check whether revising would really be of much help. I carefully polished a chapter in a book I had written, revising it again and again, and then I asked knowledgeable friends and critics to read the original and the revised version. They all preferred the original, saying it was much more spontaneous! I took the hint and have ceased to try and revise my writings, except for obvious errors, misspellings and punctuation.

"Although I am of course fluent in German, my native language, and in French (I studied in France), I find it difficult to write any lengthy reports, articles or chapters for books in either language, and prefer to have them translated. One has to be in constant contact with the language in order to preserve one's facility for writing or speaking.

"I very much enjoy writing, unlike many of my fellow scientists who find it a bore. I have always been fascinated by language, and studied literature, history, language, at both the University of Dijon in France and the University of Exeter in England, before settling down as a psychologist. In a very real sense, therefore, I feel I am a member of three cultures, which is a pleasant state to be in, but can be upsetting when you have to write for a monocultural readership!"

BIOGRAPHICAL/CRITICAL SOURCES:

BOOKS

Eysenck, Hans J., *Rebel with a Cause* (autobiography), W. H. Allen, 1990.
Gibson, H. B., *Hans Eysenck: The Man and His Works,* Peter Owen (London), 1981.
Modgil, Sohan, and Celia Modgil, editors, *Hans Eysenck: Consensus and Controversy,* Falmer Press, 1986.

PERIODICALS

New Statesman, July 2, 1971.
New York Times Book Review, May 3, 1981.
Times (London), December 12, 1980.
Times Literary Supplement, July 9, 1982; July 8, 1983.

OTHER

An Interview with Hans Eysenck (sound recording), Harper, 1976.

F

FARLEY, Carol 1936-
(Carol McDole)

PERSONAL: Born December 20, 1936, in Ludington, MI; daughter of Floyd and Thressa Moreen (Radtke) McDole; married Dennis Scott Farley (a professor), June 21, 1956; children: Denise, Elise, Roderick, Jeannette. *Education:* Western Michigan University, teacher's certificate, 1956; Michigan State University, B.A., 1980; Central Michigan University, M.A., 1983.

ADDRESSES: Home—8574 W. Higgins Lake Rd., Roscommon, MI 48653.

CAREER: Freelance writer, teacher, and lecturer, 1957—; language teacher in Seoul, Korea, 1978-79; writer-in-residence in Michigan communities, 1981—; teacher for Institute of Children's Literature, 1983-95.

AWARDS, HONORS: Franklin Watts Mystery Medal, 1966, for *Mystery of the Fog Man;* Golden Kite Award, Society of Children's Book Writers, 1975, and Wel-Met Children's Book Award, Child Study Association of America, 1976, both for *The Garden Is Doing Fine;* selection as best juvenile book by a Midwest writer, 1977, for *Loosen Your Ears, Settle Your Fidgets;* selection as a 1987 IRA/CBC Children's Choice Book, for *The Case of the Vanishing Villain.*

WRITINGS:

(Under name Carol McDole) *Yekapo of Zopo Land,* Row, Peterson, 1958.
Mystery of the Fog Man, F. Watts (New York City), 1966.
Mystery in the Ravine, F. Watts, 1967.
Sergeant Finney's Family, F. Watts, 1969.
The Bunch on McKellahan Street, F. Watts, 1971.
The Most Important Thing in the World, F. Watts, 1974.
The Garden Is Doing Fine (Junior Literary Guild selection), Atheneum (New York City), 1975.

Loosen Your Ears, Settle Your Fidgets, Atheneum, 1977.
Ms. Isabelle Cornell, Herself, Atheneum, 1979.
Twilight Waves, Atheneum, 1981.
Mystery of the Fiery Message, Avon (New York City), 1983.
Korea: A Land Divided, Dillon (Minneapolis), 1983.
Mystery of the Melted Diamonds, Avon, 1984.
The Case of the Vanishing Villain, Avon, 1986.
The Case of the Lost Lookalike, Avon, 1988.
The Case of the Haunted Health Club, Avon, 1990.
Korea: Land of the Morning Calm, Dillon, 1991.
King Sejong's Secret, Lothrop (New York City), 1996.
Tiger! Stories from Old Korea, Lothrop, in press.

Work represented in anthologies, including *2041,* edited by Jane Yolen, Delacorte (New York City), 1991; *Stories on Stage,* edited by Aaron Shepard, H. W. Wilson (Bronx, NY), 1993; and *Cross-roads,* edited by Robert Cormier, Scott, Foresman (Glenview, IL), 1995. Contributor to periodicals, including *Calliope, Cricket, Children's Playmate, Turtle, Spider, Pockets,* and *Challenge.*

WORK IN PROGRESS: A collection of short stories; a series of tales involving a sloth sleuth; a time-travel novel; a variety of topics for magazine articles.

SIDELIGHTS: Carol Farley once told *CA:* "Writing helps me bring order to what seems to be chaotic existence. I marvel that so many people seem content to float across the surface of life without ever delving deeply or trying to locate a steady anchor. When writing, I'm trying to reach out to others in hope that together we can make sense out of the emotions and events which surround us. Questions help me probe deeply, and putting feelings into words provides a much-needed anchor. I like writing for the young because they're eager to try to understand the unknowable too. Often I use a common genre, such as the mystery, in order to appeal to the most readers."

FEDDER, Norman J(oseph) 1934-

PERSONAL: Born January 26, 1934, in New York, NY; son of Abraham Herbert (a rabbi) and Harriet (Solomon) Fedder; married Deborah Pincus, November 24, 1955; children: Jordan Michael, Tamar Beth. *Education:* Attended Johns Hopkins University, 1950-52; Brooklyn College (now Brooklyn College of the City University of New York), B.A., 1955; Columbia University, M.A., 1956; New York University, Ph.D., 1962. *Religion:* Jewish.

ADDRESSES: Home—1903 Crescent Dr., Manhattan, KS 66503.

CAREER: Trenton State College, Trenton, NJ, assistant professor of English, 1960-61; Indiana State College (now Indiana University of Pennsylvania), Indiana, PA, associate professor of English, 1961-64; Florida Atlantic University, Boca Raton, associate professor of English, 1964-67; University of Arizona, Tucson, associate professor of drama, 1967-70; Kansas State University, Manhattan, associate professor, 1970-80, professor, 1980-89, distinguished professor, 1989—, University Humanities Lecturer, 1994—. Registered drama therapist, 1989—. Faculty member, Annual Religion and Arts Summer Conference, Pacific College of Religion, Berkeley, CA.

Developed Kansas Heritage Theatre to perform original plays throughout the state, 1976-77; developed touring companies, Jewish Heritage Theatre, 1978-80, and TOV (Theatre of Values), 1986. Founder/director, Drama Network, Coalition for the Advancement of Jewish Education, and Israel Summer Theatre Program; co-founder, Performing Arts in Jewish Education Conference. Member, Ecumenical Council for Drama and Other Arts, and Council of Jewish Theatres. Invited to present keynote address, Association of Kansas Theatre, 1994.

MEMBER: Association for Theatre in Higher Education (member of Religion and Theatre Program), National Association for Drama Therapy (member of board), Dramatists Guild, Association of Kansas Theatres.

AWARDS, HONORS: Winner of Sacramento State College National Drama Competition; bicentennial grant, 1976, to develop and perform *The Matter with Kansas;* National Foundation for Jewish Culture grant, 1978, to develop the Jewish Heritage Theatre, and 1984, to write *In Every Generation: A Passover Play;* fellowship to Drama-in-Education Conference in Austria, 1984; outstanding teacher award, 1989; writing commission, St. Mary of the Plains College, 1989, for one-person drama about Milburn Stone; elected to Kansas Theatre Hall of Fame, 1990; honorable mention in Charles H. Sergel Drama Competition, University of Chicago.

WRITINGS:

The Influence of D. H. Lawrence on Tennessee Williams, Mouton & Co., 1966.

PLAYS

The Eternal Kick, produced at Indiana State College, 1963.
My Old Room, produced at University of Arizona, 1968.
The Planter May Weep, produced at University of Arizona, 1968.
A Thousand at the Branches, produced at University of Arizona, fall, 1969.
Some Events Connected with the Early History of Arizona, produced by Arizona Pioneers Historical Society, 1970.
Earp! (musical), produced in Abilene at Kansas State Historical Theatre, 1971.
Monks (musical), produced at Kansas State University, 1972.
PUBA, produced at University of North Carolina, 1973.
The Betrayal (one-act), produced in Baptist churches throughout Kansas, 1974, published in *Baker's Plays,* [Boston], 1978.
The Decision, produced in Colby at Kansas Baptist Conference, 1974.
The Kansas Character and *No Place Like Kansas* (both one-acts), both produced in various communities throughout Kansas, 1976.
A Jew in Kansas (one-act) and *Next Thing to Kinfolks,* both produced in New York City at the First National Jewish Festival, 1980.
(With Richard A. Lippman) *The Buck Stops Here* (musical), produced Off-Off Broadway at AMAS Repertory Theatre, 1983.
No Other Gods: A Midrash on Moses (one-act), produced in Kansas by TOV (Theatre of Values), 1987.
Never Let 'Em Catch You at It: An Evening with Milburn Stone, produced at St. Mary of the Plains College (Kansas), 1989.
A Light to the Nations, produced at National Association for Drama Therapy Conference (Pittsburgh), 1989.
(With Lippman) *Abraham! Abraham!* (musical), produced at Kansas State University, 1990.
Custody (one-act), produced at National Association for Drama Therapy Conference (Chicago), 1993.

OTHER

Author of Readers Theatre scripts, *Proud to Be a Baptist, Tevye in the Golden Land,* and *The Matter with Kansas,* produced on tour throughout Kansas, 1975; also author of television script, *We Can Make Our Lives Sublime,* produced by Columbia Broadcasting System (CBS), Inc., 1970. Contributor to books, including *Tennessee Williams: A Tribute,* University Press of Mississippi (Jackson), 1977; *Tennessee Williams: Thirteen Essays,* University Press of Mississippi, 1980; and *Life Guidance through Literature,* American Library Association (Chicago), 1992. Theatre book reviewer, *Jewish Book World,* 1994—. Contributor of articles to periodicals, including *Kansas Speech Journal, Arts in Society, Military Chaplains Review, Theatre and Religion, Dramatics Magazine, Raayonot: A Journal of Arts and Opinion in Jewish Life,* and *Dramascope.*

WORK IN PROGRESS: From the Nile to the Jordan, a play about the "second Exodus" of the Egyptian Jews, based on a novel by Ada Aharoni.

SIDELIGHTS: Norman J. Fedder once told *CA:* "*The Buck Stops Here,* with music and lyrics by Richard Lippman, was produced at the Smithsonian Institution in Washington, D.C., in 1984, as part of the Harry S. Truman Centennial Celebration. It has received 'rave reviews' from the initial *New York Times* notice in 1983 through the present, wherever it has been produced."

He continues, "*Never Let 'Em Catch You at It: An Evening with Milburn Stone* was produced again with great success at Hutchinson Community College in Kansas, 1995, to begin a tour of the state," adding, "I have developed an annual three-week summer tour of Israeli theatre, sponsored by Kansas State University and an Israeli school of theatre arts."

BIOGRAPHICAL/CRITICAL SOURCES:

PERIODICALS

New York Times, November 1, 1983.

*   *   *

FELL, Derek (John)   1939-

PERSONAL: Born September 28, 1939, in Morecambe, England; came to the United States in 1966, naturalized citizen, 1971; son of Albert John (a restaurateur) and Mary (McCafferty) Fell; married Maria Braksal, August 20, 1964 (divorced October, 1981); married Rosemary Wilkens, February 26, 1984 (divorced July, 1987); married Elizabeth Murray, October 10, 1987 (divorced November, 1988); married Carolyn Heath, January, 1994; children: (first marriage) Christina Mary, Derek John, Jr.; (second marriage) Victoria Rose. *Education:* Attended British military school in Wilhemshaven, West Germany (now Germany). *Religion:* Church of England.

ADDRESSES: Home—53 Iron Bridge Rd., Pipersville, PA 18947. *Office*—Box 1, Gardenville, PA 18926.

CAREER: Newport Advertiser, Newport, England, reporter, 1957-59; O. D. Gallagher Ltd. (public relations agency), London, England, copywriter and account executive, 1959-66; W. Atlee Burpee Co., Philadelphia, PA, catalog manager, 1966-72; All-America Selections, Gardenville, PA, executive secretary, 1972-74; freelance photographer and writer, 1974—. Director of National Garden Bureau; consultant to the White House.

MEMBER: Garden Writers Association of America (past member of board of directors), Society of American Travel Writers, Royal Horticultural Society.

AWARDS, HONORS: Twelve awards from Garden Writers Association of America, 1982—, three for best book, six for best photography, and three for best magazine article.

WRITINGS:

How to Plant a Vegetable Garden, Countryside Books (Milwaukee), 1975.
New Ideas in Flower Gardening, Countryside Books, 1976.
How I Planned to Plant the White House Vegetable Garden, Exposition Banner, 1976.
How to Photograph Flowers, Plants, and Landscapes, H. P. Books (Tucson, AZ), 1980.
The Vegetable Spaghetti Cookbook, Pine Row (Washington Crossing, PA), 1982.
Vegetables: How to Select, Grow, and Enjoy, H. P. Books, 1982.
Annuals: How to Select, Grow, and Enjoy, H. P. Books, 1983.
Trees and Shrubs, H. P. Books, 1986.
Garden Accents, Holt (New York City), 1987.
The One-Minute Gardener, Running Press (Philadelphia), 1988.
Great Gardens (calendar), Portal, 1988.
Renoir's Garden, Frances Lincoln (London), 1991.
550 Home Landscaping Ideas, Simon & Schuster (New York City), 1991.
The Impressionist Garden, Frances Lincoln, 1994.
550 Perennial Garden Ideas, Simon & Schuster, 1994.
The Pennsylvania Gardener, Camino Press, 1995.

Also contributor to *Encyclopaedia Britannica.* Contributor of articles and photographs to magazines and newspapers, including *Architectural Digest, Woman's Day, Connoisseur,* and *New York Times Magazine.* Past editor of *Garden Writers Bulletin.*

SIDELIGHTS: "The writer who most influenced my work," Derek Fell once told *CA,* "was O. D. Gallagher, a British war correspondent whose best work appeared in the *Daily Express.* After retiring from newspapers, Gallagher started the public relations agency where I worked as a copywriter and account executive.

"At this time, I also became influenced by the work of Harry Smith, a British plant photographer. I emulated his style of horticultural photography and, as a result, I have become the world's most widely published plant photographer and owner of the Derek Fell Horticultural Color Picture Library.

"The third most important influence was meeting and working with David Burpee, president of W. Atlee Burpee Co., mail order seedsman. Before his death in 1980 I worked six years with him, learning how to communicate gardening."

BIOGRAPHICAL/CRITICAL SOURCES:

PERIODICALS

Architectural Digest, December, 1980.
Art Matters, June, 1995.
Beautiful Gardens, November/December, 1994.
Christian Science Monitor, December 17, 1982.
Doylestown Intelligencer, August 21, 1981.
Garden Design, winter, 1986; winter, 1994.
Green Scene, November/December, 1987.
Hemispheres, June, 1995.
Mother Earth News, November, 1976.
New Hope Gazette, June 10, 1982.
New York Times, May 10, 1976.

*   *   *

FINCKE, Gary (William) 1945-

PERSONAL: Born July 7, 1945, in Pittsburgh, PA; son of William A. (a janitor) and Ruth (Lang) Fincke; married Elizabeth Locker (an elementary teacher), August 17, 1968; children: Derek, Shannon, Aaron. *Education:* Thiel College, B.A., 1967; Miami University, Oxford, Ohio, M.A., 1969; Kent State University, Ph.D., 1974.

ADDRESSES: Home—3 Melody Ln., Selinsgrove, PA 17870. *Office*—Susquehanna University, Selinsgrove, PA 17870.

CAREER: Freedom Area High School, Freedom, PA, English teacher, 1968-69; Pennsylvania State University, Beaver Campus, Monaca, instructor in English, 1969-75; LeRoy Central School, LeRoy, NY, chairperson of the English department, 1975-80; Susquehanna University, Selinsgrove, PA, professor of English and director of Writers Institute, 1980—, tennis coach, 1981—. Tennis instructor, 1970—; tennis professional, 1976-80.

MEMBER: Poetry Society of America, Associated Writing Programs, Poets and Writers.

AWARDS, HONORS: Fellowships for poetry and fiction, Pennsylvania Arts Council, 1982, 1985, 1987, 1991, and 1995; syndicated fiction prize, PEN, 1984; Bess Hokin Prize, *Poetry* magazine, 1991.

WRITINGS:

Victims (poetry), Windy Row Press, 1974.
Emptied (poetry), Branden Press (Brookline Village, MA), 1974.
Permanent Season (poetry), Branden Press, 1975.
Breath (poetry chapbook), State Street, 1984.
The Coat in the Heart (poetry chapbook), Blue Buildings, 1985.
The Days of Uncertain Health (poetry), Lynx (Amherst, MA), 1988.
Handing the Self Back (poetry chapbook), Green Tower, 1990.
Plant Voices (poetry), Yardbird, 1991.
The Public Talk of Death (poetry chapbook), Two Herons, 1991.
The Double Negatives of the Living, Zoland, 1992.
For Keepsies (stories), Coffee House, 1993.
Inventing Angels (poetry), Zoland, 1994.
The Inadvertent Scofflaw (novel), Yardbird, 1995.

Also author of *The Air of Delicate Pastry* (poetry), 1995, *Emergency Calls* (stories), 1995, and *The Pagoda Sightlines* (essays), 1995. Contributor of short stories, articles, and poems to periodicals, including *Twigs, Stone Country, Green's, Wisconsin Review, Bitterroot, Wind,* and *Lake Superior Review.*

SIDELIGHTS: Gary Fincke told *CA:* "Although I began by writing poems after I received a Ph.D. in 1974, I have become a 'writer'—that is, I now write poems, short stories, novels, and creative nonfiction, usually concentrating on one genre for six to nine months. I think this is what makes the books I've published or have recently completed distinctly different from each other. Likewise, there are three months each year (tennis season) when I do no writing at all. I used to read exclusively poetry and fiction; now I read almost exclusively nonfiction—all of the sciences that I once ignored. The fact that I'm self-taught is a blessing, although my current job is teaching aspiring writers. I hope that the mix of my essentially 'blue-collar, jock' upbringing with the eventual professional educator's life proves interesting enough to sustain whatever distinctive voice I have."

*   *   *

FLEISCHER, Jane
See OPPENHEIM, Joanne

*   *   *

FORCHE, Carolyn (Louise) 1950-

PERSONAL: Surname is pronounced "for-*shay*"; born April 28, 1950, in Detroit, MI; daughter of Michael Joseph (a tool and die maker) and Louise Nada (a journalist; maiden name, Blackford) Sidlosky; married Henry E. Mattison (a news photographer), December 27, 1984; children: one son. *Education:* Michigan State University, B.A., 1972; Bowling Green State University, M.F.A., 1975.

ADDRESSES: Home—430 Greenwich St., New York, NY 10013. *Agent*—Virginia Barber, 353 West 21st St., New York, NY 10011.

CAREER: Michigan State University, Justin Morrill College, East Lansing, visiting lecturer in poetry, 1974; San Diego State University, San Diego, CA, visiting lecturer, 1975, assistant professor, 1976-78; University of Virginia, Charlottesville, visiting lecturer, 1979, visiting associate professor, 1982-83; University of Arkansas, Fayetteville, assistant professor, 1980, associate professor, 1981; New York University, New York City, visiting writer, 1983 and 1985; Vassar College, Poughkeepsie, NY, visiting writer, 1984; Writer's Community, New York City, visiting poet, 1984; State University of New York at Albany, Writer's Institute, writer in residence, 1985; George Mason University, Fairfax, VA, associate professor, 1994—. Columbia University, adjunct associate professor, 1984-85; University of Minnesota, visiting associate professor, summer, 1985. Journalist and human rights activist in El Salvador, 1978-80; correspondent for National Public Radio's *All Things Considered* in Beirut, 1983; consultant on Central America and member of Commission on U.S.-Central American Relations. Lecturer on human rights; gives poetry readings.

MEMBER: Amnesty International, PEN American Center (member of Freedom to Write and Silenced Voices committees), Poetry Society of America, Academy of American Poets, Associated Writing Programs (president, 1994—), Institute for Global Education, Coalition for a New Foreign Policy, Theta Sigma Phi.

AWARDS, HONORS: Devine Memorial fellowship in poetry, 1975; First Award in Poetry, *Chicago Review,* 1975; Yale Series of Younger Poets Award, 1975, for *Gathering the Tribes;* Tennessee Williams fellowship in poetry, Bread Loaf Writers Conference, 1976; National Endowment for the Arts fellowships, 1977 and 1984; John Simon Guggenheim Memorial fellowship, 1978; Emily Clark Balch Prize, *Virginia Quarterly Review,* 1979; Alice Fay di Castagnola Award, Poetry Society of America, 1981; Lamont Poetry Selection Award, Academy of American Poets, 1981, for *The Country between Us; Los Angeles Times* Book Award nominee, 1982, for *The Country between Us;* H.D.L., Russell Sage College, 1985; *Los Angeles Times* Book Award for Poetry, 1994, for *The Angel of History.*

WRITINGS:

(With Martha Jane Soltow) *Women in the Labor Movement, 1835-1925: An Annotated Bibliography,* Michigan State University Press (East Lansing, MI), 1972.
Gathering the Tribes (poetry), Yale University Press (New Haven, CT), 1976.
(Editor) *Women and War in El Salvador,* Women's International Resource Exchange (New York City), 1980.
The Country between Us (poetry), Copper Canyon Press (Port Townsend, WA), 1981.
(Translator) Claribel Alegria, *Flowers from the Volcano,* University of Pittsburgh Press (Pittsburgh, PA), 1982.
(Author of text) *El Salvador: The Work of Thirty Photographers,* edited by Harry Mattison, Susan Meiselas, and Fae Rubenstein, Writers and Readers Publishing Cooperative (New York City), 1983.
(Editor and author of introduction) *Against Forgetting: Twentieth-Century Poetry of Witness,* Norton (New York City), 1993.
The Angel of History (poetry), HarperCollins (New York City), 1994.

Contributing editor of *The Pushcart Prize: Best of the Small Presses,* Volume III; poetry co-editor of *The Pushcart Prize: Best of the Small Presses,* Volume VIII. Work represented in anthologies, including *The Pushcart Prize: Best of the Small Presses,* Volume VI and Volume VIII; *The American Poetry Anthology;* and *Anthology of Magazine Verse: Yearbook of American Poetry.* Contributor of poetry, articles, and reviews to periodicals, including *Parnassus: Poetry in Review, New York Times Book Review, Washington Post Book World, Ms., Antaeus, Atlantic Monthly,* and *American Poetry Review.* Poetry editor of *New Virginia Review,* 1981; contributing editor of *Tendril.*

SIDELIGHTS: "Perhaps no one better exemplifies the power and excellence of contemporary poetry than Carolyn Forche, who is not only one of the most affecting younger poets in America, but also one of the best poets writing anywhere in the world today," Jonathan Cott wrote in the introduction to his interview with Forche for *Rolling Stone.* Such praise was not new to Forche. Her first book of poetry, *Gathering the Tribes,* recounts experiences of the author's adolescence and young adult life and won the 1975 Yale Series of Younger Poets Award, and her second, *The Country between Us,* was named the 1981 Lamont Poetry Selection and became a poetry best-seller. In a critique for the *Los Angeles Times Book Review,* Art Seidenbaum maintained that the poems of the second volume "chronicle the awakening of a political consciousness and are themselves acts of commitment: to concepts and persons, to responsibility, to action." According to Joyce Carol Oates in the *New York Times Book Review,* Forche's ability to wed the "political" with the "personal" places her in the company of such poets as Pablo Neruda, Philip Levine, and Denise Levertov.

Forche began writing poetry with her mother's encouragement at the age of nine. Although she told Cott that she thought her work had little merit until she reached age nineteen—unimaginative verse initially composed in iambic pentameter because it was the only meter she knew—Forche also recalled that the activity provided her with endless hours of reverie: "I think I used writing as an escape. Writing and daydreaming. . . . I told myself narratives, and I made a parallel life to my own. . . . I suspected, when I was young, that this was madness, but I couldn't give it up."

By the time she was twenty-four, Forche had completed *Gathering the Tribes,* described by Stanley Kunitz in the book's foreword as a work centering on kinship. In these poems Forche "remembers her childhood in rural Michigan, evokes her Slovak ancestors, immerses herself in the American Indian culture of the Southwest, explores the mysteries of flesh, tries to understand the bonds of family, race, and sex," related Kunitz. "Burning the Tomato Worms," for example, deals with a young woman's sexual coming of age. But this poetic tale of "first sexual experience," Mark Harris stated in a *Dictionary of Literary Biography* essay, "is told against the larger backdrop of her grandmother's life and death and their meaning to a woman just grown."

Offering a slightly different perspective, Stanley Plumly, writing for the *American Poetry Review,* suggested that Forche's early poems involve "the initiation rites of innocence—rituals of conversion to experience. . . . What is finally learned involves the two-way perception of the spiritual in the carnal, the carnal in the spiritual." In "Kalaloch," which Kunitz appraised as quite possibly "the outstanding Sapphic poem of an era," Forche creates an erotic narrative describing a lesbian relationship. It is "one poem in particular," observed Plumly, "in which the rhythm of the natural world is realized in counterpart to the carnality of the human."

If *Gathering the Tribes* "introduced a poet of uncommon vigor and assurance," Oates wrote, then *The Country between Us* "is a distinct step forward." A *Ms.* reviewer called that second book "a poetry of dissent from a poet outraged." Forche herself told Cott: "The voice in my first book doesn't know what it thinks, it doesn't make any judgments. All it can do is perceive and describe and use language to make some sort of re-creation of moments in time. But I noticed that the person in the second book makes an utterance."

Forche's first two volumes of poetry were separated by a period of five years, during the course of which she was involved with Amnesty International and with translating the work of Salvadoran poets. In those years she also had the opportunity to go to Central America as a journalist and human rights advocate and learned firsthand of violations against life and liberty. While there, she viewed inadequate health facilities that had never received the foreign aid designated for them and discovered that sixty-three out of every thousand children died from gastrointestinal infections before age one; she saw for herself the young girls who had been sexually mutilated; she learned of torture victims who had been beaten, starved, and otherwise abused; and she experienced something of what it was like to survive in a country where baby food jars are sometimes used as bombs.

Her experiences found expression in *The Country between Us.* As reviewer Katha Pollitt observed in the *Nation,* Forche "insists more than once on the transforming power of what she has seen, on the gulf it has created between herself and those who have seen less and dared less." The poet herself admitted to the compelling nature of her Central American experience. "I tried not to write about El Salvador in poetry, because I thought it might be better to do so in journalistic articles," she told Cott. "But I couldn't—the poems just came." El Salvador became the primary subject of *The Country between Us.* In these poems Forche "addresses herself unflinchingly to the exterior, historical world," Oates explained. She did so at a time when most of her contemporaries were writing poetry in which there is no room for politics—poetry, Pollitt stated, "of wistful longings, of failed connections, of inevitable personal loss, expressed in a set of poetic strategies that suit such themes."

Forche is considered particularly adept at depicting cruelty and helpless victims, and in so doing, Paul Gray wrote in *Time,* she "makes pain palpable." More than one critic singled out her poem "The Colonel," centering on her now-famous encounter with a Salvadoran colonel who, as he made light of human rights, emptied a bag of human ears before Forche. The poem concludes: "Something for your poetry, no? he said. Some of the ears on the floor caught this scrap of his voice. Some of the ears on the floor were pressed to the ground." Pollitt remarked that "at their best, Forche's poems have the immediacy of war correspondence, postcards from the volcano of twentieth-century barbarism."

A dozen years passed between the publication of *The Country between Us* and *Against Forgetting: Twentieth-Century Poetry of Witness,* her anthology of poets speaking of human rights violations on a global level. The poems in this anthology present what Matthew Rothschild in the *Progressive* called "some of the most dramatic antiwar and anti-torture poetry written in this benighted century." The poems provide, as Gail Wronsky pointed out in the *Antioch Review,* "irrefutable and copious evidence of the human ability to record, to write, to speak in the face of those atrocities." Building on the tradition of social protest and the antiwar poems of the late 1960s, Forche presents a range of approaches: "Many of the poems here are eyes-open, horrifyingly graphic portrayals of human brutality," observed Rothschild. "But others are of defiance, demonstrating resolve and extracting hope even in the most extreme circumstances."

Against Forgetting begins with poets who witnessed the Ottoman Turk genocide of 1.5 million Armenians between 1909 and 1918. In this section the executed Armenian poet Siamento seems to speak for all the other poets in the collection: "Don't be afraid. I must tell you what I say / so people will understand / the crimes men do to men." Another section includes poems by Americans, Germans, and Japanese about the effects of World War II upon those who witnessed and recorded the events. There are also sections on the Holocaust, the Spanish Civil War, the Soviet Union, Central and Eastern Europe, the Mediterranean, the Middle East, Latin America, South Africa, and China.

Critics are divided upon both the selections in and the importance of *Against Forgetting*. Wronsky, for example, questioned why "women of all races and ethnicities are underrepresented here (124 male poets to 20 female)." But Phoebe Pettingell in the *New Leader* argued that the work's flaws were "outweighed by the anthology's breadth and scope, and by the excellence of most of its entries. *Against Forgetting* preaches the hope that humanity, after a century of unparalleled brutality met largely by helplessness, can finally learn to mend its ways." John Bayley in the *New York Review of Books* called it "a remarkable book. Not only in itself and for the poems it contains, but for the ideas that lie behind their selection as an anthology."

The year following the publication of *Against Forgetting* saw Forche bring out her own book of witness, *The Angel of History*, which won the 1994 *Los Angeles Times* Book Award for Poetry. The book is divided into five sections, dealing with the atrocities of war in France, Japan, and Germany and with references to the poet's own experiences in Beirut and El Salvador. The title figure, the Angel of History—a figure imagined by German philosopher and critic Walter Benjamin—can record the miseries of humanity yet is unable either to prevent these miseries from happening or from suffering from the pain associated with them.

Kevin Walker in the *Detroit Free Press* called the book "a meditation on destruction, survival and memory." Don Bogen in the *Nation* saw this as a logical development, since Forche's work with *Against Forgetting* was "instrumental in moving her poetry beyond the politics of personal encounter. *The Angel of History* is rather an extended poetic mediation on the broader contexts—historical, aesthetic, philosophical—which include our century's atrocities."

In an interview with Jill Taft-Kaufman in *Text and Performance Quarterly*, Forche explained that she sought to "make a form which would push my work further, breaking open the forms I had been writing on before," what she has called her "first-person lyric free verse narrative." In her new style, the work is "in long lines, but not even lines. . . . These lines go all the way to the margin, and certain thoughts are completed and certain [ones] are not. . . . It's very experimental. No closure." Forche indicated that the evolution of her new style "had something to do with the 20th Century," so that the style of the work is linked with the subject of the work. Calvin Bedient in the *Threepenny Review* praised Forche for the "new tone, at once sensitive and bleak, a new rhythm, at once prose-like and exquisite, a new line and method of sequencing, at once fluid and fragmentary." In the second section of the book, "The Notebook of the Uprising," Forche takes a "more journal-like" approach, Bogen pointed out, "loosely following a trip to Eastern Europe." The critic noted that "her lines have less of the documentary and more of the diary to them, with a focus on numinous moments and their ramifications."

Critical response to *The Angel of History* was generally supportive. Bedient claimed that *The Angel of History* is "instantly recognizable as a great book, the most humanitarian and aesthetically 'inevitable' response to a half-century of atrocities that has yet been written in English." Steven Ratiner in *Christian Science Monitor* called the collection one which "addresses the terror and inhumanity that have become standard elements in the 20th-century political landscape—and yet affirms as well the even greater reservoir of the human spirit."

Forche is a poet of social and political conscience in an era when poetry is often criticized for being self-centered and self-absorbed. But Forche's verse does not always succeed, according to some critics. Pollitt identified an "incongruity between Forche's themes and her poetic strategies," also commenting on a certain lack of "verbal energy" in her work. William Logan, critiquing for the *Times Literary Supplement*, explained that "in her attempt to offer a personal response to the horrors she has witnessed, Forche too often emphasizes herself at their expense. . . . Forche's work relies on sensibility, but she has not found a language for deeper feeling." Nevertheless, recognizing Forche's achievement, Pollitt commended the poet for "her brave and impassioned attempt to make a place in her poems for starving children and bullet factories, for torturers and victims." She might not be a reassuring poet but, in the words of Paul Gray, "she is something better, an arresting and often unforgettable voice."

BIOGRAPHICAL/CRITICAL SOURCES:

BOOKS

Contemporary Literary Criticism, Gale (Detroit), Volume 25, 1983, Volume 83, 1994, Volume 86, 1995.

Contemporary Poets, fifth edition, St. James Press (Detroit), 1991.

Dictionary of Literary Biography, Volume 5: *American Poets since World War II,* Gale, 1980.

Poetry Criticism, Volume 10, Gale, 1994.

PERIODICALS

American Poetry, spring, 1986, pp. 51-69.

American Poetry Review, November-December, 1976, p. 45; July-August, 1981, pp. 3-8; January-February, 1983, pp. 35-39; November-December, 1988, pp. 35-40.

Antioch Review, summer, 1994, p. 536.

Bloomsbury Review, September/October, 1994, p. 19.

Book Forum, 1976, pp. 369-99.

Boston Globe, July 24, 1994, p. 42.

Centennial Review, spring, 1986, pp. 160-80.

Chicago Tribune, December 13, 1982, pp. 1-3.

Christian Science Monitor, April 20, 1994, p. 20.

Commonweal, November 25, 1977.

Detroit Free Press, May 27, 1982; May 22, 1994, p. 8.

Detroit News, June 8, 1982.

Georgia Review, winter, 1982, pp. 911-22; summer, 1994, pp. 361-66.

Library Journal, May 1, 1993, p. 88.

Los Angeles Times, August 24, 1982; October 17, 1982; February 22, 1984.

Los Angeles Times Book Review, May 23, 1982; October 17, 1982.

Ms., January, 1980; September, 1982.

Nation, May 8, 1982; October 16, 1982; December 27, 1993, pp. 809, 814; October 24, 1994, p. 464.

New England Review, spring, 1994, p. 144-154.

New Leader, May 17, 1993, pp. 23-24.

New York Review of Books, June 24, 1993, pp. 20-22.

New York Times Book Review, August 8, 1976; April 4, 1982; April 19, 1982; December 4, 1983.

Parnassus, spring-summer, 1982, pp. 9-21.

Progressive, October, 1993, pp. 45-46.

Publishers Weekly, February 1, 1993, p. 78; January 31, 1994, p. 7.

Rolling Stone, April 14, 1983, pp. 81, 83-7, 110-11.

Text and Performance Quarterly, January, 1990, pp. 61-70.

Threepenny Review, summer, 1994, pp. 19-20.

Time, March 15, 1982.

Times Literary Supplement, June 10, 1983.

Triquarterly, winter, 1986, pp. 30, 32-8.

Village Voice, March 29, 1976.

Virginia Quarterly Review, autumn, 1994, p. 136.

Washington Post Book World, May 30, 1982.

Women's Review of Books, July, 1995, p. 3.

OTHER

DISCovering Authors Modules (CD-ROM product), Gale, 1996.

—*Sketch by Robert Miltner*

*   *   *

FORREST, Richard (Stockton) 1932-
(Lee Evans, Rebecca Morgan, Stockton Woods)

PERSONAL: Born May 8, 1932, in Orange, NJ; son of Williams Kraemer and Georgia (Muller) Forrest; married Frances Anne Reese, December 20, 1952 (divorced May, 1955); married Mary Bolan Brumby (a nurse), May 11, 1955 (separated, 1995); children: (first marriage) Richard; (second marriage) Christopher, Remley, Katherine, Mongin, Bellamy. *Education:* Attended New York Dramatic Workshop, 1950, and University of South Carolina, 1953-55. *Politics:* Democrat. *Religion:* Unitarian Universalist.

ADDRESSES: Home—8912 Ewing Dr., Bethesda, MD 20817. *Agent*—Phyllis Westburg, Harold Ober Associates Inc., 40 East 49th St., New York, NY 10017.

CAREER: Playwright, 1955-58; Lawyers Title Insurance Corp., Richmond, VA, state manager, 1958-68; Chicago Title Insurance Co., Chicago, IL, vice-president, 1969-72; freelance writer, 1972—. Vice-president of Connecticut Board of Title Underwriters. *Military service:* U.S. Army, Rangers, 1951-53; served in Korea; became staff sergeant.

MEMBER: Mystery Writers of America, Authors Guild, Authors League of America.

AWARDS, HONORS: Edgar Allan Poe Award, Mystery Writers of America, 1975, for *Who Killed Mr. Garland's Mistress?;* Porgie Award for best original paperback, *West Coast Review of Books,* for *The Laughing Man.*

WRITINGS:

MYSTERY NOVELS

Who Killed Mr. Garland's Mistress?, Pinnacle Books (New York City), 1974.

The Killing Edge, Tower Publications (New York City), 1980.

Lark, New American Library (New York City), 1986.

"LYON AND BEA WENTWORTH" MYSTERY SERIES

A Child's Garden of Death, Bobbs-Merrill (New York City), 1975.

The Wizard of Death, Bobbs-Merrill, 1977.

Death through the Looking Glass, Bobbs-Merrill, 1978.

The Death in the Willows, Holt (New York City), 1979.

Death at Yew Corner, Holt, 1981.

Death under the Lilacs, St. Martin's (New York City), 1985.

Death on the Mississippi, St. Martin's, 1989.

UNDER PSEUDONYM STOCKTON WOODS

The Laughing Man, Fawcett (New York City), 1980.

Game Bet, Fawcett, 1981.

The Man Who Heard Too Much, Fawcett, 1983.

(With wife, Mary Forrest) *The Complete Nursing Home Guide,* Facts on File (New York City), 1990.

(With M. Forrest) *Retirement Living,* Facts on File, 1991.

OTHER

Also author of the plays *Cry for the Spring, The Meek Cry Loud,* and *The Sandhouse.* Author of the "Lexi Lane Nautical Mystery" series under the pseudonym Rebecca Morgan and the "Randy Holden Aeronautical Adventure" series under the pseudonym Lee Evans. Contributor of short stories to periodicals, including *Northeast Magazine, Ellery Queen Mystery Magazine,* and *Mystery Monthly.*

Several editions of Forrest's work have been published in Finnish, French, German, Italian, and Swedish. His manuscript collection is part of the Twentieth-Century Archives at Mungar Memorial Library, Boston University, Boston.

WORK IN PROGRESS: The Pied Piper of Death, a suspense novel.

SIDELIGHTS: Richard Forrest once told *CA* that he "spent early years as a playwright until [a] growing family made business a necessity. Resigned position as vice-president of major insurance company on fortieth birthday to write full time—why not?"

BIOGRAPHICAL/CRITICAL SOURCES:

PERIODICALS

Chicago Tribune Book World, April 19, 1981.

New York Times Book Review, March 8, 1981.

Publishers Weekly, December 12, 1980.

Washington Post Book World, January 18, 1981.

FOSTER, David William (Anthony) 1940-

PERSONAL: Born September 11, 1940, in Seattle, WA; son of William Henry (a mechanic) and Rosamond (Pepin) Foster; married Virginia Maria Ramos (a professor), May 31, 1966. *Education:* University of Washington, Seattle, B.A. (magna cum laude), 1961, M.A., 1963, Ph.D., 1964. *Politics:* Democrat. *Religion:* Roman Catholic.

ADDRESSES: Home—928 West Palm Lane, Phoenix, AZ 85007. *Office*—Department of Foreign Languages, Arizona State University, Tempe, AZ 85281.

CAREER: University of Washington, research associate, instructor, and teaching assistant in Spanish, 1961-64; Fresno State College, visiting instructor, summer 1962; Vanderbilt University, visiting assistant professor, summer, 1964; University of Missouri—Columbia, assistant professor of Spanish, 1964-66; Arizona State University, Tempe, assistant professor, 1966-68, associate professor, 1968-70, professor of Spanish, 1970—, currently Regents' Professor of Spanish and Women's Studies and director of graduate studies, interdisciplinary humanities. Fulbright professor, Universidad Nacional de la Plata, Argentina, 1967, Instituto Nacional del Profesorado Superior, Universidad de Buenos Aires, Argentina, 1973, Universidad Federal do Parana, 1985, and Universidad Catolica del Uruguay, 1988; Inter-American Development Bank professor of linguistics, Universidad Catolica de Chile, 1975; visiting professor of Spanish, University of California, Los Angeles, 1989, and University of Arizona summer program in Guadalajara, 1989.

MEMBER: Modern Language Association of America, Hispanic Institute, Linguistic Society of America, Instituto Internacional de Literatura Iberoamericana, American Association of University Professors, Philological Association of the Pacific Coast, Rocky Mountain Council for Latin American Studies, Phi Sigma Iota.

WRITINGS:

Forms of the Novel in the Work of Camilo Jose Cela, University of Missouri Press (Columbia), 1967.

The Myth of Paraguay in the Fiction of Augusto Roa Bastos, University of North Carolina Press (Chapel Hill), 1969.

(With wife, Virginia Ramos Foster) *A Research Guide to Argentine Literature,* Scarecrow (Metuchen, NJ), 1970, 2nd revised and expanded edition published as *Argentine Literature: A Research Guide,* Garland (New York City), 1982.

Christian Allegory in Early Hispanic Poetry, University Press of Kentucky (Lexington), 1971.

The Early Spanish Ballad, Twayne (New York City), 1971.

The Marques de Santillana, Twayne, 1971.

(With V. R. Foster) *Luis de Gongora,* Twayne, 1973.

Unamuno and the Novel as Expressionistic Conceit, InterAmerican University Press (Hato Rey, Puerto Rico), 1973.

(Author of introduction) John S. Knight and German Arciniegas, *The Twilight of the Tyrants,* Arizona State University Center for Latin American Studies (Tempe), 1973.

Currents in the Contemporary Argentine Novel: Arlt, Mallea, Sabato, and Cortazar, University of Missouri Press, 1975.

Augusto Roa Bastos, Twayne, 1978.

Studies in the Contemporary Spanish-American Short Story, University of Missouri Press, 1979.

Para una lectura semiotica del ensayo latinoamericano; textos representativos, Jose Porrua Turanzas (Madrid), 1983.

Estudios sobre teatro mexicano contemporaneo; semiologia de la competencia teatral, Peter Lang (New York City), 1984.

Cuban Literature: A Research Guide, G. K. Hall (Boston), 1984.

Alternate Voices in the Contemporary Latin American Narrative, University of Missouri Press, 1985.

The Argentine Teatro Independiente, 1930-1955, Spanish Literature Publishing (York, SC), 1986.

Social Realism in the Argentine Narrative, University of North Carolina at Chapel Hill (Chapel Hill), 1986.

From Mafalda to Los Supermachos: Latin American Graphic Humor as Popular Culture, Lynne Rienner (Boulder), 1989.

The Argentine Generation of 1880: Literature, Ideology, and the Social Text, University of Missouri Press, 1990.

Gay and Lesbian Themes in Latin American Writing, University of Texas Press (Austin), 1991.

Contemporary Argentine Cinema, University of Missouri Press, 1992.

Cultural Diversity in Latin American Literature, University of New Mexico Press (Albuquerque), 1994.

EDITOR

(With V. R. Foster) *Modern Latin American Literature,* two volumes, Ungar (New York City), 1975.

Latin American Government Leaders, 2nd edition, Center for Latin American Studies, Arizona State University, 1975.

A Dictionary of Contemporary Latin American Authors, Center for Latin American Studies, Arizona State University, 1975.

Sourcebook of Hispanic Culture in the United States, American Library Association (Chicago), 1982.

Marques de Santillana: Poesia (selected poetry), Taurus (Madrid), 1982.

(With Roberto Reis) *A Dictionary of Contemporary Brazilian Authors,* Center for Latin American Studies, Arizona State University, 1982.

(With Francisco Arturo Rosales) *Hispanics and the Humanities in the Southwest: A Directory of Resources,* Center for Latin American Studies, Arizona State University, 1983.

(And contributor) *Handbook of Latin American Literature,* Garland, 1987, 2nd edition, 1992.

(And contributor) *The Redemocratization of Argentine Culture, 1983 and Beyond: An International Research Symposium,* Center for Latin American Studies, Arizona State University, 1989.

Literatura hispanoamericana; una antologia, Garland, 1994.

Latin American Writers on Gay and Lesbian Themes: A Bio-Critical Sourcebook, Greenwood Press (Westport, CT), 1994.

Mexican Literature: A History, University of Texas Press, 1994.

COMPILER OF BIBLIOGRAPHIES

(With H. L. Nostrand and Ben Christiansen) *Research on Language Teaching: An Annotated International Bibliography for 1945-1961,* University of Washington Press (Seattle), 1962, revised edition, 1965.

(With V. R. Foster) *Manual of Hispanic Bibliography: An Annotated Handbook of Basic Sources,* University of Washington Press, 1970, 2nd revised and expanded edition, Garland, 1977.

A Bibliography of the Works of Jorge Luis Borges, Center for Latin American Studies, Arizona State University, 1971.

(With Gary L. Brower) *Haiku in Western Languages: An Annotated Bibliography (with Some Reference to Senryu),* Scarecrow, 1972.

The Twentieth Century Spanish-American Novel: A Bibliography, Scarecrow, 1975.

(With Horacio Jorge Becco) *La nueva narrativa hispanoamericana, bibliografia,* Casa Pardo (Buenos Aires), 1976.

Chilean Literature: A Working Bibliography of Secondary Sources, G. K. Hall, 1978.

Peruvian Literature: A Bibliography of Secondary Sources, Greenwood Press, 1981.

Mexican Literature: A Bibliography of Secondary Sources, Scarecrow, 1981, 2nd edition, 1992.

Puerto Rican Literature: A Bibliography of Secondary Sources, Greenwood Press, 1981.

Jorge Luis Borges: An Annotated Primary and Secondary Bibliography, Garland, 1984.

(With Walter Rela) *Brazilian Literature: A Research Bibliography,* Garland, 1990.

TRANSLATOR

Enrique Medina, *The Duke: Memories and Anti-Memories of a Participant in the Repression,* Zed Books (London), 1985.

Miguel Mendez, *The Dream of Santa Maria de las Piedras,* Bilingual Press/Editorial Bilingue (Tempe), 1989.

Aristeo Brito, *The Devil in Texas: El diablo en Texas,* Bilingual Press/Editorial Bilingue, 1990.

Mendez, *Pilgrims in Aztlan,* Bilingual Press/Editorial Bilingue, 1992.

(And author of introduction) Medina, *Las tumbas,* Garland, 1993.

OTHER

Contributor to numerous books, encyclopedias, journals, and other periodicals, including *International Review of Applied Linguistics, Latin American Literary Review, World Literature Today, Revista hispanica moderna, PMLA, Hispanic Journal,* and *Anthropological Linguistics;* contributor to *Proceedings* and *Papers* of conferences and annual meetings of professional organizations. Associate editor, *Hispania,* 1975-82; editor, *Rocky Mountain Review of Language and Literature,* 1980-84; member of editorial board, *Federation Reports,* 1981-84; editor, *Chasqui; revista de literatura latinoamericana.*

*   *   *

FRADIN, Dennis Brindell 1945-

PERSONAL: Born December 20, 1945, in Chicago, IL; son of Myron (an accountant) and Selma (Brindell) Fradin; married Judith Bloom (a high school English teacher), March 19, 1967; children: Anthony, Diana, Michael. *Education:* Northwestern University, B.A., 1967; University of Illinois, graduate study, 1968. *Religion:* Jewish.

ADDRESSES: Home—2121 Dobson, Evanston, IL 60202. *Agent*—McIntosh & Otis, Inc., 475 Fifth Ave., New York, NY 10017.

CAREER: Writer.

WRITINGS:

FOR CHILDREN

Cara (fiction), Enslow (Hillside, NJ), 1977.
Cave Painter, Enslow, 1978.
Bad Luck Tony, illustrated by Joanne Scribner, Prentice-Hall (Englewood Cliffs, NJ), 1978.
North Star, illustrated by William Neebe, Enslow, 1978.

The New Spear, illustrated by Tom Dunnington, Enslow, 1979.
Beyond the Mountain, Beyond the Forest, illustrated by John Maggard, Enslow, 1979.
Young People's Stories of Our States, Enslow, 1980.
One Winter, Hastings (New York City), Enslow, 1985.
How I Saved the World (science fiction), Dillon Press (Minneapolis, MN), 1986.
Remarkable Children: Twenty Who Changed History, Enslow, 1987.
Medicine: Yesterday, Today, and Tomorrow, Enslow, 1989.
Amerigo Vespucci, F. Watts (New York City), 1991.

"DISASTER!" SERIES: PUBLISHED BY CHILDRENS PRESS (CHICAGO)

Volcanoes, 1982.
Tornadoes, 1982.
Earthquakes, 1982.
Fires, 1982.
Floods, 1982.
Hurricanes, 1982.
Blizzards and Winter Weather, 1983.
Droughts, 1983.
Famines, 1986.

"ENCHANTMENT OF THE WORLD" SERIES: PUBLISHED BY CHILDRENS PRESS

The Netherlands, 1983.
The Republic of Ireland, 1984.
Ethiopia, 1988.

"A NEW TRUE BOOK" SERIES: PUBLISHED BY CHILDRENS PRESS

Astronomy, 1983.
Archeaology, 1983.
Farming, 1983.
Movies, 1983.
Comets, Asteroids, and Meteors, 1984.
Explorers, 1984.
Movies, 1984.
Olympics, 1984.
Pioneers, 1984.
Skylab, 1984.
Hailey's Comet, 1985.
Moon Flights, 1985.
Space Colonies, 1985.
Space Lab, 1985.
The Voyager Space Probes, 1985.
Voting and Elections, 1985.
Continents, 1986.
Heredity, 1987.
Nuclear Energy, 1987.
Radiation, 1987.
Space Telescope, 1987.

The Search for Extraterrestrial Intelligence, 1987.
Cancer, 1988.
Drug Abuse, 1988.
The Cheyenne, 1988.
The Declaration of Independence, 1988.
The Flag of the United States, 1988.
The Pawnee, 1988.
The Shoshoni, 1988.
The Thirteen Colonies, 1988.
Earth, 1989.
Pluto, 1989.
Uranus, 1989.
Jupiter, 1989.
Saturn, 1989.
Mars, 1989.
Venus, 1989.
Neptune, 1990.
Mercury, 1990.

"THE THIRTEEN COLONIES" SERIES

The Virginia Colony, Enslow, 1986.
The Massachusetts Colony, Enslow, 1987.
The New Hampshire Colony, Enslow, 1988.
The New York Colony, Enslow, 1988.
The Pennsylvania Colony, Enslow, 1988.
The Rhode Island Colony, Enslow, 1989.
The Connecticut Colony, Enslow, 1990.
The Georgia Colony, Enslow, 1990.
The Maryland Colony, Enslow, 1990.
The New Jersey Colony, Enslow, 1991.
The North Carolina Colony, Childrens Press, 1991.
The Delaware Colony, Enslow, 1992.
The South Carolina Colony, Childrens Press, 1992.

"COLONIAL PROFILES" SERIES

Abigail Adams: Advisor to a President, illustrated by T. Dunnington, Enslow, 1989.
John Hancock: First Signer of the Declaration of Independence, illustrated by T. Dunnington, Enslow, 1989.
Anne Hutchinson: Fighter for Religious Freedom, illustrated by T. Dunnington, Enslow, 1990.
King Philip: Indian Leader, illustrated by T. Dunnington, Enslow, 1990.
Patrick Henry: "Give Me Liberty or Give Me Death," illustrated by T. Dunnington, Enslow, 1990.
Hiawatha: Messenger of Peace, M. K. McElderry Books, 1992.

"BEST HOLIDAY BOOKS" SERIES

Columbus Day, Enslow, 1990.
Hanukkah, Enslow, 1990.
Christmas, Enslow, 1990.
Valentine's Day, Enslow, 1990.
Halloween, Enslow, 1990.

Thanksgiving Day, Enslow, 1990.
Lincoln's Birthday, Enslow, 1990.
Washington's Birthday, Enslow, 1990.

OTHER

Author of "Words and Pictures" series on each of the fifty states and "From Sea to Shining Sea" series on North American geography, both for Childrens Press. Some of Fradin's work has also been published in Spanish.

*SIDELIGHTS:*Author of over one hundred children's books, Dennis Fradin explores a wide variety of topics in his writing, including the movies, the Olympics, geography, colonial and North American history, and Earth and space sciences. Fradin also frequently addresses Native American themes in his work.

Fradin writes realistically about his subjects. For example, *Publishers Weekly* described *Hiawatha: Messenger of Peace* as a "text [which] accurately explains the role [Hiawatha] has played in our history"; unlike other children's authors, Fradin does not depict her as "godlike" or "supernatural." Fradin declared in the *Chicago Tribune:* "I've become a fanatic about facts. I like getting obscure printed material and tracking down the real story." In a *Booklist* review, Fradin was called "scrupulous in distinguishing what is known, what is surmised, and what is legend."

Fradin's geographical series "From Sea to Shining Sea" provides introductions to the regions and states covered; each book includes a travelogue, information about distinguished people and events, photographs, reproductions, and maps. Marcia S. Rettig, in *School Library Journal,* calls Fradin's *Hawaii,* an "attractive supplemental resource." Cheryl Cufair, however, reviewing *New York* for *School Library Journal,* concludes that "the brevity of information limits its usefulness."

Fradin wrote in the *Chicago Tribune:* "At first, I was scared of reviews. Now I have enough confidence that if I feel a book is good, I don't care what anyone says. I haven't had too many bad ones. *School Library Journal* and *Booklist* are the ones people quake over in this field. I was happy when one reviewer pointed out how rhythmical my sentences are. If I make any changes, I'll type the whole manuscript over to see how the new rhythms will be because I feel in children's books rhythm is real important."

Fradin added: "I admire the beginner who is writing but not selling. This is the real thing. This is the impulse that makes someone a writer. It's what you see when kids write stories . . . . I want to keep [writing] as long as I love to do it. I want always to have a lot of that little kid in me."

Fradin once told *CA:* "From the time I was very young, I always wanted to be a writer. I wrote my first story when I was eight or so. I wrote it in longhand and my mother typed it for me. When I was in high school I had a teacher who encouraged me. He read one of my short stories to his classes and said it was the best story by a freshman he'd ever seen. I also had another teacher who looked at some of my stories and told me to forget about becoming a writer. So it was at the age of about fourteen that I realized something important: some people will like what you do and some people won't, so you'd better make sure to please the main critic in your life—yourself.

"I sold a couple of stories and won creative writing scholarships while I was in college, but it took me until my late twenties to really start selling my work. I kept sending out one story that had been rejected more than thirty times. In keeping with my idea that my opinion counted for something, I sent the story out again and again because I thought it was good. Finally, I sold it. I've been selling my work pretty regularly ever since."

BIOGRAPHICAL/CRITICAL SOURCES:

PERIODICALS

Booklist, September 15, 1992.
Chicago Tribune, December 20, 1987.
Publishers Weekly, August 31, 1992.
School Library Journal, January, 1994; February, 1994; November, 1994.

*   *   *

FRANKS, Kenny Arthur   1945-

PERSONAL: Born July 19, 1945, in Okemah, OK; son of Arthur and Christine Franks; children: Douglas William, Bryan James, Jeffery Tyler. *Education:* Attended University of Oklahoma, 1963-65; Central State College (now University of Central Oklahoma), Edmond, B.A., 1969; Oklahoma State University, M.A., 1971, Ph.D., 1973.

ADDRESSES: Home—11501 Lochwood Dr., #107, Yukon, OK 73099. *Office*—Oklahoma Heritage Association, 201 Northwest 14th St., Oklahoma City, OK 73103.

CAREER: Oklahoma Historical Society, Oklahoma City, OK, editor, 1973-75, director of publications, 1975-78; editor of education and publication at Oklahoma Heritage Association, Oklahoma City; instructor and adjunct assistant professor at Oklahoma State University, Stillwater; lecturer at University of Central Oklahoma, Edmond; adjunct instructor, Redlands Community College, El Reno, OK; adjunct member of faculty and member of graduate faculty, University of Central Oklahoma; member of adjunct faculty, Oklahoma State University, Oklahoma City.

Oklahoma Heritage Association, coordinator of museum intern program and coordinator of oral history project; Oklahoma Historical Society, research coordinator of docent program and assistant coordinator of museum intern program. City of Union City, OK, president of board of trustees, 1982-83, member of planning commission, 1982-93; member of board of directors of Canadian County Concerned Citizens Committee; member, Canadian County Industries Authority, 1990—. Research and editorial assistant to director of Will Rogers Project, Oklahoma State University. Consultant to television and radio programs, organizations, and industry, including Center for the American Indian, Exxon Oil Corp., Mobil Oil Corp., ARCO, Shell USA, OXY USA, and United States Postal Service Commemorative Stamp Series.

MEMBER: Indian Territory Posse of Westerners International, Phi Alpha Theta.

AWARDS, HONORS: Award of Merit, American Association for State and Local History, 1977, for editing "The Oklahoma Series"; Mrs. Simon Baruch University Award from United Daughters of the Confederacy, 1979, Jefferson Davis Medal from United Daughters of the Confederacy, 1979, Brigadier General Albert Pike, C.S.A. Literary Award for outstanding excellence on southern heritage of the trans-Mississippi west from Trans-Mississippi Department of the Sons of Confederate Veterans, 1979, and Southern Heritage Award from Military Order of the Stars and Bars, 1980, all for biography *Stand Watie and the Agony of the Cherokee Nation;* Distinguished Service Award from Oklahoma Petroleum Council, 1981, for *A History of the Oklahoma Petroleum Industry;* Petroleum Heritage Award, 1982, for *Early Oklahoma Oil;* elected to Okemah (OK) Hall of Fame.

WRITINGS:

(With John Stewart) *A Guide to Research at the Oklahoma Historical Society and the Oklahoma State Archives,* Oklahoma Historical Society (Oklahoma City, OK), 1975.

(With Stewart) *State Records, Manuscripts, and Newspapers at the Oklahoma State Archives and the Oklahoma Historical Society,* Oklahoma Historical Society, 1975.

(With George H. Shirk and Muriel H. Wright) *Mark of Heritage: Oklahoma's Historic Sites,* Oklahoma Historical Society, 1975.

(Editor with Odie B. Faulk and Paul F. Lambert) *Early Military Forts and Posts in Oklahoma,* Oklahoma Historical Society, 1978.

Stand Watie and the Agony of the Cherokee Nation, Memphis State University Press (Memphis, TN), 1979.

The Oklahoma Petroleum Industry, University of Oklahoma Press (Norman), 1980.

(With Lambert and Carl N. Tyson) *Early Oklahoma Oil: A Photographic History, 1859-1936,* Texas A & M University Press (College Station), 1981.

(With Lambert) *Early Louisiana/Arkansas Oil: A Photographic History,* Texas A & M University Press, 1982.

Citizen-Soldiers: A History of the Oklahoma National Guard, University of Oklahoma Press, 1984.

(With Lambert) *Voices from the Oil Field,* University of Oklahoma Press, 1984.

The Rush Begins: A History of the Cleveland, Red Ford, and Glenn Pool Oil Fields, Oklahoma Heritage Association (Oklahoma City), 1984.

You're Doin Fine Oklahoma! A History of the Diamond Jubilee, Oklahoma Historical Society, 1984.

The Legacy of Dean Julian C. Monnet and the Desegregation of the Oklahoma City School System, Western Heritage Press, 1984.

(With Lambert) *Early California Oil: A Photographic History, 1865-1940,* Texas A & M University Press, 1985.

Ragtown: A History of the Healdton-Hewitt Oil Field, Oklahoma Heritage Association, 1986.

Oklahoma Syllabus: Key to State Heritage, University of Science and Arts of Oklahoma (Chickasha), 1986.

A History of the Oklahoma Pipeline Industry, Oklahoma Heritage Association, 1987.

(With Bob Blackburn, Faulk, and Lambert) *Oklahoma City: Hub of the Sooner State,* Windsor Publications (Woodland Hills, CA), 1988.

The Osage Oil Boom, Oklahoma Heritage Association, 1989.

(With Lambert) *Oklahoma Geographic,* American and World Geographic Publishing (Helena, MT), 1994.

(With Lambert) *A History of Pawnee County,* Oklahoma Heritage Association, 1994.

Author of *Petroleum Heritage* series on KTOK-Radio. Contributor to books, including *The Civil War Era in Indian Territory,* edited by LeRoy H. Fischer, Lorrin L. Morrison (Los Angeles), 1974; *Drill Bits, Picks, and Shovels: A History of Mineral Resources in Oklahoma,* edited by John W. Morris, Oklahoma Historical Society, 1982; *Oklahoma: Land of the Fair God,* edited by Odie B. Faulk, Windsor Publications, 1986; and *Historical Homes of Lincoln Terrace,* edited by James Edwin Alexander, Southwest Heritage Publications (Oklahoma City), 1993. Contributor to *Biographical Directory of the United States Executive Branch, 1774-1977, Biographical Directory of the Governors of the United States, 1776-1976, Encyclopedia of the Confederacy, American National Biography,* and *Encyclopedia of the American Indian.* Editor of "Oklahoma Series," Oklahoma Historical Society, 1975-80; Oklahoma Heritage Association, editor of "Oklahoma Trackmaker Series," 1980-83, and "Oklahoma Horizons Series," 1980-81, and (with University of Central Oklahoma Press) "Oklahoma Statesmen Series." Contributor of numerous

articles and reviews to periodicals, including *Historical Magazine of the Protestant Episcopal Church, Western Historical Quarterly, Journal of the West, Antique Oklahoma, Arkansas Historical Quarterly, Oklahoma Women,* and *Great Plains Journal.* Editor of *Chronicles of Oklahoma,* 1973-80; book review editor, *Rural Oklahoma News,* 1991—. Creator of "Historic Oklahoma Map" series, Oklahoma Heritage Association, 1990.

BIOGRAPHICAL/CRITICAL SOURCES:

PERIODICALS

American Historical Review, April, 1985.

*   *   *

FRASER, Anthea
(Lorna Cameron, Vanessa Graham)

PERSONAL: Born in Lancashire, England; daughter of William Wallace (a director) and Mary Adelaide (a writer) Roby; married Ian Mackintosh Fraser, March 22, 1956; children: Fiona, Rosalind. *Education:* Attended Cheltenham Ladies' College. *Politics:* Conservative. *Religion:* Church of England.

ADDRESSES: Home—22 Chiltern Way, Tring, Hertfordshire HP23 5JX, England. *Agent*—Laurence Pollinger, 18 Maddox St., London W1R 0EU, England.

CAREER: Writer.

MEMBER: Society of Women Writers and Journalists, Crime Writers' Association (secretary, 1986—).

WRITINGS:

NOVELS

Designs of Annabelle, Mills & Boon (London), 1971.

In the Balance, Mills & Boon, 1973, Doubleday (New York City), 1979.

Laura Possessed (ghost story), Dodd (New York City), 1974.

Home through the Dark (thriller), Milton House Books, 1974, Dodd, 1976.

Whistler's Lane (ghost story), Dodd, 1975.

Breath of Brimstone, Dodd, 1977.

Presence of Mind, Corgi Books (London), 1978.

Island-in-Waiting, St. Martin's (New York City), 1979.

(Under pseudonym Vanessa Graham) *Time of Trial,* R. Hale (London), 1979.

(Under pseudonym Vanessa Graham) *Second Time Around,* Doubleday, 1980.

The Stone, St. Martin's, 1980.

(Under pseudonym Lorna Cameron) *Summer in France,* Mills & Boon, 1981.

A Shroud for Delilah, Collins (London), 1984, Doubleday, 1986.

(Under pseudonym Vanessa Graham) *The Stand-In,* R. Hale, 1984.

A Necessary End, Collins, 1985, Walker, 1986.

Pretty Maids All in a Row, Collins, 1986, Doubleday, 1987.

Death Speaks Softly, Collins, 1987.

The Nine Bright Shiners, Collins, 1987, Doubleday, 1988.

Six Proud Walkers, Collins, 1988, Doubleday, 1989.

The April Rainers, Collins, 1989, Doubleday, 1990.

Symbols at Your Door, Collins, 1990, Doubleday, 1991.

The Lily-White Boys, Collins, 1991, published as *I'll Sing You Two-O,* St. Martin's.

Three, Three the Rivals, Collins, 1992, St. Martin's, 1995.

The Gospel Makers, Collins, 1994, St. Martin's, 1995.

The Seven Stars, Collins, 1995.

The Macbeth Prophecy, Severn House (London), 1995.

Author of novel *One Is One and All Alone;* also author of gothic novels *Bright Face of Danger* and *Such Men Are Dangerous* under pseudonym Vanessa Graham. Some of Fraser's novels have appeared as condensed books or in magazine serializations in South Africa, Australia, Brazil, and Norway. Contributor of stories to periodicals around the world, including *Homes and Gardens, Woman's Own,* and *Cosmopolitan.* Several of Fraser's novels have been recorded by Soundings Audio Cassette, including *The Nine Bright Shiners,* 1991, *A Shroud for Delilah* and *Six Proud Walkers,* both 1992, *Symbols at Your Door,* 1993, *Pretty Maids All in a Row,* and *The Lily-White Boys.*

Several of Fraser's books have been translated into German, Danish, Spanish, Norwegian, Swedish, Italian, and Portuguese.

SIDELIGHTS: Anthea Fraser once told *CA:* "I was asked at the age of five what I wanted to be when I grew up and replied without hesitation, 'A mummy and an author.' My ambitions never altered, and I'm very thankful to have achieved them both. I was making up poetry before I could write, and my mother, who wrote novels herself, copied it out, illustrated it, and framed it.

"On average I write a novel a year, working nine to five, five days a week. It takes me about four/five months [to write a book.] Writing is a compulsion for me, and I only feel totally complete when engaged on a novel."

BIOGRAPHICAL/CRITICAL SOURCES:

PERIODICALS

Times (London), April 23, 1986.

FREELING, Nicolas 1927-
(F. R. E. Nicolas)

PERSONAL: Born March 3, 1927, in London, England; married Cornelia Termes, 1954; children: four sons, one daughter. *Education:* Attended University of Dublin. *Politics:* "Visionary." *Avocational interests:* "Planting trees. Then planting more trees."

ADDRESSES: Home—Grandfontaine, 67130 Schirmeck, Bas Rhin, France. *Agent*—Curtis Brown Ltd., 10 Astor Pl., New York, NY 10003.

CAREER: Professional cook in hotels and restaurants throughout Europe, 1948-60; novelist, 1960—. *Military service:* Royal Air Force, 1945-47.

AWARDS, HONORS: Crime Writers Award, 1963, and Grand Prix de Roman Policier, 1965, both for *Gun before Butter;* Edgar Allan Poe Award, Mystery Writers of America, 1966, for *The King of the Rainy Country.*

WRITINGS:

NOVELS

Love in Amsterdam (also see below), Gollancz (London), 1961, Harper (New York City), 1962.

Because of the Cats (also see below), Gollancz, 1962, Harper, 1963.

Gun before Butter (also see below), Gollancz, 1963, published as *Question of Loyalty,* Harper, 1964.

Valparaiso, Harper, 1964, published in England under pseudonym F. R. E. Nicolas, Gollancz, 1964.

Double Barrel (also see below), Gollancz, 1964, Harper, 1965.

Criminal Conversation, Gollancz, 1965, Harper, 1966.

The King of the Rainy Country (also see below), Harper, 1966.

The Dresden Green (also see below), Gollancz, 1966, Harper, 1967.

Strike out Where Not Applicable, Gollancz, 1967, Harper, 1968.

This Is the Castle, Hamish Hamilton (London), 1968, Harper, 1969.

The Freeling Omnibus: Comprising "Love in Amsterdam," "Because of the Cats," and "Gun before Butter," Gollancz, 1968.

Tsing-Boum, Hamish Hamilton, 1969, Harper, 1970.

The Lovely Ladies, Harper, 1970, published in England as *Over the High Side,* Hamish Hamilton, 1970.

Aupres de ma blonde, Harper, 1971, published in England as *A Long Silence,* Hamish Hamilton, 1971.

The Second Freeling Omnibus: Comprising "Double Barrel," "The King of the Rainy Country," and "The Dresden Green," Gollancz, 1972.

Dressing of Diamond, Harper, 1974.

The Bugles Blowing, Harper, 1975, published in England as *What Are the Bugles Blowing For?,* Heinemann (London), 1975.

Lake Isle, Heinemann, 1976, published as *Sabine,* Harper, 1977.

Gadget, Coward (New York City), 1977.

The Night Lords, Pantheon (New York City), 1978.

The Widow, Pantheon, 1979.

Castang's City, Pantheon, 1980.

Arlette, Pantheon, 1981, published in England as *One Damned Thing after Another,* Heinemann, 1981.

Wolfnight, Pantheon, 1982.

The Back of the North Wind, Viking (New York City), 1983.

No Part in Your Death, Viking, 1984.

A City Solitary, Viking, 1985.

Cold Iron, Viking, 1986.

Not As Far As Velma, Mysterious Press (New York City), 1989.

Sand Castles, Deutsch (London), 1989, Mysterious Press, 1990.

Those in Peril, Mysterious Press, 1990.

Flanders Sky, Mysterious Press, 1992, published as *The Pretty How Town,* 1992.

You Who Know, Mysterious Press, 1994.

The Seacoast of Bohemia, Little, Brown (London), 1995.

A Dwarf Kingdom, Little, Brown (London), 1996.

OTHER

The Kitchen: A Delicious Account of the Author's Years as a Grand Hotel Cook, Harper, 1970, published as *Kitchen Book,* Hamilton (London), 1970, published as *The Kitchen Book: The Cook Book,* Godine (Boston), 1991.

Criminal Convictions: Errant Essays on Perpetrators of Literary License, Godine, 1994.

SIDELIGHTS: Called "one of the masters" of the crime fiction genre by Newgate Callendar in the *New York Times Book Review,* Nicolas Freeling enjoys a wide popularity in England and the United States. His three detective characters—Dutch Police Inspector Piet van der Valk, private investigator Arlette van der Valk (Piet's wife) and French detective Henri Casang—have appeared in some twenty novels. Freeling has also written several non-series mysteries, *The Kitchen: A Delicious Account of the Author's Years as a Grand Hotel Cook,* about his years as a gourmet chef, and a collection of essays on the art of mystery writing, *Criminal Convictions: Errant Essays on Perpetrators of Literary License.* According to *Washington Post Book World* columnist Jean White, in his mysteries Freeling delves "into character, the malaise of society and the undercurrent of human relationships under the surface of crime and chase." Writing in the *Armchair Detective,* Cal Branche calls Freeling "a philosopher-historian-

literary critic whose writings . . . place him in the very top rank of writers."

Freeling began his writing career by introducing Inspector Van der Valk in *Love in Amsterdam.* Van der Valk, described by John R. Coyne, Jr., in *National Review* as "a cranky, gentle, bumbling, brilliant, non-conformist student of human behavior whose primary concern is why rather than how crimes are committed," was, according to Tom Sharpe in the *New Statesman,* "one of the most interesting fictional sleuths to appear in the Sixties."

Despite the popularity of Van der Valk, Freeling did something that few other mystery writers have done with a series character. In 1971's *Aupres de ma blonde,* Freeling had Van der Valk die, ending the detective's adventures—until *Sand Castles* appeared in 1990, that is. In this "prequel" novel, set before Van der Valk's demise, the Dutch inspector returns to break up a child pornography ring and a group of neo-Nazi extremists.

After killing off Van der Valk in 1971, Freeling began writing mysteries centering on the investigations of Van der Valk's wife, Arlette. Robert Goldsborough characterizes her in the Chicago *Tribune Books* as an "outspoken, independent-minded widow," and in the opinion of Jane S. Bakerman, writing in the *Armchair Detective,* Arlette is "one of Nicolas Freeling's most fully rounded, convincing creations." In addition, Arlette's adventures, Bakerman explains, provide "a refreshing, moving, beautifully crafted examination of evil from a female point of view. Not many male detective fiction writers practicing today could bring that off. Freeling can; Freeling does."

Freeling's third detective character is the French police *commissaire* Henri Castang, "whose terse and deliberate exterior belies a complex sensibility and a streaming consciousness," according to David Lehman in the *Washington Post Book World.* Castang is an introspective man who, over the course of several novels, has become "obsessed with the problem of violence," Reginald Hill writes in *Books and Bookmen.* Castang's wife, Vera, a Czech, "is herself a fully realized character, a free-speaking delight whose perceptions can be unexpectedly helpful to her husband," as Charles Champlin describes her in the *Los Angeles Times Book Review.*

Freeling's books, Hill notes, are written in a "nervous, oblique, bitty style . . . nine tenths internalized impressionistic monologue . . . and one tenth straight objective description." Complimenting Freeling's characterization and skill with language, Marilyn Stasio writes in the *New York Times Book Review* that "Freeling has few peers when it comes to the international *policier.*" T. J. Binyon, in the *Times Literary Supplement,* states that "there is no doubt that Nicolas Freeling's novels, in depth, subtlety and interest, are far superior to most other examples of the genre."

Elaborating on his career as an author of detective novels, Freeling told *CA:* "I have been writing crime fiction for more than twenty-five years. There are not many around with this experience in the genre. To pretend that I have not widely influenced crime-writing would be false modesty. Since my own beginnings I have known my ideas plagiarized, material pillaged, and my manner parodied, repeatedly. This is a compliment paid to all original writers, and one does not complain of it. Some have the grace to acknowledge their sources and others do not. Some are not even aware of it.

"Experience does not of itself confer wisdom. The writer's desire outruns performance. He and she approach the current work in a flare-up of excitement and a sense of discovery: in this country no one has yet set foot. And at the end it is so much less interesting than he had hoped. But he has merely surveyed this new patch of territory. Others will follow and mine it, to their profit, which he will be wise not to grudge them.

"Over the fifty years since the heyday of Dorothy Sayers, and thirty on from Raymond Chandler's *The Simple Art of Murder,* the genre 'crime novel' has expanded enormously, and the antiquated categories of mystery or suspense have become meaningless. Those that have survived have invariably been (as in all fiction) those with a sense of character.

"I believe that after thirty years it will be time, concurrent with the fiction I find myself at work on, to synthesize personal thinking and individual experience. In doing so I hope to understand my trade better. I hope that other writers—and readers—will find matter for thought. A critical essay? Autobiography? The portentous and self-satisfied connotations of either give pause. Elements of both will be needed: the project will be difficult. But as with fiction a notion strikes root, a crystallization occurs, and then, however flawed, the books insist upon being written. My publishers will doubtless be appalled; they've been appalled before at more or less yearly intervals and they should be accustomed to the feeling by now."

BIOGRAPHICAL/CRITICAL SOURCES:

BOOKS

Benstock, Bernard, editor, *Art in Crime Writing: Essays on Detective Fiction,* St. Martin's (New York City), 1983, pp. 159-173.
Contemporary Authors Autobiography Series, Volume 12, Gale (Detroit), 1991.
Contemporary Literary Criticism, Volume 38, Gale, 1986.

Dictionary of Literary Biography, Volume 87: *British Mystery and Thriller Writers since 1940, First Series,* Gale, 1989.

PERIODICALS

Armchair Detective, winter, 1983, pp. 348-53; winter, 1986, p. 20; fall, 1990, p. 474; winter, 1991, p. 61.
Books and Bookmen, June, 1984, p. 29.
Cosmopolitan, June, 1989, p. 48.
Globe and Mail (Toronto), June 30, 1984.
Los Angeles Times Book Review, September 20, 1992, p. 8; June 12, 1994, p. 8; July 10, 1994, p. 8.
National Review, August 24, 1971.
New Statesman, September 26, 1975; April 12, 1985, p. 25.
New York Times Book Review, August 6, 1972; July 9, 1989, p. 24; February 18, 1990, p. 23; February 10, 1991, p. 31; September 20, 1992, p. 20; July 17, 1994, p. 19; October 2, 1994, p. 35.
Observer (London), May 12, 1985, p. 21; February 20, 1994, p. 22.
Spectator, May 1, 1971.
Times Literary Supplement, May 30, 1980.
Town and Country, February, 1989, p. 154.
Tribune Books (Chicago), February 18, 1990, p. 5.
Washington Post Book World, May 19, 1974; February 19, 1978; November 19, 1978; July 4, 1982, p. 9.
Wilson Library Bulletin, March, 1990, p. 108.*

* * *

FURTADO, Celso 1920-

PERSONAL: Born July 26, 1920, in Pombal, Paraiba, Brazil; son of Mauricio Medeiros and Maria Alice (Monteiro) Furtado; married Lucia Tosi (a chemist), September 15, 1948 (divorced, 1975); married Rosa Freire d'Aguiar (a journalist), 1979; children: (first marriage) Mario, Andre. *Education:* University of Brazil, M.A., 1944; University of Paris, Ph.D., 1948; Cambridge University, postdoctoral study, 1957-58.

ADDRESSES: Home and office—Rua Conrado Niemeyer, 23, ap. 101, 22021-050 Copacabana, RJ, Brasil.

CAREER: United Nations Economic Commission for Latin America, economist, 1949-57; director, Development Bank of Brazil, 1959-60; Superintendency for the Development of the Northeast of Brazil, executive head, 1959-64; minister of planning, Brazilian government, 1962-63; Yale University, New Haven, CT, research fellow, 1964-65; Universite Pantheon, Sorbonne, Paris, France, professor of economics, 1965-79; Ecole d'Hautes Etudes en Sciences Sociales, Paris, directeur d'Etudes Associees, 1980-85; ambassador of Brazil to European Community, Brussels, Belgium, 1985-86; minister of culture for Brazilian government, 1986-88. Visiting professor, American University, Washington, DC, 1972, Cambridge University, 1973-74, and Columbia University, 1977. Member, South Commission, 1987-90, and World Commission for Culture and Development, UNO/UNESCO, 1993-95.

WRITINGS:

The Economic Growth of Brazil: A Survey from Colonial to Modern Times, University of California Press (Berkeley), 1963, reprinted, Greenwood Press (Westport, CT), 1984.

Development and Underdevelopment, University of California Press, 1964.

Diagnosis of the Brazilian Crisis, University of California Press, 1965.

Economic Development of Latin America, Cambridge University Press (Cambridge, England), 1970, 2nd edition, 1977.

Obstacles to Development in Latin America, Doubleday (New York City), 1970.

Analise do Modelo brasileiro, Civilizacao Brasileira, 1972.

O Mito do Desenvolvimento Economico, Paz e Terra, 1974.

Prefacio a Nova Economia Politica, Paz e Terra, 1976.

Criatividade e Dependencia, Paz e Terra, 1978.

Pequena Introducao ao Desenvolvimento, Editora Nacional, 1980.

O Brasil pos-"milagre", Paz e Terra, 1981.

A Nova Dependencia, Paz e Terra, 1982.

Accumulation and Development: The Logic of Industrial Civilization, St. Martin's (New York City), 1983.

Cultura e Desenvolvimento, Paz e Terra, 1984.

A Fantasia Organizada, Paz e Terra, 1985.

No to Recession and Unemployment: An Examination of the Brazilian Economic Crisis, Duke Press (North Riverside, IL), 1985.

ABC da Divida Externa, Paz e Terra, 1989.

A Fantasia Desfeita, Paz e Terra, 1989.

Os Ares do Mundo, Paz e Terra, 1991.

Brasil, a Construcao Interrompida, Paz e Terra, 1992.

G

GADNEY, Reg 1941-

PERSONAL: Born January 20, 1941, in Cross Hills, England; son of Bernard C. (a school teacher) and Margaret A. M. (Lilley) Gadney; married Annette Kobak (a writer), July 16, 1966 (divorced, 1985); children: Guy, Amy. *Education:* St. Catharine's College, Cambridge, M.A., 1966.

ADDRESSES: Office—c/o Peters Fraser and Dunlop, The Chambers, Chelsea Harbour, Lots Rd., London SW10 0XF, England.

CAREER: Massachusetts Institute of Technology, Cambridge, instructor in architecture and research fellow at School of Architecture and Planning, 1966-67; National Film Theatre, London, England, deputy controller, 1967-68; Royal College of Art, London, senior tutor and fellow, 1968-78, pro-rector, 1978-83. Consultant to American Arts Documentation Centre; editorial advisor to Paladin Books, Granada Publishing, and Lion & Unicorn Press. *Military service:* British Army, Coldstream Guards, assistant to naval, military, and air attache at British Embassy in Oslo, 1959-62; became lieutenant.

MEMBER: Marylebone Cricket Club.

WRITINGS:

NOVELS

Drawn Blanc, Heinemann (London), 1970, Coward (New York City), 1971.
Somewhere in England, St. Martin's (New York City), 1971.
Seduction of a Tall Man, Heinemann, 1972.
Something Worth Fighting For, Heinemann, 1974.
Victoria, Coward, 1975, published in England as *The Last Hours before Dawn,* Heinemann, 1976.
The Cage, Coward, 1977, published in England as *The Champagne Marxist,* Hutchinson (London), 1977.

Nightshade, St. Martin's, 1987.

NONFICTION

Constable and His World, Norton (New York City), 1976.
Kennedy, Holt (New York City), 1983.
Cry Hungary!: Uprising 1956, Atheneum (New York City), 1986.

SCREENPLAYS

Forgive Our Foolish Ways, British Broadcasting Corp. (BBC-TV), 1970.
Last Love, BBC-TV, 1983.
Kennedy, National Broadcasting Company (NBC-TV), 1983.

Also author of *The Bell,* 1982, *Last Love,* 1983, *Drummonds,* 1985, *Goldeneve,* 1989, *A Woman at War,* 1990, *444 Day,* 1990, *The Chronicles of Young Indiana Jones,* 1991, and *Iran: Days of Crisis,* 1991.

OTHER

Also author of museum catalogues, including *A Catalogue of Drawings and Watercolours by John Constable for "English Landscape Scenery" in the Fitzwilliam Museum, Cambridge,* 1976. Contributor to *Granta, Image, Broadsheet, Mosaic, Vou, Cambridge Review, London, Spectator,* and *Leonardo.* Editor, *Granta;* honorary editor, *Leonardo.*

SIDELIGHTS: English novelist and screenplay writer Reg Gadney writes suspenseful tales of espionage, usually set during World War II or the Cold War. Newgate Calendar, writing in the *New York Times Book Review,* explains that Gadney is an "experienced British writer of espionage novels."

The plot of *Victoria* concerns a widow and the man she loves, a British secret service agent captured in occupied Europe during World War II and sent to a concentration camp. Elaine Feinstein writes in the *New Statesman* that in *Victoria,* Gadney's "grasp on the realities of wartime England and France is astonishingly physical. He has gone out of his way to catch the very smell of mackintoshes in a bus at night; pale circles of torch-light on the grass in the blackout; the useless, peeling, sticky-taped glass; and the absurdity and bloody horror of blinding, and lost limbs."

In his novel *Nightshade* Gadney tells of a British Secret Intelligence Service Officer who, during an unofficial investigation into the death of his father decades earlier, stumbles onto the records of Operation Nightshade. These records reveal that London knew about the Japanese attack on Pearl Harbor in advance but concealed the information. The officer's probe causes intelligence agencies on both sides of the Atlantic to resort to extreme actions rather than risk a breakdown of relations. A *Publishers Weekly* reviewer calls *Nightshade* "a deftly handled thriller taut with attention to character and detail." Callendar claims that *Nightshade* "is Mr. Gadney at his suave best."

In addition to his novels, Gadney has also written nonfiction accounts of historical events. Perhaps the most successful of these nonfiction books has been *Cry Hungary!: Uprising 1956,* a narrative about the thirteen days, October 23 through November 4, 1956, during which students and workers revolted in Budapest, Hungary, against the Soviet-controlled communist government. Before the uprising could succeed, Soviet leader Nikita Khrushchev sent in Russian tanks and crushed the rebellion while the rest of the world stood by. Timothy Foote writes in a *Washington Post Book World* review that *Cry Hungary!* contains a "detailed and highly useful day-to-day chronology of events and quotations" along with many photographs, "more than have ever been gathered together before." Foote calls *Cry Hungary!* "stunning and memorable" and "an overwhelming record of a city and its people during a terrifying struggle."

BIOGRAPHICAL/CRITICAL SOURCES:

PERIODICALS

Armchair Detective, fall, 1993, p. 22.
British Book News, May, 1987, p. 298.
Choice, October, 1976, p. 968.
Library Journal, August, 1976, p. 1618; October 15, 1986.
New Statesman, September 10, 1971, p. 340; January 17, 1975, p. 85.
New Yorker, December 8, 1986, p. 154.
New York Review of Books, August 18, 1988, p. 45.
New York Times Book Review, May 2, 1971, p. 43; March 19, 1972, p. 41; January 15, 1989, p. 39.
Observer (London), June 7, 1987, p. 24.
Publishers Weekly, September 9, 1988, p. 18.

Saturday Review, May 13, 1972, p. 86.
Times Literary Supplement, January 1, 1971, p. 19; January 17, 1975, p. 48; February 27, 1976, p. 227.
Variety, October 7, 1991, p. 200.
Virginia Quarterly Review, spring, 1987, p. 63.
Washington Post Book World, December 21, 1986, pp. 3, 14.

* * *

GARCIA MARQUEZ, Gabriel (Jose) 1928-

PERSONAL: Born March 6, 1928, in Aracataca, Colombia; son of Gabriel Eligio Garcia (a telegraph operator) and Luisa Santiaga Marquez Iguaran; married Mercedes Barcha, March, 1958; children: Rodrigo, Gonzalo. *Education:* Attended Universidad Nacional de Colombia, 1947-48, and Universidad de Cartagena, 1948-49.

ADDRESSES: Home—P.O. Box 20736, Mexico City D.F., Mexico. *Agent*—Agencia Literaria Carmen Balcells, Diagonal 580, Barcelona 08021, Spain.

CAREER: Began career as a journalist, 1947; reporter for *Universal,* Cartegena, Colombia, late 1940s, *El heraldo,* Baranquilla, Colombia, 1950-52, and *El espectador,* Bogota, Colombia, until 1955; freelance journalist in Paris, London, and Caracas, Venezuela, 1956-58; worked for *Momento* magazine, Caracas, 1958-59; helped form Prensa Latina news agency, Bogota, 1959, and worked as its correspondent in Havana, Cuba, and New York City, 1961; writer, 1965—. Fundacion Habeas, founder, 1979, president, 1979—.

MEMBER: American Academy of Arts and Letters (honorary fellow).

AWARDS, HONORS: Colombian Association of Writers and Artists Award, 1954, for story "Un dia despues del sabado"; Premio Literario Esso (Colombia), 1961, for *La mala hora;* Chianciano Award (Italy), 1969, Prix de Meilleur Livre Etranger (France), 1969, and Romulo Gallegos prize (Venezuela), 1971, all for *Cien anos de soledad;* LL.D., Columbia University, 1971; Books Abroad/ Neustadt International Prize for Literature, 1972; Nobel Prize for Literature, 1982; *Los Angeles Times* Book Prize nomination for fiction, 1983, for *Chronicle of a Death Foretold; Los Angeles Times* Book Prize for fiction, 1988, for *Love in the Time of Cholera;* Serfin Prize, 1989.

WRITINGS:

FICTION

La hojarasca (novella; title means "Leaf Storm"; also see below), Ediciones Sipa (Bogota), 1955, reprinted, Bruguera (Barcelona), 1983.

El coronel no tiene quien le escriba (novella; title means "No One Writes to the Colonel"; also see below), Aguirre Editor (Medellin, Colombia), 1961, reprinted, Bruguera, 1983.

La mala hora (novel; also see below), Talleres de Graficas "Luis Perez" (Madrid), 1961, reprinted, Bruguera, 1982, English translation by Gregory Rabassa published as *In Evil Hour,* Harper, 1979.

Los funerales de la Mama Grande (short stories; title means "Big Mama's Funeral"; also see below), Editorial Universidad Veracruzana (Mexico), 1962, reprinted, Bruguera, 1983.

Cien anos de soledad (novel), Editorial Sudamericana (Buenos Aires), 1967, reprinted, Catedra, 1984, English translation by Rabassa published as *One Hundred Years of Solitude,* Harper, 1970.

Isabel viendo llover en Macondo (novella; title means "Isabel Watching It Rain in Macondo"; also see below), Editorial Estuario (Buenos Aires), 1967.

No One Writes to the Colonel and Other Stories (includes "No One Writes to the Colonel," and stories from *Los Funerales de la Mama Grande*), translated by J. S. Bernstein, Harper, 1968.

La increible y triste historia de la candida Erendira y su abuela desalmada (short stories; also see below), Barral Editores, 1972.

El negro que hizo esperar a los angeles (short stories), Ediciones Alfil (Montevideo), 1972.

Ojos de perro azul (short stories; also see below), Equisditorial (Argentina), 1972.

Leaf Storm and Other Stories (includes "Leaf Storm," and "Isabel Watching It Rain in Macondo"), translated by Rabassa, Harper, 1972.

El otono del patriarca (novel), Plaza & Janes Editores (Barcelona), 1975, translation by Rabassa published as *The Autumn of the Patriarch,* Harper, 1976.

Todos los cuentos de Gabriel Garcia Marquez: 1947-1972 (title means "All the Stories of Gabriel Garcia Marquez: 1947-1972"), Plaza & Janes Editores, 1975.

Innocent Erendira and Other Stories (includes "Innocent Erendira and Her Heartless Grandmother" and stories from *Ojos de perro azul*), translated by Rabassa, Harper, 1978.

Dos novelas de Macondo (contains *La hojarasca* and *La mala hora*), Casa de las Americas (Havana), 1980.

Cronica de una muerte anunciada (novel), La Oveja Negra (Bogota), 1981, translation by Rabassa published as *Chronicle of a Death Foretold,* J. Cape (London), 1982, Knopf (New York City), 1983.

Viva Sandino (play), Editorial Nueva Nicaragua, 1982, 2nd edition published as *El asalto: el operativo con que el FSLN se lanzo al mundo,* 1983.

El rastro de tu sangre en la nieve: El verano feliz de la senora Forbes, W. Dampier Editores (Bogota), 1982.

El secuestro: Guion cinematografico (unfilmed screenplay), Oveja Negra (Bogota), 1982.

Erendira (filmscript; adapted from his novella *La increible y triste historia de la candida Erendira y su abuela desalmada*), Les Films du Triangle, 1983.

Collected Stories, translated by Rabassa and Bernstein, Harper, 1984.

El amor en los tiempos del colera, Oveja Negra, 1985, English translation by Edith Grossman published as *Love in the Time of Cholera,* Knopf, 1988.

A Time to Die (filmscript), ICA Cinema, 1988.

Diatribe of Love against a Seated Man (play; first produced at Cervantes Theater, Buenos Aires, 1988), Arango Editores (Santafe de Bogota), 1994.

El general en su labertino, Mondadori (Madrid), 1989, English translation by Grossman published as *The General in His Labyrinth,* Knopf, 1990.

Collected Novellas, HarperCollins (New York City), 1990.

Doce cuentos peregrinos, Mondadori (Madrid), 1992, English translation by Grossman published as *Strange Pilgrims: Twelve Stories,* Knopf, 1993.

The Handsomest Drowned Man in the World: A Tale for Children, translated by Rabazza, Creative Education (Mankato, MN), 1993.

Del amor y otros demonios, Mondadori (Barcelona), 1994, English translation by Grossman published as *Of Love and Other Demons,* Knopf, 1995.

NONFICTION

(With Mario Vargas Llosa) *La novela en America Latina: Dialogo,* Carlos Milla Batres (Lima), 1968.

Relato de un naufrago (journalistic pieces), Tusquets Editor (Barcelona), 1970, English translation by Randolph Hogan published as *The Story of a Shipwrecked Sailor,* Knopf, 1986.

Cuando era feliz e indocumentado (journalistic pieces), Ediciones El Ojo de Camello (Caracas), 1973.

Cronicas y reportajes (journalistic pieces), Oveja Negra, 1978.

Periodismo militante (journalistic pieces), Son de Maquina (Bogota), 1978.

De viaje por los paises socialistas: 90 dias en la "Cortina de hierro" (journalistic pieces), Ediciones Macondo (Colombia), 1978.

(Contributor) *Los sandanistas,* Oveja Negra, 1979.

(Contributor) Soledad Mendoza, editor, *Asi es Caracas,* Editorial Ateneo de Caracas, 1980.

Obra periodistica (journalistic pieces), edited by Jacques Gilard, Bruguera, Volume 1: *Textos constenos,* 1981, Volumes 2-3: *Entre cachacos,* 1982, Volume 4: *De Europa y America (1955-1960),* 1983.

El olor de la guayaba: Conversaciones con Plinio Apuleyo Mendoza (interviews), Oveja Negra, 1982, English translation by Ann Wright published as *The Fragrance of Guava,* Verso, 1983.

(With Guillermo Nolasco-Juarez) *Persecucion y muerte de minorias: dos perspectivas,* Juarez Editor (Buenos Aires), 1984.

(Contributor) *La Democracia y la paz en America Latina,* Editorial El Buho (Bogota), 1986.

La aventura de Miguel Littin, clandestino en Chile: Un reportaje, Editorial Sudamericana, 1986, English translation by Asa Zatz published as *Clandestine in Chile: The Adventures of Miguel Littin,* Holt, 1987.

Primeros reportajes, Consorcio de Ediciones Capriles (Caracas), 1990.

(Author of introduction) Mina, Gianni, *An Encounter with Fidel: An Interview,* translated by Mary Todd, Ocean Press (Melbourne), 1991.

Notas de prensa, 1980-1984, Mondadori (Madrid), 1991.

Elogio de la utopia: Una entrevista de Nahuel Maciel, Cronista Ediciones (Buenos Aires), 1992.

OTHER

Author of weekly syndicated column.

ADAPTATIONS: A play, *Blood and Champagne,* has been based on Garcia Marquez's *One Hundred Years of Solitude.*

SIDELIGHTS: Winner of the 1982 Nobel Prize for Literature, Gabriel Garcia Marquez "is one of the small number of contemporary writers from Latin America who have given to its literature a maturity and dignity it never had before," asserted John Sturrock in the *New York Times Book Review.* "More than any other writer in the world," declared David Streitfeld in the *Washington Post,* "Gabriel Garcia Marquez combines both respect (bordering on adulation) and mass popularity (also bordering on adulation)." *One Hundred Years of Solitude* is perhaps Garcia Marquez's best-known contribution to the awakening of interest in Latin American literature. It has sold more than twenty million copies and has been translated into over thirty languages. According to an *Antioch Review* critic, the popularity and acclaim for *One Hundred Years of Solitude* signaled that "Latin American literature will change from being the exotic interest of a few to essential reading and that Latin America itself will be looked on less as a crazy subculture and more as a fruitful, alternative way of life." So great was the novel's initial popularity, notes Mario Vargas Llosa in *Garcia Marquez: Historia de un deicido,* that not only was the first Spanish printing of the book sold out within one week, but for months afterward Latin American readers alone exhausted each successive printing. Translations of the novel similarly elicited enthusiastic responses from critics and readers around the world.

In this outpouring of critical opinion, which *Books Abroad* contributor Klaus Muller-Bergh called "an earthquake, a maelstrom," various reviewers termed *One Hundred Years of Solitude* a masterpiece of modern fiction. For example, Chilean poet Pablo Neruda, himself a Nobel laureate, was quoted in *Time* as calling the book "the greatest revelation in the Spanish language since the *Don Quixote* of Cervantes." Similarly enthusiastic was William Kennedy, who wrote in the *National Observer* that "*One Hundred Years of Solitude* is the first piece of literature since the Book of Genesis that should be required reading for the entire human race." And Regina Janes, in her study *Gabriel Garcia Marquez: Revolutions in Wonderland,* described the book as "a 'total novel' that [treats] Latin America socially, historically, politically, mythically, and epically," adding that *One Hundred Years of Solitude* is also "at once accessible and intricate, lifelike and self-consciously, self-referentially fictive."

The novel is set in the imaginary community of Macondo, a village on the Colombian coast, and follows the lives of several generations of the Buendia family. Chief among these characters are Colonel Aureliano Buendia, perpetrator of thirty-two rebellions and father of seventeen illegitimate sons, and Ursula Buendia, the clan's matriarch and witness to its eventual decline. Besides following the complicated relationships of the Buendia family, *One Hundred Years of Solitude* also reflects the political, social, and economic troubles of South America. Many critics have found the novel, with its complex family relationships and extraordinary events, to be a microcosm of Latin America itself.

The mixture of historical and fictitious elements that appears in *One Hundred Years of Solitude* places the novel within that genre of Latin American fiction that critics have termed magical realism. Janes attributed the birth of this style of writing to Alejo Carpentier, a Cuban novelist and short story writer, and concluded that Garcia Marquez's fiction follows ideas originally formulated by the Cuban author. The critic noted that Carpentier "discovered the duplicities of history and elaborated the critical concept of 'lo maravilloso americano' the 'marvelous real,' arguing that geographically, historically, and essentially, Latin America was a space marvelous and fantastic . . . and to render that reality was to render marvels." Garcia Marquez presented a similar view of Latin America in his *Paris Review* interview with Peter H. Stone: "It always amuses me that the biggest praise for my work comes for the imagination while the truth is that there's not a single line in all my work that does not have a basis in reality." The author further explained in his *Playboy* interview with Claudia Dreifus: "Clearly, the Latin American environment is marvelous. Particularly the Caribbean. . . . The coastal people were descendants of pirates and smugglers, with a mixture of black slaves. To grow up in such an environment is to have fantastic resources for poetry. Also, in the Caribbean, we are capable of believing anything, because we have the influences of all those different cultures, mixed in with Catholicism and our own local beliefs. I think that gives us an open-mindedness to look beyond apparent reality."

But along with the fantastic episodes in Garcia Marquez's fiction appear the historical facts or places that inspired them. An episode involving a massacre of striking banana workers is based on a historical incident. In reality, Garcia Marquez told Dreifus, "there were very few deaths . . . [so] I made the death toll 3000 because I was using certain proportions in my book." But while *One Hundred Years of Solitude* is the fictional account of the Buendia family, the novel is also, as John Leonard stated in the *New York Times,* "a recapitulation of our evolutionary and intellectual experience. Macondo is Latin America in microcosm." Robert G. Mead Jr. similarly observed in *Saturday Review* that "Macondo may be regarded as a microcosm of the development of much of the Latin American continent." Mead added: "Although [*One Hundred Years of Solitude*] is first and always a story, the novel also has value as a social and historical document." Garcia Marquez responded to these interpretations in his interview with Dreifus, commenting that his work "is not a history of Latin America, it is a *metaphor* for Latin America."

The "social and historical" elements of *One Hundred Years of Solitude* reflect the journalistic influences at work in Garcia Marquez's fiction. Although known as a novelist, the author began his writing career as a reporter and still considers himself to be one. As he remarked to Stone, "I've always been convinced that my true profession is that of a journalist." Janes asserted that the evolution of Garcia Marquez's individual style is based on his experience as a correspondent. In addition, this same experience has led Janes and other critics to compare the Colombian to Ernest Hemingway. "[The] stylistic transformation between *Leaf Storm* and *No One Writes to the Colonel* was not exclusively an act of will," Janes claimed. "Garcia Marquez had had six years of experience as a journalist between the two books, experience providing practice in the lessons of Hemingway, trained in the same school." And George R. McMurray, in his book *Gabriel Garcia Marquez,* maintained that Hemingway's themes and techniques have "left their mark" on the work of the Colombian writer.

Garcia Marquez has also been compared to another American Nobel-winner, William Faulkner, who also elaborated on facts to create his fiction. Faulkner based his fictional territory Yoknapatawpha County on memories of the region in northern Mississippi where he spent most of his life. Garcia Marquez based Macondo, the town appearing throughout his fiction, on Aracataca, the coastal city of his birth. A *Time* reviewer called Macondo "a kind of tropical Yoknapatawpha County." *Review* contributor Mary E. Davis pointed out further resemblances between the two authors: "Garcia Marquez concentrates on the specific personality of place in the manner of the Mississippean, and he develops even the most reprehensible of his characters as idiosyncratic enigmas." She concluded: "Garcia Marquez is as fascinated by the capacity of things, events, and characters for sudden metamorphosis as was Faulkner."

Nevertheless, *Newsweek* writer Peter S. Prescott maintained that it was only after Garcia Marquez shook off the influence of Faulkner that he was able to write *One Hundred Years of Solitude.* Prescott argues that in this novel Garcia Marquez's "imagination matured: no longer content to write dark and fatalistic stories about a Latin Yoknapatawpha County, he broke loose into exuberance, wit and laughter." Thor Vilhjalmsson similarly observed in *Books Abroad* that while "Garcia Marquez does not fail to deal with the dark forces, or give the impression that the life of human beings, one by one, should be ultimately tragic, . . . he also shows every moment pregnant with images and color and scent which ask to be arranged into patterns of meaning and significance while the moment lasts." While the Colombian has frequently referred to Faulkner as "my master," Luis Harss and Barbara Dohmann added in their *Into the Mainstream: Conversations with Latin-American Writers* that in his later stories, "the Faulknerian glare has been neutralized. It is not replaced by any other. From now on Garcia Marquez is his own master."

In *The Autumn of the Patriarch* Garcia Marquez uses a more openly political tone in relating the story of a dictator who has reigned for so long that no one can remember any other ruler. Elaborating on the kind of solitude experienced by Colonel Aureliano Buendia in *One Hundred Years,* Garcia Marquez explores the isolation of a political tyrant. "In this fabulous, dream-like account of the reign of a nameless dictator of a fantastic Caribbean realm, solitude is linked with the possession of absolute power," described Ronald De Feo in the *National Review.* Rather than relating a straightforward account of the general's life, *The Autumn of the Patriarch* skips from one episode to another using detailed descriptions. *Times Literary Supplement* contributor John Sturrock found this approach appropriate to the author's subject, calling the work "the desperate, richly sustained hallucination of a man rightly bitter about the present state of so much of Latin America." Sturrock noted that "Garcia Marquez's novel is sophisticated and its language is luxuriant to a degree. Style and subject are at odds because Garcia Marquez is committed to showing that our first freedom—and one which all too many Latin American countries have lost—is of the full resources of our language." *Time* writer R. Z. Sheppard similarly commented on Garcia Marquez's elaborate style, observing that "the theme is artfully insinuated, an atmosphere instantly evoked like a puff of stage smoke, and all conveyed in language that generates a charge of expectancy." The critic concluded: "Garcia Marquez writes with what could be called a stream-of-consciousness technique, but the result is much more like a whirlpool."

Some critics, however, found both the theme and technique of *The Autumn of the Patriarch* lacking. J. D. O'Hara, for example, wrote in the *Washington Post Book World* that for all his "magical realism," Garcia Marquez "can only remind us of real-life parallels; he cannot exaggerate them." "For the same reason," the critic added, "although he can turn into grisly cartoons the squalor and paranoia of actual dictatorships, he can scarcely parody them; reality has anticipated him again." *Newsweek*'s Walter Clemons found the novel somewhat disappointing: "After the narrative vivacity and intricate characterization of the earlier book [*The Autumn of the Patriarch*] seems both oversumptuous and underpopulated. It is— deadliest of compliments—an extended piece of magnificent writing." Other critics believed that the author's skillful style enhances the novel. Referring to the novel's disjointed narrative style, Wendy McElroy commented in *World Research INK* that "this is the first time I have seen it handled properly. Gabriel Garcia Marquez ignores many conventions of the English language which are meant to provide structure and coherence. But he is so skillful that his novel is not difficult to understand. It is bizarre; it is disorienting . . . but it is not difficult. Moreover, it is appropriate to the chaos and decay of the general's mind and of his world." Similarly, De Feo maintained that "no summary or description of this book can really do it justice, for it is not only the author's surrealistic flights of imagination that make it such an exceptional work, but also his brilliant use of language, his gift for phrasing and description." The critic concluded: "Throughout this unique, remarkable novel, the tall tale is transformed into a true work of art."

"With its run-on, seemingly free-associative sentences, its constant flow of images and color, Gabriel Garcia Marquez's last novel, *The Autumn of the Patriarch,* was such a dazzling technical achievement that it left the pleasurably exhausted reader wondering what the author would do next," commented De Feo in the *Nation*. This next work, *Chronicle of a Death Foretold* "is, in miniature, a virtuoso performance," stated Jonathan Yardley of the *Washington Post Book World*. In contrast with the author's "two masterworks, *One Hundred Years of Solitude*

and *The Autumn of the Patriarch*," continued the critic, "it is slight . . . its action is tightly concentrated on a single event. But in this small space Garcia Marquez works small miracles; *Chronicle of a Death Foretold* is ingeniously, impeccably constructed, and it provides a sobering, devastating perspective on the system of male 'honor.' " In the novella, described Douglas Hill in the Toronto *Globe and Mail*, Garcia Marquez "has cut out an apparently uncomplicated, larger-than-life jigsaw puzzle of passion and crime, then demonstrated, with laconic diligence and a sort of concerned amusement, how extraordinarily difficult the task of assembling the pieces can be." The story is based on a historical incident in which a young woman is returned after her wedding night for not being a virgin and her brothers set out to avenge the stain on the family honor by murdering the man she names as her "perpetrator." The death is "foretold" in that the brothers announce their intentions to the entire town, but circumstances conspire to keep Santiago Nasar, the condemned man, from this knowledge, and he is brutally murdered.

"In telling this story, which is as much about the townspeople and their reactions as it is about the key players, Garcia Marquez might simply have remained omniscient," observed De Feo. But instead "he places himself in the action, assuming the role of a former citizen who returns home to reconstruct the events of the tragic day—a day he himself lived through." This narrative maneuvering, claimed the critic, "adds another layer to the book, for the narrator, who is visible one moment, invisible the next, could very well ask himself the same question he is intent on asking others, and his own role, his own failure to act in the affair contributes to the book's odd, haunting ambiguity." This recreation after the fact has an additional effect, as Gregory Rabassa noted in *World Literature Today*: "From the beginning we know that Santiago Nasar will be and has been killed, depending on the time of the narrative thread that we happen to be following, but Garcia Marquez does manage, in spite of the repeated foretelling of the event by the murderers and others, to maintain the suspense at a high level by never describing the actual murder until the very end." Rabassa explained: "Until then we have been following the chronicler as he puts the bits and pieces together ex post facto, but he has constructed things in such a way that we are still hoping for a reprieve even though we know better." "As more and more is revealed about the murder, less and less is known," wrote Leonard Michaels in the *New York Times Book Review*, "yet the style of the novel is always natural and unselfconscious, as if innocent of any paradoxical implication."

In approaching the story from this re-creative standpoint, Garcia Marquez once again utilizes journalistic techniques. As *Chicago Tribune Book World* editor John Blades maintained, "Garcia Marquez tells this grisly little fable in what often appears to be a straight-faced parody of conventional journalism, with its dependence on 'he-she-they told me' narrative techniques, its reliance on the distorted, contradictory and dreamlike memories of 'eye-witnesses.'" Blades added, however, that "at the same time, this is precision-tooled fiction; the author subtly but skillfully manipulates his chronology for dramatic impact." The *New York Times*'s Christopher Lehmann-Haupt similarly noted a departure from the author's previous style: "I cannot be absolutely certain whether in *Chronicle* Gabriel Garcia Marquez has come closer to conventional storytelling than in his previous work, or whether I have simply grown accustomed to his imagination." The critic added that "whatever the case, I found *Chronicle of a Death Foretold* by far the author's most absorbing work to date. I read it through in a flash, and it made the back of my neck prickle." "It is interesting," remarked *Times Literary Supplement* contributor Bill Buford, that Garcia Marquez chose to handle "a fictional episode with the methods of a journalist. In doing so he has written an unusual and original work: a simple narrative so charged with irony that it has the authority of political fable." Buford concluded: "If it is not an example of the socialist realism [Garcia] Marquez may claim it to be elsewhere, *Chronicle of a Death Foretold* is in any case a mesmerizing work that clearly establishes [Garcia] Marquez as one of the most accomplished, and the most 'magical' of political novelists writing today."

Despite this journalistic approach to the story, *Chronicle of a Death Foretold* does contain some of the "magical" elements that characterize Garcia Marquez's fiction. As Robert M. Adams observed in the *New York Review of Books,* there is a "combination of detailed factual particularity, usually on irrelevant points, with vagueness, confusion, or indifference on matters of more importance." The result, Adams suggested, is that "the investigation of an ancient murder takes on the quality of a hallucinatory exploration, a deep groping search into the gathering darkness for a truth that continually slithers away." But others found that this combination of journalistic detail and lack of explanation detracts from the novel. D. Keith Mano, for example, commented in the *National Review* that because the narrator "has been sequestered as a juror might be . . . he cannot comment or probe: and this rather kiln-dries the novel." The critic elaborates, noting that the primary characters "are left without development or chiaroscuro. They seem cryptic and surface-hard: film characters really. . . . Beyond a Warren Report-meticulous detective reconstruction, it is hard to care much for these people. Emotion, you see, might skew our clarity." But Edith Grossman asserted in *Review* that this reconstruction was meant to be enigmatic: "Garcia Marquez holds

onto the journalistic details, the minutiae of the factual, that constitute the great novelistic inheritance of Western realism, and at the same time throws doubt on their reliability through his narrative technique and by means of the subtle introduction of mythic elements." Grossman concluded: "Once again Garcia Marquez is an ironic chronicler who dazzles the reader with uncommon blendings of fantasy, fable and fact."

Another blending of fable and fact, based in part on Garcia Marquez's recollections of his parents' marriage, *Love in the Time of Cholera* "is an amazing celebration of the many kinds of love between men and women," according to Elaine Feinstein of the London *Times*. "In part it is a brilliantly witty account of the tussles in a long marriage, whose details are curiously moving; elsewhere it is a fantastic tale of love finding erotic fulfilment in ageing bodies." The novel begins with the death of Dr. Juvenal Urbino, whose attempt to rescue a parrot from a tree leaves his wife of fifty years, Fermina Daza, a widow. Soon after Urbino's death, however, Florentino Ariza appears on Fermina Daza's doorstep. The rest of the novel recounts Florentino's determination to resume the passionate courtship of a woman who had given him up over half a century ago. In relating both the story of Fermina Daza's marriage and her later courtship, *Love in the Time of Cholera* "is a novel about commitment and fidelity under circumstances which seem to render such virtues absurd," recounted *Times Literary Supplement* contributor S. M. J. Minta. "[It is] about a refusal to grow old gracefully and respectably, about the triumph sentiment can still win over reason, and above all, perhaps, about Latin America, about keeping faith with where, for better or worse, you started out from."

Although the basic plot of *Love in the Time of Cholera* is fairly simple, some critics have accused Garcia Marquez of over-embellishing his story. Calling the plot a "boy-meets-girl" story, Chicago *Tribune Books* contributor Michael Dorris remarked that "it takes a while to realize this core [plot], for every aspect of the book is attenuated, exaggerated, overstated." The critic also argued that "while a Harlequin Romance might balk at stretching this plot for more than a year or two of fictional time, Garcia Marquez nurses it over five decades," adding that the "prose [is] laden with hyperbolic excess." Some critics have claimed that instead of revealing the romantic side of love, *Love in the Time of Cholera* "seems to deal more with libido and self-deceit than with desire and mortality," as Angela Carter termed it in the *Washington Post Book World.* Dorris expressed a similar opinion, writing that while the novel's "first 50 pages are brilliant, provocative, . . . they are [an] overture to a discordant symphony" which portrays an "anachronistic" world of machismo and misogyny. In contrast, Toronto *Globe and*

Mail contributor Ronald Wright believed that the novel works as a satire of this same kind of "hypocrisy, provincialism and irresponsibility of the main characters' social milieu." Wright concluded: "*Love in the Time of Cholera* is a complex and subtle book; its greatest achievement is not to tell a love story, but to meditate on the equivocal nature of romanticism and romantic love."

Other reviewers have agreed that although it contains elements of his other work, *Love in the Time of Cholera* is a development in a different direction for Garcia Marquez. Author Thomas Pynchon, writing in the *New York Times Book Review,* commented that "it would be presumptuous to speak of moving 'beyond' *One Hundred Years of Solitude* but clearly Garcia Marquez has moved somewhere else, not least into deeper awareness of the ways in which, as Florentino comes to learn, 'nobody teaches life anything.'" Countering criticisms that the work is overemotional, Minta claimed that "the triumph of the novel is that it uncovers the massive, submerged strength of the popular, the cliched and the sentimental." While it "does not possess the fierce, visionary poetry of *One Hundred Years of Solitude* or the feverish phantasmagoria of *The Autumn of the Patriarch,*" as *New York Times* critic Michiko Kakutani described it, *Love in the Time of Cholera* "has revealed how the extraordinary is contained in the ordinary, how a couple of forgotten, even commonplace lives can encompass the heights and depths of grand and eternal passion." "The result," concluded the critic, "is a rich commodious novel, a novel whose narrative power is matched only by its generosity of vision." "The Garcimarquesian voice we have come to recognize from the other fiction has matured, found and developed new resources," asserted Pynchon, "[and] been brought to a level where it can at once be classical and familiar, opalescent and pure, able to praise and curse, laugh and cry, fabulate and sing and when called upon, take off and soar." Pynchon concluded: "There is nothing I have read quite like [the] astonishing final chapter, symphonic, sure in its dynamics and tempo. . . . At the very best [this remembrance] results in works that can even return our worn souls to us, among which most certainly belongs *Love in the Time of Cholera,* this shining and heartbreaking novel."

For his next novel, *The General in His Labyrinth,* Garcia Marquez chose another type of story. His protagonist, the General, is Simon Bolivar. Known as "the Liberator," Bolivar is remembered as a controversial and influential historical figure. His revolutionary activities during the early-nineteenth century helped free South America from Spanish control. The labyrinth evoked in the title consists of what John Butt described in the *Times Literary Supplement* as "the web of slanders and intrigues that surrounded [Bolivar's] decline." The book focuses on Bolivar's last months, once the leader had renounced the Colombian presidency and embarked on a long journey that ended when he died near the Caribbean coast on December 17, 1830. Even as he neared death, Bolivar staged one final, failed attempt to reassert leadership in the face of anarchy. In the *New York Times Book Review* author Margaret Atwood declared: "Had Bolivar not existed, Mr. Garcia Marquez would have had to invent him." Atwood called the novel "a fascinating literary tour de force and a moving tribute to an extraordinary man," as well as "a sad commentary on the ruthlessness of the political process."

The political process is, indeed, an integral aspect of *The General in His Labyrinth.* "Latin American politicians and intellectuals have long relied on a more saintly image of Bolivar to make up for the region's often sordid history," Tim Padgett wrote in *Newsweek.* Although Garcia Marquez presents a pro-Bolivar viewpoint in his novel, the book was greeted with controversy. Butt observed that Garcia Marquez had "managed to offend all sides. . . . From the point of view of some pious Latin Americans he blasphemes a local deity by having him utter the occasional obscenity and by showing him as a relentless womanizer, which he was. Others have detected the author's alleged 'Caribbean' tropical and lowland dislike of *cachacos* or upland and *bogotano* Colombians." The harshest criticism, Butt asserted, emanated from some Colombian historians "who claim that the novel impugns the basis of their country's independence by siding too openly with the Liberator" to the detriment of some of Bolivar's political contemporaries. Garcia Marquez earned wide praise for the quality of documentary research that contributed to the novel, although Butt, for one, lamented that the book "leaves much unexplained about the mental processes of the Liberator." He elaborated: "We learn far more about Bolivar's appearance, sex-life, surroundings and public actions than about his thoughts and motives."

In the works, off and on, for nearly two decades, *Strange Pilgrims: Twelve Stories* marked Garcia Marquez's return to the short story collection. Garcia Marquez's pilgrims are Latin American characters placed in various European settings, many of them in southern Italy. "Thematically, these dozen stories explore familiar Marquesan territory: human solitude and quiet desperation, unexpected love (among older people, between generations), the bizarre turns of fate, the intertwining of passion and death," Michael Dirda asserted in the *Washington Post Book World.* At each story's core, however, "lies a variant of that great transatlantic theme—the failure of people of different cultures, ages or political convictions to communicate with each other." In *Strange Pilgrims,* Margaret Sayers Peden asserted in the *Chicago Tribune,* "Latins do not fare well in their separation from native soil." In "The

Saint," for example, an old Colombian man has brought the intact corpse of his young daughter to Rome. For decades he journeys through the Vatican bureaucracy, trying to get his child canonized. "Absurd and oddly serene," Richard Eder wrote in the *Los Angeles Times Book Review,* "['The Saint'] says a great deal about Latin American boundlessness in a bounded Europe." In another story, "I Only Came to Use the Phone," a Mexican woman is mistakenly identified as a mental patient and is trapped in a Spanish insane asylum—no one heeds her cry that she only entered the building to place a telephone call.

"Rich with allusion and suggestion, colourful like a carnival," wrote Ian Thomson in the *Spectator,* "these short stories nevertheless lack the graceful charm of *Love in the Time of Cholera,* say, or of other novels by Marquez. There's a deadpan acceptance of the fantastic, though, which allows for a degree of comedy." In a similar vein, Dirda asserted: "Many of the stories in *Strange Pilgrims* might be classified as fantastic. . . . Still, none of them quite possesses the soul-stirring magic of Garcia Marquez's earlier short fiction." He continued: "For all their smooth execution, [the stories] don't feel truly haunted, they seldom take us to fictive places we've never been before. . . . And yet. And yet. One could hardly wish for more readable entertainments, or more wonderful detailing." Edward Waters Hood, however, declared in *World Literature Today* that these "interesting and innovative stories . . . complement and add several new dimensions to Gabriel Garcia Marquez's fictional world."

Garcia Marquez returned to his Maconderos in his next novel, *Of Love and Other Demons.* The story stems from an event the author witnessed early in his journalistic career. As a reporter in Cartagena in 1949, he was assigned to watch while a convent's tomb was opened to transfer burial remains—the convent was being destroyed to clear space for a hotel. There soon emerged twenty-two meters of vibrant human hair, attached to the skull of a young girl who had been buried for two centuries. Remembering his grandparents' stories about a twelve-year-old aristocrat who had died of rabies, Garcia Marquez began to reconstruct the life and death of a character named Sierva Maria. Jonathan Yardley remarked in the *Washington Post Book World* that the author's mood in this novel "is almost entirely melancholy and his manner is, by contrast with his characteristic ebullience, decidedly restrained." In the *Los Angeles Times Book Review,* Eder judged the novel to be "a good one though not quite among [Garcia Marquez's] best."

As the daughter of wealthy but uninterested parents, Sierva Maria grows up with the African slaves on her family's plantation. When she is bitten by a rabid dog, a local bishop determines that she requires exorcism. The girl is taken to the Convent of Santa Clara, where the bishop's

pious delegate, Father Cayetano Delaura, is charged with her case. But Delaura himself is soon possessed, by the demon of love, a forbidden love for the young woman. Yardley wrote: "Here most certainly we are in the world of Gabriel Garcia Marquez, where religious faith and human love collide in agony and passion." In *Time* magazine R. Z. Sheppard asserted that in telling "a story of forbidden love," Garcia Marquez "demonstrates once again the vigor of his own passion: the daring and irresistible coupling of history and imagination." Yardley warned, however, that "readers hoping to re-experience 'magical realism' at the level attained in the author's masterpieces will be disappointed." In the *Nation,* John Leonard stated: "My only complaint about this marvelous novella is its rush toward the end. Suddenly, [the author is] in a hurry . . . when we want to spend more time" with his characters.

The origins behind *Of Love and Other Demons* emphasize once again the dual forces of journalism and fiction in Garcia Marquez's oeuvre. The author elaborated in his interview with Dreifus: "I'm fascinated by the relationship between literature and *journalism.* I began my career as a journalist in Colombia, and a reporter is something I've never stopped being. When I'm not working on fiction, I'm running around the world, practicing my craft as a reporter." His work as a journalist has produced controversy, for in journalism Garcia Marquez not only sees a chance to develop his "craft," but also an opportunity to become involved in political issues. His self-imposed exile from Colombia was prompted by a series of articles he wrote in 1955 about the sole survivor of a Colombian shipwreck, claiming that the government ship had capsized due to an overload of contraband. In 1986, Garcia Marquez wrote *Clandestine in Chile: The Adventures of Miguel Littin,* a work about an exile's return to the repressive Chile of General Augusto Pinochet. The political revelations of the book led to the burning of almost 15,000 copies by the Chilean government. In addition, Garcia Marquez has maintained personal relationships with such political figures as Cuban President Fidel Castro, former French President Francois Mitterand, and the late Panamanian leader General Omar Torrijos.

Because of this history of political involvement, Garcia Marquez has often been accused of allowing his politics to overshadow his work, and has also encountered problems entering the United States. When asked by the *New York Times Book Review's* Marlise Simons why he is so insistent on becoming involved in political issues, the author replied that "If I were not a Latin American, maybe I wouldn't [become involved]. But underdevelopment is total, integral, it affects every part of our lives. The problems of our societies are mainly political." The Colombian further explained that "the commitment of a writer is with the reality of all of society, not just with a small part of it. If not, he is as bad as the politicians who disregard a large part of our reality. That is why authors, painters, writers in Latin America get politically involved."

Despite the controversy that his politics and work have engendered, Garcia Marquez's *One Hundred Years of Solitude* is enough to ensure the author "a place in the ranks of twentieth century masters," claimed Curt Suplee of the *Washington Post.* The Nobel-winner's reputation, however, is grounded in more than this one masterpiece. The Swedish Academy's Nobel citation states, "Each new work of his is received by critics and readers as an event of world importance, is translated into many languages and published as quickly as possible in large editions." "At a time of dire predictions about the future of the novel," observed McMurray, Garcia Marquez's "prodigious imagination, remarkable compositional precision, and wide popularity provide evidence that the genre is still thriving." And as *Chicago Tribune Book World* contributor Harry Mark Petrakis described him, Garcia Marquez "is a magician of vision and language who does astonishing things with time and reality. He blends legend and history in ways that make the legends seem truer than truth. His scenes and characters are humorous, tragic, mysterious and beset by ironies and fantasies. In his fictional world, anything is possible and everything is believable." Concluded the critic: "Mystical and magical, fully aware of the transiency of life, his stories fashion realms inhabited by ghosts and restless souls who return to those left behind through fantasies and dreams. The stories explore, with a deceptive simplicity, the miracles and mysteries of life."

BIOGRAPHICAL/CRITICAL SOURCES:

BOOKS

Bell, Michael, *Gabriel Garcia Marquez: Solitude and Solidarity,* St. Martin's Press (New York City), 1993.

Bell-Villada, Gene H., *Garcia Marquez: The Man and His Work,* University of North Carolina Press (Chapel Hill, NC), 1990.

Brotherson, Gordon, *The Emergence of the Latin American Novel,* Cambridge University Press, 1979.

Contemporary Literary Criticism, Gale (Detroit), Volume 2, 1974, Volume 3, 1975, Volume 8, 1978, Volume 10, 1979, Volume 15, 1980, Volume 27, 1984, Volume 47, 1988, Volume 55, 1989.

Dictionary of Literary Biography Yearbook: 1982, Gale, 1983.

Dictionary of Literary Biography, Volume 113: *Modern Latin-American Fiction Writers,* Gale, 1992.

Dolan, Sean, *Gabriel Garcia Marquez,* Chelsea House (New York City), 1994.

Fernandez-Braso, Miguel, *Gabriel Garcia Marquez,* Editorial Azur (Madrid), 1969.

Gabriel Garcia Marquez, nuestro premio Nobel, La Secretaria de Informacion y Prensa de la Presidencia de la Nacion (Bogota), 1983.

Gallagher, David Patrick, *Modern Latin American Literature,* Oxford University Press, 1973.

Gonzalez, Nelly S., *Bibliographic Guide to Gabriel Garcia Marquez, 1986-1992,* Greenwood Press (Westport, CT), 1994.

Guibert, Rita, *Seven Voices,* Knopf, 1973.

Harss, Luis, and Barbara Dohmann, *Into the Mainstream: Conversations with Latin-American Writers,* Harper, 1967.

Janes, Regina, *Gabriel Garcia Marquez: Revolutions in Wonderland,* University of Missouri Press (Columbia, MO), 1981.

Mantilla, Alfonso Renteria, compiler, *Garcia Marquez habla de Garcia Marquez,* Renteria (Colombia), 1979.

McGuirk, Bernard, and Richard Cardwell, editors, *Gabriel Garcia Marquez: New Readings,* Cambridge University Press, 1988.

McMurray, George R., *Gabriel Garcia Marquez,* Ungar (New York City), 1977.

Porrata, Francisco E., and Fausto Avedano, *Explicacion de Cien anos de soledad [de] Garcia Marquez,* Editorial Texto (Costa Rica), 1976.

Pritchett, V. S., *The Myth Makers,* Random House (New York City), 1979.

Rodman, Selden, *Tongues of Fallen Angels,* New Direction, 1974.

Vargas Llosa, Mario, *Garcia Marquez: Historia de un deicido,* Barral Editores, 1971.

Wood, Michael, *Gabriel Garcia Marquez: One Hundred Years of Solitude,* Cambridge University Press (Cambridge, England), 1990.

PERIODICALS

Antioch Review, winter, 1991, p. 154.

Books Abroad, winter, 1973; summer, 1973; spring, 1976.

Book World, February 22, 1970; February 20, 1972.

Chicago Tribune, March 6, 1983; October 31, 1993.

Chicago Tribune Book World, November 11, 1979; November 7, 1982; April 3, 1983; November 18, 1984; April 27, 1986.

Christian Science Monitor, April 16, 1970.

Commonweal, March 6, 1970.

Detroit News, October 27, 1982; December 16, 1984.

El Pais, January 22, 1981.

Globe and Mail (Toronto), April 7, 1984; September 19, 1987; May 21, 1988.

Hispania, September, 1976; September, 1993, pp. 439-45; March, 1994, pp. 80-81.

London Magazine, April/May, 1973; November, 1979.

Los Angeles Times, October 22, 1982; January 25, 1987; August 24, 1988.

Los Angeles Times Book Review, April 10, 1983; November 13, 1983; December 16, 1984; April 27, 1986; June 7, 1987; April 17, 1988; October 24, 1993, pp. 3, 10; May 14, 1995, pp. 3, 5.

Nation, December 2, 1968; May 15, 1972; May 14, 1983; June 12, 1995, pp. 836-40.

National Observer, April 20, 1970.

National Review, May 27, 1977; June 10, 1983.

New Republic, April 9, 1977; October 27, 1979; May 2, 1983.

New Statesman, June 26, 1970; May 18, 1979; February 15, 1980; September 3, 1982.

Newsweek, March 2, 1970; November 8, 1976; July 3, 1978; December 3, 1979; November 1, 1982; October 8, 1990, p. 70.

New York Review of Books, March 26, 1970; January 24, 1980; April 14, 1983.

New York Times, July 11, 1978; November 6, 1979; October 22, 1982; March 25, 1983; December 7, 1985; April 26, 1986; June 4, 1986; April 6, 1988.

New York Times Book Review, September 29, 1968; March 8, 1970; February 20, 1972; October 31, 1976; July 16, 1978; September 16, 1978; November 11, 1979; November 16, 1980; December 5, 1982; March 27, 1983; April 7, 1985; April 27, 1986; August 9, 1987; April 10, 1988; September 16, 1990, pp. 1, 30.

Paris Review, winter, 1981.

Playboy, February, 1983.

Publishers Weekly, May 13, 1974; December 16, 1983; March 27, 1995, pp. 72-73.

Review, number 24, 1979; September/December, 1981.

Saturday Review, December 21, 1968; March 7, 1970.

Southwest Review, summer, 1973.

Spectator, October 16, 1993, pp. 40-41.

Time, March 16, 1970; November 1, 1976; July 10, 1978; November 1, 1982; March 7, 1983; December 31, 1984; April 14, 1986; May 22, 1995.

Times (London), November 13, 1986; June 30, 1988.

Times Literary Supplement, April 15, 1977; February 1, 1980; September 10, 1982; July 1, 1988; July 14-20, 1989, p. 781; July 7, 1995.

Tribune Books (Chicago), June 28, 1987; April 17, 1988.

Washington Post, October 22, 1982; April 10, 1994, p. F1.

Washington Post Book World, November 14, 1976; November 25, 1979; November 7, 1982; March 27, 1983; November 18, 1984; July 19, 1987; April 24, 1988; October 31, 1993, p. 7; May 14, 1995, p. 3.

World Literature Today, winter, 1982; winter, 1991, p. 85; autumn, 1993, pp. 782-83.

World Press Review, April, 1982.

World Research INK, September, 1977.*

—*Sketch by Erika Dreifus*

GAY, Kathlyn 1930-

PERSONAL: Born March 4, 1930, in Zion, IL; daughter of Kenneth Charles and Beatrice (Anderson) McGarrahan; married Arthur L. Gay (an elementary school teacher), August 28, 1948; children: Martin, Douglas, Karen. *Education:* Attended Northern Illinois University, two years. *Politics:* Registered Democrat.

ADDRESSES: Home and office—1711 East Beardsley Ave., Elkhart, IN 46514.

CAREER: Church World Service, Christian Rural Overseas Program (CROP), editor and public relations writer in Elkhart, IN, and New York City, 1962-66; Juhl Advertising Agency, Elkhart, publicity and public relations writer, 1966; freelance writer, 1966—; partner in rental business, 1971—. Community relations director for Americana Healthcare Center, 1976-79; instructor in creative writing, Elkhart Area Career Center, 1970—. Past writer for political campaigns, including Mayor Richard J. Daley's political campaign in Chicago, 1967. Writing consultant to Lyons & Carnahan, 1969-70, Ginn & Co., 1971, and Science Research Associates, 1972-73.

MEMBER: Authors Guild, Society of Children's Book Writers and Illustrators, Children's Reading Round Table.

AWARDS, HONORS: Honorable mention, *Writer's Digest* short story contest, 1962; first prize in literary section, Northern Indiana Arts Festival, 1965, for one-act play; selection as "Outstanding Book," National Council for Social Studies and National Science Teachers' Association, 1983, for *Acid Rain,* and 1988, for *Silent Killers;* selection as "one of the most important books on education," National Education Association convention, 1987, for *Crisis in Education: Will the U.S. Be Ready for the Year 2000?;* selection to List of Notable Books for Young People, American Library Association, 1993, for *Global Garbage: International Trade in Toxic Waste.*

WRITINGS:

Girl Pilot, Messner (New York City), 1966.

Money Isn't Everything: The Story of Economics, Delacorte (New York City), 1967.

Meet the Mayor of Your City, Hawthorn (New York City), 1967.

Meet Your Governor, Hawthorn, 1968.

Beth Speaks Out, Messner, 1968, published as *Beth Donnis: Speech Therapist.*

Careers in Social Service, Messner, 1969.

Where the People Are: Cities and Their Future, Delacorte, 1969.

The Germans Helped Build America, Messner, 1971.

Proud Heritage on Parade, Contemporary Drama Service, 1972.

Core English: English for Speakers of Other Languages, Ginn (Lexington, MA), 1972.

A Family Is for Living, Delacorte, 1972.

Our Working World, Science Research Associates (Palo Alto, CA), 1973.

Body Talk, Scribner (New York City), 1974.

Be a Smart Shopper, Messner, 1974.

(With Ben E. Barnes) *The River Flows Backward,* Ashley Books (Port Washington, NY), 1975.

What's in a Name?, Elkhart Community Schools (Elkhart, IN), 1975.

Care and Share: Teenagers and Volunteerism, Messner, 1977.

Look Mom! No Words!, Houghton (Boston), 1977.

(With son, Martin, and Marla Gay) *Get Hooked on Vegetables,* Messner, 1978.

(Co-author) *English around the World,* Scott, Foresman (Glenview, IL), 1979.

(With Martin Gay) *Eating What Grows Naturally,* And Books (South Bend, IN), 1980.

(With Barnes) *Your Fight Has Just Begun,* Messner, 1980.

(With Barnes) *Beginner's Guide to Better Boxing,* McKay (New York City), 1980.

(Co-author) *I Like English,* Scott, Foresman, 1981.

English for a Changing World, Scott, Foresman, 1981.

Boxes and More Boxes, Houghton, 1981.

(Co-author) *Family Living,* Prentice-Hall (Englewood Cliffs, NJ), 1982, 3rd edition, 1988.

Junkyards, Enslow Publishers (Hillside, NJ), 1982.

Acid Rain, F. Watts (New York City), 1983.

Cities under Stress, F. Watts, 1985.

The Greenhouse Effect, F. Watts, 1986.

Ergonomics: Making Products and Places Fit People, Enslow Publishers, 1986.

Crisis in Education: Will the U.S. Be Ready for the Year 2000?, F. Watts, 1986.

Changing Families, Enslow Publishers, 1987.

The Rainbow Effect: Interracial Families, F. Watts, 1987.

The Science of Ancient Greece, F. Watts, 1988.

Silent Killers, F. Watts, 1988.

Bigotry, Enslow Publishers, 1989.

Ozone, F. Watts, 1989.

Adoption and Foster Care, Enslow Publishers, 1990.

They Don't Wash Their Socks!: Sports Superstitions, Walker, 1990.

Water Pollution, F. Watts, 1990.

Cleaning Nature Naturally, Walker, 1991.

Air Pollution, F. Watts, 1991.

Garbage and Recycling, Enslow Publishers, 1991.

Day Care: Looking for Answers, Enslow Publishers, 1992.

Church and State, Millbrook, 1992.

Global Garbage: International Trade in Toxic Waste, F. Watts, 1992.

Caution: This May Be an Advertisement—Teen Guide to Advertising, F. Watts, 1992.

Caretakers of the Earth, Enslow Publishers, 1993.

The Right to Die: Public Controversy, Private Matter, Millbrook, 1993.

Getting Your Message Across, Silver Burdett (Morristown, NJ)/Macmillan (New York City), 1993.

Breast Implants: Making Safe Choices, Silver Burdett/Macmillan, 1993.

Pregnancy: Private Decisions, Public Debates, F. Watts, 1994.

Rainforests of the World, American Bibliographical Center-Clio Press (Santa Barbara, CA), 1994.

The New Power of Women in Politics, Enslow Publishers, 1994.

Pollution and the Powerless: The Environmental Justice Movement, F. Watts, 1994.

I Am Who I Am: Speaking Out about Multiracial Identity, F. Watts, 1995.

Keep the Buttered Side Up: Food Superstitions from Around the World, Walker, 1995.

(With Martin Gay) *Voices from the Past,* Holt (New York City), Volumes 1-6, 1995, Volumes 7-9, 1996.

(With Martin Gay) *Encyclopedia of North American Eating and Drinking Traditions, Customs, and Rituals,* American Bibliographical Center-Clio Press, 1995.

Rights and Respect, Millbrook, 1995.

(With Martin Gay) *Emma Goldman,* Lucent Books, 1995.

(With Martin Gay) *The Information Superhighway,* Holt, 1995.

The Environment versus the Economy, F. Watts, 1996.

(With son, Douglas Gay) *The Not-So-Minor Leagues,* Millbrook, 1996.

Also author of teaching manuals, including activities and stories for numerous publishers. Contributor to books, including *Spotlights,* Houghton, 1986; and *Currents,* Houghton, 1986. Contributor to *Childcraft Annual,* Field Enterprises, 1969, *The New Book of Knowledge,* and *Collier's Encyclopedia.* Contributor to "Young America Basic Reading Series," Lyons & Carnahan. Contributor of articles and short stories to periodicals, including *Women in Business, Michiana Magazine, Better Homes and Gardens, Red Cross Journal, Success, Highlights for Children,* and *Popular Medicine.*

WORK IN PROGRESS: Cults, Communes, and Religious Communities, for Holt; *A Dictionary of Twentieth-Century Heroes of Conscience,* for American Bibliographical Center-Clio Press; *Neo-Nazis,* for Enslow Publishers.

SIDELIGHTS: Kathlyn Gay once told *CA:* "Writing, for me, is a way of life, and I could not imagine trying to function as an individual without exercising this form of communication. I have always considered myself a rather shy person, but also one who can 'walk in another's shoes.'

These traits, more than any others, have probably motivated me to write both fiction and nonfiction.

"For as long as I can remember I have been concerned about the way people get along with each other. I believe we are all of one humankind, but have differences that we can learn to respect. So, much of my writing has been about our pluralistic society—the variety of different cultures and backgrounds which shape people in this country.

"Besides human relationships, other interests have determined some types of writing I do. Since my husband (now retired) was a teacher, counselor and principal in elementary schools, I had many first-hand experiences with new educational programs. Much of this was shared in textbooks and teaching materials I helped prepare.

"Also, my husband and I were once active in amateur theater groups, and during childhood I staged my own plays in our basement or backyard. This led to writing a few plays and a variety of articles on how dramatic skills can be used in teaching, the way our bodies and facial expressions are used to send silent messages, and how to use speech effectively.

"In recent years, I have become increasingly concerned about our total environment, and this has led to involvement in various social action groups. In addition, I have been able to write about such issues as changing family life, protection of civil rights, and the effects of pollutants on the environment.

"Since the early 1990s, I have taken advantage of Internet access and online subscription services via computer and modem to do a great deal of the research needed for nonfiction books. The electronic age has also provided the means to collaborate on book projects with my two sons and a daughter who are scattered geographically. We use e-mail and file transfers to work across long distances, enabling the creation of at least a dozen books for 1995 publication.

"Finally, I consider it a real privilege to write—to share with others what arouses my curiosity and elicits my concern. I have always been eager to learn and to understand. I hope I never lose that desire to investigate and to try to make sense out of my discoveries. That is the stuff from which one keeps developing not only as a writer, but also as a productive human being."

*   *   *

GEORGE, Jonathan
See BURKE, John (Frederick)

GILLILAND, Alexis A(rnaldus) 1931-

PERSONAL: Born August 10, 1931, in Bangor, ME; son of William L. (a professor of chemistry) and Lucille (a teacher of English; maiden name, Cartmell) Gilliland; married Dorothea "Dolly" Cohle (a management consultant), August 29, 1959 (died November 27, 1991); married Elisabeth S. Uba (an interior designer), October 31, 1993; children: (first marriage) Charles D. *Education:* Purdue University, B.S., 1953; George Washington University, M.S., 1963.

ADDRESSES: Home—4030 Eighth St. S., Arlington, VA 22204.

CAREER: National Bureau of Standards, Washington, DC, thermochemist, 1956-67; Federal Supply Service, Washington, DC, chemist and specification writer, 1967-82; free-lance writer, 1982—. U.S. Army, Presidential Honor Guard, 1954-56.

MEMBER: American Association for the Advancement of Science, Science Fiction Writers of America, Washington Science Fiction Association (president, 1974-78), Smithsonian Associates, Sigma Xi.

AWARDS, HONORS: Hugo Award, World Science Fiction Convention, 1980, 1983, 1984, and 1985, for best fan artist; John W. Campbell Award, 1982, for best new science fiction writer.

WRITINGS:

The Iron Law of Bureaucracy (cartoons), Loompanics (Port Townsend, WA), 1979.
The Revolution from Rosinante (science fiction novel), Del Rey, 1981.
Long Shot from Rosinante (science fiction novel), Del Rey, 1981.
The Pirates of Rosinante (science fiction novel), Del Rey, 1982.
The End of Empire (science fiction novel), Del Rey, 1983.
Who Says Paranoia Isn't "In" Any More? (cartoons), Loompanics, 1984.
Wizenbeak (fantasy novel; also see below), Bluejay (Kokomo, IN), 1986.
The Waltzing Wizard (cartoons), Starmont House (Mercer Island, WA), 1989.
The Shadow Shaia (sequel to *Wizenbeak;* also see below), Del Rey, 1990.
Lord of the Troll-Bats (sequel to *The Shadow Shaia* and *Wizenbeak*), Del Rey, 1992.

Also author of musical comedies for amateur performance. Contributor of cartoons, essays, and reviews to periodicals, including *Science Fiction Review, Analog, Asimov's Science Fiction Magazine, The Magazine of Fantasy and Science Fiction,* and *Playboy.*

Some of Gilliland's work has been translated into German and French.

WORK IN PROGRESS: Dauvia Rising.

SIDELIGHTS: Alexis Gilliland has directed chess tournaments (and once played at the expert level). He has chaired regional science fiction conventions in and near Washington, D.C., and has hosted Washington Science Fiction Association meetings in his home for more than twenty-five years.

He explained to *CA:* "On February 19, 1982, after I had spent twenty-eight years in federal service, my job was abolished."

BIOGRAPHICAL/CRITICAL SOURCES:

PERIODICALS

Los Angeles Times Book Review, March 15, 1981.
Washington Post, September 25, 1982.
Washington Post Book World, June 28, 1981; January 29, 1984.

*   *   *

GISH, Robert F(ranklin) 1940-

PERSONAL: Born April 1, 1940, in Albuquerque, NM; son of Jesse Franklin (in business) and Lillian J. (in business; maiden name, Fields) Gish; married Judith Kay Stephenson (a teacher), 1960; children: Robin E. Gish Butzier, Timothy S., Annabeth. *Education:* University of New Mexico, B.A., 1962, M.A., 1967, Ph.D., 1972.

ADDRESSES: Home—San Luis Obispo, CA. *Office*—P.O. Box 947, San Luis Obispo, CA 93406.

CAREER: University of Northern Iowa, professor of English and literature, 1967-91; director of ethnic studies and professor of English and ethnic studies, California Polytechnic State University, 1991—. Member, Cherokee Nation of Oklahoma.

MEMBER: Screen Actors Guild (SAG), Authors Guild, PEN West.

AWARDS, HONORS: Distinguished Alumni Award, University of New Mexico, 1992.

WRITINGS:

Hamlin Garland: The Far West, Boise State University (Boise, ID), 1976.
Paul Horgan, G. K. Hall (Boston), 1983.
Frontier's End: The Life and Literature of Harvey Fergusson, University of Nebraska Press (Lincoln), 1988.
William Carlos Williams: The Short Fiction, G. K. Hall, 1989.

Songs of My Hunter Heart: A Western Kinship, Iowa State University Press (Ames), 1991.
Retold Native American Myths, Perfection Learning, 1992.
First Horses: Stories of the New West, University of Nevada Press (Reno), 1993.
When Coyote Howls: A Lavaland Fable, University of New Mexico Press (Albuquerque), 1994.
Nueva Granada: Paul Horgan and the Southwest, Texas A & M University Press (College Station), 1995.
Beyond Bounds: Cross-Cultural Essays on Anglo, American Indian, and Chicano Literature, University of New Mexico Press, 1996.

Contributor of articles and reviews to periodicals. Contributing editor, *Bloomsbury Review;* member of editorial board, *Western American Literature* and *Journal of American Indian Culture and Research.*

WORK IN PROGRESS: More short stories set in the modern West; historical research on New Mexico and the Southwest.

SIDELIGHTS: Robert F. Gish once told *CA:* "The American West and Southwest provide me with much inspiration—as places of the heart and imagination as well as geographical locales. Much of my scholarly research and writing have led me to greater discovery of my own needs and motives as an imaginative writer. Through reading and through kinship with 'place,' I have come to rediscover my family's Native American heritage in Oklahoma: a combination of Choctaw and Cherokee birthrights. I am convinced that only through the rediscovery of the land and its indigenous peoples—and through understanding of 'minority' cultures and viewpoints—will the dominant Anglo-European culture of the United States adapt and evolve. In my writing and teaching, I attempt to advance the agendas of the 'relativity of otherness' and 'thick history and ecology.' "

*   *   *

GITLIN, Todd 1943-

PERSONAL: Born January 6, 1943, in New York, NY; son of Max (a teacher) and Dorothy (a teacher; maiden name, Siegel) Gitlin. *Education:* Harvard University, B.A., 1963; University of Michigan, M.A., 1966; University of California, Berkeley, Ph.D., 1977.

ADDRESSES: Office—Department of Culture and Communication, School of Education, New York University, New York, NY 10003.

CAREER: San Francisco Express Times, San Francisco, CA, writer, 1968-69; San Jose State College (now University), San Jose, CA, lecturer, 1970-76; University of California, Santa Cruz, lecturer, 1974-77; University of California, Berkeley, assistant professor, 1978-83, associate professor, 1983-87, professor of sociology and director of mass communications program, 1987-95; New York University, New York City, professor of culture and communication, journalism, and sociology, 1995—. Holder of Chair in American Civilization, Ecole des Hautes Etudes en Sciences Sociales, French-American Foundation, Paris, 1994-95.

MEMBER: American Sociological Association, PEN American Center (co-chairperson of San Francisco branch, 1987-88).

AWARDS, HONORS: Anne Parsons Educational Trust grant, 1962; Laras Fund grant, 1976; National Endowment for the Humanities grant, 1981; Rockefeller Foundation fellowship, 1981; nonfiction award, Bay Area Book Reviewers Association, 1984, for *Inside Prime Time;* finalist, Robert F. Kennedy Book Award and Bay Area Book Reviewers Association, 1988, for *The Sixties;* grant for research and writing in international peace and security, MacArthur Foundation, 1988-89.

WRITINGS:

(With Nanci Hollander) *Uptown: Poor Whites in Chicago,* Harper (New York City), 1970.
(Editor) *Campfires of the Resistance: Poetry from the Movement,* Bobbs-Merrill (New York City), 1971.
Busy Being Born (poems), Straight Arrow Books, 1974.
The Whole World Is Watching: Mass Media in the Making and Unmaking of the New Left, University of California Press (Berkeley), 1980.
Inside Prime Time, Pantheon (New York City), 1983.
(Editor and contributor) *Watching Television,* Pantheon, 1987.
The Sixties: Years of Hope, Days of Rage, Bantam (New York City), 1987.
The Murder of Albert Einstein (novel), Farrar, Straus (New York City), 1992.
The Twilight of Common Dreams: Why America Is Wracked by Culture Wars, Metropolitan/Henry Holt, 1995.

Contributor to numerous books. Columnist, *New York Observer,* 1992—. Contributor to periodicals, including *Harper's, New York Times, Washington Post, Theory and Society, American Journalism Review, World Policy Journal,* and *Yale Review.* Member of editorial board, *Dissent.*

WORK IN PROGRESS: A novel; essays on media.

SIDELIGHTS: Todd Gitlin's writing explores myriad interconnected facets of contemporary life, including the way mass media affects society and vice versa, historical analysis of the recent past, and the changing state of American politics. He is the author or editor of three notable books on mass media: *The Whole World Is Watching: Mass Media in the Making and Unmaking of the New Left, Inside Prime Time,* and *Watching Television.* All three works reflect Gitlin's political viewpoint—the author, a New Left liberal, was for a time president of Students for a Democratic Society (SDS), well known in the 1960s as a breeding ground for countercultural activism.

In *The Whole World Is Watching,* Gitlin uses his SDS experiences to make the point that "the relationship between the media and the SDS grew from virtually nothing in 1965 . . . into something like an active partnership just a few years later," as Frank Viviano reports in a *Washington Post* review. According to the author, continues Viviano, the expectations of the media—especially television—resulted in increasing coverage of SDS activities, which brought in new members to the organization and also fulfilled the cameras' need for "good copy and photogenic media events" by the youthful activists. "That is not to say that everything that makes the airways or headlines reflects the bald interests of government and business," says Viviano. "Gitlin points out that the 'hegemonic frame' that contained SDS and the New Left for half a decade did not remain fixed. In fact, it had three stages, shifting from reasonably sympathetic coverage in 1965, . . . to denigration and implicit criticism after the escalation of the war. . . . Following the 1968 Tet Offensive in Vietnam, coverage again became sympathetic, but it was directed this time at 'moderate alternatives to the now militant New Left.' "

New York Times Book Review critic Walter Goodman praises Gitlin's thesis but also expresses some reservations. The "more readable portions of his book come when he leaves theorizing and reports on the effects that the heady attentions of reporters and cameramen had on SDS leaders," Goodman states.

Inside Prime Time "is the best book ever written about the thinking of the insulated men and women in the executive suites of Century City, Burbank and Television City," says David Crook in the *Los Angeles Times Book Review.* Gitlin infiltrated media ranks in those cities—the major network television production centers in California—to produce his study of television's power structures, tacit agreements, and dependence on advertisers' standards. "Gitlin's is a subtle, profound observation," Crook observes. "TV executives do not believe they are cultural arbiters, and certainly not political ones. Continually so accused, executives answer (honestly, given the rules where they work) that they only anticipate and reflect the social and political currents of the day. They select programs that instinct, research and ratings say people want."

The book "has many trenchant observations and an equal number of illuminating anecdotes; its account of the making and somewhat improbable success of 'Hill Street Blues' is perhaps the best of the latter," writes *Washington Post* critic Jonathan Yardley. Gitlin, he feels, "is for the most part free of the condescension with which academics often approach network television; he refrains from snide asides about [his subjects], and he also refrains from unflattering remarks about the mass audience to whom their labors are directed." Yardley notes that the author "does have one shortcoming: He believes that programs with 'politically charged themes' are desirable—which, on the evidence of most such programs, is a singularly questionable belief." But whatever drawbacks, the critic concludes, *Inside Prime Time* is "a thorough and sensitive exploration of a singularly mysterious world."

Watching Television, a book Gitlin edited and to which he contributed an essay, "consists of seven essays, each of which expresses serious complaints about the role television plays in our lives," comments Neil Postman in the *Los Angeles Times Book Review.* "Taken together, the essays may be viewed as a treatise in social psychology, with an emphasis on how television is implicated in the growing sense of impotence and fragmentation that characterize the American mood." As for Gitlin's contribution, Postman points out that the editor "provides the book with more than his trenchant essay. [Gitlin has also] given the book a coherent spirit and a unity of point of view." Brent Staples concludes in a *New York Times Book Review* article that "even though [*Watching Television*] is shrill and paranoid in places, [it] should be regarded as a prolegomenon to any further television criticism—an important step into the post-wasteland era of writing about the tube."

Departing from mass-media themes, Gitlin produced *The Sixties: Years of Hope, Days of Rage* in 1987, a year that itself saw much interest sparked in sixties recollection. "Empathetic, thoughtful, comprehensive, [the work] fuses research, personal witness and a willingness to discuss shortfalls and successes alike," according to Abe Peck in a *Tribune Books* review. "Gitlin is especially good at tracing the New Left's seesawing relationships with both the Old Left and corporate liberalism," he adds.

"In many respects, the book's most valuable parts are autobiographical," remarks *New York Times Book Review* writer Jim Miller. The critic further reports that Gitlin's reminiscences center mainly on his college days, where in the early years of the decade he "began to learn about left-wing politics. In the summer of 1960, he fell in love with a daughter of former Communists. She introduced him to folk music—perhaps the most enduring and influential artifact of the Communist Party's popular-front policies—and to 'the forbidden world of wholesale political criticism,' an 'outlaw culture' that fascinated him."

From there *The Sixties* covers events in Berkeley and Chicago, where Gitlin joined such activists as Abbie Hoffman and Thomas Hayden in movements like SDS. "At times, particularly when he is dealing with some of the most chaotic episodes of the late '60s, [the author] seems overwhelmed by his material," finds Miller. "Yet when he settles down to the work of carefully reconstructing the key events, he succeeds admirably in bringing this 'gone time' back to life."

Todd Gitlin told *CA:* "Since college days, my profession—my calling, to use the old-fashioned word—has been that of the writer, the writer before anything else. Why I took a Ph.D. in sociology and spent many years in a sociology department is a long story, the details of which are idiosyncratic, but the key element, I think, is that I wanted a certificate and a location which would permit me to write as much about whatever interested me, in the ways that interested me, as possible. In a specialized world, writing about media and popular culture gave me a way of slicing into a whole tangle of political, social, cultural, and intellectual questions. Since publishing *The Sixties: Years of Hope, Days of Rage,* I continue to write regularly on the mass media (especially as a columnist in the *New York Observer* and occasional contributor to a variety of magazines and op-ed pages), and will have in mind at least one more book about the media. But my main activity has been elsewhere. I still see studying and writing about media as a way of slicing into all kings of questions, but my main work has moved outward.

"I have been more 'writerly' than before. I published a novel, *The Murder of Albert Einstein,* a thriller set in the worlds of television, politics, and physics. In the conventions of American writing, a thriller is a low form, not taken very seriously, not regarded as 'about anything' especially, but this book, in my estimation, is an exploration of moral questions and is as serious a book as I have written. At this writing, I am at work on another novel, quite different in form and style, more inward, less compact, about which I can't say very much except that it is about the passions of fathers and sons, perhaps, and about the desire to escape.

"My other major project of recent years is a nonfiction book, *The Twilight of Common Dreams: Why American Is Wracked by Culture Wars.* This is an attempt to transcend the stale debates about American identity, multiculturalism, and so forth, and to explain why American politics has developed its distracted quality, its paralysis. The book includes some analysis of media and popular culture, but it is mostly an extended essay in American history, philosophy, social theory, and sociology.

"In fiction, I need not respect the truth of details, only the truth of the intricacy of the truth. Here I go with Picasso:

'Art is the lies by which the truth is known.' Nonfiction has other obligations. I need both."

BIOGRAPHICAL/CRITICAL SOURCES:

BOOKS

Gitlin, Todd, *The Sixties: Years of Hope, Days of Rage,* Bantam, 1987.

PERIODICALS

Chicago Tribune, February 24, 1987.
Globe & Mail (Toronto), December 19, 1987; January 16, 1988.
Los Angeles Times Book Review, October 23, 1983; March 22, 1987; December 27, 1987.
Nation, May 3, 1980.
New Republic, April 4, 1981.
New York Times Book Review, August 31, 1980; October 2, 1983; February 8, 1987; November 8, 1987.
Tribune Books (Chicago), October 25, 1987.
Village Voice, October 25, 1983.
Washington Post, September 19, 1980; October 5, 1983; February 4, 1987.
Washington Post Book World, November 29, 1987; December 20, 1987.

*   *   *

GIVNER, Joan Mary 1936-

PERSONAL: Born September 5, 1936, in Manchester, England; came to the United States in 1958, naturalized citizen, 1962; daughter of Thomas and Elizabeth (Parker) Short; married Richard Bogg, August 8, 1958 (divorced October 9, 1963); married David Aaron Givner (a professor of philosophy), April 15, 1965; children: (second marriage) Emily Jane, Jessie Louise. *Education:* University of London, B.A., 1958, Ph.D., 1972; Washington University, St. Louis, MO, M.A., 1962.

ADDRESSES: Home—2587 Seaview Rd., R.R. 1 Mill Bay, British Columbia V0R 2P0, Canada.

CAREER: St. Clair County Community College, Port Huron, MI, lecturer in English, 1960-65; University of Regina, Regina, Saskatchewan, lecturer, 1965-70, assistant professor, 1972-76, associate professor, 1976-82, professor of English, 1982-95. Fellow at Bunting Institute, Radcliffe College, 1978-79.

MEMBER: Modern Language Association of America, Rocky Mountain Modern Language Association, Saskatchewan Women Artists Association, University Women's Club.

AWARDS, HONORS: Canada Council grants, 1973-78; Humanities Endowment Fund fellow, 1978-79; citation as

one of notable books of the year, *New York Times Book Review,* for *Katherine Anne Porter: A Life;* a special issue of *Room of One's Own,* Volume 15, numbers 3 and 4, was devoted to Givner and her work.

WRITINGS:

Katherine Anne Porter: A Life, Simon & Schuster (New York City), 1982.
Tentacles of Unreason (short stories), University of Illinois Press (Champaign), 1985.
(Editor and author of introduction) *Katherine Anne Porter: Conversations,* University Press of Mississippi (Jackson), 1987.
Mazo de la Roche (biography), Oxford University Press (Canada), 1988.
Unfortunate Incidents (short stories), Oberon Press (Ottawa), 1988.
Scenes from Provincial Life (short stories), Oberon Press, 1991.
The Self-Portrait of a Literary Biographer, University of Georgia Press (Athens), 1993.

Contributor to literature journals.

BIOGRAPHICAL/CRITICAL SOURCES:

PERIODICALS

Chicago Tribune, January 30, 1983.
Los Angeles Times Book Review, February 6, 1983; December 8, 1985.
New York Times Book Review, December 15, 1985.
Time, December 6, 1982.
Times Literary Supplement, June 10, 1983.
Washington Post Book World, December 5, 1982; November 17, 1985.

*   *   *

GORDON, (Irene) Linda 1940-

PERSONAL: Born January 19, 1940, in Chicago, IL; daughter of William (a social worker) and Helen (a nursery school teacher and child-welfare activist; maiden name, Appelman) Gordon; children: Rosie Gordon Hunter. *Education:* Swarthmore College, B.A. (magna cum laude), 1961; Yale University, M.A., 1963, Ph.D. (with distinction), 1970.

ADDRESSES: Home—2121 West Lawn Ave., Madison, WI 53711. *Office*—Department of History, University of Wisconsin, Madison, WI 53706.

CAREER: University of Massachusetts, Boston, instructor, 1968-69, assistant professor, 1970-75, associate professor, 1975-81, professor of history, 1981-84; University of Wisconsin, Madison, professor of history, 1984-90,

Florence Kelley Professor of History, 1990—, Vilas Distinguished Research Professor, 1993—. Scholar in residence, Stanford University, summer, 1979, Dickinson College, summer, 1987; Bunting Institute fellow, Radcliffe College, 1983-84; visiting professor, University of Amsterdam, 1984; Bird Memorial lecturer, University of Maine, 1986; invited residency, Bellagio Center, Italy, 1992. Has given numerous academic lectures, presented papers, and participated in conferences and annual meetings throughout the world.

Member of advisory board, Margaret Sanger Papers Project, New York University and Smith College; member of advisory committee, Project on Reproductive Laws for the 1990s, American Civil Liberties Union and Rutgers University School of Law, 1985-87. Manuscript and proposal referee for many national organizations and presses, including National Endowment for the Humanities, Temple University Press, Columbia University Press, University of California Press, Northeastern University Press, University of Illinois Press, Oxford University Press, Canadian Social Science Research Council, and U.K. Social Science Research Council. Lecturer at numerous universities and colleges. Consultant/adviser to numerous local, civic, academic, media, and government organizations.

MEMBER: American Historical Association (member of program committee, 1981), Organization of American Historians (member of nominating committee, 1988-90).

AWARDS, HONORS: National Book Award in History nomination, 1976, for *Woman's Body, Woman's Right: A Social History of Birth Control in America,* and 1988, for *Heroes of Their Own Lives: The Politics and History of Family Violence, Boston, 1880-1960;* National Institute of Mental Health grant, 1979-82; American Council of Learned Societies travel grant, 1980; Outstanding Achievement Award, University of Massachusetts, 1982-83; Antonovych Prize, 1983, for *Cossack Rebellions: Social Turmoil in the Sixteenth-Century Ukraine;* Guggenheim fellowship, 1983-84, 1987; American Council of Learned Societies/Ford Foundation fellowship, 1985; University of Wisconsin graduate school research awards, 1985-95; Joan Kelley Prize for best book in women's history or theory of the American History Association, Wisconsin Library Association Award, 1988, runner-up for *Los Angeles Times* Book Award in History, nomination for Robert F. Kennedy Book Award and Merle Curti Award of the American History Association for the best book in social history, all for *Heroes of Their Own Lives: The Politics and History of Family Violence, Boston, 1880-1960;* American Philosophical Society Research Award, 1988-89; Berkshire Prize for best book in women's history, for *Pitied but Not Entitled: Single Mothers and the Origins of Welfare.*

WRITINGS:

Woman's Body, Woman's Right: A Social History of Birth Control in America, Viking (New York City), 1976.

(Editor with Rosalyn Baxandall and Susan Reverby) *America's Working Women: A Documentary History,* Random House (New York City), 1976, 2nd revised edition, 1995.

(Editor) *Maternity: Letters from Working Women* (originally published in London, 1915), Norton (New York City), 1979.

Cossack Rebellions: Social Turmoil in the Sixteenth-Century Ukraine, State University of New York Press (Albany), 1982.

Heroes of Their Own Lives: The Politics and History of Family Violence, Boston, 1880-1960, Viking, 1988.

(Editor) *Women and the State: Historical and Theoretical Essays,* University of Wisconsin Press (Madison), 1990.

(Author of introduction) *Taking Child Abuse Seriously,* Unwin Hyman (London), 1990.

Pitied but Not Entitled: Single Mothers and the Origins of Welfare, Free Press (New York City), 1994.

OTHER

Contributor to numerous books, including *Voices from Women's Liberation,* edited by Leslie Tanner, Signet Books (New York City), 1970; *Rethinking the Family,* edited by Thorne, Longman (New York City), 1981; *What Is History?,* edited by Juliet Gardiner, Macmillan (New York City), 1988; *Gendered Domains: Rethinking Public and Private Women's History,* edited by Dorothy O. Helly and Reverby, Cornell University Press (Ithaca, NY), 1992; and *American History as Women's History: Knowledge, Power, and State Formation,* revised edition, edited by Kerber and others, University of North Carolina (Chapel Hill), 1995.

Contributor to anthologies. Contributor to encyclopedias, including *Encyclopedia of the American Left, Encyclopedia of American Women's History,* and *Encyclopedia of American History.* Contributor of articles and reviews to numerous periodicals, including *National Women's Studies Association Journal, Social Research, Journal of Family History, Chronicle of Higher Education, Journal of Sociology and Social Welfare, Against the Current,* and *Nation.* Member of editorial board, *American Historical Review,* 1990-93, *Contemporary Sociology,* 1994—, *Journal of American History* and *Journal of Policy History,* both 1994-97, and of *Signs, Feminist Studies, Journal of Women's History, Contention,* and *Gender and History;* referee for many scholarly journals.

Some of Gordon's work has been translated into Italian.

BIOGRAPHICAL/CRITICAL SOURCES:

BOOKS

Dimock, editor, *Visions of History: Conversations with Radical Historians,* Pantheon (New York City), 1984.

PERIODICALS

American Historical Review, October, 1977.
Journal of American History, December, 1977.
Los Angeles Times Book Review, May 1, 1988.
New York Times Book Review, May 8, 1988.

* * *

GRAEME, Roderic
See JEFFRIES, Roderic (Graeme)

* * *

GRAHAM, Vanessa
See FRASER, Anthea

* * *

GRANT, Michael 1914-

PERSONAL: Born November 21, 1914, in London, England; son of Maurice Harold (a colonel) and Muriel E. F. (Joergensen) Grant; married Anne Sophie Beskow, August 2, 1944; children: Patrick, Antony. *Education:* Trinity College, Cambridge, B.A., 1936, M.A., 1940.

ADDRESSES: Home—Le Pitturacce, Gattaiola, 55050 Lucca, Italy.

CAREER: British Council, Ankara, Turkey, representative, 1940-45; University of Edinburgh, Edinburgh, Scotland, professor of Latin literature, 1948-59; Queen's University, Belfast, Northern Ireland, president and vice-chancellor, 1959-66; full-time writer, 1966—. Lecturer at universities in the United States, 1964—. Fellow, Trinity College, Cambridge University, 1938-49. Vice-chancellor, University of Khartoum, 1956-58. Chairperson, Advisory Council for Education in Northern Ireland, 1959-66, and Commonwealth Conference on English as a Second Language, 1960. *Military service:* British Army, 1939-40; became captain.

MEMBER: Royal Numismatic Society (president, 1953-56), Roman Society (vice-president, 1961—), Virgil Society (president, 1963-66), Classical Association (president, 1977-78), British Institute of Archaeology at Ankara (vice-president, 1961—), Athenaeum Club (London).

AWARDS, HONORS: Litt.D., Cambridge University, 1954, and Trinity College, Dublin, 1961; Commander of the Order of the British Empire, 1958; Leverhulme Research fellow, 1958; LL.D., Queen's University, Belfast, 1967; President's Gold Medal for Education, Sudan, 1977; Premio Latina, 1981; Premio del Mediterraneo, Mazara del Valo, 1984; Huntingdon Medal, American Numismatic Society; Royal Numismatic Society Medal.

WRITINGS:

From Imperium to Auctoritas: A Historical Study of Aes Coinage in the Roman Empire, 49 B.C.-A.D. 14, Cambridge University Press (Cambridge, England), 1946, reprinted, 1969.
Aspects of the Principate of Tiberius: Historical Comments on the Colonial Coinage Issued outside Spain, American Numismatic Society (New York City), 1950.
Roman Anniversary Issues: An Exploratory Study of the Numismatic and Medallic Commemoration of Anniversary Years, 49 B.C.-A.D. 375, Cambridge University Press, 1950, reprinted, Attic Books (Eastbourne, East Sussex, England), 1978.
Ancient History, Barnes & Noble (New York City), 1952.
The Six Main Aes Coinages of Augustus, Edinburgh University Press (Edinburgh, Scotland), 1953.
Roman Imperial Money, Thomas Nelson (Nashville, TN), 1954, reprinted, Hakkert, 1972.
Roman Literature, Cambridge University Press, 1954, revised edition, Penguin Books (London), 1964.
(Editor) *Roman Readings,* Penguin Books, 1958.
Roman History from Coins, Cambridge University Press, 1958.
(With Don Pottinger) *Greeks,* Thomas Nelson, 1958.
(With Pottinger) *Romans,* Thomas Nelson, 1960.
The World of Rome, World Publishing, 1960.
Myths of the Greeks and Romans, World Publishing, 1962.
(Editor) *The Birth of Western Civilization: Greece and Rome,* McGraw (New York City), 1964.
The Civilizations of Europe, New American Library (New York City), 1966, revised edition, 1971.
Cambridge, Reynal (New York City), 1966.
Gladiators, Weidenfeld & Nicolson (London), 1967, Delacorte (New York City), 1968, revised edition, Penguin Books, 1971.
The Climax of Rome: The Final Achievements of the Ancient World, A.D. 161-337, Little, Brown (Boston), 1968.
The Ancient Mediterranean, Scribner (New York City), 1969.
Julius Caesar, McGraw, 1969.
The Ancient Historians, Scribner, 1970.
The Roman Forum, Macmillan (New York City), 1970.
Nero: Emperor in Revolt, American Heritage Press, 1970.
Cities of Vesuvius: Pompeii and Herculaneum, Macmillan, 1971.
Herod the Great, American Heritage Press, 1971.

Roman Myths, Weidenfeld & Nicolson, 1971, Scribner, 1972.

Cleopatra, Weidenfeld & Nicolson, 1972, Simon & Schuster (New York City), 1973.

Ancient History Atlas, Macmillan, 1972.

The Jews in the Roman World, Scribner, 1973.

(With John Hazel) *Gods and Mortals in Classical Mythology,* Merriam, 1973.

(Editor and compiler) *Greek Literature in Translation,* Penguin Books, 1973, published as *Greek Literature, An Anthology: Translations from Greek Prose and Poetry,* 1977.

(With Hazel) *Who's Who in Classical Mythology,* Weidenfeld & Nicolson, 1973.

Caesar, Weidenfeld & Nicolson, 1974.

The Army of the Caesars, Scribner, 1974.

The Twelve Caesars, Scribner, 1975.

Eros in Pompeii: The Secret Rooms of the National Museum of Naples, Morrow (New York City), 1975, published as *Erotic Art in Pompeii: The Secret Collection of the National Museum of Naples,* Octopus Books (London), 1975.

The Fall of the Roman Empire: A Reappraisal, Annenberg School Press, 1976.

Saint Paul, Scribner, 1976.

Jesus: An Historian's Review of the Gospels, Scribner, 1977, published as *Jesus,* Weidenfeld & Nicolson, 1977.

The History of Rome, Scribner, 1978.

The Art and Life of Pompeii and Herculaneum, Newsweek (New York City), 1979.

(Editor) *Latin Literature: An Anthology,* Penguin Books, 1979.

The Etruscans, Scribner, 1980.

Greek and Latin Authors, 800 B.C.-A.D. 1000, H. W. Wilson (Bronx, NY), 1980.

Dawn of the Middle Ages, McGraw, 1981.

From Alexander to Cleopatra: The Hellenistic World, Scribner, 1982.

History of Ancient Israel, Scribner, 1984.

The Roman Emperors: A Biographical Guide to the Rulers of Ancient Rome, 31 B.C.-A.D. 476, Scribner, 1985.

Guide to the Classical World: A Dictionary of Place-Names, H. W. Wilson, 1986.

The Rise and Fall of the Greeks, Scribner, 1988.

The Classical Greeks, Scribner, 1988.

The Founders of the Western World, Scribner, 1991.

A Social History of Greece and Rome, Scribner, 1992.

Saint Peter, Scribner, 1994.

EDITOR AND TRANSLATOR

Cornelius Tacitus, *Annals of Imperial Rome,* Penguin Books, 1956, reprinted, 1982.

Marcus Tullius Cicero, *Selected Works,* Penguin Books, 1960.

Selected Political Speeches of Cicero, Penguin Books, 1969.

Cicero, *On the Good Life,* Penguin Books, 1971.

Cicero: Murder Trials, Penguin Books, 1971.

Readings in the Classical Historians, Scribner, 1992.

Cicero, *On Government,* Penguin Books, 1993.

OTHER

Also author of other books, including *Greek and Roman Historians: Information and Misinformation* and *The Severans.* Also editor of Robert Graves's translations of *The Twelve Caesars,* 1979, and *The Metamorphoses,* 1990. Contributor to professional journals.

WORK IN PROGRESS: "I have now been commissioned to write a biography of the second century A.D. doctor Galen, and am working on bringing the bibliographies of older books, about to be reprinted, up to date."

SIDELIGHTS: Michael Grant is regarded as one of the world's leading popularizers of ancient Mediterranean history. His numerous books for the general public explore the worlds of ancient Greece, Rome, and Israel with emphasis on the principal political and spiritual leaders of those times. *New York Times* contributor John Leonard calls Grant "an English academic with a gift for straddling the line between dry-eyed scholarship and popular history on matters pertaining to Mediterranean antiquity." According to a *Times Literary Supplement* reviewer, Grant most often succeeds "in combining scholarly standards with the requirements of narratives aimed at the general reader" in his illustrated volumes on life in the classical age. A critic for *Library Journal* likewise praises Grant, noting that the scholar "writes in a lucid style, has an urbane way with anecdotes and arcane information, and is sometimes very funny."

Grant's major contribution to scholarship lies in the field of Roman numismatics—the study of coins and coin-legends. Several of his early works, including *Roman Imperial Money* and *Roman History from Coins* extrapolate historical detail through the examination of ancient coinages. In a 1968 *Times Literary Supplement* review of *The Climax of Rome: The Final Achievements of the Ancient World, A.D. 161-337,* a critic describes how this scholarly perspective may apply to more popular works. "Dr. Grant is a numismatist of outstanding eminence," the critic states, "and his book is largely a numismatist's history, making much of coins, which survive in abundance. . . . And, as a good numismatist, he possesses keen aesthetic sensibility; so that what he has to say about the brilliant portraiture and architecture of the period makes good reading. . . . [*The Climax of Rome*] reveals a vast range and depth of scholarship and it is never difficult and often highly stimulating to read." Another *Times Literary Supplement* contributor maintains that Grant combines wide knowledge of written sources with the more detailed research of his academic field in order to produce thorough historical texts. In a review of Grant's biography *Julius Caesar,* the contributor claims: "Though Professor Grant, as a great polymath, is not himself a specialist in this period of [Roman] history (except where its coinage is concerned), it is evident in every sentence that he has read and evaluated the work of those who are."

Critics cite Grant's lucid style as a hallmark of his numerous popular works. *New York Review of Books* correspondent Ronald Syme contends that even though libraries are overflowing with books about the life of Julius Caesar, "Michael Grant's . . . stands out from the ruck. To an enviable skill and fluency he unites wide interests and a deep understanding of historical processes. In the course of his narration he is able to evoke the social and political background by various devices, rendering it wholly intelligible to readers of elementary pretensions." In an assessment of *The Jews in the Roman World,* a *Times Literary Supplement* contributor writes that Grant "is a fluent and skilful narrator whose prose is clear and enjoyable. . . . When he has fully mastered his sources, . . . he offers his readers penetrating insights into Jewish life."

Several other critics note, however, that at times the broad nature of Grant's subjects and the sheer volume of his published material lead to generalizations and vague footnoting. A *Times Literary Supplement* reviewer commenting on *Roman Myths* suggests that Grant "produces books at almost superhuman speed, outpacing his nearest rivals by a book or two a year, often very good books indeed." The reviewer expresses the opinion that *Roman Myths* "has all been done too fast; there are times when even the most learned and gifted of historians should observe a speed-limit." Having delivered the caveat that *Roman Myths* might prove unsatisfying for the specialist reader, the reviewer nevertheless concludes: "Like everything that Professor Grant writes, it is interesting and a reflection of great knowledge."

M. I. Finley in *The Spectator* notes that an attractive aspect of Grant's work "has been his persistent pricking, in his own words, at 'the current habit of condoning in the ancient world (unlike many ancient thinkers themselves) pernicious conduct, such as aggression, which must not be condoned today.'" Occasionally Grant draws parallels between ancient historical occurrences and modern events; his books show how European life and thought developed with influences from Greek, Roman, and Hebrew roots. "In these days, when the demands of scholarship tend to stress the necessity of knowing more about less and less," concludes a *Times Literary Supplement* reviewer, "it is sometimes difficult not to lose contact with the basic skeleton of history against which more detailed studies have to be pursued. Dr. Grant sets out to provide us with such a skeleton, covered at least with skin and muscles,

even if not always with the full allowance of flesh. . . . He undoubtedly succeeds in this aim."

Grant himself told *CA:* "My life as a writer has had two successive, though overlapping, stages. First I attempted to carry out original research in Roman numismatics, my purpose being to extract from the coinage information that contributed to our knowledge of Roman history. Since then I have been dealing with ancient historical, literary and artistic themes in books that are intended to convey the classical world to readers who are not necessarily specialists. My career has also fallen into two successive phases from another point of view as well. Until 1966 I occupied educational and administrative posts and fitted in writing whenever I could. Since then I have concentrated on writing (and preparing for more writing) as a full-time occupation."

BIOGRAPHICAL/CRITICAL SOURCES:

PERIODICALS

Best Sellers, December 15, 1971.
Books, October, 1971.
Library Journal, December 1, 1970.
Los Angeles Times, October 20, 1978.
Los Angeles Times Book Review, September 19, 1982.
New York Review of Books, January 29, 1970; January 7, 1971; April 15, 1976.
New York Times, September 3, 1977; March 6, 1981.
New York Times Book Review, October 12, 1969; December 18, 1977; August 12, 1979; August 12, 1984.
Observer, July, 1968; December 20, 1970.
Spectator, August 10, 1974; February 21, 1976; April 17, 1976; April 9, 1977; April 29, 1978; August 7, 1982.
Times Literary Supplement, December 30, 1965; July 11, 1968; September 26, 1968; October 30, 1969; October 9, 1970; January 22, 1971; September 10, 1971; January 21, 1972; November 30, 1973; March 29, 1974; October 24, 1975; August 8, 1980; October 17, 1980; April 1, 1983; May 8, 1983; May 11, 1984; August 30, 1985.
Virginia Quarterly Review, spring, 1969.
Washington Post, August 13, 1984.

*   *   *

GRIFFIN, Susan 1943-

PERSONAL: Born January 26, 1943, in Los Angeles, CA; daughter of Walden and Sarah (Colvin) Griffin; married John Levy, June 11, 1966 (divorced, 1970); children: Rebecca Siobhain. *Education:* Attended University of California, Berkeley, 1960-63; San Francisco State College (now University), B.A. (cum laude), 1965; California State University, San Francisco (now San Francisco State

University), M.A., 1973. *Politics:* "Feminist." *Religion:* None.

ADDRESSES: Home—1027 Merced, Berkeley, CA 94707. *Agent*—Frances Goldin, 305 East 11th St., New York, NY 10003.

CAREER: Poet. *Ramparts* (magazine), San Francisco, CA, assistant editor, 1966-68; San Francisco State College (now University), San Francisco, instructor in English, 1970-71; Poetry in the Schools program, teacher of poetry in Oakland, CA, high schools, 1972-73; University of California, Berkeley, extension school, instructor in English and women's studies, 1973-75; San Francisco State University, instructor, 1974-75. Visiting writer, Delta College of San Joaquin and Cazenovia College.

AWARDS, HONORS: Ina Coolbrith Prize in Poetry, 1963; National Endowment for the Arts grant, 1976; Malvina Reynolds Award for cultural achievement, 1982; Kentucky Foundation for Women grant, 1987; Commonwealth Club Silver Medal, 1988; Schumacher fellow; Ph.D., Starr King School for the Ministry.

WRITINGS:

POETRY

Dear Sky, Shameless Hussy Press (Berkeley), 1971.
(Contributor) Florence Howe and Ellen Bass, editors, *No More Masks: An Anthology of Poems by Women,* Doubleday (New York City), 1973.
Voices (a play in poetry; first produced in San Francisco, 1974), Feminist Press (Old Westbury, NY), 1975.
Like the Iris of an Eye, Harper (New York City), 1976.
Unremembered Country: Poems, Copper Canyon Press (Port Townsend, WA), 1987.

NONFICTION

Woman and Nature: The Roaring inside Her, Harper, 1978.
Rape: The Power of Consciousness, Harper, 1979.
Pornography and Silence: Culture's Revolt against Nature, Harper, 1981.
A Chorus of Stones: The Private Life of War, Doubleday, 1992.

OTHER

(Contributor) *Women Feminist Stories by New Fiction Authors,* Eakins (New York City), 1971.
Le Viol, L'Etincelle (Canada), 1972.
Let Them Be Said, Mama Press, 1973.
Letters, Twowindows Press (Berkeley), 1973.
The Sink, Shameless Hussy Press, 1973.
(Author of foreword) Karen Brodine and others, *Making the Park,* Kelsey St. Press (Berkeley), 1976.

(Author of introduction) Valerie Miner, *Movement,* Crossing Press (Trumansberg, NY), 1982.
Made from This Earth: Selections from Her Writing, 1967-82, Women's Press, 1982, published as *Made from This Earth: An Anthology of Writings,* Harper, 1983.

Contributor to numerous periodicals, including *Aphra, Los Angeles Times, Ms., Ramparts, Shocks, Sundance,* and *Whole Earth Review.*

ADAPTATIONS: Voices was adapted for television and aired in 1974.

SIDELIGHTS: Although she considers herself a poet, author Susan Griffin is also noted as a playwright and radical feminist philosopher. In addition to her well-known play *Voices,* which has helped to raise the feminist consciousness of numerous women since it was first performed in 1974, she has written several highly acclaimed social studies on subjects as diverse as pornography, anthropology, and warfare. To each of her subjects she brings a radical feminist viewpoint, setting forth a well-thought-out analysis in what have often been described as lyrical, book-length prose poems.

"If there is a stronger, better, more forceful feminist poem than Griffin's 'An Answer to a Man's Question, "What Can I Do about Women's Liberation"'" I'd like to see it," A. B. Eaglen states in a *Library Journal* review of Griffin's *Like the Iris of an Eye,* "—and that is only one excellent poem in a uniformly excellent collection by one of the most-quoted feminist poets writing today." Eaglen adds that the book is a "fine anthology of work that has been available before this only in anthologies and small press offerings, for collections serving women and/or lovers of good contemporary poetry." A later volume of poetry, *Unremembered Country,* is a poetic mosaic of female self-discovery. "All of the poems are written in a tightly controlled, minimal style," comments Bill Tremblay in *American Book Review,* "that witnesses to the most serious crises in our lives, even to the 'unspeakable' cruelties, while at the same time not becoming 'another facet of the original assault.'"

Griffin has also turned her attention to theorizing about issues important to women. In her *Ms.* review of *Woman and Nature: The Roaring inside Her,* Valerie Miner describes Griffin's task as exploring "woman's traditional identification with the earth—both as sustenance for humanity and victim of male ravage. The book is cultural anthropology, visionary prediction, literary indictment, and personal claim. Griffin's testimony about the lives of women throughout Western civilization reveals extensive research from Plato to Galileo to Freud to Emily Carr to Jane Goodall to Adrienne Rich." Concludes Miner:

"Griffin moves us from pain to anger to communion with and celebration of the survival of woman and nature."

In *Pornography and Silence: Culture's Revolt against Nature,* Griffin explores the nature and function of pornography, claiming that it is the manifestation of the male's desire to separate emotion, desire, and feeling from himself. In a dialogue related in *Women Writers of the West Coast,* Griffin elaborates on this theory: "All the qualities that women are accused of—passivity, wantonness or prudery, both the fear of sex and nymphomania—all of these qualities are human qualities, human possibilities, and they are projected onto a woman." In portraying women in this manner, pornography allows men to "disassociate these parts" from themselves and conquer them physically. For the purposes of her analysis, Griffin does not limit her definition of pornography to works that are violent or sadistic but also includes "the idea that woman is submissive; that she is pretty but dumb; that she likes to be dominated; that she's an object for somebody's pleasure; that she likes to serve." In the process of developing her thesis, Griffin refutes the concept of pornography as a sexual liberator; instead, she sees it as an attempt to deny sexuality.

Pornography and Silence has drawn a variety of responses from critics. While many critics agree that her hypothesis is interesting, they fault the author for her method. In his *New Republic* review, Irving Kristol notes that while Griffin's "polemic against pornography and its apologists . . . is shrewd, vigorous, and leaves little unsaid," he also comments that "she seems sadly unaware" of the precedents for her argument. In addition, Kristol criticizes the author's vehement attitude, remarking that "much of her book is an autodidact's brash exploration of cultural history that is occasionally very perceptive, more often painfully sophomoric." *Village Voice* contributor Robert Christgau also questions Griffin's methods, finding the details of her hypothesis lacking. "As one theory of pornography," writes Christgau, "this is fairly insightful, but it's only one theory, partial at best. First of all, it doesn't apply to all pornography, although since Griffin never defines the term . . . it's hard to pin her down." In a *Ms.* review, however, Marcia Yudkin praises the author's analysis as "surprising, deep, and unsettling. Her soundings not only connect seemingly disparate aspects of our culture; they transform one's questions and answers about sex, history, the self, and nature."

Other critics, while admiring Griffin's analysis, remark that her political, angry delivery detracts from the message of the book. In the *Washington Post Book World,* Lewis H. Lapham observes that while "*Pornography and Silence* convincingly dissects the dehumanizing character of pornography, . . . it would have been a kindness to the reader if Griffin had resisted the temptation to make of her observations a political theory." In taking an unmovable stance, Lapham writes, "she makes so many doubtful statements . . . that her more useful remarks about the nature of pornography lose their force and urgency." Critic Ellen Willis expresses a similar opinion, noting in the *New York Times Book Review* that "the passages she devotes to condemning pornography, rather than analyzing it, are reductive and heavy-handed in a way the rest of the book is not."

Whatever faults it may contain, reviewers still find that *Pornography and Silence* contains an important message. Because it refutes the myth that women enjoy being dominated and helpless, as they are often portrayed in pornographic works, *New Statesman* contributor Marion Glastonbury writes that "those of us to whom this is dangerous nonsense can take heart from Susan Griffin's subtle, lucid, and compelling book. Pornography is exposed as a system of censorship which serves not to enhance but to vilify pleasure, perpetuating error by suppressing half the evidence." Yudkin similarly concludes that the book "is profound, stimulating, sophisticated, far-reaching in its implications. Although feminists are still left wondering about the First Amendment and a conscionable strategy for making pornography disappear, we are much enriched by Susan Griffin's graceful, clear, unrhetorical book."

Griffin employed a similar approach in *A Chorus of Stones: The Private Life of War,* published in 1992. An examination of the destruction of the bond between humankind and nature that is caused by war and violence, *A Chorus of Stones* reveals a tapestry woven of personal memories, photographs, nonlinear history, and the individuals that figured in acts of warfare and social aggression in the twentieth century. Holocaust survivors like artist Kathe Kollwitz; Oscar Wilde, who was routinely persecuted for his openly "deviant" behaviors; the villainous Nazi commander Heinrich Himmler; and Royal Air Force officer Hugh Trenchard, who perfected the tactical bombing of densely populated urban areas, are but some of the individuals brought to conciousness in her work. "Griffin cinematically weaves about two dozen public lives and as many private lives around each other," comments Rosemary Keefe Curb in *Belles Lettres,* "often introducing individuals at a significant sensual moment but not naming them, gradually adding resonances, background details, and consequences."

Griffin's work is both political in its feminist approach and personal. A thesis central to her book is that forced separation or amputation from nature and mankind's capacity for denying the existence of evil or wrongdoing are each, in and of themselves, morally wrong, culpable acts. Griffin counts among such separations the conventional division between private or family history and public history, the history of warring nations. "To divide them is part of our denial," she states. Throughout *A Chorus of*

Stones Griffin similarly "makes connections, analogies—between public and private pain, between the outer spheres of military conflict and personal tragedy," notes *New Statesman and Society* reviewer Veronica Groocock. "Skilfully interweaving the historical with the autobiographical, Griffin demonstrates how these two arenas are not disparate, but inextricably linked."

Griffin attempts not to judge, but rather to understand and to illustrate these criminal motivations through her own—noncriminal—experience. "I do not see my life as separate from history," she notes in *A Chorus of Stones.* "In my mind my family secrets mingle with the secrets of statesmen and bombers. Nor is my life divided from the lives of others." Curb explains Griffin's hybrid approach to her subject this way: "*A Chorus of Stones* is not psychoanalysis but literature. Griffin gives no documentation. Instead she offers a symphony, a palimpsest of public and private memories." Such a technique gives rise to one of the central criticisms some have made to the work. In *Women's Review of Books,* Lise Weil states: "Unlike *Woman and Nature,* which wove disparate voices into a seamless whole, this book is shapeless and unwieldy; it rambles, it sprawls, it jerks and strays and sometimes completely bogs down." Richard Restak in the *New York Times Book Review,* however, finds Griffin's creative approach to her subject ultimately satisfying. "While writing graphic and haunting descriptions of battle[, she] sets a standard few authors could meet: she enters the psyches of people known to her only through books and photographs, getting everything somehow just right, and yet she retains a firm grasp on her own singularity."

Summing up her philosophy of writing, Griffin once told *CA:* "As a woman, I struggle to write from my life, to reflect all the difficulties, angers, joys of my existence in a culture that attempts to silence women, or that does not take our work, our words, or our lives seriously. In this, I am a fortunate woman, to be published, to be read, to be supported, and I live within a cultural and social movement aiming toward the liberation of us all. And within and also beyond all this I experience the transformations of my soul through the holy, the ecstatic, the painfully born or joyously made *word.* I know now that never when I begin to write will I truly know what or how my vision will become."

BIOGRAPHICAL/CRITICAL SOURCES:

BOOKS

Griffin, Susan, *A Chorus of Stones: The Private Life of War,* Doubleday (New York City), 1992.
Shima, Alan, *Skirting the Issue: Pursuing Language in the Works of Adrienne Rich, Susan Griffin, and Beverly Dahlen,* Uppsala University Press (Uppsala, Sweden), 1993.

Yalom, Marilyn, editor, *Women Writers of the West Coast,* Capra (Santa Barbara), 1983.

PERIODICALS

American Book Review, November, 1988, p. 22.
Belles Lettres, winter, 1992-93, pp. 7-9.
Library Journal, December 1, 1976.
Los Angeles Times Book Review, January 17, 1993, pp. 4, 10.
Ms., April, 1979; January, 1982.
New Republic, July 25, 1981.
New Statesman, November 6, 1981.
New Statesman and Society, May 22, 1994, pp. 40-41.
New York Times Book Review, July 12, 1981; November 22, 1992, p. 14.
Quill and Quire, September, 1981.
San Francisco Review of Books, winter, 1992, pp. 27, 38.
Times Literary Supplement, January 1, 1982.
Village Voice, July 15, 1981.
Wall Street Journal, January 5, 1993, p. A12.
Washington Post Book World, June 21, 1981.
Women's Review of Books, December, 1993, pp. 12-13.*

*   *   *

GRIFFITH, Aline
See QUINTANILLA, (Maria) Aline (Griffith y Dexter)

*   *   *

GROOM, Winston 1943-

PERSONAL: Born March 23, 1943, in Washington, DC; son of Winston Francis (an attorney) and Ruth (Knudsen) Groom; married Ruth Noble (an importer), 1969 (divorced, 1974); married Anne-Clinton Bridges, 1987. *Education:* University of Alabama, A.B., 1965.

ADDRESSES: Agent—Theron Raines, Raines & Raines, 71 Park Ave., New York, NY 10016.

CAREER: Washington Star, Washington, DC, 1967-76, began as reporter, became columnist; novelist, 1976—. *Military service:* U.S. Army, 1965-67, served in Vietnam; became captain.

MEMBER: Authors League of America, Authors Guild.

AWARDS, HONORS: Best fiction award, Southern Library Association, 1980, for *As Summers Die;* Pulitzer Prize nomination, 1984, for *Conversations with the Enemy: The Story of PFC Robert Garwood.*

WRITINGS:

NOVELS

Better Times Than These, Summit Books (New York City), 1978.

As Summers Die, Summit Books, 1980.

Only, Putnam (New York City), 1984.

Forrest Gump, Doubleday (New York City), 1986.

Gone the Sun, Doubleday, 1988.

Gumpisms: The Wit and Wisdom of Forrest Gump, Pocket Books (New York City), 1994.

NONFICTION

(With Duncan Spencer) *Conversations with the Enemy: The Story of PFC Robert Garwood,* Putnam, 1983.

Shrouds of Glory: From Atlanta to Nashville; The Last Great Campaign of the Civil War, Atlantic Monthly Press (Boston), 1994.

ADAPTATIONS: The film adaptation of *Forrest Gump,* directed by Robert Zemeckis and starring Tom Hanks, was released by Paramount in 1994; *Forrest Gump* was recorded as an audiocassette, read by Groom; *Bubba Gump Shrimp Co. Cookbook: Recipes and Reflections from Forrest Gump,* based on Groom's character Forrest Gump, was published by Oxmoor House, 1994.

WORK IN PROGRESS: A sequel to *Forrest Gump.*

SIDELIGHTS: Winston Groom is not a household name, but the character he created in a 1986 novel has become an American icon. That character took Groom six weeks to create, but it was nine years before he really came to life, and then it was on the silver screen. Groom is the creator of Forrest Gump. The 1994 movie version of the novel *Forrest Gump,* directed by Robert Zemeckis and starring Tom Hanks, grossed almost $300 million dollars. That made it the second biggest moneymaker for 1994 and the fifth biggest moneymaker of all time. The film won six Academy Awards, including best picture, best director, and best actor. It also "triggered a multimillion-dollar sideshow in T-shirts, chocolate and cookbook sales," reports Michele Bearden in *Publishers Weekly.*

"As Mr. Groom tells it," William Grimes writes in the *New York Times,* "pretty much everything about the Gump phenomenon has been a surprise, including the writing of the novel." The original idea for the character came from Groom's father. Groom told Robert Epstein in a *Los Angeles Times* interview that one day over lunch his father "reminisced about this fellow he once knew, an older man who was slow-witted but whose mother had taught him to play the piano. His story struck something inside me and then I saw a '60 Minutes' show about idiot savants. After Daddy left I started making notes and by midnight I had the first chapter of *Forrest Gump.*" Six

weeks later, Groom had *Forrest Gump,* the book. "The result," comments Grimes, "was an unusual blend of farce, satire and the picaresque, told in Forrest's voice." Doubleday bought the book and published it in 1986. Warner Brothers bought the rights to the movie; Paramount later acquired the rights in a turnaround deal.

Groom's biggest-selling book did not start out on the fast track. It sold about 40,000 books in the 1980s, combining hardcover and paperback sales. At the time, reviews were mixed. *Los Angeles Times* contributor Tom Nolan pointed out that "the notion of a fictional 'idiot' enduring various real-life regional and national idiocies with folkwise equanimity is not without charm. . . . Part Candide, part Huck Finn and a whole lot of Andy Griffith, [Forrest] makes his case in a voice all his own." Nolan continued, "The generous reader will not be unmoved by certain wispy sentences that tug at the heart like hound dog pups that are starved for love." Yet, as Jonathan Baumbach observes in the *New York Times Book Review,* "A novel like *Forrest Gump* relies on revved-up pace and nonstop narrative invention. When the invention goes stale, when it becomes predictable and familiar, as it does at times in the second half, the novel falters." Baumbach concludes, "If charm were everything, *Forrest Gump* might be some kind of masterpiece. This light satiric novel has many pleasures to offer. As a serious work, which is its sometime ambition, it is too ingratiating, too lacking in genuine surprise, to undemanding of itself."

The 1994 film version of *Forrest Gump* reincarnated the novel and elevated it to the status of bestseller. Pocket Books, a division of Paramount which had acquired the rights to the novel from Doubleday, sold over 1.7 million paperbacks, capitalizing on movie audiences' desire to find out more about this unlikely hero. And, as Grimes points out, they do find out more. "Fans of the movie may be surprised to find out that in addition to being a champion Ping-Pong player," he writes, "the Forrest of the novel is a professional wrestler, a chess grandmaster and an astronaut." *New York Times* reviewer Janet Maslin calls Groom's rediscovered work a "tart, playful novel." Audiences wanting more Gump also purchased Groom's small companion to the novel and movie, *Gumpisms: The Wit and Wisdom of Forrest Gump.* This collection of the world according to Gump sold over 500,000 copies in the few months after the film's release.

Though surprised by the Gump phenomenon, Groom refused to take it too seriously. As he explained to Robert Epstein, "I wasn't delivering any messages other than showing that a man doesn't have to be rich or smart to be dignified." He also kept his writing career in perspective. He told Michele Bearden, "If you get hit by a load of hay, you better make hay, because the time will come when they'll forget you and move on."

Before the Forrest Gump phenomena forced him into the spotlight, fielding interviewers' questions, signing books at bookstores across the country, and making appearances at the Academy Awards, Groom had already built a moderately successful career as a writer. "Two landscapes loom large in the work of Winston Groom," writes Nicholas Proffitt in the *Washington Post Book World*, "both of them green, both of them hothouses for chicanery and violence: Vietnam and the American South." The Gulf Coast native has borrowed liberally from his experiences in those two milieus yet has produced a rather diverse body of writing. Groom told *CA:* "Like most writers, I write about what I see and feel about the human race in the hope that it might help them understand their lives a little better."

Groom's first novel, *Better Times Than These,* depicts the trials of an ill-fated company of the Seventh Calvary in Vietnam. He draws heavily upon personal experience in that conflict to create what *New York Times Book Review* contributor Thomas R. Edwards terms an "authentic" Vietnam novel. However, Edwards criticizes Groom's usage of generalizations that tend towards stereotype: "We hear almost nothing about military profiteering; atrocities are committed only by soldiers who are naturally vicious or insane. The Vietnamese are all spongers, racketeers, buffoons or spies, and all the Vietcong can finally be assessed . . . as 'a core of scraggly, . . . brown-skinned men with vague and inarticulate hopes and dreams.' " L. J. Davis expressed similar reservations in the *Washington Post Book World,* but added that familiarity is the hallmark of the "war novel" genre and character depictions are necessarily made "in the interest of universalizing them, not to render them troublesomely unique." He notes that the characters in *Better Times Than These* are "made to wear their backgrounds like some triplets wear their clothes—so that we can tell them apart," but nevertheless called the book "a perfectly adequate war novel."

In his second novel, *As Summers Die,* Groom relates a tale of southern social politics in the 1950s: a poor black family's attempt to retain their oil-rich land and the do-good lawyer who takes up their struggle against a wealthy white family. Beverly Lowry finds the plot "rigged" but enjoys Groom's writing, especially in his hunting and fishing scenes. In the *Washington Post Book World* she writes: "Here, Winston Groom explores the memory of the senses, nostalgia. The book comes alive in these pages. Groom's ear tunes up and finally, the language sings." In the *New York Times,* Christopher Lehmann-Haupt offers different impressions. He finds Groom's writing suspect at times, citing occasional "failures of syntax, diction, and tone," but praises the storyline as "sure-handedly plotted." "Winston Groom's *As Summers Die* has an element of the moral fable about it," wrote Elizabeth Wheeler in

the *Los Angeles Times.* "His world is constructed with certain immutable laws. Characters are either good or bad—not both, not neither. When they are put to the test, the good obey those laws and are rewarded. The bad disobey them and are punished." Groom discounts the moral qualities of his work, however. He told *CA:* "I tend to think of my writing as more traditional, in the sense that I want to tell a good story first, and any meanings assigned to it by anyone are pretty much incidental."

In his novel *Gone the Sun,* "Groom has mixed themes from his earlier books into a cohesive whole," observes Timothy Bay in *Publishers Weekly.* "Again tackling the subject of moral corruption in the Deep South, the novel has as protagonist a Vietnam vet who returns to his Southern coastal home town and becomes embroiled in a scandal within the community." Beau Gunn discovers corruption and murder in the Gulf Coast oil town of Bienville, and, as the local newspaper editor, he sets out to expose all. He also discovers some of his own sins. Nicholas Proffitt finds *Gone the Sun* "a well written and engrossing novel of lost illusions, buried dreams, fresh starts, retribution and lives cut short." And, as Gary Dretzka offers in the *Chicago Tribune,* "Much of the book provides an effective portrait of how a group of boys grow up in the South of Spanish-moss memories and then get sucked into the overgrown swamps of the real world."

Gone the Sun is a complicated novel which weaves together many elements and genres. "As his earlier novels *Better Times Than These* and *Forrest Gump* demonstrated," comments Michiko Kakutani in the *New York Times,* "Mr. Groom has a gift for orchestrating large numbers of characters and incidents, a talent for narrative invention." Yet, the reviewer continues, "Unfortunately, in the case of *Gone the Sun,* the thriller-like aspects of the story undermine Mr. Groom's more serious aspirations, while his more literary ambitions hobble his action-packed plot." And, according to *Los Angeles Times Book Review* contributor Keith Love, despite all that it attempts, the book comes up short. "It fails," suggests Love, "because Groom walks away from the chance to explore the disturbing transformation of the South, and from the chance to more deeply explore Beau Gunn as tormented Southerner come home." Still, Love concedes that this novel "does confirm my opinion that Groom is one of the best writers of dialogue today. That and his story-telling ability keep you going in *Gone the Sun* even as the book fails." Proffitt concludes that "*Gone the Sun* can be enjoyed purely for its considerable entertainment value, as a whodunit of sorts. But there is a moral core to Winston Groom's novels, this one included, and it is this that elevates them."

In addition to his novels, Groom has also written nonfiction. *Conversations with the Enemy: The Story of PFC Gar-*

wood was Groom's second book based on the Vietnam experience. With co-author Duncan Spencer he attempts to reveal the facts of Private Robert Garwood's capture in Vietnam, fourteen-year imprisonment by the Viet Cong, eventual release, and dishonorable discharge from the Marines on allegations of desertion and collaboration with the enemy. "What is fascinating about *Conversations with the Enemy,*" writes C. D. B. Bryan in the *New York Times Book Review,* "is its detailed and vivid reconstruction of Private Garwood's 14 years of internment—his isolation, physical deprivations, confinement in urine-soaked pits; his learning to scrounge for scraps of food and clothing; his endurance of torture by the Vietnamese and his surviving of bombings by the Americans; his becoming fluent in Vietnamese and his undergoing a personality change so complete that when he returned to this country he spoke English with an Oriental accent. . . . He thought in Vietnamese, spoke Vietnamese when upset and was uncomfortable sitting in chairs and sleeping in beds." In a review for the *Washington Post Book World* Webster Schott calls the book "a testament to everything dark, everything wondrous about human beings."

In *Shrouds of Glory: From Atlanta to Nashville; The Last Great Campaign of the Civil War,* his first book following the resurgence of *Forrest Gump,* Groom turns to history. Specifically, the book chronicles "Confederate Gen. John Bell Hood's quixotic invasion of Tennessee in the war's final months," explains Fritz Buckallew in *Library Journal.* As Groom told interviewer Michele Bearden, "My intention was to write something that appealed to a wider audience than Civil War nuts. This story was perfect because it had all the elements: sex, violence, honor." *New York Times* reviewer Christopher Lehmann-Haupt notes that "Hood's campaign turned out to be a catastrophe for the Confederacy." "Still," concludes the reviewer, "despite the ignominy of the story's outcome from the South's point of view, Mr. Groom's book effectively evokes the overwhelming momentousness of the war."

BIOGRAPHICAL/CRITICAL SOURCES:

PERIODICALS

Atlanta Journal-Constitution, August 9, 1994, p. D20.
Chicago Tribune, July 24, 1988, sec. 14, pp. 6-7.
Library Journal, April 1, 1995, p. 108.
Los Angeles Times, November 4, 1980; August 7, 1994, p. 24.
Los Angeles Times Book Review, October 23, 1983; April 6, 1986, p. 3; September 11, 1988, pp. 1, 10.
New York Times, June 28, 1978; October 6, 1980; April 12, 1984; August 3, 1988, p. C21; July 6, 1994; July 27, 1994, p. C9; September 1, 1994, p. C13; April 10, 1995, p. B5.

New York Times Book Review, July 9, 1978; October 16, 1983; March 16, 1986, p. 31; September 10, 1995, p. 15.
People, September 18, 1978; September 5, 1994, pp. 79-80.
Publishers Weekly, August 12, 1988, pp. 430-31; April 17, 1995, p. 34-35.
Washington Post, November 17, 1980; March 26, 1984.
Washington Post Book World, July 9, 1978; September 25, 1983; March 16, 1986, p. 5; August 14, 1988, p. 6.

—*Sketch by Bryan Ryan*

*   *   *

GROSS, Michael (Robert) 1952-
(Robert Alexander; D. G. Devon, a joint pseudonym)

PERSONAL: Born July 16, 1952, in New York, NY; son of Milton (a sports columnist) and Estelle (a registered nurse; maiden name, Murov) Gross. *Education:* Vassar College, B.A., 1974.

ADDRESSES: Office—*Esquire,* 1790 Broadway, New York, NY 10019. *Agent*—Ellen Levine Literary Agency, 15 East 26th St, #1801, New York, NY 10010.

CAREER: Zakin & Comerford Advertising, New York City, copywriter, 1975-76; *Rock,* New York City, editor-in-chief, 1976-77; *Fire Island News,* Ocean Beach, NY, editor-in-chief, 1978; Bantam Books, New York City, copywriter, beginning 1978; *Esquire,* New York City, senior writer.

MEMBER: Authors Guild, Authors League of America.

AWARDS, HONORS: Andy Award from New York Advertising Club, 1975, for radio commercials.

WRITINGS:

I, a Groupie (novel), Pinnacle Books (New York City), 1975.
Robert Plant (biography), Popular Library, 1975.
Bob Dylan: An Illustrated History, Grosset, 1978.
The Hits Just Keep Coming In, Ace Books (New York City), 1980.
(Editor with Maxim Jakubowski) *The Rock Year Book, 1981,* Delilah (New York City), 1980.
Model: The Ugly Business of Beautiful Women, Morrow (New York City), 1995.

WITH STEPHEN DEMOREST; UNDER JOINT PSEUDONYM D. G. DEVON

Temple Kent, Ballantine (New York City), 1982.
Shattered Mask, Ballantine, 1983.
Precious Objects, Ballantine, 1984.

OTHER

Contributor, under pseudonym Robert Alexander, to *American Mass Media: Industry and Issues,* edited by Robert Atwan, Barry Orton, and William Vesterman, Random House (New York City), 1978. Also author with Stephen Demorest of screenplay "Lucky's Strike," 1977. Also author of radio commercials. Columnist for *Interview,* 1973-74, and *New York,* 1988-92. Contributing editor, *Circus,* 1974-76, *Rush,* 1976-77, and *Swank,* 1976-79; music editor, *Club,* 1975-76. Contributor to *New York Times, Chicago Tribune, Interview,* and *Town and Country.*

SIDELIGHTS: In *Model: The Ugly Business of Beautiful Women,* New York fashion writer Michael Gross offers an insider's view of the big business of fashion modeling. Because, as Michele Ingrassia points out in *Newsweek,* the book "names names and dishes dirt, the sort of on-the-record kiss-and-tell that tab TV would die for," it created a stir in the fashion world upon publication. Despite the controversy it created, however, Ingrassia contends that Gross's main concern is not to tarnish the image of the fashion world, but to chronicle the growth of that industry. To this end, Gross follows the history of modeling from the early part of the twentieth century through the 1940s and 1950s, when models were part of high society and the photographer set. He continues through the 1960s, when for the first time, models such as Twiggy attained success and recognition both for their modeling careers and entrepreneurial ventures. The book then traces developments in the modeling industry right up to the 1990s, a decade most identified with the "supermodel," where models have become enormously successful and have, in turn, helped the photographers and designers associated with them. Additionally, the book also relates stories of legendary rivalries between such well-established modeling agencies as Ford and Elite.

Reviewing the book for *Maclean's,* contributor Nora Underwood says that, despite the sometimes racy content of *Model,* Gross "remains non-judgmental throughout almost 500 pages of scandal, sex, greed, betrayal, big money, power and girls." Underwood adds, "In the end, the only truly disappointing aspect of the book is mediocre, black-and-white photographs. Despite that, *Model* is perfect summer fare—and cautionary reading for any parent of a beautiful girl."

BIOGRAPHICAL/CRITICAL SOURCES:

BOOKS

Gross, Michael, *Model: The Ugly Business of Beautiful Women,* Morrow, 1995.

PERIODICALS

Los Angeles Times Book Review, September 12, 1982, p. 6; January 8, 1984, p. 4.
Maclean's, July 10, 1995, p. 45.
Newsweek, April 3, 1995, p. 75.
Publishers Weekly, April 24, 1995, p. 55.
Time, April 17, 1995, p. 66; June 5, 1995, p. 58.*

*   *   *

GZAY, Victor
   See CONQUEST, (George) Robert (Acworth)

H

HADDAD, Yvonne Y(azbeck) 1935-

PERSONAL: Born March 23, 1935, in Alexandretta, Syria; came to the United States in 1963, naturalized citizen, 1976; daughter of Wadi and Catherine (Basha) Yazbeck; married Wadi Zaidan Haddad, November 2, 1958; children: Susan, Ramsey. *Education:* Beirut College for Women, B.A., 1958; Boston University, M.R.E., 1966; University of Wisconsin—Madison, M.A., 1971; Hartford Seminary, Ph.D., 1979.

ADDRESSES: Home—60 Burnwood, Bloomfield, CT 06002. *Office*—Department of History, University of Massachusetts, Amherst, MA 01003.

CAREER: Teacher in the Middle East, 1956-63; Mercer County Community College, Trenton, NJ, adjunct lecturer in social studies, 1968-69; McGill University, Montreal, Quebec, research associate at Institute of Islamic Studies, 1976-78; Colgate University, Hamilton, NY, visiting assistant professor of philosophy and religion, 1978-80; Hartford Seminary, Hartford, CT, associate professor, 1980-85, professor of Islamic studies, 1985-86; University of Massachusetts, Amherst, MA, professor of Islamic history, 1986—. Lecturer at Northeastern University, summers, 1974-75, Vassar College, spring, 1975, Hartford Seminary, autumn, 1976, and University of Calgary, summer, 1977; visiting lecturer at Andover-Newton Theological Seminary, autumn, 1980; visiting adjunct professor at University of Connecticut, spring, 1981; visiting professor, Yale University, 1987, West Virginia University, and Marshall University, both summer, 1988; visiting adjunct faculty member, Georgetown University, 1994-95. Has presented papers at numerous professional meetings. Member of American Council for the Study of Islamic Societies, American Research Center in Egypt, American Institute of Maghribi Studies, and Middle East Outreach Council.

MEMBER: Middle East Studies Association, American Academy of Religion.

AWARDS, HONORS: University of Wisconsin—Madison grant, 1969-70; Fund for the Study of World Religions grant, 1979-80; grants from Connecticut Humanities Council, United Technologies, Exxon, and Islamic Science Foundation, 1982, to host a lecture series; Hartford Consortium for Higher Education grant, 1983, for symposium; grants from Hartford Consortium on Higher Education, National Endowment for the Humanities, Aetna Foundation, Connecticut Humanities Council, and Jodik Foundation, 1983, to host a conference; National Endowment for the Humanities grant, 1983-85; Islamic Civilization grant, 1985; Fulbright senior research fellowship, 1985; Social Science Research Council grant, 1985; American Institute of Maghribi Studies grants, 1986 and 1989; Massachusetts Foundation for Humanities and Public Policy grant, 1988; grants from National Endowment for the Humanities, Mobil Oil Corp., Five Colleges Inc., and Arabian American Oil Co., 1988, to convene a conference on the Muslims of America; University of Massachusetts, faculty research grant, 1988, faculty fellowship award, 1990-91, and Chancellor's Medal for Excellence in Research, 1993; grants from National Endowment for the Humanities and Connecticut Humanities Council, 1990, to host international conference on "Christian-Muslim Encounter"; grants from Connecticut Humanities Council, National Council on U.S.-Arab Relations, and Middle East Institute, 1991, to direct a summer institute; Rockefeller residency fellowship, 1992.

WRITINGS:

(With Jane Idleman Smith) *The Islamic Understanding of Death and Resurrection,* New York University Press (New York City), 1981.

Contemporary Islam and the Challenge of History, New York University Press, 1982.

(Editor with Ellison Findly and Byron Haines) *The World of Islam,* Syracuse University Press (Syracuse, NY), 1983.

(Co-editor with Haines and Findly) *The Islamic Impact,* Syracuse University Press, 1984.

(Co-editor with Findly) *Women, Religion and Social Change,* State University of New York Press (Albany), 1985.

(With Adair Lummis) *Islamic Values in the United States: A Comparative Study,* Oxford University Press (New York City), 1987.

The Muslim Experience in North America, Oxford University Press, 1988.

(With others) *The Contemporary Islamic Revival: A Critical Survey and Bibliography,* Greenwood Press (Westport, CT), 1991.

(Editor) *The Muslims of America,* Oxford University Press, 1991.

(With Smith) *Mission to America: Five Islamic Sectarian Movements in the United States,* University Presses of Florida (Gainesville), 1993.

(Editor with Smith) *Muslim Communities in the North America,* State University of New York Press (Albany), 1994.

(Editor with husband, Wadi Zaidan Haddad) *Christian-Muslim Encounters,* University Presses of Florida, 1995.

(Associate editor) *The Oxford Encyclopedia of the Modern Islamic World,* 4 volumes, Oxford University, 1995.

Contributor to numerous books, including *Religion and Ethnicity,* edited by Harold Coward and Leslie Kawamura, Wilfrid Laurier University Press, 1977; *Islam: The Religious and Political Life of a Community,* edited by Marjorie Kelly, Praeger (New York City), 1984; *Living among Muslims,* International Reformed Center (Switzerland), 1987; *Beyond the Storm: A Gulf Crisis Reader,* edited by Phillys Bennis, Interlink Books (New York City), 1991; and *The United States and the Middle East: A Historical Reassessment,* edited by David Lesch, Westview (Boulder, CO), 1996. Contributor to encyclopedias, including *The Canadian Encyclopedia* and *Encyclopedia of the Modern Islamic World.* Contributor of articles and reviews to numerous periodicals, including *Women's Studies International Forum, Religious Studies Review, Arab-American Affairs, National Catholic Reporter, Journal of the American Academy of Religion, Journal of Ecumenical Studies,* and *Middle East Journal.* Editor, *Muslim World,* 1980-88.

Some of Haddad's work has been translated into Arabic.

HALLAM, Elizabeth M. 1950-

PERSONAL: Born November 5, 1950, in Somerset, England; married in 1976; children: two. *Education:* Westfield College, London, B.A. (with first class honors), 1972, Ph.D., 1975.

ADDRESSES: Office—Public Record Office, Ruskin Ave., Kew, Richmond, Surrey TW9 4DV, England.

CAREER: University of Reading, Reading, Berkshire, England, tutor, 1975-76; Public Record Office, London, England, assistant keeper of public records, 1976—. Part-time tutor at Open University, London Region, 1974-78.

MEMBER: Royal Historical Society (fellow), Society of Antiquaries of London (fellow).

WRITINGS:

Capetian France, 987-1328, Longman (London), 1980.

The Itinerary of Edward I and His Household, 1307-1328, List and Index Society (London), 1984.

The Domesday Project Book, Hodder & Stoughton (London), 1986.

Domesday Book through Nine Centuries, Thames & Hudson (London), 1986.

(Author of introduction) *Domesday Heritage: Towns and Villages of Norman England through Nine Hundred Years,* Arrow Books (London), 1986.

(Author of introduction) Thomas Hinde, editor, *The Domesday Book: England's Heritage, Then and Now,* Hutchinson (East Sussex, England), 1986.

(Author of introduction) D. Parsons, editor, *Eleanor of Castile, 1290-1990,* Paul Watkins (Stamford), 1991.

(Author of transcriptions and translations) *Domesday Book, Middlesex,* Alecto Historical Editions (London), 1992.

EDITOR

The Plantagenet Chronicles, Weidenfeld & Nicolson (London), 1986.

Chronicles of the Age of Chivalry, Weidenfeld & Nicolson, 1987.

Chronicles of the Wars of the Roses, Weidenfeld & Nicolson, 1988.

Chronicles of the Crusades, Weidenfeld & Nicolson, 1989.

The Plantagenet Encyclopaedia, Weidenfeld & Nicolson, 1990.

Saints: More Than 150 Patron Saints for Today, Simon & Schuster (New York City), 1994.

OTHER

Author of museum pamphlet *English Royal Marriages,* Public Record Office, HMSO (London), 1981. Contributor to books, including *Domesday Book: Special Studies,* edited by A. Williams and R. W. H. Erskine, Alecto Historical Editions, 1987; and *Records of the Nation*, edited by G. H. Martin and P. Spufford, Boydell & Brewer (Woodbridge, Suffolk, England), 1990. Contributor to periodicals, including *Journal of Medieval History, History Today, Studies in Church History, Journal of Ecclesiastical History, Bulletin of the Institute of Historical Research, Journal of the Society of Archivists,* and *Museums Journal.*

Some of Hallam's work has been translated into French and Japanese.

WORK IN PROGRESS: Entries for *The New Dictionary of National Biography,* for Oxford University Press; contributing to *Sir Robert Cotton and His Circle,* edited by C. Wright, for British Library Publications; research on medieval English historical topics.

SIDELIGHTS: Elizabeth M. Hallam once told *CA:* "My work in the Public Record Office (particularly in the departments which help members of the public with their historical and genealogical studies) has convinced me of the importance of producing carefully researched but widely intelligible history, which appeals to an audience beyond that of the specialized scholar. At the same time, meticulously researched monographs and editions of texts are vital to the continuation of historical studies as an academic discipline."

Much of Hallam's writing has been connected to the Domesday Book, which was begun at the order of William the Conqueror in the year 1086. This record of England's government administration was used continuously until the sixteenth century; it has also served the needs of British property holders into the twentieth century. H. R. Loyn praised Hallam's *Domesday Book through Nine Centuries* in the *Times Literary Supplement* as "an attractive and well-illustrated book . . . alive with information." The reviewer added: "It is good to have the antiquarian details so well presented." Loyn also described *Domesday Heritage* as a popular survey of sites that housed the Domesday Book at various times in its nine-hundred-year history.

Hallam's *The Plantagenet Chronicles* is a lavishly illustrated work covering the English Plantagenet kings of the twelfth and thirteenth centuries. In the first volume of this book, she supports her historical entries with numerous excerpts from contemporary accounts.

BIOGRAPHICAL/CRITICAL SOURCES:

PERIODICALS

Times Literary Supplement, May 16, 1986.

HAMLET, Ova
See LUPOFF, Richard A(llen)

*　　　*　　　*

HART, Sandra Lynn Housby 1948-
(Samantha Harte)

PERSONAL: Born March 24, 1948, in Aurora, IL; daughter of William J. (a lithographer) and Patricia (Watson) Housby; married William Michael Hart, December 16, 1967 (divorced November 25, 1987); children: Laura, Robert, Kathleen. *Education:* Attended Colorado Woman's College, 1966-67. *Avocational interests:* Drawing, oil and acrylic painting, sewing, needlecraft, quilting, miniature houses and furnishing, dolls, piano, history, travel.

ADDRESSES: Home—107 North Orr Dr., Unit C, Normal, IL 61761. *Agent*—Jane Jordan Browne, 410 South Michigan Ave., Suite 724, Chicago, IL 60605.

CAREER: Artist in Frankfurt, West Germany, 1970-71; dressmaker in Atchison, KS, 1971-73; writer, 1974—. Workshop leader at Philadelphia Writers Conference, 1978, 1981, 1982, and 1985, and at Mississippi Valley Writers Conference, 1985 and 1986.

WRITINGS:

UNDER PSEUDONYM SAMANTHA HARTE

HISTORICAL ROMANCE NOVELS

Kiss of Gold, Paperjacks, 1985.
Sweet Whispers, Paperjacks, 1986.
Vanity Blade, Paperjacks, 1987.
Summer Sea, Paperjacks, 1989.
Autumn Blaze, Diamond Books, 1993.
Sunflower Sky, Harper Monogram, 1994.

OTHER

The Snows of Craggmoor (gothic novel), Avalon, 1978.
Angel (historical novel), Pinnacle Books (New York City), 1982.
Hurricane Sweep (novel), Pinnacle Books, 1983.
Tears of Flame (historical suspense), Paperjacks, 1988.

Also author of *Timberhill* (historical gothic romance), Paperjacks. Contributor of nearly two hundred stories to periodicals, including *True Story, True Confessions, Modern Romances, Secrets, Intimate Story,* and *Personal Romances.*

WORK IN PROGRESS: Historical romance novels.

SIDELIGHTS: Sandra Lynn Housby Hart once told *CA:* "Becoming a writer sometimes carries a high price. Putting aside hobbies, friendships and family needs in my quest to sell novels and stories, I woke to find one day that my marriage was over and my life was taking a very unexpected turn.

"But a writer uses all experience to create fiction, and so as I learn to be a single person after twenty years, I find my writing changing. I'm still writing romance and I still write 'happily ever after,' but it's with the knowledge now that there is no guarantee of forever in today's changing world.

"Love is more precious than ever. The relationship between a man and a woman is more complex than I ever dreamed. So I think my writing will reflect this change in my perception. I still dream of writing bestselling fiction but I hope perhaps more to understand the world around me and convey that new understanding in my work.

"There is a happily ever after, not in romantic love necessarily, but in the growth of self, understanding and deep friendship. If a writer's job is to interpret life, I hope this unexpected alteration in the course of my own life can lead to greater wisdom in my fiction. Perhaps through that I will realize some of my dreams, and in the meantime I will lead a richer, fuller life from which I can draw new characters and fictional situations."

*   *   *

HARTE, Samantha
See HART, Sandra Lynn Housby

*   *   *

HASKELL, John Duncan, Jr. 1941-

PERSONAL: Born January 3, 1941, in Providence, RI; son of John Duncan (an accountant) and Grace (Johanson) Haskell; married Mary Binkowski (a librarian), October 8, 1966; children: Sarah Elizabeth. *Education:* University of Rhode Island, A.B., 1962; Rutgers University, M.L.S., 1964; George Washington University, M.Phil., 1972, Ph.D., 1977. *Politics:* Democrat. *Religion:* Episcopalian.

ADDRESSES: Home—Williamsburg, PA. *Office*—Earl Gregg Swem Library, College of William and Mary, Williamsburg, VA 23187-8794.

CAREER: University of Maryland, Baltimore County, Baltimore, library director, 1965-69; U.S. Naval Ordnance Laboratory, Silver Spring, MD, part-time cataloguer, 1969-72; Committee for a New England Bibliography, Boston, MA, editor, 1972-78; College of William

and Mary, Earl Gregg Swem Library, Williamsburg, VA, associate dean of university libraries, 1978—. Member of Williamsburg Bibliophiles, Williamsburg Historic Records Association, Bibliographical Society of the University of Virginia, Friends of the Library of the College of William and Mary, and Associates of the John Carter Brown Library. *Military service:* U.S. Army Reserve, 1964-70.

MEMBER: American Library Association, Association for the Bibliography of History, American Printing History Association, Bibliographical Society of America, John Russell Bartlett Society, Society for Commercial Archaeology, Manuscript Society, Virginia Library Association, Grolier Club (New York).

AWARDS, HONORS: Manuscript Society Award of Distinction, 1993.

WRITINGS:

(Editor) *Massachusetts: A Bibliography of Its History,* G. K. Hall (Boston), 1976.
(Editor) *Maine: A Bibliography of Its History,* G. K. Hall, 1977.
(Editor with T. D. Bassett) *New Hampshire: A Bibliography of Its History,* G. K. Hall, 1979.
Americana, Science, Art, and Politics: The Worlds of John Russell Bartlett, John Carter Brown Library, 1985.
(Compiler with M. C. Cook) *Treasures of the College of William and Mary Library,* College of William and Mary (Williamsburg, VA), 1988.

Contributor to books, including *Advances in Library Administration and Organization,* edited by Gerard B. McCabe and Barnard Kreissman, JAI Press (Greenwich, CT), 1984. Contributor to *Papers of the Bibliographical Society of America.* Contributor to periodicals, including *Poe Studies, Modern Drama, AB Bookman's Weekly, Bulletin of Bibliography, Choice, New England Quarterly,* and *William and Mary Quarterly.*

WORK IN PROGRESS: A book on drive-in theaters in America.

*   *   *

HASS, Robert 1941-

PERSONAL: Surname rhymes with "grass"; born March 1, 1941, in San Francisco, CA; son of Fred (in business) and Helen (Dahling) Hass; married Earline Leif (a psychotherapist), September 1, 1962; children: Leif, Kristin, Luke. *Education:* St. Mary's College of California, B.A., 1963; Stanford University, M.A., 1965, Ph.D., 1971.

ADDRESSES: Home—576 Santa Barbara Rd., Berkeley, CA 94707. *Office*—c/o Ecco Press, 26 West 17th St., New York, NY 10011.

CAREER: State University of New York at Buffalo, assistant professor, 1967- 71; St. Mary's College of California, Moraga, professor of English, 1971-74, 1975-89; University of California, Berkeley, professor of English, 1989—. Visiting lecturer at University of Virginia, 1974, Goddard College, 1976, and Columbia University, 1982. Poet in residence, The Frost Place, Franconia, NH, 1978.

AWARDS, HONORS: Woodrow Wilson fellow, 1963-64; Danforth fellow, 1963-67; Yale Series of Younger Poets Award from Yale University Press, 1972, for *Field Guide;* U.S.-Great Britain Bicentennial Exchange Fellow in the Arts, 1976-77; William Carlos Williams Award, 1979, for *Praise;* Guggenheim fellow, 1980; National Book Critics Circle Award in criticism, 1984, and Belles Lettres Award, Bay Area Book Reviewers Association, 1986, for *Twentieth Century Pleasures: Prose on Poetry;* award of merit, American Academy of Arts and Letters, 1984; MacArthur Foundation grant, 1984.

WRITINGS:

POETRY

Field Guide, Yale University Press (New Haven, CT), 1973.
Winter Morning in Charlottesville, Sceptre Press, 1977.
Praise, Ecco Press (Hopewell, NJ), 1979.
The Apple Trees at Olema, Ecco Press, 1989.
Human Wishes, Ecco Press, 1989.

Contributor of poetry to various anthologies, including *The Young American Poets,* edited by Paul Carroll, Follett (New York City), 1968, and *Five American Poets,* Carcanet (Manchester, England), 1979.

TRANSLATOR

(With Robert Pinsky) Czeslaw Milosz, *The Separate Notebooks,* Ecco Press, 1983.
(With Milosz) Milosz, *Unattainable Earth,* Ecco Press, 1986.
(With Louis Iribarne and Peter Scott) Milosz, *Collected Poems, 1931-1987,* Ecco Press, 1988.
(With Milosz) Milosz, *Provinces,* Ecco Press, 1993.
(And editor and author of introduction) *The Essential Haiku: Versions of Basho, Buson, and Issa,* Ecco Press, 1994.

OTHER

Twentieth Century Pleasures: Prose on Poetry, Ecco Press, 1984.

(Editor) *Rock and Hawk: A Selection of Shorter Poems by Robinson Jeffers,* Random House (New York City), 1987.
(Co-editor with Bill Henderson and Jorie Graham) *The Pushcart Prize XII,* Pushcart (Wainscott, NY), 1987.
(Editor with Charles Simic) Tomaz Salamun, *Selected Poems* (translations from the Slovene), Ecco Press, 1988.
(Editor) May Swenson and others, translators, *Selected Poems of Tomas Transtroemer, 1954-1986,* Ecco Press, 1989.
(Editor with Stephen Mitchell) *Into the Garden: A Wedding Anthology, Poetry and Prose on Love and Marriage,* HarperCollins (New York City), 1993.

SIDELIGHTS: Despite Robert Haas's success as a translator and critic, Forrest Gander declares in a *Dictionary of Literary Biography* essay that "it is for his own musical, descriptive, meditative poetry that Robert Hass is primarily recognized." Critics celebrate Hass's poetry for its clarity of expression, its conciseness, and its imagery, often drawn from everyday life. "Robert Hass," states Carolyn Kizer in the *New York Times Book Review,* "is so intelligent that to read his poetry or prose, or to hear him speak, gives one an almost visceral pleasure." "Hass has noted his own affinity for Japanese haiku," Gander continues, "and his work similarly attends to the details of quotidian life with remarkable clarity." "Poetry," Hass tells interviewer David Remnick in the *Chicago Review,* "is a way of living . . . a human activity like baking bread or playing basketball."

With his first collection of poems, *Field Guide,* Hass won the 1973 Yale Series of Younger Poets Award and established himself as an important American poet. Many critics noted that Hass drew on his native California countryside and his background in Slavic studies to provide much of the imagery for the volume. "The poems in *Field Guide,*" writes Gander, "are rich with Russian accents, aromas of ferny anise and uncorked wines, and references to plant and animal life: the green whelks and rock crabs, tanagers and Queen Anne's lace, sea spray and pepper trees of the Bay Area." "He is a fine poet," Michael Waters relates in *Southwest Review,* "and his book is one of the very best to appear in a long time. . . . *Field Guide* is a means of naming things, of establishing an identity through one's surroundings, of translating the natural world into one's private history. This is a lot to accomplish, yet Robert Hass manages it with clarity and compassion." In the *Ontario Review* Linda W. Wagner agrees that "*Field Guide* is an impressive first collection. . . . Hass's view of knowledge is convincing. As we read the sonorous and generally regular poems, we are aware that the poet has achieved his apparent tranquility by living close to the edge. . . . One can be reminded only of the best of Hemingway."

Hass confirmed his ability with *Praise,* his second volume of poems, which won the William Carlos Williams Award in 1979. "In many ways," Gander explains, "*Praise* addresses the problems implicit in the first book: Can the act of naming the world separate us from the world? How is it possible to bear grief, to accept death, and how can the spirit endure?" According to William Scammell in the *Times Literary Supplement,* these poems "unite freshness and wonder with a tough, inventive imagination." Writing in the *Chicago Review,* Ira Sadoff remarks that *Praise* "might even be the strongest collection of poems to come out in the late seventies." Sadoff notes that *Field Guide* "was intelligent and well-crafted; it tapped Hass's power of observation carefully and engagingly." Nevertheless the reviewer had "reservations" about *Field Guide* that "stemmed from some sense of chilliness that seemed to pervade a number of poems, as if the poems were wrought by an intellect distant from its subject matter." Sadoff continued: "I have no such problems with *Praise.* . . . [It] marks Hass's arrival as an important, even pivotal, young poet."

Hollins Critic reviewer Robert Miklitsch expresses similar feelings about *Praise,* which he feels "marks the emergence of a major American poet. If his first book, *Field Guide,* . . . did not provoke such acclaim, the second book will." Still more applause comes from *Ontario Review* contributor Charles Molesworth, who writes that Hass is "slowly but convincingly becoming one of the best poets of his generation. . . . [*Praise*] is about language, its possibilities and its burdens, its rootedness in all we do and its flowering in all we hunger for and fear. . . . But the loving tentativeness, the need to see and to save, these are Hass's own gifts. He is that extremely rare person: a poet of fullness."

In 1984, Hass published *Twentieth Century Pleasures: Prose on Poetry,* a collection of previously published essays and reviews. In the volume, the author examines American writers (including Robert Lowell and James Wright) as well as European and Japanese poets. Many critics appreciated the book, honoring it with the 1984 National Book Critics Circle award, among others. "Mr. Hass's style balances conversational directness and eloquent complexity," notes *New York Times Book Review* contributor Anthony Libby. He concludes, "Mr. Hass believes that poetry is what defines the self, and it is his ability to describe that process that is the heart of this book's pleasure."

Since the publication of *Twentieth Century Pleasures,* Hass has continued to write both poetry and prose. His third collection, *Human Wishes,* "is a distinct joy to expe-

rience in this time when so many published works deal with violence, aberration, and alienation," declares Daisy Aldan in *World Literature Today.* "His elegant gleanings of essence, often impressionist in tone, make us aware once again that beauty and meaningful silence still exist." *Nation* critic Don Bogen explains that *Human Wishes* "reveals [Hass's] basic concerns: He is a student of desire, of what we want and how likely we are to get it." "In *Human Wishes,*" Bogen concludes, "Robert Hass captures both the brightness of the world and its vanishing."

Hass paid tribute to some of his non-Western mentors in *The Essential Haiku: Versions of Basho, Buson, and Issa,* translations of short works by the most famous seventeenth- and eighteenth-century masters of the short Japanese poem. According to Mark Ford in the *New Republic,* the verse form known as *haiku* was developed in the nineteenth century from an older form named *hokku.* Hokku in turn was only part of a larger verse form known as *haikai,* which was practiced as a sort of game by several collaborating poets. Each of the three *haiku* masters (Basho, Buson, and Issa) used the short verse form to record commonplace images in an uncommon way. "Hass's language is unflashy, his interpretations sensible and his pacing effective," Ford declares. The three chosen writers in Hass's book "demonstrate the ways in which great art may intensify and illuminate our engagements with the real, the experience of art."

BIOGRAPHICAL/CRITICAL SOURCES:

BOOKS

Contemporary Literary Criticism, Volume 18, Gale (Detroit), 1981.
Dictionary of Literary Biography, Volume 105: *American Poets since World War II, Second Series,* Gale, 1991.

PERIODICALS

Atlantic Monthly, June, 1979.
Boston Globe, September 24, 1989.
Chicago Review, spring, 1981, pp. 17-26.
Hollins Critic, February, 1980.
Los Angeles Times Book Review, November 18, 1984.
Nation, May 19, 1979; December 11, 1989, pp. 722-23.
New England Review, Volume 2, number 2, 1979, pp. 295-314.
New Republic, March 16, 1992, pp. 34-5; October 31, 1994, pp. 48-51.
New York Review of Books, November 7, 1985, pp. 53-60.
New York Times Book Review, March 3, 1985, p. 37; November 12, 1989, p. 63.
Ontario Review, fall, 1974; fall-winter, 1979-80.
Parnassus, February, 1988, pp. 189-95.
Poetry, March, 1985, pp. 345-48; January, 1993, pp. 223-26.

Southwest Review, June, 1975.
Times Literary Supplement, May 28, 1982; March 15, 1985, p. 293.
Voice Literary Supplement, December, 1989, pp. 5-6.
Washington Post Book World, August 19, 1979.
World Literature Today, winter, 1985, p. 163; spring, 1990, p. 313.*

*   *   *

HASTINGS, Graham
See JEFFRIES, Roderic (Graeme)

*   *   *

HAYMAN, Ronald 1932-

PERSONAL: Born May 4, 1932, in Bournemouth, Hampshire, England; son of John (an antique dealer) and Sadie (Morris) Hayman. *Education:* Trinity Hall, Cambridge, B.A., 1954, M.A., 1963.

ADDRESSES: Home—Flat 1, 68 Fellows Rd., London NW3 3LJ, England. *Agent*—Literistic, 264 Fifth Ave., New York, NY 10001; and Peters Fraser & Dunlop, 503-4 The Chambers, Chelsea House, London SW10 0XF, England.

CAREER: Stage and television actor, 1957-61, director, 1961—. Director of Jean Genet's *Deathwatch,* Arts Theatre, 1961; Bertolt Brecht's *Jungle of the Cities,* Stratford East, Theatre Royal, 1962; *An Evening with G.B.S.,* later titled *Max Adrian as G.B.S.,* Edinburgh Festival, 1966, and later on the West End; Peter Handke's *My Foot My Tutor* and Martin Walser's *Home Front,* both at Open Space Theatre, 1971; Rainer Werner Fassbinder's *Bremen Coffee,* Traverse Theatre, Edinburgh, and Hampstead Theatre Club, both 1974; and Robin Maugham's *The Servant,* Yvonne Arnaud Theatre, Guildford; directed his own play *The Last Real Thing* at Three Horseshoes, 1976. *Military service:* Royal Air Force, 1950-51.

WRITINGS:

Techniques of Acting, Methuen (New York City), 1969.
Tolstoy, Humanities (Atlantic Highlands, NJ), 1970.
Arguing with Walt Whitman, Covent Garden Press, 1971.
John Gielgud, Random House (New York City), 1971.
Playback, Horizon Press (New York City), 1973.
Playback II, Horizon Press, 1974.
The Set-up: An Anatomy of English Theatre Today, Methuen, 1974.
The First Thrust, Davis-Poynter, 1975.
Leavis, Rowman & Littlefield (Totowa, NJ), 1976.
The Last Real Thing (play), first produced in England at Three Horseshoes, February, 1976.

How to Read a Play, Grove (New York City), 1977.
De Sade: A Biography, Crowell (New York City), 1978.
Nietzsche: A Critical Life, Oxford University Press (New York City), 1980.
Kafka: A Biography, Oxford University Press, 1981, published in England as *K: A Biography of Kafka,* Weidenfeld & Nicolson (London), 1981.
Brecht: A Biography, Oxford University Press, 1983.
Fassbinder: Film Maker, Simon & Schuster (New York City), 1984.
Secrets: Boyhood in a Jewish Hotel, 1932-1954 (autobiography), Peter Owen, (London), 1985.
Guenter Grass, Methuen, 1985.
Writing Against: A Biography of Sartre, Weidenfeld and Nicolson, 1986, published as *Sartre: A Biography,* Simon & Schuster, 1987, and as *Sartre: A Life,* Carroll & Graf (New York City), 1992.
Proust: A Biography, HarperCollins (New York City), 1990.
The Death and Life of Sylvia Plath, Carol Publishing Group (Secaucus, NJ), 1991.
Tennessee Williams: Everyone Else Is an Audience, Yale University Press (New Haven, CT), 1993.
Thomas Mann: A Biography, Scribner, 1995.
Playing the Wife (play), first produced in 1992 in Belfast, Northern Ireland, produced on West End, November, 1995.

"CONTEMPORARY PLAYWRIGHTS" SERIES: PUBLISHED BY HEINEMANN EDUCATIONAL (LONDON)

John Osborne, 1968.
Harold Pinter, 1968.
Samuel Beckett, 1968.
John Arden, 1968.
John Whiting, 1969.
Robert Bolt, 1969.
Arthur Miller, 1970.
Arnold Wesker, 1970.
Edward Albee, 1971.
Eugene Ionesco, 1972.
Tom Stoppard, 1977.
Bertolt Brecht: The Plays, 1984.

EDITOR

The Collected Plays of John Whiting, two volumes, Heinemann Educational, 1969.
The Art of the Dramatist and Other Pieces, Alan Ross, (London), 1970.
The German Theatre (textbook), Barnes & Noble (New York City), 1975.
(With Ann Thwaite) *My Oxford, My Cambridge,* Robson Books (London), 1977.

OTHER

Also author of *The Novel Today, 1967-75,* published by Longman (London). Contributor of articles and reviews to *Drama, Encounter, New Review, Obliques* (Paris), *Partisan Review,* and *Plays International.*

WORK IN PROGRESS: A biography of Carl Jung and a book entitled *Hitler and Geli.*

SIDELIGHTS: Ronald Hayman is a biographer of subjects as diverse as John Gielgud and the Marquis de Sade; he is especially notable for his critical studies of philosopher Friedrich Nietzsche, writer Franz Kafka, and playwright Bertolt Brecht, each of whom suffered from physical or mental ailments which affected their work. Nietzsche and Kafka, for example, were plagued by chronic illness and depression, while Brecht's emotional problems caused him and others to suffer for his vision of a new German theater. In their biographies Hayman examines how each artist dealt with these obstacles and even used them as inspiration. Hayman has continued his study of controversial, creative thinkers who led seemingly doomed lives with biographical explorations of director Rainer Werner Fassbinder, philosopher Jean-Paul Sartre, novelist Marcel Proust, poet Sylvia Plath, and playwright Tennessee Williams.

Nietzsche: A Critical Life is an example of this type of analysis. "The principal theme of Hayman's biography is Nietzsche's tendency 'to take sides against himself' in all he did and thought—to value any experience, even illness, for its ability to militate against his own self-satisfaction and complacency," said Henry McDonald in a *Washington Post Book World* article. *New Republic* critic Glenn Tinder believed the author had "written an interesting and useful book—unpretentious, intelligent, and balanced. And he has done something even the most ambitious biographers often fail to accomplish. He has brought his subject to life. He makes the reader feel the heavy burden of Nietzsche's days." However, Tinder criticized Hayman for failing "to bring out Nietzsche's importance as forcefully as he might, [and] his critical comments upset the scales. Thus he passes psychoanalytical judgments that are too casual and assured and that make Nietzsche seem merely a pathetic victim of his drives." While *New York Review of Books* critic J. M. Cameron found fault with Hayman's comparison of Nietzsche's work to that of Ludwig Wittgenstein, the reviewer called the study "brilliant in its portrayal" of the subject's life. "Combining remarkable philosophical sophistication with solid scholarship and a detached but effective narrative style," remarked McDonald, "Hayman sounds for us the shrill blessing with which Nietzsche, through the oracle of his life and work, sought to shatter the ears of the modern world."

While Nietzsche used the despair in his life to form the basis of a conquering ideal, Franz Kafka saw in his sad existence—a lonely childhood, repressed sexuality—a symbol for the degradation to which the human spirit can descend. In one story, Kafka imagines himself as a piece of raw meat, cut up and thrown to a dog. Hayman's *Kafka: A Biography* is considered the first comprehensive English-language study of the novelist since Kafka's literary executor, Max Brod, published a biography in 1937. Hayman's work "is possibly the most exhaustive in any language," declared John Simon in a *New Republic* review, adding, "It is certainly the most exhausting to read, though, given the subject, this must be taken not as derogation but as a compliment." The author "collects really all there is to be known," *Observer* reviewer Neal Ascherson wrote, "quotes only what is necessary . . . and proposes ideas about the relation of Kafka's psyche to his life which are independent of Freudian orthodoxies." To Theodore Ziolkowski in the *Washington Post Book World,* Hayman showed strength in his "sense for the apt quotation—almost 2,000 quotations or paraphrases by my count," but weakness in his tendency to "[heap] up his material with little selectivity, little drama, and little hint of the controversies concerning Kafka's life and the interpretation of his work." Likewise, Simon found that Hayman's "reasoning is sometimes circular and naive," but ultimately recommended *Kafka* as "a full-length portrait worth hanging alongside the writings; it is not, however, a key to hidden locks or an epiphany of genius." *Christian Science Monitor* critic Bruce Allen predicted that Hayman's portrayal of Kafka "may surprise readers who thought [the writer's] obsessive cravings for solitude and complete quiet cut him off from personal relationships. And it helps greatly that this biographer is a surpassingly graceful writer, capable of a consistent display of elegant phrasemaking."

Bertolt Brecht poses a problem for biographers, according to some critics. The architect of modern German theater, he was as well known for his ruthlessness and opportunism as he was for the revolutionary "distancing" mode of drama he created in such works as *Mother Courage and Her Children.* Hayman received some criticism for the tone of his book *Brecht: A Biography.* The author's point of view "combines lack of deep interest in either artistic or social questions with straight-forward personal dislike," Erika Munk wrote in the *Voice Literary Supplement.* While *New York Review of Books* critic James Fenton acknowledged that he "would certainly not envy anyone the task of doing justice to Brecht," he found that Hayman "appears to have put his head down and charged through the material. He never loses his temper, although sometimes one feels it would have been healthier if he had done so. . . . In general he is reasonable—and his book is no more than reasonable." On the other hand, Peter

Gay, in the *New York Times Book Review,* saw a "cool and generally competent" quality in *Brecht:* Hayman "has tried to narrate Brecht's unsettled existence at such a brisk trot that his book appears rather shorter than it is. With good reason, he devotes a full fifth of the biography to Brecht's early years in Bavaria, sketching in his family roots, his hometown of Augsburg, his voracious reading and his precocious, no less voracious, sexuality." *New Statesman* reviewer Nicholas Jacobs concluded that "for all [Hayman's] basic, though on the whole self-disciplined, political antipathy, it is a great credit to him that his biography is so sympathetic."

Fassbinder: Film Maker details the life of German motion picture director Rainer Werner Fassbinder, who died at age thirty-seven with forty-three films to his credit. As David Thomson noted in *New Republic,* "It seems fatuous to ponder whether Fassbinder was a great director or a great artist; he had so little time for such loftiness. He was unique and misanthropic, pledged to little more than excess. There was a flagrant punk in Fassbinder who wanted to offend. . . . Yet there was a mawkish romantic there, too, a mother's boy who could get drunk on Fine Women, True Love, Beauty, whatever other intoxicants he was shoveling down." While a *Los Angeles Times Book Review* critic believed Hayman "records Fassbinder's pain with high fidelity in stereophonic sound," Thomson determined the author had neglected his subject in several crucial areas: "His book keeps a prim, tense distance. . . . Hayman is the author already of biographies of de Sade, Nietzsche, Kafka, and Brecht, but he never goes far in tracing those influences on Fassbinder." Further, Thomson felt the author "doesn't seem to know the films well enough. He accepts a format in which they are bound to be neglected, . . . and he lacks the abandon or the drunken style to descend into this world where flowers grew in the trash."

Writing Against: A Biography of Sartre explores French philosopher Jean-Paul Sartre, founder of the Existentialism movement. Sissela Bok, reviewing *Writing Against* and two other Sartre biographies in the *London Review of Books,* observed, "Anyone undertaking to write Sartre's biography . . . faces an unusual challenge. What new ground could one possibly break in studying a life so thoroughly documented by the subject himself? And how could one best get behind the facade that he had so laboriously constructed to outwit biographers?" Bok commended Hayman's "careful attention to each of the works, considering their roots in Sartre's reading, teaching, and reflection," but faulted his "adversarial tone": "Hayman's criticisms of Sartre as a thinker and as a human being so pervade his book as to overwhelm his account of Sartre's life." Bok concluded, "Although the book contains intriguing trains of thought and interpretation, it hammers

in its judgments relentlessly." *Observer* critic John Sturrock asserted that in *Writing Against* Hayman presented much interesting anecdotal material but fell short in his analysis of Sartre's influence. "Sartre is seen only in close-up, as represented by what he or his associates have earlier recorded about him, and the book is full of variously appealing trivialities. . . . On this intimate side, Hayman's book is diligent and interesting. . . . But we need to be helped to *understand* Sartre as well (if not the complicated man then his multitudinous ideas) rather than merely to follow him groupie-like through a vagrant, positive but not so dramatic life." Reviews of the U.S. release of *Writing Against* entitled *Sartre: A Life,* however, contained opposing views: Michael Liccione of *National Review* found "little of the merely trivial" in the work, and asserted that Hayman's "smooth prose is laced with shrewd insights"; Tom Bishop in the *New York Times Book Review* concluded, "Mr. Hayman successfully counterpoints the public and the private man and highlights the frequent contradictions that mark Sartre's actions and writings." *Wall Street Journal* reviewer Richard Locke deemed the book "certainly clear and hard-working," and Beverly Fields, in *Tribune Books,* declared, "Hayman is a match for the powerful figure he is up against here. He has turned out an orderly, objective and analytical study, tough enough to present the grittiness, flexible enough to follow the turns and returns, paradoxes and ambiguities in Sartre's search for authenticity in thought and action."

French novelist Marcel Proust presented further challenges for Hayman in *Proust: A Biography.* Proust, whose *A la Recherche du Temps Perdu* (*Remembrance of Things Past*) is considered by many critics one of the supreme achievements of world literature, was "a delicate bird of paradise in one of history's weirdest aviaries, prewar Paris," according to Donald Lyons in the *Wall Street Journal.* Lyons acknowledged Hayman's earlier biographies and remarked, "Now it's Proust's turn, and a mighty sorry figure he cuts under Mr. Hayman's rigidly clinical eye." Lyon asserted that "no book about [Proust] can fail to offer a cornucopia of baroque anecdotes," and Hayman delivers these, "but local color cannot outweigh the clumsily reductivist psychologizing of this book, or its floundering inarticulateness about Proust's, or any, art." *Los Angeles Times Book Review's* Charles Solomon, however, judged *Proust* "well written and scrupulously documented." Paul Binding of *New Statesman* said, "Hayman shows extremely clearly the progression of Proust's great and all-demanding work: how rejection in fact stimulated him, enabling him to write at the necessary slower narrative pace" that his magnum opus demanded, and "reveals the way in which his friends and acquaintances passed from life into literature." Peter Brooks writing in the *New York Times Book Review* deemed the book "highly readable . . . consistently entertaining, well informed and instructive," and added, "Mr. Hayman has the great merit of leaving his readers freer to intuit the connections between life and art [than other biographers]. And he has deftly gathered all the most recent Proustian scholarship and woven it into a lively narrative." In the *Times Literary Supplement,* David Coward lauded *Proust:* "What makes his biography so absorbing is the sympathetic, nuanced portrait which he has teased with such industry out of the vast secondary literature. . . . Observing not simply from without, Hayman helps us to understand something of the inner vision which Proust considered more important than mere technique."

The Death and Life of Sylvia Plath is a "biographical study," rather than a traditional biography, of the life of poet Sylvia Plath, considered by many a prime voice of the women's movement and a major feminist martyr who committed suicide at age thirty in 1963. Biographies concerning the full details of her life and work have been hampered by control of rights to reproduce the text of all her writings, both published and unpublished, by her estranged husband, Poet Laureate Ted Hughes, and his sister, Olwyn Hughes, agent of her estate. The impetus of Plath's suicide is widely attributed to depression over an affair between her husband and Assia Gutmann Wevill, wife of Canadian poet David Wevill, leading observers to note an obvious motive for the Hughes family to suppress documents which could shed light on the subject. As an *Economist* critic observed: "In practice [Ted Hughes] has kept the facts of his life with Sylvia quite closely guarded, even destroying one of her journals. He has often met authorial speculation with threats of legal action or refusal of permission to publish excerpts from Plath's work." Hayman succeeds despite such hindrances, M. C. Dalton, writing in *Bloomsbury Review,* asserted: "For readers who are curious about the details of Plath's personal legacy, *The Death and Life of Sylvia Plath* is an eye-opening study." *Spectator* critic Frances Spalding condemned Hayman's approach, however, remarking that the author "works as if facts come independent of their context or speaker." Elizabeth Frank of the *New York Times Book Review* said, "Mr. Hayman has evident tenderness and compassion toward his subject. He isn't blind to her faults, and he handles the psychoanalytic discussion that seems to be the inescapable lingua franca of Plath studies with restraint and insight. He does, however, have an ax to grind: he states that he wants to 'help to correct some of the imbalance created by writers who have been unfair to Sylvia Plath,' but he doesn't identify them by name, as he ought to."

Hayman's biography of American playwright Tennessee Williams received mixed reviews. A *Publishers Weekly* reviewer noted that the author acknowledged Williams's talent in *Tennessee Williams: Everyone Else Is an Audience,*

but predicted that the book would "strike some readers as basically unsympathetic and as focusing excessively on the playwright's worst qualities." This was precisely the complaint of several reviewers, including *Los Angeles Times Book Review* contributor David Ehrenstein, who described the book as "little more than a rehash of every canard that has been volleyed at the playwright." *New York Times* reviewer Michiko Kakutani expressed disappointment with the "decidedly mediocre collection of biographies and memoirs" of Williams published so far, and described Hayman's as "a particularly depressing contribution" that provides much information about Williams's health problems and troubled relationships, but "tells us nothing . . . about the artistic vision that fueled his writing, nothing about the emotional contradictions that animated his life and his work."

Hayman does, however, "succeed admirably at tracing various causes and consequences of Williams's lifelong bouts with paranoia, hypochondria, depression, and self-doubt," according to Kurt Eisen in *American Literature.* J. Hafley, writing in *Choice,* also acknowledged Hayman's tendency to "lean heavily on Williams's vices, but only grudgingly to admit his many virtues," but nonetheless described the book as an "engaging, absorbing biography that stresses relationships between Williams's art and life."

Thomas Mann was the first complete biography of the German Nobel Prize-winning author of *Buddenbrooks, The Magic Mountain,* and *Doctor Faustus,* and draws heavily on Mann's recently published diaries, according to Theodore Ziolkowski in the *New York Times Book Review. New York Times* reviewer Kakutani wrote, "In contrast to Mr. Hayman's last biography, a hasty and highly unsympathetic portrait of Tennessee Williams, . . . *Thomas Mann* is an energetically researched work that tries to penetrate Mann's public mask of bourgeois decorum without ever becoming prurient or sensationalistic." In fact, the author may have been too conservative, according to a *Kirkus Reviews* critic who remarked that in "striving nobly not to speculate," the author failed "to make the educated guesses biographers can best supply." The reviewer nonetheless described *Thomas Mann* as an "important, accomplished work."

Many reviewers remarked on the level of detail Hayman employed in *Thomas Mann. Booklist* reviewer Ron Antonucci noted the "almost day-to-day examination of Mann's life" in what he deemed a "heavy, heady work, worthy of this German master," but *Los Angeles Times Book Review* contributor Mark Harman was less appreciative of the author's comprehensive approach, commenting, "Ronald Hayman has a good eye for apt detail, but he often spoils the effect through clutter." An *Atlantic Monthly* reviewer concluded, "Admirers of Mann's fiction will find no reason in this extremely detailed biography to shift their ground."

BIOGRAPHICAL/CRITICAL SOURCES:

BOOKS

Contemporary Literary Criticism, Volume 44, Gale (Detroit), 1987.

Hayman, Ronald, *Nietzsche: A Critical Life,* Oxford University Press, 1980.

Hayman *Secrets: Boyhood in a Jewish Hotel, 1932-1954,* Peter Owen, 1985.

PERIODICALS

American Literature, December, 1994, pp. 860-61.

American Spectator, January, 1992, p. 52.

Antioch Review, fall, 1987, p. 501.

Atlanta Journal-Constitution, November 3, 1991, p. N10.

Atlantic Monthly, April, 1995, pp. 141-42.

Bloomsbury Review, June 12, 1992, p. 21.

Booklist, March 15, 1995, p. 1301.

Books and Bookmen, August, 1978; May, 1980.

Boston Globe, June 21, 1987, p. 53; November 4, 1990, p. B16; September 22, 1991; May 3, 1994, p. 65.

Chicago Tribune, June 7, 1987, s. 14, p. 6; December 22, 1991, s. 14, pp. 4, 6.

Chicago Tribune Book World, January 17, 1982.

Choice, May, 1994, p. 1435.

Christian Science Monitor, April 9, 1982.

Economist, August 10, 1991, p. 78.

Entertainment Weekly, April 1, 1994, p. 49.

Guardian Weekly, August 18, 1985, p. 21; November 22, 1987, p. 28; July 7, 1991, p. 29.

Kirkus Reviews, February 1, 1995, p. 132.

Listener, August 29, 1985, p. 20; October 23, 1986, p. 25.

London Review of Books, October 3, 1985, p. 20; September 1, 1988, pp. 11-12.

Los Angeles Times Book Review, December 16, 1984, p. 9; November 11, 1990, p. 6; June 26, 1994, pp. 4-5; June 18, 1995, p. 12.

National Review, September 25, 1987, pp. 58-59.

New Republic, July 26, 1980; March 10, 1982; December 31, 1984, pp. 36-38, 40.

New Statesman, September 30, 1983; October 3, 1986, p. 39; November 14, 1986, p. 27; October 5, 1990, pp. 40, 43; June 21, 1991, pp. 43-44.

Newsweek, February 1, 1982.

New Yorker, December 24, 1990, p. 99; August 23, 1993, p. 84.

New York Review of Books, October 9, 1980; February 4, 1982; March 15, 1984; August 13, 1987, pp. 42-46.

New York Times, July 25, 1980; November 26, 1983; June 7, 1987, p. 11; November 13, 1990, p. C17; February 4, 1994, p. C23; March 24, 1995, p. C31.

New York Times Book Review, November 4, 1979; January 17, 1982; November 27, 1983; June 7, 1987, p. 11; December 23, 1990, p. 8; October 6, 1991, pp. 14-15, 53; July 19, 1992, p. 13; February 27, 1994, p. 21.

Observer, November 15, 1981; September 18, 1983; December 2, 1984, p. 25; July 28, 1985, p. 24; August 24, 1986, p. 20; November 9, 1986, p. 28; April 26, 1987, p. 25; June 23, 1991, p. 53; April 26, 1992, p. 57; December 26, 1993, p. 20.

Publishers Weekly, January 24, 1994, p. 46.

Sewanee Review, summer, 1993, p. R101.

Sight and Sound, April, 1994, p. 32.

Spectator, April 2, 1977; October 31, 1981; October 25, 1986, p. 34; July 13, 1991, p. 27.

Times (London), April 30, 1980; October 29, 1981; August 11, 1985.

Times Educational Supplement, April 25, 1986, p. 30; October 17, 1986, p. 24; December 19, 1986, p. 20; September 28, 1990, p. R2; July 12, 1991, p. 23.

Times Literary Supplement, June 9, 1972; April 5, 1974; August 8, 1975; February 5, 1982; August 2, 1985, p. 844; December 12, 1986, p. 1404; October 26-November 1, 1990, p. 1144.

Theatre Journal, May, 1985, p. 255.

Tribune Books (Chicago), June 7, 1987, p. 6; December 22, 1991, p. 4; December 27, 1992, p. 2.

USA Today, August 4, 1987, p. 6D; September 13, 1991, p. D6.

Voice Literary Supplement, April, 1984; November, 1987, pp. 14-15.

Wall Street Journal, June 23, 1987, p. 28; October 26, 1990, p. A13.

Washington Post, December 30, 1990, p. 5.

Washington Post Book World, January 12, 1980; September 7, 1980; March 7, 1982; June 21, 1987, p. 1487; December 30, 1990, p. 5; July 26, 1992, p. 12; December 27, 1992, p. 12; January 30, 1994, p. 13.

West Coast Review of Books, July, 1985, p. 51.

*　　　*　　　*

HELGESEN, Sally 1948-

PERSONAL: Born July 1, 1948, in St. Cloud, MN. *Education:* Received B.A. from Hunter College of the City University of New York.

ADDRESSES: Home—271 West 11th St., New York, NY 10014. *Agent*—Georges Borchardt Inc., 136 East 57th St., New York, NY 10022.

CAREER: Journalist.

MEMBER: Authors Guild.

WRITINGS:

Wildcatters: A Story of Texans, Oil, and Money, Doubleday (New York City), 1981.

The Female Advantage: Women's Ways of Leadership, Doubleday, 1990.

Contributor to periodicals, including *Vogue* and *Glamour.* Past contributing editor of *Harper's.*

WORK IN PROGRESS: A novel, for Doubleday.

SIDELIGHTS: Sally Helgesen's *The Female Advantage: Women's Ways of Leadership* "reassures women that their style is perfectly acceptable in today's business world, is distinctly different from men's styles and can positively influence the manner in which business in conducted," comments Sue M. Barkley in *Perspectives on Political Science.* The book analyzes the management techniques of women executives, focusing on four top female executives. Helgesen kept a diary of the activities of Dorothy Brunson, Frances Hesselbein, Barbara Grogan, and Nancy Badore over a period of several months; she based her investigative approach on a study published in 1973 by Henry Mintzberg (using research conducted in 1968), *The Nature of Managerial Work,* which examined the management methods of top male executives. A *Business Week* reviewer remarks that "Helgesen's thesis—that women have a unique perspective that companies should encourage—raises serious issues," adding that she "has an eye for the telling detail."

Helegesen noted several differences between male and female administrative practices. For example, the four female executives she studied all utilize "the circle or web approach to management," explains Barkley. "Women tend to see themselves as being in the *center* of things rather than at the top. . . . The companies of Helgesen's female executives were structured as networks or grids instead of hierarchies." Suzanne B. Laporte writes in *Working Woman,* "Each of the women described her place in the organization as being in the center reaching out, rather than at the top reaching down." Treatment of information varies by gender as well. Helgesen argues that top-level females share information readily, facilitated by the web structure of management, unlike men whom Mintzberg identified as hoarding information with the belief that information equals power.

Another significant contrast observed by Helgesen involves the scheduling of time: women tend to plan periodic small breaks into their daily schedule, rather than working steadily all day long. " 'The women didn't give the impression that they only had so much time to talk to someone before they had to get on to their next appointment,' " Helgesen states in *Working Woman.* Barkley concludes that Helgesen's work successfully compares the differ-ences between the male and female styles "not to 'bash' male executives," but to "learn from one another."

BIOGRAPHICAL/CRITICAL SOURCES:

PERIODICALS

Business Week, June 25, 1990, p. 14.
Christian Science Monitor, February 15, 1991, p. 13.
Perspectives on Political Science, fall, 1991, pp. 230-31.
Working Woman, September, 1990, p. 143.*

*   *   *

HENSON, Margaret Swett 1924-

PERSONAL: Born January 3, 1924, in Chicago, IL; daughter of William Claude (a civil engineer) and Clara L. (a teacher; maiden name, Kaufman) Swett; married W. A. Nowotny, October 2, 1943; married James Scott Henson, September 14, 1951; children: (first marriage) Kathleen Nowotny Duncan, Patricia (deceased); (second marriage) Mike, Peter, Steve. *Education:* University of Houston, B.S., 1962, M.A., 1967, Ph.D., 1974. *Religion:* Presbyterian.

ADDRESSES: *Home*—6723 Richwood, Houston, TX 77087.

CAREER: Housewife, 1943-60; Houston Independent School District, Houston, TX, high school teacher of history, 1962-69; Houston Metropolitan Archives Project, Houston, archivist, 1974-76; Southwest Center for Urban Research, Houston, director of humanities research program, 1975-77; University of Houston at Clear Lake City, Houston, assistant professor of history, 1977-85; writer, 1985—. Member of Harris County Historical Commission, 1976—.

MEMBER: Texas State Historical Association (fellow; member of board of editors, 1982—), East Texas Historical Association (fellow; member of board of directors, 1980-84), Harris County Historical Society (president, 1978).

AWARDS, HONORS: Summerfield G. Roberts Award from Sons of the Republic of Texas, 1976, for *Samuel May Williams;* T. R. Fehrenboch Award for Best County History, 1988, for *A Pictorial History of Chambers County.*

WRITINGS:

Samuel May Williams: Early Texas Entrepreneur, Texas A & M University Press (College Station, TX), 1976.

Juan Davis Bradburn: A Reappraisal of the Mexican Commander of Anahuac, Texas A & M University Press, 1982.

Anahuac in 1832: Cradle of the Texas Revolution, Chambers County Historical Commission, 1982.

Anglo-American Women in Texas, 1820-1850, American Press (Boston), 1982.

(Contributor) Donald W. Whisenhunt, editor, *Texas: A Sesquicentennial Celebration,* Eakin Publications (Austin), 1985.

Baytown: A History, Bay Area Heritage Society, 1986.

A Pictorial History of Chambers County, Wallisville Heritage Park, 1987.

The Cartwrights of San Augustine: Three Generations of Agricultural Entrepreneurs in Nineteenth Century Texas, Texas State Historical Association (Austin), 1993.

Lorenzo de Zavala, First Vice-President of Texas, Texas Christian University Press (Fort Worth), 1995.

Contributor to *Southwestern Historical Quarterly* and *American Archivist.*

SIDELIGHTS: Margaret Swett Henson once told *CA:* "I am considered a revisionist historian of nineteenth-century Texas. I used Mexican sources as well as the usual glorifying accounts of Anglo-Texans.

"Samuel May Williams was Stephen F. Austin's associate during the Anglo colonization of Texas in the 1820s. He was a founder of the Galveston City Company in 1838, and he was the first banker in 1848. He and partner T. F. McKinney used ninety thousand dollars of their credit to finance the Texas Revolution, which peaked in 1836 with that state declaring its independence from Mexico."

BIOGRAPHICAL/CRITICAL SOURCES:

PERIODICALS

Houston Post, January 21, 1986.

*   *   *

HERMALYN, Gary 1952-

PERSONAL: Born July 10, 1952, in New York, NY; son of Sol Montcalm (a sales executive) and Isabelle Lee (a sales executive) Hermalyn; married Elizabeth Beirne (a philosopher), January 11, 1981. *Education:* City College of the City University of New York, B.A., 1972; Long Island University, M.A., 1980; Columbia University, Ed.D., 1985. *Avocational interests:* Hiking and mountaineering in Alaska, Greenland, the continental United States, and Mexico; exploration; music; basketmaking; and organic farming.

ADDRESSES: Home—New York, NY. *Office*—The Bronx County Historical Society, 3309 Bainbridge Ave., New York, NY 10467. *Agent*—P.O. Box 104, Bronx, New York City, NY 10463.

CAREER: The Bronx County Historical Society, New York City, executive director, 1973—. Adjunct associate professor at New York University, 1979—; adjunct lecturer at Teachers College, Columbia University, 1983-89. Founder and president of History of New York City Project, Inc., 1981—; chair of Museums Council of New York City, 1982-85; founder and chair of Exploration of Bygone Waterways and Pathways in New York City, 1975—; member of advisory board of Bronx Arts Ensemble, 1977—; chair of Greater New York Centennial Commission, 1994-; member of board of directors of Society of the National Shrine of the Bill of Rights at St. Paul's Church.

MEMBER: American Association of Museums, Authors Guild, American Forestry Association, Metropolitan Historic Structures Association (founder), Bronx Cultural Institutions Association (founder; chair, 1978—), Earthwatch, Explorers Club, NOFA.

AWARDS, HONORS: Media Award from National Society of Colonial Dames, 1986, for radio show *Out of the Past.*

WRITINGS:

Genealogy of the Bronx, The Bronx County Historical Society, 1977, revised edition, 1986.

(With Lloyd Ultan) *The Bronx in the Innocent Years,* Harper (New York City), 1985.

Landmarks of the Bronx, The Bronx County Historical Society, 1989.

The Bronx: It Was Only Yesterday, The Bronx County Historical Society, 1994.

Morris High School and the Creation of the First Public High Schools in New York City, The Bronx County Historical Society, 1995.

EDITOR

John McNamara, History in Asphalt, The Bronx County Historical Society, 1978, third edition, 1989.

The Bronx in Print, The Bronx County Historical Society, 1980.

Edna Mead, *The Bronx Triangle,* The Bronx County Historical Society, 1982.

Elizabeth Beirne, *Poems of Edgar Allan Poe at Fordham,* The Bronx County Historical Society, 1982.

Lloyd Ultan, *Legacy of the Revolution,* The Bronx County Historical Society, 1983.

Ed Quinn, *Signers of the U.S. Constitution,* The Bronx County Historical Society, 1987.

Jeffrey Wisotsky, *Movies of the Bronx,* The Bronx County Historical Society, 1987.

Sydney Horenstein, *On Tap: The Story of the New York City Water System,* The Bronx County Historical Society, 1987.

Lisa Garrison, *The U.S. Constitution Teacher and Student Activities Workbook,* The Bronx County Historical Society, 1987.

Ron Roth, *Starlight Amusement Park,* The Bronx County Historical Society, 1987.

McNamara, *McNamara's Guide to the Old Bronx,* The Bronx County Historical Society, 1988.

Ed Quinn, *Signers of the Declaration of Independence,* The Bronx County Historical Society, 1989.

Lloyd Ultan, *History of the Bronx, Volume I: The Colonial Period,* The Bronx County Historical Society, 1994.

(Associate editor) *Encyclopedia of New York City,* Yale University Press (New Haven, CT), 1995.

George Lankevich, *Chief Justices of the Supreme Court,* The Bronx County Historical Society, 1995.

Richard Streb, *The First Senate of the U.S.,* The Bronx County Historical Society, 1995.

Lankevich, *The First U.S. House of Representatives,* The Bronx County Historical Society, in press.

Also editor of *Presidents of the U.S.,* by Ultan. Editor-in-chief of "U.S. Constitution" series, Grolier, 1995—, and of ten-volume "History of the U.S. Supreme Court," Grolier Education Corp., 1994—. Author of radio scripts, 1973-90. Contributor of articles to *The Bronx County Historical Society Journal* and to publications of the Museum of the American Indian, The Bronx Realty Board, and The Poe Foundation. Editor of *The Bronx County Historical Society Journal,* 1973—; editor of audio-visual shows "The Life and Times of Edgar Allan Poe," "Newspapers of New York City," and "Time and the Calendar," produced by The Bronx County Historical Society.

WORK IN PROGRESS: A History of New York City, completion expected in 1995; with Ultan, *The Birth of the Bronx.*

SIDELIGHTS: Gary Hermalyn told *CA:* "My work results from historical and scientific curiosity and discovery. With regard to my New York City-related work, there is a tremendous lack of information on the city and its boroughs. For example, there is no modern, comprehensive history of the city of New York. The last published was in the 1920's. The city is an extraordinary place, and it behooves us to know its parts, its ethnicity, its rapid change, its enduring history. My role is to fill the gaps where I can."

BIOGRAPHICAL/CRITICAL SOURCES:

PERIODICALS

New Yorker, June 7, 1982.
New York Post, May 4, 1984.
New York Times, April 24, 1977; December 8, 1985.

HERMES, Patricia 1936-

PERSONAL: Born February 21, 1936, in Brooklyn, NY; daughter of Frederick Joseph (a bank vice-president) and Jessie (Gould) Martin; married Matthew E. Hermes (a research and development director for a chemical company), August 24, 1957 (divorced, 1984); children: Paul, Mark, Timothy, Matthew, Jr., Jennifer. *Education:* St. John's University, B.A., 1957.

ADDRESSES: Home and office—1414 Melville Ave., Fairfield, CT 06430. *Agent*—Dorothy Markinko (juvenile books) and Julie Fallowfield (adult books), McIntosh & Otis, Inc., 310 Madison Ave., New York, NY 10017.

CAREER: Rollingcrest Junior High School, Takoma Park, MD, teacher of English and social studies, 1957-58; Delcastle Technical High School, Delcastle, DE, teacher of home-bound children, 1972-73; Norfolk Public School System, Norfolk, VA, writer-in-residence, beginning 1981; Sacred Heart University, Fairfield, CT, teacher of English and writing, 1986-87.

MEMBER: Authors Guild, Authors League of America, Society of Children's Book Writers.

AWARDS, HONORS: Best Book for Young Adults from American Library Association, 1985, for *A Solitary Secret,* and 1992, for *Mama, Let's Dance;* Hodge-Podger Award, 1993, for *Mama, Let's Dance; Someone to Count On* named one of Best Books for the Teen Years by New York Library, 1993; *You Shouldn't Have to Say Goodbye* won California Young Reader Medal, Hawaii Nene Award, Pine Tree Book Award, and Iowa Young Reader Medal; several of Hermes' books have received Children's Choice awards.

WRITINGS:

JUVENILE NOVELS

What If They Knew?, Harcourt (New York City), 1980.
Nobody's Fault?, Harcourt, 1981.
You Shouldn't Have to Say Goodbye, Harcourt, 1982.
Who Will Take Care of Me?, Harcourt, 1983.
Friends Are Like That, Harcourt, 1984.
A Solitary Secret, Harcourt, 1985.
Kevin Corbett Eats Flies, illustrations by Carol Newsom, Harcourt, 1986.
A Place for Jeremy, Harcourt, 1987.
Mama, Let's Dance, Little, Brown (Boston), 1991.
Take Care of My Girl, Little, Brown, 1992.
Someone to Count On, Little, Brown, 1993.
Nothing But Trouble, Trouble, Trouble, Scholastic Inc. (New York City), 1994.

Also author of *Heads I Win,* Harcourt, *Be Still My Heart,* Putnam, and *I Hate Being Gifted,* Putnam.

OTHER

A Time to Listen: Preventing Youth Suicide, Harcourt, 1987.

My Girl (movie novelization), Simon & Schuster (New York City), 1991.

Also author of *My Girl II*, 1994. Contributor to magazines, including *Woman's Day, Life and Health, Connecticut, County, American Baby, Mother's Day*, and to newspapers.

Some of Hermes' books have been translated into French, Italian, Japanese, Danish, and Portuguese.

SIDELIGHTS: Patricia Hermes once told *CA:* "Although I have done many nonfiction articles and essays for adults, I write primarily for children and young adults. I think I have chosen writing for young people because I remember what it was like to be a child, and remember more than anything how painful it was. As adults, we often try to deceive ourselves that childhood is a safe, pleasant place to be. It isn't—at least, not all of the time. For me, it is important to say this to young people, to let them know they are not alone and that others share their feelings, their dreams and fears and hopes. It is important for them to know that things aren't always great in other children's lives either, because I have long believed that anything is bearable when we know that we are not alone. This does not mean that my books must be sad—not at all. What it means is that I need to tell young people that there are tough things going on in their lives but other kids share those problems, and that there is HOPE. Hope is the most important thing I can hold out to them. The pleasure and joy that I find in writing is in expressing how I feel in a way with which young readers can identify.

"Most of the subjects of my books come, in some small way at least, from my own background. Jeremy, in my first book, has epilepsy. When I was a child, I too had epilepsy, and it was a very painful thing emotionally. I wanted to write about it to tell children today what it's like, to help young people who might have the disease, or children who might know someone who has it. But that is not all. One does not have to have epilepsy to have the feelings that Jeremy had, to feel lonely, frightened, rejected. All children feel that way at times, so in writing about those feelings, I hope I can help them cope with their feelings. It is up to my readers to decide if I achieve that goal.

"In *Nobody's Fault?*, a young child dies in an accident. That accident did not really happen, not to my children nor to anyone I know. But many years ago, one of my children did die from a disease when she was just an infant. In some ways then, I am talking about my own feelings in that book, my feelings about losing a child in death.

These are feelings I believe a child can identify with, because children have strong feelings. They know about death and separation and loneliness."

She added: "Children live in the world and are part of the world, and they need books that reflect their world. Adults often forget this. And in trying to present a sanitized version of life, we cheat children. Kids are gutsier and more courageous than we give them credit for. They need honest books. So many good books are removed from libraries because *adults* fear their content. And the content is often not threatening, but something as harmless as slang or normal kids' speech."

*   *   *

HESS, Beth B(owman)

PERSONAL: Born in Buffalo, NY; daughter of Albert A. (an advertising executive) and Yetta (a social worker; maiden name, Lurie) Bowman; married Richard C. Hess (in business), April 26, 1953; children: Laurence Albert, Emily Frances. *Education:* Radcliffe College, B.A. (magna cum laude), 1950; Rutgers University, M.A., 1966, Ph.D., 1970. *Politics:* Democrat. *Religion:* Jewish.

ADDRESSES: Home—14 Sherwood Dr., Mountain Lakes, NJ 07046. *Office*—Department of Social Sciences, County College of Morris, Dover, NJ 07801.

CAREER: County College of Morris, Dover, NJ, assistant professor, 1969-73, associate professor, 1973-79, professor of social sciences, 1979—. Adjunct professor at Graduate Center, City University of New York, 1979; visiting professor at Gerontology Center, Boston University, 1980-81; lecturer at Douglass College, 1981.

MEMBER: American Sociological Association (secretary, 1989-92), Sociologists for Women in Society (president, 1987-89), Association for Humanist Sociology (president, 1987), Society for the Study of Social Problems (vice-president, 1994-95), Gerontological Society (fellow), Eastern Sociological Society (executive secretary, 1978-81; president, 1988-89).

AWARDS, HONORS: Peter I. Gellman Distinguished Service Award from Eastern Sociological Society, 1982; faculty recognition award, New Jersey Department of Higher Education, 1989.

WRITINGS:

(With Matilda White Riley and Anne Foner) *Aging and Society*, Volume I, Russell Sage Foundation, 1968.
(Editor) *Growing Old in America*, Transaction Books, 1976, 4th edition (with Elizabeth W. Markson), 1991.
(With Markson) *Aging and Old Age: An Introduction to Social Gerontology*, Macmillan, 1980.

(Editor with Kathleen Bond) *Leading Edges: Recent Research on Psychological Aging,* U.S. Government Printing Office, 1981.

(With Markson and Peter J. Stein) *Sociology,* Macmillan, 1982, 5th edition, Allyn & Bacon, 1995.

(Editor with Marvin B. Sussman) *Women and the Family: Two Decades of Change,* Haworth Press, 1984.

(With Myra Marx Ferree) *Controversy and Coalition: The New Feminist Movement,* G. K. Hall, 1985, revised edition, 1994.

(With Ferree) *Analysing Gender,* Sage Publications, 1987.

(Editor with Riley and Bettina Huber) *Social Structure and Human Lives,* Sage, 1988.

Contributor to books, including *Aging and Society,* Volume III, edited by Riley, Foner, and Marilyn Johnson, Russell Sage Foundation, 1971; *Proceedings of Association for Gerontology in Higher Education,* 1975; *Public Policies for an Aging Population,* edited by Markson and G. R. Batra, Lexington Books, 1980; *Gender and the Life Course,* edited by A. Rossi, Aldine, 1984; *Encyclopedia of Sociology,* edited by E. and M. Borgatta, Macmillan, 1992; and *Individual Voices, Collective Visions: Fifty Years of Women in Sociology,* edited by A. Goetting and S. Fenstermaker, Temple University Press, 1994. Contributor of reviews and articles to scholarly journals, including *Contemporary Sociology, The Gerontologist, Sociological Forum,* and *Social Policy.* Associate editor of *Society, Research on Aging, Contemporary Sociology,* and *Teaching Sociology.*

SIDELIGHTS: Beth B. Hess told *CA:* "It seems that the theme which best describes my adulthood, as for so many older women today, is 'balance'; that is, managing the demands of scholarship, teaching, parenthood and marriage. This has been a richly rewarding mix, one which I hope will increasingly characterize the lives of both men and women.

"I have also sought to balance my commitment to sociology with an obligation to social activism. My biography in this respect is no doubt similar to that of most academics my age: active involvement at the community level in the major movements of the last two decades: civil liberties, civil rights, antiwar, and, most significantly, the feminist movement.

"Admittedly, this balancing act can strain one's abilities and energies; to achieve all one wishes in all these roles is perhaps impossible. So, while there is much that I regret not doing better, there is little to which I would not commit myself again."

HEWISON, Robert 1943-

PERSONAL: Born June 2, 1943, in Surrey, England; son of Robert J. P. (a civil servant) and Nancy (Henderson) Hewison. *Education:* Brasenose College, Oxford, M.A., 1965, B.Litt., 1972.

ADDRESSES: Home—82 Fetter Lane, London EC4, England. *Agent*—Michael Sissons, A. D. Peters & Co., 10 Buckingham St., London WC2N 6BU, England.

CAREER: Freelance radio journalist, 1967—. Part-time lecturer at Winchester School of Art, 1976-77; guest curator at J. B. Speed Art Museum in Kentucky, 1977-78; theater critic for *Sunday Times,* 1981—.

MEMBER: Writers' Guild of Great Britain.

WRITINGS:

The Gentle Art of Making Enemies (documentary film), British Broadcasting Corp., 1969.
John Ruskin: The Argument of the Eye, Princeton University Press (Princeton, NJ), 1976.
(With Chris Orr) *Chris Orr's John Ruskin,* Signford, 1976.
Under Siege: Literary Life in London, 1939-45, Oxford University Press (New York City), 1977.
Ruskin and Venice, Thames & Hudson (London), 1978.
In Anger: British Culture in the Cold War, 1945-1960, Oxford University Press (New York City), 1981.
Monty Python, The Case Against, Grove (New York City), 1981.
Footlights: A Hundred Years of Cambridge Comedy, Methuen (London), 1983.
Too Much: Art and Society in the Sixties, 1960-75, Oxford University Press, 1986.
The Heritage Industry: Britain in a Climate of Decline, Methuen, 1987.
Future Tense: A New Art for the Nineties, Methuen, 1990.

Contributor to *Review of English Studies* and *New Statesman.*

SIDELIGHTS: Robert Hewison once told *CA:* "As a professional writer, I am very concerned that all authors should be properly rewarded for their work, by the granting of a payment through the Public Lending Right for the free use of their work in the public library system. Hence my firm belief in the value of the Writers' Guild of Great Britain. Although the study of Ruskin has been (and will continue to be) a specialty, I find it helpful to alternate this with work in a more contemporary field. There is nonetheless a connection between the two areas of study, since Ruskin was one of the pioneers of the genre of cultural history which I am trying to develop."

BIOGRAPHICAL/CRITICAL SOURCES:

PERIODICALS

New York Times, July 21, 1978.
Observer (London), July 31, 1977.
Punch, July 27, 1977.
Times Literary Supplement, August 12, 1977; October 17, 1986; August 17-23, 1990.
Washington Post, December 26, 1977.*

*   *   *

HIGGINS, Reynold Alleyne   1916-1993

PERSONAL: Born November 26, 1916, in Weybridge, England; died April 18, 1993; son of Charles Alleyne (a lawyer) and Marjorie Edith (Taylor) Higgins; married Patricia Mary Williams (a physiotherapist), 1947; children: Jenny, Michael, Nicolas, Thomas, Katherine. *Education:* Attended Pembroke College, Cambridge, 1935-38, M.A., 1960, Litt.D., 1963. *Religion:* Church of England.

CAREER: British Museum, Department of Greek and Roman Antiquities, London, England, assistant keeper, 1947-65, deputy keeper, 1965-77, acting keeper, 1976. British School of Archaeology at Athens, visiting fellow, 1969, chairperson of managing committee, 1975-79; Norton lecturer, Archaeological Institute of America, 1982-83. Guest speaker on Hellenic cruises, beginning 1963. *Military service:* British Army, 1939-46; became captain; prisoner of war, 1940-45.

WRITINGS:

Greek and Roman Jewelry, Methuen (London), 1961, 2nd edition, University of California Press (Berkeley), 1980.
Greek Terracotta Figures, Trustees of the British Museum (London), 1963.
Jewelry from Classical Lands, Trustees of the British Museum, 1965.
Minoan and Mycenean Art, Praeger (New York City), 1967, revised edition, Oxford University Press (New York City), 1981.
Greek Terracottas, Barnes & Noble (New York City), 1967.
The Archaeology of Minoan Crete, Walck, 1973.
The Aegina Treasure: An Archaeological Mystery, British Museum Publications (London), 1979.
Tanagra and the Figurines, Princeton University Press (Princeton, NJ), 1986.

Also author of *Catalogue of the Terracottas in the British Museum,* Volume 1, 1954, and Volume 2, 1959, and of *The Greek Bronze Age,* 1970.

OBITUARIES:

PERIODICALS

Times (London), April 28, 1993, p. 19.*

*   *   *

HIGHLAND, Monica
See ESPEY, John (Jenkins) and SEE, Carolyn (Penelope)

*   *   *

HIJUELOS, Oscar   1951-

PERSONAL: Surname is pronounced "E-way-los"; born August 24, 1951, in New York, NY; son of Pascual (a hotel worker) and Magdalena (a homemaker; maiden name, Torrens) Hijuelos; divorced. *Education:* City College of the City University of New York, B.A., 1975, M.A., 1976. *Religion:* Catholic. *Avocational interests:* Pen-and-ink drawing, old maps, turn of the century books and graphics, playing musical instruments, jazz ("I absolutely despise modern rock and roll").

ADDRESSES: Home—211 West 106th St., New York, NY 10025. *Agent*—Harriet Wasserman Literary Agency, 137 East 36th St., New York, NY 10016.

CAREER: Transportation Display, Inc., Winston Network, New York City, advertising media traffic manager, 1977-84; writer, 1984—.

MEMBER: International PEN.

AWARDS, HONORS: Received "outstanding writer" citation from Pushcart Press, 1978, for the story "Columbus Discovering America"; Oscar Cintas fiction writing grant, 1978-79; Bread Loaf Writers Conference scholarship, 1980; fiction writing grant from Creative Artists Programs Service, 1982, and from Ingram Merrill Foundation, 1983; Fellowship for Creative Writers award from National Endowment for the Arts, and American Academy in Rome Fellowship in Literature from American Academy and Institute of Arts and Letters, both 1985, both for *Our House in the Last World;* National Book Award nomination, National Book Critics Circle Prize nomination and Pulitzer Prize for fiction, all 1990, all for *The Mambo Kings Play Songs of Love.*

WRITINGS:

NOVELS

Our House in the Last World, Persea Books (New York City), 1983.
The Mambo Kings Play Songs of Love, Farrar, Straus (New York City), 1989.

The Fourteen Sisters of Emilio Montez O'Brien, Farrar, Straus, 1993.

Mr. Ives' Christmas, HarperCollins (New York City), 1995.

Work represented in anthology *Best of Pushcart Press III,* Pushcart, 1978.

ADAPTATIONS: The Mambo Kings Play Songs of Love was filmed in 1992.

SIDELIGHTS: Award-winning novelist Oscar Hijuelos turns the characters and experiences of his Cuban-American heritage into fictional works that have won both critical and popular praise. As Marie Arana-Ward explains in the *Washington Post Book World,* "once in a great while a novelist emerges who is remarkable not for the particulars of his prose but for the breadth of his soul, the depth of his humanity, and for the precision of his gauge on the rising sensibilities of his time. . . . Oscar Hijuelos is one of these."

Hijuelos explains to *CA* that his first novel, *Our House in the Last World,* "traces the lives of a Cuban family who came to the United States in the 1940s and follows them to the death of the father and subsequent near collapse of the family. In many ways a realistic novel, *Our House in the Last World* also reflects certain Latin attributes that are usually termed 'surreal' or 'magical.' Although I am quite Americanized, my book focuses on many of my feelings about identity and my 'Cubanness.' I intended for my book to commemorate at least a few aspects of the Cuban psyche (as I know it)."

Reviewing *Our House in the Last World* for the *New York Times Book Review,* Edith Milton affirms that Hijuelos is concerned "with questions of identity and perspective," especially those concerning family. Hijuelos is "especially eloquent," lauds *Cleveland Plain Dealer* critic Bob Halliday, "in describing the emotional storms" that transform the Santinio family of his novel as they "try to assimilate the rough realities of Spanish Harlem in terms of the values and personal identities they have inherited from their homeland." There is a "central tension," Milton explains, between the "lost, misremembered Eden [Cuba]" and the increasing squalor of the family's new life in their "last world"—New York. "Opportunity seems pure luck" to these well-intentioned immigrants, observes *Chicago Tribune Book World* reviewer Pat Aufderheide, and, in the absence of hope, each ultimately succumbs to the pressures that "work against the [American] dream of upward mobility." Hijuelos' "elegantly accessible style," Aufderheide states, "combines innocence and insight" in creating the individual voices of his characters. Beyond that, notes the reviewer, there is a "feel for the way fear . . . pervades" the Santinios' lives. The characters and the "sheer energy" of the narrative are the book's strengths, Milton

concludes, adding that Hijuelos "never loses the syntax of magic, which transforms even the unspeakable into a sort of beauty." Critic Roy Hoffman in the *Philadelphia Inquirer* calls *Our House in the Last World* a "vibrant, bitter and successful" story and compares Hijuelos to an "urban poet" who creates a "colorful clarity of life." Halliday likewise deems the book to be a "wonderfully vivid and compassionate" first novel.

But it was Hijuelos' Pulitzer Prize-winning second novel, *The Mambo Kings Play Songs of Love,* that moved him to the first rank of American novelists. Telling the story of two brothers, Cesar and Nestor Castillo, who leave their native Cuba and make careers as singers in the Spanish Harlem of the 1950s, the novel traces their rise to an appearance on *The I Love Lucy Show* before fading away from public attention again, like the mambo dance their band played.

The Mambo Kings, Cathleen McGuigan explains in *Newsweek,* "isn't conventionally plotted; it slides back and forth in time and meanders into dreams and fantasies." The novel is comprised of the dreams and fantasies of Cesar Castillo at the end of his career when he lives in a run-down hotel called the Splendour and drinks away his days. McGuigan notes that Cesar "is a classic portrait of machismo: he's in closest touch with his feelings when they originate below the waist." But she acknowledges that "Hijuelos has a tender touch with his characters, and Cesar is more than a stereotype." Despite the novel's flaws, McGuigan finds *The Mambo Kings Play Songs of Love* to be a "vibrant tragicomic novel." Joseph Coates of *Tribune Books* finds echoes of magical realism in the novel and feels that it "achieves the long backward look" of novels such as *One Hundred Years of Solitude,* "dealing as fully with the old worlds the migrants left as with the new ones they find." Writing in the *Washington Post Book World,* novelist Bob Shacochis also remarks upon Hijuelos' skilled contrasts between Cuban and American life, observing that "his *cu-bop* music scene gathers credibility as a grand metaphor for the splitting of a national family that took place [with the Cuban revolution] in 1959." Finally, Margo Jefferson of *the New York Times Book Review* observes that Hijuelos alternates "crisp narrative with opulent musings," achieving a "music of the heart."

Hijuelos' 1993 novel, *The Fourteen Sisters of Emilio Montez O'Brien,* takes a very different tack from its predecessor. Whereas *The Mambo Kings Play Songs of Love* is told by one male narrator, *The Fourteen Sisters of Emilio Montez O'Brien* is told from a number of female viewpoints and spans several generations in the life of a Cuban-Irish family in Pennsylvania. Writing in *Time,* Janice E. Simpson praises the novel's warmth, suggesting that reading it "is like leafing through the pages of a treasured family album," but laments that "the fate of the sisters is determined and defined by their relationships with men." Jane Mendelsohn, writing in the *London Review of Books,* generally admires the way Hijuelos characterizes his female characters, observing that "the novel skillfully chronicles the lives" of all the sisters and that Margarita, in particular, is an embodiment of the "women's movement . . . in the 20th century." At the same time, Mendelsohn faults the novel for its sentimentality and concluded that there is "nothing of the glorious flame which set *The Mambo Kings* on fire." Nick Hornby of the *Times Literary Supplement* calls the novel "at all times readable and diverting" but finds that its many characters bog down its pacing. Even so, Arana-Ward praises the story for its celebration of "human diversity and its promise of vitality," and for its compelling characters, who "hold us captive until the very last page of this generous novel."

BIOGRAPHICAL/CRITICAL SOURCES:

BOOKS

Contemporary Literary Criticism, Gale (Detroit), Volume 65, 1990.
Dictionary of Literary Biography, Volume 145: *Modern Latin-American Fiction Writers, Second Series,* Gale, 1994.

PERIODICALS

Americas Review, Volume 22, number 1-2, pp. 274-276.
Bloomsbury Review, May, 1990, p. 5.
Boston Globe, November 18, 1990, p. 21.
Chicago Tribune, August 9, 1990, p. 1; January 3, 1993; May 30, 1993, Section 6, p. 5.
Chicago Tribune Book World, July 17, 1983.
Cleveland Plain Dealer, July 17, 1983.
Cosmopolitan, March, 1993, p. 16.
Entertainment Weekly, March 19, 1993, p. 57.
Insight on the News, October 23, 1989, p. 56.
London Review of Books, September 23, 1993, p. 23.
Los Angeles Times, April 16, 1990, p. 1.
Los Angeles Times Book Review, September 3, 1989, p. 1; March 14, 1993, pp. 3, 8.
Los Angeles Times Magazine, April 18, 1993, pp. 22-28, 54.
New Republic, March 22, 1993, pp. 38-41.
New York, March 1, 1993, p. 46.
New Yorker, March 29, 1993, p. 107; August 21, 1995, pp. 126-127.
New York Times, September 11, 1989, p. C17; April 1, 1993, p. C17.
New York Times Book Review, May 15, 1983; August 27, 1989, pp. 1, 30; March 7, 1993, p. 6; December 3, 1995, p. 9.
Newsweek, August 21, 1989, p. 60.
Observer (London), July 25, 1993, p. 53.
People, April 5, 1993, p. 26.

Philadelphia Inquirer, July 17, 1983.
Publishers Weekly, July 21, 1989, pp. 42, 44.
New Republic, March 22, 1993, p. 38.
Time, August 14, 1989, p. 68; March 29, 1993, pp. 63, 65.
Times Literary Supplement, August 6, 1993, p. 19.
Tribune Books (Chicago), August 13, 1989, p. 6; January 3, 1993, p. 6.
Village Voice, May 1, 1990, p. 85.
Washington Post Book World, August 20, 1989; March 14, 1993, pp. 1, 10.
World Literature Today, winter, 1994, p. 127.

*   *   *

HILL, Donna (Marie)

PERSONAL: Born in Salt Lake City, UT; daughter of Clarence Henry (a U.S. Customs official) and Emma (Wirthlin) Hill. *Education:* Attended Phillips Gallery Art School, Washington, 1940-43; George Washington University, A.B., 1948; Columbia University, M.L.S., 1952. *Religion:* Church of Jesus Christ of Latter-day Saints. *Avocational interests:* Travel, playing the recorder, opera, theater, reading, swimming.

ADDRESSES: Agent—Kidde, Hoyt & Picard, c/o 530 East 23rd St., Apt. 6B, New York, NY 10010.

CAREER: U.S. Department of State, Washington, DC, code clerk, 1944-49; U.S. Department of State, U.S. Embassy, Paris, France, code clerk, 1949-51; New York Public Library, New York City, librarian, 1952-59; City University of New York, New York City, City College Library, assistant to librarian, 1962-63, Hunter College Library, assistant to librarian, 1964-70, instructor, 1970-75, assistant professor, 1975-79, associate professor, 1980-84, named professor, professor emeritus, 1984—, head of Teachers Central Laboratory, 1974-84. Member of Professional Staff of Congress and of the Academy for the Humanities and Sciences. Painter, with work exhibited in several Paris shows, and in U.S. Information Services exhibition touring Europe, 1950-51.

MEMBER: American Recorder Society (national secretary, 1959-61), Women's National Book Association (chair of New York City chapter, 1991-93), Phi Beta Kappa, Kappa Delta, Pi Gamma Mu, Delta Kappa Gamma (president, Gamma Alpha Chapter, 1988-90).

AWARDS, HONORS: Maurice Fromkes painting scholarship to international workshop, Segovia, Spain, summer, 1953; Staten Island Writers Conference, weekly reader fellow, 1957; *New York Times Book Review* selection as one of "One Hundred Outstanding New Books for the Younger Reader," for *Not One More Day;* research fellowship to Huntington Library, summer, 1970; nomination for Colorado Children's Book Award, for *Ms. Glee Was Waiting;* City University of New York, Scholar Incentive Award, 1981-82; Alumni Association of Central High School, certificate of distinction, 1984; Lolabel Hall Award, 1988; Ruth Mack Havens Award, 1991.

WRITINGS:

(Self-illustrated) *Not One More Day* (juvenile), Viking (New York City), 1957.

(Illustrator) Janet Konkle, *The Sea Cart* (juvenile), Abingdon (Nashville, TN), 1961.

Catch a Brass Canary (novel), Lippincott (Philadelphia, PA), 1965.

(Editor with Doris de Montreville) *The Third Book of Junior Authors,* H. W. Wilson (Bronx, NY), 1972.

The Picture File: A Manual and Curriculum Related Subject Heading List, Shoe String (Hamden, CT), 1975, 2nd edition, 1978.

Joseph Smith: The First Mormon (adult), Doubleday (New York City), 1977.

Ms. Glee Was Waiting (juvenile; Junior Literary Guild selection), Atheneum (New York City), 1978.

Mr. Peeknuff's Tiny People (juvenile), Atheneum, 1981.

(Self-illustrated) *Eerie Animals: Seven Stories,* Atheneum, 1983.

First Your Penny (teen novel), Atheneum, 1985.

Murder Uptown, Carroll & Graf (New York City), 1992.

Contributor to books, including *More Stories to Dream On,* Houghton (Boston), 1993. Also contributor to periodicals, including *Delta Kappa Gamma Bulletin.* Editor-in-chief, *American Recorder,* 1962-63.

Some of Hill's works have been published in the Netherlands.

The "Donna Hill Collection," consisting of papers, manuscripts, diaries, letters, drafts, books, art, gallery proofs, and other pertinent material, was established at Marriott Library, University of Utah, 1994.

WORK IN PROGRESS: A teen novel about the U.S. Life Saving Service in 1880 entitled *Surfman!;* another teen novel, *Trouble Next Door;* a juvenile biography of Ida Lewis.

SIDELIGHTS: In a review of Donna Hill's *Joseph Smith: The First Mormon,* a biography of the founder of the Church of Jesus Christ of Latter-day Saints, a *New York Review of Books* critic writes: "What is special about this book is its balanced character. Though hedged by Hill's own allegiance, it does for Smith what Samuel Taylor's book on Brigham Young . . . did for one of his less complicated followers—puts the subject in a full, and fresh, perspective." Alden Whitman of the *New York Times* comments: "Conceding that Joseph Smith was perhaps a 'less-than-perfect man' and that he did indeed have plural wives, Miss Hill nevertheless accepts the divinity of his religious role. This rests on Smith's presumed visions, in which Jesus or God or an angel appeared to instruct him. . . . Joseph Smith was, in her view, an inspired prophet seeking to cope with the difficult problems of founding both a church and a churchly society in the midst of scoffers, ruffians and murderers. . . . Hill's book should be instructive to Mormons and to many others disposed to religious belief." John Seelye writes in the *New Republic* that Hill's "book is the most detailed study of Joseph Smith and the religion he founded yet to be published. . . . Her attitude is fair minded and her handling of the questions is tactful and balanced; though coming out generally on the side of Mormonism and Joseph Smith, she readily admits that prophets are only human, and are thereby subject to errors of the flesh, a truth which Smith himself voiced when he said: 'A prophet is only a prophet when he is acting as such.' "

Hill once told *CA:* "I started out in life expecting to be an artist, an author, and a great many other things as well, including inventor, detective, and puppeteer, but at about age twelve I began to concentrate on art and writing. Of course it is sad that every choice means the loss of something else, but in a way, as author, one can do and be anything one wishes.

"I suppose my pleasure in doing a variety of things is reflected in my writing, since I have done picture books for children, novels and short stories for teens, and fiction and nonfiction for adults. While I enjoy every aspect of writing, from research to rough drafts to rewriting and revising, I find it all very hard work.

"What I enjoy above all is writing fiction. I love imagining scenes and characters and hearing dialogue in my head. It is especially astonishing and gratifying when people I thought I had made up take on a life of their own, speak their own minds and evolve their own destinies. I feel very close to the people I write about, whether real, such as Joseph Smith, or fictional. After I have lived with characters for a year or sometimes for several years (and with Joseph Smith for more than eight years), they become as substantial to me as my associates and neighbors, sometimes more so, because I usually know more about them.

"I like to read books of every sort, novels, history, biographies, how-to, and I still dearly love good children's books. I do not like jokes, slapstick, or (with some notable exceptions) comedians, but I love wit, especially when it is spontaneous, or when, through the art and sensitivity of the writer, it is made to seem so. My favorite authors are ones that bring joy and raise the spirits through a delicious sense of life's absurdities."

BIOGRAPHICAL/CRITICAL SOURCES:

PERIODICALS

American Historical Review, April, 1978.
Angelos of Kappa Delta, May, 1957; March, 1965; fall, 1985.
Art d'Aujourd'hui, October, 1950.
Best Sellers, October, 1985.
Chicago Tribune, April 4, 1977.
Civil War History, June, 1978.
Day Care: The Magazine of the Child Growth-Movement, fall, 1978.
Interracial Books for Children Bulletin, Volume 17, number 2, 1986.
Look, August 29, 1950.
Los Angeles Times, April 23, 1977.
New Republic, May 7, 1977.
New York Review of Books, April 14, 1977.
New York Times, April 9, 1977.
New York Times Book Review, January 10, 1965; April 30, 1978.
Parents Choice, September/October, 1978.
PSCcuny Clarion, November, 1981.
Reading Teacher, October, 1979.

*　　　*　　　*

HILL, M(elba) Anne 1953-

PERSONAL: American citizen born abroad; born September 30, 1953, in Osaka, Japan; daughter of William (an engineer) and Kathleen (a lawyer; maiden name, Jordan) Hill; married Edward Vermont Blanchard (an investment banker), February 28, 1976; children: Lydia Hill, Catherine Anne, Cordelia Jordan. *Education:* University of Chicago, B.A., 1974; Duke University, M.A., 1977, Ph.D., 1980.

ADDRESSES: Home—1158 Fifth Ave., #11C, New York, NY 10029. *Office*—Department of Economics, 300B Powdermaker Hall, Queens College of the City University of New York, Flushing, NY 11367.

CAREER: National Bureau of Economic Research, Cambridge, MA, research assistant, 1974-75; Research Triangle Institute, Research Triangle Park, NC, economist, 1975-76, economic consultant, 1976-77; Duke University, Durham, NC, lecturer in mathematical economics, 1977-78; Yale University, New Haven, CT, postdoctoral fellow at Economic Growth Center, 1979-81, lecturer in economics, 1980; Rutgers University, New Brunswick, NJ, assistant professor of economics, 1981-89, fellow of Rutgers College, 1982—, member of Institute for Health Care Policy and Aging Research, member of Council for Asian Economic Research, 1985—, chairperson of Labor

and Human Resources Workshop, 1985-87; Queens College of the City University of New York, Flushing, NY, associate professor, 1989-92, professor of economics 1993—, acting chairperson of department, 1994-95. Baruch College of the City University of New York, senior research associate, 1988—, visiting assistant professor, 1988-89; visiting research associate at Keio Economic Observatory, 1981. Consultant to Princeton Economic Research, Inc.

MEMBER: American Economic Association, Industrial Relations Research Association, Population Association of America, Econometric Society.

AWARDS, HONORS: Fellow of Japan Foundation, 1981; Rutgers University, Research Council summer fellowship, 1982, faculty academic study program, 1985; Henry Rutgers research fellowship, 1985-87; book award, President's Committee on Employment of the Handicapped, 1987, for *Disability and the Labor Market: Economic Problems, Programs, and Policies.*

WRITINGS:

(Editor with Monroe Berkowitz, and contributor) *Disability and the Labor Market: Economic Problems, Programs, and Policies,* ILR Press (Ithaca, NY), 1986.
(Editor with Mark Killingsworth) *Comparable Worth: Analyses and Evidence,* ILR Press, 1989.
(With Carol Harvey and Berkowitz) *Disability Counts,* New Jersey Demographics of Disability Survey, 1992.
(With June E. O'Neill) *Underclass Behaviors in the United States: Measurement and Analysis of Determinants,* Department of Health and Human Services, 1993.
(Editor with Elizabeth M. King) *Women's Education in Developing Countries: A Review of Barriers, Benefits, and Policy,* Johns Hopkins University Press (Baltimore, MD), 1993.

Contributor to books, including *Environmental Controls,* edited by Robert A. Leone, Lexington Books, 1976; and *Disability in the U.S.: A Review of National Data,* edited by Susan Thompson-Hoffman and Inez Fitzgerald Storck, Springer Publishing (New York City), 1991. Contributor of articles and reviews to economic journals, including *International Review of Comparative Public Policy, American Economic Review, Journal of Human Resources, Research in Labor Economics, Research in Asian Economics, Review of Economics and Statistics,* and *Southern Economic Journal.*

WORK IN PROGRESS: Research on effects of health and disability on work and earnings of men and women; research on determinants of underclass behaviors; research on the effectiveness of welfare-to-work programs.

HOOGENBOOM, Ari (Arthur) 1927-

PERSONAL: Born November 28, 1927, in Richmond Hill, NY; son of Ari (a carpenter) and Clara (Behn) Hoogenboom; married Olive Gwendoline Youngberg (an author), August 28, 1949; children: Lynn Cordelia, Ari Arthur, Jr., Jan Margaret. *Education:* Atlantic Union College, A.B., 1949; Columbia University, A.M., 1951, Ph.D., 1958. *Politics:* Democrat. *Religion:* Unitarian Universalist.

ADDRESSES: Home—1451 East 21st St., Brooklyn, NY 11210; and Heron Island, South Bristol, ME 04568. *Office*—Department of History, Brooklyn College of the City University of New York, Brooklyn, NY 11210.

CAREER: University of Texas, El Paso, instructor, 1956-57, assistant professor of history, 1957-58; Pennsylvania State University, University Park, instructor, 1958-60, assistant professor, 1960-62, associate professor, 1962-66, professor of history, 1966-68; Brooklyn College of the City University of New York, Brooklyn, NY, professor of history, 1968—, head of department, 1968-74. Visiting lecturer at University of Wisconsin—Milwaukee, summer, 1960; visiting associate professor at University of Oregon, summer, 1965; George Bancroft Professor of American History at University of Goettingen, Germany, 1991-92.

MEMBER: American Historical Association, Organization of American Historians, Pennsylvania Historical Association (secretary, 1960-65), New York Historical Society, Brooklyn Historical Society.

AWARDS, HONORS: Guggenheim fellowship, 1965-66; commendation from American Association for State and Local History, 1975; Fulbright Award, 1991-92.

WRITINGS:

Outlawing the Spoils: A History of the Civil Service Reform Movement, 1865-1883, University of Illinois Press (Champaign), 1961, reprint, Greenwood Press (Westport, CT), 1982.

(Editor) *Spoilsmen and Reformers,* Rand McNally (Chicago), 1964.

(With William S. Sachs) *The Enterprising Colonials: Society on the Eve of the Revolution,* Argonaut, 1965.

(Editor with wife, Olive Hoogenboom) *The Gilded Age,* Prentice-Hall (Englewood Cliffs, NJ), 1967.

(With Philip S. Klein) *A History of Pennsylvania,* McGraw (New York City), 1973, 2nd enlarged edition, Pennsylvania State University Press (University Park), 1980.

(Editor with O. Hoogenboom) *An Interdisciplinary Approach to American History,* two volumes, Prentice-Hall, 1973.

(With O. Hoogenboom) *A History of the I.C.C.: From Panacea to Palliative,* Norton (New York City), 1976.

(Editor with Abraham S. Eisenstadt and Hans L. Trefousse) *Before Watergate: Problems of Corruption in American Society,* Brooklyn College Press (Brooklyn, NY), 1978.

The Presidency of Rutherford B. Hayes, University Press of Kansas (Lawrence), 1988.

Rutherford B. Hayes: Warrior and President, University Press of Kansas, 1995.

Contributor to *Dictionary of American Biography, American National Biography,* and *Encyclopedia of American Political History.* Also contributor to periodicals, including *American Historical Review, Journal of American History, Historian,* and *Pennsylvania History.*

WORK IN PROGRESS: Gustavus Vasa Fox and the Union Navy, "a biography of Lincoln's assistant secretary of the Navy who was, in effect, his chief of naval operations."

SIDELIGHTS: Ari Hoogenboom told *CA:* "Reading the correspondence of someone like Rutherford B. Hayes is fascinating. It helps a biographer establish an intimacy with his subject that under normal conditions would be impossible. Indeed, when there is voluminous material available, a biographer (peering as it were through an open window) becomes better acquainted with the person he is writing about than were that person's friends. Before I become too enthralled by the voyeuristic aspect of my research, I force myself to write up my findings. My subsequent research is more focused and often leads me to revisions of what I have written.

"Since research is fun and writing is hard work, I mix the two as much as possible. As I get deeper into a writing project, however, distilling the material, making connections, and gaining insights makes writing a less onerous and more rewarding task. Because of the fulfillment they bring, research and writing have become my main interests in life. My work has become my hobby and my therapy. My happiness, equanimity—even my mental stability—depend on a steady diet of research and writing."

*　　*　　*

HOOPER, Walter (McGehee) 1931-

PERSONAL: Born March 27, 1931, in Reidsville, NC; son of Arch Boyd (an engineer) and Madge (Kemp) Hooper. *Education:* University of North Carolina, B.A., 1954, M.A., 1957; St. Stephen's House, Oxford, England, Diploma in Theology, 1964; Wadham College, Oxford, additional study, 1965.

ADDRESSES: Home and office—30 St. Bernard's Rd., Oxford 0X2 6EH, England. *Agent*—Curtis Brown Ltd., 162-168 Regent St., London W1R 5TB, England.

CAREER: Private secretary to C. S. Lewis, Oxford, England, 1963, literary advisor to the estate of C. S. Lewis, 1969—. University of Kentucky, Lexington, instructor in English literature, 1960-62. Oxford University, Oxford, chaplain of Wadham College, 1965-67, assistant chaplain of Jesus College, 1967-70; St. Mary Magdalen, assistant priest, 1970-88. *Military service:* U.S. Army, 1954-56.

MEMBER: Athenaeum Club (London).

WRITINGS:

(With Roger Lancelyn Green) *C. S. Lewis: A Biography,* Harcourt (San Diego, CA), 1974, revised edition, 1994.
Past Watchful Dragons, Macmillan (New York City), 1979.
Through Joy and Beyond: A Pictorial Biography of C. S. Lewis, Macmillan, 1982.

EDITOR OR COMPILER OF WORKS BY C. S. LEWIS

Poems, Bles, 1964, Harcourt, 1965.
Studies in Medieval and Renaissance Literature, Cambridge University Press (Cambridge, England), 1966.
Of Other Worlds: Essays and Stories, Bles, 1966, Harcourt, 1967.
Christian Reflections, Eerdmans (Grand Rapids, MI), 1967.
The Dark Tower and Other Stories, Collins (London), 1967, Harcourt, 1977.
Narrative Poems, Bles, 1969, Harcourt, 1972.
Selected Literary Essays, Cambridge University Press, 1969.
God in the Dock: Essays on Theology, Eerdmans, 1970, published in England as *Undeceptions,* Bles, 1971.
Fern-Seed and Elephants, Collins, 1975.
They Stand Together: The Letters of C. S. Lewis to Arthur Greeves, 1914-1963, Macmillan, 1979.
The Weight of Glory, revised edition (Hooper was not associated with earlier editions), Macmillan, 1980.
Mere Christianity: An Anniversary Edition, Macmillan, 1981.
Of This and Other Worlds, Collins, 1982, published as *On Stories,* Harcourt, 1982.
The Business of Heaven: Daily Readings from C. S. Lewis, Harcourt, 1984.
Spirits in Bondage: A Cycle of Lyrics, Harcourt, 1984.
Boxen: The Imaginary World of the Young C. S. Lewis, Harcourt, 1985.
First and Second Things, Collins, 1985.
Present Concerns, Collins, 1986, Harcourt, 1987.
Timeless at Heart, Collins, 1987.

Letters of C. S. Lewis, revised and enlarged edition (Hooper was not associated with the first edition), Collins, 1988.
Christian Reunion and Other Essays, Collins, 1990.
All My Roads before Me: The Diary of C. S. Lewis, 1922-1927, HarperCollins (New York City), 1991.
Daily Readings with C. S. Lewis, HarperCollins, 1992.
Collected Poems, HarperCollins, 1994.

OTHER

Contributor to books, including *Light on C. S. Lewis,* Bles, 1965, Harcourt, 1966; *Imagination and the Spirit,* edited by C. A. Huttar, Eerdmans, 1971; *The Longing for a Form,* edited by P. J. Schakel, Kent State University Press (Kent, OH), 1977; and *Essays on C. S. Lewis and George MacDonald,* edited by Cynthia Marshall, Edwin Mellen (Lewiston, NY), 1991. Creator (with A. F. Marchington) of *Through Joy and Beyond,* (film script for three-part documentary about C. S. Lewis), Lord and King Associates (Chicago, IL), 1978.

WORK IN PROGRESS: A Handbook to C. S. Lewis, for HarperCollins.

BIOGRAPHICAL/CRITICAL SOURCES:

PERIODICALS

Christian Century, November 20, 1991.
Library Journal, July, 1991.
National Review, December 2, 1991.
Publishers Weekly, May 24, 1991.

*   *   *

HOROWITZ, Irving Louis   1929-

PERSONAL: Born September 25, 1929, in New York, NY; son of Louis and Esther (Tepper) Horowitz; married Ruth Lenore Narowlansky, 1950 (divorced, 1963); married Mary Ellen Curtis, 1979; children: (first marriage) Carl Frederick, David Dennis. *Education:* College of the City of New York (now City College of the City University of New York), B.S.S., 1951; Columbia University, M.A., 1952; University of Buenos Aires, Ph.D., 1957; Brandeis University, postdoctoral fellow, 1958-59.

ADDRESSES: Home—Blawenburg-Rocky Hill Rd., 1247 State Rd., Route 206, Princeton, NJ 08540. *Office*—Rutgers University, Department of Sociology, Lucy Stone Hall, P.O. Box 5072, New Brunswick, NJ 08903; Transaction Publishers, Building 4051, Kilmer Campus, New Brunswick, NJ 08903.

CAREER: College of the City of New York, graduate assistant, 1952; University of Buenos Aires, Buenos Aires, Argentina, assistant professor of social theory, 1956-58;

Bard College, Annandale-on-Hudson, NY, assistant professor of sociology, 1959-60; Hobart and William Smith Colleges, Geneva, NY, assistant professor of sociology and chair of department of sociology and anthropology, 1960-63; Washington University, St. Louis, MO, associate professor, 1963-65, professor of sociology, 1965-69; Rutgers University, New Brunswick, NJ, graduate professor of sociology and chair of department of sociology at Livingston College, 1969-73, chair of sociology section for all campuses, 1975-85, Hannah Arendt Professor of sociology and political science, 1979—. Visiting professor at Central University of Venezuela, Caracas, 1957, State University of New York at Buffalo, 1960, University of Buenos Aires, 1961, 1963, Syracuse University, 1961, University of Rochester, 1962, University of California, Davis, 1966, University of Wisconsin, Madison, 1967, Stanford University, 1968-69, University of Calgary, 1970, American University, 1972, Queen's University, 1973, Princeton University, 1976, Boston College, 1976, University of Mexico, 1978, Tokyo University, 1980, and Hosei University, 1980; visiting lecturer at London School of Economics and Political Science, University of London, 1962; Fulbright-Hays lecturer in Argentina, 1961, in Israel, 1969, and in India, 1977. Advisory staff member, Latin American Research Center, 1964-67, 1967-70. Consultant to International Education Division, Ford Foundation, 1959-60; member of advisory board, Institute for Scientific Information, Inc., 1969-73. Consulting editor, Oxford University Press, 1964-69, and Aldine-Atherton Publishers, 1969-72. Founding president of Transaction/ SOCIETY. External board member of Radio Marti and Television Marti programs of U.S. Information Agency, 1985—. Chair of board of Hubert Humphrey Center, Ben Gurion University, 1990-92. Has served as external board member of methodology section of research division of U.S. General Accounting Office.

MEMBER: Council of Foreign Relations, Carnegie Council, American Association of Publishers, American Political Science Association, American Association for the Advancement of Science (fellow, 1983-87), New York State Sociological Society (president, 1961-62).

AWARDS, HONORS: Special citation, Carnegie Endowment for International Peace, 1957, for *Idea of War and Peace in Contemporary Philosophy;* Man of the Year in Behavioral Science, *Time,* 1970; Centennial Medallion, St. Peters College, 1971, for outstanding contribution to a humanistic social science; presidential outstanding achievement award, Rutgers University, 1985; National Jewish Book Award, Jewish Book Council, 1991, for *Daydreams and Nightmares: Reflections on a Harlem Childhood.*

WRITINGS:

Claude Helvetius: Philosopher of Democracy and Enlightenment, Paine-Whitman (New York City), 1955.

Idea of War and Peace in Contemporary Philosophy, Paine-Whitman, 1957, 2nd edition, Humanities, 1973.

Philosophy, Science and the Sociology of Knowledge, C. C. Thomas (Springfield, IL), 1960, revised edition, Greenwood, 1978.

Radicalism and the Revolt against Reason: The Social Theories of Georges Sorel, Humanities, 1961, revised edition, Southern Illinois University Press (Carbondale, IL), 1968.

The War Game: Studies of the New Civilian Militarists, Ballantine (New York City), 1963.

Historia y elementos de la sociologia del conocimiento, University of Buenos Aires Press (Buenos Aires, Argentina), 1963.

Revolution in Brazil: Politics and Society in a Developing Nation, Dutton (New York City), 1964.

Three Worlds of Development: The Theory and Practice of International Stratification, Oxford University Press (New York City), 1966, revised edition, 1972.

Professing Sociology: The Life Cycle of a Social Science, Aldine (Chicago, IL), 1968, revised edition, Southern Illinois University Press, 1972.

The Struggle Is the Message: The Organization and Ideology of the Anti-War Movement, Boyd and Fraser (Berkeley, CA), 1970.

(With William H. Friedland) *The Knowledge Factory: Student Activism and American Crisis,* Aldine, 1970, revised edition, Southern Illinois University Press, 1974.

Foundations of Political Sociology, Harper (New York City), 1972.

Israeli Ecstasies and Jewish Agonies, Oxford University Press, 1974.

(With James Everett Katz) *Social Science and Public Policy in the United States,* Praeger (New York City), 1975.

Taking Lives: Genocide and State Power, Transaction (New Brunswick, NJ), 1976, 3rd revised edition, 1980.

Ideology and Utopia in the United States, 1956-1976, Oxford University Press, 1977.

(With Seymour Martin Lipset) *Dialogues on American Politics,* Oxford University Press, 1978.

Beyond Empire and Revolution: Militarization and Consolidation in the Third World, Oxford University Press, 1982.

C. Wright Mills: An American Utopian, Free Press/ Macmillan (New York City), 1983.

Winners and Losers: Social and Political Polarities in America, Duke University Press (Durham, NC), 1984.

Communicating Ideas: The Crisis of Publishing in a Post-Industrial Society, Oxford University Press, 1986, expanded edition published as *Communicating Ideas: The Politics of Scholarly Publishing,* Transaction, 1991.

Persuasions and Prejudices: An Informal Compendium of Modern Social Science, 1953-1988, Transaction, 1989.

Daydreams and Nightmares: Reflections on a Harlem Childhood, University Press of Mississippi (Jackson, MS), 1990.

The Conscience of Worms and the Cowardice of Lions: Cuban Politics and Culture in an American Context, University of Miami North-South Center (Coral Gables, FL), 1993.

The Decomposition of Sociology, Oxford University Press, 1993.

EDITOR

Conference on Conflict, Consensus and Cooperation, Hobart and William Smith Colleges, 1962.

The New Sociology: Essays in Social Science and Social Values in Honor of C. Wright Mills, Oxford University Press, 1964.

The Anarchists, Dell, 1964.

The Rise and Fall of Project Camelot, M.I.T. Press, 1967, revised edition, 1974.

(And author of introduction) *Power, Politics and People: The Collected Papers of C. Wright Mills,* Oxford University Press, 1968.

(With John Gerassi and Josue deCastro) *Latin American Radicalism: A Documentary Report on Left and Nationalist Movements,* Random House, 1969.

Sociological Self-Images: A Collective Portrait, Pergamon, 1969.

Cuban Communism, Aldine, 1970, 8th edition, Transaction, 1994.

Masses in Latin America, Oxford University Press, 1970.

(With others) *Sociological Realities: A Guide to the Study of Sociology,* Harper, 1971, 2nd edition published as *Sociological Realities II: A Guide to the Study of Society,* Van Nostrand, 1975.

The Troubled Conscience, Center for the Study of Democratic Institutions, 1971.

The Use and Abuse of Social Science, Dutton, 1971, 2nd edition, 1975.

Equity, Income, and Policy: Comparative Studies in Three Worlds of Development, Praeger, 1977.

Science, Sin and Scholarship: The Politics of Reverend Moon and the Unification Church, M.I.T. Press, 1978.

(With John C. Leggett and Martin Oppenheimer) *The American Working Class: Prospects for the 1980s,* Transaction, 1979.

(And author of introduction) *Constructing Policy: Dialogues with Social Scientists in the National Political Arena,* Praeger, 1979.

(With H. S. Thayer) *Ethics, Science and Democracy: The Philosophy of Abraham Edel,* Transaction, 1987.

Member of editorial board, *Sociological Abstracts,* 1962-73, *Transaction/SOCIETY,* 1963—, *Indian Sociological Bulletin,* 1963-69, *Studies in Comparative International Development,* 1964-79, *International Studies Quarterly,* 1966-70, *Journal of Conflict Resolution,* 1966-72, *Social Theory and Practice,* 1970-75, *Indian Journal of Sociology,* 1971-75, *Social Praxis,* 1973-77, *Social Indicators,* 1973-79, *Journal of Jazz Studies,* 1973-82, *Journal of Political and Military Sociology,* 1973-89, *Civil Liberties Review,* 1976-79, *Journal of Contemporary Jewry,* 1976-81, *Third World Review,* 1976-83, *Policy Studies Review Annual,* 1976-85, *Journal of Symbolic Interaction,* 1977-80, *Journal of Interamerican Studies and World Affairs,* 1980—, *Orbis,* 1985—, *Academic Questions,* 1988—, *North-South,* 1994—.

SIDELIGHTS: Irving Louis Horowitz is a social scientist, editor, publisher, and writer who, through his books, has analyzed the political implications of forces as diverse as communism in Cuba, the changing landscape of publishing technology, the Reverend Sun Myung Moon of the Unification Church, and the work of American sociologist C. Wright Mills. Described as a "neo-conservative and a 'left' academic" by Jeff Greenfield in the *New York Times Book Review,* the New York-born Horowitz began his career at the University of Buenos Aires in Argentina and continued his international role in social theory through posts in Venezuela, India, and Tokyo. He received a special citation from the Carnegie Endowment for International Peace in 1957 for his first book, *Idea of War and Peace in Contemporary Philosophy.*

Writing in the *New York Review of Books,* Francine du Plessix Gray noted that the Horowitz-edited *Science, Sin, and Scholarship: The Politics of Reverend Moon and the Unification Church* warned of Moon's growing influence on American politics and scholarship. Gray described the book as a "carefully edited" work "documenting the persistence with which Moon has infiltrated powerful groups in America from the federal government to the universities."

Published in the same year was *Dialogues on American Politics,* a debate between coauthors Horowitz and Seymour Martin Lipset on polity, equality, presidency, and development. Faulting it for its "narrowly construed boundaries" and its tendency toward simplification, Jean

Bethke Elshtain, writing in the *Nation,* nevertheless found in it the "occasional insight or interesting tidbit." Greenfield described the discussions of polity and equality as "provocative" in the *New York Times Book Review,* while taking exception to the description of "post-Watergate Democratic Congressmen as adherents of the 'new politics.' "

In the *New York Times Book Review,* Steven Lukes lauded *C. Wright Mills: An American Utopian* as an "excellent book" for its illumination of the "complex interplay between man and image, creation and reception." Some argument surrounded Horowitz's portrayal of Mills, however—a portrayal which Dan Wakefield, writing in the *Nation,* characterized as having "shifted drastically" from the author's earlier assertion that Mills was "'the greatest sociologist the United States has ever produced.' " Although Robert Westbrook wished for a fuller biographical portrayal of Mills, he wrote in the *New Republic* that Horowitz did "effectively debunk the Mills myth."

In 1986, Horowitz's *Communicating Ideas: The Crisis of Publishing in a Post-Industrial Society* explored the future of publishing in an era of rapid technological advancement, raising issues both practical and ideological, including the consequences of the easy reproduction of documents and the potential political influence of a wider communication of knowledge. While Robert T. Golembiewski, writing in the *Times Literary Supplement,* questioned some of the book's underlying premises, he applauded Horowitz for failing to "pander to his audience with facile anti-technology talk." Joseph Gusfield described *Communicating Ideas* as an "intelligent book" in the *Los Angeles Times Book Review,* finding Horowitz "alive to the possibilities and barriers for academics to reach wider audiences and for lay-persons to utilize scholarship."

Horowitz received the National Jewish Book Award for his autobiography, *Daydreams and Nightmares: Reflections on a Harlem Childhood.* "Horowitz calls his work a 'sociological biography—in contrast to an intellectual or intimate biography,' " George Ritzer observed in *Contemporary Sociology,* and concluded that as such, the book succeeds in illuminating the relationships between race, ethnicity, age, religion, and social class. "The book is well written, and I think even readers raised elsewhere, in other social classes, and with other religious and ethnic backgrounds, will find it engaging," Ritzer remarked. A *Kirkus Reviews* critic bemoaned the "academic objectivity" which "frequently overrules experiential immediacy" in the book, and asserted that the "personal warmth that should be a part of any memoir is deliberately condensed and cooled." The reviewer pronounced the book "a unique, child's-eye view of Harlem in the 1930s, with surprisingly frank glimpses into a Jewish family life in that

context, but with many of the sharp edges reasoned away." *Social Forces* reviewer Raymond W. Mack, however, described *Daydreams and Nightmares* as "a hard-edged personal history. It is soft only at the core. The memoir is sentimental without being sentimentalized; it is touching without being treacly."

BIOGRAPHICAL/CRITICAL SOURCES:

PERIODICALS

America, May 4, 1974; April 16, 1977.
American Journal of Sociology, September, 1974; September, 1975.
American Political Science Review, June, 1974.
Choice, January, 1973; September, 1974; June, 1977.
Christian Century, March 20, 1974.
Chronicle of Higher Education, October 16, 1978, pp. 10-11.
Comparative Literature Studies, December, 1973.
Contemporary Sociology, January, 1991, pp. 10-12.
Jerusalem Post, March 4, 1991, p. 7.
Kirkus Reviews, April 1, 1990, pp. 480-81.
Los Angeles Times Book Review, December 14, 1986, p. 4.
Miami Herald, September 24, 1991, p. 13.
Motive, February, 1968.
Nation, March 3, 1969; March 24, 1979, pp. 310-312; September 15, 1984, pp. 212-213.
New Leader, April 28, 1969.
New Republic, March 26, 1984, pp. 40-42.
New York Review of Books, October 25, 1979, p. 8.
New York Times Book Review, February 25, 1979, p. 18; November 13, 1983, p. 11.
Political Science Quarterly, summer, 1977.
Progressive, April, 1974.
Saturday Review, June 7, 1969.
Social Forces, December, 1991, p. 524.
Time, January 5, 1970.
Times Literary Supplement, August 3, 1967; June 24, 1977; June 12, 1987, p. 646.
University Bookman, Volume 31, number 2, pp. 29-31.
Virginia Quarterly Review, spring, 1977.

*   *   *

HOUSTON, Douglas (Norman)   1947-

PERSONAL: Born March 18, 1947, in Cardiff, Wales; son of Norman Douglas (a sales executive) and Mary Elizabeth (a homemaker; maiden name, Batten) Houston; common law marriage to Sophy Carrington (an antiques dealer; separated, 1984); married Karen Mary Pearce (a painter and counselor), 1986; children: (first marriage) Samuel Summers, Alexander Gavin; (second marriage) Lloyd Robert, Manon Elizabeth, Eleanor Johnson (step-daughter). *Education:* University of Hull, B.A., English, 1969, Ph.D., 1985. *Politics:* "More-or-less Socialist." *Religion:* "More-or-less Christian." *Avocational interests:* Mountain walking, basic rock-climbing, flying control-line model aircraft.

ADDRESSES: "Brynheulog," Cwmbrwyno, Aberystwyth, Dyfed, Wales.

CAREER: Teacher at schools in Hull and London, England, 1969-72; Julian Hodge Ltd., Cardiff, Wales, credit controller, 1973-74; British Army of the Rhine, Duesseldorf, Germany, civilian chauffeur for liaison officer, 1975-77; freelance teacher of English, Duesseldorf, 1977-78; Oxford University Press, writer, consultant, 1979—; University of Wales, Aberystwyth, part-time tutor, 1979—; manager of prints/greetings cards business based on work by wife Karen Pearce, 1979—. Aberystwyth Arts Center, organizer, with Clive Meachen, of "Verbals" poetry readings, 1990—.

MEMBER: Welsh Academy, elected member, 1987—; Welsh Union of Writers.

AWARDS, HONORS: Welsh Arts Council, poetry prize, 1987, for *With the Offal Eaters;* Arts Council of Wales, enabling grant, 1988, writer's bursary, 1990-91.

WRITINGS:

(Contributor) Dunn, Douglas, editor, *A Rumoured City: New Poets from Hull,* Bloodaxe (Newcastle, England), 1982.
With the Offal Eaters, Bloodaxe, 1986.
Myths of Place: Landscape in the Poetries of W. H. Auden and Seamus Heaney, University of Hull (Hull, England), 1986.
(Contributor) Stephens, Meic, editor, *The Bright Field: Contemporary Poetry from Wales,* Carcanet Press (Manchester), 1991.
The Hunters in the Snow, Bloodaxe, 1994.

Also reviewer of poetry to periodicals including *Poetry Review, Times Literary Supplement, Poetry Wales,* and *International Review of Children's Literature.*

SIDELIGHTS: Douglas Houston told *CA:* "I have been writing poetry more or less in earnest since I was about eighteen, though none of my published work was written before 1978, when I began to achieve some competence in the techniques and disciplines of verse. While much of my work is 'free,' the traditions of rhyme and metre are very important to me as rich sources of the musicality that is the defining characteristic of poetry. I increasingly seek to combine comparatively plain language with highly wrought forms and hope to produce a poetry of emotional power and authenticity that has some bearing on social or cultural common experience. I am also fond of bizarrely

imaginative effects, especially when they succeed in being amusing.

"The status and functions of poetry are problematic to me, largely because of the vexed question of who reads it and why. My reluctance to produce a cultural style accessory for the novel-reading classes can seem like the best excuse I've got for not making the considerable and ludicrously underpaid effort that's needed to finish a poem. I can't define here the more absolute value of poetry, but it's deeply central to my experience and I know it [and] I feel it when I've done it."

BIOGRAPHICAL/CRITICAL SOURCES:

PERIODICALS

New Statesman, September, 1986.
Observer (London), October 5, 1986.
Times (London), February 26, 1995.

*   *   *

HOWE, Irving   1920-1993

PERSONAL: Born June 11, 1920, in New York, NY; died of complications following a stroke, May 5, 1993, in New York, NY; son of David and Nettie (Goldman) Howe; married Arien Hausknecht; married Ilana Wiener; children: Nina, Nicholas. *Education:* City College of New York (now City College of the City University of New York), B.Sc., 1940; Brooklyn College (now Brooklyn College of the City University of New York), graduate study. *Politics:* Socialist.

ADDRESSES: Office—English Programs, Graduate Center, City University of New York, 33 West 42nd St., New York, NY 10036.

CAREER: Brandeis University, Waltham, MA, 1953-61, began as associate professor, became professor of English; Stanford University, Stanford, CA, professor of English, 1961-63; Hunter College of the City University of New York, New York City, professor of English, 1963-70, distinguished professor, 1970-86, distinguished professor emeritus, 1986-93. Visiting professor, University of Vermont and University of Washington; Christian Gauss Seminar Chair Professor, Princeton University, 1953. *Military service:* U.S. Army, 1942-45.

MEMBER: Modern Language Association of America.

AWARDS, HONORS: Indiana University, School of Letters, fellow; Longview Foundation prize for literary criticism; *Kenyon Review* fellow, 1953; Bollingen Award, 1959-60; National Institute of Arts and Letters award, 1960; Guggenheim fellow, 1964-65, 1971; Jewish Heritage Award, 1975, for excellence in literature; Brandeis University Creative Arts Award, 1975-76; National Book Award, 1976, for *World of Our Fathers: The Journey of the Eastern European Jews to America and the Life They Found and Made.*

WRITINGS:

LITERARY CRITICISM

Sherwood Anderson: A Critical Biography, Sloane, 1951.

William Faulkner: A Critical Study, Random House (New York City), 1952, 4th edition, Ivan R. Dee (Chicago), 1991.

Politics and the Novel, Horizon Press (New York City), 1957, with new epilogue, New American Library (New York City), 1987, with new preface, Columbia University Press (New York City), 1992.

A World More Attractive: A View of Modern Literature and Politics, Horizon Press, 1963.

Thomas Hardy: A Critical Study, Macmillan (New York City), 1967.

Decline of the New, Harcourt (New York City), 1970.

The Critical Point: On Literature and Culture, Horizon Press, 1973.

Celebrations and Attacks: Thirty Years of Literary and Cultural Commentary, Horizon Press, 1978.

A Critic's Notebook: Essays, edited by Nicolas Howe, Harcourt, 1994.

EDITOR

Leo Baeck, *The Essence of Judaism,* Schocken (New York City), 1948.

Modern Literary Criticism: An Anthology, Beacon Press (Boston), 1958.

Edith Wharton, *The House of Mirth,* Holt (New York City), 1962.

Edith Wharton: A Collection of Critical Essays, Prentice-Hall (Englewood Cliffs, NJ), 1962.

George Gissing, *New Grub Street,* Houghton (Boston), 1962.

George Orwell, *Nineteen Eighty-Four: Text, Sources, Criticism,* Harcourt, 1963.

Leon Trotsky, *Basic Writings,* Random House, 1963.

(And author of introduction) *The Radical Papers,* Doubleday (New York City), 1966.

Isaac Bashevis Singer, *Selected Short Stories,* Modern Library (New York City), 1966.

Thomas Hardy, *Selected Writings: Stories, Poems, and Essays,* Fawcett (New York City), 1966.

The Radical Imagination: An Anthology from Dissent Magazine, New American Library, 1967.

Student Activism, Bobbs Merrill (Indianapolis), 1967.

Literary Modernism, Fawcett, 1967.

The Idea of the Modern in Literature and the Arts, Horizon Press, 1968.

Classics of Modern Fiction: Eight Short Novels, Harcourt, 1968, 3rd edition published as *Classics of Modern Fiction: Ten Short Novels,* 1980, 5th edition (with S. Welch), 1993.

(With Jeremy Larnier) *Poverty: Views from the Left,* Morrow (New York City), 1968.

A Dissenter's Guide to Foreign Policy, Praeger (New York City), 1968.

Beyond the New Left: A Confrontation and Critique, McCall, 1970.

Essential Works of Socialism, Holt, 1970 (published in England as *A Handbook of Socialist Thought,* Gollancz (London), 1972).

The Literature of America: Nineteenth Century, McGraw (New York City), 1970.

(With Carl Gershman) *Israel, the Arabs, and the Middle East,* Quadrangle Books, 1972.

(With Michael Harrington) *The Seventies: Problems and Proposals,* Harper (New York City), 1972.

The World of the Blue-Collar Worker, Times Books (New York City), 1973.

Saul Bellow, *Herzog,* Viking, 1976.

Jewish-American Stories, New American Library, 1977.

Fiction as Experience: An Anthology, Harcourt, 1978.

(With others) *Literature as Experience: An Anthology,* Harcourt, 1979.

(With Ruth Wisse) *The Best of Sholom Aleichem,* Simon & Schuster (New York City), 1980.

The Portable Kipling, Viking, 1982, published as *The Portable Rudyard Kipling,* Penguin (New York City), 1982.

(With wife, Ilana W. Howe) *Short Shorts: An Anthology of the Shortest Stories,* David Godine (Boston), 1982.

"1984" Revisited: Totalitarianism in Our Century, Harper, 1983.

Alternatives: Proposals for America from the Democratic Left, Pantheon (New York City), 1984.

(With Wisse and Khone Shmeruk) *The Penguin Book of Modern Yiddish Verse,* Viking, 1987.

EDITOR WITH ELIEZER GREENBERG

A Treasury of Yiddish Stories, Viking, 1954, revised edition, Viking, 1989.

A Treasury of Yiddish Poetry, Holt, 1969.

Voices from the Yiddish: Essays, Memoirs, Diaries, University of Michigan Press (Ann Arbor), 1972.

Yiddish Stories Old and New, Holiday House (New York City), 1974.

Ashes Out of Hope: Fiction by Soviet-Yiddish Writers, Schocken, 1978.

OTHER

The U.A.W. and Walter Reuther, Random House, 1949.

(With Lewis Coser) *The American Communist Party: A Critical History, 1919-1957,* Beacon Press, 1957, reprinted, Da Capo Press (New York City), 1974.

Steady Work: Essays in the Politics of Democratic Radicalism, 1953-1966, Harcourt, 1966.

(Author of introduction) William O'Neill, editor, *Echoes of Revolt: The Masses, 1911-1917,* Quadrangle Books, 1967.

(Author of introduction) Henry James, *The American Scene,* Horizon Press, 1968.

(With Coser) *The New Conservatives: A Critique from the Left,* Quadrangle Books, 1968.

World of Our Fathers: The Journey of the Eastern European Jews to America and the Life They Found and Made, Harcourt, 1976 (published in England as *The Immigrant Jews of New York: 1881 to the Present,* Routledge, 1976).

Leon Trotsky, Viking, 1978.

(With Kenneth Libo) *How We Lived: A Documentary History of Immigrant Jews in America, 1880-1930,* Marek, 1979.

(Author of introduction) *Images of Labor,* Pilgrim Press (New York City), 1981.

A Margin of Hope: An Intellectual Autobiography, Harcourt, 1982.

Beyond the Welfare State, Schocken, 1982.

(With Libo) *We Lived There, Too: In Their Own Words and Pictures, Pioneer Jews and the Westward Movement of America,* St. Martin's, 1984.

Socialism and America, Harcourt, 1985.

The American Newness: Culture and Politics in the Age of Emerson, Harvard University Press, 1986.

(Contributor) Susan L. Braunstein and Jenna Weissman Joselit, editors, *Getting Comfortable in New York: The American Jewish Home, 1880-1950,* Jewish Museum (New York City), 1990.

Irving Howe: Selected Writings, 1950-1990, Harcourt, 1990.

Also author of *Favorite Jewish Stories,* 1992. Contributor to *Partisan Review, New Republic, New York Review of Books, Harper's, New York Times Book Review,* and other publications. Editor and co-founder, *Dissent,* 1953-93.

SIDELIGHTS: Irving Howe was known in a variety of roles. He was a distinguished literary critic; the editor of *Dissent,* an influential left-wing journal of opinion; an historian whose *World of Our Fathers: The Journey of Eastern European Jews to America and the Life They Found and Made* was a winner of the National Book Award and a bestseller; and a prominent spokesperson for the democratic socialist position in the United States. Julian Symons, writing in the *Times Literary Supplement,* defined Howe as "a man primarily involved throughout much of his adult life with politics who has retained a deep interest in literary creation."

Howe first joined the socialist movement as a teenager in 1934, following the faction led by Russian revolutionary leader Leon Trotsky. He wrote for the leftist newspaper *Labor Action* and participated in political debates on behalf of the Trotskyists and the Independent Socialist League. As he explained in *A Margin of Hope: An Intellectual Autobiography,* "Only radicalism seemed to offer the prospect of coherence, only radicalism could provide a unified view of the world."

With the advent of the Second World War, Howe's political activity was cut short. He was drafted into the United States army and for three years was stationed at a military base in Alaska. "Enforced isolation and steady reading together brought about a slow intellectual change . . . ," Howe wrote in *A Margin of Hope.* "I lost the singleness of mind that had inspired the politics of my youth." Howe turned to a less dogmatic socialist position which emphasized the necessity for democracy.

When the war ended Howe began to write for *Partisan Review, Commentary,* and other leftist political journals of the late 1940s. This led him in 1953 to co-found the magazine *Dissent,* a political and literary journal. "Despite its circulation of about 5,000," Peter Steinfels wrote in the *New York Times Book Review,* "*Dissent* ranks among the handful of political journals read most regularly by American intellectuals. And it is virtually alone in its explicit affirmation of democratic socialism."

Howe also wrote a number of books about American radicalism, including *The American Communist Party: A Critical History, 1919-1957* and *Socialism and America.* Howe's history of the American Communist Party, written with Lewis Coser, was the first complete party history to be published. Although several reviewers cite the authors' obvious prejudice against the party—Robert Claiborne of the *Nation* admitted that the "lively account is biased, as any book on the subject must be"—most observers found the work to be of great value. "The major merit of this new book," Michael Harrington stated in *Commonweal,* "is that it puts the question of the Communist Party into some kind of a historical and political perspective. . . . As history . . . this is a first-rate introduction to a stormy and important subject." Philip Green, writing in the *New Republic,* called it "a brilliant book, entertaining, lucid, and composed with real style. Though marred by occasional defects of historical method, it remains the most penetrating analysis of the subject matter that I have seen." Harry Schwartz of the *New York Times* concluded that "there is no other single volume of comparable merit and scope available."

Socialism and America is a related study in which Howe wrote the history of socialism in the United States, documenting its evolution from the heyday of Eugene Debs at the turn of the century to its present eclipse on the political scene. It is, wrote Nicholas Xenos of the *Nation,* "a history of defeat and decline." Howe cited the distinctive nature of American culture, with its strong belief in individualism, for the failure of socialism in the United States. His vision of socialism's future in America was a modest one: to be a moderating force in a capitalist society, curbing the system's worst excesses. Howe "has culled the voluminous scholarship available and summarized it with superb economy, maintaining a level of commentary that nearly always strikes a judicious balance between criticism of the errors and the shortcomings of the socialists of the past and a large-spirited allowance for the particular historical constraints under which they acted," Dennis Wrong stated in the *New Republic.*

In *Leon Trotsky,* Howe examined the life and thought of a major figure in the Russian Revolution. The book is, Howe stated in the introduction, a "political essay." As a one-time Trotskyist, Howe brought a unique perspective to his account, sympathetic to many of Trotsky's goals but critical of his methods. Trotsky and Vladimir Lenin were the primary leaders of the Russian Revolution of 1917 which brought the Communist Party to power. During the subsequent civil war Trotsky led the Red Army to ultimate victory, displaying great skill as a military tactician. The author of seventeen books of socialist theory and a spellbinding orator, Trotsky was "one of the two founding fathers of Soviet Russia, and one of the greatest political thinkers of the century," W. Warren Wagar maintained in the *Saturday Review.* "Trotsky," Webster Schott explained in the *Washington Post Book World,* "was much of the brains, most of the voice, and all of the arms of the revolution."

After the communists assumed control of Russia, it was Trotsky who "provided the ideological base for Lenin's exclusion of other parties from the ruling center," Schott wrote. By excluding from power other socialist parties, Trotsky and Lenin created the political framework for an all-encompassing dictatorship. "Trotsky," Wagar explained, "helped construct the Soviet state as a bureaucratized one-party dictatorship in which all dissent, and ultimately even his own, was crushed." In the struggle for power following Lenin's death, Trotsky lost to Joseph Stalin and was forced into exile. He was assassinated by a Soviet agent in Mexico in 1940.

Because of his struggle against Stalin and his forced exile, Trotsky's role in the Russian Revolution is not mentioned in official Soviet histories of the period. Trotsky's life "has been completely obliterated in Soviet historical works," Alexander Rabinowitch wrote in the *Nation.* Howe's ac-

count is one of the few scholarly works published to deal seriously with Trotsky's life and thought. "*Leon Trotsky* is the kind of work one expects from Irving Howe," Schott believed. "It is wise, beautifully written, and emotionally informed. . . . He gives us a man, a time, a condition." The critic for the *New York Review of Books* described the biography as "a tough-minded and fair introduction both to the life of Trotsky and to issues surrounding 'Trotskyism'." Jack Beatty of the *New Republic* believed that "what Howe has given us here is an admirably compact account of Trotsky's life as well as something far more urgent: he has subjected the political ideas of Trotsky to a discriminating historical and political criticism . . . from the social-democratic point of view. The result is a work full of the rarest sort of political wisdom."

Howe claimed that his long political involvement prepared him to write about his other great interest, modern literature. The socialist movement, Howe wrote in *A Margin of Hope,* "taught us to grasp the structure of an argument . . . to speak and think, and to value discipline of mind." Symons believed that "it was a training that prepared the young Howe . . . for entry into the literary world as critic and social commentator." In his role as critic, Howe approached literature as a social phenomenon. He insisted, Robert Towers explained in the *New Republic,* "upon the rootedness of literature in history, society, and psychology, upon its connection with ideas and the use that has been made of them." Howe was also, Towers wrote, a critic who refused "to insulate his literary concerns from his social and political commitments."

In the late 1940s Howe began to contribute essays and book reviews to journals, becoming one of the New York Jewish intelligensia. Howe made, James Atlas wrote in the *New York Times Book Review,* "the familiar pilgrimage through an American literary vocation, making all the stops: He contributed to *Partisan Review,* became a book reviewer for *Time,* wrote ambitious literary essays, eventually got a teaching job at Brandeis, edited *Dissent,* and is now a professor at the City University of New York." Howe wrote studies of Sherwood Anderson, William Faulkner, and Thomas Hardy, several collections of essays, and the study *Politics and the Novel.*

A continuing concern in Howe's literary criticism was the conflict between modernist literature, with its conservative and even reactionary basis, and his own leftist political beliefs. As John Leonard of the *New York Times* wrote, "No American critic has struggled more manfully in the last 30 years to reconcile the taste for high art and the temptation to radical politics. Can't we have Ezra Pound and socialism, too?" "To appreciate Howe's critical faculty to its fullest," C. David Heymann admitted in the *Chicago Tribune Book World,* "it is perhaps necessary to identify to some degree with his political sympathies.

Throughout the years he has adamantly maintained his strong political views in which he continues to admire the dissident in history . . . and to profess his libertarian socialism without rancor toward those of alternate persuasion."

Howe's usually unerring ability to discern the merits and demerits of a literary work, along with his distinguished writing style, made him a respected critic. "Those who read, write or think about literature turn to Irving Howe," Schott maintained. "He is what we mean by 'critic' instead of 'reviewer'. . . . Howe writes magnificently and has exquisite sensibilities." Towers believed that Howe "has a trained eye for what is meretricious, flashy or merely crackpot in literary discourse and goes after it with the speed and assurance of a leopard." Heymann called Howe "a literary stylist of the first order" and "unique among his contemporaries for his amazing intellectual versatility."

In his National Book Award-winning *World of Our Fathers,* Howe traced the history of Eastern European Jewish immigrants in America. In so doing, he recreated the history of his own family and friends. Writing in *National Review,* Jacob Neusner praised *World of Our Fathers.* "In this stunning, elegant, monumental work—a triumph of sustained and brilliant narrative—Irving Howe recaptures the intense and vivid life of the immigrant generation," Neusner wrote. "His book is, quite simply, the finest work of historical literature ever written on American Jews."

Howe began the book by recounting Jewish life in Eastern Europe in the 1880s and the conditions that led Jews to immigrate to the United States. Between 1880 and the outbreak of the First World War, some 2 million Jews came to the United States from Eastern Europe, most of them to escape a series of bloody pogroms. "Their story," Peter Shaw wrote in the *Saturday Review,* "is recounted masterfully by the distinguished literary critic Irving Howe, who marshals the major elements—history, politics, culture, life-style—in a narrative that serves as both a chronicle and an interpretation." Howe drew upon published memoirs, scholarly studies, personal interviews, and official government records for his story. "Massive as it is," Walter Clemons wrote in *Newsweek,* "Howe's epic history is a model of distillation and clarity."

After covering the decades of Jewish immigration to America at the turn of the century, Howe spoke of the assimilation of Jews into American society since that time and the resultant disintegration of traditional Jewish culture that this entailed. Howe, Christopher Lehmann-Haupt explained in the *New York Times,* "is both hopeful about the future and surprisingly forgiving for the watering-down that Jewish culture has undergone in the present. . . . All the same, one can't ignore the scope and energy and richness of anecdotal detail with which Mr. Howe has recalled every aspect of the East European immigrant past. . . . This speaks a love far more powerful than the sympathy he grants the Jewish present. Obviously he mourns the death of this past. So he has built a monument to it." Writing in the *New York Review of Books,* Leon Wieseltier called *World of Our Fathers* "a masterly social and cultural history, a vivid, elegiac, and scrupulously documented portrait of a complicated culture, from its heroic beginnings to its unheroic end."

In *A Margin of Hope* Howe traced the course of his own career, recalling the ideas and issues with which he had been engaged. It is not a personal account, Symons explained: "This is the life of an American radical, not of a husband or father." The publication of the book gave several reviewers occasion to evaluate Howe's contributions over the years. Vivian Gornick, writing in the *Nation,* believed that "*A Margin of Hope* reveals a man for whom idea is event, position engagement. The life of the mind fills these pages, and within that life this man has struggled to be serious, to cohere, to make sense of things; he has risen from the bed seven mornings out of seven to grapple, in his thoughts, with history. Such a person may not necessarily compel love, but he commands recognition and respect." Symons called *A Margin of Hope* "the record of an admirable life, the testimony of a decent, honest man." "As he has grown older," Monroe K. Spears wrote in the *Washington Post Book World,* "[Howe] has come to appreciate the ideal of the gentleman, of being quiet and unassertive, and modest."

The American Newness: Culture and Politics in the Age of Emerson contains three essays on Emerson based on a series of lectures Howe delivered at Harvard. In this collection Howe examined what he considered Emerson's vision of an ideal America (a democratization of culture based on individualism), discussed the possible realization of that vision in contemporary culture, and proceeded to apply it to a new interpretation of the works of four major American novelists: Mark Twain, James Fenimore Cooper, Nathaniel Hawthorne and Herman Melville. Leo Marx in the *New York Review of Books* stated that Howe "fails to distinguish between Emerson as a guide to an intellectual vocation and to a politics, and he ultimately adopts a position of considered ambivalence." At the same time, Marx praises *The American Newness* as "a graceful, engaging essay." Brian Lee in the *Times Literary Supplement* believed that the book was "out of phase with the best of Irving Howe." He concluded that it was "impossible to guess what would have been forthcoming, had the freshest and least conventional gifts of this critic been summoned for the engagement . . . We might or might not have been able to see connections between the Emersonian project and the striking styles of individualism emerging in contemporary culture."

Irving Howe: Selected Writings, 1950-1990 is composed of 34 essays spanning the length and breadth of Howe's career both as a literary and political scholar. Essays in the collection deal with a wide range of English, European and American novelists, as well as with such American political figures as Whitaker Chambers, Lillian Hellman and Ronald Reagan, yet mostly relating these individuals to American socialism since the 1930s. Writing in the *Chicago Tribune,* Robert Alter believed that these essays "abundantly demonstrate the breadth of Howe's interests, his ability to confront complex issues with blessed clarity and to strike the right tone and muster vivifying stylistic energy for very different subjects." Howe's "unflagging curiosity, commitment, dispassionateness and independence of mind," Alter continued, "have enabled him to produce a body of criticism that repeatedly wins our attention, compels us to reflection and honors us as readers." Walter Kendricks noted in the *New York Times Book Review* that "Howe does not write 'academic' criticism. He writes to be read by anyone who cares about literature and life." Dennis Donoghue, in the *New York Review of Books,* is more reserved in his praise of the collection, basing his observations on the fact that all of Howe's work, both literary and political, employs social worth as its primary criterion. "I don't know what readers would make," he stated, "of Irving Howe's *Selected Works 1950-1990* if they didn't place a high valuation on the axiom of society; if they didn't regard social considerations as of the first importance." Donoghue believed that all of Howe's work is filtered through his lifelong vision of socialism. However, he goes on to point out that even when "a social vision . . . has no chance of establishing itself in political life," it can still lead to edifying criticism.

A Critic's Notebook: Essays, which Howe had begun prior to his death, was published posthumously. His aim was to put together a collection of what he called *shtiklakh* (Yiddish for "morsels")—short literary observations and criticisms compiled from notes he had made over the years. Howe's son Nicolas completed the editing and compilation of the volume, holding true to his father's intent. Covering works from English, American and European fiction, the essays in *A Critic's Notebook* examine various aspects of the fiction-writing craft. David Bromwich in the *New York Times Book Review* described the collection as a "sequence of free-standing essays on the art of fiction—from Defoe to Kundera, from the nature of anecdotes to the social function of the storyteller . . . mainly a record of the pleasure of thinking about novels." Bromwich found that the book is "full of diversions, in the favorable sense of the word, and often it moves to the larger puzzles of fiction by way of smaller ones." A reviewer in the *New*

Yorker found that "the book is unified by Howe's assumption that the reading and writing of fiction matters, and it sparkles with the sense that serious works are somehow fun." A reviewer in *Kirkus Reviews* concluded that the collection was "a delightful potpourri in which Howe displays an essayist's ease, a critics incisiveness, and, when necessary, an academic's scholarship."

Summing up Howe's career, a reviewer in the *New Republic,* where Howe was a frequent contributor, stated: "As a critic, Howe was versatile and various and had what Henry James called 'a liberal heart.' He did not condescend to art, and he did not worship it. Indeed, he took a special pleasure in the imperfections of the masters: their flaws ratified his humanism, and were an occasion for the wryness with which he diversified his seriousness. He championed modernism without a moment's preciousness, and tradition without a moment's piousness. When he wrote about Yiddish literature, certainly, he was one of the great rescuers."

Other evaluations of Howe's career also praise his varied accomplishments. Lehmann-Haupt characterized him as "one of our leading historians and theoreticians of the Left," while Clemons called him "our most capable man of letters since Edmund Wilson." In the *New York Times Book Review,* Roger Sales stated that "Irving Howe has had a long, admirable and increasingly enviable career. An academic who is never musty and a journalist who is never merely quick or content with flash, he seems to have grown over the years, and his prose is sharper, his insights more precise and flexible." Towers saw Howe as one of "a line of honorable, engaged, incisive and pugnacious critics that includes Edmund Wilson and [F. R.] Leavis and reaches back to Dr. Johnson—a line that has done as much to invigorate the literary life as any number of theorists or aestheticians." Irving Howe, R. Z. Sheppard stated in *Time,* "is one of those writers for whom the designation 'a gentleman and a scholar' was minted."

BIOGRAPHICAL/CRITICAL SOURCES:

BOOKS

Contemporary Literary Criticism, Volume 85, Gale (Detroit), 1995.
Dictionary of Literary Biography, Volume 67: *Modern American Critics Since 1955,* Gale, 1988.
Howe, Irving, *A Margin of Hope: An Intellectual Autobiography,* Harcourt, 1982.
Howe, *Leon Trotsky,* Viking, 1978.

PERIODICALS

Atlantic, November, 1985, pp. 138-42.
Boston Review, February/March, 1995, pp. 23-25.
Chicago Tribune, November 10, 1991.

Chicago Tribune Book World, May 20, 1979; March 6, 1983; June 7, 1992, sec. 14, p. 2.

Christian Science Monitor, April 25, 1957; October 27, 1966; July 22, 1967.

Commentary, February, 1969.

Commonweal, August 1, 1958.

Kirkus Reviews, July 1, 1994, p. 904.

Los Angeles Times Book Review, November 3, 1985, p. 26.

Nation, September 24, 1949; September 20, 1958; September 23, 1978; January 1-8, 1983; November 16, 1985, pp. 498-502.

National Review, May 14, 1976; December 10, 1982.

New Republic, January 26, 1959; October 28, 1978; June 2, 1979; November 1, 1982; November 25, 1985, pp. 31-35; October 17, 1994, pp. 56-59.

New York Review of Books, July 15, 1976; September 28, 1978; January 30, 1986, pp. 26-29; March 12, 1987, pp. 36-38; October 15, 1991, pp. 53-56.

New York Times, September 28, 1949; April 8, 1951; June 22, 1958; March 18, 1970; February 5, 1976; January 29, 1979; March 27, 1979; October 28, 1982.

New York Times Book Review, April 12, 1970; January 6, 1974; November 26, 1978; January 13, 1980; October 31, 1982; October 20, 1985, p. 11; June 29, 1986, p. 17; October 28, 1990, p. 12; October 30, 1994, p.7.

New York Times Magazine, June 17, 1984.

New Yorker, May 26, 1986, p. 107; November 21, 1994, p. 132.

Newsweek, February 2, 1976; December 20, 1982.

Partisan Review, winter, 1975; fall, 1976.

Saturday Review, February 21, 1976; September 2, 1978.

Time, January 26, 1976.

Times Literary Supplement, August 4, 1978; March 4, 1983; January 2, 1987, p. 8.

Village Voice, January 12, 1967.

Wall Street Journal, November 13, 1990, p. A20.

Washington Post Book World, September 24, 1978; June 10, 1979; December 26, 1982.

World Literature Today, autumn, 1983.

OBITUARIES:

PERIODICALS

Chicago Tribune, May 12, 1993, p. 1-19.

Los Angeles Times, May 6, 1993, p. A28.

Nation, June 14, 1993, p. 822.

New Republic, May 31, 1993, p. 10.

New York Times, May 6, 1993, p. D22; May 10, 1993, p. 18.

New York Times Book Review, May 23, 1993, p. 31.

Time, May 17, 1993, p. 25.

Times (London), May 8, 1993, p. 19.

Wall Street Journal, May 6, 1993, p. A1.

Washington Post, May 6, 1993, p. C4; May 11, 1993, p. A19.*

HSIA, Hsiao
See LIU, Wu-chi

*   *   *

HUGHES, Colin A(nfield) 1930-

PERSONAL: Born May 4, 1930, on Harbour Island, Bahamas; son of John Anfield (a civil servant) and Byrle (Johnson) Hughes; married Gwen Glover, August 6, 1955; children: John Anfield. *Education:* Attended George Washington University, 1946-48; Columbia University, B.A., 1949, M.A., 1950; London School of Economics and Political Science, Ph.D., 1952.

ADDRESSES: *Home*—23 Arrabri Ave., Jindalee, Queensland 4074, Australia.

CAREER: McKinney, Bancroft & Hughes (attorneys), Nassau, Bahamas, counsel and attorney, 1954-56, 1959-61; University of Queensland, St. Lucia, Australia, lecturer, 1956-59, professor of political science, 1965-74; Australian National University, Canberra, Australian Capital Territory, fellow, 1961-65, professional fellow, 1975-84; Australian Electoral Commission, electoral commissioner, 1984-89.

WRITINGS:

(Editor with David G. Bettison and Paul W. van der Veur) *The Papua-New Guinea Elections, 1964,* Australian National University Press (Jannali), 1965.

(With John S. Western) *The Prime Minister's Policy Speech,* Australian National University Press, 1966.

(Editor) *Readings in Australian Government,* University of Queensland Press (Saint Lucia), 1968.

(With B. D. Graham) *A Handbook of Australian Government and Politics 1890-1964,* Australian National University Press, 1968.

Issues and Images, Australian National University Press, 1969.

(Editor with D. J. Murphy and R. B. Joyce) *Prelude to Power,* Jacaranda Press (Queensland), 1970.

(With Western) *The Mass Media in Australia,* University of Queensland Press, 1971, 2nd edition, 1982.

(With Graham) *Voting for the Australian House of Representatives, 1901-1964,* Australian National University Press, 1974.

Mr. Prime Minister: Australian Prime Ministers, 1901-1972, Oxford University Press (Melbourne), 1976.

A Handbook of Australian Government and Politics, 1965-1974, Australian National University Press, 1977.

(Editor with Murphy and Joyce) *Labor in Power: The Labor Party and Governments in Queensland, 1915-1957,* University of Queensland Press, 1980.

The Government of Queensland, University of Queensland Press, 1980.

Race and Politics in the Bahamas, St. Martin's (New York City), 1981.

(Editor with Brian Costar) *Labor to Power: Victoria 1982,* Drummond, 1983.

Handbook of Australian Government and Politics: 1975-1984, Australian National University Press, 1986.

(Editor with Rosemary Whip) *Political Crossroads: The 1989 Queensland Election,* University of Queensland Press, 1991.

Also editor of *The Australian University,* 1975-77.

*   *   *

HUMPHREYS, J(ohn) R(ichard Adams) 1918-

PERSONAL: Born June 7, 1918, in Mancelona, MI; son of John C. and Blanche Belle (Beam) Adams, adopted by stepfather, Harold Llewellyn Humphreys; married June Tolton, 1942 (divorced, 1953); married Joan Aucourt, 1955 (divorced, 1958); married Peggy Frink, 1959; children: (first marriage) Catherine. *Education:* University of Michigan, A.B., 1940; New York Institute of Photography, additional study, 1955. *Avocational interests:* Photography, theater, antiques, travel.

ADDRESSES: Home—622 1/2 A Canyon Road, Santa Fe, NM 87501. *Office*—Department of English, School of General Studies, Columbia University, 116th St., New York, NY 10027.

CAREER: Detroit Free Press, Detroit, MI, feature writer, 1940-41; Columbia University, School of General Studies, New York City, member of English department, 1946-88, director of creative writing program, 1962-88, senior lecturer, 1967-88; Cane Hill Press, Santa Fe, NM, editor, 1988—. Paddock Studios, photographer and color technician, 1957-59; Dingee Studio, photographer, 1959. KTRC, disc jockey, 1960. Literary consultant to Doubleday (New York City), 1973-77, and to writing program for Humphreys fellowship, 1990—. *Military service:* U.S. Army, Signal Corps; became first lieutenant.

MEMBER: PEN, Author's League of America, Lambda Chi Alpha.

AWARDS, HONORS: Guggenheim fellow, 1947; *New York Times Book Review,* Notable Books of the Year selection, 1977, for *Subway to Samarkand;* National Endowment of the Arts fellow, 1979; Columbia University, Distinguished Teacher, 1981; Bancroft Award for distinguished retiring professor, 1988; Columbia University, Humphreys fellowship established in his name, 1990; two University of Michigan Avery Hopwood Awards in fiction; MacDowell fellow; Huntington Hartford fellow; Wurlitzer Foundation fellow.

WRITINGS:

Vandameer's Road, Scribner (New York City), 1946.

The Dirty Shame, Dell (New York City), 1955.

The Lost Towns and Roads of America (nonfiction), Doubleday (New York City), 1961, revised edition, Harper (New York City), 1967.

The Last of the Middle West (nonfiction), Doubleday, 1966.

Subway to Samarkand, Doubleday, 1977.

Maya Red, Cane Hill Press (Santa Fe, NM), 1989.

Timeless Towns and Haunted Places (nonfiction), St. Martin's (New York City), 1989.

Also editor of *Pushcart Prize: The Best of the Small Presses.* Contributed short story "Michael Finney and the Little Men" to *Best Short Stories of 1947,* edited by Martha Foley, Houghton (Boston), 1947. Contributor of articles and fiction to periodicals, including *Argosy, Collier's, Cosmopolitan, Harper's Bazaar, Holiday, Mademoiselle,* and *Vogue.* Associate editor of *Beachcomber,* 1960-61.

Some of Humphreys's work has been translated into Swedish.

ADAPTATIONS: Humphreys's story "Michael Finney and the Little Men" was dramatized on *The Big Show.*

WORK IN PROGRESS: Bad Road North (fiction).

SIDELIGHTS: J. R. Humphreys told *CA:* "I was aware I had a certain facility with words that I'd picked up from my extensive reading while I was in grade school, but my spelling was so miserable no one thought to encourage me. At that time I was interested in a career in the theater and received a fellowship at a New York dramatic school (Lucy Fagin's) and appeared as a bit player in a movie, *Gigolette.* In college, as a freshman, my English composition instructor spotted the writer in me (my spelling was still atrocious and still is), and in short order I was winner of two Hopwood Awards in fiction. This was enough for me to decide to switch from theater to fiction writing.

"My early influence was *Ballyhoo* magazine (Dada and Surrealism) and then the Surrealist art movement. Add Lewis Carroll to early and lasting influences, and then came [William] Faulkner, Henry Miller, and [Louis-Ferdinand] Celine. At one time I knew Morley Callaghan personally. He was a family friend who supported and encouraged me, although he said he saw the seeds of my destruction in my interest in surrealism. And he may have been right because I could write with either hand. I drifted away from Callaghan's solid influence because I could not help myself. But my other hand, from time to time, wants control, and I now find myself drifting away from Postmodern, or dream stories toward a residual form of Realism. My work, as a whole, tends to mix the two. There is,

I believe, an element of fantasy, or disorder, in all of reality, for all of us."

*   *   *

HUNTER, Beatrice Trum 1918-

PERSONAL: Born December 16, 1918, in New York, NY; daughter of Gabriel (a foreman) and Martha (Engle) Trum; married John Frank Hunter (a craftsman in pewter and wood), August 2, 1943 (died, 1985). *Education:* Brooklyn College (now Brooklyn College of the City University of New York), B.A., 1940; Columbia University, M.A., 1943; graduate study at State University of New York at Buffalo, Harvard University, and New York University. *Politics:* Independent. *Religion:* Nondenominational.

ADDRESSES: Home—R.F.D. 1, Box 223, Hillsboro, NH 03244.

CAREER: Teacher of visually handicapped children in Belleville, NJ, 1940-42, Newark, NJ, 1942-45, and New York, NY, 1945-55; lecturer and freelance writer, 1955—. Columbia University, summer demonstration teacher, 1942, 1943; Consumers' Research, Inc., food editor. Honorary board member, Nutrition for Optimal Health, 1980, and Nutritional Division, Nassau County Mental Health Clinic; member of Council for Agricultural Science and Technology. Conducts workshops at Learning Institute of New England College, 1989—; gives speeches and addresses to professional organizations, including Martha R. Jones Lectureship in Nutrition at Ashbury Theological Seminary, 1973 and 1974. Exhibitions of ice crystal photography at New England art galleries and museums, including Currier Museum of Fine Arts, Manchester, NH, 1991-93, and Thorne Sagendorph Art Gallery, Keene, NH, 1992.

MEMBER: International Society for the Study of Fatty Acids and Lipids, Natural Food Associates (director of New Hampshire chapter), Federation of Homemakers (honorary vice-president), American Academy of Applied Nutrition (honorary vice-president), American Academy of Environmental Medicine (honorary member), Institute of Food Technologists, Price-Pottenger Nutrition Foundation (honorary member), Land Fellowship (Canada), Soil Association (England).

AWARDS, HONORS: Friends of Nature award, 1961, for public education on pesticides; Tastemaker's Award, 1973, for *The Natural Foods Primer*; Jonathan Forman Award, Society for Clinical Ecology (now American Academy of Environmental Medicine), 1980; Costello Award for ice crystal photography, 1992.

WRITINGS:

The Natural Foods Cookbook, Simon & Schuster (New York City), 1961.
Gardening without Poisons, Houghton (Boston, MA), 1964, 2nd edition, 1971.
Consumer Beware!, Simon & Schuster, 1971.
The Natural Foods Primer, Simon & Schuster, 1972.
The Whole-Grain Baking Sampler, Keats (New Canaan, CT), 1972.
Food Additives and Your Health, Keats, 1972, revised edition, 1980.
Yogurt, Kefir, and Other Milk Cultures, Keats, 1972.
Fermented Foods and Beverages, Keats, 1972.
Beatrice Trum Hunter's Favorite Natural Foods, Simon & Schuster, 1974.
The Mirage of Safety: Food Additives and Federal Policy, Scribner (New York City), 1975.
The Great Nutrition Robbery, Scribner, 1978.
The Sugar Primer, Garden Way Publishing (Charlotte, VT), 1979.
How Safe Is Food in Your Kitchen?, Scribner, 1981.
The Sugar Trap and How to Avoid It, Houghton, 1982.
Be Kitchen Wise! Allen & Unwin (Winchester, MA), 1986.
Gluten Intolerance, Keats, 1987.
Sugar and Sweeteners, Storey/Garden Way, 1989.
The Family Whole Grain Baking Book, Keats, 1993.
Grain Power, Keats, 1994.

Contributor to *Cambridge History and Culture of Human Nutrition,* three volumes, 1994. Contributor to periodicals, including *Herald of Health, Consumer Bulletin, Consumer's Research Magazine, Handbook of Buying, Health News, Natural Food and Farming,* and other magazines.

BIOGRAPHICAL/CRITICAL SOURCES:

PERIODICALS

Washington Post Book World, August 22, 1982.

*   *   *

HURLEY, F(orrest) Jack 1940-

PERSONAL: Born August 28, 1940, in Fort Worth, TX; son of Forrest L. G. and Amelia (Deffebach) Hurley; married Mary Catherine Moses, September 1, 1961 (divorced, 1971); married Anne Banks (an editor), October 28, 1972; children: (first marriage) Catherine Elizabeth, Forrest James; (second marriage) Michael Banks Hurley. *Education:* Austin College, B.A., 1962; Tulane University, M.A., 1966, Ph.D., 1971.

ADDRESSES: Home—5300 Shady Grove Rd., Memphis, TN 38120. *Office*—Department of History, University of Memphis, Memphis, TN 38152.

CAREER: Memphis State University (now University of Memphis), Memphis, TN, instructor, 1966-71, assistant professor, 1971-76, associate professor, 1976-81, professor of history, 1981—, chairperson of history department, 1992—. Member of board of directors of Appalachian Oral History Project, 1972-73; National Ornamental Metal Museum, Memphis, member of board of trustees, 1980-92, president of board, 1984-92. Humanist in residence, International Museum of Photography George Eastman House, Rochester, NY, 1974-75; visiting professor, Austin College, summer, 1980.

MEMBER: Organization of American Historians, Southern Historical Association.

AWARDS, HONORS: Distinguished Southern Book Award, 1972, for *Portrait of a Decade: Roy Stryker and the Development of Documentary Photography in the Thirties;* National Endowment for the Humanities, Young Humanist summer grant, 1973, Bicentennial Award, 1974-75, Lyndhurst Foundation Prize, 1990; SPUR (Superior Performance in University Research) Award, 1990.

WRITINGS:

(With Robert Doherty) *Portrait of a Decade: Roy Stryker and the Development of Documentary Photography in the Thirties,* Louisiana State University Press (Baton Rouge), 1972.

Russell Lee: Photographer, introduction by Robert Coles, Morgan & Morgan (Dobbs Ferry, NY), 1978.

(Editor) *Industry and the Photographic Image: One Hundred Fifty-Three Great Prints from 1850 to the Present,* Dover (New York City), 1980.

(Co-author) *Tennessee Traditional Singers,* University of Tennessee Press (Knoxville), 1980.

(Co-editor) *Southern Eye, Southern Mind: A Photographic Inquiry,* Memphis Academy of the Arts (Memphis, TN), 1981.

Marion Post Wolcott: A Photographic Journey, introduction by Coles, University of New Mexico Press (Albuquerque), 1989.

*   *   *

HURWITZ, Johanna 1937-

PERSONAL: Born October 9, 1937, in New York, NY; daughter of Nelson (a journalist and bookseller) and Tillie (a library assistant; maiden name, Miller) Frank; married Uri Levi Hurwitz (a writer and college teacher), February 19, 1962; children: Nomi, Benjamin. *Education:* Queens College (now Queens College of the City University of New York), B.A., 1958; Columbia University, M.L.S., 1959. *Politics:* Liberal. *Religion:* Jewish.

ADDRESSES: Home—10 Spruce Pl., Great Neck, NY 11021.

CAREER: New York Public Library, New York City, children's librarian, 1959-63; Queen's College of the City University of New York, Flushing, NY, lecturer on children's literature, 1965-68; Calhoun School, New York City, children's librarian, 1968-75; Manor Oaks School, New Hyde Park, NY, children's librarian, 1975-77; Great Neck Library, Great Neck, NY, children's librarian, 1978-92; writer. New York Public Library, visiting storyteller, 1964-67.

MEMBER: PEN, Authors Guild, Society of Children's Book Writers, American Library Association, Amnesty International, Beta Phi Mu.

AWARDS, HONORS: Parents' Choice Award, Parents' Choice Foundation, 1982, for *The Rabbi's Girls,* and 1984, for *The Hot and Cold Summer;* Texas Bluebonnet Award and Wyoming Indian Paintbrush Award, both 1987, both for *The Hot and Cold Summer;* Kentucky Bluegrass Award, West Virginia Children's Book Award, and Mississippi Children's Book Award, all 1989, all for *Class Clown;* Florida Sunshine State Award, 1990, and New Jersey Garden State Award, 1991, both for *Teacher's Pet;* New Jersey Garden State Award, 1994, for *School's Out!*

WRITINGS:

FICTION FOR CHILDREN AND YOUNG ADULTS

Busybody Nora, illustrated by Susan Jeschke, Morrow (New York City), 1976, published with new illustrations by Lillian Hoban, 1990.

Nora and Mrs. Mind-Your-Own-Business, illustrated by Jeschke, Morrow, 1977, published with new illustrations by Hoban, 1991.

The Law of Gravity, illustrated by Ingrid Fetz, Morrow, 1978, published as *What Goes Up Must Come Down,* Scholastic Inc./Apple (New York City), 1983.

Much Ado about Aldo, illustrated by John Wallner, Morrow, 1978.

Aldo Applesauce, illustrated by Wallner, Morrow, 1979.

New Neighbors for Nora, illustrated by Jeschke, Morrow, 1979, published with new illustrations by Hoban, 1991.

Once I Was a Plum Tree, illustrated by Fetz, Morrow, 1980.

Superduper Teddy, illustrated by Jeschke, Morrow, 1980, published with new illustrations by Hoban, 1990.

Aldo Ice Cream, illustrated by Wallner, Morrow, 1981.

Baseball Fever, illustrated by Ray Cruz, Morrow, 1981.

The Rabbi's Girls, illustrated by Pamela Johnson, Morrow, 1982.

Tough-Luck Karen, illustrated by Diane de Groat, Morrow, 1982.

Rip-Roaring Russell, illustrated by Hoban, Morrow, 1983.

DeDe Takes Charge!, illustrated by de Groat, Morrow, 1984.

The Hot and Cold Summer, illustrated by Gail Owens, Morrow, 1985.

The Adventures of Ali Baba Bernstein, illustrated by Owens, Morrow, 1985.

Russell Rides Again, illustrated by Hoban, Morrow, 1985.

Hurricane Elaine, illustrated by de Groat, Morrow, 1986.

Yellow Blue Jay, illustrated by Donald Carrick, Morrow, 1986, published as *Bunk Mates,* Scholastic (New York City), 1988.

Class Clown, illustrated by Sheila Hamanaka, Morrow, 1987.

Russell Sprouts, illustrated by Hoban, Morrow, 1987.

The Cold and Hot Winter, illustrated by Carolyn Ewing, Morrow, 1988.

Teacher's Pet, illustrated by Hamanaka, Morrow, 1988.

Hurray for Ali Baba Bernstein, illustrated by Owens, Morrow, 1989.

Russell and Elisa, illustrated by Hoban, Morrow, 1989.

Class President, illustrated by Hamanaka, Morrow, 1990.

Aldo Peanut Butter, illustrated by de Groat, Morrow, 1990.

"E" Is for Elisa, illustrated by Hoban, Morrow, 1991.

School's Out!, illustrated by Hamanaka, Morrow, 1991.

Roz and Ozzie, illustrated by Eileen McKeating, Morrow, 1992.

Ali Baba Bernstein: Lost and Found, illustrated by Karen Milone, Morrow, 1992.

Make Room for Elisa, illustrated by Hoban, Morrow, 1993.

New Shoes for Sylvia, illustrated by Jerry Pinkney, Morrow, 1993.

The Up and Down Spring, illustrated by Owens, Morrow, 1993.

School Spirit, illustrated by Karen Dugan, Morrow, 1994.

A Llama in the Family, illustrated by Mark Graham, Morrow, 1994.

Ozzie on His Own, illustrated by McKeating, Morrow, 1995.

Elisa in the Middle, illustrated by Hoban, Morrow, 1995.

NONFICTION FOR CHILDREN AND YOUNG ADULTS

Anne Frank: Life in Hiding, illustrated by Vera Rosenberry, Jewish Publication Society (Philadelphia, PA), 1988.

Astrid Lindgren: Storyteller to the World, illustrated by Michael Dooling, Viking (New York City), 1989.

Leonard Bernstein: A Passion for Music, illustrated by Sonia O. Lisker, Jewish Publication Society, 1993.

OTHER

(Editor) *A Word to the Wise: And Other Proverbs,* illustrated by Robert Rayevsky, Morrow, 1993.

(Editor) *Birthday Surprises: Ten Great Stories to Unwrap,* Morrow, 1995.

Contributor to periodicals, including *Horn Book.*

WORK IN PROGRESS: Even Stephen and *The Down and Up Fall.*

SIDELIGHTS: Johanna Hurwitz is the author of more than forty books for young people. Among her most popular works are lighthearted novels for elementary and junior high school readers that are characterized by endearing and eccentric protagonists who face the universal difficulties of childhood. Hurwitz's books share loose connections, as a minor character in one novel will often become the central figure of another. *Aldo Applesauce,* for instance, is about a fourth-grader, while *Tough-Luck Karen* and *Hurricane Elaine* feature his older sisters. Though Hurwitz tackles some serious issues, such as divorce in *DeDe Takes Charge!* and prejudice in *The Rabbi's Girls,* her fiction is laced with trademark humor and irony, and her protagonist's main problems are often resolved by book's end. Hurwitz's optimistic approach, fast-paced narratives, and frequent depictions of strong family relationships have made her books appealing to readers and reviewers alike.

Many of Hurwitz's works have been praised for their light, humorous glimpses into the world of children, replete with minor disasters and triumphant successes. The books are considered especially suitable for reading aloud, as their chapters are short and self-contained while relating to a more general plot. In a *Bulletin of the Center for Children's Books* review of *Russell and Elisa,* Ruth Ann Staitl commented: "Hurwitz excels in conveying the young child's point of view without any condescension. The moments of laughter in this family story ring true."

Some critics have praised Hurwitz's works where, as in *Tough-Luck Karen* and *Hurricane Elaine,* the protagonist achieves noticeable personal growth. Another example is *School's Out,* in which class clown Lucas Cott delights in getting the best of his new French babysitter, Genevieve, during summer vacation. As the weeks go by, however, Lucas comes to like Genevieve and decides that he must become a better influence on his younger twin brothers.

In addition to fiction, Hurwitz has published two nonfiction works. *Anne Frank: Life in Hiding* introduces Anne and the Frank family to elementary school readers, gives an explanation of the political and economic background of the Holocaust of World War II, and describes the significance of the diary that was published after Anne's death. And in *Astrid Lindgren: Storyteller to the World*

Hurwitz recounts the life and career of the creator of the beloved character Pippi Longstocking.

Though she has penned a variety of works for young readers, Hurwitz does not expect to write for adults someday. "I get angry when people ask me when am I going to write a book for adults," the author once commented to *CA*. "I do not feel that my writing for children is practice for that. I write for children because I am especially interested in that period of life. There is an intensity and seriousness about childhood which fascinates me."

BIOGRAPHICAL/CRITICAL SOURCES:

BOOKS

Sixth Book of Junior Authors, H. W. Wilson (Bronx, NY), 1989, pp. 144-146.

PERIODICALS

Booklist, October 15, 1988, p. 409.
Bulletin of the Center for Children's Books, January, 1980; June, 1980; November, 1984; June, 1985; October, 1985; December, 1986; April, 1987; January, 1990, p. 111; April, 1991, p. 197.
Publishers Weekly, January 30, 1981; June 29, 1984, p. 104; July 8, 1988, p. 56; March 30, 1990, p. 62; August 10, 1990, p. 444.
School Library Journal, October, 1978, pp. 129, 134; September, 1979, p. 113; February, 1980, p. 57; December, 1980, p. 53; January, 1983, p. 76; May, 1984, p. 81; November, 1984, p. 126; September, 1988, p. 183; March, 1989, p. 163; August, 1989, p. 146; February, 1990, p. 103; May, 1990, p. 106; May, 1991, p. 93.

*   *   *

HUTCHINS, Hazel J. 1952-

PERSONAL: Born August 9, 1952, in Calgary, Alberta, Canada; daughter of Bill (a cowboy and farmer) and Peggy (a farmer; maiden name, McKinnon) Sadler; married James Edward Hutchins, January 13, 1973; children: Wil, Leanna, Ben Brodie. *Education:* Attended University of Calgary. *Avocational interests:* Travel, skiing, hiking, visiting high alpine lakes.

ADDRESSES: Home—Box 185, 521 4th St., Canmore, Alberta T0L 0M0, Canada.

CAREER: Writer. Visiting author and speaker in schools.

AWARDS, HONORS: Selection for the Read Magic Awards List, *Parenting* magazine, for *The Three and Many Wishes of Jason Reid;* Award for Children's Literature, Alberta Writer's Guild, for *A Cat of Artimus Pride.*

WRITINGS:

FOR CHILDREN; PICTURE BOOKS EXCEPT AS NOTED

The Three and Many Wishes of Jason Reid (novel), illustrated by John Richmond, Annick (Ontario, Canada), 1983.
Anastasia Morningstar and the Crystal Butterfly (novel), illustrated by Barry Trower, Annick, 1984.
Leanna Builds a Genie Trap, illustrated by Catherine O'Neill, Annick, 1986.
Ben's Snow Song, illustrated by Lisa Smith, Annick, 1987.
Casey Webber, the Great (novel), illustrated by Richmond, Annick, 1988.
Norman's Snowball, illustrated by Ruth Ohi, Annick, 1989.
Nicholas at the Library, illustrated by Ohi, Annick, 1990.
A Cat of Artimus Pride (novel), illustrated by Ohi, Annick, 1991.
Katie's Babbling Brother, illustrated by Ohi, Annick, 1991.
And You Can Be the Cat, illustrated by Ohi, Annick, 1992.
The Best of Arlie Zack (novel), illustrated by Ohi, Annick, 1993.
The Catfish Palace, illustrated by Ohi, Annick, 1993.
Within a Painted Past, illustrated by Ohi, Annick, 1994.
Tess, Annick, 1995.
Believing Sophie, Albert Whitman (Niles, IL), 1995.

WORK IN PROGRESS: Preschool storybooks, pre-teen fiction, and adult short stories.

SIDELIGHTS: Hazel J. Hutchins, who grew up on a farm in southern Alberta, Canada, told *CA:* "I like words—how they sound and feel. I love the way ideas in fiction open so many doors in my mind. The most rewarding part is making the words say exactly what I want. When that happens, it's wonderful." Hutchins credits her family with story inspiration and writes first drafts longhand, followed by editing and printing on a computer. She advises aspiring writers: "Always write about things you're intrigued by, not just about things you know. Don't talk about your stories, write about them. And don't be discouraged. It takes time to be a good writer."

*   *   *

HYMAN, Ronald T. 1933-

PERSONAL: Born October 16, 1933, in Chicago, IL; son of Maurice H. and Matilda (Grossman) Hyman; married Suzanne Linda Katz, February 13, 1958; children: Jonathan, Elana, Rachel. *Education:* University of Miami, Coral Gables, B.A., 1955; Vanderbilt University and George Peabody College for Teachers, M.A.T., 1956; Columbia University, Ed.D., 1965; Rutgers University,

Newark Campus, J.D., 1986. *Politics:* Liberal. *Religion:* Jewish.

ADDRESSES: Home—227 Lincoln Ave., Highland Park, NJ 08904. *Office*—Graduate School of Education, Rutgers University, New Brunswick, NJ 08903.

CAREER: Public school teacher, 1956-62; Columbia University, New York City, research assistant, 1962-64; Queens College of the City University of New York, Flushing, NY, assistant professor, 1964-66; Rutgers University, New Brunswick, NJ, associate professor, 1966-74, professor of education, 1974—, chair of department of science and humanities education in Graduate School of Education, 1977-80. Visiting summer professor at Hofstra University, 1965 and 1966. Attorney at law of the State of New Jersey, 1986—. Member of State Advisory Council for Gifted and Talented Education. Conductor of workshops on teaching strategies and teacher supervision and evaluation.

MEMBER: Association for Supervision and Curriculum Development, American Association of University Professors, National Organization on Legal Problems of Education, New Jersey Association for Supervision and Curriculum Development (member of executive board), New Jersey School Development Council (member of executive board), New Jersey State Bar Association.

WRITINGS:

The Principles of Contemporary Education, Monarch (New York City), 1966.

(With A. A. Bellack, H. M. Kliebard, and F. L. Smith) *The Language of the Classroom,* Teachers College Press, Columbia University (New York City), 1966.

(Editor) *Teaching: Vantage Points for Study,* Lippincott (Philadelphia), 1968, 2nd edition, 1974.

Ways of Teaching, Lippincott, 1970, 2nd edition, 1974.

(Editor) *Contemporary Thought on Teaching,* Prentice-Hall (Englewood Cliffs, NJ), 1971.

(Editor with Maurice Hillson) *Change and Innovation in Elementary and Secondary Organization,* 2nd edition (Hyman was not associated with previous edition), Holt (New York City), 1971.

(Editor) *Approaches in Curriculum,* Prentice-Hall, 1973.

(Editor with Samuel L. Baily, and contributor) *Perspectives on Latin America,* Macmillan (New York City), 1974.

School Administrator's Handbook of Teacher Supervision and Evaluation Methods, Prentice-Hall, 1975.

(With Alan Teplitsky) *Walk in My Shoes,* Prentice-Hall, 1976.

Paper, Pencils, and Pennies: Games for Learning and Having Fun, Prentice-Hall, 1977.

(With Allan Pessin) *The Securities Industry,* New York Institute of Finance (New York City), 1977.

(With Kevin Goldstein-Jackson and Norman Rudnick) *Experiments with Everyday Objects: Science Activities for Children, Parents, and Teachers,* Prentice-Hall, 1978.

Simulation Gaming for Values Education: The Prisoner's Dilemma, University Press of America (Lanham, MD), 1978.

Strategic Questioning, Prentice-Hall, 1979.

Improving Discussion Leadership, Teachers College Press, Columbia University, 1980.

(Editor) *Thinking Processes in the Classroom: Prospects and Programs,* New Jersey Association for Supervision and Curriculum Development, 1985.

School Administrator's Faculty Supervision Handbook, Prentice-Hall, 1986.

School Administrator's Staff Development Manual, Prentice-Hall, 1986.

(With Charles Rathbone) *Corporal Punishment in Schools: Reading the Law,* National Organization on Legal Problems of Education (Topeka, KS), 1993.

(With Rathbone) *The Principal's Decision: A Teaching Monograph on Corporal Punishment,* National Organization on Legal Problems of Education, 1993.

Co-general editor of "Latin America Social Studies" series for Macmillan, 1974-75; advisory editor of "Spectrum Series in Applied Education" for Prentice-Hall. Contributor of articles and reviews to numerous periodicals, including *Elementary School Journal, Journal of Teacher Education, Teachers College Record, Education Law Reporter, Religious Education, Educational Leadership,* and *Hebrew Studies.*

WORK IN PROGRESS: Connecting education law with current problems facing education; connecting the Bible with the act of questioning in education.

I-K

IGLESIAS, Mario 1924-

PERSONAL: Born September 8, 1924, in Havana, Cuba; naturalized U.S. citizen in 1968; son of Daniel (a tailor) and Consola (Frade) Iglesias; married Alicia R. Armas, April 1, 1950; children: Alicia, Amalia M. *Education:* University of Havana, P.D., 1949; Western Reserve University (now Case Western Reserve University), M.A., 1967.

ADDRESSES: Home—347 Colonial Ave., Worthington, OH 43085. *Office*—Department of Spanish and Portuguese, Ohio State University, Columbus, OH 43210.

CAREER: Ruston Academy, Havana, Cuba, teacher, supervisor, and headmaster, 1946-61; junior high school teacher of Spanish in Lakewood, OH, 1961-64; Elmira College, Elmira, NY, assistant professor of Spanish, 1964-67; Ohio State University, Columbus, assistant professor, 1967-73, associate professor of romance languages, 1973-95, professor emeritus, 1995—.

MEMBER: American Association of Teachers of Spanish and Portuguese (secretary of northern Ohio chapter, 1963-64), Midwest Modern Language Association, Ohio Modern Language Association.

WRITINGS:

(Editor and contributor) Agnes M. Brady and Harley D. Oberhelman, *Espanol Moderno,* two volumes, C. E. Merrill (Columbus, OH), 1970.
Spanish Testing Program: Level I, C. E. Merrill, 1971.
(With Walter Meiden) *Cuaderno de Ejercicios* (to accompany Richard Armitage and Meiden, *Beginning Spanish*), Houghton (Boston), 1972, 2nd edition, 1979.
(With Meiden) *Spanish for Oral and Written Review,* Holt (New York City), 1975, new edition, 1995.
(With Nancy Humbach and others) *Spanish Today 2,* Houghton, 1982.

En Contacto: Workbook/Lab Manual, Houghton, 1985, new edition, 1992.

WORK IN PROGRESS: Writing advanced Spanish language textbooks on grammar, composition, and conversation.

SIDELIGHTS: Mario Iglesias told *CA:* "My academic and professional training was always directed toward the production of teaching materials for the elementary, secondary, and college levels. This production was for me a most serious and creative task. With the intense demands for scholastic output placed upon the younger as well as the experienced professor, writing textbooks has been looked down upon by academia to the point that there are very few scholars willing to undertake the task of writing good teaching materials, including that maligned teaching instrument known as the textbook.

"I have given up the opportunity to produce significant empirical research, and, instead, I have directed my efforts to creating textbooks that will open for the student a promising world of basic—although for him or her, new—knowledge and new horizons."

*　　*　　*

JASSEM, Kate
See OPPENHEIM, Joanne

*　　*　　*

JEFFRIES, Roderic (Graeme) 1926-
(Peter Alding, Jeffrey Ashford, Hastings Draper, Roderic Graeme, Graham Hastings)

PERSONAL: Born October 21, 1926, in London, England; son of Graham Montague (a writer) and Lorna Helene (Louch) Jeffries; married Rosemary Powys Wood-house, March 13, 1958; children: Xanthe Kathleen, Crispin John. *Education:* University of Southampton, navigation studies, 1942-43; Gray's Inn, Barrister-at-Law, 1953. *Avocational interests:* Shooting, training gun dogs, vintage Bentleys, travel, gardening, drinking local wines when in Spain.

ADDRESSES: Home—Apartado 5, Ca Na Paiaia, 07460 Pollenca, Mallorca, Spain. *Office*—c/o HarperCollins, 77-85 Fulham Palace Rd., Hammersmith, London W6 8JB.

CAREER: Writer. British Merchant Navy, 1943-49, went to sea as apprentice, became second mate; began part-time writing and study of law, 1950; practiced law, 1953-54. Former part-time dairy farmer.

MEMBER: Paternosters.

WRITINGS:

Evidence of the Accused, Collins, 1961, British Book Center, 1963.
Exhibit No. Thirteen, Collins for the Crime Club, 1962.
Police and Detection, Brockhampton Press, 1962, published as *Against Time!,* Harper (New York City), 1963.
The Benefits of Death, Collins for the Crime Club, 1963, Dodd (New York City), 1964.
An Embarrassing Death, Collins for the Crime Club, 1964, Dodd, 1965.
Dead against the Lawyers, Dodd, 1965.
Police Dog, Harper, 1965.
Death in the Coverts, Collins for the Crime Club, 1966.
A Deadly Marriage, Collins, 1967.
Police Car, Brockhampton Press, 1967, published as *Patrol Car,* Harper, 1967.
A Traitor's Crime, Collins for the Crime Club, 1968.
River Patrol, Harper, 1969.
Dead Man's Bluff, Collins, 1970.
Police Patrol Boat, Brockhampton Press, 1971.
Trapped, Harper, 1972.
Mistakenly in Mallorca, Collins for the Crime Club, 1974.
Two Faced Death, Collins, 1976.
The Riddle in the Parchment, Hodder & Stoughton (London), 1976.
The Boy Who Knew Too Much, Hodder & Stoughton, 1977.
Troubled Deaths, Collins, 1977.
Murder Begets Murder, St. Martin's (New York City), 1978.
Eighteen Desperate Hours, Hodder & Stoughton, 1979.
The Missing Man, Hodder & Stoughton, 1980.
Just Deserts, St. Martin's, 1980.
Unseemly End, St. Martin's, 1981.
Voyage into Danger, Hodder & Stoughton, 1981.

Peril at Sea, Hodder & Stoughton, 1983.
Deadly Petard, Collins, 1983.
Three and One Make Five, Collins, 1984.
Layers of Deceit, Collins, 1985.
Sunken Danger, Hodder & Stoughton, 1985.
Meeting Trouble, Hodder & Stoughton, 1986.
Almost Murder, Collins, 1986.
Relatively Dangerous, Collins, 1987.
The Man Who Couldn't Be, Hodder & Stoughton, 1987.
Death Trick, Collins, 1988.
Dead Clever, HarperCollins (London), 1989.
Too Clever by Half, St. Martin's, 1990.
A Fatal Fleece, St. Martin's, 1991.
Murder's Long Memory, St. Martin's, 1992.
Murder Confounded, St. Martin's, 1993.
Death Takes Time, St. Martin's, 1994.
An Arcadian Death, HarperCollins, 1995.
An Artistic Way to Go, HarperCollins, 1996.

UNDER PSEUDONYM PETER ALDING

The C.I.D. Room, John Long (London), 1967, published as *All Leads Negative,* Harper, 1967.
Circle of Danger, John Long, 1968.
Murder among Thieves, John Long, 1969, McCall Publishing Co., 1970.
Guilt without Proof, John Long, 1970, McCall Publishing Co., 1971.
Despite the Evidence, John Long, 1971, Saturday Review Press, 1972.
Call Back to Crime, John Long, 1972.
Field of Fire, John Long, 1973.
The Murder Line, Walker & Co. (New York), 1974.
Six Days to Death, Walker & Co., 1975.
Murder Is Suspected, Walker & Co., 1978.
Ransom Town, Walker & Co., 1979.
A Man Condemned, R. Hale (London), 1981.
Betrayed by Death, R. Hale, 1982.

UNDER PSEUDONYM JEFFREY ASHFORD

Counsel for the Defence, John Long, 1960, Harper, 1961.
Investigations Are Proceeding, John Long, 1961, published as *The D.I.,* Harper, 1962.
The Burden of Proof, Harper, 1962.
Will Anyone Who Saw the Accident . . . , Harper, 1963.
Enquiries Are Continuing, John Long, 1964.
The Superintendent's Room, John Long, 1964, Harper, 1965.
The Hands of Innocence, John Long, 1965, Walker & Co., 1966.
Consider the Evidence, Walker & Co., 1966.
Hit and Run, Arrow Books (London), 1966.
Forget What You Saw, Walker & Co., 1967.
Grand Prix Monaco, Putnam (New York City), 1968.
Prisoner at the Bar, Walker & Co., 1969.

Grand Prix Germany, Putnam, 1970.
To Protect the Guilty, Walker & Co., 1970.
Bent Copper, Walker & Co., 1971.
Grand Prix United States, Putnam, 1971.
A Man Will Be Kidnapped Tomorrow, Walker & Co., 1972.
Grand Prix Britain, Putnam, 1973.
The Double Run, Walker & Co., 1973.
Dick Knox at Le Mans, Putnam, 1974.
The Color of Violence, Walker & Co., 1974.
Three Layers of Guilt, John Long, 1975.
Slow Down the World, Walker & Co., 1976.
Hostage to Death, Walker & Co., 1977.
The Anger of Fear, Walker & Co., 1978.
A Recipe for Murder, Walker & Co., 1979.
The Loss of the Culion, Walker & Co., 1981.
Guilt with Honour, Collins, 1982.
Presumption of Guilt, Collins, 1984.
An Ideal Crime, Collins, 1985.
A Question of Principle, Collins, 1986.
A Crime Remembered, Collins, 1987.
The Honourable Detective, HarperCollins, 1988.
A Conflict of Interests, St. Martin's, 1989.
An Illegal Solution, St. Martin's, 1990.
Deadly Reunion, St. Martin's, 1991.
Twisted Justice, St. Martin's, 1992.
Judgement Deferred, St. Martin's, 1993.
The Bitter Bit, HarperCollins, 1994.
The Price of Failure, HarperCollins, 1995.

UNDER PSEUDONYM HASTINGS DRAPER

Wiggery Pokery, W. H. Allen (London), 1956.
Wigged and Gowned, W. H. Allen, 1958.
Brief Help, W. H. Allen, 1961.

UNDER PSEUDONYM RODERIC GRAEME

Brandy Ahoy!, Hutchinson (London), 1951.
Concerning Blackshirt, Hutchinson, 1952.
Where's Brandy?, Hutchinson, 1953.
Blackshirt Wins the Trick, Hutchinson, 1953.
Blackshirt Passes By, Hutchinson, 1953.
Salute to Blackshirt, Hutchinson, 1954.
Brandy Goes a Cruising, Hutchinson, 1954.
Blackshirt Meets the Lady, Hutchinson, 1956.
Paging Blackshirt, John Long, 1957.
Blackshirt Helps Himself, John Long, 1958.
Double for Blackshirt, John Long, 1958.
Blackshirt Sets the Pace, John Long, 1959.
Blackshirt Sees It Through, John Long, 1960.
Blackshirt Finds Trouble, John Long, 1961.
Blackshirt Takes the Trail, John Long, 1962.
Blackshirt on the Spot, John Long, 1963.
Call for Blackshirt, John Long, 1963.
Blackshirt Saves the Day, John Long, 1964.

Danger for Blackshirt, John Long, 1965.
Blackshirt at Large, John Long, 1966.
Blackshirt in Peril, John Long, 1967.
Blackshirt Stirs Things Up, John Long, 1969.

UNDER PSEUDONYM GRAHAM HASTINGS

Twice Checked, R. Hale, 1959.
Deadly Game, R. Hale, 1961.

ADAPTATIONS: Several of Jeffries's books have been adapted for films, television, radio, and audio cassettes.

SIDELIGHTS: Roderic Jeffries's books have been published in seventeen countries and translated into fifteen languages.

BIOGRAPHICAL/CRITICAL SOURCES:

PERIODICALS

Armchair Detective, spring, 1986, p. 192; summer, 1987, p. 330; winter, 1993, p. 107.
Kirkus Reviews, July 15, 1990, p. 966; February 15, 1993, p. 183; April 15, 1994, p. 505; October 15, 1995, p. 1372.
Los Angeles Times Book Review, August 4, 1985, p. 9.
Observer (London), October 21, 1984, p. 24; April 14, 1985, p. 23.
Publishers Weekly, July 13, 1990, p. 43; July 19, 1993, p. 238; May 16, 1994, p. 54.
Times Literary Supplement, July 17, 1987, p. 778; August 12, 1988, p. 893; May 19, 1989, p. 536.
Tribune Books (Chicago), September 5, 1993, p. 6.

*   *   *

JOCELYN, Richard
See CLUTTERBUCK, Richard

*   *   *

JONES, Joanna
See BURKE, John (Frederick)

*   *   *

JONES, Rebecca C(astaldi) 1947-

PERSONAL: Born September 10, 1947, in Evergreen Park, IL; daughter of Lawrence J. (an accountant) and Ruth (Speitel) Castaldi; married Christopher Jones (a research manager), August 8, 1970; children: Amanda, David. *Education:* Northwestern University, B.S., 1969, M.S., 1970. *Religion:* Roman Catholic.

ADDRESSES: Home—130 Pinecrest Dr., Annapolis, MD 21403. *Office*—*American School Board Journal,* 1680 Duke St., Alexandria, VA 22314.

CAREER: *Warsaw Times-Union,* Warsaw, IN, reporter, 1965-66; Illinois Children's Home and Aide Society, Chicago, public relations aide, 1967; *Cue,* New York City, staff intern, 1968; *Ingenue,* New York City, staff intern, 1968; Newark Advocate, Newark, OH, reporter, 1970-71; WBNS-TV, Columbus, OH, assignment editor and reporter, 1971-72; Ohio State University, Columbus, instructor in journalism, 1972-75; University of Maryland, University College, College Park, MD, professor of journalism, 1975-93; Anne Arundel Community College, Arnold, MD, English instructor, 1977, 1984-86.

AWARDS, HONORS: Excellence in Teaching Award, University of Maryland University College, 1992; Outstanding Faculty Award, National Universities Continuing Education Association, 1993.

WRITINGS:

Angie and Me (juvenile), Macmillan (New York City), 1981.

The Biggest, Meanest, Ugliest Dog in the Whole Wide World (juvenile), Macmillan, 1982.

Madeline and the Great (Old) Escape Artist (juvenile), Dutton (New York City), 1983.

I Am Not Afraid, Concordia (St. Louis, MS), 1986.

Germy Blew It (juvenile), Dutton, 1987.

The Biggest (and Best) Flag That Ever Flew, Tidewater (Centreville, MD), 1988.

Germy Blew It—Again! (juvenile), Henry Holt, 1988.

The Believers, Arcade, 1989.

Germy Blew the Bugle (juvenile), Arcade, 1990.

Down at the Bottom of the Deep Dark Sea (juvenile), Bradbury (Scarsdale, NY), 1991.

Matthew and Tilly (juvenile), Dutton, 1991.

Germy in Charge (juvenile), Dutton, 1993.

Great Aunt Martha, Dutton, 1994.

Also author of screenplay *Germy Blew It,* based on her book of the same title, 1989. Author of weekly column "A Woman's Words," in *Catholic Times,* 1970-72. Contributor of hundreds of stories and articles to periodicals, including *Washington Post, Young Miss,* and *Army.* Associate editor, *American School Board Journal* and *Executive Educator,* 1993—.

Some of Jones's books have been published in foreign editions.

WORK IN PROGRESS: *The President Has Been Shot,* for Dutton.

SIDELIGHTS: Rebecca C. Jones once told *CA:* "I was sick a great deal as a child, and our parish priest used to warn me of the dangers of 'playing with yourself' when alone in bed. I wasn't sure what that meant but interpreted it to be the same as 'playing *by* yourself.' I avoided the evil by creating great imaginary characters to keep me company in the sickroom. Today many of those imaginary characters stand by my computer and wait for me to tell their stories."

* * *

KAELLBERG, Sture 1928-

PERSONAL: Born March 29, 1928, in Upplands Vaesby, Sweden. *Education:* Attended public schools in Sweden and Denmark.

ADDRESSES: *Home*—Slupskjulsv. 3, 11149 Stockholm, Sweden.

CAREER: Journalist. Has worked on a farm, in factories, in shipyards, and as a docker.

MEMBER: Swedish Union of Authors (board member, 1975-80), Swedish Pen Club.

AWARDS, HONORS: Guaranteed annual author's coin, Swedish Author's Fund, 1977—.

WRITINGS:

Kamrat med 700 miljoner (nonfiction; title means "Comrade with 700 Millions"), Raben & Sjoegren (Stockholm), 1964.

Uppror-Budapest 1956 (memoirs; title means "Rebellion—Budapest 1956"), Raben & Sjoegren, 1966.

Ho Chi Minh i urval (title means "Ho Chi Minh Selection and Biography"), Norstedt (Stockholm), 1967.

Rapport fraan medelsvensk stad: Vaesteraas, PAN/Norstedt (Stockholm), 1969, translation by Angela Gibb published as *Off the Middle Way: Report from a Swedish Village,* Pantheon (New York City), 1972.

Marx och Engels till vardags (nonfiction; title means "Everyday Life of Marx and Engels"), Norstedt, 1970.

Ackord (short stories; title means "Piece-Work"), Norstedt, 1972.

Samtal med Cahun: Episod fraan en kommande tid (radio play; first broadcast September 28, 1974, on Sveriges Radio; title means "Talk with Cahun: Episode from a Coming Time"), Gidlund (Stockholm), 1973.

Iakttagelser (articles; title means "Observations"), Norstedt, 1973.

Vandringen till staederna (fiction trilogy; title means "The Wandering to the Cities"), Norstedt, Volume I: *Agnarna i vinden* (title means "The Chaffs in the Wind"), 1976, Volume II: *I flock och ensam* (title means "In Flock and Alone"), 1977, Volume III: *Den roeda alven* (title means "The Red River"), 1979.

Upprorets dagar: Kortare aen en vaarblommas liv (title means "Days of Rebellion—Shorter Than the Life of a Spring Flower"), Norstedt, 1982.

I Dankos hus (nonfiction; title means "In Danko's House"), Norstedt, 1984.

Ut ur skogen (autobiographical stories; title means "Out of the Forest"), Norstedt, 1988.

Ut pa torget (autobiographical stories; title means "Out on the Square"), Norstedt, 1990.

Stalan (nonfiction; title means "Steely"), Carlsson (Stockholm), 1994.

SIDELIGHTS: Sture Kaellberg told *CA:* "I have worked or traveled in about forty countries in Europe, Africa, Asia, and South America for approximately nine years altogether. During that time I picked up English and German and parts of other languages. I am interested especially in the long-range transformations of social orders and cultures and am also anxious to learn about the everyday life of common people both here and abroad."

*   *   *

KAUFMAN, Stuart Bruce 1942-

PERSONAL: Born February 15, 1942, in New York. *Education:* University of Florida, B.A., 1962, M.A., 1964; Emory University, Ph.D., 1970.

ADDRESSES: Office—Department of History, University of Maryland at College Park, College Park, MD 20742.

CAREER: Morris Brown College, Atlanta, GA, lecturer in U.S. history, 1965-66; Texas A & M University, College Station, instructor in history, 1967-69; University of Maryland at College Park, visiting lecturer, 1969-70, assistant professor, 1970-74, associate professor, 1974-92, professor of history, 1992—. Instructor at George Meany Center for Labor Studies, Antioch University, MD, 1977-89; director, George Meany Memorial Archives, MD, 1987-89. Acting historian for U.S. Department of Labor, 1974.

AWARDS, HONORS: National Historical Publishing Commission fellow in advanced editing of documentary sources of U.S. history, 1969-70; distinguished achievement award from National Capital Labor History Society, 1986.

WRITINGS:

(Assistant editor) *Booker T. Washington Papers,* Volumes II-IV, University of Illinois Press (Champaign), 1972-75.

Samuel Gompers and the Origins of the American Federation of Labor, 1848-1896, Greenwood Press (Westport, CT), 1973.

(Editor) *The Samuel Gompers Papers,* University of Illinois Press, Volume I: *The Making of a Union Leader, 1850-1886,* 1986, Volume II: *The Early Years of the American Federation of Labor, 1887-1890,* 1987, Volume III: *Unrest and Depression, 1891-1894,* 1989, Volume IV: *A National Labor Movement Takes Place, 1895-1898,* 1991.

Challenge and Change: The History of the Tobacco Workers International Union, Bakery, Confectionery, and Tobacco Workers International Union, 1986.

A Vision of Unity: The History of the Bakery and Confectionery Workers International Union, Bakery, Confectionery, and Tobacco Workers International Union, 1986.

Contributor to history journals. Founder and editor, *Labor's Heritage,* 1988—.

WORK IN PROGRESS: Editing *The Samuel Gompers Papers,* Volumes V-XII, for University of Illinois Press.

BIOGRAPHICAL/CRITICAL SOURCES:

PERIODICALS

American Historical Review, April, 1975.
Annals of the American Academy of Political and Social Science, May, 1974.

*   *   *

KENEALLY, Thomas (Michael) 1935-

PERSONAL: Born October 7, 1935, in Sydney, Australia; son of Edmund Thomas and Elsie Margaret (Coyle) Keneally; married Judith Martin, August 15, 1965; children: Margaret Ann, Jane Rebecca. *Education:* Attended St. Patrick's College, New South Wales.

ADDRESSES: Office—International Creative Management, West 57th St., New York, NY 10019.

CAREER: Novelist. High school teacher in Sydney, Australia, 1960-64; University of New England, New South Wales, Australia, lecturer in drama, 1968-70; University California Irvine, visiting professor school of writing, 1985, distinguished professor 1991-95; New York University, distinguished professor, 1991-95. Member of Australia-China Council, 1978-88; advisor, Australian Constitutional Committee, 1985-88; member, Literary Arts Board of Australia, 1985-88; chairman, Australian Republican Movement, 1991-93. *Military service:* Served in Australian Citizens Military Forces.

AWARDS, HONORS: Miles Franklin Award, 1967, 1968; Captain Cook Bi-Centenary Prize, 1970; Heinemann Award for Literature, Royal Society of Literature, 1973, for *The Chant of Jimmie Blacksmith;* notable book citation, American Library Association, 1980, for *Confederates;* Booker McConnell Prize for Fiction, and fiction prize, *Los Angeles Times,* both 1982, both for *Schindler's List;* named Officer, Order of Australia.

MEMBER: Australian Society of Authors (chairman, 1987-90), National Book Council of Australia (president, 1985-90); Australian Society of Authors; PEN, Royal Society of Literature (fellow), American Academy of Arts and Sciences (fellow).

WRITINGS:

NOVELS

The Place at Whitton, Cassell (London), 1964, Walker & Co. (New York City), 1965.
The Fear, Cassell, 1965.
Bring Larks and Heroes, Cassell Australia, 1967, Viking (New York City), 1968.
Three Cheers for the Paraclete, Angus & Robertson (Sydney), 1968, Viking, 1969.
The Survivor, Angus & Robertson, 1969, Viking, 1970.
A Dutiful Daughter, Viking, 1971.
The Chant of Jimmie Blacksmith, Viking, 1972.
Blood Red, Sister Rose: A Novel of the Maid of New Orleans, Viking, 1974, published as *Blood Red, Sister Rose,* Collins (London), 1974.
Gossip from the Forest, Collins, 1975, Harcourt (New York City), 1976.
Moses the Lawgiver, Harper (New York City), 1975.
Season in Purgatory, Collins, 1976, Harcourt, 1977.
A Victim of the Aurora, Collins, 1977, Harcourt, 1978.
Ned Kelly and the City of the Bees (juvenile), J. Cape (London), 1978, Penguin (New York City), 1980.
Passenger, Harcourt, 1979.
Confederates, Collins, 1979, Harper, 1980.
The Cut-Rate Kingdom, Wildcat Press, 1980.
Bullie's House, Currency Press (Sydney), 1981.
Schindler's List, Simon & Schuster (New York City), 1982, published as *Schindler's Ark,* Hodder & Stoughton (London), 1982.
A Family Madness, Hodder & Stoughton, 1985, Simon & Schuster, 1986.
The Playmaker, Simon & Schuster, 1987.
To Asmara: A Novel of Africa, Warner Books (New York City), 1989, published as *Towards Asmara,* Hodder & Stoughton, 1989.
By the Line, University of Queensland Press (St. Lucia), 1989.
Flying Hero Class, Warner Books, 1991.
Woman of the Inner Sea, Hodder & Stoughton, 1992; Doubleday (Garden City, New York), 1993.
Jacko the Great Intruder, Hodder & Stoughton, 1994.
A River Town, Doubleday, 1995.

NONFICTION

Outback, Hodder & Stoughton, 1983, Rand McNally (Chicago), 1984.
Australia, Facts on File (New York City), 1987.

Now and in Time to Be: Ireland & the Irish, Norton (New York City), 1992, HarperCollins (London), 1993.
The Place Where Souls Are Born: A Journey into the Southwest, Simon & Schuster, 1992, published as *The Place Where Souls Are Born: A Journey into the American Southwest,* Hodder & Stoughton, 1992.
Memoirs from a Young Republic, Heinemann (London), 1993.

PLAYS

Halloran's Little Boat (produced in Sydney, 1966), Penguin, 1975.
Childermass, produced in Sydney, 1968.
An Awful Rose, produced in Sydney, 1972.

Also author of television play, *Essington,* produced in England, 1974.

ADAPTATIONS: Schindler's List was adapted for film by Steven Zaillian for Amblin Entertainment, 1993. *Playmaker* and *Woman of the Inner Sea* are being adapted for film.

WORK IN PROGRESS: The Great Shame, a nonfiction work about Irish political prisoners who were sent to Australia and later immigrated to the United States.

SIDELIGHTS: Best known for his novel *Schindler's List,* which served as the basis for an award-winning motion picture in 1993, Thomas Keneally has become one of Australia's most well-known authors. In works characterized by their sensitivity to style, their objectivity, their suspense, and diversity, this "honest workman"—as Raymond Sokolev calls Keneally in the *New York Times*—has explored subjects as diverse as the history of his native Australia and war-torn Ethiopia.

While discussions of Keneally often emphasize his years spent as a seminary student, only one of his novels focuses directly on the subject. In *Three Cheers for the Paraclete* his protagonist is a "doubting priest," Father James Maitland, who "runs afoul of the local taboos" in a Sydney seminary. As in many of his novels, Keneally presents his characters objectively and compassionately; priests and bishops are seen in the fullness of their humanity. Richard Sullivan writes in the *Washington Post Book World:* "Though this admirably sustained novel makes it clear that some structures are too rigid, that the Church is not unflawed in its members, both clerical and lay, and that more windows need opening, at the same time it reveals with fine objectivity that it is human beings who are at fault, each in his own way, Maitland as much as any."

A similar example of Keneally's desire for objectivity is evident in his account of the St. Joan of Arc story, *Blood Red, Sister Rose.* Bruce Cook of the *Washington Post Book World* claims Keneally's "intent, in fact, seems to be to reduce her and her legend to recognizably human dimensions." Placing Keneally's Joan of Arc in a historical perspective, *Time*'s Melvin Maddocks saw her standing between the "Joan-too-spiritual" of the original legend and the "Joan-too-earthy" of George Bernard Shaw. She is "less spectacular than the first two but decidedly more convincing and perhaps, at last, more moving."

Though the subjects of Keneally's novels are wide-ranging, war is often used as a backdrop in his work. After *Blood Red, Sister Rose,* wherein, Cook states, Keneally "seemed determined to write a sort of antihistorical novel, one that would expose the pettiness of war's political basis," Keneally wrote two more wartime novels, *Season in Purgatory* and *Gossip from the Forest.* The first book tells the story of a young English surgeon transferred to a Yugoslavian medical unit during World War II. *Gossip from the Forest,* one of Keneally's most highly praised works, combines fiction with the historical events surrounding the signing of the armistice ending World War I.

Perhaps Keneally's most ambitious historical novel is *Confederates,* set during the American Civil War and told from a Southern perspective. The book has no central character, but rather focuses on a group of characters who are involved in the preparations for the Second Battle of Antietam, fought in 1862. Keneally "keeps his canvas as vast as possible," writes John Higgins in the *Times Literary Supplement,* "and his concern is as much with the conscripts as with the captains; the volunteers get just as large a show as the likes of Robert E. Lee and Stonewall Jackson."

Several critics find that Keneally's portrayal of the American South is surprisingly realistic. Jeffrey Burke of the *New York Times Book Review,* for example, writes that it "is almost necessary to remind oneself that the author is Australian, so naturally, intrinsically Southern is the narrative voice." Robert Ostermann of the *Detroit News* states that Keneally's account of the Second Battle of Antietam "deserves comparison . . . to Tolstoy's rendering of the Russian defeat and retreat at Borodino and to Hemingway's of the retreat from Caporetto in *Farewell to Arms.... * The fact that this massive, absorbing narrative is the work of an Australian—not a Southerner, not even a native American—testifies even further to the stature of his achievement."

With the publication of *Schindler's List*—published in England as *Schindler's Ark*—Keneally found himself embroiled in a controversy over whether his book was fiction or nonfiction, an important point since the book was nominated for England's prestigious Booker McConnell Prize for Fiction. Although the story of Oskar Schindler, a German industrialist during World War II who saved the

Jews assigned to work in his factory from Nazi gas chambers, is historical truth, Keneally wrote the book as a novel. "The craft of the novelist," Keneally explains in the *London Times,* "is the only craft to which I can lay claim, and . . . the novel's techniques seem suited for a character of such ambiguity and magnitude as Oskar [Schindler]." After deliberation, the judges deemed the work a novel and awarded it the Booker Prize in 1982.

The controversy over *Schindler's List* is understandable. As Richard F. Shepard points out in the *New York Times,* the real-life story of Oskar Schindler "is indeed stranger than fiction." The owner of a German armaments factory staffed with forced Jewish laborers from nearby concentration camps, Schindler made a fortune during the war by supplying the German army with war materials. But when the Nazi regime decided to solve the "Jewish question" through mass extermination of Jewish prisoners, Schindler acted to save as many of his workers as possible. He convinced the local S.S. chief to allow him to house his Jewish workers in a compound built on his factory grounds rather than at a concentration camp "so that their labor [could] be more fully exploited," as Schindler explained it. Through the use of bribes and favors, Schindler worked to reunite his workers with their families, provided them with adequate food and medical care, and even managed to get a particularly murderous S.S. officer transferred to the Russian front. When the Russian army threatened to capture the area of southern Poland where Schindler's factory was located—and the German army made plans to execute the Jewish workers before retreating—Schindler moved his company and his workers to safety in German-held Czechoslovakia. By the end of the war, Schindler had some thirteen hundred Jewish workers under his protection—far more than he needed to operate his factory—and had spent his entire fortune on bribes and favors.

But despite the singular nature of Schindler's wartime activities, few people after the war knew of Schindler or what he had done. Keneally only learned of the story through a chance meeting with Leopold Pfefferberg, one of the Jews Schindler had saved. "With Pfefferberg's constant help," Keneally told the *New York Times,* "I interviewed almost fifty people who survived, thanks to Schindler." From these interviews Keneally pieced together the full story of Schindler's life for the first time.

Critical reaction to *Schindler's List* was generally favorable. Keneally, writes Christopher Lehmann-Haupt in the *New York Times,* "does not attempt to analyze in detail whatever made Oskar Schindler tick," which the reviewer finds "a little disconcerting, considering the novelistic technique he employs to tell his story. But this restraint increases the book's narrative integrity. Because the story doesn't try to do what it can't honestly do, we trust all the more what it does do." Jonathan Yardley of the *Washington Post Book World* feels that the book's major flaw is "the author's insistence on employing devices of the 'new' journalism. . . . But *Schindler's List* has about it a strong, persuasive air of authenticity, and as an act of homage it is a most emphatic and powerful document." Phillip Howard of the London *Times* agrees: "The book is a brilliantly detailed piece of historical reporting. It is moving, it is powerful, it is gripping."

In 1985's *A Family Madness,* Keneally again returns to World War II, this time exploring its repercussions upon later generations; the book was inspired by a real-life tragedy in Sydney during the summer of 1984, in which a family of five willingly ended their lives. The author's rugby-playing protagonist, Terry Delaney, goes to work for a security firm owned by a Byelorussian named Rudi Kabbel. Haunted by traumatic memories of his childhood in Russia during the War and his father's wartime journals, which reveal countless horrors inflicted upon his family, Kabbel is mentally unstable. When Delaney, who is married, falls in love with Kabbel's daughter and fathers her child, the Kabbel family closes ranks—not only against Delaney but against the world. As Blake Morrison explains in the *Observer,* "They sell up the business, surround themselves with heavy weaponry, and wait for the new dawn."

Writing in the *Times Literary Supplement,* Michael Wood says *A Family Madness* conveys the idea that "even here, in this comfort-loaded and forward-looking Australia, history will get you one way or another." Wood praises the novel, calling it "an ambitious and successful book that makes connections we need to think about." John Sutherland of the *London Review of Books,* lauds the novel as "better than its applauded predecessor [*Schindler's List*]" and notes that the nobility of the characters makes a genuine claim on the reader. However, in a review for the *New York Times Book Review,* Robert Towers criticizes Keneally's characterization, writing that "the lack of an adequately realized psychological dimension" in the character of Rudi Kabbel "is . . . crippling to the novel's aspirations."

In 1989, with the publication of *To Asmara,* as with *Schindler's List,* Keneally found himself once again accused of writing, not a novel, but an impassioned journalistic tribute. A fictionalized portrayal of the brutal African guerilla warfare of the 1980s, *To Asmara* focuses on the Eritrean Peoples Liberation Front's struggle to break free from an Ethiopia dominated by tyrants. Assisted by Russian military aid, the Ethiopian army was permitted to commit a form of genocide against the Eritreans, in the course of which Ethiopian troops destroyed the beautiful ancient city of Asmara.

Protagonist and narrator Tim Darcy is an Australian freelance journalist on "loose assignment" from the London *Times,* "one of those tentative, self-despising dreamers drawn to the empty quarters and violent margins of the West's known world," according to Robert Stone in the *New York Times Book Review.* Stone has high praise for both the character of Darcy and the novel as a whole: "Not since *For Whom the Bell Tolls* has a book of such sophistication, the work of a major international novelist, spoken out so unambiguously on behalf of an armed struggle." In contrast, Andrew Jaffe, reviewing the book for the *Los Angeles Times Book Review,* takes issue with Keneally's advocacy of the Eritrean cause. Jaffe writes, "The nobility of the rebels shouldn't be the concern of the novelist. His job is to sketch an intriguing story against an exotic backdrop. Keneally forgot to leave his commitment to the cause behind in Port Sudan."

Keneally uncharacteristically moves away from the sweeping panoramas of his earlier fiction and limits the action to the confines of one airplane in 1991's *Flying Hero Class.* Frank McCloud, tour manager for a troupe of Australian aboriginal dancers, finds himself involved in a hijacking on a flight from New York to Frankfurt following the troupe's performance. Describing *Flying Hero Class* as a "thoughtful and exciting novel," Richard Lipez points out in the *Washington Post Book World* that Keneally examines with ease two complex issues: the issue of Israeli security versus Palestinian justice and the issue of the territorial rights of the Australian aboriginal tribe versus U.S. and international mining interests. Although finding some fault with the novel, Edward Hower of the *New York Times Book Review* shares Lipez's positive opinion. "Keneally's people are fascinating, and so are the ideas his plot generates, making the hijacking a metaphor for the complex relationship between the West and the third world peoples deprived of land and dignity," Hower states, ending his review with the conclusion that "*Flying Hero Class* gives original insights into the way one man learns to reclaim responsibility for his own fate."

With *Woman of the Inner Sea,* Keneally returns to his native Australian turf and bases his plot on a real-life incident. In the 1992 work, Kate Gaffney-Kozinski, wife of a wealthy construction-empire scion, loses her husband to another woman, and her two precious children to the fire that levels the family's expensive beach home near Sydney. In an effort to forget, Kate boards a train for the interior. The place Kate chooses for her "self-annihilation" is Myambagh, a town built on the hard, flat rock of what was once an immense inland sea. Donna Rifkind, in the *Los Angeles Times Book Review,* writes, "[The Australian outback], with its miles of empty red earth, stringybark and eucalyptus, savage storms and eccentric wildlife, represents more than just external landscape . . . the fluid unpredictability of the land also mirrors Kate's transformation."

In commending the novel, Rifkind writes that "[in] the tragedy of her dead children and her subsequent pilgrimage, Kate represents a nation on a perpetual search for reinvention, a nation hardened by countless histories of hunger, tough luck and untimely death." Susan Fromberg Schaeffer echoes Rifkind's praise in the *New York Times Book Review*: "*Woman of the Inner Sea* succeeds on many fronts. It is a picaresque and often hilarious adventure story, recounting one woman's unforgettable if improbable travels. It is a series of love stories . . . and it is a mystery story as well. But the novel is also very much an exploration of ethics."

Drawing on his family background again, Keneally's novel *River Town* is based on his Irish grandparent's immigration to Australia. In *River Town*, Keneally relates the experiences of a turn-of-the-century Irishman, Tim Shea, who immigrates to Australia when he tires of the confining mores of his own country. While happy to be rid of the restraints he experienced in Ireland, Tim discovers through a series of adverse events many of the same problems with the social conventions of the Australian frontier. In his new hometown of Kempsey, New South Wales, Tim becomes a community hero when he rescues two children from a cart accident. Shortly after he finds himself being ostracized by the same community for his opposition to the Boer War—a position which ends in near economic disaster for Tim and his family when town members boycott his general store. As unfortunate events continue to plague Tim, he uncovers more of the very same social conventions he had hoped to leave behind in Ireland.

In general, critics were impressed with *River Town*. "This is truly a compassionate novel, full of vividly portrayed outcasts," commends reviewer David Willis McCullough in the *New York Times Book Review*, noting the characters are "outsiders in a nation of outsiders who are only beginning to define themselves in their new home, people who thought that 'if they traveled 12,000 miles, they might outrun original sin.' " Also finding the novel full of compassion and a well depicted historical background, a *Publishers Weekly* contributor concluded: "The story is haunting because it is both commonplace and universal. Keneally looks clearly at moral rot, but he is cautiously optimistic about the survival of good people and the uplifting heritage they bequeath." "Keneally has marvelous descriptive powers," finds *Detroit News* reviewer Barbara Holiday, lauding the author's ability to "[bring] the community alive." Holiday summarizes: "Kenneally has written an absorbing homespun account of ordinary people who are heroic in spite of themselves." Pointing out that Keneally's "use of language is a fresh breeze on a hot day,"

Time's John Skow opines that "Thomas Keneally is a builder, a gifted, painstaking maker of books." While commenting that the "final pages seem a bit hurried," McCullough deems *River Town* a "finely told novel. It is fired with the passion and hidden poetry that only a sure and experienced novelist can bring to fiction."

While reviews of his fiction have been generally favorable, several of Keneally's works of nonfiction have been received with less enthusiasm. In 1992's *Now and in Time to Be: Ireland and the Irish*, for example, the author attempts to describe the land of his grandparents. In the *New York Times Book Review* Katharine Weber writes that "dazzled by his adventure" in Ireland, Keneally fails to discern what is significant and what is not. And, reviewing Keneally's study of Australian independence entitled *Memoirs from a Young Republic*, for the *Observer*, Peter Conrad cites the author's carelessness, writing that: "Grammar and syntax frequently slump out of control." Many critics would agree that the novel is Keneally's forte: his impressive body of fiction, as Schaffer writes in the *New York Times Book Review*, "makes convincing the very serious belief that each of us has a necessary place—and that our most important task is to find it."

BIOGRAPHICAL/CRITICAL SOURCES:

BOOKS

Contemporary Literary Criticism, Gale, Volume 27, 1984, pp. 231-34, Volume 43, 1987, pp. 229-37.

PERIODICALS

America, November 13, 1976; May 28, 1977.
Best Sellers, July 15, 1968; April 1, 1969; July 1, 1971; August 15, 1972; February 1, 1975; August 1976; July 1978.
Books and Bookmen, April 1968; October 1972; March 1974; March 1979.
Chicago Tribune Book World, December 20, 1980; November 14, 1982.
Commonweal, October 24, 1969.
Detroit News, September 28, 1980; November 21, 1982; May 21, 1995, p. 8J.
Guardian Weekly, March 7, 1976; September 12, 1976.
Kirkus Reviews, March 15, 1971; July 1, 1972; February 1, 1976; November 1, 1976.
Library Journal, February 15, 1995, pp. 122-124.
London Review of Books, November 7, 1985, pp. 24-26.
Los Angeles Times Book Review, October 15, 1989, pp. 2, 13; May 16, 1993, p. 7.
Nation, November 6, 1972.
National Review, April 29, 1977.
New Statesman, September 1, 1972; October 26, 1973; October 11, 1974; September 19, 1975; September 3,

1976; September 9, 1978; January 19, 1979; November 2, 1979; September 29, 1985; September 12, 1993.

Newsweek, April 19, 1976; February 7, 1977; June 18, 1979.

New Yorker, February 10, 1975; August 23, 1976; May 23, 1977; May 8, 1978; May 19, 1986, pp. 118-19.

New York Times, April 4, 1970; September 9, 1972; October 18, 1982; November 22, 1982.

New York Times Book Review, September 27, 1970; September 12, 1971; January 16, 1972; August 27, 1972; December 3, 1972; February 9, 1975; April 11, 1976; February 27, 1977; October 14, 1977; March 26, 1978; July 8, 1979; October 5, 1980; September 20, 1987, pp. 7, 9; October 1, 1989, pp. 1, 42; April 7, 1991, p. 9; April 26, 1992, p. 12; April 18, 1993, p. 9; March 16, 1986; April 19, 1992; April 26, 1992, p. 22; May 14, 1995, p. 12.

Observer, April 25, 1971; September 10, 1971; November 24, 1974; September 21, 1975; December 14, 1975; September 5, 1976; September 4, 1977; January 21, 1979; October 21, 1979; September 29, 1985, p. 23; September 6, 1987, p. 25; March 10, 1991, p. 60; July 19, 1992, p. 58; September 12, 1993, p. 53.

Publishers Weekly, January 18, 1983, p. 447; August 7, 1987, p. 434; January 6, 1992, p. 60.

Punch, February 28, 1968.

Saturday Review, April 12, 1969; July 24, 1971.

Spectator, March 1, 1968; November 25, 1972; September 7, 1974; November 15, 1975; September 4, 1976; September 3, 1977.

Time, May 15, 1995, p. 80.

Times (London), August 16, 1968; June 7, 1971; August 28, 1972; February 10, 1975; March 7, 1981; October 20, 1982; October 21, 1982.

Times Literary Supplement, May 7, 1970; April 23, 1971; September 15, 1972; October 26, 1973; October 11, 1974; September 19, 1975; September 3, 1976; October 14, 1977; November 2, 1979; November 23, 1979; October 18, 1985, p. 1169; October 20, 1989, p. 1147; January 29, 1993, p. 28; March 18, 1994, p. 13.

Washington Post Book World, April 27, 1969; April 19, 1970; August 29, 1971; August 13, 1972; January 26, 1975; February 20, 1977; March 26, 1978; August 31, 1980; October 4, 1981; October 20, 1982; March 24, 1991, p. 8.

West Coast Review of Books, July 1978.

World Literature Today, winter 1977; autumn 1978; spring 1980.

* * *

KING, Margaret L(eah) 1947-

PERSONAL: Born October 16, 1947, in New York, NY; daughter of Reno C. (an engineer) and Marie (a teacher; maiden name, Ackerman) King; married Robert E. Kessler (a journalist), 1976; children: David King, Jeremy King. *Education:* Sarah Lawrence College, B.A., 1967; Stanford University, M.A., 1968, Ph.D., 1972. *Religion:* Protestant.

ADDRESSES: Home—324 Beverly Rd., Douglaston, NY 11363. *Office*—Ph.D. Program in History, Graduate Center of the City University of New York, 33 West 42nd St., New York, NY 10036.

CAREER: California State College, Fullerton, assistant professor of history, 1969-70; Brooklyn College of the City University of New York, Brooklyn, NY, assistant professor, 1972-76, associate professor, 1977-85, professor of history, 1986—; Graduate Center of the City University of New York, New York City, professor of history, 1986—.

MEMBER: American Historical Association, Renaissance Society of America.

AWARDS, HONORS: Danforth Foundation fellowship, 1967-72; City University of New York research awards, 1973, 1973-74, 1977-78, 1980, and 1990; grant from American Council of Learned Societies, 1976, fellow, 1977-78; grants from Gladys Krieble Delmas Foundation, 1977-78, 1980-81,and 1990, and National Endowment for the Humanities, 1984, and 1986-87; Howard R. Marraro Prize from the American Catholic Historical Association, 1986; grant from American Philosophical Society, 1991; Tow Award for distinction in scholarship, Brooklyn College of the City University of New York, 1994-95.

WRITINGS:

(Editor and translator with Albert Rabil, Jr.) *Her Immaculate Hand: Humanists of the Early Italian Renaissance,* Center for Medieval and Early Renaissance Studies, 1983, 2nd revised edition, 1992.

Venetian Humanism in an Age of Patrician Dominance, Princeton University Press (Princeton, NJ), 1986.

Women of the Renaissance, University of Chicago Press (Chicago, IL), 1991.

The Death of the Child Valerio Marcello, University of Chicago Press, 1994.

Contributor of about twenty articles and reviews to scholarly journals and essay collections. Editor of *Renaissance Quarterly,* 1984-88.

WORK IN PROGRESS: The Meaning of the West, completion expected in 1997.

SIDELIGHTS: Margaret L. King's 1986 book, *Venetian Humanism in an Age of Patrician Dominance,* is a study of the state and society of fifteenth-century Venice. While supporting the controversial myth that the city was a "uniquely wise and harmonious polity," wrote B. S. Pullan in the *Times Literary Supplement,* King takes care to not confuse the mythical view with reality. With "rare thoroughness . . . [and] great skill," judged the reviewer, King "manages to draw out the significance of [Venetian humanism's] unenterprising character, to be honest about its limitations, and to reveal it for what it became." Overall, this "sensitively written, lucid and well planned" book, determined Pullan, contributes to a "comprehensive view of the most stable of Renaissance states."

King told *CA:* "I am interested in humanism because I am a humanist, in the child Valerio Marcello because I am a mother, in Venice because—more than any place I know—it is now as it was in the fifteenth century, and I am interested in death because it is our future."

BIOGRAPHICAL/CRITICAL SOURCES:

PERIODICALS

New York Review of Books, April 6, 1995.
New York Times Book Review, October 30, 1994.
Times Literary Supplement, August 22, 1986.

*　　*　　*

KLIMA, Ivan 1931-

PERSONAL: Born September 14, 1931, in Prague, Czechoslovakia; son of Ing Vilem and Marta (Synkova) Klima; married Helena Mala (a psychotherapist), September 24, 1958; children: Michal, Hana. *Education:* Charles University, M.A., 1956. *Avocational interests:* Lawn tennis, picking mushrooms.

ADDRESSES: Agent—(books) Brombergs Bokforlag Industrigatan, 4a Box 12886 S-11298 Stockholm, Sweden; (plays) Projekt, Theater & Medien Verlag, Karolimgerring 31, 5000 Cologne 1, Germany.

CAREER: Writer. Ceskoslovensky Spisovatel (publishers), Prague, Czechoslovakia, editor, 1959-63; *Literarni noviny* (weekly publication of Union of Writers), Prague, deputy and editor in chief, 1963-69; University of Michigan, Ann Arbor, visiting professor, 1969-70. Member of editorial board, *Lidove Noviny* (daily newspaper).

MEMBER: Union of Czechoslovak Writers (central committee 1963-70, when the union was banned by the Czech government; council member, 1989—), Club of Rome (Czech branch), Czech PEN Centre (president, 1990-93), Ambassador Club.

AWARDS, HONORS: Awards from Ministry of Culture, 1960, 1965, and from Ceskoslovensky Spisovatel, 1963; Hostovsky Award, New York, 1986, for *My First Loves;* George Theiner Prize, for *My Golden Trades,* 1993; Best Books of 1995 citation from *Publisher's Weekly,* for *Waiting for the Dark, Waiting for the Light.*

WRITINGS:

NONFICTION

Mezi tremi hranicemi (book on Slovakia), Ceskoslovensky Spisovatel (Prague), 1960.
Karel Chapek (essay), Ceskoslovensky Spisovatel, 1962.
The Spirit of Prague (essays), Granta (London), 1994.

SHORT STORIES

Bezvadny den (short stories; title means "The Wonderful Day"), Ceskoslovensky Spisovatel, 1962.
Milenci na jednu noc (short stories; title means "Lovers for One Night"), Ceskoslovensky Spisovatel, 1964.
Ma vesela jitra, Ceskoslevensky Spisovatel, 1978, translation by George Theiner published as *My Merry Mornings: Stories from Prague,* Readers International, 1985.
My First Loves, translation by Ewald Osers, Chatto and Windus, 1987, Harper (New York City), 1988, originally published in Czech as *Moje prvni lasky.*
Ostrov mrtvych kralu (title means "The Island of Death Kings"), Rozmluvy (Prague), 1991.
My Golden Trades, translation by Paul Wilson, Granta, 1992, originally published in Czech as *Moje zlata remesla.*

FICTION

Hodina ticha (fiction; title means "The Hour of Silence"), Ceskoslovensky Spisovatel, 1963.
Lod jmenem nadeje, Ceskoslovensky Spisovatel, 1969, translation by Edith Pargeter published as *A Ship Named Hope,* Gollancz (London), 1970.
Milostne leto, Sixty-Eight Publishers, 1973, translation by Osers, published as *A Summer Affair,* Chatto & Windus, 1987.
Love and Garbage, Chatto & Windus, 1990, Knopf (New York City), 1991, originally published in Czech as *Laska a smeti.*
Judge on Trial, translation by A. G. Brain, Chatto & Windus, 1991, Knopf, 1993, originally published in Czech as *Soudce z milosti.*
Waiting for the Dark, Waiting for the Light, translation by Wilson, Granta, 1994, originally published in Czech as *Cekani na tmu, cekani na svetlo.*

PLAYS

Zamek, first produced in Prague, Czechoslovakia, at Theatre Na Vinohradech, 1964, produced as *The Castle* in Ann Arbor, MI, at Lydia Mendelssohn Theatre, University of Michigan, December 3, 1968, produced for television in Austria, Finland, and the Netherlands.
Porota (title means "The Jury"), first produced in Prague, April 17, 1969, adaptation for radio produced by

NDR Radio, West Germany, English radio version produced by the British Broadcasting Corporation (BBC), London, England, 1970.

Zenich pro Marcelu (title means "A Bridegroom for Marcelo"), translation by Ruth Willard first produced Off-Broadway, spring, 1969, produced for television in Austria and West Germany.

Klara, translation by Willard first produced Off-Broadway, spring, 1969, produced for television in Austria and West Germany.

Ministr a andel (title means "President and the Angel"), broadcast by BBC, London, 1973.

Hry (title means "The Games"), first produced in Vancouver, Canada, 1975.

Also author of *Mistr* (title means "The Master"), 1967; *Cafe Myrian* (title means "The Sweetshoppe Myriam"), 1968; and *Franz a Felice,* translation by Yan Drabak as *Kafka and Felice,* 1985.

OTHER

Uz Se Blizi Mece: Eseje, Fejetony, Rozhovory, Novinar (Prague), 1990.

(With others) *Uzel Pohadek: Pohadky, Soucasnych Cesky-chautoru,* Lidove Noviny, 1991.

Contributor to periodicals, including *New York Review of Books, National, Granta,* and *Index on Censorship.* Klima's works have been translated into various languages, including German, Swedish, Italian, Spanish, Hebrew, French, Korean, Norwegian, Russian, Danish, Dutch, Polish, Portuguese, and Serbocroation.

SIDELIGHTS: Ivan Klima is a Czech writer who was banned in his own country after the 1968 Prague Spring reforms. One of about two hundred banned Czech writers, Klima chose not to emigrate, unlike his fellow dissidents Milan Kundera and Josef Skvorecky, preferring to stay at home and write as best he could under the existing constraints. "Ivan Klima," according to Eva Hoffman in the *New York Times Book Review,* "is among those urbane, plain-spoken literary spirits whose work travels successfully across political systems, as well as across continents."

During the communist government's ban on writers' work, an underground movement was formed in Czechoslovakia to circulate photocopied manuscripts among interested readers. The Russian term for writing circulated in this fashion is *samizdat,* generally translated as "writing for the desk-drawer." Circulating and reading *samizdat* writings were considered criminal offenses, so the reader as well as the writer took a risk in participating in the movement. After the collapse of the Czech communist government, restrictions loosened and efforts were made to reintegrate banned writers into Czech society and liber-

alize controls on the arts. Klima was an active member and spokesperson for the revived Czech branch of PEN; in 1990 he became its president.

Both Michiko Kakutani of the *New York Times* and *Los Angeles Times* reviewer Richard Eder have discussed the effects that government bans can have on writing style. Eder observed that "writing accomplished through censorship and the prospect of punishment can take on a primal urgency. There is a nerviness to it. It comes partly from the act of defiance, and partly from the hunger of readers to hear voices and messages denied them by the official monopoly." As an example, Eder pointed to Klima's short-story collection *My Merry Mornings,* which he called "a work of jittery truth . . . gritty, passionate and starved." Kakutani noted that "in the work of . . . Milan Kundera and Ivan Klima, people *do* make an attempt to create a personal life that will be free from state control. They do so mainly by engaging in frenetic and promiscuous sex, but they discover that even sex has been colored by the duplicities and manipulations of the political life around them. For them, too, the line between the public and the personal has been erased."

The plot of Klima's *A Summer Affair* supports Kakutani's point, at least in part. It is the story of a research scientist who, in the words of *Times Literary Supplement*'s Lesley Chamberlain, "shamelessly and unreasonably . . . abandons his family and his work for a humiliating and temperamental sexual arrangement." Summing up the author's treatment of his protagonist's behavior, Chamberlain states: "Though Ivan Klima does not quite condone, these are facts, not matters inviting judgment. Love is a condition, not a controllable sin, and Klima writes about it with disconcerting Flaubertian wisdom."

My First Loves, a collection of four stories, was published in the United States in 1988. "At first glance," Eder remarks, "the tone is delicately nostalgic, even pastoral. . . . The longings, delusions and losses of young love become a code language for an alien and crimped reality. The code works sporadically; the result is writing that is haunting at times, but that can be cloudy and bland." Jack Sullivan, writing in the *New York Times Book Review,* comments that "Klima is most compelling when he is willing to trust the power and odd lucidity of his hero's adolescent musing. He is least so when he occasionally . . . explains the work's symbolism and significance. No explanations are necessary, for these stories carry the burning authority and desperate eloquence of a survivor."

Several reviewers unhesitatingly labeled the stories autobiographical. Andrew Sinclair points out in the London *Times* that Klima spent several of his childhood years in the Czech barracks camp of Terezin. In one story of the collection, a boy is emotionally attracted to and then disappointed by the young woman who doles out the daily milk rations and initially gives the child an extra portion every day. In the *New York Review of Books,* D. J. Enright gives the example of another story in which the boy's father—like Klima's, an engineer—"voices the idealistic Communist vision of a future in which poverty and exploitation will be no more, heavy labor will be done by marvelous machines, the people will govern, and, since there is no reason for war, an age of universal peace and trust will dawn."

Klima's novel *Love and Garbage* focuses on a middle-aged dissident writer in Prague who had lived in the Terezin camp as a child. Unable to make a living at his profession because his work is banned, he becomes a street-sweeper. The tales of his fellow laborers become part of the material for his fiction, along with memories of people who were close to him and an account of his present struggle to choose between his wife and his mistress. The book turns on many allegories, most of which are centered around the question of what is trash. In the London *Times,* Barbara Day explains that "Klima was writing before the 'gentle revolution' which swept away the tainted ideals of his country's old government, and brought in a new one. Now he is amongst those who are working—a little less gently—to clear up the rubbish of the past." In the opinion of Alberto Manguel in the *Washington Post Book World,* "*Love and Garbage* announces [the] world's essential dichotomy: We create in order to destroy, and then build from the destruction. Our emblem is the phoenix."

In the *New Republic,* Stanislaw Baranczak criticizes the author's style, noting that "Klima does his thing with utmost seriousness, with heavy-handed directness; even his symbols seem to have a sign that reads ATTENTION: SYMBOL attached to them, lest we overlook their exfoliating, larger-than-life implications. . . . It is . . . the arbitrariness, the sententiousness and the priggishness of Klima's observations, which leave no room for the reader's own interpretation of the matters under discussion." Hoffman finds that the author's "sincerity sometimes slides toward banality. The novel's fragmentary method makes for a certain stasis." She concludes, however, that these defects "do not substantially affect the import or the impact of Mr. Klima's work," which "affords the experience, rare in today's fiction, of being in the presence of a seasoned, measured perspective, and a mind that strives honestly to arrive at a wisdom sufficient to our common condition."

Judge on Trial centers around a judge who earlier in his career wrote against the death penalty and withdrew from the Community Party, acts that have brought his loyalty to the government increasingly into question. As he presides over the trial of a petty criminal accused of gassing his landlady and her granddaughter, the judge realizes that he is equally on trial. "The novel's subject is suffocation. Like all of Ivan Klima's fiction," writes Peter Kemp in the *Times Literary Supplement,* "it takes you into an atmosphere of choking oppressiveness." Kemp concludes that Klima demonstrates in this novel how, "even in a climate thickly polluted by cynicism, integrity can't be entirely asphyxiated." In a *Times Literary Supplement* review, Roger Scruton calls *Judge on Trial* "one of the saddest novels to have been written in contemporary Czechoslovakia."

BIOGRAPHICAL/CRITICAL SOURCES:

BOOKS

Goetz-Stankiewicz, Marketa, *The Silenced Theatre,* University of Toronto Press, 1979.
Kienzle: Modernes Welttheatre, Kroner Verlag, 1966.

PERIODICALS

London Review of Books, December 19, 1991.
Los Angeles Times, June 19, 1985; January 13, 1988.
Los Angeles Times Book Review, May 19, 1991.
Nation, December 30, 1991.
New Republic, July 29, 1991.
New York Review of Books, May 18, 1989; April 12, 1990; July 15, 1993.
New York Times, August 4, 1989; February 8, 1990.
New York Times Book Review, February 21, 1988; May 12, 1991; April 18, 1993.
Times Literary Supplement, July 5, 1985; January 23, 1987; August 28, 1987; March 30, 1990; October 25, 1991; October 16, 1992.
Times (London), November 30, 1986; April 5, 1990.
Washington Post Book World, June 23, 1991; April 18, 1993.

*   *   *

KRIEGER, Murray 1923-

PERSONAL: Born November 27, 1923, in Newark, NJ; son of Isidore and Jennie (Glinn) Krieger; married Joan Stone, 1947; children: Catherine Leona, Eliot Franklin. *Education:* Attended Rutgers University, 1940-42; University of Chicago, A.M., 1948; Ohio State University, Ph.D., 1952.

ADDRESSES: Home—407 Pinecrest Dr., Laguna Beach, CA 92651-1471. *Office*—Department of English and Comparative Literature, University of California, Irvine, CA 92717.

CAREER: Kenyon College, Gambier, OH, instructor, 1948-49; Ohio State University, Columbus, instructor, 1951-52; University of Minnesota, Minneapolis, assistant professor, 1952-55, associate professor, 1955-58; University of Illinois at Urbana-Champaign, professor of English, 1958-63; University of Iowa, Iowa City, Carpenter Professor of Literary Criticism, 1963-66; University of California, professor at Irvine campus, 1967-85, professor of English at Los Angeles campus, 1973-82, university professor, 1974—. Director, School of Criticism and Theory at University of California, Irvine, 1976-79, honorary senior fellow, 1981—, and at Northwestern University, 1980-81. Director, University of California Humanities Research Institute, 1987-89. Associate member, Center for Advanced Study, University of Illinois, 1961-62. Regents lecturer, University of California, Davis, 1966. *Military service:* U.S. Army, 1942-46.

MEMBER: International Association of University Professors of English, Academy of Literary Studies, American Academy of Arts and Sciences (fellow; council and executive committee member, 1987-88), Modern Language Association of America, Phi Beta Kappa.

AWARDS, HONORS: Guggenheim fellowships, 1956-57, 1961-62; American Council of Learned Societies fellowship, 1966-67; National Endowment for the Humanities research grant, 1971-72; Rockefeller Foundation humanities fellowship, 1978; Humboldt Foundation (Germany) research prize, 1986; medal from University of California, Irvine, 1991.

WRITINGS:

(Co-editor) *The Problems of Aesthetics,* Rinehart (New York City), 1953.

The New Apologists for Poetry, University of Minnesota Press (Minneapolis), 1956.

The Tragic Vision: Variations on a Theme in Literary Interpretation (also see below), Holt (New York City), 1960.

A Window to Criticism: Shakespeare's Sonnets and Modern Poetics, Princeton University Press (Princeton, NJ), 1964.

(Editor) *Northrop Frye in Modern Criticism,* Columbia University Press (New York City), 1966.

(Co-editor) *Directions for Criticism: Structuralism and Its Alternatives,* University of Wisconsin Press (Madison), 1977.

Arts on the Level: The Fall of the Elite Object, University of Tennessee Press (Knoxville), 1981.

(Editor and author of introduction) *The Aims of Representation: Subject, Text, History,* Columbia University Press, 1987.

A Reopening of Closure: Organicism against Itself, Columbia University Press, 1989.

The Ideologial Imperative: Repression and Resistance in Recent American Theory, Academia Sinica (Taipei, Taiwan), 1993.

PUBLISHED BY JOHNS HOPKINS UNIVERSITY PRESS (BALTIMORE. MD)

The Play and the Place of Criticism, 1967.

The Classic Vision: The Retreat from Extremity in Modern Literature (also see below), 1971.

Visions of Extremity in Modern Literature, 1973, Volume 1: *The Tragic Vision: Variations on a Theme in Literary Interpretation,* Volume 2: *The Classic Vision: The Retreat from Extremity in Modern Literature,* 1973.

Theory of Criticism: A Tradition and Its System, 1976.

Poetic Presence and Illusion: Essays in Critical History and Theory, 1979.

Words about Words about Words: Theory, Criticism, and the Literary Text, 1988.

Ekphrasis: The Illusion of the Natural Sign, illustrated by Joan Krieger, 1992.

The Institution of Theory, 1994.

OTHER

Contributor to numerous books of collected essays. Also contributor of numerous articles to critical and scholarly journals. Contributor of introductions for paperback reprints of novels in "New American Library of World Literature" series.

SIDELIGHTS: An influential literary critic and theoretician of literary criticism, Murray Krieger defends the notion that literature—especially poetry—is uniquely different from other uses of language. For Krieger, wrote *Dictionary of Literary Biography* contributor Paul B. Armstrong, "the special language of poetry is an unrivalled repository of existential insight." Armstrong added that the controversial Krieger has defended his views against a variety of opponents, especially the New Critics who tend to "cut literature off from the reader and the lived world."

Krieger received his Ph.D. from Ohio State University in 1952 and established his professional reputation shortly thereafter with the publication of *The New Apologists for Poetry* in 1956 and *The Tragic Vision: Variations on a Theme in Literary Interpretation* in 1960. He was offered the Carpenter Chair in Literary Criticism at the University of Iowa in 1963, becoming the first American chaired professor in the field of literary criticism. As Armstrong noted, "Long before the theory of criticism became recognized as a central discipline in literary study, Krieger insisted on its importance." In fact, the scholar went on to found the School of Criticism and Theory, an association that "refused allegiance to any particular critical dogma but gained a reputation for unusual rigor and penetration in the scrutiny to which it subjected all theoretical positions," according to Armstrong.

Since 1974 Krieger has been a university professor for the entire University of California system. His many books use aesthetics, existential philosophy, and criticism to approach and explore poetry's paradoxes. According to Armstrong, "Krieger has set for himself the goal of accounting intelligibly for the inconsistencies of literature and life without lapsing into nonsense or falling into chaos." In a *Modern Fiction Studies* review of *Ekphrasis: The Illusion of the Natural Sign,* John B. Vickery commended Krieger for "the care and subtlety with which the arguments are developed, . . . the strikingly relevant implications they possess for critical theory's being grounded in its own history, and . . . the vital importance which an open, thoughtful, rigorous mind has to the scholarly study of both."

BIOGRAPHICAL/CRITICAL SOURCES:

BOOKS

Dictionary of Literary Biography, Volume 67: *Modern American Critics since 1955,* Gale (Detroit), 1988, pp. 213-20.
Henricksen, Bruce, editor, *Murray Krieger and Contemporary Critical Theory,* Columbia University Press (New York City), 1986.
Lentricchia, Frank, *After the New Criticism,* University of Chicago Press, 1980, pp. 213-54.
Morris, Wesley, *Toward a New Historicism,* Princeton University Press, 1972.

PERIODICALS

English Journal, November, 1992, p. 75.
Georgia Review, summer, 1968.
Modern Fiction Studies, summer, 1982, p. 345; winter, 1988, pp. 729-30; summer, 1993, pp. 433-35.
New Orleans Review, spring, 1983, pp. 13-17.
Saturday Review, May 19, 1956.
Times Literary Supplement, December 16, 1988, p. 1399; August 28, 1992, p. 20.
World Literature Today, winter, 1995.

*   *   *

KRLEZA, Miroslav 1893-1981

PERSONAL: Born July 7, 1893, in Zagreb, Yugoslavia; died December 29, 1981, in Zagreb, Yugoslavia; son of Miroslav (a city clerk) and Ivanka Krleza; married Bela Kangrga (an actress). *Education:* Educated at Lucoviceum military academy in Budapest, Hungary.

CAREER: Dramatist, novelist, poet, and essayist. Yugoslav Lexicographical Institute, Zagreb, Yugoslavia, director, 1950-81. Founder of periodicals *Plamen* (literary review; title means "Flame"), 1919, *Knjizevna republika* (title means "Literary Republic"), 1924, *Danas* (title means "Today"), 1934, *Pecat* (title means "Seal"),

1939-40, and *Republika* (title means "Republic"), 1945-46. *Military service:* Austrian Army, 1914-18.

MEMBER: Yugoslav Writers' Union (former president), Yugoslav Academy of Science and Art (former vice president), Yugoslav National Assembly (former deputy).

AWARDS, HONORS: Received numerous Yugoslavian literary prizes after World War II and several international awards, including the Heder Prize.

WRITINGS:

IN ENGLISH TRANSLATION

Povratek Filipa Latinovicza (also see below), Minerva (Zagreb), 1932, translation by Zora Depolo published as *The Return of Philip Latinovicz,* Lincolns-Prager, 1959, Vanguard (New York City), 1969.
Na rubu pameti (also see below), Biblioteka nezavisnih pisaca (Zagreb), 1938, translation by Depolo published as *On the Edge of Reason,* Vanguard, 1976.
The Cricket beneath the Waterfall, and Other Stories, translated by Branko Lenski from the original *Cvrcak pod vodopadom,* Vanguard, 1972.
Selected Correspondence, Oslobodenje, 1988.

IN CROATIAN: POETRY

Pan, Naklada autora (Zagreb), 1917.
Tri simfonije (title means "Three Symphonies"), Drustvo hrvatskih knjizevnika (Zagreb), 1917.
Pjesme (title means "Poems"), volumes 1 and 2, Naklada autora, 1918, volume 3, Jug (Zagreb), 1919.
Lirika (title means "Lyric Poems"), Jug, 1919.
Knjiga pjesama (title means "The Book of Poems"), Izdavacka knjizarnica Geca Kona (Belgrade), 1931.
Knjiga lirike (title means "A Book of Lyric Poetry"), Minerva, 1932.
Simfonije (title means "Symphonies"), Minerva, 1933.
Balade Petrice Kerempuha (title means "The Ballads of Petrica Kerempuh"), Akademska zalozba (Ljubljana, Yugoslavia), 1936.
Pjesme u tmini (title means "Poems in the Darkness"), Biblioteka nezavisnih pisaca, 1937.

PROSE

Tri kavalira gospodice Melanije (title means "Three Suitors of Miss Melania"), Matica hrvatska (Zagreb), 1920.
Magyar Kiralyi honved novela (title means "Short Story on the Royal Hungarian Homeguards"), Naklada Josipa Caklovica (Zagreb), 1921.
Hrvatski bog Mars (title means "The Croatian God Mars"; also see below), Narodna knjiznica (Zagreb), 1922, 2nd edition, Minerva, 1934.

Novele (title means "Short Stories"), Nakladna knjizara Vinka Vosickog (Koprivnica, Yugoslavia), 1923, new edition, Biblioteka nezavisnih pisaca, 1937.

Sabrana djela (collection), 3 volumes, Vinko Vosicki, 1923-26, edition in 9 volumes, Minerva, 1932-34, edition in 27 volumes, Zora, 1952-72.

Vrazji otok (title means "Devil's Island"), Neva (Zagreb), 1924.

Izlet u Rusiju (title means "Excursion to Russia"), Narodna knjiznica, 1926.

Hiljadu i jedna smrt (title means "A Thousand and One Deaths"), Minerva, 1933.

Djela Miroslava Krleze, eleven volumes, Biblioteka nezavisnih pisaca, 1937-39.

Banket u Blitvi (title means "Banquet in Blitva"), Volumes I and II, Biblioteka nezavisnih pisaca, 1938 and 1939, Volume III, Zora (Zagreb), 1956, published in two volumes, 1964.

Knjiga proze (title means "The Book of Prose"), Biblioteka nezavisnih pisaca, 1938.

Djela (collection; includes *Hrvatski bog Mars* and *Povratek Filipa Latinovicza*), Nakladni zavod Hrvatska, 1946.

Djetinjstvo u Agramu, 1902-1903 (title means "Childhood in Agram in 1902-1903"), Zora, 1952.

Davni dani (title means "Days Long Gone"), Zora, 1956.

Zastave I-IV (title means "Banners I-IV"), Zora, 1967.

Miroslav Krleza (collected works), five volumes, Zora, 1973.

Baraka Pet Be i druge novele (collection), Mladost, 1976.

Zastave I-V (title means "Banners I-V"), Oslobodenje (Sarajevo), 1976.

Dnevnik I-V (title means "Diary I-V"), Oslobodenje, 1977.

Stari i novi razgovori s Krlezom, Spektar (Zagreb), 1982.

Iz nase knjizevne krcme, Oslobodenje, 1983.

Ratne teme, Oslobodenje, 1983.

Sa urednickog stola, Oslobodenje, 1983.

Gdje smo i kako smo: Suvremene politicke teme, Oslobodenje, 1988.

Svjedocanstva vremena: Knjizevno-estetske varijacije, Oslobodenje, 1988.

COLLECTIONS OF ESSAYS AND CRITICISM

Eseji (title means "Essays"), Minerva, 1932, new edition, Prosveta, 1958, edition in several volumes, Zora, 1961-67.

Moj obracun s njima (title means "Getting Even"), Naklada autora, 1932.

Podravski motivi (title means "Motifs of Podravina"), Minerva, 1933.

Evropa danas (title means "Europe Today"), Biblioteka aktuelnih pitanja (Zagreb), 1935.

Deset krvavih godina (title means "Ten Years in Blood"), Biblioteka nezavisnih pisaca, 1937.

Eppur si muove: Studije i osvrti, Biblioteka nezavisnih pisaca, 1938.

Dijalekticki antibarbarus (title means "Dialectic Antibarbarus"), Biblioteka nezavisnih pisaca, 1939.

Knjiga studija i putopisa (title means "The Book of Studies and Travels"), Biblioteka nezavisnih pisaca, 1939.

Racic, Nakladni zavod Hrvatske (Zagreb), 1947.

Goya, Nakladni zavod Hrvatske, 1948.

O Marinu Drzicu (title means "On Marin Drzic"), Prosveta (Belgrade), 1949.

Kalendar jedne bitke, 1942 (title means "An Almanac of a Battle in 1942"), Zora, 1953.

Kalendar jedne parlamentarne komedije (title means "An Almanac of a Parliamentary Comedy"), Zora, 1953.

O Erazmu Rotterdamskom (title means "On Desiderius Erasmus"), Zora, 1953.

99 varijacija lexicographica (title means "Ninety-Nine Lexicographic Variations"), Duga, 1972.

Djetinjstvo 1902-1903 i drugi zapisi, Zora, 1972.

Krleza o religiji, Oslobodenje, 1982.

Svjetiljke u tmini: Knjizevni eseji, Oslobodenje, 1988.

PLAYS

Hrvatska rapsodija (title means "Croatian Rhapsody"; includes *Kraljevo* and *Cristoval Colon* [also see below]), Djordje Celap, 1918.

Vucjak (three-act; title means "The Village of Wolfhound"; first produced in Zagreb, 1922; also see below), Nakladna Knjizara Vinka Vosickog, 1923.

Mikelandjelo Buonaroti (one-act; title means "Michelangelo Buonarroti"; also see below), first produced in Zagreb, 1925.

Adam i Eva (one-act; title means "Adam and Eve"; also see below), first produced in Zagreb, 1925.

Gospoda Glembajevi (three-act; title means "The Glembay Family"; first produced in Zagreb, 1929; also see below), Drustvo hrvatskih knjizevnika, 1928.

U agoniji (two-act; title means "In Agony"; first produced in Zagreb, 1928; produced as three-act play in Serbia, Yugoslavia, 1959), Srpska knjizevna zadruga (Belgrade), 1931, eighth edition, in three acts, 1962.

Leda (four-act), first produced in Zagreb, 1930.

Glembajevi (title means "The Glembays"), Minerva, 1932.

Legende (title means "Legends"; includes *Legenda* [first published in *Knjizevne novosti,* 1914], *Michelangelo Buonarotti, Kristofor Kolumbo, Maskerata, Kraljevo,* and *Adam i Eva*), Minerva, 1933.

U logoru [and] *Vucjak* (*U logoru* was originally titled *Galicija,* published in 1922 and produced in 1924; also see below), Minerva, 1934.

Golgota (title means "Golgotha"), Biblioteka nezavisnih pisaca, 1937.

Maskerata (title means "Mascherata: A Carnival Poem"), first produced in Ljubljana, 1955.

Kraljevo (title means "The Kermess"), first produced in Ljubljana, 1955.

Kristofor Kolumbo (two-part legend; title means "Christopher Columbus"; sometimes listed as *Cristoval Colon*), first produced in Ljubljana, 1955.

Aretej; ili, Legenda o Svetoj Ancili (five-scene fantasy; title means "Aretaios; or, The Legend of St. Ancilla"; first produced in Zagreb, 1959), Zora, 1959.

Saloma (one-act; title means "Salome"), first produced in Serbia, 1963.

Tri drame: U logoru, Vucjak, Golgota (title means "Three Dramas: In the Camp, The Village of Wolfhound, Golgotha"), Zora, 1964.

Put u raj (two-part fantasy; title means "Journey to Paradise"; first produced in Zagreb, 1973), JAZU, 1970.

Drame (includes *Galicija* and *Saloma*), [Sarajevo], 1981.

Also author of plays *U predvecerje,* 1919, and *Krokodilina ili razgovor o istini,* 1945.

OTHER

Govor na Kongresu knjizevnika u Ljubljani, Zora, 1952.

Pijana noc cetrnaestog novembra 1918, Zora, 1952.

O parlamentarizmu i demokraciji kod nas, Zora, 1953.

Kako stoje stvari, Zora, 1953.

Izbrannoe, Izd-vo inostrannoi lit-ry, 1958.

Izbor, two volumes, edited by Petar Dzadzic, Svjetlost, 1960.

(Editor with Milan Bogdanovic, Stanko Lasie, and Vera Sevecic) *Danas,* two volumes, [Zagreb], 1971.

Krleza u skoli, Zavod za izadvanje udzbenika, 1972.

(With Edvard Kardelj) *Tito i Savez komunista Jugoslavije,* Radnicka stampa (Belgrade), 1972.

Panorama pogleda, pojava i pojmova I-V, Oslobodjenje, 1975.

Author of introduction, Petar Dobrovic, *Petar Dobrovic,* Zora, 1954; Miljenko Stancic, *Miljenko Stancic: Mapa reprodukeija,* [Zagreb], 1964; *Zlato i srebro Zadra i Nina,* Turistkomerc, 1972. Contributor to books, including *Kervave kronika glas,* [Zagreb], 1972. Editor of *Pomorska enciklopedija,* 1954-64, *Enciklopedija Jugoslavije,* Leksikografski zavod, 1955-71, and, with Marko Kostrencic, *Enciklopedija Leksikografskog zavoda,* 1955-64.

SIDELIGHTS: When Ivo Andric received the 1961 Nobel Prize for Literature and was asked what his Swedish publisher could do for him, he replied: "Publish Krleza." Although Miroslav Krleza wrote over five dozen books and is considered the major Croatian literary voice in the twentieth century, only a small portion of his work has been published in English. Some critics have attributed this neglect partly to the narrow-mindedness of Western publishers and their public and partly to the ambiguities of Krleza's themes and politics. As Ante Kadic explained in the *Dictionary of Literary Biography,* Krleza's "materi-

alistic convictions—conveyed with strong emotional impetus, his Marxist and liberal philosophy, his socialism mingled with a sincere defense of personal freedom, and his readiness to defend his point of view with his own life—made Krleza highly controversial."

Krleza was committed to radical humanism, a belief that led the Yugoslav government to ban most of his work until 1940. Indeed, in 1920 *Galicija,* his first play accepted for production, was shut down an hour before it was scheduled to open (although it was later produced in 1924 as *O logoru*). Despite official restrictions, Krleza proceeded to turn out not only plays but novels, poetry, short stories, and essays, and by the early 1950s, related Kadic, he had become a "driving force in liberalizing Yugoslav culture."

Krleza's earliest models were such figures as Arthur Schopenhauer, Friedrich Nietzsche, and Feuerbach, through whom he replaced his Catholic upbringing with atheistic existentialism. His distaste for literal realism led some to compare his work to the writings of Franz Kafka and Louis-Ferdinand Celine. Krleza's other influences included Karl Marx, Charles Darwin, and especially Vladimir Lenin, "because he was the first to bring to fruition Marx's thesis that philosophy should no longer merely interpret the world but seek to change it," observed Dragan M. Jeremic.

Critics have differed in their opinions of the link between Krleza's politics and writings. Jeremic maintained that all of Krleza's work should be regarded from an "activist, revolutionary perspective," for even as it embodies the philosophical principles of Marxism, Leninism, and Darwinism, it must be "understood as the criticism of the ethical hypocrisy and political short-sightedness of the European bourgeoisie." Others, however, have countered this point of view by saying that Krleza's only insurgent tendency was his constant faith in the power of humanity, a belief that was repeatedly proclaimed in his many works.

It was this duality in Krleza's vision—his simultaneous attachment both to socialist revolutionary ideals and to moral and artistic integrity—that, critics have contended, distinguished him among Yugoslavian writers, earning him both adulation and condemnation. He expressed his convictions on artistic and intellectual liberties in a famous speech at a writer's conference in Ljubljana in 1952: "Our mission is to open doors, to prove by our works that we have always struggled for freedom of artistic expression, for the simultaneous existence of differing schools and styles, for liberty of choice and independence of moral and political convictions." This attack on socialist realism and Stalinist aesthetics strengthened his following among younger Yugoslavian artists.

One of the first of Krleza's books to appear in English was *The Return of Philip Latinovicz,* the story of a has-been painter who returns to the small town of his childhood after an absence of twenty years. Another English translation of Krleza's work is *The Cricket beneath the Waterfall, and Other Stories,* which consists of six stories about Eastern Europe during the early part of the twentieth century. *On the Edge of Reason* is a first-person narrative, a story about a Zagreb lawyer's alienation from his society, which progresses until "he loses his wife, his friends, his job, and, eventually, his sanity," explained a reviewer for the *New Yorker.*

In addition to books and short stories, Krleza also wrote several plays depicting the hardships of Croatian peasants and the decadence of the aristocratic class. His most acidic portrait of capitalist society appears in eleven stories and three plays about the Glembay family, whose gradual movement from peasantry to affluence is accompanied by moral degeneration. Reviewing this series of works in the *Dictionary of Literary Biography,* Kadic wrote of the Glembays: "They can prosper only in the antinational and antisocialist Austro-Hungarian monarchy, of which they are obedient servants." Using them as examples, says Kadic, Krleza presents a powerful indictment of the capitalist system they epitomize.

Krleza also wrote numerous essays on subjects ranging from politics to literary criticism, vehemently defending and proclaiming his beliefs in his nonfiction writing as he had done through his novels and plays. According to Kadic, while Krleza was not always accurate and unbiased in his essays, they did illustrate his "persuasive and expressive power" and his "encyclopedic" knowledge of the issues and people he wrote about. And while he was a controversial writer, often descredited by his contemporaries and critics, Kadic said that "Krleza was and shall remain a pivotal figure, and no one interested in twentieth-century Croatian and South Slavic literature can ignore him. . . . He fully deserves to be ranked among the luminaries of contemporary world literature. The future generations of his countrymen will rightly be proud of his contributions to their cultural heritage."

BIOGRAPHICAL/CRITICAL SOURCES:

BOOKS

Bogert, Ralph Baker, *The Writer as Naysayer: Miroslav Krleza and the Aesthetic of Interwar Central Europe,* Slavica (Columbus, OH), 1991.
Contemporary Croatian Literature, Croatian P.E.N. Club (Zagreb), 1966.
Contemporary Literary Criticism, Volume 8, Gale (Detroit), 1978.
Dictionary of Literary Biography, Volume 147: *South Slavic Writers before World War II,* Gale, 1994.
Jeremic, Dragan M., *Esejisti i kriticari,* Prosveta (Belgrade), 1966.

Leitner, Andreas, *Die Gestalt des Kunstlers bei Miroslav Krleza,* C. Winter (Heidelberg), 1986.
Marinkovic, Nada, *Secanja na Krlezu,* Prosveta, 1987.
Matkovic, Marijan, *La Vie et l'oeuvre de Miroslav Krleza,* UNESCO (Paris), 1977.
Ocak, Ivan, *Krleza-Partija,* Spektar (Zagreb), 1982.
Spiro, Gyorgy, *Miroslav Krleza,* Gondolat (Budapest), 1981.
Wierzbicki, Jan, *Miroslav Krleza,* Sveucilisna naklada Liber (Zagreb), 1980.

PERIODICALS

Antioch Review, fall, 1975.
Books Abroad, autumn, 1970.
Canadian Slavic Studies, fall, 1968.
Knjizevne novine, July 12, 1963.
Mosaic, Volume 6, number 4, 1973, pp. 169-83.
New York Times Book Review, February 23, 1969; February 15, 1970.
New Yorker, April 11, 1977.
Partisan Review, fall, 1967.
Saturday Review, November 15, 1969.
Times Literary Supplement, May 6, 1960.
World Literature Today, autumn, 1984, p. 632; winter, 1989, p. 133.

OBITUARIES:

PERIODICALS

Times (London), December 30, 1981.*

*   *   *

KROLL, Steven 1941-

PERSONAL: Born August 11, 1941, in New York, NY; son of Julius (a diamond merchant) and Anita (a business executive; maiden name, Berger) Kroll; married Edite Niedringhaus (a children's book editor), April 18, 1964 (divorced, 1978); married Abigail Aldridge (a milliner), June 3, 1989 (divorced, 1994). *Education:* Harvard University, B.A., 1962. *Politics:* "Committed to change." *Religion:* Jewish. *Avocational interests:* Walking, traveling, and playing squash and tennis.

ADDRESSES: Home and office—64 West Eleventh St., New York, NY 10011.

CAREER: Transatlantic Review, London, England, associate editor, 1962-65; Chatto & Windus Ltd., London, reader and editor, 1962-65; Holt, Rinehart & Winston, New York City, acquiring editor, adult trade department, 1965-69; free-lance writer, 1969—. Instructor in English, University of Maine at Augusta, 1970-71.

MEMBER: PEN American Center (chairman of children's book committee and member of executive board),

Authors Guild, Authors League of America, Harvard Club (New York).

WRITINGS:

FOR CHILDREN

Is Milton Missing? (Junior Literary Guild selection), illustrated by Dick Gackenbach, Holiday House (New York City), 1975.

That Makes Me Mad!, illustrated by Hilary Knight, Pantheon (New York City), 1976.

The Tyrannosaurus Game, illustrated by Tomie de Paola, Holiday House, 1976.

Gobbledygook, illustrated by Kelly Oechsli, Holiday House, 1977.

If I Could Be My Grandmother, illustrated by Lady McCrady, Pantheon, 1977.

Sleepy Ida and Other Nonsense Poems, illustrated by Seymour Chwast, Pantheon, 1977.

Santa's Crash-Bang Christmas, illustrated by Tomie de Paola, Holiday House, 1977.

T. J. Folger, Thief, illustrated by Bill Morrison, Holiday House, 1978.

Fat Magic, illustrated by Tomie de Paola, Holiday House, 1979.

The Candy Witch, illustrated by Marylin Hafner, Holiday House, 1979.

Space Cats, illustrated by Friso Henstra, Holiday House, 1979.

Amanda and the Giggling Ghost, illustrated by Dick Gackenbach, Holiday House, 1980.

Dirty Feet, illustrated by Toni Hormann, Parents Magazine Press (New York City), 1980.

Monster Birthday, illustrated by Dennis Kendrick, Holiday House, 1980.

Friday the 13th, illustrated by Dick Gackenbach, Holiday House, 1981.

Giant Journey, illustrated by Kay Chorao, Holiday House, 1981.

Are You Pirates?, illustrated by Marylin Hafner, Pantheon, 1982.

Banana Bits, illustrated by Maxie Chambliss, Avon (New York City), 1982.

Bathrooms, illustrated by Maxie Chambliss, Avon, 1982.

The Big Bunny and the Easter Eggs, illustrated by Janet Stevens, Holiday House, 1982.

The Goat Parade, illustrated by Tim Kirk, Parents Magazine Press, 1982.

One Tough Turkey, illustrated by John Wallner, Holiday House, 1982.

The Hand-Me-Down Doll, illustrated by Evaline Ness, Holiday House, 1983.

Otto, illustrated by Ned Delaney, Parents Magazine Press, 1983.

Pigs in the House, illustrated by Tim Kirk, Parents Magazine Press, 1983.

Toot! Toot!, illustrated by Anne Rockwell, Holiday House, 1983.

Woof, Woof!, illustrated by Nicole Rubel, Dial (New York City), 1983.

The Biggest Pumpkin Ever (Junior Literary Guild selection), illustrated by Jeni Bassett, Holiday House, 1984.

Loose Tooth, illustrated by Tricia Tusa, Holiday House, 1984.

Happy Mother's Day, illustrated by Marylin Hafner, Holiday House, 1985.

Mrs. Claus's Crazy Christmas, illustrated by John Wallner, Holiday House, 1985.

Annie's Four Grannies, illustrated by Eileen Christelow, Holiday House, 1986.

The Big Bunny and the Magic Show, illustrated by Janet Stevens, Holiday House, 1986.

I'd Like to Be, illustrated by Ellen Appleby, Parents Magazine Press, 1987.

I Love Spring, illustrated by Kathryn E. Shoemaker, Holiday House, 1987.

It's Groundhog Day!, illustrated by Jeni Bassett, Holiday House, 1987.

Don't Get Me in Trouble!, illustrated by Marvin Glass, Crown (New York City), 1988.

Happy Father's Day, illustrated by Marylin Hafner, Holiday House, 1988.

Looking for Daniela: A Romantic Adventure, illustrated by Anita Lobel, Holiday House, 1988.

Newsman Ned Meets the New Family, illustrated by Denise Brunkus, Scholastic Inc. (New York City), 1988.

Oh, What a Thanksgiving!, illustrated by S. D. Schindler, Scholastic Inc., 1988.

Big Jeremy, illustrated by Donald Carrick, Holiday House, 1989.

The Hokey-Pokey Man, illustrated by Deborah Kogan Ray, Holiday House, 1989.

Newsman Ned and the Broken Rules, illustrated by Denise Brunkus, Scholastic Inc., 1989.

Branigan's Cat and the Halloween Ghost, Holiday House, 1990.

Gone Fishing, illustrated by Harvey Stevenson, Crown, 1990.

It's April Fools' Day!, illustrated by Jeni Bassett, Holiday House, 1990.

Annabelle's Un-Birthday, illustrated by Gail Owens, Macmillan (New York City), 1991.

Howard and Gracie's Luncheonette, illustrated by Michael Sours, Holt (New York City), 1991.

Mary McLean and the St. Patrick's Day Parade, illustrated by Michael Dooling, Scholastic Inc., 1991.

Princess Abigail and the Wonderful Hat, illustrated by Patience Brewster, Holiday House, 1991.

The Squirrels' Thanksgiving, illustrated by Jeni Bassett, Holiday House, 1991.

The Magic Rocket, illustrated by Will Hillenbrand, Holiday House, 1992.

Andrew Wants a Dog, illustrated by Molly Delaney, Hyperion Books (Westport, CT), 1992.

The Hit and Run Gang, volumes 1-4, illustrated by Meredith Johnson, Avon, 1992.

The Pigrates Clean Up, illustrated by Jeni Bassett, Henry Holt (New York City), 1993.

Queen of the May, illustrated by Patience Brewster, Holiday House, 1993.

Will You Be My Valentine?, illustrated by Lillian Hoban, Holiday House, 1993.

I'm George Washington and You're Not!, illustrated by Betsy Lewin, Hyperion Books, 1994.

By the Dawn's Early Light: The Story of the Star-Spangled Banner, illustrated by Dan Andreasen, Scholastic, Inc., 1994.

Patrick's Tree House, illustrated by Roberta Wilson, Macmillan, 1994.

The Hit and Run Gang, volumes 5-8, illustrated by Meredith Johnson, Avon, 1994.

Lewis and Clark: Explorers of the American West, illustrated by Richard Williams, Holiday House, 1994.

Doctor on an Elephant, illustrated by Michael Chesworth, Henry Holt, 1994.

YOUNG ADULT BOOKS

Take It Easy, Four Winds (Bristol, FL), 1983.
Breaking Camp, Macmillan, 1985.
Multiple Choice, Macmillan, 1987.

OTHER

Contributor of book reviews to *Book World, Commonweal, Village Voice, Listener, New York Times Book Review, Spectator, Times Literary Supplement,* and *London Magazine.* Contributor to poetry anthologies. Some of Kroll's works have been translated into French, Spanish, and Japanese.

ADAPTATIONS: The Biggest Pumpkin Ever and Other Stories (includes *The Biggest Pumpkin Ever; Sleepy Ida and Other Nonsense Poems; T. J. Folger, Thief;* and *Woof, Woof!*) have been recorded on audiocassette for Caedmon, 1986; *The Biggest Pumpkin Ever* and *The Big Bunny and the Easter Eggs* have been recorded on audiocassette for Scholastic.

WORK IN PROGRESS: A picture book about Ellis Island for Holiday House and a chapter book about a boy who is a vegetarian for Hyperion, both to be published in the fall of 1995. Also a picture book about the Pony Express,

illustrated by Dan Andreasen, to be published by Scholastic in the spring of 1996.

SIDELIGHTS: Children's author Steven Kroll possesses a unique ability to view his stories as a child would, so he understands what interests and entertains his young audience. Even though it took him years to commit himself to writing and he fell into children's writing by chance, the author has never regretted his career choice. Writing for children affords Kroll a special connection with his own youth—something he values. "What is most important is the feeling that I am somehow in touch with my own childhood," Kroll has said. "To be in touch with your own childhood is to be, in some way, touched with wonder, and when I write for children, that is what I feel."

Following work as an editor in London, England, and New York City, Kroll went off to Maine to write full-time and began writing for children in the early 1970s upon the suggestion of his former wife, then a children's book editor, and other friends in children's book publishing. Although he resisted the idea at first, once he began writing for children he discovered he loved it. His first book, *Is Milton Missing?,* was published in 1975, and since then Kroll has steadily produced at least two books per year, sometimes as many as six, for Holiday House and other publishers. As a result, with his fall, 1994, publication of *Doctor on an Elephant* and *Lewis and Clark,* the prolific author has written seventy-three children's books.

For his story ideas and settings Kroll sometimes recalls places and instances from his own childhood. "When I write about a child's room, that room is often my own—the one in the Manhattan apartment house where I grew up," Kroll commented. "When I write about an urban street or an urban school, it is often my street or my school, taken out of time into a situation I have invented. And sometimes," the author continued, "if I'm writing about a suburb or a small town, that place will resemble the home of a summer camp friend I visited once, and longed to see again."

Kroll's stories appeal greatly to young readers, evidenced by the great number of letters the author constantly receives. His favorites are those from children who particularly enjoyed one of his books, but "the best letter I ever got was from a first grader in Connecticut where I was going to speak the following week," Kroll recollected in *Behind the Covers.* "This one read, 'Dear Mr. Kroll, My heart is beating because it's so anxious to see what you look like.' The little girl was wonderful! She signed everything she wrote with her name and 'Made in U.S.A.' "

Kroll never regrets leaving his full-time job to become a children's author. "I really love writing for children," he remarked. "I love starting the fireworks, love that explosion of emotion, of excitement, terror, and enthusiasm that comes with putting those words on paper and sometimes, if the mood is right, doing a draft of a whole picture-book story in one sitting. I've been doing a lot more picture books, but I've also become much more involved in writing chapter books for middle grade readers." Writing for children is what Kroll feels most content doing. "It's part of me now," the author concluded, "and I'd like other adults to let down the barriers and feel the wonder in their own lives that I feel in these books."

BIOGRAPHICAL/CRITICAL SOURCES:

BOOKS

Behind the Covers: Interviews with Authors and Illustrators of Books for Children and Young Adults, Libraries Unlimited (Littleton, CO), 1985.
Something about the Author Autobiography Series, Volume 7, Gale (Detroit, MI), 1989.

PERIODICALS

Junior Literary Guild, September, 1975.
Wilson Library Bulletin, January, 1985.

*   *   *

KURTZ, Katherine (Irene) 1944-

PERSONAL: Born October 18, 1944, in Coral Gables, FL; daughter of Fredrick Harry (an electronics technician) and Margaret Frances (an educator; maiden name, Carter) Kurtz; married Scott MacMillan; children: Cameron. *Education:* University of Miami—Coral Gables, B.S., 1966; University of California, Los Angeles, M.A., 1971. *Avocational interests:* Counted cross-stitch embroidery, costuming, calligraphy, protocol and heraldry, restoration of period architecture, riding, hypnosis.

ADDRESSES: Home—Holybrooke Hall, Kilmacanogue, Bray, County Wicklow, Ireland.

CAREER: Los Angeles Police Department, Los Angeles, CA, junior administrative assistant, 1969-71, training technician, 1971-74, senior training technician, 1974-80; full-time writer, 1980—.

MEMBER: Science Fiction Writers of America, Swordsmen and Sorcerers' Guild of America, Authors Guild, Society for Creative Anachronism, Irish Heraldry Society, Order of St. John of Jerusalem (Knights Hospitaller; Dame of Honour), Order of St. Lazarus of Jerusalem (Dame), Order of the Temple of Jerusalem (Dame Grand Cross), Companion of the Royal House of O'Conor, Noble Company of the Rose (Dame of Honour), Augustan and Octavian Societies (fellow), Phi Alpha Theta, Alpha Epsilon Delta, Pi Kappa Phi, Mortar Board.

AWARDS, HONORS: Edmund Hamilton Memorial Award, 1977, for *Camber of Culdi;* Gandalf Award nomination for best book-length fantasy, World Science Fiction Convention, 1978, for *Saint Camber;* Balrog Award, 1982, for *Camber the Heretic;* Best Science Fiction Titles of 1986 citation, *Voice of Youth Advocates*, 1986, for *The Legacy of Lehr.*

WRITINGS:

FANTASY NOVELS

"CHRONICLES OF THE DERYNI" SERIES

Deryni Rising, Ballantine (New York City), 1970.
Deryni Checkmate, Ballantine, 1972.
High Deryni, Ballantine, 1973.
The Chronicles of the Deryni (contains *Deryni Rising, Deryni Checkmate*, and *High Deryni*), Science Fiction Book Club, 1985.

"LEGENDS OF SAINT CAMBER" SERIES

Camber of Culdi, Ballantine, 1976.
Saint Camber, Del Rey, 1978.
Camber the Heretic, Del Rey, 1981.

"HISTORIES OF KING KELSON" SERIES

The Bishop's Heir, Del Rey, 1984.
The King's Justice, Del Rey, 1985.
The Quest for Saint Camber, Del Rey, 1986.

"HEIRS OF SAINT CAMBER" SERIES

The Harrowing of Gwynedd, Del Rey, 1989.
King Javan's Year, Del Rey, 1992.
The Bastard Prince, Del Rey, 1994.

"SCOTTISH" SERIES; NOVELS; WITH DEBORAH TURNER HARRIS

The Adept, Ace (New York City), 1991.
Adept II: The Lodge of the Lynx, Ace, 1992.
Adept III: The Templar Treasure, Ace, 1993.
Adept IV: Dagger Magic, Ace, 1995.
Adept V, Ace, 1996.

OTHER

Lammas Night (World War II thriller), Ballantine, 1983.
The Legacy of Lehr (science fiction), Walker & Co. (New York City), 1986.
The Deryni Archives (short stories), Del Rey, 1986.
Codex Derynianus: Stories, Essays, and Poems, Borgo (San Bernardino, CA), 1987.
Deryni Magic: A Grimoire, Del Rey, 1991.
(Editor) *Tales of the Knights Templar*, Warner (New York City), 1995.
Two Crowns for America, Bantam (New York City), 1996.
(With Robert Reginald) *Codex Derynianus*, Del Rey, 1996.

King Kelson's Bride, Del Rey, 1997.

Contributor to anthologies, including *Flashing Swords #4: Warriors and Wizards,* edited by Lin Carter, Dell (New York City), 1977; *Hecate's Cauldron,* edited by Susan Schwartz, DAW (New York City), 1982; *Nine Visions,* edited by Andrea LaSonde Melrose, Seabury Press (New York City), 1983; *Moonsinger's Friends,* edited by Schwartz, Bluejay (Kokomo, IN), 1985; *Once upon a Time,* edited by Lester Del Rey and Risa Kessler, Del Rey, 1991; *Crafter I,* edited by Bill Fawcett and Christopher Stasheff, Ace, 1991; *The Gods of War,* edited by Fawcett and Stasheff, Baen Books (Riverdale, NY), 1992; *Battlestation Book II; Vanguard,* edited by Fawcett and Stasheff, Ace, 1992.

Some of Kurtz's works have been translated into German, Spanish, Dutch, Italian, Swedish, Polish, French, and Japanese.

SIDELIGHTS: Katherine Kurtz once told *CA:* "Obviously, one of the important themes that runs through most of [my] books is the reality of spiritual dimensions to one's life, and examples of how various characters handle this element in their day to day living. I like to think that we all have a little Deryni in us, that could be developed to make us better human beings. In a way, perhaps the Deryni are an archetype for the perfected human being—what we would all be like, if we have the courage to stand by our convictions and actively enlist on the side of the Light. And also, I obviously have a lot to say about the stupidity and destructiveness of blind prejudice. There's a lot happening, on many different levels. Mostly, though, I want to tell stories about interesting, multi-dimensional characters who will get my readers involved. If those readers get something in addition to a good read, then that's best of all!"

BIOGRAPHICAL/CRITICAL SOURCES:

BOOKS

Clarke, Boden, and Mary A. Burgess, *The Work of Katherine Kurtz: An Annotated Bibliography and Guide,* Borgo Press, 1993.

Spivack, Charlotte, *Merlin's Daughters: Contemporary Women Writers of Fantasy,* Greenwood Press (Westport, CT), 1987.

L

LANG, T. T.
See TAYLOR, Theodore

* * *

LANSDALE, Joe R(ichard) 1951-
(Ray Slater)

PERSONAL: Born October 28, 1951, in Gladewater, TX; son of Alcee Bee (a mechanic) and Reta (in sales; maiden name, Wood) Lansdale; married Cassie Ellis, June 25, 1970 (divorced, 1972); married Karen Ann Morton, August 25, 1973; children: (second marriage) Keith Jordan, Kasey JoAnn. Education: Attended Tyler Junior College, 1970-71, University of Texas at Austin, 1971-72, and Stephen F. Austin State University, 1973, 1975, 1976.

ADDRESSES: Home and office—113 Timber Ridge, Nacogdoches, TX 75961. Agent—Barbara Puechner, 3121 Portage Rd., Bethlehem, PA 18017.

CAREER: Transportation manager, Goodwill Industries, 1973-75; custodian, Stephen F. Austin State University, Nacogdoches, TX, 1976-80; foreman, LaBorde Custodial Services, Nacogdoches, 1980-81; writer, 1981—. Also worked variously as a bouncer, bodyguard, factory worker, carpenter, ditch digger, plumber's helper, and karate instructor.

MEMBER: Horror Writers of America (vice president, 1987-88), Western Writers of America (treasurer, 1987).

AWARDS, HONORS: Bram Stoker Award, Horror Writers of America, 1988, 1989; American Horror award, 1989; British Fantasy Award, 1989, for novella.

WRITINGS:

MYSTERY/SUSPENSE NOVELS

Act of Love, Zebra (New York City), 1981, CD Publications (Edgewood, MD), 1993.
The Nightrunners, Dark Harvest (Arlington Heights, IL), 1987.
Cold in July (also see below), Bantam (New York City), 1989.
Savage Season (also see below), Bantam, 1990.
Lansdale's Limited Edition: Cold in July & Savage Season, (as boxed set), Ziesing (Shingletown, CA), 1990.
Mucho Mojo, Mysterious Press (New York City), 1994.
The Two-Bear Mambo, Mysterious Press, 1995.

SCIENCE-FICTION/FANTASY/HORROR NOVELS

The Drive In: A B-Movie with Blood and Popcorn, Made in Texas, Bantam, 1988.
The Drive In 2: Not Just One of Them Sequels, Bantam, 1989.
Batman: Captured by the Engines, Warner (New York City), 1991.
On the Far Side of the Cadillac Desert with Dead Folks (chapbook), Roadkill Press (Denver, CO), 1991.
Terror on the High Skies (juvenile), Little, Brown (Boston), 1992.

WESTERN NOVELS

(Under pseudonym Ray Slater) Texas Night Riders, Leisure Press (Champaign, IL), 1983.
Dead in the West, Space & Time Books (New York City), 1986.
The Magic Wagon, Doubleday (New York City), 1986.
Jonah Hex: Two-Gun Mojo, DC Comics (New York City), 1994.

SHORT STORIES

By Bizarre Hands, Ziesing, 1989.
Stories by Mama Lansdale's Youngest Boy, Pulphouse (Eugene, OR), 1991.
Best Sellers Guaranteed, Ace (New York City), 1993.

EDITOR

Best of the West, Doubleday, 1986.
The New Frontier: Best of the West 2, Doubleday, 1989.
(With Pat Lo Brutto) *Razored Saddles,* Dark Harvest, 1989.
(With wife, Karen Lansdale) *Dark at Heart,* Dark Harvest, 1992.

OTHER

Contributor to several anthologies, including *Fears,* 1984, and *Book of the Dead,* Bantam, 1989. Contributor of articles, stories, and reviews to magazines, including *Horror Show, Modern Stories, Espionage,* and *Mike Shayne.*

WORK IN PROGRESS: Tarzan: The Lost Adventure, a four-part series to be collected as a book for Dark Horse Comics.

SIDELIGHTS: Joe R. Lansdale once told *CA:* "The Martian series by Edgar Rice Burroughs got me started, and I've been writing my own stories ever since. My work ranges from popular to literary. I believe the purpose of fiction is to entertain. Enlightening the reader is nice, but secondary. If you don't have a good tale to tell, no one is listening anyway.

"My preferred genre is the fantastic, but suspense runs a close second, followed by mystery, westerns, and the mainstream. Actually, much of my work and intended work is a combination of these things. I am also interested in screenplays, and hope to work in that medium on occasion.

"I like all kinds of horror and fantasy writing, especially the contemporary horror tale. I am not too fond, though, of the vague ending that seems so popular in many publications today. Much of what I write, although it is called horror, is really just oddball or weird fantasy, perhaps never becoming scary, but certainly striking a note of the unusual."

Horror, fantasy, science fiction, mystery, suspense, western: Lansdale's fiction encompasses all of the above, frequently combining several genres in the same story or novel while at the same time defining a distinctive voice of its own. Writing in the *New York Times Book Review,* Daniel Woodrell has characterized Lansdale's work as "country noir," likening him to such authors as James M. Cain and Erskine Caldwell (Lansdale, himself, has listed Cain as a major influence). The "country" in this case is

East Texas, where Lansdale was born, raised, and continues to reside. The "noir" refers to the dark vision of human nature and contemporary life that pervades nearly all of his work. Other writers that Lansdale mentions as influential include Ray Bradbury, Robert Bloch, Flannery O'Connor, Dashiell Hammett, Raymond Chandler, and Richard Matheson.

Lansdale departs from these literary icons on at least two counts, each of which reflects one of his stated non-literary influences: B-movies and comic books. No matter the genre in which he is writing, graphic horror and violence are usually present. No matter how dark the vision he is rendering, satirical and humorous elements often abound.

Author of well over one hundred stories, short fiction was the arena where Lansdale first made his mark. "I prefer the short story medium," he told Stanley Wiater in *Dark Dreamers: Conversations with the Masters of Horror.* "I think if I could make a living as a short story writer, I would do that primarily." Lansdale's stories began appearing widely in both commercial and alternative publications by the late 1970s. Some of this work is collected in *By Bizarre Hands* and *Stories by Mama Lansdale's Youngest Boy. Best Sellers Guaranteed* combines the stories from the second collection with "The Events Concerning a Nude Fold-Out Found in a Harlequin Romance," a previously anthologized novella. Writing in *Locus,* Ed Bryant describes *Best Sellers Guaranteed* as "a first-rate retrospective, particularly of Lansdale's earlier career." He goes on to characterize "Lansdale's strong suit" as "whacked-out humorous melodrama with a distinctive voice (East Texas) and a keen sense of place (ditto)." Writing in the *Bloomsbury Review,* Bryant also credits Lansdale with having "a universal grasp of humankind's terrors."

Lansdale's novels began appearing in the early 1980s. Although marketed within particular genres, they transcend traditional genre definitions. Typical of a Lansdale western is *Dead in the West.* Set in pioneer days in Mud Water, Texas (a fictionalized version of Lansdale's own Gladewater) it relates a series of events involving animated corpses that would seem more at home in a contemporary horror tale than in a western. The more recent *Magic Wagon,* set in East Texas in 1909, tells of a traveling medicine show that includes a wrestling chimpanzee and the corpse of Wild Bill Hickok. Writing on *The Magic Wagon* for the *New York Times Book Review,* Anne Roston offers another example of how Lansdale's work defies simple categorization: "Behind this entertaining and seemingly innocent western . . . lies a subtle discussion of racism and the myths people create for themselves."

Prime examples of Lansdale's science fiction and fantasy/ horror fiction can be found in *The Drive In: A B-Movie with Blood and Popcorn, Made in Texas,* and *The Drive In 2: Not Just One of Them Sequels.* In the first novel, the patrons of a Texas drive-in movie are whisked into another universe where the horror films they have been watching and the drive-in itself become the sum of their reality. Scenes of rape, cannibalism, and necrophilia are portrayed. In the sequel, the patrons leave the drive-in to enter the strange world surrounding it, where they encounter both dinosaurs and vampires. Richard Gehr in the *Village Voice* sees these two books as "semiparodistic novels" that "turn the horror spectacle upon itself."

Lansdale's mystery and suspense novels tend to adhere more closely to genre conventions. *Savage Season,* set in the nineties, relates the story of Hap Collins, a sixties draft-dodger who is lured by his ex-wife Trudy into a scheme to locate stolen money at the bottom of the Sabine River in East Texas. Accompanied by his friend Leonard, a gay Vietnam veteran, Hap must eventually confront the nefarious gang with whom Trudy has become involved. Liz Currie in *Armchair Detective* says: "When 1960s idealism meets 1990s cynicism, the stage is set for a violent confrontation between good intentions and evil results." Hap Collins and Leonard return in *Mucho Mojo.* After Leonard inherits a house from his uncle, the skeleton of a murdered child is discovered under the floorboards. Hap and Leonard proceed to track down the killer. Daniel Woodrow in the *Village Voice* states: "Mr. Lansdale sets his story in motion and carries through with great, sneaky skill. The individual scenes are sometimes not only funny, but also slyly offer acute commentary on matters of race, friendship and love in small-town America."

Lansdale's fiction has often been praised and blamed for the same reasons. The extreme, graphic violence he depicts can be viewed as gratuitous, shock for its own sake, or as a pointed exaggeration of the violence in America. Depending on one's perspective and sensibilities, his humor on the darkest subjects can be perceived as poor taste or as satire on American popular culture. Critics do agree that there is far more to his work than run-of-the-mill genre fiction written for the sake of entertainment. In summing up *Mucho Mojo* for *Locus,* Edward Bryant feels that what "Lansdale proceeds to spin is not only a top-drawer thriller, but a social portrait of a society in painful evolution. His East Texas is a place of entrenched tradition in painful conflict with new ideas about race relations, gender politics, and more open choices in sexual preference."

Lansdale told Kevin E. Proulx in *Fear to the World: Eleven Voices in a Chorus of Horror:* "Good fiction can actually tell you how people relate to one another. How they really feel about things. What life is all about. What makes it worth living, or, for some people, not worth living. I find a lot more truth in fiction than nonfiction, and that's why I prefer to write it."

Lansdale also told *CA:* "My writing is done to entertain and to please me. And to put bread on the table. I like to think my work has something going for it besides momentum. That there is some thematic depth that will ring in the reader's head afterwards like an echo. I'm attempting to blend the pacing and color of genre fiction with the character and style of the mainstream. And maybe doing a damn bad job of it. But I'm trying."

BIOGRAPHICAL/CRITICAL SOURCES:

BOOKS

Proulx, Kevin E., *Fear to the World: Eleven Voices in a Chorus of Horror* (interview), Starmont House (Mercer Island, WA), 1992, pp. 43-58.
Wiater, Stanley, *Dark Dreamers: Conversations with the Masters of Horror* (interview), Avon (New York City), 1990, pp. 111-18.

PERIODICALS

Antioch Review, winter, 1987, p. 117.
Armchair Detective, fall, 1989, p. 435; spring, 1991, p. 227.
Bloomsbury Review, December, 1991, p. 27; June, 1992, p. 17.
Deathrealm, fall/winter, 1988, pp. 42-44.
Horror Show, January, 1987.
Locus, April, 1993, p. 21; May, 1993, p. 23; July, 1993, p. 23; May, 1994, p. 25.
Mystery Scene, August, 1987.
New York Times Book Review, December 14, 1986, p. 24; October 2, 1994, p. 37.
Small Press Review, April, 1990, p. 27.
Village Voice, February 6, 1990, pp. 57-58.

*   *   *

LAPPIN, Peter 1911-

PERSONAL: Born April 29, 1911, in Ireland; son of John (a railroad employee) and Sarah (Barrett) Lappin. *Education:* Fordham University, M.A., 1953; also attended Salesian Studentate, Hong Kong, International School of Theology, Shanghai, China, Belfast School of Technology, Salesian College, Cowley, Oxford, England, Pallaskenry College, and Columbia School of Writing. *Avocational interests:* Preaching, lecturing, conferences, production of television documentaries.

ADDRESSES: Home and office—Marian Shrine, Filors Lane, West Haverstraw, NY 10993.

CAREER: Ordained Roman Catholic priest; Marian Shrine, West Haverstraw, NY, public relations agent, editor of *Salesian Bulletin*, and member of editorial board of *Biographic Memoirs of St. John Bosco*. Lecturer on the Far East, South America, and other topics.

MEMBER: International Order of the Alhambra, Catholic Press Association, Cambridge Society of Biographers, Ancient Order of Hibernians, Knights of Columbus.

AWARDS, HONORS: Recipient of Venice Festival awards, Catholic Family Club award, two Catholic Literary Foundation awards, and awards for service to various organizations.

WRITINGS:

General Mickey, Salesiana Publishers (New Rochelle, NY), 1952, reprinted, Don Bosco Publications (New Rochelle, NY), 1977.
Bible Stories, Doubleday (New York City), 1953.
Dominic Savio: Teenage Saint, Don Bosco Publications, 1954.
Conquistador!, Salesiana Publishers, 1957.
Stories of Don Bosco, Irish Press, 1958, 2nd edition, Don Bosco Publications, 1979.
Land of Cain, Doubleday, 1958.
Mighty Samson (juvenile), [Garden City, NY], 1961.
The Wine in the Chalice, Salesiana Publishers, 1972.
Bury Me Deep, Our Sunday Visitor (Huntington, IN), 1974.
Give Me Souls!: Life of Don Bosco, Our Sunday Visitor, 1977.
Halfway to Heaven, Don Bosco Publications, 1980.
Sunshine in the Shadows: Mama Margaret, Mother of St. John Bosco, Don Bosco Publications, 1980.
The Challenge of Mornese, F.M.A. Publications, 1982.
The Falcon and the Dove, Patron Book (New Rochelle, NY), 1982.
Zatti!, Salesiana Publishers, 1987.
First Lady of the World, Don Bosco Multimedia (New Rochelle, NY), 1988.

WORK IN PROGRESS: The Challenge and the Change, a biography of the A.F.C. movement; a history of the B.A.C. movement in Birmingham, Alabama; a history of the Marian Shrine in New York.

SIDELIGHTS: Several of Peter Lappin's books have been translated into foreign languages.

*   *   *

LEAMING, Barbara

PERSONAL: Born in Philadelphia, PA; daughter of James F. and Muriel (Neville) Leaming; married David Packman (a professor), February 21, 1975. *Education:* Re-

ceived B.A. from Smith College, and Ph.D. from New York University.

ADDRESSES: Home—New York, NY. *Office*—Department of Theatre and Film, Hunter College of the City University of New York, 695 Park Ave., New York, NY 10021. *Agent*—Wallace & Sheil Agency, Inc., 177 East 70th St., New York, NY 10021.

CAREER: Professor of theater and film at Hunter College of the City University of New York, New York City; writer.

WRITINGS:

BIOGRAPHIES

Grigori Kozintsev, Twayne (Boston), 1980.
Polanski: The Filmmaker as Voyeur, Simon & Schuster (New York City), 1982 (published in England as *Polanski: His Life and Films*, Hamish Hamilton, 1982).
Orson Welles: A Biography, Viking Penguin (New York City), 1985.
If This Was Happiness: A Biography of Rita Hayworth, Viking (New York City), 1989.
Bette Davis: A Biography, Simon & Schuster (New York City), 1992.

SIDELIGHTS: Biographer Barbara Leaming's *Polanski: The Filmmaker as Voyeur* details the life and work of the controversial filmmaker who fled the United States while being tried for statutory rape in 1977. Leaming traces Roman Polanski's years as an abandoned child in World War II Europe. She also analyzes the possible influence his tragic experiences—such as the murder of his wife, actress Sharon Tate, by Charles Manson's clan—may have had on his work, including the gruesome *Macbeth* and the pessimistic *Chinatown*. *Los Angeles Times* critic Irwin R. Blacker views the biography as "an insightful and useful study of both the artist and his work." A reviewer for the *Fort Worth Star-Telegram* agrees, calling *Polanski* "an appreciative but hardly gentle study."

Following the Polanski biography, Leaming turned her attention to the legendary cinematic giant Orson Welles. The appearance of *Orson Welles: A Biography* was timely, for it was published within weeks of his death in 1985. Reviewer Louis Parks sees it as a triumph in the *Houston Chronicle*: "The book is not only timely, it is also unusual and fascinating, an exceptionally intimate, personal look at a remarkable public figure. Leaming achieves what all biographers want but few manage—she gets at her subject from the inside."

Initially, when Leaming approached Welles to write his authorized biography, he refused. She pursued him for a number of years, all the while accumulating information on him from a multitude of sources. Leaming was on the verge of composing an unauthorized biography when Welles decided to speak. The meetings to follow were not mere interviews, for it is said by various reviewers that Welles slowly opened his soul to Leaming. According to Leaming, it is the achievement of such closeness which has made her work a success. Parks quotes Leaming: "If Orson Welles had died without talking, the private man just never would have appeared. There were hints (of him) in things people told me, but he just wasn't there. . . . That legend of his is so entrenched—a larger-than-life figure, arrogant and terrifying, unreachable and cold. But when you know him, he's shy and vulnerable. He's the most approachable, warm, amusing person you can imagine. It's something I would never have known if Orson hadn't decided to take the chance."

The fact that Leaming was able to get so close to Welles is viewed favorably by some critics and skeptically by others. Whereas *Financial Times* critic Nigel Andrews professes that Leaming "obtained near limitless access to the Master, and has repaid the privilege with a biography that is as revealing, confiding and sumptuously wide-ranging as any autobiography," Jay Scott notes in the Toronto *Globe and Mail:* "Leaming wooed and won the recalcitrant Welles and, at the same time, one suspects, fell in love with him. . . . We are told in [others' biographies of Welles] that Welles could charm birds out of trees; he certainly charmed Leaming out of her critical faculties and with a few exceptions she accepts his memories as Holy Writ and his rationalizations as fact." Other reviewers express opinions similar to Scott's, asserting that Leaming was so taken in by Welles that he moved her to plead for all of his life's mistakes. *Detroit News* commentator Bruce Cook calls it a "singular lack of objectivity" and believes Welles found the ideal biographer, "so protective of him that very often she seems more an amanuensis than a biographer." Nevertheless, in spite of this, Cook feels the biography is a "good and wonderfully readable book." Others are also pleased with Leaming's work. According to David Elliott in the *Chicago Sun Times,* "Welles is alive in [Leaming's] book as he has never been before in print. . . . Here is Welles as a talking, eating, sexing, stirringly emotive man. . . . Leaming should have spent more time on the films and plays, a little less with 'look what I found' stuff (courtesy of Welles, mostly) on his prodigious sex life. But for the first time his wives, and not just Rita Hayworth, are more than mere appendages. . . . Leaming has written the best of the Welles books, full of body heat, and a generosity that rarely blunts insight." Sarah Bradford in *Spectator* believes Welles's life is told in a "fascinating, skillfully assembled biography."

In her next two books, Leaming looked at two other film legends: Welles's former wife and World War II pin-up girl Rita Hayworth, and the combative Bette Davis, flamboyant star of the Warner Brothers studio during the 1940s. Both women, according to Leaming, were products of abusive upbringings, and both of them reflected this damage in their later histories. Both Davis and Hayworth were unable to keep their public images—Hayworth as a "sex kitten," Davis as a feisty, strong-willed feminist—from influencing their offscreen lives.

Rita Hayworth, according to *If This Was Happiness: A Biography of Rita Hayworth,* was sexually abused by her sometime dance partner and father, Eduardo Cansino, who recruited his teenaged daughter to work with him in his nightclub act. "According to Ms. Leaming," writes Susan Braudy in the *New York Times Book Review,* "her father's abusive treatment was the key to her emotional development and led to a lifetime of disastrous relationships." Hayworth married five times: the first, at age 18, to a much older man who exploited her, states Braudy, by "threaten[ing] her with physical abuse and disfigurement," and "offer[ing] her to any man he thought would advance her career." Her second husband was Orson Welles, who married her in 1943. However, Welles was unable to meet Hayworth's emotional needs and soon sought solace outside the marriage. Three other marriages—to Prince Aly Khan, heir to the throne of the Aga Khan, to the singer Dick Haymes, and to the director James Hill—also ended in divorce. Hayworth became an alcoholic and in 1980 was diagnosed with Alzheimer's disease. Her daughter, Princess Yasmin Khan, cared for her until her death in 1987.

Many critics celebrated Leaming's convincing portrayal of Hayworth. "The meticulous research," states Braudy, "makes the painful story of Hayworth's personal problems vivid, which may diminish some envy of her public successes. The book teaches a harder lesson: Rita Hayworth's tortured childhood . . . shaped her. . . . Hollywood did not destroy her." "Leaming's prose can gush," declares Paul Gray in *Time,* " . . . and regularly descends to write-by-the-numbers cliche. But the material is poignant, another reminder of the chasm that can exist between public images and private pain." Hayworth "claimed to have been happy with Welles," Gray concludes, "at least before his infidelities became too blatant. 'If this was happiness,' Welles told Leaming years later, 'imagine what the rest of her life had been.' "

Leaming also presents Bette Davis as a person haunted by her childhood. Davis's father, a Boston lawyer, deserted his family when Bette was ten years old. Bette's mother, Ruthie, compensated by pushing her older daughter into an acting career and making personal sacrifices to maintain Bette's schooling. "When Bette ultimately achieved success," writes James Kotsilibas-Davis in the *Washington Post Book World,* "Ruthie would exact her toll, living like a queen on her daughter's earnings." In part because of these troubles, Davis evolved into a woman and an actress who practiced what *Los Angeles Times Book Review* contributor David Elliott calls "empress tactics." Elliott continues, "A friend said later, 'She began to imitate herself as an actress and to refuse to know that she was doing that.'" Davis's self-destructive practices helped to end all four of her marriages—including those to abusive husbands such as William Grant Sherry and Gary Merrill—and to alienate her daughter. "Leaming's biography," declares Richard Christiansen in the *Chicago Tribune*, "walks delicately between pity and scorn for its subject. The author records the traumas Davis inflicted on her daughter B.D., yet she carefully notes the deep pain that B.D., a born-again Christian, inflicted on her mother with the publication of *My Mother's Keeper*," her tell-all vituperative autobiography.

Leaming once told *CA*: "I am a professor of film history and aesthetics. Both the Kozintsev and Polanski books were written out of my long-term study of Soviet and East European cinema and culture. I also have a special interest in the relationship between American film and its cultural context."

BIOGRAPHICAL/CRITICAL SOURCES:

BOOKS

Leaming, Barbara, *Orson Welles: A Biography*, Viking Penguin, 1985.

PERIODICALS

Chattanooga Times, February 13, 1982.
Chicago Sun Times, September 8, 1985.
Chicago Tribune, May 17, 1992, p. 3.
Contemporary Review, March, 1986.
Detroit Free Press, October 13, 1985.
Detroit News, October 13, 1985.
Financial Times, October 19, 1985.
Fort Worth Star-Telegram, February 14, 1982.
Globe and Mail (Toronto), October 5, 1985; November 2, 1985.
Houston Chronicle, October 20, 1985.
Los Angeles Times, April 11, 1982; September 9, 1985.
Los Angeles Times Book Review, May 17, 1992, pp. 2, 8.
New Republic, March 17, 1986.
New York Review of Books, June 10, 1982.
New York Times, September 6, 1985.
New York Times Book Review, September 15, 1985; November 19, 1989, pp. 7, 9.
Seattle Times, April 11, 1982.
Spectator, April 3, 1982; November 9, 1985.
Time, October 7, 1985; December 4, 1989, pp. B8, 97.
Times Literary Supplement, November 28, 1986.
Village Voice, October 15, 1985.

Village Voice Literary Supplement, March, 1982.
Washington Post Book World, September 17, 1992, p. 8.*

*   *   *

LEAVITT, David   1961-

PERSONAL: Born June 23, 1961, in Pittsburgh, PA; son of Harold Jack (a professor) and Gloria (a homemaker; maiden name, Rosenthal) Leavitt. *Education:* Yale University, B.A., 1983.

ADDRESSES: Agent—Andrew Wylie, Wylie, Aitken and Stone, Inc., 250 W. 57th Street, Suite 2114, New York, NY, 10107.

CAREER: Writer. Viking-Penguin, Inc., New York City, reader and editorial assistant, 1983-84.

MEMBER: PEN, Phi Beta Kappa.

AWARDS, HONORS: Willets Prize for fiction, Yale University, 1982, for "Territory"; O. Henry Award, 1984, for "Counting Months"; nomination for best fiction, National Book Critics Circle, 1984, and for PEN/Faulkner Award for best fiction, PEN, 1985, both for *Family Dancing;* National Endowment for the Arts grant, 1985; Visiting Foreign Writer, Institute of Catalan Letters, Barcelona, Spain, 1989; Guggenheim Fellow, 1990.

WRITINGS:

Family Dancing (short stories), Knopf (New York City), 1984.
The Lost Language of Cranes (novel), Knopf, 1986.
Equal Affections (novel), Weidenfeld & Nicolson (London), 1989.
A Place I've Never Been (short stories), Viking (New York City), 1990.
While England Sleeps (novel), Viking, 1993, reprinted with a new preface by the author, Houghton (Boston), 1995.
(Co-editor Mark Mitchell) *Penguin Book of Gay Short Stories*, Viking, 1994.

Contributor to periodicals, including *Esquire, Harper's, New Yorker, New York Times Book Review, New York Times Magazine*, and *Village Voice*.

ADAPTATIONS: The Lost Language of Cranes was made into a film by the British Broadcasting Corp. (BBC) in 1991.

SIDELIGHTS: Lauded for his insightful and empathetic characterizations, author David Leavitt has been at the leading edge of the gay literature movement in the United States for over a decade. Daniel J. Murtaugh noted in *Dictionary of Literary Biography:* "While Leavitt has converted the experiences of gay men and women into a matter of interest for the mainstream reader, he remains one of the most poignant and subjective tellers of what it means to be gay and how a gay person survives in a world of family, education, or business not necessarily receptive to sexual difference." Leavitt published his first story, "Territory," in the *New Yorker* at the age of twenty-one. The story of a mother and her homosexual son, it was the first of its kind to be published in that magazine, and it created "a small stir in the city's more conservative circles," according to an *Interview* writer. Leavitt also published pieces in other various periodicals, including *Esquire* and *Harper's,* and in 1984 he published his first book, a collection of short stories entitled *Family Dancing.*

Family Dancing showcased Leavitt's insights into some of the more offbeat, troubling aspects of domestic life. Among the stories noted by critics are "Radiation," about a slowly dying cancer victim, "Out Here," which concerns sibling guilt, and "Aliens," in which a young girl believes herself to be an extraterrestrial creature. The story "Territory" is included in this collection, and several other works in the volume also address homosexual concerns, including "Dedicated," and "Out Here," in which one of the characters is a lesbian.

Family Dancing earned acclaim as an impressive debut volume. *Newsweek*'s David Lehman, hailing the 1980s boom in short story writing, called Leavitt's book "a first collection of unusual finesse," and Michiko Kakutani wrote in the *New York Times* that *Family Dancing* is "an astonishing collection" with "the power to move us with the blush of truth." In a review for the *Washington Post,* Dennis Drabelle praised Leavitt as "remarkably gifted," and reserved particular commendation for Leavitt's tales of homosexuality. Leavitt, Drabelle contended, "captures the deep-rooted tensions between adult gays and their families and the efforts of childless gays to carve out families among their peers." Drabelle concluded that Leavitt's insights had "only just been tapped."

Leavitt devoted his first novel, *The Lost Language of Cranes,* to a further depiction of homosexual life. While the main character's romantic experiences are rather typical—he falls in love, loses his lover, and finds a more suitable mate—a subplot involving the protagonist's father delves into traumas specific to homosexuality. The father is a married man who spends Sunday afternoons indulging in his passion for patronizing pornography theaters. After learning that his son is a homosexual, he too makes his own difficult confession.

The Lost Language of Cranes, however, chronicles more than just the elements of a homosexual life. It also addresses more universal issues regarding love and traces the hope, pain, ecstasy, and suffering that are all a part of ro-

mantic involvement. Other issues explored in the novel include the notion of family life, and Leavitt narratively delineates the tensions and disappointments of the family as it is altered by the son's and the father's revelations. In addition, the anguish of the wife and mother is also evoked through her increased withdrawal from familial crises. Her disappointment, together with the father's anguish and the son's alternately exhilarating and crushing experiences with love, adds another dimension to Leavitt's work.

The Lost Language of Cranes garnered much critical acclaim. Susan Wood wrote in the *Washington Post* that Leavitt's novel "has much to recommend it," and Philip Lopate noted in the *New York Times Book Review* that the book is "readable and literate." An enthusiastic reviewer for Chicago *Tribune Books* described the novel as "well-written and frankly interesting," and added that "Leavitt's style is compelling, and the subject matter . . . is equally elucidative." Similarly, Dorothy Allison wrote in the *Village Voice* that "Leavitt catches beautifully the terror and passion of new love" and shows a profound understanding of love's "tentativeness." She further declared that *The Lost Language of Cranes* "places David Leavitt firmly among the best young authors of his generation," and concluded that his novel gave her "new hope for modern fiction."

Critics of *The Lost Language of Cranes* were especially impressed with Leavitt's skill in portraying compelling characters and his ability to evoke the tension and turmoil, as well as the fulfillment and ecstasy, of love. The reviewer for *Tribune Books* declared that "Leavitt opens up the gay world to readers" and added that the narrative is "mature, quick-paced and fascinating." Likewise, Allison wrote that the novel's various characters are "so fully realized" that she found herself "tense with fear for each of them." Allison commended Leavitt for his artistry in evincing such a response from readers. "It is David Leavitt's strength that he could inspire that kind of fear in me and win me back when his characters did not find true love or happiness," Allison noted. "At every moment I believed in them, and these days that is so rare as to suggest genius."

Leavitt's second novel, *Equal Affections,* which *Listener* reviewer John Lahr called a "tale of the extraordinariness of ordinary family suffering," centers around Louise Cooper, who is dying of cancer, and the members of her family who must deal with this reality. Louise's husband, Nat, is a computer visionary whose visions have never amounted to much. Her son Danny is a gay lawyer living in bland, immaculate monogamy in the suburbs with Walter, who has not fully committed to the relationship. Daughter April is a famous folk singer who "discovers" her true lesbian nature and turns her singing to feminist issues. Louise's bitterness over lost opportunities, her crisis of faith, and her impending death color her interactions with her husband and family. As Louise's twenty-year bout with cancer draws to a close, the family deals with this strain as well as their individual problems: Nat is having an affair with another woman, Danny endures Walter's on-line computer philandering, and April is artificially inseminated with donor sperm from a culturally aware San Francisco homosexual.

Equal Affections received mixed reviews. Acknowledging her disappointment in Leavitt's first novel, *The Lost Language of Cranes,* Beverly Lowry wrote in the *New York Times Book Review* that "*Equal Affections* does not compromise itself with easy answers. It is a gritty, passionate novel that should settle the question of David Leavitt's abilities. . . . He has the talent for a lifelong career." Lahr called the novel "adroit," while a *New York* writer found it to be "limp, dreary business." The *Washington Post Book World*'s Alan Hollinghurst praised Leavitt's characterizations but observed that the "emotional drama . . . is distinctly soggy. Leavitt's characters are notoriously lachrymose, but here there's really too much tearful sentiment, spunky goodness and curtain-line corniness: this is a sleepie that turns into a weepie." The London *Observer*'s Candia McWilliam, however, called it an "attentive, unsparing book."

Leavitt followed *Equal Affections* with a second collection of short stories, *A Place I've Never Been,* in which a majority of the stories include gay characters dealing with relationships. "When You Grow to Adultery" finds the protagonist leaving an old lover for a new one, and in "My Marriage to Vengeance," a lesbian character's former lover marries a man. In the title story, a woman finally realizes that her gay friend Nathan is too wrapped up in his own self-pity to contribute to their friendship. A mother tests the limits of her AIDS-stricken son's waning strength in "Gravity," and a heterosexual couple who have lost their respective spouses to cancer begin an affair in "Spouse Night."

Many critics praised *A Place I've Never Been.* Charles Solomon of the *Los Angeles Times Book Review* called Leavitt's writing "fine, polished prose that is refreshingly free of the drip-dry nihilism of his Brat Pack contemporaries." James N. Baker of *Newsweek* summarized that "Leavitt is not an oracle nor is he a groundbreaker. . . . he remains what he has always been: a writer of conventional stories who casts an incisive, ironic eye on families and lovers, loyalty and betrayal." Reviewer Harriet Waugh wrote in the *Spectator:* "Short stories, unlike novels, have to be perfect. *A Place I've Never Been* . . . very nearly is." Waugh further declared, "I do not think I have read short stories that have given me greater pleasure or satisfaction in the last couple of years than *A Place I've Never Been.*" Wendy Martin of the *New York Times Book*

Review called the book a "fine new collection of short fiction," and Clifford Chase described the stories as "at once wrenching and satisfying" in his review for the *Village Voice Literary Supplement.*

Leavitt's third novel, *While England Sleeps,* is set in the 1930s against the backdrop of the Spanish Civil War, and follows the love story between Brian Botsford, a literary aristocrat, and Edward Phelan, a lower-class ticket-taker on the London Underground. Brian ends the affair, and in an attempt to deny his homosexuality marries a woman whom his wealthy aunt thinks is suitable. Distraught, Edward joins the fight in Spain, but soon deserts the military and lands in prison. Brian follows his lover to Spain and secures Edward's release, but Edward dies of typhoid on the voyage home.

While England Sleeps borrowed a segment of its plot from Sir Stephen Spender's 1948 autobiography, *World within World,* a fact first revealed by Bernard Knox in his review for the *Washington Post.* Leavitt admitted using an episode from Spender's life as a springboard for his novel and wrote in the *New York Times Magazine* that he had initially included an acknowledgement to Spender, "but had been advised by an in-house lawyer at Viking to omit the reference." He also defended his book on the basis that it is a historical novel and maintained that it "diverged from Spender's account in many more ways than it converged with it." Spender brought suit in London against Leavitt for copyright infringement. Viking agreed to withdraw the book until Leavitt had revised some seventeen points cited in the Spender suit; once this had been done, however, Viking declined to publish the revised version. But in the fall of 1995, Houghton-Mifflin released the new version with an added preface by Leavitt that addressed the book's legal controversy.

Despite this controversy, the *Los Angeles Times* shortlisted the book for its fiction prize after it had been withdrawn from its initial publication, and *While England Sleeps* continued to receive much publicity from reviewers. In a *New York Times* review, Christopher Lehmann-Haupt lauded the book's authentic portrayal of the prewar European era and its depiction of divergent social classes. In the scenes which take place in Spain, Lehmann-Haupt added that "the theme of sexual deception is chillingly replicated in the way the Communist leaders treat their followers," and concluded that *While England Sleeps* should be credited for "[climbing] out of its preoccupation with sex and [making] a significant comment on the political issues of its time." Conversely, Jeremy Treglown noted in the *Times Literary Supplement* that "style is one thing about which Spender hasn't complained, yet the book's main offence lies in its novelettishness." D. T. Max concluded in the *Los Angeles Times Book Review* that "A careful reading of *World within World* shows Spender's charge of plagiarism to be over the top—all the novel's words seem Leavitt's own—but a charge of laziness would be far harder to disprove, and the knowledge of it mars an otherwise graceful, romantic novel."

Leavitt's success has made him one of the few mainstream writers whose work deals primarily with homosexual themes. As Martin explained in the *New York Times Book Review:* "Leavitt has the wonderful ability to lead the reader to examine heterosexist assumptions without becoming polemical. In prose that is often spare and carefully honed, he sensitizes us to the daily difficulties of homosexual life—of negotiating public spaces, for example, where holding hands or a simple embrace becomes problematic." She added: "Leavitt's insight and empathy serve . . . to enlighten, to make us realize that human sexuality is a continuum of possibilities that encompasses the subtle as well as the sensational." Leavitt once told *CA:* "I think the labeling as a gay writer can be a form of ghettoizing, of saying that now the work will only be read by gay people. That hasn't happened to me. The work has had a larger appeal. . . . More aptly, perhaps, I would say that the sexuality of the characters is less important than the situation that they're in, which may be caused by their sexuality but is ultimately more interesting than that fact itself."

BIOGRAPHICAL/CRITICAL SOURCES:

BOOKS

Contemporary Literary Criticism, Volume 34, Gale (Detroit), 1985.
Dictionary of Literary Biography, Volume 130: *American Short Story Writers Since World War II,* Gale, 1993.

PERIODICALS

Advocate, October 19, 1993, pp. 51-55; December 28, 1993, p. 76.
Esquire, May, 1985.
Harper's, April, 1986.
Interview, March, 1985.
Library Journal, June 1, 1995.
Listener, June 15, 1989, p. 25.
London Review of Books, May 23, 1991, pp. 22-23.
Los Angeles Times Book Review, March 5, 1989, p. 6; August 4, 1991, p. 1991; October 3, 1993, pp. 3, 12.
National Review, December 27, 1993, p. 72.
New Statesman & Society, November 12, 1993, p. 38; March 11, 1994, p. 41.
Newsweek, January 14, 1985; February 13, 1989, p. 78; September 3, 1990, p. 66; November 8, 1993, p. 81.
New York, January 30, 1989; October 18, 1993, pp. 139-140.
New York Times, October 30, 1984; October 14, 1993, p. C20; February 20, 1994, p. D14.

New York Times Book Review, September 2, 1984; October 5, 1986; February 12, 1989, p. 7; August 26, 1990, p. 11; October 3, 1993, p. 14; September 4, 1994, p. 10.
New York Times Magazine, July 9, 1989, pp. 28-32; April 3, 1994, p. 36.
Observer (London), May 28, 1989, p. 46.
Partisan Review, winter, 1994, pp. 80-95.
Publishers Weekly, August 24, 1990, pp. 47-48; February 21, 1994.
Spectator, March 9, 1991, p. 28.
Time, November 8, 1993, p. 27.
Times Literary Supplement, June 9-15, 1989, p. 634; October 29, 1993, p. 20.
Tribune Books (Chicago), September 21, 1986.
Village Voice, October 14, 1986.
Village Voice Literary Supplement, December, 1990, pp. 10-11.
Washington Post, November 19, 1984; March 2, 1985; October 7, 1986; February 17, 1994, p. A1.
Washington Post Book World, January 22, 1989, p. 4; October 7, 1990, p. 7; September 12, 1993, p. 5.*

—*Sketch by Ellen Dennis French*

*   *   *

LEUCI, Bob
See LEUCI, Robert

*   *   *

LEUCI, Robert   1940-
(Bob Leuci)

PERSONAL: Born February 28, 1940, in New York, NY; son of James (a pipe-factory foreman and union organizer) and Lucy (an office worker, telephone operator, and sewing-machine plant laborer; maiden name, Tuccitto) Leuci; married Regina Manarin (an insurance administrator), May 11, 1963; children: Anthony James, Santina. *Education:* Attended Baker University, 1957-58; Fordham University, 1979-80, and New School for Social Research. *Politics:* "A small step left." *Religion:* Roman Catholic; humanist.

ADDRESSES: Agent—Esther Newberg, International Creative Management, 40 West 57th St., New York, NY 10019.

CAREER: New York Police Department, New York City, police officer, 1961-63, detective in Special Investigations Unit of Narcotics Division, 1963-72, detective in First Deputy Commissioner's Special Force, 1972-76, internal affairs officer, 1976-80, Civil Complaint Review

Board officer, 1980-81, retired, 1981. Writer. 1981—. Adjunct at Western Connecticut State University, 1983-84. Resident and lecturer at universities, law schools, and police departments nationwide.

MEMBER: Amnesty International (anti-capital punishment co-ordinator for Danbury, CT, group), International Association of Crime Writers, Mystery Writers of America, Authors Guild.

WRITINGS:

CRIME NOVELS: UNDER NAME BOB LEUCI

Doyle's Disciples, Freundlich Books (New York City), 1984.
Odessa Beach, Freundlich Books, 1985.
Captain Butterfly, New American Library (New York City), 1988.
Double Edge, Dutton (New York City), 1991.

WORK IN PROGRESS: Writing the screenplay for a motion picture adaptation of *Captain Butterfly,* for Lorimar Productions; adapting *Doyle's Disciples* as a television series; a novel, tentative title *Marimbero;* a play, tentative title "Slapper."

SIDELIGHTS: Robert Leuci draws much of his subject matter from his experience as a detective in a special narcotics investigating unit of the New York City Police Department during the 1960s and early 1970s. It was Leuci who, caught between his sense of ethics and his loyalty to his fellow officers, became the subject of the best-selling book and film *Prince of the City,* a study of the dangers of undercover police work and the temptations offered by a corrupt system. A *Chicago Tribune Books* contributor notes that, in the wake of the "Prince of the City" scandal, "ostracized by his peers for his ethical stance, Leuci . . . has committed himself to fighting criminals and corrupt cops in novels." Leuci's vast experience in the criminal justice system informs all of his work.

A choice, self-directed group whose independence and citywide jurisdiction earned its members the label "princes of the city," the special narcotics investigating unit to which Leuci belonged in the 1960s also reflected the corruption present in the police department at the time. To investigate the rumors of drug dealing and other illegal activities in the police department, a special commission was formed, headed by Whitman Knapp. At that time, Leuci recalled for *CA,* he believed that "the concept of the Knapp Commission was outrageous, [because it] was focusing only on the police." He remembered telling counsel for the commission "that I could, if I wanted, expose corruption in lawyers, judges, district attorneys, bail-bondsmen, organized crime types, and a slew of others, none of whom were policemen." The counsel asked him

to prove it, Leuci said, and "it was then that I realized that I'd told him too much."

Leuci agreed to work undercover for a federal team investigating the New York City criminal justice system. "Ultimately, I was convinced that I had to tell the truth about my own involvement in corruption," he told *CA.* This admission produced unfortunate repercussions, however. "In admitting my own misdeeds I implicated several men who had been close friends," Leuci recalled. His actions led some colleagues and observers to consider the detective a hero and others to call him a traitor, and it necessitated the protection of Leuci and his family, for a time, by armed guards. He refused the government's offer of a new identity and relocation, however, because "to run away or change my identity. . . would be to admit to myself that I was worthless," as he told Tom Zito in the *Washington Post.* "What I set out to do was not hypocritical," he explained to *CA,* "but really a noble ambition that unraveled and turned tragic."

Leuci's story was retold by Robert Daley in the book *Prince of the City* and in director Sidney Lumet's motion picture of the same title. The former policeman reflected: " 'Prince of the City' is truly a sad and tragic story. Looked at in its broadest sense, it is simply the tale of a group of basically good and decent men that lost sight of who they were and what they were about, as people and as policemen. The setting is the police world, but what is true for those described in that story is also true for anyone who loses sight of what is best in them."

Leuci turned to writing after retiring from the police force in 1981.

His first novel, *Doyle's Disciples,* echoed his own story and acted as "a bit of a catharsis," Leuci was quoted as saying in the *Los Angeles Times.* Protagonist Bobby Porterfield is a New York City detective who uncovers a bloody payoff scandal that involves top police officials; the officer grapples with whether to expose department criminality or to accept the workings of a pervasively errant system. "The resulting climax threatens his profession, his marriage, his friendships and his self-respect, as well as his life," described Carl Sessions Stepp in the *Washington Post.* "Unlike the author, Leuci's fictional hero recoils from his magic opportunity to combat police corruption."

Doyle's Disciples was praised by some reviewers for its potent realism. "The backgrounds and police routines are meticulously depicted," wrote *New York Times Book Review* critic Newgate Callendar. "Mr. Leuci knows his way around the city, the court, [and] the precinct houses." As for his protagonist's moral dilemma, the critic continued, "it will be up to the reader to decide if he has solved it." Stepp commended Leuci's "skill in pacing the action and in penetrating those gritty inner-city subcultures and nerve-jangling street terrors police face daily," and he called the novel's theme "provocative and disturbing—a disheartening testament to the fruitlessness of reform and the fragility of relationships." While deciding that "the novel does draw its authority more from who Leuci is and where he has been than from how he writes," Stepp concluded, "Leuci seems to have deeper possibilities within."

Attempting to realize these possibilities, Leuci wrote *Odessa Beach,* a thriller concerning a Russian black marketeer and New York's Mafia. Callendar observed: "Mr. Leuci is a very good technician. . . . Everything rings true." Judging it "a fascinating yarn told vulgarly, yet compellingly," Nick B. Williams, Sr., in the *Los Angeles Times Book Review,* placed the novel "among the most exciting that I've read this year." *Captain Butterfly,* Leuci's 1989 novel, is about an ambitious precinct captain in Brooklyn and a feisty female inspector from the city's Internal Affairs Division who is sent to investigate unorthodox questioning procedures at the precinct. According to Randall Short in the *New York Times Book Review,* Leuci "has a flawless ear for the several varieties of street talk, bureaucratese and casual conversation that subtly distinguish his characters."

In 1991 Leuci released another crime novel, *Double Edge.* Set in the nation's capital, the story follows a weary homicide detective named Scott Ancelet as he tries to solve the brutal execution-style murder of a black teenager who may or may not have been involved in high-level drug-dealing. A *Washington Post Book World* reviewer notes: "There's a fine line between excitement and exploitation; Leuci, a talented writer, stays on the right side of it most of the time." The critic adds that Leuci's portraits of jaded police officers working together "have real juice. . . . It takes a writer to bring so many desperate characters to life."

In addition to his writing, Leuci lectures on criminal justice and other issues. He told *CA:* "The pleasure of my work comes from giving readers the opportunity to see the world through the eyes of street people and the police. This is the arena I know best: law officers and street people—the disenfranchised, the set upon, the predators. We live in a violent world. Why? That's the question that interests me most.

"I have been a fan all my conscious life of a certain crew of writers. Each of them has something to say, and it's in the way they say it that makes you jump off the tracks. No one here has mastered a formula, few have best-sellers. They are not self-conscious or tedious; they are simply wonderful writers of prose whose words are fine poetry. Most rely on dialogue to disclose character, and all dramatize the various ways individuals and nations sin. For me this is writing, this is what I strive to do."

BIOGRAPHICAL/CRITICAL SOURCES:

BOOKS

Daley, Robert, *Prince of the City: The True Story of a Cop Who Knew Too Much,* Houghton (Boston, MA), 1979.

PERIODICALS

Booklist, October 15, 1991, p. 414.
Chicago Tribune, October 9, 1984.
Chicago Tribune Books, July 2, 1989, p. 5.
Los Angeles Times, November 23, 1984.
Los Angeles Times Book Review, August 19, 1984; February 16, 1986; April 21, 1991.
New York Times Book Review, January 6, 1985; January 4, 1987; November 12, 1989, p. 55.
Washington Post, January 17, 1979; August 24, 1984.
Washington Post Book World, December 15, 1991, p. 6.*

* * *

LEVERTOV, Denise 1923-

PERSONAL: Born October 24, 1923, in Ilford, Essex, England; came to the United States in 1948, naturalized in 1955; daughter of Paul Philip (an Anglican priest) and Beatrice Adelaide (Spooner-Jones) Levertoff; married Mitchell Goodman (a writer), December 2, 1947 (divorced, 1972); children: Nikolai Gregor. *Education:* Privately educated; also studied ballet.

ADDRESSES: Home—5535 Seward Park Avenue South, Seattle, WA 98118. *Office*—c/o New Directions, Inc., 80 Eighth Ave., New York, NY 10011.

CAREER: Poet, essayist, editor, translator, and educator. Worked in an antique store and a bookstore in London, 1946; taught English in Holland, three months; Young Men and Women's Christian Association (YM-YWCA) poetry center, New York City, teacher of poetry craft, 1964; Drew University, Madison, NJ, visiting lecturer, 1965; City College of the City University of New York, New York City, writer in residence, 1965-66; Vassar College, Poughkeepsie, NY, visiting lecturer, 1966-67; University of California, Berkeley, visiting professor, 1969; Massachusetts Institute of Technology (M.I.T), Cambridge, visiting professor and poet in residence, 1969-70; Kirkland College, Clinton, NY, visiting professor, 1970-71; University of Cincinnati, Cincinnati, OH, Elliston Lecturer, 1973; Tufts University, Medford, MA, professor, 1973-79; Brandeis University, Waltham, MA, Fannie Hurst Professor, 1981-83; Stanford University, Stanford, CA, professor of English, 1981—. Co-initiator of Writers and Artists Protest against the War in Vietnam, 1965; active in the anti-nuclear movement. *Wartime ser-*

vice: Trained and worked in several London hospitals, 1943-45.

MEMBER: American Academy and Institute of Arts and Letters.

AWARDS, HONORS: Bess Hokin Prize from *Poetry,* 1959, for poem "With Eyes at the Back of Our Heads"; Longview Award, 1961; Guggenheim fellowship, 1962; Harriet Monroe Memorial Prize, 1964; Inez Boulton Prize, 1964; American Academy and Institute of Arts and Letters grant, 1965; Morton Dauwen Zabel Memorial Prize from *Poetry,* 1965; D.Litt., Colby College, 1970, University of Cincinnati, 1973, Bates College, 1984, Saint Lawrence University, 1984; Lenore Marshall Poetry Prize, 1976; Elmer Holmes Bobst Award in poetry, 1983; Shelley Memorial Award from Poetry Society of America, 1984.

WRITINGS:

POETRY

The Double Image, Cresset (Philadelphia, PA), 1946, Brooding Heron Press (Waldron Island, WA), 1991.
Here and Now, City Lights (San Francisco, CA), 1957.
Overland to the Islands, Jargon, 1958.
Five Poems, White Rabbit (Santa Barbara, CA), 1958.
With Eyes at the Back of Our Heads, New Directions Press (New York City), 1959.
The Jacob's Ladder, New Directions Press, 1961.
O Taste and See: New Poems, New Directions Press, 1964.
City Psalm, Oyez (Kensington, CA), 1964.
Psalm Concerning the Castle, Perishable Press, 1966.
The Sorrow Dance, New Directions Press, 1967.
(With Kenneth Rexroth and William Carlos Williams) *Penguin Modern Poets 9,* Penguin (London), 1967.
(Editor) *Out of the War Shadow: An Anthology of Current Poetry,* War Resisters League, 1967.
A Tree Telling of Orpheus, Black Sparrow Press (Santa Barbara, CA), 1968.
A Marigold from North Vietnam, Albondocani Press-Ampersand (Everett, WA), 1968.
Three Poems, Perishable Press, 1968.
The Cold Spring and Other Poems, New Directions Press, 1969.
Embroideries, Black Sparrow Press, 1969.
Relearning the Alphabet, New Directions Press, 1970.
Summer Poems 1969, Oyez (Kensington, CA), 1970.
A New Year's Garland for My Students, MIT 1969-1970, Perishable Press, 1970.
To Stay Alive, New Directions Press, 1971.
Footprints, New Directions Press, 1972.
The Freeing of the Dust, New Directions Press, 1975.
Chekhov on the West Heath, Woolmer/Brotherston (Revere, PA), 1977.
Modulations for Solo Voice, Five Trees Press, 1977.

Life in the Forest, New Directions Press, 1978.
Collected Earlier Poems, 1940-1960, New Directions Press, 1979.
Pig Dreams: Scenes from the Life of Sylvia, Countryman Press (Woodstock, VT), 1981.
Wanderer's Daysong, Copper Canyon Press (Port Townsend, WA), 1981.
Candles in Babylon, New Directions Press, 1982.
Poems, 1960-1967, New Directions Press, 1983.
Oblique Prayers: New Poems with Fourteen Translations from Jean Joubert, New Directions Press, 1984.
El Salvador: Requiem and Invocation, William B. Ewert, 1984.
The Menaced World, William B. Ewert, 1984.
Selected Poems, Bloodaxe Books (England), 1986.
Breathing the Water, New Directions Press, 1987.
Poems, 1968-1972, New Directions Press, 1987.
A Door in the Hive, New Directions Press, 1989.
Evening Train, New Directions Press, 1992.
Tesserae: Memories and Suppositions, New Directions Press, 1995.

OTHER

(Translator and editor with Edward C. Dimock, Jr.) *In Praise of Krishna: Songs from the Bengali,* Doubleday (New York City), 1967.
In the Night: A Story, Albondocani Press, 1968.
(Contributor of translations) Jules Supervielle, *Selected Writings,* New Directions Press, 1968.
(Translator from French) Eugene Guillevic, *Selected Poems,* New Directions Press, 1969.
The Poet in the World (essays), New Directions Press, 1973.
Light Up the Cave (essays), New Directions Press, 1981.
(Translator with others from Bulgarian) William Meredith, editor, *Poets of Bulgaria,* Unicorn Press (Greensboro, NC), 1985.
(Translator from French) Jean Joubert, *Black Iris,* Copper Canyon Press (Port Townsend, WA), 1988.
El paisaje interior (essays translated to Spanish by Patricia Gola), Universidad Autonoma de Tlaxcala (Tlaxcala, Mexico), 1990.
New & Selected Essays, New Directions, 1992.

Also author of *Lake, Mountain, Moon,* 1990. Translator from French of Jean Joubert's *White Owl and Blue Mouse,* 1990.

Contributor to poetry anthologies, such as *The New American Poetry, Poet's Choice, Poets of Today,* and *New Poets of England and America.* Sound recordings of Levertov's poetry include, "Today's Poets 3," Folkways, and "The Acolyte," Watershed, 1985. Poetry editor, *Nation,* 1961-62, and *Mother Jones,* 1976-78.

Main manuscript collection is housed at the Green Library, Stanford University, Stanford, CA. Other collections housed in the following locations: Humanities Research Center, University of Texas at Austin; Washington University, St. Louis, MO; Indiana University, Bloomington; Fales Library, New York University, New York City; Beinecke Library, Yale University, New Haven, CT; Brown University, Providence, RI; University of Connecticut, Storrs, CT; Columbia University, New York City; and State University of New York at Stony Brook.

SIDELIGHTS: World Literature Today contributor Doris Earnshaw describes poet and essayist Denise Levertov as being "fitted by birth and political destiny to voice the terrors and pleasures of the twentieth century. . . . She has published poetry since the 1940s that speaks of the great contemporary themes: Eros, solitude, community, war." Although born and raised in England, Levertov came to the United States when she was twenty-five years old and all but her first few poetry collections have been described as thoroughly American. Early on, critics and colleagues alike detected an American idiom and style to her work, noting the influences of writers like William Carlos Williams, H. D. (Hilda Doolittle), Kenneth Rexroth, Wallace Stevens, and the projectivist Black Mountain poets. With the onset of the turbulent 1960s, Levertov delved into socio-political poetry and has continued writing in this sphere; in *Modern American Women Poets*, for instance, Jean Gould calls her "a poet of definite political and social consciousness." In the end, however, Levertov refuses to be labeled, and Rexroth in *With Eye and Ear* says she is "in fact classically independent."

Because Levertov never received a formal education, her earliest literary influences can be traced to her home life in Ilford, England, a suburb of London. Levertov and her older sister, Olga, were educated by their Welsh mother Beatrice Adelaide Spooner-Jones until the age of thirteen. The girls further received sporadic religious training from their father Paul Philip Levertoff, a Russian Jew who converted to Christianity and subsequently moved to England and became an Anglican minister. In the *Dictionary of Literary Biography*, Carolyn Matalene explains that "the education [Levertov] did receive seems, like Robert Browning's, made to order. Her mother read aloud to the family the great works of nineteenth-century fiction, and she read poetry, especially the lyrics of Tennyson. . . . Her father, a prolific writer in Hebrew, Russian, German, and English, used to buy secondhand books by the lot to obtain particular volumes. Levertov grew up surrounded by books and people talking about them in many languages." Many of Levertov's readers favor her lack of formal education because they see it as an impetus to verse that is consistently clear, precise, and accessible. According to Earnshaw, "Levertov seems never to have had to shake

loose from an academic style of extreme ellipses and literary allusion, the self-conscious obscurity that the Provencal poets called 'closed.' "

Levertov had confidence in her poetic abilities from the beginning, and several well-respected literary figures believed in her talents as well. Gould records Levertov's "temerity" at the age of twelve when she sent several of her poems directly to T. S. Eliot: "She received a two-page typewritten letter from him, offering her 'excellent advice'. . . . His letter gave her renewed impetus for making poems and sending them out." Other early supporters included critic Herbert Read, editor Charles Wrey Gardiner, and author Kenneth Rexroth. When Levertov had her first poem published in *Poetry Quarterly* in 1940, Rexroth professed: "In no time at all Herbert Read, Tambimutti, Charles Wrey Gardiner, and incidentally myself, were all in excited correspondence about her. She was the baby of the new Romanticism. Her poetry had about it a wistful *Schwarmerei* unlike anything in English except perhaps Matthew Arnold's 'Dover Beach.' It could be compared to the earliest poems of Rilke or some of the more melancholy songs of Brahms."

During World War II, Levertov pursued nurse's training and spent three years as a civilian nurse at several hospitals in the London area, during which time she continued to write poetry. Her first book of poems, *The Double Image*, was published just after the war in 1946. Although a few poems in this collection may focus on the war, there is no direct evidence of the immediate events of the time. Instead, as noted above by Rexroth, the work is very much in keeping with the British neo-romanticism of the 1940s, for it contains formal verse that some consider artificial and overly sentimental. Some critics detect the same propensity for sentimentality in Levertov's second collection, *Here and Now*. In the *National Review*, N. E. Condini comments in retrospect on both of these volumes: "In *The Double Image*, a recurrent sense of loss prompts [Levertov] to extemporize on death as not a threat but a rite to be accepted gladly and honored. This germ of personal mythology burgeons in *Here and Now* with a fable-like aura added to it. . . . [*Here and Now*] is a hymn to 'idiot' joy, which the poet still considers the best protection against the aridity of war and war's memories. Her weakness lies in a childish romanticism, which will be replaced later by a more substantial concision. Here the language is a bit too ornate, too flowery." Criticism aside, Gould says *The Double Image* revealed one thing for certain: "the young poet possessed a strong social consciousness and . . . showed indications of the militant pacifist she was to become."

Levertov came to the United States in 1948, after marrying American writer Mitchell Goodman, and began developing the style that was to make her an internationally respected American poet. Some critics maintain that her first American poetry collection, *Here and Now,* contains vestiges of the sentimentalism that characterized her first book, but for some, *Here and Now* displays Levertov's newly-found American voice. Rexroth, for one, insists in his 1961 collection of essays entitled *Assays* that "the *Schwarmerei* and lassitude are gone. Their place has been taken by a kind of animal grace of the word, a pulse like the footfalls of a cat or the wingbeats of a gull. It is the intense aliveness of an alert domestic love—the wedding of form and content. . . . What more do you want of poetry? You can't ask much more." By the time *With Eyes at the Back of Our Heads* was published in 1959, Gould claims Levertov was "regarded as a bona fide American poet."

Levertov's American poetic voice is, in one sense, indebted to the simple, concrete language and imagery, and also the immediacy, characteristic of Williams Carlos Williams' art. Accordingly, Ralph J. Mills, Jr., remarks in his essay in *Poets in Progress* that Levertov's verse "is frequently a tour through the familiar and the mundane until their unfamiliarity and otherworldliness suddenly strike us. . . . The quotidian reality we ignore or try to escape, . . . Levertov revels in, carves and hammers into lyric poems of precise beauty." In turn, *Midwest Quarterly* reviewer Julian Gitzen explains that Levertov's "attention to physical details permits [her] to develop a considerable range of poetic subject, for, like Williams, she is often inspired by the humble, the commonplace, or the small, and she composes remarkably perceptive poems about a single flower, a man walking two dogs in the rain, and even sunlight glittering on rubbish in a street."

In another sense, Levertov's verse exhibits the influence of the Black Mountain poets, such as Robert Duncan, Charles Olson, and Robert Creeley, whom Levertov met through her husband. Creeley was among the first to publish Levertov's poetry in the United States in *Origin* and *Black Mountain Review* in the 1950s. Unlike her early formalized verse, Levertov now gave homage to the projectivist verse of the Black Mountain era, whereby the poet "projects" through content rather than through strict meter or form. Although Levertov was assuredly influenced by several renowned American writers of the time, Matalene believes Levertov's "development as a poet has certainly proceeded more according to her own themes, her own sense of place, and her own sensitivities to the music of poetry than to poetic manifestos." Indeed, when Levertov became a New Directions author in 1959, Matalene explains that this came to be because the editor James Laughlin had detected in Levertov's work her own unique voice.

With the onset of U.S. involvement in the Vietnam War in the 1960s, Levertov's social consciousness began to

more completely inform both her poetry and her private life. With poet Muriel Rukeyser and several fellow poets, Levertov founded the Writers and Artists Protest against the War in Vietnam. She took part in several anti-war demonstrations in Berkeley, California, and elsewhere, and was briefly jailed on numerous occasions for civil disobedience. More recently she has spoken out against nuclear weaponry and U.S. aid to El Salvador. *The Sorrow Dance, Relearning the Alphabet, To Stay Alive,* and, to an extent, *Candles in Babylon,* as well as other poetry collections, address many socio-political themes, like the Vietnam War, the Detroit riots, and nuclear disarmament. Her goal has been to motivate others into an awareness on these various issues, particularly the Vietnam War and ecological issues.

In contrast with the generally favorable criticism of her work, commentators tend to view the socio-political poems with a degree of distaste, often noting that they resemble prose more than poetry. In *Contemporary Literature,* Marjorie G. Perloff writes: "It is distressing to report that . . . Levertov's new book, *To Stay Alive,* contains a quantity of bad confessional verse. Her anti-Vietnam War poems, written in casual diary form, sound rather like a versified *New York Review of Books.*" Gould mentions that some consider these poems "preachy," and Matalene notes that in *Relearning the Alphabet* Levertov's "plight is certainly understandable, but her poetry suffers here from weariness and from a tendency toward sentimentality. . . . *To Stay Alive* is a historical document and does record and preserve the persons, conversations, and events of those years. Perhaps, as the events recede in time, these poems will seem true and just, rather than inchoate, bombastic, and superficial. History, after all, does prefer those who take stands."

In an interview with Levertov in *Los Angeles Times Book Review* just prior to the publication of *Candles in Babylon,* contributor Penelope Moffet explains that "[Levertov] probably would not go so far as to describe any of her own political work as 'doggerel,' but she does acknowledge that some pieces are only 'sort-of' poems." Moffet then quotes Levertov: "If any reviewer wants to criticize [*Candles in Babylon*] when it comes out, they've got an obvious place to begin—'well, it's not poetry, this ranting and roaring and speech-making.' It [the 1980 anti-draft speech included in *Candles in Babylon*] *was* a speech." Nevertheless, others are not so quick to find fault with these "sort-of" poems. In the opinion of Hayden Carruth for the *Hudson Review, To Stay Alive* "contains, what so annoys the critics, highly lyric passages next to passages of prose—letters and documents. But is it, after *Paterson,* necessary to defend this? The fact is, I think Levertov has used her prose bits better than Williams did, more prudently and economically. . . . I also think that *To Stay*

Alive is one of the best products of the recent period of politically oriented vision among American poets." In turn, James F. Mersmann's lengthy analysis of several years of Levertov's poetry in *Out of the Vietnam Vortex: A Study of Poets and Poetry against the War* contains remarkable praise for the social protest poems. For contrast, Mersmann first analyzes Levertov's early poetry: "*Balanced* and *whole* are words that have perhaps best characterized the work and the person of Denise Levertov—at least until the late sixties. . . . There are no excesses of ecstasy or despair, celebration or denigration, naivete or cynicism; there is instead an acute ability to find simple beauties in the heart of squalor and something to relish even in negative experiences. . . . Through poetry she reaches to the heart of things, finds out what their centers are. If the reader can follow, he is welcomed along, but although the poetry is mindful of communication and expression, its primary concern is discovery." However, claims Mersmann, the chaos of the war disrupted the balance, the wholeness, and the fundamental concern for discovery apparent in her work—"the shadow of the Vietnam War comes to alter all this: vision is clouded, form is broken, balance is impossible, and the psyche is unable to throw off its illness and sorrow. . . . A few notes of *The Sorrow Dance* sound something like hysteria, and later poems move beyond desperation, through mild catatonia toward intransigent rebellion. . . . In some sense the early poems are undoubtedly more perfect and enduring works of art, more timeless and less datable, but they are, for all their fineness, only teacups, and of sorely limited capacities. The war-shadowed poems are less clean and symmetrical but are moral and philosophical schooners of some size. . . . The war, by offering much that was distasteful and unsightly, prompted a poetry that asks the poet to add the light and weight of her moral and spiritual powers to the fine sensibility of her palate and eye."

Diane Wakoski, reviewing Levertov's volume of poems *Breathing the Water,* for the *Women's Review of Books,* stresses the religious elements in Levertov's work. "Levertov's poetry," Wakoski states, "like most American mysticism, is grounded in Christianity, but like Whitman and other American mystics her discovery of God is the discovery of God in herself, and an attempt to understand how that self is a 'natural' part of the world, intermingling with everything pantheistically, ecologically, socially, historically and, for Levertov, always lyrically." Doris Earnshaw seems to echo Wakoski in her review of Levertov's volume *A Door in the Hive* for *World Literature Today.* Earnshaw feels that Levertov's poems are "truly lyrics while speaking of political and religious affairs." The central piece of *A Door in the Hive* is "El Salvador: Requiem and Invocation," a libretto composed as a requiem for Archbishop Romero and four American woman who were killed by death squads in El Salvador in the early eighties.

Emily Grosholz in the *Hudson Review* states that while this is "not a poem, [it] is a useful kind of extended popular song whose proceeds served to aid important relief and lobbying efforts; such writing deserves a place side by side with Levertov's best poetry. And indeed, it is flanked by poems that rise to the occasion."

In a discussion of Levertov's volume *Evening Train, World Literature Today* reviewer Daisy Aldan believes the "collection reveals an important transition toward what some have called 'the last plateau': that is, the consciousness of entering into the years of aging , which she experiences and expresses with sensitivity and grace." Mark Jarman in the *Hudson Review* describes the book as "a long sequence about growing older, with a terrific payoff. This is the best writing she has done in years." *Evening Train* consists of individually titled sections, beginning with the pastoral "Lake Mountain Moon" and ending with the spiritually-oriented "The Tide." In between, Levertov deals both with problems of personal conscience and social issues, such as AIDS, the Gulf War, pollution, the ongoing threat of nuclear annihilation. Jarman sees the more topical poems as the weakest in the book, a viewpoint shard by Elizabeth Lund in the *Christian Science Monitor.* However, Amy Gerstler in the *Los Angeles Times Book Review* feels that all of the poems "blend together to form one long poem . . . ," and credits Levertov with possessing "a practically perfect instinct for picking the right distance to speak from: how far away to remain from both reader and subject, and how much of an overt role to give herself in the poem." Aldan concludes that the poems in *Evening Train* "manifest a new modesty, a refinement, sensibility, creative intelligence, compassion and spirituality."

In addition to being a poet, Levertov has taught her craft at several colleges and universities nationwide; she has translated a number of works, particularly those of the French poet Jean Joubert; she was poetry editor of the *Nation* from 1961-62 and *Mother Jones* from 1976-78; and she has authored several collections of essays and criticism, including *The Poet in the World, Light Up the Cave,* and *New & Selected Essays.*

According to Carruth, *The Poet in the World* is "a miscellaneous volume, springing from many miscellaneous occasions, and its tone ranges from spritely to gracious to, occasionally, pedantic. It contains a number of pieces about the poet's work as a teacher; it contains her beautiful impromptu obituary for William Carlos Williams, as well as reviews and appreciations of other writers. But chiefly the book is about poetry, its mystery and its craft, and about the relationship between poetry and life. . . . It should be read by everyone who takes poetry seriously." Other reviewers also recommend the work to those interested in the craft of poetry since, as *New Republic* commentator

Josephine Jacobsen puts it, "Levertov speaks for the reach and dignity of poetry. . . . [The book] makes . . . large claims for an art form so often hamstrung in practice by the trivial, the fake and the chic. It is impossible to read this book, to listen to its immediacy, without a quickening."

The essays in *Light Up the Cave,* in turn, are considered "a diary of our neglected soul," by *American Book Review* critic Daniel Berrigan: "Norman Mailer did something like this in the sixties; but since those heady days and nights, he, like most such marchers and writers, has turned to other matters. . . . Levertov is still marching, still recording the march . . ." *Library Journal* contributor Rochelle Ratner detects much maturation since the earlier *Poet in the World* and Ingrid Rimland, in the *Los Angeles Times Book Review,* remarks that "the strong impression remains that here speaks a poet intensely loyal to her craft, abiding by an artist's inner rules and deserving attention and respect. . . . This volume is a potpourri: assorted musings, subtle insights, tender memories of youth and strength, political passions, gentle but respectful accolades to other writers. The prose is utterly free of restraints, save those demanded by a fierce, independent spirit insisting at all times on honesty."

New & Selected Essays brings together essays dating from 1965 to 1992 and includes topics such as politics, religion, the influence of other poets on Levertov, the poetics of free verse, the limits beyond which the subject matter of poetry should not go, and the social obligations of the poet. Essays on poets who have influenced Levertov cover William Carlos Williams, Robert Duncan, and Rilke. Mary Kaiser, writing in *World Literature Today,* says of the collection: "Wide-ranging in subject matter and spanning three decades of thought, Levertov's essays show a remarkable coherence, sanity, and poetic integrity." Ray Olsen, in *Booklist,* feels that some of the best essays included are the ones on technical aspects of poetry, singling out four essays on William Carlos Williams' variable foot as "some of the most illuminating, sensible, exciting Williams commentary ever written." He concludes: "Next to poetry itself, this is ideal reading for lovers of poetry." However, Belle Randall in *American Book Review* takes strong exception to Levertov's essay criticizing certain types of confessional writing. Randall believes that such attempts "are probably always doomed." Referring to Levertov's own work, Randall argues that such "constraint limits the range and depth of her poetry, especially in view of her express desire to be exploratory and inclusive."

In her review of *Evening Train* for the *Los Angeles Times Book Review,* Amy Gerstler begins with a succinct summary of Levertov's career. According to Gerstler: "*Dignity, reverence* and *strength* are words that come to mind as one gropes to characterize not only this 21st volume by one of America's most respected poets but also her writing over the span of a nearly 50-year-career. . . . [A] reader poking her nose into any Levertov book at random finds herself in the presence of a clear uncluttered voice—a voice committed to acute observation and engagement with the earthly, in all its attendant beauty, mystery and pain." Discussing Levertov's social and political consciousness in his review of *Light Up the Cave,* Berrigan states: "[O]ur options [in a tremulous world], as they say, are no longer large. . . . [We] may choose to do nothing; which is to say, to go discreetly or wildly mad, letting fear possess us and frivolity rule our days. Or we may, along with admirable spirits like Denise Levertov, be driven sane; by community, by conscience, by treading the human crucible."

BIOGRAPHICAL/CRITICAL SOURCES:

BOOKS

Breslin, James E. B., *From Modern to Contemporary: American Poetry, 1945-1965,* University of Chicago Press, 1984, pp. 143-55.

Capps, Donald, *The Poet's Gift: Toward the Renewal of Pastoral Care,* Westminister/John Knox (Louisville, KY), 1993.

Contemporary Literary Criticism, Volume 66, Gale (Detroit), 1991.

Dictionary of Literary Biography, Volume 5: *American Poets Since World War II,* Gale, 1980.

Gelpi, Albert, editor, *Denise Levertov: Selected Criticism,* University of Michigan Press (Ann Arbor), 1993.

Gould, Jean, *Modern American Women Poets,* Dodd (New York City), 1985.

Hungerford, Edward, editor, *Poets in Progress,* Northwestern University Press (Evanston, IL), 2nd edition, 1967.

Kinnahan, Linda A., *Poetics of the Feminine: Authority and Literary Tradition in William Carlos Williams, Mina Loy, Denise Levertov, and Kathleen Fraser,* Cambridge University Press (Cambridge), 1994.

Marten, Harry, *Understanding Denise Levertov,* University of South Carolina Press (Columbia), 1988.

Mersmann, James, *Out of the Vietnam Vortex: A Study of Poets and Poetry against the War,* University Press of Kansas (Lawrence, KS), 1974.

Rexroth, Kenneth, *Assays,* New Directions Press, 1961.

Rexroth, *With Eye and Ear,* Herder & Herder, 1970.

Rodgers, Audrey T., *Denise Levertov: The Poetry of Engagement,* Fairleigh Dickinson University Press (Rutherford, NJ), 1993.

Slaughter, William, *The Imagination's Tongue: Denise Levertov's Poetic,* Aquila, 1981.

Wagner, Linda W., *Denise Levertov,* Twayne (New Haven, CT), 1967.

Wagner, Linda W., editor, *Denise Levertov: In Her Own Province,* New Directions Press, 1979.

Wagner-Martin, Linda W., editor, *Critical Essays on Denise Levertov,* G. K. Hall (Boston), 1990.

PERIODICALS

America, November 13, 1993, p. 19.

American Book Review, January-February, 1983; October, 1993, p. 7.

Booklist, October 15, 1992, p. 394.

Christian Science Monitor, June 3, 1993, p. 16.

Contemporary Literature, winter, 1973.

Hudson Review, summer, 1990, pp. 328-29; summer, 1993, pp. 415-24.

Library Journal, September 1, 1981.

Los Angeles Times Book Review, June 6, 1982; July 18, 1982; December 27, 1992, p. 5.

Michigan Quarterly Review, fall, 1985.

Midwest Quarterly, spring, 1975.

Nation, August 14, 1976.

National Review, March 21, 1980.

New Republic, January 26, 1974.

New York Times Book Review, January 7, 1973; November 30, 1975.

Village Voice, September 29, 1987.

Women's Review of Books, February, 1988, pp. 7-8.

World Literature Today, winter, 1981; spring, 1983; summer, 1985; autumn, 1990, p. 640-41; autumn, 1993, p. 832; winter, 1994, p. 132-33.

*   *   *

LEVIN, Betty 1927-

PERSONAL: Born September 10, 1927, in New York, NY; daughter of Max (a lawyer) and Eleanor (a musician; maiden name, Mack) Lowenthal; married Alvin Levin (a lawyer), 1947; children: Katherine, Bara, Jennifer. *Education:* University of Rochester, A.B., 1949; Radcliffe College, M.A., 1951; Harvard University, A.M.T., 1951.

ADDRESSES: Home—Old Winter St., Lincoln, MA 01773. *Office*—Center for the Study of Children's Literature, Simmons College, Boston, MA 02115.

CAREER: Museum of Fine Arts, Boston, MA, assistant in research, 1952; Pine Manor Open College, Chestnut Hill, MA, instructor in literature, 1970-75; Simmons College, Center for the Study of Children's Literature, Boston, MA, adjunct professor, 1975-87; member of faculty, Radcliffe Seminars, 1987—. Instructor at Emmanuel College, 1975, and Radcliffe College, beginning 1976.

MEMBER: Authors Guild, Authors League of America.

AWARDS, HONORS: Fellowship in creative writing at Radcliffe Institute, 1968-70.

WRITINGS:

YOUNG ADULT

The Sword of Culann (fiction), Macmillan (New York City), 1973.

A Griffon's Nest (historical fiction), Macmillan, 1975.

The Forespoken (historical fiction), Macmillan, 1976.

Landfall, Atheneum (New York City), 1979.

A Beast on the Brink, Avon (New York City), 1980.

The Keeping-Room, Greenwillow (New York City), 1981.

JUVENILE FICTION

The Zoo Conspiracy, Hastings House (New York City), 1973.

A Binding Spell, Lodestar/Dutton (New York City), 1984.

Put on My Crown, Lodestar/Dutton, 1985.

The Ice Bear, Greenwillow, 1986.

The Trouble with Gramary, Greenwillow, 1988.

Brother Moose, Greenwillow, 1990.

Mercy's Mill, Greenwillow, 1992.

Starshine and Sunglow, Greenwillow, 1994.

Away to Me, Moss, Greenwillow, 1994.

Fire in the Wind, Greenwillow, 1995.

Gift Horse, Greenwillow, in press.

Contributor to *Proceedings for Travelers in Time,* Green Bay Press, 1990. Also contributor of articles to education journals and to *Horn Book.*

Levin's manuscripts are housed in the Kerlan Collection, University of Minnesota, Minneapolis.

WORK IN PROGRESS: A biography; a children's novel; a novel for young adults.

BIOGRAPHICAL/CRITICAL SOURCES:

BOOKS

Something about the Author Autobiography, Volume 11, Gale (Detroit), 1991.

PERIODICALS

Times Literary Supplement, July 24, 1987.

*   *   *

LEWIN, Ted 1935-

PERSONAL: Born May 6, 1935, in Buffalo, NY; son of Sidney (a retail jeweler) and Bernece (Klehn) Lewin; married Betsy Reilly (an artist). *Education:* Pratt Institute of Art, B.F.A., 1956. *Avocational interests:* Outdoor life, scuba diving, birdwatching, wildlife observation, world travel.

ADDRESSES: Home and office—152 Willoughby Ave., Brooklyn, NY 11205.

CAREER: Professional wrestler, 1952-65; artist and free-lance illustrator, 1956—. Conducted one-man shows in Laboratory of Ornithology, Cornell University, 1978, and Central Park Zoo Gallery. Group show, Brooklyn Botanic Garden. *Military service:* U.S. Army, 1958.

AWARDS, HONORS: Booklist Editor's Choice List citation, *School Library Journal* Best Books Citation, and ALA Notable Book citation, all 1993, all for *I Was a Teenage Professional Wrestler;* Caldecott Honor award, 1994, for *Pepe the Lamplighter;* ALA Notable Book citations for *Bird Watch* and *The Day of Ahmed's Secret;* Texas Bluebonnet Award, for *Cowboy Country;* Sydney Taylor Award, Association of Jewish Libraries, and National Jewish Book Award, Jewish Council, both for *The Always Prayer Shawl.*

WRITINGS:

AUTHOR AND ILLUSTRATOR

World within a World: Everglades, introduction by Don R. Eckelberry, Dodd (New York City), 1976.
World within a World: Baja, Dodd, 1978.
World within a World: Pribilofs, Dodd, 1980.
Tiger Trek, Macmillan (New York City), 1990.
When the Rivers Go Home, Macmillan, 1992.
Amazon Boy, Macmillan, 1993.
I Was a Teenage Professional Wrestler, Orchard Books, 1993.
The Reindeer People, Macmillan, 1994.
Sacred River, Clarion (New York City), 1995.

ILLUSTRATOR

Jack McClellan, Millard Black, and Sid Norris, adapters, *A Blind Man Can!,* Houghton (Boston, MA), 1968.
Wyatt Blassingame, *The Look-It-Up Book of Presidents,* Random House (New York City), 1968.
George S. Trow, *Meet Robert E. Lee,* Random House, 1969.
Margaret T. Burroughs, *Jasper the Drummin' Boy,* Follett, 1970.
Janet H. Ervin, *More Than Half Way There,* Follett, 1970.
Donald Cox, *Pioneers of Ecology,* Hammond (Maplewood, NJ), 1971.
Nellie Burchardt, *Surprise for Carlotta,* F. Watts (New York City), 1971.
Gene Smith, *Visitor,* Cowles, 1971.
Betty Horvath, *Not Enough Indians,* F. Watts, 1971.
Maurine H. Gee, *Chicano, Amigo,* Morrow (New York City), 1972.
Rose Blue, *Grandma Didn't Wave Back,* F. Watts, 1972.
Michael Capizzi, *Getting It All Together,* Delacorte (New York City), 1972.

Blue, *A Month of Sundays,* F. Watts, 1972.
Rita Micklish, *Sugar Bee,* Delacorte, 1972.
Darrell A. Rolerson, *In Sheep's Clothing,* Dodd, 1972.
Charlotte Gantz, *Boy with Three Names,* Houghton, 1973.
William MacKellar, *The Ghost of Grannoch Moor,* Dodd, 1973.
Marian Rumsey, *Lion on the Run,* Morrow, 1973.
Blue, *Nikki 108,* F. Watts, 1973.
Marjorie M. Prince, *The Cheese Stands Alone,* Houghton, 1973.
Rolerson, *A Boy Called Plum,* Dodd, 1974.
Jean Slaughter Doty, *Gabriel,* Macmillan, 1974.
Gene Smith, *The Hayburners,* Delacorte, 1974.
Matt Christopher, *Earthquake,* Little, Brown (Boston, MA), 1975.
Patricia Beatty, *Rufus, Red Rufus,* Morrow, 1975.
Charles Ferry, *Up in Sister Bay,* Houghton, 1975.
Doty, *Winter Pony,* Macmillan, 1975.
Blue, *The Preacher's Kid,* F. Watts, 1975.
S. T. Tung, *One Small Dog,* Dodd, 1975.
Scott O'Dell, *Zia,* Houghton, 1976.
Lynne Martin, *Puffin: Bird of the Open Seas,* Morrow, 1976.
Laurence Pringle, *Listen to the Crows,* Crowell, 1976.
Patricia Edwards Clyne, *Ghostly Animals of America,* Dodd, 1977.
Mildred Teal, *Bird of Passage,* Little, Brown, 1977.
Rumsey, *Carolina Hurricane,* Morrow, 1977.
Nigel Gray, *The Deserter,* Harper (New York City), 1977.
Robert Newton Peck, *Patooie,* Knopf (New York City), 1977.
Philippa Pearce, *The Shadow-Cage and Other Tales of the Supernatural,* Crowell, 1977.
Helen Hill, Agnes Perkins, and Althea Helbig, compilers, *Straight on Till Morning: Poems of the Imaginary World,* Crowell, 1977.
Blue, *The Thirteenth Year: A Bar Mitzvah Story,* F. Watts, 1977.
Lee Bennett Hopkins, *Mama,* Knopf, 1977.
Leslie Norris, *Merlin and the Snake's Egg: Poems,* Viking (New York City), 1978.
MacKellar, *The Silent Bells,* Dodd, 1978.
Peck, *Soup for President,* Knopf, 1978.
MacKellar, *The Witch of Glen Gowrie,* Dodd, 1978.
Anne E. Crompton, *A Woman's Place,* Little, Brown, 1978.
David Stemple, *High Ridge Gobbler: A Story of the American Wild Turkey,* Collins & World, 1979.
Margaret Goff Clark, *Barney and the UFO,* Dodd, 1979.
Clyne, *Strange and Supernatural Animals,* Dodd, 1979.
Peck, *Hub,* Knopf, 1979.
Doty, *Can I Get There by Candlelight?,* Macmillan, 1980.
Blue, *My Mother the Witch,* McGraw (New York City), 1980.

Francine Jacobs, *Bermuda Petrel: The Bird That Would Not Die,* Morrow, 1981.

Clark, *The Boy from the UFO Returns,* Scholastic Book Services (New York City), 1981.

Mark Twain, *The Adventures of Tom Sawyer,* Wanderer Books (New York City), 1982.

Clark, *Barney on Mars,* Dodd, 1983.

Eleanor Clymer, *The Horse in the Attic,* Bradbury (Scarsdale, NY), 1983.

Priscilla Homola, *The Willow Whistle,* Dodd, 1983.

Mary Francis Shura, *The Search for Grissi,* Dodd, 1985.

R. R. Knudson, *Babe Didrikson: Athlete of the Century,* Viking, 1985.

Enid Bagnold, *National Velvet,* Morrow, 1985.

Frances Wosmek, *A Brown Bird Singing,* Lothrop (New York City), 1986.

Elizabeth Simpson Smith, *A Dolphin Goes to School: The Story of Squirt, a Trained Dolphin,* Morrow, 1986.

P. R. Giff, *Mother Teresa,* Viking, 1986.

Susan Saunders, *Margaret Mead,* Viking, 1987.

O'Dell, *The Serpent Never Sleeps,* Houghton, 1987.

Faithful Elephants, Houghton, 1988.

Kathleen Kudlinski, *Rachel Carson,* Viking, 1988.

Bruce Coville, *Herds of Thunder, Manes of Gold,* Doubleday, 1989.

O'Dell, *Island of the Blue Dolphins,* Houghton, 1990.

Jane Yolen, *Bird Watch,* Philomel, 1990.

F. P. Heide and J. H. Gilliland, *The Day of Ahmed's Secret,* Lothrop, 1990.

Frances Ward Weller, *I Wonder if I'll See a Whale?,* Philomel, 1991.

Megan McDonald, *The Potato Man,* Orchard Books, 1991.

Margaret Hodges, *Brother Francis and the Friendly Beasts,* Scribner (New York City), 1991.

Heide and Gilliland, *Sami and the Time of the Troubles,* Clarion Books, 1992.

Corinna Damas Bliss, *Matthew's Meadow,* Harcourt, 1992.

Weller, *Matthew Wheelock's Wall,* Macmillan, 1992.

McDonald, *The Great Pumpkin Switch,* Orchard Books, 1992.

Elisa Bartone, *Pepe the Lamplighter,* Lothrop, 1993.

Ann Herbert Scott, *Cowboy Country,* Clarion Books, 1993.

Sheldon Oberman, *The Always Prayer Shawl,* Boyds Mills Press (Honesdale, PA), 1993.

Louise Borden, *Just in Time for Christmas,* Scholastic, Inc., 1994.

Jan Slepian, *Lost Moose,* Philomel, 1994.

WORK IN PROGRESS: Illustrating and writing *Market,* a picture book on markets around the world, for Lothrop, Lee & Shepard; illustrating Elisa Bartone's *American, Too,* a companion volume to *Pepe the Lamplighter;* two books set in Botswana, one about the Okavango Delta, and the other about the Bushmen of the Kalahari Desert; *Something Special, Fair, Milo and the Tortoise,* set in the Galapagos Islands, and *Billabong,* set in Australia's Northern Territory.

SIDELIGHTS: Ted Lewin told *CA:* "I grew up in an old frame house in Buffalo, New York, with two brothers, one sister, two parents, a lion, an iguana, a chimpanzee, and an assortment of more conventional pets. The lion was given to my brother Donn while he was traveling as a professional wrestler and he shipped it home. We kept Sheba in the basement fruit cellar until Donn returned and my mother convinced him to give it to the Buffalo Zoo.

"I always wanted to be an illustrator, and as a kid I spent endless hours by myself drawing and copying the work of artists I admired: N. C. Wyeth, Winslow Homer, and John Singer Sargent. My whole family encouraged what they saw as a gift. I was the only one in the family who could draw. I read every volume of my brother's first edition set of Edgar Rice Burroughs' *Tarzan* and copied those illustrations, too. When it came time to earn money for art school at Pratt Institute, I followed in Donn's footsteps and took a summer job as a professional wrestler. This marked the beginning of a fifteen year part-time career that eventually inspired my memoir *I Was a Teenage Professional Wrestler.*

"After art school I began freelancing, doing illustrations for adventure magazines. An agent, Elizabeth Armstrong, introduced me to children's books, and I did many illustrations for textbooks and book jackets. I married, and with my wife, Betsy, also an illustrator, took our first trip to East Africa in 1975. It was a dream come true for both of us, and it set the tenor of our lives. I'm having more fun putting these experiences down in words and pictures than anything I've ever done before. My first picture book, *Faithful Elephants,* gave me the chance not only to draw animals but to make a strong statement about man's cruelty to them in certain circumstances. I realized then that the picture book was the best possible world for an illustrator, and I've devoted my full time to it ever since. As well as writing and illustrating my own books, I enjoy illustrating the work of other authors. It gives me the chance to do things I might never have done on my own.

"My studio is the entire top floor of our hundred and ten-year-old brownstone in the historic Clinton Hill section of Brooklyn, near Pratt Institute. I'm very disciplined and work almost every day from eight until one. Four times a week I work out in the gym for two hours to stay fit for our excursions into the bush. One of these excursions, a trip to India, produced *Tiger Trek* and *Sacred River.* A trip to Brazil inspired *Amazon Boy* and *When the Rivers Go Home.* A journey to Lapland produced *The Reindeer*

People. One day I was sketching a pair of lions in the Oka-vango Delta in Botswana and thought, 'This isn't such a great leap from that little kid surrounded by Tarzan books, sketching his big brother's lion cub.' "

*   *   *

LEWIS, David L(evering)   1936-

PERSONAL: Born May 25, 1936, in Little Rock, AR; son of John H. (an educator) and Urnestine (Bell) Lewis; married Sharon Siskind, April 15, 1966 (divorced October, 1988); married Ruth Ann Stewart, April 15, 1994; children: (first marriage) Eric Levering, Allison Lillian, Jason Bradwell; (second marriage) Allegra. *Education:* Fisk University, B.A., 1956; Columbia University, M.A., 1958; London School of Economics and Political Science, Ph.D., 1962. *Politics:* Liberal Democrat.

ADDRESSES: Office—Department of History, Van Dyck Hall, Rutgers University, New Brunswick, NJ 08903.

CAREER: University of Ghana, Accra, lecturer in modern French history, 1963-64; Howard University, Washington, DC, lecturer in modern French history, 1964-65; University of Notre Dame, Notre Dame, IN, assistant professor of modern French history, 1965-66; Morgan State College, Baltimore, MD, associate professor of modern French history, 1966-70; Federal City College, Washington, DC, associate professor of modern French history, 1970-74; University of the District of Columbia, Washington, DC, professor of history, 1974-80; University of California at San Diego, La Jolla, professor of history, 1981-85; Rutgers University, New Brunswick, NJ, Martin Luther King Jr. Professor of History, 1985—. Fellow, Drug Abuse Council of Ford Foundation, 1972-73. *Military service:* U.S. Army, Medical Corps, 1961-63.

MEMBER: American Historical Association, Society for French Historical Studies, American Association of University Professors, Organization of American Historians, African Studies Association, Southern Historical Association, Authors Guild, Phi Beta Kappa.

AWARDS, HONORS: Grants from American Philosophical Society, 1967, Social Science Research Council, 1971, and National Endowment for the Humanities, 1975; Woodrow Wilson International Center for Scholars fellow, 1977-78; National Book Award nomination, 1993, Pulitzer Prize for biography, 1994, Bancroft Prize, Columbia University, 1994, and Francis Parkman Prize, Society of American Historians, 1994, all for *W. E. B. Du Bois: Biography of a Race, 1868-1919.*

WRITINGS:

Martin Luther King: A Critical Biography, Praeger (New York City), 1971, 2nd edition, University of Illinois Press (Champaign, IL), 1978.

Prisoners of Honor: The Dreyfus Affair, Morrow (New York City), 1973.

District of Columbia: A Bicentennial History, Norton (New York City), 1977.

When Harlem Was in Vogue: The Politics of the Arts in the Twenties and Thirties, Knopf (New York City), 1981.

(With others) *Harlem Renaissance: Art of Black America,* Abrams (New York City), 1987.

The Race to Fashoda: European Colonialism and African Resistance in the Scramble for Africa, Weidenfeld & Nicolson (New York City), 1988.

W. E. B. Du Bois: Biography of a Race, 1868-1919, Holt (New York City), 1994.

(Editor) *The Portable Harlem Renaissance Reader,* Viking (New York City), 1994.

(Editor) *W. E. B. Du Bois: A Reader,* Holt, 1995.

SIDELIGHTS: David L. Lewis is an American historian best known for his works on the twentieth-century African-American experience. He has written biographies of two of the most important figures in the push for civil rights, Martin Luther King Jr. and W. E. B. Du Bois. He has also written a history and edited a reader on the Harlem Renaissance of the 1920s. Yet, Lewis has not confined his scholarship to the United States. A long-time professor of modern French history, he has explored events on the European continent and written a book on the Dreyfus Affair. In the late 1980s, Lewis turned to Africa. "It became a personal and intellectual challenge to move from European and American history to African history," he told Anne Zusy in the *New York Times Book Review.* "I'm glad I persevered because the real bottom line for me is to do comparative history—this is the whole frontier for historians today."

Lewis's 1988 book *The Race to Fashoda: European Colonialism and African Resistance in the Scramble for Africa* tells the story of an encounter between the French and British at Fashoda in the southern Sudan along the White Nile late in the nineteenth century. As William Boyd explains in the *New York Times Book Review,* "The situation in the 1880s was as follows: Britain was trying to establish an area of influence that stretched south to north, from the Cape of Good Hope to the Mediterranean. France was working west to east, from the Atlantic to the Indian Ocean." Boyd continues, "The area where these swaths crossed was the Sudan, and it was the Sudan where the final act in the colonization of Africa—the Fashoda incident—was played out."

At Fashoda, the French were represented by Captain Jean-Baptiste Marchand, seven French officers, and 100 Senegalese soldiers. The British were represented by General Herbert Kitchener and 25,000 English, Egyptian, and Sudanese soldiers. The French force had crossed the continent from the French Congo on the Atlantic to take control of a region abandoned by Egypt. They had arrived at Fashoda in July of 1898 and taken control of a mud fort. Marchand believed that the French could dam the Nile and thereby exert control over Egypt. The British had come down the Nile from Omdurman to extend their influence into the heart of Africa; Kitchener and his men had arrived in September of 1898. The standoff lasted little over a month. In November, the French government ordered Marchand to turn over Fashoda to the superior British force. In *The Race to Fashoda,* Lewis explores this European confrontation for control of Africa. "Lewis writes with gusto about the intricacies and absurdities of the colonial scramble for Africa," comments Thomas Pakenham in the *Washington Post Book World.*

Lewis also probes deeper, beyond the European story, and uncovers African resistance to this partitioning of its continent. "Unlike that of most of his predecessors," notes Pakenham, "his main interest in writing on Fashoda is Afrocentric, not Eurocentric. Fashoda, he says, is a 'superb paradigm' of the interaction between Africans and Europeans during the partition." Pakenham adds that "Lewis cites numerous . . . examples of African resistance and claims it was 'broader, deeper, and more effective' than it is usually given credit for." While his inclusion of the African perspective is a significant feature of *The Race to Fashoda,* "Mr. Lewis does not claim too much for that resistance but makes us appreciate its importance," observes a *New Yorker* reviewer. Boyd finds that the historian's African perspective "is a worthy aim, but Mr. Lewis is hampered by the paucity of sources on the African side."

In the estimation of *American Historical Review* contributor M. W. Daly, *The Race to Fashoda* "succeeds in surveying the complex political, diplomatic, and military interactions of European intruders and African polities." Yet, the reviewer also offers reservations: "David Levering Lewis's uncritical use of sources is ironically the book's greatest weakness; enthusiasm for the subject and a style of breezy assurance are unsupported by a command of the subject." William Boyd also has reservations: "The Fashoda incident, however stirring and intriguing, is merely that. . . . It was a watershed in the colonization of Africa but not a global one." Even so, Boyd concludes that "any reservations over Mr. Lewis's wider claims in no way devalue the achievement of his elegantly written and thoroughly researched book. He has illuminated aspects of the 'scramble for Africa' that were shadowy, misunderstood or ignored."

W. E. B. Du Bois: Biography of a Race, 1868-1919 is the first part of Lewis's two-volume biography of William Edward Burghardt Du Bois, the African-American scholar, writer, editor, and civil rights leader. Du Bois was born just after the Civil War in Massachusetts. He attended Fisk University in Tennessee and then returned to Massachusetts where he enrolled at Harvard. In 1896, he became the first black to earn a Ph.D. from that institution. He had a long career as a professor of sociology at various American universities, helped found the National Association for the Advancement of Colored People (NAACP), and also edited *Crisis,* the journal of the NAACP. In his work and life, he struggled for over 70 years to change the attitudes of whites and fellow blacks. He died in 1963 in Ghana, where he had gone to make a new home. "Du Bois was cut out to be a modern intellectual," R. Z. Sheppard points out in *Time,* "conflicted, inconsistent and alienated from the conditions and customs of the race he strove to transform."

Du Bois had his greatest impact on American society through his large body of written works: novels, poetry, plays, histories, and sociological studies of blacks in America. As Sean Wilentz observes in the *New Republic,* "Writing in a melange of genres—history, fiction, biography, autobiography—Du Bois turned the everyday racist characterizations of the black peasantry on their heads." In books such as *The Souls of Black Folk,* Du Bois argued against other African-American movements and called for immediate racial equality across the United States. "Instead of settling for a choice of nationalism over assimilationism," explains Wilentz, "Du Bois offered up a dialectic of doubleness; he wrote of a divided American Negro soul, part American, part Negro, the two parts ever in conflict with each other but headed toward an eventual merging."

In *W. E. B. Du Bois,* Lewis chronicles the first half of the civil rights leader's long and full life. "Mr. Lewis examines a tremendous amount of information, but never overwhelms the reader," comments Waldo E. Martin Jr. in the *New York Times Book Review.* The reviewer adds that Lewis "carefully analyzes the historical, sociological, literary and journalistic works of Du Bois, including the often self-contradictory autobiographical volumes, without confusing the reader. Likewise, he reveals the political, economic and social development of the nation in a way that illuminates Du Bois's life and the history of his era."

A number of reviewers of *W. E. B. Du Bois* make note of Lewis's handling of a complicated and challenging subject. "Nothing and no one escapes Lewis's scrutiny" comments Richard Blackett in *American Historical Review.* "Like his subject, Lewis leaves nothing to chance. Even on the rare occasions when the records are silent, Lewis has a knack for employing reasonable speculation to round out his portrait or analysis. It is without doubt the tidiest biography I have read." David J. Garrow offers a different view in his review in *Journal of American History*. He states, "*W. E. B. Du Bois* is a richly informative but often frustrating book. Reading it is work, not pleasure. While it presents an intriguingly complex portrait of Du Bois, a reader's appreciation of Du Bois's life is sometimes hindered by Lewis's peculiar interpretive speculations."

In addition to its scholarship and organization, *W. E. B. Du Bois* has received critical attention for Lewis's presentation and style. Blackett finds that "Although [Lewis] is careful to keep Du Bois center stage, there exists a perfect and constant tension between all the characters and events in this high drama." The reviewer concludes, "There is possibly no higher praise for any biographer of Du Bois than to say that he has matched his subject, the master of the lyrical emotive prose, with a style that at times is almost rhapsodic." In the opinion of John Egerton of the *Progressive*, "History is never better—more enlightening, satisfying, inspiring—than when it flows from the mind and hand of a writer like Lewis. Du Bois is finally getting his due."

BIOGRAPHICAL/CRITICAL SOURCES:

PERIODICALS

American Historical Review, October, 1989, p. 1144; April, 1994, p. 510.
Journal of American History, September, 1994, p. 620.
Los Angeles Times Book Review, January 1, 1989, p. 10.
New Republic, April 4, 1994, pp. 28-35.
New Yorker, March 21, 1988, p. 120.
New York Times, February 3, 1988, p. C21.
New York Times Book Review, February 28, 1988, pp. 11-12; December 12, 1993, p.7.
Progressive, October, 1994, p. 52.
Time, November 15, 1993, p. 98.
Times Literary Supplement, April 22, 1988, p. 443.
Washington Post Book World, January 17, 1988, pp. 1, 8.

—*Sketch by Bryan Ryan*

*   *   *

LEWIS, Gordon R(ussell)   1926-

PERSONAL: Born November 21, 1926, in Johnson City, NY; son of Frederick C. and Florence E. (Winn) Lewis; married Doris Jane Berlin, June 19, 1948; children: Nancy, Cynthia, Scott. *Education:* Gordon College, A.B., 1948; Faith Theological Seminary, B.Th., 1951; Syracuse University, A.M., 1953, Ph.D., 1959. *Politics:* Republican.

ADDRESSES: Home—7925 West Layton, No. 519, Littleton, CO 80123-1329. *Office*—Denver Conservative Baptist Seminary, P.O. Box 10000, Denver, CO 80250.

CAREER: Baptist Bible Seminary, Johnson City, NY, instructor, 1951-53, professor of apologetics, 1954-58; Conservative Baptist Theological Seminary (now Denver Conservative Baptist Seminary), Denver, CO, associate professor, 1958-61, professor of systematic theology and Christian philosophy, 1962-93, senior professor, 1993—. Visiting professor of theology, Union Biblical Seminary, Yavatmal, India, 1973. Member of advisory board of International Council on Biblical Inerrancy and Christian Research Associates.

MEMBER: American Philosophical Association (Western division), American Academy of Religion, Evangelical Philosophical Society (president, 1978), Evangelical Theological Society (president, 1992), Theta Beta Phi.

WRITINGS:

Confronting the Cults, Presbyterian & Reformed (Black Mountains, NC), 1966.
Decide for Yourself: A Theological Workbook, Inter-Varsity Press (Downers Grove, IL), 1970.
Judge for Yourself: A Workbook on Contemporary Challenges to Christian Faith, Inter-Varsity Press, 1974.
What Everyone Should Know about Transcendental Meditation, Regal Books (Glendale, CA), 1975.
Testing Christianity's Truth Claims: Approaches to Christian Apologetics, Moody (Chicago, IL), 1976.
(Editor) *Challenges to Inerrancy: A Theological Response*, Moody, 1984.
Integrative Theology, Zondervan (Grand Rapids, MI), Volume I, 1987, Volume II, 1990, Volume III, 1994.

Contributor to theological collections and anthologies, including Bruce Shelley, editor, *A Call to Christian Character*, Zondervan, 1970; Geehan, editor, *Jerusalem and Athens*, Presbyterian & Reformed, 1970; Harish D. Merchant, editor, *Encounter with Books: A Guide to Christian Reading*, Inter-Varsity Press, 1972; Josh McDowell, editor, *More Evidence That Demands a Verdict*, Campus Crusade for Christ, 1975; John W. Montgomery, editor, *Demon Possession*, Bethany Fellowship (Minneapolis, MN), 1976; Norman Geisler, editor, *Inerrancy*, Zondervan, 1979; Kenneth Kantzer and Stanley Gundry, editors, *Perspectives on Evangelical Theology*, Baker Book (Grand Rapids, MI), 1981; Ronald Youngblood, editor, *Evangelicals and Inerrancy*, Thomas Nelson (Nashville, TN), 1984; Earl D. Rademacher and Robert D. Preus, editors, *Hermeneutics, Inerrancy, and the Bible*, Zondervan, 1984; R. Laird Harris, editor, *Interpretation and History*, Singapore Christian Life Publications, 1986; Ronald W. Ruegsegger, editor, *Reflections on Francis Schaeffer*, Zondervan, 1986; Walter A. Elwell, editor, *Handbook of Evangelical Theologians*,

Baker, 1993. Also contributor to religious publications, including *Christianity Today, Foundations, Journal of the Evangelical Theological Society, Christian Research Journal, Trinity Journal,* and *His.*

SIDELIGHTS: Gordon R. Lewis wrote *CA:* "In the midst of a literally explosive world we have three basic choices of general perspective upon the whole human enterprise: a naturalistic secular humanism, a pantheistic, cosmic occult humanism and a theistic, Christian humanism. I argue that there should be open, free, unthreatened exchange of ideas among all three in our pluralistic societies and public schools.

"In order for such tolerance to be enjoyed we need to interpret our lives with some objectivity by criteria of truth such as logical consistency, factual adequacy and existential viability. A critical realism and verificational methodology are established and used in my writings.

"The most coherent and viable account of inner and outer human experiences, in my judgment, is Christian theistic humanism. A Christian belief system provides the values of human dignity, human rights, the demand for justice, and the need as well as empirical and logical realities. Evangelical Christianity offers the only just basis for alleviating human injustice and the only power adequate to give people a new heart and way of life."

*   *   *

LIFSHIN, Lyn (Diane) 1944-

PERSONAL: Born July 12, 1944, in Burlington, VT; daughter of Ben and Frieda (Lazarus) Lipman; married Eric Lifshin, 1963. *Education:* Syracuse University, B.A., 1960; University of Vermont, M.A., 1963; also attended Brandeis University, Waltham, MA, and State University of New York at Albany.

ADDRESSES: Home—2719 Baronhursht Dr., Vienna, VA 22181-6158.

CAREER: Poet and writing instructor. State University of New York at Albany, teaching fellow, 1964-66; educational television writer, Schenectady, NY, 1966; State University of New York, Cobleskill, instructor, 1968, 1970; writing consultant to New York State Mental Health Department, Albany, 1969, and to Empire State College of the State University of New York, 1973; Mansfield State College, Mansfield, PA, poet-in-residence, 1974; University of Rochester, Rochester, NY, poet-in-residence, 1986; Antioch Writers' Conference, Antioch, OH, poet-in-residence, 1987. Has also taught at Cornell University, Dartmouth College, University of Chicago, University of New Mexico, and Syracuse University.

AWARDS, HONORS: Hart Crane Award; Bread Loaf scholarship; Harcourt Brace poetry fellowship; Boulder poetry award; San Jose Bicentennial Poetry Award; Yaddo fellowship, 1970, 1971, 1975, 1979, and 1980; MacDowell fellowship, 1973; Millay Colony fellowship, 1975 and 1979; New York Creative Artists Public Service grant, 1976; Jack Kerouac Award, 1984, for *Kiss the Skin Off; Centennial Review* poetry prize, 1985; Madeline Sadin Award, *New York Quarterly,* 1986; *Footwork* (magazine) Award, 1987; Bring Back the Stars Award, 1987; Estersceffler Award, 1987, for poem "Hiroshima."

WRITINGS:

POETRY COLLECTIONS

Why Is the House Dissolving?, Open Skull Press (San Francisco, CA), 1968.

Femina 2, Abraxas Press (Madison, WI), 1970.

Leaves and Night Things, Baby John Press (West Lafayette, IN), 1970.

Black Apples, New Books, 1971, revised edition, Crossing Press (Trumansburg, NY), 1973.

Lady Lyn, Morgan Press (Milwaukee, WI), 1971.

I'd Be Jeanne Moreau, Morgan Press, 1972.

The Mercurochrome Sun, Charas Press (Tacoma, WA), 1972.

Tentacles, Leaves, Hellric Publications (Bellmont, MA), 1972.

Moving by Touch, Cotyledon Press (Traverse City, MI), 1972.

Undressed, Cotyledon Press, 1972.

Love Poems, Zahir Press (Durham, NH), 1972.

Forty Days, Apple Nights, Morgan Press, 1972.

Museum, Conspiracy Press (Albany, NY), 1973.

The First Week Poems, Zahir Press, 1973.

All the Women Poets I Ever Liked Didn't Hate Their Fathers, Konglomerati Press (Gulfport, FL), 1973.

The Old House on the Croton, Shameless Hussy Press (San Lorenzo, CA), 1973.

Poems, Konglomerati Press, 1974.

Selected Poems, Crossing Press, 1974.

Thru Blue Post, New Mexico, Basilisk Press (Fredonia, NY), 1974.

Blue Fingers, Shelter Press (Bolinas, CA), 1974.

Mountain Moving Day, Crossing Press, 1974.

Plymouth Women, Morgan Press, 1974.

Walking Thru Audley End Mansion Late Afternoon and Drifting into Certain Faces, Mag Press (Long Beach, CA), 1974.

Green Bandages, Hidden Springs (Genesco, NY), 1975.

Upstate Madonna: Poems, 1970-1974, Crossing Press, 1975.

Old House Poems, Capra Press (Santa Barbara, CA), 1975.

Paper Apples, Wormwood Review Press (Stockton, CA), 1975.

North Poems, Morgan Press, 1976.

Shaker House Poems, Sagarin Press (Chatham, NY), 1976.

Naked Charm, Fireweed Press, 1976, revised edition published as *Op 15 Second Ed.* Illuminati (Los Angeles, CA), 1984.

Some Madonna Poems, White Pine Press (Buffalo, NY), 1976.

Crazy Arms, Ommation Press (Chicago, IL), 1977.

The January Poems, Waters Journal of the Arts (Cincinatti, OH), 1977.

More Waters, Waters Journal of the Arts, 1977.

Pantagonia, Wormwood Review Press, 1977.

Mad Girl Poems, Out of Sight Press (Wichita, KS), 1977.

Leaning South, Red Dust (New York City), 1977.

Blue Dust, New Mexico, Basilisk Press, 1978.

Glass, Morgan Press, 1978.

Early Plymouth Women, Morgan Press, 1978.

35 Sundays, Ommation Press, 1979.

More Naked Charm, Illuminati, 1979.

Lips on the Blue Rail, Lion's Breath (San Francisco, CA), 1980.

Doctors and Doctors of English, Mudborn Press (Santa Barbara, CA), 1981.

Colors of Cooper Black, Morgan Press, 1981.

In the Dark with Just One Star, Morgan Press, 1982.

Want Ads, Morgan Press, 1982.

Mad Girl, Blue Horse Publications, 1982.

Lobster and Oat Meal, Pinchpenny (Boston, MA), 1982.

Finger Prints, Wormwood Review Press, 1982.

Reading Lips, Morgan Press, 1982.

Hotel Lifshin, Poetry Now (Eureka, CA), 1982.

Leaving the Bough, New World Press (New York City), 1982.

Madonna Who Shifts for Herself, Applezaba (Long Beach, CA), 1983.

The Radio Psychic Is Shaving Her Legs, Planet Detroit (Detroit, MI), 1984.

Remember the Ladies, Ghost Dance Press (East Lansing, MI), 1985.

Kiss the Skin Off, Cherry Valley Editions (Silver Spring, MD), 1985.

Blue Horses Nuzzle Thursday, Illuminati, 1985.

Camping Madonna at Indian Lake, MAF (Portlandville, NY), 1986.

(With others) *Eye of the Beast,* Vergin Press (El Paso, TX), 1986.

Madonna (bound with *Vergin' Mary* by Belinda Subraman), Vergin Press, 1986.

Red Hair and the Jesuit, Trout Creek Press (Parkdale, OR), 1987.

Raw Opals, Illuminati, 1987.

Rubbed Silk, Illuminati, 1987.

The Daughter May Be Let Go, Clock Radio Press (Harbor Beach, FL), 1987.

Many Madonnas, Kindred Spirit Press (St. John, KS), 1988.

Dance Poems, Ommation Press, 1988.

(With Belinda Subraman) *Skin Divers,* Krax (Leeds, Yorkshire), 1989.

The Doctor Poems, Applezaba, 1989.

Blood Road, Illumanati, 1989.

Under Velvet Pillows, Four Zoas Press (Ashvelot Village, NH), 1989.

Reading Lips, Morgan Press, 1989.

Not Made of Glass: Poems, 1968-1988, edited by Mary Ann Lynch, introduction by Laura Chester, Combinations Press (Greenfield Center, NY), 1989.

(With Subraman) *The Innocents,* Buzzard's Roost Press, 1991.

The Jesuit Is Dying, Big Head Press, 1992.

Tammy Says, Big Head Press, 1992.

Appleblossoms, Ghost Dance Press, 1993.

Marilyn Monroe, Quiet Lion Press (Portland, OR), 1994.

Parade, Wormwood, 1994.

Blue Tattoo, Event Horizon (Desert Hot Springs, CA), 1995.

My Mother's Fire, Glass Cherry Press, 1995.

Color and Light, Lilliput Press, 1995.

Mad Girl Drives in a Daze, JVC, 1995.

Mad Girl Poems, Morgan Press, 1995.

Also author of *Some Voices,* 1993, *The 527th Poem about Me Comes in the Mail,* 1993, *Feathers in the Wind,* 1994, *Shooting Kodachromes in the Dark,* 1994, *Pointe Shoes,* 1995, *Mad Girls, Dead Men, The Jesuit Poems, Between My Lips, White Horse Cafe, Lobsters and Oatmeal, The Radio Shrink, Sunday Poems, More Madonnas, He Wants His Meat, Appletree Lane, Cars and Men, Auddley End, Sotto Voce, Mad Windows,* and *Sulphur River.*

EDITOR

Tangled Vines: A Collection of Mother and Daughter Poems, Beacon Press (Boston, MA), 1978, new edition, Harcourt (San Diego, CA, and New York City), 1992.

Ariadne's Thread: A Collection of Contemporary Women's Journals, Harper (New York City), 1982.

Lips Unsealed, Capra, 1990.

OTHER

Lyn Lifshin Reads Her Poems (recording), Women's Audio Exchange, 1977.

Offered by Owner (recording with booklet of poems), Natalie Slohm Associates, 1978.

Mint Leaves at Yappo (prose), Writers Digest (Cincinnati, OH), 1994.

Hints for Writers (prose), Writers Digest, 1995.
On the Outside (autobiography), 1995.

Contributor to anthologies, including, *New American and Canadian Poetry,* edited by John Gill, Beacon Press, 1971; *Writing While Young and Seeing Thru Shucks,* Ballantine (New York City), 1972; *Rising Tides,* Simon & Schuster (New York City), 1973; *Psyche,* Dell (New York City), 1974; *In Youth,* Ballantine, 1974; *Pictures That Storm inside My Head,* Avon (New York City), 1975; *I Hear My Sisters Saying,* Crowell, 1976; *Six Poets,* Vagabond (Ellensburg, WA), 1978; *Editor's Choice,* Spirit That Moves Us (Jackson Heights, NY), 1980; *Woman: An Affirmation,* D. C. Heath (Lexington, MA), 1980; *Contents under Pressure,* edited by Fred H. Laughter, Moonlight Publications, 1981; *Poetry: Sight and Insight,* Random House (New York City), 1982; *Deep Down,* Dutton (New York City), 1988. Also contributor to several hundred publications, including *Chicago Review, Rolling Stone, Ms., Chelsea, American Poetry Review,* and *Massachusetts Review.*

SIDELIGHTS: One of the most prolific poets in the United States, Lyn Lifshin has published some seventy collections of her work and has appeared in "virtually every poetry and literary magazine," as she tells *CA.* A critic for the *San Francisco Review of Books* calls Lifshin "one of the most distinctive, prolific, and widely published poets of all time . . . and very popular with readers." She is also recognized for editing two critically-acclaimed collections of women's writings and for her many poetry readings and writing workshops.

A typical Lifshin poem is a small work, consisting of a few words per line and rarely more than thirty lines in length. Her poems, Gerald Burns comments in the *Southwest Review,* are "long thin things." Enjambed phrases intensify the single emotion or event with which each poem is concerned, and humor is never far from the surface. Lifshin's poems, a writer for the *San Francisco Review of Books* believes, are "a quick, fun read, and [she] seems to strive for that effect." Kenneth Funsten of the *Los Angeles Times Book Review* explains that Lifshin "writes poems both spontaneous and sure of their mark." A critic for the *North American Review,* speaking of the speed with which a Lifshin poem can be read, calls her "Queen of the quickies."

Speaking to Hugh Fox in the *Greenfield Review* about her views on poetry, Lifshin explains that in the Eskimo language "the words 'to breathe' and 'to make a poem' are the same. I mean poetry is that central, essential, as much a part of me as breathing is." She tells Theodore Bouloukos II in *Albany* that "when a great deal of time goes by and I haven't written, I begin to feel edgy. I think it's probably like somebody who has an addiction or an obsession."

Lifshin began writing at the age of three, but it wasn't until the late 1960s that she thought of publishing her work. Her 1968 collection, *Why Is the House Dissolving?,* is "a scathing, angry, iconoclastic, shocking, vituperative book," according to Fox. Part of this early anger was caused by Lifshin's failure to pass her oral examination for a doctorate degree, Fox believes. This anger led her to reject formal, academic writing in favor of personal poetry. "She maintains," Fox writes, "a high degree of *voluminous spontaneity* . . . [because she] doesn't see poetry as academic watch-making, but rather [as] an important expression of a primal interior *howl.*"

Similar to haiku and other short poetic forms, Lifshin's lean and concise poems are especially suited for re-creating a single moment or emotion, or describing a particular place. Her best work, many critics believe, is found in her poems about historical subjects. Some of these pieces are collected in *Shaker House Poems,* in which Lifshin writes about the women of the Shaker religious communities of early America, having visited many of the original historical settlements. A *Choice* critic remarks, Lifshin "very successfully captures the spirit, the mood, the mystique of the Shakers, through magnificently crafted poems, terse as needlework." Her collection *Leaning South* contains poems about sites in New England and about the early Eskimo culture of the Arctic. Peter Schjeldahl, reviewing the book for the *New York Times Book Review,* finds the Eskimo poems to be especially well done. These poems, Schjeldahl writes, evoke "in fantasy, but with a lot of anthropological detail, the world of the ancient Eskimos. Here [Lifshin's] clipped line takes on a chantlike undertone, as of native voices themselves singing from the beyond, that is very pleasing." Fox explains that what Lifshin is doing in her historical poems is "creating a psycho-historical large canvas that traces the evolution of woman within the Occident."

Lifshin's feminist concerns are also evident in her popular "Madonna" poems, each of which describes a modern female archetype in a terse, often humorous manner. Titles in the series include *Madonna Who Shifts for Herself, Many Madonnas* and *More Madonnas.* Speaking to Bouloukos, Lifshin explains: "Sometimes to be a little more flippant or satirical I use the Madonna as a metaphor. I'm relying on some of my own feelings and reactions which are often totally fictionalized and fantastic." A critic for the *Small Press Review* says of the Madonna poems: "Many have the quick, throw-away humor of the epigram, the pun," but also possess "the irony and resentment that provides much of the energy of Lifshin's poetry."

In addition to writing poetry, Lifshin teaches classes and workshops in journal and diary writing. She keeps a diary herself and has drawn upon its entries for some of her poems. In 1982, she edited *Ariadne's Thread: A Collection of Contemporary Women's Journals,* which presents a wide spectrum of women's emotions and ideas on such subjects as relationships, work, families, death, and birth. "Most of the journals," Ursula Hegi writes in the *Los Angeles Times,* "are spontaneous, fascinating, and often painfully honest. . . . Lifshin has woven a living tapestry of women's voices—often angry and sad, sometimes joyful and content, yet never self-pitying."

Lifshin has emerged as one of the most recognized woman poets in the United States. She has given over 500 poetry readings and participated in mixed media theater performances as well. In 1988, Karista Films released a documentary on Lifshin, "Not Made of Glass," which shows her typical working day, a visit she made to the Yaddo writing colony, and a reading she gave at a local coffeehouse. Lifshin also appears on the "First American Poetry Disc," a Laserdisc recording of readings given by contemporary American poets. Her manuscripts are being collected by the University of Texas at Austin and by Temple University. A *Choice* reviewer claims that she "has slowly moved up among the ranks of her peers . . . until . . . she comes practically to the top." Janice Eidus notes in the *Small Press Review* that Lifshin "continues to explore her poetic obsessions with her unique poetic voice and her unique sensibility." Speaking of Lifshin's writing career, Fox describes it as "an artistically rich embattled journey into the fragile clarity of the Here and Now."

BIOGRAPHICAL/CRITICAL SOURCES:

BOOKS

Fox, Hugh, *Lifshin: A Critical Study,* Whitiston Press (Troy, NY), 1985.

PERIODICALS

Albany, December, 1986.
Booklist, April 1, 1978; July 15, 1978; April 15, 1990; January 1, 1991.
Bookwatch, January, 1991.
Choice, March, 1977; December, 1978.
Greenfield Review, summer/fall, 1983.
Library Journal, June, 1971; December, 1972; June 1, 1976.
Little Magazine, summer/fall, 1972.
Los Angeles Times, October 18, 1982.
Los Angeles Times Book Review, September 23, 1984; October 13, 1985.
Minneapolis Star, April 18, 1972.
Ms., September, 1976; July, 1978; July, 1983.
New York Times Book Review, December 17, 1978.
North American Review, fall, 1978; March, 1985.
Northeast, fall/winter, 1971-72.
Poetry Now, spring, 1980.

Review of Contemporary Fiction, fall, 1990.
Road Apple Review, summer/fall, 1971.
San Francisco Review of Books, spring, 1985; fall, 1985.
Small Press Book Review, March, 1991.
Small Press Review, September, 1983; March, 1984; January, 1985; May, 1990.
Southwest Review, winter, 1983.
Utne Reader, spring, 1990.
Village Voice, September 24, 1979.
Windless Orchard, summer, 1972.
Wormwood Review, Volume XII, number 3, 1971.
Writers Digest, September, 1994.

OTHER

Lynch, Mary Ann, *Lyn Lifshin: Not Made of Glass* (film), Women Make Movies, 1990.

*   *   *

LIJPHART, Arend   1936-

PERSONAL: Surname rhymes with "Capehart"; born August 17, 1936, in Apeldoorn, Netherlands; son of Anthonius (a corporation executive) and Mathilde T. (d'Angremond) Lijphart; married Eva Tamm, August 10, 1959 (divorced, 1980); married Gisela Meyers, June 24, 1988; children (first marriage): Antony Sune, Anna Margaretha. *Education:* Principia College, B.A., 1958; Yale University, M.A., 1959, Ph.D., 1963.

ADDRESSES: Home—4276 Caminito Terviso, San Diego, CA 92122. *Office*—Department of Political Science, University of California, San Diego, La Jolla, CA 92093-0521.

CAREER: Elmira College, Elmira, NY, instructor in political science, 1961-63; University of California, Berkeley, assistant professor, 1963-68, associate professor of political science, 1968-69; University of Leiden, Leiden, Netherlands, professor of international relations, 1968-78, chairman of department of political science and international relations, 1972-74, 1976-78; University of California, San Diego, La Jolla, professor of political science, 1978-94, acting chairman of department, 1979-80, research professor, 1994—. Visiting professor of government, Harvard University, 1970; visiting research fellow, Institute of Advanced Studies, Australian National University, 1971-72; fellow of Netherlands Institute for Advanced Study, 1974-75; fellow, Science Center, Berlin, Germany, fall, 1991; visiting fellow, Rajiv Gandhi Institute for Contemporary Studies, New Delhi, India, 1993.

MEMBER: American Academy of Arts and Sciences, International Political Science Association (member of committee on political sociology), International Studies Association (vice-president, 1976-77), European Consortium for Political Research (member of executive committee, 1976-78), Council for European Studies (member of executive committee, 1983-85), Royal Netherlands Academy of Sciences, Netherlands Institute for Advanced Studies Fellows Association, American Political Science Association (secretary, 1983-84, president, 1995—), American Association for Netherlandic Studies, Canadian Political Science Association, Nederlandse Kring voor Wetenschap der Politiek (member of executive committee, 1977-78), Nederlands Genootschap voor Internationale Zaken, Comparative Interdisciplinary Studies Section (member of council, 1980-82), Western Political Science Association, Southern Political Science Association, Midwest Political Science Association, Center for the Study of Democratic Institutions, Phi Beta Delta.

AWARDS, HONORS: Ralph J. Bunche Award from American Political Science Association, 1979; Excellence in Teaching Award from University of California, San Diego, 1982; German Marshall Fund of the United States fellowship, 1983-84; Guggenheim fellowship, 1984-85; Hendrik Muller Prize in Social and Behavioral Sciences, Royal Netherlands Academy of Sciences, 1992; George H. Hallett Prize, Representation and Electoral Systems Section, American Political Science Association, 1995.

WRITINGS:

The Trauma of Decolonization: The Dutch and West New Guinea, Yale University Press (New Haven, CT), 1966.

The Politics of Accommodation: Pluralism and Democracy in the Netherlands, University of California Press (Berkeley), 1968, 2nd edition, 1975.

Verzuiling, pacificatie en kentering in de Nederlandse politiek, De Bussy (Amsterdam), 1968, 9th edition, 1992.

Democracy in Plural Societies: A Comparative Exploration, Yale University Press, 1977.

(With G. D. L. Schreiner, L. Schlemmer, and others) *Buthelezi Commission Report,* Inkatha Institute (Durban, South Africa), 1982.

(With others) *The Requirements for Stability and Development in KwaZulu and Natal,* H & H Publications (Durban), 1982.

Democracies: Patterns of Majoritarian and Consensus Government in Twenty-one Countries, Yale University Press, 1984.

Power-Sharing in South Africa, Institute of International Studies, University of California Press, 1985.

(With Thomas C. Bruneau, P. Nikiforos Diamandouros, and Richard Gunther) *Los democracias contemporaneas: Un estudio comparativo,* translated by Elena de Grau, Editorial Ariel (Barcelona, Spain), 1987, 2nd edition, 1991.

Electoral Systems and Party Systems: A Study of Twenty-Seven Democracies, 1945-1990. Oxford University Press (New York City), 1994.

EDITOR

World Politics: The Writings of Theorists and Practitioners, Classical and Modern, Allyn & Bacon (Newton, MA), 1966, 2nd edition, 1971.

Politics in Europe: Comparisons and Interpretations, Prentice-Hall (Englewood Cliffs, NJ), 1969.

Conflict and Coexistence in Belgium: The Dynamics of a Culturally Divided Society, Institute of International Studies, University of California Press, 1981.

(With Bernard Grofman, Robert McKay, and Howard Scarrow) *Representation and Redistricting Issues,* Lexington Books (Lexington, MA), 1982.

(With Grofman, and contributor) *Choosing an Electoral System: Issues and Alternatives,* Praeger (New York City), 1984.

(With Grofman, and contributor) *Electoral Laws and Their Political Consequences,* Agathon Press (New York City), 1986.

Parliamentary versus Presidential Government, Oxford University Press, 1992.

(With Seymour Martin Lipset et al) *The Encyclopedia of Democracy,* 4 volumes, Congressional Quarterly Press (Washington, DC), 1995.

(With Carlos H. Waisman) *Institutional Design in New Democracies,* Westview Press (Boulder, CO), 1996.

Contributor to collections, including *Paradigmata in de Leer der Internationale Betrekkingen,* De Bussy, 1969; Robert J. Jackson and Michael B. Stein, editors, *Issues in Comparative Politics: A Text with Readings,* St. Martin's (New York City), 1971; Andries Hoogerwerf, editor, *Verkenningen in de politiek,* Volume II, Alphen aan den Rijn, 1971, 3rd edition, 1976; Kenneth McRae, editor, *Consociational Democracy: Political Accommodation in Segmented Societies,* McClelland & Stewart (Toronto, Ontario), 1974; Louis J. Cantori, editor, *Comparative Political Systems,* Holbrook (Oxford, MA), 1974; Richard Rose, editor, *Electoral Behavior: A Comparative Handbook,* Free Press (New York City), 1974; Roy C. Macridis and Bernard E. Brown, editors, *Comparative Politics: Notes and Readings,* 5th edition, Dorsey (Homewood, IL), 1977; Milton J. Esman, editor, *Ethnic Conflict in the Western World,* Cornell University Press (Ithaca, NY), 1977; Nic Rhoodie, editor, *Intergroup Accommodation in Plural Societies,* Macmillan (New York City), 1978; *Werkboek Staatkunde,* Alphen aan den Rijn, 1979, 2nd edition, 1982; Mattei Dogan and Dominique Pelassy, editors, *La comparaison internationale en sociologie politique: Une selection de textes sur la demarche du comparatiste,* Libraries Techniques (Paris), 1980; Rhoodie, editor, *Conflict Resolution in South Africa: The Quest for Accommodation-*

ist *Policies in a Plural Society*, Institute for Plural Societies, University of Pretoria, 1980; Robert I. Rotberg and John Barratt, editors, *Conflict and Compromise in South Africa*, Lexington Books, 1980; Gabriel A. Almond and Sidney Verba, editors, *The Civic Culture Revisited*, Little, Brown (Boston, MA), 1980; Georgina Ashworth, editor, *World Minorities in the Eighties*, Quartermaine, 1980; Rose, editor, *Electoral Participation: A Comparative Analysis*, Sage (Beverly Hills, CA), 1980; Richard L. Merritt and Bruce M. Russett, editors, *From National Development to Global Community: Essays in Honor of Karl W. Deutsch*, Allen & Unwin (Winchester, MA), 1981; David Butler, Howard R. Penniman, and Austin Ranney, editors, *Democracy at the Polls: A Comparative Study of Competitive National Elections*, American Enterprise Institute (Washington, DC), 1981; J. J. A. Thomassen, editor, *Democratie: Theorie en praktijk*, Alphen aan den Rijn, 1981; Desmond Rea, editor, *Political Co-operation in Divided Societies: A Series of Papers Relevant to the Conflict in Northern Ireland*, Gill & McMillan (Dublin), 1982; Bolivar Lamounier, editor, *A ciencia politica nos anos 80*, Editora Universidade de Brasilia, 1982; John Chapman, editor, *The Western University on Trial*, University of California Press, 1983; Jacques Cadart, editor, *Les modes de scrutin des dixhuit pays libres de l'Europe occidentale, leurs resultats et leurs effects compares: Elections nationales et europeennes*, Presses Universitaires de France (Paris), 1983; Nerio Rauseo, editor, *Simposio sistemas electorales comparados con especial referencia a nivel local*, Consejo Supremo Electoral (Caracas, Venezuela), 1984; Domenico Fisichella, editor, *Metodo scientifico e ricerca politica*, La Nuova Italia Scientifica (Rome), 1985; Adam Kuper and Jessica Kuper, editors, *The Social Science Encyclopedia*, Routledge & Kegan Paul (Boston, MA), 1985; Theodor Hanf, Antoine N. Messarra, and Hinrich R. Reinstrom, editors, *La societe de concordance: Approche comparative*, Librairie Orientale (Beirut), 1986; Peter Haungs and Eckhard Jesse, editors, *Parteien in der Krise?*, Verlag Wissenschaft und Politik (Cologne), 1987; Robert Schrire, editor, *Critical Choices for South African Society*, Institute for the Study of Public Policy (Rondebosch, South Africa), 1987; Herman Bakvis and William Chandler, editors, *Federalism and the Role of the State*, University of Toronto Press (Ontario), 1987; Vernon Bogdanor, editor, *The Dictionary of Political Institutions*, Basil Blackwell (London), 1987.

OTHER

Contributor to professional journals, including *Asian Survey, American Political Science Review, Internationale Spectator, Canadian Journal of Political Science, Comparative Politics, British Journal of Political Science, World Politics*, and *Government and Opposition*. Editor of *European Journal of Political Research*, 1971-75; member of

editorial advisory board, *Civis Mundi*, 1969-73, *Journal of Conflict Resolution*, 1972-77, *Jerusalem Journal of International Relations*, 1973—, *Government and Opposition*, 1974—, *Studies in International Political Science*, 1980—, *Review of Politics*, 1984—, *Companion to Politics of the World*, Oxford University Press, 1989-93, and *Democratization*, 1993—; member of editorial board, *British Journal of Political Science*, 1975-78, *American Political Science Review*, 1976-81, *Comparative Political Studies*, 1981—, *Electoral Studies: An International Journal*, 1981—, *Comparative European Politics*, 1986—, *Journal of Theoretical Politics*, 1986—, *Publications of the American Association for Netherlandic Studies*, 1989-94, *Democratization and Democratic Politics*, Cambridge University Press, 1992—, and *Journal of Democracy*, 1993—.

* * *

LINDSEY, Robert (Hughes) 1935-

PERSONAL: Born January 4, 1935, in Glendale, CA; son of Robert Hughes (an engineer) and Claire Elizabeth (Schulz) Lindsey; married Sandra Jean Wurts, September 29, 1956; children: Susan, Steven. *Education:* San Jose State University, B.A., 1956. *Avocational interests:* Music, photography, restoring antique sports cars.

ADDRESSES: Office—900 Wilshire Blvd., Los Angeles, CA 90017.

CAREER: San Jose Mercury News, San Jose, CA, reporter, 1956-68; *New York Times*, New York City, reporter, 1968-75, Los Angeles bureau chief, 1975-86, chief West Coast correspondent, beginning 1986; writer.

AWARDS, HONORS: Edgar Allan Poe Award from Mystery Writers of America, 1980, for *The Falcon and the Snowman: A True Story of Friendship and Espionage*.

WRITINGS:

The Falcon and the Snowman: A True Story of Friendship and Espionage (nonfiction), Simon & Schuster (New York City), 1979.
(With others) *Reagan: The Man, the President*, Macmillan (New York City), 1981.
The Flight of the Falcon (nonfiction), Simon & Schuster, 1983.
A Gathering of Saints: A True Story of Money, Murder, and Deceit (nonfiction), Simon & Schuster, 1988.
Irresistible Impulse: A True Story of Blood and Money (nonfiction), Simon & Schuster, 1992.
(With Marlon Brando) *Brando: Songs My Mother Taught Me*, Random House (New York City), 1994.

ADAPTATIONS: A movie version of *The Falcon and the Snowman* was released by Orion Pictures in 1985.

SIDELIGHTS: Robert Lindsey has made a career of writing true crime stories. Former chief West Coast correspondent for the *New York Times*, Lindsey is the author of *The Falcon and the Snowman* and *The Flight of the Falcon*, two highly acclaimed bestsellers that together constitute what *Los Angeles Times* critic Gladwin Hill calls "one of the strangest criminal odysseys of our time."

Lindsey's first book, *The Falcon and the Snowman: A True Story of Friendship and Espionage*, relates the true story of two friends who pulled off "one of the most damaging espionage conspiracies against the U.S. in the postwar era," as Lindsey describes it. Involved were Christopher Boyce and Andrew Daulton Lee, two young men who grew up in affluent Palos Verdes, California, served together as altar boys, and shared an interest in falconry. After high school these "all-American" boys moved in different directions. Boyce, "the falcon," drifted from job to job before ending up as a clerk at TRW Systems Group, a CIA contractor that specialized in making intelligence-collection satellites. Meanwhile, Lee, "the snowman," became a drug dealer in southern California. In April, 1975, the two teamed up and began selling secret information to the Russians at their embassy in Mexico. Boyce stole the documents while Lee delivered them. The pair were arrested in January of 1977 but the information they so easily spirited out of TRW was so sensitive that the United States was reluctant to prosecute as the stolen information would be openly discussed in court. For their roles as spies Boyce and Lee were each sentenced to forty-year prison terms.

Lindsey's portrayal of the espionage case met with an enthusiastic reception. Writing in *Newsweek*, Walter Clemons declares *The Falcon and the Snowman* to be "a book quite unlike any other spy story you have ever read. . . . The story Lindsey tells is spellbinding." *New York Times Book Review* contributor Robert Sherrill concurs, claiming, "Lindsey has written an absolutely smashing real life spy story." In addition to the exciting story line, critics also praised Lindsey's writing style in *The Falcon and the Snowman*. "Lindsey has told this sad story adeptly, unraveling a complicated sequence of events with clarity and sensitivity," writes Michael Collins in the *Washington Post Book World*. Christopher Lehmann-Haupt of the *New York Times* praises Lindsey's "skillful handling" in portraying the story's two main characters and calls *The Falcon and the Snowman* "the first book of the last two decades that makes us understand how the boy next door could become a superspy." *Newsweek* critic Donald Morrison extols the thoroughness of Lindsey's account, noting: "*The Falcon and the Snowman* omits no telling detail about falconry, the drug trade, spy satellites, the duo's stoned bumbling, and their tortuous legal battles after capture. But there are enough tantalizing loose ends in the

book to make it clear that Lindsey is describing life, not art."

A number of reviewers commend Lindsey's lack of sentimentality and overall objectivity in presenting Boyce's and Lee's story. In a *Chicago Tribune Book World* review, Peter Wyden writes: "Lindsey dissects this horror with insight, occasional brilliance, and a few lapses into journalese. His explanations work." Similarly, claiming Lindsey writes with "considerable restraint," Sherrill adds, "*The Falcon* is such a balanced, objective, powerful story, which pulls you so deeply into the lives of these young felons, that you simply won't be able to dismiss them (or at least I couldn't, though that was my first impulse) as just a couple of mindless, spoiled dudes who got what they deserved." Aaron Latham, writing in the *New York Times Book Review*, calls *The Falcon and the Snowman* "one of the best non-fiction stories ever to appear in this country."

In 1983 Lindsey published a sequel to *The Falcon and the Snowman* entitled *The Flight of the Falcon*. The book begins with Boyce's dramatic escape from a federal prison in Lompoc, California, on January 21, 1980. *The Flight of the Falcon* follows Boyce from this date until nearly nineteen months later, and recounts the efforts made to capture him. Upon escaping from Lompoc, Boyce, an experienced woodsman, hid out in the chaparral of southern California before making his way to a remote section of the Idaho panhandle region. There he established a new identity and took a job at a nursery. He might have remained there indefinitely but, for money as well as excitement, he began robbing small-town banks in Idaho, Montana, and Washington. Boyce eventually settled in Puget Sound, Washington. There he took flying lessons, apparently with the hope of going over the Bering Strait to the Soviet Union. In spite of an intensive manhunt involving both the FBI and the U.S. Marshals Service, Boyce was able to elude capture for over a year and a half. He was aided in part by false information provided by inmate friends and people who had read of his plight in newspaper articles. False leads sent officials to such faraway places as Australia, Costa Rica, and South Africa. In the end, however, it was Boyce's own bravado that did him in when an informer who had heard Boyce boasting of his exploits led authorities to his capture.

The Flight of the Falcon was held up to its predecessor and found worthy of comparison. "In *The Flight of the Falcon* Robert Lindsey . . . again exhibits his storytelling mastery," writes *Washington Post Book World* contributor Dan Moldea, who adds, "Lindsey's second major work yields nothing less than an action-packed, roller-coaster ride, twisting and turning through an array of international scenes and settings." Hill concurs, calling the book "an exciting account" and a sequel "as gripping as the original." There is, however, one fundamental stylistic difference between the two books. Whereas Lindsey arranged *The Falcon and the Snowman* in a chronological manner, in *The Flight of the Falcon* he employs an unusual method of storytelling, devoting the first portion of the book to Boyce, then introducing his pursuers in the next section, and finally alternating between the two as Boyce's capture becomes imminent. This narrative structure attracted a good deal of critical attention. Comparing Lindsey's composition to that of "a skillful playwright working in a three-act format," *New York Times* contributor Evan Hunter writes, "As the story hurtles toward its breathless climax, it is virtually impossible to turn the pages fast enough." Some critics, among them Moldea, praise in particular the way Lindsey's method draws the reader into the story.

Notes Moldea: "Lindsey's technique of building up suspense and then letting the reader down time and time again does not ultimately detract from the book. To the contrary, Lindsey's integrity and adherence to the facts enhance the story and prove his effectiveness as a storyteller. In lieu of feeling manipulated by the author, one has the sensation of being part of the chase." Similarly, after praising Lindsey for the way he "deftly interweaves three stories," Hill adds, "Only Lindsey could tell the Boyce story in all the dramatic detail in which it now appears."

Lindsey details another tale of true-life crime in *A Gathering of Saints: A True Story of Money, Murder, and Deceit.* This strange case came to public attention in October of 1985 when three bombs exploded in Salt Lake City, Utah. Two people were killed; another was seriously wounded. All three had important ties to the Mormon church. At the time, some believed that the bombs were the work of religious terrorists. In the end, however, investigators discovered that the survivor of the third bomb was actually the bomber. In *A Gathering of Saints,* Lindsey probes the record to uncover the events that led to the bombings and the scandal that unfolded afterwards surrounding the Mormon church. At the center of this storm was the bomber, Mark Hofmann. "The tale of Mark Hofmann, a returned Mormon missionary who was a closet heretic, makes for a superb crime book," comments David Johnston in the *Los Angeles Times Book Review.* "There is intrigue, a terrific detective story and politics aplenty."

Hofmann turned away from the Mormon faith as a teen, but he remained in the church. Sometime later, he began to forge diaries, letters, and other documents related to Joseph Smith, the founder of Mormonism, and the early history of the church. He then sold these documents to collectors or to the church itself. Hofmann's "documents duped the Library of Congress, the Church of Jesus Christ of Latter-day Saints (Mormon), and the FBI," observes Bryce Nelson in the *Washington Post Book World.* "Hofmann could convince almost anyone that his fictions were

fact, and elite news organizations, including the *New York Times* and *Los Angeles Times,* headlined his 'discoveries.' " Hofmann's deception was doubly damaging to the Mormon church, for his aim was not only to defraud the church of its money. John Katzenbach points out in the *New York Times Book Review* that "the key to this scheme was Mr. Hofmann's ability to forge documents that cast the early days of the Mormon Church into disrepute." Church officials concerned about the effect such documents might have on the faith scrambled to buy them and lock them away in archives. As Hofmann's scam grew larger and more tangled, he found it increasingly difficult to sustain the ruse. "The murders that Mr. Hofmann committed . . . were designed primarily to divert attention from his forgeries," explains Katzenbach.

On one level, *A Gathering of Saints* is an expose of Mark Hofmann and his crime; Nelson commends Lindsey for this aspect of his book. "Lindsey is an excellent reporter and writer, as demonstrated in every chapter," he comments. *Christian Century* contributor David S. Cunningham calls "this well-organized, rapid-fire book a real page-turner." However, the reviewer adds that "when Lindsey tries to add literary ornamentation to the news, he nearly ruins it. The fictional dialogue is melodramatic, the characters shallow and cosmetic and the scenes of violence . . . have all the subtlety of a horror film."

On another level, *A Gathering of Saints* is an expose of the Mormon church. Of this aspect, Johnston writes, Lindsey's "graceful book, written with thoughtful sympathy for Mormons and his subjects and rigorously reported, is easily the best single volume ever written to explain the church to outsiders as it is, not as it wants to be seen." Katzenbach concludes: "*A Gathering of Saints* does not read like the majority of books that seek to illuminate the hows and whys of a particular crime and criminal. . . . It ultimately becomes a study not merely of a crime but of a society, a way of life and how fragile belief can be. In a tale of deception, Mr. Lindsey sought out truths, and that makes for potent reading."

In addition to his true-crime stories, Lindsey has also helped in the writing of two celebrity "autobiographies." In his first, *Reagan: The Man, the President,* Lindsey and a group of other writers help organize Ronald Reagan's memoir of his rise from small-town midwestern boy to the presidency of the United States. In *Brando: Songs My Mother Taught Me,* Lindsey adds his professional touches to Marlon Brando's memoir. Caryn James comments in the *New York Times Book Review* that "the autobiography is so shrewdly put together that no one can accuse Brando of ignoring the sensational aspects of his past, however glancing his responses. . . . Mr. Lindsey . . . presumably deserves credit for the book's coherence."

BIOGRAPHICAL/CRITICAL SOURCES:

PERIODICALS

Chicago Tribune, January 25, 1985.
Chicago Tribune Book World, November 18, 1979.
Christian Century, March 8, 1989, p. 264.
Entertainment Weekly, September 23, 1994, pp. 60-61.
Los Angeles Times, December 20, 1983; January 25, 1985.
Los Angeles Times Book Review, December 18, 1988, p. 7.
Nation, December 24, 1983.
Newsweek, November 26, 1979; September 12, 1994, pp. 54-56.
New York, September 19, 1994, pp. 74-75.
New York Review of Books, May 11, 1995, pp. 12-14.
New York Times, November 7, 1979; November 23, 1983; January 25, 1985.
New York Times Book Review, November 4, 1979; November 27, 1983; October 9, 1988, p. 28; October 18, 1992, p. 39; September 11, 1994, p. 3.
People, October 10, 1994, p. 31.
Time, December 31, 1979; September 12, 1994, p. 91.
Times (London), April 19, 1985.
Times Literary Supplement, June 9, 1989, p. 629.
Washington Post, November 29, 1983; January 25, 1985.
Washington Post Book World, December 16, 1979; October 9, 1988, p. 4.

*   *   *

LINDSKOOG, Kathryn (Ann) 1934-

PERSONAL: Born December 27, 1934, in Petaluma, CA; daughter of John Welby (a Navy bandmaster) and Margarete (Zimmerman) Stillwell; married John Samuel Lindskoog (a history teacher), August 15, 1959; children: Jonathan, Peter. *Education:* University of Redlands, B.A. (magna cum laude), 1956; University of London, graduate study, 1956; California State University, Long Beach, M.A. (with high honors), 1957. *Politics:* "Common Cause." *Religion:* Christian. *Avocational interests:* "Humanities (especially psychology, ethics, public affairs, the arts—and art frauds), natural science (especially biological aspects of cognition and behavior—and science frauds), metaphysics (especially the fascinating interface between nature and supernature—and spiritual frauds)."

ADDRESSES: Home—1344 East Mayfair Ave., Orange, CA 92667.

CAREER: High school teacher of English in Orange, CA, 1957-63; writer and freelance lecturer, 1965—. Part-time instructor at Rancho Santiago College, Santa Ana, CA, 1982-89, and Biola University, La Mirada, CA, 1984-89; occasional adjunct at Fuller Theological Seminary, Pasadena, CA, 1978-89.

MEMBER: Mythopoeic Society, PEN.

AWARDS, HONORS: Mythopoeic Society scholarship award, 1974; first prize in national essay contest sponsored by Norman Vincent Peale, 1975; Gold Medallion book award, Christian Booksellers Association, 1993; *Cornerstone* magazine book award for investigative reporting, 1995.

WRITINGS:

C. S. Lewis: Mere Christian, Regal Books (Ventura, CA), 1973, revised edition, Harold Shaw (Wheaton, IL), 1987.
The Lion of Judah in Never-Never Land, Eerdmans (Grand Rapids, MI), 1973.
Up from Eden, David Cook (Elgin, IL), 1976.
Loving Touches, Regal Books, 1976.
How to Grow a Young Reader, David Cook, 1978, revised edition, Harold Shaw, 1989.
The Gift of Dreams, Harper (New York City), 1979.
A Child's Garden of Christian Verses, Regal Books, 1983.
(Contributor) Stephen Schofield, editor, *In Search of C. S. Lewis,* Bridge Publishing (South Plainfield, NJ), 1984.
Around the Year with C. S. Lewis and His Friends, C. R. Gibson (Norwalk, CT), 1986.
(Contributor) John Timmerman, editor, *In the World,* Baker (Grand Rapids, MI), 1987.
(Contributor) Dave Jackson, editor, *Storehouse of Family-Time Ideas,* David Cook, 1987.
(Contributor) Bruce Edwards, editor, *The Taste of the Pineapple,* Popular Press, 1988.
The C. S. Lewis Hoax, Multnomah (Portland, OR), 1988.
(Co-author) *Over the Counter,* Focus on the Family (Colorado Springs, CO), 1989.
Creative Writing for People Who Can't Not Write (textbook), Zondervan (Grand Rapids, MI), 1989.
(Contributor) Doug Peterson, editor, *Fearfully and Wonderfully Weird,* Zondervan, 1990.
Fakes, Frauds and Other Malarkey, Zondervan, 1993.
Light in the Shadowlands: Protecting the Real C. S. Lewis, Questar (Sisters, OR), 1994.
Finding the Landlord: A Guidebook to C. S. Lewis's "Pilgrim's Progress," Cornerstone (Virginia Beach, VA), 1995.
Journey into Narnia, Hope (Carol Stream, IL), 1996.

Contributor of approximately 300 items on a wide range of topics to magazines and journals. Contributing editor of *Wittenburg Door* and *Reformed Journal.* Editor and publisher of *The Lewis Legacy* (quarterly newsletter), 1989—; editor of seven volumes of the *Young Reader's Library* series for Multinomal Press, 1991-93.

WORK IN PROGRESS: Dante's Divine Comedy, a new annotated version; a book on the "Enneagram" titled *Patches from Paradise;* a chapbook of poems called *Written to That End.*

SIDELIGHTS: Kathryn Lindskoog told *CA:* "When I was nine years old my heart's wish was to become a detective like Nancy Drew or a published author like her creator Carolyn Keene, but I figured that the former was improbable and the latter was impossible. (Almost 30 years later I learned to my surprise that there was no Carolyn Keene. By then I had published quite a bit myself, primarily good-humored scholarship, general nonfiction, and satire.) Almost 50 years after my infatuation with Nancy Drew and Carolyn Keene, a reporter happened to call me a literary sleuth. That's when I first noticed that both parts of the long-forgotten childhood wish came true long ago.

"One can't be too careful about choosing favorite books and making wishes. I fell in love with the books of C. S. Lewis in 1954, met him in 1956, and sent him my thesis in 1957. He answered, 'You are in the center of the target everywhere. For one thing, you know my work better than anyone else I've met; certainly better than I do myself. . . . But secondly you (alone of the critics I've met) realize the connection or even the unity of all the books—scholarly, fantastic, theological—and make me appear a single author, not a man who impersonates half a dozen authors, which is what I seem to most. This wins really very high marks indeed. . . .' "

In her books *The C. S. Lewis Hoax* and *Light in the Shadowlands: Protecting the Real C. S. Lewis,* Lindskoog looks at posthumously-published writings attributed to C. S. Lewis and comes to the conclusion that many of them are in fact forgeries, created by the operators of Lewis's estate in order to profit from his reputation. "I think I've proved my case so thoroughly that the truth is bound to prevail, as it did eventually in the Piltdown hoax," she told *CA.* "But it usually takes time for people who were duped to admit to gullibility. (As famous art forger Eric Hebborn chuckled in his booklength confession *Drawn to Trouble,* 'How embarrassing to be duped by bad fakes rather than good ones.' ") Lindskoog also suggests that elements of Mark Twain's novel *Huckleberry Finn* originally appeared in his friend George MacDonald's novel *Sir Gibbie.* Twain, however, she states, "turned MacDonald's religious message upside down." Lindskoog concludes, "My writing life is high adventure, although I am now paralyzed by advanced multiple sclerosis. Writing is slower, but thanks to my computer I can still write."

LIU, Wu-chi 1907-
(Hsiao Hsia)

PERSONAL: Born July 27, 1907, in Wu-chiang, Kiangsu, China; came to United States in 1946, naturalized in 1972; son of Ya-tzu (a poet) and Pei-ni (Cheng) Liu; married Helen Gaw (a librarian), April 20, 1932; children: Shirley (Mrs. Raymond Clayton). *Education:* Tsing Hua College, Peking, China, graduate, 1927; Lawrence College (now University), B.A., 1928; Yale University, Ph.D., 1931; University of London, post-doctoral study, 1931-32.

ADDRESSES: Home—2140 Santa Cruz Ave., Menlo Park, CA 94025.

CAREER: Nankai University, Tientsin, China, professor of English and chairman of department, 1932-41; National Central University, Chunking, China, professor of foreign languages, 1941-45; Rollins College, Winter Park, FL, visiting professor of English and Chinese culture, 1946-48; Yale University, New Haven, CT, visiting professor of Chinese, 1951-53, associate director of research, Human Relations Area Files, 1955-60; Hartwick College, Oneonta, NY, chairman of department of Chinese studies, 1953-55; University of Pittsburgh, Pittsburgh, PA, professor of Chinese language and literature and director of Chinese Language and Area Center, 1960-61; Indiana University—Bloomington, professor of East Asian languages and literature, 1961-76, professor emeritus, 1976—, chairman of department, 1962-67. Director of Far Eastern Language Institute, Committee on Institutional Co-operation (CIC), 1964. Consultant to National Endowment for the Humanities, 1969-71.

MEMBER: International Association for Nan-shi (Southern Society) Studies (president, 1989—).

AWARDS, HONORS: Bollingen Foundation fellowship, 1948-51; National Endowment for the Humanities senior fellowship, 1967-68; distinguished service award, Lawrence University, 1978.

WRITINGS:

A Collection of Wartime Essays, translation of original Chinese manuscript by the author, Commercial Press (Chang-sha, China), 1940.

A Short History of Confucian Philosophy, Penguin (England), 1955, Dell, 1964, reprinted, Hyperion Press (Westport, CT), 1979.

Confucius: His Life and Time, Philosophical Library, 1955, reprinted, Greenwood Press, 1972.

An Introduction to Chinese Literature, Indiana University Press, 1966.

(Author of supplement) H. A. Giles, *A History of Chinese Literature,* Ungar, 1966.

Su Man-shu, Twayne, 1972.

EDITOR

(With Tien-yi Li) *Readings in Contemporary Chinese Literature,* five volumes, Far Eastern Publications, Yale University, 1953-58, revised edition, three volumes, 1964-68.

(Under pseudonym Hsiao Hsia) *China: Its People, Its Society, Its Culture,* Human Relations Area File Press, 1960.

(With Freiderich Bischoff, Jerome Seaton, and Kenneth Yasuda) *K'uei Hsing: A Repository of Asian Literature in Translation,* Indiana University Press, 1974.

(With Irving Y. C. Lo) *Sunflower Splendor: Three Thousand Years of Chinese Poetry,* Doubleday, 1975.

IN CHINESE

A Chronology of Su Man-shu's Life and Other Essays, Pai-hsing Book Co. (Shanghai, China), 1927, 2nd edition, 1928.

The Young Goethe, Pai-hsing Book Co., 1929.

(With Liu Wu-fei and Liu Wu-kou) *Rosaries* (essays), Pai-hsing Book Co., 1936.

(With Liu Wu-fei and Liu Wu-kou) *Appleton* (essays), Liangyu Book Store (Shanghai, China), 1936.

Selected Lyrics from Shakespeare and Others, Ta Shih-tai Book Co., 1942, reprinted, Tien-tung Publishing (Taiwan), 1959.

Cast Bricks to Find Gems (poetry), Chien-wen Book Co. (Kweilin, China), 1943.

Literature Tomorrow (essays), Chien-wen Book Co., 1943.

Literature of India, China Culture Service Co. (Chungking, China), 1945, reprinted, Lien-ching Publishing (Taipei, Taiwan), 1982.

Studies in Western Literature, Ta-tung Book Co. (Shanghai, China), 1946, reprinted, China Friendship Publishing (Peking), 1985.

Reminiscences at Age Seventy, Lien-ching Publishing, 1980.

Retired and Regenerated, Times Publishing (Taipei, Taiwan), 1983.

A Chronology of Liu Ya-tzu's Life, China Social Sciences Press (Peking, China), 1983.

Selected Essays by Liu Wu-chi, China Friendship Press, 1984.

From Sharpened Sword Studio to Swallow's Mausoleum, Times Publishing, 1986.

(With Liu Wu-fei and Liu Wu-kou) *Our Father Liu Ya-tzu,* China Friendship Press, 1989.

IN CHINESE: EDITOR

Two Newly Discovered Works by (Su) Man-shu, Pai-hsing Book Co., 1927.

(With father, Liu Ya-tzu) *Complete Works of Su Man-shu,* 5 volumes, Pai-hsing Book Co., 1928.

Su Man-shu: A Memorial Volume, Cheng-feng Publishing (Chungking, China), 1943.

(With Tsen-chung Fan) *Modern English Prose* (textbook), Institute of Foreign Languages, National Central University (Chungking, China), 1944, reprinted, Kiangsu Education Press (Nanking, China), 1986.

(With Tsen-chung Fan) *Contemporary English Prose* (textbook), Institute of Foreign Languages, National Central University, 1945.

(With Chang Ching-tan and Li Tien-yi) *Modern English Readers* (textbook), six volumes, Kaiming Book Co. (Chungking, China), 1945, 4th edition, 1947.

The World's Treasury of Short Stories, Cheng-feng Publishing, 1948, reprinted, Chung-liu Book Co. (Hong Kong), 1974.

A Treasury of T'ang Poetry, Cheng-feng Publishing, 1948, reprinted, World Book Co. (Taipei, Taiwan), 1972.

(With Liu Wu-fei and others) *Liu Ya-tzu's Collected Works,* 9 volumes, Shanghai People's Publishing House, 1983-93.

TRANSLATIONS INTO CHINESE

Selected Lyrics from Shakespeare and Others, Ta Shih-tai Book Co. (Kweilin, China), 1942, reprinted, Tien-teng Publishing Co. (Taiwan), 1959.

Joseph Conrad, *Almayer's Folly,* Ku-chin Publishing Co. (Kweilin, China), 1943.

(With Ts'ao Hung-chao) William V. Moody and Robert M. Lovett, *A History of English Literature,* Commercial Press, 1947.

Also translator of Shakespeare's *Julius Caesar,* Ta Shih-tai Book Co.

OTHER

(Translator into English) *Liu Ya-tzu and Su Man-shu,* Shanghai Foreign Language Education Press, 1993.

Also translator into English of *Sharpened Sword and Resonant Strings: Poems of Two Southern Society Friends,*

Contributor to dictionaries and encyclopedias, including *Biographical Dictionary of Republican China,* Columbia University Press (New York City), *Dictionary of Oriental Literatures,* Allen & Unwin (Winchester, MA), *Encyclopedia of World Biography,* McGraw (New York City), *Encyclopedia of World Literature in the Twentieth Century,* Ungar (New York City), and *Encyclopedia of Philosophy,* Macmillan (New York City); consultant to *Funk & Wagnalls Encyclopedia,* 1969—. Contributor to Chinese periodicals and newspapers. Co-editor of periodicals, including *Life and Literature,* 1935-37, *I-shih Pao Literary Supplement,* 1935-37, *World Literature,* 1940s, and *Literature, History, and Philosophy Quarterly,* 1943-45; *Tsing-hua Journal of Chinese Studies,* member of editorial board, 1956-76, chairman, 1976-86; member of editorial board, *K'uei Hsing: A Journal of Translations from East and Central Asian Literature,* 1975. Contributing editor, *Books Abroad,* 1964-66.

SIDELIGHTS: Wu-chi Liu told *CA:* "Looking back into my long career as teacher and writer, I realize I am fortunate to have the benefit of two worlds, having spent the first half of my life to bring Western culture to my fellow countrymen at the time of the Chinese Renaissance, and since 1950 to promote Chinese studies among students and readers of my adopted country. I am happy to witness in the United States during the last [several] decades a widespread interest in Chinese literature and philosophy, which are no longer regarded as exotic subjects fit only for the pursuit of a handful of sinologists, the chinoiserie lovers, but as legitimate fields of scholarly research. With a sense of deep gratification, I find myself an active participant in the serious endeavor to initiate a rising generation of impressionable and broadminded young American intellectuals into the rich cultural traditions of one quarter of the world's population.

"From the viewpoint of a Chinese cultural missionary, which I consider myself to be, it seems the time is now ripe for the further enrichment of Western civilization, built upon a combination of both Hellenic and Hebraic heritage, by things Oriental, literature and art, philosophy and religion. The resultant 'melting pot' of the world's greatest traditions, I envision, will produce a truly universal outlook and kinship, transcending language barriers and racial biases, a cultural continuum, and a genial warmth of humanity that will perpetuate itself in the works of contemporary as well as of future authors."

*   *   *

LOEWEN, James W. 1942-
(James Lyons)

PERSONAL: Born February 6, 1942, in Decatur, IL; son of David Frank (a physician) and Winifred (a librarian; maiden name, Gore) Loewen; married Judith Murphy (a teacher), September 16, 1978 (divorced); children: (from previous marriage) Bruce Nicholas, Lucy Catherine. *Education:* Attended Mississippi State University, 1963; Carleton College, B.A. (cum laude), 1964; Harvard University, M.A., 1967, Ph.D., 1968. *Politics:* Independent. *Religion:* Unitarian Universalist.

ADDRESSES: Home—46 Central Ave., South Burlington, VT 05403. *Office*—Department of Sociology, University of Vermont, Burlington, VT 05405.

CAREER: Tougaloo College, Tougaloo, MS, assistant professor, 1968-70, associate professor of sociology, 1970-75, chair of sociology and anthropology department, 1969-73, chair of Division of Social Science, 1972-74; University of Vermont, Burlington, associate professor, 1975-83, professor of sociology, 1984—. Director of research, Center for National Policy Review, Washington, DC, 1978-80. Has served as an expert witness in numerous civil rights cases for Department of Justice, Lawyers Committee for Civil Rights, and others, beginning 1969; has lectured and presented papers to various professional organizations.

MEMBER: American Sociological Association, American Studies Association.

AWARDS, HONORS: Distinguished Teacher Award, Tougaloo College, 1970-71, 1972-73; National Science Foundation postdoctoral fellowship, 1975; Lillian Smith Award for southern nonfiction, 1975, for *Mississippi: Conflict and Change;* First Annual Sidney Spivack Award, American Sociological Association, 1978; Fulbright scholarship to Australia, 1981; fellow, Smithsonian Institution, 1990-91, 1993.

WRITINGS:

The Mississippi Chinese: Between Black and White, Harvard University Press (Cambridge, MA), 1971, 2nd edition, Waveland Press (Prospect Heights, IL), 1988.
(With Charles Sallis and others) *Mississippi: Conflict and Change,* Pantheon (New York City), 1974, revised edition, 1980.
Social Science in the Courtroom, Heath (Lexington, MA), 1983.
Truth about Columbus: A Subversively True Poster Book for a Dubiously Celebration Occasion, New Press, 1992.
Lies My Teacher Told Me: Everything Your American History Teacher Got Wrong, New Press (New York City), 1995.

Also author of booklet "Sociology at Vermont (How, Maybe Even Why, to Major in It)," 1977, resource packet "If Your State History Is Dull and Boring, Here's How to Fix It," 1977, and script for documentary film *The Spirit of Kake Walk,* 1978. Contributor to national journals and professional publications, including *Monthly Review,* sometimes under pseudonym James Lyons. Editor, *Clearinghouse for Civil Rights Research,* 1978-80.

ADAPTATIONS: The Mississippi Chinese: Between Black and White was adapted as a motion picture and produced under the title *Mississippi Triangle* by Third World Newsreel, 1984.

WORK IN PROGRESS: Visitation in Divorce, a "how to" book and review of social science literature for parents without custody; several articles for professional journals.

SIDELIGHTS: James W. Loewen told *CA:* "One of my most vivid memories is of a freshman social science seminar at predominantly black Tougaloo College one morning in the early 1970s. Afro-American history was the subject of the semester, and I needed to find out what my students already knew about it. 'What was Reconstruction?' I asked. 'What images come to your mind about that era?' The class consensus, with but one exception, went like this: Reconstruction was the time when blacks took over the governing of several Southern states, including Mississippi, but they were too soon out of slavery, so they messed up, and the whites had to take back control of the state governments themselves.

"So many misconceptions of fact mar that statement that it's hard to know where to start rebutting it. But the crucial question is: why would a group of black Americans believe a myth about the past that connoted such tragic incapability about their own people? (And whites who believe this myth conclude erroneously that it is only right that blacks be governed by whites, unless the colored races can be helped along toward citizenship via the elixir of education.)

"Their answers were programmed, of course, by their prior 'education.' *Any* history book that celebrates, rather than examines, our heritage has the by-product, intended or not, of alienating all those in the 'out group,' those who have not become affluent, and denies them a tool for understanding their own group's lack of success. Seems as though, incredible as it sounds, the old cliche is correct: the truth will make you free. It's this truth that social science, including history, is hopefully about, and that I've tried to capture in my own writing. 'Performance,' as a previous writer on the South observed, 'is another matter.' "

*   *   *

LoMEDICO, Brian T.
See MONTELEONE, Thomas F(rancis)

*   *   *

LORENZO, Carol Lee 1939-

PERSONAL: Born February 28, 1939, in Atlanta, GA; daughter of Henry George (a grocer) and Freddye Lee (a supervisor of beauty salons; maiden name, Williams) Newman; married Samuel Lorenzo (a lawyer and exhibiting photographer), November 21, 1964. *Education:* Attended American Theatre Wing, 1957-58, Herbert Berghof Acting Studio, 1959, and New School for Social Research, 1970—. *Avocational interests:* Natural history,

animals (especially dogs), reading, walking, sketching with charcoal.

CAREER: Writer for children. Has worked as an actress on Off-Off Broadway.

AWARDS, HONORS: Flannery O'Connor Award for Short Fiction, 1995, for *Nervous Dancer.*

WRITINGS:

Nervous Dancer (short stories), University of Georgia Press (Athens, GA), 1995.

Contributor of articles and reviews to magazines.

YOUNG ADULT NOVELS

Mama's Ghosts, Harper (New York City), 1974.
Heart-of-Snowbird, Harper, 1975.
The White Sand Road, Harper, 1978.

SIDELIGHTS: Carol Lee Lorenzo offers portraits of adolescents in transition in her three novels for young adults. In *Mama's Ghosts,* a young girl named Ellie becomes deeply involved with her grandmother's memories of days gone by. As her grandmother approaches death, Ellie struggles to maintain her own memories, yet transcends her childhood in order to become an adult. In *The White Sand Road,* a brother and sister unwillingly accompany their mother when she runs away from an unhappy marriage. *Heart-of-Snowbird,* praised as "warm and vivid" by a reviewer for *Horn Book,* focuses on a small Appalachian town and one girl who longs to leave it. In time, however, an outsider teaches her to love the place enough to stay.

Numerous reviewers commented on the dreamy quality of Lorenzo's books for children. The stories in *Nervous Dancer,* a collection aimed at adult readers, also feature "the ephemerality of troubling dreams," according to a reviewer for *Publishers Weekly,* including the unsettling images of a dog killed on the highway, a one-armed man, and an idling car with locked doors and no driver. Susannah Hunnewell, commenting on *Nervous Dancer* in the *New York Times Book Review,* admitted that although Lorenzo's imagery was startling, she "doesn't so much tell a story as connect sentences that are meant to jar." A *Publishers Weekly* contributor commented that although the subject matter was weighty enough for intense exploration, "Lorenzo favors imagery over narrative consequence, [thus] they contract into well-wrought miniatures."

Lorenzo once told *CA* that she regrets that she "never learned to do anything tangible—neither writing nor acting deals with known quantities. . . . At writing's most frustrating times, I dream of being a chemist and putting A and B together and making Alka Seltzer (but that's only because I don't understand what's involved in chemistry)."

BIOGRAPHICAL/CRITICAL SOURCES:

PERIODICALS

Booklist, July 1, 1974, p. 1201; June 15, 1975, p. 1076.
Horn Book, August, 1975, p. 388.
Library Journal, May 15, 1974, p. 1474.
New York Times Book Review, May 4, 1975, p. 30; April 16, 1995, p. 16.
Publishers Weekly, March 20, 1995, p. 45.
School Library Journal, May, 1978, p. 69.*

*   *   *

LUPOFF, Dick
   See LUPOFF, Richard A(llen)

*   *   *

LUPOFF, Richard A(llen) 1935-
   **(Dick Lupoff; pseudonyms: Ova Hamlet,
   Addison Steele II, Del Marston; joint
   pseudonyms: Dick O'Donnell, Pascal
   Pascudniak)**

PERSONAL: Born February 21, 1935, in Brooklyn, NY; son of Sol J. (an accountant) and Sylvia (Feldman) Lupoff; married Patricia Loring, August 27, 1958; children: Kenneth Bruce, Katherine Eve, Thomas Daniel. *Education:* University of Miami, Coral Gables, FL, B.A., 1956. *Politics:* None. *Religion:* Jewish.

ADDRESSES: Home—3208 Claremont Ave., Berkeley, CA 94705. *Agent*—Henry Morrison, Inc., P.O. Box 235, Bedford Hills, NY 10507.

CAREER: Remington Rand Univac, New York City, technical writer, 1958-63; International Business Machines Corp., New York City and Poughkeepsie, NY, writer and director of technical films, 1963-70; full-time writer, 1970-82 and 1986—. KPFA-FM, interviewer and book reviewer, 1977—; held various office positions, 1982-85. *Military service:* U.S. Army, 1956-58; became first lieutenant.

AWARDS, HONORS: Hugo Award, World Science Fiction Convention, 1961, for amateur science fiction magazine *Xero;* Hugo Award nominations, 1975, for novelette "After the Dreamtime," and 1976, for short story "Sail the Tide of Mourning"; Nebula Award nominations, Science Fiction Writers of America, 1972, for novella "With the Boomer Boys on Little Old New Alabama," 1975, for short story "Sail the Tide of Mourning," and 1978, for novel *Sword of the Demon.*

WRITINGS:

NONFICTION

Edgar Rice Burroughs: Master of Adventure, Canaveral (Santa Monica, CA), 1965, revised edition, Ace Books (New York City), 1974.
(Editor under name Dick Lupoff, with Don Thompson) *All in Color for a Dime,* Arlington House (New York City), 1969.
(Editor with Thompson, and contributor with Thompson under joint pseudonym Dick O'Donnell) *The Comic-Book Book,* Arlington House, 1973.
Barsoom: Edgar Rice Burroughs and the Martian Vision, Mirage (Manchester, MD), 1976.

FICTION

One Million Centuries, Lancer Books, 1967.
Sacred Locomotive Flies, Ballantine (New York City), 1971.
Into the Aether (adaptation of his comic strip "Into the Aether"; also see below), Dell (New York City), 1974.
The Crack in the Sky, Dell, 1976.
The Triune Man, Berkley Publishing (New York City), 1976.
Sandworld, Berkley Publishing, 1976.
Lisa Kane: A Novel of the Supernatural (juvenile), Bobbs-Merrill (New York City), 1976.
(With Robert E. Howard) *The Return of Skull-Face,* Fax, 1977.
Sword of the Demon, Harper (New York City), 1977.
Space War Blues, Dell, 1978.
The Ova Hamlet Papers (contains material originally published under pseudonym Ova Hamlet), Pennyfarthing Press (Berkeley, CA), 1979.
Stroka Prospekt: A Story, illustrated by Ann Mikolowski, Toothpaste Press (Westbranch, IA), 1982.
Circumpolar!, Simon & Schuster (New York City), 1984.
Sun's End, Berkley Publishing, 1984.
The Digital Wristwatch of Philip K. Dick, Canyon Press, 1985.
Lovecraft's Book, Arkham House (Sauk City, WI), 1985.
Countersolar!, Arbor House (New York City), 1987.
The Forever City, Walker (Louisville, KY), 1988.
The Black Tower, Bantam (New York City), 1988.
Galaxy's End, Ace Books, 1988.
The Comic Book Killer, Offspring Press, 1988.
The Final Battle, Bantam, 1990.
The Classic Car Killer, Offspring Press, 1991.
Night of the Living Gator, Ace, 1992.
The Bessie Blue Killer, St. Martin's (New York City), 1994.
Hyperprism, Gryphon Books (Mt. Rainier, MD), 1994.
The Sepia Siren Killer, St. Martin's, 1994.
The Cover Girl Killer, St. Martin's, 1995.

OTHER

(Editor) *What If? Stories That Should Have Won the Hugo* (anthology), Pocket Books (New York City), Volume I, 1980, Volume II, 1981.

Professor Thintwhistle (adaptation of his *Into the Aether;* originally published in *Heavy Metal,* 1980-81), Phantagraphics Books, 1991.

Also editor of five volumes of previously unpublished miscellaneous writings of Edgar Rice Burroughs, 1963-64; author, occasionally under pseudonym Pascal Pascudniak, with Stephen W. Stiles, of comic strips, including "The Amazing Adventures of Professor Thintwhistle and His Incredible Ether Flyer," *Horib,* 1964-65, and "The Adventures of Isidore," *Jive Comics,* 1969.. Contributor to anthologies, including *Again, Dangerous Visions,* edited by Harlan Ellison, Doubleday (New York City), 1972, and *New Dimensions, 4* and *5.*

Contributor of short stories and articles to newspapers and magazines; contributor of book reviews to *San Francisco Chronicle,* 1979-81; contributor with Michael Kurland of short story "The Square Root of Dead" to *Mike Shayne's Mystery Magazine;* contributor under pseudonym Addison Steele II of short story "The Wedding of Ova Hamlet" to *Fantastic.* Coeditor with wife, Patricia Lupoff, of *Xero,* 1960-63; book editor and reviewer, *Starship* (formerly *Algol*), 1968-79; West Coast editor, *Crawdaddy,* 1970-71, and *Changes,* 1971-72; contributing editor of *Organ,* 1972.

WORK IN PROGRESS: The Silver Chariot Killer, before 12:01 PM . . . and After: Collected Fiction, 1952-1995, and, under pseudonym Del Marston, *Death in the Ditch.*

SIDELIGHTS: Richard A. Lupoff told *CA:* "I've spent most of my intellectual life trying to become a 'good' writer (in the artistic sense) and a successful one (in the sense of making a living at it). I made my first sale (as a sports reporter) while still in my teens, sold my first book in 1965, and became a full-time author in 1970.

"In 1981, economic conditions left me with a drawerful of cancelled contracts and no income whatsoever. After a year of hanging on desperately, I gave up the struggle and took a dreadful job working in a government office. By the end of 1985, happily, I was able to leave that job and return to writing. In a strange way, that interval may have been beneficial to my writing. It represented a fallow period, and during this period, my creative batteries recharged themselves. Since the end of 1985, I have been in the most productive period of my career, and both the commercial and the critical response has been excellent. In recent years I have reduced my level of association with science fiction and have concentrated on crime and mainstream writing. As the Duke of Milan said, 'What is past

is prologue.' As far as I'm concerned, I'm a new writer and my *real* career has just begun."

Lupoff's *Countersolar!* is about a duplicate Earth discovered orbiting on the other side of the sun and the attempts to make contact with that differently evolved planet. Writing in the *Los Angeles Times Book Review,* science fiction novelist Orson Scott Card observes that Lupoff abandons the "respectable" strain of contemporary science fiction that parodies the thrillers of the 1930s and creates "not the scientific wonders that our jaded '80s sensibility expects, but rather the limitless possibilities that people in the '30s once imagined." Noting that Lupoff "knows his cosmos, his history," Card suggests that what Lupoff believes and subtly conveys is "not the details of his story, but its underlying hope."

BIOGRAPHICAL/CRITICAL SOURCES:

PERIODICALS

Analog Science Fiction/Science Fact, July, 1977; February 2, 1981.
Fantasy Review, January, 1987.
Los Angeles Times Book Review, February 15, 1987.
Magazine of Fantasy and Science Fiction, September, 1981.
Science Fiction Chronicle, March, 1987.
Science Fiction Review, November, 1981.

*　　　*　　　*

LURIE, Alison 1926-

PERSONAL: Born September 3, 1926, in Chicago, IL; daughter of Harry and Bernice (Stewart) Lurie; married Jonathan Peale Bishop (a professor), September 10, 1948 (divorced, 1985); children: John, Jeremy, Joshua. *Education:* Radcliffe College, A.B., 1947.

ADDRESSES: Office—Department of English, Cornell University, Ithaca, NY 14853.

CAREER: Cornell University, Ithaca, NY, lecturer, 1969-73, associate professor, 1973-76, professor of English, 1976—, Frederic J. Whiton Professor of American Literature, 1989—. Has also worked as a ghostwriter and librarian.

AWARDS, HONORS: Yaddo Foundation fellow, 1963, 1964, 1966; Guggenheim grant, 1965-66; Rockefeller Foundation grant, 1967-68; New York State Cultural Council Foundation grant, 1972-73; American Academy of Arts and Letters award in literature, 1978; American Book Award nomination in fiction, 1984, National Book Critics Circle Award nomination for best work of fiction, 1984, and Pulitzer Prize in fiction, 1985, all for *Foreign Af-*

fairs; Radcliffe College Alumnae Recognition Award, 1987; Prix Femina Etranger, 1989.

WRITINGS:

V. R. Lang: A Memoir, privately printed, 1959.

V. R. Lang: Poems and Plays, Random House (New York City), 1974.

The Heavenly Zoo (juvenile), Farrar, Straus (New York City), 1980.

Clever Gretchen and Other Forgotten Folk Tales (juvenile), Crowell (New York City), 1980.

Fabulous Beasts (juvenile), Farrar, Straus, 1981.

The Language of Clothes (nonfiction), Random House, 1981, 2nd edition, 1992.

Don't Tell the Grown-Ups: Subversive Children's Literature, Little, Brown (Boston), 1990.

(Editor) *The Oxford Book of Modern Fairy Tales,* Oxford University Press (Oxford, England), 1993.

Women and Ghosts (short stories), Doubleday (New York City), 1994.

NOVELS

Love and Friendship, Macmillan (New York City), 1962.

The Nowhere City, Coward, 1965.

Imaginary Friends, Coward, 1967.

Real People, Random House, 1969.

The War between the Tates, Random House, 1974.

Only Children, Random House, 1979.

Foreign Affairs, Random House, 1984.

The Truth about Lorin Jones, Little, Brown, 1988.

OTHER

Also editor, with Justin G. Schiller, of "Classics of Children's Literature, 1631-1932" series, Garland Publishing. Contributor of articles and reviews to periodicals, including *New York Review of Books, New York Times Book Review, New Statesman,* and *New Review.*

ADAPTATIONS: Imaginary Friends, The War between the Tates, and *Foreign Affairs* were filmed for television.

SIDELIGHTS: Although she has written children's books and several works of nonfiction, Alison Lurie is best known for her novels, especially *The War between the Tates* and *Foreign Affairs,* each one a finely structured comedy of manners about people from an academic milieu. As Sara Sanborn states in a *New York Times Book Review* critique of *The War between the Tates,* from the beginning of her career Lurie "has regularly produced insightful and witty novels about The Way We Live Now, drawing on a large talent for social verisimilitude." Her work has been praised by a London *Times* reviewer as "formidably well made," while Christopher Lehmann-Haupt declares in the *New York Times* that Lurie "has quietly but surely established herself as one of this coun-

try's most able and witty novelists." "I can think of no other writer who so thoroughly embodies the [Henry] Jamesian spirit as Alison Lurie," comments Edmund White in the *New York Times Book Review.* "Like him she can excavate all the possibilities of a theme. Like his, her books seem long, unbroken threads, seamless progressions of effects."

In the opinion of several critics, *The War between the Tates* and Lurie's Pulitzer Prize-winning *Foreign Affairs* are examples of the author at her best. A London *Times* reviewer explains that *The War between the Tates,* a comic novel about the marital difficulties of a professor and his wife in an era of campus unrest, "caught, just on the instant, the conflict between radical passions and more conventional moralities that raged like foreign wars in the early 1970s. It could now seem a period piece, its targets, with the hindsight of the 1980s and the new conservatism, almost too easy to pick off. But, reread, its toughness and satirical precision hold it together; its satirical object is not just the age but contradictory human nature." *Foreign Affairs,* the story of two American academics on sabbatical in England, "should help propel Alison Lurie into the forefront of American novelists, where she clearly belongs," according to William French in the Toronto *Globe and Mail.*

Lurie's characters are usually well-educated, sophisticated members of the upper middle class. Everett Wilkie and Josephine Helterman describe her in the *Dictionary of Literary Biography* as "a highly intelligent writer, perhaps too intelligent for popular tastes since much of her satire is of a cerebral sort aimed at persons in academic life, especially those in prestigious colleges." As Sanborn relates, "Miss Lurie's protagonists are always academics or writers, well-read and well-controlled, thoughtful and successful, people of good taste—and hence people especially susceptible to the Call of the Wild and the perfectly rational processes of self-deception. In each case, their carefully constructed lives and self images, glowing with conscious enlightenment, break up on the rocks of the irrational, to which they have been lured by the siren song of sheer sexual energy."

Extramarital sex is a recurring element in the tendency of Lurie's characters to depart from the carefully controlled, rational path; it figures prominently in almost every novel. *Love and Friendship,* for example, is a comedy set in academia that centers around the dissolution of a young couple's marriage, just as *The Nowhere City* contrasts the values of the northeastern United States with those of California against the backdrop of another marriage that is coming apart. In *Imaginary Friends,* described by a London *Times* reviewer as "a classic comedy about the desire to command knowledge," a sociologist becomes influenced by a millenarian cult he has infiltrated, while *Real*

People satirizes Illyria, a pastoral artists' retreat. In each book, Sanborn writes, "the protagonists leave home and journey into the bizarre, where they learn their own mettle or come to terms with their lack of it. Thus each of these novels is marked to a greater or lesser degree by a certain laboriousness of invention, an intrusive quality of the special case."

In *The War between the Tates,* however, Lurie raises "The Way We Live Now into the Human Comedy" with "the effortless grace of a real ironic gift," to use Sanborn's words. The book examines the midlife crisis of Brian Tate, a professor of political science at Corinth University who is just beginning to realize that he will never be a great man outside of his department. He becomes involved with a student whom he later impregnates, and this affair precipitates the rebellion of his wife, Erica, who experiments briefly with sex, drugs, and Eastern philosophy.

The Tates' marital difficulties and the student's pregnancy are not the only sources of discontent in the Tate household, however. Their best friends, Danielle and Leonard Zimmern, have just weathered their own divorce and are adopting radically different ways of life—Danielle is becoming an abrasive feminist, and Leonard is turning into an outspoken bachelor with an apartment in New York City—and Brian and Erica are forced to align themselves against one or the other. Furthermore, the much-glorified Tate children are growing into unpleasant, rebellious adults. Well into the novel Lurie draws an elaborate parallel between the war in Vietnam and the continuing battle between sexes and generations that is taking place in the Tate household. "This metaphor, of Miltonic grandeur and epic absurdity, ascends from the embattled Tate home and floats over the campus of Corinth University like a majestic balloon," Walter Clemons claims in *Newsweek.* The book climaxes with a feminist demonstration during which Brian Tate has to rescue a colleague from the wrath of his girlfriend and the other protesters.

Overall, reviewers have high praise for the novel. The book "represents a breakthrough into ease in the handling of the author's favorite themes," says Sanborn. Many of the incidents in the book are exaggerated or heightened for comic effect, with the plot often bordering on the preposterous, but unlike many of Lurie's earlier works, "no one goes anywhere; the Tates meet their destiny and the truth about themselves in their own back yard, on their daily rounds," Sanborn observes. "The whole plot unfolds, with the inevitability of a round dance once the first steps are taken in the college of Corinth."

Roger Sale adds in the *New York Review of Books* that Lurie "cheerfully takes on the standard plot—an ambitious professor, his well-educated wife, their domestic boredom and strain, a student mistress for the husband,

futile attempts at retaliation and freedom by the wife, and whenever these figures and actions move into the surrounding community, we have clarity and brightness where others usually have managed murky expositions and cute tricks." In *The War between the Tates,* notes Doris Grumbach in the *Washington Post Book World,* Lurie "has taken a set of ordinary characters, or at least not exceptional ones, submitted them to the strains and battles of time, sex, legal alliances, generation gaps, politics and work: all the ingredients of a popular novel. But her sensibility and talent are so superior that she has given us an artistic work, which every one will read because it is 'common' to us all, but which some will perceive to have the crafted look and feel of a first-rate work."

Some reviewers criticize Lurie's tendency to distance herself from the characters in *The War between the Tates,* finding various portraits overly satirical and unsympathetic. In general, however, most regard the novel as a real accomplishment, primarily due to the author's familiarity with her subject matter. Lurie is a professor of children's literature at Cornell University, the campus that is the source of much of her inspiration, and as Sale sums up, Lurie creates a convincing fictional world "by means of her quickness, her efficiency, her lightness of touch, with lots of subjects that others manage only with ponderousness or self-regarding wit: The Department, The Book, The Cocktail Party, the Young, both children and students." Sanborn points out that the book is "a novel not only to read, but to reread for its cool and revealing mastery of a social epoch."

Only Children concerns itself with some of the same subjects as *The War between the Tates,* most notably the conflict between the sexes and the generations, but whereas *The War between the Tates* depicts children as rude interlopers, *Only Children* takes a more sympathetic view in that the story unfolds through the eyes and voices of two eight-year-old girls. The novel also reflects Lurie's interests in children's literature and gender discrimination, a theme she also addresses in *Clever Gretchen and Other Forgotten Folk Tales,* a collection of retold fairy tales that present women in a positive light.

Only Children relates the events of a Depression-era Fourth of July holiday that two couples and their daughters spend on a farm owned by the headmistress of the progressive school the girls attend. (Leonard Zimmern also appears in the story as the adolescent son from a previous marriage of one of the adults.) The author's preoccupation in *Only Children* is with sexual role dynamics and the flirtations that occur among the parents as observed and puzzled over by their daughters. In the process, notes *Time* critic John Skow, Lurie also depicts "the narrow range of adult female behavior that was on view to a girl of four decades ago." During the course of the long weekend, the adults' actions become more and more childish, while the girls' sensibilities take on a more mature awareness. Only the headmistress, independent and manless, but sexually experienced, remains an adult.

The book has garnered significant praise from reviewers. An *Atlantic Monthly* critic calls it Lurie's "gentlest, most sympathetic satire," while Mary Gordon describes it in the *New York Review of Books* as "the most interior of Lurie's novels, the most reflective, the most lyrical." And in the opinion of Ann Hulbert in the *New Republic,* "this novel about love and its disorderly ways in unexamined lives is a thoughtfully crafted and traditionally unified comic drama. In *Only Children* Lurie draws deftly from her academic literary discipline, without cramping her ironic and sympathetic imagination, which ranges as easily and fruitfully as ever."

Lurie's work "is triumphantly in the comic mode, and she knows its contours and idiosyncrasies and its meticulous pacing exceptionally well," writes Joyce Carol Oates in the *New York Times Book Review.* The *Atlantic Monthly* reviewer adds that Lurie's "lovely evocations of the natural world nicely offset the minutely observed artificiality of her adult characters, and she deftly avoids the obvious pitfalls of writing about children."

Other critics also laud the author's descriptive abilities in *Only Children.* Gabriele Annan comments in the *Listener* that "Lurie is superb at describing nature, weather, interiors, sandwich cutting, stewing in a traffic jam, swimming in a sand-bottomed creek," while a *West Coast Review of Books* critic remarks that "one can almost feel the Unguentine as it spreads over a firecracker burn, or taste the homemade lemon-coconut cake (and later the baking soda for the indigestion), or smell the insides of the new DeSoto sedan, or see the designs made with the Gyro Art machine."

Some reviewers find the style of *Only Children* didactic and the work less fulfilling as a novel than *The War between the Tates,* but still noteworthy. Gordon feels that the attempt to tell the story through the eyes of children is not always successful, but maintains that Lurie "is doing something different from what she has already done successfully, and has tried to go deeper." As Lynne Sharon Schwartz in *Saturday Review* indicates, "one must admire her willingness to risk this quite different and difficult conception." *Only Children* "is not so free-wheeling and inventive as *The War between the Tates,*" Oates concludes, "but it is a highly satisfactory achievement and should be read with enthusiasm by Miss Lurie's many admirers."

Lurie's Pulitzer Prize-winning comedy of manners *Foreign Affairs* returns to more familiar subject matter for the author, as it "reassemble[s] her Corinth cast in a new setting," states James McGrath Morris in the *Washington Post.* Two members of the faculty of Corinth University's English department, 54-year-old Vinnie Miner and young, handsome Fred Turner, "spend a semester in London and learn a great deal more about love than about their intended scholarly pursuits," says Morris.

As the book opens, Vinnie Miner has boarded the plane and is settling into her seat in preparation for an uneventful flight to England. Vinnie is a professor of children's literature, single, childless, and plain-looking, who is researching the difference between American and English playground rhymes for a forthcoming book. She is a selfish woman, but also afflicted with self-pity; she realizes that, though she has been married and has always had an active sex life, she has never really been loved, probably because she is not pretty, and now she is growing too old. Furthermore, her work, which is funded by a not-so-secure grant, has just been ridiculed in a national magazine by a critic she has never heard of (Leonard Zimmern from *The War between the Tates* and *Only Children*). As Charles Champlin relates in the *Los Angeles Times Book Review,* "Vinnie Miner is accompanied by a small invisible dog that is the tangible embodiment of her self-pity (an allowable conceit in an imaginative 54-year-old academic, I expect, although I didn't so much accept it as admire Lurie's daring in making it almost credible)." Despite the fact that Vinnie feels sorry for herself, she is still excited about the trip, being an Anglophile with a wide circle of friends in London.

Seated next to Vinnie on the plane is Chuck Mumpson, a loud, retired waste disposal engineer from Tulsa, dressed cowboystyle and accompanied by a group of noisy tourists on a package tour. Though Vinnie initially finds Chuck annoying, he and Vinnie eventually become friends and passionate lovers. (Mumpson even develops an interest in researching his genealogy.) He dies of a heart attack before Vinnie figures out a way to make him fit in with her English friends and reconcile him with her career, but she gradually comes to the conclusion that, with Mumpson, she has finally loved and been loved in return.

Alternating chapters relate in counterpoint the experiences of youthful and handsome Fred Turner, who is an untenured member of Vinnie's faculty. Fred is in London researching John Gay, the 18th-century poet and playwright, and he's having a considerably worse time than Vinnie. Penniless between paychecks and recently separated from his feminist wife, Roo (Leonard Zimmern's daughter), he spends some of his time with a poor, complaining university couple who are having an equally miserable time in London. He has an affair with a spoiled, titled English actress who introduces him to her trendy friends, but it does not improve the quality of the time he spends in London wrapped up in his personal problems.

The book examines the differences between the English and the Americans while at the same time exploring a recurring theme in Lurie's novels, the line between illusion or appearance and reality. "For the real inspiration of Miss Lurie's entertaining fables is her fascination with levels of truth, with the war between fact and fantasy," says a *Times Literary Supplement* reviewer. According to William French in the Toronto *Globe and Mail,* "the characters in the novel of both nationalities simultaneously have their illusions shattered and prejudices confirmed, proving that generalizations about national traits are superficial and dangerous." And as French reports, Lurie "is sardonic, droll, intelligent and literary, in the best sense of that word, with a sure grasp of her characters and the social and cultural conditioning that has made them what they are."

The novel contains references to novelist Henry James and echoes of his work. And as Annan points out, even the fable itself is Jamesian: "Against a background of alluring, repellent London society a sophisticated American learns from an unsophisticated one that, contrary to appearances, true goodness exists and matters more than beauty, wit or grace." But Joel Conarroe adds in the *Washington Post Book World* that "although her plot is concerned with the confrontation of American naivete and European sophistication, a major Jamesian theme, she resists the temptation to explore various levels of ironic correspondence."

Foreign Affairs also has some elements of the fairy tale; *Voice Literary Supplement* writer Maureen Corrigan finds extensive borrowings from "The Frog Prince" in the love story of Vinnie and Chuck. A more direct theme of the narrative, though, is the extent to which it is assumed that only the young and the beautiful have sex lives. Although some reviewers believe that the author states this a little too forthrightly in the novel, and others regard the portrait of Chuck Mumpson as more of a caricature than a characterization, Dorothy Wickenden in the *New Republic* indicates that "Lurie is as deft as ever when she turns to the mortifications of romance. She is an uncannily accurate observer of the ambivalent emotions that enter into unconventional sexual alliances."

Another criticism of the novel is its busy, formulaic, and often incredible plot, as *Chicago Tribune Book World* reviewer Peter Collier describes it. Lurie's novels tend to be "programmatic," with the author relying upon "formal contrivances to heighten irony, to create startling juxtapositions, and to make a larger point about the individual's accommodations to the demands of society," says Wickenden, who considers *Foreign Affairs* to be an extreme case. And Anne Bernays in the *New York Times Book Review* would have preferred a less intrusive omniscient narrator. But Collier disagrees, claiming that "this narrative voice—by turns wicked and insightful, ironic and

aloof—is the primary source of pleasure" in the novel. Wickenden also qualifies her criticism as she points out that when Lurie "abandons her gimmicky plot devices and moral posturing, *Foreign Affairs* is funny, touching, and even suspenseful."

In the opinion of some reviewers, the novel is perfectly constructed. "Besides amusing us with its story," Lehmann-Haupt writes, "[*Foreign Affairs*] is wonderfully stimulating for its sheer performance as a novel. Perhaps by stressing this I'm admitting nostalgia for a classical approach to literature, but as I read *Foreign Affairs* I couldn't help visualizing a diagram with the rise of Vinnie's fortunes superimposed on the decline of Fred Turner's. There's something almost musical in the way the two plots interplay, like two bands marching toward each other playing consonant music." The book's construction "is so neat, so ingenious and satisfying, with no loose ends anywhere, that you barely notice its two stories operating on different levels of truth and entertainment," Annan finds.

Writing in the *Times Literary Supplement,* Lorna Sage also refers to the novel's classical structure, indicating that *Foreign Affairs* is "warm, clever and funny—the kind of novel that elicits a conspiratorial glow from the start because it flatters the reader unmercifully. You're assumed to be witty and literate, you're told (indirectly, of course) how very wide awake you are, and you're congratulated for being (on the other hand and after all) so sensible as to prefer your metafiction in traditional form." The book is "one of those rare novels," remarks French, "in which the author's vision is perfectly realized, and the reader finishes it with a sense of shared triumph and generous benediction." According to Conarroe, "it also earns the gratitude of all of us who admire literacy, wit, and the underrated joys of ironic discourse." And as Anthony Thwaite declares in the *Observer,* "let no one suppose that [Lurie's] field of social observation is a restricted one, or in any way slight: she makes a world, commands it, and is a mistress not only of wit but of passion."

In *The Truth about Lorin Jones,* Lurie draws again from her familiar pool of characters to create what *Nation* contributor Brina Caplan calls an "energetic, gossipy romantic comedy-cum-mystery, lively with incidents and revelations, sexual ambiguities and twists of fate." The title character was born Laurie "Lolly" Zimmern (a member of the Zimmern family, found throughout Lurie's fiction.) As Lorin Jones, Zimmern became a painter who gained a measure of success in the New York art world for her abstract paintings before dying of pneumonia in Key West. But, the novel is only indirectly about Lorin Jones. At its heart is Polly Alter, a museum curator who has organized an exhibit of Lorin's work. Drawn to the painter by her works, Alter decides to do a biography of Lorin to uncover the story of her life and untimely death. Alter pursues the biography through Lorin's family, ex-husband, lover, art dealers, and other players in her life. Along the way, she loses herself in her subject and then finds the flaws in her preconceptions.

What Alter finally discovers is that Lorin Jones had not been the product of exploitative fathers, brothers, lovers, and colleagues. Instead, as Francis King points out in the *Spectator,* Lorin "was prepared to exploit her menfolk in precisely the manner in which Polly's feminist, lesbian friends claim that men exploit their womenfolk." King adds that "the secondary theme of the book is precisely this 'exploitation,' handled with the rueful irony to which this novelist so often subjects not merely the opposite but her own sex." In addition to skewering Lorin, Lurie also turns a critical eye on Alter. As King suggests, "The book has something arresting to say about the writing of biography as an instrument both of self-discovery and of envy." True, the novel shines a spotlight on exploitative women and the dangers of biography; yet as Caplan writes, "*The Truth about Lorin Jones* is ultimately not about Lorin Jones nor about truth—it's about laughs." According to this reviewer, "Lurie has simplified the terms of reality so that pretensions bring prat-falls and sexual confusions resolve under the irresistible sway of love. No character gets treated in greater depth than the conventions of a middle-brow, say a Neil Simon screenplay, demand." Edmund White offers greater praise in the *New York Times Book Review.* He writes, "This book is funny, intelligent, and packed with incident arranged in a suspenseful plot—which makes it one of the most entertaining novels I've read in a long time. It is also a relentless comedy about the sin of pride and the folly it can inspire."

Lurie's comic and satirical look at women and biographers has drawn a variety of responses from reviewers. Barbara Griffith Furst writes in *Belles Lettres* that *The Truth about Lorin Jones* is the "usual snappy Lurie commentary on trendy contemporary life, and the characters are virtually all exaggerated and self-serving." Furst admits that "the book will no doubt annoy some feminists. However, Lurie is describing a journey many women make from traditional wives and mothers to angry, aggressive, and lonely career women, followed by a mellowing and appreciation of their own femaleness and the vulnerability of men." Others feel that this novel does not represent Lurie's best effort. According to *Wall Street Journal* contributor Donna Rifkind, "The only hints of Ms. Lurie's characteristic sparkle are a clever structure (she alternates action with 'transcriptions' of Polly's interviews) and one or two funny passages."

Barbara A. Bannon tempers this judgement in a *Commonweal* review. She comments, "Although *The Truth about Lorin Jones* is not up to the high standards set by Lurie

herself in *The War between the Tates* and the Pulitzer Prize-winning *Foreign Affairs,* it is quirky, zesty, and funny enough to give enjoyment and amusement to its readers, most of whom will undoubtedly be women." And, Anthony Thwaite suggests that Lurie has more at work in the novel than might seem on its surface. He writes in the *London Review of Books,* "Alison Lurie is a very adept novelist, manipulating plot and characters with such consummate ease that it's only after finishing the book one notices how cunningly she has brought together her strands, establishing suspense here and exhaustion there, allowing one to make discoveries and be faced with puzzles as abruptly and with as much bewilderment as Polly."

Women and Ghosts is a short story collection in which Lurie offers up nine contemporary ghost stories featuring women who are haunted by figments from their own psyches. In one, a poet is tormented by a double who begins to take her place at literary events. In another, a young foreign service officer, never serious about men, has her love life interrupted by the spirit of a dead ex-lover. Yet another finds fat ghosts hounding a dieting woman. As Lurie told John Blades in the *Chicago Tribune, Women and Ghosts* "can be read either as realistic or supernatural . . . about people in desperate situations who begin to see things that aren't there." She added, "Ambiguity is part of the charm of ghost stories. . . . We seem to like not being sure whether something is imagined or supernatural. The gray area between reality and the imagination has always been intriguing." The results of Lurie's foray into the ambiguity of the ghost story, comments David Leavitt in the *New York Times Book Review,* "are simultaneously funny (in the Lurie tradition) and unsettling (in the ghost story tradition): Dorothy Parker meets Edgar Allan Poe."

Lurie's artistry in balancing humor and horror is at the center of the critical response to *Women and Ghosts.* "In this collection of nine ghost stories," writes Alex Clark in the *Times Literary Supplement,* "[Lurie's] talent for subtlety and equivocation is to the fore, making its force felt in the sheer range and diversity of characters and in the inventiveness of the situations they find themselves in." He continues that "the stories are at their best when they combine this sense of mistrust for empirical data with the self-deceptions and vanities of their characters." D. J. Taylor is not so generous in his *Spectator* review. He finds the stories "fatally winded by groaning explanations and laboured dialogue. . . . There are plenty of good ideas here—a pretentious poet with a mysterious double, a dieting woman haunted by sinister fat familiars: invariably, though, the execution is flat and unsatisfactory." In the estimation of Susan Salter Reynolds in the *Los Angeles Times Book Review,* "the voices of [Lurie's] haunted women . . . are so deadpan, so matter-of-fact, and the objects and situations endowed with ghostly spirits are so everyday that the stories end up being funnier than they are scary." However, counters Christopher Lehmann-Haupt in the *New York Times,* "these are not so much tales of ectoplasmic terror as stories of right and wrong and of character disorder. . . . Instead of fear, these stories provoke one's sense of decorum, with the ghosts reflecting good sense or silliness." The element of humor, Clark suggests, is what elevates these ghost stories above the standard genre fare. "Lurie is an accomplished enough satirist to have crafted these stories without an overarching theme. If one occasionally wonders whether the self-imposed structure of 'ghost story' is always necessary, or indeed desirable," he writes, "a faultless touch and delicate sense of irony carry the day."

Lurie's manuscripts are collected at the Cornell University Library.

BIOGRAPHICAL/CRITICAL SOURCES:

BOOKS

Contemporary Literary Criticism, Gale, Volume 4, 1975, Volume 5, 1976, Volume 18, 1980, Volume 39, 1986.
Costa, Richard Hauer, *Alison Lurie,* Twayne, 1992.
Dictionary of Literary Biography, Volume 2: *American Novelists since World War II,* Gale, 1978.

PERIODICALS

America, August 10, 1974; October 18, 1975.
Atlanta Journal and Constitution, October 16, 1988, p. M11.
Atlantic Monthly, September, 1974; May, 1979; December, 1981; April, 1990, p. 108.
Belles Lettres, spring, 1989, p. 8.
Best Sellers, March 1, 1966; November 15, 1967; September 1, 1974.
Bloomsbury Review, March, 1990, p. 11.
Books and Bookmen, April, 1970.
Book Week, January 23, 1966.
Book World, September 24, 1967; May 18, 1969.
Boston Globe, September 13, 1988, p. 66; March 18, 1990, p. B46.
Chicago Sunday Tribune, April 8, 1962.
Chicago Tribune, August 5, 1993, sec. 5, p. 3; October 31, 1994, sec. 5, p. 2; November 15, 1994, sec. 5, p. 4.
Chicago Tribune Book World, November 4, 1984.
Christian Science Monitor, October 26, 1967; May 22, 1969; September 18, 1974; May 14, 1979; May 12, 1980.
Commentary, August, 1969; January, 1975.
Commonweal, January 12, 1968; December 16, 1988, p. 690.
Encounter, August, 1979.
Globe and Mail (Toronto), September 15, 1984.

Harper's, July, 1979.
Hudson Review, spring, 1966; spring, 1975.
Life, November 24, 1967; May 23, 1969.
Listener, February 19, 1970; June 20, 1974; April 19, 1979; May 6, 1982.
London Magazine, December, 1974-January, 1975.
London Review of Books, February 21, 1985, p. 5; September 1, 1988, p. 24; July 22, 1993, p. 19.
Los Angeles Times, October 21, 1988, p. V12; October 28, 1994, p. E4.
Los Angeles Times Book Review, October 21, 1984, p. 1; March 11, 1990, p. 6; May 20, 1990, p. 14; October 3, 1993, p. 1; September 11, 1994, p. 6.
Maclean's, October 10, 1988, p. 48A.
Ms. Magazine, October, 1988, p. 88.
Nation, November 21, 1981; November 21, 1988, p. 540.
National Review, December 7, 1979.
New Leader, September 2, 1974.
New Republic, August 10-17, 1974; December 21, 1974; May 12, 1979; December 7, 1979; December 23, 1981; October 8, 1984, p. 34; November 15, 1993, p. 39.
New Statesman, February 5, 1965; June 30, 1967; June 21, 1974; April 20, 1979; July 8, 1988, p. 39; May 25, 1990, p. 32; June 26, 1992, p. 40; May 28, 1993, p. 40; June 17, 1994, p. 38.
Newsweek, January 10, 1966; November 6, 1967; May 26, 1969; August 5, 1974; December 30, 1974; April 23, 1979; September 24, 1984, p. 80; October 10, 1988, p. 74.
New Yorker, March 23, 1968; October 11, 1969; August 19, 1974; May 14, 1979; November 5, 1984.
New York Review of Books, February 3, 1966; December 7, 1967; August 8, 1974; June 14, 1979; April 15, 1982; October 11, 1984; April 26, 1990, p. 45.
New York Times, May 27, 1969; November 18, 1981; September 13, 1984, p. C21; September 12, 1988, p. C18; February 27, 1990, p. C17; August 19, 1993, p. C15; October 3, 1994, p. C14.
New York Times Book Review, April 1, 1962; January 16, 1966; October 15, 1967; May 25, 1969; July 28, 1974; April 22, 1979; April 27, 1980; July 13, 1980; January 17, 1982; June 6, 1982; November 7, 1982; September 16, 1984, p. 9; September 4, 1988, p. 3; March 11, 1990, p. 13; September 18, 1994, p. 12.
Observer, May 16, 1965; February 15, 1970; June 16, 1974;, July 31, 1977; April 16, 1978; July 23, 1978; April 15, 1979; December 9, 1979; January 20, 1985.
Progressive, April, 1975; September, 1979.
Publishers Weekly, August 19, 1974.
Punch, February 17, 1965; January 23, 1985, p. 52.
Saturday Review, January 29, 1966; June 9, 1979; November, 1981; November, 1984.

Spectator, July 7, 1967; February 21, 1970; June 29, 1974; April 21, 1979; January 26, 1985; July 16, 1988, p. 31; June 16, 1990, p. 30; June 18, 1994, p. 34.

Time, March 4, 1966; June 6, 1969; July 29, 1974; June 11, 1979; November 30, 1981; October 15, 1984; September 19, 1988, p. 95.

Times (London), May 27, 1982; January 19, 1985; January 31, 1985.

Times Literary Supplement, February 4, 1965; July 6, 1967; February 10, 1970; February 19, 1970; June 21, 1974; November 23, 1979; July 18, 1980; November 20, 1981; May 14, 1982; February 1, 1985, p. 109; July 30, 1993, p. 7; June 17, 1994, p. 23.

Tribune Books (Chicago), March 4, 1990, p. 6; June 9, 1991, p. 6.

USA Today, April 25, 1985, p. D4; April 18, 1986, p. A13; September 23, 1988, p. D9.

Village Voice, August 8, 1974.

Voice Literary Supplement, October, 1984, p. 5; May, 1990, p. 41.

Wall Street Journal, October 30, 1967; October 11, 1988, p. A20.

Washington Post, April 25, 1985.

Washington Post Book World, August 11, 1974; September 7, 1975; April 29, 1979; July 13, 1980; November 29, 1981; September 30, 1984, p. 6; April 8, 1990, p. 8; May 9, 1993, p. 2; October 9, 1994, p. 5.

West Coast Review of Books, September, 1979.

Yale Review, October, 1979.*

*   *   *

LYONS, James
  See LOEWEN, James W.

M

MACK, Maynard 1909-

PERSONAL: Born October 27, 1909, in Hillsdale, MI; son of Jesse Floyd and Pearl (Vore) Mack; married Florence Brocklebank, August 5, 1933; children: Prudence Allen (Mrs. T. Cuyler Young), Sara Bennett, Maynard. *Education:* Yale University, B.A., 1932, Ph.D., 1936. *Religion:* Episcopalian. *Avocational interests:* Gardening, photography.

ADDRESSES: Home—273 Willow St., New Haven, CT 06511. *Office*—No. 206, 305 Crown St., New Haven, CT 06511; and 1314 Yale Station, Yale University, New Haven, CT 06520.

CAREER: Yale University, New Haven, CT, instructor, 1936-40, assistant professor, 1940-45, associate professor, 1945-48, professor, 1948-65, Sterling Professor of English, 1965-78, became Sterling Professor emeritus, director of humanities division, 1962-64, chair of English department, 1965-68. Shakespeare Institute, associate director, 1953-62; New Haven Board of Education, vice president, 1954-59; University of Washington, Seattle, Walker-Ames Lecturer, 1956; "College English," consultant in comparative literature, 1961; University of Toronto, Alexander Lecturer, 1963; University of California, Berkeley, Beckman Visiting Professor, 1964-65; University of London, Lord Northcliffe Lecturer, 1972; National Humanities Institute, director, 1974-77; American Council on Education, member of committee on academic affairs; trustee of Hopkins Grammar School, Berkeley Divinity School, Shakespeare Association of America (president, 1976), and American Shakespeare Festival Theatre Association. Commentator in documentary film *Dying,* for WGBH (Boston).

MEMBER: International Shakespeare Association (vice-president, 1976-86), International Association of University Professors of English, Modern Humanities Research Association (member of advisory council, 1971—; president, 1984), American Academy of Arts and Sciences, Modern Language Association of America (president, 1970), Renaissance Society of America, Elizabethan Club, Malone Society, Phi Beta Kappa.

AWARDS, HONORS: Yale University prize for poems, 1932, for *For All Our Fathers, Gentlemen!,* and 1934, for *Mister Scoggins' Saturday Night;* Guggenheim fellow, 1943, 1965, and 1978; Ford faculty fellow, 1952-53; Fulbright senior research fellow, University of London, 1959-60; senior fellow, National Endowment for the Humanities, 1968-69; certificate of honor for "distinguished contributions to the humanities and to humanistic education," National Council of Teachers of English, 1970; fellow, Center for Advanced Study in the Behavioral Sciences, 1971-72; senior research fellow, Clark Library, Los Angeles, 1974, and Huntington Library, 1979-80; Wilbur Cross Award for outstanding contributions to the humanities in Connecticut, Connecticut Humanities Council, 1986; Christian Gauss Award, Phi Beta Kappa, and *Los Angeles Times* Book Prize, both 1986, for *Alexander Pope: A Life.* Honorary degrees include LL.D., Duke University, Kalamazoo College, University of Northern Michigan, Oberlin College, and Lawrence University, and D.H.L., Towson State University.

WRITINGS:

EDITOR

(And author of introduction and notes) Henry Fielding, *The History of the Adventures of Joseph Andrews and His Friend, Mr. Abraham Adams,* Rinehart (Boulder, CO), 1949, paperback edition published as *Joseph Andrews.*

(General editor) *English Masterpieces: An Anthology of Imaginative Literature from Chaucer to T. S. Eliot,* eight volumes, Prentice-Hall (Englewood Cliffs, NJ), 1950, 2nd edition, 1961.

Alexander Pope, *An Essay on Man*, Twickenham edition, Volume 3, part 1, Yale University Press (New Haven, CT), 1951, reprinted, Methuen (New York City), 1982.

(General editor, with others) *The Norton Anthology of World Masterpieces*, two volumes, Norton (New York City), 1956, revised edition, 1992, continental edition (non-English literature), 1962, enlarged continental edition, 1995.

Milton, Prentice-Hall, 1957, 2nd edition, 1961.

The Augustans, Prentice-Hall, 1957, 2nd edition, 1961.

(With Leonard Dean and William Frost) *Modern Poetry*, Prentice-Hall, 1958, 2nd edition, 1961.

William Shakespeare, *The Tragedy of Antony and Cleopatra*, Penguin (New York City), 1960, revised edition, 1970.

(And author of introduction and notes) *The Morgan and Houghton Library Manuscripts of Alexander Pope's "Essay on Man"* (Roxburghe Club), Oxford University Press (New York City), 1962.

Essential Articles for the Study of Alexander Pope, Archon Books (Hamden, CT), 1964, revised and enlarged edition, 1968.

(With Boynton) *Images of Man*, Prentice-Hall, 1964.

(And author of introduction and notes) Shakespeare, *The History of Henry IV: Part One*, New American Library (New York City), 1965.

(And author of introduction and notes) *The Poems of Alexander Pope: Translations of Homer*, Twickenham edition, Yale University Press, Volumes 7-8: *The Iliad*, 1967, Volumes 9-10: *The Odyssey*, 1967, index, 1969.

(With Ian Gregor) *Imagined Worlds: Essays on Some English Novels and Novelists in Honour of John Butt*, Barnes & Noble (New York City), 1968.

(And author of introduction and notes) Shakespeare, *The First Part of King Henry the Fourth*, Hayden Book (Rochelle Park, NJ), 1973.

(And author of introduction and notes) Shakespeare, *The Tragedy of Hamlet*, Hayden Book, 1973.

(And author of introduction and notes) Shakespeare, *The Tragedy of Julius Caesar*, Hayden Book, 1973.

(And author of introduction and notes) Shakespeare, *The Tragedy of Macbeth*, Hayden Book, 1973.

Contexts One: The Beggar's Opera, Shoe String (Hamden, CT), 1976.

William Kinsley, *Contexts Two: The Rape of the Lock*, Shoe String, 1979.

Rescuing Shakespeare, Oxford University Press, 1979.

(With George deForest Lord) *Poetic Traditions of the English Renaissance*, Yale University Press, 1982.

(And author of introduction and notes, and decipherer of manuscript text) *The Last and Greatest Art: Some Unpublished Poetical Manuscripts of Alexander Pope*, University of Delaware Press (East Brunswick, NJ), 1982.

Contexts Three: Absalom and Achitophel, Shoe String, 1983.

Also editor in chief of "Twentieth Century Views" essay series, Prentice-Hall, 1962—, and of "Twentieth Century Interpretations" series, Prentice-Hall, 1968—; coeditor in chief of "New Century Views," 1993—.

OTHER

For All Our Fathers, Gentlemen! (poem), Profile Press (New Haven), 1932.

Mister Scoggins' Saturday Night (poem), City Printing (New Haven), 1934.

King Lear in Our Time (three Beckman lectures given at University of California, 1964-65), University of California Press (Berkeley, CA), 1965.

(With Robert Whitney Boynton) *Introduction to the Poem*, Hayden Book, 1965, 2nd revised edition, 1972.

(With Boynton) *Introduction to the Short Story*, Hayden Book, 1965, 2nd revised edition, 1972.

(With Boynton) *Introduction to the Play*, Hayden Book, 1969, 2nd revised edition, 1976.

The Garden and the City: Retirement and Politics in the Later Poetry of Pope, 1731-1743, University of Toronto Press (Toronto), 1969.

(With Boynton) *Sounds and Silences: Poems for Performing*, Hayden Book, 1975.

(With Boynton) *Whodunits, Farces, and Fantasies: Ten Short Plays*, Hayden Book, 1976.

A History of Scroll and Key, 1842-1942, The Society (New Haven, CT), 1978.

(With James A. Winn) *Pope: Recent Essays by Several Hands*, Shoe String, 1980.

Collected in Himself: Essays Critical, Biographical, and Bibliographical on Pope and Some of His Contemporaries, University of Delaware Press, 1982.

Alexander Pope: A Life, Yale University Press, 1985.

The World of Alexander Pope: Exhibitions in the Beinecke Rare Book Library and the Yale Center for British Art in Honor of His 300th Birthday, Yale University Press, 1988.

Pros and Cons: Monologues on Several Occasions, [privately printed], 1989.

Everybody's Shakespeare Reflections, Chiefly on the Tragedies, University of Nebraska Press (Lincoln), 1993.

Contributor to collections, including *Pope and His Contemporaries*, edited by James L. Clifford and Louis A. Landa, Clarendon Press, 1949; *Jacobean Theatre*, edited by John Russell Brown and Bernard Harris, Edward Arnold, 1960, St. Martin's, 1961; *Shakespeare's Art: Seven Essays,* edited by Milton Crane, University of Chicago Press (Chicago, IL), 1973; *Augustan Worlds,* Leicester University Press, 1978; and *Evidence in Literary Scholarship,* edited by Rene Wellek and A. Ribeiro, Clarendon Press, 1979.

Member of editorial board, *Studies in English Literature,* 1962-75. Script writer and teacher for four films on *Hamlet,* Council for a Television Course in the Humanities, under the auspices of the Ford Foundation.

WORK IN PROGRESS: A children's story.

SIDELIGHTS: Maynard Mack has devoted a lifetime to the study of seventeenth- and eighteenth-century English literature, particularly the works of William Shakespeare and Alexander Pope. Indeed, many critics consider Mack the world's foremost Pope scholar, an author who is able to recreate "in richly imagined historical context the controversial figure of Alexander Pope, the most important poet of his time," in the words of *Chicago Tribune Book World* contributor Patricia Meyer Spacks. From 1951, when he edited Pope's *Essay on Man* for the prestigious Twickenham edition, to 1985, when he published *Alexander Pope: A Life,* Mack has concerned himself with assessments of the poet's works, both well-known and obscure, and with investigations of Pope's private life from remaining primary sources. In the *New Republic,* Ronald Paulson contends that as autobiographer and literary critic, Mack has "defended Pope against the image of a malicious 'monkey ladling boiling oil' on innocent victims by distinguishing the biographical Pope from the conventional 'satirist.' He defended him against the charge of being 'a classic of our prose' by showing how powerfully metaphoric and ironic, how polysemous and ambiguous, was the operation of the Popean couplet."

George Dimock of the *Yale Review* expresses admiration for Mack's 1967 volumes of *The Poems of Alexander Pope: Translations of Homer.* Praising Mack's "heroic task of editorship," the critic writes: "Now, after some fifteen years of effort by many hands, the experience of reading Pope's Homer as he meant to have it read is available to all." The critic commends Mack's introduction and notes that he "has been able to chase down all but a very few of Pope's vague, not to say lordly, references to other writers in his notes. There are more than four thousand of these and Mack writes that if he had to do it again he is not sure he would make the effort. If he means this, we can only be grateful that he has come through on his first attempt."

Mack's critical study *The Garden and the City: Retirement and Politics in the Later Poetry of Pope, 1731-1743* has drawn similar acclaim. "Most books fit into categories," notes a reviewer for *Spectator,* "but this one not readily."

The critic observes that while the volume resembles a handsome but superficial book suitable for adorning a coffee table, it actually offers much more than a glossy overview. "Mack adroitly interweaves much erudition with a little avowed speculation, so as at least to suggest that Pope's loving attention to his villa had its Palladian and indeed perhaps its Platonic overtones," writes the reviewer. "There is a beautiful completeness in the synthesis this book creates: in a certain sense, its varied learning comes out with something that is almost a poetic vision of Pope's last phase. This is indeed far from the coffee-table."

Alexander Pope: A Life, Mack's 1985 biography, won both the 1986 *Los Angeles Times* Book Prize and the Christian Gauss Award from Phi Beta Kappa. The work explores Pope's life and art from cradle to grave; *New York Times* correspondent John Gross calls it "the crowning achievement of a life that has been largely devoted to the poet." Gross also claims that the biography "bears witness to the ease with which [Mack] moves among 18th-century surroundings; it is the product of patient scholarship and undimmed affection." In the *Los Angeles Times Book Review,* John Hummel contends that Mack regrets the passing of Pope's age—when poets and writers were cultural heroes and significant political commentators. "He pictures Pope as one of the last poets who tried to conceive of themselves as integral to the workings of their society," Hummel writes, "poets who shared the concerns and the cultural preconceptions of the ruling class, who were consulted and whose opinions counted, and who translated a fundamentally social vision into a poetic language read and understood by those whose business was running the state." Paulson praises *Alexander Pope: A Life* for its "analysis of the poetry, which is as good as the biography and the history. Mack has distilled his critical as well as his textual findings into the larger unity of the writer's character." He finds that the book's greatest accomplishment, however, "is finally to make Pope an understandable human being as well as a great artist, as 'realized' as a character in a novel and yet plainly one of our half-dozen most important and, as Mack certainly proves, exemplary poets."

In addition to his duties as author and editor, Mack served as a professor of English at Yale University for more than forty years. Paulson observes that Mack's writings and lectures "established the poet 'Pope' who was read by students of the 1950s and 1960s," and his more recent works "opened up the submerged aspects of Pope that have been explored by students since." Hummel offers a similar opinion: "Wherever Pope is studied seriously and taught enthusiastically, it is often one of Mack's former students doing the teaching. Insofar as anyone under 50 reads Pope at all, their Pope is already likely to be Mack's Pope. This is Maynard Mack's real legacy."

Mack told *CA:* "I first engaged in a piece of 'serious' writing when I was chosen to give the address of welcome, followed by a topic more substantial, to my assembled seventh-grade classmates and their parents at one of those always-awkward parent-teacher meetings now blissfully forgotten by everyone concerned but me. The speech must have been stunning in the root sense, for when I got up to give it my mind went even blanker than is normal at that age, and I had to return to my seat—and the acute embarrassment of my parents. I have never since in my life been without a script. Not to be read from—a practice I deplore—but to buoy me up if I start to crash and ballast me down when I begin to float away. Thanks to the comforting presence of a script I got through my next piece of 'serious' writing, a high school valedictory, without a hitch.

"In due course I plunged into scholarly writing because that turned out to be my trade. It is a troubling trade with two built-in perils. One is that if you are at all self-aware, common sense may keep breaking in to tell you that it might be a kindness to your readers and your own reputation if you knocked off and went fishing. The other, if you are not self-aware, is that you will probably produce one of those amorphous masses of adipose tissue oozing with self-importance increasingly found these days in professional quarterlies and even the output of reputable academic presses.

"My own, possibly eccentric, conviction is that even the weariest material can be reawakened with a suitable application of blood, sweat, and tears, and that the first duty of 'scholarship,' at least in the literary-critical and literary-historical fields, is to be accessible to the general educated public as well as one's peers. No newcomer to the trade, however, should be unaware that in the current professional climate it is not as uncommon as it ought to be for hard-won clarity of exposition to be airily dismissed as shallowness of thought."

BIOGRAPHICAL/CRITICAL SOURCES:

BOOKS

Dictionary of Literary Biography, Volume 111: *American Literary Biographers, Second Series,* Gale (Detroit), 1992.

PERIODICALS

Atlantic Monthly, December, 1985.
Chicago Tribune Book World, February 9, 1986.
Globe and Mail (Toronto), June 14, 1986.
Los Angeles Times Book Review, November 24, 1985.
Nation, March 1, 1986.
New Haven Register, April 8, 1959.

New Republic, March 3, 1986.
New York Review of Books, May 12, 1966; March 13, 1986.
New York Times, February 14, 1986.
New York Times Book Review, March 2, 1986.
Sewanee Review, autumn, 1967.
Spectator, February 28, 1970; August 24, 1985.
Times (London), August 22, 1985.
Times Literary Supplement, August 25, 1966; December 7, 1967; May 15, 1969; April 30, 1970; May 6, 1983; April 13, 1984; September 13, 1985.
Washington Post Book World, February 9, 1986.
Yale Alumni Magazine, February, 1959.
Yale Review, winter, 1964; summer, 1967; autumn, 1968.

*   *   *

MACKAY, Claire 1930-

PERSONAL: Born December 21, 1930, in Toronto, Ontario, Canada; daughter of Grant McLaren (an accountant) and Bernice (a secretary and bereavement counselor; maiden name, Arland) Bacchus; married Jackson F. Mackay (an economist, chemical engineer, and jazz musician), September 12, 1952; children: Ian, Scott, Grant. *Education:* University of Toronto, B.A. (with honors), 1952; University of British Columbia, B.S.W., 1969; University of Manitoba, Certificate in Rehabilitation Counseling, 1971. *Avocational interests:* Bird-watching, collecting dictionaries.

ADDRESSES: Home and office—6 Frank Cres., Toronto, Ontario, Canada M6G 3K5.

CAREER: Polysar Corp., Sarnia, Ontario, library assistant in research department, 1952-55; Plains Hospital (now Wascana Hospital), Regina, Saskatchewan, medical social worker, 1969-71; United Steelworkers, Toronto, Ontario, research librarian, 1972-78; freelance researcher and writer, 1978—. Writer-in-the-School, John Wanless School, Toronto, 1986; Writer-in-the-Library, Toronto and Borough libraries, 1987. Trustee, judge, or juror for various literature and arts competitions. Consultant and editor, Houghton Mifflin Canada, 1986-91.

MEMBER: International PEN, International Board on Books for Young People (Canadian section), Canadian Authors Association, Writers Union of Canada, Canadian Society of Children's Authors, Illustrators, and Performers (CANSCAIP; founding member; secretary, 1977-79; president, 1979-81), Children's Book Centre (board member, 1985-89), Writers' Development Trust, Children's Literature Round Table of Toronto, Friends of the National Library of Canada, Town of York Historical Society.

AWARDS, HONORS: Writing grants from Ontario Arts Council, 1980, 1983, 1984, 1985, 1986 and 1989; second prize from *Toronto Star* short story contest, 1980, for "Important Message: Please Read"; Ruth Schwartz Foundation Award for best children's book, 1982; honorable mention, Children's Literature Prize competition, Canada Council, 1982; Canadian Authors Association, Vicky Metcalf Award, 1983, for body of work for children, and Vicky Metcalf Short Story Award, 1988, for "Marvin and Me and the Flies"; notable book selection, Canadian Library Association, 1987, for *Pay Cheques and Picket Lines: All about Unions in Canada,* and 1990, for *The Toronto Story;* Award of Excellence competition, Parenting Publications of America, honorable mention in column/regular feature category, 1989, and first prize in column/humor category, 1990; finalist in Mr. Christie Book Award, 1990 and City of Toronto Book Awards, 1991, both for *The Toronto Story;* Civic Award of Merit, City of Toronto, 1992.

WRITINGS:

JUVENILE

Mini-Bike Hero, Scholastic (New York City), 1974, revised edition, 1991.
Mini-Bike Racer, Scholastic, 1976, revised edition, 1991.
Exit Barney McGee, Scholastic, 1979, revised edition, 1992.
(With Marsha Hewitt) *One Proud Summer* (historical novel), Women's Educational Press, 1981.
Mini-Bike Rescue, Scholastic, 1982, revised edition, 1991.
The Minerva Program, James Lorimer, 1984, Houghton (Boston), 1992.
Pay Cheques and Picket Lines: All about Unions in Canada, Kids Can Press, 1987, revised edition, 1988.
The Toronto Story, Annick Press, 1988.
Touching All the Bases: Baseball for Kids of All Ages, illustrated by Bill Slavin, Boardwalk Books/Scholastic, 1994.
(With Jean Little) *Bats about Baseball,* illustrated by Kim LaFave, Viking (New York City), 1994.

OTHER

Contributor to *Canadian Writers' Guide,* and *Writers on Writing.* Contributor of articles, speeches, short stories, poetry and book reviews to periodicals, including *Canadian Children's Literature, Canadian Women's Studies, Chatelaine, Writers' Quarterly, Quill and Quire, Toronto Star,* and *Globe and Mail* (Toronto). Editor of *CANSCAIP News,* 1978-83, associate editor, 1983-85. Author of "Women's Words," a monthly feminist column in *Steel Labour,* 1975-78, and of regular column in *Kids Toronto,* 1986-93.

Some of Mackay's works have been published in French, Swedish, Japanese, and Norwegian.

ADAPTATIONS: One Proud Summer has been filmed for Les Productions Barbara Schrier, Inc., Montreal, Quebec; a film of *Pay Cheques and Picket Lines: All about Unions in Canada* is in production.

WORK IN PROGRESS: A novel about a radical family in the Great Depression.

SIDELIGHTS: Claire Mackay told *CA:* "My entry into the field of writing (though a secret dream for years) came about largely by fluke. My youngest son nagged me into writing the book *Mini-Bike Hero.* It altered my life profoundly. I'm still in a bemused state, but now thoroughly hooked on writing.

"One of the great—and occasionally the only—rewards in writing for children is the fan mail from kids to whom you're the best writer who ever lived. I've accumulated many letters, answered all, and find them a powerful antidote to a bad review! I regard each letter as an honor greater than any prize awarded by adult peers and judges and as a gift of confidence when my own has wavered badly. Someday I hope to write that one excellent book that will merit that honor and that gift."

BIOGRAPHICAL/CRITICAL SOURCES:

BOOKS

Aitken, Johan L., *Masques of Morality: Females in Fiction,* Woman's Press, 1987, pp. 120-23.
Moss, John, editor, *A Reader's Guide to the Canadian Novel,* McClelland & Stewart (Toronto), 2nd edition, 1987, pp. 446, 451-52.

PERIODICALS

Canadian Literature, fall, 1993, p. 172.
CANSCAIP News, September, 1982.
Classroom, March/April, 1986.
Emergency Librarian, November-December, 1987, pp. 59-64.
Quill & Quire, April, 1994, p. 38.
Sunday Star, August 17, 1986.
Toronto Star, June 23, 1984.
Writers' Quarterly, May, 1986.

OTHER

Claire Mackay: Meet the Author Series (filmstrip, cassette, and videotape), Mead Sound Filmstrip and Children's Book Centre (Toronto), 1985.

MACKEY, Mary 1945-

PERSONAL: Born January 21, 1945, in Indianapolis, IN; daughter of John Edward (a physician) and Jean (an art museum director; maiden name, McGinness) Mackey. *Education:* Radcliffe College, B.A. (magna cum laude), 1966; University of Michigan, M.A., 1967, Ph.D., 1970. *Avocational interests:* Cooking, swimming, hiking, travel.

ADDRESSES: Home—P.O. Box 8524, Berkeley, CA 94707. *Office*—Department of English, California State University, 6000 J St., Sacramento, CA 95819. *Agent*—Barbara Lowenstein, 250 West 57th St., New York City, NY 10107.

CAREER: Indianapolis Star, Indianapolis, IN, feature writer, 1965; California State University, Sacramento, assistant professor, 1972-76, associate professor, 1976-80, professor of English, 1980—, writer in residence.

MEMBER: PEN American Center West (president, 1989-92), Feminist Writers Guild (founder and member of national steering committee), Media Alliance, Writers Guild of America.

AWARDS, HONORS: Woodrow Wilson fellowship, 1966-67; Exceptional Merit Service award, California State University, Sacramento, 1984.

WRITINGS:

Immersion (novella), Shameless Hussy Press (Berkeley, CA), 1972.

Split Ends (poems), Ariel Press (Columbus, OH), 1974.

One Night Stand (poems), Effie's Press (Emeryville, CA), 1977.

(Editor with Mary MacArthur) *Chance Music* (anthology) Gallimaufry (Cambridge, MA), 1977.

Skin Deep (poems), Gallimaufry, 1978.

McCarthy's List (novel), Doubleday (New York City), 1979.

The Last Warrior Queen (novel), Putnam (New York City), 1983.

A Grand Passion (novel), Simon & Schuster (New York City), 1986.

The Kindness of Strangers (novel), Simon & Schuster, 1988.

Season of Shadows (novel), Bantam (New York City), 1991.

The Year the Horses Came (novel), Harper (San Francisco), 1993.

The Horses at the Gate (novel; sequel to *The Year the Horses Came*), Harper, 1996.

Also author of *Silence* (screenplay), 1974; *As Old As You Feel* (television documentary), Columbia Broadcasting System, 1978; *Dark Oceans* (screenplay), 1980; *The Dear Dance of Eros* (poems). Contributor to periodicals, including *New Age Journal, Saturday Evening Post, Yellow Silk, Ms., New American Review,* and *Harvard Advocate.*

Mackey's works have been translated into eleven foreign languages including Japanese, Hebrew, and Finnish.

SIDELIGHTS: Mary Mackey told *CA:* "While my poetry has mainly centered around the traditional lyric themes of love, death, and nature, my novels have ranged from the Midwestern United States to neolithic Europe, from comedy to tragedy." Her first novel, *McCarthy's List,* is a dark comedy about a paranoid schizophrenic woman wrongly sentenced to death. It details the wrongs done her by various men in her life and suggests, according to *New York Times Book Review* writer Michael Malone, that at certain times madness might be "a perfectly rational adjustment to an insane situation." And while *Los Angeles Times Book Review* critic Christopher Rauber does not share in the author's sense of humor—"Easy targets abound, and laughter is expected . . . [but] the intensity and wit of true satire are absent"—Malone finds Mackey's imagination "inventive" and praises her "crisp style that only occasionally trips over its own nimbleness."

BIOGRAPHICAL/CRITICAL SOURCES:

PERIODICALS

Los Angeles Times Book Review, December 9, 1979; June 12, 1983.

New York Times Book Review, October 14, 1979, pp. 15, 28.

*　　　*　　　*

MADSEN, Richard (Paul) 1941-

PERSONAL: Born April 2, 1941, in Alameda, CA; son of Harold Paul (a steel foundry worker) and Gazella (a homemaker; maiden name, Matjasic) Madsen; married Judith Rosselli (a teacher), January 12, 1974. *Education:* Maryknoll College, Glen Ellyn, IL, B.A., 1963; Maryknoll Seminary, Ossining, NY, B.D., 1967, M.Th., 1986; Harvard University, M.A. (Asian studies), 1972, Ph.D., 1977. *Politics:* Democrat. *Religion:* Roman Catholic.

ADDRESSES: Home—5521 Dalen Ave., San Diego, CA 92122. *Office*—Department of Sociology, University of California, San Diego, La Jolla, CA 92093.

CAREER: Ordained Roman Catholic priest, 1968; Maryknoll missioner in Taiwan, 1968-71; left priesthood, 1974; Harvard University, Cambridge, MA, lecturer in sociology, 1977-78; University of California, San Diego, La Jolla, assistant professor, 1978-83, associate professor, 1983-85, professor of sociology, 1985—, chairman of Chinese studies program, 1984-88.

MEMBER: American Sociological Association, Association of Asian Studies.

AWARDS, HONORS: C. Wright Mills Award, Society for the Study of Social Problems, 1985, for *Morality and Power in a Chinese Village;* current interest book award, *Los Angeles Times,* 1985, and Association of Logos Bookstores Book Award, 1986, both for *Habits of the Heart: Individualism in American Life.*

WRITINGS:

(With Anita Chan and Jonathan Unger) *Chen Village: The Recent History of a Peasant Community in Mao's China,* University of California Press (Berkeley), 1984, revised and expanded edition published as *Chen Village under Mao and Deng,* 1992.

Morality and Power in a Chinese Village, University of California Press, 1984.

(With Robert N. Bellah, William M. Sullivan, Ann Swidler, and Steven M. Tipton) *Habits of the Heart: Individualism in American Life,* University of California Press, 1985.

(With Bellah, Sullivan, Swidler, and Tipton) *Individualism and Commitment in American Life: A Habits of the Heart Reader,* Harper (New York City), 1987.

(Editor with Perry Link and Paul Pickowicz) *Unofficial China,* Westview (Boulder, CO), 1989.

(With Bellah, Sullivan, Swidler, and Tipton) *The Good Society,* Knopf (New York City), 1991.

China and the American Dream: A Moral Inquiry, University of California Press, 1995.

WORK IN PROGRESS: The World of God: Catholicism and the Civil Society in China, a study of the Catholic Church in contemporary China, with an analysis of the contribution Catholicism is making to social cohesion and fragmentation.

SIDELIGHTS: In *Chen Village: The Recent History of a Peasant Community in Mao's China* Anita Chan, Richard Madsen, and Jonathan Unger look at the effect of the Chinese Communist Party's continuously changing policies—from the mid-1960s through the early 1980s—on the inhabitants of the southern Chinese village of Chen. Based on interviews conducted in Hong Kong with village emigres, the study reveals how the Cultural Revolution eroded rural productivity and collective cooperation and helps to explain why the Deng Xiaoping leadership has dramatically decollectivized much of Chinese society. Reviewing the work for the *New York Times Book Review,* Merle Goldman pointed out that "the absence of official constraints" in the Hong Kong interviews provides "a richer, more in-depth view of Chinese society." The critic continued: " 'Chen Village' . . . depict[s] in rich detail the background against which reforms are being carried out. . . . Although the authors . . . were unable to deal with the social implications of the economic reforms of the Deng Xiaoping leadership, their [book helps] us . . . appreciate the magnitude of what is being attempted."

Madsen told *CA:* "Much of my education was in Catholic seminaries, where I studied Latin and Greek and Thomistic philosophy in preparation for life as a Maryknoll missionary priest. After I was ordained I was sent to Taiwan, where I learned to speak fluent Chinese—and became both fascinated by the culture and politics of modern Asia and deeply confused by the inability of my religious training to make any sense out of that culture and politics. Disillusioned, I left the priesthood and went to graduate school in Asian studies and sociology at Harvard. My writing since has been a way for me to understand human realities that my earlier religious training had rendered obscure—and to link that new understanding with the philosophical and religious quests of my earlier life. Thus, my books on China not only analyze the roles of Marxism and Confucianism in that society but also attempt to dramatize the moral dilemmas created in the lives of ordinary people by the clash between these different world views. And my books on America, *Habits of the Heart* and *The Good Society,* probe the tension between individualism and commitment in American morality.

"I have recently attempted to combine my interests in China and America by writing a book on the moral bases of U.S.-China relations: *China and the American Dream: A Moral Inquiry.* I hope that this book will help to stimulate public conversations on both sides of the Pacific on how to search for justice and peace in the frightening new world disorder that seems to be upon us. Saint Thomas Aquinas once said that hope is a divine virtue, optimism a human vice. In that spirit, I have tried in my books to engender hopefulness, though I am not optimistic for the short term prospects of peace and justice in most of the world."

BIOGRAPHICAL/CRITICAL SOURCES:

PERIODICALS

New York Times Book Review, October 7, 1984.
Washington Post Book World, July 20, 1986.

*   *   *

MAEHLQVIST, (Karl) Stefan 1943-

PERSONAL: Born August 7, 1943, in Nykoeping, Sweden; son of Alexis (a bath attendant) and Asta (a clerk; maiden name, Persson) Maehlqvist; married Karin Johannisson (a university lecturer), July 26, 1967 (divorced, 1990); children: Andreas Sergej, Aksel Sebastian. *Education:* University of Uppsala, B.A., 1967, Ph.D., 1977. *Avo-*

cational interests: "I went through a whole lot of avocational interests in my youth and suppose I left them there."

ADDRESSES: Home—Haellbygatan 32 B, S-752 28 Uppsala, Sweden. *Office*—Schloss Westerwinkel D-59387 Ascheberg, Germany. *Agent*—Foreign Rights' Manager, Raben & Sjoegren, Box 45022, S-1403, Stockholm 45, Sweden.

CAREER: Early in career worked as an actor; University of Uppsala, Uppsala, Sweden, assistant, 1969-73, research assistant, 1974-76, lecturer in comparative literature, 1978-93, associate professor, 1994—; Swedish Institute for Children's Books, Stockholm, information secretary, 1976-78; author of books for children.

MEMBER: Swedish Union of Authors (secretary of children's literature section, 1978-85; board member, 1983-93).

WRITINGS:

Boecker foer Svenska barn 1870-1950, Gidlunds, 1977.
Biggles i sverige (a study of the writings of W. E. Johns; title means "Biggles in Sweden"), Gidlunds, 1983.
Den andra roesten (title means "The Second Voice"), Haber, 1984.
(Editor) *Foerfattaren fran Fattigmannagatan. En bok om Harry Kullman* (title means "Author from Poor Man's Street: A Book about Harry Kullman"), Raben & Sjoegren, 1989.
Barnboken i braennpunkten (title means "Children's Books in Focus: Landings in the Critical Debate on Children's Literature in Sweden after World War II"), Litteratur och samhaelle (Uppsala), 1992.
Kaos i tiden. En laesning av Alan Garners Red Shift (title means "Chaos in Time: A Reading of Alan Garner's Red Shift"), Haber, 1992.

FOR CHILDREN

Inte farligt pappa, krokodilerna klarar jag, illustrations by Tord Nygren, Raben & Sjoegren, 1977, translation by author and Margaret McElderry published as *I'll Take Care of the Crocodiles,* Atheneum, 1978.
Kom in i min natt, kom in i min droem, illustrations by Nygren, Raben & Sjoegren, 1978, translation by Anthea Bell published as *Come into My Night, Come into My Dream,* Pepper Press, 1981.
Drakberget (title means "Dragon's Mountain"), illustrations by Nygren, Raben & Sjoegren, 1981.
Apan i arken (title means "The Ape in the Ark"), illustrations by Pia Forsberg, Raben & Sjoegren, 1982.
Ett hart paket (title means "A Hard Parcel"), Raben & Sjoegren, 1983.
Nattens svarta flagga (title means "The Black Flag of Night"), AWE/Gebers, 1985.

Ga pa stenar (title means "Walk on Stones"), AWE/Gebers, 1986.
Jag goer som jag vill—och lite till (title means "I Make What I Want—And a Little More"), Norstedts, 1988.

Author of teleplays for Swedish television, including "Ram tam tagger," a series of four pantomimes, aired in 1970-71, and "Circus tagger," a series of three programs, aired in 1972. Author of more than two hundred "Boktipset," short book promotions for television, aired beginning in 1976. Children's book critic and translator, *Dagens Nyheter* (newspaper), 1973—. Contributor of essays on children's literature and children's authors to periodicals, including *Barn och Kultur* and *De skriver foer barn och ungdom.*

SIDELIGHTS: Stefan Maehlqvist told *CA:* "I came into children's books through criticism and research. My theoretical background was well grounded before I suddenly, rather unintentionally, found myself in practice. A story came upon me while I was trying to keep awake for a nighttime work session, waiting for my boy to fall asleep. It came out in two hours, and I revised it by changing one word." For his latest book, "this one sentence came to me: 'As Arman went out of his house this morning heaven fell down over his head.' I got curious and wrote a little story called *I Make What I Want—And a Little More.*"

Maehlqvist continued: "My first three children's books, in collaboration with artist Tord Nygren, now form a thematic trilogy, 'excursions from a room.' The first is a daydream at bedtime, with a humorous slice of wish fulfillment; the second is a nightmare with streams of dark fantasy; the third contains a historical setting, and it enters into a pair of parallel fairy tales. I hope that my stories leave the door open to a wider social context.

"In general, the text for many picture books is, for my taste, much too simple, pedagogical, and idyllic. Picture books are usually read by a grownup to a preschool child. They are in a unique situation of direct communication—I try to make use of that, working with text and pictures on many levels. As a boy, I wrote and directed films, and later I went into acting. So dialogue and visual sensuality are of great importance to my writing. Some layers of meaning may be hidden from the child but engage the adult reader. My books are meant to reach these two readers at the same time. Unfortunately, these textual overtones are lost in the English translations, where I have found a very conservative and anxious attitude still very much alive.

"Nygren makes the same congenial references in his pictures that I make in my text, although the relationship between the two is different in each of the three parts of the trilogy. In *I'll Take Care of the Crocodiles,* the scenes take an active part in the telling of the story; things left out of the text are acted out visually. In *Come into My Night,*

Come into My Dream, every scene tries to give a new emotional response by the use of a different dominant color. In *Dragon's Mountain,* the pictures differ according to the historical setting of the story. A tale about a medieval knight is illustrated with imitations of woodcuts, and the next tale about early industrial mining is illustrated with xylographs.

"Creative work for me means a lot of brooding about, collecting little pieces here and there, until it finally bursts out in fairly rapid writing sessions. But never again have I been so lucky as with my first story!

"Every new book is a new adventure for me, not only in the sense that I produce a new story—I try to find a new scheme for the story as such. *Walk on Stones* is a novel for young adults where narration collapses in broken images. It had to be done that way in the eye of a new world picture as drawn by quantum mechanics. It's a meeting of stones (experiences) picked up by the I (subjective filter). The centre of the book contains a fictional discussion between Albert Einstein and Niels Bohr in front of the dead Victor Frankenstein. I don't like to lead the reader by the hand, I like to open up a conversation."

BIOGRAPHICAL/CRITICAL SOURCES:

PERIODICALS

Bonniers Litterara Magasin, Number 4, 1980.
Dagens Nyheter, November 11, 1982.
Opsis Kalopsis, Number 2, 1987.

*   *   *

MAHLER, Gregory S. 1950-

PERSONAL: Born August 12, 1950, in Palo Alto, CA; son of Irwin (a college professor) and Eleanor (Schwartz) Mahler; married Marjorie Ward, August 18, 1973; children: Alden, Darcy (daughters). *Education:* Oberlin College, B.A. (cum laude), 1972; Duke University, M.A., 1974, Ph.D., 1976.

ADDRESSES: Home—404 Country Club Rd., Oxford, MS 38655. *Office*—Department of Political Science, University of Mississippi, University, MS 38677.

CAREER: Metropolitan State College, Denver, CO, 1977, member of faculty, 1977-78; University of Vermont, Burlington, assistant professor, 1978-83, associate professor of political science, 1983-90; University of Mississippi, Oxford, professor and chair, Department of Political Science, 1990—. Visiting scholar, Commonwealth Parliamentary Association Headquarters Secretariat, Palace of Westminster, London, England, 1984-85; visiting instructor at Duke University, 1986-88.

MEMBER: American Political Science Association, Association for Canadian Studies in the United States, Association for Israel Studies, Middle East Studies Association.

AWARDS, HONORS: Fulbright-Hays dissertation fellow, 1974-75; Canadian Studies fellow, Duke University, 1975-76; Faculty enrichment grant, Government of Canada, 1981, 1984; Bush Foundation scholar in residence, Canadian Politics, Bemidji State College, Bemidji, MI, 1983; Faculty research grant, Government of Canada, 1985, 1988, 1992; Organization of American States research grant (to six Caribbean nations), 1986-88; Fulbright American Republics Program, research grant (to six Caribbean nations), 1988; Academy of Sciences of the U.S.S.R. Institute for the Study of the U.S.A. and Canada, visiting scholar, 1989; Peoples' Republic of China, Chinese Association for Canadian Studies, guest scholar, 1990; National Council on U.S.-Arab Relations, Malone Fellowship for Arab and Islamic Studies, travel grant (to United Arab Emirates/Bahrain), 1991; Government of Israel, travel grant (to Jerusalem), 1992; Gouvernement du Quebec, Quebec Studies grant, 1992; U. S. Information Agency U. S. Speakers Program speaker in Mauritania, Liberia, Ivory Coast, and Senegal, 1993; International Council for Canadian Studies Programme for International Research Linkages research grant, 1994.

WRITINGS:

The Knesset: Parliament in the Israeli Political System, Fairleigh Dickinson University Press (New Brunswick, NJ), 1981.
Readings on the Israeli Political System, University Press of America (Lanham, MD), 1982.
Comparative Politics: An Institutional and Cross-National Approach, Schenkman (Cambridge, MA), 1983, 3rd edition, Prentice-Hall (Englewood Cliffs, NJ), 1995.
Bibliography of Israeli Politics, Westview Press (Boulder, CO), 1985.
New Dimensions of Canadian Federalism, Fairleigh Dickinson University Press, 1987.
Contemporary Canadian Politics: An Annotated Bibliography, 1970-1987, Greenwood Press (Westport, CT), 1988.
The Israeli Political System: Government and Politics in a Maturing State, Harcourt (New York City), 1989.
Contemporary Canadian Politics: An Annotated Bibliography, 1987-1993, Greenwood Press, 1995.

CO-EDITOR (WITH OTHERS UNLESS NOTED)

Canadian Politics 90/91, Dushkin Publishing (Guilford, CT), 1989.
(Editor) *Israel after Begin,* State University of New York Press, 1990.
Canadian Politics 91/92, Dushkin Publishing, 1991.

Canadian Politics 92/93, Dushkin Publishing, 1993.
Israel at the Crossroads, I. B. Taurus Press, 1994.
Israel in the Nineties, University of Florida Press, 1995.

WORK IN PROGRESS: Caribbean Legislatures: Democratic Politics in Small Settings, expected completion date, December, 1995.

*   *   *

MALOUF, (George Joseph) David   1934-

PERSONAL: Surname is pronounced "Ma-*louf*"; born March 20, 1934, in Brisbane, Queensland, Australia; son of George and Welcome (Mendoza) Malouf. *Education:* University of Queensland, B.A. (with honors), 1954. *Politics:* Socialist.

ADDRESSES: Home—53 Myrtle St., Chippendale, New South Wales 2008, Australia. *Agent*—Rogers, Coleridge and White, 20 Powis Mews, London W11, England; and Barbara Mobbs, P.O. Box 126, Edgecliff, New South Wales 2027, Australia.

CAREER: University of Queensland, Brisbane, Australia, assistant lecturer in English, 1955-57; St. Anselm's College, Birkenhead, Cheshire, England, schoolmaster, 1962-68; University of Sydney, Sydney, Australia, lecturer in English, 1968-77. Member of the Literature Board of the Australia Council, 1972-74.

AWARDS, HONORS: Grace Leven Prize for Poetry and Australian Literature Society Gold Medal, both 1974, and James Cook University of North Queensland Award from the Foundation for Australian Literary Studies, 1975, all for *Neighbours in a Thicket: Poems;* Australian Council fellowship, 1978; New South Wales Premier's Fiction Award, 1979, for *An Imaginary Life; The Age* Book of the Year Award and *The Age* award for fiction, both 1982, both for *Fly Away Peter;* Victorian Premier's Award, 1985, for *Antipodes;* New South Wales Premier's award for drama, 1987, for *Blood Relations;* Miles Franklin Award, Commonwealth Prize for Fiction, and Prix Femina Etranger, all 1991, for *The Great World; Los Angeles Times* Book Prize for fiction and Booker Prize nomination, both 1994, for *Remembering Babylon.*

WRITINGS:

(Contributor) *Four Poets: David Malouf, Don Maynard, Judith Green, Rodney Hall,* Cheshires, 1962.
Bicycle and Other Poems, University of Queensland Press (St. Lucia, Australia), 1970, published as *The Year of the Foxes and Other Poems,* Braziller (New York City), 1979.
(Co-editor) *We Took Their Orders and Are Dead: An Anti-War Anthology,* Ure Smith, 1971.

Neighbours in a Thicket: Poems, University of Queensland Press, 1974.
Johnno (novel), University of Queensland Press, 1975, Braziller, 1978.
(Editor) *Gesture of a Hand* (anthology of Australian poetry), Holt (New South Wales), 1975.
Poems, 1975-1976, Prism (Sydney, Australia), 1976.
An Imaginary Life (novel), Braziller, 1978.
(With Katharine Brisbane and R. F. Brissenden) *New Currents in Australian Writing,* Angus & Robertson (North Ryde, New South Wales), 1978.
Wild Lemons (poems), Angus & Robertson, 1980.
First Things Last (poems), University of Queensland Press, 1981.
Selected Poems, Angus & Robertson, 1981.
Child's Play [and] *The Bread of Time to Come* (novellas), Braziller, 1981, *The Bread of Time to Come* published as *Fly Away Peter,* Chatto & Windus (London), 1982.
Child's Play [and] "Eustace" [and] "The Prowler," Chatto & Windus, 1982.
Harland's Half Acre (novel), Knopf (New York City), 1984.
Twelve Edmondstone Street (memoir), Chatto & Windus, 1985.
Antipodes (short stories), Chatto & Windus, 1985.
Blood Relations (play), Currency Press, 1988.
David Malouf: Johnno, Short Stories, Poems, Essays, and Interview (selected works), edited by James Tulip, University of Queensland Press, 1990.
The Great World (historical novel), Chatto & Windus, 1990, Pantheon (New York City), 1990.
Selected Poems, Angus & Robertson, 1991.
Poems 1959-89, University of Queensland Press, 1992.
Remembering Babylon (historical novel), Pantheon, 1993.

Also author of opera librettos, including *Voss,* 1986; *La Mer de Glace,* 1991; and *Baa Baa Black Sheep,* 1993. Contributor to periodicals, including *The Australian, New York Review of Books, Poetry Australia, Southerly,* and *Sydney Morning Herald.*

SIDELIGHTS: A prize-winning poet before he published his first novel, David Malouf was born and raised in Australia, lived for some years in Italy, and now resides in his native Australia. Many critics believe Malouf writes as comfortably about cosmopolitan Europe as he does about his childhood home, and the author's favored themes and literary devices also traverse his poetry and prose. Reviewers have praised the vivid, sensuous descriptions and evocative settings of his works, throughout which Malouf weaves an awareness of the distinct cultures and the diverse characters within them. Malouf often combines the past, present, and future to create an all-inclusive, multidirectional point of reference, is interested in dualities that repel and compel, and searches for perfect unities with nature.

Fleur Adcock commented in a *Times Literary Supplement* review of Malouf's 1980 poetry collection, *First Things Last,* that the author "has a strong visual consciousness with a sense of joyful absorption in the natural world which makes the overworked word 'celebration' irresistible." Malouf revels in nature's various forms—from paradisiacal gardens to wilderness, from life in the ocean to wild lemon trees—in attempts to harmonize with nature. For example, in "The Crab Feast" the poet searches for crabs so that he can ingest, embody, and join with them. Music harmonizes with nature as well; and in the poem "An die Musik," man, music, and nature integrate: "We might have known it always: music / is the landscape we move through in our dreams," Adcock quoted the poet.

In *First Things Last* Malouf also experiments with time, creating a present contemporaneously with the past and future. As Adcock explained: "In an elegy for his father he writes of the dead being buried in the living and looking out through their eyes, as do the not yet born." And in the poem "Deception Bay" Malouf writes of his ancestors viewing the future through the eyes of the present generation. Malouf also experiments with prose-poetry and other free verse forms, yet he generally emphasizes his content more than technique. Critics have called his poetry mature, elegant, fine, and lavish, and have lauded Malouf for his sensitivity and emotion. Adcock concluded that "Malouf's powerful imagination allows a certain amount of surrealism. . . . [He] can be playful . . . but he is a serious poet concerned with serious things."

Malouf's first novel, *Johnno,* was published in 1975. Reviewing the work for the *Times Literary Supplement,* Frank Pike commended the author for his resonant depiction of place and atmosphere: Malouf creates "an unaffected and densely detailed evocation of a particular way of life at a particular time; urban, unspectacular." According to Pike, the novel commences "with a convincing account, finely written without fine writing, of childhood and early adolescence" in suburban Brisbane during World War II. The story follows the rocky friendship of the honorable but impressionable narrator, Dante, and Johnno, an intriguing, disturbed, fatherless youth. Dante is attracted to Johnno's fondness for carousing and heavy drinking and tries unsuccessfully to mimic his behavior. After Johnno departs for the Congo the youths meet again in Paris, but by now the narrator is more wary of his old hero's unstable behavior. Afterward in Australia, Dante receives news of Johnno's death by drowning, an event that confirms Dante's early suspicions that Johnno was suicidal. Dante then receives an angst-ridden note from Johnno written prior to his death, in which he cites Dante's emotional indifference and restraint as reasons for his suicide.

In 1979 Malouf was awarded the New South Wales Premier's prize for fiction for his second novel, *An Imaginary Life,* a fictionalized account of the ancient Roman poet Ovid's mature life. From the sketchy information available on the Roman's later years, Malouf created a life for the poet as he imagined it to have transpired after Ovid was exiled from Rome in 8 A.D. The circumstances which led to Ovid's banishment are unclear. Many historians hold that the poet was banished as punishment for ridiculing the Emperor Augustus's wife Livia in his just-completed epic poem "Metamorphoses," others believe he was exiled for arranging a lovers' tryst for Augustus's granddaughter Julia, and still more suspect it was Ovid's writing of the intemperate "Art of Love" at a time when Augustus was calling for virtue in Roman society. Nonetheless, Malouf fills in the blanks to create what Katha Pollitt, writing for the *New York Times Book Review,* deemed "an extraordinary novel" and "a work of unusual intelligence and imagination, at once sensuous and quirky, full of surprising images and intriguing insights."

Malouf depicts an aging Ovid who was once at the heart of pleasure-seeking Roman society but is now forced to the desolate reaches of the known world. He settles at Tomis, a grim village of one hundred huts in modern Romania on the Black Sea, whose barren land supports vegetation the poet cannot even identify. Malouf makes such a setting seemingly tangible in *An Imaginary Life,* prompting Pollitt to comment: "Mr. Malouf's [prose] is indeed fine: a spare yet evocative English that captures both the bleak monochromes of Tomis and the sunny humanized landscape of Ovid's remembered Italy, without ever losing the distinctive voice, now caustic, now dreamlike, in which Ovid tells his own story." Kate Eldred, writing for *New Republic,* asserted: "Malouf shows us the mind of a great wordsmith struck dumb in his surroundings trying to adjust to a new life." Carole Horn, reviewing the novel for the *Washington Post,* pointed out that "the story works on emotional and philosophical planes. Malouf maintains a fine consistency of tone, and his language is hauntingly lovely." Pollitt agreed, stating that *An Imaginary Life* is "one of those rare books you end up underlining and copying out into notebooks and reading out loud to your friends." Eldred, impressed with Malouf's manipulation of time, remarked that the author "interplays the historical present, [which is] clumsy in English, with a narrative present and an anecdotal past tense, interweaving them so gracefully that the techniques aren't obvious, only the aftertaste of grandeur in certain passages, of a facile rhythm in others."

Harland's Half Acre, Malouf's 1984 novel, also garnered critical praise. It opens with protagonist Frank Harland living with his brothers and bemused father at Killarney, the remainder of what was once an expansive farm in the Australian countryside. Jim Crace, in a review for the *Times Literary Supplement,* commended Malouf for his polished descriptions: the "opening chapters are . . . stunningly artful evocations of Queensland and Queenslanders. The Harland acres ('lush country but of the green, subtropical kind, with sawmills in untidy paddocks') are squandered with 'extravagant folly' through drink, gambling, debt and neglect." Hearing fantastic tales of the glory of Killarney spun by his father, Frank dreams to restore the farm to its original grandeur as a gift to his family. Jonathan Yardley in *Book World* called *Harland's Half Acre* "a rewarding book . . . long on intelligence and feeling" and commended the author for writing "a meditation on the subtle, mysterious relationship between life and art. . . . He has written it with great sensitivity."

Malouf 's 1982 novella, *Fly Away Peter,* for which he won the Book of the Year Award and a fiction award from the Australian literary journal *The Age,* also commences in Australia. After spending twelve years in England, protagonist Ashley Crowther returns to a thousand-acre plantation he inherited in his native Queensland, unsure of what to do with it or his future. Already inhabiting this land is Jim Saddler, a young man who is content with a simple existence among nature observing the numerous species of birds that migrate to the swamps there. Ashley decides to make the estate a wildlife reserve and hires Jim to manage it. They befriend a nature photographer, Imogen Harcourt, and the three settle into a serene life until World War I disrupts the calm.

The men enlist and at the front encounter the horrors of war. "The scenes in the trenches," wrote Alan Brownjohn in the *Times Literary Supplement,* "are much the finest in *Fly Away Peter:* men passing down the slope from fields where peasants continue to till the ground and birds continue to sing, to enter that labyrinth of mud, rats and twitching bodies from which they will never return, or never return the same." Ashley, far removed from the individualistic living practiced at the plantation, becomes disillusioned, concluding that men are as cogs in machines—indistinct and replaceable. Imogen, still in Australia, thinks the fighting is absurd and senseless and concludes that a purpose is not necessary in life. David Guy in *Book World* wrote: "She understands that the life of men should be as Jim's once was, like the life that the birds lead. 'A life wasn't *for* anything. It simply was.' " And Jim reacts to the war by cultivating a tranquil plot of land in an attempt to reclaim the innocence he left behind in Australia.

Malouf made Italy the setting for his 1982 novella *Child's Play,* a first-person narrative told by a young terrorist preparing to assassinate an internationally acclaimed author.

Times Literary Supplement reviewer Peter Kemp described the work as "surreally hard-edged," adding that "the world *Child's Play* projects is one where details have a hallucinatory vividness and patterns stand out with stark clarity: only significance remains creepily opaque." Guy stressed that Malouf 's depiction of the brilliant, influential writer is "masterful" and that Malouf again employs the concept of a simultaneous past, present, and future. Guy explained that in his preparation the terrorist envisions the near and distant future and his own place in history: "Already he sees the photographs of the piazza where the assassination will take place as those of a historic site; he imagines it in newsprint and news photograph, media which distort and deaden an event but also in some ways create it; he sees himself as the hand of fate toward which a life's work has been leading, as a figure in the writer's biography." *Child's Play* prompted the critic to conclude: "Malouf is something of a primitive narrator, rough around the edges, but he is also a deeply serious writer, not to be taken up lightly . . . [and] a genuine artist."

The two short stories bound with *Child's Play,* "Eustace" and "The Prowler," take place in Australia. They, like *Child's Play* and *Johnno,* focus on society's fascination with elusive, sordid characters and demonstrate the author's preoccupation with the interaction of opposites. "Conformity, community, security are repeatedly set against anarchy, loneliness, danger," Peter Kemp observed in the *Times Literary Supplement.* "Obsessively, [Malouf 's] work juxtaposes order and disturbance, light and dark. Those positives and negatives can unexpectedly change places. And always in Malouf 's stories the powerful attraction between seemingly opposed poles is used to generate some shock effects." Also focusing on disparities is Malouf 's 1985 collection of thirteen short stories, *Antipodes.* The tales follow new Australian immigrants and the problems they encounter in their attempts to assimilate into a new culture, and examine the tribulations of Australians in Europe as well.

Malouf 's 1990 *The Great World,* an epic spanning some seventy years, examines the intertwined lives of two Australians, Vic Curran and Digger Keen, in a structure "juxtaposing scenes of past and future as a kind of continuous present," noted Ray Willbanks in *World Literature Today.* The two men are first drawn together in 1942 as prisoners of the Japanese during World War II, surviving three and a half years of brutal captivity together in Malaya and Thailand, assigned to a workgang laboring in construction of the infamous Bangkok-Rangoon Railway, and encamped in an abandoned amusement park, "The Great World." *New York Review of Books* critic Ian Buruma described *The Great World* as "superb new novel" containing "one of the most horrifying and vivid descriptions of the death railroad camps I have read. The rotting wounds, the maddening fevers, the casual sadism of the Japanese and Korean guards, the terror of cholera, of giving in to fate, of becoming what in Auschwitz camp jargon was called a *Musulman,* a doomed man already in the grip of death." Elizabeth Ward, writing in *Washington Post Book World,* noted their experience results in "a profound alteration in these men's sense of reality," and "both carry the horror of their memories—dormant but never dead, like malaria—permanently." Even more, perhaps, than the physical abuse and deprivation is their loss of identity, Malouf told *Observer* reviewer Ed Thomason: "Everything was taken away from those POWs—their white skin, their privileges, their manhood in some kind of way. They had to find out what it was they had to hang on to, in what way you could lose things without losing them. Really, that's what the book is about—loss, in every possible meaning of the word."

"The experience of the war itself is, in Malouf's way of storytelling, known both through the bare language of prisoners' speech and the spare but poetic language of their thoughts," assessed Peter Campbell in *London Review of Books.* Writing in *Wall Street Journal,* Bruce Bawer praised Malouf's prose: "Lean, evocative and rich with localisms . . . , it is a marvel, at once vigorous and reflective, colloquial and elegant." Bawer described Malouf as "a first-rate writer" of a "passionate, penetrating and remarkably powerful book about nothing less than what it means to be human."

Remembering Babylon, set in the 1840s, "examines the fragility of identity from within a band of 19th-century British colonials, who have scratched out a home in the Australian bush," according to Suzanne Berne in the *New York Times Book Review.* The group is transformed with the arrival of Gemmy Fairley, a British-born young man who survived being thrown overboard from a British ship at age thirteen, washed up on a Queensland shore, and lived a wandering existence with the Aborigines for sixteen years before stumbling into the colony. "There's little plot," Catherine Foster observes in *Christian Science Monitor.* "Malouf roams from mind to mind of the various town residents as they react to Gemmy or try to make sense of him. Malouf generously lets us see as much of the other residents as of this gibberish-spouting character whose other, British, self slowly reemerges." Gemmy develops into a richly "multifaceted" character, "at turns human, at turns brutal," noted Berne, and in *Remembering Babylon* the author "adroitly limns each of these shifting projections, sympathetically portraying the desperation of human exile with its terrors, its possibilities, its unlikely opportunities for grace." Gemmy, "a white man with Aboriginal ways, represents a primitive immigrant's worst confusion: the man in the right skin but the wrong

tribe," *Time* contributor R. Z. Sheppard assessed. "He is a reminder of instincts caged but not tamed by civilization. That such a creature has much to teach can be even more upsetting."

Los Angeles Times staff writer John J. Goldman noted that Malouf, who is "of Lebanese and British ancestry, has focused on issues of Australian identity during his thirty-five-year literary career." Malouf once told *CA:* "I write out of a strong sense of time and place, a past that is continuously present, and of continuities within change. Wholeness is what I see myself as being concerned with—which means, of course, disruption. As an Australian I am especially concerned with what is unique to that place, but as it is also seen from within a whole culture of which ours is a dialect—that is, my work frequently shifts back and forth, as I do, between Queensland and Europe, and attempts to hold the hemispheres in a single view."

BIOGRAPHICAL/CRITICAL SOURCES:

BOOKS

Hansson, Karin, *Sheer Edge: Aspects of Identity in David Malouf's Writing,* Lund University Press (Lund, Sweden), 1991.
Indyk, Ivor, *David Malouf,* Oxford University Press (Melbourne, Australia), 1993.
Malouf, David, *First Things Last,* University of Queensland Press, 1981.
Malouf, David, *Fly Away Peter,* Chatto & Windus, 1982.
Malouf, David, *Harland's Half Acre,* Knopf, 1984.
Neilsen, Philip, *Imagined Lives: A Study of David Malouf,* University of Queensland Press, 1990.

PERIODICALS

Boston Globe, April 4, 1991, p. 68; October 17, 1993, p. A15.
Boston Review, fall, 1994, p. 32.
Chicago Tribune, November 28, 1993, sec. 14. p. 6.
Christian Science Monitor, October 21, 1993, p. 15.
Guardian Weekly, August 8, 1993, p. 29.
Listener, January 9, 1986, p. 29; February 13, 1986, p. 28; April 5, 1990, p. 32.
London Review of Books, May 8, 1986, p. 19; April 19, 1990, p. 20; June 10, 1993, pp. 28-29.
Los Angeles Times, May 13, 1991, p. E3; October 31, 1993, p. BR3; September 23, 1994, p. A13.
Los Angeles Times Book Review, October 31, 1993, p. 3.
Meanjin, spring, 1993, pp. 545-548.
New Republic, May 13, 1978.
New Statesman, May 7, 1993, p. 40.
New Yorker, August 12, 1991, p. 79; November 1, 1993, p. 131.
New York Review of Books, July 19, 1990, pp. 43-45; December 2, 1993, pp. 13-15.

New York Times, July 14, 1978; October 19, 1993, p. C19.

New York Times Book Review, April 23, 1978; February 10, 1985, p. 40; June 22, 1986, p. 34; July 19, 1990, p. 43-45; March 31, 1991, p. 20; October 17, 1993, pp. 7, 52; December 5, 1993, p. 64.

Observer (London), February 10, 1985, p. 26; February 2, 1986, p. 28; April 8, 1990, p. 58; May 5, 1991, p. 61; May 30, 1993, p. 63.

Punch, March 13, 1985, p. 76.

Time, October 25, 1993, pp. 82, 84; January 3, 1994, p. 79.

Times (London), June 17, 1982; January 31, 1985.

Times Literary Supplement, April 9, 1976; September 22, 1978; January 29, 1982; May 21, 1982; October 15, 1982; June 15, 1984; February 8, 1985, p. 140; April 6, 1990, p. 375; May 7, 1993, p. 20.

Tribune Books, November 28, 1993, p. 6.

USA Today, November 19, 1993, p. D14.

Wall Street Journal, May 8, 1991, p. A10; October 25, 1993, p. A18.

Washington Post, May 12, 1978; May 2, 1982; September 26, 1984; September 23, 1993, p. D3.

Washington Post Book World, March 24, 1991, pp. 8-9; September 5, 1993, p. 9; October 31, 1993, p. 12.

World Literature Today, summer, 1991, p. 543.

*   *   *

MANGO, Karin N.   1936-

PERSONAL: Born January 11, 1936, in Riga, Latvia; daughter of Manfred R. (a British civil engineer) and Helen (a broadcasting monitor; maiden name, Libertal) Nowak; married Anthony Mango (a United Nations official), February 27, 1960; children: Alexander Nicholas, Helen Natalie. *Education:* University of Edinburgh, M.A., 1958; Pratt Institute, M.L.S., 1975. *Avocational interests:* Travel, theater, books and book collecting, walking.

ADDRESSES: Home—83 Hillside Ave., Mount Kisco, NY 10549. *Agent*—McIntosh & Otis, Inc., 310 Madison Ave., New York, NY 10017.

CAREER: George H. Harrap & Co. Ltd. (publisher), London, England, assistant head of education department, 1958-60; McGraw-Hill Book Co., New York City, education correspondent, 1960; Long Island Historical Society, Brooklyn, NY, part-time librarian and researcher, 1975-79; R. R. Bowker Co., New York City, freelance copy editor and proofreader, 1979-82; Suzanne Pathy Speak-Up Institute, New York City, staff writer, 1981-86; freelance writer, 1986—. League for the Hard of Hearing, librarian, 1990—.

MEMBER: Authors Guild, Beta Phi Mu.

WRITINGS:

Cantering Through (juvenile), Harrap, 1951.

The Children's Book of Russian Folktales, Harrap, 1961.

The Children's St. Francis, Harrap, 1963.

New York Holiday (juvenile), Harrap, 1971.

(Editor) M. V. Doggett, *Long Island Printing: A Checklist of Imprints,* Long Island Historical Society, 1979.

(Editor) *Calendar of Manuscripts of the Revolutionary Period,* Long Island Historical Society, 1980.

Armor: Yesterday and Today (juvenile), Messner (New York City), 1980.

A Various Journey (young adult novel), Macmillan (New York City), 1983.

Mapmaking (juvenile), Messner, 1984.

Somewhere Green (young adult novel), Macmillan, 1987.

Codes, Ciphers and Other Secrets (juvenile), F. Watts (New York City), 1988.

Just for the Summer (young adult novel), Harper (New York City), 1990.

Hearing Loss, F. Watts, 1991.

Portrait of Miranda (young adult novel), HarperCollins (New York City), 1993.

Contributor to New York University School of Education Videomath Project, 1993; contributor to *No Walls of Stone* (an anthology of literature by deaf and hard of hearing writers), edited by J. Jepson, Gallaudet University Press, 1992, and to *World Book Encyclopedia.* Contributor to magazines for the hearing impaired.

WORK IN PROGRESS: Getting to Know You, a work on the integration of hearing-impaired children in mainstream schools.

SIDELIGHTS: Karin N. Mango's first book was published when she was fourteen years old. The author told *CA:* "Some of the most influential events in my life took place before I was really aware of them. I came to England as a baby, just before World War II. We were bombed out of our house in London, and I was evacuated to the countryside. I was an only child and lived with different families, learning to adapt to different environments. I spent most of the war, however, at a hostel that was situated in a country manor house in beautiful surroundings. I wrote my first book, *Cantering Through,* with that as a setting. A later book, *A Various Journey,* is set in the more normal provincial town atmosphere in which I spent my teenage years. The story grew out of classic teenage problems and anxieties, but the heroine's wartime experiences color the story.

"I have lived in New York for most of my adult life because my husband worked for the United Nations here until his retirement. New York provides me with access to almost anything I want to know. I have written books on subjects as varied as armor, mapmaking, and St. Francis of Assisi.

"Local history has always interested me; one of my latest young adult novels is set in the brownstone renovation area of Brooklyn, where I lived, and another in Brooklyn Heights. I worked for a while at the Long Island Historical Society and enjoyed most locating and researching their revolutionary manuscripts. I hunted through the archives of the landmark building from attic to cellar. I handled land deeds, shopping receipts, war documents, and manuscripts written by such people as Benedict Arnold and Benjamin Franklin.

"Over the past ten years I have become deaf. I write for hearing impaired people, to inform and encourage and also to entertain and amuse them. People with hearing loss tend to withdraw and become isolated and depressed as their ability to communicate with the normal world decreases. I try to use my own experiences and writing to encourage them to rejoin the world and to use all available help. I now live about an hour north of New York City in a late Victorian house. The area has much interesting history that I hope to use in future writing."

*   *   *

MARKIE, Peter J(oseph) 1950-

PERSONAL: Born April 4, 1950, in New York, NY; son of Stanley Joseph (a civil servant) and Mary Frances (a nurse; maiden name, Killeen) Markie; married Kathleen Murphy (an attorney), May 24, 1975; children: Elizabeth, Robert. *Education:* Washington Square College, New York University, B.A. (summa cum laude), 1972; University of Massachusetts at Amherst, M.A., 1975, Ph.D., 1977.

ADDRESSES: Home—316 East Briarwood Ln., Columbia, MO 65203. *Office*—Department of Philosophy, University of Missouri—Columbia, Columbia, MO 65211.

CAREER: University of Missouri—Columbia, assistant professor, 1976-82, associate professor, 1982-88, professor of philosophy, 1988—.

MEMBER: American Philosophical Association, Southern Society for Philosophy and Psychology, Phi Beta Kappa.

WRITINGS:

Descartes's Gambit, Cornell University Press (Ithaca, NY), 1987.
A Professor's Duties, Rowman & Littlefield (Totowa, NJ), 1994.

WORK IN PROGRESS: Research in epistemology (theories of justification) and ethics (theories of rights).

MARON, Margaret

PERSONAL: Surname rhymes with "baron"; born in Greensboro, NC; daughter of C. O. and Claudia (Stephenson) Brown; married Joseph J. Maron, June 20, 1959; children: John J.

ADDRESSES: Agent—The Vicky Bijur Literary Agency, 333 West End Ave., New York, NY 10023.

MEMBER: Mystery Writers of America (former board of directors), America Crime Writers League, Sisters in Crime (former president), Carolina Crime Writers (steering committee).

AWARDS, HONORS: Agatha Christie Award nomination, Best Mystery Novel, 1989, American Mystery Award nomination, Best Mystery Novel, 1989, Anthony Boucher Award nomination, Best Mystery Novel, 1989, all for *Corpus Christmas;* Edgar Allan Poe Award, Best Mystery Novel, 1992, Agatha Christie Award, Best Mystery Novel, 1992, Anthony Boucher Award, Best Mystery Novel, 1992, Macavity Award, Best Mystery Novel, 1992, all for *Bootlegger's Daughter;* Agatha Christie Award nomination, Best Mystery Novel, 1993, Anthony Boucher Award nomination, Best Mystery Novel, 1993, both for *Southern Discomfort.*

WRITINGS:

MYSTERY NOVELS

One Coffee With, Raven House, 1981.
Death of a Butterfly, Doubleday (New York City), 1984.
Death in Blue Folders, Doubleday, 1985.
Bloody Kin, Doubleday, 1985.
The Right Jack, Bantam (New York City), 1987.
Baby Doll Games, Bantam, 1988.
Corpus Christmas, Doubleday, 1988.
Past Imperfect, Doubleday, 1991.
Bootlegger's Daughter, Mysterious Press (New York City), 1992.
Southern Discomfort, Mysterious Press, 1993.
Shooting at Loons, Mysterious Press, 1994.
Fugitive Colors, Mysterious Press, in press.

OTHER

Contributor of stories to magazines, including *Redbook, McCall's, Alfred Hitchcock's Mystery Magazine, Mike Shayne's Mystery Magazine,* and *Readers' Digest.* Contributor of stories to anthologies, including *Sisters in Crime 2,* Berkley Publishing, 1989; *Sisters in Crime 4,* Berkley Publishing, 1990; *A Woman's Eye,* edited by Sara Paretsky; *Christmas Stalkings,* edited by Charlotte MacLeod; *Deadly Allies,* edited by Marilyn Wallace and Robert Randall; *Crimes of the Heart,* edited by Carolyn G. Hart.

WORK IN PROGRESS: Editing an anthology of original short mystery stories by fellow North Carolina authors.

*　　*　　*

MARSHALL, I(an) Howard 1934-

PERSONAL: Born January 12, 1934, in Carlisle, England; son of Ernest and Ethel Marshall; married Joyce Elizabeth Proudfoot, 1961; children: three daughters, one son. *Education:* University of Aberdeen, M.A., 1955; B.D., 1959, Ph.D., 1963; Cambridge University, B.A., 1959; attended University of Goettingen, 1959-60.

ADDRESSES: Office—c/o Department of Divinity with Religious Studies, University of Aberdeen, Aberdeen AB9 2UB, Scotland.

CAREER: Ordained Methodist minister, 1962; minister at Methodist church in Darlington, England, 1962-64; University of Aberdeen, Aberdeen, Scotland, lecturer in New Testament exegesis, 1964-70, senior lecturer, 1970-77, reader, 1977-79, professor, 1979—.

WRITINGS:

Christian Beliefs: A Brief Introduction, Inter-Varsity Press (Downers Grove, IL), 1963, 3rd edition published as *Pocket Guide to Christian Beliefs,* 1978.

The Books of Kings and Chronicles, Scripture Union (Philadelphia), 1967, reprinted as *Understanding the Old Testament: I and II Kings, I and II Chronicles, Ezra, Nehemiah, Esther, Job,* 1978.

St. Mark, Scripture Union, 1967, published as *Mark,* A. J. Holman (Nashville, TN), 1978, also published as *Understanding the New Testament: Mark,* Scripture Union, 1982.

Kept by the Power of God: A Study of Perseverance and Falling Away, Epworth Press (London), 1969, Bethany House (Minneapolis, MN), 1975.

The Work of Christ, Haynes Publishers, 1969.

Luke: Historian and Theologian, Paternoster Press, 1970, 2nd edition, 1979, Zondervan (Grand Rapids, MI), 1971.

I Believe in the Historical Jesus, Eerdmans (Grand Rapids, MI), 1977.

(Editor) *New Testament Interpretation: Essays on Principles and Methods,* Eerdmans, 1977, 3rd edition, 1985.

The Origin of New Testament Christology, Inter-Varsity Press, 1977.

The Gospel of Luke: A Commentary on the Greek Text, Eerdmans, 1978.

The Epistles of John, Eerdmans, 1978.

The Acts of the Apostles: An Introduction and Commentary, Eerdmans, 1980.

Last Supper and Lord's Supper, Paternoster Press, 1980, Eerdmans, 1981.

I and II Thessalonians, Eerdmans, 1983.

Biblical Inspiration, Hodder & Stoughton (London), 1982, Eerdmans, 1983.

Jesus the Saviour, Inter-Varsity Press, 1990.

I Peter, Inter-Varsity Press, 1991.

The Epistle to the Phillipians, Epworth Press, 1992.

The Acts of the Apostles, Sheffield Academic Press, 1992.

(With K. P. Donfried) *The Theology of the Shorter Pauline Letters,* Cambridge University Press (New York City), 1993.

Contributor to *The New Bible Dictionary* and *The New Bible Commentary Revised.* Contributor to theology journals. Editor of *The Evangelical Quarterly.*

*　　*　　*

MARSTON, Del
See LUPOFF, Richard A(llen)

*　　*　　*

MARTIN, Mario, Jr.
See MONTELEONE, Thomas F(rancis)

*　　*　　*

MARTIN, Ralph G(uy) 1920-

PERSONAL: Born March 4, 1920, in Chicago, IL; son of Herman and Tillie (Charno) Martin; married Marjorie Jean Pastel, June 17, 1944; children: Maurice Joseph, Elizabeth Ruth, Tina Suzanne. *Education:* University of Missouri, B.J., 1941. *Avocational interests:* Traveling, walking.

ADDRESSES: Home—135 Harbor Road, Westport, CT 06880. *Agent*—Sterling Lord Agency, 660 Madison Avenue, New York, NY 10021.

CAREER: Box Elder News Journal, Brigham, UT, managing editor, 1941; *New Republic,* New York City, associate editor, 1945-48; freelance writer for magazines, 1945-53; *Newsweek,* New York City, associate editor, 1953-55; *House Beautiful,* New York City, executive editor, 1955-57; publisher and president of Bandwagon, Inc. *Wartime service:* Combat correspondent, *Stars and Stripes* and *Yank,* in Europe and Mediterranean, 1941-45.

MEMBER: Overseas Press Club, Dramatists Guild, Authors Guild, Century Association.

WRITINGS:

BIOGRAPHY

A Man for All People: Hubert H. Humphrey, introduction by Adlai E. Stevenson III, Grosset & Dunlap, 1968.

Jennie: The Life of Lady Randolph Churchill, Prentice-Hall (Englewood Cliffs, NJ), Volume 1: *The Romantic Years, 1854-1895,* 1969, Volume 2: *The Dramatic Years, 1895-1921,* 1971.

The Woman He Loved: The Story of the Duke and Duchess of Windsor, Simon & Schuster (New York City), 1973.

Cissy: The Life of Elenor Medill Patterson, Simon & Schuster, 1979.

A Hero for Our Time: An Intimate Study of the Kennedy Years, Macmillan (New York City), 1983.

Charles and Diana, Putnam (New York City), 1985.

Golda: Golda Meir, the Romantic Years, Scribner (New York City), 1988.

Henry and Clare: An Intimate Portrait of the Luces, Putnam, 1991.

Seeds of Destruction: Joe Kennedy and His Sons, Putnam, 1995.

WITH RICHARD HARRITY

Eleanor Roosevelt: Her Life in Pictures, Duell, Sloan & Pearce, 1958.

The Human Side of FDR, Duell, Sloan & Pearce, 1959.

Man of Destiny: Charles de Gaulle, Duell, Sloan & Pearce, 1962.

World War II: From D-Day to VE-Day, Fawcett (New York City), 1962.

The Three Lives of Helen Keller, Doubleday (New York City), 1962.

OTHER

Boy from Nebraska, Harper (New York City), 1946.

The Best Is None Too Good, Farrar, Straus (New York City), 1948.

(With Ed Plaut) *Front Runner, Dark Horse,* Doubleday, 1960.

(With Morton Stone) *Money, Money, Money,* Rand McNally (Chicago), 1961.

Ballots and Bandwagons, Rand McNally, 1964.

The Bosses, Putnam, 1964.

President from Missouri, Messner (New York City), 1964.

Skin Deep (novel), McKay (New York City), 1964.

World War II: Pearl Harbor to V-J Day, Fawcett, 1965.

Wizard of Wall Street, Morrow (New York City), 1965.

The GI War: 1941-1945, Little, Brown (Boston), 1967.

Lincoln Center for the Performing Arts, Prentice-Hall, 1971.

Contributor to books, including *Yank: The GI Story of the War,* Duell, Sloan & Pearce, 1946; *Stevenson Speeches,* Random House (New York City), 1952; *Social Problems in America,* Holt (New York City), 1955; *The Stars and Stripes,* McKay, 1962; and *Democracy in Action,* Macmillan, 1963. Work has appeared in *Harper's, Look,* *McCall's, Ladies' Home Journal, New York Times,* and other publications.

Jennie: The Life of Lady Randolph Churchill has been translated into a number of languages.

WORK IN PROGRESS: A play based on *Jennie: The Life of Lady Randolph Churchill.*

SIDELIGHTS: Ralph G. Martin is a biographer of politicians and celebrities as well as the author of several popular histories. Among his best-known works is *Jennie: The Life of Lady Randolph Churchill,* a bestselling two-volume biography of Winston Churchill's mother. The first volume, subtitled *The Romantic Years, 1854-1895,* describes Jennie Jerome's childhood in Brooklyn and her marriage to Lord Randolph Henry Spencer Churchill of England. In *Book World,* official Winston Churchill biographer Martin Gilbert wrote that Martin "has produced a volume in which not only Jennie, but the world in which she lived, dance before the reader in magnificent display." Similarly, Paul D. Zimmerman, writing in *Newsweek,* commended Martin for bringing "to his sympathetic, balanced and always absorbing chronicle an easy working knowledge of Victorian history." Gilbert noted that the most surprising parts of the biography are its implication that Winston Churchill was conceived out of wedlock and Martin's speculation that pregnancy was the only way that Jennie and Randolph, the son of a duke, could obtain parental permission to marry.

Jennie was known as a great beauty, and her many lovers included the Prince of Wales (later King Edward VII). The second volume of Martin's biography, subtitled *The Dramatic Years, 1895-1921,* chronicles Jennie's successive marriages to two younger men, George Cornwallis-West and Montagu Porch, after her first husband's death; it also relates how she launched a literary magazine, sailed to South Africa in order to tend the sick in the Boer War, and advanced her son Winston's political career. Edward Weeks, writing in the *Atlantic Monthly,* observed: "This second volume of uninhibited biography, covering the years 1895 to 1921, shows Jennie as she rode the crest, passionate, versatile, and devoted in her concern for her young sons, Winston and Jack. As the biographer well says, she was a woman 'of so many facets that it seemed she needed a variety of men to suit them.'"

Several reviewers commented upon Martin's research for the two books. Reviewing the first volume in the *Washington Post,* Kay Halle said, "Martin's research is so extensive that even the footnotes are intriguing (they keep the reader constantly whipsawed between the back of the book and the text, where they properly belong.)" Some expressed reservations about weaknesses in his scholarship, notably Martin's willingness to accept as truth the word of a known prevaricator. Still, more than one critic praised his inclusion of correspondence related to his subject, and Alden Whitman, assessing the second volume in *Saturday Review,* labeled Martin "a scrupulous researcher and an excellent writer."

In *A Hero for Our Time: An Intimate Study of the Kennedy Years,* his portrait of President John F. Kennedy, Martin emphasizes personality and psychology over political issues. Harry S. Ashmore, a contributor to the *Los Angeles Times Book Review,* said that Martin's book presents "no pretense of formal scholarship" but instead consists largely of quotations from Kennedy intimates. The work received mixed reviews, with some writers complaining of inaccuracies, gossip, and rambling structure. In a review for the *Detroit News,* Bernard A. Weisberger opined that although *A Hero for Our Time* might be loosely structured and light on analysis, it succeeds in reminding readers of Kennedy's finer qualities and the appeal of his presidency without bowing to sentimentality. Eliot Fremont-Smith of the *Village Voice* found the book preferable to William Manchester's *One Brief Shining Moment: Remembering Kennedy,* published the same year, remarking that he came to Martin's work "ready to rage . . . and couldn't."

Although Martin has selected a wide range of subjects for his biographies, he has often focused on strong women who played a major role in politics. In the mid-1980s he realized that no full biography had been written about Golda Meir, and so he began researching the personal history of the former prime minister of Israel. He completed *Golda: Golda Meir, the Romantic Years* in 1988. Raised in Milwaukee after having fled Russia with her family at age eight, Meir married Morris Meyerson at age nineteen, and in addition to promoting Zionism and helping to found Israel, she carried on relationships with a number of leaders of the Zionist movement. Wrote Dorothy Herrmann in Chicago *Tribune Books:* "Although Martin . . . provides a great deal of new information about Meir's private life, he writes with taste and perspective. Wisely, he weaves the accounts of her various liaisons into the far more dramatic story of her most passionate love affair, which was not with any man but with an entire country."

In *Henry and Clare: An Intimate Portrait of the Luces,* Martin chronicled the lives of Henry Luce, the powerful publisher and cofounder of *Time* magazine, and his wife, Clare Boothe Luce, a talented writer and editor who was twice elected to Congress and served as ambassador to Italy. Scott Donaldson described the tone of the biography this way in *Tribune Books:* "[Martin] characterizes the union of Henry and Clare Boothe Luce as 'a royal American marriage,' the royalty deriving from their status as international celebrities, and this book is for those curious about celebrities and eager to discover how unhappy they are." Writing in the *New York Times Book Review,* Eileen Shanahan commented that although some of the sources

documenting the couple's numerous affairs are dubious, the whole is a compassionate and diverting look at the Luces' marriage. Wrote Shanahan: "Although flaw after flaw, personal and professional, of both Luces is spread over the pages of Mr. Martin's book, his tone is sympathetic, much like the tone of people discussing the defects of a beloved relative or dear friend."

Although the public figures that Martin has written about lived and worked within a range of social and political milieus, in each case he has been able to unearth sometimes controversial details about their private lives. Barbara Seaman, writing about *Golda* in *Washington Post Book World,* commented upon this aspect of his work: "Martin, biographer of Jennie Churchill, has a genius for uncovering the private lives of public women."

BIOGRAPHICAL/CRITICAL SOURCES:

PERIODICALS

Atlantic Monthly, November, 1971.
Book World, January 19, 1969; July 26, 1970; January 2, 1972.
Chicago Tribune, January 15, 1989.
Christian Science Monitor, June 12, 1969.
Commonweal, March 9, 1984.
Detroit News, September 18, 1983.
Globe and Mail (Toronto), August 5, 1995.
Guardian Weekly, November 20, 1983.
Listener, December 11, 1969; December 7, 1972.
Los Angeles Times, October 24, 1979.
Los Angeles Times Book Review, September 18, 1983, p. 1; September 8, 1991.
Maclean's, December 10, 1979.
Newsweek, February 3, 1969; November 21, 1983.
New Yorker, February 22, 1969; November 5, 1979.
New York Review of Books, July 10, 1969.
New York Times, February 27, 1969; June 14, 1969; November 19, 1971; September 25, 1979.
New York Times Book Review, February 16, 1969; June 8, 1969; November 28, 1971; December 5, 1971; August 25, 1974, p. 7; September 23, 1979; September 25, 1983; August 18, 1991.
Observer (London), November 19, 1972; October 27, 1974.
Observer Review, November 2, 1969.
Saturday Review, March 8, 1969; November 28, 1970; November 6, 1971.
Time, August 26, 1991.
Times Literary Supplement, January 5, 1973; November 1, 1974.
Tribune Books (Chicago), December 11, 1988; August 4, 1991.
Village Voice, November 29, 1983.
Washington Post, February 12, 1969; November 2, 1985.

Washington Post Book World, September 15, 1974; December 8, 1974; December 16, 1979; October 30, 1983; November 13, 1988.

*   *   *

MASUDA, Takeshi 1944-
(Warabe Aska)

PERSONAL: Born February 3, 1944, in Kagawa, Japan; immigrated to Canada, 1982; son of Satoru (an office worker) and Miyoko (a dressmaker; maiden name, Fujimoto) Masuda; married Keiko Inouye (a homemaker), October 17, 1979; children: Haydn Yohyoh, Anne Mari, Michael Kohta. *Education:* Attended Takamatsu Technological School. *Politics:* None. *Religion:* Shintoist.

ADDRESSES: Home—1019 Lorne Park Rd., Mississauga, Ontario, Canada L5H 2Z9.

CAREER: Ad House (design studio), Tokyo, Japan, founder and president, 1964-78; artist and writer, 1979—. Paintings exhibited in solo and group shows in Japan, Europe, and Canada.

AWARDS, HONORS: UNESCO Exhibition Prize from Japan's minister of education, 1966; *Dandelion Puffs* and *P-yororo O-yororo* were accepted for exhibition at the Biennale of Graphic Design, 1984; City of Toronto Book Award, 1985, for *Who Goes to the Park;* Society of Graphic Designers of Canada named *Who Goes to the Park* one of the best books of the eighties, 1985; work selected for UNICEF greeting card, 1985; poster design accepted for exhibition at International Youth Year, 1985; International Book Design exhibition, Leipzig, East Germany, honorable mention as one of the best designed books from all over the world, 1986, for *Who Goes to the Park,* and 1989, for *Who Hides in the Park;* Gold Medal, Studio Magazine Awards, Toronto, and Governor General's Literary Awards nomination, both 1990, Mr. Christie's Book Award in children's illustration, 1991, and Diploma Gold Pen, Belgrade, Yugoslavia, 1992, all for *Seasons;* Biennale of Graphic Design Silver Medal, Brno, Czech Republic, and Canadian Library Association Book of the Year Award runner-up, both 1992, for *Aska's Animals;* first prize, Tehran International Biennale of Illustration, Iran, 1993, for *Aska's Birds.*

WRITINGS:

SELF-ILLUSTRATED JUVENILES, UNDER NAME WARABE ASKA

Discovering Japan in Eighty Days, Alice Kan (Tokyo), 1973.
Dandelion Puffs, Liblio Publishing (Tokyo), 1981.
P-yororo O-yororo, Liblio Publishing, 1982.

Who Goes to the Park, Tundra Books (Montreal and New York City), 1984.
Who Hides in the Park, Tundra Books, 1986.

ILLUSTRATOR; UNDER NAME WARABE ASKA

A Midsummer Night's Dream, Alice Kan, 1976.
Ma Vlast, Alice Kan, 1977.
Harry Janos, Alice Kan, 1977.
Seasons, Doubleday (Toronto and New York City), 1990.
Aska's Animals, Doubleday, 1991.
Aska's Birds, Doubleday, 1992.
Aska's Sea Creatures, Doubleday, 1994.

SIDELIGHTS: Takeshi Masuda, best known as Warabe Aska, immigrated to Canada after extensive travel and numerous exhibitions of his work in England, France, Italy, Spain, and Germany. His books have received international acclaim. *Who Goes to the Park,* a collection of paintings and poems about Toronto's High Park, has been recommended by critics as a delightful and refreshing tribute that should appeal equally to adults and young people. Aska's next book, *Who Hides in the Park,* is a similar tribute to Stanley Park in Vancouver. Critics have praised the work, which is trilingual in English, French, and Japanese, as imaginative, breathtaking, and unique.

Aska told *CA:* "In my childhood I became interested in reading, writing, and painting when, in junior high school, a friend invited me to the activities of an art club. At the age of twenty-eight I had my first exhibit at a gallery in Tokyo. After traveling around Japan I had the chance to write and illustrate for various monthly magazines, and a year later I wrote and illustrated my first book, *Discovering Japan in Eighty Days.* It was a turning point in my career as I began to focus on the book world instead of on commercial artwork.

"I have traveled extensively in Western and Eastern Europe, a world I've found very different from the Japan I know, and I have developed many new ideas from my discoveries there. My next five picture books for children are based on my experiences in countries as varied as England, Czechoslovakia, Spain, and Canada.

"Many of my ideas come to me during my time spent in airplanes, trains, buses, boats, and cars. I also find that sitting out in the open air inspires me. Natural objects like trees, flowers, birds, animals, the sun and moon, clouds, water, and cheerful children trigger my ideas. My imagination has been expanding greatly since I immigrated to Canada in 1979 because of the many interesting subjects that motivate me here, such as the people, Canada's multicultural aspect, and its nature.

"The readers of my books are gradually beginning to include adults. I never think of a particular age group while creating a book."

BIOGRAPHICAL/CRITICAL SOURCES:

PERIODICALS

Booklist, January 1, 1994.
Canadian Bookseller, April, 1985.
Children's Book Review Service, January, 1994.
Gazette (Montreal), April 13, 1985.
Quill and Quire, August, 1990.
School Library Journal, January, 1994.
Toronto Star, March 1, 1985.

* * *

MATTHIESSEN, Peter 1927-

PERSONAL: Surname is pronounced "*Math*-e-son"; born May 22, 1927, in New York, NY; son of Erard A. (an architect) and Elizabeth (Carey) Matthiessen; married Patricia Southgate, February 8, 1951 (divorced, 1958); married Deborah Love, May 16, 1963 (deceased, 1972); married Maria Eckhart, November 28, 1980; children: (first marriage) Lucas, Sara C.; (second marriage) Rue, Alexander. *Education:* Attended Sorbonne, University of Paris, 1948-49; Yale University, B.A., 1950.

ADDRESSES: Home—Bridge Lane, Box 392, Sagaponack, Long Island, NY 11962. *Agent*—Candida Donadio Associates, Inc., 231 West 22nd St., New York, NY 10011.

CAREER: Writer, 1950—; *Paris Review,* New York City (originally Paris, France), co-founder, 1951, editor, 1951—. Former commercial fisherman; captain of deep-sea charter fishing boat, Montauk, Long Island, NY, 1954-56; member of expeditions to Alaska, Canadian Northwest Territories, Peru, Nepal, East Africa, Congo Basin, Siberia, India, Bhutan, China, Japan, Namibia, Botswana, and Outer Mongolia and of Harvard-Peabody Expedition to New Guinea, 1961; National Book Awards judge, 1970. *Military service:* U.S. Navy, 1945-47.

MEMBER: American Academy and Institute of Arts and Letters, New York Zoological Society (trustee, 1965-78).

AWARDS, HONORS: Atlantic Prize, 1951, for best first story; permanent installation in White House library, for *Wildlife in America;* National Institute/American Academy of Arts and Letters grant, 1963, for *The Cloud Forest: A Chronicle of the South American Wilderness* and *Under the Mountain Wall: A Chronicle of Two Seasons in the Stone Age;* National Book Award nomination, 1966, for *At Play in the Fields of the Lord;* Christopher Book Award, 1971, for *Sal si puedes: Cesar Chavez and the New American Revolution;* National Book Award nomination, 1972, for *The Tree Where Man Was Born/The African Experience;* elected to National Institute of Arts and Letters,

1974; "Editor's Choice" citation, *New York Times Book Review,* 1975, for *Far Tortuga;* Brandeis Award and National Book Award for contemporary thought for *The Snow Leopard,* both 1979; American Book Award, 1980, for paperback edition of *The Snow Leopard;* John Burroughs Medal and African Wildlife Leadership Foundation Award, both 1982, both for *Sand Rivers;* gold medal for distinction in natural history, Academy of Natural Sciences, Philadelphia, 1985; Ambassador Award, English-speaking Union, 1990, for *Killing Mister Watson;* John Steinbeck Award, Long Island University, Southampton, elected to Global 500 Honour Roll, United Nations Environment Programme, and designated fellow, Academy of Arts and Science, all 1991.

WRITINGS:

NOVELS

Race Rock, Harper (New York City), 1954.
Partisans, Viking (New York City), 1955.
Raditzer, Viking, 1961.
At Play in the Fields of the Lord, Random House (New York City), 1965.
Far Tortuga, Random House, 1975.
Midnight Turning Gray, Ampersand, 1984.
Killing Mister Watson, Random House, 1990.

NONFICTION

Wildlife in America, Viking, 1959, Penguin (London), 1977, revised edition, Viking, 1987.
The Cloud Forest: A Chronicle of the South American Wilderness, Viking, 1961.
Under the Mountain Wall: A Chronicle of Two Seasons in the Stone Age, Viking, 1962.
Oomingmak: The Expedition to the Musk Ox Island in the Bering Sea, Hastings House (New York City), 1967.
(With Ralph S. Palmer and Robert Verity Clem) *The Shorebirds of North America,* edited by Gardner D. Stout, Viking, 1967, published as *The Wind Birds,* illustrated by Robert Gillmor, 1973.
Sal si puedes: Cesar Chavez and the New American Revolution, Random House, 1970.
Blue Meridian: The Search for the Great White Shark, Random House, 1971.
Everglades: With Selections from the Writings of Peter Matthiessen, edited by Paul Brooks, Sierra Club-Ballantine (New York City), 1971.
The Tree Where Man Was Born/The African Experience, photographs by Eliot Porter, Dutton (New York City), 1972.
The Snow Leopard, Viking, 1978.
Sand Rivers, photographs by Hugo van Lawick, Viking, 1981.
In the Spirit of Crazy Horse, Viking, 1983.
Indian Country, Viking, 1984.

Men's Lives: The Surfmen and Baymen of the South Fork, Random House, 1986.

Nine-Headed Dragon River: Zen Journals 1969-1982, Shambhala (Boulder, CO), 1986.

African Silences, Random House, 1991.

Shadows of Africa, illustrated by Mary Frank, Abrams (New York City), 1992.

Baikal, Sacred Sea of Siberia, photographs by Boyd Norton, Sierra Club Books (San Francisco), 1992.

JUVENILES

Seal Pool, illustrated by William Pene Du Bois, Doubleday (Garden City, NY), 1972, published as *The Great Auk Escape,* Angus & Robertson (London), 1974.

OTHER

On the River Styx, and Other Stories, Random House, 1989.

Contributor to *The American Heritage Book of Natural Wonders,* edited by Alvin M. Josephy, American Heritage Press, 1972. Contributor of numerous short stories, articles and essays to popular periodicals, including *Atlantic, Audubon, Conde Nast Traveler, Esquire, Geo, Harper's, Nation, Newsweek, New Yorker, New York Review of Books,* and *Saturday Evening Post.*

ADAPTATIONS: At Play in the Fields of the Lord was produced as a motion picture by Saul Zaentz, directed by Hector Babenco, starring Aidan Quinn, Tom Berenger, Tom Waits, Kathy Bates, and John Lithgow, and released by Metro-Goldwyn-Mayer, 1992; *Men's Lives* was adapted by Joe Pintauro and was performed on Long Island at the Bay Street Theater Festival on July 28, 1992.

WORK IN PROGRESS: A novel.

SIDELIGHTS: Peter Matthiessen is widely considered one of the most important wilderness writers of the twentieth century. In fiction and nonfiction alike, he explores endangered natural environments and human cultures threatened by encroaching technology. As Conrad Silvert notes in *Literary Quarterly,* Matthiessen "is a naturalist, an anthropologist and an explorer of geographies and the human condition. He is also a rhapsodist who writes with wisdom and warmth as he applies scientific knowledge to the peoples and places he investigates. Works of lasting literary value and moral import have resulted." Matthiessen also writes of the inner explorations he has undertaken as a practitioner of Zen Buddhism. His National Book Award-winning memoir *The Snow Leopard* combines the account of a difficult Himalayan trek with spiritual autobiography and contemplations of mortality and transcendence. According to Terrance Des Pres in the *Washington Post Book World,* Matthiessen is "a visionary, but he is very hardminded as well, and his attention is wholly with

abrupt detail. This allows him to render strangeness familiar, and much that is menial becomes strange, lustrous, otherworldly." *Dictionary of Literary Biography* contributor John L. Cobbs concludes: "In fiction and in nonfiction, Peter Matthiessen is one of the shamans of literature. He puts his audience in touch with worlds and forces which transcend common experience."

Matthiessen has journeyed through numerous foreign locales, including the far North, the Amazon rain forest, Siberia, East Africa, the high country of Nepal, and the jungles of New Guinea. His works hardly conform to the standard notion of travelogue, however. Des Pres writes: "Matthiessen is not an adventurer, nor have his voyages been impelled by some silly man-against-the-elements ideal. His central thrust has been to celebrate the virtues of lost cultures, to praise the excellence of life apart from human life, to bear witness to creation vanishing. And in this pursuit he has been quietly obsessed with one of the uglier truths of our age: that nothing lasts, that no place, culture, bird or beast can survive in the path of Western—and now Eastern—greed." This theme pervades Matthiessen's fiction in *At Play in the Fields of the Lord, Far Tortuga,* and *Killing Mister Watson* and forms the basis of a good portion of his nonfiction, including *Indian Country, Sand Rivers, African Silences,* and *Men's Lives: The Surfmen and Baymen of the South Fork.* "Anyone who has really read his nature writing knows that Matthiessen's attitude toward the natural world is hardly that of a fatuous admirer in his dotage," notes Cobbs. "He brings to his work a skeptical, wary professionalism, the uncompromising eye of a scientist, and an almost cynical and often bitter knowledge of the vulnerability of nature."

Critics contend that despite his pessimistic forecasts for the future of natural areas and their inhabitants, Matthiessen imbues his work with descriptive writing of high quality. According to Vernon Young in the *Hudson Review,* Matthiessen "combines the exhaustive knowledge of the naturalist . . . with a poet's response to far-out landscapes. . . . When he pauses to relate one marvel to another and senses the particular merging into the general, his command of color, sound and substance conjures the resonance of the vast continental space." *New York Times Book Review* contributor Jim Harrison feels that Matthiessen's prose has "a glistening, sculpted character to it. . . . The sense of beauty and mystery is indelible; not that you retain the specific information on natural history, but that you have had your brain, and perhaps the soul, prodded, urged, moved into a new dimension." Robert M. Adams offers a concurrent assessment in the *New York Review of Books.* Matthiessen, Adams writes, "has dealt frequently and knowingly with natural scenery and wild life; he can sketch a landscape in a few vivid, unsentimental words, capture the sensations of entering a wild, windy

Nepalese mountain village, and convey richly the strange, whinnying behavior of a herd of wild sheep. His prose is crisp, yet strongly appealing to the senses; it combines instinct with the feeling of adventure."

Although Matthiessen was born in New York City, he spent most of his youth in rural New York State and in Connecticut, where he attended the Hotchkiss School. His father, an architect, was a trustee of the National Audubon Society, and Matthiessen took an early interest in the fascinations of the natural world. "I had always been interested in nature," he remembered in *Publishers Weekly.* "My brother and I started with a passion for snakes, and he went into marine biology, while I took courses in [zoology and ornithology] right up through college." After service in the U.S. Navy, Matthiessen attended Yale University, spending his junior year at the Sorbonne in Paris. Having realized that a writing vocation drew him strongly, he began writing short stories, one of which won the prestigious *Atlantic* Prize in 1951—several of his works of short fiction would be collected in *On the River Styx, and Other Stories,* published in 1989. Matthiessen also received his degree in 1950, and after teaching creative writing for a year at Yale, he returned to Paris.

In Paris Matthiessen became acquainted with a number of expatriate American writers, including James Baldwin, Richard Wright, Terry Southern, and Irwin Shaw. Cobbs quotes Gay Talese, who described Matthiessen's apartment as "as much a meeting place for young American literati as was Gertrude Stein's apartment in the Twenties." A discussion about the critical pretentiousness of little magazines led Matthiessen and Harold L. Humes to found the *Paris Review* in 1951 with an initial investment of three hundred dollars. Matthiessen still serves as an editor of the magazine that has become one of the best known literary periodicals in English. While living in Paris Matthiessen also completed his first novel, *Race Rock,* a psychological study of four upper-middle-class Americans.

When *Race Rock* was published in 1954, Matthiessen returned to the United States, where he continued to write while eking out a livelihood as a commercial fisherman on Long Island. Reflecting on the early stages of his writing career in the *Washington Post,* Matthiessen said: "I don't think I could have done my writing without the fishing. I needed something physical, something non-intellectual." The friendships Matthiessen formed with Long Island's fishermen enabled him to chronicle their vanishing lifestyle in his book *Men's Lives: The Surfmen and Baymen of the South Fork.* Although tourism threatens the solitude of the far reaches of Long Island, Matthiessen still makes his home there when he is not travelling.

Matthiessen embarked on his first lengthy journey in 1956. Loading his Ford convertible with textbooks, a shot-

gun and a sleeping bag, he set off to visit every wildlife refuge in the United States. He admitted in *Publishers Weekly* that he brought more curiosity than expertise to his quest. "I'm what the 19th century would call a generalist," he said. "I have a lot of slack information, and for my work it's been extremely helpful. I've always been interested in wildlife and wild places and wild people. I wanted to see the places that are disappearing." Nearly three years of work went into Matthiessen's encyclopedic *Wildlife in America,* published in 1959 to high critical acclaim. A commercial success as well, *Wildlife in America* initiated the second phase of Matthiessen's career, a period of two decades during which he undertook numerous expeditions to the wild places that captured his curiosity. Since 1959, he has supported himself solely by writing.

The popularity of Matthiessen's nonfiction somewhat overshadows his equally well-received fiction. Three of his first four books are novels, and critics have found them commendable and promising works. In a *New York Herald Tribune Book Review* piece about *Race Rock,* Gene Baro comments: "Mr. Matthiessen's absorbing first novel, apart from being a good, well-paced story, offers the reader some depth and breadth of insight. For one thing, *Race Rock* is a vivid but complex study of evolving character; for another, it is a narrative of character set against a variously changed and changing social background. Mr. Matthiessen has succeeded in making from many strands of reality a close-textured book." *New York Times* contributor Sylvia Berkman contends that with *Race Rock,* Matthiessen "assumes immediate place as a writer of disciplined craft, perception, imaginative vigor and serious temperament. . . . He commands also a gift of flexible taut expression which takes wings at times into a lyricism beautifully modulated and controlled." Cobbs feels that although *Race Rock* "does not anticipate the experimental techniques or exotic subject matter of Matthiessen's later fiction, the novel shows the author's early concern with fundamental emotions and with the tension between primitive vitality and the veneer of civilization."

Partisans and *Raditzer,* Matthiessen's second and third novels, have garnered mixed reviews. According to M. L. Barrett in the *Library Journal,* the action in *Partisans,* "notable for its integrity and dramatic quality, is realized in real flesh-and-blood characters." *New York Times* contributor William Goyen conversely states: "The characters [in *Partisans*] seem only mouthpieces. They are not empowered by depth of dramatic conviction—or confusion. They do, however, impress one with this young author's thoughtful attempt to find answers to ancient and serious questions." Critics have been more impressed with the title character in *Raditzer,* a man Cobbs finds "both loathsome and believable." In the *Nation,* Terry Southern describes *Raditzer*'s anti-hero as "a character distinct from those in literature, yet one who has somehow figured, if but hauntingly, in the lives of us all. It is, in certain ways, as though a whole novel had been devoted to one of [Nelson] Algren's sideline freaks, a grotesque and loathsome creature—yet seen ultimately, as sometimes happens in life, as but another human being." Cobbs concludes: "A skillful ear for dialect and an immediacy in sketching scenes of violence and depravity saved *Raditzer*'s moral weightiness from being wearisome, and the novel proved Matthiessen's ability to project his imagination into worlds far removed from that of the intellectual upper-middle class."

At Play in the Fields of the Lord enhanced Matthiessen's reputation as a fiction writer when it was issued in 1965; the novel would increase his renown still further after it was filmed as a motion picture directed by Hector Babenco in 1992. Set in a remote jungle village in the Amazon region, the work is, in the words of *New York Times Book Review* contributor Anatole Broyard, "one of those rare novels that satisfy all sorts of literary and intellectual hungers while telling a story that pulls you along out of sheer human kinship." The story recounts the misguided efforts of four American missionaries and an American Indian mercenary to "save" the isolated Niaruna tribe. Cobbs suggests that the book shows "a virtuosity and richness that few traditional novels exhibit. There is immense stylistic facility in shifting from surreal dream and drug sequences to scrupulous realistic descriptions of tropical nature." *Nation* contributor J. Mitchell Morse voices some dissatisfaction with *At Play in the Fields of the Lord*, claiming that Matthiessen "obviously intended to write a serious novel, but . . . he has unconsciously condescended to cheapness." Conversely, Granville Hicks praises the work in the *Saturday Review:* "[Matthiessen's] evocation of the jungle is powerful, but no more remarkable than his insight into the people he portrays. He tells a fascinating story, and tells it well. . . . It is this firm but subtle evocation of strong feeling that gives Matthiessen's book its power over the imagination. Here, in an appallingly strange setting, he sets his drama of familiar aspirations and disappointments." In the *New York Times Book Review,* Emile Capouya concludes that the novel "is never less than a very superior adventure story, and often a good deal more than that. . . . Where it counts most, the story is well conceived and beautifully written—all in all, a most unusual novel."

Matthiessen's 1975 novel, *Far Tortuga,* presents a stylistic departure from his previous fictional works. As Cobbs describes it, "the deep penetration of character and psychology that characterized *At Play in the Fields of the Lord* yields to an almost disturbing objectivity in *Far Tortuga,* an absolute, realistic reproduction of surface phenomena—dialogue, noises, colors, shapes." In *Far Tortuga*

Matthiessen creates a fictitious voyage of a Caribbean turtling schooner, using characters' conversations and spare descriptions of time, weather and place. "The radical format of *Far Tortuga* makes the novel a structural tour de force and assured a range of critical reaction," Cobbs notes. Indeed, the novel's use of intermittent blank spaces, wavy lines, ink blots and unattributed dialogue has elicited extreme critical response. *Saturday Review* contributor Bruce Allen calls the work an "adventurous failure. . . . It exudes a magnificent and paradoxical radiance; but beneath the beautiful surface [it lacks] anything that even remotely resembles a harmonious whole." Most reviewers express a far different opinion, however. *Newsweek*'s Peter S. Prescott praises the book as "a beautiful and original piece of work, a resonant, symbolical story of nine doomed men who dream of an earthly paradise as the world winds down around them. . . . This is a moving, impressive book, a difficult yet successful undertaking." And *New York Review of Books* contributor Thomas R. Edwards feels that the novel "turns out to be enthralling. Matthiessen uses his method not for self-display but for identifying and locating his characters. . . . What, despite appearances, does *not* happen in *Far Tortuga* is a straining by literary means to make more of an acutely observed life than it would make of itself."

Killing Mister Watson, published in 1990, details, through the linked recollections of ten individuals, life in the Florida Everglades a century ago. Basing his story on actual events, Matthiessen novelizes the life of Edgar J. (Jack) Watson, who settled in the area in 1892 and became a successful sugar-cane farmer. Tales of a dark past begin to circulate among his neighbors: tales of murder, of past wives, of illegitimate children. People are mysteriously murdered and Watson's volatile temper and mean streak are common knowledge. Despite, or perhaps because of, his wealth, strong physical charisma, and the golden tongue of a born politician, Watson eventually becomes the object of resentment and even fear in his community—a man approached with submission. Eventually, Watson is killed by a group of his neighbors—shot with thirty-one bullets—upon returning to town after the hurricane of 1910. "Aggressive and gregarious, without ethics or introspection, both hugely talented and dangerously addicted to untamed power, Edgar Watson finally seems to represent great potential gone awry, or America at its worst," notes Ron Hansen in the *New York Times Book Review*. But the act of his murder remains incomprehensible: "since accounts of the man differ so radically, we are left, like the detective-historian, with more questions than answers, and with a sense of frustration," remarks Joyce Carol Oates in the *Washington Post Book World*. "The more we learn about Watson, this 'accursed' figure, the less we seem to know."

Critical reception to *Killing Mister Watson* was overwhelmingly positive. Calling it "a nightmare of a novel, intricately structured, richly documented, utterly convincing," Oates praises the work as "one which is certain to linger in the memory like an experience we have lived through but cannot, for all our effort at analysis, comprehend." And Tim McNulty, in a review for the *Bloomsbury Review,* extols the novel as "a deeply historic narrative that touches the very roots of our culture's attitude towards the land, the native people who dwelled there, and the rich tapestry of life that once graced it. Peter Matthiessen has returned to what may prove his most powerful genre, but if this historic snapshot of our national character is fiction, it is a fiction that, a century later, still troubles our world." McNulty notes Matthiessen's characteristic obsessions: throughout *Killing Mister Watson* the author's ecological passions provide a compelling subtext to the events surrounding Watson's murder. The destruction of the swamplands of the Florida Everglade region was rampant during that period, due to the wholesale slaughter of native birds like the egret by hunters. "It is as though, when they look at Watson, they have in view their own dying world," John Clute contends of Watson's killers in the *Times Literary Supplement.* "While alive, he stands as an intolerable symptom of a tragedy they cannot comprehend. *Killing Mister Watson,* like every story Matthiessen has told for decades, is a tale of the planet."

In an interview for *Publishers Weekly,* Matthiessen discussed his preference for weaving a story: "I prefer writing fiction; I find it exhilarating. Your battery is constantly being recharged with the excitement of it. I find that with nonfiction, it may be extremely skillful, it may be cabinetwork rather than carpentry, but it's still assembled from facts, from research, from other people's work. It may be well made or badly made, but it's still an assemblage." "In a sense," he added, "I've always thought of nonfiction as a livelihood, my way of making a living so I could write fiction."

Matthiessen may view his nonfiction as the means to a livelihood, but his critics have a different conception of the stature of his factual works. In the *New York Times Book Review,* Jim Harrison contends that the reading public "should feel indebted to this man who has taken the earth, of all things, as his literary territory. In a curious reversal of a century of modernist dogma, Mr. Matthiessen appears to think that what he writes about is more important than how he writes about it; he does not mine and re-mine the narcissistic mode that so long has provided the energy of modern literature."

"To judge from references in his work," Des Pres writes of the growing list of nonfiction works by the author, "there seems no place on earth Matthiessen has not at least passed through." Matthiessen's extensive travels are sometimes partially underwritten by the *New Yorker,* a magazine that regularly publishes the author's work. This funding has enabled him to spend extended periods of time in the environments he portrays, from that of the Caribbean turtle fishermen to the world of New Guinea's Kurelu tribe. Though critics such as *New Republic* contributor Paul Zweig contend that "no one writes more vividly about the complex sounds and sights of a world without man," human beings and their vagaries invariably figure in Matthiessen's works, no matter how far afield he travels. Zweig feels that in some of Matthiessen's books, the naturalist "has also been an elegist, chronicling the decline of an older earth of sparse populations hunting and gathering, or planting according to modest needs, in a ritual of respect for the cycles of the year." Quite a few of Matthiessen's nonfiction books and essays address the prerogative of saving cultural groups whose livelihood derives from cultivation of land or sea. Often these human cultures are as endangered as the many species of animal and plant life Matthiessen illuminates in his writings. According to Robert Sherrill in the *Atlantic,* "death and violence have often inspired [Matthiessen]; . . . victims have stirred him to some of his finest writing."

Human victims form the core of Matthiessen's most recent writings about the United States. In his 1970 title, *Sal si puedes: Cesar Chavez and the New American Revolution,* Matthiessen chronicles the efforts of migrant worker Cesar Chavez to organize farm laborers in California. In a review for the *Nation,* Roy Borngartz expresses the opinion that in *Sal si puedes* Matthiessen "brings a great deal of personal attachment to his account of Chavez and his fellow organizers. . . . He makes no pretense of taking any objective stand between the farm workers and the growers. . . . But he is a good and honest reporter, and as far as he was able to get the growers to talk to him, he gives them their say. . . . Matthiessen is most skillful at bringing his people to life." A similar sympathy for oppressed cultures provides the focus for *Indian Country* and *In the Spirit of Crazy Horse.*

Zweig notes that the author "has two subjects in *Indian Country:* the destruction of America's last open land by the grinding pressure of big industry, in particular the energy industry; and the tragic struggle of the last people on the land to preserve their shrinking territories, and even more, to preserve the holy balance of their traditions, linked to the complex, fragile ecology of the land." According to David Wagoner in the *New York Times Book Review,* what makes *Indian Country* "most unusual and most valuable is its effort to infuse the inevitable anger and sorrow with a sense of immediate urgency, with prophetic warnings. . . . Few people could have been better equipped than Mr. Matthiessen to face this formidable task. He has earned the right to be listened to seriously on the ways in which tribal cultures can teach us to know ourselves and the earth."

The focus of *In the Spirit of Crazy Horse,* while still directed towards the historic treatment of Native Americans, was much more journalistic in nature than *Indian Country.* In fact, the book itself was the subject of much press when it became the subject of a lawsuit the year after its publication. Claiming that they were libelled in the book, both an FBI agent and then-governor of South Dakota, William Janklow, sued both Matthiessen and Viking, the book's publisher, for a combined $49 million. While the two lawsuits were eventually thrown out by a Federal appeals court, the actions of the two men effectively kept the book out of circulation for several years. A reading of the work makes their efforts understandable: *In the Spirit of Crazy Horse* presents an effective indictment of the FBI and other government offices in crushing the efforts of the American Indian Movement (AIM) to recover sacred Sioux lands illegally confiscated by the U.S. government. The discovery of uranium and other mineral deposits on the land prompted federal officials to go to desperate lengths—including, Matthiessen claims, framing AIM activist Leonard Peltier for murder. *In the Spirit of Crazy Horse* was reissued by Matthiessen in 1991, after new evidence came to light further enforcing the author's contentions. As attorney Martin Garbus notes in the new edition's afterword: "The republication of *In the Spirit of Crazy Horse* makes a great victory against a new kind of censorship: the attempt by present and former public officials to suppress books that criticize them or disagree with their policies. Libel suits are the vehicle for this censorship, and they can be just as effective as government injunctions or physical threats."

The Snow Leopard integrates many of Matthiessen's themes—the abundance and splendor of nature, the fragility of the environment, the fascinations of a foreign culture—with contemplations of a more spiritual sort. The book is an autobiographical account of a journey Matthiessen took, in the company of wildlife biologist George Schaller, to a remote part of Nepal. *New York Times* columnist Anatole Broyard writes of Matthiessen: "On this voyage he travels to the outer limits of the world and the inner limits of the self. . . . When he looks in as well as outward, the two landscapes complement one another." Harrison likewise notes in a review in the *Nation:* "Running concurrent to the outward journey in *The Snow Leopard* is an equally torturous inward journey, and the two are balanced to the extent that neither overwhelms the other." As part of that "inward journey," Matthiessen remembers his second wife's death from cancer and opens himself to the spiritual nourishment of Zen. Des Pres suggests that as a result of these meditations, Matthiessen "has expressed, with uncommon candor and no prospect

of relief, a longing which keeps the soul striving and alert in us all."

The Snow Leopard elicited wide critical respect as well as a National Book Award and an American Book Award. In the *Saturday Review,* Zweig comments that the book "contains many . . . passages, in which the naturalist, the spiritual apprentice, and the writer converge simply and dramatically." *Atlantic* contributor Phoebe-Lou Adams concludes of the work: "It is as though [Matthiessen] looked simultaneously through a telescope and a microscope, and his great skill as a writer enables the reader to share this double vision of a strange and beautiful country." Harrison contends that the author "has written a magnificent book: a kind of lunar paradigm and map of the sacred for any man's journey." As a conclusion to his review, Des Pres calls *The Snow Leopard* "a book fiercely felt and magnificently written, in which timelessness and 'modern time' are made to touch and join."

Though Matthiessen writes about Zen in *The Snow Leopard* and his more recent *Nine-Headed Dragon River: Zen Journals 1969-1982,* he still expresses reservations about offering his personal philosophies for public perusal. "One is always appalled by the idea of wearing your so-called religion on your sleeve," he told *Publishers Weekly.* "I never talked about Zen much. . . . If people come along and want to talk about Zen, that's wonderful, but I don't want to brandish it. It's just a quiet little practice, not a religion . . . just a way of seeing the world. . . . And I find myself very comfortable with it." He elaborated briefly: "Zen is a synonym for life, that's all. Zen practice is life practice. If you can wake up and look around you, if you can knock yourself out of your customary way of thinking and simply see how really miraculous and extraordinary everything around you is, that's Zen."

Joseph Kastner offers an analogy for Matthiessen's writing career in a *Washington Post Book World* review. Kastner records: "A famous photographer once remarked that, for him, the ideal camera would be a lens screwed into his forehead and focused by his brain so that he could take pictures without any intervention. In a sense, Matthiessen, the writer, is equipped with that ideal camera. The things he sees are captured with the click of a thought on his mind and later fixed and printed by a prose rich with specific imagery." With Peter Matthiessen, concludes Styron, "we behold a writer of phenomenal scope and versatility."

BIOGRAPHICAL/CRITICAL SOURCES:

BOOKS

Contemporary Literary Criticism, Gale (Detroit), Volume 7, 1977, Volume 11, 1979, Volume 32, 1985, Volume 64, 1991.

Dictionary of Literary Biography, Volume 6: *American Novelists since World War II,* second series, Gale, 1980.

Dowie, William, *Peter Matthiessen,* Twayne (Boston), 1991.

Matthiessen, Peter, *In the Spirit of Crazy Horse,* Viking, 1983.

Matthiessen, Peter, *Nine-Headed Dragon River: Zen Journals 1969-1982,* Shambhala, 1986.

Matthiessen, Peter, *The Snow Leopard,* Viking, 1978.

Nicholas, D., *Peter Matthiessen: A Bibliography,* Orirana (Canoga Park, CA), 1980.

Parker, William, editor, *Men of Courage: Stories of Present-Day Adventures in Danger and Death,* Playboy Press, 1972.

Styron, William, *This Quiet Dust and Other Writings,* Random House, 1982.

PERIODICALS

Atlantic, June, 1954; March, 1971; November, 1972; June, 1975; September, 1978; March, 1983.

Bloomsbury Review, September-October, 1990, pp. 22, 24.

Book World, December 10, 1967; April 18, 1971.

Chicago Tribune Book World, April 5, 1981; March 13, 1983; June 24, 1990, pp. 1, 5; July 28, 1991, pp. 6-7.

Christian Science Monitor, March 11, 1983.

Commonweal, October 28, 1955.

Critic, May-June, 1970.

Esquire, May, 1989, p. 118.

Georgia Review, winter, 1981.

Globe and Mail (Toronto), July 28, 1984.

Hudson Review, winter, 1975-76; winter, 1981-82.

Library Journal, August, 1955.

Listener, October 19, 1989, pp. 30-31.

Literary Quarterly, May 15, 1975.

Los Angeles Times, March 22, 1979; November 16, 1990, p. E4; May 30, 1991, p. E1; November 8, 1992, p. L9.

Los Angeles Times Book Review, May 10, 1981; March 6, 1983; May 18, 1986; August 24, 1986; May 14, 1989, pp. 2, 11; July 8, 1990, pp. 1, 5; July 28, 1991, p. 4; December 6, 1992, p. 36.

Maclean's, August 13, 1990, p. 59; July 22, 1991, p. 41.

Nation, February 25, 1961; December 13, 1965; June 1, 1970; May 31, 1975; September 16, 1978.

National Review, October 13, 1978.

Natural History, January, 1968.

New Leader, June 9, 1975.

New Republic, June 7, 1975; September 23, 1978; March 7, 1983; June 4, 1984; November 5, 1990, pp. 43-35.

New Statesman, January 10, 1986, p. 26.

Newsweek, April 26, 1971; May 19, 1975; September 11, 1978; December 17, 1979; April 27, 1981; March 28, 1983; August 11, 1986; June 11, 1990, p. 63.

New York, July 22, 1991, p. 50.

New Yorker, May 19, 1975; April 11, 1983; June 4, 1984.

New York Herald Tribune Book Review, April 4, 1954.

New York Review of Books, December 23, 1965; January 4, 1968; August 31, 1972; January 25, 1973; August 7, 1975; September 28, 1978; April 14, 1983; September 27, 1984; January 31, 1991, p. 18.

New York Times, April 4, 1954; October 2, 1955; November 8, 1965; April 23, 1971; August 24, 1978; March 19, 1979; May 2, 1981; March 5, 1983; June 19, 1986; October 11, 1986; July 7, 1990, p. A16; August 22, 1991; July 26, 1992.

New York Times Book Review, April 4, 1954; October 2, 1955; November 22, 1959; October 15, 1961; November 18, 1962; November 7, 1965; December 3, 1967; February 1, 1970; November 26, 1972; May 25, 1975; May 29, 1977; August 13, 1978; November 26, 1978; May 17, 1981; March 6, 1983; July 29, 1984; June 22, 1986; May 14, 1989, p. 11; June 24, 1990, p. 7; August 18, 1991, p. 3; December 6, 1992, p. 52.

New York Times Magazine, June 10, 1990, pp. 30, 42, 94-96.

Paris Review, winter, 1974.

Parnassus, fall, 1984, pp. 21-71.

Progressive, April, 1990, pp. 28-29.

Publishers Weekly, May 9, 1986; September 1, 1989, p. 8; November 9, 1990, p. 12.

San Francisco Chronicle, April 9, 1954; October 10, 1955.

Saturday Review, April 10, 1954; November 6, 1965; November 25, 1967; March 14, 1970; October 28, 1972; June 28, 1975; August, 1978; April, 1981.

Sierra, January-February, 1992, p. 141.

Spectator, June 13, 1981; May 23, 1992, p. 34.

Time, May 26, 1975; August 7, 1978; March 28, 1983; July 7, 1986; July 16, 1990, p. 82; January 11, 1993, pp. 42-43.

Times Literary Supplement, October 23, 1981; March 21, 1986, p. 299; September 22, 1989, p. 1023; August 31, 1990; July 17, 1992, p. 6.

Vanity Fair, December, 1991, p. 114.

Village Voice, June 2, 1975.

Washington Post, December 13, 1978.

Washington Post Book World, August 20, 1978; April 19, 1981; March 27, 1983; May 20, 1984; June 29, 1986; June 24, 1990, p. 5; July 14, 1991, p. 1.

Wilson Library Bulletin, March, 1964.

OTHER

Peter Matthiessen Interview with Kay Bonetti (audio cassette), American Audio Prose Library, 1987.

MAX, Nicholas
See ASBELL, Bernard

*　　*　　*

McCABE, Patrick 1955-

PERSONAL: Born March 27, 1955, in Clones, County Monaghan, Ireland; son of Bernard (a clerk) and Dympna (a homemaker; maiden name, Maguire) McCabe; married Margot Quinn (a receptionist), December, 1981; children: Ellen, Katy. *Education:* Attended St. Patrick's Training College, Dublin, Ireland, 1971-74. *Politics:* None. *Religion:* Roman Catholic.

ADDRESSES: Office—Kingsbury Day Special School, Kingsbury, London NW9, England.

CAREER: Kingsbury Day Special School, London, teacher, 1980—.

AWARDS, HONORS: Hennessy Award from *Irish Press*, 1979, for short story "The Call"; Booker Prize nomination, 1992, and *Irish Times*-Aer Lingus Award for best novel by an Irish writer, 1992, both for *The Butcher Boy.*

WRITINGS:

Ulster Final (one-act play), first broadcast by RTE-Radio, 1984.
Frontiers (one-act play), first broadcast by RTE-Radio, 1984.
The Adventures of Shay Mouse (four-part series for children; broadcast by RTE-Radio, 1983), Raven, 1985.
Music on Clinton Street, Raven, 1986.
Carn, Aidan Ellis (Oxford, England), 1989.
The Butcher Boy, Fromm International (New York City), 1993.
Frank Pig Says Hello! (play; adaptation of *The Butcher Boy*), first produced in Dublin, Ireland, 1993, produced in London at Royal Court Theatre, 1993.
Psychobilly (play), produced in London, 1994.
The Dead School, Dial (New York City), 1995.

Also author of one-act plays *Belfast Days, The Outing*, and *The Butcher Boy*, all broadcast by RTE Dublin, the film script *Madeleine's Eyes*, and the short story collection *Apaches*. Work represented in anthologies, including *The Dolmen Book of Christmas Stories*. Contributor to periodicals, including the *Irish Press, Irish Times*, and *Panurge*.

WORK IN PROGRESS: A film adaptation of *The Butcher Boy*, to be directed by Neil Jordan; two novels.

SIDELIGHTS: A longtime teacher at schools for the learning-disabled in his native Ireland and London, Patrick McCabe turned his talents to writing plays and novels in the mid-1980s. He once told *CA:* "I am particularly interested in writing about contemporary Ireland, against which background all my work is set. The world is an insoluble enigma. Each novel written, each play completed is another step on the road to silencing the furies within." His work has steadily gained recognition from critics and prompted a *Kirkus Reviews* contributor to call him "as skilled and significant a novelist as Ireland has produced in decades."

In his novel *The Butcher Boy*, McCabe offers a vision of life in a small Irish town. As such it recounts "the cruelties, betrayals and other repressions of small-town life," notes James Hynes in the *Washington Post Book World*. And as Julian Moynahan describes it in the *New York Review of Books*, "This much discussed and prize-winning novel is full of social shaming but is full also of so many appalling other things—family breakdown, suicide, alcoholism, a priest's sexual abuse of a male child, hallucination, psychosis, and murder."

As Moynahan suggests, *The Butcher Boy* is also the story of a murder. The title refers to Francie Brady, a lower-class Irish lad who works in a slaughterhouse. Francie's psyche and behavior have been devastated by a childhood with alcoholic and disturbed parents. He has spent time in a reform school and a madhouse. He returns to his little town and eventually exacts revenge on his parents, his town, and everybody who has darkened his life by murdering Mrs. Nugent. The Nugents, as Moynahan explains, "epitomize the decent Irish middle-class family and Catholic values from which Francie is forever barred." Also, Mrs. Nugent had once humiliated Francie and his mother, calling them "pigs." Francie's tale "is startlingly original," comments Hynes. "McCabe has . . . given us a protagonist who is nastier and scarier than any of the petty autocrats [of his small town]."

McCabe has Francie tell his own story, looking back at a personal history of decades ago through the distorting lens of psychosis. As David Mehegan explains in the *Boston Globe*, "The whole story is a continuous interior monologue, shifting seamlessly among Francie's narration, his often screamingly funny analysis of what is happening and his fantasies . . . , his own adventures . . . and his poignant image of himself as a bird on the wing above the town." The character that emerges from this monologue is what has attracted the greatest critical attention to McCabe's book. According to Mehegan, "The book has a compelling and terrible beauty that grows from Francie's convincing character and the truthfulness of his responses to the awful things that befall him."

In the estimation of *New York Times Book Review* contributor Rosemary Mahoney, "With eerie accuracy, Mr. McCabe has captured the machinations of a deranged young mind. Francie is a lovable villain, a semisweet psychotic who elicits from the reader much the same affectionate interest that Perry Smith did in Truman Capote's 'In Cold Blood.' " Mahoney adds that Francie is "part Huck Finn, part Holden Caulfield, part Hannibal Lecter. It is precisely Mr. McCabe's ability to capture the warring states of Francie's mind that elevates this book from the level of the absurd to that of art." Moynahan expresses some reservations about Francie's character: "*The Butcher Boy* has several flaws which come to light once the shock of its Grand Guignol sensationalism wears off. One is Francie's sentimentality. . . . Another problem is that Francie has too much charm."

In addition to McCabe's story and his characterization, critics have remarked upon the author's ability to create Francie's unique voice. "McCabe's slyest move is to make Francie's voice as engaging and funny as it is frightening," observes Hynes. He adds that McCabe's work is a "small masterpiece of literary ventriloquism—a Beckett monologue with a plot by Alfred Hitchcock." As Mahoney puts it: "Despite its Gothicism and its gruesome ending, *The Butcher Boy* crackles with humor, much of it generated by the remarkable authenticity of Francie's voice, the running, skipping, epic fashion in which he tells his story."

Even with its skillful characterization and portrayal of Francie's captivating voice, Scott Turow wonders if McCabe's novel and Francie's story will appeal to American readers. "What *The Butcher Boy* reveals probably was more of a shock to the straitened Irish conscience than it will be to the American one," he writes in Chicago *Tribune Books.* "Sad to say, but I think our per capita population of Francie Bradys is far higher than Ireland's, and as a result many Americans are more accustomed to imagining the sad course of events that overcome such children." Yet, in Rosemary Mahoney's opinion, "*The Butcher Boy* is the side of the murder story never revealed in the newspapers: a map of a murderer's mind, a revelation of a murder's reason. It is the story of the heritage of madness and loneliness, a stunning picture of the desperation of the unloved."

BIOGRAPHICAL/CRITICAL SOURCES:

PERIODICALS

America, April 30, 1994, pp. 22-24.
Boston Globe, June 9, 1993, p. 65.
Kirkus Reviews, March 1, 1995, p. 258.
Los Angeles Times Book Review, June 13, 1993, p. 6.
New York Review of Books, October 7, 1993, pp. 28-29; June 8, 1995, pp. 45-48.
New York Times Book Review, May 30, 1993, p. 9.
Times Literary Supplement, May 19, 1989.
Tribune Books (Chicago), July 11, 1993, sec. 14, pp. 4-5.
Washington Post Book World, May 16, 1993, p. 4.

McCARTHY, Mary (Therese) 1912-1989

PERSONAL: Born June 21, 1912, in Seattle, WA; died of cancer, October 25, 1989, in New York, NY; daughter of Roy Winfield (a lawyer) and Therese (Preston) McCarthy; sister of the actor Kevin McCarthy; married Harold Johnsrud (an actor and playwright), June 21, 1933 (divorced August, 1936); married Edmund Wilson (a writer and critic), February, 1938 (divorced December, 1946); married Bowden Broadwater, December, 6, 1946 (divorced, 1961); married James Raymond West (a U.S. State Department official), April 15, 1961; children: (second marriage) Reuel Kimball Wilson. *Education:* Vassar College, A.B., 1933. *Politics:* Libertarian socialist.

CAREER: Novelist, literary critic, and essayist. Founder while at Vassar, with Elizabeth Bishop, Muriel Rukeyser, and Eleanor Clark, of a literary magazine to protest the policies of the *Vassar Review* (the two magazines later merged). Book reviewer for the *Nation* and the *New Republic,* typist and editor for Benjamin Stolberg, and brochure writer for an art gallery, all New York City, 1933-36; editor, Covici Friede (publisher), New York City, 1936-37; ghostwriter for H. V. Kaltenborn, 1937; *Partisan Review,* New York City, editor, 1937-38, drama critic, 1937-62. Bard College, Annandale-on-Hudson, NY, instructor in literature, 1945-46, Charles P. Stevenson Chair of Literature, 1986-89; Sarah Lawrence College, Bronxville, NY, instructor in English, 1948; University College, University of London, Northcliffe Lecturer, 1980.

MEMBER: National Institute of Arts and Letters, Authors League of America, Phi Beta Kappa.

AWARDS, HONORS: Horizon prize, 1949, for *The Oasis;* Guggenheim fellowship, 1949-50 and 1959-60; National Institute of Arts and Letters grant in literature, 1957; Doctor of Letters, Syracuse University, 1973, University of Hull, 1974, Bard College, 1976; Doctor of Laws, University of Aberdeen, 1979; D.Litt., Bowdoin College, 1981, University of Maine at Orono, 1982; Edward MacDowell Medal, MacDowell Colony, 1984, for outstanding contributions to literature; National Medal for Literature, Harold K. Guinzburg Foundation, 1984, for a distinguished and continuing contribution to American letters.

WRITINGS:

FICTION

The Company She Keeps (novel), Simon & Schuster (New York City), 1942, 2nd edition, Weidenfeld & Nicolson (London), 1957.
The Oasis (novel; first published in *Horizon;* also see below), Random House (New York City), 1949, published in England as *A Source of Embarrassment,* Heinemann (London), 1950.

Cast a Cold Eye (short stories; also see below), Harcourt (New York City), 1950, expanded edition published as *The Hounds of Summer and Other Stories: Mary McCarthy's Short Fiction,* Avon, 1981.

The Groves of Academe (novel), Harcourt, 1952.

A Charmed Life (novel), Harcourt, 1955.

The Group (novel), Harcourt, 1963.

Winter Visitors (excerpt from *Birds of America;* also see below), Harcourt, 1970.

Birds of America (novel), Harcourt, 1971.

Cast a Cold Eye [and] *The Oasis,* New American Library (New York City), 1972.

Cannibals and Missionaries (novel), Harcourt, 1979.

NONFICTION

Sights and Spectacles, 1937-1956 (theater criticism), Farrar, Straus (New York City), 1956, augmented edition published as *Sights and Spectacles, 1937-1958,* Heinemann, 1959, augmented edition published as *Mary McCarthy's Theatre Chronicles, 1937-1962* (also see below), Farrar, Straus, 1963.

Venice Observed (also see below), Reynal (New York City), 1956, 2nd edition, 1957.

Memories of a Catholic Girlhood, Harcourt, 1957.

The Stones of Florence (also see below), Harcourt, 1959.

On the Contrary (essays; also see below), Farrar, Straus, 1961.

The Humanist in the Bathtub (selected essays from *Mary McCarthy's Theatre Chronicles, 1937-1962* and *On the Contrary*), New American Library, 1964.

Vietnam (reportage; also see below), Harcourt, 1967.

Hanoi (reportage; also see below), Harcourt, 1968.

The Writing on the Wall and Other Literary Essays, Harcourt, 1970.

Medina (reportage; also see below), Harcourt, 1972.

Venice Observed [and] *The Stones of Florence,* Penguin, 1972.

The Mask of State: Watergate Portraits (reportage), Harcourt, 1974.

The Seventeenth Degree (reportage; includes *Vietnam, Hanoi,* and *Medina*), Harcourt, 1974.

Ideas and the Novel (literary essays), Harcourt, 1980.

Occasional Prose (essays), Harcourt, 1985.

How I Grew, Harcourt, 1987.

Intellectual Memoirs: New York, 1936-1938, foreword by Elizabeth Hardwick, Harcourt, 1992.

Between Friends: The Correspondence of Hannah Arendt and Mary McCarthy, 1949-1975, edited by Carol Brightman, Harcourt, 1995.

OTHER

(Translator) Simone Weil, *The Iliad; or, The Poem of Force,* Politics Pamphlets, 1947.

(Translator) Rachel Bespaloff, *On the Iliad,* Pantheon (New York City), 1948.

Author of afterword to *Without Marx or Jesus: The New American Revolution Has Begun,* by Jean-Francois Revel, Doubleday (New York City), 1971, and *Portugal,* by Neal Slavin, Lustrum Press (New York City), 1971. Also contributor of essays to periodicals, including *New York Review of Books, New York Times Book Review, Observer, Partisan Review,* and *Sunday Times.*

McCarthy's books have been translated into French, Spanish, Italian, Dutch, Finnish, Danish, Swedish, Romanian, Serbo-Croatian, Hebrew, Japanese, German, and Polish.

ADAPTATIONS: The Group was filmed by United Artists in 1966.

SIDELIGHTS: Mary McCarthy, one of America's most prominent intellectuals, was renowned for her outspokenness and her opposition to what she perceived as hypocrisy. She rose to prominence in the 1930s as part of a group of New York City intellectuals that included literary critic Edmund Wilson (her second husband), *Partisan Review* editor Philip Rahv, and writer Lillian Hellman. "Her uniqueness," Doris Grumbach noted in *The Company She Kept: A Revealing Portrait of Mary McCarthy,* "lies partly in her readiness to do battle, her willingness to attack in every direction, without concern for the barriers of established reputation." McCarthy's effort brought her to the heart of contemporary issues. "[This] need to strip away facades and to uncover what she considers to be the truth," Barbara McKenzie noted in her book *Mary McCarthy,* "is the result of the unusually high value she places on honesty."

With this honesty guiding her pen, McCarthy set out to restore to the individual the capacity for understanding. "All of us, she supposes, are engaged for a multitude of reasons in a conspiracy to escape reality, to tame and falsify it," wrote Arthur Schlesinger Jr. in the *New Republic.* In such a world, McCarthy explained in "Settling the Colonel's Hash" (collected in *On the Contrary*), "the writer must be, first of all, a listener and observer, who can pay attention to reality, like an obedient pupil, and who is willing, always, to be surprised by the messages reality is sending through to him." Armed with the lessons of reality, McCarthy exposed the falseness of what seems to be and illuminated, Schlesinger observed, the "reality [that] exists in the spontaneities and unpredictabilities of human experience."

McCarthy was orphaned at the age of six and spent several years in the care of abusive relatives, an experience she later recounted in the much-praised memoir *Memories of a Catholic Girlhood.* Rescued from her plight by sympathetic grandparents, she eventually became an aspiring young writer studying at Vassar College, a journey toward personal fulfillment that she described in what some called her intellectual autobiography, *How I Grew.* In 1933 she graduated and moved to New York, where she quickly became a professional writer whose essays and sometimes scathing reviews appeared in many respected publications, including the *New Republic, Nation,* and *Partisan Review.* "Pointed sharply to the weaknesses, foolishness, and ineptitude of critics," Grumbach observed in *The Company She Kept,* these articles "suggested the very real injustices that stupid but compassionate critics committed against the public by recommending second-rate, weak-minded pap and ignoring really excellent work."

Her work at the *Nation* earned McCarthy some recognition, but it was freelance work. She found regular work as an editor for Covici Friede (John Steinbeck's publisher) from 1936 to 1937 and then joined the staff of the *Partisan Review.* She worked as an editor for the magazine only until 1938, but she continued to contribute drama criticism in a column entitled "Theatre Chronicle" for several years. To these roles of drama critic and literary critic McCarthy would soon add those of journalist, short story writer, and novelist. She began writing fiction at the encouragement of her second husband, Edmund Wilson, shortly after their marriage in 1938. Rather than sacrifice her personal commitment to honesty in order to create fiction, McCarthy developed a fiction style rooted in this honesty.

Her first novel came about when McCarthy noticed a relationship between several stories that she had originally written separately. She worked these stories into the same framework; the result was *The Company She Keeps.* The novel reveals Margaret Sargent, a young woman much like McCarthy herself, engaged in a quest for her one true identity. But more than this, Irvin Stock suggested in *Fiction as Wisdom: From Goethe to Bellow* that *The Company She Keeps* conveys Sargent's moral dilemma, her "increasingly desperate struggle, against all the temptations to falsehood in the intellectual life of her time, to stop lying and to live by the truth." Because the novel parallels the life of its author, one might expect from it a measure of protective distortion; however, Stock noted, "The book is remarkable for the honesty of its self-exposure, an exposure which dares to include the ignoble and the humiliating and which shows a kind of reckless passion for the truth that is to remain an important element of [McCarthy's] talent."

By 1960 McCarthy had written three other novels, *The Oasis, The Groves of Academe,* and *A Charmed Life.* These novels established McCarthy as a writer with a keen critical sense, a social satirist whose eye focused on the intellectual elite. Together with *The Company She Keeps,* they

received considerable attention in literary circles. Those critical of the novels cite too much autobiographical material within the fiction and a preoccupation with intellectuals and their ideas. McCarthy herself responded to these charges in an interview with Elisabeth Niebuhr published in *Writers at Work: The "Paris Review" Interviews:* "What I really do is take real plums and put them in an imaginary cake. If you're interested in the cake, you get rather annoyed with people saying what species the real plum was." She elaborated, "I do try . . . to be as exact as possible about the essence of a person, to find the key that works the person both in real life and in the fiction." Commenting on McCarthy's portrayal of intellectuals and their ideas, Stock wrote, "Though she has written mainly about her own class of American intellectuals, people who try to live by ideas or to give the appearance of doing so, and has, therefore, naturally admitted the play of ideas into her stories, her chief concerns have always been psychological, emotional, and above all, moral, the concerns of the novelist."

With the publication of *The Group,* her 1963 novel, McCarthy became known to a wider audience. This novel, which chronicles the lives of a group of Vassar graduates from the time of their graduation until seven years later, became a bestseller and was made into a motion picture starring Candice Bergen and Joan Hackett. Because the book details the lives of eight upper-middle-class women, their careers, loves, and sexual attitudes, it was accused by some reviewers of playing up to the women's magazine audience. Norman Mailer, writing in the *New York Review of Books,* called the novel "good but not nearly good enough." Mailer recognized the value of *The Group* as a sociological study, and admitted: "It is skillful, intricately knitted as a novel, its characters while not always distinguishable from one another are true in their reactions, or at least are true in the severe field of limitation she puts on their comings and goings, their paltry passions, their lack of grasp, their lack of desire to grasp." Even so, he faulted McCarthy for not following through on her theme. He commented, "She failed out of profound timidity . . . she is afraid to unloose the demons." Stock also identified shortcomings in *The Group,* but found it nonetheless a pleasure to read. He noted, "The pleasure comes from the characters (most of them), so pathetic and comic, so true, in their struggle to live up to their advanced ideas or to cling to reality amid the general falsenesses; from the continuous vivifying detail of their setting, appearance, tone, and gesture; and from the sheer quantity of people and experiences the story brings to life."

McCarthy's deeply felt personal concern for the fate of nature is the central issue of her sixth novel, *Birds of America.* The author told Jean-Francois Revel in an interview for the *New York Times Book Review:* "Nature for centuries has been the court of appeals. It will decide one way or another. Not always justly; but nevertheless . . . the appeal is always to this court, to Nature's court. And if this is gone, we're lost. And I think we're lost, I'm not an optimist." Stock discussed how *Birds of America* illustrated McCarthy's pessimism in his book *Fiction as Wisdom:* "The tragedy at the heart of her novel is not only that Nature is dead, but that it has been murdered by an ideal she also values, the ideal of Equality." Stock added that the servant of equality—technology—has not only "replaced Nature . . . with life-reducing conveniences and abstractions, but, far worse, by giving man control over what once controlled and educated him, it has put our whole world at the mercy of the ego-driven human will."

The novel follows nineteen-year-old Peter Levi, student and bird watcher, from the coast of New England, where he and his mother are spending the summer, to Paris, the site of Peter's foreign studies. In New England, Peter discovers that the great horned owl that had captivated him during a previous visit is dead. Gone also is the quaint old-fashioned atmosphere of the small town, replaced by the technology of the 1960s. Paris is no better; it is alien and as an environment, unnatural. When Peter retreats to a zoo upon learning of the bombing of North Vietnam, he is struck by a black swan. Later, having been rushed to the hospital, Peter sees the philosopher Immanuel Kant appear in his hospital room. His mentor tells him, "Nature is dead, *mein kind*." "The didacticism of Miss McCarthy's theme in no way blunts her wit," wrote a *Times Literary Supplement* reviewer; "indeed, the challenge of the *philosophes* and the attempt to make her Candide a convincingly likable as well as serious fall-guy hero seem to have stimulated her into some of the funniest scenes she has ever written."

The critical debate surrounding *Birds of America* often centered on the characters in the book. Some reviewers found Peter Levi and the others who populate his world inadequately developed and unbelievable. "No creature more devoid of existential reality ever lived than this so-carefully-documented Peter Levi," commented Helen Vendler in the *New York Times Book Review*. The weakness of the characters is due, in Hilton Kramer's opinion, to a flaw in their creator. Kramer wrote in the *Washington Post Book World*, "She lacks the essential fictional gift: She cannot imagine *others*. Missing from the powerful arsenal of her literary talents is some fundamental mimetic sympathy." The result, Vendler added, is that "stereotypes take over where her own knowledge leaves off." John Thompson expressed a different opinion in his review in *Commentary:* "This mother and her son [are] two people I liked very much and found completely credible." And of Peter Levi, Foster Hirsch wrote in *Commonweal,*

"At the beginning of the novel, his idealizing vision is truly innocent, at the end, it is open-eyed, alert to the world: that he retains his sense of the potential fineness of life is his (and the book's) special triumph."

As a novel about coming of age, some critics believed *Birds of America* ran the risk of too closely mirroring its predecessors in the genre. Yet, Hirsch observed, "More often than not the cliches are overturned, reworked into fresh, life-giving terrain. . . . Pleasant surprises and reversals almost continuously enrich the narrative." The author's insights into her character and his dilemma set this novel apart from similar novels. Melvin Maddocks, writing in *Life,* called *Birds of America* "a profoundly thoughtful and finally moving book, a cumulative book that seems to bring to bear upon every page all that Miss McCarthy has ever learned or hoped for from art and civilization." Maddocks concluded, "McCarthy has performed the small miracle of the major artist, treating tragedy with such clarity, such range that it becomes for the reader a healing act."

As *Birds of America* reflects the social turbulence of the war in Vietnam, McCarthy's next novel, *Cannibals and Missionaries,* reflects the political unrest of the 1970s. McCarthy's novel "is pure pleasure," Grumbach noted in the *Chicago Tribune Book World,* "a psychological thriller, a suspense story, a brilliant ideological parable, all wrapped in a strong coat of the kind of witty and intelligent talk she has always been capable of." While confronting one of the central issues of our time, terrorism and the psychology of terror, McCarthy also offered for scrutiny another older question, as Robert M. Adams put it, "the value of major works of art, relative to human life." In examining these issues, Adams wrote in the *New York Review of Books,* "McCarthy writes crisp, unsentimental prose, with a cruel eye for weakness and inauthenticity."

In *Cannibals and Missionaries,* a group of liberals—politicians and concerned citizens—are on their way to Iran to investigate accusations that the Shah's secret police are engaged in the torture of dissidents. On the same flight, in first class, is a group of wealthy art collectors. Terrorists hijack the airplane, hoping to use the liberals as bargaining chips, but in time, they realize that the collectors are more valuable. A scheme is concocted to exchange the collectors for their most precious possessions; an irreplaceable work of art, the terrorists reason, will command a higher price than any human hostage. *Cannibals and Missionaries* captures the tension of the hijack situation, observed Anne Tyler in her *Washington Post Book World* review: "There are the psychological quirks . . . that the hostages show under stress: unexpected examples of cowardice and bravery, comic adherences to the old 'normal' rituals, illogical urges to protect the terrorists from defeat."

As with *Birds of America, Cannibals and Missionaries* has been faulted by some reviewers because of McCarthy's manipulation of the elements of the novel. "As a work of fiction," wrote an *Atlantic Monthly* reviewer, "*Cannibals and Missionaries* suffers from a lack of focus. . . . The characters are maddeningly banal." "Her cast is so large," suggested *Time* reviewer R. Z. Sheppard, "that [McCarthy] is forced to try to bring them to life with unwieldy dossiers rather than with dialogue and action."

Other reviewers, however, regarded *Cannibals and Missionaries* in terms of its thematic concerns. In the *Times Literary Supplement,* for example, T. J. Binyon noted, "This is very much a novel of ideas." In presenting ideas, Binyon reasoned, in confronting issues and uncovering their underlying implications, McCarthy challenged the reader. "A remorseless, powerful intellect has burst open the seams of the novelist's kid glove," Binyon wrote. "No longer allowed to laze in the groves of fiction, we are forced to exercise our minds on a series of philosophical problems." *New York Times Book Review* contributor Mary Gordon believed "the most important achievement of *Cannibals and Missionaries* is McCarthy's understanding of the psychology of terrorism, the perception . . . that terrorism is the product of despair." Gordon concluded, "In response to the truly frightful prospect of anarchic terrorism, Mary McCarthy has written one of the most shapely novels to have come out in recent years: a well-made book. It is delightful to observe her balancing, winnowing, fitting in the pieces of her plot."

Given her high regard for truthfulness, McCarthy's approach to writing fiction is not surprising. In "Settling the Colonel's Hash" from *On the Contrary,* she compares story writing to discovery: "A cluster of details presents itself to my scrutiny, like a mystery that I will understand in the course of writing or sometimes not fully until afterward, when, if I have been honest and listened to these details carefully, I will find that they are connected and that there is a coherent pattern. This pattern is *in* experience itself; you do not impose it from the outside and if you try to, you will find that the story is taking the wrong tack, dribbling away from you into artificiality or inconsequence."

But as McCarthy pointed out in the *New York Times Book Review,* the author needs more than an accepting and understanding eye; the author also needs faith. McCarthy commented: "In any novel (in my experience) there is a crisis of faith for the author. This generally occurs toward the end of Chapter Two, when the first impetus has gone; occasionally in Chapter Three. . . . The crisis can last a night or a few hours; with *The Group* it lasted years, during which I put the manuscript aside. . . . There is no use going on till the crisis is resolved. . . . A moment comes, though, about three-quarters of the way through the book,

when you know you are going to finish it; this is the moment when it has gained your belief."

As an author who seeks to understand the lessons of reality and remain faithful to the vision of that reality contained in her writing, McCarthy strives to offer readers poignant insights into the nature of humankind. As Stock wrote in *Fiction as Wisdom,* "Though Mary McCarthy's novels are not all equally successful, each has so much life and truth, and is written in a prose so spare, vigorous, and natural, and yet at the same time so witty, graceful, and, in a certain way, poetic, that it becomes a matter for wonder that she is not generally named among the finest American novelists of her period."

In the late 1960s, McCarthy interrupted a novel in progress to take action against the war in Vietnam. "Though she had tried to hide behind a novelist's detachment . . . Vietnam [had] finally gotten inside her and produced an 'identity crisis,' " Lee Lockwood observed in the *Nation.* McCarthy visited Southeast Asia twice; she travelled to Saigon in 1967 and later, in 1968, she went to Hanoi. McCarthy wrote several essays based upon these trips which first appeared in the *New York Review of Books* and were later collected in her books *Vietnam* and *Hanoi.* "Her moral sensibility . . . led her to Vietnam where she experienced the anguish of societies in war," wrote Marcus Raskin in the *Partisan Review.* "She was not there as an adventurer or as a journalist. She was there as a committed person who happened to write. Her visit to Vietnam led her to believe that the American system itself was decaying."

McCarthy not only opposed the war, she rejected its purpose, an opinion upon which she expounded in an exchange with Diana Trilling published in the *New York Review of Books:* "Nor frankly do I think it admirable to try to stop Communism even by peaceful subversion. The alternatives to Communism offered by the Western countries are all ugly in their own ways and getting uglier. What I would hope for politically is an internal evolution in the Communist states toward greater freedom and plurality of choice." Her first trip, to a Saigon filled with the by-products of an American presence, prompted her to write in *Vietnam:* "The worst thing that could happen to our country would be to win this war." As she commented in her exchange with Trilling, an essay entitled "On Withdrawing from Vietnam," "The imminent danger for America is not of being 'taken in' by Communism . . . but of being taken in by itself. If I can interfere with that process, I will."

McCarthy's criticism of the American war effort that appeared in *Vietnam* was well-received by reviewers. "This is . . . tight and excellent writing, and constitutes perhaps the most piercing wound delivered to America's conception of itself since the war," wrote Neal Ascherson in the *Listener*. From McCarthy's essays on Vietnam, a sort of literary journalism, emerged a truth greater than that obtained from the mere reporting of facts. Ascherson commented, "She is not the first to record the grotesque terminology of the war, but as a professional with words, her understanding of what these phrases actually mean, as well as of what they conceal, is unrivalled."

Her essays reveal the physical products of the war—the pollution of the jungle, the squalor of the refugee camps—as well as the malaise that accompanies its inefficiency and corruption. Yet, despite her preconceived mission to return from her trip with "material damaging to the American interest," she refrained from prescribing quick remedies. "Mary McCarthy wisely does not offer a solution," observed George Woodstock in *Canadian Forum*. "That the war is too appalling, too materially destructive to the Vietnamese, too morally destructive to the Americans, for it to be continued; this is what she sets out to present." Woodstock concluded, "Her argument on this point is a model lesson in the need to keep great moral issues simple and sharp to the point."

McCarthy found a much different environment when she visited North Vietnam in 1968. Her essays published in *Hanoi* conveyed her view of the contrast between the North and the South. Moved by what she saw, McCarthy strengthened her demand for an American withdrawal. Tom Buckley found in *Hanoi* evidence that McCarthy's experience affected her position as a dispassionate observer. He wrote in the *Washington Post Book World*, "The clear voice has been muted, indeed almost strangled, by rage and shame over the bombing of North Vietnam and by the author's compassion and admiration for its people and its leaders." Buckley added, "The author's protective . . . attitude toward the North Vietnamese, her expressed concern to do or say nothing that might prove injurious to them, seem excessive." Similarly, Peter Shaw indicated in *Commentary* that McCarthy's bias distorted her image of the situation. "When, in Mary McCarthy's books, a corrupt, Americanized South Vietnam and its people is contrasted with a utopian, inspiriting North," Shaw noted, "it becomes impossible for the most sympathetic reader, if he has the slightest sensitivity to the truth, not to mistrust the reality of what is being described." Concluded Ward Just in the *Washington Post*, "This book is very shrill and very shrill and very polemical, and as a result is almost useless as a guide to North Vietnam."

In 1971, McCarthy attended the trial of Captain Ernest Medina, Lieutenant William Calley's company commander in 1968 when South Vietnamese civilians were massacred at the village of My Lai. The trial and Medina's acquittal furnished McCarthy with the material for her third book of essays on the Vietnam War. In *Medina*,

commented Fredrica S. Friedman in the *Saturday Review*, McCarthy "uses the trial of Capt. Ernest L. Medina to comment on America's resolution of the issue of wartime guilt." The account focuses on the former soldiers who testified and on the proceedings more than on the defendant, offering in McCarthy's literary journalism her vision of what happened. "The novelist's cold eye surveys the scene and in the language that made her famous, she freezes the protagonists in their failures and venalities and evasions," Stephen Koch wrote in the *Nation*.

As Basil T. Paquet noted in the *New York Review of Books*, McCarthy's "keen moral sensibility" allowed her to see not only what happened but also the underlying significance of this trial. From *Medina*, he observed, "what emerges is not a document that vilifies the rather shallow figures of the trial but a polemic that tries to pull us closer to recognition of the nature of our involvement in this action." Such is the value of this style of reporting, indicated Friedman: "In her fine-drawn observations on the ineptness of the prosecution and, more importantly, on the country's psyche at that time, she adds to our understanding."

In a review of *The Seventeenth Degree* (a collection of the essays previously published in *Vietnam, Hanoi*, and *Medina*) and of *The Mask of State: Watergate Portraits*, Harold Rosenberg discussed how McCarthy's approach to journalism, founded upon her dedication to honesty, succeeded where others failed. During the war in Vietnam and the Senate Watergate hearings, Rosenberg believed, "The problem was not to gather the 'news' but to get behind it or see through it." He observed in the *New York Review of Books*, "The news media, applying their traditional techniques, could only present a mixture of data and distortion." McCarthy, by seeing through to the meaning behind the facts succeeded in capturing the social impact of that period. "Her constantly sparking style makes historical events as tangible to her readers as they are to her, instead of pushing off these events into the dead space of the media," observed Rosenberg. Writing in the *New York Times Book Review*, Richard Goodwin called McCarthy "one of America's finest journalists."

McCarthy's commitment to honesty, her intolerance of deception and distortion, served as the standard for her critical writing. McCarthy first found an opportunity to exercise her critical talents in the book reviews she wrote for the *Nation* and the *New Republic* and then more regularly in her "Theatre Chronicles" for *Partisan Review*. "Although a Trotskyist view of art's relationship to society provided a foundation for her remarks about current theatrical productions," Julian Symons pointed out in *Critical Occasions*, "it was her native wit and sharp perceptiveness that made these monthly chronicles the most notable dramatic criticism of the period." These essays were first collected and published in book form in 1956 as *Sights and Spectacles, 1937-1956.*

On the Contrary, which contained social commentary as well as literary criticism, appeared in 1961, but her first book devoted exclusively to literary criticism was *The Writing on the Wall and Other Literary Essays,* published in 1970. Reviewing this book in *Esquire,* Malcolm Muggeridge commented, "Like all her writing in this genre, [*The Writing on the Wall* is] extremely readable, if at times vaguely irritating; a characteristic blend of shrewd observations, imaginative insight and occasional lapses into naivete." In this collection of essays, McCarthy offered her views of a large selection of literary works and their authors—Shakespeare, Flaubert, Hannah Arendt, William Burroughs, George Orwell, J. D. Salinger, and others. "She certainly locates that 'false and sentimental' element in Salinger but her attack on Orwell is patently unfair and sometimes silly," wrote Derek Stanford in *Books and Bookmen.* "Orwell has been called 'the conscience of his generation,' " Stanford points out, "and one has the feeling that Miss McCarthy is revolting against that conscience . . . when she writes the title essay of her book upon him."

McCarthy found more to identify with in the writing of Ivy Compton-Burnett, the novelist whose works observe upperclass life in pre-World War I England. McCarthy noted, "What flashes out of her work is a spirited, unpardoning sense of injustice, which becomes even sharper in her later books. In her own eccentric way, Compton-Burnett is a radical thinker, one of the rare modern heretics." McCarthy also viewed favorably the work of some of the experimental novelists of the twentieth century, including Nathalie Sarraute, Monique Wittig, and Vladimir Nabokov. "She calls Nabokov's *Pale Fire* 'one of the very great works of this century' and, with awesome powers of explication, supported by scholarly resources, shows why," wrote a *Newsweek* contributor.

Although some reviewers found fault with the opinions and conclusions McCarthy expressed in *The Writing on the Wall,* they agreed for the most part that it was a valuable addition to critical literature. *New York Times* writer Christopher Lehmann-Haupt commented, "Her prose is economical without being austere, witty without extravagance, tense and dramatic in its development from sentence to paragraph, clean as a chime. . . . Her intelligence and learning are dazzling." Moreover, Diana Loercher observed in the *Christian Science Monitor,* "This group of essays would be interesting even if one had not read the authors, for Miss McCarthy is superb at provoking thought well beyond the ostensible subject." Loercher concluded, "McCarthy deserves credit for the rectitude of her criticism, for she clearly possesses the verbal skill to be captious and vicious, but she has chosen to style herself

as a champion of truth rather than a dragoness of destruction."

Ideas and the Novel offers McCarthy's vision of the modern novel and its fate. She long considered it the tendency of the modern novel to minimize the role of the traditional elements: plot, character, and setting; trends that she maintained betrayed a low regard for facts. In addition, the central point of *Ideas and the Novel* is her accusation that for twentieth-century authors ideas are "unsightly in a novel." McCarthy believed that the modern novelist, taking Henry James as a model, feels a duty "to free himself from the workload of commentary and simply, awesomely, to show: his creation is beyond paraphrase or reduction."

McCarthy felt that James's descendants had overaestheticized the novel. As John Leonard pointed out in the *New York Times,* the novel had lost its sense of audience, its sense of place, and its sense of society. "What [Mary McCarthy] mourns most," he said, "is a modern failure of curiosity, a missing texture. . . . The details are what make life interesting; ideas are what makes the brain interesting; plot implies that something happens, and something always does."

To emphasize her dissatisfaction with the contemporary novels, McCarthy contrasted the twentieth-century novel with its nineteenth-century counterpart. For McCarthy, the novels of Dostoevsky and other nineteenth-century novelists revealed the "fascination of ideas." The vision of empire created by Napoleon permeates these novels, affecting them and informing them. The authors of these books were highly regarded by their readers; she noted that at that time the author was considered "an authority on . . . medicine, religion, capital punishment, the right relations between the sexes."

Ideas and the Novel received a mixed response. Loosely defined lengthy plot summaries were cited as weak points by some reviewers. Others found the book self-indulgent or judgmental. Yet, noted Herbert Gold in the *Los Angeles Times Book Review,* "Sometimes she has seemed malevolent in judgment . . . but at her best she is redeemed by wit, cogency, conviction." Moreover, reviewers admitted McCarthy's collection does remind the reader of the value of the traditional elements of the novel; it does much to restore the acceptability of a close relationship between the idea and the novel. It also expresses the author's feeling that "emergency strategies [are necessary] to disarm and disorient reviewers and teachers of literature, who as always," she wrote, "are the reader's main foe." Gold concluded, "It's a pleasure to praise this mind as it casts about elegantly in the desire to understand a matter congenial to her and important to all good readers and serious writers."

In the twenty-one essays that make up *Occasional Prose,* McCarthy put her critical eye and formidable pen to marking occasions of personal, literary, social, political, and linguistic significance. As Stefan Kanfer wrote in *Time,* "All of the works are reminiscent of, in Stendhal's memorable phrase, 'a mirror walking along a main road.' " And, as Kanfer noted, "Although *Occasional Prose* ranges back to 1968, none of it is dated, and little seems forced by headlines." The book offers obituaries of lost friends, an exploration of the novel and some of its notable practitioners, a description of an anti-war demonstration, an explication of Richard Nixon's doublespeak, an opera guide, and observations of McCarthy as gardener. For *Village Voice* contributor Jacqueline Austin, "McCarthy provides an education in transforming the external into the personal, whether I agree with her or not. She makes each moment of reading, experiencing, remembering into an occasion." To Webster Schott, writing in the *Washington Post Book World, Occasional Prose* is a reminder of the character of McCarthy's thought and writing. "To read Mary McCarthy is often sheer pleasure," he commented. "Her mind works like bright light, showing us details that redefine what we thought we had seen before. Her sentences are displays of grace."

The personal pieces collected in this book, especially the obituaries, suggested that McCarthy may have mellowed as she matured. As Gordon put it in *Esquire,* "The eye of *Occasional Prose,* . . . is not cold but tender, the reflective vision beautifully matured." The literary criticism still reflects McCarthy's characteristic hard edge, but it also shows her unique insight into works. "As a literary critic Miss McCarthy often likes to lay down rules and devise categories . . . , but her finest talent is for unraveling difficult texts by paying the closest possible attention to the actual twists and turns of words on the page," Julian Moynahan observed in the *New York Times Book Review.* McCarthy's essay on the demonstrations held in London in 1968 to protest the Vietnam War harkens back to her books on that war published in the late 1960s and early 1970s. "This description [of the London protest] is typical of her reportorial style—a quick eye for the telling and anomalous detail, along with a tendency to view public events, or at least public events in the 1960's, as theater," Moynahan observed.

The essays of *Occasional Prose* continued McCarthy's exploration of issues found in her previous fiction and nonfiction, but a number of reviewers questioned the coherence and depth of this collection. Schott recognized that "Mary McCarthy's purpose in writing is exactly this: to find meaning, to make order of human expression and action." Even so, he added, "I do wish in this particular book she had left out her rewrite of the plot of *La Traviata* for a Metropolitan Opera guide book and had passed up the temptation to memorialize her garden pieces. They're geese among swans." In the *San Francisco Review of Books,* Robert Linkous called *Occasional Prose* "a grab-bag of trivialities and occasional treasures. . . . The compilation is eclectic, if not eccentric." Jeffrey Meyers noted that "these essays have a common manner and style, but are rather arbitrarily arranged." He wrote in the *National Review,* "They would be more effective if they were divided into sections on literature and politics, as in her collection *On the Contrary.*" Yet, despite its weaknesses, Schott found that *Occasional Prose* reinforced McCarthy's standing among the American literati. He contended, "She is a clear-eyed, cool-voiced analyst of human behavior and one of the few commentators on the arts for whom the term 'critic' seems barely adequate. She is nearly a national cultural asset, and the pieces retrieved for *Occasional Prose* show us why once again."

McCarthy wrote *How I Grew* as the first installment of her intellectual autobiography. As such, it does not detail the sensational events of her life, many of which can be found in her novels. Instead of her exploits as the bad girl of the New York intellectuals, the author's character shines through in this book. As Richard Eder observed in the *Los Angeles Times Book Review,* "McCarthy, for all her lucid critical mind and moral sensibility, is not an autobiographer by nature, any more than she is a novelist by nature. To a reader, the details of growing up are not usually interesting in themselves; it is the quality of the writer's remembrance that holds us." Eder suggested that those who may have expected more of McCarthy's hard yet insightful analysis will be disappointed with *How I Grew.* "And yet," he concluded, "the book, with its many details and anecdotes that remain undigested and untransformed because the temperature is too low for such a process, is redeemed by intelligence."

When she died in 1989, McCarthy was at work on the second book of her intellectual autobiography. The finished material was collected and published as *Intellectual Memoirs: New York, 1936-1938.* As Robert Cummings pointed out in the *Journal of American History,* "The dates of this memoir . . . were the years during which McCarthy made her literary debut as an astringent book reviewer and critic for the *Nation* and, briefly, the *New Republic.*" Because of the tell-all nature of many of McCarthy's novels, much of the terrain covered in this book may not be new to a reader familiar with the author's work. Cummings explained, "Just as *How I Grew* somewhat overlapped with *Memories of a Catholic Girlhood,* so too this memoir returns to a place and time that McCarthy had already treated in such essays as 'My Confession' (1953) and in her first book of fiction, *The Company She Keeps.*"

Although it has historical value as the final piece of McCarthy's oeuvre and it offers her final look back at her literary beginnings, some critics believed that *Intellectual Memoirs: New York, 1936-1938* does not seem representative of the work that made her a force in literary circles. In a *Nation* review, Marianne Wiggins characterized the book in this way: "This volume also offers us Miss McCarthy, in her own words, yakking, and the effect is often like sitting down beside a chatty dowager on speed." "Her once vivid and original voice now sounds thin, mannered, dryly self-important," Jean Strouse wrote in the *New York Times Book Review*, "listing the names of people, credentials, cocktails and clothes, but telling almost nothing of her emotional experience."

Throughout her career, McCarthy wrote on a broad range of subjects in a number of different forms, and in each case she proved her ability to cut through the surface clutter to expose the underlying reality. As Gordon wrote, "McCarthy's voice has always been reliable; the stirring and disturbing tone of the born truth-teller is hers, whether she is writing essays or fiction." Remembering McCarthy in remarks from a memorial service published in the *Partisan Review*, Arthur Schlesinger Jr. observed, "Whatever the contemporary equivalent of the old phrase ['man of letters'], it applied vividly to Mary. She wrote with analytical power, startling clarity, keen human insight, silken wit, dispassionate ruthlessness, on an enviable diversity of subjects: the novel, painting, architecture, opera, theater, politics, manners, tastes, religion, language, museums, universities, Vassar, Venice, Florence, France, America, Vietnam. Her novels, stories and essays constitute a brilliant commentary, interpretation, panorama of our disordered age."

BIOGRAPHICAL/CRITICAL SOURCES:

BOOKS

Bennett, Joy, and Gabriella Hochmann, *Mary McCarthy: An Annotated Bibliography*, Garland (New York City), 1992.

Brightman, Carol, *Writing Dangerously: Mary McCarthy and Her World*, C. N. Potter (New York City), 1993.

Brightman, Carol, editor, *Between Friends: The Correspondence of Hannah Arendt and Mary McCarthy, 1949-1975*, Harcourt, 1995.

Contemporary Literary Criticism, Gale (Detroit), Volume 1, 1973, Volume 3, 1975, Volume 5, 1976, Volume 14, 1980, Volume 24, 1983.

Dictionary of Literary Biography, Volume 2: *American Novelists since World War II*, Gale, 1978.

Dictionary of Literary Biography Yearbook: 1981, Gale, 1982.

Gelderman, Carol, *Mary McCarthy: A Life*, St. Martin's (New York City), 1989.

Gelderman, Carol, editor, *Conversations with Mary McCarthy*, University Press of Mississippi (Jackson, MS), 1991.

Grumbach, Doris, *The Company She Kept: A Revealing Portrait of Mary McCarthy*, Coward, 1976.

McCarthy, Mary, *Memories of a Catholic Girlhood*, Harcourt, 1957.

McCarthy, Mary, *On the Contrary*, Farrar, Straus, 1961.

McCarthy, Mary, *Ideas and the Novel*, Harcourt, 1980.

McKenzie, Barbara, *Mary McCarthy*, Twayne (New York City), 1966.

Moore, Harry T., editor, *Contemporary American Novelists*, Southern Illinois University Press (Carbondale, IL), 1964.

Stock, Irvin, *Fiction as Wisdom: From Goethe to Bellow*, Pennsylvania State University Press (University Park, PA), 1980.

Stock, Irvin, *Mary McCarthy*, University of Minnesota Press (Minneapolis, MN), 1968.

Symons, Julian, *Critical Occasions*, Hamish Hamilton (London), 1966.

Wald, Alan M., *The New York Intellectuals: The Rise and Decline of the Anti-Stalinist Left, from the 1930s to the 1980s*, University of North Carolina Press (Chapel Hill, NC), 1987.

Writers at Work: The "Paris Review" Interviews, second series, Viking (New York City), 1963.

PERIODICALS

America, January 14, 1989, pp. 14-19.

Atlantic Monthly, July, 1971; November, 1979; May, 1993, p. 107.

Best Sellers, March 1, 1970; June 15, 1971.

Books and Bookmen, August, 1970.

Boston Globe, December 20, 1992, p. B15; January 29, 1995, p. 53.

Canadian Forum, February, 1968.

Chicago Tribune, March 30, 1980; May 19, 1985, section 14, p. 43; May 3, 1987, section 14, p. 6; November 19, 1992, section 1, p. 22.

Chicago Tribune Book World, October 14, 1979.

Christian Science Monitor, March 12, 1970.

Commentary, July, 1969; June, 1970; October, 1971; May, 1981; May, 1993, pp. 41-47.

Commonweal, September 3, 1971; December 21, 1979.

Descant, fall, 1968.

Esquire, October, 1970; November, 1985, pp. 249, 251.

Hudson Review, spring, 1972; spring, 1980; spring, 1981.

Interview, January, 1990, p. 88.

Journal of American History, March, 1994, pp. 1518-1520.

Life, May 21, 1971.

Listener, November 2, 1967.

Los Angeles Times, May 13, 1985; May 12, 1992, p. E5.

Los Angeles Times Book Review, November 23, 1980; May 10, 1987, pp. 3-4; May 7, 1993, p. 9; July 25, 1995, p. 12.

Modern Fiction Studies, winter, 1981.

Nation, March 24, 1969; September 18, 1972; November 10, 1979; May 19, 1984; November 16, 1992, pp. 569-572.

National Review, October 8, 1971; May 16, 1980; August 8, 1980; September 6, 1985, pp. 55-56; February 5, 1990, p. 24; August 17, 1992, p. 50.

New Leader, January 20, 1969; March 2, 1970; June 1, 1992, p. 22.

New Republic, October 9, 1961; February 28, 1970.

New Statesman, September 17, 1971; March 6, 1981.

Newsweek, February 16, 1970; October 8, 1979.

New York Review of Books, January 18, 1968; March 13, 1969; August 13, 1970; June 3, 1971; September 21, 1972; October 31, 1974; October 25, 1979; March 26, 1992, p. 3.

New York Times, February 9, 1970; May 19, 1971; July 31, 1979; October 4, 1979; November 18, 1980; March 29, 1987, section 6, p. 60; April 19, 1987, section 7, p. 5; December 4, 1988, section 1, p. 90; October 27, 1989, p. A34; May 14, 1992, p. C20.

New York Times Book Review, October 17, 1963; November 26, 1967; March 8, 1970; May 16, 1971; August 13, 1972; June 30, 1974; September 30, 1979; November 25, 1979; May 11, 1980; January 18, 1981; May 5, 1985, p. 15.; April 13, 1987, p. C16; May 8, 1988, p. 46; May 24, 1992, p. 1.

Observer Review, May 24, 1970.

Partisan Review, winter, 1975; Volume 57, number 1, 1990, pp. 14-15.

People, November 12, 1979.

San Francisco Review of Books, summer, 1985, p. 10.

Saturday Review, May 8, 1971; July 15, 1972; December, 1979.

Spectator, November 15, 1968; May 23, 1970; November 3, 1979; October 19, 1985, pp. 31-32.

Time, October 1, 1979; April 15, 1985, pp. 101-102.

Times (London), October 29, 1989, p. G7.

Times Literary Supplement, November 9, 1967; January 16, 1969; June 4, 1970; September 17, 1971; March 16, 1973; December 7, 1979; March 6, 1981.

Village Voice, February 11, 1981; June 4, 1985, p. 47.

Washington Post, November 21, 1968; August 21, 1971.

Washington Post Book World, December 1, 1968; October 14, 1979; November 30, 1980; May 12, 1985, pp. 5, 8; May 17, 1992, p. 2; November 29, 1992, p. 1; January 29, 1995, p. 3.

OBITUARIES:

PERIODICALS

Boston Globe, October 26, 1989, p. 53.

Chicago Tribune, October 26, 1989.

Detroit Free Press, October 26, 1989.

Los Angeles Times, October 26, 1989, p. A3, A36.

National Review, November 24, 1989, p. 14.

Newsweek, November 6, 1989, p. 91.

New York, November 6, 1989, p. 87.

New York Times, October 26, 1989, pp. A1, B10; November 9, 1989, p. D27.

People, November 13, 1989, p. 75.

Time, November 6, 1989, p. 87.

U.S. News and World Report, November 6, 1989, p. 16.

Variety, November 1, 1989, p. 85.

Wall Street Journal, October 26, 1989, p. A1.

Washington Post, October 26, 1989, p. B11.*

—*Sketch by Bryan Ryan*

*   *   *

McCAULEY, Carole Spearin   1939-

PERSONAL: Born April 18, 1939, in Great Barrington, MA; daughter of Kenneth Waldo and Elizabeth (LaPrise) Spearin; married Arthur Leo McCauley (a technical writer), November 14, 1964; children: Brendan Spearin. *Education:* Attended University of Montpellier, 1959, and University of Besancon, 1959-60; Antioch College, A.B., 1962; graduate study at New School for Social Research, 1965-66, and at Manhattanville College, 1973-74. *Politics:* "Saddened liberal." *Religion:* "Saddened Catholic."

ADDRESSES: Home—23 Buena Vista Dr., Greenwich, CT 06831-4210.

CAREER: NIH Record, Bethesda, MD, medical reporter, 1961; Antioch College, Yellow Springs, OH, secretary-assistant in extramural department, 1962; Grailville, Loveland, OH, staff member, 1962-64; Grail Art and Bookshop, New York City, assistant, 1966-74, manager, 1972; Woman's Salon (writer's group), New York City, coordinator of public programs, 1976-80; medical editor, Southwest Connecticut Health Systems Agency, 1979; International Business Machines Corp. (IBM), technical writer in Warwick, England, 1987-88, editor of technical publications in White Plains, NY; Vantage Press, New York City, proofreader, 1992—. A. P. John Institute for Cancer Research, member of public relations staff; *Orthopaedic Index,* staff writer. Has conducted writing workshops at Dialogue House, 1974, 1977, The Womanschool, 1976, and International Women's Writing Guild; participant in computer conferences in data processing and APL and BASIC programming languages. Does public speaking on numerous topics.

MEMBER: Grail Movement, National Writers Union (officer), Publishing Triangle (member of steering committee), Sisters in Crime.

AWARDS, HONORS: Short story prize, *Writer's Digest,* 1968, for "Monty Montgomery Knorr"; short story prize, *Analecta,* 1968, for "Hello to All My Readers"; short story prize, Contemporary Connecticut Writers, 1979; short story prize, Writers of the Future, for "Misty, Moisty Morning"; poetry prize from *Work-Out* (London).

WRITINGS:

(Translator from the French) Pierre Babin, *Crisis of Faith,* Herder (Rome), 1963.

(Translator from the French) Maurice Bellet, *Facing the Unbeliever,* Herder, 1967.

Six Portraits (computer-assisted fiction), Cantz'sche, 1973.

Computers and Creativity (nonfiction), Praeger (New York City), 1974.

Happenthing in Travel On (novel with computerized sections), Daughters, Inc., 1975.

Pregnancy after Thirty-five, Dutton (New York City), 1976.

Surviving Breast Cancer, Dutton, 1979, revised edition, Bantam (Canada), 1986.

AIDS: Prevention and Healing with Nutrition, New Science Press, 1985.

The Honesty Tree (novel), Frog in the Well (East Palo Alto, CA), 1986.

(With Robert Schacter) *Why Your Child Is Afraid: Understanding the Normal Fears of Childhood from Birth to Adolescence and Helping to Overcome Them,* Simon & Schuster (New York City), 1988.

Cold Steal (novel), Womens Press, 1991.

Contributor to collections, including *Women: Omen,* Connecticut Feminists in the Arts, 1971; *In Youth,* edited by Richard Kostelanetz, Ballantine (New York City), 1972; *Changes of the Day,* edited by Diane Kruchkow, New England Small Press Association, 1975; *The New Fiction: Interviews with Innovative American Writers,* edited by Joe David Bellamy, University of Illinois Press (Champaign), 1975; and *Spaced Out* (computer prose), edited by Adele Aldridge, Magic Circle (Weston, CT), 1975. Contributor of articles, interviews, poetry, stories, and reviews to various periodicals, including *Partisan Review, North American Review, Creative Computing, Omni, Self, Writer's Digest, Child, Family Circle,* and *New Women's Times.* Associate editor, *Panache* (literary magazine), 1969-74.

WORK IN PROGRESS: The Twisted Crystal, a medieval mystery novel with a sorceress heroine, set in Norse Iceland; new erotica pieces.

SIDELIGHTS: Carole Spearin McCauley told *CA:* "Although I earn a living writing, proofreading, or editing various kinds of nonfiction, the novel and fiction are my first love. By this time I have a core of people who care and understand what I am doing, whether experimenta-

tion in form (computer-assisted work) or in content (sexual variations), but it saddens me to see how addicted to 'blockbusters' most large publishers are and how eager to publish only their friends' work many small publishers are. How do 'tweenies'—fiction writers between these two categories—survive? Does anyone care?

"Because the characters in my books care passionately about vital topics (human cooperation and survival, honest medical research, better treatment of cancer patients, civil and personal rights for minorities, feminist consciousness), I hope to embed within exciting plots a variety of such characters who learn to cope with their worlds, even triumph above them. I want especially to construct characters with whom contemporary women can identify. Subjects such as androgyny or better care in medical settings seem to choose me, and I try to honor them by careful constructions because they will matter to the history of human thought and evolution. A century from now, for example, will we all be androgynous or bisexual? Will the human lifespan have doubled, reducing or at least postponing the degradation of chronic illness (cancer, stroke, and so on)?

"My computer texts have appeared in art shows in the United States, Canada, and Germany. I give illustrated talks on computer arts to school groups and speak on women's writing to suburban groups, writers' conferences, and book fairs."

*   *   *

McCURDY, Michael 1942-

PERSONAL: Born February 17, 1942, in New York, NY; son of Charles E. (an artist) and Beatrice (Beatson) McCurdy; married Deborah Lamb (a social worker), September 7, 1968; children: Heather, Mark. *Education:* Boston School of the Museum of Fine Arts, student, 1960-66; Tufts University, B.F.A., 1964, M.F.A., 1971. *Politics:* Democrat. *Religion:* Protestant.

ADDRESSES: Home—66 Lake Buel Rd., Great Barrington, MA 01230.

CAREER: Illustrator, 1965—. Former director of Penmaen Press; designer of artwork for various book publishers, magazines, and corporations; work has been widely exhibited throughout the United States and in England.

MEMBER: Society of Printers.

AWARDS, HONORS: New York Times Best Illustrated Children's Book Award, 1986, for *The Owl-Scatterer;* Notable Children's Trade book citation, National Council for the Social Studies, 1988, for *Hannah's Farm: The Seasons on an Early American Homestead;* has also won many awards at New England Book Show.

WRITINGS:

(With Michael Peich) *The First Ten: A Penmaen Press Bibliography,* Penmaen Press (Great Barrington, MA), 1978.

Toward the Light: Wood Engravings by Michael McCurdy, self-illustrated, Porcupine's Quill (Erin, Ontario), 1982.

The Illustrated Harvard: Harvard University in Wood Engravings and Words, self-illustrated, Globe Pequot (Chester, CT), 1986.

The Devils Who Learned to Be Good (juvenile), self-illustrated, Little, Brown (Boston), 1987.

Hannah's Farm: The Seasons on an Early American Homestead (juvenile), self-illustrated, Holiday House (New York City), 1988.

McCurdy's World, self-illustrated, Capra Press (Santa Barbara, CA), 1992.

The Old Man and the Fiddle, self-illustrated, Putnam (New York City), 1992.

Escape from Slavery: The Boyhood of Fredrick Douglass in His Own Words, self-illustrated, Knopf (New York City), 1994.

ILLUSTRATOR

The Brick Moon, Imprint Society, 1971.

Amauskeeg Falls, Barre (New York City), 1971.

This Quiet Place, Little, Brown, 1971.

Narrative of Alvar Nunez Cabeza de Vaca, Imprint Society, 1972.

Madam Knight, David Godine (Boston), 1972.

Isaac Asimov, *Please Explain* (juvenile), Houghton (Boston), 1973.

Dove at the Windows: Last Letters of Four Quaker Martyrs, Penmaen Press, 1973.

William Ferguson, *Light of Paradise* (poetry), Penmaen Press, 1973.

X. J. Kennedy, *Celebrations after the Death of John Brennan* (poetry), Penmaen Press, 1974.

Linda Grant De Pauw, *Founding Mothers: Women in America in the Revolutionary Era,* Houghton, 1975.

Richard Eberhart, *Poems to Poets,* Penmaen Press, 1975.

Pardee Lowe, Jr., translator, *King Harald and the Icelanders,* Penmaen Press, 1979.

John Gilgun, *Everything That Has Been Shall Be Again: The Reincarnation Fables of John Gilgun,* Bieler (St. Paul, MN), 1981.

Kennedy, editor, *Tygers of Wrath: Poems of Hate, Anger, and Invective,* University of Georgia Press (Athens), 1981.

Vicente Aleixandre, *Mundo a solas/World Alone* (bilingual edition), translations by Lewis Hyde and David Unger, Penmaen Press, 1982.

Philip Dacey, *Gerard Manley Hopkins Meets Walt Whitman in Heaven and Other Poems,* Penmaen Press, 1982.

May Sarton, *A Winter Garland: New Poems,* W. B. Ewert, 1982.

Susan Efird, *The Eye of Heaven: A Narrative Poem,* Abattoir Editions, University of Nebraska at Omaha, 1982.

B. A. King, *The Very Best Christmas Tree* (juvenile), David Godine, 1983.

William Edgar Stafford, *Listening Deep: Poems,* Penmaen Press, 1984.

Weldon Kees, *Two Prose Sketches,* Aralia Press, 1984.

Chet Raymo, *The Soul of the Night: An Astronomical Pilgrimage,* Prentice-Hall (Englewood Cliffs, NJ), 1985.

Jean Giono, *The Man Who Planted Trees,* Chelsea Green Publishing, 1985.

Henry David Thoreau, *The Winged Life: The Poetic Voice of Henry David Thoreau,* Sierra Books (San Francisco), 1986.

Howard A. Norman, *The Owl-Scatterer* (juvenile), Atlantic Monthly Press (New York City), 1986.

King, *The Christmas Junk Box* (juvenile), David Godine, 1987.

Eva A. Wilbur-Cruce, *A Beautiful, Cruel, Country,* University of Arizona Press (Tucson), 1987.

Mary W. Freeman, *The Revolt of Mother,* Redpath Press, 1987.

Somerset Maugham, *The Three Fat Women of Antibes,* Redpath Press, 1987.

Charles Dickens, *A Christmas Carol: Bah! Humbug!,* Redpath Press, 1987.

John Muir, *My First Summer in the Sierra,* Yolla-Bolly Press (Covelo, CA), 1988.

Muir, *The Yosemite,* Sierra Books, 1988.

Muir, *Travels in Alaska,* Sierra Books, 1988.

Scott Hastings, *Goodbye Highland Yankee,* Chelsea Green Publishing, 1988.

Villy Sorenson, *Downfall of the Gods,* University of Nebraska Press (Lincoln), 1988.

Louisa May Alcott, *An Old-Fashioned Thanksgiving,* Holiday House, 1989.

Norman, *How Glooskap Outwits the Ice Giants and Other Tales of the Maritime Indians,* Little, Brown, 1989.

Nathan Smith, *Sermon to the Birds,* Oxzimoron Press, 1990.

Mary Pope Osborne, *American Tall Tales,* Knopf, 1991.

David Peterson, *Racks,* Capra Press, 1991.

Noel Perrin, *Last Person Rural,* David Godine, 1991.

David Mamet, *American Buffalo,* Arion Press (San Francisco), 1992.

Richard Nunley, editor, *The Berkshire Reader,* Berkshire House, 1992.

Sally Ryder Brady, *A Yankee Christmas,* Yankee Press (Emmaus, PA), 1992.

Diana Appelbaum, *Giants in the Land,* Houghton, 1993.

Amelia Knight, *The Way West: Journal of a Pioneer Woman,* Simon & Schuster (New York City), 1993.

Clarissa Pinkola Estes, *The Gift of Story,* Ballantine (New York City), 1993.

Donald Hall, *Lucy's Christmas,* Harcourt (San Diego and New York City), 1994.

Ralph L. Voss and Michael L. Keene, *The Heath Guide to College Writing,* 2nd edition, D. C. Heath & Co. (Lexington, MA), 1994.

Neil Philip, editor, *Singing America,* Viking Press (New York City), 1995.

Hall, *Lucy's Summer,* Harcourt, 1995.

Mamet, *Passover,* St. Martin's (New York City), 1995.

Abraham Lincoln, *The Gettysburg Address,* Houghton, 1995.

Harry Crews, *A Childhood: The Biography of a Place,* University of Georgia Press, 1995.

Ann Whitford Paul, *The Seasons Sewn: A Year in Patchwork,* Harcourt, 1996.

Philip, editor, *American Fairy Tales,* Hyperion Books (Westport, CT), 1996.

WORK IN PROGRESS: Illustrations for *The Bone Man,* by Laura Simms, for Hyperion Books, 1997; also *Trapped by the Ice: Shackleton's Amazing Journey,* for Walker & Co. (New York City), 1997.

SIDELIGHTS: Illustrator Michael McCurdy told *CA:* "My first freelance commission was given to me in 1965, a book jacket wood engraving for a Harvard University Press book. Since then, I have continued as a freelance book illustrator and writer, with occasional forays into corporate and magazine illustration. For some years I also printed and published Penmaen Press books, working directly with some of America's best writers and poets. Keeping my hand into the fine press concurrently, I have created wood engravings for illustrated editions by John Muir, Henry David Thoreau, and David Mamet. And consistent with my desire to have diversity in my work, I also illustrate children's books along with a healthy mix of adult material. At the same time, I have written four books for young readers. My technique for these has gone from wood engraving to scratchboard—and now a try at acrylic painting. For me, as I am certain with most book artists, inspiration comes from a text, from words. It's the desire to participate in all branches of the book arts that brings to me the most satisfaction."

McDOLE, Carol
See FARLEY, Carol

*   *   *

McFEELY, William S(hield)   1930-

PERSONAL: Born September 25, 1930, in New York, NY; son of William C. and Marguerite (Shield) McFeely; married Mary Drake (a librarian), September 13, 1952; children: William Drake, Eliza, Jennifer. *Education:* Amherst College, B.A., 1952; Yale University, M.A., 1962, Ph.D., 1966.

ADDRESSES: Home—445 Franklin St., #25, Athens, GA 30606. *Office*—301 LeConte Hall, University of Georgia, Athens, GA 30602.

CAREER: First National City Bank, New York City, assistant cashier, 1952-61; Yale University, New Haven, CT, assistant professor, 1966-69, associate professor of history, 1969-70; Mount Holyoke College, South Hadley, MA, professor of history, 1970-80, Rodman Professor of History, 1980-82, Andrew W. Mellon Professor in the Humanities, 1982-86, dean of faculty, 1970-73; University of Georgia, Athens, Richard B. Russell Professor of American History, 1986-94, Franklin Professor of History, 1994—. Visiting professor of history, University College, London, 1978-79, and Amherst College, 1980-81; University of Massachusetts, visiting professor, 1984-85, and John J. McCloy Professor, 1988-89; W. E. B. DuBois Institute, Harvard University, visiting scholar, 1992—; associate fellow, Charles Warren Center, 1991-92; affiliated with Huntington Library, 1976, 1983. Teacher, Yale/Harvard/Columbia intensive summer studies program, 1967-69. Consultant to U.S. House of Representatives committee on the judiciary, 1974.

MEMBER: PEN, Authors Guild, American Historical Association, Association for the Study of Afro-American Life and History, Organization of American Historians, Southern Historical Association, Century Association.

AWARDS, HONORS: Morse fellow, 1968-69; American Council of Learned Societies fellow, 1974-75; Pulitzer Prize in biography, 1982, for *Grant: A Biography;* L.H.D., Amherst College, 1982; Francis Parkman Prize, 1982; Guggenheim fellow, 1982-83; National Endowment for the Humanities grant, 1986-87; Lincoln Prize, 1992; Avery O. Craven Award, 1992.

WRITINGS:

Yankee Stepfather: General O. O. Howard and the Freedmen, Yale University Press (New Haven, CT), 1968.
(With Thomas J. Ladenburg) *The Black Man in the Land of Equality,* Hayden, 1969.
Grant: A Biography, Norton (New York City), 1981.

(Author of introduction) *Memoirs of General William T. Sherman,* Norwood (Norwood, PA), 1984.

(Editor with wife, Mary Drake McFeely) *Ulysses S. Grant: Memoirs and Selected Letters, 1839-1865,* Library of America, 1990.

Frederick Douglass, Norton, 1991.

Sapelo's People, Norton, 1994.

Also author of introduction for *Personal Memoirs of U. S. Grant,* 1983. Contributor to books, including *The Black Experience in America,* edited by J. C. Curtis and C. C. Gould, University of Texas Press (Austin), 1970; *Key Issues in the Afro-American Experience,* edited by N. I. Huggins and M. Kilson, Harcourt (San Diego, CA), 1971; and *Region, Race and Reconstruction: Essays in Honor of C. Vann Woodward,* edited by J. Morgan Kousser and James M. McPherson, Oxford University Press, 1982.

SIDELIGHTS: William S. McFeely captured the ironic life of General Ulysses S. Grant, whose remarkable leadership won the Civil War for the Union yet who was beset by personal and professional failure during his non-military career, in his Pulitzer Prize-winning book *Grant: A Biography.* As noted by Christopher Lehmann-Haupt in his *New York Times* review of *Grant,* McFeely describes Grant's "unpromising" childhood and "mediocre" scholastic record at West Point, as well as his uneventful early career as peacetime army officer, farmer, bill collector, and clerk. Lehmann-Haupt states that McFeely records "the sudden change that the outbreak of the Civil War effected in him; his astonishing rise from adviser to a Galena [Illinois] unit of volunteers to commanding general of the Union forces; his gloriously empty and corruption-ridden two-term Presidency; his late disastrous attempts to succeed as a businessman, and the final race against death to produce what turned out to be his great and best-selling military memoirs—all of this amounts to an archetypal saga of American failure and success."

In analyzing the reasons why such a brilliant general would meet with almost overwhelming defeat as America's Reconstruction-era president, McFeely fills his study with "revealing pointers and subtle theorizing," according to Marcus Cunliffe in the *New York Times Book Review.* "The main themes of his book are that Grant, though never a crusader for good causes, once had a fellow feeling for the ordinary citizen but gradually lost it as fame led him to depend upon the applause of the people en masse."

To *Newsweek* critic Peter S. Prescott, "McFeely's entirely plausible conclusion is that Grant, the former failure, was exceedingly disillusioned about his subordinates, as much in war as in peace. He expected little from them, but in war he could give an order and see it obeyed; coping with the members of his Cabinet was another matter." While the post-Civil War life of Ulysses S. Grant could never

compare with his success in the military, Grant's last project—his wartime *Memoirs,* written while the ex-president was battling throat cancer—is acknowledged by critics to be the finest book ever written by a chief of state, demonstrating that for all his faults Grant was an extraordinary military strategist.

"McFeely's biography is the first full-scale treatment of all aspects of Grant's life," says *Newsweek*'s Prescott, "the first to attempt a reconciliation of the warrior and the statesman, to explain the psychology that produced such astonishing success and failure. The portrait that emerges—sympathetic yet firm about its subject's shortcomings—seems to me entirely successful."

The author sees in his subject "a man of his time, beset by the terrible fear of failure and hardship that swallowed so many around him, especially those who, like him, did not do well at the all-absorbing game of getting," states *Washington Post Book World* reviewer Bernard S. Weisberger. Grant "sought a presidency for which he was unqualified because 'he could not risk giving up an inch for fear that he might fall all the way back.' "

McFeely's next biography deals with the life of ex-slave Frederick Douglass, renowned orator and freedom fighter. *Frederick Douglass* focuses on Douglass's early life, which he spent on a Maryland plantation with his maternal grandmother, until his death in 1895. McFeely covers material the abolitionist himself treated in his own three autobiographies, yet he has assimilated research—some previously undiscovered—from an abundant variety of sources. Louis S. Gerteis comments in the *Journal of American History* that the author "brings to the familiar Frederick Douglass story an engaging sensitivity to the complex interactions of middle-class Victorian sexuality, the evolving American culture of race, and the class distinctions of the early industrial era." Gerteis adds that McFeely's book provides "a richness of resources never before assembled." Ishmael Reed observes in the *Los Angeles Times,* "This engaging and well-written work of literature suggests that the Age of Douglass was this nation's greatest epoch."

Sapelo's People offers insight into black American history through the perspective of contemporary descendants of slaves. An island off the Georgia coast, Sapelo is home today to a small population of blacks whose ancestors were abducted from Africa and the West Indies and who served owners on plantations and in cotton fields. While the Civil War ended the stronghold of property owners on the island, General William Sherman's Special Field Order 15, later supported by Congress, allowed for the habitation of the Sea Islands for newly-freed black slaves, beginning in 1865. "Using the stories the Sapelo people told him, the advice of a professional genealogist for the

Georgia Department of Natural Resources and the tools of the historian's trade, McFeely delineates a spare trail from slaves like Bilali—the great-great-great-grandfather of one of his sources on Sapelo—to the poor and decent lives led by the few remaining inhabitants," comments Roger Wilkins in the *Los Angeles Times Book Review.* Malcolm Jones, Jr. notes in *Newsweek* that McFeely "interweaves accounts of slavery and Reconstruction's treacheries with the testimony of the fishermen and basket-making artisans who currently abide on Sapelo." Wilkins concludes that he is "deeply grateful for McFeely's magnificent effort of thought, empathy, scholarship, and imagination."

BIOGRAPHICAL/CRITICAL SOURCES:

PERIODICALS

African American Review, fall, 1994, pp. 473-79.
Chicago Tribune Book World, March 15, 1981.
Journal of American History, March, 1992, pp. 1448-49.
Los Angeles Times, June 4, 1981; February 3, 1991.
Los Angeles Times Book Review, July 24, 1994, pp. 1, 11.
New Republic, February 18, 1991, pp. 61-65.
Newsweek, April 13, 1981; July 18, 1994, p. 61.
New York Review of Books, February 27, 1969.
New York Times, April 9, 1972, May 18, 1981.
New York Times Book Review, March 22, 1981.
Time, May 4, 1981.
Washington Post Book World, February 22, 1981.
Yale Review, July, 1992, pp. 186-97.*

*   *   *

McGOWEN, Thomas E. 1927-
(Tom McGowen)

PERSONAL: Born May 6, 1927, in Evanston, IL; son of William Robert (a salesperson) and Helene (Nelson) McGowen; married Loretta Swok; children: Alan, Gayle, Maureen, Kathleen. *Education:* Attended Roosevelt College of Chicago (now Roosevelt University), 1947 and 1948, and American Academy of Art, 1948-49. *Avocational interests:* War-gaming, gourmet cooking, classical music, historical research, travel.

ADDRESSES: Home—4449 North Oriole Blvd., Norridge, IL 60656.

CAREER: Sidney Clayton & Associates (advertising firm), Chicago, IL, production manager, 1949-53; Justrite Manufacturing Co., Chicago, advertising manager, 1953-54; National Safety Council, Chicago, sales promotion director, 1954-59; Hensley Co. (advertising firm), Chicago, creative director, 1959-69; World Book, Inc. (publishers), Chicago, senior editor, 1969—. *Military ser-*

vice: U.S. Navy, member of hospital corps during World War II.

MEMBER: Authors League of America, Authors Guild, Children's Reading Round Table, Society of Midland Authors.

AWARDS, HONORS: Notable Children's Book in the Field of Social Studies citation, Association of Social Sciences Teachers, 1975, for *Album of Prehistoric Man;* Outstanding Science Book for Children citations, National Science Teachers Association/Children's Book Council Joint Committee, 1980, for *Album of Whales,* and 1986, for *Radioactivity: From the Curies to the Atomic Age;* *Booklist* Children's Editors Choice Award and nominations for Rebecca Caudill Young Readers Book Award, Sequoyah Young Readers Award, and Young Hoosier Book Award, all 1987, for *The Magician's Apprentice;* Children's Reading Round Table Annual Award for Outstanding Contributions to the Field of Children's Literature, 1990; Book for the Teen Age citation, New York Public Library, 1991, for *The Great Monkey Trial: Science versus Fundamentalism in America;* Children's Book of the Year citation, Child Study Children's Book Committee, 1992, for *A Trial of Magic.*

WRITINGS:

UNDER NAME TOM McGOWEN; JUVENILE

The Only Glupmaker in the U.S. Navy, self-illustrated, Albert Whitman (Niles, IL), 1966.
The Apple Strudel Soldier, Follett, 1968.
Dragon Stew, Follett, 1969.
Last Voyage of the Unlucky Katie Marie, Whitman, 1969.
The Biggest Toot in Toozelburg, Reilly & Lee, 1970.
Hammett and the Highlanders, Follett, 1970.
Sir MacHinery, Follett, 1970.
The Fearless Fossil Hunters, Whitman, 1971.
Album of Dinosaurs, Rand McNally (Chicago), 1972.
Album of Prehistoric Animals, Rand McNally, 1974.
Odyssey from River Bend, Little, Brown (Boston), 1975.
Album of Prehistoric Man, Rand McNally, 1975.
The Spirit of the Wild, Little, Brown, 1976.
Album of Sharks, Rand McNally, 1977.
Album of Reptiles, Rand McNally, 1978.
Album of Astronomy, Rand McNally, 1979.
Album of Whales, Rand McNally, 1980.
Album of Rocks and Minerals, Rand McNally, 1981.
Encyclopedia of Legendary Creatures, Rand McNally, 1981.
Album of Birds, Rand McNally, 1982.
Album of Space Flight, Rand McNally, 1983.
Midway and Guadalcanal, F. Watts (New York City), 1984.
King's Quest, TSR (Lake Geneva, WI), 1984.
War Gaming, F. Watts, 1985.

George Washington, F. Watts, 1986.

Radioactivity: From the Curies to the Atomic Age, F. Watts, 1986.

The Magician's Apprentice, Lodestar (New York City), 1987.

The Circulatory System: From Harvey to the Artificial Heart, F. Watts, 1987.

Chemistry: The Birth of a Science, F. Watts, 1988.

The Time of the Forest, Houghton (Boston), 1988.

The Magician's Company, Lodestar, 1988.

The Magicians' Challenge, Lodestar, 1989.

Epilepsy, F. Watts, 1989.

The Great Monkey Trial: Science versus Fundamentalism in America, F. Watts, 1990.

The Shadow of Fomor, Lodestar, 1990.

The Magical Fellowship, Lodestar, 1991.

A Trial of Magic, Lodestar, 1992.

The Korean War, F. Watts, 1992.

A Question of Magic, Lodestar, 1993.

World War I, F. Watts, 1993.

World War II, F. Watts, 1993.

Lonely Eagles and Buffalo Soldiers: African-Americans in World War II, F. Watts, 1995.

"Go for Broke": Japanese-Americans in World War II, F. Watts, 1995.

Yearbooks in Science: 1900-1919, Holt (New York City), 1995.

Yearbooks in Science: 1960-1969, Holt, 1995.

The Black Death, F. Watts, 1995.

SIDELIGHTS: Thomas E. McGowen told *CA:* "I began writing books for children in 1964, when in my late thirties, with the feeling that this was the most meaningful and important work I could possibly do. Now, I still feel the same. My fiction, mainly fantasy, is designed to entertain; my nonfiction, mainly in the area of general science, is intended both to entertain and to help children understand the reasons for things, whether the behavior of a particular kind of wild animal or the twinkle of a star. I believe that if children can come to understand the why and how of things going on around them, from the interrelated activities of animals and plants to the unseen movement of molecules, they'll be more likely to grow into comfortable, confident, *civilized* adults, unencumbered by superstition and irrationality. If one of my fiction books can turn just *one* child on to the imagination-stimulating world of fantasy; if one of my nonfiction books can make just *one* child aware of the equally stimulating world of nature and natural science, I'll have achieved my personal goal."

*   *   *

McGOWEN, Tom
   See McGOWEN, Thomas E.

McWHIRTER, Norris (Dewar) 1925-

PERSONAL: Born August 12, 1925, in London, England; son of William Allan (former editor, *London Daily Mail*) and Margaret M. (Williamson) McWhirter; married Carole Eckert, December 29, 1957; children: Jane Margaret, Alasdair William. *Education:* Trinity College, Oxford, B.A. and M.A., 1948. *Politics:* Conservative. *Religion:* Church of England. *Avocational interests:* Tennis, skiing, athletics.

ADDRESSES: *Office*—Guinness Superlatives Ltd., 2 Cecil Court, London Road, Enfield, Middlesex EN2 6DJ, England.

CAREER: Athletics correspondent for *Observer,* London, 1949, *Star,* London, 1950; McWhirter Twins Ltd., London, chairperson, beginning 1951; Guinness Superlatives Ltd., London, managing director, 1954-75, director, beginning 1975; Dreghorn Publications Ltd., London, director, beginning 1962; Redwood Press, Trowbridge, England, founder and chairperson, 1967-72; Gieves Group Ltd., London, director, beginning in 1972. British Broadcasting Corp. (BBC), commentator, beginning 1951 (announced first four-minute mile by Roger Bannister, 1954), television commentator of Olympic track and field events, 1952-72, guest, as "memory man" on facts and figures, on other radio and television programs, including *What's in the Picture,* 1957, and *The Record Breakers,* beginning in 1972. Athletics correspondent for the London *Star,* 1951-60, and for the London *Observer,* 1951-67. Vice president, Guinness Museums, Inc., beginning in 1976; Chairperson of Royal Freedom Association, beginning in 1983. Contested 1964-66 general elections for Conservatives. *Military service:* Royal Naval Volunteer Reserve, 1943-46; became sub-lieutenant.

MEMBER: Royal Institution of Great Britain, Association of Track and Field Statisticians, Society of Genealogists, Achilles Club, Vincent's Club (Oxford).

WRITINGS:

EDITOR/COMPILER WITH TWIN BROTHER, ROSS McWHIRTER

Get to Your Marks, Kaye, 1950.

Guinness Book of Records, Guinness Superlatives (London), 1954, 21st edition, 1974.

Guinness Book of World Records, Sterling, 1956, 5th edition, 1975.

Guinness Book of Olympic Records: Complete Roll of Olympic Medal Winners (1886-1964, including 1906) for the 28 Sports (7 Winter and 21 Summer) Contested in the 1964 Celebrations and Other Useful Information, Sterling, 1964.

Dunlop Book of Facts, Dreghorn (London), 1964, 2nd edition, 1966.

Dunlop Illustrated Encyclopedia of Facts, Doubleday (London), 1969.

Guinness Sports Record Book, Sterling, 1972-75.

Guinness Book of Olympic Records: Complete Roll of Olympic Medal Winners (1886-1972, including 1906) for the 28 Sports (7 Winter and 21 Summer) Contested in the 1972 Celebrations and Other Useful Information, Penguin (New York City), 1975, revised edition, 1976.

Guinness Book of Amazing Achievements, illustrated by Kenneth Laager, Sterling, 1975.

Guinness Book of Astounding Feats and Events, illustrated by Laager, Sterling, 1975.

Guinness Book of Surprising Accomplishments, illustrated by Laager, Sterling, 1977.

Guinness Book of Daring Deeds and Fascinating Facts, illustrated by Bill Hinds and Alex Chin, Sterling, 1979.

EDITOR/COMPILER WITH OTHERS

Guinness Book of Records, Guinness Superlatives, 1976, 30th edition, 1983.

Guinness Book of World Records, Sterling, 1976, 22nd edition, 1983.

Guinness Sports Record Book, revised editions, Sterling, 1976-82.

Ross, Story of a Shared Life, Churchill (London), 1977.

Guinness Book of Women's Sports Records, Sterling, 1979.

Guinness Book of Superstunts and Staggering Statistics, illustrated by Bill Hinds, 1980.

Guinness Book of Olympic Records: Complete Roll of Olympic Medal Winners (1886-1980, including 1906) for the 28 Sports (7 Winter and 21 Summer) Contested in the 1980 Celebrations and Other Useful Information, Bantam (New York City), 1980, revised edition, 1983.

Guinness Book of Sports Records, Guinness Superlatives, 1980, revised edition published as *Guinness Book of Sports Records, Winners and Champions,* Bantam, 1981.

Guinness Book of Amazing Animals, Sterling, 1981.

Guinness Book of Answers: A Handbook of General Knowledge, Guinness Superlatives, 1982, 5th edition, 1985.

Guinness: The Stories behind the Records, Sterling, 1982.

Contributor to *Encyclopaedia Britannica, Encyclopaedia Britannica Year Book, Modern Athletics,* and *Encyclopaedia of Sport.* Statistics editor, *News of World Almanac,* 1950-57; editor, *Athletics World,* 1952-57.

SIDELIGHTS: Sales of the *Guinness Book of Records* passed the 1 million mark in 1964, 25 million in 1975, and 40 million in 1981.

BIOGRAPHICAL/CRITICAL SOURCES:

BOOKS

Ross, Story of A Shared Life, Churchill, 1977.

PERIODICALS

Reader's Digest, May, 1965.
Sports Illustrated, February 8, 1965.
Time, January 19, 1963.*

*   *   *

MEE, Charles L., Jr.   1938-

PERSONAL: Born September 15, 1938, in Evanston, IL; son of Charles Louis and Sarah (Lowe) Mee; married Claire Lu Thomas (an actress), June, 1959 (divorced, 1962); married Suzi Baker (a poet), November, 1962 (divorced); married Kathleen Tolan (a playwright), December, 1983; children: (second marriage) Erin, Charles; (third marriage) Sarah, Alice. *Education:* Harvard University, B.A. (cum laude), 1960.

ADDRESSES: Agent—Lois Wallace, 177 East 70th St., New York, NY 10021; (plays) Helen Merrill, 361 W. 17th Street, New York, NY 10011.

CAREER: Horizon magazine, New York City, editor, 1961-71; editor-in-chief, 1971-75; full-time writer, 1975—.

MEMBER: Urban Institute, Theatre Communications Group, En Garde Artes.

AWARDS, HONORS: National Book Critics Circle nomination for best literary work, general non-fiction, for *The Genius of the People,* 1987; *Meeting at Potsdam* was a Literary Guild selection.

WRITINGS:

POPULAR HISTORY

(With editors of *Horizon*) *Lorenzo de Medici and the Renaissance,* American Heritage Press (New York City), 1968.

(Translator with Edward L. Greenfield) *Dear Prince: The Unexpurgated Counsels of N. Machiavelli to Richard Milhous Nixon,* American Heritage Press, 1969.

(Editor) *Horizon Bedside Reader,* American Heritage Press, 1971.

White Robe, Black Robe, Putnam (New York City), 1972.

Erasmus: The Eye of the Hurricane, Coward, 1973.

The Horizon Book of Daily Life in Renaissance Italy, American Heritage Publishing, 1975.

Meeting at Potsdam, M. Evans (New York City), 1975.

(With Ken Munowitz) *Happy Birthday, Baby Jesus* (children's), Harper (New York City), 1976.

(With Munowitz) *Moses, Moses* (children's), Harper, 1977.

A Visit to Haldeman and Other States of Mind, M. Evans, 1977.

(With Munowitz) *Noah,* Harper, 1978.

Seizure, M. Evans, 1978.

The End of Order: Versailles, 1919, Dutton (New York City), 1980.

The Marshall Plan: The Launching of the Pax Americana, Simon & Schuster (New York City), 1982.

The Ohio Gang: The World of Warren G. Harding, M. Evans, 1983.

The Genius of the People, Harper, 1987.

Rembrandt's Portrait: A Biography, Simon & Schuster, 1988.

Playing God: Seven Fateful Moments When Great Men Met to Change the World, Simon & Schuster, 1993.

PLAYS

Players' Repertoire, first produced in Cambridge, MA, 1960.

Constantinople Smith (one-act), first produced Off-Broadway, May, 1961.

The Gate (one-act), produced Off-Broadway, 1961.

Three by Mee, produced in New York City, 1962.

Anyone! Anyone!, produced Off-Broadway, 1964.

The Investigation of the Murder in El Salvador, produced in New York City, 1989.

Orestes, produced in New York City, 1993.

Also author of plays *God Bless Us Everyone, The Life of the Party, Wedding Night, Vienna: Lusthaus, The War to End War,* and *Imperialists at the Club Cave Canem.* Contributor of articles to periodicals including *Smithsonian* and *New York Times.*

ADAPTATIONS: *Meeting at Potsdam* was made into a television production by David Susskind.

SIDELIGHTS: First as editor of *Horizon* magazine, then as a freelance writer, Charles L. Mee, Jr., has made history his specialty. Though his early works in this field focused primarily on Renaissance and Reformation-era figures and history, his 1975 analysis of the post-World War II strategy meeting of Truman, Stalin, and Churchill signaled his interest in more recent events. A revisionist view of the origins of the Cold War, *Meeting at Potsdam* attempts to demonstrate that the "Big Three," each greedy for power and with a perverse love of conflict, deliberately worked out their agreements not to ensure peace, but to virtually guarantee war in the years ahead.

Critics have lined up on both sides of Mee's thesis, some commending the author for his insight, others questioning his grasp of history. Walter Clemons remarks in *Newsweek* that "sheer pleasure would be low on my list of

expectations from a book about the meeting of Truman, Churchill and Stalin in a suburb of Berlin during the summer of 1945 to redraw the map of the world. But Charles Mee . . . treats this unpromising subject with wit and a sharply satirical eye for the discrepancies between public gas and the horse-trading realities of the conference table." Claude Cockburn of the *New York Times Book Review* is equally impressed, asserting that in this "masterpiece of factual research, dramatic narration and vigorous analysis of global realities, Charles L. Mee . . . brilliantly illuminates the width and depth of the gap between what the general public supposed to be happening and what was in fact going on. . . . The nervous reader . . . might indulge in the hope that Mr. Mee is exaggerating. . . . Unfortunately for everyone's peace of mind, Mr. Mee is soon seen to have based his grisly story on irrefutable data and documented it to the point where it is useless to ask anyone to say it wasn't so."

On the other hand, *National Review*'s Allen G. Weakland said just that. Calling the book a "popular synthesis of scholarly writings" or a "sort of history as pop art," Weakland says that it is "not that the facts are not there. Indeed they are—in profusion. . . . [But] anyone desiring to sink his teeth into some good, chewy history had best look elsewhere." In addition, he notes, "Mee takes the no-footnote route, leaving the reader to plod through bibliographical essays at the rear of the book." The *New Republic*'s James Chace points out that what sources Mee does cite show that "he is acquainted with the literature but he has misread the information," resulting in an account which "is absorbing reading but highly misleading because its selective use of scholarly sources seriously distorts the historical realities in order to buttress the author's thesis."

"Here is a book that professes to have, finally, the answer to the question of why the Cold War started," begins Vojtech Mastny in his *New Leader* review of *Meeting at Potsdam.* "It doesn't, really, but the twist it gives to the old controversy is original enough to warrant a close examination. . . . Mee presents his thesis exceedingly well—with force, elegance and a special flair for pertinent and entertaining detail. Although not a professional historian, he knows his sources and treats them with respect. Without doubt, his analysis of the conference is the most serious so far." At the same time, Mastny says that Mee's work does have its shortcomings. He faulted Mee for imputing "superhuman foresight" to the participants of this gathering, and for therefore concluding that these men wanted events to turn out as they did. "The case is not nearly as clearcut as Mee would have us believe. . . . [His] principal thesis, no matter how alluring in its starkest simplicity, simply fails to do justice to all [the] considerations." Thomas G. Paterson, writing in the *Washington Post Book World,* summarizes the conclusions of several reviewers when he observes that "*Meeting at Potsdam* does not give us much that is new, but Mee tells a familiar story with verve and authority. It is first-rate reading."

In *The Marshall Plan: The Launching of the Pax Americana,* Mee discusses another historical event that shaped the U.S. attitude toward the Soviet Union—the massive program launched by U.S. Secretary of State George C. Marshall in the late '40s to aid Europe in its recovery from the devastation of World War II. Many reviewers noted that the $13 billion that the U.S. poured into Europe from 1947 to 1951 fueled a sense of national beneficence on the part of American citizens, but Mee observes that the plan also had a negative result: it spurred the Soviet Union to isolate its satellites from the European nations. Noting that a revisionist history of this chapter in American history was long overdue, Martin J. Sherwin quotes Mee in his *Nation* review: " 'Foreign policy is a grand and prolonged revelation of national character.' " Sherwin said that Mee "has designed his concise, fast-paced history of the Marshall Plan to aid of understanding of American statesmanship during the early cold war."

Although for the most part critics agreed that a popular, revisionist history of this type was important, some found fault with aspects of Mee's book. For instance, in the *New Republic,* Robert J. Samuelson states that the Marshall Plan has, for Americans, become synonymous with a vision of national abundance, generosity and farsightedness. He faults Mee for not penetrating this type of mythology and for failing to critically examine whether the Marshall Plan accomplished all that its proponents now claim. A. W. DePorte, writing in the *New York Times Book Review,* raises another issue. As he points out: "The sober theme that underlies this book contrasts sharply with some of its concessions to readability." DePorte further comments that although all books have mistakes, the factual errors in *The Marshall Plan* are frequent and grave enough to raise doubts about the credibility of the whole.

Critics were divided over whether the style in which Mee wrote *The Marshall Plan* suits the subject matter. In his *Los Angeles Times* review, Neil M. Heyman notes that "*The Marshall Plan* is heavy with character sketches of the story's leading figures, and it bristles with accounts of their most dramatic verbal exchanges. Mee confidently paints in the motives of all his key characters (one motive per character). The result is a disappointing hash." On the other hand, Robert Lekachman, writing in the *Washington Post Book World,* describes the book as "a brilliant volume of diplomatic history," in which major performers are characterized "with a novelist's precision." He concludes: "Mee tells the complex chronicle of maneuver between American and Europeans with grace, elegance, and epigrammatic brevity. A first-rate performance."

Reaching back to an earlier point in American history with *The Genius of the People,* published in 1987, Mee offers a popular history of the Constitutional Convention and of what the Founding Fathers sought to achieve as they drafted the document in Philadelphia in 1787. Mee points out that many present-day Americans would find fault with the intentions of the framers of the Constitution: to protect the institution of slavery; to prevent the emergence of a strong chief executive; and to guard against the creation of a standing army, which was believed to lead to war and despotism. *New York Times Book Review* writer Jack N. Rakove calls *The Genius of the People* "overheated" and says that too many of Mee's readings rest on speculations for which no substantiation is provided. "Since," writes Rakove, "errors on points minor and major recur throughout the book, I am not inclined to trust Mr. Mee's imagination too far." John Denvir offers a much different appraisal in the *Los Angeles Times Book Review;* he maintains that "Mee makes skillful use of detail to highlight the cavernous gulf that separates us from the late 18th Century." He further comments that "Mee has written the type of book which gives popularization a good name. He tells his story clearly and simply without making it simplistic."

In addition to writing historical novels, Mee is also a playwright. *The Investigation of the Murder in El Salvador,* produced in New York City by the New York Theatre Workshop, is the story of a group of aristocrats having a cocktail party in a beach house in El Salvador while gunshots and explosions are heard off-stage. Mel Gussow in the *New York Times,* compares Mee's play with T. S. Eliot's *The Cocktail Party,* but notes that Mee's version is a "*Cocktail Party* with a contemporary political punch— Eliot crossbred with Wallace Shawn. In Mr. Mee's El Salvador, the world ends with a loud bang." Gussow calls Mee's dialogue "as literate as it is self-revealing," and comments that Mee has "a keen eye for verbal imagery."

In Mee's novel *Playing God: Seven Fateful Moments When Great Men Met to Change the World,* Mee discusses seven incidents involving the meetings or confrontations of world leaders that became historical events of great impact. These include Attila the Hun's confrontation with Pope Leo, the meeting of Cortez and Montezuma, Henry VIII's meeting with Francis I, the Congress of Vienna, the Paris Peace Conference of 1919, and the G7 meeting of 1991. Edwin M. Yoder, Jr. of the *Washington Post Book World* comments that "the cogency of Mee's retelling of these episodes varies. . . . The connection between the historical episodes and the lesson allegedly to be drawn from them is usually strained, arbitrary or elusive." He concludes that Mee is "for the most part . . . unpersuasive."

Mee's 1993 play, *Orestes,* humorously critiques contemporary society by way of the Atreus family, each generation of which either kills its parents or children. Orestes Atreus has killed his mother (at the urging of his sister Electra) because she had killed his father. Throughout the play, Mee makes reference to highly publicized contemporary murders and the defenses subsequently presented for them. D. J. R. Bruckner, in the *New York Times,* notes that Mee "borrows from many sources, including *Soap Opera Digest* and the serial killer John Wayne Gacy." Bruckner concludes that Mee's "dark vision of society . . . is not brighter than his other plays, but his humor is sharper."

Mee told *CA* that his life-long interest has been politics "dealt with not as a scholar but as a citizen." In a *Publishers Weekly* interview with Robert Dahlin, Mee said: "I think the only reason to write popular history in a republic is to engage in a communication. That's my motivation, to talk politics with my fellow citizens."

BIOGRAPHICAL/CRITICAL SOURCES:

PERIODICALS

Chicago Tribune, April 3, 1983.
Chicago Tribune Book World, May 28, 1972.
Commonweal, July 18, 1975.
Journal of American History, March, 1988.
Listener, February 12, 1981.
Los Angeles Times, August 29, 1984; July 27, 1990.
Los Angeles Times Book Review, August 30, 1981; September 20, 1987; May 29, 1988.
Nation, June 22, 1985.
National Review, March 19, 1976.
New Leader, June 23, 1975.
New Republic, April 19, 1975; February 28, 1981; September 9, 1981; June 25, 1984; June 29, 1987; August 22, 1988.
Newsweek, March 24, 1975.
New Yorker, February 9, 1981.
New York Review of Books, June 24, 1982.
New York Times, November 16, 1978; June 6, 1988; July 3, 1988; May 23, 1989; June 30, 1993.
New York Times Book Review, March 9, 1975; April 17, 1983; September 9, 1984; March 15, 1987; May 15, 1988; May 29, 1988.
Publishers Weekly, June 26, 1981; August 9, 1993.
Saturday Review, March 8, 1975.
Spectator, August 2, 1975.
Time, May 5, 1975; May 15, 1978; July 27, 1981.
Village Voice, June 27, 1977.
Virginia Quarterly Review, spring, 1981; summer, 1987.
Washington Post Book World, May 4, 1969; March 9, 1975; March 27, 1977; April 3, 1983; June 3, 1984; May 17, 1987; December 26, 1993.

MIALL, Robert
See BURKE, John (Frederick)

*   *   *

MILL, C. R.
See CRNJANSKI, Milos

*   *   *

MITCHELL, Daniel J(esse) B(rody)   1942-

PERSONAL: Born September 7, 1942, in Brooklyn, NY; married in 1966. *Education:* Columbia University, B.A., 1964; Massachusetts Institute of Technology, Ph.D., 1968.

ADDRESSES: Office—Anderson Graduate School of Management, University of California-Los Angeles, 405 Hilgard Ave., Los Angeles, CA 90095-1481.

CAREER: University of California, Los Angeles, professor, 1968—, research associate at Institute for Industrial Relations, 1971—, director, 1979-90. Chief economist with U.S. Pay Board, 1972-73. Senior fellow, Brookings Institute, 1978-79.

MEMBER: International Industrial Relations Association, North American Economic and Finance Association, American Economic Association, Industrial Relations Research Association.

AWARDS, HONORS: Fellow at University of Aix-Marseille, 1971.

WRITINGS:

Essays on Labor and International Trade, University of California-Los Angeles (UCLA) Institute of Industrial Relations, 1970.
(Author of introduction to reprint) Bessie Van Vorst, *The Woman Who Toils: Being the Experiences of Two Ladies as Factory Girls,* UCLA Institute of Industrial Relations, 1974.
(With Ross E. Azevedo) *Wage-Price Controls and Labor Market Distortions,* UCLA Institute of Industrial Relations, 1976.
Labor Issues of American International Trade and Investment, Johns Hopkins University Press (Baltimore, MD), 1976.
(With Arnold R. Weber) *The Pay Board's Progress: Wage Controls in Phase II,* Brookings Institution (Washington, DC), 1978.
(With John Clapp) *Legal Constraints on Teenage Employment: A New Look at Child Labor and School Leaving Laws,* UCLA Institute of Industrial Relations, 1979.
Unions, Wages, and Inflation, Brookings Institution, 1980.

(With Barry Bosworth and Laurence Seidman) *Controlling Inflation: Studies in Wage/Price Policy,* Center for Democratic Policy (Washington, DC), 1981.

Industrial Relations Research in the 1970's, Industrial Relations Research Association, 1982.

(Editor) *The Future of Industrial Relations,* UCLA Institute of Industrial Relations, 1987.

Human Resource Management: An Economic Approach (with instructor's manual), PWS-Kent Publishing (Boston, MA), 1989, revised edition, Southwestern, 1995.

(Editor with M. A. Zaidi) *The Economics of Human Resource Management,* Basil Blackwell (London), 1990.

(Editor with J. Wildhorn) *The Effective Use of Human Resources: A Symposium on New Research Approaches,* UCLA Institute of Industrial Relations, 1990.

(Editor with D. Lewin) *International Perspectives and Challenges in Human Resource Management,* UCLA Institute of Industrial Relations, 1994.

Contributor to economic and industrial relations journals.

BIOGRAPHICAL/CRITICAL SOURCES:

PERIODICALS

Annals of the American Academy of Political and Social Science, November, 1978.
Business Economics, July, 1985.
California Management Review, spring, 1992.
Canada-U.S. Outlook, May, 1993.
Industrial Relations, winter, 1993.
Journal of Economic Literature, September, 1992; December, 1992.
Journal of Labor Research, spring, 1995.
Labour, spring, 1993.
Personnel Journal, August, 1986.
Political Science Quarterly, winter, 1978-79; summer, 1981.
Public Personnel Management, spring, 1986.

*   *   *

MONTELEONE, Thomas F(rancis) 1946-
(Brian T. LoMedico, Mario Martin Jr.)

PERSONAL: Born April 14, 1946, in Baltimore, MD; son of Mario Martin (a machinist) and Marie (in sales; maiden name, Krauch) Monteleone; married Natalie Cohen (a librarian and flamenco dancer), 1969 (divorced, 1980); married Linda J. Smith, May 22, 1981; children: (first marriage) Damon Andrei; (second marriage) Brandon Thomas. *Education:* University of Maryland at College Park, B.S., 1968, M.A., 1973, further graduate study, 1973-74. *Politics:* "Fairly apolitical but leaning towards libertarian." *Religion:* "Agnostic, at best."

ADDRESSES: Agent—Howard Morhaim Agency, 175 Fifth Ave., New York, NY 10010.

CAREER: Clifton T. Perkins Hospital Center, Jessup, MD, psychotherapist, 1969-78; writer.

MEMBER: Horror Writers of America (vice president, 1987-88).

AWARDS, HONORS: Nebula Award nominations for best short story, Science Fiction Writers of America, 1973, for "Agony in the Garden," 1977, for "Breath's a Ware That Will Not Keep," and 1978, for "Camera Obscura"; Nebula Award nomination for best short novel, 1977, for *The Time-Swept City;* John W. Campbell Memorial Award finalist for Best New Writer of 1973, 32nd World Science Fiction Convention, 1974; finalist in Maryland Theatrical Association One-Act Play Tournament, 1978, for "Mister Magister"; Bronze Award, International Film and TV of New York, 1984, for *Mister Magister;* Bram Stoker Award, 1992, for *Blood of the Lamb.*

WRITINGS:

SCIENCE FICTION AND FANTASY NOVELS

Seeds of Change, Laser, 1975.
The Time Connection, Popular Library, 1976.
The Time-Swept City, Popular Library, 1977.
The Secret Sea, Popular Library, 1979.
Guardian, Doubleday (Garden City, NY), 1980.
Night Things, Fawcett (New York City), 1980.
Ozymandias, Doubleday, 1981.
(With David F. Bischoff) *Day of the Dragonstar* (originally serialized as *Dragonstar* in *Analog Science Fiction-Science Fact,* 1981), Berkley Publishing (New York City), 1983.
Night Train, Pocket Books (New York City), 1984.
(With Bischoff) *Night of the Dragonstar,* Berkley Publishing, 1985.
(With John DeChancie) *Crooked House,* Tor Books (New York City), 1987.
Lyrica, Berkley Publishing, 1987.
The Magnificent Gallery, Tor Books, 1987.
Fantasma, Tor Books, 1989.
(With Bischoff) *Dragonstar Destiny,* Berkley Publishing, 1989.
The Apocalypse Man, St. Martin's (New York City), 1991.
The Blood of the Lamb, Tor Books, 1992.
The Resurrectionist, Warner Aspect, 1995.

OTHER

(With others) *Writing and Selling Science Fiction,* Writer's Digest (Cincinnati, Ohio), 1976.
(Editor) *The Arts and Beyond: Visions of Man's Aesthetic Future* (science fiction short stories), Doubleday, 1977.

(With Grant Carrington) *U.F.O.!* (three-act play), first produced in Ashton, MD, 1977.

Dark Stars and Other Illuminations (collected science fiction; contains "The Star-Filled Sea Is Smooth Tonight," "The Curandeiro," "Present Perfect," "Just in the Niche of Time," "Mister Magister" [story; also see below], "Mister Magister" [play; first produced in Silver Spring, MD, at Maryland Theatrical Association One-Act Play Tournament, 1978], "Camera Obscura," "Where All the Songs Are Sad," "The Dancer in the Darkness," and "Taking the Night Train"), Doubleday, 1981.

Mister Magister (teleplay; adapted from the short story of the same name), WMPB-TV, 1984.

(Editor) *Random Access Messages of the Computer Age* (short stories), Hayden Book (Hasbrouck Heights, NJ), 1984.

(Editor) *Borderlands* (short stories), Avon, 1990.

(Editor) *Borderlands Two* (short stories), Avon, 1991.

Also author of "Spare the Child" for the CA-TV anthology series *Dark Sides;* editor of anthologies *Fearful Symmetries,* 1991, and *Borderlands Three,* 1992. Contributor of articles to periodicals, including *Cerberus, Nickelodeon,* and *Omni;* author of a column about publishing genre fiction. Author of numerous stories, sometimes written under pseudonyms Mario Martin Jr. or Brian T. LoMedico, and published in anthologies, including *Future City,* edited by Elwood, Trident, 1973; *New Voices,* edited by George R. R. Martin, Jove, 1979; *Masters of Darkness II,* Tor Books, 1987; *Slashers,* Avon Books, 1990; and *Year's Best Horror Stories XVII,* DAW Books. Contributor of stories to periodicals, including *Algol, Cemetery Dance, Comet, Fantastic Stories, Grue, Horror Show, Magazine of Fantasy and Science Fiction, Night Voyages, Pulphouse, Stardate,* and *Sun.*

SIDELIGHTS: Described in *Science Fiction and Fantasy Book Review* as "a veteran writer who's often nominated for the Nebula Awards," Thomas F. Monteleone has written science fiction for both adults and children since 1972. Although he concentrated on short stories during the early years of his writing career, Monteleone has since gone on to write novels, stage plays, and teleplays.

Monteleone is often labeled a science fiction writer, but he told *CA:* "I am not only (nor even primarily) a science fiction writer. I prefer to be known under the broader title of fantasist, which includes fiction of the surreal, the bizarre, and the unusual, as well as the story of modern horror. I work from the tradition of Edgar Allan Poe and Herman Melville, up through Harlan Ellison rather than Jules Verne or Robert Heinlein. Even my science fiction is conspicuously lacking in formulae, spanners, and grommets."

His first novel, *Seeds of Change,* deals with revolution in a future society; it was the first title published by Laser Books and was given free of charge to libraries and booksellers to promote later titles. Monteleone's subsequent novels include *The Time-Swept City,* a Nebula Award finalist about a future city and the effects of technology on men. *Guardian* makes use of Greek mythology in a tale about four men, living in a postholocaust society, who find the only remaining computer of an earlier, lost civilization. In *Ozymandias,* a sequel to *Guardian,* the computer takes on a mobile life of its own, in a special body, and embarks on a quest to improve the planet. He experiences human love and fathers a son, but eventually the machine-man is forced to take military action and descends into bitterness.

Monteleone has long been active in the short fiction market. As he once told *CA:* "I find it much more difficult to write a great short story than a fine novel—I think you have to be at the top of your form to write good short fiction, and I'm glad I started out with stories. . . . In books you have more freedom to change and shift things around, to add and fill in. You don't have that leeway with a short story. Every word has to count. Short stories are like the poetry of novels. And poetry really is the ultimate condensation of image and feeling." Monteleone's first collection of short stories, *Dark Stars and Other Illuminations,* includes such previously published works as "The Star-Filled Sea Is Smooth Tonight," about a space traveler pondering life back home, and "The Dancer in the Darkness," about a woman passionately pursuing dance. The author has also edited several short story anthologies, including *The Arts and Beyond: Visions of Man's Aesthetic Future* and two *Borderlands* collections, which *Locus* reviewer Edward Bryant deemed "very much the dark fantasy series to follow."

In *Fantasma,* a novel of dark fantasy, Monteleone delves into the Italian-American crime world of New York City, focusing on the Manzarra and Candelotto families. Peopling his story with demons of hate and vengeance conjured by Sicilian witches, he propels the reader into a frightening world. Bryant, who expressed mild criticism of some scenes that he felt had been underwritten, nonetheless maintained that the book's merits outweighed its weaknesses. "The real strength of the book," he wrote, is the authentic feel of its view of Italian American experience.

In *The Blood of the Lamb* Monteleone uses what *New York Times Book Review* writer Newgate Callendar identified as "a bit of science fiction and a great deal of fantasy" to tell a "gripping" story of a new Messiah. Years after a secret Vatican experiment in genetics, a youthful priest in Brooklyn's future discovers he has supernatural powers. The man gains worldwide renown and multitudes of followers, but some of his actions begin to alarm the Church officials who created him. While Callendar expressed doubts about the believability of the author's premise, he also recommended the book and called Monteleone "a thoroughly professional stylist who grabs the reader with his first paragraph and never relaxes the tension."

BIOGRAPHICAL/CRITICAL SOURCES:

PERIODICALS

Analog Science Fiction-Science Fact, January, 1976; June, 1978; September, 1979.
Commonweal, March 17, 1978.
Dead of Night, winter, 1995.
Locus, December 17, 1975; August, 1989, p. 21; November, 1990, p. 26; May, 1992, p. 21; July, 1992, p. 19.
Magazine of Fantasy and Science Fiction, July, 1972; June, 1978; September, 1979; December, 1979, p. 16.
New York Times Book Review, August 30, 1992, p. 25.
Science Fiction and Fantasy Book Review, April, 1979; January, 1982.
Science Fiction Review, February, 1975; February, 1982.
Thrust, fall, 1979.
Unearth, winter, 1978.
Universe, November/December, 1975.
Voice of Youth Advocates, June, 1981.

*   *   *

MORGAN, Cary
  See CUTLER, Roland

*   *   *

MORGAN, Rebecca
  See FORREST, Richard (Stockton)

*   *   *

MORRIS, Sara
  See BURKE, John (Frederick)

*   *   *

MOSCOVITZ, Judy   1942-

PERSONAL: Born January 16, 1942, in Montreal, Quebec, Canada; daughter of Jack (in needle trade) and Bess (a secretary; maiden name, Saul) Moscovitz. *Education:* McGill University, B.A., 1962, teaching certificate, 1968,

M.Ed. (counseling), 1978. *Politics:* "Messianic." *Religion:* Jewish.

ADDRESSES: Home—P.O. Box 61333, Durham, NC 27715. *Agent*—Mort Janklow, 598 Madison Ave., New York, NY 10022.

CAREER: The Counseling Center, Montreal, Quebec, director, 1978-82; teacher at Lakeshore School Board, Montreal. Founder of The Single Gourmet.

WRITINGS:

The Rice Diet Report, Putnam (New York City), 1986.
The Dieter's Companion, Avon (New York City), 1988.

WORK IN PROGRESS: A book, workbook, cookbook, and video documentary on the Structure House Diet.

SIDELIGHTS: Judy Moscovitz told *CA:* "Life continues its ups and downs—much like dieting. Indeed, I consider dieting to be a metaphor for life. Would that it were not also an obsession, an addiction and the destroyer of millions of lives. This work continues to be my passion. I consider it part of my mission in a world that needs to be healed. That having been said, I don't always pontificate and have even been known to laugh."

*   *   *

MULLAN, Bob
  See MULLAN, Robert

*   *   *

MULLAN, Robert   1950-
  (Bob Mullan)

PERSONAL: Born December 11, 1950, in Nuneaton, England; son of William and Jane (McGuckin) Mullan; married Michele Allen (a writer; divorced); children: Jessica, Alex, Sean. *Education:* University of Newcastle upon Tyne, B.A. (with honors), 1975; London School of Economics and Political Science, London, Ph.D., 1979. *Politics:* Socialist. *Religion:* Roman Catholic.

ADDRESSES: Office—Department of Applied Social Studies, University of Wales, Singleton Park, Swansea SA2 8PP, Wales.

CAREER: University of East Anglia, Norwich, England, lecturer in sociology, 1978-86; freelance television producer, 1986-95; University of Wales, Swansea, Wales, lecturer in applied social studies, 1995—.

WRITINGS:

UNDER NAME BOB MULLAN

Stevenage Ltd.: Aspects of the Planning and Politics of Stevenage New Town, 1946-1978, Routledge & Kegan Paul (London), 1980.

(With E. Ellis Cashmore) *Approaching Social Theory,* cartoons by Mick Davis, Heinemann Educational Books (London), 1983.

Life as Laughter: Following Bhagwan Shree Rajneesh, Routledge & Kegan Paul, 1983.

The Mating Trade, Routledge & Kegan Paul, 1984.

(With Laurie Taylor) *Uninvited Guests: The Intimate Secrets of Television and Radio,* Chatto & Windus (London), 1986.

Sociologists on Sociology, Croom Helm (London), 1987.

The Enid Blyton Story, Boxtree, 1987.

(With Garry Marvin) *Zoo Culture,* Weidenfeld & Nicolson (London), 1987.

Are Mothers Really Necessary?, Weidenfeld & Nicolson, 1987.

Mad to Be Normal: Conversations with R. D. Laing, Free Association Press, 1995.

WORK IN PROGRESS: A semiological study of the psychotherapeutic enterprise in the United Kingdom.

* * *

MURPHY, Jill (Frances) 1949-

PERSONAL: Born July 5, 1949, in London, England; daughter of Eric Edwin (an engineer) and Irene (Lewis) Murphy; children: Charles. *Education:* Attended Chelsea, Croydon, and Camberwell art schools.

ADDRESSES: Home—London, England. *Agent*—A. P. Watt Ltd., 20 St. John St., London WC1N 2DR, England.

CAREER: Writer and illustrator, 1976—. Worked in a children's home for four years, and as a nanny for one year.

AWARDS, HONORS: Kate Greenaway Award nomination, British Library Association, 1981, and Children's Choice Book of 1981, Children's Book Council and International Reading Association, for *Peace at Last; Parents* Best Books for Babies award, 1987, for *Five Minutes' Peace;* Kate Greenaway Award nominations, c. 1988, for *All in One Piece,* and 1994, for *A Quiet Night In.*

WRITINGS:

SELF-ILLUSTRATED: FOR CHILDREN

The Worst Witch, Allison & Busby (London), 1974, Schocken (New York City), 1980.

The Worst Witch Strikes Again, Schocken, 1980.

Peace at Last, Dial (New York City), 1980, published as *Peace at Last—In Miniature!,* Macmillan (New York City), 1987.

A Bad Spell for the Worst Witch, Puffin (New York City), 1982.

On the Way Home (picture book), Macmillan, 1982.

Whatever Next!, Macmillan (London), 1983, published as *What Next, Baby Bear!,* Dial, 1984.

Five Minutes' Peace, Putnam (New York City), 1986.

All in One Piece, Putnam, 1987.

Worlds Apart, Walker (London), 1988.

A Piece of Cake, Putnam, 1989.

Geoffrey Strangeways, Walker, 1990, published as *Jeffrey Strangeways,* Candlewick Press (Cambridge, MA), 1992.

A Quiet Night In, Candlewick Press, 1994.

ILLUSTRATOR

Fiona Macdonald, *The Duke Who Had Too Many Giraffes, and Other Stories,* Allison & Busby, 1977.

Brian Ball, *The Witch in Our Attic,* British Broadcasting Corp., 1979.

ADAPTATIONS: The Worst Witch and *Peace at Last* were adapted for television in 1978 and 1984, respectively. *The Worst Witch* and *A Bad Spell for the Worst Witch* were recorded on cassette.

SIDELIGHTS: Jill Murphy has been writing and drawing since she was very young. She once told *CA:* "I inherited the ability to draw from my father and I had a mother who *liked* being a mother. She encouraged me to be observant and to write from the age of three. I have drawn and written little books stapled together ever since I can remember. I always had a difficult time at school because I never wanted to do anything except write stories and draw pictures, which drove my teachers to distraction. . . . It never occurred to me that I would be anything [but a writer/illustrator.] Now I write and draw because I always have. It was a choice of making a success of it or working in a shop. I can't think of a more satisfying career and feel very fortunate that I am able to do it."

Murphy explained to *CA* that she still creates her illustrations in an exercise book, just as she did when she was a child, adding: "I always use coloured pencils. You can get lovely light effects very softly with coloured pencils. Also I hate all the mess of paints and inks and I always seem to knock things over!" Several reviewers have commented that Murphy's illustrations enhance her tales. One of Murphy's books about a family of elephants called the Larges drew praise from Christopher Lehmann-Haupt in the *New York Times.* Although he observes that *All in One Piece* is "predictable enough," Lehmann-Haupt also writes: "The author's appealing paintings of [the Larges] keep yielding up comic surprises." According to Virginia

E. Jeschelnig in a *School Library Journal* review of *A Piece of Cake*, "Murphy's skillful illustrations feature rich color, amusing detail, and an engaging blend of elephantine and human characteristics."

Felicity Trotman, writing in *Twentieth-Century Children's Writers*, says that "Jill Murphy has a particular talent for writing stories that appeal to children who have learned the basic skill of reading, and want something bright and enticing to make them enjoy books thenceforward."

BIOGRAPHICAL/CRITICAL SOURCES:

BOOKS

Twentieth-Century Children's Writers, 3rd edition, St. James Press (London), 1989, p. 706.

PERIODICALS

Los Angeles Times Book Review, June 13, 1982, p. 8.
New Yorker, December 1, 1980, pp. 103-104, 220.
New York Times, December 28, 1986, p. 20; December 3, 1987.
New York Times Book Review, December 30, 1984, p. 19.
School Librarian, February, 1991, p. 24.
School Library Journal, January, 1988, p. 68; January, 1990, pp. 86-87.
Times (London), March 16, 1991.
Times Literary Supplement, November 21, 1980, p. 1328; November 20, 1987, p. 1284; June 9-15, 1989, p. 648.
Voice Literary Supplement, December, 1989.
Washington Post Book World, February 14, 1982, p. 12.

* * *

MUTHESIUS, Stefan 1939-

PERSONAL: Born July 30, 1939, in Berlin, Germany; son of Karl Volkmar (a journalist) and Helene (Rossbach) Muthesius; married Katarzyna Murawska (a museum curator and art historian; marriage ended); married Anna Maria Butterworth, 1971; children: Bianca Helena. *Education:* University of Marburg and University der Lahn, D.Phil., 1969; also studied at University of Munich and Courtauld Institute of Art, University of London.

ADDRESSES: Home—72 Helena Rd., Norwich NR2 3BZ, England. *Office*—School of World Art Studies, University of East Anglia, Norwich NR4 7TJ, England.

CAREER: University of East Anglia, Norwich, England, lecturer in fine arts, 1968—. Member of faculty at Johns Hopkins University, spring, 1972.

MEMBER: Society of Architectural Historians, Verband Deutscher Kunsthistoriker, Norwich Society (member of committee).

WRITINGS:

The High Victorian Movement in Architecture, 1850-1870, Routledge & Kegan Paul (London), 1972.
Das englische Vorbild: Eine Studie zu den deutschen Reformbewegungen in Architektur, Wohnbau und Kunstgewerbe imspaeteren 19, Jahrhundert (title means "England as a Model: A Study of German Reform Movements in Architecture, Domestic Architecture and Applied Arts in the Later 19th Century"), Prestel Verlag Muenchen (Munich, Germany), 1974.
(With Bridget Wilkins) *Europe, 1900-1914*, Milton Keynes, 1975.
(With Roger Dixon) *Victorian Architecture*, Thames & Hudson (London), 1978.
The English Terraced House, Yale University Press (London), 1982.
(With Miles Glendinning) *Tower Block Modern Public Housing in England, Scotland, Wales and Northern Ireland*, Yale University Press, 1994.
Art, Architecture and Design in Poland, 1960-1990, Koenigstein/Taunus (Klosteneuburg, Austria), 1994.

Contributor to English and German language art history journals.

WORK IN PROGRESS: Research on nineteenth-century domestic architecture in England and Europe.

* * *

MYERS, Edward 1950-

PERSONAL: Born April 1, 1950, in Denver, CO; son of Francis Milton Myers (a college professor) and Estela (a college professor, maiden name Montemayor) Myers; married Edith Poor (a writer and writing consultant), June 29, 1985; children: two. *Education:* Attended Grinnell College, 1968-70, and University of Denver, 1973-75. *Religion:* "Theologically polymorphous."

ADDRESSES: Home—Maplewood, NJ. *Agent*—Faith Hamlin, Sanford J. Greenburger Associates, 55 Fifth Avenue, New York, NY 10003.

CAREER: Worked variously as a bricklayer, language instructor, greenhouse worker, baker, librarian, hospital orderly, secretary, administrator at two mental health clinics, editor, proofreader, and cabinetmaker; full-time writer, 1982—.

WRITINGS:

The Chosen Few (nonfiction), And Books (South Bend, IN), 1982.
When Parents Die: A Guide for Adults, Viking (New York City), 1986.

Mind Movies (fiction), American Health Foundation, 1986.

The Mountain Made of Light (fiction, first novel in "The Mountain Trilogy"), New American Library (New York City), 1992.

(With Jane Greer) *Adult Sibling Rivalry: Understanding the Legacy of Childhood* (nonfiction), Crown (New York City), 1992.

Fire and Ice (fiction, second novel in "The Mountain Trilogy"), New American Library, 1992.

Climb or Die (juvenile), Hyperion (New York City), 1994.

The Summit (fiction, third novel in "The Mountain Trilogy"), New American Library, 1994.

Forri the Baker (juvenile), illustrated by Alexi Natchev, Dial (New York City), 1995.

WORK IN PROGRESS: The Renaissance Man, a novel about a classical musician adrift in the 1960s; *Fever,* a novella about a survivalist holed up in the Colorado Rockies; and *My House Is Your House,* a young-adult novel about a teenager who spends his summer vacation with a poor family in Mexico.

SIDELIGHTS: Edward Myers told *CA:* "*The Chosen Few* is a study of the so-called survivalist movement in the United States. Based on interviews with men and women of greatly differing backgrounds and orientations, the book explores their plans and preparations for surviving nuclear war and other disasters.

"I wrote *When Parents Die* to fill a need that has gone largely unrecognized. Despite the many books available about bereavement, few address the specific issues facing adults following a parent's final illness. This is ironic; the death of a parent is the most common form of loss in this country. Perhaps the lack of information is a side effect of Americans' continuing (though diminishing) reluctance to discuss death and bereavement.

"Because I feel that a book like this should be useful in tangible ways, *When Parents Die* contains chapters about dealing with both the emotional and practical consequences of experiencing the loss of a parent. The book contains listings of resources that can help readers deal with issues ranging from Alzheimer's disease to probate to sibling conflicts. My hope is that *When Parents Die* will help Americans come to terms with one of the most complex issues of our time: the aging of the older generation.

"My major efforts during the past five years or so have focused on three novels collectively titled 'The Mountain Trilogy,' an adventure story—more in the 19th-century style of Kipling and Melville than in the current fantasy mode—that operates as well on levels other than external action."

The first novel of the trilogy, *The Mountain Made of Light,* introduces the character Jesse O'Keefe, an anthropology student in the Peruvian Andes climbing and doing field work in the 1920s. He is told about expert local climbers by an old man who leads him to discover the airy, alpine realm of the Rixtirra. "There is a strange quality to this book early on, a wistful innocent thirst for knowledge," comments a reviewer for *Locus,* who praised this first novel's "wonderful sense of place" that illuminates "both culture and character."

Involving himself in the conflicts of the civilization he finds, O'Keefe befriends the lovely native Aeslu. When a new climber—the spoiled, upper-class Forster Beckwith—intrudes, the two outsiders fulfill an ancient prophecy that tells of two strangers: one who will lead Rixtirra to salvation on the Mountain Made of Light, the other to calamity. Myers explained that " 'The Mountain Trilogy' is at once nonautobiographical and deeply rooted in my past; I've undergone nothing like what I have written in these novels, yet I can trace almost everything there to personal experience. First, a complex heritage. My father's clan was Scottish and German, and my mother's was Mexican. I am a one-man cultural collision.

"Another influence on my life was travel. My parents decided in 1957 to move to Mexico. We ended up living near Guanajuato in a run-down hacienda without electricity or running water. It was rough going in some ways but paradise for a seven-year-old boy. I played hide-and-seek in the hills overlooking a 400-year-old town, hunted lizards with slingshots, learned from playmates how to cuss in Spanish, and ate tortillas given to me by an old hag purported to be a witch. Although we ended up staying only part of that year, I returned to Denver as changed as if I'd been off to Mars and back.

"A few years later, when my father received a Fulbright grant, we moved to Peru for a longer stay. That first year in Peru jolted me in ways I've never gotten over. The change of time-sense was especially bewildering. In Colorado, a miner's shack built in 1880 is considered ancient; in Peru, the Spanish Conquest in 1532 is a fairly recent event. The Incas themselves, having done to neighboring and far older tribes essentially what the Spaniards did to them, were Johnnie-come-latelies. Some of the archaeological sites I visited as a kid were the remains of civilizations that had fallen around 500 A.D.

"During the summer of 1965, when I was fifteen, my family stayed for several days in Yungay, a small city right at the base of Peru's highest peak. It was there, with a massive double-dome of rock and ice rising to an altitude of 22,300 feet above me, that I first started musing not about just mountains themselves but also about their tenacious hold on my imagination."

In *Fire and Ice,* the second novel of Myers's "Mountain Trilogy," rival adventurers Jesse and Forster both fall in love with the native guide woman Aeslu as they play out their predestined roles in the mountaintop world's mythology. One Rixtirran faction favors the playboy Forster and the other Jesse, so they compete to be the first to reach the top of the Mountain of Light. Reviewer Faren Miller, writing in *Locus,* is intrigued that "despite Forster's frequent caddishness, the roles of hero and villain are not entirely clear-cut" and that "the rival factions . . . also resist being categorized." This ability to present more than one point of view, says Miller, "allows Myers a degree of subtlety unusual in a Lost Race adventure."

BIOGRAPHICAL/CRITICAL SOURCES:

PERIODICALS

Locus, December, 1991, p. 33; January, 1992; November, 1992, p.17.
New York Review of Science Fiction, April, 1992.
Publishers Weekly, January 13, 1992, p. 52; November 23, 1992, p. 58; March 20, 1995.
School Library Journal, February, 1995.

N

NEWMAN, John Kevin 1928-

PERSONAL: Born August 17, 1928, in Bradford, England; immigrated to United States, 1969, naturalized citizen, 1984; son of Willie (a watchmaker) and Agnes (a civil servant; maiden name, Shee) Newman; married Frances Stickney (a professor of classics), September 8, 1970; children: Alexandra, John, Victoria. *Education:* Oxford University, B.A. (humane letters), 1950, B.A. (Russian), 1952, M.A., 1953; University of Bristol, Ph.D., 1967. *Religion:* Roman Catholic.

ADDRESSES: Home—703 West Delaware Ave., Urbana, IL 61801. *Office*—Department of Classics, University of Illinois at Urbana-Champaign, Urbana, IL 61801.

CAREER: Master of classics at school in Bath, England, 1955-69; University of Illinois at Urbana-Champaign, associate professor, 1970-80, professor of classics, 1980—, chairman of department, 1981-85.

MEMBER: American Philological Association.

AWARDS, HONORS: Vatican International Latin Poetry Competition prizes, 1960, for "Mors et Vita," 1963, for "Ad Posteritatum Epistula," and 1966, for "Navigatio in Incognitum"; Certamen Capitolinum Awards, Instituto di Studi Romani (Rome), 1968, for "Romanitas," 1980, for "De Novo Galli Fragmento in Nubia Eruto," and 1987, for *The Classical Epic Tradition;* fellowship, University of Edinburgh Institute for Advanced Studies in the Humanities, 1986-87.

WRITINGS:

Augustus and the New Poetry, Latomus, 1967.
The Concept of Vates in Augustan Poetry, Latomus, 1967.
Latin Compositions, Ex Aedibus, 1976.
Golden Violence: Poems for Proclamation, Ex Aedibus, 1976.

Dislocated: An American Carnival (novel), Ex Aedibus, 1977.
(With wife, F. S. Newman) *Pindar's Art,* Weidmann, Hildesheim, 1984.
The Classical Epic Tradition, University of Wisconsin Press (Madison), 1986.
Roman Catullus, Weidmann, Hildesheim, 1990.
(With Newman) *Lelio Guidiccioni, Latin Poems,* Weidmann, Hildesheim, 1992.
(With P. Fehl) *Durer, Passio Christi (1511),* Pennsylvania State University Press (University Park), in press.

Editor of series "Illinois Classical Studies," Scholars Press (Decatur, GA), 1981—. Contributor to *Princeton Encyclopedia of Poetry and Poetics.*

WORK IN PROGRESS: Ingenium Properti: The Nature of an Augustan Poet; H. B. de Saussure, De Geographia Physica Excerpta, with A. Carozzi.

SIDELIGHTS: John Kevin Newman told *CA:* "My aim as a scholar is to live out the title of the degree I took at Oxford in 'humane letters.' The Greco-Roman authors are not to be viewed as an arcane mystery accessible only to the few, but as the first surveyors and mappers of an intellectual and imaginative terrain that we are still exploring. Great writers know this by instinct, and it is very often to them rather than to professional academics that we must look for real guidance about what we are doing in our civilization and where we are to find our links with the past. Hence the need to study more than the classics in order to understand the classics.

"European and all Western civilization (including that of the Slavic peoples) constitutes a unity because of its roots in the Greco-Roman past. But that past must be studied in its entirety, not selected portions artificially singled out for admiration. There are indispensable clues in religious language, popular survivals, and that is why anthropology must also form part of our interests.

"I see an age of specialization so narrow that scholars are now no longer experts even on a single century of a given literature, but on particular aspects of one author. It is the death of education. There are some hopeful signs that others see this, too.

"I do not claim expertise in any language, but *Pindar's Art* quotes from material in ten languages apart from Latin and Greek, and *The Classical Epic Tradition* discusses epics written in Italian, English, German, and Russian, again apart from Latin and Greek. This is deliberate.

"In recent years, I have been increasingly aware of the importance of Hebrew as part of the Renaissance ideal of studies embracing the three languages of the Bible. My

edition of the Latin poems of Lelio Guidiccioni especially emphasizes this point.

"I was brought up in an England hit by the Depression of the thirties and still reeling from the First World War. I entered grammar school as the Second World War was beginning. Poor education, poor social conditions, poor grasp of history have dire personal consequences. Humane education, classical education, could be such a weapon in the only battle worth fighting, that against impoverishment of the imagination and intellect."

*   *   *

NICOLAS, F. R. E.
    See FREELING, Nicolas

O

OAKLEY, Ann (Rosamund) 1944-
(Rosamund Clay)

PERSONAL: Born January 17, 1944, in London, England; daughter of Richard Morris (a university professor) and Kathleen (a social worker; maiden name, Miller) Titmuss; children: Adam, Emily, Laura. *Education:* Somerville College, Oxford, M.A. (with honors), 1965; Bedford College, London, Ph.D., 1974. *Politics:* Feminist.

ADDRESSES: Office—Social Science Research Unit, 18 Woburn Sq., London WC1H 0NS, England. *Agent*—Tessa Sayle Ltd., 11 Jubilee Place, London SW3, England.

CAREER: University of London, Bedford College, London, England, research officer in Social Research Unit, 1974-79; Radcliffe Infirmary, National Perinatal Epidemiology Unit, Oxford, England, Wellcome Research Fellow, 1980-83; University of London, professor of sociology and social policy, 1991—, Thomas Coram Research Unit, deputy director, 1985-90, Social Science Research Unit, director, 1990—.

WRITINGS:

Sex, Gender and Society, Maurice Temple Smith, 1972, Harper (New York City), 1973.

The Sociology of Housework, Martin Robertson, 1974, Pantheon (New York City), 1975.

Housewife, Allen Lane (London), 1974, published as *Woman's Work: A History of the Housewife,* Pantheon, 1975.

(Contributor) David Tuckett, editor, *Medical Sociology,* Tavistock (London), 1975.

(Editor with Juliet Mitchell) *The Rights and Wrongs of Women,* Penguin (London), 1976.

Becoming a Mother, Martin Robertson, 1979, Schocken (New York City), 1980.

Women Confined, Schocken, 1980.

Subject Women, Pantheon, 1981.

(With A. McPherson and H. Roberts) *Miscarriage,* Fontana (London), 1984.

Taking It Like a Woman, Random House (New York City), 1984.

The Captured Womb: A History of the Medical Care of Pregnant Women, Blackwell (London), 1984, Oxford University Press (New York City), 1985.

Telling the Truth about Jerusalem, Blackwell, 1986.

(Editor with Mitchell) *What Is Feminism,* Blackwell, 1986.

The Men's Room (fiction), Virago (London), 1988.

(Under pseudonym Rosamund Clay) *Only Angels Forget* (fiction), Virago, 1990.

Matilda's Mistake (fiction), Virago, 1990.

(With S. Houd) *Helpers in Childbirth: Midwifery Today,* Hemisphere Books (London), 1990.

The Secret Lives of Eleanor Jenkinson (fiction), HarperCollins (London), 1992.

Social Support and Motherhood: The Natural History of a Research Project, Blackwell (Oxford), 1992.

Essays on Women, Medicine and Health, Edinburgh University Press (Edinburgh, England), 1992.

Scenes Originating in the Garden of Eden (fiction), HarperCollins (London), 1993.

(With J. Brannen, K. Dodd, and P. Storey) *Young People, Health and Family Life,* Open University Press (Buckingham, England), 1994.

(Editor with S. Williams) *The Politics of the Welfare State,* University College Press (London), 1994.

WORK IN PROGRESS: Editor with J. Popay, *Researching Welfare: A Critique of Theory and Method,* for University College Press; *Public Visions, Private Lives: Richard and Kathleen Titmuss; The Early Years,* for HarperCollins; *A Proper Holiday,* fiction, for HarperCollins.

BIOGRAPHICAL/CRITICAL SOURCES:

PERIODICALS

Globe & Mail (Toronto), April 13, 1985.
Newsweek, January 20, 1975.
New York Times Book Review, June 3, 1984.
Spectator, January 21, 1984.
Times (London), January 12, 1984; January 17, 1985.
Times Literary Supplement, March 2, 1972; February 28, 1975; June 28, 1985.
Village Voice, November 4, 1981.

* * *

OATES, Stephen B(aery) 1936-

PERSONAL: Born January 5, 1936, in Pampa, TX; son of Steve Theodore and Florence (Baer) Oates; married Marie Philips; children (from previous marriage): Gregory Allen, Stephanie. *Education:* University of Texas at Austin, B.A. (magna cum laude), 1958, M.A., 1960, Ph.D., 1969.

ADDRESSES: Home—10 Bridle Path, Amherst, MA 01002-1632. *Office*—Department of History, University of Massachusetts, Amherst, MA 01003.

CAREER: Arlington State College (now University of Texas at Arlington), instructor, 1964-67, assistant professor of history, 1967-68; University of Massachusetts, Amherst, assistant professor, 1968-70, associate professor, 1970-71, professor of history, 1971-80, adjunct professor of English, 1980-85, Paul Murray Kendall Professor of Biography, 1985—. Guest lecturer at numerous colleges, universities, societies and associations throughout the United States; has made numerous guest appearances on radio and television programs. Honorary member of board of directors, Abraham Lincoln Association. American history and biography consultant to various commercial and university presses, and consultant to National Endowment for the Humanities for various book, museum, television, and motion-picture projects.

MEMBER: Society of American Historians, American Antiquarian Society, Texas Institute of Letters, Phi Beta Kappa.

AWARDS, HONORS: Texas State Historical Association fellow, 1968; Texas Institute of Letters fellow, 1969; Guggenheim fellow, 1972; Chancellor's Medal for Outstanding Scholarship, University of Massachusetts, 1976; Christopher Award, 1977, and Barondess/Lincoln Award, New York Civil War Round Table, 1978, both for *With Malice toward None: The Life of Abraham Lincoln;* National Endowment for the Humanities senior summer fellow, 1978; Distinguished Teaching Award, University

of Massachusetts, 1981; Litt.D., Lincoln College, 1981; graduate faculty fellowship, University of Massachusetts, 1981-82; Christopher Award, 1982, Robert F. Kennedy Memorial Book Award, 1983, and Chancellor's Certificate of Recognition, University of Massachusetts, 1983, all for *Let the Trumpet Sound: The Life of Martin Luther King, Jr.;* Institute for Advanced Studies in the Humanities fellow, 1984; Author's Award for best article of the year, *Civil War Times Illustrated,* 1984, for "Abraham Lincoln: Man and Myth"; University of Massachusetts Presidential Writers Award, 1985; Master Teacher Award, University of Hartford, 1985; Silver Medal winner and semi-finalist in national professor of the year competition, Council for Advancement and Support of Education, 1986 and 1987; Kidger Award, New England History Teachers Association, 1992; Nevins-Freeman Award, Chicago Civil War Round Table, 1993.

WRITINGS:

Confederate Cavalry West of the River, University of Texas Press (Austin, TX), 1961.
(Editor and author of introduction and commentary) John Salmon Ford, *Rip Ford's Texas,* University of Texas Press, 1963.
(General editor and contributor) *The Republic of Texas,* American West Publishing, 1968.
Visions of Glory: Texas on the Southwestern Frontier, University of Oklahoma Press (Norman, OK), 1970.
To Purge This Land with Blood: A Biography of John Brown, Harper (New York City), 1970, revised 2nd edition, University of Massachusetts Press (Amherst, MA), 1984.
(Editor) *Portrait of America,* Volume 1: *From the European Discovery to the End of Reconstruction,* Volume 2: *From Reconstruction to the Present,* Houghton (Boston, MA), 1973, 6th edition, 1994.
The Fires of Jubilee: Nat Turner's Fierce Rebellion, Harper, 1975.
With Malice toward None: The Life of Abraham Lincoln, Harper, 1977.
Our Fiery Trial: Abraham Lincoln, John Brown, and the Civil War Era, University of Massachusetts Press, 1979.
Let the Trumpet Sound: The Life of Martin Luther King, Jr., Harper, 1982.
Abraham Lincoln: The Man behind the Myths, Harper, 1984.
(Editor, author of prologue, and contributor) *Biography as High Adventure: Life-Writers Speak on Their Art,* University of Massachusetts Press, 1986.
William Faulkner: The Man and the Artist; A Biography, Harper, 1987.
A Woman of Valor: Clara Barton and the Civil War, Free Press (New York City), 1994.

OTHER

Editor with Paul Mariani of the "Commonwealth Classics in Biography" series for University of Massachusetts Press, 1986—. Contributor to numerous periodicals, including *American Heritage, American History Illustrated, American West, Civil War History, Timeline, Nation, American History Review, Journal of American History,* and *Southwestern Historical Quarterly.*

WORK IN PROGRESS: Another biographical history of the Civil War era.

SIDELIGHTS: Distinguished biographer and educator Stephen B. Oates links his lifelong dual interests in history and literature not only by assuming professorial posts in both disciplines, but by crafting biographies of historical and literary figures as well; and as the Paul Murray Kendall Professor of Biography at the University of Massachusetts, he guides others in that art. "Inevitably," Oates recalls in *Biography as High Adventure: Life-Writers Speak on Their Art,* "biography appealed to me as the form in which I wanted to write about the past, because the best biography—pure biography—was a storytelling art that brought people alive again, eliciting from the coldness of fact 'the warmth of a life being lived,' as Paul Murray Kendall expressed it." Oates explains that unlike other biographical approaches such as the critical study, with its "appropriate detachment and skepticism," or the scholarly chronicle, with its "straightforward recitation of facts," pure biography is the narration or "simulation" of an individual's life. Describing the pure biographer as "both a historian who is steeped in his material and an artist who wields a deft and vivid pen," Oates says that "by telling a story, the pure biographer hopes to engage our hearts as well as our minds."

Oates is especially recognized for what he refers to in *Biography as High Adventure* as "a biographical quartet on the Civil War era and its century-old legacies, a quartet that sought to humanize the monstrous moral paradox of slavery and racial oppression in a land based on the ideals of the Declaration of Independence." In these four biographies, *To Purge This Land with Blood: A Biography of John Brown, The Fires of Jubilee: Nat Turner's Fierce Rebellion, With Malice toward None: The Life of Abraham Lincoln,* and *Let the Trumpet Sound: The Life of Martin Luther King, Jr.,* Oates examines the lives of men profoundly committed to the struggle for equality. "All four were driven, visionary men, all were caught up in the issues of slavery and race, and all devised their own solutions to those inflammable problems," writes Oates. "And all perished, too, in the conflicts and hostilities that surrounded the quest for equality in their country." A former civil rights activist himself, Oates considers these men "martyrs of our racial hatred," states Genevieve Stutta-

ford in *Publishers Weekly,* "martyrs of what he describes as the hateful thing they hated." Complementing this biographical quartet of historical figures is Oates's *William Faulkner: The Man and the Artist; A Biography,* about one of America's most esteemed literary figures who was a voice in the turbulent South for the cause of equality of opportunity, and whose fiction frequently concerns the Civil War and its legacies. Based upon his own native Mississippi, the fictional world that Faulkner created spanned generations and microcosmically mirrored the South's changing landscape while exploring the capacity of the human spirit to not only "endure" but "prevail."

John Brown, the subject of *To Purge This Land with Blood,* Oates's first book in his biographical quartet, was a "white northerner who hated slavery from the outside," explains Oates in *Biography as High Adventure.* Resolved to forcefully abolish slavery by leading an armed insurrection, Brown seized the government's arsenal in Harpers Ferry, Virginia, in 1859, but was ultimately captured, tried, and executed. In the *Saturday Review,* T. Harry Williams calls the book "a major work, based on research in a wide variety of sources . . . that treats in detail Brown's career before he went to Kansas and his actions in that territory, as well as the blazing climax at Harpers Ferry." Noting in the *New York Times Book Review* that "Brown's activities and motivations . . . have been the subject of heated historiographical debate," Eric Foner observes that unlike previous biographers who have set out "either to vindicate or demolish" Brown's legend as an American folk hero, thereby losing "sight of the man himself," Oates neither indicts nor eulogizes Brown. "Brown's life was filled with drama," says Foner, "and Oates tells his story in a manner so engrossing that the book reads like a novel, despite the fact that it is extensively documented and researched."

While acknowledging the "almost complete acceptance and much praise" with which *To Purge This Land* has met, Truman Nelson suggests in a *Nation* review that Oates misunderstands and even maligns his subject by creating a portrait of "a hate-filled man." Nelson disagrees with the premise that Brown's actions derived from his religious beliefs, and feels that to instill "the false consciousness of orthodox Calvinism in Brown diminishes him as a revolutionary." Foner maintains, though, that while Oates's portrait of Brown is "not wholly flattering," neither does it "denigrate the genuinely heroic aspects of Brown's life," and that "about all we can say with certainty is that Brown was fanatic about both his religious and antislavery convictions, but in this he was hardly alone." Willie Lee Rose points out in the *New York Review of Books* that "biographers of men who lived in violent times have the special problem of dealing with the abstractions about means and ends that clutter the rhetoric of political systems in a state of polarization. When do men mean what they say?" Rose also feels that Oates has examined the "whole of John Brown's life as carefully and thoroughly as the end of it . . . and has given us the most objective and absorbing biography of John Brown ever written."

Nat Turner, the subject of *The Fires of Jubilee,* Oates's second biography, was a "victim of human bondage, a brilliant and brooding slave preacher blocked from his potential by an impregnable wall," writes Oates in *Biography as High Adventure.* Oates adds that he "tried to narrate Nat's story as graphically and as accurately" as he could, hoping to "convey how the insurrection rocked the South to its foundations and pointed the way to civil war thirty years later." Assessed as "vivid and convincing" by a *Publishers Weekly* contributor, *The Fires of Jubilee* "presents as complete a narrative account of this affair as we are likely to get," remarks Henry Mayer in the *New York Times Book Review.* Oates recreates the violent and doomed 1831 uprising in which more than fifty whites "were murdered by Turner's insurgents, a band that grew from its nucleus of six to more than forty black men," explains Mayer, adding that Oates also devotes much attention to the "indiscriminate reprisals directed by vengeful whites against blacks" in which almost two hundred blacks died during "the several weeks' reign of terror that followed Turner's two-day uprising."

Mayer argues, however, that the attempt "to present a rational, secularized explanation of the deeply emotional and religious forces" at work in Turner's ability to organize and lead the rebellion "makes Turner's claim of freedom depend more upon merit than right and does not lay adequate stress upon Nat Turner's role as an avenging Messiah." In a *Nation* essay about Turner, Oates deems him "a complex and paradoxical man, a victim of a violent system who in the end struck back with retributive violence," and suggests that "the historical Turner with all his strength and human frailty, his loves and hatreds, his family cares and Messianic posturings, his liberating visions and bloody doom, lived a life that affords profound insight into the tragic consequences of man's inhumanity to his fellow man."

Discussing the subject of his third biography, *With Malice toward None,* Oates indicates in *Biography as High Adventure* that "one of the supreme ironies of Lincoln's life—and of my quartet—was that he who spurned violence, he who placed his reverence for the system above his loathing of slavery, ended up smashing the institution in a violent civil war, a war that began because southerners equated Lincoln with John Brown and Nat Turner and seceded from the very system that protected slavery from Lincoln's grasp." Reviewing *With Malice toward None* in the *Washington Post Book World,* Bernard Weisberger asserts

that "what [Oates] has done in this admirable book is to synthesize basic source materials with an array of new scholarly writing on slavery, Republicanism, the Civil War and Lincoln," a synthesis that Luther Spoehr in *Saturday Review* refers to as "both comprehensive and tightly focused."

Translated into French, Spanish, and Polish, *With Malice toward None* "is an impressive performance," David Herbert Donald comments in the *New York Times Book Review.* "Full, fair and accurate, it does, as its author boasts, cover all significant aspects of Lincoln's life." Oates carefully probes the obfuscatory legends about Lincoln to reveal the man himself. Noting that the Lincoln of *With Malice toward None* is neither Carl Sandburg's "hard-scrabble folk-hero, voicing the soul of a lost frontier," nor the "too overrated" figure perceived by the revisionists, Weisberger thinks that Oates "has made Lincoln recognizably human instead of homespun saint—moody, unusual, inner-directed, but very successful in the world at large." Donald observes that "what most distinguishes Oates from all previous Lincoln biographers is the fact that he is consistently nonjudgmental."

Although Donald believes that *With Malice toward None* represents "the most objective biography of Lincoln ever written," he suggests that "the most crippling consequence of Oates's objectivity is that he is prevented from reflecting about his materials, from raising interesting new questions and attempting fresh answers to old questions." Similarly, Esmond Wright declares in a *Times Literary Supplement* review, "It is all here, without much pause for analysis or assessment, and without any new revelations or discoveries." In the *Spectator,* though, Hugh Brogan interprets Oates's method somewhat differently: "Oates is content to state his own view of every point persuasively, and to move on. Nor does he provide an explicit analysis of Lincoln's character, policies, achievements and significance: he leaves all that to his reader. Of course, his view of Lincoln emerges; but it is not stated outright in any page or sentence. He seems to hold that the story, well-told, will interpret itself, itself fascinate the reader. He is right, of course; and he narrates the extraordinary saga very well."

In a conference paper presented in 1990, an Illinois professor broached the possibility that portions of *With Malice toward None* had been plagiarized from *Abraham Lincoln: A Biography,* written by Benjamin P. Thomas. Oates called the accusation "absurd" and "reckless." As Paul Gray writes in *Time,* Oates "argued that any resemblances between his book and Thomas' were due simply to a reliance on the same historical documents or to an inevitable and entirely innocent overlap between separate descriptions of the same scene or event." Several fellow historians came to his defense, but amid ongoing complaints, the

American Historical Association (AHA) undertook a year-long investigation. In a split decision announced in May of 1992, the AHA found that Oates relied too heavily on other scholars without giving them sufficient attribution, but did not specifically state he had plagiarized.

Let the Trumpet Sound, the last book in Oates's biographical quartet, examines Martin Luther King Jr.'s life "from Montgomery to Memphis," says Roger Wilkins in the *Washington Post Book World;* Oates traces King's development from the "enormously bright . . . and sensitive" child and the youthful "serious scholar" to an adulthood spent "reshaping and refining against hard experience the moral and intellectual view of the world he had developed in his student days." In the *New York Times Book Review,* Foner finds that "King emerges as a charismatic leader, a brilliant tactician of the civil rights struggle, but also a deeply troubled man, subject to periodic bouts of depression and indecisiveness and, like Lincoln, wracked by premonitions of his own death." Calling it "by far the most complete examination of the progression of King's movement and of the crosscurrents that beset it," Harry S. Ashmore notes in a *Chicago Tribune Book World* review that Oates has "remained faithful to his conviction that biography is a storytelling art" by capturing "the high drama and moving tragedy of King's brief passage through our time."

Let the Trumpet Sound, which has been translated into French, German, and Arabic, "succeeds very well in describing King's intellect" and represents a "good place to begin for the facts of King's own life," says Wilkins, a nephew of the late NAACP executive director Roy Wilkins, but it fails to adequately treat the movement's other prominent figures as more than "shadows in King's play." Suspecting that the biography is too uncritical of its subject, Elliott Rudwick similarly suggests in *American Historical Review* that "Oates pictures King as more heroic than he probably was and greatly overstates the importance of his role in the movement." However, Foner declares that the book "provides more than just a chronicle of King's life; as his story is unfolded, the roles of other prominent personalities of the period become clearer." Concerning such criticism, Oates indicates to Stuttaford, "I never leave anything out. And I certainly showed King's warts, showed when he had hatred, when he was angry. He overcame all that, and he showed other blacks how to overcome." Ashmore thinks that "as Oates portrays him, King was not only mortal but, for all his great gifts, essentially humble. It was this quality that allowed him to inspire the lowliest blacks and touch the conscience of guiltridden whites."

A Woman of Valor: Clara Barton and the Civil War evolved from Oates's research into the Civil War for his previous books. He had initially planned to include Barton in his biographical quartet since she was well known for her efforts to aid and save wounded soldiers on the battlefield during the Civil War and for founding the American Red Cross. Once he became fascinated by Barton, however, Oates decided to devote an entire book to her. Writing in the *New York Times Book Review,* Andrew Delbanco says of *A Woman of Valor* that though "we . . . catch glimpses of some of Barton's less attractive features . . . somehow a fully human Clara Barton does not quite come into focus in the book." Delbanco nonetheless finds that the biography, "by attempting a close-up view of one woman's efforts to salve the casualties, reveals just how adept Americans became between 1861 and 1865 at killing one another. . . . What Mr. Oates has written is a kind of chronicle of man-made horror, with one appalled but undaunted woman at the center." Suzanne Gordon notes in the *Washington Post Book World* that "for those who are intrigued by battle, this biography will give them what they want and a taste of Clara Barton as well. For those who want to learn more about Barton, they will have to wait for another book, or refer to earlier ones."

Oates's examination of the Civil War and its legacies continues in an ongoing project he tells *CA* will be his "magnum opus." *Voices of the Storm: A Biographical History of the Civil War Era,* says Oates, will be a "biographical history of the antebellum and Civil War era that tries to capture its human experiences, that presents the entire period through the perceptions and feelings of some twenty-three significant figures whose lives and destinies intersected on many levels." Oates hopes to reinfuse that fratricidal war with the passion that he thinks has been wrung out of it through "dry, scholarly analysis." Oates discusses the two parts that comprise the book: the first part addresses the coming war and demonstrates "in human terms, which is the strength of biography, America's tragic failure to find a peaceful solution to slavery"; and the second part addresses the war itself and explores "what it was like, through various individual perceptions, to fight and suffer in that conflict and to make the human decisions that determined the outcome."

Suggesting that a more meaningful term for this genre might be "*literary* biography," Oates explains in *Biography as High Adventure* that "the term would encompass biographies that attempt to create a life through the magic of language, that seek to illuminate universal truths about humankind through the sufferings and triumphs of a single human being." Oates points out in a *Publishers Weekly* interview with William Goldstein that "biography is an exercise in the art of omission," explaining that in his biography *William Faulkner: The Man and the Artist,* he tried to suggest the writer's art as well as his life through "the use of telling detail alone." He also expresses to Goldstein why he chose a literary figure as a biographical subject:

"I am attracted to figures who have [a profound] sense of history, and Faulkner shares this with the men I have already written about. Faulkner's imagination was fired to incandescence by the history of the South."

Calling Oates's *William Faulkner* "romantic and absorbing," *New York Times*'s Christopher Lehmann-Haupt likens reading it to "racing through a streamlined version" of the more massive, two-volume, fact-filled, scholarly biography by Joseph Blotner: "Suddenly, instead of being the sum of a million particles, Faulkner's life assumes terrific motion. His personality coalesces—the courtliness, the obdurate eyes, the impenetrable silences. There is action to his story." Liberating Faulkner from a "marble block of information," says Lehmann-Haupt, enables him "to live out his life at twice its normal rate and degree of drama." And praising Oates's "streamlined storytelling techniques," John Blades concludes in the *Chicago Tribune Book World* that "with considerable narrative skill, Oates navigates the muddy, turbulent currents of Faulkner's life, so that few readers will come away unmoved by his tragedy and his glory."

Translated into French and German, *William Faulkner* is aimed at a broad audience; however, it has generated a somewhat mixed critical reception. Some critics who fault the biography feel that it suffers from a lack of critical commentary on Faulkner's life as well as his work; Louis D. Rubin Jr., for instance, ponders in the *New York Times Book Review,* "What *is* the point of literary biography . . . if not to illuminate the sources—historical, familial, geographical, social—of the author's literary imagination, and to interpret, as best possible, the ties between an author's life and what he or she wrote?" However, in *Biography as High Adventure* Oates discusses the importance of restraint in the crafting of a biography, indicating that the pure biographer is "careful not to lapse into critical commentary or psychoanalytical speculation" lest the narrative itself be destroyed.

Other critics who fault Oates's *William Faulkner* tend to believe that Faulkner was not an autobiographical writer and that the life, therefore, does not inform the work; Jonathan Yardley, for example, suggests in the *Washington Post Book World* that although "Faulkner was the great American novelist of the century . . . his life's story is essentially irrelevant to his work." Oates, however, finds "Faulkner's inner life . . . illuminated by his fiction" and tells Goldstein that "even an artist as reticent as Faulkner reveals a lot about his personal life and conflicts in his art." Moreover, Oates also thinks that "the themes that troubled him in art and life are universal themes: man's suffering as well as his triumph, his trouble with alcohol, with depression, with feeling unloved, unappreciated, especially by the literary establishment. Toiling in loneliness and solitude, only partly by choice. He was the only

American writer of his generation who chose to go back home and write about that." Faulkner wrote about the Mississippi of his birth "because he knew its history," says Oates. "He sensed [the] problems there were a microcosm of the human race."

In *Biography as High Adventure,* Oates speaks about the current popularity of biography and offers a possible explanation for why it "may now be the preferred form of reading" in America. Aside from a certain natural curiosity about the lives of others, he says that in an increasingly complex and technical society like our own, biography's ability to personalize events "demonstrates that the individual does count—which is reassuring to people . . . who often feel caught up in vast impersonal forces beyond their control." Oates indicates that for him, biography has not only served as "high literary and historical adventure, but deep personal experience as well." Having lived vicariously through the several lives he has documented biographically, Oates believes that he has been enriched "beyond measure as a writer and a man," adding that the experience of writing biographies has "reenforced my lifelong conviction that the people of the past have never really died. For they enjoy a special immortality in biography, in our efforts to touch and understand them and so to help preserve the human continuum. Perhaps this is what Yeats meant when he said that 'nothing exists but a stream of souls, that all knowledge is biography.'"

BIOGRAPHICAL/CRITICAL SOURCES:

BOOKS

Oates, Stephen B., *Biography as High Adventure: Life-Writers Speak on Their Art,* University of Massachusetts Press, 1986.

PERIODICALS

American Historical Review, October, 1983.
American History Illustrated, January, 1986; April, 1988, p. 19.
Antioch Review, summer, 1970; fall, 1984.
Atlantic Monthly, July, 1987.
Biography, spring, 1987, p. 167.
Book Forum, Volume 7, number 4, 1986.
Boston Globe, May 2, 1991, p. 77; May 23, 1992, p. 24; December 18, 1993, p. 13; April 17, 1994, p. A16.
Chicago Tribune, July 26, 1987; December 11, 1990, section 2C, p. 1.
Chicago Tribune Book World, August 8, 1982; September 18, 1983; April 22, 1984.
Christian Science Monitor, February 28, 1977.
Chronicle of Higher Education, November 3, 1982; May 12, 1993, p. A16; June 2, 1993, p. A12; January 5, 1994, p. A17.
Contemporary Review, January, 1983.

Globe and Mail (Toronto), August 23, 1986.
Journal of American History, June, 1987, p. 148.
Library Journal, April 1, 1994, p. 108.
Los Angeles Times Book Review, August 29, 1982.
Nation, March 29, 1971; May 31, 1975.
National Review, October 23, 1987, p. 58.
New Republic, September 13, 1982.
Newsweek, July 6, 1970.
New York Review of Books, December 3, 1970; October 27, 1983.
New York Times, March 12, 1977; August 25, 1982; August 3, 1987.
New York Times Book Review, November 1, 1970; October 5, 1975; March 13, 1977; September 12, 1982; October 28, 1984; September 20, 1987, p. 18; June 12, 1994, p. 14.
Publishers Weekly, January 13, 1975; August 27, 1982; June 28, 1985; February 21, 1994, pp. 240-241.
Saturday Review, August 22, 1970; February 5, 1977.
Spectator, February 25, 1978.
Time, April 26, 1993, pp. 59-60.
Times Literary Supplement, April 28, 1978.
USA Today, July 31, 1987, p. 5D.
Washington Post, January 8, 1994, p. A12.
Washington Post Book World, March 6, 1977; August 8, 1982; April 29, 1984; August 16, 1987; May 1, 1994, p. 4.

*　　*　　*

O'DONNELL, Dick
See LUPOFF, Richard A(llen)

*　　*　　*

OE, Kenzaburo 1935-

PERSONAL: Surname is pronounced "*Oh*-ey"; born January 31, 1935, in Ehime, Shikoku, Japan; married, wife's name, Yukari; children: two, elder named Hikari Pooh. *Education:* Tokyo University, degree in French literature, 1959.

ADDRESSES: Home—585 Seijo-machi, Setagaya-Ku, Tokyo, Japan.

CAREER: Novelist and short story writer, 1952—.

AWARDS, HONORS: Akutagawa Prize from Japanese Society for the Promotion of Literature, 1958, for novella *Shiiku;* Shinchosha Literary Prize from Shinchosha Publishing Co., 1964; Tanizaki Prize, 1967; Europelia Arts Festival Literary Prize, 1989; Nobel Prize for Literature, 1994; Order of Culture, Japanese government, 1994 (declined).

WRITINGS:

IN ENGLISH

Shiiku (novella; title means "The Catch"), [Japan], 1958, translation by John Bester published in *The Shadow of Sunrise,* edited by Saeki Shoichi, [Palo Alto], 1966.
Memushiri kouchi (fiction), [Japan], 1958, translation by Paul St. John Mackintosh and Maki Sugiyama published as *Nip the Buds, Shoot the Kids,* Marion Boyars (New York City), 1995.
Kojinteki na taiken (fiction), [Japan], 1964, translation by John Nathan published as *A Personal Matter,* Grove (New York City), 1968.
Man'en gannen no futtoboru (fiction), [Japan], 1967, translation by Bester published as *The Silent Cry,* Kodansha (New York City), 1974, reprinted, 1989.
Pinchi ranna chosho (fiction), [Japan], 1976, translation by Michiko N. Wilson and Michael K. Wilson published as *The Pinch Runner Memorandum,* M. E. Sharpe (Armonk, NY), 1995.
Teach Us to Outgrow Our Madness (contains "The Day He Himself Shall Wipe My Tears Away," "Prize Stock," "Teach Us to Outgrow Our Madness," and "Aghwee the Sky Monster"), translation and introduction by Nathan, Grove, 1977.
The Crazy Iris and Other Stories of the Atomic Aftermath, translation by Ivan Morris and others, Grove, 1984.
Japan, the Ambiguous, and Myself: The Nobel Prize Speech and Other Lectures, translation by Hisaaki Yamanouchi and Kunioki Yanagishita, Kodansha, 1995.

FICTION; IN JAPANESE

Warera no jidai (title means "Our Age"), [Japan], 1959.
Okurete kita seinen (title means "Born Too Late"), [Japan], 1961.
Sakebigoe (title means "Screams"), [Japan], 1962.
Nichijo seikatsu no boken, [Japan], 1971.
Kozui wa waga tamashii ni oyobi, [Japan], 1973.
Seinen no omei, [Japan], 1974.

SHORT STORIES; IN JAPANESE

Oe Kenzaburo shu, [Japan], 1960.
Kodoku na seinen no kyuka, [Japan], 1960.
Seiteki ningen, [Japan], 1968.
Warera no hyoki o ikinobiru michi o oshieyo, [Japan], 1969, enlarged edition, 1975.
Oe Kenzaburo (volume from "Gendai no bungaku" series), [Japan], 1971.
Mizukara waga namida o nugui-tamau hi, [Japan], 1972.
Sora no kaibutsu Agui, [Japan], 1972.

ESSAYS: IN JAPANESE

Jizokusuru kokorozashi, [Japan], 1968.

Kakujidai no sozoryoku, [Japan], 1970.
Kowaremono to shite no ningen, [Japan], 1970.
Okinawa noto, [Japan], 1970.
Kujira no shimetsusuru hi, [Japan], 1972.
Dojidai to shite no sengo, [Japan], 1973.
Jokyo e, [Japan], 1974.
Bungaku noto, [Japan], 1974.
Genshuku na tsunawatari, [Japan], 1974.
Kotoba no yotte, [Japan], 1976.

OTHER

Sekai no wakamonotachi, [Japan], 1962.
Oe Kenzaburo zensakuhin, [Japan], 1966-67.
Oe Kenzaburo shu (volume from "Shincho Nihon bungaku" series), [Japan], 1969.
(Editor) Mansaku Itami, *Itami Mansaku essei shu,* [Japan], 1971.

Also author of *Hiroshima Notes* (essays), 1963, *The Perverts* (fiction), 1963, and *Adventures in Daily Life* (fiction), 1964.

SIDELIGHTS: Kenzaburo Oe became one of Japan's first authors ever to receive national recognition for his writing while still a university student. When he was awarded the prestigious Akutagawa Prize in 1958 for his novella *Shiiku* ("The Catch"), the twenty-three-year-old "automatically became Japan's *number one* young writer," Josh Greenfeld states. "And with each succeeding work, both fictional and journalistic, his reputation as *number one* has grown to the point where . . . he is touted by the Japanese as their answer to [Norman] Mailer, their send-up on [Jean-Paul] Sartre, their oriental version of Henry Miller."

Despite his popularity, Oe has offended some Japanese critics with his controversial writing style, which, according to translator John Nathan, "treads a thin line between artful rebellion and mere unruliness." Rejecting the delicacy and elegant simplicity of traditional Japanese writers, Oe incorporates elements of Western style into his work. His long sentences, "crammed with adjectives and similes, . . . prod the reader along, constantly forcing him to make unexpected associations, or emphasizing the author's analytical self-awareness," John Bester writes. In the preface to *A Personal Matter,* Nathan points out: "Oe consciously interferes with the tendency to vagueness which is considered inherent in the Japanese language. He violates its natural rhythms; he pushes the meaning of words to their furthest acceptable limits. . . . But that is to be expected: his entire stance is an assault on traditional values. The protagonist of his fiction is seeking his identity in a perilous wilderness, and it is fitting that his language should be just what it is—wild, unresolved, but never less than vital."

Oe has been politically engaged since his student days when he led demonstrations against the re-establishment of the U.S.-Japan Security Treaty. He has consistently protested war, nuclear weapons, racism, even the nearly sacrosanct "Emperor system." Masao Miyoshi writes in the *San Francisco Review of Books* that Oe's "passion for the underclass of the earth cannot be challenged." Shortly after Oe won the Nobel Prize, the Japanese government offered the author its Order of Culture. Oe refused to accept the award on the grounds that it violated his ideals of democracy, and he could not accept an award from the "Emperor system," which he holds accountable for atrocities abroad and suffering at home during World War II. He also cited the government's discrimination among its own citizens as an additional reason for refusing the award.

Western literature has greatly influenced Oe's writings. At Tokyo University he studied the existentialist philosophy of Jean-Paul Sartre, as well as the works of Blaise Pascal and Albert Camus. His favorite American authors are those whose heroes search for "personal freedom beyond the borders of safety and acceptance"—authors such as Herman Melville, William Faulkner, and Norman Mailer. Oe was most inspired by Mark Twain's character Huckleberry Finn, whom Nathan calls "the model for Oe's existential hero."

Two pivotal events in Oe's life have also had a strong impact on his writing. The first incident occurred on August 15, 1945, when Emperor Hirohito announced over the radio that Japan had surrendered to the Allies, thus ending World War II. The Japanese citizens, who believed that the emperor was a living god, had never heard the Emperor's voice before. In *Portrait of a Postwar Generation,* Oe writes: "How could we believe that an august presence of such awful power had become an ordinary human being on a designated summer day?" The cognitive dissonance of hearing that "ordinary" human voice has informed Oe's work: one is never quite sure when the bizarre, the grotesque or the merely incredible will afflict the comfortable.

The second pivotal event in Oe's life and work was the birth of his brain-damaged son Hikari ("Light") in 1963. As a strong bond developed between Oe and his son, he wrote several partially autobiographical novels in which the protagonist is the father of a brain-damaged child. The first of these was *A Personal Matter,* the story of a twenty-seven-year-old man nicknamed Bird, whose wife gives birth to a deformed baby. The boy, looking like a two-headed monster, appears to have a brain hernia, and the doctors tell Bird that the baby will probably die or be a vegetable for life. Bird is so horrified that he chooses to let the baby die rather than face life tied to a retarded son. While his wife and child are in the hospital, Bird runs off to the apartment of a young widow friend, where he escapes into a world of fantasy, sex, and alcohol. He loses his teaching job after being so hung over that he vomits during a lecture. Meanwhile, the baby, being fed only on sugar water, refuses to die, so Bird takes him to an abortionist to have him killed. Suddenly, however, he changes his mind and returns the baby to the hospital. Doctors discover that the hernia is only a benign tumor and after successfully operating, they announce that the baby will be normal, though with a low IQ. Bird finds a new job and is reunited once more with his wife and child.

The novel is not as pretty as its ending might suggest. *Washington Post* reviewer Geoffrey Wolff declares that *A Personal Matter* "reeks of vomit and spilled whisky. Its surreal characters are all vegetables, cut off from history and hope. They define themselves by their despair. They use sex to wound and humiliate one another. They trick themselves with hopeless dreams of a new life, far away." Alan Levensohn surmises that this representation of humanity is Oe's way of suggesting that "the stunted existence Bird's baby will probably have, if Bird allows him to live, comes to seem terribly close to the existence which Bird and the others are making for themselves."

Several critics note that Oe compares Bird's personal disaster to World War II's nuclear holocaust. Wolff reflects: "Like the survivors of Hiroshima whose children were crippled in their mothers' wombs, Bird asks: Why? Who is to blame? Am I polluted? What grotesque signal has been delivered to me from Heaven?" Webster Schott states that "Oe makes certain we understand that he is addressing the larger world beyond Bird's 'personal matter' by projecting his plot against nuclear tests, the defection of a Balkan diplomat and suicides galore." Oe also uses many symbols in the novel, adds Schott, including Bird's baby, whose ruptured brain represents "a Japan that Burst its intellectual shell with a trauma."

Some reviewers are disappointed with *A Personal Matter*'s ending. "It is simply inconceivable that Bird could turn over so many new leaves in the space of the book's last few pages," Enright points out. James A. Phillips comments that the epilogue undermines Oe's frank descriptions of sex and emotional turmoil. "To negate all this candor with a story-book ending leaves the reader with the feeling that being honest and baring your psyche is meaningless because ultimately you return to wishy-washy conventionality."

Wayne Falke theorizes that the negative reactions of Western critics to Bird's final decision are due to cultural disparities. "Japan has a long tradition of accepting the inevitable which, in the West, is called resignation. . . . For the Japanese, to assume the responsibilities imposed upon one by one's superiors, by filial piety and the like, is an act

of virtue. To maintain existent orders is preferable to change." Thus, when Bird chooses to remain with his wife and child, he is making the proper decision according to his own social structure. His actions are seen by Westerners as taking the easy way out, according to Falke, because "a more or less cheerful acceptance of circumstances is beyond our comprehension." Despite their criticism of the book's ending, reviewers are receptive to the book as a whole. John Hearsum remarks: "The prose is hard and brittle, the images like tiny nightmares. . . . It communicates the full terror of such a predicament, and confronts the arbitrary horror of the universe without any recourse to fancy techniques."

The real-life situation that inspired *A Personal Matter* has turned out "more surprisingly than any denouement in Oe's fiction," *Publishers Weekly* interviewer Sam Staggs notes. Hikari Oe is now a successful musical composer in Japan. In spite his language impairments, he has a thorough talent for music and has released two CDs in Japan that have sold well.

Oe's interest in the political and the absurd are reflected in two of his earlier novels which have been recently translated into English. *Nip the Buds, Shoot the Kids* is set on the island of Shikoku, Oe's "peripheral" birthplace, during World War II, when a group of juvenile delinquents are evacuated from a reformatory to a remote village. The boys are mistreated by hostile peasants until the villagers, fearing plague, abandon them. The adolescent narrator tells how the boys band together, caring for each other and an abandoned girl and a Korean boy. When the villagers return, they attempt to hush the boys about their abandonment at the hands of those meant to protect them. All but the narrator give in, and he is hounded and chased out of the village "insanely angry, tearful, shivering with cold and hunger." Julian Duplain of the *Times Literary Supplement* writes: "As a story of misled innocents, Oe's novel draws clear parallels with imperialistic Japanese military policy in the Second World War, as well as providing a rallying cry for anti-authoritarian resistance. To Western readers, the directness of emotion—for example, the boys' honest esteem for one another—sometimes sounds simplistic." A *Kirkus Reviews* writer finds *Nip the Buds, Shoot the Kids* to be "more shaded, more graphic, and angrier than *Lord of the Flies,* but the fierce anger is transmuted by Oe's art into literary gold—an anguished plea for tolerance more wrenching than any rant could ever be."

The Pinch Runner Memorandum tells the story of a group of student radicals who construct their own atomic bomb. The brain-damaged boy Mori and his father, a former nuclear physicist, work with Oe and his own son to avert disaster. "The invention of this 'pinch runner' double," Masao Miyoshi writes in the *Nation,* "suggests the increasing complexity of a writer in positioning himself in his story—and the world." A critic for the *New Yorker* finds that "Oe's writing is bold, savage, and often very funny. . . . This complicated book is above all a heartening display of the explosively constructive power of imagination."

Describing how his son Hikari had once been "awakened by the voices of birds to the music of Bach and Mozart," Oe concluded his Nobel Prize acceptance speeh thus: "Herein I find the grounds for believing in the exquisite healing power of art. . . . As one with a peripheral, marginal, and off-center existence in the world, I would like to seek how. . . . I can be of some use in a cure and reconciliation of mankind."

BIOGRAPHICAL/CRITICAL SOURCES:

BOOKS

Contemporary Literary Criticism, Gale (Detroit), Volume 10, 1979, Volume 36, 1986, Volume 86, 1995.
Oe, Kenzaburo, *A Personal Matter,* translation by John Nathan, Grove, 1968.
Oe, Kenzaburo, *Teach Us to Outgrow Our Madness,* translation by Nathan, Grove, 1977.

PERIODICALS

Best Sellers, July 1, 1968; October, 1977.
Books Abroad, winter, 1969.
Boundary 2, fall, 1991; summer, 1993.
Christian Science Monitor, August 8, 1968; October 18, 1994, p. 13.
Critique: Studies in Modern Fiction, Volume 15, number 3, 1974.
Hudson Review, autumn, 1968.
Japan Quarterly, October-December, 1973.
Kirkus Reviews, March 1, 1995, p. 261.
Life, August 16, 1968.
London Magazine, June, 1969.
Los Angeles Times, October 14, 1994, p. A1; October 19, 1994, p. B7.
Nation, August 5, 1968; May 15, 1995, pp. 696-701.
New Republic, August 17, 1968.
New Yorker, June 8, 1968; November 14, 1994, p. 147.
New York Review of Books, October 10, 1968.
New York Times, November 6, 1994, p. 5.
New York Times Book Review, July 7, 1968; September 8, 1985.
Publishers Weekly, October 17, 1994, p. 17; March 27, 1995, p. 48; August 7, 1995, pp. 438-39.
San Francisco Review of Books, March/April, 1995, pp. 8-9.
Studies in Short Fiction, fall, 1974.
Time, October 24, 1994, p. 64.
Times (London), May 16, 1995, p. 35.
Times Literary Supplement, October 26, 1984, p. 1227; April 28, 1989; May 12, 1995, p. 21.
Voice Literary Supplement, October, 1982.
Washington Post, June 11, 1968.
Washington Post Book World, August 25, 1968; September 11, 1977.
World Literature Today, spring, 1978; spring, 1985, p. 318; winter, 1995, pp. 5-16.

*　　*　　*

OPPENHEIM, Joanne 1934-
(Jane Fleischer, Kate Jassem)

PERSONAL: Born May 11, 1934, in Middletown, NY; daughter of Abe P. (an electrical engineer) and Helen (Jassem) Fleischer; married Stephen Oppenheim (a lawyer), June 27, 1954; children: James, Anthony, Stephanie. *Education:* Sarah Lawrence College, B.A., 1960; Bank Street College of Education, M.S., 1980.

ADDRESSES: Home—Sackett Lake Rd., Box 29, Monticello, NY. *Office*—Oppenheim Toy Portfolio, 40 East 9th St., #14M, New York, NY 10003; and 55 East 9th St., New York, NY 10003.

CAREER: Teacher in primary grades, Monticello, NY, 1960-80; Bank Street College of Education, New York City, member of Writer's Laboratory, 1962—, senior editor in publications department, 1980-90; president and cofounder of Oppenheim Toy Portfolio, 1990—.

AWARDS, HONORS: Outstanding Teachers of America award, 1973; Children's Choice IRA, 1980, for *Mrs. Peloki's Snake,* and 1984, for *Mrs. Peloki's Class Play;* Canadian Picture Book Award and Outstanding Science Book Award, both 1987, both for *Have You Seen Birds?;* Outstanding Science Book citation, 1994, for *Oceanarium.*

WRITINGS:

FOR CHILDREN

Have You Seen Trees?, Young Scott/Addison Wesley, 1967.
Have You Seen Birds?, illustrated by Barbara Reid, Young Scott/Addison Wesley, 1968.
(With G. Nook) *Have You Seen Roads?,* Young Scott/ Addison Wesley, 1969.
Have You Seen Boats?, Young Scott/Addison Wesley, 1971.
On the Other Side of the River, F. Watts (New York City), 1972.
Have You Seen Houses?, Young Scott/Addison Wesley, 1973.
Mrs. Peloki's Snake, Dodd (New York City), 1980.
James Will Never Die, Dodd, 1982.
Mrs. Peloki's Class Play, Dodd, 1984.

Barron's Bunny Activity Books, Barron's (Woodbury, NY), 1985.

KidSpeak about Computers, Ballantine (New York City), 1985.

Can't Catch Me!, illustrated by Andrew Shachat, Houghton (Boston, MA), 1986.

The Storybook Prince, illustrated by Rosanne Litzinger, Harcourt (San Diego, CA, and New York City), 1987.

Mrs. Peloki's Substitute, illustrated by Joyce A. Zarins, Dodd, 1987.

Left and Right, Harcourt, 1988.

Not Now, Said the Cow, Bantam (New York City), 1989.

Follow That Fish, Bantam, 1989.

Left and Right, Harcourt, 1989.

Could It Be?, Bantam, 1990.

Wake Up, Baby!, Bantam, 1990.

Rooter Remembers, Viking (New York City), 1990.

Eency-Weency Spider, Bantam, 1991.

(With B. Brenner and others) *No Way, Slippery Slick!,* HarperCollins (New York City), 1991.

Two Fools and a Donkey, Bantam, 1991.

One Gift Deserves Another, Dutton (New York City), 1992.

Show and Tell Frog, Bantam, 1992.

Floatorium, Bantam, 1993.

Do You Like Cats?, Bantam, 1993.

Uh-oh, Said Crow, Bantam, 1993.

Christmas Witch, Bantam, 1993.

Row Your Boat, Bantam, 1993.

Oceanarium, Bantam, 1994.

Have You Seen Bugs?, Scholastic, 1995.

FOR ADULTS

(Contributor) *Pleasure of Their Company,* Chilton (Radnor, PA), 1980.

Kids and Play, Ballantine, 1984.

Raising a Confident Child, Pantheon (New York City), 1984.

Choosing Books for Kids, Ballantine, 1986.

Buy Me! Buy Me! The Bank Street Guide to Choosing Toys for Children, Pantheon, 1987.

The Elementary School Handbook: Making the Most of Your Child's Education, Pantheon, 1989.

The Best Toys, Books and Videos for Kids: The 1996 Guide to 1,000+ Classic and New Products for Kids 0-10, HarperCollins, 1995.

OTHER

Also author of ten young people's biographies of Native Americans, written under original name and pseudonyms Kate Jassem and Jane Fleischer, 1977-78; author of six activity books for children on maps, time, money, communications, and safety. Contributor of stories and poems to "Bank Street Readers" basal series, Macmillan (New York City), 1965.

Contributor of articles to magazines, including *Working Mother, Parent and Child,* and *Baby Talk.*

BIOGRAPHICAL/CRITICAL SOURCES:

PERIODICALS

Christian Science Monitor, May 1, 1987.
Quill and Quire, December, 1986.

*   *   *

OSCEOLA
See BLIXEN, Karen

P

PAPE, D. L.
See PAPE, Donna (Lugg)

* * *

PAPE, Donna (Lugg) 1930-
(D. L. Pape)

PERSONAL: Surname is pronounced "poppy"; born June 21, 1930, in Sheboygan, WI; daughter of Arthur Phillip and Ruth (Fenninger) Lugg; married William Pape (a carpet mechanic), June 16, 1951; children: Diane Ruth, Jan Lynn, Jean Carol. *Avocational interests:* Music, art, nature, and nutrition.

ADDRESSES: Home—1734 South 15th St., Sheboygan, WI 53081.

CAREER: Freelance writer, 1960—; photojournalist, 1960-64; writes verse for various greeting card companies.

MEMBER: Society of Children's Book Writers and Illustrators, Wisconsin Regional Writers' Association, Sheboygan County Writers' Club.

AWARDS, HONORS: First Prize in Wisconsin Regional Writers' Association juvenile writing contest, 1965; *The Mouse at the Show* was included in "Children's Choices for 1982"; first place award, Juvenile Wisconsin Council of Arts, 1988, for *The Book of Foolish Machinery.*

WRITINGS:

The Best Surprise of All, Whitman Publishing (Racine, WI), 1961.
Splish, Splash, Splush, Whitman Publishing, 1962.
Tony Zebra and the Lost Zoo, Whitman Publishing, 1963.
I Play in the Snow, Whitman Publishing, 1967.
Mary Lou, the Kangaroo, E. M. Hale, 1967.
The Seal Who Wanted to Ski, E. M. Hale, 1967.

Catch That Fish, L. W. Singer, 1969.
Leo Lion Looks at Books, Garrard (Easton, MD), 1972.
Mrs. Twitter, the Sitter, Garrard, 1972.
Mr. Mogg in the Log, Garrard, 1972.
Handy Hands, Standard Publishing (Cincinnati, OH), 1973.
A Special Way to Travel, Standard Publishing, 1973.
Big Words for Little People, Standard Publishing, 1973.
A Gerbil for a Friend, Prentice-Hall (Englewood Cliffs, NJ), 1973.
(With daughter, Jan Pape, and Jeanette Grote) *Puzzles and Silly Riddles,* Scholastic Book Service (New York City), 1973.
Count on Leo Lion, Garrard, 1973.
The Kangaroo Who Leaped in Her Sleep, Garrard, 1973.
A Bone for Breakfast, Garrard, 1974.
Promises Are Special Words, Moody (Chicago, IL), 1975.
(With Grote) *Pack of Puzzles,* Scholastic Book Service, 1975.
(With John McInnes) *Taffy Finds a Halloween Witch,* Garrard, 1975.
(With McInnes) *The Big White Thing,* Garrard, 1975.
(With Grote) *Puzzle Panic,* Scholastic Book Service, 1976.
(With Grote) *Fun Puzzles for One,* Xerox Education Publications (Middletown, CT), 1976.
(With Grote and Carol Karle) *Puzzle Party,* Reader's Digest Press (New York City), 1977.
Snowman for Sale, Garrard, 1977.
Where Is My Little Joey?, Garrard, 1978.
(With Grote) *All Kinds of Puzzles,* Scholastic Book Service, 1978.
The Peek-a-Boo Book, Golden Press (New York City), 1978.
(With Grote) *A Turn for the Words,* Grosset & Dunlap (New York City), 1979.
(With Grote) *Puzzle Parade,* Xerox Education Publications, 1979.

Dog House for Sale, Garrard, 1979.

The Snoino Mystery, Garrard, 1980.

(With Leonard Kessler) *Play Ball, Joey Kangaroo,* Garrard, 1980.

(With Virginia Mueller) *Think-Pink Solve and Search Puzzles,* Xerox Education Publications, 1980.

(With Mueller and Karle) *Bible Activities for Kids,* Books 1-6, Bethany House (Minneapolis, MN), 1980-82.

The Mouse at the Show, Elsevier-Nelson, 1981.

(With Mueller and Karle) *Texas Puzzle Book,* Eakin Publications (Austin, TX), 1981.

Jack Jump under the Candlestick, Albert Whitman, 1982.

(With Mueller and Karle) *Arkansas Puzzle Book,* Rose Publishing (Little Rock, AR), 1983.

(With Mueller and Karle) *Wisconsin Puzzle Book,* Bess Press (Honolulu, HI), 1984.

(With Mueller and Karle) *Hawaii Puzzle Book,* Bess Press, 1984.

(With Mueller and Karle) *California Trivia Puzzle Book,* Bess Press, 1984.

(With Mueller and Karle) *Tennessee Puzzle Book,* Winston-Derek (Nashville, TN), 1985.

(With Mueller and Karle) *Vermont Puzzle Book,* Countryman Press (Woodstock, VT), 1987.

The Book of Foolish Machinery, Scholastic Inc., 1988.

Who Will Read to Me?, Houghton, 1991.

Let's Jump, Houghton, 1991.

Hamid's Surprise, Houghton, 1995.

The Little Bird, Newbridge Communications, 1995.

(With Grote and Karle) *Florida Puzzle Book,* Pineapple Press (Englewood, FL), 1996.

"PAPE SERIES OF SPEECH IMPROVEMENT AND READING"

The Three Thinkers of Thay-Lee, Oddo (Fayetteville, GA), 1965.

Professor Fred and the Fid-Fuddlephone, Oddo, 1965.

Scientist Sam, Oddo, 1965.

King Robert, the Resting Ruler, Oddo, 1965.

Liz Dearly's Silly Glasses, Oddo, 1965.

Shoemaker Fooze, Oddo, 1965.

OTHER

Contributor to *Parades* (reader), Houghton (Boston, MA), 1986. Also author, with Grote, of *Puzzling Pastimes* and *Packet of Puzzles,* 1973; author, with Mueller and Karle, of *Country Music Puzzle Book,* for Winston-Derek. Contributor to speech therapy workbooks for Word-Making Productions, and of stories to Whitehaven Game Co. (a speech therapy game publisher). Contributor to juvenile magazines, including *Humpty Dumpty Magazine, Jack and Jill, Highlights, Our Little Messenger,* and *Junior World.*

PARKER, J(ohn) Carlyle 1931-

PERSONAL: Born October 14, 1931, in Ogden, UT; son of Levi C. (a farmer and guard) and Marietta (a maker of sewn goods; maiden name, Parkinson) Parker; married Janet C. Greene, May 31, 1956; children: Denise, Nathan, Bret. *Education:* Brigham Young University, B.A., 1957; University of California, Berkeley, M.L.S., 1958; Humboldt State College (now University), graduate study, 1959-60. *Politics:* Democrat. *Religion:* Church of Jesus Christ of Latter-day Saints (Mormon). *Avocational interests:* Birding, travel, singing "solos, duets, and in choirs."

ADDRESSES: Home—2115 North Denair Ave., Turlock, CA 95382.

CAREER: Humboldt State College (now University), Arcata, CA, librarian, 1958-60; Church College of Hawaii (now Brigham Young University, Hawaii), Laie, assistant and acting librarian, 1960-63; California State University library, Stanislaus, Turlock, head of public services, 1963-83 and 1985—, assistant director, 1968-83 and 1985-90, acting director, 1983-84, archivist, 1990-94, librarian and university archivist emeritus, 1994—. Modesto California Branch Genealogical Library, founder and librarian, 1968-90; Turlock Centennial Foundation Board, secretary, 1971-75; Turlock Community Concert Association, president, 1973-75; Turlock Family History Center, founder and director, 1990—. *Military service:* U.S. Army, 1953-55.

MEMBER: American Library Association (chair of genealogy committee, Reference and Adult Services Division of the History Section, 1989-92), American Association of University Professors, National Education Association, Congress of Faculty Associations, California Teachers' Association, Stanislaus County Historical Society, Genealogical Society of Stanislaus County.

AWARDS, HONORS: American Library Association fellowship, 1965; Award of Merit, National Genealogical Society, 1984; Utah Genealogical Association fellow, 1984; Meritorious Performance and Professional Promise Award, California State University, Stanislaus, 1986 and 1990; American Library Association History Section/Genealogical Publishing Company award, 1994.

WRITINGS:

EDITOR

A Personal Name Index to Orton's "Records of California Men in the War of the Rebellion, 1861 to 1867," Gale (Detroit), 1978.

City, County, Town, and Township Index to the 1850 Federal Census Schedule, Gale, 1979.

An Index to the Biographees in 19th-Century California County Histories, Gale, 1979.

Genealogy in the Central Association of Libraries: A Union Catalog Based on Filby's "American and British Genealogy and Heraldry," Library, California State College, Stanislaus, 1981.

Pennsylvania and Middle Atlantic States Genealogical Manuscripts: A User's Guide to the Manuscript Collections of the Genealogical Society of Pennsylvania, as Indexed in Its Manuscript Materials Index, Microfilmed by the Genealogical Department, Salt Lake City, Marietta, 1986.

(With wife, Janet G. Parker) *Nevada Biographical and Genealogical Sketch Index,* Marietta, 1986.

Rhode Island Biographical and Genealogical Sketch Index, Marietta, 1991.

OTHER

(Compiler) *An Annotated Bibliography of the History of Del Norte and Humboldt Counties,* Humboldt State College Library (Arcata, CA), 1960.

Sources of Californiana: From Padron to Voter Registration, Genealogical Society (Salt Lake City), 1969.

Library Service for Genealogists, Gale, 1979.

(Contributor) David F. Trask and Robert W. Pomeroy III, editors, *The Craft of Public History: An Annotated Select Bibliography,* Greenwood Press (Westport, CT), 1983.

(Compiler) *Directory of Archivist and Librarian Genealogical Instructors,* Marietta, 1985, second edition, 1990.

(Compiler) *Music Directors' and Accompanists' Index to "Hymns" (1985) and "Simplified Accompaniments" (1986),* Marietta, 1988.

Going to Salt Lake City to Do Family Research, 2nd edition, Marietta, 1993.

Documents of Library History, California State University, Stanislaus and Other Whatnots and War Stories from the Career of the Author, Library, California State University, Stanislaus, 1994.

Editor of "Genealogy and Local History" series, Gale, 1978-81. Contributor of articles and reviews to genealogy, history, and library journals.

WORK IN PROGRESS: A third edition of *Going to Salt Lake City to Do Family History Research;* a second edition of *Library Service for Genealogists;* several additional biographical sketch indexes and genealogical reference works, to be published by Marietta.

SIDELIGHTS: J. Carlyle Parker told *CA:* "The majority of my early writing was an attempt to assist librarians in their understanding of how to help patrons in biographical, genealogical, and local history research; how to use and obtain these research materials; and to make some of these research materials easier to use and more accessible. Some time ago my attention also turned to helping genealogists do their research through the preparation of in-

dexes, guides, book and microform reviews, and how-to-do-it works."

*   *   *

PASCAL, Francine 1938-

PERSONAL: Born May 13, 1938, in New York, NY; daughter of William and Kate (Dunitz) Rubin; married John Robert Pascal (a journalist and author), August 18, 1965 (died, 1981); children: Jamie (daughter), Laurie, Susan. *Education:* New York University, B.A., 1958. *Avocational interests:* Travel, reading.

ADDRESSES: Home—New York, NY, and France. *Agent*—Amy Berkower, Writers House, 21 West 26th St., New York, NY 10010.

CAREER: Writer and lecturer.

MEMBER: PEN, International Creative Writers League, Dramatist's Guild, National Organization for Women.

AWARDS, HONORS: "Books for the Teenage, 1978-1985" citation, New York Public Library, for *Hangin' Out with Cici;* best book for young adults citation, American Library Association, 1979, for *My First Love and Other Disasters;* Dorothy Canfield Fisher Children's Book Award, Vermont Congress of Parents and Teachers, *Publishers Weekly* Literary Prize list, both 1982, and Bernard Versele Award, Brussels, 1988, all for *The Hand-Me-Down Kid;* Milner Award, Atlanta Public Library, 1988.

WRITINGS:

(With husband, John Pascal, and brother, Michael Stewart) *George M!* (musical; also see below), produced on Broadway, 1968.

(With J. Pascal) *George M!* (television special based on musical of same title), American Broadcasting Companies, Inc. (ABC-TV), 1970.

(With J. Pascal) *The Strange Case of Patty Hearst,* New American Library (New York City), 1974.

Hangin' Out with Cici, Viking (New York City), 1977, paperback edition published as *Hangin' Out with Cici; or, My Mother Was Never a Kid,* Dell (New York City), 1985.

My First Love and Other Disasters (also see below), Viking, 1979.

The Hand-Me-Down Kid, Viking, 1980.

Save Johanna! (adult novel), Morrow (New York City), 1981.

Love and Betrayal and Hold the Mayo! (sequel to *My First Love and Other Disasters*), Viking, 1985.

If Wishes Were Horses (adult novel), Crown (New York City), 1994.

"*SWEET VALLEY HIGH*" SERIES

Double Love, Bantam (New York City), 1984.

Secrets, Bantam, 1984.

Playing with Fire, Bantam, 1984.

Power Play, Bantam, 1984.

All Night Long, Bantam, 1984.

Dangerous Love, Bantam, 1984.

Dear Sister, Bantam, 1984.

Heartbreaker, Bantam, 1984.

Racing Hearts, Bantam, 1984.

Wrong Kind of Girl, Bantam, 1984.

Too Good to Be True, Bantam, 1984.

When Love Dies, Bantam, 1984.

Kidnapped!, Bantam, 1984.

Deceptions, Bantam, 1984.

Promises, Bantam, 1985.

Rags to Riches, Bantam, 1985.

Love Letters, Bantam, 1985.

Head over Heels, Bantam, 1985.

Showdown, Bantam, 1985.

Crash Landing!, Bantam, 1985.

Runaway, Bantam, 1985.

Too Much in Love, Bantam, 1986.

Say Goodbye, Bantam, 1986.

Memories, Bantam, 1986.

Nowhere to Run, Bantam, 1986.

Hostage!, Bantam, 1986.

Lovestruck, Bantam, 1986.

Alone in the Crowd, Bantam, 1986.

Bitter Rivals, Bantam, 1986.

Jealous Lies, Bantam, 1986.

Taking Sides, Bantam, 1986.

The New Jessica, Bantam, 1986.

Starting Over, Bantam, 1987.

Forbidden Love, Bantam, 1987.

Out of Control, Bantam, 1987.

Last Chance, Bantam, 1987.

Rumors, Bantam, 1987.

Leaving Home, Bantam, 1987.

Secret Admirer, Bantam, 1987.

On the Edge, Bantam, 1987.

Outcast, Bantam, 1987.

Caught in the Middle, Bantam, 1988.

Pretenses, Bantam, 1988.

Hard Choices, Bantam, 1988.

Family Secrets, Bantam, 1988.

Decisions, Bantam, 1988.

Slam Book Fever, Bantam, 1988.

Playing for Keeps, Bantam, 1988.

Troublemaker, Bantam, 1988.

Out of Reach, Bantam, 1988.

In Love Again, Bantam, 1989.

Against the Odds, Bantam, 1989.

Brokenhearted, Bantam, 1989.

Teacher Crush, Bantam, 1989.

Perfect Shot, Bantam, 1989.

White Lies, Bantam, 1989.

Two-Boy Weekend, Bantam, 1989.

That Fatal Night, Bantam, 1989.

Lost at Sea, Bantam, 1989.

Second Chance, Bantam, 1989.

Ms. Quarterback, Bantam, 1990.

The New Elizabeth, Bantam, 1990.

The Ghost of Tricia Martin, Bantam, 1990.

Friend against Friend, Bantam, 1990.

Trouble at Home, Bantam, 1990.

Who's to Blame, Bantam, 1990.

The Parent Plot, Bantam, 1990.

Boy Trouble, Bantam, 1990.

Who's Who?, Bantam, 1990.

The Love Bet, Bantam, 1990.

Amy's True Love, Bantam, 1991.

Miss Teen Sweet Valley, Bantam, 1991.

The Perfect Girl, Bantam, 1991.

Regina's Legacy, Bantam, 1991.

Rock Star's Girl, Bantam, 1991.

Starring Jessica!, Bantam, 1991.

Cheating to Win, Bantam, 1991.

The Dating Game, Bantam, 1991.

The Long-Lost Brother, Bantam, 1991.

The Girl They Both Loved, Bantam, 1991.

Rosa's Lie, Bantam, 1992.

Kidnapped by the Cult, Bantam, 1992.

Steven's Bride, Bantam, 1992.

The Stolen Diary, Bantam, 1992.

Soap Star, Bantam, 1992.

Jessica against Bruce, Bantam, 1992.

My Best Friend's Boyfriend, Bantam, 1992.

Love Letters for Sale, Bantam, 1992.

Elizabeth Betrayed, Bantam, 1992.

Don't Go Home with John, Bantam, 1993.

In Love with a Prince, Bantam, 1993.

She's Not What She Seems, Bantam, 1993.

Stepsisters, Bantam, 1993.

Are We in Love?, Bantam, 1993.

The Morning After, Bantam, 1993.

The Arrest, Bantam, 1993.

The Verdict, Bantam, 1993.

The Wedding, Bantam, 1993.

Beware the Babysitter, Bantam, 1993.

The Boyfriend War, Bantam, 1994.

Almost Married, Bantam, 1994.

Operation Love Match, Bantam, 1994.

Love and Death in London, Bantam, 1994.

A Date with a Werewolf, Bantam, 1994.

Jessica's Secret Love, Bantam, 1994.

Left at the Altar, Bantam, 1994.

Double-Crossed, Bantam, 1994.

Death Threat, Bantam, 1994.
Jessica Quits the Squad, Bantam, 1995.
The Pom-Pom Wars, Bantam, 1995.
"V" for Victory, Bantam, 1995.
The Treasure of Death Valley, Bantam, 1995.

"SWEET VALLEY HIGH" SUPER EDITIONS

Perfect Summer, Bantam, 1985.
Malibu Summer, Bantam, 1986.
Special Christmas, Bantam, 1986.
Spring Break, Bantam, 1986.
Spring Fever, Bantam, 1987.
Winter Carnival, Bantam, 1987.

"SWEET VALLEY HIGH" SUPER THRILLER SERIES

Double Jeopardy, Bantam, 1987.
On the Run, Bantam, 1988.
No Place to Hide, Bantam, 1988.
Deadly Summer, Bantam, 1989.
Murder on the Line, Bantam, 1992.
Beware the Wolfman, Bantam, 1994.
A Deadly Christmas, Bantam, 1994.
Murder in Paradise, Bantam, 1995.

"SWEET VALLEY HIGH" SUPER STAR SERIES

Lila's Story, Bantam, 1989.
Bruce's Story, Bantam, 1990.
Enid's Story, Bantam, 1990.
Olivia's Story, Bantam, 1991.
Todd's Story, Bantam, 1992.

"SWEET VALLEY" MAGNA EDITIONS

The Wakefields of Sweet Valley, Bantam, 1991.
The Wakefield Legacy: The Untold Story, Bantam, 1992.
A Night to Remember, Bantam, 1993.
The Evil Twin, Bantam, 1993.
Elizabeth's Secret Diary, Bantam, 1994.
Jessica's Secret Diary, Bantam, 1994.

"SWEET VALLEY TWINS" SERIES

Best Friends, Bantam, 1986.
Teacher's Pet, Bantam, 1986.
The Haunted House, Bantam, 1986.
Choosing Sides, Bantam, 1986.
Sneaking Out, Bantam, 1987.
The New Girl, Bantam, 1987.
Three's a Crowd, Bantam, 1987.
First Place, Bantam, 1987.
Against the Rules, Bantam, 1987.
One of the Gang, Bantam, 1987.
Buried Treasure, Bantam, 1987.
Keeping Secrets, Bantam, 1987.
Stretching the Truth, Bantam, 1987.
Tug of War, Bantam, 1987.

The Bully, Bantam, 1988.
Playing Hooky, Bantam, 1988.
Left Behind, Bantam, 1988.
Claim to Fame, Bantam, 1988.
Center of Attention, Bantam, 1988.
Jumping to Conclusions, Bantam, 1988.
Second Best, Bantam, 1988.
The Older Boy, Bantam, 1988.
Out of Place, Bantam, 1988.
Elizabeth's New Hero, Bantam, 1989.
Standing Out, Bantam, 1989.
Jessica on Stage, Bantam, 1989.
Jessica the Rock Star, Bantam, 1989.
Jessica's Bad Idea, Bantam, 1989.
Taking Charge, Bantam, 1989.
Big Camp Secret, Bantam, 1989.
Jessica and the Brat Attack, Bantam, 1989.
April Fool!, Bantam, 1989.
Princess Elizabeth, Bantam, 1989.
Elizabeth's First Kiss, Bantam, 1990.
War between the Twins, Bantam, 1990.
Summer Fun Book, Bantam, 1990.
The Twins Get Caught, Bantam, 1990.
Lois Strikes Back, Bantam, 1990.
Mary Is Missing, Bantam, 1990.
Jessica's Secret, Bantam, 1990.
Jessica and the Money Mix-Up, Bantam, 1990.
Danny Means Trouble, Bantam, 1990.
Amy's Pen Pal, Bantam, 1990.
Amy Moves In, Bantam, 1991.
Jessica's New Look, Bantam, 1991.
Lucky Takes the Reins, Bantam, 1991.
Mademoiselle Jessica, Bantam, 1991.
Mansy Miller Fights Back, Bantam, 1991.
The Twins' Little Sister, Bantam, 1991.
Booster Boycott, Bantam, 1991.
Elizabeth the Impossible, Bantam, 1991.
Jessica and the Secret Star, Bantam, 1991.
The Slime That Ate Sweet Valley, Bantam, 1991.
The Big Party Weekend, Bantam, 1991.
Brooke and Her Rock-Star Mom, Bantam, 1992.
The Wakefields Strike It Rich, Bantam, 1992.
Big Brother's in Love!, Bantam, 1992.
Elizabeth and the Orphans, Bantam, 1992.
Barnyard Battle, Bantam, 1992.
Ciao, Sweet Valley, Bantam, 1992.
Jessica the Nerd, Bantam, 1992.
Sarah's Dad and Sophia's Mom, Bantam, 1992.
Poor Lila!, Bantam, 1992.
The Charm School Mystery, Bantam, 1992.
Patty's Last Dance, Bantam, 1993.
The Great Boyfriend Switch, Bantam, 1993.
Jessica the Thief, Bantam, 1993.
The Middle School Gets Married, Bantam, 1993.

Won't Someone Help Anna?, Bantam, 1993.
Psychic Sisters, Bantam, 1993.
Jessica Saves the Trees, Bantam, 1993.
The Love Potion, Bantam, 1993.
Lila's Music Video, Bantam, 1993.
Elizabeth the Hero, Bantam, 1993.
Jessica and the Earthquake, Bantam, 1994.
Yours for a Day, Bantam, 1994.
Todd Runs Away, Bantam, 1994.
Steven the Zombie, Bantam, 1994.
Jessica's Blind Date, Bantam, 1994.
The Gossip War, Bantam, 1994.
Robbery at the Mall, Bantam, 1994.
Steven's Enemy, Bantam, 1994.
Amy's Secret Sister, Bantam, 1994.
Romeo and Two Juliets, Bantam, 1995.
Elizabeth the Seventh-Grader, Bantam, 1995.
It Can't Happen Here, Bantam, 1995.
The Mother-Daughter Switch, Bantam, 1995.

"SWEET VALLEY TWINS" SUPER SERIES

Class Trip, Bantam, 1988.
Holiday Mischief, Bantam, 1988.
The Big Camp Secret, Bantam, 1989.
The Unicorns Go Hawaiian, Bantam, 1991.
Lila's Secret Valentine, Bantam, 1994.

"SWEET VALLEY TWINS" SUPER CHILLER SERIES

The Christmas Ghost, Bantam, 1989.
The Carnival Ghost, Bantam, 1990.
The Ghost in the Graveyard, Bantam, 1990.
The Ghost in the Bell Tower, Bantam, 1992.
The Curse of the Ruby Necklace, Bantam, 1993.
The Curse of the Golden Heart, Bantam, 1994.
The Haunted Burial Ground, Bantam, 1994.

"SWEET VALLEY TWINS" MAGNA EDITIONS

The Magic Christmas, Bantam, 1992.
A Christmas without Elizabeth, Bantam, 1993.
BIG for Christmas, Bantam, 1994.

"SWEET VALLEY KIDS" SERIES

Surprise! Surprise!, Bantam, 1989.
Runaway Hamster, Bantam, 1989.
Teamwork, Bantam, 1989.
Lila's Secret, Bantam, 1990.
Elizabeth's Valentine, Bantam, 1990.
Elizabeth's Super-Selling Lemonade, Bantam, 1990.
Jessica's Big Mistake, Bantam, 1990.
Jessica's Cat Trick, Bantam, 1990.
Jessica's Zoo Adventure, Bantam, 1990.
The Twins and the Wild West, Bantam, 1990.
Starring Winston, Bantam, 1990.
The Substitute Teacher, Bantam, 1990.

Sweet Valley Trick or Treat, Bantam, 1990.
Crybaby Lois, Bantam, 1990.
Bossy Steven, Bantam, 1991.
Carolyn's Mystery Dolls, Bantam, 1991.
Fearless Elizabeth, Bantam, 1991.
Jessica and Jumbo, Bantam, 1991.
The Twins Go to the Hospital, Bantam, 1991.
Jessica the Babysitter, Bantam, 1991.
Jessica and the Spelling Bee Surprise, Bantam, 1991.
Lila's Haunted House Party, Bantam, 1991.
Sweet Valley Slumber Party, Bantam, 1991.
Cousin Kelly's Family Secret, Bantam, 1991.
Left-Out Elizabeth, Bantam, 1992.
Jessica's Snobby Club, Bantam, 1992.
The Sweet Valley Cleanup Team, Bantam, 1992.
Elizabeth Meets Her Hero, Bantam, 1992.
Andy and the Alien, Bantam, 1992.
Jessica's Unburied Treasure, Bantam, 1992.
Elizabeth and Jessica Run Away, Bantam, 1992.
Left Back!, Bantam, 1992.
Caroline's Halloween Spell, Bantam, 1992.
The Best Thanksgiving Ever, Bantam, 1992.
Elizabeth's Broken Arm, Bantam, 1993.
Elizabeth's Video Fever, Bantam, 1993.
The Big Race, Bantam, 1993.
Good-bye, Eva, Bantam, 1993.
Ellen Is Home Alone, Bantam, 1993.
Robin in the Middle, Bantam, 1993.
The Missing Tea Set, Bantam, 1993.
Jessica's Monster Nightmare, Bantam, 1993.
Jessica Gets Spooked, Bantam, 1993.
The Twins Big Pow-Wow, Bantam, 1993.
Elizabeth's Piano Lessons, Bantam, 1994.
Get the Teacher!, Bantam, 1994.
Elizabeth the Tattletale, Bantam, 1994.
Lila's April Fool, Bantam, 1994.
Jessica's Mermaid, Bantam, 1994.
Steven's Twin, Bantam, 1994.
Lois and the Sleepover, Bantam, 1994.
Julie the Karate Kid, Bantam, 1994.
The Magic Puppets, Bantam, 1994.
Star of the Parade, Bantam, 1994.
The Jessica and Elizabeth Show, Bantam, 1995.
Jessica Plays Cupid, Bantam, 1995.
No Girls Allowed, Bantam, 1995.
Lila's Birthday Bash, Bantam, 1995.

"SWEET VALLEY KIDS" SUPER SNOOPER SERIES

The Case of the Secret Santa, Bantam, 1990.
The Case of the Magic Christmas Bell, Bantam, 1991.
The Case of the Haunted Camp, Bantam, 1992.
The Case of the Christmas Thief, Bantam, 1992.
The Case of the Hidden Treasure, Bantam, 1993.
The Case of the Million-Dollar Diamonds, Bantam, 1993.

The Case of the Alien Princess, Bantam, 1994.

"SWEET VALLEY UNIVERSITY" SERIES

College Girls, Bantam, 1993.
Love, Lies, and Jessica Wakefield, Bantam, 1993.
What Your Parents Don't Know . . . , Bantam, 1994.
Anything for Love, Bantam, 1994.
A Married Woman, Bantam, 1994.
The Love of Her Life, Bantam, 1994.
Home for Christmas, Bantam, 1994.
Sorority Scandal, Bantam, 1995.
No Means No, Bantam, 1995.
Take Back the Night, Bantam, 1995.

"SWEET VALLEY UNIVERSITY" THRILLER EDITIONS

Wanted for Murder, Bantam, 1995.
He's Watching You, Bantam, 1995.

"UNICORN CLUB" SERIES

Save the Unicorns, Bantam, 1994.
Maria's Movie Comeback, Bantam, 1994.
The Best Friend Game, Bantam, 1994.
Lila's Little Sister, Bantam, 1994.
Unicorns in Love, Bantam, 1994.

"UNICORN CLUB" SUPER EDITIONS

The Unicorns at War, Bantam, 1995.

"CAITLIN" SERIES

The Love Trilogy, Volume 1: *Loving,* Volume 2: *Love Lost,* Volume 3: *True Love,* Bantam, 1986.
The Promise Trilogy, Bantam, Volume 1: *Tender Promises,* 1986, Volume 2: *Promises Broken,* 1986, Volume 3: *A New Promise,* 1987.
The Forever Trilogy, Volume 1: *Dreams of Forever,* Volume 2: *Forever and Always,* Volume 3: *Together Forever,* Bantam, 1987.

ADAPTATIONS: Hangin' Out with Cici was filmed by ABC-TV and broadcast as "My Mother Was Never a Kid," an *ABC Afterschool Special,* 1981; *The Hand-Me-Down Kid* was filmed by ABC-TV and broadcast as an *ABC Afterschool Special,* 1983. Books that have been recorded onto audio cassette and released by Warner Audio include: *Double Love, Secrets,* and *Playing with Fire,* all 1986, *All Night Long, Dangerous Love,* and *Power Play.* In 1994 *Sweet Valley High* was adapted for television.

WORK IN PROGRESS: Monthly plot outlines for the "Sweet Valley High," "Sweet Valley Twins," "Sweet Valley Kids," "Sweet Valley University," and "Unicorn Club" series; another series, *Sam O'Malley and the See-Through Kids,* written with Richard Wenk, centers on an eleven-year-old boy with an extraordinary imagination; *The Poison Tree,* an adult novel.

SIDELIGHTS: Francine Pascal made publishing history in 1985 when *Perfect Summer,* the first "Sweet Valley High" super edition, became the first young adult novel to make the *New York Times* bestseller list. With over sixty-five million books in print, Pascal and the mythical middle-class suburb of Sweet Valley, California, are a publishing phenomenon. Although many critics maintain that the various "Sweet Valley" series are simplistic, unbelievable, and sexist, their popularity with young adults is undeniable. The various series revolve around Elizabeth and Jessica Wakefield, beautiful and popular identical twins with completely opposite personalities—while Elizabeth is sweet, sincere, and studious, Jessica is arrogant, superficial, and devious. The events in each story usually focus on relationships with boys or other personal issues, and adults are nearly nonexistent. "Sweet Valley is the essence of high school," asserts Pascal in a *People* interview with Steve Dougherty. "The world outside is just an adult shadow going by. The parents barely exist. Action takes place in bedrooms, cars and school. It's that moment before reality hits, when you really do believe in the romantic values—sacrifice, love, loyalty, friendship—before you get jaded and slip off into adulthood."

Born in New York City, Pascal moved from Manhattan to Jamaica, Queens, when she was five. This new neighborhood had houses with yards and children were able to play outside unattended. Movies, adventure comics, and fairy tales were among Pascal's many passions, and because there was no young adult literature at the time, she read the classics. "I have always had a very active imagination—my retreat when things don't go right," explains Pascal in an interview with Marguerite Feitlowitz for *Authors and Artists for Young Adults* (*AAYA*). "I realized early that this set me apart from most people. For example, it wasn't my habit to confide in others very much, particularly my parents. As far back as I can recall, I kept a diary. Important thoughts, imaginings, and events were recounted in my diaries, not to people."

Other forms of writing that Pascal attempted at an early age included poetry and plays. Her brother was a writer, so Pascal wanted to write too, but her parents did not take her writing as seriously as they did his. Her teachers and classmates encouraged her, though, and she even performed her plays, casting and directing her friends for neighborhood audiences. Moving from childhood into adolescence, Pascal, unlike her "Sweet Valley" characters, had a less than ideal high school experience. "Going to high school in the fifties, as I did, was not appreciably different from going to high school in the eighties," points out Pascal in her *AAYA* interview. "Both decades are conservative and full of nostalgia. Adolescence is pretty awful no matter when you go through it. And all of us think high school is wonderful for everyone else. The 'Sweet Valley' series came out of what I fantasized high school was like for everyone but me."

College, on the other hand, was something Pascal looked forward to and thoroughly enjoyed. It was a couple days after her last class that she met her future husband, John Pascal, who was then a journalist working for a number of papers. "He was an excellent writer," recalls Pascal in her *AAYA* interview, "and in many ways my mentor. He loved everything I wrote and encouraged me unceasingly." In their early years together, Pascal's husband freelanced while she began her own writing career with articles for such magazines as *Ladies' Home Journal* and *Cosmopolitan.* They began working together. The musical *George M!* and the nonfiction work *The Strange Case of Patty Hearst* were among the other writings they collaborated on before Pascal turned her attention to the young adult audience.

The idea for Pascal's first young adult novel, *Hangin' Out with Cici,* came to her early one morning while she was lying in bed. She had never written a novel before, and at the time had no idea what young adult novels were. Upon hearing her idea, Pascal's husband encouraged her to sit down and begin writing immediately, so she did. When the manuscript was finished she mailed it off to three agents, and the book sold within two weeks. *Hangin' Out with Cici* introduces Victoria, a spoiled and selfish young girl who has just been caught smoking a joint during a weekend visit to her aunt. On the train ride home, Victoria somehow wishes herself back in time to 1944, where she makes friends with a girl named Cici. Even wilder than Victoria, Cici shoplifts and sneaks cigarettes before being caught trying to buy a science test with stolen money. Over time, Victoria realizes that Cici is really her mother as a young girl and urges her to confess to her crime. She then wakes up to find herself on the train, where she had been all along—everything was just a dream. From that point on, however, Victoria and her mother have a stronger relationship. "The story contains some funny episodes," comments Ann A. Flowers in *Horn Book,* adding that *Hangin' Out with Cici* is "an amusing fantasy with realistic adolescent characters."

A few other novels followed before Pascal came up with the idea for the "Sweet Valley High" series. *My First Love and Other Disasters,* published in 1979, is the story of Victoria as she takes a summer job as a mother-helper on Fire Island to be close to her first love. Barbara Elleman, writing in *Booklist,* maintains that the novel is "wittily told in the first person vernacular of a 15-year-old" and "captures the kaleidoscopic complexities of living through a first love." *The Hand-Me-Down Kid* offers a younger protagonist. Eleven-year-old Ari Jacobs is the youngest child in her family, and has a distinctly negative view of life until she meets Jane, who is in the same position as herself, yet

exudes positiveness. "Narrated in the slightly skewed grammatical style typical of today's adolescent, the story is an amusing contemporary novel with an urban setting, which maintains a perspective on everything from training bras to older brothers and sisters and offers hand-me-down kids a believable example of assertiveness training," remarks Mary M. Burns in *Horn Book.*

Pascal's husband died in 1981, shortly after the 1980 publication of *The Hand-Me-Down Kid.* "It seems unfair that he isn't alive to enjoy the success of my 'Sweet Valley' series," relates Pascal in her interview with Feitlowitz. "He would have gotten a real kick out of it, and could have retired on the money I've made. The house is too quiet now." The idea for this incredibly successful series was not a completely new one. In the late 1970s, Pascal wanted to do something similar, but in the form of a television soap opera for teenagers. No one was interested, but a few years later one of Pascal's editors suggested she try a teenage book series instead, maybe something similar to the television show *Dallas.*

When this first attempt failed, Pascal examined the reasons why, coming up with the elements she thought must be present to make a teenage series work. "Each book, I concluded," explains Pascal in her *AAYA* interview, "would have to be a complete story in itself, but with a hook ending to lead you to the sequel. The series would have to have vivid continuing characters. When I came up with the idea for Elizabeth and Jessica, the Jekyll and Hyde twins, I was off and running. I did a proposal over the course of several days, wrote about six pages and that was that." Bantam immediately bought the project and, with successful marketing and packaging, made it a publishing sensation. At the beginning of the series, Pascal presented Sweet Valley as a completely idealized fantasy world. But when she started getting letters from readers telling her how "real" the books were to them, Pascal decided to include some aspects of reality, such as minority characters. "I didn't intend Sweet Valley to be realistic," admits Pascal in her interview with Feitlowitz, "so I'm a little puzzled. It is a soap opera in book form, after all. I guess what these readers mean is that there is emotional reality in the relationship between the characters."

Despite the success of the various "Sweet Valley" series, Pascal has received a great deal of criticism. She argues, however, that her "books encourage young people to read. 'Sweet Valley High' opened a market that simply didn't exist before," points out Pascal in her *AAYA* interview. "It is not that those millions of girls were not reading my books, they weren't reading any books. I have gotten many, many letters from kids saying that they never read before 'Sweet Valley High.' If nine out of ten of those girls go on to read Judith Krantz and Danielle Steel, so be it, they are still reading. . . . The reality is that not everyone is able, or wishes to read great literature. There should be books for all types of readers. Reading time is precious; it's a time for privacy, fantasy, learning, a time to live in our imaginations. No one should be denied that."

The popularity of the "Sweet Valley High" series prompted a number of spin-off series, including "Sweet Valley Twins," which aims at younger readers by placing Elizabeth and Jessica in sixth grade, "Sweet Valley Kids," which presents the twins as six-year-olds, "Sweet Valley High" super thriller series, which attempts to compete with other young adult mystery and horror writers, "Sweet Valley University," aimed at high schoolers, which tells the story of the twins' life at college, and "The Unicorn Club," featuring the stars from "Sweet Valley Twins" as they enter the seventh grade. In 1991, Pascal brought a new twist to the series with the publication of *The Wakefields of Sweet Valley.* This full-length novel covers one hundred years as it traces five generations of the Wakefield family. It begins in 1860 with the sea voyage of sixteen-year-old Alice Larson of Sweden and eighteen-year-old Theodore Wakefield from England, following the family through wagon trains, earthquakes, the Roaring Twenties, love, courage and heartbreak. In 1994, *Sweet Valley High* became the television series Pascal had originally envisioned it to be. Once a week the Wakefield twins and all the other characters come to life on the screen.

With so many series going, Pascal is unable to write the books herself. "It would be impossible to do them without a stable of writers," remarks Pascal in her interview with Feitlowitz. "They come out at the rate of one a month plus periodic super editions. I do all the plot outlines, descriptions of characters, time setting, and so forth. I love plot twists and the conflicts between the good and bad twin. Creating Sweet Valley was a real 'high.' I loved making up the history of the place, visualizing it in great detail. We have a stable of authors each of whom generally does one title every three months. I maintain artistic control over every aspect of these novels. I may not write every word, but they are very much mine."

BIOGRAPHICAL/CRITICAL SOURCES:

BOOKS

Children's Literature Review, Volume 25, Gale, 1991, pp. 175-182.
Pascal, Francine, in an interview with Marguerite Feitlowitz for *Authors and Artists for Young Adults,* Volume 1, Gale, 1989, pp. 189-202.

PERIODICALS

Booklist, February 15, 1979, p. 936.
Chicago Tribune, June 1, 1987.
Growing Point, September, 1984, pp. 4311-12.
Horn Book, October, 1977, p. 541; June, 1980, pp. 302-03.

Library Journal, June 15, 1981, pp. 1323-24.
Los Angeles Times, April 20, 1986, section 6, pp. 1, 10-11.
New York Times Book Review, April 29, 1979, p. 38.
People, March 30, 1981; July 11, 1988, pp. 66-68.
Publishers Weekly, January 8, 1979, p. 74; July 26, 1985; May 29, 1987, p. 30.
School Library Journal, September, 1977, p. 134; March, 1979, pp. 149-50; September, 1980, p. 76; September, 1984, p. 136; September, 1985, p. 148; March, 1990, pp. 137-40.
Voice of Youth Advocates, October, 1980, p. 27; August, 1984, p. 146; October, 1985, p. 264; December, 1986, p. 231-32; June, 1987, p. 87.

*   *   *

PASCUDNIAK, Pascal
See LUPOFF, Richard A(llen)

*   *   *

PAUKER, Ted
See CONQUEST, (George) Robert (Acworth)

*   *   *

PERRY, Anne 1938-

PERSONAL: Given name, Juliet Marion Hulme; born October 28, 1938, in London, England; daughter of Walter A. B. (an industrial engineer) and H. Marion (a teacher of the mentally handicapped; maiden name, Reavley) Hulme. *Education:* Educated privately. *Politics:* Liberal. *Religion:* Church of Jesus Christ of Latter-day Saints (Mormon).

ADDRESSES: Home—Tyrn Vawr, Seafield, Portmahomack, Rossshire IV20 1RE, Scotland. *Agent*—Meg Davies, MBA Literary Agents Ltd., 45 Fitzroy St., London W1P 5HR, England.

CAREER: Flight attendant, Northumberland, England, 1962-64; assistant buyer for department store, Newcastle, England, 1964-66; Muldoon & Adams, Los Angeles, CA, property underwriter, 1967-72; writer, 1972—. Volunteer driver for hospital automobile service.

WRITINGS:

"CHARLOTTE" MYSTERY NOVEL SERIES

The Cater Street Hangman, St. Martin's (New York City), 1979.
Callander Square, St. Martin's, 1980.
Paragon Walk, St. Martin's, 1981.

Resurrection Row, St. Martin's, 1982.
Rutland Place, St. Martin's, 1983.
Bluegate Fields, St. Martin's, 1984.
Death in the Devil's Acre, St. Martin's, 1985.
Cardington Crescent, St. Martin's, 1987.
Silence in Hanover Close, St. Martin's, 1988.
Bethlehem Road, St. Martin's, 1990.
Highgate Rise, Fawcett Columbine (New York City), 1991.
Belgrave Square, Fawcett Columbine, 1992.
Farriers' Lane, Fawcett Columbine, 1993.
The Hyde Park Headsman, Fawcett Columbine, 1994.
Traitors Gate, Fawcett Columbine, 1995.

"MONK" MYSTERY NOVEL SERIES

The Face of a Stranger, Fawcett Columbine, 1990.
A Dangerous Mourning, Fawcett Columbine, 1991.
Defend and Betray, Fawcett Columbine, 1992.
A Sudden, Fearful Death, Fawcett Columbine, 1993.
The Sins of the Wolf, Fawcett Columbine, 1994.
Cain His Brother, Fawcett Columbine, 1995.

OTHER

Also author of *Death in the Devil's Acre* and *Riders Ready!;* contributor to a book on the history of the Church of Jesus Christ of Latter-day Saints in the British Isles, published by Cambridge University Press.

WORK IN PROGRESS: A fantasy saga called *Sadokhar;* additional mystery novels for the "Charlotte" series.

SIDELIGHTS: Anne Perry's distinctive mysteries are notable for their representation of Victorian England, independent and industrious female sleuths well ahead of their time, and their preoccupation with morality and the motives behind human behavior.

In all her mysteries, Perry employs an investigative team made up of a man and a woman. In the so-called "Charlotte" novels the team is comprised of the blue-blooded Charlotte Pitt and her husband, Inspector Thomas Pitt. Herbert Mitgang, reviewing *Belgrave Square* for the *New York Times,* notes that while the Pitts "came from different stations in society, they are happily married and form an ideal detective team." With her husband working through official channels, Charlotte pulls the strings of her highborn status to bring Victorian England's villains to task.

Through both her "Charlotte" and "Monk" series, Perry presents the rigidity and pomposity of Victorian society with a keen eye for detail and an indulgent sense of humor. Yet she doesn't forget the painful social inequities of that era, a condition that she often highlights in her books. In *Bethlehem Road,* for example, the Pitts investigate a series of political assassinations, turning their suspicious eyes on

an avenging suffragette who had lost her child and property because of England's punishing divorce laws. In other books, the author examines child abuse, sexual exploitation, slum landlords, and the confined lives of ambitious, talented women with no outlet for their gifts. Rosemary Herbert writes in her review of *The Face of a Stranger* for the *New York Times Book Review* that "[Perry's] intent has been to entertain the reader with well-paced action and strong plot lines while uncovering societal woes."

The first novel in the "Monk" series, *The Face of a Stranger* also marks the debut of the second Perry team: private detective William Monk and Nurse Hester Latterly. The couple's first case is that of a dead nobleman, whose murder offers Monk the chance to rediscover lost memories of his own life following a carriage accident. The ending offers a revelatory solution to both plot lines.

In *A Sudden, Fearful Death,* Monk and Latterly are presented with the case of a murdered hospital nurse which puts a prominent physician under suspicion. Their investigative work continues during a thoroughly detailed courtroom drama. Maria Brolley of *Armchair Detective* writes of the trial, "the reader could not find a more riveting description of the procedure plus the emotional and tactical maneuvers of the prosecution and the defense."

In *Cain His Brother,* Monk's task is to locate Genevieve Stonefield's missing husband. Genevieve fears her husband has been killed by his violent twin brother. The further Monk delves into the case, the greater the obstacles he must overcome. *Booklist*'s Emily Melton praises Perry's work and calls for "high marks for superb plotting, fine writing, intriguing characters, and outstanding historical detail." But *New York Time Book Review*'s Martin Seymour-Smith faults Perry's historical setting as being "not quite of the sort to attract a student of Victorian England" and claims "the plot is patently impossible, the solution is obvious."

Throughout her works, Perry reveals an interest in the internal lives of her characters, wielding acute psychological insight that adds to the great appeal of her books. "My major interest is in conflict of ethics," Perry once told *CA,* "especially involving honesty with oneself, which is why the Victorian scene, with its layers of hypocrisy, appeals to me. My other favorite periods are the Spanish Inquisition and the French Revolution, because of the question of free agency and the use of force to make others believe as we do, in what we believe to be their best interest.

"I am not sure what motivates me; a fascination with people, motives, the belief that the written word is the means by which we can give something of ourselves, hopefully the best of our pleasures and beliefs, to everyone else who can read, in any country, and in the present or the future. My own joy in reading, and the wealth gained, has been immeasurable. The world never stops growing, becoming more complex and more marvelous to one who can read."

In 1994 Perry's own true-life mystery was revealed. Due to the release of the film *Heavenly Creatures,* Perry was pressured to admit that in 1954, as a British teenager living in New Zealand under her real name, Juliet Marion Hulme, she was convicted of helping her best friend murder the friend's mother. The film is based on the newspaper account of the incident. The disclosure, which came just as Perry was to embark on a twenty-three-city tour to promote *Traitors Gate,* surprised the publishing world and her legions of readers. Perry told John Darnton of the *New York Times* that admitting her past to her friends and business associates was "one of the worst days of my life." She shared her story in numerous interviews, even while she expressed surprise that anyone would find it of interest. She told Darnton, "It never occurred to me that 40 years on, something that had been dealt with and paid for, that anybody would care anymore."

Eventually attention turned once again to Perry's work. Reviewing *Traitors Gate* for the *New York Times Book Review,* Marilyn Stasio writes, "Ms. Perry's infallible feeling for the historical moment yields animated political debate over the colonization of Africa, glittering views of Victorian society at play and tantalizing glimpses of a confident, assertive creature known as the 'new woman'. . . . Along with deeply affecting scenes as a funeral in the country, these are the true wonders and pleasures of Ms. Perry's art."

BIOGRAPHICAL/CRITICAL SOURCES:

PERIODICALS

Armchair Detective, summer, 1993, p. 75; spring, 1994, pp. 235-6; summer, 1994, pp. 363-4.
Booklist, March 1, 1987, p. 983; March 15, 1993, p. 1308; August, 1995.
Globe and Mail (Toronto), September 24, 1988; June 22, 1991, p. C6; September 14, 1991, p. C7.
Kirkus Reviews, January 1, 1995.
New York Times, June 12, 1992, p. C21; February 14, 1995, pp. B1-2; November 5, 1995, p. 20.
New York Times Book Review, August 5, 1990, p. 29; November 18, 1990, p. 40; June 16, 1991, p. 21; October 18, 1992, p. 36; March 20, 1994, p. 22; October 2, 1994, p. 32; March 19, 1995, p. 29.
Publishers Weekly, February 6, 1987, p. 87; September 14, 1990, p. 113; April 5, 1991, p. 138; February 17, 1992, p. 49; January 24, 1994, p. 42; January 2, 1995, p. 61; March 27, 1995, pp. 64-65; July 31, 1995.
School Library Journal, September, 1991, p. 294; March, 1994, p. 246.
Washington Post Book World, December 20, 1992.*

PETERSON, Christmas
See CHRISTMAS, Joyce

* * *

PHILLIPS, Jayne Anne 1952-

PERSONAL: Born July 19, 1952, in Buckhannon, WV; daughter of Russell R. (a contractor) and Martha Jane (a teacher; maiden name, Thornhill) Phillips; married Mark Brian Stockman (a physician), May 26, 1985; children: one son, two stepsons. *Education:* West Virginia University, B.A. (magna cum laude), 1974; University of Iowa, M.F.A., 1978.

ADDRESSES: Home—Brookline, MA. *Agent*—Lynn Nesbit, International Creative Management, 40 West 57th St., New York, NY 10019.

CAREER: Writer. Boston University, Boston, MA, adjunct associate professor of English, 1982—; Brandeis University, Waltham, MA, Fanny Howe Chair of Letters, 1986-87.

MEMBER: Authors League of America, Authors Guild, PEN.

AWARDS, HONORS: Pushcart Prize, Pushcart Press, 1977, for *Sweethearts,* 1979, for short stories "Home" and "Lechery," and 1983, for short story "How Mickey Made It"; Fels Award in fiction, Coordinating Council of Literary Magazines, 1978, for *Sweethearts;* National Endowment for the Arts fellowship, 1978 and 1985; St. Lawrence Award for fiction, 1979, for *Counting;* Sue Kaufman Award for first fiction, American Academy and Institute of Arts and Letters, 1980, for *Black Tickets;* O. Henry Award, Doubleday & Co., 1980, for short story "Snow"; Bunting Institute fellowship, Radcliffe College, 1981, for body of work; National Book Critics Circle Award nomination, American Library Association Notable Book citation, and *New York Times* Best Books of 1984 citation, all 1984, all for *Machine Dreams.*

WRITINGS:

FICTION

Sweethearts, Truck Press, 1976.
Counting, Vehicle Editions (New York City), 1978.
Black Tickets, Delacorte (New York City), 1979.
How Mickey Made It, Bookslinger (St. Paul, MN), 1981.
Machine Dreams, Dutton (New York City), 1984.
Fast Lanes, Vehicle Editions, 1984.
Shelter, Houghton (Boston), 1994.

RECORDINGS

Jayne Anne Phillips Interview with Kay Bonetti, American Audio Prose Library (Columbia, MO), 1991.

Jayne Anne Phillips Reads Souvenir and Machine Dreams, American Audio Prose Library, 1991.

OTHER

Contributor of short stories to magazines, including *Granta, Grand Street, Esquire,* and *Rolling Stone.*

SIDELIGHTS: Jayne Anne Phillips "stepped out of the ranks of her generation as one of its most gifted writers," writes Michiko Kakutani in the *New York Times.* "Her quick, piercing tales of love and loss [demonstrate] a keen love of language, and a rare talent of illuminating the secret core of ordinary lives with clearsighted unsentimentality," Kakutani continues.

The short stories in *Black Tickets,* Phillips' first effort for a commercial press, fall into three basic categories: short stylistic exercises, interior monologues by damaged misfits from the fringes of society, and longer stories about family life. In these stories, notes Michael Adams in the *Dictionary of Literary Biography Yearbook: 1980,* "Phillips explores the banality of horror and the horror of the banal through her examination of sex, violence, innocence, loneliness, illness, madness, various forms of love and lovelessness," and lack of communication. These stories were drawn, observes James N. Baker of *Newsweek,* "from observations she made in her rootless days on the road," in the mid-1970s when she wandered from West Virginia to California and back again, "then developed in her imagination."

"Most of the stories in *Black Tickets,*" states Thomas R. Edwards in the *New York Review of Books,* "examine the lives of people who are desperately poor, morally deadened, in some way denied comfort, beauty, and love." While some of these stories deal with alienation within families, others are "edgy, almost hallucinatory portraits of disaffected, drugged out survivors of the 60s," according to Kakutani. Stories of this genre in the collection include "Gemcrack," the monologue of a murderer driven by a voice in his head that he calls "Uncle," and "Lechery," the story of a disturbed teenaged girl who propositions adolescents. These are "brittle episodes of despair, violence and sex," declares *Harper's* reviewer Jeffrey Burke, characterized by "economy and fierceness [and] startling sexuality," in the words of Walter Clemons of *Newsweek.*

Other stories focus on less unique individuals. They are about "more or less ordinary people, in families, who are trying to love each other across a gap," according to Edwards. Stories such as "Home," "The Heavenly Animal," and "Souvenir" all deal with the problems of grown-up children and their aging parents: a young woman's return home forces her divorced mother to come to terms with both her daughter's and her own sexuality; a father at-

tempts to share his life—Catholic senior citizens meals, car repairs—with his daughter and fails; a mother slowly dying of cancer still has the courage to comfort her daughter. In them, Edwards states, "Phillips wonderfully captures the tones and gestures in which familial love unexpectedly persists even after altered circumstances have made [that love] impossible to express directly."

While some reviewers—like Carol Rumens in the *Times Literary Supplement,* who calls the dramatic monologues in *Black Tickets* "dazzling"—enjoy Phillips' richly sensuous language, others feel the author's best work is found in the more narrative stories concerning the sense of alienation felt by young people returning home. Stone calls these stories "the most direct and honest of the longer works in the collection" and states that "the language in these stories serves character and plot rather than the other way around." "The strength in these stories," says Mary Peterson in the *North American Review,* "is that even narrative gives way to necessity: honesty gets more time than forced technique; language is simple and essential, not flashy; and even the hard truth, the cruel one, gets telling."

Machine Dreams, Phillips' fifth book, is the first of her two novels. According to John Irving, writing in the *New York Times Book Review,* the novel is the prose format in which Phillips excels. He states that Phillips is at her best "when she sustains a narrative, manipulates a plot, and develops characters through more than one phase of their lives or behaviors." In *Machine Dreams,* the author uses the family in much the same way she had in some of the stories in *Black Tickets.* The sprawling novel tells the story of the Hampson family—Mitch, Jean, their daughter Danner and son Billy—focusing on the years between World War II and the Vietnam War, although it does show glimpses of an earlier, quieter time in Jean's and Mitch's reminiscences. It is the story of the family's collapse, told from the point of view of each of the family members.

In a larger sense, however, *Machine Dreams* is about disorientation in modern life, tracing, in the words of Allen H. Peacock in the *Chicago Tribune Book World,* "not only [the Hampsons'] uneasy truce with contemporary America but contemporary America's unending war with itself." Mitch and Jean were raised in the days of the Depression, hard times, "but characterized by community, stability and even optimism. You could tell the good guys from the bad ones in the war Mitch fought," says Jonathan Yardley in the *Washington Post Book World. Machine Dreams* is, he concludes, "a story of possibility gradually turning into disappointment and disillusion," in which the Hampson family's dissolution mirrors "the simultaneous dissolution of the nation." Peacock echoes this analysis, declaring, "This is the stuff of tragedy: disintegration of a family, disintegration by association of a society." Toronto *Globe and Mail* contributor Catherine Bush points out that the machine dreams of the title, "the belief in technology as perpetual onward-and-upward progress; the car as quintessential symbol of prosperity; the glamour of flight . . . become nightmares. Literally, the dream comes crashing down when Billy leaps out of a flaming helicopter in Vietnam." Bush notes that Vietnam itself, however, is not the cause of the dissolution; appropriately, she observes, Phillips "embeds the war in a larger process of breakdown."

Part of this tragedy lies in the characters' inability to understand or control what is happening to them. Kakutani explains: "Everywhere in this book there are signs that the old certainties, which Miss Phillips's characters long for, have vanished or drifted out of reach. Looking for love, they end up in dissonant marriages and improvised relationships; wanting safety, they settle for the consolation of familiar habits." For them, there are no answers, there is no understanding. "This fundamental inexplicability to things," states Nicholas Spice in the *London Review of Books,* "is compounded for Phillips's characters by their uncertainty about what it is exactly that needs explaining. Emerson's dictum 'Dream delivers us to dream, and there is no end to illusion' might aptly stand as the motto of the book."

Many reviewers recognize the strength and power of Phillips' prose in *Machine Dreams.* Anne Tyler writes in the *New York Times Book Review* that "the novel's shocks arise from small, ordinary moments, patiently developed, that suddenly burst out with far more meaning than we had expected. And each of these moments owes its impact to an assured and gifted writer." Phillips also rises to the technical challenge of using more than one point of view. As John Skow of *Time* magazine declares, "Phillips . . . expresses herself in all four [character] voices with clarity and grace." Geoffrey Stokes writes in the *Voice Literary Supplement,* "That *Machine Dreams* would be among the year's best written novels was easy to predict," and Yardley calls the novel "an elegiac, wistful, rueful book."

Like *Machine Dreams,* Phillips' next work—another collection of short stories—concerns itself with discontinuity and isolation from the past. *Fast Lanes* begins with "stories of youthful drift and confusion and gradually moves, with increasing authority, into the past and what we might call home," comments Jay McInerney in the *New York Times Book Review.* Many of the characters "are joined more by circumstances than by relationships"; they "lack purpose and authority," says Pico Iyer of *Time* magazine. "Their world is fluid, but they do not quite go under. They simply float." These are people, adds Kakutani, for whom "rootlessness has become the price of freedom, alienation the cost of self-fulfillment."

In some reviewers' opinions, *Fast Lanes* suffers in comparison with *Machine Dreams.* For instance, Kakutani states that although "these [first] pieces remain shiny tributes to [the author's] skills, they rarely open out in ways that might move us or shed light on history the way that . . . *Machine Dreams* did." David Remnick, writing for the *Washington Post Book World,* does find that the last two stories in the book—the ones most reminiscent of the novel—are "such strong stories that they erase any disappointment one might have felt in the other five. They are among the best work of one of our most fascinating and gritty writers, and there can be little disappointment in that." Chicago *Tribune Books* contributor Alan Cheuse similarly says that in these stories "you can see [Phillips'] talent grow and flex its muscles and open its throat to reach notes in practice that few of us get to hit when trying our hardest at the height of our powers."

Some of Phillips' best writing, concludes Marianne Wiggins of the *Times Literary Supplement,* concerns "the near-distant, fugitive past—life in the great USA fifteen years ago," reflecting the unsettledness of that period in American life. In some ways Phillips' writing returns to themes first expounded by the poets and novelists of the Beat generation; *Los Angeles Times Book Review* contributor Richard Eder calls *Fast Lanes* "the closing of a cycle that began over three decades ago with Kerouac's 'On the Road,'" the novel about the post-World War II generation's journey in search of the ultimate experience. "It is the return trip," Eder concludes, "and Phillips gives it a full measure of pain, laced with tenderness." McInerney echoes this assessment, calling Phillips "a feminized Kerouac."

Unlike her expansive *Machine Dreams,* Phillips' second novel is "a tighter, smaller book, limited to a few voices and a few days; but what it lacks in scope, it gains in intensity," according to Andrew Delbanco in the *New Republic.* In this novel Phillips once again examines human loss, this time the loss of childhood innocence. Set in 1963 in a West Virginia summer camp for girls, *Shelter,* like Phillips' earlier fiction, renders a full range of voices. As Delbanco notes, Phillips "writes in the idiom of the trailer-park Mama as comfortably as in that of the bookish dreamer." He adds, "In *Shelter,* where each chapter amounts to an interior monologue belonging to a different consciousness, [Phillips'] virtuosity is on full display. The result is a novel that has the quality of an extended eavesdrop."

Shelter tells the connected stories of four of the campers—15-year-old Lenny Swenson, her 11-year-old sister Alma, Lenny's friend Cap Briarley, and Alma's friend Delia Campbell—as well as those of Buddy, the 8-year-old son of the camp's cook, and Carmody, his ex-con stepfather. But as Gail Caldwell states in the *Boston Globe,* "it is [the character of] Parson, a holy madman living on the fringes of the camp, who is Phillips' great creation." Parson has come to the camp ostensibly to lay pipe with a road crew, but actually in pursuit of Carmody, whom he met in prison. "I wanted to think about evil," Phillips tells Delbanco in explaining her motivation for writing *Shelter,* "about whether evil really exists or if it is just a function of damage, the fact that when people are damaged, they damage others."

The children in *Shelter,* Deb Schwartz explains in the *Nation,* are "confused, lonely, struggling to temper a barrage of information and emotions with only the crudest of skills. They are slightly grotesque, clumsily chasing their half-formed desires and attempting to outrun their fears." The four young girls have more than summer camp in common: Lenny's and Alma's mother was in the midst of a love affair with Delia's father at the time he committed suicide. "Phillips," Schwartz writes, "goes straight and true into their hearts and illuminates how children make sense of what they can."

Kakutani also commends Phillips' characterization: "In delineating the girls' relationships to one another and to their families, Ms. Phillips manages to conjure up the humid realm of adolescence: its inchoate yearnings, its alternately languid and hectic moods of expectation." Kakutani points out, too, the skillful way in which child molestation and incest are alluded to and "covered over with layers of emotional embroidery that transform the event even while setting it down in memory."

Though most reviews contain accolades for *Shelter,* R. Z. Sheppard's review in *Time* finds fault. Describing the novel as "overwritten and trendy," Sheppard notes that its treatment of sexual abuse will undoubtedly prove "a hot selling point." By contrast, Ann Hulbert writes in the *New York Times Book Review:* "To be sure, Ms. Phillips plays skillfully with the rich metaphoric implications of violated children—the religious overtones of creatures being cast out, the mythic dimensions of generational rivalry and decay." Hulbert concludes that Phillips is "an astute chronicler of American preoccupations."

BIOGRAPHICAL/CRITICAL SOURCES:

BOOKS

Contemporary Literary Criticism, Gale (Detroit), Volume 15, 1980, Volume 33, 1985.
Dictionary of Literary Biography Yearbook: 1980, Gale, 1981.
Short Story Criticism, Volume 16, Gale, 1994.

PERIODICALS

Afterimage, October, 1985, p. 20.
Books and Arts, November 23, 1979.

Books and Bookmen, December, 1984, p. 25.
Boston Globe, April 5, 1987, p. 100; September 4, 1994, p. A12.
Boston Magazine, September, 1994, p. 70.
Boston Review, August, 1984; June, 1987, p. 25.
Chicago Tribune Book World, June 24, 1984; July 22, 1984.
Chicago Tribune, September 30, 1979.
Christian Science Monitor, June 7, 1985, p. B7.
Commonweal, October 19, 1984.
Detroit News, January 27, 1980; December 13, 1984.
Elle, April, 1987.
Encounter, February, 1985, p. 45.
Entertainment Weekly, December 2, 1994, p. 66.
Esquire, December, 1985.
Globe and Mail (Toronto), July 28, 1984.
Harper's, September, 1979.
Harper's Bazaar, September, 1994, p. 306.
Horizon, October, 1987, p. 63.
Kirkus Reviews, February 15, 1987.
Listener, December 13, 1984, p. 30.
London Review of Books, February 7, 1985, p. 20; October 1, 1987, p. 23.
Los Angeles Times, April 24, 1986.
Los Angeles Times Book Review, July 9, 1984; April 19, 1987, p. 3; September 4, 1994.
Ms., June, 1984; June, 1987, p. 18.
Nation, November 14, 1994, pp. 585-588.
New Leader, December 3, 1979.
New Republic, December 24, 1984; September 2, 1985; December 26, 1994, pp. 39-40.
New Statesman, November 9, 1984.
Newsweek, October 22, 1979; July 16, 1984.
New Yorker, October 24, 1994, p. 111.
New York Review of Books, March 6, 1980.
New York Times, June 12, 1984; June 28, 1984; January 6, 1985; April 4, 1987; April 11, 1987, p. 11; June 19, 1988; January 12, 1992; August 30, 1994, p. C19.
New York Times Book Review, September 30, 1979; July 1, 1984; March 17, 1985; May 5, 1985; May 3, 1987, p. 7; March 6, 1988, p. 32; September 18, 1994, p. 7.
North American Review, winter, 1979.
Observer (London), October 28, 1984; September 6, 1987, p. 25; October 30, 1988, p. 44.
Publishers Weekly, May 9, 1980; June 8, 1984; March 1, 1985; February 27, 1987, p. 152; December 4, 1987, p. 68.
Quill and Quire, September, 1984.
San Francisco Chronicle, July 22, 1984; April 5, 1987.
Spectator, November 3, 1984.
Threepenny Review, spring, 1981.
Tikkun, January-February, 1990, p. 68.
Time, July 16, 1984; June 1, 1987, p. 70; September 19, 1994, p. 82.

Times Literary Supplement, November 14, 1980; November 23, 1984; September 11, 1987, p. 978.
Tribune Books (Chicago), April 19, 1987, p. 6.
USA Today, April 10, 1987, p. D8.
Village Voice, October 29, 1979.
Virginia Quarterly Review, winter, 1985, p. 23.
Voice Literary Supplement, June, 1984; February, 1986.
Wall Street Journal, July 25, 1984.
Washington Monthly, March, 1985, p. 42.
Washington Post, September 4, 1994, p. 5.
Washington Post Book World, December 21, 1979; June 24, 1984; April 26, 1987.
West Coast Review of Books, November, 1984.
Women's Review of Books, July, 1987, p. 24.

*   *   *

PORTER, David L(indsey) 1941-

PERSONAL: Born February 18, 1941, in Holyoke, MA; son of Willis Hubert and Lora Frances (Bowen) Porter; married Marilyn Esther Platt (an elementary school teacher), November 28, 1970; children: Kevin, Andrea. *Education:* Franklin College, B.A. (magna cum laude), 1963; Ohio University, M.A., 1965; Pennsylvania State University, Ph.D., 1970. *Religion:* United Methodist.

ADDRESSES: Home—2314 Ridgeway Ave., Oskaloosa, IA 52577. *Office*—Department of Social Science, William Penn College, Oskaloosa, IA 52577.

CAREER: Rensselaer Polytechnic Institute, Troy, NY, assistant professor of history, 1970-75, codirector of American studies program, 1972-74; State of New York Civil Service, Troy, educational administrative assistant, 1975-76; William Penn College, Oskaloosa, IA, assistant professor, 1976-77, associate professor of history, 1977-82, professor of history and political science, 1982-86, Louis Tuttle Shangle Professor of History and Political Science, 1986—, supervisor of pre-law program, 1979—. Chair of Troy Bicentennial Committee, 1975-76, Sperry & Hutchinson Foundation lectureship series, 1980-82, and annual assembly of Iowa State United Nations Association, 1982; supervisor of Iowa General Assembly legislative internship program, 1978—, Mahaska County records inventory project, 1978-79, and Washington Center internship program, 1985—.

MEMBER: North American Society for Sport History, American Association of University Professors, American Historical Association, Organization of American Historians, Center for the Study of the Presidency, College Football Historical Society, College Football Researchers Association, Popular Culture Association, Professional Football Researchers Association, Society for American Baseball Research, Society for the History of American Foreign Relations, State Historical Society of Iowa, Mahaska County Historical Society, Mahaska County United Nations Association, Alpha, Phi Alpha Theta, Kappa Delta Pi.

AWARDS, HONORS: National Science Foundation grant, 1967; faculty travel grant, Rensselaer Polytechnic Institute, 1974; National Endowment for the Humanities grant, 1979; Eleanor Roosevelt Institute grant, 1981; United Nations Association distinguished service award, 1981; professional development grants, William Penn College, 1986, 1989, and 1992; *Choice* Outstanding Academic Book Award, 1989.

WRITINGS:

EDITOR AND CONTRIBUTOR

The Biographical Dictionary of American Sports: Baseball, Greenwood Press (Westport, CT), 1987.
The Biographical Dictionary of American Sports: Football, Greenwood Press, 1987.
The Biographical Dictionary of American Sports: Outdoor Sports, Greenwood Press, 1988.
The Biographical Dictionary of American Sports: Basketball and Other Indoor Sports, Greenwood Press, 1989.
The Biographical Dictionary of American Sports: 1989-1992 Supplement for Baseball, Football, Basketball, and Other Sports, Greenwood Press, 1992.
The Biographical Dictionary of American Sports: 1992-1995 Supplement for Baseball, Football, Basketball, and Other Sports, Greenwood Press, 1995.

OTHER

The Seventy-sixth Congress and World War II, 1939-1940, University of Missouri Press (Columbia), 1979.
Congress and the Waning of the New Deal, Kennikat (Port Washington, NY), 1980.
(Compiler) *A Cumulative Index to the Biographical Dictionary of American Sports,* Greenwood Press (Westport, CT), 1993.

Contributor to books. Contributor to *Aerospace Historian, American Heritage, American Historical Association Perspectives, Foundations, National Pastime, Palimpsest, Senate History, Chicago Tribune, Des Moines Register, Annals of Iowa, Chicago History, Journal of American History,* and *Midwest Review.* Author of weekly column, *Oskaloosa Herald,* 1994—. Associate editor, *American National Biography* series, Oxford University Press, 1989—.

WORK IN PROGRESS: Congress and Foreign Policy, 1941; America's Greatest Figures; Representative Mary T. Norton of New Jersey; Cap Anson: Baseball's First Superstar; San Diego Padres Baseball Club; editing *Supplement for Baseball, Football, and Other Sports* and *Afro-*

American Sports Greats for *Biographical Dictionary of American Sports,* Greenwood Press.

SIDELIGHTS: David L. Porter told *CA:* "My writing primarily has concerned American politics and foreign policy in the Franklin D. Roosevelt era, biography, and American sports history. I have written two books and numerous articles on the role of the U.S. Congress in the Franklin D. Roosevelt era.

"During the last decade, I have edited a multivolume *Biographical Dictionary of American Sports* series for Greenwood Press. The series is designed to provide readers with quick access to biographical information on athletic figures without having to spend a lot of time consulting various sources. Each volume contains 300- to 500-word biographies of around 600 major figures from baseball, football, basketball, and other major sports. Entries describe the figure's biographical background, career records, accomplishment, and significance, and include pertinent bibliographical sources. Sports historians, educators, and journalists contributed most entries.

"I have nearly completed editing *Afro-American Sports Greats* for Greenwood Press. The book, designed for junior high school, high school, and public libraries, contains 800- to 1,000-word profiles of nearly 170 Afro-American sports greats from baseball, football, basketball, track and field, boxing, and other sports. Entries include information on the personal background and struggles of the athletic figures as well as their career accomplishments and records. Quotations by or about the athletic figures are included."

*   *   *

PORTER, Theodore M(ark)   1953-

PERSONAL: Born December 3, 1953, in Kelso, WA; son of C. Clinton (a teacher) and Shirley (a teacher; maiden name, Tolle) Porter; married Diane R. Campbell (a professor of biology), August 19, 1979. *Education:* Stanford University, A.B., 1976; Princeton University, Ph.D., 1981.

ADDRESSES: Home—18 Virgil Court, Irvine, CA 92715. *Office*—Department of History, University of California, Los Angeles, Los Angeles, CA 90095.

CAREER: California Institute of Technology, Pasadena, A. W. Mellon Instructor in History, 1981-84; University of Virginia, Charlottesville, assistant professor, 1984-90, associate professor of history, 1990-91; University of California at Los Angeles, associate professor, 1991-95, professor of history, 1995—. Research fellow at University of Bielefeld, 1982-83.

MEMBER: American Historical Association, History of Science Society.

AWARDS, HONORS: John Simon Guggenheim Memorial Foundation award, 1989-90; National Science Foundation award, 1991-93, 1994-96.

WRITINGS:

The Rise of Statistical Thinking, 1820-1900, Princeton University Press (Princeton, NJ), 1986.
(With John Beatty, Lorraine Daston, Gerd Gigerenzer, Lorenz Krueger, and Zeno Swijtink) *The Empire of Chance: How Probability Changed Science and Everyday Life,* Cambridge University Press (New York City), 1988.
Trust in Numbers: The Pursuit of Objectivity in Science and Public Life, Princeton University Press, 1995.

OTHER

Contributor to books. Contributor to *Encyclopedia Americana* and *Encyclopedia of the History and Philosophy of the Mathematical Sciences.* Contributor to science and history journals, including *Annals of Science, British Journal for the History of Science, Historical Studies in the Physical Sciences, Poetics Today, Revue de Synthese,* and *Social Studies of Science.*

SIDELIGHTS: Theodore M. Porter told *CA:* "I aim to promote public understanding of the scientific enterprise, in hope that awe and fear of science may in some measure be replaced by critical respect for it. I am currently at work on the broader cultural influences of science since the nineteenth century. I am particularly interested in the sources and effects of quantification in economic and political life and objectivity as a scientific and cultural phenomenon."

Since modern statisticians date the history of their branch of science from about 1890, it is the precursors of this century's statisticians who form the topic of Porter's largely nontechnical book, *The Rise of Statistical Thinking, 1820-1900.* The earliest statisticians, according to the author, were the Germans of the eighteenth century, who attempted to ascertain those facts that concerned the state. Their studies did not consistently rely on mathematics, or even numbers. In the nineteenth century, so-called statisticians began to concern themselves with the collection of numerical data, usually for purposes of social reform. Although they, too, used little mathematics, their investigations provided a model for what has come to be known as the statistical method—that is, reasoning about large numbers of individuals or events without trying to explain particular occurrences. Porter explained that Adolphe Quetelet was the first of the reformers to consider mathematical probability as a valuable tool for the social scientist, and it was Quetelet who first applied what we now know as the bell-shaped "normal curve" to variation in nature and society. Mathematician Morris Kline writes in the *New York Times Book Review:* "An outstanding feature of Mr. Porter's book is its depiction of the interrelationships between statistics and certain intellectual and social movements," such as determinism. Kline describes the author's work as "unfailingly interesting" and praised the book, which he deemed "succeeds admirably in what it sets out to do."

BIOGRAPHICAL/CRITICAL SOURCES:

PERIODICALS

New York Times Book Review, October 5, 1986.

*   *   *

PRIME, Derek (James) 1931-

PERSONAL: Born February 20, 1931, in London, England; son of James Henry (a company director) and Lilian Mabel (a secretary; maiden name, Carpenter) Prime; married Betty Kathleen Martin, April 9, 1955; children: Esther, Timothy, Jonathan, Priscilla. *Education:* Emmanuel College, Cambridge, M.A., 1954; received S.Th. diploma from Archbishop of Canterbury. *Avocational interests:* Reading, stamps, travel, golf.

ADDRESSES: Home—44 Spottiswoode St., Edinburgh EH9 1DG, Scotland.

CAREER: Battersea Grammar School, London, England, head of religious instruction, 1954-57; ordained minister of Fellowship of Independent Evangelical Free Churches, 1957, president, 1965-67; minister of Lansdowne Evangelical Free Church in London, 1957-69; Charlotte Baptist Chapel, Edinburgh, Scotland, minister, 1969-87.

WRITINGS:

"TELL ME THE ANSWER" SERIES

Tell Me the Answer about the Bible and about God, Victory Press (Carlton, OR), 1965, published as *Tell Me about the Bible and about God,* Moody, 1967.

Tell Me the Answer about the Lord Jesus Christ, Victory Press, 1965, published as *Tell Me about the Lord Jesus Christ,* Moody, 1967.

Tell Me the Answer about the Holy Spirit and the Church, Victory Press, 1965.

Tell Me the Answer about the Lord's Prayer, Victory Press, 1965, published as *Tell Me about the Lord's Prayer,* Moody, 1967.

Tell Me the Answer about Becoming a Christian, Victory Press, 1967.

Tell Me the Answer about the Ten Commandments, Victory Press, 1967, published as *Tell Me about the Ten Commandments,* 1969.

OTHER

A Christian's Guide to Prayer, Hodder & Stoughton (London), 1963.

A Christian's Guide to Leadership, Hodder & Stoughton, 1964, Moody (Chicago, IL), 1966, published in England as *Christian Leadership,* Pickering & Inglis, 1980.

Questions on the Christian Faith Answered from the Bible, Hodder & Stoughton, 1967, Eerdmans (Grand Rapids, MI), 1968.

This Way to Life, Hodder & Stoughton, 1968, Moody, 1970.

Bible Guidelines, Hodder & Stoughton, 1979.

Created to Praise, Inter-Varsity Press (Downers Grove, IL), 1981.

From Trials to Triumphs, Regal Books (Ventura, CA), 1982.

Baker's Bible Study Guide, Baker Book (Grand Rapids, MI), 1982.

Practical Prayer, Hodder & Stoughton, 1985.

Directions for Christian Living, Marshall Pickering, 1986.

Pastors and Teachers, Highland Books, 1989.

Drawing Power: Evangelism in the Acts, Scripture Union (Philadelphia, PA), 1991.

Women in the Church, Crossway Books (Westchester, IL), 1992.

Let's Say the Grace Together, Day One Publications, 1994.

Focus on the Bible: James, Christian Focus Publications (Fearn, Tain, England), 1995.

Gofors and Grumps: An A-Z of Bible Characters, Day One, 1995.

Also series editor of "Christian Guide" series, Hodder & Stoughton.

WORK IN PROGRESS: The Lord's Prayer for Today.

*   *   *

PULLMAN, Philip (Nicholas) 1946-

PERSONAL: Born October 19, 1946, in Norwich, Norfolk, England; son of Alfred Outram (an airman) and Audrey Evelyn (Merrifield) Pullman; married Judith Speller (a therapist), August 15, 1970; children: James, Thomas. *Education:* Oxford University, B.A., 1968. *Politics:* Left. *Avocational interests:* Music, drawing.

ADDRESSES: Home—24 Templar Rd., Oxford OX2 8LT, England. *Agent*—Ellen Levine, Ellen Levine Literary Agency Inc., 15 E. 26th Street, Suite 1801, New York, NY 10010; A. P. Watt, 20 John St., London WC1N 2DR, England.

CAREER: Writer. Oxfordshire Education Authority, Oxford, England, teacher, 1972-88; Westminster College,

Oxford, part-time lecturer, 1988—. Public speaker and lecturer.

AWARDS, HONORS: Children's Book Award for Older Readers from International Reading Association, 1988, Best Book for Young Adults from American Library Association, and Preis der Leseratten from West German television station 2DF, all for *The Ruby in the Smoke.*

WRITINGS:

Ancient Civilizations (juvenile), Wheaton (Exeter, England), 1978.
Galatea (adult novel), Dutton (New York City), 1979.
Count Karlstein, or the Ride of the Demon Huntsman (picture book), Chatto & Windus (London), 1982.
The Ruby in the Smoke (young adult novel; first novel of trilogy; also see below), Knopf (New York City), 1987.
How to Be Cool (juvenile), Heinemann (London), 1987.
The Shadow in the Plate (young adult novel; second novel in trilogy; also see below), Oxford University Press (Oxford, England), 1987, published as *Shadow in the North,* Knopf, 1988.
Spring-Heeled Jack: A Story of Bravery and Evil (young adult novel), Transworld Publishers (London), 1989, Knopf, 1991.
The Tiger in the Well (young adult novel; third novel in trilogy; also see above), Knopf, 1990.
The Broken Bridge (young adult novel), Macmillan (London), 1990, Knopf, 1992.
The White Mercedes (young adult novel), Macmillan (London), 1992, Knopf, 1993.
The Tin Princess (young adult novel; sequel to trilogy; also see above), Knopf, 1994.
The Firework Maker's Daughter, Doubleday, 1995.
Northern Lights (first novel in a young adult fantasy trilogy), Scholastic (U.K.), 1995, published in the U.S. as *The Golden Compass,* Knopf, 1996.

Author of numerous stage adaptations, including *The Three Musketeers,* produced by Polka Children's Theatre, Wimbledon, England, *Frankenstein,* and the original stage play *The Adventure of the Sumatian Devil,* a new adventure of Sherlock Holmes; also author of an adaptation of *Aladdin* for Scholastic in England and a version of *Frankenstein* for Oxford University Press.

ADAPTATIONS: How to Be Cool was adapted and broadcast by Granada TV as a television show, 1988.

WORK IN PROGRESS: The second novel in *His Dark Materials,* a young adult science fantasy trilogy.

SIDELIGHTS: An author in numerous genres, British writer Philip Pullman first achieved renown in the United States with his young adult trilogy—*The Ruby in the Smoke, Shadow in the North,* and *The Tiger in the Well*—

"set in [his] quirky, gothic version of nineteenth-century England and starring the staunchly independent Sally Lockhart," explains Kit Alderdice in *Publishers Weekly.* The trilogy offers commentary on numerous levels, including melodrama, social analysis, and historical insight. *The Ruby in the Smoke,* the first of the trilogy, "weaves together two dark intrigues" involving the disappearance of an important ruby and the sinking of a schooner in the Far East, writes Peter Hollindale in *British Book News Children's Books.* Sixteen-year-old Sally Lockhart finds herself embroiled in these two seemingly-unrelated events and must draw on her somewhat extraordinary and unusual resources to avoid sinister repercussions. Hollindale maintains that *The Ruby in the Smoke* "is a splendid book, full of memorable characters, furious action and heroic deeds in murky London settings."

Shadow in the North continues Sally Lockhart's mystery adventures and reunites her with another character from *The Ruby in the Smoke,* Frederick Garland. While some reviewers consider the plot events too graphic and disturbing for younger readers, other critics relish the lurid twists and turns. M. Crouch remarks in *Junior Bookshelf* that the book "is the kind of tale in which the reader willingly suspends critical judgment in favour of a wholehearted good 'read.' "

The final novel in the trilogy, *The Tiger in the Well,* again visits London's corrupt neighborhoods. Sally finds herself the subject of a well-orchestrated plot to steal her identity and her life, leaving her homeless and victimized. In other parts of London, Russian Jews experience the same tactics undermining Sally's existence; much of the plot revolves around London's shadowy underworld as Sally attempts to learn the identity of the mastermind of this villainous and dangerous scam. A *Publishers Weekly* reviewer comments that "this thought-provoking romp is as rich and captivating as a modern-day Dickens novel."

The Broken Bridge signifies a departure from Pullman's previous young adult fiction. Instead of describing Victorian England, *The Broken Bridge* turns to current life and times, examining a teenager's growth to maturity. Set in Wales in the summertime, the novel introduces adolescent Ginny Howard, a Haitian-English sixteen-year-old determined to establish an identity as an artist while searching for answers to family questions and secrets. According to Michael Dorris in the *New York Times Book Review,* "It's a credit to the storytelling skill of Philip Pullman . . . that this contemporary novel succeeds as well as it does. As the plot tumbles forward, full of red herrings, coincidences and dramatic encounters, the writing remains fresh, the settings original and the central characters compelling." About the conclusion of the novel, a *Books for Keeps* reviewer notes, "It's an uncompromising, trustworthy climax from a writer who will excite, delight and disturb many young readers."

In *The Tin Princess,* Pullman returns to Sally Lockhart's era. Instead of centering on Sally, however, the book resurrects characters from earlier volumes in the trilogy. Alderdice remarks in *Publishers Weekly* that *The Tin Princess* "focuses instead on the exploits of Sally's old ally Jim Taylor and his long-lost true love, the orphan Adelaide, last seen in *The Ruby in the Smoke.*" Pullman related to Alderdice that "people kept asking me what happened to Adelaide after the first book. . . . And I thought it would be nice to do a book which gave Jim a bit of a bigger part, because I put him on the sidelines in *The Tiger in the Well.*" The action, set some years after *The Tiger in the Well,* occurs in Central Europe.

Pullman once told *CA:* "I am first and foremost a storyteller. Whatever form I write in, whether it's the novel or the screenplay or the stage play, or even if I tell stories (as I sometimes do), I am always the servant of the story that has chosen me to tell it, and I have to discover the best way of doing that. I believe there's a pure line that goes through every story, and the closer the telling approaches that pure line, the better it will be.

"I have other values as well as those of a storyteller, though I don't think they actually conflict. I believe passionately in social justice and in the right of every citizen to live a decent life, to be well educated, to be part of a society that does not regard the acquisition of money as the most important thing in life—a society that has a proper human regard for the well being of all its members, not just the strongest. I find that as I grow older I'm getting more angry, not less, and no doubt this is reflected in the things I'm now writing about; my stories are becoming less fantastic and more realistic. Real things spark off stories: an incident in a shopping mall; a friend's difficulty in getting hospital treatment; a vagrant in a local park. And although I've been writing historical fiction, which might seem remote from the present day, I've begun to see parallels between such things as the condition of the poor in the East End of London in the 1880s and the growing contrast between rich and poor today.

"But I don't write stories to a plan or to make a political point. I've tried, and it doesn't work. The story must tell me. If a story isn't there, no amount of research, analysis, or passion will make it come. If, when it does come, it's quite different from the one I thought I ought to tell, so be it. And despite what I say above about the fantastic and the realistic, I have found myself recently possessed by a story that is entirely fantastic, which is to form a trilogy called *His Dark Materials.* But whatever I write, I continue to rely on my wife, who is and always has been my first and best critic."

BIOGRAPHICAL/CRITICAL SOURCES:

PERIODICALS

Books for Keeps, May 7, 1992, p. 25.
British Book News Children's Books, March, 1986, pp. 33-34.
Junior Bookshelf, December, 1986, pp. 229-30.
New York Times Book Review, May 17, 1992, p. 24.
Publishers Weekly, October 12, 1990, pp. 65-66; May 30, 1994, pp. 24-25.
Times Educational Supplement, July 21, 1995.

Q-R

QUINTANILLA, (Maria) Aline (Griffith y Dexter) 1921-
(Aline, Countess of Romanones; Aline Griffith)

PERSONAL: Born May 22, 1921, in Pearl River, NY; daughter of William F. (in real estate) and Marie (Dexter) Griffith; married Luis Figueroa y Perez de Guzman el Bueno, Count of Romanones (an artist), 1947 (died, 1987); children: Alvaro, Luis, Miguel. *Education:* College of Mont St. Vincent, B.A. *Religion:* Catholic.

ADDRESSES: Home—Castellon de la Plana 23, Madrid 6, Spain. *Agent*—Julian Bach, Jr., 3 East 48th St., New York, NY 10017.

CAREER: Worked as a model in the early 1940s; worked as a code clerk and espionage agent for the Office of Strategic Services (OSS) in Madrid, Spain, during World War II, and as an espionage agent for the Central Intelligence Agency (CIA) on various occasions during the 1960s and 1970s; author and lecturer, 1987—.

AWARDS, HONORS: Lazo de Dama of Isobel; decoration of the Venezuelan Institute of Hispanic Culture.

WRITINGS:

UNDER NAME ALINE, COUNTESS OF ROMANONES

The Spy Wore Red: My Adventures as an Undercover Agent in World War II, Random House, 1987.
The Spy Went Dancing, Putnam, 1990.
The Spy Wore Silk, Putnam, 1991.

OTHER

The Story of Pascualete, J. Murray, 1963, published under name Aline Griffith as *The Earth Rests Lightly,* Holt, 1964.

Contributor to *Estudios Extremenos.*

ADAPTATIONS: A television movie and a Broadway musical, both based on *The Spy Wore Red,* are planned.

WORK IN PROGRESS: A historical biography on the half-sister of Isobel the Catholic.

SIDELIGHTS: Aline Quintanilla is best-known for her autobiographical books *The Spy Wore Red, The Spy Went Dancing,* and *The Spy Wore Silk,* written under the name Aline, Countess of Romanones. These nonfiction works chronicle her experiences as an undercover agent for first the Office of Strategic Services (OSS) and later the Central Intelligence Agency (CIA). During World War II Quintanilla became a member of the Spanish nobility by marriage, meeting her husband while she was posted to Madrid to unmask Heinrich Himmler's main Spanish agent and other secret Nazi sympathizers. The Countess of Romanones writes about her code names (among them "Tiger," "Sugarlump," and "Butch") and contacts, about glamorous European soirees and weekends with guests such as Jacqueline Kennedy Onassis, the Duchess of Windsor, Malcolm Forbes, and Elizabeth Taylor. She also details specific espionage situations for which the OSS and CIA brought her out of retirement, including a 1966 search for a KGB agent and an assignment in 1971 to thwart a plot to assassinate King Hassan II of Morocco.

About *The Spy Wore Red: My Adventures as an Undercover Agent in World War II,* Michael Gross of the *New York Times Book Review* notes: "It is not the adventure, nor the romance, nor the rather simple brand of espionage Aline Romanones engaged in, that makes *The Spy Wore Red* so delightful. . . . Rather, the best parts . . . are the glimpses the author offers of the sophisticated, sometimes amoral world in which she spied." Rhoda Koenig of *New York* magazine opines that the book "sounds impossibly novelettish," but she points out that it "was endorsed as accurate by no less than [former CIA director] William

Casey." Joanne Kaufman observes in the *New York Times Book Review* that while "it's hard to resist an espionage story, especially a true one," *The Spy Went Dancing,* the Countess's second book about her spy experiences, "reads too often like a Judith Krantz novel." In *The Spy Wore Silk,* the third book in the autobiographical espionage series, Ann Banks of the *New York Times Book Review* comments that "plots, counterplots and betrayals figure prominently." Banks also describes the action as "thrilling," noting that "there are periodic brushes with death, roughly one every 50 pages."

Despite Casey's support, some critics question the veracity of the author's accounts. In *Newsweek,* Barbara Kantrowitz explains that *Women's Wear Daily* asserted in a February 28, 1991, article that her books "may be more fiction than fact." The controversy arises from supposed documents—allegedly written by the countess while working undercover and later filed at the National Archives in Washington, D.C.—which hint at a much more pedestrian espionage career than that presented in her books. The countess has admitted in her author's notes that some of the events and characters were altered to "simplify the story line . . . while keeping the 'core' of the tale," Kantrowitz reports. Several publishers had rejected her initial manuscript as "too documentary." The critic writes that "even the countess's fans concede that readers should not take every word of her books literally"; Kantrowitz quotes Ray Cline, a former deputy CIA director: "Espionage is mostly boredom. . . . In order to get her books published, she decided to glamorize." The countess, however, maintains her honor and dismisses the controversial files, noting that they only tell part of the story, that in the interest of secrecy, many things could not be written down.

BIOGRAPHICAL/CRITICAL SOURCES:

PERIODICALS

Life, October 2, 1964.
Newsweek, March 25, 1991, p. 59.
New York, June 27, 1988, p. 97.
New York Herald Tribune, May 25, 1964.
New York Times, December 4, 1964.
New York Times Book Review, June 21, 1987, p. 10; March 4, 1990, p. 25; March 17, 1991, p. 23.*

*   *   *

REED, Michael   1930-

PERSONAL: Born April 25, 1930, in Aylesbury, Buckinghamshire, England; son of Victor Harold (a clerk) and Gertrude (South) Reed; married Gwynneth Vaughan (a librarian), October 1, 1955; children: Philip. *Education:* University of Birmingham, B.A., 1954, M.A., 1958; University of London, LL.B., 1966; University of Leicester, Ph.D., 1973.

ADDRESSES: Home—1 Paddock Close, Quorn, Leicestershire LE12 8BJ, England. *Office*—Department of Library and Information Studies, Loughborough University of Technology, Loughborough, Leicestershire, England.

CAREER: Schoolteacher in Kent, Yorkshire, and Leicestershire, England, 1955-73; Loughborough University of Technology, Loughborough, England, lecturer in library studies, 1973-76, senior lecturer, 1976-84, reader in landscape studies, 1984-88, professor of archives and topography, 1988—. *Military service:* Royal Air Force, 1948-50.

MEMBER: Royal Historical Society (fellow), Society of Antiquaries of London (fellow).

WRITINGS:

The Buckinghamshire Landscape, Hodder & Stoughton (London), 1979.
(Contributor) Margaret Gelling, editor, *The Early Charters of the Thames Valley,* Leicester University Press (London), 1979.
(Contributor) Peter Clark, editor, *Country Towns in Pre-Industrial England,* Leicester University Press, 1981.
Ipswich Probate Inventories, 1583-1631, Suffolk Records Society, 1981.
The Georgian Triumph, 1700-1830, Routledge & Kegan Paul (London), 1983.
(Editor and contributor) *Discovering Past Landscapes,* Croom Helm (London), 1984.
The Age of Exuberance, Routledge & Kegan Paul, 1986.
Buckinghamshire Probate Inventories, 1600-1714, Buckinghamshire Record Society, 1987.
The Landscape of Britain, Routledge & Kegan Paul, 1990.
A History of Buckinghamshire, Phillimore (West Sussex), 1993.
(Contributor) Peter Clark, editor, *Small Towns in Early Modern Europe,* Cambridge University Press (Cambridge), 1995.

Contributor to library and history journals.

SIDELIGHTS: In *The Georgian Triumph, 1700-1830,* Michael Reed focuses on the significant aspects of eighteenth-century society in England, Scotland, and Wales, discussing the relationship between geography and the built environment, agrarian development in rural Britain, and urban and industrial contributions to British history. To critic Penelope J. Corfield, the book brought to life a century that has traditionally been considered complacent and dull. She wrote in the *Times Literary Supplement* that Reed's study is "lucidly written, pleasantly illustrated and well researched," adding that it is "aimed at the intelligent general reader, who is treated with proper respect."

Reed once told *CA:* "I am particularly interested in the ways in which men shape and mold their environment over time. I am curious about the ideas that inform their motives and actions, not only in Britain, but also in Western Europe and more especially in France.

"The landscape is for me a palimpsest, a writing surface that has been used again and again by succeeding generations of men and women to record thereon their own authentic and unself-conscious social autobiography, without totally erasing that of previous generations. Thus a monastic ruin is today a picturesque element in the English landscape, but it is also a silent witness to an ancient ideal that has passed away into history, while the care now lavished upon its preservation is evidence of another range of ideas that have replaced those to which the building owes its origins. It is this sense of the incredibly rich historical density of the landscape that makes its exploration so rewarding and so fascinating. I hope that through my books I can convey at least something of my pleasure to others."

BIOGRAPHICAL/CRITICAL SOURCES:

PERIODICALS

Daily Telegraph (London), July 18, 1986.
Times Literary Supplement, August 12, 1983.

*   *   *

RICOU, Laurence (Rodger) 1944-

PERSONAL: Born October 17, 1944, in Brandon, Manitoba, Canada; son of Reginald Thomas (an advertising agent) and Gladys (Hawke) Ricou; married Treva Carolyn Clendenning (a librarian), June 5, 1966; children: Marc Laurence, Liane Adele. *Education:* Brandon College, University of Manitoba, B.A., 1965; University of Toronto, M.A., 1967, Ph.D, 1971.

ADDRESSES: Home—5115 Cypress St., Vancouver, British Columbia, Canada V6M 4L5. *Office*— Department of English, University of British Columbia, No. 397, 1873 East Mall, Vancouver, British Columbia, Canada V6T 1Z1.

CAREER: University of Lethbridge, Lethbridge, Alberta, assistant professor, 1970-75, associate professor of English, 1975-78, chair of department, 1973-78; University of British Columbia, Vancouver, associate professor, 1978-89, professor of English, 1989—, associate dean of graduate studies, 1990-96.

MEMBER: Association of Canadian University Teachers of English, Association for Canadian and Quebec Literatures, Western Literature Association.

AWARDS, HONORS: Humanities Research Council of Canada grant, 1973, for *Vertical Man/Horizontal World: Man and Landscape in Canadian Prairie Fiction;* Ontario Arts Council grant, 1976; Canada Council leave fellowship, 1976-77 and 1982-83; Canadian Federation for the Humanities grant, 1986, for *Everyday Magic: Child Languages in Canadian Literature.*

WRITINGS:

Vertical Man/Horizontal World: Man and Landscape in Canadian Prairie Fiction, University of British Columbia Press (Vancouver), 1973.
(Editor and author of introduction) *Twelve Prairie Poets* (anthology), Oberon Press, 1976.
Everyday Magic: Child Languages in Canadian Literature, University of British Columbia Press, 1987.

Contributor to books, including *The Twenties in Western Canada,* edited by S. M. Trofimenkoff, National Museum of Man, 1972; *A Candle to Light the Sun,* by Patricia Blondal, McClelland & Stewart (Toronto), 1976; *RePlacing,* edited by Dennis Cooley, ECW Press, 1980; *Profiles in Canadian Literature 2,* edited by Jeffrey M. Heath, Dundurn Press (Toronto), 1980; *Violence in the Canadian Novel since 1960,* edited by Terry Goldie and Virginia Harger-Grinling, Memorial University of Newfoundland, 1981; *Voices from Distant Lands: Poetry in the Commonwealth,* edited by Konrad Gross and Wolfgang Klooss, Koenigshausen & Neumann, 1983; *Canada: The Verbal Creation/La Creazione Verbale,* edited by Alfredo Rizzardi, Piovan Editore, 1985; *The Annotated Bibliography of Canada's Major Authors,* edited by Robert Lecker and Jack David, ECW Press, 1985; and *Writing Canadian Women Writing,* edited by Shirley Neuman and Smaro Kamboureli, NeWest Press (Edmonton), 1986. Contributor of articles and reviews to literary journals, including *Essays on Canadian Writing, NeWest Review, Canadian Plains Studies 6: Man and Nature on the Prairies, Mosaic,* and *Canadian Children's Literature.* Associate editor, *Canadian Literature,* 1983—.

*   *   *

RIDENOUR, Fritz 1932-

PERSONAL: Surname is pronounced with a short "i"; born January 19, 1932, in Waukegan, IL; son of Leo Leroy (a chiropractor) and Viola (a secretary and office manager; maiden name, Kasten) Ridenour; married Jackie Cosman (an executive secretary), September 6, 1953; children: Kimberly Jean, Jeffrey Robert, Todd Steven. *Education:* Whitworth College, B.A., 1955; Pasadena College (now Point Loma College), M.A. *Politics:* Republican. *Religion:* Protestant.

ADDRESSES: Home and office—28710 Indies Lane, Santa Clarita, CA 91351.

CAREER: Gospel Light Publications, Glendale, CA, managing editor, 1957-79; acquisitions editor, Zondervan, 1979-80; senior acquisitions editor, Fleming H. Revell, 1980-85; self-employed writer and ghost writer, 1985—. *Military service:* U.S. Naval Air Reserve, photographer, 1951-58.

MEMBER: Christian Writers Guild.

AWARDS, HONORS: Named best periodical editor of the year by Evangelical Press Association, 1960, for *Teach;* book award from *Campus Life,* 1974, for *How to Be a Christian without Being Religious;* named author of the year by Gospel Literature International, 1975, for foreign translations of his books; Gold Medallion Book Award, E.C.P.A., 1987, for *How to Be a Christian without Being Perfect.*

WRITINGS:

How to Be a Christian without Being Religious, Gospel Light Publications (Ventura, CA), 1967, revised edition, 1972.
So What's the Difference?, Gospel Light Publications, 1967, revised edition, Regal Books (Ventura, CA), 1979.
Who Says?, Gospel Light Publications, 1967.
(Editor) *Tell It Like It Is,* Gospel Light Publications, 1968.
It All Depends, Gospel Light Publications, 1969.
Right or Wrong, Gospel Light Publications, 1969.
I'm a Good Man, But . . . , Gospel Light Publications, 1969.
It's Your Move, Gospel Light Publications, 1970.
Take Your Choice, Gospel Light Publications, 1970.
How to Be a Christian in an Un-Christian World, Gospel Light Publications, 1971.
How Do You Handle Life?, Regal Books, 1976.
Faith It or Fake It?, Regal Books, 1978.
How to Decide What's Really Important, Regal Books, 1978.
Lord, What's Really Important?, Regal Books, 1978.
What Teen-Agers Wish Their Parents Knew about Kids, Word, Inc. (Waco, TX), 1982.
How to Be a Christian without Being Perfect, Regal Books, 1986.
How to Be a Christian and Still Enjoy Life, Regal Books, 1988.

Editor of *Teach.*

SIDELIGHTS: Fritz Ridenour once told *CA:* "The motivation for all my books to date has been a desire to help Christians—particularly young people—understand their faith and what the Bible teaches. I am a strong proponent of the theological concept of 'grace'—the unmerited favor of God. I believe that a happy and secure relationship with God is attainable through His grace, not through a religious system of works, or trying to please a policeman type of God who is constantly watching to see how many mistakes you make or rules you break.

"I am also deeply aware of the many paradoxes in human existence—especially in the Christian faith. The Gospel presented in Holy Scripture is simple, and yet it is deeply profound and highly complex. Living life as a Christian is a simple matter of 'walking in faith,' yet it is also a difficult, baffling, and confusing experience on many occasions. I have tried to grapple with these paradoxes as I've dealt with such issues as situation ethics, the new morality, science and the Bible, evolution, philosophy, and psychology. Always, I try to write at a popular, layman's level, for maximum understanding by the typical person."

*　　　*　　　*

RIFAAT, Alifa
See RIFAAT, Fatma Abdulla

*　　　*　　　*

RIFAAT, Fatma Abdulla　1930-
(Alifa Rifaat)

PERSONAL: Born June 5, 1930, in Cairo, Egypt; daughter of Abdulla (an architect) and Zakia (a homemaker; maiden name, Ali Rifaat) Rifaat; married Hussien Rifaat (a police officer), July 3, 1952 (died in 1979); children: Amany (daughter) and Mamdouh and Moustafa (sons). *Education:* Domestic Arts School, diploma, 1946; attended British Institute, Cairo, 1946-49. *Religion:* Muslim.

ADDRESSES: Home—4 Mahmoud Ahmad El-Meligi St., Flat 3, El-Nozha, Heliopolis, Cairo, Egypt.

CAREER: Homemaker, 1952-55 and 1960-73; writer, 1955-60 and 1973—. Volunteer worker for Red Crescent, 1948 and 1973. Attendee at conferences and seminars, including First Feminist International Book Fair (London, England), 1984, Arabic Literature Seminar (Berlin, Bonn, and Nuremberg, Germany), 1990, UNISECO—Reality and Horizons (Casablanca, Morocco), 1990, Al-Salam Al-ikom Islamic Conference (Graz, Austria), and many seminars in Egypt.

MEMBER: Union of Egyptian Writers, Story Club, Authors Assembly of Egypt, Modern Literature Association, Literal Akkad Assembly, Zaky Mubarak Assembly.

AWARDS, HONORS: Excellence Award from Modern Literature Assembly, 1984, for excellence in body of work.

WRITINGS:

UNDER PSEUDONYM ALIFA RIFAAT

Hawatandbi-Adam (short stories; title means "Eve Returns with Adam to Paradise"), Ministry of Culture (Egypt), 1975.

Jawharah Farum (novel; title means "The Jewel of Pharaoh"), Ministry of Culture, 1978, translation published as *Pharaoh's Jewel,* Dar Al-Helal, 1991.

Man Ya Kun al-rajul? (short stories; title means "Who Can This Man Be?"), Ministry of Culture, 1981.

Salat Al-hubb (short stories; title means "The Prayer of Love"), Ministry of Culture, 1983.

Distant View of a Minaret, translation by Denys Johnson-Davies, Quartet Books, 1983, from the Arabic, published as *Leil Al-Shetaa Al-taweel* (title means "The Long Night of Winter and Other Stories"), Dar El-Asema, 1985.

Kad Lia al-Hawa (title means "Love Conspired on Me"), Ministry of Culture, 1985, translation published as *Love Made a Trap for Me,* Nile Press, 1991.

Girls of Baurdin (novel), Dar Al-Helal, 1995.

Also author of about ninety short stories in Arabic and English magazines, some of which have been broadcast by the British Broadcasting Corporation (BBC), the Egyptian broadcasting service, and German radio and television.

SIDELIGHTS: Fatma Abdulla Rifaat once told *CA* that several significant childhood experiences as well as growing up in a traditional Arab society profoundly influenced her life and her writings. Rifaat explained: "I had wanted to go on to university education by enrolling in the College of Fine Arts, but my father's refusal was decisive; he made me stay at home and married me off to my maternal uncle's son, a police officer. All decisions in our family are made by the menfolk; we are proud of our Arab origin and hold on to certain Arab customs, among which is the belief that the marriage of girls and their education remains the business of the man. The men taught us to be ladies in society and mistresses of the home only. As for the arts and literature, they were a waste of time and even forbidden.

"I wrote a short story when I was nine. It was about despair in our village. However I was punished for this effort. Then I tried oil painting and studied music and song writing. Finally I went back to writing short stories, a thing which clashed with my marriage. It is significant that my husband should have created a storm when I published my first short story in 1955. Even though I published under a pseudonym until 1960, he discovered it and made me swear on God's book that I stop publishing, or else he would divorce me. I actually did stop writing for about fifteen years during which time I studied literature and read many books on Sufism, history, astronomy, and the sciences, until finally he allowed me, after I had fallen ill, to go back to writing. It was then that I wrote the story 'My World of the Unknown,' which attracted attention, and I began to publish. My husband died, God rest him, in 1979. I then met translator Denys Johnson-Davies, who encouraged me to change my style by abandoning some of the romantic aspects. He also convinced me to write the dialogues in colloquial.

"Death has always been one of the main subjects about which I write, due to the emotional impact of the death of a close childhood friend. Most of my stories, however, revolve around a woman's right to a fully affective and complete sexual life in marriage; that and the sexual and emotional problems encountered by women in marriages are the most important themes of my stories. When I married I found my sexual life unfulfilling because nobody talked to me about the subject or taught me anything. I believe there should be more education for women, even if only through books. In my view, it is wrong to look to the West for sexual education for young people. Our society does not allow us to experience sex freely as Western women may. We have our traditions and our religion in which we believe."

*　　*　　*

RIFKIN, Jeremy 1945-

PERSONAL: Born January 26, 1945, in Denver, CO; son of Milton and Vivette Rifkin; married Donna Wulkan (an attorney), March 12, 1983 (divorced); married Carol Grunewald (a writer and activist). *Education:* Received B.A. from University of Pennsylvania; received M.A. from Fletcher School of Law and Diplomacy (part of Tufts University).

ADDRESSES: Office—Foundation on Economic Trends, 1130 17th St. N.W., Suite 630, Washington, DC 20036. *Agent*—Michael Carlisle, William Morris Agency, 1350 Avenue of the Americas, New York, NY 10019.

CAREER: Lecturer, activist, and author, 1967—; worker for Volunteers in Service to America in Harlem, NY, and activist against Vietnam War, 1967-71; founder and leader of People's Bicentennial Commission, 1971-76; cofounder and president of People's Business Commission (name changed to Foundation on Economic Trends in 1977), 1976—. Guest on television programs, including *Nightline.*

WRITINGS:

(Editor with John Rossen) *How to Commit Revolution American Style—[The] Bicentennial Declaration: An Anthology,* Lyle Stuart (Secaucus, NJ), 1973.

(Editor with Rossen) *Common Sense II: The Case against Corporate Tyranny,* Bantam (New York City), 1975.

(With Ted Howard) *Who Should Play God? The Artificial Creation of Life and What It Means for the Future of the Human Race,* Delacorte (New York City), 1977.

Own Your Own Job: Economic Democracy for Working Americans, Bantam, 1977.

(With Randy Barber) *The North Will Rise Again: Pensions, Politics, and Power in the 1980s,* Beacon Press (Boston, MA), 1978.

(With Howard) *The Emerging Order: God in the Age of Scarcity,* Putnam (New York City), 1979.

(With Howard) *Entropy: A New World View,* afterword by Nicholas Georgescu-Roegen, Viking (New York City), 1980.

(With Nicanor Perlas) *Algeny,* Viking, 1983.

Declaration of a Heretic, Routledge & Kegan Paul (Boston), 1985.

Time Wars: The Primary Conflict in Human History, Holt (New York City), 1987.

(Editor) *The Green Lifestyle Handbook,* Holt, 1990.

Biosphere Politics: A New Consciousness for a New Century, Crown (New York City), 1991, reprinted as *Biosphere Politics: A Cultural Odyssey from the Middle Ages to the New Age,* Harper (San Francisco, CA), 1992.

Beyond Beef: The Rise and Fall of the Cattle Culture, Dutton (New York City), 1992.

(With wife, Carol Grunewald Rifkin) *Voting Green: Your Complete Environmental Guide to Making Political Choices in the 90's,* Doubleday (New York City), 1992.

The End of Work: The Decline of the Global Labor Force and the Dawn of the Post-Market Era, Putnam, 1994.

Contributor of articles and editorials to newspapers and periodicals, including *New York Times, U.S.A. Today,* and *Garden.*

SIDELIGHTS: As head of the Foundation on Economic Trends in Washington, D.C., social activist Jeremy Rifkin has organized demonstrations, formed coalitions, and initiated lawsuits against persons, groups, and institutions whose activities in biotechnology—especially genetic engineering—he sees as a potential threat to life. While to his supporters Rifkin stands as a public crusader against impending disaster, his detractors, including members of the business, government, and scientific communities, characterize him as a nuisance and a doomsayer. Indeed, much of Rifkin's criticism concerns the pressing need to define—politically, socially, economically, culturally, and ethically—exactly what constitutes humanity's responsibility to present and future generations. In his writings Rifkin calls for nothing less than a radical revision in the

way human beings see themselves in relation to their environment.

Rifkin received a B.A. in economics from the prestigious Wharton School of Finance at the University of Pennsylvania and a master's degree in international affairs from the Fletcher School of Law and Diplomacy in the 1960s. He became an activist in 1967 when he helped organize the first national protest against the Vietnam War. After working in New York City's Harlem ghetto as a member of Volunteers in Service to America, Rifkin moved to Washington, D.C., where in 1971 he became disillusioned by initial planning for what he saw as a frivolous and commercialized celebration of the nation's 1976 bicentennial anniversary. He founded the People's Bicentennial Commission and promoted ceremonies and activities that he hoped would help Americans reaffirm the democratic ideas on which the country was established. Dubbed "Declaration of Independence fundamentalists" by *Newsweek* magazine, Rifkin and his organization led protests against large corporations, distributed pamphlets, and called for the redistribution of America's wealth. Rifkin published his first books at this time, assembling an anthology titled *How to Commit Revolution American Style—[The] Bicentennial Declaration: An Anthology* and presenting his personal views on the bicentennial in *Common Sense II: The Case against Corporate Tyranny.*

Remaining in Washington after the festivities ended, Rifkin turned his attention to the business world, urging reforms through which workers would have a greater say in company policies, more autonomy in the workplace, and a larger share of corporate profits. With Randy Barber, he founded the People's Business Commission, an organization committed to confronting corporate exploitation, and in the late 1970s he published two works, *Own Your Own Job: Economic Democracy for Working Americans* and, with Barber, *The North Will Rise Again: Pensions, Politics, and Power in the 1980s.* The latter book's suggestion that labor unions in the industrialized northern states regain control over the investment of their pension funds received widespread attention and the work itself garnered generally favorable reviews. The authors asserted that these pension funds, a major source of American capital, were being invested by corporations in new ventures in the southern United States and overseas, causing loss of jobs and diminishing influence for the northern labor unions. "The story is laid out for all of us to read and to weep over the years of wasted opportunities," commented *Nation* reviewer Henry Foner, who was nevertheless encouraged by Rifkin's new perspective and proposals. Although cautious about what he called "minor flaws born of overenthusiasm," *New Republic*'s Matt Witt also praised the book, remarking that "by raising in a coherent argument the broad issue of control of pension funds, and by linking it to the future of the labor movement and the northern states, Rifkin and Barber could fundamentally change the game plan of those who seek to defeat the conservative forces in the U.S."

Rifkin established the Foundation on Economic Trends, successor to the People's Business Commission, in 1977. The foundation has focused on the issues surrounding genetic engineering and biotechnology, fields that explore and develop medical and agricultural applications for improvements made to living organisms through alterations of their genetic structures. Rifkin, alarmed by these advances, envisioned a future in which humankind could control and exploit the genetic composition of all life forms—including its own—through cloning, selective breeding, gene transference, and discrimination based on genetic constitution. Further worried that biotechnology was outpacing society's ability to assess, and perhaps even identify, its negative social, moral, and economic implications, Rifkin began voicing his concerns in lectures and on television programs. He also outlined his position against genetic experimentation in his 1977 book *Who Should Play God? The Artificial Creation of Life and What It Means for the Future of the Human Race.* The first of his works to achieve best-seller status, *Who Should Play God?* established Rifkin as one of the most important dissenters in the debate on the merits of genetic engineering.

Rifkin further advanced his opposition to genetic engineering in the early 1980s with a series of lawsuits against the National Institute of Health and the University of California, Berkeley. Concerned that the release of genetically altered organisms into the environment posed a potential danger to surrounding areas, he enlisted the support of local residents and environmentalists to prevent university researchers from field testing a form of bacteria designed to deter frost formation on potatoes. The foundation argued that experiments should not be performed outside the laboratory before sufficient research regarding the environmental risks is conducted. Rifkin also charged that researchers should be required to file an Environmental Impact Statement before undertaking such experiments and asked that the Environmental Protection Agency regulate future public and private research.

Rifkin gained more publicity in 1983 with his opposition to human genetic research, insisting that no human being has the right to dispose of "undesirable" genes in human reproductive cells. "Once we decide to begin the process of human genetic engineering, there is really no logical place to stop," Rifkin told Philip J. Hilts in the *Washington Post*. "If diabetes, sickle cell anemia and cancer are to be cured by altering [the] genetic makeup of an individual, why not proceed to other 'disorders': myopia, color blindness, left-handedness?" He enlisted the support of a diverse range of America's religious leaders, from Jewish rabbis to Christian ministers including fundamentalist leader Jerry Falwell, in opposing further genetic experiments. His petition to the U.S. Congress titled "Theological Letter Concerning the Moral Arguments against Genetic Engineering of the Human Germline Cells" was signed by more than sixty religious leaders and opposed interference in natural human reproduction on both ecological and ethical grounds.

In 1986 Rifkin focused his efforts on preventing the Department of Defense from building a new biological weapons laboratory. Rifkin and his followers stridently opposed the use of genetic engineering for military purposes, averring that genetically altered viruses have a potential for human disaster on a par with nuclear holocaust. In addition, Rifkin questioned security procedures for military biological testing labs, submitted recommendations to an international conference reviewing the 1972 Biological Weapons Agreement, and established a "Whistleblowers Fund" to provide financial support to military or scientific personnel sacrificing jobs, security, or reputations by disclosing information about illegal biological weapons testing.

Rifkin also used his administrative skills to coordinate the activities of diverse factions concerned about the implications of genetic engineering. In 1987 he established a coalition—made up of an assortment of farming organizations, academics, and animal protection groups such as the Humane Society—to protest the government's decision to issue patents for new animal species created by gene splicing. Rifkin's opposition to surrogate parenthood contracts, in which a woman is paid to bear a child for another person or couple, prompted him to join with feminists to form the National Coalition Against Surrogacy. Appalled and frightened by what he saw as man's increasing interference in the natural biological reproduction processes of all living things, Rifkin called for legislation against surrogate parenthood. "This cheapening of life to the status of a commercial product represents one of the greatest threats to human dignity of our time," Rifkin declared in an editorial for New Jersey's Toms River *Observer*.

Rifkin's critics accused him of catering to people's fears by exaggerating biotechnology's dangers and ignoring potential benefits such as the elimination of deformity and hereditary diseases and the creation of hardier, more nutritious livestock and crops. Rifkin has also been accused of holding anti-scientific attitudes, and many critics believed that his nonscientific background has prevented him from making a realistic assessment of the issues. Eliot Marshall, in the *New Republic*, wondered whether Rifkin's pleas to stop genetic experimentation showed more bad faith in humanity than the research itself. "Rifkin is really asking that we give up hope of understanding or improving the material world. In this sense it is Rifkin—not the gene-splicers—who would diminish the human spirit in a premature confession of failure," Marshall pointed out.

It is precisely Western society's notion of progress, however, that Rifkin has sought to change. In his writings, which since 1979 have typically addressed the wider philosophical issues that underlie his views toward biotechnology, Rifkin has attacked the modern concept of progress and argued that human attitudes toward civilization must change in order for life to continue much longer. *Entropy: A New World View,* written in collaboration with Ted Howard in 1980, places modern world problems, mainly resource depletion and conservation, in the context of entropy—a law in thermodynamics explaining that the matter in the universe is slowing towards an ultimate state of inertia. According to Rifkin, Western civilization must recognize that its technologies are consuming the planet's remaining energy; it must adjust its notion of progress from one of mastery over the earth to one of conserving its resources and protecting the environment, before the world finds itself in a disastrous condition of decline, scarcity, and stasis. The adjustment, Rifkin theorized, amounts to a profound change in basic attitudes and entails the decentralization of most social institutions, a return to a labor-intensive, rather than a capital- or technology-intensive economy, and, as noted by Richard Woods in *Critic,* "the massive redistribution of wealth and power."

Several of *Entropy*'s reviewers admired Rifkin's message, but felt that the metaphorical framework of his opinions was simplistic and unnecessary. "Rifkin's excursion into the implications of entropy is wild and undisciplined in its evangelical fervor. It is probably wrong on a score of points. But for all its faults, [*Entropy*] is an important book and a stimulating one," assessed Woods, who believed Rifkin was "fundamentally . . . correct in his appraisal of the dilemmas confronting Western society and also right in pointing the way to a likely remedy for our ailments." "It is as a prophetic jeremiad that this book should be read," remarked *New York Times Book Review*'s Carroll Pursell Jr., who similarly believed Rifkin to be "profoundly correct" in stating that Western civilization should, in Pursell's words, "abandon pride for humility, and use not more than our fair share of the world's remaining energy so that there can be a future."

Rifkin's next book, *Algeny,* was written with Nicanor Perlas and extended *Entropy*'s futuristic outlook. Its title is a play on the word alchemy, from the medieval quest to convert ordinary metals into gold, and refers to the process by which future scientists will design the genetic structures of living things. According to Rifkin, Western man's Judeo-Christian heritage of believing himself to have dominion over the earth provides the rationale for his

attempts to control all facets of life. But pointing to advances made in animal breeding and human reproductive technology, Rifkin describes a future in which parents have the option, and perhaps even the obligation, to design their offspring's genetic composition. He claims that such control over progeny marks the replacement of the natural process of evolution by new paradigms of human control and efficiency—paradigms which regard life as little more than a manufactured product. "Genetic engineering is a grasp at more power than human beings can or ought to handle," Rifkin told Harry Cook in a *Detroit Free Press* interview. "Why can't we just learn to live with God's creation?"

Algeny proved to be one of Rifkin's most controversial books, eliciting often emotional responses from its reviewers. In widely varying reactions, several critics acknowledged Rifkin's position, but some vehemently rejected its intellectual validity. While an *Esquire* reviewer deemed *Algeny* "an unusually intelligent book," David Graber wrote in the *Los Angeles Times Book Review* that the work "is a shameless potpourri of misinformation and faulty logic," scoffing that the author "misrepresents the discipline of biology when he baldly states that the central thesis of biology has been tossed out." "Everything in *Algeny* is possible, but little is real," complained Mark Czarnecki in *Maclean's,* venturing that "the book is pop science at its best and worst, provocative in conception and thoroughly banal in execution." The most scathing response, however, came in a *Discover* article titled "On the Origin of Specious Critics," written by Stephen Jay Gould, a respected Harvard biologist who took issue with Rifkin's arguments. Gould accused Rifkin of using, as quoted in *Time,* "every debater's trick in the book to mischaracterize and trivialize his opposition, and to place his own dubious claims in a rosy light." Although the scientist said he did not disagree with Rifkin's appeal to science to maintain the evolutionary lineages of all living things, Gould judged *Algeny* "a cleverly constructed tract of anti-intellectual propaganda masquerading as scholarship."

Undaunted by the harsh criticism, Rifkin followed *Algeny* with *Time Wars: The Primary Conflict in Human History,* a work he considers the culmination of his previous efforts. Rifkin identifies the frantic pace of modern life epitomized by the split-second processing capabilities of computers as the source of anxiety and stress-related disease. "You cannot press the human species into a nanosecond-programmed future without tremendous rebellion, biologically, emotionally and spiritually," Rifkin contended. On a global scale, Rifkin linked environmental devastation to contemporary preoccupation with speed and competition: "We have reached a point at which we are producing and consuming at such an accelerated rate that nature can't possibly recycle and replenish at the pace we're demanding." Again critical response was mixed, with reviewers appreciating the importance of Rifkin's ideas while questioning the adequacy of his scholarship.

Rifkin remains philosophical about the often negative appraisals of his work and responses to the controversial lawsuits, petitions, and coalitions he has generated. "It all boils down to faith. . . . I know I'm in the minority. What I believe is heresy today," he said in the *New Republic.* But Rifkin continues to advance his ideas publicly, he told *Science Digest*'s Andrew Revkin, because of his conviction that genetic engineering is "a question for the human species to deal with. . . . If we can't engage the entire human race in this set of discussions, then there's never going to be another discussion worthy of public comment."

In recent years Rifkin has joined the growing number of ecologist-writers who have tried to draw attention to issues of resource management in what they consider to be a time of global crisis. In Rifkin's case his concerns led to the publication of his 1992 book *Beyond Beef: The Rise and Fall of the Cattle Culture.* This work attacks the cattle industry as one of the world's most egregious sources of environmental waste and ecosystem destruction. Rifkin demonstrates that more grain is grown in America to feed cattle than to feed people, that rain forests in both Africa and South America have been felled to graze cattle, and that the production of beef depletes soil and wastes water and energy. In a *Washington Post Book World* review of *Beyond Beef,* Colman McCarthy wrote: "If fresh thinking and well-reasoned arguments can cause conversions, [Rifkin's] will do it. Combining reliable research with logical conclusions, he offers enough economic, medical, environmental and ethical arguments to persuade any open-minded person to pass by the meat (en)-counter." Other critics, however, stated that while Rifkin's topic is relevant, he uses faulty reasoning, exaggeration, and over-generalizations in his arguments.

Several of Rifkin's other works enlarge upon his environmental concerns. *Voting Green: Your Complete Environmental Guide to Making Political Choices in the 90's,* co-authored with his wife Carol Grunewald Rifkin, publicizes the voting records of politicians on any issue that has an effect on the environment, including pollution legislation, labor laws, farm policy, and foreign policy. The author explained in *Publishers Weekly* that "when we talk green, it's a framework for reassessing a whole range of issues that affect human beings." *The Green Lifestyle Handbook,* edited by Rifkin, offers practical suggestions for energy conservation within middle-class American homes. *Biosphere Politics: A New Consciousness for a New Century,* the most wide-ranging of Rifkin's environmental works, examines how the modern worldview has impacted the earth's dwindling resources. Rifkin told *Publishers*

Weekly: "I'm using a whole range of cultural and anthropological markers in the last five centuries to understand how we've enclosed ourselves step by step from the world, our own bodies and then our own consciousness. The reason I did that book was to suggest that at the next stage of history we have to reopen the commons."

Rifkin turns to technological issues in *The End of Work: The Decline of the Global Labor Force and the Dawn of the Post-Market Era.* In this work Rifkin asserts that computers and other advanced technologies are displacing millions of workers throughout the world and that they could, in turn, cause widespread unemployment. While most critics agreed that Rifkin raises some legitimate concerns, they noted that he often does not support or document his claims and that he fails to address the positive economic aspects of computer technology. Philip Mattera of *Nation,* for example, stated that "the problem for Rifkin is that the immediate evidence seems to go against him. . . . The U.S. labor force does not appear to be shrinking. The number of employed persons is at the highest level ever." *Los Angeles Times Book Review* critic James Flanigan stated that while the book is "full of rhetorical statistics and misleading arguments" it is "worth considering because it addresses a question that has aroused widespread anxiety: Will advancing technology bring good jobs and decent pay for all workers?"

In an interview with *CA,* Rifkin described the goals of his writings and political activities: "What we're trying to do is take a critical look at the world view of Western civilization; ask some fundamental questions about how well it is working; make a reflective, introspective examination of its components, the values and the principles; and, if need be, redefine some of the values thoughtfully and respectfully," he said. "Our goal is to help develop a new kind of value framework for a new philosophy of science technology and economic policy. We take a look at the major transitions in science, technology, and economics and look at their broad cultural, social and ethical impacts." He noted, "It is possible to develop a philosophy of science and technology that is quite different from the one we entertain in the modern age but is nevertheless sophisticated, intelligent, thoughtful, and, in the end, respectful to the dignity of living things on the planet."

BIOGRAPHICAL/CRITICAL SOURCES:

BOOKS

Rifkin, Jeremy, *Time Wars: The Primary Conflict in Human History,* Holt, 1987.

PERIODICALS

Business Week, July 28, 1986.
Chicago Tribune, September 23, 1987.
Critic, March 15, 1981.

Detroit Free Press, August 30, 1983.
Discover, January, 1985.
Esquire, August, 1983.
Harper's, September, 1987.
Journal and Courier (West Lafayette, IN), September 20, 1987.
Los Angeles Times, July 31, 1987.
Los Angeles Times Book Review, June 19, 1983; March 22, 1992, p. 1; March 12, 1995, pp. 2-3.
Maclean's, August 1, 1983.
Nation, November 4, 1978; February 9, 1980; April 3, 1995, pp. 463-65.
New Republic, September 16, 1978; December 10, 1984.
New Statesman & Society, August 5, 1994, pp. 37-38.
Newsweek, May 19, 1975; May 4, 1987.
New York Review of Books, April 9, 1992, pp. 9-13.
New York Times, May 17, 1984; August 20, 1986; April 2, 1987; April 26, 1987; June 9, 1987; September 1, 1987; October 16, 1988, p. 38.
New York Times Book Review, October 26, 1980; April 22, 1990, p. 44.
Observer (Toms River, NJ), September 18, 1987.
Progressive, May, 1991, pp. 38-41.
Publishers Weekly, February 24, 1992, pp. 33-34; November 28, 1994, p. 49.
Science, June 24, 1983; October 10, 1986.
Science Digest, May, 1985.
Time, April 21, 1986; September 14, 1987.
Times Literary Supplement, May 13, 1988.
U.S. Medicine, November, 1986.
U.S. News & World Report, October 8, 1984.
Washington Post, May 27, 1983; June 8, 1983; July 16, 1986; September 26, 1986; January 19, 1988.
Washington Post Book World, May 31, 1992, p. 7.
Washington Post Magazine, January 17, 1988.*

*   *   *

RODGERS, Harrell R(oss), Jr. 1939-

PERSONAL: Born August 25, 1939, in Columbus, MS; son of Harrell Ross and Eunice Rodgers; married Lynne Wyatt Parsons (a district attorney). *Education:* University of Houston, B.A., 1963, M.A., 1964; University of Iowa, Ph.D., 1968.

ADDRESSES: Home—138 Whipple, Bellaire, TX 77401. *Office*—Department of Political Science, University of Houston, Houston, TX 77004.

CAREER: Sam Houston State College (now University), Huntsville, TX, instructor in political science, 1964-65; University of Georgia, Athens, assistant professor, 1968-70, associate professor of political science, 1970-71; University of Missouri—St. Louis, associate professor,

1971-73, professor of political science, 1974-75, chair of department, 1974-75; University of Houston, Houston, TX, professor, 1975—, chair of department of political science, 1983-86, dean of College of Social Sciences, 1986-94. Visiting lecturer, University of Houston, summer, 1965. Has presented numerous research papers at conventions; regularly reviews grant proposals for National Science Foundation; regularly reviews manuscripts and proposals for publishing houses.

MEMBER: American Political Science Association, Policy Studies Association, Midwest Political Science Association, Southern Political Science Association, Western Political Science Association, Southwestern Political Science Association (member of awards committee, 1976-77; chair of awards committee, 1977-78), Alpha Chi, Phi Gamma Mu, Phi Sigma Alpha.

AWARDS, HONORS: Research grants from National Science Foundation, 1967, 1973, Meyer Foundation, 1969, Social Science Institute, and Ford Foundation; Phi Sigma Alpha Award, Southwestern Political Science Foundation, for best paper presented at 1972 meetings, co-winner for second best paper presented at 1973 meetings, and for second best paper (with Charles S. Bullock) presented at 1974 meetings; selected as outstanding teacher by students, University of Missouri, 1972, 1973, 1974, 1975.

WRITINGS:

Community Conflict, Public Opinion and the Law, C. E. Merrill (Columbus, OH), 1969.
(Editor with Robert Golembiewski and Charles S. Bullock) *The New Politics: Polarization or Utopia?,* McGraw (New York City), 1970.
(With Bullock) *Law and Social Change: Civil Rights and Their Consequences,* McGraw, 1972.
(Editor with Bullock) *Black Political Attitudes: Implications for Political Support,* Markham (Chicago), 1972.
(With Bullock) *Racial Equality in America: In Search of an Unfulfilled Goal,* Goodyear Publishing (Pacific Palisades, CA), 1975.
(Editor and contributor) *Racism and Inequality: The Policy Alternatives,* W. H. Freeman (San Francisco), 1975.
(With Bullock) *Coercion to Compliance: A Cost-Benefit Analysis,* Lexington Books (Lexington, MA), 1976.
Crisis in Democracy: A Policy Analysis of American Government, Addison-Wesley (Reading, MA), 1978.
Poverty amid Plenty: A Political and Economic Analysis, Random House (New York City), 1979.
(Editor and contributor) *The Sunbelt Society,* Foundation for the Study of Independent Social Ideas (New York), 1980.

(With Michael Harrington) *Unfinished Democracy: The American Political Process,* Scott, Foresman (Glenview, IL), 1981, 2nd edition, 1985.

The Cost of Human Neglect: America's Welfare Failure, M. E. Sharpe (Armonk, NY), 1982.

(With Howard Leichter) *American Public Policy in a Comparative Context,* McGraw, 1984.

(Editor and contributor) *Public Policy and Social Institutions,* JAI Press (Greenwich, CT), 1984.

Poor Women, Poor Families: The Economic Plight of America's Female-Headed Households, M. E. Sharpe, 1986, 2nd edition, 1990.

(Editor) *Beyond Welfare: New Approaches to the Problem of Poverty in America,* M. E. Sharpe, 1988.

(Editor with Gregory Weiher) *Rural Poverty: Special Causes and Policy Reforms,* Greenwood Press (Westport, CT), 1989.

(Editor with Tom DeGregori) *Poverty Policy in Developing Nations,* JAI Press, 1995.

Poor Women, Poor Children: American Poverty in the '90s, M. E. Sharpe, 1996.

OTHER

Contributor to numerous books, including *Political Attitudes and Public Opinion,* edited by Dan Nimmo and Charles Bonjean, McKay (New York City), 1972; *Desegregation to Integration: A Method,* edited by Angelo Puricelli, University of Missouri at St. Louis Extension Division, 1975; *American Political Institutions in the 1970s,* edited by Demetrios Caraley, Columbia University Press (New York City), 1976; *Public Law and Public Policy,* edited by John Gardiner, Praeger, 1977; *The American Court System: Readings in Judicial Process and Behavior,* by Sheldon Goldman and Austin Sarat, W. H. Freeman, 1978; *Elite Deviance,* by D. Stanley Eitzen and David Simon, Allyn & Bacon (Newton, MA), 1981; *Encyclopedia of Public Policy,* edited by Stuart Nigel, Dekker (New York City), 1983; *Implementation of Civil Rights Policy,* edited by Bullock and Charles M. Lamb, Brooks/Cole (Monterey, CA), 1984; *Futures for the Welfare State,* edited by Norman Furniss, Indiana University Press (Bloomington), 1986; *Rural Poverty and Public Policy: A Comparative Perspective,* edited by Aruna N. Michie, Greenwood Press, 1987; *Perspectives on American and Texas Politics,* edited by Donald Lutz and Kent Tedin, Kendall-Hunt (Dubuque, IA), 1989; *Encyclopedia of Policy Studies,* edited by Stuart Nagel, Dekker, 1994; and *Encyclopedia of the Future,* edited by George T. Kurian and Graham Molitor, Macmillan (New York City), 1995.

Contributor of articles and reviews to numerous periodicals, including *International Journal of Group Tensions, Dissent, Journal of Black Studies, American Journal of Political Science, Integrated Education, American Politics Quarterly,* and *Politics and Society.* Member of editorial board, *Youth and Society,* 1975-93, *Journal of Politics,* 1978-84, and *Policy Studies Journal,* 1989—.

* * *

RODITI, Edouard Herbert 1910-1992

PERSONAL: Born June 6 (one source says June 5), 1910, in Paris, France; died of injuries sustained in an accident, May 10, 1992, in Paris, France (one source says Cadiz, Spain); son of Oscar and Violet (Waldheim) Roditi. *Education:* Attended Balliol College, Oxford, England, 1927-28; University of Chicago, B.A., 1939; graduate study at University of California, Berkeley.

CAREER: Writer and translator. Served as interpreter at war crimes trial in Nuremberg, Germany, following World War II. Affiliated with Voice of America in New York.

AWARDS, HONORS: Grant from Gulbenkian Foundation, 1969.

WRITINGS:

Oscar Wilde: A Critical Guidebook, New Directions, 1947, revised edition, 1987.

Dialogues on Art (collection of interviews; also see below), Secker & Warburg (London), 1960, Horizon Press (New York City), 1961.

Joachim Karsch, Verlag Gebr. Mann, 1960.

Selbstanalyse eines Sammlers, Galerie der Spiegel (Cologne), 1960.

De l'Homosexualite, Editions Sedimo, 1962.

(Editor) Ambrose Bierce, *Mein Lieblingsmord,* Insel (Frankfurt), 1963.

Magellan of the Pacific (biography), Faber (London and Winchester, MA), 1972, McGraw (New York City), 1973.

The Delights of Turkey: Twenty Tales (short stories), New Directions, 1974.

(Editor) Hamri, *Tales of Joujouka,* Capra (Santa Barbara, CA), 1975.

The Disorderly Poet (essays), Capra, 1975.

Meetings with Conrad, Press Pegacycle (Los Angeles), 1977.

More Dialogues on Art (also see below), Ross-Erikson (Santa Barbara, CA), 1983.

Propos sur l'Art, Jose Corti, 1987.

Dialogues (contains revised selections from *Dialogues on Art* and *More Dialogues on Art),* Bedford Arts (San Francisco, CA), 1990.

Dialoge uber Kunst, Suhrkamp (Frankfurt), 1991.

Art critic for *L'Arche.* Contributing editor of *Antaeus, European Judaism, Expatriate Review,* and *Shantih.* Cofounder of literary journal, *Das Lot,* 1947.

POETRY

Poems for F, Editions du Sagittaire, 1935.

Prison within Prison: Three Elegies on Hebrew Themes, J. A. Decker, 1941.

(With Paul Goodman and Meyer Liben) *Pieces of Three,* 5 x 8 Press, 1942.

Poems, 1928-1948, New Directions, 1949.

New Hieroglyphic Tales: Prose Poems, Kayak (Santa Cruz, CA), 1968.

Surrealist Poetry and Prose, Black Sparrow Press (Santa Barbara, CA), 1973.

Thrice Chosen: Poems on Jewish Themes, Tree Books (Berkeley, CA), 1974.

Emperor of Midnight, Black Sparrow Press, 1974.

In a Lost World, Black Sparrow Press, 1978.

The Temptations of a Saint (prose poem), Ettan Press, 1980.

New and Old Testaments (prose poems), Red Ozier Press, 1983.

Etre un Autre, privately printed, 1983.

The Journal of an Apprentice Cabbalist, CLOUD, 1991.

Aphorisms: (Or Life with God the Father), Invisible-Red Hill, 1991.

Choose Your Own World (prose poems), Asylum Arts Press (Santa Maria, CA), 1993.

TRANSLATOR

Andre Breton, *Young Cherry Trees Secured against Hares,* View Editions, 1946.

Albert Memmi, *The Pillar of Salt,* Elek, 1956.

Ernest Namenyi, *The Essence of Jewish Art,* Yoseloff, 1960.

Yashar Kemal, *Memed, My Hawk,* Harvill Press, 1961.

Pablo Picasso, *Toros y Toreros,* Thames & Hudson (London), 1961.

Robert Schmutzler, *Art Nouveau,* Thames & Hudson, 1964.

Carlos Suares, *Genesis Rejuvenated,* Menard Press, 1973.

(With Paul Celan) Fernando Pessoa, *Selected Poems,* Suhrkamp, 1983.

Yunus Emre, *The Wandering Fool: Sufi Poems of a Thirteenth-Century Turkish Durvish* (selected poems of a medieval Turkish Sufi mystic), Cadmus Editions (Santa Barbara, CA), 1984.

Horace Walpole, *Contes Hieroglyphiques,* Jose Corti (Paris), 1985.

No Matter No Fact, New Directions, 1988.

Suleiman the Magnificent, *Soliman le Magnifique, Poete* (selected poems), Dost Yayinlari (Istanbul), 1989.

Alain Bosquet, *God's Torment: Poems,* Ohio University Press (Columbus, OH), 1994.

SIDELIGHTS: During his lifetime, Edouard Herbert Roditi was rarely accorded recognition for his own poetry.

He was primarily identified as the friend, translator, and editor of many better-known Surrealist poets of the 1930s. Roditi wrote fluently in several languages and was able to translate from more than a dozen. He produced the first English translation of the French poet Andre Breton's works, and this version is still considered the finest edition available in English. Yet as Thomas Epstein pointed out in *Alea,* "Roditi was not merely 'associated' with Surrealism but, at the very least, stands as one of America's most important authentic Surrealists. Equally underappreciated are his several hundred essays on art and literature, his scholarly studies of Ladino and Medieval literature and culture, his fine prose fiction, and his biographies of Wilde and Magellan."

Choose Your Own World, a book of prose poems, was published the year after Roditi's death and has been praised by reviewers as some of the author's finest writing. "Absurdity and dream were central concerns for Roditi," noted Epstein, "and no more so than in [this] remarkable collection of prose poems, stories, and fables." In one typical piece, "Roditi's Metamorphosis," the narrator falls asleep as a bachelor, awakes as an unhappily married man, and continues through a series of transformations that render him a monogamous homosexual, a bum, a baby awaiting a diaper change, a fighting cat, a plant, and finally, a word. "In this story all the qualities of Roditi's mind and art are at work; his literariness, his ironic sense of humor, his despair, his persistent philosophical probings of identity," stated Epstein. A writer for *Review of Contemporary Fiction* called the collection "playful and serious, fantastic and reflective, sad and hilarious, satiric and gentle, political and remote." Nanos Valaoritis declared in *American Book Review:* "All told and said, *Choose Your Own World* has to be one of the most macabre and decadent pieces of surrealist writing of this century." Valaoritis further emphasized that he could not imagine "anyone trying to outdo or continue this style or genre after [Roditi. The pieces in *Choose Your Own World*] seem to me to seal their species once and for all in a variegated and colorful mausoleum of ingenious ideas and devices, whose eccentricity cannot be surpassed."

Roditi was born in Paris to parents who held American citizenship, although neither of them had ever been in the United States. Born an Italian citizen in Constantinople, Roditi's Jewish father was educated in France and obtained his U.S. citizenship through his father, who moved to America and left his family behind. Roditi's mother, born in France, was of French-Catholic and German-Jewish extraction; she became a British subject as a young girl, then gained American citizenship through her marriage. Roditi himself never set foot in the United States until he was an adult. In a *Contemporary Authors Autobiography Series* essay, he commented: "Was I originally destined to be Christian or Jew, heterosexual or homosexual, French, English, or American? And what have I finally become? As an American poet, I'm consistently neglected by nearly all American anthologists, who appear to believe erroneously that I'm either English or French. French and Italian anthologists, on the other hand, sometimes include me in their anthologies of contemporary American poetry. Only the FBI and its sinister offspring, the CIA . . . have at all times considered me American enough to deserve the dubious privilege of their attentions."

BIOGRAPHICAL/CRITICAL SOURCES:

BOOKS

Contemporary Authors Autobiography Series, Volume 14, Gale, 1991, pp. 237-87.

PERIODICALS

Alea, fall, 1993, pp. 132-43.
American Book Review, August-September, 1993, pp. 16-30.
Review of Contemporary Fiction, summer, 1992, pp. 210-11.
World Literature Today, summer, 1993, p. 616.

OBITUARIES:

PERIODICALS

New York Times, May 23, 1992, p. 11.
Times (London), May 18, 1992, p. 15.

* * *

ROOD, Ronald (N.) 1920-

PERSONAL: Surname rhymes with "food"; born July 7, 1920, in Torrington, CT; son of Nellis Frost (a life insurance underwriter) and Bessie (Chamberlain) Rood; married Margaret Bruce (a teacher), December 21, 1942; children: Janice, Thomas Elliot, Alison, Roger Warren. *Education:* University of Connecticut, B.S., 1941, M.S., 1949.

ADDRESSES: Home and office—R. R. 1, Box 740, Lincoln, VT 05443.

CAREER: Writer. Long Island Agricultural and Technical Institute, Farmingdale, NY, instructor in biology, 1949-53; Grolier Enterprises, New York City, research editor, 1954-64; Middlebury College, Middlebury, VT, instructor in biology, 1956-58; commentator on Vermont Public Radio program *The Human Touch,* 1989—. Church choir director. *Military service:* U.S. Army Air Forces, fighter pilot, World War II; received Air Medal.

MEMBER: Forest and Field, American Forestry Association, National Wildlife Federation, Outdoor Writers As-

sociation of America, League of Vermont Writers (president, 1965-67, 1975), Vermont Natural Resources Council, Vermont Academy of Arts and Sciences.

WRITINGS:

The How and Why Wonder Book of Insects, Grosset, 1960.
The How and Why Wonder Book of Ants and Bees, Grosset, 1962.
Land Alive: The World of Nature at One Family's Door, Stephen Greene (Brattleboro, VT), 1962.
The How and Why Wonder Book of Butterflies and Moths, Grosset, 1963.
The Loon in My Bathtub, Stephen Greene, 1964, revised edition, New England Press (Shelburne, VT), 1986.
The Sea and Its Wonderful Creatures, Whitman Publishing (Racine, WI), 1965.
Bees, Bugs and Beetles: The Arrow Book of Insects, Four Winds (New York City), 1965.
Hundred Acre Welcome: The Story of a Chincoteague Pony, Stephen Greene, 1967.
Vermont Life Book of Nature, Stephen Greene, 1967.
How Do You Spank a Porcupine?, Trident, 1969, revised edition, New England Press, 1983.
Animal Champions, Grosset, 1969.
Answers about Insects, Grosset, 1969.
Animals Nobody Loves, Stephen Greene, 1971, revised edition, New England Press, 1987.
Who Wakes the Groundhog?, Norton (New York City), 1973.
May I Keep This Clam, Mother? It Followed Me Home, Simon & Schuster (New York City), 1973.
Good Things Are Happening, Stephen Greene, 1975.
It's Going to Sting Me, Simon & Schuster, 1976.
Possum in the Parking Lot, Simon & Schuster, 1977.
Elephant Bones and Lonely Hearts, Stephen Greene, 1977.
Laska, Norton, 1980.
Ron Rood's Vermont: An Easygoing Guide to the Outdoors in the Green Mountain State, New England Press, 1987.
Beachcombers All, New England Press, 1990.
Tide Pools, HarperCollins (New York City), 1993.
Wetlands, HarperCollins, 1994.

Contributor to numerous periodicals, including *Reader's Digest, Coronet, Audubon Magazine, Christian Herald, New York Times, Pageant,* and *Vermont Life.*

SIDELIGHTS: Ronald Rood once told *CA:* "I paid $5.00 for my typewriter years ago. Now, two dozen books later, I'm still trying to get my money back!"

ROOT, Phyllis 1949-

PERSONAL: Born February 14, 1949, in Fort Wayne, IN; daughter of John Howard and Esther (Trout) Root; married James Elliott Hansa; children: Amelia Christin Hansa, Ellen Rose Root. *Education:* Valparaiso University, B.A., 1971.

ADDRESSES: Home—3842 Bloomington Ave. S., Minneapolis, MN 55407.

CAREER: Writer. Worked as architectural drafter, costume maker, bicycle repair person, and administrative assistant.

MEMBER: Authors League of America, Authors Guild, Society of Children's Book Writers and Illustrators.

WRITINGS:

FOR JUVENILES

Hidden Places, Carnival Press (Minneapolis, MN), 1983.
(With Carol A. Marron) *Gretchen's Grandma,* Carnival Press, 1983.
(With Marron) *Just One of the Family,* Carnival Press, 1984.
(With Marron) *No Place for a Pig,* Carnival Press, 1984.
My Cousin Charlie, Carnival Press, 1984.
Moon Tiger, Holt (New York City), 1985.
Soup for Supper, Harper (New York City), 1986.
Galapagos, Carnival/Crestwood, 1988.
Great Basin, Carnival/Crestwood, 1988.
Glacier, Carnival/Crestwood, 1989.
The Old Red Rocking Chair, Arcade (New York City), 1991.
The Listening Silence, Harper, 1992.
Coyote and the Magic Words, Lothrop (New York City), 1993.
Sam Who Was Swallowed by a Shark, Candlewick, 1994.

Contributor to *Cricket* and *Children's Magic Window.*

WORK IN PROGRESS: Paula Bunyan, a tall tale.

SIDELIGHTS: Phyllis Root told *CA:* "As far back as I can remember, I made up stories, poems, and songs. I had a wonderful fifth-grade teacher who encouraged my writing. It wasn't until I was thirty, however, that I learned how to write. I took a class in writing for children and young adults taught by Marion Bauer. She taught me both the tools of writing and also how to write from the heart. For me this is the most important part of writing, this chance to share a little bit of who I am and what I care about with whoever reads my stories.

"I have been writing ever since, whenever I get the chance. I write at my word processor, I write on the backs of old envelopes, I write in my head when I can't sleep at night. *Coyote and the Magic Words* is really a story about story-telling, about how to create worlds with nothing more than our words.

"Some stories come after endless work and rewrites. A few come almost unbidden out of wherever it is stories come, like gifts waiting to be unwrapped. They are like my children—I don't necessarily understand them, but I feel blessed to have been given them."

*   *   *

ROSEN, Charles (Welles) 1927-

PERSONAL: Born May 5, 1927, in New York, NY; son of Irwin and Anita (Gerber) Rosen. *Education:* Attended Juilliard School of Music, 1933-1938; Princeton University, B.A. (summa cum laude), 1947, M.A., 1949, Ph.D., 1951.

ADDRESSES: Home—New York, NY. *Office*—Department of Music, State University of New York at Stony Brook, Stony Brook, NY 11790.

CAREER: Concert pianist, 1951—; Massachusetts Institute of Technology, Cambridge, MA, assistant professor of modern languages, 1953-55; State University of New York at Stony Brook, Stony Brook, NY, professor of music, 1971—; writer. Messenger Lecturer at Cornell University, 1975; University of California, Berkeley, Ernest Bloch Professor, 1977; Harvard University, Charles Eliot Norton Professor of Poetry, 1980-81; University of Chicago, professor of music and social thought, 1986; Oxford University, George Eastman Professor, 1987-88. Pianist in solo recital and with numerous orchestras in both concert performances and recordings.

MEMBER: National Academy of Arts and Sciences.

AWARDS, HONORS: Fulbright fellowship, 1951-53; American Society of Composers, Authors, and Publishers, Deems Taylor Award, and National Book Award in arts and letters, both 1972, both for *The Classical Style: Haydn, Mozart, Beethoven;* Guggenheim fellowship, 1973; Edison Prize, 1974; D.Mus., from Trinity College (Dublin), 1976, University of Leeds, 1978, and Durham University, 1980.

WRITINGS:

The Classical Style: Haydn, Mozart, Beethoven, Viking (New York City), 1971.
Arnold Schoenberg (monograph), Viking, 1975 (published in England as *Schoenberg,* Calder & Boyars (London), 1975).
Sonata Forms, Norton (New York City), 1982.
(With Henri Zerner) *Romanticism and Realism: The Mythology of Nineteenth-Century Art* (essays), Viking, 1984.

The Frontiers of Meaning: Three Informal Lectures on Music, Hill & Wang (New York City), 1994.

Contributor to periodicals, including *New York Review of Books.*

SIDELIGHTS: Charles Rosen has distinguished himself as both a concert pianist and a National Book Award-winner in a career that includes performances, lectures, and written studies of such composers as Beethoven, Haydn, Chopin, and Schoenberg. *Washington Post* critic Joseph McLellan calls Rosen "a thinking man's performer who uses his brain as much as his muscles," adding that in his books, recordings and lectures, the artist "has harmonized the work of a scholar with that of a well-equipped performer."

Born in New York City, Rosen attended the Juilliard School of Music as a child. In adolescence he studied piano under the celebrated instructor Moritz Rosenthal, a former pupil of Franz Liszt. Rosen continued his musical training while at Princeton University, where he earned a doctorate in French literature in 1951. That same year he made his professional debut as a concert pianist in New York's Town Hall, and he recorded his first album, *Debussy Etudes.* Since that time, Rosen has been recognized as a pianist of commanding technique and sensitivity. He has also earned respect for his wide-ranging repertoire, which stretches from works of Baroque master Johann Sebastian Bach to those of modern composers such as Pierre Boulez. In addition, Rosen has assayed the staples of piano literature— compositions by Ludwig van Beethoven and those of Romantics such as Robert Schumann—and has thus been seen as an artist of great versatility as well as one of great technical and interpretative mastery. McLellan notes that, perhaps by virtue of his academic background, Rosen "sometimes can sound more analytic than deeply involved, more perceptive than technically dazzling."

Though probably best known as a performer, Rosen has also gained recognition as a critic. His first book, 1971's *The Classical Style: Haydn, Mozart, Beethoven,* is an analysis of musical language as developed by three great composers. He argues that the development of each artist's musical language was predicated on the "symmetrical resolution of opposing forces," and he illustrates his thesis through detailed analysis of examples from genres such as symphonies, string quartets, and even operas. Alan Tyson, writing in the *New York Review of Books,* deemed Rosen's effort "a formidable task: first to describe and then to explain and trace the development and maturation of what has so far proved the richest stylistic achievement in Western music." Tyson wrote that the book succeeds "in such a way and on such a scale as to make it hard for anyone who cares about the music characterized here to remain without illumination." Similarly, E. T. Cone reported in the *New York Times Book Review* that *The Classical Style* is a "thoughtful and illuminating study." *Nation* reviewer Robert Lilienfeld, who complained that Rosen's rhetoric was "elusive and allusive," nonetheless conceded that the book contains "brilliant observations on particular works." Lilienfeld added that *The Classical Style* is "genuinely valuable for its details, for its incidental insights." *The Classical Style* won the National Book Award in 1972.

In 1975 Rosen completed the monograph *Arnold Schoenberg,* which he wrote for Viking's "Modern Masters" series. In this short book, Rosen considered Schoenberg's development from expressionism to atonality and from serialism to neoclassicism. He also assessed the composer's entire career within the context of European musical history. Some reviewers of *Arnold Schoenberg* argued that the book offered an incisive analysis of the composer and his work. Donal Henahan affirmed in the *New York Times Book Review,* "What Mr. Rosen does, far better than one could reasonably expect in so concise a book, is not only to elucidate Schoenberg's composing techniques and artistic philosophy but to place them in history." Robert Craft, in his commentary for the *New York Review of Books,* noted that *Arnold Schoenberg* would prove most useful to musicians and musicologists, but he praised Rosen's exposition as "admirably lucid" and commended his "directness in identifying and confronting central issues." Craft ultimately commended *Arnold Schoenberg* as "one of the most brilliant monographs ever to be published on any composer."

In Rosen's third book, *Sonata Forms,* he traces the development of the sonata structure. He argues that the nineteenth-century definition of the sonata is woefully imprecise and that a proper definition of the term encompasses several interdependent forms. In addition, he analyzes stylistic differences, illustrating how the first movements from different sonatas may differ substantially. *Sonata Forms* was praised by some reviewers as a provocative and compelling volume. "After studying such analyses," wrote Edward Rothstein in the *New York Times Book Review,* "one's ears return to the music more educated, more aware of the life behind the forms." Joseph Kerman, writing in the *New York Review of Books,* was even more enthusiastic, contending that "to familiar and unfamiliar music alike Rosen brings not only an uncommonly refined ear and sensibility but also . . . unerring insight into just the features that make the music special and fine."

Rosen's *Romanticism and Realism: The Mythology of Nineteenth-Century Art* presents a wide-ranging assessment of artistic schools including the present avant-garde. With collaborator Henri Zerner, a museum curator, Rosen explores the development of nineteenth-century art—music, painting and sculpture, and literature—as the result of artists' continual effort to avoid convention. This pursuit of the unknown and socially unacceptable is traced from romanticism to realism to today's avant-garde art. Marina Vaizey, writing in the *New York Times Book Review,* described Rosen and Zerner's volume as a collection of "audacious, ambitious essays." *Spectator* reviewer Marc Jordan found the volume appealing and refreshing, observing that "what is most impressive about the articles which make up *Romanticism and Realism* is their sense of engagement." Jordan added, "At a time when art criticism and art history seem to have drawn away in to opposite corners, it is healthy to be reminded that serious writing about the art of the past can be in the best sense 'partial, passionate, and political.' "

In 1993 Rosen delivered a series of lectures in Rome that were sponsored by the *New York Review of Books.* Three of these were published in 1994 as *The Frontiers of Meaning: Three Informal Lectures on Music.* In this work Rosen tackles the difficult question of how we understand music. Arguing that since each new style of music creates its own meaning, methods of musical analysis must change with the times. He illustrates his points with examples from Beethoven, Mozart, and Schubert, as well as the challenging musical art of today. A *Kirkus Reviews* contributor writes of the work: "For wit, intelligence, and original thought . . . Rosen has few rivals."

Despite enjoying some prominence as a critic, Rosen insists that he is primarily a pianist. Interviewed by the *New York Times* in 1977, Rosen referred to writing as "a sort of hobby." He explained: "At the piano, if you practice 10 hours a day, then you have no time to write. I really can't

practice more than about four to five. I can play the piano for eight to 10 hours a day, but I can't practice for that long. So I have to do something with my time."

BIOGRAPHICAL/CRITICAL SOURCES:

BOOKS

Dubal, David, *Reflections from the Keyboard: The World of the Concert Pianists,* Summit Books (New York City), 1984.

Rosen, Charles, *The Classical Style: Haydn, Mozart, Beethoven,* Viking (New York City), 1971.

PERIODICALS

Christian Century, October 22, 1975; May 30, 1984.
Christian Science Monitor, May 24, 1976.
Clavier, March 1984.
Kirkus Reviews, May 1, 1994, p. 617.
Library Journal, June 15, 1994, p. 71.
Nation, December 6, 1971.
Newsweek, May 3, 1971.
New York Review of Books, June 15, 1972; September 18, 1975; October 23, 1980.
New York Times, October 16, 1977.
New York Times Book Review, May 23, 1971; December 28, 1975; December 21, 1980; April 1, 1984.
Observer (London), May 23, 1976.
Publishers Weekly, June 27, 1994, p. 66.
Spectator, May 26, 1984.
Time, December 29, 1952.
Times Literary Supplement, April 16, 1971; June 10, 1977.
Village Voice, January 4, 1983.
Washington Post, July 17, 1989, p. 12B.*

S

SACK, John 1930-

PERSONAL: Born March 24, 1930, in New York, NY; son of John Jacob (a clerk) and Tracy Rose (Levy) Sack. *Education:* Harvard University, A.B., 1951; Columbia University, graduate study, 1963-64.

ADDRESSES: *Home*—2005 La Brea Ter., Los Angeles, CA 90046. *Agent*—Lois Wallace, Wallace & Sheil Agency, Inc., 177 East 70th St., New York, NY 10021.

CAREER: Writer and journalist. United Press, correspondent in Peru, 1950, Japan and Korea, 1953-54, and Albany, NY, 1954-55; Columbia Broadcasting System, CBS News, documentary writer and producer in New York City and Paris, France, 1961-66; *Esquire*, New York City, correspondent in Vietnam, 1966-67, contributing editor, 1967-78; *Playboy*, Chicago, IL, contributing editor in Los Angeles, 1978—; KCBS-TV, Los Angeles, newswriter and producer, 1982-84. *Military service:* U.S. Army, 1951-53; served in Korea; war correspondent, *Pacific Stars and Stripes*, 1952-55.

MEMBER: Writers Guild of America, Screen Actors Guild, American Federation of Television and Radio Artists.

WRITINGS:

The Butcher, Rinehart, 1952 (published in England as *The Ascent of Yerupaja,* Jenkins [Lancaster, England], 1954).
From Here to Shimbashi, Harper (New York City), 1955.
Report from Practically Nowhere, Harper, 1959.
M, New American Library (New York City), 1967.
Lieutenant Calley, Viking (New York City), 1971 (published in England as *Body Count,* Hutchinson, 1971).
The Man-Eating Machine, Farrar, Straus (New York City), 1973.
Fingerprint, Random House (New York City), 1983.

An Eye for an Eye, Basic Books (New York City), 1993.

Author of television documentaries. Contributor to magazines, including *Harper's, Atlantic Monthly, Holiday, Town and Country, Playboy, Eros,* and *New Yorker.*

WORK IN PROGRESS: "Searching in the People's Republic of the Congo for the last living dinosaurs," and writing about them for the Associated Press, CBS News, *Playboy,* and Random House.

SIDELIGHTS: John Sack told *CA* that his "best or best-known book" is "*M,* which was excerpted in 1966 as the cover story in *Esquire,* the longest article in *Esquire's* history." *M* is the story of "M" Company of the 1st Advanced Infantry Training Brigade. "John Sack followed the company from the inanity of a training inspection at Fort Dix to the senseless killing of a seven-year-old girl in Viet Nam," writes Stewart Kampel in the *New York Times.* "He has produced a gripping, honest account, compassionate and rich, colorful and blackly comic, but with that concerned objectivity that makes for great reportage." Writing in *Book Week,* Dan Wakefield praises *M* as "one of the finest, most perceptive books of reportage in recent years. One must go back to Orwell for appropriate comparisons of journalistic excellence." And Robert Kirsch's *Los Angeles Times* review names *M* as "the whole story, one of the most compelling ever told about men in war. This is the way it is." Sack's *Lieutenant Calley* is the story of the My Lai massacre in Viet Nam. In a letter to *CA,* the author notes that it is his "most infamous book . . . in the course of writing which the federal government arrested and indicted me but never prosecuted me." *Lieutenant Calley* has been translated into German, Spanish, French, Portuguese, Italian, and Finnish.

The 1983 book *Fingerprint* has been compared by reviewers to Laurence Sterne's *Tristam Shandy.* Like that classic, writes Michiko Kakutani in the *New York Times, Fin-*

gerprint "begins with the events leading up to the author's conception and birth, and it similarly boasts a narrative positively crammed with digressions and asides." Kakutani continues: "Gifted with an eye for physical detail and a canny ear for dialogue, Mr. Sack is at his best when he sticks closely to the facts of his own life. . . . It is when he attempts to pontificate on the large evils of society that he becomes trite and moralistic." Reviewing *Fingerprint* in the *Washington Post Book World,* Joseph McLellan criticizes Sack's "polemic, which is . . . a diatribe against what he calls 'efficiency'. . . . In a sense, his complaints resemble what one of his beard follicles might have to say about his efficient habit of shaving. Still, he does write well and there is a germ of truth in what he has to say. . . . In an age when we are teaching computers to become more and more 'user-friendly,' we may hope to see better days ahead—speeded, perhaps, by amorphous howls such as *Fingerprint.*"

"Sack has hung about since the '50's, participating in the kinks and enthusiasms of the succeeding times while writing about them critically but on the whole amiably," notes Richard Eder in the *Los Angeles Times Book Review.* "He is a sunny man, or a sunny writer, at least: *Fingerprint,* though a concentrated denunciation of what he sees as the central fallacy of our civilization, draws its originality not so much from the fierceness or cogency of the denunciation as from its exuberance."

In 1993 Sack became the center of controversy again with the publication of *An Eye for an Eye,* a story of abuse in the internment camps set up by the postwar Communist Polish government to hold ethnic Germans and Poles suspected of collaborating with the Nazis. Some of the commandants of these camps were Polish Communist Jews—including people who had themselves been held in concentration camps during World War II—who took out their resentments on their German prisoners. In a series of interviews with some of these commandants, Sack presented a drastic picture of anti-German brutality that, according to some reviewers, distorted historical truth. In addition, historians complained that Sack's free, journalistic style and the unorthodoxy of his documentation made it difficult or impossible to check his sources.

Basic Books, Sack's publisher, attracted criticism for its sensational marketing of the book and its hurried publication. Sack's book was very nearly never published; according to the author, reports Jon Wiener in the *Nation,* "no one else [but Basic Books] would publish the book: It was rejected by something like a dozen publishers, until Steve Fraser of Basic Books signed it up." One of the reasons that Basic Books accepted *An Eye for an Eye* so quickly was because *60 Minutes* was doing a piece on one of Sack's interviewees. The book was rushed through publication within two months, about one-fourth of the time normally

taken. "The publication date of the book did coincide with the *60 Minutes* broadcast," Wiener explains, "but the result was that the book that Basic published, as Fraser says, was virtually identical to the text that Sack submitted. A manuscript that desperately needed editing got virtually none."

A number of critics agree that the events Sack describes in *An Eye for an Eye* did happen—that some Communist Polish Jews who had been held by the Nazis in concentration camps during World War II were appointed by the Communist government of Poland in 1945 to command camps interning ethnic Germans and suspected German collaborators, and that some of these Polish Jews took their frustrations out on their prisoners. However, they question his conclusions and implications as well as his methods. Daniel Jonah Goldhagen, an assistant professor at Harvard University's school of government and one of Sack's earliest and harshest critics, declares in his review for the *New Republic* that *Eye for an Eye* "strings together facts and pseudo-facts about individual Jews in the aftermath of the Holocaust with the effect of creating a sometimes subtle and sometimes not so subtle indictment of Jews in general." "The book fails disgracefully in much of what it does present—misshapen stories and wild innuendo—and in all of what it does not present, namely a serious consideration of the context and the meaning of the events that it describes," Goldhagen concludes, "and the analytical and moral concepts that it employs." "There's one more problem with Sack's claim that the Jews in his book 'became like Nazis'—they didn't," asserts Wiener. "The Holocaust was not just sadistic SS men whipping and killing Jews; it was bureaucratic, scientific and comprehensive in its mobilization of the resources of Europe's leading industrial society for the purposes of extermination."

Some reviewers attacked Sack's critics, claiming that the Jewish community objected to the presentation of Jews as persecutors of Germans at the end of World War II. According to John Lombardi in *New York* magazine, "Alarms went off that Sack had produced a tract that would prove useful to . . . traditional anti-Semites and right-wing crazies interested in denying the Holocaust and showing that Jews were as 'bad as Nazis': and excitement grew at Basic Books, which signed Sack up, and *60 Minutes,* which dispatched its own researchers to verify Sack's reporting." Carolyn Toll Oppenheim writes in *Progressive* that, although she "questioned the book's failure to blast the Polish Communists" who may have placed the abusive camp commanders in their positions, and objected to the fact that "Sack never refers to the ultimate fate of many of those Polish Jewish Communists," she nonetheless felt that "rather than take on the task of supplying such context, some of Sack's critics chose simply to discredit his entire story." In particular, Oppenheim refers to a *60 Minutes* interview with "Elan Steinberg, director of the World Jewish Congress, [who] told Sack . . . 'You'd better be damn sure you have your evidence there. Because if you don't you're . . . insulting the memory of six million martyrs.' "

Oppenheim herself took a less harsh view of Sack's conclusions. "Inside," she concludes, "the book is far more balanced and empathetic toward the Jewish avengers than the jacket advertises. Sack, a literary journalist, records his interviews and archival research in a novel-like, 'in-your-face' style with recreated dialogue that packs the brutal punch of a war story. . . . What comes out is not nice, and it wasn't meant to be nice. It's meant to try to get to the truth about war, violence, and other ugly things most of us want to ignore."

BIOGRAPHICAL/CRITICAL SOURCES:

PERIODICALS

Book Week, March 12, 1967.
Christian Science Monitor, April 6, 1967.
Los Angeles Times, March 8, 1967.
Los Angeles Times Book Review, January 2, 1983.
Nation, October 23, 1967; June 20, 1994, pp. 878-82.
New Republic, December 27, 1993, pp. 28-34.
New York, May 9, 1994, pp. 18-21.
New York Times, March 7, 1967; January 31, 1983.
New York Times Book Review, May 14, 1967.
Progressive, September, 1994, pp. 39-44.
Washington Post Book World, March 5, 1983.*

*   *   *

SACKS, Oliver (Wolf) 1933-

PERSONAL: Born July 9, 1933, in London, England; immigrated to United States, 1960; British citizen; son of Samuel (a physician) and Muriel Elsie (a physician; maiden name, Landau) Sacks. *Education:* Queen's College, Oxford, B.A., 1954, M.A., B.M., and B.Ch., all 1958; attended University of California, Los Angeles, 1962-65. *Avocational interests:* Swimming, scuba diving, cycling, mountaineering.

ADDRESSES: Office—299 West 12th St., No. 14, New York, NY 10014-1801. *Agent*—International Creative Management, 40 West 57th St., New York, NY 10019.

CAREER: Middlesex Hospital, London, England, intern in medicine, surgery, and neurology, 1958-60; Mt. Zion Hospital, San Francisco, CA, rotating intern, 1961-62; University of California, Los Angeles, resident in neurology, 1962-65; Yeshiva University, Albert Einstein College of Medicine, Bronx, NY, fellow in neurochemistry and neuropathology, 1965-66, instructor, 1966-75, assistant professor, 1975-78, associate professor, 1978-85, clinical professor of neurology, 1985; Beth Abraham Hospital, Bronx, staff neurologist, 1966—. University of California, Santa Cruz, visiting professor, 1986. Consultant neurologist at Bronx State Hospital, beginning 1966, and at Little Sisters of the Poor, New York City; affiliated with Bronx Psychiatric Center, until 1991.

MEMBER: American Academy of Neurology (fellow), New York State Medical Society, New York Institute for the Humanities, Alpha Omega Alpha.

AWARDS, HONORS: Hawthornden Prize, 1974, for *Awakenings;* Felix Mart-Ibanez book award, *MD* magazine, 1987; Oskar Pfister Award, American Psychiatric Association, 1988; Guggenheim fellowship, 1989; Harold D. Vursell Memorial Award, American Academy and Institute of Arts and Letters, 1989; Odd Fellows book award, 1990; D.H.L., Georgetown University, 1990, and College of Staten Island, City University of New York, 1991; honorary D.S., Tufts University and New York Medical College, both 1991; Scriptor Award, University of Southern California, 1991; Professional Support Award, National Headache Foundation, 1991; presidential citation, American Academy of Neurology, 1991.

WRITINGS:

Migraine: Evolution of a Common Disorder, University of California Press (Berkeley), 1970, revised and enlarged edition published as *Migraine: Understanding a Common Disorder,* 1985.
Awakenings, Duckworth (London), 1973, Doubleday (New York City), 1974, published with a new foreword by the author, Summit Books (New York City), 1987.
A Leg to Stand On, Summit Books, 1984.
The Man Who Mistook His Wife for a Hat, and Other Clinical Tales, Duckworth, 1985, Summit Books, 1986.
Seeing Voices: A Journey into the World of the Deaf, University of California Press, 1989, new revised edition, Picador (London), 1991.
An Anthropologist on Mars: Seven Paradoxical Tales, Knopf (New York City), 1995.

Contributor to *New York Review of Books, New Yorker, Discover, New York Times,* and to various journals.

ADAPTATIONS: Harold Pinter's play *A Kind of Alaska* was based on one of the case histories from *Awakenings; Awakenings* was adapted into a movie with the same title, starring Robin Williams and Robert De Niro, and directed by Penny Marshall, 1990; the title case study from *The Man Who Mistook His Wife for a Hat, and Other Clinical Tales* was adapted into an opera with the same title by Michael Nyman and into the play *The Man Who* by Peter Brook; a case history from *An Anthropologist on Mars: Seven Paradoxical Tales* was adapted into the play *Molly Sweeney* by Brian Friel.

WORK IN PROGRESS: A study of the residents of Pingelap Island in Micronesia, where there is a high incidence of color blindness and leprosy.

SIDELIGHTS: Oliver Sacks is one of the best-known and well respected neurologists in the country. He first made a name for himself among his peers in the field of neurology with his work in the hospitals of the Bronx, New York, and gained a wider audience with the publication of his case histories. "Sacks has consistently offered us fascinating, intense, thoughtful chronicles of the bizarre and the freakish—a kind of 'Ripley's Believe It or Not' for the intellectual and artistic set," Wendy Lesser observes in the *New York Times Book Review.* "In books like 'Awakenings,' 'Seeing Voices,' and 'The Man Who Mistook His Wife for a Hat' he has explored the terrain where physical and mental ailments blur into spiritual quandaries, moral inquiries and exemplary tales about the infinite variety of the human organism. Oliver Sacks has become our modern master of the case study, an artistic form whose antecedents lie in the scientific work of practitioners like A. R. Luria and Sigmund Freud." Sacks's work has also reached other audiences through adaptations for the stage and screen. Three of his case histories have been made into plays, one into an opera, and *Awakenings* was the subject of a major motion picture starring Robin Williams and Robert De Niro.

In his work as a physician, professor, and author, Sacks has become a leading proponent of the rehumanization of the medical arts. Working day-to-day in the hospitals and nursing homes of the New York City area exploring organic disorders of the brain and their symptoms, Sacks resembles a general practitioner, "a medical man in the old-fashioned humanist tradition," in the words of *New York Times* reviewer Michiko Kakutani. "He sees medicine as part of the continuum of life." Sacks is unhurried by an overly ambitious schedule and, therefore, able to give time to patients, time for listening and discussing their conditions. He is also free of the technical bias characteristic of much medical practice, so he involves patients in developing their own treatments. "His outstanding quality is wonder," writes Douglas Hill in the Toronto *Globe and Mail,* "a constant amazed appreciation of how men and women afflicted with frustrating or terrifying handicaps can cope with them and even help themselves to master them."

Sacks's approach to his work is reflected in his writing. He avoids the technical language and biochemical analyses common in medical treatises. Instead, in journal articles and such books as *Migraine: Evolution of a Common Dis-* order, *Awakenings, A Leg to Stand On,* and *The Man Who Mistook His Wife for a Hat, and Other Clinical Tales,* he uses a case history approach to write straightforward clinical biographies that go beyond medical analysis to capture the human side of illness. These human stories also chronicle Sacks's discovery of health as a complex interaction of mind, body, and lifestyle that requires a concerted effort on the part of patient and physician in order to arrive at an appropriate cure. As Walter Kendrick puts it in a *Voice Literary Supplement* article, "Sacks's aim in all his books has been to show that neuropsychologists are wrong when they confine themselves to dry tabulations of symptoms and dosages. Just as the subject ought to be the full human brain, not half of it, so the method should account for the human being—emotions, personal relationships, everything."

In his book *Migraine,* first published in 1970 and later updated and enlarged for publication in 1985, Sacks examines a condition known to mankind for thousands of years. As Sacks points out, though it is a common affliction, migraine is little understood, its cycles of agony and euphoria often different with each episode. Headache is but one of many symptoms that include convulsions, vomiting, depression, and hallucinations. Drawing upon his observation of the numerous patients he treated, Sacks focuses not on cures but on an explanation of the function migraine serves for its human sufferers. As Israel Rosenfield relates in the *New York Times Book Review,* Sacks maintains that the disorder "is part of the human repertory of passive reactions to danger. The complexity of human social activities often necessitates passivity—neuroses, psychosomatic reactions and the varieties of migraine—when the individual confronts essentially unsolvable problems."

Though particularly useful to migraine sufferers for the answers it provides, Sacks's book has attracted a varied readership. Kakutani finds that "his commentary is so erudite, so gracefully written, that even those people fortunate enough to never have had a migraine in their lives should find it equally compelling." Rosenfield maintains that *Migraine* "should be read as much for its brilliant insights into the nature of our mental functioning as for its discussion of migraine."

Upon his arrival at Beth Abraham Hospital in the late 1960s, Sacks discovered a group of patients suffering from a range of debilitating symptoms, the worst of which was a "sleep" so deep the sufferer was beyond arousal. The patients, he learned, were survivors of a sleeping sickness epidemic that had occurred between 1916 and 1927. In his second book, *Awakenings,* Sacks tells of his attempts to help this group. Recognizing the similarities between the symptoms exhibited by his patients and those of sufferers of Parkinson's disease, Sacks decided to begin administering L-dopa, a drug proven effective in treating Parkinson's. L-dopa initially produced dramatic results; patients out of touch with the world for over four decades suddenly emerged from their sleep. Sacks discovered, however, that the drug was not a miracle cure. Side-effects and the shock of waking a changed person in a changed world proved too much for some in the group. Some died; others withdrew into trancelike states. Still others succeeded, but only by achieving a balance between the illness and the cure, the past and the present.

Sacks's portrayal of the complexities of this episode has earned him considerable praise from readers of *Awakenings.* "Well versed in poetry and metaphysics, [Sacks] writes from the great tradition of Sir Thomas Browne," writes *Newsweek* reviewer Peter S. Prescott, "probing through medicine and his own observations of fear, suffering and total disability toward an investigation of what it means not only to be, but to become a person." "Some would attribute this achievement to narrative skill, others to clinical insight," comments Gerald Weissman in the *Washington Post;* "I would rather call this feat of empathy a work of art."

A Leg to Stand On is a doctor's memoir of his experience as a patient. As Jerome Bruner explains in the *New York Review of Books,* Sacks's book "is about a horribly injured leg, his own, what he thought and learned while living through the terrors and raptures of recovering its function." In 1976 while mountaineering in Scandinavia, Sacks fell and twisted his left knee. Although surgery repaired the physical damage—torn ligaments and tendons—the leg remained immobile. Sacks found he had lost his inner sense of the leg; it seemed to him detached and alien, not his own. His inability to recover disturbed him, and the surgeon's dismissal of his concerns only heightened his anxiety.

"By describing his experience and its resolution," comments Vic Sussman in the *Washington Post Book World,* "Sacks shows how patients rapidly become isolated (even physician-patients) when medicine regards them as 'invalids, in-valid.' " Critics observe that this reflection on the doctor/patient relationship is what makes *A Leg to Stand On* more than a personal story. As Bruner notes, "It is also a book about the philosophical dilemma of neurology, about the philosophy of mind, about what it might take to create a 'neurology of the soul' while still hanging on to your scientific marbles." And, Sussman concludes, "Sacks' remarkable book raises issues of profound importance for everyone interested in health care and the humane application of science."

In his bestselling collection of case histories entitled *The Man Who Mistook His Wife for a Hat,* "Sacks tells some two dozen stories about people who are also patients, and who manifest strange and striking peculiarities of percep-

tion, emotion, language, thought, memory or action," observes John C. Marshall in the *New York Times Book Review.* "And he recounts these histories with the lucidity and power of a short-story writer." One of the case histories Sacks presents is that of an instructor of music who suffers from a visual disorder. While able to see the component parts of objects, he is unable to perceive the whole they compose. Leaving Sacks's office after a visit, this patient turns to grab his hat and instead grabs his wife's face. Another history features two autistic twins unable to add or subtract but capable of determining the day of the week for any date past or present and of calculating twenty-digit prime numbers. "Blessed with deep reserves of compassion and a metaphysical turn of mind," comments Kakutani, "Sacks writes of these patients not as scientific curiosities but as individuals, whose dilemmas—moral and spiritual, as well as psychological—are made as completely real as those of characters in a novel."

As it demonstrates the variety of abnormal conditions that can arise from damage to the brain, *The Man Who Mistook His Wife for a Hat* also touches larger themes. *Nation* contributor Brina Caplan is taken by the book's portrayal of "men and women [who] struggle individually with a common problem: how to reconcile being both a faulty mechanism and a thematic, complex and enduring self." As Walter Clemmons suggests in *Newsweek,* "Sacks's humane essays on these strange cases are deeply stirring, because each of them touches on our own fragile 'normal' identities and taken-for-granted abilities of memory, attention and concentration."

Seeing Voices: A Journey into the World of the Deaf is a departure from Sacks's case studies of neurological disorders. Yet, as in his other works, in this exploration of deafness and the deaf Sacks continues to challenge readers' assumptions of what is normal. As Simon J. Carmel explains in *Natural History,* "When Sacks started to read books on the deaf, he was so enraptured that he began a journey into their silent world." The result is a book in three parts. In the first part, Sacks outlines the history of the deaf. As he points out, prior to the mid-1700s, those who were born deaf were generally considered uneducable and were neglected. Then the French Abbe Charles-Michel de l'Epee shattered these assumptions. He learned the sign language of some of the deaf in Paris and adapted it to teach the deaf to read. His school for the deaf, which opened in 1755, trained teachers who spread deaf education throughout Europe and America. During the years since, two approaches to deaf education have persisted. The focus of education in oralist schools is on teaching deaf students to speak, lip read, and to use signed English. The focus of Sign schools (those using American Sign Language, or ASL) is on helping deaf students to learn Sign as a native language and use it to learn other things. The remaining two parts of the book, notes Prescott, are "an examination (and celebration) of the complexity and richness of Sign, the true language of the deaf; and an account of [the March 1988] uprising at Gallaudet University, which for the first time placed a deaf president in charge."

"Presenting himself as a traveler to a foreign land," comments David M. Perlmutter in the *New York Review of Books,* "Sacks enables readers to experience vicariously his discovery of the contrasting lives of the signing Deaf and the nonsigning deaf." And, as Perlmutter adds, "his book's greatest contribution is in making accessible to the general reader a sympathetic portrayal of the linguistic-cultural view of deafness and of the discoveries that led him to it." In addition to his discovery of the Deaf culture within the larger American mosaic, Sacks revels in his discovery of the language of Sign in a world of speech. In Prescott's words, "Sacks's enthusiasm for Sign is contagious. His excitement over the ways in which the deaf have overcome their tragic past is reflected in his narrative. . . . *Seeing Voices* is a searching book." Perlmutter offers reservations, however. "Although Sacks has performed a valuable service in introducing the general reader to the linguistic-cultural view of deafness," writes the reviewer, "much of what he says about ASL is seriously flawed. . . .. He realizes that sign language is central to the lives of the Deaf and he grasps the intellectual interest of the fact that language exists in sign, but depends too much on what he can see with his own eyes." He continues, "The result is a strange blend of personal reactions to signing and speculations that run the risk of creating new myths to replace those he has helped to dispel."

Even with such reservations and with weaknesses like those expressed by Paul West that Sacks overuses footnotes, *Seeing Voices* challenges the assumptions of the hearing. As West puts it in the *New York Times Book Review,* "Sacks, whose heart is in the right place, wants the deaf to have all they need, but most of all, their own natural and private language. He brings afresh to our attention a problem that is never easily going to be solved." And Carmel (himself deaf, an anthropologist of deaf folklore and culture) concludes, "Above all, I must admit that Sacks's book is most informative and stimulating, and I must praise his intense research and crystal-clear understanding of the deaf world. So I strongly recommend that his book be read by those individuals who want a better understanding of the cultural, educational, historical, linguistic, psychological, and sociological discipline of deafness."

Sacks returns to his examination of how people cope with neurological disorders in *An Anthropologist on Mars: Seven Paradoxical Tales.* In these seven case histories

Sacks again probes what it means to be normal through the lives of people who seem anything but normal. He includes the story of a painter who has lost the ability to see anything but black and white, a surgeon with Tourette's syndrome, an autistic boy who can draw buildings in great detail after only briefly viewing them, an autistic zoologist, and a man who has regained his eyesight after decades of blindness. With each, Sacks shows the balance of science and humanity that characterizes all of his writing. Ethan Canin observes this quality in the *Washington Post Book Review:* "Sacks possesses the physician's love for classification and logical dissection, but once again we see that he is also blessed with the humanist's wonder at character and grace, at the ineffable sadness and wondrous joy of art." In Lesser's opinion, *An Anthropologist on Mars* is "Sacks's best book to date because it very self-consciously explores both the physician's and the patients' peculiar ways of thinking."

Commenting on his work and writing, Sacks once told an interviewer for *U.S. News and World Report,* "You get an idea of how much is given to us by nature when you see what happens if it's taken away and how the person—the human subject—survives its loss, sometimes in the most extraordinary and even creative ways." This creativity is what Sacks attempts to capture in his case histories and memoirs. *New York Times* reviewer Benedict Nightingale characterizes Sacks as "a most unusual man, as much a metaphysician as physician: passionate, inquiring, generous, imaginative and supremely literate, a sort of Isaac Bashevis Singer of the hospital ward." Paul Baumann offers a similar view in a *Commonweal* review but compares Sacks to a different author. "Sacks possesses the gifts of a speculative philosopher and the subtler, rarer skills of an old-fashioned doctor who was taught how to take a history," writes Baumann. "He knows a good story when he treats one, and propounds a conundrum with the same vigor of expression, eye for detail, and vivid sense of character that made Sir Arthur Conan Doyle, another English physician-writer with a profound regard for the spiritual properties of intelligence, a master storyteller. Sacks shares with the creator of Sherlock Holmes a fascination with what we might call cerebral mysteries."

Yet Sacks's writing also serves his larger purpose. "What he's arguing for is a set of neglected values: empathetic, emotional, individual, storylike," notes Caplan. "To ignore those values, he suggests, means constructing a science of cold, rigid design." As Baumann sums it up, "Sacks's larger ambition is to develop what he calls an 'existential neurology' or 'romantic science' that will shed the rigid computational paradigms of traditional neurology and open itself up to the dynamic 'powers' of the mind."

BIOGRAPHICAL/CRITICAL SOURCES:

BOOKS

Contemporary Literary Criticism, Volume 67, Gale (Detroit), 1992, pp. 284-309.
Sacks, Oliver, *A Leg to Stand On,* Summit Books (New York City), 1984.
Sacks, *Awakenings,* Summit Books, 1987.

PERIODICALS

Boston Globe, December 29, 1985, p. A13; March 24, 1986, p. 23; August 27, 1989, p. 87; November 12, 1989, p. M8; January 25, 1991, p. 29.
Chicago Tribune, August 20, 1989, section 14, p. 5; November 3, 1989, section 5, p. 1.
Commonweal, March 28, 1986; February 9, 1990, p. 88.
Globe and Mail (Toronto), February 21, 1987.
Interview, October, 1989, p. 24.
JAMA: The Journal of the American Medical Association, July 8, 1988, p. 273; February 9, 1994, p. 478.
Los Angeles Times, March 18, 1986, p. V1; September 24, 1989, p. B7.
Los Angeles Times Book Review, March 23, 1986; September 6, 1987, p. 14.
Nation, February 22, 1986.
Natural History, November, 1989, pp. 88-92, 94-95.
New England Journal of Medicine, November 9, 1989, p. 1347.
New Statesman and Society, February 9, 1990, p. 35.
Newsweek, July 15, 1974; August 20, 1984; December 30, 1985; March 2, 1986; March 13, 1986; March 27, 1986; October 2, 1989, p. 72.
New York Review of Books, September 27, 1984; March 2, 1986; March 13, 1986; March 27, 1986; January 29, 1987, p. 39; March 28, 1991, p. 65.
New York Times, May 24, 1984; June 19, 1985; January 25, 1986; September 30, 1989, p. A14; February 7, 1995, pp. C13, C18; February 14, 1995, p. C19.
New York Times Book Review, July 7, 1985; March 2, 1986; October 8, 1989, pp. 17-18; February 19, 1995, p. 1.
People, March 17, 1986; February 11, 1991, p. 91.
Psychology Today, November, 1989, p. 75.
Times Literary Supplement, December 14, 1973; June 22, 1984; February 7, 1986.
USA Today, January 31, 1986, p. D4; September 29, 1989, p. D4; January 11, 1991; January 14, 1991, p. D1.
U.S. News and World Report, July 14, 1986; October 16, 1989, p. 86.
Voice Literary Supplement, February, 1986; November, 1990, p. 12.
Wall Street Journal, June 17, 1986, p. 26.
Washington Post, October 30, 1987; January 13, 1991, pp. F1, F6.
Washington Post Book World, August 26, 1984; February 16, 1986; September 10, 1989, p. 1; March 5, 1995, p. 2.
Yale Review, winter, 1988, p. 172.*

—*Sketch by Bryan Ryan*

*   *   *

SANDS, Martin
See BURKE, John (Frederick)

*   *   *

SANFORD, John 1904-
(John B. Sanford, Julian L. Shapiro)

PERSONAL: Name originally Julian Lawrence Shapiro; name legally changed, 1940; born May 31, 1904, in New York, NY; son of Philip D. (an attorney) and Harriet E. (a homemaker; maiden name, Nevins) Shapiro; married Marguerite Roberts (a screenwriter), December 30, 1938 (died February 17, 1989). *Education:* Attended Lafayette College, 1922-23; Fordham University, LL.B., 1927. *Politics:* Democratic. *Religion:* Jewish.

ADDRESSES: Home—812 Buena Vista Rd., Santa Barbara, CA 93108.

CAREER: Poet, novelist, and historian, 1928—. Attorney, 1928-36.

AWARDS, HONORS: Award from the Los Angeles chapter of PEN, 1986, for *The Color of the Air.*

WRITINGS:

Seventy Times Seven (novel), Knopf (New York City), 1939.
The People from Heaven (novel), Harcourt (San Diego, CA), 1943.
Every Island Fled Away (novel), Norton (New York City), 1964.
The $300 Man (novel), Prentice-Hall (Englewood Cliffs, NJ), 1967.
A More Goodly Country: A Personal History of America, Horizon Press (New York City), 1975.
Adirondack Stories, Capra (Santa Barbara, CA), 1976.
View from This Wilderness: American Literature as History, foreword by Paul Mariani, Capra, 1977.
To Feed Their Hopes: A Book of American Women, foreword by Annette K. Baxter, University of Illinois Press (Champaign), 1980.
The Winters of That Country: Tales of the Man-Made Seasons, Black Sparrow Press (Santa Barbara, CA), 1984.
(With William Carlos Williams) *A Correspondence,* foreword by Paul Mariani, Oyster (Santa Barbara, CA), 1984.

Scenes from the Life of an American Jew (autobiography), Black Sparrow Press, Volume 1: *The Color of the Air,* 1985, Volume 2: *The Waters of Darkness,* 1986, Volume 3: *A Very Good Land to Fall With,* 1987, Volume 4: *A Walk in the Fire,* 1989, Volume 5: *The Season, It Was Winter,* 1991.

Maggie! A Love Story (autobiographical), Barricade, 1993.

The View from Mt. Morris: A Harlem Boyhood (autobiographical), Barricade, 1994.

UNDER NAME JOHN B. SANFORD

The Old Man's Place (novel), A. & C. Boni, 1935.

A Man without Shoes (novel), Plantin (Los Angeles), 1951, published under name John Sanford, Black Sparrow Press, 1982.

The Land That Touches Mine (novel), Doubleday (New York City), 1953.

We Have a Little Sister, Capra, 1995.

UNDER NAME JULIAN L. SHAPIRO

The Water Wheel (novel), Dragon Press, 1933.

OTHER

Contributor to periodicals, including *Contact, New Review, Pagany,* and *Tambour.*

WORK IN PROGRESS: The New World.

SIDELIGHTS: Julian L. Shapiro had barely begun a career as a lawyer when a conversation with author Nathanael West, one of his old school friends, convinced him that he had to be a writer. An increasing commitment to the art led him to leave the legal profession completely. Associated with what Morris Dickstein labeled in the *New York Times Book Review* as "the left-wing popular front of the late [19]30's and early [19]40's," Shapiro has written for more than half a century as John or John B. Sanford, adopting his pseudonym as his legal name in 1940. A writer of fiction, history, and autobiography, Sanford's work in all genres exhibits a concern for the poor and oppressed in America.

Sanford's first four novels were well received, but an increasingly conservative climate culminating with the 1950s Senate investigations of allegedly subversive activities, headed by Senator Joseph McCarthy, made it difficult to find a publisher for his fifth, *A Man without Shoes.* Though Sanford had the novel printed privately after approximately thirty rejections, the political atmosphere so disheartened him—he and his wife, screenwriter Marguerite Roberts, were blacklisted and therefore unable to get work—that he placed the printed copies in storage. Sanford began rebuilding the reputation he had enjoyed earlier, however, with the 1975 publication of his unusual historical work, *A More Goodly Country: A Personal History of America.* The critical acclaim accorded *A More Goodly*

Country and subsequent books in Sanford's historical series probably paved the way for the reissuance of *A Man without Shoes* by Black Sparrow Press in 1982, which gave Sanford even wider exposure. In 1985, Sanford turned to autobiography, publishing *The Color of the Air,* the first volume of *Scenes from the Life of an American Jew,* which won him a PEN award in 1986.

A Man without Shoes is the story of Dan Johnson, a man born of working-class parents in New York City. Spanning the years from 1909 to 1938, the novel details Dan's growth from an innocent boy to a hardened crusader against injustice. He works in vain to stay the executions of political activists Nicola Sacco and Bartolomeo Vanzetti, then later marries and finds a job in depression-era New York at an employment agency. In the words of Robert W. Smith in the *Washington Post Book World,* "Dan finds that the sometime love and goodness he meets fail to mitigate the terrible distress permeating Depression-era America." The protagonist becomes increasingly concerned with the Spanish Civil War of the late 1930s, but rather than leave to fight on the Loyalist side in that conflict—as other idealists of the time did—he elects to stay in America, depressed though it is. Calling the novel "a lyrical love affair with words and their arrangement," Smith praised Sanford's ability as an author, declaring, "compared to many writers today, his brilliance is a lantern on a dark lawn of lightning-bugs." Even Dickstein, who criticized the novel as "deeply flawed" because "Sanford lets his characters down when he allows them to fall into radical slogans, Marx for the masses," admitted that it is "beautifully written."

The applause that greeted the reissuing of *A Man without Shoes* added to the critical approval Sanford had begun to receive for his unique historical works, whose titles are taken from a passage in Puritan leader William Bradford's *History of Plymouth Plantation.* When *A More Goodly Country: A Personal History of America,* the first of these, was published in 1975, it sparked great enthusiasm. Paul L. Mariani announced in the *Nation:* "In this, our Bicentennial year . . . one very important literary work, dealing in a serious, deeply considered and profoundly imaginative way with [the American experience] has entered the arena so modestly among . . . more widely publicized events that, like so much else that is truly in the American grain, it is in danger of being overlooked while all the hoopla goes merrily on its way." Richard M. Dorson in the *New Republic* declared *A More Goodly Country* to be "refreshing . . . as a relief from . . . historical monographs and literary studies of conventional scholarship." As Dorson puts it, Sanford's method of writing history is "to relate [it] through the imagined tongues and eyes of its actors." What results is an often unconventional view of familiar historical events. George Washington's crossing of the Delaware River with the American Army is presented thus by Sanford in the guise of an eyewitness: "Once over, they had nine white miles to Trenton [New Jersey], but the boozing snake [f—king] bastards made it, and even as the legend goes, they left bloody tracks in the snow. They lost four men to wounds (none died), but of the fancy-Dan Dutchmen [Hessians], some nine hundred never saw home. . . . *Fifty thousand pounds should not induce me again to undergo what I have done,* the C.-in-C. [Washington] said."

Aside from its originality, *A More Goodly Country* was praised for the power of its prose. Mariani lauded the book's approximately two hundred "independent sections," which are "executed in so masterful a manner, so extraordinary in lyric intensity, so without slack or even brief sketches of uninspired writing, that one discovers very early on that he is reading a prose epic of America." Dorson averred that Sanford "has the [James] Joycean virtuosity with language" and asserted that the author "can assume the speech and posture of Americans in four centuries and from all walks, yet write his own prose, verse and dialogue, eloquent and searing, salted with slang and puns."

Sanford's other historical works, which include *View from This Wilderness: American Literature as History, To Feed Their Hopes: A Book of American Women,* and *The Winters of That Country: Tales of the Man-Made Seasons,* also concern themselves with a wide variety of personalities. Not only do traditional historical figures such as presidents George Washington, Thomas Jefferson, and Abraham Lincoln walk Sanford's pages, but also striking miners, authors, and even fictional characters. Each book spans a period from before America's independence—one even goes back to the Viking exploration of North America—to modern times. Two of them specialize: *View from This Wilderness* centers on literary figures, *To Feed Their Hopes* on women. Collectively, they have been compared to works by such writers as William Carlos Williams, John Dos Passos, and D. H. Lawrence. Robert Atwan concluded in the *Los Angeles Times Book Review* that "Sanford is completely at ease with the American idiom and—unlike most professional historians—he sees history as inseparable from the verbal texture of the past."

Though Sanford ostensibly turned from history after writing *The Winters of That Country* to work on his autobiography, *Scenes from the Life of an American Jew,* the first volume of the latter—*The Color of the Air*—exhibits similarities to his previous books. As Elaine Kendall noted in the *Los Angeles Times Book Review,* "Like his four volumes of American history, the autobiography is written as a series of compressed vignettes." Interspersed among incidents from Sanford's personal life are depictions of historical events that had great influence on him in his youth.

The Color of the Air also contains commonplace elements of autobiography such as descriptions of family and friends, but, as Kendall pointed out, "everything [is] seen from an unexpected oblique angle, so even the familiar seems freshly invented. The method is metaphysical in its intensity, each image wrenching the imagination and forcing a new perspective upon the reader."

Sanford's vignette style is continued in the second volume of his autobiography, *The Waters of Darkness,* which chronicles his early adult life against a backdrop of history. Discussed in this book are Sanford's fellow writers, who, deeply influenced by the Depression and the World Wars, became part of what Kendall described in the *Los Angeles Times* as "a liberal 20th-Century consciousness." Sanford's friendship with novelist Nathanael West is a particularly important facet detailed in *The Waters of Darkness,* but, as Kendall explained, "central to the book is the candid account of the making of a writer by trial and error, delight and disappointment, accolade and derogation, nothing spared or rationalized in the retelling."

Another of Sanford's autobiographical books is *Maggie! A Love Story,* about his wife Marguerite Roberts, who died in 1989. Sanford met her on a Hollywood film studio lot, after he moved to the West Coast in 1936 upon receiving a writing contract with Paramount Pictures. A successful screenwriter for Metro-Goldwyn-Mayer for thirteen years, Maggie was officially blacklisted for ten years, following an appearance before McCarthy's House Un-American Activities Committee in 1951 during the senator's anti-communism investigations. Maggie had attended meetings with Sanford, and they both pled the Fifth Amendment (so as not to incriminate other meeting attendees) during questioning, leading to their censure. A *Publishers Weekly* reviewer remarked that Sanford's description of his wife's "courageous" appearance before the Senate in 1951 "is vividly told." Maggie was well-known for many of her screenplays, including *True Grit,* which she produced upon her return to employment in the 1960s. She supported Sanford and herself with her screenwriting earnings while Sanford worked on his novels and memoirs. In *Review of Contemporary Fiction,* Joe Napora described *Maggie: A Love Story* as "as honest a portrait of a writer at work as we have gotten." The critic further labeled their marriage "that of life and literature," adding, "We desperately need his story, which is everything that is not perverse."

Sanford's *The View from Mt. Morris: A Harlem Boyhood* continues in his autobiographical vein. The book "is both a boy's-eye view of adult life and homage to a distant age, an altogether charming collection of portraits from Jewish life in Harlem, between 1910 and 1920," commented Chris Goodrich in the *Los Angeles Times Book Review.* A *Publishers Weekly* reviewer noted that the book "evokes the horsecar era" and captures Sanford's childhood neighborhood. Describing the author's characterizations of family and friends as "engaging," the reviewer further observed that Sanford's words "pay loving tribute" to his now-deceased wife, Maggie. Goodrich concludes that the reminiscences contain "much more than you typically find in a memoir, and with much less dross."

Sanford's five volumes of *Scenes from the Life of an American Jew* inspired Robert W. Smith to comment in the *Bloomsbury Review* on the overall impact and importance of the body of the author's work: "This wonderfully wrought autobiography caps Sanford's career by showing a man in love with a woman and words, doing beautifully for both. Undiminished by age, he continues to write with a brilliance that, compared to most writers today, is like a lantern on a dark lawn of lightning bugs."

BIOGRAPHICAL/CRITICAL SOURCES:

BOOKS

Sanford, John, *A More Goodly Country: A Personal History of America*, Horizon Press, 1975.
Sanford, John, *Scenes from the Life of an American Jew*, Black Sparrow Press, Volume 1: *The Color of Air*, 1985, Volume 2: *The Waters of Darkness*, 1986, Volume 3: *A Very Good Land to Fall With*, 1987, Volume 4: *A Walk in the Fire*, 1989, Volume 5: *The Season, It Was Winter*, 1991.
Sanford, John, *Maggie! A Love Story*, Barricade, 1993.
Sanford, John, *The View from Mt. Morris: A Harlem Boyhood*, Barricade, 1994.

PERIODICALS

Bloomsbury Review, December, 1991, pp. 17-18.
Los Angeles Times, August 22, 1986.
Los Angeles Times Book Review, July 15, 1984; November 24, 1985; December 25, 1994, p. 7.
Nation, September 13, 1975.
New Republic, February 14, 1976.
New York Times Book Review, July 7, 1982.
Publishers Weekly, August 2, 1993, p. 72; August 29, 1994, p. 57.
Review of Contemporary Fiction, summer, 1994, pp. 218-19.
Washington Post Book World, June 6, 1982; August 12, 1984.

*　　　*　　　*

SANFORD, John A.　1929-

PERSONAL: Born July 26, 1929, in Camden, NJ; son of Edgar L. II (an Episcopal clergyman) and Agnes Mary (White) Sanford; married Adaline Hawkins, August 21, 1954; children: Kathryn, John Stuart. *Education:* Kenyon College, B.A., 1950; Episcopal Theological School, B.D., 1955.

CAREER: Member of clergy of Episcopal Church; rector in Los Angeles, CA, 1958-65; St. Paul's Episcopal Church, San Diego, CA, rector, 1965-74; currently private counselor, lecturer, and writer. *Military service:* U.S. Army Reserve, chaplain, nine years.

MEMBER: American Association of Pastoral Counselors.

WRITINGS:

Gottes Vergessene Sprache, Rascher Verlag, 1966, translation published as *God's Forgotten Language*, Lippincott (Philadelphia), 1968.
Kingdom Within: A Study of the Inner Meaning of Jesus' Sayings, Lippincott, 1970, revised edition published as *The Kingdom Within: The Inner Meaning of Jesus' Sayings*, Harper (San Francisco), 1987.
The Man Who Wrestled with God, Religious Publishing Co., 1974, revised edition published as *The Man Who Wrestled with God: Light from the Old Testament on the Psychology of Individuation*, Paulist Press (New York City), 1987.
Healing and Wholeness, Paulist/Newman, 1977.
Dreams and Healing, Paulist/Newman, 1979.
The Invisible Partners, Paulist/Newman, 1980.
Evil: The Shadow Side of Reality, Crossroad Publishing (New York City), 1981.
Between People: Communicating One-to-One, Paulist/Newman, 1982.
Ministry Burnout, Paulist/Newman, 1982.
The Man Who Lost His Shadow (novelette), Paulist/Newman, 1983.
King Saul, the Tragic Hero: A Study in Individuation, Paulist Press, 1985.
Song of the Meadowlark: The Story on an American Indian and the Nez Perce War, Harper (New York City), 1986.
The Strange Trial of Mr. Hyde: A New Look at the Nature of Human Evil, Harper (San Francisco), 1987.
Running with Your Dog, edited by William W. Denlinger and R. Annabel Rathman, Denlingers (Fairfax, VA), 1987.
(With George Lough) *What Men Are Like*, Paulist Press, 1988.
Dreams: God's Forgotten Language, Harper (San Francisco), 1989.
Soul Journey: A Jungian Analyst Looks at Reincarnation, Crossroad Publishing, 1991.
Healing Body and Soul: The Meaning of Illness in the New Testament and in Psychotherapy, Gracewing (Leominster, England), 1992.

Mystical Christianity: A Psychological Commentary on the Gospel of John, Crossroad Publishing, 1993.

SIDELIGHTS: John A. Sanford's *The Song of the Meadowlark: The Story of an American Indian and the Nez Perce War* "is an ambitious historical novel based on the Nez Perce War of 1877," comments Edward Halsey Foster in *Western American Literature.* The novel follows the narrator, Nez Perce warrior Teeto Hoonod, and his spiritual growth through the brutalities of the war. As his tribe is forced from their ancestral lands in Washington State, they decide to migrate northeast to Canada. A white soldier kills Hoonod's brother, and the brutalities of war eventually causes him to abandon his tribe as he seeks inner peace from the revenge which has scarred his soul. While Foster questions Sanford's lack of character development throughout the novel, he notes that the author "is a capable writer, and when he writes about the war itself, or about Indian myths and customs, he does quite well." In the *Library Journal,* W. Keith McCoy describes the book as "an evocative portrait of an honest people faced with protecting their way of life." A *Publishers Weekly* reviewer comments that Sanford is "skilled at depicting Nez Perce values, customs and myths."

Soul Journey: A Jungian Analyst Looks at Reincarnation examines numerous issues related to reincarnation and past life memories. Reviewer A. McDowell observes in *Choice* that despite several flaws involving theological precepts, Sanford "has commendably culled many important passages about these two concepts [the soul and reincarnation] from Hindu, Buddhist, Greek, Jewish, Christian, Gnostic, and modern sources." In *Healing Body and Soul: The Meaning of Illness in the New Testament and in Psychotherapy,* "John A. Sanford presents a kind of mini-Jungian view of healing in the New Testament and in analytical (Jungian) psychotherapy, modified by some of the useful insights of Fritz Kunkel, as well as his own," claims James N. Lapsley in *Theology Today.* The reviewer mentions that Sanford disregards certain implications of Jesus's healing, yet he concedes that Sanford is "generally well informed about New Testament and classical Greek scholarship." *Mystical Christianity: A Psychological Commentary on the Gospel of John* investigates instances of Jungian theory throughout John's gospel writings. In *Library Journal,* W. Alan Froggatt perceives substantive critical theological and psychological fallacies with Sanford's conclusions. About the organization of the book, the reviewer remarks that "the text uses successive Johannine pericopes (extracts) as touch points for psychological reflection, at times bordering on free association."

BIOGRAPHICAL/CRITICAL SOURCES:

PERIODICALS

Choice, November, 1992, p. 487.

Library Journal, May 1, 1986, p. 132; April 1, 1993, p. 104.
Publishers Weekly, March 21, 1986, p. 75.
Theology Today, January, 1994, p. 663.
Western American Literature, spring, 1987, p. 62.*

*   *   *

SANFORD, John B.
  See SANFORD, John

*   *   *

SCHOEPS, Karl-Heinz 1935-

PERSONAL: Born December 8, 1935, in Dinslaken, Germany (now West Germany); son of Karl G. (a teacher) and Ella (Gruhl) Schoeps; married Dorothy Sturdivant, August, 1965. *Education:* University of Bonn, Staatsexamen, 1962; attended Universities of Freiburg, 1956-57, Junsbruck, 1957-58, University of London King's College, 1958-59, University of Kansas, 1962-64; University of Wisconsin—Madison, Ph.D., 1971. *Avocational interests:* Travel, classical music, opera, tennis, skiing, soccer.

ADDRESSES: Office—Department of Germanic Languages and Literature, 3072 Foreign Languages Building, University of Illinois at Urbana—Champaign, Urbana, IL 61801.

CAREER: Gymanisium Wipperfurth and Wuppertal, Wuppertal, West Germany, English teacher, 1964-67; University of Illinois at Urbana—Champaign, assistant professor, 1971-76, associate professor, 1977-89, professor of German, 1989—. Mount Holyoke College, South Hadley, MA, assistant professor, 1977.

MEMBER: International Brecht Society (secretary-treasurer, 1979—), Modern German Studies Association, American Association of Teachers of German.

WRITINGS:

Bertolt Brecht und Bernard Shaw, Bouvier, 1974.
Bertolt Brecht, Ungar, 1977.
(With Richard Zipser) *DDR-Literatur in Tauwetter* (anthology), three volumes, Peter Lang, 1985.
Bertolt Brecht: Life, Work, and Criticism, York Press, 1989.
(Editor and contributor with Christopher Wickham) *Neue Interpretationen vou der Aufklarung zur Moderne,* Peter Lang, 1991.
Literature im Dritten Reich, Peter Lang, 1992.

Contributor of articles on Bertolt Brecht and East German literature to periodicals, including *Germanic Review,*

Comparative Literature Studies, Books Abroad, Monatshefte, and *German Quarterly.* Also associate editor of *German Quarterly,* 1991-94.

SIDELIGHTS: Karl-Heinz Schoeps told *CA:* "Apart from the aesthetics of literature, I am very interested in the interaction of literature with society, history, and politics. My other professional interests are modern German literature (including East Germany), drama, and comparative literature, especially the relationships among English, American, and German literature. Besides my native German and English, I have some Latin, French, and Spanish."

BIOGRAPHICAL/CRITICAL SOURCES:

PERIODICALS

German Quarterly, November, 1977; March, 1979; fall, 1993.
Modern Language Review, July, 1977.
New Boston Review, April/May, 1979.

*   *   *

SCHULTES, Richard Evans   1915-

PERSONAL: Born January 12, 1915, in Boston, MA; son of Otto Richard and Maude Beatrice (Bagley) Schultes; married Dorothy Crawford McNeil, March 26, 1959; children: Richard Evans II, Neil Parker and Alexandra Ames (twins). *Education:* Harvard University, A.B., 1937, A.M., 1938, Ph.D., 1941. *Religion:* Unitarian-Universalist.

ADDRESSES: Home—78 Larchmont Rd., Melrose, MA 02176. *Office*—Botanical Museum, Harvard University, Cambridge, MA 02138.

CAREER: Botanist. Harvard University, Cambridge, MA, research fellow at Botanical Museum, 1941-42, research associate, 1941-53, curator of Orchid Herbarium of Oakes Ames, 1953-58, curator of economic botany of Botanical Museum, beginning 1958, executive director of museum, 1967-70, director, beginning 1970, professor of biology, 1970-72, Paul C. Mangelsdorf Professor of Natural Sciences, 1973-80, Edward G. Jeffrey Professor of Biology, 1980—. Instituto Agronomico do Notre, collaborator, 1948-50; Universidad Nacional de Colombia, honorary professor, 1953—; Morris Arboretum, Laura L. Barnes Annual Lecturer, 1969; Rho Chi society, Koch Memorial Lecturer, 1971 and 1974; Jardin Botanico, visiting professor, 1973; University of British Columbia, Cecil and Ida M. Queen Visiting Lecturer, 1974; Museo del Oro, associate in ethnobotany, 1974—; University of Illinois at Chicago Circle, adjunct professor, 1975—; Macalester College, Hubert Humphrey Visiting Professor, 1979;

Rockefeller Foundation, member of survey of Mexican agriculture, 1941, resident scholar at Study and Conference Centre, 1980; participant in seminars and symposia; chair of workshops.

Plant explorer for National Research Council, 1941-42, and U.S. Department of Agriculture (in the Amazon Valley), 1945-53; Rubber Development Corp. of the United States, field agent in South America, 1943-44; Alpha-Helix Amazon Expeditions, member in Brazil, 1967, chief scientist in Peru, 1977; conducted field studies in Mexico, Costa Rica, Colombia, Trinidad, Cuba, Brazil, Peru, Argentina, Ceylon, Afghanistan, and Malaysia; conducted studies in botanical centers in Great Britain, Denmark, Sweden, France, Germany, the Netherlands, Belgium, Spain, Switzerland, Oman, and the U.S.S.R. Member of selection committee for Latin American Guggenheim fellowships, 1964—; member of advisory panels and boards, National Institutes of Health, 1964, Fitz Hugh Ludlow Library, 1974—, and Palm Oil Research Institute of Malaysia, 1980-82; chair of National Research Council panels. Botanical consultant to Smith, Kline & French, 1954-65.

MEMBER: International Association of Plant Taxonomy, Phytochemical Society of North America, American Academy of Arts and Sciences (fellow), American Association for the Advancement of Science, American College of Neuropsychopharmacology (fellow), American Orchid Society (honorary life member), American Society of Pharmacognosy, National Academy of Sciences, Association of Tropical Biology, Society for Economic Botany, Indian Ethnobotany Society (founding and honorary member), Academia Colombiana de Ciencias Exactas, Fisico-Quimicas y Naturales, Sociedad Colombiana de Orquideologia, Association Colombiana de Ingenieros Agronomos, Sociedad Cubana de Botanica, Academia de Ciencias Argentina, Instituto Ecuadoriano de Ciencias Naturales, Sociedad Cientifica Antonio Alzate (Mexico), Asociacion de Amigos de Jardines Botanicos (life member), Linnean Society of London (foreign member), Pan-American Society of New England, New England Botanical Club (president, 1954-60), Phi Beta Kappa, Sigma Xi (president of Harvard chapter, 1971-72), Phi Sigma (Beta Nu chapter).

AWARDS, HONORS: Guggenheim fellow, 1942-43; M.H., Universidad Nacional de Colombia, 1953; Orden de la Victoria Regia, Government of Comisaria del Amazonas, Colombia, 1969; named distinguished economic botanist by Society for Economic Botany, 1979; Cross of Boyaca, Republic of Colombia, 1983; Annual Gold Medal, World Wildlife Fund, 1984; Tyler Prize for Environmental Achievement, University of Southern California, 1987, for outstanding research in environmental science; Linnean Medal, Linnean Society of London, 1992.

WRITINGS:

(With P. A. Vestal) *Economic Botany of the Kiowa Indians,* Botanical Museum, Harvard University (Cambridge, MA), 1941.

A Contribution to Our Knowledge of Rivea Corymbosa: The Narcotic Ololiuqui of the Aztecs, Botanical Museum, Harvard University, 1941.

Native Orchids of Trinidad and Tobago, Pergamon (Elmsford, NY), 1960.

(With A. F. Hill) *Plants and Human Affairs,* Botanical Museum, Harvard University, 1960, 2nd edition, 1968.

(With A. S. Pease) *Generic Names of Orchids: Their Origin and Meaning,* Academic Press (New York City), 1963.

(With Albert Hofmann) *The Botany and Chemistry of Hallucinogens,* C. C Thomas (Springfield, IL), 1973, 2nd edition, 1980.

Hallucinogenic Plants, Western Publishing (New York City), 1976.

Atlas des plantes hallucinogenes du monde (title means "Atlas of Hallucinogenic Plants of the World"), L'Aurore, 1978.

(With Hofmann) *Plants of the Gods: Origins of Hallucinogenic Use,* McGraw (New York City), 1979.

(With William A. Davis) *The Glass Flowers at Harvard,* Dutton (New York City), 1982.

El reino de los dioses: Paisajes, plantas, y pueblos de la Amazonia Colombiana (title means "Where the Gods Reign: Plants and People of the Colombian Amazon"), El Navegante Editores, 1989.

(With R. E. Raffauf) *The Healing Forest: Medicinal and Toxic Plants of the Northwest Amazonia,* Dioscorides Press, 1990.

Los medicos tradicionales de la Amazonia Colombiana, sus plantos y sus rituales, Ediciones Uniandes, 1994.

(Editor with S. von Reis) *Ethnobotany: Evolution of a Discipline,* Dioscorides Press, 1995.

Also author, with Raffauf, of *Vine of the Soul: Medicine Men, Their Plants and Rituals in the Colombian Amazonia,* 1992. Contributor to books, including *A Quarter-Century of Publications of the Botanical Museum of Harvard University: 1940-1965,* Botanical Museum, Harvard University, 1966; *Plants in the Development of Modern Medicine,* edited by T. Swain, Harvard University Press, 1972; *The Shaman and the Jaguar,* by Gerardo Reichel-Dolmatoff, Temple University Press (Philadelphia), 1975; *Principles of Psychopharmacology,* 2nd edition, edited by W. G. Clark and J. del Guidice, Academic Press, 1978; and *Ethnobotany and the Search for New Drugs,* Ciba Foundation, 1994.

Also contributor to *Encyclopedia of the Biological Sciences, Encyclopaedia Britannica, International Encyclope-*

dia of Veterinary Medicine, Encyclopedia of Biochemistry, and *McGraw-Hill Yearbook of Science and Technology.* Editor of "Botanical Museum Leaflets," Harvard University, 1957-85. Contributor of about four hundred fifty articles and reviews to scientific journals. Assistant editor, *Chronica Botanica,* 1947-52; editor, *Economic Botany,* 1962-79; member of editorial board, *Lloydia,* 1965-76, *Altered States of Consciousness,* 1973—, *Journal of Psychedelic Drugs,* 1974—, *Journal of Latin American Folklore,* 1975—, *Horticulture,* 1976-78, *American Journal of Chinese Medicine,* 1977—, and *Journal of Ethnopharmacology,* 1978—.

Some of Schultes's work has been translated into French, Spanish, Italian, and German.

WORK IN PROGRESS: A series of approximately thirty papers on the economic flora of the Amazon; a textbook on economic botany; *Ethnopharmacology of the Northwest Amazon; Psychoactive Drugs of South America,* with J. Wilbert and T. Plowman; *Where the Gods Reign,* a photographic volume; translation of the recently discovered complete *Relacion historica del viage que hizo el botanico Ruiz al Peru y Chile.*

SIDELIGHTS: Plants of the Gods: Origins of Hallucinogenic Use is "a lavishly illustrated coffee-table guide to hallucinogenic plants," declares I. M. Lewis in the *Times Literary Supplement.* Written by Richard Evans Schultes and Albert Hofmann, the chemist who discovered LSD (lysergic acid diethylamide), *Plants of the Gods* identifies ninety-one plants with known or assumed hallucinogenic properties. The book also contains a discussion of "the controversial use of hallucinogenic drugs in psychiatric treatment and in helping terminally ill patients to come to terms with death through drug-induced religious experience." According to *Los Angeles Times* reviewer Lee Dembart, *Plants of the Gods* "contains a fair amount of pure science, chemical structures and the like and speculation about why these substances have the effect on people that they do. Much of the writing is academic and flat, intentionally, no doubt, given the subject matter." Dembart further notes the author's respect for hallucinogens and concludes, "At a time of public hysteria over the use of drugs, it takes guts to bring out this book." In the opinion of *Los Angeles Times Book Review* contributor Jeff Bailey, *Plants of the Gods* is "the finest overall volume available on the subject."

BIOGRAPHICAL/CRITICAL SOURCES:

PERIODICALS

Los Angeles Times, August 25, 1987.
Los Angles Times Book Review, July 6, 1980.
Times Literary Supplement, January 23, 1981.

SCHULZ, Phillip Stephen 1946-

PERSONAL: Born December 23, 1946, in Omaha, NE; son of Herold A. (a Lutheran minister) and Mildred (a homemaker; maiden name, Moehlenbrink) Schulz. *Education:* Attended Colorado State University, 1964-65, and Columbia University, 1972-74. *Politics:* "Democrat, bordering on liberal." *Religion:* "Biological Lutheran." *Avocational interests:* Travel, literature, theater, gardening.

ADDRESSES: Home—65 Montague St., No. 4A, Brooklyn, NY 11201. *Agent*—Judith Weber, Sobel Weber Associates, 146 East 19th St., New York, NY 10003.

CAREER: State Highway Department, Golden, CO, surveyor, 1965-66; Hartford Insurance Co., accounts in Denver and New York City, 1968-71; The Store in Amagansett, Amagansett, NY, pastry chef, 1971-76; general associate to Bert Greene, 1974-81; freelance writer, 1982—. Cooking teacher. *Military service:* U.S. Army, 1966-68.

MEMBER: International Association of Culinary Professionals.

AWARDS, HONORS: International Association of Culinary Professionals Cookbook award for an illustrated book and James Beard Award (Americana Category), both 1990, for *America the Beautiful Cookbook.*

WRITINGS:

(With Bert Greene) *Pity the Poor Rich,* Contemporary Books (Chicago), 1978.
Vodka'n Vittles, Irena Chalmers (New York City), 1982.
(With Greene) *Cooking for Giving,* Irena Chalmers, 1984.
Cooking with Fire and Smoke, illustrations by Richard Pracher, Simon & Schuster (New York City), 1986.
As American as Apple Pie, Simon & Schuster, 1990.
America the Beautiful Cookbook, Collins (New York City), 1990.
Celebrating America, a Cookbook, Simon & Schuster, 1994.
(With Judith Blahnik) *Mud Hens and Mavericks,* Viking Studio Books, 1995.

Contributor to numerous periodicals, including *Family Circle, Food and Wine, Chocolatier, Good Food, Cook's, New York Daily News,* and *Los Angeles Times.*

WORK IN PROGRESS: A historical work on American food; a second barbecue book.

SIDELIGHTS: Commenting on *Mud Hens and Mavericks,* an illustrated travel guide to minor league baseball, Phillip Stephen Schulz told *CA* that although he usually writes about food, "the book is not as far afield as one might think. Baseball lingo is loaded with food related terms. For example, a 'hot dog' is a show-off player; a 'pickle' is a rundown; a 'rhubarb' is a fight; 'cheese' is a fastball with zing; and a 'can of corn' is an easy pop-up."

*   *   *

SCHWERNER, Armand 1927-

PERSONAL: Born May 11, 1927, in Antwerp, Belgium; son of Elie (in manufacturing) and Sarah (Bartnowski) Schwerner; married Doloris Holmes (an art ecologist), January 13, 1961 (divorced, 1978); children: Adam, Ari. *Education:* Attended Cornell University, 1945-47, and Universite de Geneve, 1947-48; Columbia University, B.S., 1950, M.A., 1964. *Religion:* Buddhist.

ADDRESSES: Home—20 Bay St. Landing, Apt. B-3C, Staten Island, NY 10301. *Office*—College of Staten Island, City University of New York, 2800 Victory Blvd., Staten Island, NY 10314.

CAREER: Eron Preparatory School, New York City, teacher, 1955-59; Barnard School for Boys, Riverdale, NY, instructor in English and French, 1959-64; Long Island University, New York City, instructor in English, 1963-64; Staten Island Community College (now College of Staten Island) of the City University of New York, Staten Island, NY, instructor, 1964-66, assistant professor, 1966-69, associate professor, 1969-73, professor of English and speech, 1973—. Attended National Endowment for the Humanities seminar, Princeton University, 1978. Also does "sound poetry and music in the context of avant-garde, aleatoric music/poetry/sound combinations." *Military service:* U.S. Navy, 1945-46.

AWARDS, HONORS: National Endowment for the Arts grant, 1973; creative writing fellowships, New York State Council on the Arts, 1973 and 1975; National Education Association creative writing fellowships, 1973 and 1979; National Endowment for the Arts creative writing fellowship, 1987; two research fellowships from State University of New York; research fellowship from City University of New York.

WRITINGS:

POETRY

The Lightfall, Hawk's Well Press (New York City), 1963.
The Tablets I-VIII, Cummington Press (West Branch, IA), 1968.
(if personal), Black Sparrow Press (Los Angeles), 1968.
Seaweed, Black Sparrow Press, 1968.
The Tablets I-XV, Grossman (New York City), 1971.
Bacchae Sonnets, Abattoir (Omaha, NE), 1974.
The Tablets XVI, XVII, XVIII, Heron Press (Deerfield, MA), 1975.
Triumph of the Will, Perishable Press (Mount Horeb, WI), 1976.

This Practice: Tablet XIX and Other Poems, Permanent Press (London), 1976.

Bacchae Sonnets 1-7, Pod Press (Baltimore, MD), 1977.

The Work, The Joy, and the Triumph of the Will, New Rivers Press (New York City), 1977.

Sounds of the River Naranjana [and] *The Tablets I-XXIV,* Station Hill (Barrytown, NY), 1983.

The Tablets I-XXVI, Atlas (London), 1989.

RECORDINGS

The Tablets I-XVIII, S-Press, 1974, Black Box, 1978.

Recent Poetry 1977, Black Box, 1978.

Philoctetes, New Wilderness Audiographics, 1978.

OTHER

Stendahl's "The Red and the Black": Notes and Criticism, Study Master (New York City), 1963.

(With Donald M. Kaplan) *The Domesday Dictionary,* Simon & Schuster (New York City), 1963.

A Farewell to Arms: A Critical Commentary, Study Master, 1963.

Billy Budd and Typee: Critical Commentary, American R.D.M. (New York City), 1964.

(With Jerome Neibrief) *The Sound and the Fury: A Critical Commentary,* American R.D.M., 1964.

John Steinbeck's "Of Mice and Men," Monarch Press (New York City), 1965.

John Steinbeck's "The Red Pony" and "The Pearl," Monarch Press, 1965.

Andre Gide's "The Immoralist," "Strait Is the Gate," and Other Works: A Critical Commentary, Monarch Press, 1966.

Dos Passos's "U.S.A." and Other Works, Monarch Press, 1966.

Albert Camus' "The Stranger": A Critical Commentary, Monarch Press, 1970.

(Translator) *Redspell: Eleven American Indian Adaptations,* Perishable Press, 1975.

Poetry appears in anthologies, including *Conditions of Man,* edited by Willoughby Bonnette and Dale Johnson, Houghton (New York City), 1968; *A Treasury of Yiddish Poems,* edited by Irving Howe and Eliezer Greenberg, Holt (New York City), 1969; *A Caterpillar Anthology,* edited by Clayton Eshleman, Doubleday (New York City), 1971; *The New Open Poetry,* edited by Ronald Gross and George Quasha, Simon & Schuster, 1973; *The Roses Race around Her Name,* edited by Jonathan Cott, Stonehill, 1974; *CAPstan: Poems by CAPS Poetry Fellows, 1970-1975,* edited by Darcy Ryser and Bruce Benderson, Creative Artists Public Service Program, 1976.

Contributor to *Nation, Beloit Poetry Review, Trobar, Accent, West Wind, Nomad,* and other literary publications, and to professional journals.

ADAPTATIONS: The Tablets, a stage adaptation of Schwerner's poetry sequence by Hanon Reznikov, was first presented at Living Theater, June, 1989.

WORK IN PROGRESS: Workings and adaptations drawn from American Indian, Yiddish, French, and Tibetian sources.

SIDELIGHTS: Armand Schwerner's poetry is poetry that is meant to be heard—"the closest thing," writes Diane Wakoski in *Contemporary Poets,* "to a theatrical or oral poetry produced today." In addition to his own work, Schwerner has translated and adapted oral and dramatic poetry from other languages, including Greek and American Indian tongues. Writing about Schwerner's adaptation of the Greek dramatist Sophocles' *Philoctetes,* a *New York Times Book Review* critic states that "if Schwerner generally prefers the damped to the vibrating string, his sense of pace and pause wards off monotony."

Schwerner's satirical sequence of poems *The Tablets* "make up a wonderful, riddling text on illusion and reality, on communication and misunderstanding and the limits of speech," declares D. J. R. Bruckner, writing in the *New York Times.* "These imaginative puzzles are dramatic gestures even when they only lie silent on the page." The poet began the sequence in the 1960s, loosely basing their structure on the texts of clay tablets uncovered by archaeologists on the sites of ancient Sumerian and Akkadian cities of Iraq and Iran. In the process, he parodied the tendency among some poets of the 1960s and 1970s to incorporate anthropological motifs in their works. The poems mimic the ancient originals, using "commentary" from the supposed translator, missing lines, and holes where the text was damaged or made untranslatable. In these poems, states Wakoski, Schwerner "has taken the absurd and ridiculous world he lives in and creat[ed] . . . a beautiful religious and love poetry, as well as a witty game."

BIOGRAPHICAL/CRITICAL SOURCES:

BOOKS

Bowles, Jerry, editor, *This Book Is a Movie,* Delta (New York City), 1972.

Contemporary Poets, St. James Press, 1980.

Kostelanetz, Richard, editor, *Possibilities of Poetry,* Delta, 1970.

Kostelanetz, editor, *The End of Intelligent Writing,* Sheed & Ward (London), 1973.

Language and Structure in North America (exhibition catalogue), [Toronto], 1976.

PERIODICALS

American Poetry Review, March, 1973.

Chelsea, May, 1969; July, 1971.

Choice, September, 1978.

Hudson Review, autumn, 1964.

Nation, June 19, 1972.

New York Times, June 11, 1989.

New York Times Book Review, February 12, 1978, pp. 13, 23; June 4, 1978.

Parnassus, fall/winter, 1972; spring, 1973; spring/summer, 1979.

Performing Arts Journal, winter, 1978.

San Francisco Review of Books, September, 1978.*

*   *   *

SCOTT, Elaine 1940-

PERSONAL: Born June 20, 1940, in Philadelphia, PA; daughter of George Jobling (a banker) and Ethel (Smith) Watts; married Parker Scott (a geophysical engineer), May 16, 1959; children: Cynthia Ellen, Susan Elizabeth. *Education:* Attended Southern Methodist University, 1957-59, and Southern Methodist University and University of Houston, 1979-81. *Religion:* Methodist.

ADDRESSES: Home—13042 Taylorcrest, Houston, TX 77079. *Agent*—Jean V. Naggar, 216 East 75th St., New York, NY 10021.

CAREER: Writer, 1975—. Teacher of leadership workshops for Texas Conference of the United Methodist Church, 1978; teacher of writing workshops at Southwest Writer's Conference, Houston, TX, 1979, and at Trinity University, San Antonio, TX, 1980. Volunteer teacher of leadership workshops at United Methodist Church, Houston, 1959-77; volunteer publicity director for Camp Fire Girls of America, 1973-74. Board member and chair of committee on international adoptions, Homes of St. Mark (a private non-profit adoption agency), Houston, TX.

MEMBER: Authors Guild, Authors League of America, Society of Children's Book Writers and Illustrators.

AWARDS, HONORS: Parenting Magazine Reading Magic Award and American Library Association Notable Book citation, both for *Ramona: Behind the Scenes;* School Library Journal 'Best Books of 1995' Award for *Adventure in Space: The Flight to Fix the Hubble.*

WRITINGS:

CHILDREN'S NONFICTION

Adoption, F. Watts (New York City), 1980.

The Banking Book (illustrated by Kathie Abrams), Warne (New York City), 1981.

Doodlebugging for Oil: The Treasure Hunt for Oil, Warne, 1982.

Oil! Getting It, Finding It, Selling It, Warne, 1984.

Stocks and Bonds, Profits and Losses, F. Watts, 1985.

Ramona: Behind the Scenes of a Television Show, Morrow (New York City), 1987.

Could You Be Kidnapped?, F. Watts, 1988.

Safe in the Spotlight: The Dawn Animal Agency and the Sanctuary for Animals, Morrow Junior Books, 1991.

Look Alive: Behind the Scenes of an Animal Film, Morrow Junior Books, 1992.

From Microchips to Movie Stars: The Making of Super Mario Brothers, Hyperion (New York), 1993.

Funny Papers: Behind the Scenes of the Comics, Morrow Junior Books, 1993.

Adventure in Space: The Flight to Fix the Hubble, Hyperion, 1995.

Movie Magic: Behind the Scenes with Special Effects (photo essay), Morrow Junior Books, 1995.

YOUNG ADULT FICTION

Choices, Morrow, 1988.

WORK IN PROGRESS: Close Encounters with the Universe: What the Hubble Saw and *Becoming an Astronaut,* for Hyperion.

SIDELIGHTS: Elaine Scott told *CA* that she first considered a career as an author at age ten: "Our teacher decided on a dreary, early March afternoon that the entire class would write a poem during recess instead of sliding around the frozen turf of the school yard. Along with the rest of the class, I agonized as I stared at the blank piece of paper that lay in front of me on the desk. What to write about? What did I have to say about anything? Any writer, no matter how young, writes about what he knows, and I was no exception. That very morning as I left for school, I noticed the sorry state of the snowman I had built the week before. The thirty-two-degrees-plus temperature was playing havoc with his physique, pulling him steadily toward his demise, so I wrote my poem called 'A Tale of Woe' about three snowmen whose fate it was to melt with the coming of spring. I got an 'A' for my efforts and that grade thrilled me, but not nearly as much as the thrill I received when I heard that my teacher had entered my poem in a state-wide contest in Pennsylvania, and it won second prize." Her creative writing career was put on hold when her family moved to Texas a few months later, "and for the next twenty-five years I wrote nothing creative other than term papers and letters home," Scott related. "I never really thought about writing for children until I went to the Southwest Writer's Conference at the University of Houston. Because of a lull in my schedule, I dropped into a workshop on writing nonfiction for children. As I listened to an editor speak about the need for good philosophical books for children, the idea for my book *Adoption* began to form in my subconscious. By the end of the day, the idea had forced itself into my conscious thought and was no longer merely an idea, but a tangible form—a rough outline of the book. I plucked up the courage to approach Jean Naggar, a literary agent who was appearing at the university, and asked her what she thought of my book proposal. Jean was enthusiastic and agreed to represent me. She quickly sold that book proposal and has sold all my other books as well. Jean continues to represent me now.

"As I think about the books I have written up to now, I realize I haven't travelled too far from the child of ten who wrote about her melting snowmen. I still write about subjects I know and care about. I believe that without caring (and caring can mean hating, as well as loving) about his subject, the writer is in real danger of becoming nothing but a flesh and blood word processor—spitting out facts and nothing more. I think a writer should share himself, as well as his information, with his reader. . . . For me that is the essence of writing—it's really a dialogue between me and my reader. I am grateful for the reader, and out of that gratitude comes a willingness to share myself and my experience of life with him."

BIOGRAPHICAL/CRITICAL SOURCES:

PERIODICALS

Houston Chronicle, November 30, 1980, January 8, 1981.
Profile, August, 1982.
Texas Association for Childhood Education News, fall, 1981.

*   *   *

SCOTT, John M(artin)   1913-

PERSONAL: Born April 8, 1913, in Omaha, NE; son of Patrick John (a civil engineer) and Nettie (a clerk; maiden name, Martin) Scott. *Education:* St. Louis University, M.A., 1935, S.T.L., 1945, M.S., 1948. *Politics:* "Not bound to one party." *Avocational interests:* Hiking, travel ("from the Arctic Circle to Australia and New Zealand, and from Hong Kong to Egypt").

ADDRESSES: Home—2500 California St., Omaha, NE 68178. *Office*—Creighton University, Omaha, NE 68178.

CAREER: Entered Society of Jesus (Jesuits), 1931, ordained Roman Catholic priest, 1944; assigned to mission on Sioux Indian reservation in South Dakota, 1938-41; Campion High School, Prairie du Chien, WI, physics teacher, 1948-75; Creighton University, Omaha, NE, conducted science workshops, summers, 1949-75, visiting lecturer, 1950-82, chaplain, 1978—. Regional chair of Wisconsin Junior Academy of Science.

AWARDS, HONORS: Wisconsin Physics Teacher of the Year citation, 1959; citation as one of forty "Impact

Teachers" in the United States, National Education Association, 1967; *The Senses* was named one of the Outstanding Science Books for Children, 1976; Alumni Merit Award, College of Philosophy and Letters, St. Louis University, 1994.

WRITINGS:

Wonderland (juvenile), Loyola University Press (Chicago), 1958.
Adventures in Science (high school text), Loyola University Press, 1963.
Rain: Man's Greatest Gift, Culligan, 1967.
Our Romance with Sun and Rain, Culligan, 1968.
Adventure Awaits You, Culligan, 1968.
The Everyday Living Approach to Teaching Elementary Science, Parker Publishing, 1970.
What Is Science? (juvenile), Parents' Magazine Press (New York City), 1972.
What Is Sound? (juvenile), Parents' Magazine Press, 1973.
Heat and Fire (juvenile), Parents' Magazine Press, 1973.
The Senses (juvenile), Parents' Magazine Press, 1975.
To Touch the Face of God, Our Sunday Visitor (Huntington, IN), 1975.
Phenomena of Our Universe: Mysteries that Influence Our Lives, Our Sunday Visitor, 1976.
The Last Word in Lonesome Is Me, Our Sunday Visitor, 1978.
Countdown to Encounter: Von Braun and the Astronauts, Our Sunday Visitor, 1979.
Why a Gift on Sunday?, St. Paul Editions, 1979.
Electricity, Electronics, and You, J. Weston Walch, 1981.
Beyond Earth, J. Weston Walch, 1983.
Something of the Wonderful, St. Paul Editions, 1986.
How to Start Your Romance with God, Franciscan Herald (Chicago), 1987.
Without Thorns, It's Not a Rose, Our Sunday Visitor, 1988.
Activities that Prove Science Is Fun-damental, J. Weston Walch, 1988.
Discovering God: Life's Adventure, Our Sunday Visitor, 1992.
Everyday Science, Real-Life Activities, J. Weston Walch, 1994.

Author of column, "Talking It over with Fr. John," in *Treasure Chest,* 1959-63. Author of about twenty pamphlets for adults and young people. Contributor to *Educators Guide.* Contributor of more than one hundred articles to magazines and newspapers, including *Arizona Highways.* Science editor for *Queen's Work* and *Young Catholic Messenger,* 1949-63.

SIDELIGHTS: John M. Scott told *CA* why he writes about science: "Every moment of our lives we live in a wonder world. If we see not the magic, the fault must be our own. 'To me,' said Walt Whitman, 'every hour of light and dark is a miracle. Every cubic inch of space is a miracle.' According to Albert Einstein, 'The most beautiful thing we can experience is the mysterious. It is the source of all true art and science. He to whom this emotion is a stranger, who can no longer pause to wonder and stand rapt in awe, is as good as dead; his eyes are closed.' Dag Hammarskjold would have us keep in mind that 'we die on the day when our lives cease to be illumined by the steady radiance, renewed daily, of a wonder, the source of which is beyond all reason.' 'Always around,' says E. Merrill Root, 'lies a world that can become either dull with habit and sleep, or magical with marvel and wonder.' According to G. K. Chesterton, 'The world will never perish for lack of wonders, but only for lack of wonder.'

"Because I find the whole world a place of magic and mystery and surprise and delights, of glorious revelations of man's wonderful nature, of astounding glimpses of glory and beauty, I wish to share my delight with others—through the magic of the printed page."

BIOGRAPHICAL/CRITICAL SOURCES:

PERIODICALS

Blackrobe, March, 1973.

*   *   *

SEARLE, Ronald (William Fordham) 1920-

PERSONAL: Born March 3, 1920, in Cambridge, England; son of William James and Nellie (Hunt) Searle; married Kaye Webb, 1946 (divorced, 1967); married Monica Koenig (a theater designer), 1967; children: (first marriage) Kate, John. *Education:* Cambridge School of Art, diploma, 1939.

ADDRESSES: Agent—Tessa Sayle, 11 Jubilee Place, London SW3 3TE, England; and John Locke Studio, 15 East 76th St., New York, NY 10021.

CAREER: Graphic artist, cartoonist, medalist, designer, and animator, 1935—. One man shows at galleries in many cities, including London; New York; San Francisco; Paris; Vienna; Berlin-Dahlem; Munich; Philadelphia; Zurich; Bremen; West Germany; Tolentino, Italy; Linz, Austria; Soedertaelje, Sweden; Lausanne, Switzerland; and Hannover, West Germany. Film designer, 1957—; films designed include *John Gilpin,* 1951, *On the Twelfth Day,* 1954, *Energetically Yours,* 1957, *Germany,* 1960, and *The King's Breakfast,* 1963; designer of animated sequences for the films *Those Magnificent Men in Their Flying Machines,* 1964, *Monte Carlo or Bust,* 1968, and *Scrooge,* 1970. Designer of commemorative medals for the French Mint, 1974—, and British Art Medal Society, 1983—. Ed-

itorial director, Perpetua Books, 1951-62. *Military service:* British Army, Royal Engineers, 1939-46; Japanese prisoner of war, 1942-45; Allied Force Headquarters, Department of Psychological Warfare, Port Said Operations, 1956.

MEMBER: Alliance Graphique Internationale, Garrick Club (London).

AWARDS, HONORS: Eleven awards, including Stratford (Ontario) Festival award, International Film Festival award, and Art Directors Club of Los Angeles medal, for animated film *Energetically Yours,* 1958-59; Art Directors Club of Philadelphia award, 1959; National Cartoonists Society of America, Reuben Award, 1960; III Biennale, Tolentino, Italy, gold medal, 1965; Prix de la Critique Belge, 1968; Festival d'Avignon, Prix d'Humour, 1971; Medaille de la ville d'Avignon, 1971; Grand Prix de l'Humour Noir "Grandville," 1971; Prix Internationale Charles Huard de dessin de presse, 1972; La Monnaie de Paris Medal, 1974; named Royal Designer for Industry, 1988.

WRITINGS:

Forty Drawings, foreword by Frank Kendon, Cambridge University Press (Cambridge, England), 1946, Macmillan (New York City), 1947.

Le Nouveau ballet anglais (picture album), Editions Montbrun, 1946.

Hurrah for St. Trinian's! and Other Lapses (also see below), foreword by D. B. Wyndham Lewis, Macdonald & Co. (London), 1948.

The Female Approach, with Masculine Sidelights (also see below), foreword by Max Beerbohm, Macdonald & Co., 1949.

Back to the Slaughterhouse and Other Ugly Moments (also see below), Macdonald & Co., 1951.

Souls in Torment, preface and short dirge by C. Day Lewis, Perpetua (London), 1953.

Medisances, Editions Neuf, 1953.

The Female Approach: Cartoons, introduction by Malcolm Muggeridge, Knopf (New York City), 1954.

The Rake's Progress, Perpetua, 1955, new edition published as *The Rake's Progress: Some Immoral Tales,* Dobson (Durham, England), 1968.

Merry England, Etc., Perpetua, 1956, Knopf, 1957.

(Editor and author of introduction) *The Biting Eye of Andre Francois,* Perpetua, 1960.

The Penguin Ronald Searle, Penguin (Middlesex, England, and New York City), 1960.

(Editor) Henri Perruchot, *Toulouse-Lautrec: A Definitive Biography,* translated by Humphrey Hare, Perpetua, 1960, World Publishing, 1961.

(Editor) Perruchot, *Cezanne: A Definitive Biography*, translated by Hare, Perpetua, 1961, World Publishing, 1962.

Which Way Did He Go? Perpetua, 1961, World Publishing, 1962.

Toulouse-Lautrec (television script), British Broadcasting Corporation, 1961.

From Frozen North to Filthy Lucre: With Remarks by Groucho Marx and Commentaries by Jane Clapperton, Viking (New York City), 1964.

Searle in the Sixties, Penguin, 1964.

Pardong, M'sieur: Paris et autres, Denoel, 1965.

Searle's Cats, Dobson, 1967, Greene, 1968, revised and redrawn edition, Souvenir Press, 1987.

The Square Egg, Greene, 1968.

Take One Toad: A Book of Ancient Remedies, Dobson, 1968.

Hello—Where Did All the People Go?, Weidenfeld & Nicolson (London), 1969, Greene, 1970.

Hommage a Toulouse-Lautrec, introduction by Roland Topor, Edition Empreinte, 1969, published in England as *The Second Coming of Toulouse-Lautrec*, Weidenfeld & Nicolson, 1970.

Filles de Hambourg, J. J. Pauvert, 1969, published in England as *Secret Sketchbook: The Back Streets of Hamburg*, Weidenfeld & Nicolson, 1970.

The Addict: A Terrible Tale, Greene, 1971.

Weil noch das Laempchen glueht (contains selections from *Hurrah for St. Trinian's! and Other Lapses*, *The Female Approach, with Masculine Sidelights*, and *Back to the Slaughterhouse and Other Ugly Moments*), Diogenes, 1972.

Gilbert & Sullivan: A Selection from Ronald Searle's Original Designs for the Animated Feature Film "Dick Deadeye" (picture album), Entercom Productions, 1975.

Dick Deadeye; or, Duty Done, Harcourt (San Diego, CA, and New York City), 1975.

More Cats, Dobson, 1975, Greene, 1976.

Searle's Zoodiac, Dobson, 1977, published as *Zoodiac*, Pantheon (New York City), 1978.

Ronald Searle (monograph), Deutsch, 1978, Mayflower Books (New York City), 1979.

The King of Beasts and Other Creatures, Allen Lane, 1980, published as *The Situation Is Hopeless*, Viking, 1981.

Ronald Searle's Big Fat Cat Book, Little, Brown (Boston, MA), 1982.

The Illustrated Winespeak: Ronald Searle's Wicked World of Winetasting, Souvenir Press, 1983, Harper (New York City), 1984.

Ronald Searle in Perspective, New English Library, 1984, Atlantic Monthly Press, 1985.

Ronald Searle's Golden Oldies, 1941-1961, Pavilion, 1985.

To the Kwai—and Back: War Drawings, 1939-1945, Atlantic Monthly Press, 1986.

Something in the Cellar: Ronald Searle's Wonderful World of Wine, Souvenir Press, 1986, Ten Speed Press (Berkeley, CA), 1988.

Ah Yes, I Remember It Well . . . : Paris 1961-1975, Pavilion, 1987, Salem House, 1988.

Ronald Searle's Non-Sexist Dictionary, Ten Speed Press, 1988.

Slightly Foxed—but Still Desirable: Ronald Searle's Wicked World of Book Collecting, Souvenir Press, 1989.

Carnet de Croquis: Le Plaisir du trait, Editions La Nompareille (Paris), 1992.

The Curse of St. Trinian's: The Best of the Drawings, Pavilion, 1993.

Marquis de Sade Meets Goody Two-Shoes, Pavilion, 1994.

CO-AUTHOR

(With Kaye Webb) *Paris Sketchbook*, Saturn Press, 1950, revised edition, Perpetua, 1957.

(With Timothy Shy, pseudonym of D. B. Wyndham Lewis) *The Terror of St. Trinian's; or, Angela's Prince Charming*, Parrish, 1952.

(With Geoffrey Willans) *Down with Skool!: A Guide to School Life for Tiny Pupils and Their Parents* (also see below), Parrish, 1953, Vanguard, 1954.

(With Webb) *Looking at London and People Worth Meeting*, News Chronicle (London), 1953.

(With Willans) *How to Be Topp: A Guide to Sukcess for Tiny Pupils, Including All Is to Kno about Space* (also see below), Vanguard, 1954.

(With Willans) *Whizz for Atomms: A Guide to Survival in the 20th Century for Fellow Pupils, Their Doting Maters, Pompous Paters and Any Others Who Are Interested* (also see below), Parrish, 1956, published as *Molesworth's Guide to the Atomic Age*, Vanguard, 1957.

(With Willans) *The Dog's Ear Book: With Four Lugubrious Verses*, Crowell (New York City), 1958.

(With Alex Atkinson) *The Big City; or, The New Mayhew*, Perpetua, 1958, Braziller (New York City), 1959.

(With Willans) *The Compleet Molesworth* (includes *Down with Skool!: A Guide to School Life for Tiny Pupils and Their Parents*, *How to Be Topp: A Guide to Sukcess for Tiny Pupils, Including All Is to Kno about Space*, *Whizz for Atomms: A Guide to Survival in the 20th Century for Fellow Pupils, Their Doting Maters, Pompous Paters and Any Others Who Are Interested*, and *Back in the Jug Agane*; also see below), Parrish, 1958, reprinted, Pavilion, 1984.

(With Willans) *Back in the Jug Agane*, Parrish, 1959, published as *Molesworth Back in the Jug Agane*, Vanguard, 1960.

(With Atkinson) *USA for Beginners,* Perpetua, 1959, published as *By Rocking Chair across America,* Funk (New York City), 1959.

(With Atkinson) *Russia for Beginners: By Rocking Chair across Russia,* Perpetua, 1960, published as *By Rocking Chair across Russia,* World Publishing, 1960.

(With Webb) *Refugees 1960,* Penguin, 1960.

(With Atkinson) *Escape from the Amazon!,* Perpetua, 1964.

(With Heinz Huber) *Anatomie eines Adlers: Ein Deutschlandbuch,* Desch, 1966, translation by Constantine Fitz Gibbon published as *Haven't We Met Before Somewhere?: Germany from the Inside and Out,* Viking, 1966.

(With Kildare Dobbs) *The Great Fur Opera: Annals of the Hudson's Bay Company, 1670-1970,* Greene, 1970.

(With Irwin Shaw) *Paris! Paris!,* Harcourt, 1977.

ILLUSTRATOR

W. Henry Brown, *Co-operation in a University Town,* Co-operative Printing Society, 1939.

Ronald Hastain, *White Coolie,* Hodder & Stoughton, 1947.

Douglas Goldring, *Life Interests,* Macdonald & Co., 1948.

W. E. Stanton Hope, *Tanker Fleet,* Anglo-Saxon Petroleum Co., 1948.

Gillian Olivier, *Turn But a Stone,* Hodder & Stoughton, 1949.

Audrey Hilton, *This England 1946-1949,* Turnstile Press, 1949.

Meet Yourself on Sunday, Naldrett Press, 1949.

Meet Yourself at the Doctor's, Naldrett Press, 1949.

Patrick Campbell, *A Long Drink of Cold Water,* Falcon Press, 1949.

Noel Langley, *The Inconstant Moon,* Arthur Barker, 1949.

Campbell, *A Short Trot with a Cultured Mind,* Falcon Press, 1950.

Oliver Philpott, *Stolen Journey,* Hodder & Stoughton, 1950.

Russell Braddon, *The Piddingtons,* Laurie, 1950.

Bernard Darwin and others, *The British Inn,* Naldrett Press, 1950.

Campbell, *Life in Thin Slices,* Falcon Press, 1951.

Harry Hearson and John Courtenay Trewin, *An Evening at the Larches,* Elek, 1951.

Braddon, *The Naked Island* (includes drawings made in Changi prison camps by Searle), Laurie, 1952.

Winifred Ellis, *London—So Help Me!,* Macdonald & Co., 1952.

William Cowper, *The Diverting History of John Gilpin,* Chiswick Press, 1952.

Frank Carpenter, *Six Animal Plays,* Methuen (New York City), 1953.

Denys Parsons, *It Must Be True,* Macdonald & Co., 1953.

Richard Haydn, *The Journal of Edwin Carp,* Hamish Hamilton (London), 1954.

Campbell, *Patrick Campbell's Omnibus,* Hulton Press, 1954.

Geoffrey Gorer, *Modern Types,* Cresset Press, 1955.

Reuben Ship, *The Investigator: A Narrative in Dialogue,* Sidgwick & Jackson (London), 1956.

Kaye Webb, compiler, *The St. Trinian's Story: The Whole Ghastly Dossier,* Perpetua, 1959.

Christopher Fry, *Phoenix Too Frequent: A Comedy,* Oxford University Press, 1959.

Anger of Achilles: Homer's Iliad, translated by Robert Graves, Doubleday (New York City), 1959.

Ted Patrick and Silas Spitzer, *Great Restaurants of America,* Lippincott (Philadelphia), 1960.

Charles Dickens, *A Christmas Carol,* Perpetua, 1961, World Publishing, 1961.

Dickens, *Great Expectations,* abridged edition, edited by D. Dickens, Norton (New York City), 1962.

Dickens, *Oliver Twist,* abridged edition, edited by D. Dickens, Norton, 1962.

James Thurber, *The Thirteen Clocks and the Wonderful O,* Penguin, 1962.

Allen Andrews and William Richardson, *Those Magnificent Men in Their Flying Machines; or, How I Flew from London to Paris in 25 Hours, 11 Minutes,* Norton, 1965.

Mr. Rothman's New Guide to London: Together with a Guide to Some Londoners of the Eighteen-Nineties, Rothmans of Pall Mall, 1968.

Rudolf Eric Raspe and others, *The Adventures of Baron Munchausen,* introduction by S. J. Perelman, Pantheon, 1969.

Jack Davies, Ken Annakin, and Andrews, *Those Daring Young Men in Their Jaunty Jalopies: Monte Carlo or Bust!* (screenplay; also see below) Putnam (New York City), 1969, published in England as *Monte Carlo or Bust!: Those Daring Young Men in Their Jaunty Jalopies,* Dobson, 1969.

E. W. Hildick, *Monte Carlo or Bust!* (novelization of the screenplay *Those Daring Young Men in Their Jaunty Jalopies: Monte Carlo or Bust!*), Sphere Books, 1969.

Leslie Bricusse, *Scrooge* (juvenile), Aurora Publications (Nashville), 1970.

Frank Whitbourn, *Mr. Lock of St. James's Street: His Continuing Life and Changing Times,* Heinemann (London), 1971.

Oliver Philpot, *Stolen Journey,* Morley Books, 1971.

George Rainbird, *The Subtle Alchemist,* revised edition, Michael Joseph, 1973.

Michael Flanders and Donald Swan, *The Songs of Michael Flanders and Donald Swan,* St. Martin's (New York City), 1978.

Tom Lehrer, *Too Many Songs by Tom Lehrer: With Not Enough Drawings by Ronald Searle,* Pantheon, 1981.

Kingsley Amis and James Cochrane, *The Great British Songbook,* Pavilion, 1986.

Lee Wardlaw, *The Tales of Grandpa Cat,* Dial (New York City), 1994.

Sarah Kortum, *The Hatless Man,* Viking, 1995.

OTHER

Contributor to *Encyclopedia Britannica.* Contributor of illustrations to *New York Times, Le Monde, Life, TV Guide, New Yorker,* and numerous other periodicals. Member of editorial board, *Punch,* 1956-61. Searle was twice featured on BBC television in 1975, in the documentary *A Step in the Jungle,* and on the program *Omnibus.*

Searle's books have been translated into many languages, including French and German.

ADAPTATIONS: A series of cartoons on a fictitious girls' school became the "St. Trinian's" film series. Film versions of *The Belles of St. Trinian's,* starring Alastair Sim, British Lion Film Production, 1954; *Blue Murder at St. Trinian's,* starring Joyce Grenfell, Terry-Thomas, and Sim, John Harvel Productions, 1957; *The Pure Hell of St. Trinian's,* starring Cecil Parker and Grenfell, Vale Film Productions, 1960; *The Great St. Trinian's Train Robbery,* starring Frankie Howerd and Dora Bryan, Braywild Films, 1965; *The Wildcats of St. Trinian's,* starring Sheila Hancock and Michael Hordern, Wildcat Film Productions, 1980, all produced by Frank Launder and Sidney Gilliat.

SIDELIGHTS: Ronald Searle is an artist who "can do anything," claims Malcolm Muggeridge in the introduction to *The Female Approach: Cartoons,* "—illustrate, expound or embellish an idea, convey a scene or person. His talent extends to illustrating Boswell's Grand Tour as finely and sufficiently as it does to his weekly theatre drawing, or to a Hogarthian treatment of the contemporary scene." Famous in England and America for his blackly humorous drawings of animals in books such as *The King of Beasts and Other Creatures* (later published as *The Situation Is Hopeless*) and people, especially the wicked little girls of his "St. Trinian's" series, Searle expresses, in Muggeridge's opinion, a wit which "moves far beyond the field of the merely funny. It is sharp, satirical, cruel and belongs essentially to these strange and disconcerting times. Like all artists, particularly humourous ones, he is basically anarchistic. Beneath the skin he sees the skull."

In some ways, states Bill Mauldin in the *New York Times Book Review,* Searle's work resembles Picasso's because "he makes [drawing] look so easy." Searle's highly individual style "created a new approach to caricature by combining the highly conventionalized, two-dimensional drawing that came out of French modernism with a peculiarly British attention to details of costume, furniture, architecture, ornament, facial expression, gesture and the bric-a-brac of social life," says Tom Wolfe in the *New York Times Book Review.* "The contradiction between the simplicity of the line and the clutter of the content," he continues, "tends to make even the most pointless Searle drawing funny." The artist's widespread popularity "spawned a massive school of admirers and imitators," according to Mauldin, making him a source of inspiration for three generations of political cartoonists and satirists. Searle's comic artwork has influenced graphic artists such as Jeff MacNelly and Pat Oliphant in America, and Gerald Scarfe and Ralph Steadman in England.

Perhaps the most significant period of Searle's life was the time he spent in Japanese prison camps in Southeast Asia during the Second World War. He told Robert Osborn in *Saturday Review:* "That was the turning point for me . . . I was captured when Singapore fell, and for four years I stayed a prisoner, drawing like mad. You learn how to feel things in a prisoncamp, and I was lucky enough to learn how to draw what I feel." This work—some of it done with burnt matches and other improvised material—would have cost Searle his life had it been discovered, says Mauldin. Sometimes his pictures were concealed by fellow prisoners suffering from cholera, who depended on Japanese dread of the disease to prevent discovery. "Such an experience," states Muggeridge, "was bound to have a profound effect on someone as sensitive and imaginative as Searle. It might easily have destroyed him. Actually, he survived, not only in body (itself a considerable achievement) but, what was even more important, in spirit. The drawings he made during his confinement are haunting in their tenderness, and . . . miraculous in the sureness and soundness of their line."

Searle's wartime sketches formed the basis of an exhibition at the Cambridge School of Art in 1946, a show which, says Wolfe, made the artist famous. A selection of these drawings was published as his first book, *Forty Drawings.* Many years later, Searle added reminiscences to his artwork and published the full three hundred sketches with text as *To the Kwai—and Back: War Drawings, 1939-1945.* Mauldin, himself a famous war artist, sums up his feeling about Searle's work: "For me one of the greatest things about this book is its demonstration that the only chance for survival in truly impossible circumstances is to have a sense of humor so ingrained that it can't be kicked out of you. . . . Most of war seems to be a double image, harrowing and often tragic on one face, ennobling and sometimes whimsical on the flip side. This book of Ronald Searle's has it all. It will be rewarding for any serious art student, war buff or hardy but sensitive soul."

BIOGRAPHICAL/CRITICAL SOURCES:

BOOKS

Davies, Russell, *Ronald Searle: A Biography,* Sinclair-Stevenson (London), 1990.
Feaver, William, *Masters of Caricature,* Knopf, 1981.
Heller, Steven, *Man Bites Man: Two Decades of Satiric Art,* A & W, 1981.
Miller, Bertha, and others, compilers, *Illustrators of Children's Books: 1946-1956,* Horn Book (Boston), 1958.
Searle, Ronald, *The Female Approach: Cartoons,* introduction by Malcolm Muggeridge, Knopf, 1954.
Searle, *Ronald Searle in Perspective,* New English Library, 1984.

PERIODICALS

American Artist, September, 1955.
Bulletin C.E.M. of La Monnaie de Paris, June, 1974.
Cartoonist Profiles, fall, 1969.
Chicago Tribune Book World, November 1, 1981; December 5, 1982.
Connaissance des Arts, June, 1979.
Das Schoenste, July, 1962.
Elseviers Weekblad, May 18, 1957.
Gebrauschgraphic, December, 1961.
Graphis, number 23, 1948; number 80, 1958; number 109, 1963.
Graphis 36, 1980/81.
Idea, number 78, 1966.
International Herald Tribune, February 17, 1973.
La Quinzaine Litteraire, December, 1967.
Le Monde, January 3, 1970; February 2, 1973.
Les Lettres Francaises, December 22, 1966; November 15, 1967.
Les Nouvelles Litteraires, December, 1966.
Library Journal, June 1, 1969.
Life, October 31, 1960.
L'oeil, November, 1974.
Los Angeles Times Book Review, April 19, 1981.
Natural History, June, 1971.
New Statesman, November 17, 1978.
New York Times Book Review, March 8, 1981; November 1, 1981; August 8, 1986.
Opus, January, 1972.
Paris Match, February 3, 1973.
P. N. Review, number 50, 1986.
Publimondial, number 76, 1955; number 82, 1956.
Quest, March, 1981.
Saturday Review, November 23, 1957.
Studio, March, 1963.
Texas Quarterly, number 4, 1960.
Times (London), February 12, 1973; May 8, 1973; November 24, 1978.
Times Literary Supplement, April 6, 1973; June 15, 1973.

Vogue, November 1, 1957.
Washington Post Book World, December 12, 1981.

*   *   *

SECREST, Meryle
See DOMAN, June

*   *   *

SEE, Carolyn (Penelope)   1934-
   (Monica Highland, a joint pseudonym)

PERSONAL: Born January 13, 1934, in Pasadena, CA; daughter of George Newton Bowland (a writer) and Kate (Sullivan) Laws; married Richard Edward See (an anthropologist), February 27, 1954 (divorced); married Tom Sturak (an editor and teacher), April 11, 1960 (divorced); currently lives with John Espey; children: (first marriage) Lisa; (second marriage) Clara. *Education:* Los Angeles State College of Applied Arts and Sciences (now California State University, Los Angeles), B.A., 1957; University of California, Los Angeles, M.A., 1961, Ph.D., 1963. *Politics:* Democrat.

ADDRESSES: Home—P.O. Box 107, Topanga, CA 90290. *Agent*—Janklow Nesbit Agency, 598 Madison Ave., New York, NY 10022.

CAREER: Writer. Loyola University of Los Angeles, Los Angeles, CA, began as associate professor, became professor of English; currently professor of English at University of California, Los Angeles.

MEMBER: Writers Guild of America, Modern Language Association of America, PEN.

AWARDS, HONORS: Samuel Goldwyn Award, 1963; Sidney Hillman Award, 1969; grant from National Endowment for the Arts, 1974; Proclamation from City of Los Angeles and Long Beach Literary Hall of Fame Award, both 1983, both for *Lotus Land;* runner-up, Olive Branch Award, Writers' and Publishers' Alliance for Nuclear Disarmament/Editors' Organizing Committee, 1987, and Bread and Roses Award, National Women's Political Caucus, 1988, both for *Golden Days;* Robert Kirsch Body of Work Award, *Los Angeles Times,* 1993.

WRITINGS:

The Rest Is Done with Mirrors, Little, Brown (Boston, MA), 1970.
Blue Money (nonfiction), McKay (New York City), 1973.
Mothers, Daughters, Coward, 1977.
Rhine Maidens, Coward, 1981.
(With John Espey and daughter, Lisa See Kendall, under joint pseudonym Monica Highland) *Lotus Land,* Coward, 1983.

(With Espey and Kendall under joint pseudonym Monica Highland) *110 Shanghai Road*, McGraw-Hill (New York City), 1986.

Golden Days, McGraw-Hill, 1986.

(With Espey and Kendall under joint pseudonym Monica Highland) *Greetings from Southern California* (nonfiction), Graphic Arts Press, 1988.

(With Espey) *Two Schools of Thought: Tales of Education and Romance*, John Daniel, 1991.

Making History, Houghton (Boston), 1991.

Dreaming: Hard Luck and Good Times in America, Random House (New York City), 1995.

Regular contributor to *TV Guide;* also contributor to *Atlantic, Los Angeles Times Magazine, McCall's, Ms., Esquire, Sports Illustrated,* and *California Magazine.* Weekly book reviewer, *Los Angeles Times,* 1981-93, *Washington Post,* 1993—.

ADAPTATIONS: Lotus Land and *110 Shanghai Road* have been optioned for television miniseries. *Golden Days* has been optioned for a feature film by producer Arnold Glimcher.

SIDELIGHTS: A native Californian who wrote her doctoral thesis on the "Hollywood" novel, Carolyn See's novels contribute to the genre by using settings, characters, and ideas that illustrate the unique West Coast lifestyle. Her earliest works are "obscure novels on Los Angeles," as she told John F. Baker in a *Publishers Weekly* interview. *The Rest Is Done with Mirrors* relates the story of two UCLA graduate students, or "unpersons," remarked a *New York Times Book Review* critic. The two "are described in detail and patronized continually—but characterized inadequately." *Mothers, Daughters* is a novel about "the commonplace conjugal recklessness of our dwindling decade," summarized Jane Larkin Crain in the *New York Times Book Review.* Written after her second divorce, See remarked to Charles Trueheart in a *Washington Post* interview that she "should have waited another year. . . . I was still awfully mad at Tom, so I wrote it as a sorrowful woman's book. It's pretty silly, although there's some good writing in it." Crain echoed See's assessment, writing that although the book begins with "bite and tension . . . [it] never really achieves dramatic plausibility."

With her third novel *Rhine Maidens,* however, See "has written a book about women that is agreeably free from passive self-pity and humorless hand-wringing," according to Judith Chettle in the *Washington Post Book Review.* *Rhine Maidens* "hands us a bittersweet slice of California living and introduces two characters who pull us in to share their shoes, their eyes, their insides," observed Rhea Kohan in the *Los Angeles Times Book Review.* These two characters are a mother and daughter who, as Nora Johnson described in the *New York Times Book Review,* "have

nothing in common but a chance biological connection and an eerie penchant for losing husbands." Although Clancy Sigal, in the *Chicago Tribune Book World,* found See's book "hugely funny and entertaining," he also remarked that it is "a breeze—perhaps a little too much so. See is so at pains not to bore her readers that [the characters] do not fully engage." Kohan feels otherwise; although the two women are "pathetic," the author "makes us care, really care about them," commented the critic. "She makes us root for them. . . . See's depiction of life styles is so vivid the reader sees, smells, feels, weeps, even laughs along with the characters." As Chettle put it, *Rhine Maidens* "is a book in the best tradition of comedy, where laughter is close to tears."

Many critics found *Rhine Maidens* successful because of the quality of its writing. Chettle noted that See "has an eye for the little details that give a place authenticity. . . . The data are noted with affection and tolerant amusement." Johnson had a similar assessment: "Carolyn See is a skillful writer. . . . [She] looks at that well-trodden territory, Southern California, from some new angles." And Peter S. Prescott in *Newsweek* called the author "a clever writer; whenever her story stumbles into stridency or distemper, she gives it a shake and then her wit falls back glittering onto the page."

In *Golden Days,* a post-doomsday novel set in California, See "has taken The Unthinkable and turned it into a tale that is almost inspirational," commented Johnson in the *Los Angeles Times Book Review.* As See told Trueheart, her book considers and confronts "The Unthinkable": "I don't have to think about it'—that's a failure of imagination. The people who survive will be the ones who like their life enough that they want to see what's going to happen next." What happens next is "an absolute refusal by . . . California weirdos—particularly in the graduates of positive-thinking workshops—to accept the end of the world," in the words of *New York Times Book Review* contributor Carol Sternhell.

See has explained that after writing *Rhine Maidens* she intended to make her work less generic; as she told Trueheart, "I don't think I'm interested in writing women's novels anymore." This claim to the contrary, some critics detected a distinctly "female" outlook in *Golden Days.* Ursula K. LeGuin, writing in the *Washington Post Book World,* thought that the novel contained "the strength of feminism [that] enables it to take the risk of being vulnerable. It isn't safe, but it's fearless." Sternhell also observed a "wicked feminist skewering of 'grim-lipped men' and their missiles" while Johnson saw an "intricate connection between male fear of failure and ever bigger payloads and bigger bangs." While the author does not view the book as feminist, there is within it a demonstration of "the female principle, not confined to women," as Johnson described it, "the kind of thinking that could—were it in higher places—save our lives."

This "female," less incendiary way of thinking is also reflected in the more flexible West Coast viewpoint of the novel: "The sophistication of thought in the novel is considerable, cool and Californian," said LeGuin. "The rigid European fixation of much East Coast thinking doesn't encompass the real West at all." Helen Byatt, writing for the *Times Literary Supplement,* felt this regional viewpoint is confusing: "We are mostly unaware of any direction. It is also difficult to distinguish the other characters. . . . One needs to be finely tuned to the Californian idiom to recognize [them]." LeGuin believed, however, that this uniquely western idiom "may be invisible to readers to whom they're just foreign words. . . . No harm in that, unless it leaves the book underestimated by critics who should know better."

As with her previous novel, *Golden Days* demonstrates See's skillful writing; in the London *Times,* for example, John Nicholson noted that the author "writes tautly and with scathing elegance about contemporary Californian mores." The critic also called *Golden Days* "one of the most original and entertaining books to come out of America for a very long time." R. Z. Sheppard of *Time* characterized See's writing as "strikingly gnomic," although he criticized her "impatience with novelistic invention." He also commented that much of the novel "reads like a catchall of California behaviors." Johnson, however, believed that this impatience is consistent with the book; although *Golden Days* "seems hastily put together, as though written in a race against the last deadline of all . . . this perhaps unintentional mood of haste works."

Although Sheppard did not think *Golden Days* will "pass for serious fiction in the 80's," LeGuin saw in it a vision of "crazy majesty . . . [and] stinging exactness." While "an inspirational novel about nuclear war seems, well, a bit perverse," Sternhell contended that "this may be the most life-affirming novel I've ever read." "Anybody who cares about anything should read this," suggested Johnson, concluding that *Golden Days* " . . . is a very, very, important book."

The pseudonym Monica Highland, responsible for *Lotus Land* and *110 Shanghai Road,* is used by See, her longtime companion, John Espey, and her daughter, Lisa See Kendall. The trio began writing with the intention of creating an epic novel better than the typical mini-series they were seeing on television. The first Monica Highland novel, *Lotus Land,* is a "rich and well-researched story," according to Audrey C. Foote in the *Washington Post Book World.* Although at first "the author drones portentously," said the critic, Highland "then mercifully gets

down to business . . . in brief, serviceable prose." Linda Rolens, in the *Los Angeles Times Book Review,* found that the three authors "build a sense of place and character and a feel that is somehow historically accurate." Even when "characterization turns vague and the details . . . are ignored," noted Rolens, the book "manages to imitate the nature of the [Los Angeles] it chronicles—often unashamedly tacky, frequently fun."

110 Shanghai Road, another Monica Highland chronicle, is a "plot-heavy book . . . [that] contains a great deal more intelligence and elan than most historical sagas," remarked Dennis Drabelle in the *Washington Post Book World.* "There is nothing dull about *110 Shanghai Road,*" wrote Harrison E. Salisbury in the *Los Angeles Times Book Review.* The novel "roars over continents, time zones, the years from 1913 to 1983, in a panorama of murder, incest, rape, torture, passion, high crime, jealousy, billions, betrayal, and all the furies known to humanity and even a few hitherto unknown. If hilariously out-of-sync chronologies of the last few decades satisfy your taste, no zanier one is likely to be pasted together." "Although the authors might try fleshing out their characters more," suggested Drabelle, " . . . on the whole their amalgamated talents do justice to their rich material."

See has not allowed the success of "Monica Highland" to interfere with her own more serious fiction. In 1991 she published another California novel, *Making History.* Set in the affluent neighborhood of Pacific Palisades, *Making History* presents a family that must deal with a series of harsh blows and sudden catastrophes. One character, a teen named Robin, narrates sections from the afterlife. Another, the gracious housewife Wynn, questions her reliance on the "safety nets" of marriage and financial prosperity. *Los Angeles Times Book Review* reviewer Bette Pesetsky wrote that, in *Making History,* "the family drama is the focus, the driving force—but we are not about to be trapped in any banal suburban malaise. See is too good for that, and she knowingly explores the facade of civility with which her characters interact." Pesetsky concluded that the book is "perceptive in its details and ambitious in its daring . . . *Making History* is a satisfying and remarkable book." In the *New York Times Book Review,* Susan Fromberg Schaeffer declared: "To read *Making History* is to hear what Thea, the book's seer, perceives—it is to tune in to a kind of cosmic television on whose channels one can see and hear the living and the dead, the animate and the inanimate. . . . Ms. See sets out to catch the sound of our world singing its way into the future. The miracle is how well she has succeeded."

From writing fiction about the American family, See turned in 1995 to a nonfiction account of her own eccentric relatives and their history of self-destructive behavior. *Dreaming: Hard Luck and Good Times in America,* a well-received memoir, has been cited for its emotional bravery and clear writing. "Carolyn See's is the kind of American voice you can fall in love with," maintained Geoffrey Wolff in his *Washington Post Book World* review of the work. "This is not a celebration of the self or a limning of the self 's prison walls. *Dreaming* is the systematic disclosure of a process of understanding . . . in the sense of figuring out, making sense." Wolff further praised the book as "unflinching, reflective, sassy, building a house from bad cards, creating a voice and vision from the raw material of shouting and mess."

Comparing her work with the epics of "Monica Highland," See told Baker: "The main difference between me and Monica Highland is that I write about people the way they are, which means my books are comparatively plotless, whereas Monica writes of them as they should be, which means there's lots of plot." She once told *CA:* "I hope someday to see California literature become a part of mainstream American literature. And I hope to be part of that process."

BIOGRAPHICAL/CRITICAL SOURCES:

PERIODICALS

Booklist, February 1, 1995.
Chicago Tribune Book World, October 18, 1981.
Los Angeles Times Book Review, September 27, 1981; March 20, 1983; July 13, 1986; October 12, 1986; September 15, 1991, pp. 1, 9; March 5, 1995, pp. 2, 11.
Newsweek, October 5, 1981.
New York Times Book Review, May 10, 1970; January 15, 1978; October 18, 1981; November 30, 1986; September 15, 1991, p. 7.
Publishers Weekly, February 4, 1983; November 14, 1986; January 2, 1995.
San Francisco Review of Books, May/June 1995, pp. 16-7.
Time, November 24, 1986.
Times (London), October 8, 1987.
Times Literary Supplement, November 12, 1987.
Tribune Books, October 6, 1991, p. 6.
Washington Post, December 30, 1986.
Washington Post Book World, November 2, 1981; March 6, 1983; July 26, 1986; August 31, 1986; November 9, 1986; August 2, 1987; September 15, 1991, p. 9; March 5, 1995, pp. 1, 10.

*   *   *

SEGAL, Harriet 1931-

PERSONAL: Born October 10, 1931, in Wilkes-Barre, PA; daughter of Albert Robins (a physician) and Madeline (Schas) Feinberg; married Sheldon J. Segal (a scientist and foundation officer), May 22, 1961; children: Amy R.,

Jennifer A., Laura J. *Education:* Wellesley College, B.A., 1953. *Religion:* Jewish.

ADDRESSES: Home—Westchester County, NY; and Woods Hole, MA. *Agent*—Ellen Levine, Ellen Levine Literary Agency, 15 East 26th St., New York, NY 10010.

CAREER: McCann-Erickson, Inc., New York City, assistant account executive, 1954-55, art buyer, 1955-57; Albert Frank-Guenther Law, Inc., San Francisco, CA, assistant account executive/copywriter, 1958-60; *SHOW* (magazine), New York City, assistant to art director, 1960-61; U.S. Information Service, New Delhi, India, writer and editor, 1962-63; free-lance writer and editor, 1963-80; writer, 1980—. Reporter for *Greenburgh Independent,* 1969-72. Member of executive board of Associates of the Marine Biological Laboratory, Woods Hole, MA, 1982—.

MEMBER: PEN, Authors Guild, Authors League of America, National Writers Union, MBL Club, Scarsdale Woman's Club, Wellesley in Westchester, New York Wellesley Club.

AWARDS, HONORS: Susquehanna selected as one of the five best novels of 1984 by *Pittsburgh* magazine; Washington Irving Book List, 1991 for *Shadow Mountain,* and 1995, for *The Skylark's Song.*

WRITINGS:

NOVELS

Susquehanna, Doubleday (New York City), 1984, published in England as *On Flows the River,* Piatkus, 1985.
Catch the Wind, Doubleday, 1987.
Shadow Mountain, Donald Fine, 1990, reprinted as *Magnolia Dreams,* Avon (New York City).
The Skylark's Song, Donald Fine, 1994.

Some of Segal's books have been translated into Slovene, French, Norwegian, and German.

WORK IN PROGRESS: Northern Lights, a contemporary novel set in England, Austria, Switzerland, Russia, and the United States.

SIDELIGHTS: Harriet Segal told *CA:* "When I wrote my first novel, it had long been my dream to write a book about the place where I was born, the Wyoming Valley of Pennsylvania, in the heart of the anthracite coal regions. *Susquehanna* is the story of four generations of an American Jewish family. I wanted to tell a story about nonstereotypical immigrants in a section of the country that has been largely neglected in American literature.

"*Catch the Wind* depicts the world of the international medical and scientific community. It has as its background the smallpox eradication campaign of the 1970s.

Its heroine, a young woman doctor, becomes a victim of the repressive military dictatorship in Peru. For the settings, I've drawn on my experience while living in India and traveling in the developing world.

"For my third novel, I turned to the American South. My mother was a Southerner, and I spent many summers during my childhood visiting her family in the Blue Ridge Mountains of North Carolina. *Shadow Mountain* is a family saga about Southern Jews, focusing on two women who are linked by ties of love and jealousy. *The Skylark's Song* is a generational story centering on the widow of a Gershwin-like composer and her complex family relationships.

"Settings and details are very important to my work. I make use of my own experiences to create authentic details of background and setting. I will spend a long time researching a novel—on average, a year. Sometimes I travel abroad for research; but often, no further than the library. There is always a serious theme behind the main tale in my books. In each book I have explored something different, although 'commitment' has been a continuing motif. Character and plot are my strengths as a novelist. I am basically a storyteller. And I believe that the most dramatic stories result when ordinary people are placed in extraordinary circumstances."

*　　*　　*

SETH, Vikram 1952-

PERSONAL: Surname is pronounced "sate"; born June 20, 1952, in Calcutta, India; son of Premnath (a consultant) and Leila (a judge; maiden name, Seth) Seth. *Education:* Corpus Christi College, Oxford, B.A. (with honors), 1975, M.A., 1978; Stanford University, M.A., 1977; Nanjing University, China, graduate diploma, 1982.

ADDRESSES: Home—8 Rajaji Marg, New Delhi, India 110 011. *Agent*—Irene Skolnick, Curtis Brown Inc., 10 Astor Pl., New York, NY 10003.

CAREER: Poet, novelist, and travel writer. Stanford University Press, Stanford, CA, senior editor, 1985-86.

AWARDS, HONORS: Thomas Cook Travel Book Award, 1983, for *From Heaven Lake: Travels through Sinkiang and Tibet;* Commonwealth Poetry Prize, Asian Region, 1985, for *The Humble Administrator's Garden;* Ingram Merrill fellowship, 1985-86; Quality Paperback Book Club New Voice Award and Commonwealth Poetry Prize, both 1986, for *The Golden Gate: A Novel in Verse;* Guggenheim fellowship, 1986-87; W. H. Smith Award, 1994, for *A Suitable Boy: A Novel.*

WRITINGS:

Mappings (poems), Writers Workshop (Calcutta), 1980.

From Heaven Lake: Travels through Sinkiang and Tibet, illustrated with own photographs, Chatto & Windus (London), 1983, Vintage (New York City), 1987.

The Humble Administrator's Garden (poems), Carcanet (Manchester, England), 1985.

The Golden Gate: A Novel in Verse, Random House (New York City), 1986.

All You Who Sleep Tonight: Poems, Knopf (New York City), 1990.

Beastly Tales from Here and There, illustrated by Ravi Shankar, Viking (New Delhi), 1992, HarperCollins (New York City), 1994.

(Translator) *Three Chinese Poets: Translations of Poems by Wang Wei, Li Bai, and Du Fu,* HarperPerennial (New York City), 1992.

A Suitable Boy: A Novel, HarperCollins, 1993.

WORK IN PROGRESS: Lynch & Boyle, a play in verse about an English publishing firm.

SIDELIGHTS: Vikram Seth will "no doubt . . . be proclaimed the reinventor of narrative verse in America," predicted X. J. Kennedy in a review of *The Golden Gate: A Novel in Verse* for the *Los Angeles Times Book Review.* "I don't know when a versifier has proved better versed in verse-form than Seth," continued the reviewer, declaring that such mastery of poetry "probably hasn't been heard in English since Alexander Pope." Seth's studies in economics and literature, in addition to travel and residency in eastern Asia and west-coast America, have given him ample and uncommon background for his writings, and he has acquired a reputation as a skillful poet who exhibits unique cultural understanding in all of his works.

From Heaven Lake: Travels through Sinkiang and Tibet is Seth's account of his 1981 hitchhiking adventure from Nanjing University in eastern China through Tibet and Nepal to his home in Delhi, India. In what Jonathan Mirsky in *New Statesman* deemed "the perfect travel book," Seth tells of his episodes of loneliness, illness, and danger as well as the pleasures he took from visiting various civilizations, encountering interesting people along the way. Intermittently, he reflects—with both lament and satire—on the Chinese Cultural Revolution, the annihilation of Tibetan temples, and the treatment of foreigners by the Chinese. Mirsky noted that with his ability to read and speak Chinese, his attention to detail, and his acceptance of cultural differences, Seth is "a wonderful companion," able to manage better than the average tourist. "Very few foreigners have spent the night in Chinese truck parks and country inns," the reviewer added. "Few have had even a meal with a Chinese family. . . . Seth has, and he notices everything and tells us about it." Further remarking on the uniqueness of *From Heaven Lake,* Larry Kart in the *Chicago Tribune* commented that the author "manages to turn the conventional notions of travel writing inside out." Because Seth is "a multiply foreign figure from a Western reader's point of view," continued Kart, "what he sees along the way is filtered through several cultural prisms, an effect that adds greatly to the meaning of his book."

Critics were also charmed by the personality of *From Heaven Lake*'s narrator. Nicholas Garland in *Spectator* assessed that Seth is "adventurous, restless and inquisitive. When opportunity knocks he grabs at it, and when it doesn't he gives it a little push." Additionally, many reviewers liked Seth's self-deprecating humor, his modesty, and his treatment of himself as a somewhat comical figure throughout his travels. Garland, however, found fault with this aspect of the narration, maintaining that Seth "mars his account of this wonderful journey by an attempt to emphasize his poetic and dreamy side." Seth, continued the critic, sometimes concentrates too much on "the intensity of his feelings, not realizing that his material is so good it does not require more than honest telling. . . . His image of himself as a gentle pilgrim leads him to sacrifice too much straightforward reporting." Observations like Andrew Robinson's in the *British Book News*, though, were more common: "[Seth] is a phlegmatic but sensitive traveller, delightfully alive to all that he sees and hears." *From Heaven Lake*, he added, is filled with "lively descriptions" and "interesting reflections."

Seth conveys more of his cultural diversity through the medium of poetry in *The Humble Administrator's Garden*. Like his previous book, the collection of poems contains material gleaned from Seth's visits to both Eastern and Western countries. "Given the exotic nature of his background," noted Tom D'Evelyn in the *Christian Science Monitor*, the poet could have gone "toward the specialized feeling and idea, toward myth and cultural arcana, toward anthropology." Instead Seth goes in the other direction, continued the reviewer, choosing "to represent in his poems feeling of the widest applicability." Divided into three sections—on China, India, and California (with occasional references to England)—the book was hailed by Raymond Tong in *British Book News* as an "impressive" collection in which "a high level is generally maintained throughout."

As with *From Heaven Lake*, critics liked *The Humble Administrator's Garden* for the unassuming tone Seth presents in the work. Dick Davis in the *Listener*, for example, found the collection to be "modest, ordered, well-mannered and well-planned, with a trace of deprecatory self-pity." In his review in the *Times Literary Supplement*, Claude Rawson praised Seth's "fastidious probing language," noting that the work includes "small masterpieces of delicate verbal and emotional discipline, observant of pathos, of ironies of behaviour, of the unexpected small exuberances of life." Extolling Seth's talent as a disci-

plined poet, the critic observed that "Seth focuses on the mundane with unusual clarity," and he added that Seth "is one of the few young poets who has taken the trouble to learn, really learn, the disciplines of meter."

"I've always enjoyed reading poetry," Seth once told *CA* interviewer Jean W. Ross, "perhaps for the reason that I've never had to study English literature! I like a great deal of poetry from the past, but if you want to talk about this century, the poets who most affect me on this side of the Atlantic are Edwin Arlington Robinson and Robert Frost and Timothy Steele. I dedicated *The Golden Gate* to Timothy Steele, and if you read his poetry, you'll see why. On the other side of the Atlantic, Thomas Hardy and Edward Thomas—who was a friend of Frost's, incidentally—and Philip Larkin. All of them write profoundly about ordinary life, and that's what I find moves me the most, even though I admire a great deal of other poetry: [William Butler] Yeats, for instance, I very much admire, and early [T. S.] Eliot. But what speaks nearest to me, really, is poetry of ordinary life somehow made poignant through expressivity."

Seth's widest acclaim as a technically solid poet came with *The Golden Gate*, his 1986 verse novel, which many critics hailed as a tour de force. Containing nearly six hundred sonnets of iambic tetrameter, Seth's long narrative poem is set in present-day San Francisco and concerns the lives of young, urban professionals, or "yuppies." The story introduces John Brown, a twenty-six-year-old computer expert working for a defense contractor, who suddenly comes to the realization that his life is meaningless. He has lunch with his old girlfriend Janet Hayakawa—a sculptor and a drummer in a punk-rock band called Liquid Sheep—after which Janet, unbeknownst to John, submits an advertisement on John's behalf to a lonely hearts column. The action is a catalyst for the presentation of *The Golden Gate*'s other characters: Liz Dorati, an attractive lawyer; Phil Weiss, a divorced single parent, philosopher, and peace demonstrator; and Ed, an advertising executive. In addition to incorporating timely concerns within the novel—such as a long scene at an anti-nuclear demonstration and a dialogue between two homosexual men on sex and celibacy—Seth places his characters in typically modern situations, such as singles bars and wine-making parties. Seth "knows these people inside out," noted Kennedy, and he consequently "conducts us on a psychological safari through five interesting souls."

Deemed "one of the curiosities of the season" by John Gross in the *New York Times*, *The Golden Gate* struck many critics as unusual in its portrayal of modern yuppies conveyed through narrative verse, a form that is a "throwback to our literary past," Raymond Mungo pointed out in the *New York Times Book Review*. Seth told Ross that he patterned the style of *The Golden Gate* after Russian poet Aleksandr Pushkin's *Eugene Onegin,* a work exhibiting intricately rhymed and metered sonnets. Expecting little, Seth found in reading *Eugene Onegin* that "I was reading it as I would read a novel. That was something that intrigued me, because the idea of a novel in verse had at first struck me as some curious hybrid, something that would not work. Here was something that *did* work, and that not only worked, but moved me and amused me and made me want to write something in a similar form set in my time and in a place that I knew." According to Alan Hollinghurst in the *Times Literary Supplement,* the Pushkin stanza is "a form whose inner counterpoint gives it both gravity and levity." Moreover, the reviewer judged the unconventionality of Seth's novel entirely appropriate, declaring, "It is hard to imagine a better vehicle for social verse narrative which aims to be both reflective and lightly comic."

Many critics, originally wary that Seth was attempting a literary stunt by writing a novel in verse, admitted that poetry is the most effective medium for Seth's modern subjects and for his intention to inject social commentary. David Lehman in *Newsweek* stated, "None of this may have worked in prose; in verse it's a nonstop pleasure. Seth makes us care about his characters, proposes a moral criticism of their lives and captures his California setting with a joyous wit little seen in narrative poetry this side of Lord Byron." *The Golden Gate,* then, was hailed for both its form and content. "In setting out to revitalize verse as a storytelling medium, Seth fulfills all the requirements of first-rate fiction," explained Lehman. Thomas M. Disch in the *Washington Post Book World* proclaimed the novel a thing of "anomalous beauty: . . . a rhyming poem in strict meter that is a 'good read.'" In addition to crediting Seth for creating what Kennedy labeled a "mountain of technical virtuosity," Gross noted that Seth "is witty, dexterous and imaginative" in a work where "incidental pleasures abound."

It took Seth years to complete and publish his next novel, *A Suitable Boy,* described by Michele Field of *Publishers Weekly* as "the longest single-volume work of English fiction since Samuel Richardson's *Clarissa* was published in 1747." At a dense 1,349 pages and weighing four pounds, *A Suitable Boy* is Seth's "magnum opus," according to Robert Worth of *Commonweal.* Seth completed several other works while *A Suitable Boy* was in progress: the poetry collections *Beastly Tales from Here and There* and *All You Who Sleep Tonight,* and the translation of a collection of Chinese poetry entitled *Three Chinese Poets: Translations of Poems by Wang Wei, Li Bai, and Du Fu.*

A Suitable Boy is the story of the arranged marriage of Lata Mehra, an upper-class Indian woman rebelling against the traditional customs imposed upon her by her mother and Indian society at large. The widow Mehra, Lata's mother, is determined to find her daughter a husband of appropriate caste, color, religion, and financial stability—a "suitable boy." However, after attending her older sister's wedding at the beginning of the novel, Lata becomes skeptical of marriage and of the Indian traditions inherent in arranged matrimony. The plot centers on four families—the Mehras, Kapoors, Chatterjis, and Khans—yet Seth reaches beyond the limits of their experiences: "He chose to tell the whole story, producing for all time the whole world of Lata Mehra, with all the intermingled levels of North Indian culture," Schuyler Ingle remarked in the *Los Angeles Times Book Review.* While the action in *A Suitable Boy* takes place in the fictional northern city of Brahmpur in the 1950s, not long after India's 1947 independence from England, Seth describes in great detail the political, religious, and cultural shifts gripping postcolonial India in a multitude of subplots.

Reviews of the content of *A Suitable Boy* were mixed. *New Republic* reviewer Richard Jenkyns acknowledged the tendency of long books to "be spoken of, whether for praise or blame, in superlatives," which may seem to leave only one conclusion: "since *A Suitable Boy* is not obviously a bad book, it must be a marvel. What we do not expect, with something so massive, is to speak in neutral, colorless terms: pleasant, mostly unpretentious, some pale charm, some gentle humor, readable but a bit flat and dull. But such, I think, is the judgment that we should return on this book." *Vanity Fair*'s Christopher Hitchens noted, "Those who aren't so keen on Seth's blockbuster say that it's more like [English writer John] Galsworthy than [Russian epic novelist Leo] Tolstoy, a jolly giant of a saga with lots of characters and speaking parts but no darkness or depth and no real consciousness of evil and suffering." Robert Towers, writing in the *New York Times Book Review,* found that "in his drive toward inclusiveness" the author "has sacrificed intensity," and he concluded, "In the end, *A Suitable Boy* succeeds less as a novel than as a richly detailed documentary focused upon a crucial era in the history of an endlessly fascinating country." *London Review of Books* contributor John Lanchester found, however, that the author succeeds in his quest for "complete transparency: all his energies are concentrated on making the prose a vehicle for the characters and the action." He further added, "The prose is intended not to distract. The resulting structural clarity is remarkable—you never don't know what's happening, why, where, and to whom. . . . It's a considerable technical feat." In the *Los Angeles Times Book Review,* Ingle noted the many hours required to read a novel of such length but concluded that "*A Suitable Boy* is a book that pays readers back, and richly, for their nightly effort."

As critics debated the issue of the book's length, some found it a hindrance, and others deemed it appropriate, though unwieldy. According to Jill Rachlin of *People,* although the author intended *A Suitable Boy* to be the first novel of a set of five, his first draft was close to two thousand pages. "After cutting it by a third," Rachlin reported, "he tried to divide it into two or three separate books. 'It didn't break in any right point,' he says with a laugh, 'so I was stuck with this monster.' " In a *Newsweek* review entitled "Easy Reading, Heavy Lifting," Laura Shapiro remarked, "Surprisingly, it makes very easy reading. What you can't do is *hold* the damn thing." She further observed, "Very few novels demand extraordinary length, and this isn't one of them. But Seth's publishers aren't entirely crazy: there is something strangely appealing about *A Suitable Boy.*" Pico Iyer, writing for the *Times Literary Supplement,* observed, "Every single page of *A Suitable Boy* is pleasant and readable and true; but the parts are better crafted, and so more satisfying, than the whole. . . . [I]t is not immediately evident that its some 1,400 pages make it four times better than it would have been at 350." Yet Ingle found the book's length logical: "In a land of 900 million people, Seth seems to be saying, no one person can possibly be singled out: Their connections must be taken into account as well."

BIOGRAPHICAL/CRITICAL SOURCES:

BOOKS

Contemporary Literary Criticism, Volume 43, Gale (Detroit), 1987, pp. 386-94.
Dictionary of Literary Biography, Volume 120: *American Poets since World War II, Third Series,* Gale, 1992, pp. 281-85.

PERIODICALS

British Book News, November, 1983; September, 1985.
Chicago Tribune, April 20, 1986; February 3, 1988.
Christian Science Monitor, August 21, 1985.
Commonweal, May 21, 1993, pp. 25-26.
Listener, December 5, 1985.
London Review of Books, April 22, 1993, p. 9.
Los Angeles Times Book Review, April 6, 1986; May 23, 1993, pp. 4, 11.
New Republic, April 21, 1986; June 14, 1993, pp. 41-44.
New Statesman, October 7, 1983.
Newsweek, April 14, 1986; May 24, 1993, p. 62.
New Yorker, July 14, 1986.
New York Times, April 14, 1986.
New York Times Book Review, May 11, 1986; May 9, 1993, pp. 3, 16.
Observer (London), September 12, 1993, p. 54.
People, June 30, 1986; May 24, 1993, pp. 29-30.
Publishers Weekly, May 10, 1993, pp. 46-7.
Spectator, February 11, 1984.

Times Literary Supplement, February 7, 1986; July 4, 1986; September 21-27, 1990, p. 1007; March 19, 1993, p. 20.
Vanity Fair, June, 1993, pp. 36-40.
Washington Post, May 17, 1986.
Washington Post Book World, March 23, 1986; July 22, 1990, p. 4; December 2, 1990, p. 9.
World Literature Today, spring, 1993, pp. 447-48.*

* * *

SHAPIRO, Julian L.
See SANFORD, John

* * *

SIEGEL, Robert (Harold) 1939-

PERSONAL: Born August 18, 1939, in Oak Park, IL; son of Frederick William (a personnel manager) and Charlotte Lucille (Chance) Siegel; married Roberta Ann Hill, August 19, 1961; children: Anne Lenaye, Lucy Blythe, Christine Elizabeth. *Education:* Attended Denison University, 1957-59; Wheaton College, Wheaton, IL, B.A., 1961; Johns Hopkins University, M.A., 1962; Harvard University, Ph.D., 1968. *Religion:* Christian. *Avocational interests:* Hiking, camping, travel.

ADDRESSES: Office—Department of English, University of Wisconsin—Milwaukee, P. O. Box 413, Milwaukee, WI 53201.

CAREER: Trinity College, Bannockburn, IL, instructor in English, 1962-63; Dartmouth College, Hanover, NH, assistant professor of English, 1968-75; University of Wisconsin—Milwaukee, assistant professor, 1976-79, associate professor, 1979-83, professor of English, 1983—, coordinator of graduate program in creative writing, 1992—. Visiting lecturer in creative writing, Princeton University, 1975-76; poet-in-residence and visiting professor of English, Wheaton College, 1976; visiting professor of English and American studies, Johann Wolfgang von Goethe University, 1985. Resident poet, Greenlake Writers' Conference, 1974, 1976, and Wheaton College Summer Writers' Institute, 1980; faculty poet, Wesleyan Writers Conference, 1982, 1983. Teaching fellow, Breadloaf Writers' Conference, 1974.

MEMBER: Authors Guild, Authors League of America, Modern Language Association of America, Conference on Christianity and Literature (director, 1969-72), Associated Writing Programs, Council for Wisconsin Writers.

AWARDS, HONORS: Foley Award for poetry, *America Magazine,* 1970; Dartmouth faculty fellowship, 1971-72;

Transatlantic Review fellow, Breadloaf Writers' Conference, 1974; Yaddo resident, 1974, 1975; Chicago Poetry Prize, Society of Midland Authors and Illinois Council for the Arts, and Cliff Dwellers Arts Foundation award, both 1974, for *The Beasts and the Elders;* Borestone Mountain Poetry Award, 1976, for "To Market, to Market"; Jacob Glatstein Memorial Prize, *Poetry,* 1977; *Prairie Schooner* poetry prize, 1977; research grants for poetry, University of Wisconsin—Milwaukee, 1978 and 1984; Ingram Merrill Foundation award, 1979; National Endowment for the Arts creative writing fellowship, 1980; Council for Wisconsin Writers award and first prize for poetry, Society of Midland Authors, both 1981, both for *In a Pig's Eye;* gold medallion from Evangelical Christian Publishers Association, book of the year award from *Campus Life,* and first prize for juvenile fiction from Council for Wisconsin Writers, all 1981, all for *Alpha Centauri;* Matson Award from Friends of Literature, 1982, for *Whalesong;* Golden Archer Award, School of Library Science, University of Wisconsin—Oshkosh, 1986, for *Whalesong;* sabbatical grant, University of Wisconsin, 1988-89; Pushcart Prize nomination, 1990; Milton Center Poetry Prize, 1994.

WRITINGS:

POETRY

The Beasts and the Elders, University Press of New England (Hanover, NH), 1973.
In a Pig's Eye, University Presses of Florida (Gainesville), 1980.

FICTION

Alpha Centauri, Cornerstone Books, 1980.
Whalesong, Crossway (Westchester, IL), 1981.
The Kingdom of Wundle, Crossway, 1982.
White Whale, Harper (San Francisco), 1991.
The Ice at the End of the World, Harper, 1993.

Contributor to poetry anthologies. Contributor of articles and over 250 poems to magazines and journals, including *Poetry, Prairie Schooner, Atlantic Monthly, Carolina Quarterly, Poetry Northwest, Ploughshares, Beloit Poetry Journal, Sewanee Review,* and *New York Quarterly.*

Whalesong has been translated into German, Dutch, Japanese and Czech; *White Whale* has been translated into German and Dutch.

WORK IN PROGRESS: Two collections of poems, *The Waters under the Earth* and *The Book of Beasts,* and a novel.

SIDELIGHTS: Robert Siegel once told *CA:* "When asked what it is that moves me to write a poem, I confess it is the desire to call things up into words. This is the alchemy that fascinates me. Whether things are common or secret (and all things are both common and secret), I wish to call

them up by the power of words—or rather, as words. A sensation, impression, or image will step out from its surroundings and demand my total attention. The thing itself will appear to rise up as words. Here is the wonder of the magic, what Keats called 'natural magic.' As the image reaches up toward the words, the words become the image, the thing itself. For one happy moment they are fused. Thing becomes word and word becomes thing in a process perhaps far more central to the workings of the universe than we have up to now thought. Substance and meaning are fused. The terrible gap between experience and the articulation of experience is closed. The mind is one with what it perceives.

"This union, or participation, with the universe is perhaps one implication of St. John's infinitely suggestive phrase, 'the Word became flesh'—though he is referring to something at once more mysterious and more specific. Fantasy stories, like poems, may bring about an experience of participation, since they arise from the sense of a reality behind appearances that is nevertheless expressed through appearances. At least for me, writing fantasy is another way of discovering the fusion of spirit and matter in an incarnational universe."

A *Times Literary Supplement* reviewer remarks about *The Beasts and the Elders:* "To meet the unpretentious versatility of Robert Siegel after the single-mindedness of other poets is like returning to the mainland after a tour of the islands; . . . his expression is lively and compact, fresh and concrete."

BIOGRAPHICAL/CRITICAL SOURCES:

PERIODICALS

Chicago Tribune Book World, October 11, 1981.
Christianity Today, November 21, 1980; November 25, 1991.
Fantasy Review, January, 1986, p. 25.
Los Angeles Times, December 10, 1981.
Milwaukee Journal, October 6, 1991; July 10, 1994.
Poetry, September, 1974; May, 1982.
Times Literary Supplement, March 29, 1974.
Voice of Youth Advocates, February, 1992, p. 376.
Western Humanities Review, summer, 1974.
Wisconsin Academy Review, June, 1982.

*   *   *

SIMPSON, O(renthal) J(ames)   1947-

PERSONAL: Born July 9, 1947, in San Francisco, CA; son of Jimmie (a chef) and Eunice (a hospital administrator; maiden name, Durton) Simpson; married Marguerite Whitley (an artist), June 24, 1967 (divorced, 1980); married Nicole Brown, 1985 (divorced, 1992); children: first marriage: Arnelle, Jason, Aaren (deceased); second marriage: Sydney, Justin. *Education:* Attended San Francisco City College, 1966-67; University of Southern California, B.A., 1969.

ADDRESSES: Home—Los Angeles, CA. *Office*—11661 San Vincente Blvd., Los Angeles, CA 90049.

CAREER: Buffalo Bills, Orchard Park, NY, running back, 1969-77; San Francisco 49'ers, San Francisco, CA, running back, 1977-79. Actor in motion pictures, including *The Towering Inferno,* 1974, *Killer Force,* 1975, *Cassandra Crossing,* 1976, *Firepower,* 1978, *The Naked Gun,* 1988, *The Naked Gun 2 1/2,* 1991, and *The Naked Gun 33 1/3,* 1994. Executive producer of Orenthal Productions, 1978—. Actor in TV films, including *A Killing Affair,* 1977, and *The Golden Moment,* 1980. Television sports commentator for *Summer Olympics,* Montreal, Quebec, 1976, *Wide World of Sports* (ABC-TV); co-host, *NFL Live on NBC,* 1990-94; guest on television variety shows, specials, and dramatic series.

AWARDS, HONORS: Named All-American collegiate football player, 1965-68; named outstanding player in Rose Bowl game, 1967; Walter Camp Memorial Trophy, Maxwell Memorial Trophy, and Heisman Trophy for collegiate football player of the year from New York Downtown Athletic Club, all 1968; named Man of the Year by *Sport* magazine, 1969; named College Player of the Decade by American Broadcasting Co. (ABC-Sports), 1970; named to American Football Conference All-Star team, 1970, and to ProBowl team, 1972-76; named Most Valuable Player in American Football Conference, 1972, 1973, 1975, and National Football League, 1973; Hickok Belt for professional athlete of the year, 1973; named National Football League (NFL) Player of the Decade by *Pro Football Monthly,* 1979; inducted into Pro Football Hall of Fame, 1985.

WRITINGS:

(With Pete Axthelm) *O. J.: The Education of a Rich Rookie,* Macmillan (New York City), 1970.
(With Lawrence Schiller) *I Want to Tell You: My Responses to Your Letters, Your Messages, Your Questions,* Little, Brown (Boston), 1995.

SIDELIGHTS: As a child, O. J. Simpson had to wear leg braces because he suffered from a calcium deficiency. The children in his neighborhood nicknamed him "pencil legs," never suspecting that he would one day be a star running-back in both collegiate and professional football, holding the record for most yards rushing gained in a season and in a game. They also never suspected, as did the thousands of Americans who idolized this affable athlete, that his renown in the world of sports would be eclipsed

when he stood trial for the brutal 1994 murders of his second wife, Nicole Simpson, and her friend Ronald Goldman, in what would become one of the most amazing media circuses in the history of the American judicial system.

Simpson began his collegiate career at San Francisco City College, where he scored fifty-four touchdowns in two years, including six in a single game. He continued setting records at the University of Southern California (USC), rushing for 3,295 yards and thirty-four touchdowns in twenty-two games. After the final game of the 1968 season, USC Coach John McKay praised Simpson, saying, "This is not only the greatest player I ever had, but the greatest anyone ever had." *Sport* magazine dubbed him the greatest running back in the history of college football; in 1969 Simpson was chosen as *Sport's* Man of the Year, the first time that honor had ever been awarded to a collegiate player. In his last year playing college football, Simpson carried the ball an average of thirty-five times a game, gaining a record 1,709 yards and a Heisman Trophy.

Simpson's professional football career was as illustrious as his collegiate career. In 1969 he signed with the Buffalo Bills, and during the eight years he spent with the club he continued making football history. From 1972 through 1976 he rushed for over one thousand yards per season, and he was named annually to the Pro Bowl team. In 1975 he led the American Football Conference in both rushing and scoring. Six times between 1975 and 1976, he rushed two hundred yards or more in a single game; his game high was 273 yards. Simpson retired from the sport in 1979, two years after he was traded to the San Francisco 49'ers.

People magazine credited a mid-1970s ad campaign for Hertz Rent-a-Car with making Simpson's one of the most recognizable faces in America, pointing out that more Americans watched him sprint across crowded airports on television commercials than ever saw him make his famous runs down a football field. "The Hertz commercials gave me more national recognition in one year than I had received after playing football for fourteen years," Simpson commented. Whatever the source of his growing fame and fortune, by 1979 Simpson's estimated annual income was over two million dollars. He had successfully made the transition from retired athlete to media celebrity.

Roles in several motion pictures followed, including the popular *Naked Gun* films, which found Simpson playing for laughs alongside costar Leslie Nielson. But in 1994 the laughter stopped when he was arrested in June for the brutal murders of ex-wife Nicole Brown Simpson and her friend Ronald L. Goldman outside her home in Brentwood, Los Angeles. The trial that followed made Simpson's former celebrity status seem tame by comparison; his profile appeared on numerous periodicals ranging from the *National Enquirer* to *Time,* while the legal proceedings wore on amid massive media hype and exhaustive television coverage.

In early January of 1995 it was announced that Simpson had signed a book deal with the publisher Little, Brown in the previous month, a move that predated the initiation of a California law designed to prevent criminals from profiting from their crimes through books or other moneymaking ventures. Simpson declared that the book was written to respond to the 300,000 pieces of mail that he had received while awaiting trial. "One of the things O. J. said to me in my first meeting with him about the book was 'This is not my biography,'" co-author Lawrence Schiller is quoted as saying in the *New York Times.* "'This is my response to the public's response to me, to my pain, to my suffering.'"

I Want to Tell You: My Responses to Your Letters, Your Messages, Your Questions, which hit bookstores the following month, coincided with the opening days of what would soon be touted as the "Trial of the Century." Simpson's book is a mosaic of letters, family photographs, and personal commentary focused on proclaiming his innocence. As David Margolick notes in the *New York Times,* Simpson "repeatedly maintains his innocence . . . [and] . . . lambastes the press for murdering him as surely as someone else murdered Nicole Brown Simpson and Ronald L. Goldman." *I Want to Tell You* became the fastest selling book in Little, Brown's esteemed history. "The thin volume, the issue of a fat-figured deal ($1 million), is a brilliant sliver of disgeniousness," commented Gregory Jaynes in *Time,* noting that many small, independent booksellers around the United States "did not want to be seen as contributing to the author's defense fund" by stocking large quantities of Simpson's book.

Simpson's life became the subject of made-for-TV films like the FOX network's *O.J. Simpson Story,* and other books, including journalist Sheila Weller's *Raging Heart,* written with the help of Nicole's family, and former friend Faye Resnick's *Nicole Brown Simpson,* a startling expose acusing the football hero of abuse, infidelity, and assorted other transgressions that ended, presumably, in murder. Simpson was, however, acquitted of all charges in the fall of 1995.

BIOGRAPHICAL/CRITICAL SOURCES:

BOOKS

Durant, John, and Les Elter, *Highlights of College Football,* Hastings House (New York City), 1970.
Libby, Bill, *Heroes of the Heisman Trophy,* Hawthorn (New York City), 1973.

PERIODICALS

Ebony, December, 1968.
Life, October 27, 1967.
Look, October 15, 1968.
New York Times, January 8, 1995, p. 24; January 28, 1995, p. 6; February 1, 1995, p. C14.
New York Times Magazine, July 30, 1978.
People, June 12, 1978; April 2, 1979.
Sport, November, 1978.
Sports Illustrated, November 20, 1967; December 25, 1967; July 14, 1969; August 25, 1969; November 26, 1979.
Time, February 6, 1995, pp. 64-65.*

*   *   *

SINGER, Robert N.

PERSONAL: Education: Brooklyn College of the City University of New York, B.S., 1961; Pennsylvania State University, M.S., 1962; Ohio State University, Ph.D., 1964.

ADDRESSES: Home—712 Northeast Fifth Place, Gainesville, FL 32601. *Office*—302 Florida Gym, Department of Exercise and Sports Sciences, University of Florida, Gainesville, FL 32611.

CAREER: Ohio State University, Columbus, 1963-65, began as instructor, became assistant professor; Illinois State University, Normal, 1965-69, began as assistant professor, became associate professor, assistant dean of College of Applied Science and Technology, 1968-69; Michigan State University, East Lansing, associate professor, 1969-70; Florida State University, Tallahassee, professor and director of Motor Learning Research Laboratory, 1970-72, 1975-88, director of Division of Human Performance, 1972-75, director of Motor Behavior Resource Center, 1975-88, assistant dean for graduate programs and research, College of Education, 1983-84; University of Florida, Gainesville, chair of exercise and sports sciences department, 1988—. Consulting editor to Holt, Rinehart & Winston for health, physical education, and recreation, 1970-77; head of sport psychology area, Sports Medicine Committee, U.S. Olympic Committee, 1978-80; has lectured and presented papers to various professional organizations worldwide.

MEMBER: International Society of Sport Psychology (member of managing council, 1977—, president, 1985-89; 1989-93; 1994-97), American Academy of Kinesiology and Physical Education (president, 1994-96), American Psychological Association (president of division of exercise and sport psychology, 1995-96), American Educational Research Association, American Alliance for

Health, Physical Education, Recreation and Dance, North American Society for the Psychology of Sport and Physical Activity, Omicron Delta Kappa, Phi Epsilon Kappa.

AWARDS, HONORS: Named one of the ten leading sport psychologists in North America in the 1980s by *The Sport Psychologist;* Bulgarian Medal for International Cooperation in Sport Psychology, 1987; fellowship from Association for the Advancement of Applied Sport Psychology, 1988; Brooklyn College, Distinguished Alumnus Award, 1989; fellowship from International Society of Sport Psychology, 1989; named one of ten most notable contemporary American physical educators by *Journal of Physical Education, Recreation, and Dance,* 1989; American Alliance for Health, Physical Education, Recreation and Dance, R. Tait McKenzie Award, 1991 and International Service Award, 1994; Ministry of Higher Education of Russia medal for scientific achievement, 1994; medal from National Olympic Committee of Russia, 1994, for recognition of contributions to the science of sport; Association for Research, Administration, Professional Councils, and Societies International Relations Council Honor Award, 1994.

WRITINGS:

Motor Learning and Human Performance, Macmillan (New York City), 1968, 3rd edition, 1980.
(Editor) *Readings in Motor Learning,* Lea & Febiger (Philadelphia, PA), 1972.
Coaching, Athletics, and Psychology, McGraw (New York City), 1972.
(With others) *Physical Education: An Interdisciplinary Approach,* Macmillan, 1972.
(Editor) *The Psychomotor Domain: Movement Behavior,* Lea & Febiger, 1972.
(Co-author) *Teaching Physical Education: A Systems Approach,* Houghton (Boston, MA), 1974, 2nd edition, 1980.
Myths and Truths in Sport Psychology, Harper (New York City), 1975.
(Co-author) *Laboratory and Field Experiments in Motor Learning,* C. C Thomas (Springfield, IL), 1975.
Physical Education: Foundations, Holt (New York City), 1976.
Sustaining Motivation in Sports, Sports Consultants International, 1984.
Peak Performance . . . and More, Mouvement (Ithaca, NY), 1986.
(With others) *Handbook of Research on Sport Psychology,* Macmillan, 1993.

Contributor to books, including *The Psychomotor Domain,* Gryphon Press, 1972; *Research Methods,* American Association for Health, Physical Education, and Recre-

ation, 1973; *Physical Education: A View toward the Future,* edited by R. Welsh, Mosby (St. Louis, MO), 1977; *Cognitive and Affective Learning Strategies,* edited by H. F. O'Neil and C. D. Speilberger, Academic Press (New York City), 1979; and *International Perspectives in Sport and Exercise Psychology,* edited by S. Serpa and others, Fitness Information Technology (Morgantown, WV), 1994. Also contributor to *Encyclopedia of Sport Sciences and Medicine.*

Editor of series, "Issues in Contemporary Physical Education," published by Harper. Co-editor of *Completed Research in Health, Physical Education, and Recreation,* American Association of Health, Physical Education, and Recreation, 1968-74. Abstractor for *Psychological Abstracts.* Contributor of more than sixty articles to professional journals. Member of editorial board of *International Journal of Sport Psychology, Sport Psychologist, Journal of Applied Sport Psychology, Journal of Motor Behavior, Research Quarterly for Exercise and Sport,* and *Journal of Sport and Exercise Psychology.* Special reader for *Journal of Physical Education and Recreation, Journal of Personality and Social Psychology, American Psychologist, Perceptual and Motor Skills, Journal of Applied Psychology, Medicine and Science in Sports,* and *Educational Psychology.*

SIDELIGHTS: Robert N. Singer told *CA:* "Writing and sports participation are addictions of mine: a day doesn't go by without a degree of fulfillment through both outlets. The sports I enjoy vary as much as the contents of the books and articles I write. If excessiveness is a vice, then I am guilty. I believe that my ability to think, concentrate, and persevere has helped me to author what I have; my dedication to excellence in movement skills has contributed to my various athletic accomplishments, primarily through continuous effort."

*   *   *

SISTER MARY TERESE
    See DONZE, Mary Terese

*   *   *

SLATER, Ray
    See LANSDALE, Joe R(ichard)

*   *   *

SMILEY, Jane (Graves) 1949-

PERSONAL: Born September 26, 1949, in Los Angeles, CA; daughter of James Laverne (in U.S. Army) and Frances Nuelle (a writer; maiden name, Graves) Smiley; married John Whiston, September 4, 1970 (divorced November, 1975); married William Silag (an editor), May 1, 1978 (divorced February, 1986); married Stephen Mortensen (a screenwriter), July 25, 1987; children: (second marriage) Phoebe Graves Silag, Lucy Gallagher Silag. *Education:* Vassar College, B.A., 1971; University of Iowa, M.A., 1975, M.F.A., 1976, Ph.D., 1978. *Politics:* "Skeptical." *Religion:* "Vehement agnostic." *Avocational interests:* Cooking, swimming, playing piano, quilting.

ADDRESSES: Office—Department of English, Iowa State University, 201 Ross, Ames, IA 50011-1401. *Agent*—Molly Friedrich, Aaron Priest Agency, 122 East 42nd St., New York, NY 10168.

CAREER: Iowa State University, Ames, professor of English, 1981—. Visiting assistant professor at University of Iowa, spring, 1981.

MEMBER: Authors Guild, Authors League of America, Screenwriters Guild.

AWARDS, HONORS: Fulbright fellowship, 1976-77; grants from National Endowment for the Arts, 1978 and 1987; Friends of American Writers Prize, 1981, for *At Paradise Gate;* O. Henry awards, 1982, 1985, and 1988; National Book Critics Circle Award nomination, 1987, for *The Age of Grief;* Pulitzer Prize, National Book Critics Circle Award, and Heartland Award, all 1991, all for *A Thousand Acres;* Midland Authors Award, 1992; Amb. Award, 1992.

WRITINGS:

Barn Blind (novel), Harper (New York City), 1980.
At Paradise Gate (novel), Simon & Schuster (New York City), 1981.
Duplicate Keys (mystery novel), Knopf (New York City), 1984.
The Age of Grief (story collection), Knopf, 1987.
Catskill Crafts: Artisans of the Catskill Mountains (nonfiction), Crown (New York City), 1987.
The Greenlanders (novel), Knopf, 1988.
Ordinary Love and Good Will (novellas), Knopf, 1989.
The Life of the Body (short story), Coffee House Press (Minneapolis, MN), 1990.
A Thousand Acres (novel), Knopf, 1991.
(With others) *The True Subject: Writers on Life and Craft,* Graywolf Press (St. Paul, MN), 1993.
Moo (novel), Knopf, 1995.

Work represented in anthologies, including *The Pushcart Anthology, Best American Short Stories, 1985, Best of the Eighties,* and *The True Subject: Writers on Life and Craft,* 1993. Contributor of stories to *Redbook, Atlantic, Mademoiselle, Fiction, TriQuarterly,* and *Playgirl.*

SIDELIGHTS: Even before her Pulitzer-prize winning novel *A Thousand Acres,* Jane Smiley's fiction has shared a concern for families and their troubles. As Joanne Kaufman remarks in *People,* Smiley "has an unerring, unsettling ability to capture the rhythms of family life gone askew." Smiley also possesses what Jane Yolen in the *Washington Post* calls a "spare, yet lyric" prose. In addition, Yolen finds Smiley to be "a true storyteller."

The theme of family life was present in Smiley's first book, *Barn Blind,* a "pastoral novel of smooth texture and—like the Middle Western summer in which it is set—rich, drowsy pace," as Michael Malone describes it in the *New York Times Book Review.* The story revolves around Kate Karlson, a rancher's wife, and her strained relationships with her four teenaged children. "Smiley handles with skill and understanding the mercurial molasses of adolescence, and the inchoate, cumbersome love that family members feel for one another," according to Malone.

In her next book, *At Paradise Gate,* Smiley looked again at conflict between family members. In this story, elderly Anna Robinson faces the imminent death of her husband, Ike. The couple have had a rough marriage; Ike is an emotionally cold and violent person. When Anna's three daughters arrive to visit their dying father, old sibling rivalries are revived, tensions between the parents are renewed, and Anna must confront the failures and triumphs of her life. The story, explains Valerie Miner in the *New York Times Book Review,* "is not so much about Ike's death as about Anna's life—a retrospective on her difficult past and a resolution of her remaining years." *At Paradise Gate,* Susan Wood maintains in the *Washington Post,* "is a sensitive study of what it means to grow old and face death, and of the courage to see clearly what one's life has meant."

Smiley took a different tack with *Duplicate Keys,* a mystery novel set in Manhattan; and yet even in this book her concern for family relations holds firm. Laura Marcus of the *Times Literary Supplement* calls *Duplicate Keys* a story about "marriages, affairs, friendships, growing up and growing older. . . . Smiley demonstrates a considerable sensitivity in the treatment of love and friendship." Lois Gould in the *New York Times Book Review* calls the book only incidently a mystery. "More important and far more compelling," Gould notes, "is the anatomy of friendship, betrayal, the color of dusk on the Upper West Side, the aroma of lilacs in Brooklyn's Botanic Garden, of chocolate tortes at Zabar's, and the bittersweet smell of near success that is perhaps the most pungent odor in town." Alice Cromie in the *Chicago Tribune Book World* concludes that *Duplicate Keys* is "a sophisticated story of friendships, loves, jealousies, drugs, celebrities and life in the fastest lane in Manhattan."

In 1987 Smiley published *The Age of Grief,* a collection of five stories and a novella, focusing on the joys and sorrows of married life. The title novella, according to Kaufman, "is a haunting view of a marriage from the inside, a tale told by a betrayed husband full of humor and sadness and sound and quiet fury." Michiko Kakutani, writing in the *New York Times,* finds that the novella "opens out, organically, from a comic portrait . . . into a lovely and very sad meditation on the evanescence and durability of love." Speaking of the book as a whole, Roz Kaveney writes in the *Times Literary Supplement* that "one of the major strengths of this quiet and unflashy collection . . . is that in [Smiley's] stories things actually do happen. These events are entirely in keeping with her strong vein of social realism, but they have too a quality of the unpredictable, a quality which gives an uninsistent but pervasive sense of the pain and surprise which lie beneath even the most conventional of lives." Anne Bernays, in her review for the *New York Times Book Review,* concludes: "The stories are fine; the novella is splendid." John Blades in the *Chicago Tribune* finds that Smiley "speaks most confidently and affectingly [about] the delicate mechanics of marriage and family life, the intricate mysteries of love."

In 1988 Smiley published *The Greenlanders,* a "prodigiously detailed, haunting novel," as Howard Norman describes it in the *New York Times Book Review.* A 500-page historical novel set in fourteenth-century Greenland, the novel took Smiley five years to research and write. *The Greenlanders* is "a sprawling, multi-generational, heroic Norse narrative," according to Richard Panek in *Tribune Books.* Based on old Viking sagas and, in particular, on surviving accounts of the colonies the Vikings established in Greenland, the story blends fact and fiction to create a modern novel with a traditional flavor. As Norman explains, the book "employs a 'folkloristic' mode—with its stories overlapping other stories, folded into yet others." The technique, Yolen finds, presents "more than an individual's story. It is the community's story, the land's." By telling the community's story, Smiley contrasts the tragic failure of the Greenland colonies to survive with our contemporary society and its problems. "The result," Panek writes, "is a novel that places contemporary conflicts into the context of the ages."

As in her other novels, Smiley also focuses on family relations in *The Greenlanders,* tracing the effects of a curse on several generations of the Gunnarsson family, well-to-do farmers in Greenland. "Family matters . . . ," Yolen states, "become both the focus and the subtext of the novel: the feuds, the curses, the marriages, the passions and the brutal deaths." Norman notes the complexity of the novel, citing the "hundreds of episodes and tributary episodes: the seasonal seal hunts and rituals, the travels over hazardous yet awe-inspiring terrain, the births and

deaths. . . . Given the vast template of History, it is impressive how Ms. Smiley is able to telescope certain incidents, unravel personalities in a few paragraphs, [and] delve into a kind of folkloric metaphysics." Norman concludes that Smiley "is a diverse and masterly writer."

After the publication the novellas *Ordinary Love and Good Will,* and a short story, *The Life of the Body,* Smiley published *A Thousand Acres.* The subtle account of a family's disintegration emerges through a painstakingly detailed portrait of Midwestern farm life, just before much of it was lost during the wave of foreclosures in the 1980s. Donna Rifkind comments in her *Washington Post* review that the novel "has all the stark brutality, if not the poetic grandeur, of a Shakespearean tragedy."

The correlation to Shakespeare is no accident, as Smiley admits that the novel is a deliberate recasting of *King Lear,* the Elizabethan playwright's drama of an aged king bordering on madness and conspired against by three daughters plotting to take control of his kingdom. Reinterpreting the motivations of the daughters through a more jaundiced view of patriarchal control and feminine subjugation, Smiley puts the character of Lear's eldest daughter, Goneril in Shakespeare's work, now Ginny in her own, at the center of her family narrative. "Her feminist re-writing of Shakespeare's plot replaces the incomprehensibly malign sisters with real women who have suffered incomprehensible malignity," notes Diane Purkiss in a review for the *Times Literary Supplement.* "In giving Goneril a voice, Smiley joins the distinguished line of women's writers who have written new parts for Shakespeare's women."

For Jack Fuller, reworking the plot of *King Lear* has its dangers. "The large risk that Smiley runs, of course, is using the Lear story so explicitly," Fuller notes in Chicago *Tribune Books.* "It could have turned the book into a kind of precious exercise or a literary curiosity. But Smiley avoids this by the mounting brilliance of her close observations and delicate rendering of human behavior."

Through Ginny's eyes, Smiley shows the deleterious impact of her father Larry's decision to divide his multimillion dollar farm among his three daughters, which includes the embittered Rose and the emotionally distant Caroline. As the divided enterprise deteriorates, marriages fall apart and family relationships are crippled by suspicion and betrayal. Describing *A Thousand Acres* as "powerful" and "poignant," Ron Carlson writes in the *New York Times Book Review* that "Ms. Smiley brings us in so close that it's almost too much to bear. She's good in those small places, with nothing but the family, pulling tighter and tighter until someone has to leave the table, leave the room, leave town."

Smiley also brings her knack for detail in her descriptions of Iowa farm life. Carlson observes, "Ms. Smiley's portrait of the American farm is so vivid and immediate—the way farmers walk, what the corn looks like, the buzz of conversation at the community dinners—that it causes a kind of stunning nostalgia." Not all critics are as enamored of the rural tableau. In his review of the book for the *London Review of Books,* James Woods complains that "we learn far too much about hogs and slurry systems and combine harvesters. . . . This is a very American kind of writing, partly inherited and partly invented by creative-writing programmes."

As the Cook family saga unfolds, Smiley gently yet skillfully reveals her feminist and environmentalist sympathies. "In *A Thousand Acres,* men's dominance of women takes a violent turn, and incest becomes an undercurrent in the novel," writes Martha Duffy in *Time.* "The magic of [the novel] is that it deals so effectively with both the author's scholarship and her dead-serious social concerns in an engrossing piece of fiction."

In her next work, *Moo,* Smiley leaves the strains of family relationships to poke some fun at campus life, which she explores at the fictitious Midwestern agricultural college, nicknamed Moo U. *Moo* received mixed reactions from reviewers. While critics found moments of brilliance in the work, some considered it flawed. In a review appearing in *Washington Post Book World,* the writer compares *Moo* with another satire of academia, *Pictures from an Institution* by Randall Jarrell. "Stylistically, [Smiley] employs a prose and tone reminiscent of the dry, ironic, distanced manner Jarrell so masterfully adopted. . . . When it comes down to the essential business of satire, though, Smiley is ill-equipped to follow in Jarrell's train. This is not because she lacks humor but because, more tellingly, she lacks malice." While commenting that Smiley wields a "considerable wit" and "provocative intelligence," Richard Eder's review in the *Los Angeles Times Book Review* takes the novel to task for being "a playful takeoff on too many things, all crowded together and happening at once." In contrast *New York Review of Books'* Cathleen Schine finds *Moo* a social comedy closer to Anthony Trollope's work than Jarrell's satire. Schine notes, "Smiley subverts satire, making it sweeter and ultimately more pointed. She has written a generous and, therefore daring book. . . . Smiley has transformed the genre by embracing a different tradition altogether. . . . Jane Smiley has created what modern novel readers have until now been able only to dream about, that elusive, seemingly impossible thing: a fresh literary, modern twentieth-century nineteenth-century novel." A reviewer for *Publishers Weekly,* offers praise for the work, writing that in *Moo* "Smiley delivers a surprising tour de force, a satire of university life that leaves no aspect of contemporary academia un-

scathed." Joanne Wilkinson sounds a similar positive note in her review for *Booklist* in her appreciation of the novel's ending. She writes, "Smiley's great gift here is the way she gently skewers any number of easily recognizable campus fixtures . . . while never failing to show their humanity."

BIOGRAPHICAL/CRITICAL SOURCES:

BOOKS

Contemporary Literary Criticism, Volume 76, Gale (Detroit), 1993.

PERIODICALS

Belles Lettres, summer, 1992, pp. 36-38.
Booklist, February 1, 1995, p. 971.
Chicago Tribune, November 6, 1987; November 24, 1991.
Chicago Tribune Book World, July 8, 1984.
English Journal, March, 1994, p. 94.
London Review of Books, November 19, 1992, October 19, 1995, p. 38.
Los Angeles Times Book Review, March 18, 1984; October 18, 1987; April 2, 1995, pp. 3, 8.
New York Review of Books, August 10, 1995, pp. 38-9.
New York Times, August 26, 1987.
New York Times Book Review, August 17, 1980; November 22, 1981; April 29, 1984; September 6, 1987; May 15, 1988; November 3, 1991.
People, January 18, 1988.
Publishers Weekly, April 1, 1988; February 6, 1995, pp. 75-6.
Time, November 11, 1991.
Times (London), February 4, 1988.
Times Literary Supplement, August 24, 1984; March 18, 1988; October 30, 1992.
Tribune Books (Chicago), April 3, 1988; November 3, 1991.
Washington Post, October 27, 1981; May 13, 1988; October 27, 1991.
Washington Post Book World, March 26, 1995.*

* * *

SMITH, Bonnie G(ene) 1940-

PERSONAL: Born June 30, 1940, in Bridgeport, CT; daughter of William Wallace (a minister) and Harriet Amanda (Howard) Sullivan; married Donald R. Kelley (a historian). *Education:* Smith College, A.B., 1962; University of Rochester, Ph.D., 1976.

ADDRESSES: Home—45 Jefferson Ave., New Brunswick, NJ 08901. *Office*—Department of History, Rutgers University, New Brunswick, NJ 08903-5059.

CAREER: University of Rochester, Rochester, NY, instructor in history, 1976-77; University of Wisconsin—

Parkside, Kenosha, assistant professor of history, 1977-81; University of Rochester, assistant professor, 1981-84, associate professor, 1984-88, professor of history, 1988-90; Rutgers University, New Brunswick, NJ, professor of history, 1990—.

MEMBER: American Historical Association, French Historical Society.

AWARDS, HONORS: Fellowships from American Philosophical Society, 1978, American Council of Learned Societies, 1979-80 and 1984-85, National Humanities Center, 1984, Shelby Cullam Davis Center of Princeton University, 1992-93, Guggenheim Foundation, 1993.

WRITINGS:

Ladies of the Leisure Class: The Bourgeoises of Northern France in the Nineteenth Century, Princeton University Press (Princeton, NJ), 1981.

Confessions of a Concierge: Madame Lucie's History of Twentieth-Century France, Yale University Press (New Haven, CT), 1985.

Changing Lives: Women in European History, 1700-1985, D. C. Heath (Lexington, MA), 1988.

(Translator, with Donald R. Kelley, and editor) P. J. Proudhon, *What Is Property?,* Cambridge University Press (New York City), 1994.

(Co-author with Lynn Hunt and others) *The Challenge of the West: Peoples and Cultures from the Stone Age to the Global Age,* D. C. Heath (Lexington, MA), 1995.

Contributor to history journals.

WORK IN PROGRESS: Gender and Historiography in the West, 1800-1940.

SIDELIGHTS: Unlike history that limits itself to the recording of extraordinary events or lives, Bonnie G. Smith's *Confessions of a Concierge: Madame Lucie's History of Twentieth-Century France* is premised upon what James F. McMillan refers to in the *Times Literary Supplement* as the "valid assumption that the key events in an individual's private life may bear little relation to the public events which constitute the stuff of 'official history.' " *Confessions of a Concierge* documents the difficult life of a woman born in Normandy during the 1890s to a prosperous family of tradespeople who lose their wealth through the two world wars. The financial upheaval in her life compels her to marry beneath the social class into which she was born and she survives as a Paris concierge. "Mme. Lucie Lemaire deplores her reduced circumstances, but in the best tradition of concierges she's a keen observer of the world that passes her door, and she is willing to re-create her difficult life," says a *Newsweek* contributor. Considering her story "worth the telling," McMillan adds that "Smith, working in miniature, restores

a welcome human dimension to the exploration of the French past."

The *New York Times*'s Christopher Lehmann-Haupt believes that one of *Confessions of a Concierge*'s "most striking effects is the way it transforms what is lively incident in Part I into the fading memories and obsessions of the old lady in Part II. In the twinkling of an eye, biography becomes psychology. In barely 150 pages, we are made to feel the weight of Madame Lucie's more than 80 years." Although Lehmann-Haupt questions whether "piecing together . . . quotations so that they read like a 19th-century novel" is appropriate, he concludes: "In the long run, history will decide whether *Confessions of a Concierge* is history. What matters for now is that Bonnie G. Smith has taken an actual character and through artifice has made her seem timeless." McMillan concludes: "These *Confessions* remain valuable, not because they are remarkable but because they are ordinary; not because they are typical, but because they are unique."

BIOGRAPHICAL/CRITICAL SOURCES:

PERIODICALS

Atlantic, September, 1985, p. 114.
Ms., December, 1985, p. 14.
Newsweek, September 23, 1985.
New York Times, July 31, 1985.
New York Times Book Review, August 9, 1987, p. 32.
Signs, summer, 1987, p. 818.
Times Literary Supplement, January 17, 1986.

*   *   *

SOTO, Gary 1952-

PERSONAL: Born April 12, 1952, in Fresno, CA; son of Manuel and Angie (Trevino) Soto; married Carolyn Sadako Oda, May 24, 1975; children: Mariko Heidi. *Education:* California State University, Fresno, B.A., 1974; University of California, Irvine, M.F.A., 1976. *Avocational interests:* Karate, reading, Aztec dancing, travel.

ADDRESSES: Home—43 The Crescent, Berkeley, CA 94708.

CAREER: University of California, Berkeley, assistant professor 1979-85; associate professor of English and ethnic studies, 1985-92, part-time senior lecturer in English department, 1992-93; University of Cincinnati, Elliston Poet, 1988; Wayne State University, Martin Luther King/Cesar Chavez/Rosa Parks Visiting Professor of English, 1990; full-time writer, 1993—.

AWARDS, HONORS: Academy of American Poets Prize, 1975; *Discovery/The Nation* prize, 1975; United States

Award, International Poetry Forum, 1976, for *The Elements of San Joaquin;* Bess Hokin Prize from *Poetry,* 1978; Guggenheim Fellowship, 1979-80; National Endowment for the Arts fellowships, 1981 and 1991; creative writing fellowship, National Education Association, 1982; Levinson Award, *Poetry,* 1984; American Book Award, Before Columbus Foundation, 1985, for *Living up the Street;* California Arts Council fellowship, 1989; Best Book for Young Adults citation, American Library Association, 1990, Beatty Award, California Library Association, 1991, and Reading Magic Award, *Parenting* magazine, all for *Baseball in April, and Other Stories;* George G. Stone Center Recognition of Merit, Claremont Graduate School, 1993; Carnegie Medal, 1993; National Book Award and *Los Angeles Times* Book Prize nominations, both 1995, both for *New and Selected Poems.*

WRITINGS:

The Elements of San Joaquin (poems), University of Pittsburgh Press (Pittsburgh, PA), 1977.
The Tale of Sunlight (poems), University of Pittsburgh Press, 1978.
Where Sparrows Work Hard (poems), University of Pittsburgh Press, 1981.
Black Hair (poems), University of Pittsburgh Press, 1985.
Living up the Street: Narrative Recollections (prose memoirs), Strawberry Hill (San Francisco, CA), 1985, reprinted, Dell (New York City), 1993.
Small Faces (prose memoirs), Arte Publico (Houston, TX), 1986, reprinted, Dell, 1994.
Lesser Evils: Ten Quartets (memoirs and essays), Arte Publico, 1988.
(Editor) *California Childhood: Recollections and Stories of the Golden State,* Creative Arts Book Company (Berkeley, CA), 1988.
A Fire in My Hands (poems), Scholastic (New York City), 1990.
A Summer Life (autobiography), University Press of New England (Hanover, NH), 1990, reprinted, Dell, 1992.
Baseball in April and Other Stories (short stories), Harcourt (San Diego, CA), 1990.
Who Will Know Us? (poems), Chronicle Books (San Francisco, CA), 1990.
Home Course in Religion (poems), Chronicle Books, 1991.
Taking Sides, Harcourt, 1991.
Neighborhood Odes, Harcourt, 1992.
Pacific Crossing, Harcourt, 1992.
The Skirt, Delacorte (New York City), 1992.
Too Many Tamales (picture book), Putnam (New York City), 1992.
(Editor) *Pieces of the Heart: New Chicano Fiction,* Chronicle Books, 1993.
Local News (short stories), Harcourt, 1993.
The Pool Party, Delacorte, 1993 (also see below).

Crazy Weekend, Scholastic, 1994.
Jesse, Harcourt, 1994.
Boys at Work, Delacorte, 1995.
Canto Familiar/Familiar Song (poetry), Harcourt, 1995.
The Cat's Meow, Scholastic, 1995.
Chato's Kitchen, Putnam, 1995.
(Editor) *Everyday Seductions,* Ploughshare Press (Sea Bright, NJ), 1995.
New and Selected Poems, Chronicle Books, 1995.
Summer on Wheels, Scholastic, 1995.
The Old Man and His Door, Putnam, 1996.
Snapshots of the Wedding, Putnam, 1996.

SHORT FILMS

The Bike, Gary Soto Productions, 1991.
The Pool Party, Gary Soto Productions, 1993.
Novio Boy, Gary Soto Productions, 1994.

Contributor of poetry to periodicals, including *American Poetry Review, Antaeus, Nation, New Chicano Writing, New Republic, New Yorker, North American Review, Paris Review, Partisan Review, Poetry,* and *Revista Chicano-Riquena.* Contributor of articles to *Bloomsbury Review, Image, Los Angeles Times, MELUS, Parnassus, San Francisco Review of Books, Washington Post,* and *Zyzzyvz.* Author of forewords to *Condor Dreams and Other Fictions* (Reno, University of Nevada Press, 1994) and *Folk Wisdom of Mexico* (Chronicle Books, 1994).

WORK IN PROGRESS: Buried Onions, for Harcourt, due 1997.

SIDELIGHTS: Gary Soto is an American poet and prose writer influenced by his working-class Mexican-American background. Born in Fresno, California, in the agricultural San Joaquin Valley, he worked as a laborer during his childhood. In his writing, as Raymund Paredes noted in the *Rocky Mountain Review,* "Soto establishes his acute sense of ethnicity and, simultaneously, his belief that certain emotions, values, and experiences transcend ethnic boundaries and allegiances." Many critics have echoed the assessment of Patricia De La Fuente in *Revista Chicano-Requena* that Soto displays an "exceptionally high level of linguistic sophistication."

In his first volume of poetry, *The Elements of San Joaquin,* Soto offers a grim portrait of Mexican-American life. His poems depict the violence of urban life, the exhausting labor of rural life, and the futility of trying to recapture the innocence of childhood. In the book *Chicano Poetry* Juan Bruce-Novoa likened Soto's poetic vision to T. S. Eliot's bleak portrait of the modern world, *The Waste Land.* Soto uses wind-swept dust as a dominant image, and he also introduces such elements as rape, unflushed toilets, a drowned baby, and, as Bruce-Novoa quotes him, "men / Whose arms / Were bracelets / Of burns." Soto's skill with the figurative language of poetry has been noted by reviewers throughout his career, and in *Western American Literature* Jerry Bradley praised the metaphors in *San Joaquin* as "evocative, enlightening, and haunting." Though unsettled by the negativism of the collection, Bruce-Novoa felt the work "convinces because of its well-wrought structure, the craft, the coherence of its totality." Moreover, he thought, because it brings such a vivid portrait of poverty to the reading public, *San Joaquin* is "a social as well as a literary achievement."

Soto's social concerns and aspects of his poetic style have led several critics to compare him to poet Philip Levine, who taught Soto at the Fresno campus of California State University. Levine's poetry focuses on the degraded lives of American working people, and, as Vicki Armour-Hileman noted in *Denver Quarterly*, its plain language and short, run-on lines are similar to Soto's work. When Soto spoke to *CA* in a 1986 interview, he acknowledged Levine's influence but stressed his familiarity with other poets too.

Many critics have also observed that Soto's writing transcends social commentary. Bruce-Novoa said that one reason why the author's work has "great significance within Chicano literature" is because it represents "a definite shift toward a more personal, less politically motivated poetry." As Alan Williamson suggested in *Poetry*, Soto avoids either idealizing the poor for their oppression or encouraging their violent defiance. Instead, he focuses on the human suffering that poverty engenders. When Peter Cooley reviewed Soto's second volume of poetry, *The Tale of Sunlight*, in *Parnassus*, he praised the author's ability to temper the bleakness of *San Joaquin* with "imaginative expansiveness." The poems in *Sunlight*, many of which focus on a child named Molina or on the owner of a Hispanic bar, display both the frustrations of poverty and what Williamson called "a vein of consolatory fantasy which passes beyond escapism into a pure imaginative generosity toward life." Williamson cited as an example "the poem in which an uncle's gray hair is seen as a visitation of magical butterflies."

In the poems of *Black Hair*, Soto focuses on his friends and family. He portrays fondly the times he shared with his buddies as an adolescent and the more recent moments he has spent with his young daughter. Some critics, such as David Wojahn in *Poetry*, argued that Soto was moving away from his strengths as a writer. While acknowledging that "by limiting his responses to a naive aplomb, Soto enables himself to write with a freshness that is at times arresting," Wojahn considered the work "a disappointment." He praised *San Joaquin* and *Tale of Sunlight* as "thematically urgent . . . and ambitious in their scope" and said that "compared to them, *Black Hair* is a distinctly minor achievement." Others, such as Ellen Lesser

in *Voice Literary Supplement*, were charmed by Soto's poetic tone, "the quality of the voice, the immediate, human presence that breathes through the lines." Lesser contended that Soto's celebration of innocence and sentiment is shaded with a knowledge of "the larger, often threatening world." In the *Christian Science Monitor*, Tom D'Evelyn hailed Soto's ability to go beyond the circumstances of his own life and write of "something higher," concluding, "Somehow Gary Soto has become not an important Chicano poet but an important American poet. More power to him."

When Soto discusses American racial tensions in the prose collections *Living up the Street: Narrative Recollections* and *Small Faces*, he uses vignettes drawn from his own childhood. One vignette shows the anger the author felt upon realizing that his brown-skinned brother would never be considered an attractive child by conventional American standards. Another shows Soto's surprise at discovering that, contrary to his family's advice to marry a Mexican, he was falling in love with a woman of Japanese ancestry. In these deliberately small-scale recollections, as Paredes noted, "it is a measure of Soto's skill that he so effectively invigorates and sharpens our understanding of the commonplace." With these volumes Soto acquired a solid reputation as a prose writer as well as a poet; *Living up the Street* earned him an American Book Award.

Soto's autobiographical prose continued with *Lesser Evils: Ten Quartets* and *A Summer Life*. The first of these, as Soto explained in an unpublished 1988 interview, reflects the author's experience with Catholicism—in the same interview Soto declared himself a reconciled Catholic. *A Summer Life* consists of thirty-nine short essays. According to Ernesto Trejo in the *Los Angeles Times Book Review*, these pieces "make up a compelling biography" of Soto's youth. As he had done in previous works, Soto here "holds the past up to memory's probing flashlight, turns it around ever so carefully, and finds in the smallest of incidents the occasion for literature." Writing in the *Americas Review*, Hector Torres compared *A Summer Life* with Soto's earlier autobiographical texts and asserted that the later book "moves with greater stylistic elegance and richer thematic coherence."

During the early 1990s Soto turned his attentions in a new direction: children's literature. A first volume of short stories for young readers, *Baseball in April and Other Stories*, was published in 1990. The eleven tales depict Mexican-American boys and girls as they enter adolescence in Hispanic California neighborhoods. In the *New York Times Book Review*, Roberto Gonzalez Echevarria called the stories "sensitive and economical." Echevarria praised Soto: "Because he stays within the teenagers' universe . . . he manages to convey all the social change and stress without bathos or didacticism. In fact, his stories are moving, yet humorous and entertaining." In the *Americas Review,* Torres suggested that *Baseball in April* was "the kind of work that could be used to teach high school and junior high school English classes."

One of Soto's juvenile characters, a boy named Lincoln Mendoza, appears as a protagonist in two works: *Taking Sides* and *Pacific Crossing.* As a Mexican-American eighth-grader in *Taking Sides,* Lincoln is confronted with challenges and insecurities when he and his mother move from San Francisco's Mission District to a predominantly Anglo suburb. He works to keep his heritage intact in his new environment. *Pacific Crossing* finds Lincoln and one of his friends facing cultural challenges in another context: they embark on a voyage to Japan as exchange students. Writing in the *Multicultural Review,* Osbelia Juarez Rocha called *Pacific Crossing* "cleverly crafted" and "entertaining."

Soto has also written poetry for younger readers, most notably the volumes *A Fire in My Hands* and *Neighborhood Odes,* both of which focus on growing up in the Mexican neighborhoods of California's Central Valley. Soto has ventured as well into the arena of children's picture books. *Too Many Tamales* depicts the story of Maria, a young girl who misplaces her mother's wedding ring in tamale dough while helping to prepare a Christmastime feast. Maria— with her cousins' help—embarks on a futile effort to recover the ring by consuming vast quantities of tamales. *Chato's Kitchen* introduces a cat whose efforts to entice the local "ratoncitos"—little mice—lead him to prepare abundant portions of fajitas, frijoles, enchiladas, and other foods.

In a 1989 volume of the *Dictionary of Literary Biography,* Hector Avalos Torres declared: "Soto's consistent attention to the craft of writing and his sensitivity to his subject matter have earned him an indisputable place in American and Chicano literature." Torres noted that critical response to Soto's work has been "overwhelmingly positive." He attributed that respect and admiration to Soto's ability to represent his experience "in a manner that shows his talent at creating poetry and prose that, through simple and direct diction, expresses the particulars of everyday life and simultaneously contains glimpses of the universal."

BIOGRAPHICAL/CRITICAL SOURCES:

BOOKS

Bruce-Novoa, Juan, *Chicano Poetry: A Response to Chaos,* University of Texas Press, (Austin) 1982.
Contemporary Literary Criticism, Gale (Detroit), Volume 32, 1985, Volume 80, 1994.

Dictionary of Literary Biography, Volume 82: *Chicano Writers,* Gale, 1989.

PERIODICALS

American Book Review, July-August, 1982.
Americas Review, spring, 1991, pp. 111-15.
Christian Science Monitor, March 6, 1985.
Denver Quarterly, summer, 1982.
Los Angeles Times Book Review, August 5, 1990, pp. 1, 9.
Multicultural Review, June 1993, pp. 76, 78.
Nation, June 7, 1993, pp. 772-74.
New York Times Book Review, May 20, 1990, p. 45.
Parnassus, fall-winter, 1979.
Poetry, March, 1980, June, 1985.
Publishers Weekly, March 23, 1992, p. 74; April 12, 1993, p. 64; August 16, 1993, p. 103; February 6, 1995, pp. 84-85.
Revista Chicano-Riquena, summer, 1983.
Rocky Mountain Review, Volume 41, numbers 1-2, 1987.
San Francisco Review of Books, summer, 1986.
Voice Literary Supplement, September, 1985.
Western American Literature, spring, 1979.

—*Sketch by Erika Dreifus*

*   *   *

SPURLING, John   1936-

PERSONAL: Born July 17, 1936, in Kisumu, Kenya; son of Antony Cuthbert (a barrister) and Elizabeth (Stobart) Spurling; married Hilary Forrest (a writer), April 4, 1961; children: Amy Maria, Nathaniel Stobart, Gilbert Alexander. *Education:* St. John's College, Oxford, B.A., 1960.

ADDRESSES: Home—London, England. *Agent*—MLR Ltd., 200 Fulham Rd., London SW10 9PN, England; and Christopher Little, 48 Walham Grove, London SW6 1QR, England.

CAREER: Playwright, novelist, and art critic. British Government, Kumba, Southern Cameroons, plebiscite officer, 1960-61; British Broadcasting Corp., London, England, announcer, 1963-66. *Military service:* British Army, Royal Artillery, 1955-57; became second lieutenant.

AWARDS, HONORS: Henfield writing fellowship, University of East Anglia, 1973.

WRITINGS:

PLAYS

MacRune's Guevara (as Realised by Edward Hotel) (first produced in London by the National Theatre at Jeanetta Cochrane Theatre, February 8, 1969; produced in New York, 1975), Calder & Boyars, 1969.

In the Heart of the British Museum (first produced in Edinburgh, Scotland, at Traverse Theatre, August 5, 1971), Calder & Boyars, 1971.
Shades of Heathcliff [and] *Death of Captain Doughty* (contains *Shades of Heathcliff* [first produced in Sheffield, at Lucky's, December 8, 1971] and *Death of Captain Doughty* [television play; first broadcast in 1973]), Marion Boyars, 1975.
The British Empire, Part One: A Play (first produced in Birmingham, England, February, 1980), Marion Boyars, 1982.

UNPUBLISHED PLAYS

Char, first produced in Oxford, England, 1959.
Romance (musical), music and lyrics by Charles Ross, first produced on the West End, at Duke of York's Theatre, September 28, 1971.
Peace in Our Time, first produced in Sheffield, England, at Crucible Theatre, November 16, 1972.
McGonagall and the Murderer, first produced in London, 1974.
While Rome Burns, first produced in Canterbury, England, at Marlowe Theatre, 1976.
Antigone through the Looking Glass, first produced in London, at King's Head Theatre, September, 1979.
Coming Ashore in Guadeloupe, first produced in England at Harrogate and Edinburgh Festivals, summer, 1982.
Racine at the Girls' School, first produced in England at Cheltenham Literary Festival, October 17, 1992.
The Butcher of Baghdad, first produced in England at the Grace at the Latchemere, London, June 21, 1993.
Achilles on the Beach at Troy, first produced in England at New Theatre, Bretton Hall College, November 17, 1994.

Also author of television plays *Hope,* 1970, *Faith,* 1971, *Silver,* 1973, and radio plays *Where Tigers Roam,* 1976, the "British Empire" trilogy (*Dominion over Palm and Pine,* 1982, *The Christian Hero,* 1982, *The Day of Reckoning,* 1985), *Fancy Picture: A Portrait after Gainsborough,* 1988, *Discobolus,* 1989, *The Butcher of Baghdad,* 1993, and *MacRune's Guevara,* 1993. Author of six-part radio play of I. Compton-Burnett's novel *Daughters and Sons,* 1985.

NOVELS

The Ragged End, Weidenfeld & Nicolson, 1989.
After Zenda, Andre Deutsch, 1995.

OTHER

(With John Fletcher) *Beckett: A Study of His Plays,* Hill & Wang (New York City), 1972, 3rd revised edition published as *Beckett, the Playwright,* 1985.
(Editor and contributor) J. G. Farrell, *The Hill Station,* Weidenfeld & Nicolson (London), 1981.

Graham Greene, Methuen (New York City), 1983.

Contributor to books, including *Best Plays of 1969-70,* edited by Otis Guernsey, Jr., Dodd (New York City), 1970; *Best Plays of 1971-72,* edited by Guernsey, Dodd, 1972; *New Stories I,* edited by Margaret Drabble and Charles Osborne, Arts Council of Great Britain, 1976; and *Contemporary Dramatists,* St. James Press (New York City). Art critic for *New Statesman,* 1976-88. Contributor to periodicals, newspapers, radio programs, and art catalogs.

SIDELIGHTS: Martin Seymour-Smith, in a *Spectator* review, calls John Spurling's *MacRune's Guevara (as Realised by Edward Hotel)* "consistently intelligent . . . and entertaining." He goes on to say that comparison of the play to "a many-layered cake is tempting but misleading. It is primarily an intellectual play, a witty double-barrelled discharge at abstractionism and uninformed political passion; but the author allows his own passionate emotional involvement with South America to be reflected in a structure that much more resembles a delicately constructed mathematical model than an object with simple layers." Seymour-Smith also notes that "Mr. Spurling has made use of techniques employed by [George Bernard] Shaw, Pirandello and—I would suggest—such experimental plays of Eugene O'Neill as *The Great God Brown;* he has also drawn upon the available literature on the Bolivian campaign. The author's originality is apparent in his savage and subtle exploitation of cliche, his rueful but satirical recognition of the power of theatrical rhetoric, and the bad effect it may have—and, most strikingly, in the dazzling manner in which he counterpoints his characters against one another to raise truly Borgesian . . . issues about identity."

BIOGRAPHICAL/CRITICAL SOURCES:

PERIODICALS

New Statesman, February 29, 1980; April 7, 1989.
Radio Three Magazine, November, 1982.
Spectator, February 28, 1969; February 25, 1995.
Stage, July 9, 1970; December 30, 1971.
Times Literary Supplement, March 3, 1995.

*   *   *

STEELE, Addison, II
  See LUPOFF, Richard A(llen)

*   *   *

STEELE, Timothy (Reid) 1948-

PERSONAL: Born January 22, 1948, in Burlington, VT; son of Edward William (a teacher) and Ruth (a nurse;

maiden name, Reid) Steele; married Catherine Fuller, September 27, 1969 (divorced 1973); married Victoria Lee Erpelding (a librarian), January 14, 1979. *Education:* Stanford University, B.A., 1970; Brandeis University, Ph.D., 1977.

ADDRESSES: Home—1801 Preuss Rd., Los Angeles, CA 90035.

CAREER: California State University, Hayward, lecturer, 1973-74; Stanford University, Stanford, CA, Jones Lecturer in Poetry, 1975-77; University of California, Los Angeles, lecturer in English, 1977-83; University of California, Santa Barbara, lecturer, 1986; California State University, Los Angeles, professor, 1987—.

MEMBER: Academy of American Poets, Modern Language Association.

AWARDS, HONORS: Wallace Stegner Fellowship in Creative Writing, Stanford University, 1972-73; Guggenheim fellow, 1984-85, Peter I. B. Lavan Younger Poets Award, Academy of American Poets, 1986; Medal for Poetry, Commonwealth Club of California, 1986; Literary Award for Poetry, Los Angeles Center of PEN, 1987.

WRITINGS:

(Editor) *The Music of His History: Poems for Charles Gullans on His Sixtieth Birthday,* Robert L. Barth (Florence, KY), 1990.

Missing Measures: Modern Poetry and the Revolt against Meter (nonfiction), University of Arkansas Press (Fayetteville), 1990.

POETRY

Uncertainties and Rest, Louisiana State University Press (Baton Rouge), 1979.

The Prudent Heart, Symposium Press (Los Angeles), 1983.

Nine Poems, Robert L. Barth, 1984.

On Harmony, Abattoir Editions (Lincoln, NE), 1984.

Short Subjects, Robert L. Barth, 1985.

Sapphics against Anger and Other Poems, Random House (New York City), 1986.

Beatitudes, Words (Child Okeford, England), 1988.

The Color Wheel, Johns Hopkins University Press (Baltimore, MD), 1994.

Sapphics and Uncertainties: Poems, 1970-1986, University of Arkansas Press, 1995.

OTHER

Contributor of poems, reviews, essays to *Poetry, Threepenny Review, Paris Review,* and other publications.

SIDELIGHTS: In an era when free verse has largely been the dominant mode of poetic expression, Timothy Steele has emerged as one of the major practitioners of the New Formalism movement. Along with poets such as Thom Gunn, Richard Wilbur, Janet Lewis, Edgar Bowers and Vikram Seth, he has chosen to write in traditional meter and rhyme. Likewise in his critical work Steele has argued for the return to traditional forms to revitalize poetry in the modern world. Steele stated in a poetry symposium in *Crosscurrents:* "My keenest pleasure in reading poetry has from the beginning been bound up with the metrical experience; and I write in meter because only by doing so can I hope to give someone else the same degree of pleasure that the poetry I most love has given me."

Like many contemporary poets, Steele's career has been firmly rooted in the academic world. He took his undergraduate degree at Stanford in 1970, at a time when the influence of the major formalist poet Yvor Winters was still felt very strongly. Steele's graduate degree is from Brandeis, where he studied under J. V. Cunningham, another well-known formalist and a friend of Winters. Steele has taught at a number of colleges and universities in California, including Stanford, UCLA, and California State University, Los Angeles. Many of his poems employ the Los Angeles and Southern California environments as their setting; others hearken back to his boyhood days in New England.

Although Steele's modes of poetic expression are formal, even classical, he often departs from this tradition in terms of subject matter. He tends to write private poems about the personal and the everyday, nearly always in contemporary settings. Reviewing his second collection, *The Prudent Heart,* for the *Ontario Review,* Dana Gioia states: "What one notices . . . is a carefully cultivated sensibility flawlessly translated into words. . . . Steele believes he can command the reader's attention by writing well about ordinary things. . . . He writes about the beauties of the everyday world, the abiding love in marriage, the forgiveness and self-knowledge that can come from anger." In addition to praising Steele's technical skill, Gioia feels that his tone is valid and his subject matter worthy. However, other reviewers have often criticized his work for what's been called a lack of intensity and a failure to address larger issues of the day.

Steele's major nonfiction work, *Missing Measures: Modern Poetry and the Revolt against Meter,* is a 343-page treatise discussing the history of poetry from the Greeks to the present. It examines why the moderns—Ezra Pound, T. S. Eliot, William Carlos Williams—revolted against and abandoned traditional verse in favor of free verse. Steele proposes that what began as an attempt to free poetry from its traditional structures has somewhat evolved into a destructive movement, often tearing down the old without offering anything worthwhile in its place. Meg Schoerke states in *The American Scholar:* "According to Steele, free verse results in a wholly subjective poetry that is divorced from human experience, solipistic, and therefore immoral; its adherents, who refuse to abide by universal standards of judgment, persistently indulge in irrationality and illusory novelty and . . . are guilty of automatic writing. Steele does not admit that free verse can lead to anything other than these vices . . . ''

Writing in *Modern Language Review* Stephen Matterson sees *Missing Measures* as a "polemical essay" rather than a scholarly thesis, going on to note that it is "inordinately long, and there are inevitably repetitions. More seriously, in spite of the length of the book, it never really comes face to face with the modernists." Matterson feels that Steele's technique is "to criticize selected passages necessarily isolated from context." Matterson concludes: "Overall, there is too much in the book that is similarly equivocal for it to be convincing. Too many ideas are introduced then left undeveloped . . . ''

Reactions from some other quarters to *Missing Measures* have been more supportive. Although Schoerke criticizes the book on many of the same counts as Matterson, she also credits Steele with voicing "the legitimate complaint that many poets of the last few decades have done little more than parrot the surface characteristics of modern poetry. . . ." Thomas D'Evelyn, writing in the *Christian Science Monitor,* offers a far more positive evaluation of Steele's work: "*Missing Measures* is ultimately a hopeful book. Returning to Aristotle's recognition that although all metered language (verse) need not be poetry, all poetry is metered, we see that the way forward is plain." D'Evelyn concludes his essay with a glowing evaluation of Steele's own poem entitled "Summer": "Here, iambic meter is no 'straitjacket,' but an imitation, with carefully weighed syllables, of great beauty and truth."

Steele's poetry has generated less controversy than his critical stance, but as much difference of opinion. His first collection, *Uncertainties and Rest,* received mixed responses, often within the same review. Wyatt Prunty, writing in the *Southern Review,* praises Steele's "technical mastery" and calls the collection "a strong book." At the same time, he feels that the poems are often too private, having "less significance for an outsider who reads them than they apparently have for Steele and the various people he addresses." John N. Miller, in the *Chowder Review,* also complains of the poems' "unrelieved privatism," calling this the "more pervasive shortcoming of Steele's poetry." Yet, in another display of the mixed feelings shared by many critics, Miller concludes his review by stating "the craftsmanship and controlled detail in *Uncertainties and Rest* admirably demonstrate that traditional poetry still lives in America." Mary Kinzie in the *Partisan Review* levels some of the same criticisms as Miller and Prune, yet nevertheless concludes that the collection is "one of the

most exciting first books of poems to appear in the past decade."

Steele's second full-length collection, *Sapphics against Anger and Other Poems,* set mainly in the milieu of Southern California, advanced his reputation considerably as a formalist poet. Again, critical response to the book varies widely, even with regard to Steele's technical mastery of traditional form. For example, writing in the *Times Literary Supplement,* Brad Leithauser refers to the "weighted gracefulness" of Steele's style, while, in stark contrast, William Logan in the *New York Times Book Review* feels that Steele "handles his meters like a mannequin." The only fault that Leithauser finds with the collection is that "Steele rarely startles the reader, rarely lets illogic have its say." Logan, on the other hand, believes that "Steele's passions are domestic, his sorrows what the suburban tract house inspires . . . " Logan finds Steele at his best when he is dealing with historical subjects rather than contemporary ones. In these poems Logan feels that Steele "finds occasions that promise a maturing of talent beyond the conventions of 'needless invention, needless thrift.' "

Judging from some reviews, Steele's third full-length collection of poems may have fulfilled this promise. Writing in the *Southern Review,* Donald E. Stanford states: "There are thirty-five poems in *The Color Wheel,* and not one is badly written. . . . The excellence of the poems is in their language. The phrasing is adroit, the poetic detail precise and memorable." Stanford is particularly taken with the poem from which the book's title is drawn, "Portrait of the Artist as A Young Child," describing Steele's astonishment on first seeing a color wheel. A reviewer in *Publisher's Weekly* also gives unreserved affirmation to the collection, explaining that a reader may be so impressed with the technical aspect of the poems, that he/she could miss Steele's "thematic range, from satirizing urge to wistfulness and a more profound consciousness of pain."

Response to Steele's poetry varies widely, from high praise to disdain, perhaps reflecting in part the controversy between formal verse and free verse he has helped to generate. Clearly, Steele has already made his mark as a major poet writing in the traditional style of rhyme and meter. At the same time, the eventual outcome of his call for a return to rhyme and meter as the dominant form of expression in contemporary poetry has yet to be decided.

In an effort to clarify his views concerning his own poetry and that from the "experimental school," Steele wrote *CA:* "Because comparatively few poets today write in meters, rhymes, and stanzas, my use of these has resulted in my being labeled a 'formalist.' But I find this term meaningless and even objectionable. It suggests, among other things, an interest in style rather than substance, whereas I believe that the two are mutually vital in any successful poem. I employ the traditional instruments of verse simply because I love the symmetries and surprises that they produce and because meter especially allows me to render feelings and ideas more flexibly and precisely than I otherwise could. This preference is personal and aesthetic, however; I have never imagined that it provided me with access to cultural or spiritual virtue. And despite allegations to the contrary about *Missing Measures,* I have never said that *vers libre* is somehow wrong and immoral or that meter is somehow right and pure. The experimental school of Pound, Eliot, Lawrence, and Williams has its own beauties and achievements. But we can prize them justly and build on them, it seems to me, only if we retain a knowledge and appreciation of the time-tested principles of standard versification. Free verse cannot be free, unless there is something for it to be free of."

BIOGRAPHICAL/CRITICAL SOURCES:

BOOKS

Contemporary Literary Criticism, Volume 45, Gale (Detroit), 1987.
Dictionary of Literary Biography, Volume 120: *American Poets Since World War II,* Gale, 1992.

PERIODICALS

American Poetry Review, March-April, 1982, pp. 13-17.
American Scholar, summer, 1991, pp. 457-58, 460-63.
Brandeis Review, summer, 1992, pp. 28-33.
Choice, November, 1990.
Chowder Review, spring-summer, 1980, pp. 60-62.
Christian Science Monitor, May 2, 1990, p. 12.
Crosscurrents, no. 8, 1989.
Library Journal, April 1, 1990.
Los Angeles Times, November 3, 1985, p. B2; June 10, 1991, p. B1; January 19, 1995, p. E1.
Los Angeles Times Book Review, September 21, 1986, p. 2.
Modern Language Review, April, 1993, pp. 440-42.
New York Times Book Review, January 18, 1987, p. 13.
Ontario Review, fall-winter, 1983-84, pp. 101-103.
Partisan Review, March-April, 1982, pp. 13-17.
Poetry, March, 1987, pp. 342-44; May 1995, pp. 112-15.
Publishers Weekly, August 22, 1986, p. 91; November 28, 1994. p. 55.
Southern Review, summer, 1981, pp. 634-41; spring, 1995, pp. 385-86.
Threepenny Review, winter, 1988, p. 32.
Times Literary Supplement, February 19, 1988, p. 180; February 1, 1991.
Virginia Quarterly Review, autumn, 1987, p. 138.

STEINHEIMER, Richard (V.) 1929-

PERSONAL: Born August 23, 1929, in Chicago, IL; son of Virgil (a salesman) and Frances (a secretary; maiden name, Sandstedt) Steinheimer; married Nona Dean, 1955 (divorced, 1967); married Shirley Burman (a photographer), November 4, 1984; children: Alan, Marilyn, Sally. *Education:* Glendale College, A.A., 1949; attended City College of San Francisco, 1949-50, and San Jose State College (now University), 1953-54.

ADDRESSES: P.O. Box 8188, Sacramento, CA 95818.

CAREER: Glendale News-Press, Glendale, CA, photographer, 1950-51, writer, 1954-56; *Marin County Independent-Journal,* San Rafael, CA, photographer, writer, and part-time editor of *Marin Magazine* section, 1956-62; Fairchild Semiconductor Corp., Mountain View, CA, chief photographer and senior member of creative staff, 1962-70; Bender & Steinheimer Design Studio, Palo Alto, CA, partner, 1970-72; commercial photographer in Palo Alto, 1972-75; Ford Aerospace and Communications Corp., Palo Alto, Audiovisual photographer and writer, 1975-78; Associated Ad-Ventures Agency, Los Altos, CA, creative director, photographer, and writer, 1978-80; commercial photographer, 1980—. Photographs exhibited at New York City's Grand Central Station, George Eastman House, California State Railroad Museum, and Southern Methodist University; speaker at seminars. *Military service:* U.S. Navy, journalist, 1951-53.

AWARDS, HONORS: First prize for news feature photography from California/Nevada Associated Press, 1958; Western Art Directors Club, four awards of merit, 1968, award of distinctive merit, 1969, award of distinction and four awards of merit, 1970, award of merit, 1971 and 1973; San Francisco Society of Communicating Arts, San Francisco Medal, 1971, award of excellence for photography, 1973; award of excellence from *Communicating Arts,* 1971; certificates of merit from Art Directors Club of Los Angeles, 1972 and 1974; award of excellence from Simpson Paper Co., 1980, for design of *The Electric Way Across the Mountains;* Railroad History Senior Achievement Award from Railway and Locomotive Historical Society, 1983.

WRITINGS:

AND PHOTOGRAPHER

Backwoods Railroads of the West, Kalmbach (Milwaukee, WI), 1963.
(With Donald Sims) *Western Trains,* privately printed, 1965.
The Electric Way Across the Mountains, Carbarn Press, 1980.
(With Sims) *Growing Up With Trains,* Interurban (Glendale, CA), 1982.

Southern California in the Diesel Age Portfolio, Westrail (Glendora, CA), 1982.

(With Ted Benson) *Growing Up With Trains II,* Interurban, 1983.

(With Dick Dorn) *Diesels over Donner,* Interurban, 1989.

(With wife, Shirley Burman) *Whistles across the Land,* Cedco, 1994.

Also photographer for *Up the Swiftwater* by Sandra A. Crowell and David O. Asleson. Contributing photographer to numerous books, including Lucius Beebe and Charles Clegg, *The Age of Steam,* Rinehardt, 1957; Jeffrey Moreau, *Glendale and Montrose,* Pacific Bookwork, 1966; Oliver Jensen, *Railroads in America,* American Heritage Publishing (New York City), 1975; John R. Signor, *Rails in the Shadow of Mount Shasta,* Howell-North (Burbank, CA), 1982; Thomas Mahon, *Charged Bodies,* New American Library (New York City), 1985; and George H. Drury, *The Historical Guide to North American Railroads,* Kalmbach, 1986. Also contributor to magazines, including *Trains.*

Negatives of Steinheimer's work between 1946 and 1971 are housed in the DeGolyer Library of Southern Methodist University in Dallas, TX.

SIDELIGHTS: Richard Steinheimer told *CA:* "It was fun having successful careers in electronics and newspapers. What's thrilling today is the growth of family relationships and my ability to continue to develop a great body of photography and written work dealing with railroading in America. It's an amazing industry—the target of government for most of this century, yet still the lowest cost producer of land surface transportation. The way they fight to do this is great drama."

BIOGRAPHICAL/CRITICAL SOURCES:

BOOKS

Beebe, Lucius, *Great Railroad Photographs U.S.A.,* Howell-North, 1964.

Mahon, Thomas, *Charged Bodies,* New American Library, 1985.

Styffe, David and Ted Benson, editors, *Wheels Rolling West,* Westrail, 1979.

PERIODICALS

Railroad, January, 1978.
Trains, November, 1955.

*　　　*　　　*

STERN, Robert A. M. 1939-

PERSONAL: Born May 23, 1939, in New York, NY; son of Sidney S. and Sonya (Cohen) Stern; married Lynn G.

Solinger, May 22, 1966 (divorced, 1977); children: Nicholas S. G. *Education:* Columbia University, B.A., 1960; Yale University, M.Arch., 1965.

ADDRESSES: Home—177 East 77th St., New York, NY 10021. *Office*—460 West 34th St., New York, NY 10001.

CAREER: Architectural League of New York, New York City, program director, 1965-66; Richard Meier, Architect, New York City, designer, 1966; Housing and Development Administration, New York City, assistant to assistant administrator and urban designer, 1966-70; Robert A. M. Stern and John S. Hagmann (architects and designers), New York City, partner, 1969-77; Robert A. M. Stern, Architects, New York City, principal, 1977—. Columbia University, lecturer, 1970-73, assistant professor, 1973-77, associate professor, 1977-82, professor of architecture, 1982—, professor and director of Temple Hoyne Buell Center for American Architecture, 1984-88, director of Program in Historic Preservation, 1990—. Visiting lecturer, Yale University, 1972, 1973; visiting critic, Rhode Island School of Design, 1976, University of Pennsylvania, 1977, North Carolina State University, 1978; William Henry Bishop Visiting Professor of Architecture, Yale University, fall, 1978. One-man exhibit at Neuberger Museum, State University of New York at Purchase; participant in exhibitions in galleries and universities across the United States, including the Museum of Modern Art, the Metropolitan Museum of Art, the Art Institute of Chicago, the Drawing Center, the Cooper-Hewitt and Whitney museums in New York City, and the Walker Center in Minneapolis, Minnesota. Member, Mayor's Task Force on Urban Design, New York City, 1966-67; consultant, Small Parks Program, Department of Parks, New York City, 1966-70; trustee, American Federation of Arts, 1967-76; Cunningham Dance Foundation, member of board of directors, 1968-75, vice-president, 1969-73; member of building committee, Whitney Museum, 1970-76; member, advisory commission of architectural section for Venice Biennale, 1980; member of board of directors, Walt Disney Company, 1992—. Host of eight-part documentary television series, *Pride of Place: Building the American Dream,* Public Broadcasting Service (PBS), 1986.

MEMBER: American Institute of Architects (director, New York chapter, 1976-78), Society of Architectural Historians (director, 1975-78), Architectural League of New York (president, 1973-77), Century Association, Coffee House.

AWARDS, HONORS: Medal of Honor, New York chapter, American Institute of Architects, 1984; nominee with Gregory Gilmartin and Thomas Mellins for National Book Award in nonfiction, 1987, for *New York 1930: Architecture and Urbanism between the Two World Wars.*

WRITINGS:

40 Under 40: Young Talent in Architecture (catalog), American Federation of Arts (New York City), 1966.

New Directions in American Architecture, Braziller (New York City), 1969, revised edition, 1977.

George Howe: Toward a Modern Architecture, Yale University Press (New Haven, CT), 1975.

(With Deborah Nevins) *The Architect's Eye: American Architectural Drawings from 1799-1978,* Pantheon (New York City), 1979.

(Author of commentary) Philip Johnson, *Writings,* Oxford University Press, 1979.

(Editor) *American Architecture: After Modernism,* A & U Publishing (Tokyo), 1981.

(Editor with John Massengale) *The Anglo American Suburb,* St. Martin's (New York City), 1981.

(With Clay Lancaster and Robert Hefner) *East Hampton's Heritage,* Norton (New York City), 1982.

(With Thomas P. Catalano) *Raymond Hood,* Institute for Architecture and Urban Studies (New York City), 1982.

The Residential Works of Robert A. M. Stern, A & U Publishing, 1982.

(Editor with Richard W. Longstreth) *On the Edge of the World: Four Architects in San Francisco at the Turn of the Century,* MIT Press (Cambridge, MA), 1983.

(With Gregory Gilmartin and Massengale) *New York 1900: Metropolitan Architecture and Urbanism, 1890-1915,* Rizzoli International (New York City), 1983.

(Editor) *International Design Yearbook,* Abbeville Press (New York City), 1983.

Pride of Place: Building the American Dream (companion to PBS series), Houghton (Boston), 1986.

(Editor with David G. De Long and Helen Searing) *American Architecture: Innovation and Tradition,* Rizzoli International, 1986.

(With Gilmartin and Thomas Mellins) *New York 1930: Architecture and Urbanism between the Two World Wars,* Rizzoli International, 1987.

(With Raymond W. Gastil) *Modern Classicism,* Rizzoli International, 1988.

The House that Bob Built, Rizzoli International, 1991.

(With Thomas Mellins and David Fishman) *New York 1960: Architecture and Urbanism between the Second World War and the Bicentennial,* Monacelli Press, 1995.

Also editor of *Perspecta: The Yale Architectural Journal,* 1965.

SIDELIGHTS: By the age of 45, Robert A. M. Stern already had "an established reputation as a master house builder," comments Carol Vogel in the *New York Times Magazine.* An architect who involves himself with every aspect of a project, including landscaping and interiors,

Stern creates designs that "have come to embody the spirit of 'contextual architecture'—architecture that respects the established building styles of a place," says Vogel. Stern's work has been exhibited in universities and museums all over the country, including the Metropolitan Museum of Art, and his visibility as a proponent of the "American vernacular" style of architecture has increased since the debut of his documentary series *Pride of Place: Building the American Dream* on PBS.

Although Stern has made his name by designing houses that fit within a historical context, many of his earliest architectural designs were thought of as too "heavy-handed," as art historian Vincent Scully told Vogel. "Stern himself concedes that much of his early work was overly didactic," Vogel wrote. "He was so caught up in theories and in the idea of using historical references in an original way . . . that his buildings were rhetorical and stiff." Today Stern recognizes the dangers of relying too much on theory. "In today's world, we've become fascinated with technique at the expense of content," he told *Interiors* editor-in-chief Beverly Russell. " 'Experts' have replaced real people. We're trapped by a jargon of expertise and drowned in documents." In order to use architecture in a manner appropriate to its purpose, the architect believes that "we need to get rid of this vast layering of technique that separates us from the actual task."

Communication is an important purpose of architecture, believes Stern; his role as architect includes helping his clients express themselves. "The dialogue between client and architect is about as intimate as any conversation you can have," he told Vogel, "because, when you're talking about building a house, you're talking about dreams." He believes that like art, architecture can be a medium for ideas: "[It] is as much a language as the spoken or written word," the architect commented to Russell. "It may have even preceded the development of writing as a way of passing on ideas from one generation to the next." Even when speaking of his own work, Stern uses terms of communication rather than "style": "I prefer to think I have a voice within a language," he told Vogel, "just as F. Scott Fitzgerald and Ernest Hemingway had different voices."

Because the "American Vernacular" style of design is grounded in historic ideas of architecture, Stern's is a voice that echoes the language of others. But although he is not noted for originating many new ideas, "as an interpreter, Stern is tops," commented colleague Stanley Tigerman to Vogel. Stern claims that part of the artistry of architecture lies in the interpretation of the past. As Stern commented to *CA:* "Americans do not have a native architectural tradition, but one that is essentially a hybrid between European and Oriental traditions and American circumstances." Because of this, the architect believes that "our greatest responsibility is not to . . . simply copy the old, but to interpret these ideas and make them our own. . . . Imitation is [part of] what an artist does," he told Vogel. Those architects who eliminate detail and ignore background in an effort to make their designs more "fundamental" work against the purpose of architecture. "The act of reduction is *part* of the artistic experience—but distillation is not the same as eradication," Stern told Russell. "It is one thing to bring a beautiful shape down to its essence, and quite another to forget that beauty is the ultimate goal of architecture."

Like some of his early work in architecture, one of Stern's earliest books shows a tendency toward didacticism. Writing for the *Times Literary Supplement,* Reyner Banham finds *George Howe: Toward a Modern Architecture* difficult in its "apparent inability to mention any building—or even detail of building—by Howe without immediately citing a building by someone else from which it may . . . have been plagiarized." Stern's persistent focus on finding precedents for Howe's work leads him to overlook "some important extensions of the precedent game in which Howe appears as progenitor, not borrower," says Banham. The architect's response to this opinion reflects his theories about architectural artistry; as he told *CA,* "the point of Howe's achievement was in his capacity to interpret, not to innovate."

With *New York 1900: Metropolitan Architecture and Urbanism, 1890-1915,* Stern turns to "something more than architectural history, something less than social and political history," states Paul Goldberger of the *New York Times Book Review.* In combination with over 500 pictures of different buildings, Stern and his co-authors' detailed text produces a "solid portrait of a city coming into greatness," says Sam Hall Kaplan in the *Los Angeles Times Book Review.* Goldberger criticizes the book's emphasis on the "greatness" of New York City, however, finding that "it gives us a skewed picture. For while there was more grand public presence in the 'Age of Metropolitanism,' there was also more private poverty." Nevertheless, the critic calls *New York 1900* "lavish, celebratory and, for all its shortcomings, . . . truly appealing."

Pride of Place, a documentary series and companion book conceived by Stern, represents "an attempt to convey the American experience through architecture, to use our buildings as a way of drawing conclusions about our culture," comments Goldberger about the television series in the *New York Times.* Although Judith Weinraub describes the companion volume in *Washington Post Book World* as a "highly personal and interesting view of the progress of American architecture," Goldberger thinks that in the series "Stern's revisionist history has a bit too much revising." In a *New York Times Book Review* critique of the book, Martin Filler contends that the architect has "a myopic social outlook. . . . Stern's obsessive interest in the

superficialities of style limits his insights." He feels Stern presents an America that is "elitist, self-aggrandizing, ostentatious, and above all escapist," avoiding a presentation of the harsher side of reality.

Instead of showing an "elitist" America, however, *New York 1930: Architecture and Urbanism between the Two World Wars,* "does much to correct the implicit tendency of extravagantly illustrated architecture books to list toward the right—to ignore the city of the middle class in favor of the city of the rich," according to Goldberger in the *New York Times Book Review.* "This is not, thank heavens, one of those stuffy architecture books that divorces buildings from the manners and mores of the people for whom they were designed," echoes Paul Gapp of the *Chicago Tribune.* Like its predecessor *New York 1900, New York 1930* presents an architectural history complete with hundreds of period photographs and an elaborate text that Goldberger calls "good enough to be read on its own."

In *New York 1960: Architecture and Urbanism between the Second World War and the Bicentennial,* Stern continues his survey of the American architectural tradition, noting how post-war structures sought to convey New York City as the center of the world's power and prestige. In addition, Stern discusses how parks, streets, bridges, and other facets of urban planning also played a role in the formulation of the city's international image of urban life and spirit. The rise of interior decorating and design was also an important part of this era, and Stern spends sufficient time commenting on the interior spaces of many of the era's influential public buildings. Though it lauds the human achievements of this era, the "book is not wholly celebratory," as Thomas S. Hines states in the *New York Times Book Review.* For example, in discussing the razing of Pennsylvania Station, Hines continues, "the authors can be forcefully critical and sometimes melancholy" when it comes to the issue of historic preservation. These sentiments also come into play when the authors write about proposed buildings that were never erected and the effect of zoning laws on the landscape of particular neighborhoods. "*New York 1960* should be read and pondered by all who value architecture and who understand, or wonder about, its importance in their lives," concludes Hines, who praises the book as one that "fairly crackles with energy and purpose."

With his work, Stern has "successfully bridged the gap between public acceptance and architectural respect," commented architect Philip Johnson to Vogel. "When I design a house," Stern told Vogel, "it looks like a house, not a dry run for a bank or a frustrated airport." Although Stern has started branching out into commercial design, he still attempts to fit his plans within the "vernacular" of the site's surroundings. "Architects are perhaps the last doers who are also humanists in the best sense," he told Russell. "They are the mediators between realities and intuitions."

BIOGRAPHICAL/CRITICAL SOURCES:

BOOKS

Arnell, Peter and Ted Bickford, editors, *Robert A. M. Stern, 1966-1980: Toward a Modern Architecture after Modernism,* Rizzoli International (New York), 1981.

Arnell, Peter and Ted Bickford, editors, *Robert A. M. Stern, 1965-1980: Buildings and Projects,* Rizzoli International (New York), 1982.

Dunster, David, editor, *Robert Stern,* with an introduction by Vincent Scully, Academy Editions, 1981.

Rueda, Luis F., editor, *Robert A. M. Stern: Buildings and Projects 1981-1985,* Rizzoli International (New York), 1986.

PERIODICALS

Chicago Tribune, May 21, 1987.

Interiors, July, 1984.

Los Angeles Times Book Review, February 5, 1984.

Newsweek, December 21, 1981; December 10, 1984.

New York Times, March 30, 1986.

New York Times Book Review, March 18, 1984; May 18, 1986; May 31, 1987, March 19, 1995, p. 12-16.

New York Times Magazine, January 13, 1985.

Times Literary Supplement, November 27, 1969; September 19, 1975.

Washington Post Book World, December 7, 1986.

*   *   *

STONE, Albert E(dward) 1924-
(Albert E. Stone, Jr.)

PERSONAL: Born January 1, 1924, in New London, CT; son of Albert E. (a Navy officer) and Rebecca (Rollins) Stone; married Grace Woodbury (a social activist), July 5, 1954; children: Albert Edward, Jr., Rebecca Rollins Stone-Miller. *Education:* Yale University, B.A., 1949, Ph.D., 1957; Columbia University, M.A., 1955. *Politics:* Democrat. *Religion:* Episcopalian. *Avocational interests:* Golf, gardening, music, art, travel.

ADDRESSES: Home—Spinney Mill Rd., Arrowsic, ME 04530.

CAREER: Casady School, Oklahoma City, OK, instructor in English, 1949-52; Yale University, New Haven, CT, instructor, 1955-59, assistant professor of English, 1959-62; Emory University, Atlanta, GA, professor of English and chairman of department, 1962-68, professor of English and American studies, 1968-77; University of Iowa, Iowa City, professor of American studies and chairman of department, 1977-91. Fulbright lecturer, Charles University, Prague, Czechoslovakia, 1968-69; visiting professor, Universite Paul Valery, Montpellier, France, 1986-87. Member of advisory council, Danforth Foundation graduate fellowship program, 1965-68. *Military service:* U.S. Army, Military Intelligence, 1943-46, served in Southwest Pacific; became master sergeant; received Purple Heart and Bronze Star.

MEMBER: American Studies Association, Genesis Fund (Wiscasset, ME), Literacy Volunteers of America, Maine Maritime Museum.

AWARDS, HONORS: Morse fellowship, Yale University, 1960-61; E. Harris Harbison Award for distinguished teaching, 1965-66; National Endowment for the Humanities fellowship, 1976-77; senior faculty fellowship from University of Iowa, 1983-84; *Choice* award, 1983; Bode-Pearson Prize, American Studies Association, 1988.

WRITINGS:

(Under name Albert E. Stone, Jr.) *The Innocent Eye: Childhood in Mark Twain's Imagination,* Yale University Press (New Haven, CT), 1961.

(Editor and author of introduction under name Albert E. Stone, Jr.) St. John de Crevecoeur, *Letters from an American Farmer,* New American Library (New York City), 1963, revised edition (under name Albert E. Stone) published as *Letters from an American Farmer* [and] *Sketches of Eighteenth-Century America,* Penguin (New York City), 1981.

(Editor under name Albert E. Stone, Jr.) *Twentieth-Century Interpretations of "The Ambassadors,"* Prentice-Hall (Englewood Cliffs, NJ), 1969.

(Editor) *The American Autobiography: A Collection of Critical Essays,* Prentice-Hall, 1981.

Autobiographical Occasions and Original Acts: Versions of American Identity from Henry Adams to Nate Shaw, University of Pennsylvania Press (Philadelphia), 1982.

The Return of Nat Turner, University of Georgia Press (Athens, GA), 1992.

Literary Aftershocks: American Writers, Readers, and the Bomb, Twayne (Boston), 1994.

Also editor of *Singular Lives: The Iowa Series in North American Autobiography,* eleven volumes, 1988-. Contributor to *Oxford Companion to African American Literature.* Contributor to periodicals, including *Prospects: An Annual of American Cultural Studies, American Heritage, American Literature, American Quarterly, Genre, New England Quarterly,* and *College Language Association Journal.*

SIDELIGHTS: Albert E. Stone told *CA:* "As your garden-variety teacher-scholar, I have been drawn to writing books on four different aspects of American culture and literature. My interests in Mark Twain, childhood, slavery and slave revolts, and the nuclear age in literature are ongoing, and even in retirement I continue to review books, edit them, and lecture on these topics."

*   *   *

STONE, Albert E., Jr.
    See STONE, Albert E(dward)

*   *   *

STROZIER, Charles B(urnett) 1944-

PERSONAL: Born February 16, 1944, in Athens, GA; son of Robert M. (a university president) and Margaret (an academic administrator; maiden name, Burnett) Strozier; married Carol A. Kelly (a medical administrator), September 4, 1965, (divorced, 1983); married Cathryn C. Compton-Strozier, January 21, 1985; children: Michael, Matthew, Christopher, Alison. *Education:* Harvard University, B.A., 1966; University of Chicago, M.A., 1967, Ph.D., 1971; Training and Research Institute in Self Psychology, clinical graduate, 1992.

ADDRESSES: Home—300 Washington Ave., Brooklyn, NY 11205. *Office*—John Jay College, 899 10th Ave., New York, NY 10019.

CAREER: Sangamon State University, Springfield, IL, assistant professor, 1972-76, associate professor, 1976-82, professor of history, 1982-86; John Jay College of Criminal Justice and the Graduate Center, City University of New York, professor of history, 1986—, co-director of the Center on Violence and Human Survival, 1986—. Visiting assistant professor of psychiatry, Department of Psychiatry, Rush Medical School, Chicago, IL, 1977-86; consultant to Department of Psychiatry, Michael Reese Hospital, Chicago, 1980-86; practicing and senior psychoanalyst, Training and Research Institute in Self Psychology, 1986—.

MEMBER: American Historical Association (executive officer, Group for the Use of Psychology in History, 1972—).

AWARDS, HONORS: Named writer of the year by the Lincoln Library, Springfield, 1981.

WRITINGS:

(Editor with Cullom Davis, Rebecca Veach, and Geoffrey Ward) *The Public and Private Lincoln: Contemporary*

Perspectives, Southern Illinois University Press (Carbondale), 1979.

Lincoln's Quest for Union: Public and Private Meanings, Basic Books (New York City), 1982.

(With Daniel Offer) *The Leader,* Plenum (New York City), 1985.

(Editor) *Self Psychology and the Humanities,* Norton (New York City), 1985.

Apocalypse: On the Psychology of Fundamentalism in America, Beacon Press (Boston), 1994.

Founding editor of *Psychohistory Review,* 1947-86. Contributor of articles to journals, including *American Heritage* and *Illinois Issues.*

SIDELIGHTS: In *Lincoln's Quest for Union: Public and Private Meanings,* Charles B. Strozier discusses Lincoln's emotional crises and relates them to decisions made in his public life. Among the emotional conflicts Strozier considers crucial are Lincoln's guilt over his mother's death and a period of upheaval that occurred between his two engagements to Mary Todd. Strozier states in his conclusion that "after 1854 Lincoln discovered, remarkably enough, that his private concerns found reflection in the country as a whole. . . . In the idea of a house divided, Lincoln found a way of creatively enlarging his private concerns to fill the public space."

In a *New York Times* article, Christopher Lehmann-Haupt finds that Strozier's psychohistorical work says "some new and original things about one of the most exhaustively investigated subjects in human history. . . . His line of reasoning is sensitive, cautious, entirely free of psychiatric jargon, and surpassingly eloquent." Edwin M. Yoder, Jr., in a *Washington Post* review, was less enthusiastic about the book's psychohistorical approach but states, "Strozier's treatment of Lincoln, while also 'psychobiographical' to a degree, shows a firmer command of the tangled political literature without which Lincoln's emerging purposes and politics, messianic or not, can hardly be understood. . . . He does not ignore . . . the grainy texture of events."

In his *Apocalypse: On the Psychology of Fundamentalism in America,* Strozier reports on some 25 religious adherents who believe an apocalypse is due soon. His account, Marty E. Marty writes in the *New York Times Book Review,* "brings down to earth and to our time believers who say they cannot wait for an end to that earth and the beginning of God's new time."

BIOGRAPHICAL/CRITICAL SOURCES:

PERIODICALS

Los Angeles Times Book Review, July 4, 1982.
New York Times, April 29, 1982.
New York Times Book Review, May 8, 1994.

Washington Post Book World, May 16, 1982.

* * *

STRUTZ, Henry 1932-

PERSONAL: Born October 31, 1932, in New York, NY; son of Henry F. W. and Barbara (Laches) Strutz. *Education:* City College (now City College of the City University of New York), B.A., 1955; Brown University, M.A., 1961; doctoral study at Rutgers University.

ADDRESSES: Home—P.O. Box 250, Hornell, NY 14843.

CAREER: New York College of Music, New York City, instructor in German, 1957-62, acting registrar, 1961; City College (now City College of the City University of New York), New York City, instructor in German, 1958-62; Yeshiva University, New York City, instructor in German, 1960-61; Rutgers University, New Brunswick, NJ, instructor in German, 1962-65; Skidmore College, Saratoga Springs, NY, instructor in German, 1965-70; State University of New York Agricultural and Technical College at Alfred, associate professor of languages, 1970-76.

WRITINGS:

The Flower and the Flame, Terrier Press, 1960.
Moon Howls, Terrier Press, 1962.
Dancing with Shiva (poetry and short essays), Vega Press, 1981.
1001 Pitfalls in German, Barron's, 1981, 2nd edition, 1986.
German at a Glance, Barron's, 1984, 2nd edition, 1992.
Express Track to German, Barron's, 1992.
German for the Business Traveler, Barron's, 1994.
English Idioms and German Idioms, Barron's, 1995.
French Vocabulary, Barron's, 1995.

EDITOR

201 German Verbs, Barron's, 1963, 2nd edition, 1965.
501 German Verbs, Barron's, 1972.
(With H. K. Thompson, Jr.) *Doenitz at Nuremberg: A Re-Appraisal,* Amber Publishing, 1976.
301 German Verbs, Barron's, 1981.

Also author of *Consolations* and *Talking Business* (a German-English/English-German commercial dictionary). Contributor of articles, short stories, and poetry to numerous periodicals, including *Third Eye, Kansas Quarterly, Vega, Golden Isis, Parnassus, Lapis,* and *Tempest.*

SIDELIGHTS: Henry Strutz told *CA:* "I try to relate and integrate into language study as many aspects of human life as possible, particularly emphasizing music as a tool in language learning. I believe that in teaching a language, and most other things, an attempt should be made to con-

vey cultural values as well as information about the human condition. Unfortunately, editors have not always been able to appreciate some of the more basic and racy aspects of the human condition which I felt should be included, and therefore the spectrum is not as broad as I would have wished.

"In literature, too, I admire a broad spectrum, such as the Renaissance fusion and confusion of Judeo-Christian myth with the classical tradition called 'pagan' by some. This fusion is fruitful as a source of literary material and metaphor, but it can be broadened. Islam should, of course, be included as the other branch of the Judeo-Christian complex it is. Perhaps all three can be subsumed into the far more vast, and to me esthetically and philosophically richer and more comprehensive, traditions of India and the Orient. The Trimurti can easily absorb the Trinity. Vishnu, for instance, has had so many interesting avatars (among them the Buddha, some say) that perhaps the prophets of the Judeo-Christian-Islamic systems should be counted among them.

"Although I am not committed to any one specific system, I do affirm the mythic impulse behind all of them. I find it vitalizing to create and craft out of the debris of the occidental myth system in which I was raised, while combining it with other mythologies. In a world 'yearning to be one', as Thomas Mann put it, I find this a revealing and rewarding approach. In my poems, short stories, and in the several novels I'm working on, I draw from this syncretistic mythmaking of my own. Thus, for example, the great god-bird Garuda can merge with the Holy Ghost dove, which can in turn become Aphrodite's doves. Poe's and Woden's ravens fly with the Phoenix. Various forms of the rook of the Arabian Nights consort with Pallas Athena's owls and Zeus's eagles, while whole flocks of very particular parakeets congregate with all kinds of comforting paracletes.

"This kaleidoscopic and constant recycling is not confined to an avian world but tries to embrace the whole (usually) beautifully evolving world, inside us and all around us. Chinese celestial dancers or 'apsaras' along with Mohammedan houris can traipse with Terpsichore and join Shiva for a schottische or for any dance he pleases in any number of possible configurations of choreographed atoms.

"I think I keep my writing from getting too exuberant, high-flown, Baroque, and 'poetic' (as the preceding might lead a reader to believe) by trying to touch all the bases, including the basic. As far as literary exploration and investigation is concerned, no taboos as to language or subject matter exist for me. Like other writers, I delight in the many surprising revelations granted to me concerning myself and the world, which occur during the course of creating characters or developing themes."

T

TAYLOR, Dawson 1916-

PERSONAL: Born November 14, 1916, in Detroit, MI; son of George M. and Florence (Dawson) Taylor; married Mary Ellen Connolly, May 21, 1941; children: Ellen Denise, Mary Christine, Dawson. *Education:* University of Detroit, A.B., 1936, LL.B., 1939.

ADDRESSES: Home—Florida. *Office*—4722 Holly Lake Dr., Lake Worth, FL 33463.

CAREER: Admitted to Michigan bar, 1940. Practicing attorney in state of Michigan, 1940-43; Dawson Taylor Chevrolet, Inc., Detroit, MI, president, 1957-69; *National Enquirer,* Lantana, FL, book editor, 1969-82; Globe Communications, Boca Raton, FL, book editor, 1983—. *Military service:* U.S. Navy, 1942-45, served in Pacific; became lieutenant, junior grade; received Navy Unit Commendation.

MEMBER: American Society of Composers, Authors, and Publishers; Michigan Bar Association; Detroit Bar Association.

AWARDS, HONORS: Nathan Burkan Memorial Award from American Society of Composers, Authors, and Publishers, 1939.

WRITINGS:

The Secret of Bowling Strikes, A. S. Barnes (San Diego, CA), 1959.
The Secret of Holing Putts, A. S. Barnes, 1960.
(With Horton Smith) *The Secret of Perfect Putting,* Wilshire (North Hollywood, CA), 1961.
The Making of the Pope, A. S. Barnes, 1962.
Your Future in the Automotive Industry, Rosen, 1962.
(With James Bradley) *Aim for a Job in Automotive Service,* Rosen, 1968, 2nd edition published as *Your Future in Automotive Service,* 1971, revised edition published under the original title, 1977.
The Masters: Profile of a Tournament, A. S. Barnes, 1973, 3rd revised edition, 1981.
St. Andrews: Cradle of Golf, A. S. Barnes, 1974, 2nd edition, Baseball Magazine, 1986.
(With Earl Anthony) *Winning Bowling,* Contemporary Books (Chicago), 1977.
Inside Golf, Contemporary Books, 1978.
Mastering Bowling, Contemporary Books, 1980.
The Masters: An Illustrated History, A. S. Barnes, 1981.
(With Smith) *The Master's Secrets of Putting,* A. S. Barnes, 1982.
(With Anthony) *Earl Anthony's Championship Bowling,* Contemporary Books, 1983.
(With Gary Wiren) *Super-Power Golf: Technique for Increasing Distance,* Contemporary Books, 1985.
(With Taylor Jones) *How to Talk Golf,* Dembner (New York City), 1985.
The Masters: Golf's Most Prestigious Tradition, Contemporary Books, 1986.
How to Improve Your Memory Instantly, Globe Books, 1986.
(With Wiren) *Sure Shot: 100 Common Errors and How to Correct Them,* Contemporary Books, 1986.
(With Jones) *How to Talk Bowling,* Contemporary Books, 1987.
(With Gary Patterson) *Spare Me: The Insanity of Bowling,* Contemporary Books, 1987.
(With Craig Stadler) *Craig Stadler's Secrets of the Short Game,* Contemporary Books, 1987.

Also author of *Bowling Strikes,* Contemporary Books.

MUSICAL COMPOSITIONS

I Turn the Corner of Prayer, words by Dylan Thomas, Chappell Music, 1964.

An Empty Cottage, Boosey & Hawkes, 1964.

Also composer of words and music for the songs "They Said You'd Come Back Running" and "Stars Over My Shoulder" on the Dinah Washington album *In Tribute,* Roulette, 1960; composer of music for the songs "The Other Side of the Moon," "Touch o' the Moon," "Moon Madness," "Moonstruck," and "Nuit D'Amour" on the album *Moonstruck,* Dot, and the Steve Allen song "I Will Bring You a Rainbow" on *The Sound Is All Around Us,* Murbo Records, 1965.

CALENDARS

(Compiler) *Amazing But True Golf Facts 1993,* Andrews & McMeel (Fairway, KS), 1993.
(Compiler) *Amazing But True Golf Facts 1994,* Andrews & McMeel, 1994.
(Compiler) *Amazing But True Golf Facts 1995,* Andrews & McMeel, 1995.

*   *   *

TAYLOR, Peter (Hillsman)   1917-1994

PERSONAL: Born January 8, 1917, in Trenton, TN; died of pneumonia, November 2, 1994, in Charlottesville, VA; son of Matthew Hillsman (a lawyer) and Katherine Taylor; married Eleanor Lilly Ross (a poet), June 4, 1943; children: Katherine Baird, Peter Ross. *Education:* Attended Vanderbilt University, 1936-37, and Southwestern at Memphis, 1937-38; Kenyon College, A.B., 1940.

CAREER: University of North Carolina at Greensboro, 1946-67, became professor of English; University of Virginia, Charlottesville, professor of English, 1967-94. Visiting lecturer, Indiana University, 1949, University of Chicago, 1951, Kenyon College, 1952-57, Oxford University, 1955, Ohio State University, 1957-63, Harvard University, 1964 and 1972-73, and University of Georgia, 1985. *Military service:* U. S. Army, 1941-45; served in England; became sergeant.

MEMBER: National Academy and Institute of Arts and Letters, American Academy of Arts and Sciences.

AWARDS, HONORS: Guggenheim fellowship in fiction, 1950; National Institute of Arts and Letters grant in literature, 1952; Fulbright fellowship to France, 1955; first prize, O. Henry Memorial Awards, 1959, for short story "Venus, Cupid, Folly and Time"; Ohioana Book Award, 1960, for *Happy Families Are All Alike;* Ford Foundation fellowship, to England, 1961; Rockefeller Foundation grant, 1964; second prize, *Partisan Review-Dial* for short story "The Scoutmaster"; National Academy and Institute of Arts and Letters gold medal for literature, 1979; Ritz Paris Hemingway Award and PEN/Faulkner Award

for fiction, both 1986, and Pulitzer Prize for fiction, 1987, all for *A Summons to Memphis.*

WRITINGS:

NOVELS

A Woman of Means, Harcourt (New York City), 1950.
A Summons to Memphis, Knopf (New York City), 1986.
In the Tennessee Country, Knopf, 1994.

SHORT STORIES

A Long Fourth and Other Stories, introduction by Robert Penn Warren, Harcourt, 1948.
The Widows of Thornton (includes a play), Harcourt, 1954.
Happy Families Are All Alike: A Collection of Stories, Astor Honor (New York City), 1959.
Miss Leonora When Last Seen and Fifteen Other Stories, Astor Honor, 1963.
The Collected Stories of Peter Taylor, Farrar, Straus (New York City), 1969.
In the Miro District and Other Stories, Knopf, 1977.
The Old Forest and Other Stories, Dial (Garden City, NY), 1985.
The Oracle at Stoneleigh Court, Knopf, 1993.

Contributor of stories to numerous anthologies, including *The Best American Short Stories,* edited by Martha Foley, Houghton (Boston, MA), 1945-46, 1950, 1959, 1965, edited by Foley and David Burnett, 1960, 1961; *Prize Stories of 1950: The O. Henry Awards,* edited by Herschell Bricknell, Doubleday (New York City), 1950; *The Literature of the South,* edited by R. C. Beatty and others, Scott, Foresman (Glenview, IL), 1952; *Stories from the Southern Review,* edited by Cleanth Brooks and Robert Penn Warren, Louisiana State University Press (Baton Rouge, LA), 1953; *Prize Stories 1959: The O. Henry Awards,* edited by Paul Engle, Doubleday, 1959; *Prize Stories 1961: The O. Henry Awards,* edited by Richard Poirier, Doubleday, 1961; *Prize Stories 1965: The O. Henry Awards,* edited by Poirier and William Abrahams, Doubleday, 1965; and *The Sense of Fiction,* edited by Robert L. Welker and Herschel Gover, Prentice-Hall (Englewood Cliffs, NJ), 1966.

Contributor of short stories to *Sewanee Review, Virginia Quarterly Review, Kenyon Review, New Yorker,* and numerous other journals.

PLAYS

Tennessee Day in St. Louis, Random House (New York City), 1959.
A Stand in the Mountains (produced Abingdon, VA, 1971), published in *Kenyon Review,* 1965.
Presences: Seven Dramatic Pieces (contains "Two Images," "A Father and a Son," "Missing Person,"

"The Whistler," "Arson," "A Voice through the Door," and "The Sweethearts"), Houghton, 1973.

OTHER

(Editor with Robert Lowell and Robert Penn Warren) *Randall Jarrell, 1914-1965,* Farrar, Straus, 1967.

(Editor) *The Road and Other Modern Stories,* Cambridge University Press, 1979.

Peter Taylor Reading and Commenting on His Fiction (audio tape), Archive of Recorded Poetry and Literature, 1987.

Contributor of an essay to *Tennessee: A Homecoming,* edited by John Netherton, Third National, 1985.

ADAPTATIONS: "The Old Forest" was adapted into a short motion picture of the same name, directed by Steven John Ross, Pyramid Films, 1984.

SIDELIGHTS: Although author Peter Taylor received critical acclaim for his novels *A Woman of Means, In the Tennessee Country,* and the Pulitzer Prize-winning *A Summons to Memphis,* he is best known for his work in short fiction. He was called "one of the most accomplished short-story writers of our time" by Gene Baro in the *New York Herald Tribune Book Review,* and John Leonard of the *New York Times* praised Taylor by saying that he "makes stories the way Mercedes-Benz makes automobiles: to last."

Born in Trenton, Tennessee, the grandson of one of that state's former governors, Taylor is considered by many critics to be a Southern writer in the tradition of William Faulkner and Flannery O'Connor; as a *Village Voice* reviewer observed, he "often writes about the decay of the gentrified South (something he has observed firsthand)." In the *Times Literary Supplement,* Zachary Leader agreed, noting that Taylor's "roots in the Southern literary tradition are deep, . . . [and an understanding of his] complex relation to the tradition this background fostered is helpful to an appreciation of his stories."

Taylor was conscious of drawing his inspiration from the recollections of his childhood. As he once told *CA:* "My theory is that you listen to people talk when you're a child—a Southerner does especially—and they tell stories and stories and stories, and you feel those stories must mean something. So, really, writing becomes an effort to find out what these stories mean in the beginning, and then you want to find out what *all* the stories you hear or think of mean. The story you write is interpretation. People tell the same stories over and over, with the same vocabulary and the same important points, and I don't think it ever crosses their minds what they mean. But they do mean something, and I'm sure that is what influenced me. Then too, you just inherit a storytelling urge."

Poet Allen Tate and novelist Andrew Lytle were two of Taylor's early literary influences. As an undergraduate at Vanderbilt University, the young author also met and became friends with several proponents of the Southern Agrarian movement, including Randall Jarrell and Robert Penn Warren. Taylor, Jarrell, and another friend, Robert Lowell, later studied under well-known poet and critic John Crowe Ransom, then the acknowledged leader of the Agrarians, who advocated, among other things, a return to a non-industrialized South free of Northern influence and exploitation. "It was my great luck to have come along at the time when those people were in the part of the world I was growing up in," recalled Taylor. "And they did influence me very much. . . . Tate was simply my freshman English teacher, and at once he liked my writing, and he gave me the feeling that writing was important. That's the big thing he did. . . . He made me feel that literature was important. And then he and I became great friends. I learned more from him as a friend than formerly as a teacher.

"I studied with Ransom, too, for several years, and I think he had a real influence on the form my writing has taken. He made me write poetry and discouraged me from writing fiction. I think that made my fiction more compressed and made me turn to short stories more than to novels, because I did write poetry. And not only was my studying under Ransom an influence in that way, but some other fellow students who became my lifelong friends were poets—Jarrell and Lowell."

Out of Taylor's early exposure to the philosophy of the Agrarian movement through Ransom, Jarrell, and Warren "grew the dream of the 'Old South,' or what Taylor calls 'the old times,'" according to Leader. "These writings look past the South's supposedly aristocratic origins to the pre-settlement wilderness, an Eden whose native inhabitants were as unspoilt and unspoiling as the surroundings from which they drew their character." Yet, despite his grounding in the traditions of Southern culture and literature, Taylor is often praised for the universality of his short fiction. When his first collection, *A Long Fourth and Other Stories,* appeared in 1948, a *New Yorker* critic commented that the stories were "particularly notable for a vein of unobtrusive humor and for a complete lack of the regional chauvinism that Southern authors so frequently exhibit when writing about their own." Coleman Rosenberger, in the *New York Herald Tribune Book Review,* wrote: "These seven short stories by Peter Taylor are a little island of excellence in the flood of books from the South. They have the qualities of permanence: a fine craftsmanship, integrity, and the imprint of a subtle and original intelligence."

Taylor himself believed that he wrote in "response" to his experiences of people and place, seeking through his writing to discover *how* he felt rather than *what* he felt in regards to a certain subject. "I don't think of myself as a regional writer," he told *CA*, "and I don't really like it when people say, 'He writes about the urban South.' I'm writing about people under certain circumstances, but I'm always concerned with the individual experience and the unique experience of that story. Goodness knows I don't have any political vision for the South, in retrospect or in the future, but I have strong feelings about it. And I think that's the main thing that you have to write about, not only what you have ideas about but what you feel about most keenly. My earliest recollections are a sense of the past in the South, and that's what I think has been responsible for a lot of Southern writing. There was the great turning point: before 1865 is the past; after that, the present. That's dramatic, and it's bound to create stories."

Critical response to Taylor's second collection of Southern-based short fiction, 1954's *The Widows of Thornton*, solidified his reputation as a master in his field. Mack Morriss, in a *Saturday Review* article, called the collection of nine stories "as free of ugliness as the lingering nutmeg and as unpretentious as coldwater cornbread. . . . [Taylor] has created a wistful, clinging, but utterly non-depraved image of the Deep South that some of us, his regional contemporaries, have been trying to recall from our childhood." F. H. Lyell of the *New York Times* commented that "The stories in [this book] are outwardly simple but psychologically complex and powerful, and under the surface of events in the regions he knows best the author discloses the universal longings of the human heart." And *Bloomsbury Review* critic Mimi MacFarland noted that "Wit, grace, and humor are abundant in the anachronistic possibilities created by Taylor's Southerners as they are transported to faraway places, even into the future, dragging along their traditions like so much excess baggage."

Taylor continued to examine the lives and culture of the gentry of the "Upper South" in *In the Miro District and Other Stories*, and *The Old Forest and Other Stories*, each of which contain works of drama in addition to short fiction. The lives of his Southern nobility are drawn into a more ghostly milieu in Taylor's *The Oracle at Stoneleigh Court*, a collection of short stories published in 1993. "After 53 years of practicing his craft, [Taylor] has obviously chosen to keep growing, rather than to repeat elegant past triumphs," stated Gail Godwin in the *New York Times Book Review*. "In this volume he seems to have been seized by the necessity to refine out of existence some of his more rarefied specimens—specimens who were becoming ghosts in our society even as he precisely chronicled them—in order to make room for new characters and fresh perspectives that have emerged from their ruins and their genes." As in gothic-inspired stories like "Demons,"

in which a grown man looks back fondly on the inner voices he heard as a child, and "The Witch of Owl Mountain Springs," about a jilted bride who lives in eccentric seclusion until she dies in a fire of questionable origins, the ghosts inhabiting Taylor's fiction are not "floating wraiths and extraneous horrors," according to Godwin, but are "all those ghosts we have to face before we can rendezvous with the ghost of the person we can still become."

A Summons to Memphis was, according to Taylor, "a story that got out of hand." Scarcely more than novella-length, its two hundred pages are filled with what Jonathan Yardley described in the *Washington Post Book World* as "the sly depiction of contrasting folkways in Memphis and Nashville, the nostalgic yet unsentimental excursions into a lost way of life, the rich yet precise and unadorned prose. . . . Prose of such subtlety, taste and clarity—prose that so poignantly and exactly evokes a moment, and makes it real." In the genteel Upper South of Memphis, Phillip Carver and his sisters face their mother's death and the change of heart of a father who had undermined their youthful attempts at romance and marriage. With Phillip as narrator, Taylor's Pulitzer Prize-winning novel draws the reader into the many facets of revenge and family loyalties as the eighty-year-old father's attempts to both remarry and resolve a long-standing dispute with a former friend are thwarted by his frustrated, middle-aged offspring. "Mr. Taylor's sympathy for the chiaroscuro of familial emotion, combined with his command of naturalistic detail, remains so assured, so persuasive," stated *New York Times* critic Michiko Kakutani, "that we finish the novel feeling we've not only come to know his characters, but also come to share their inner truth."

Taylor's final novel, *In the Tennessee Country*, was published in 1994, the year of his death. Born into a Southern family that prides itself on roots buried deep in the milieu of the Civil War, Nathan Longfort maintains a lifelong obsession with his elusive cousin Aubrey, an illegitimate relative who had once courted Nathan's mother but for a reason Nathan is not privy to was shunned at family gatherings, a treatment that drove him away to make a life for himself independent of his family. Nathan's obsession with Aubrey and his whereabouts eventually destroys his relationship with his own son, a painter who ultimately seeks Aubrey out and joins him in isolation from his father. While Mary Flanagan stated in the *New York Times Book Review* that she "missed the delicious slyness of . . . *A Summons to Memphis*, its flash and bite, its malice," she goes on to say that *In the Tennessee Country* is, on the whole, "unnerving and, on reflection, closer to life. . . . Aubrey and [Nathan's son] fulfill the dream of transformation, of becoming better men. They escape history, Mr. Taylor sagely implies, because they understand that the pursuit of happiness involves a spell in the wilderness."

Praise for Taylor's fiction was sustained by critics throughout his long career: His natural ear for dialogue, his smooth, finely paced style, and especially his sensitive character portrayal have been consistently lauded. A *Times Literary Supplement* critic described him as "a cautious writer with an intellectual respect for his characters. Every change of mood and feeling is something he considers worth recording." And, in *Saturday Review*, William Peden wrote: "[Taylor's] stories succeed because his characters and their words are real, moving, and convincing. In each story there is always at least one character who becomes 'finely aware' (the phrase is Henry James's) of the situations in which they find themselves. It is this fine awareness that gives the 'maximum of sense' to what befalls them, which makes these quietly effective stories so meaningful to the reader." In a *Washington Post* remembrance of the author, Jonathan Yardley described Taylor as a writer whose "world was not my own and whose narrative voice possessed an elegance to which I could never hope to aspire, yet who spoke to my innermost self with a depth of feeling and psychological insight that I had never before encountered. . . . [Taylor's] interest was kind rather than censorious; human faults were to be understood, even liked, rather than mocked or vilified. . . . Some of those to whom he was mentor went on to accomplished writing careers of their own, while others merely cherished the personal acquaintance they had been given with literary genius; but all are bound by their devotion and gratitude to this remarkable man."

For a previously published interview, see entry in *Contemporary Authors New Revision Series*, Gale, Volume 9, 1983, pp. 489-91.

BIOGRAPHICAL/CRITICAL SOURCES:

BOOKS

Contemporary Literary Criticism, Gale (Detroit), Volume 1, 1973, Volume 4, 1975, Volume 18, 1981; Volume 37, 1986; Volume 44, 1987; Volume 50, 1988; Volume 71, 1992.

Eisinger, Charles E., *Fiction of the Forties*, University of Chicago Press (Chicago), 1963.

Graham, Catherine Clark, *Southern Accents: The Fiction of Peter Taylor*, Lang (New York City), 1993.

Griffith, Albert, *Peter Taylor*, Twayne (Boston), 1970, revised, 1990.

Kramer, Victor A., *Andrew Lytle, Walker Percy, Peter Taylor: A Reference Guide*, G. K. Hall (Boston, MA), 1983.

McAlexander, Hubert H., *Conversations with Peter Taylor*, University Press of Mississippi (Jackson), 1987.

McAlexander, Hubert H., *Critical Essays on Peter Taylor*, G. K. Hall, 1993.

Robinson, James Curry, *Peter Taylor: A Study of the Short Fiction*, Twayne, 1988.

Rubin, Louis D., Jr., and Robert D. Jacobs, *South: Modern Southern Literature in Its Cultural Setting*, Doubleday, 1961.

PERIODICALS

Bloomsbury Review, July/August, 1994, p. 22.
Book Week, March 8, 1964.
Boston Globe, August 21, 1994, p. 61.
Chicago Tribune, May 14, 1950; December 6, 1959; October 26, 1986, sec. 14, p. 4; February 28, 1993, sec. 14, p. 6; September 11, 1994.
Christian Science Monitor, August 26, 1994, p. 13.
Critique, Volume 9, number 3, 1967.
Georgia Review, winter, 1970.
Hudson Review, winter, 1994, pp. 765-72.
Los Angeles Times, October 3, 1994, p. E4.
Los Angeles Times Book Review, February 21, 1993, p. 6.
New Republic, March 8, 1948; June 26, 1950; October 18, 1969; May 7, 1977.
New Statesman, August 6, 1960.
Newsweek, October 20, 1969.
New Yorker, March 13, 1948.
New York Herald Tribune Book Review, March 14, 1948; May 2, 1950; May 2, 1954; December 6, 1959.
New York Review of Books, June 11, 1964.
New York Times, March 21, 1948; June 11, 1950; May 2, 1954; October 11, 1969; April 7, 1977; September 24, 1986, p. C23; April 7, 1987, p. C15; November 2, 1994, p. C17.
New York Times Book Review, November 22, 1959; March 29, 1964; October 19, 1969; February 12, 1970; April 3, 1977; September 14, 1986, p. 3; February 21, 1993, p. 13; August 28, 1994, p. 6.
New York Times Magazine, January 1, 1995, p. 23.
San Francisco Chronicle, May 13, 1954.
Saturday Review, May 8, 1954; November 28, 1959; October 18, 1969; May 14, 1977; March 15, 1980.
Saturday Review of Literature, March 27, 1948.
Sewanee Review, autumn, 1962.
Shenandoah, winter, 1973; winter, 1977; summer, 1978.
Southern Review, winter, 1979; winter, 1994, pp. 156-164.
Spectator, September 3, 1994, p. 35-36.
Time, May 15, 1950; August 22, 1994, p. 84.
Times Literary Supplement, August 19, 1960; September 30, 1977; January 22, 1982.
Village Voice, April 28, 1980.
Virginia Quarterly Review, spring 1978.
Washington Post, March 15, 1980; May 9, 1993, p. 12; August 21, 1994, p. 3.
Washington Post Book World, September 14, 1986, p. 3.

OBITUARIES:

PERIODICALS

Boston Globe, November 13, 1994, p. A5.
Los Angeles Times, November 5, 1994, p. A32.
New York Times, November 4, 1994, p. A33.
Washington Post, November 4, 1994, p. B7; November 7, 1994, p. D2.*

*   *   *

TAYLOR, Theodore 1921-
(T. T. Lang)

PERSONAL: Born June 23, 1921, in Statesville, NC; son of Edward Riley (a molder) and Elnora Alma (Langhans) Taylor; married Gweneth Goodwin, October 25, 1946 (divorced, 1977); married Flora Gray Schoenleber (a library clerk), April 18, 1981; children: (first marriage) Mark, Wendy, Michael. *Education:* Attended Fork Union Military Academy, VA, 1939-40, U.S. Merchant Marine Academy, Kings Point, NY, 1942-43, and Columbia University, 1948; studied with American Theater Wing, 1947-49. *Politics:* Republican. *Religion:* Protestant. *Avocational interests:* Ocean fishing and foreign travel.

ADDRESSES: Home—1856 Catalina St., Laguna Beach, CA 92615. *Agent*—Gloria Loomis, Watkins Loomis Agency, Inc., 150 East 35th St., Suite 530, New York, NY 10016.

CAREER: Portsmouth Star, Portsmouth, VA, cub reporter, 1934-39, sports editor, 1941-42; *Washington Daily News,* Washington, DC, copyboy, c. 1942; National Broadcasting Co. Radio (NBC), New York City, sports writer, 1942; *Sunset News,* Bluefield, WV, sports editor, 1946-47; New York University, New York City, assistant director of public relations, c. 1947-48; YMCA schools and colleges, New York City, director of public relations, c. 1948-50; *Orlando Sentinel Star,* Orlando, FL, reporter, 1949-50; Paramount Pictures, Hollywood, CA, publicist, 1955-56; Perlberg-Seaton Productions, Hollywood, story editor, writer and associate producer, 1956-61; freelance press agent for Hollywood studios, 1961-68; Twentieth Century-Fox, Hollywood, writer, 1965-68; writer, 1961—. Producer and director of documentary films. *Military service:* U.S. Merchant Marine, 1942-44; U.S. Naval Reserve, active duty, 1944-46, 1950-55; became lieutenant.

MEMBER: Academy of Motion Picture Arts and Sciences, Writers Guild, Authors League of America, Mystery Writers of America, Society of Children's Book Writers.

AWARDS, HONORS: Commonwealth Club of California Silver Medal, 1969, Jane Addams Children's Book Award from Women's International League for Peace and Freedom (returned, 1975), Lewis Carroll Shelf Award, Southern California Council on Literature for Children and Young People Notable Book Award, Woodward Park School Annual Book Award, California Literature Medal Award, and Best Book Award from University of California, Irvine, all 1970, all for *The Cay; Battle in the Arctic Seas* was selected one of *New York Times* Outstanding Books of the Year, 1976; Spur Award for Best Western for Young People, Western Writers of America, and Commonwealth Club of California Silver Medal for the best juvenile book by a California author, both 1977, both for *A Shepherd Watches, a Shepherd Sings;* Southern California Council on Literature for Children and Young People Award, 1977, for distinguished contribution to the field of children's literature and body of work; George G. Stone Center for Children's Books Recognition of Merit Award, 1980, for body of work; Young Reader Medal from the California Reading Association, 1984, for *The Trouble with Tuck;* Jefferson Cup Honor Book, Virginia Library Association, 1987, for *Walking Up a Rainbow: Being the True Version of the Long and Hazardous Journey of Susan D. Carlisle, Mrs. Myrtle Dessery, Drover Bert Pettit, and Cowboy Clay Carmer and Others;* American Library Association Best Book Award, 1989, for *Sniper;* Young Reader Medal for best young adult book, California Reading Association, 1992, for *Sniper;* Edgar Allan Poe Award, Mystery Writers of America, Best Book Award, American Library Association, and New York Public Library Award for Best Book, all 1992, all for *The Weirdo;* Best Book Award, American Library Association, 1993, for *Timothy of the Cay;* Best Young Adult Book Award, Maryland Reading Association, 1995, for *Sniper.*

WRITINGS:

JUVENILE FICTION

The Cay (*Horn Book* honor list), Doubleday (New York City), 1969.
The Children's War, Doubleday, 1971.
The Maldonado Miracle, Doubleday, 1973.
Teetoncey, illustrated by Richard Cuffari, Doubleday, 1974.
Teetoncey and Ben O'Neal, illustrated by R. Cuffari, Doubleday, 1975.
The Odyssey of Ben O'Neal, illustrated by R. Cuffari, Doubleday, 1977.
The Trouble with Tuck, Doubleday, 1981.
Sweet Friday Island, Scholastic Inc. (New York City), 1984.
Walking Up a Rainbow: Being the True Version of the Long and Hazardous Journey of Susan D. Carlisle, Mrs. Myrtle Dessery, Drover Bert Pettit, and Cowboy Clay Carmer and Others, Delacorte (New York City), 1986.

The Hostage, illustrated by Darrell Sweet, Delacorte, 1987.

Sniper, Harcourt (New York City), 1989.

Tuck Triumphant, Doubleday, 1991.

The Weirdo, Harcourt, 1992.

Maria, Harcourt, 1992.

Timothy of the Cay, Harcourt, 1993.

The Bomb, Harcourt, 1995.

JUVENILE NONFICTION

People Who Make Movies, Doubleday, 1967.

Air Raid—Pearl Harbor! The Story of December 7, 1941, illustrated by W. T. Mars, Crowell (New York City), 1971.

Rebellion Town: Williamsburg, 1776, illustrated by R. Cuffari, Crowell, 1973.

Battle in the Arctic Seas: The Story of Convoy PQ 17 (Junior Literary Guild selection), illustrated by Robert Andrew Parker, Crowell, 1976.

(With Louis Irigaray) *A Shepherd Watches, a Shepherd Sings*, Doubleday, 1977.

The Battle off Midway Island, illustrated by Andrew Glass, Avon (New York City), 1981.

H.M.S. Hood vs. Bismarck: The Battleship Battle, illustrated by A. Glass, Avon, 1982.

Battle in the English Channel, illustrated by A. Glass, Avon, 1983.

Rocket Island, Avon, 1985.

ADULT FICTION

The Stalker, D. I. Fine, 1987.

Monocolo, D. I. Fine, 1989.

To Kill the Leopard, Harcourt, 1993.

ADULT NONFICTION

The Magnificent Mitscher (biography), foreword by Arthur W. Radford, Norton (New York City), 1954.

Fire on the Beaches, Norton, 1958.

The Body Trade, Fawcett (New York City), 1968.

(With Robert A. Houghton) *Special Unit Senator: The Investigation of the Assassination of Senator Robert F. Kennedy*, Random House (New York City), 1970.

(With Kreskin) *The Amazing World of Kreskin*, Random House, 1973.

Jule: The Story of Composer Jule Styne, Random House, 1979.

(With Tippi Hedren) *The Cats of Shambala*, Simon & Schuster (New York City), 1985.

OTHER

Author of television plays, including *Tom Threepersons*, for *TV Mystery Theatre*, 1964, *Sunshine, the Whale* (juvenile), 1974, and *The Girl Who Whistled the River Kwai*, 1980, and of screenplays, including *Night without End*,

1959, *Showdown*, Universal, 1973, *The Hold-Up*, and seventeen documentaries. Also author of books under the pseudonym T. T. Lang. Contributor of short stories and novelettes to magazines, including *Redbook, Argosy, Ladies' Home Journal, McCall's* and *Saturday Evening Post*.

Taylor's manuscripts are held at the Kerlan Collection of the University of Minnesota.

ADAPTATIONS: The Cay was adapted as a movie by NBC-TV, 1974, and as a filmstrip by Pied Piper Productions, 1975. *The Trouble with Tuck* was adapted as a filmstrip by Pied Piper Productions, 1986.

WORK IN PROGRESS: Rainbow's End, a collection of short stories for boys; *Naughty, Naughty Knifework*, for adults.

SIDELIGHTS: Author Theodore Taylor does not have a very good imagination, or so he contends in his autobiographical sketch in *Something about the Author Autobiography Series* (*SAAS*). The creator of nearly thirty books, both fiction and nonfiction, adult and juvenile, insists that he is "basically a reporter, finding it easier to work from real-life models." Luckily for his readers, his real-life experiences are vast and varied: Taylor has worked for numerous newspapers, has served as a sailor in two wars, assisted in the production of Hollywood movies, and traveled the world making his own documentary films. These experiences, together with various childhood exploit, provide him with fodder for his many books.

Taylor was born in Statesville, North Carolina, on June 23, 1921, to a father who worked in a Pittsburgh foundry and a religious mother. His father left the family in search of work during the depression—not deserting his family, but doing his best to provide for them without exacerbating their circumstances. To help out, the young Taylor performed odd jobs and delivered newspapers. Childhood was not all work for Taylor, however. Though he was not an exceptional student, he says in *SAAS* that he "excelled in the practice of freedom, a brand of which is not known to many of today's children of six or seven." When his father got a job in the Naval Yard in Portsmouth, Virginia, Taylor had a whole new world to explore, a world of salt marshes, fishing docks, and coal-burning side-wheeler ferries. Taylor's "unwitting accomplice" in these adventures was his mother; "I do not remember," says Taylor, "at this age of seven and upward, her ever asking, 'Where are you going?' She trusted in God that I'd always be safe."

Taylor recreates this adventurous self-reliance in the characters of many of his books for young people. Ben O'Neal and Teetoncey (from *Teetoncey, Teetoncey and Ben O'Neal*, and *The Odyssey of Ben O'Neal*), Phillip (from *The Cay*), and Jose (from *The Maldonado Miracle*) "are the kind of peer models children can like and respect,"

Taylor tells *Language Arts* interviewer Norma Bagnall. "All of them are self-reliant; all are self-sufficient. They find their own way without constant reference to adults. I like that kind of kid; I think kids like that kind too, and if it helps them aim toward self-reliance, then I've done a good job."

Taylor secured his first writing job when he was thirteen years old when he was offered the chance to write a sports column for the *Portsmouth Star*. After graduating from high school, he convinced the managing editor of the *Washington Daily News* in Washington, D.C., to hire him as a copyboy. Soon he was writing theater and concert reviews, and within a few months was given the chance to write a profile of a local boxer. Thus, he traded college experience for real-life experience—as he writes in *SAAS,* the newspapers "were to be my college, my seamy-side university, my graduate school. I've often regretted I didn't attend college. City rooms were the substitutes, newsmen were the teachers."

In the fall of 1942, Taylor joined the merchant marine and the naval reserve, and although he did not see the likes of the action he wrote about in *Air Raid—Pearl Harbor! The Story of December 7, 1941,* and *The Battle off Midway Island,* during these years he developed a love for naval war history that made those books possible. Drew Middleton, writing in the *New York Times Book Review,* says that in *The Battle off Midway Island* "Taylor has provided readers of any age with a splendid picture of the naval battles that turned the Pacific War around." By carefully selecting revealing episodes in the war of the Pacific, and by providing background on the major figures in those battles, Taylor maintains the kind of pace that, according to Middleton, makes his "depiction of the men, the aircraft and the ships . . . seem as vivid as it was that day when the Navy took its first step on the long road to victory." *Air Raid—Pearl Harbor!* also elicited positive reviews: Wilson Sullivan, reviewing the book in *New York Times Book Review,* comments that "with the scenarist's eye for the effective fadeout, closeup and symbolic detail, Theodore Taylor has presented a vividly credible account of the attack on Pearl Harbor."

Taylor wrote his first book, a biography of Admiral "Pete" Mitscher entitled *The Magnificent Mitscher,* during his five-year tour of duty with the naval reserve during the Korean War. Late in that tour he found himself stationed in the Caribbean providing hurricane relief to many small islands. These experiences formed the basis of his award-winning book, *The Cay.* The book, written years after Taylor left the Caribbean, tells the story of a young white boy and an old black West Indian sailor who are marooned on an island, the only survivors of a shipwreck that left the boy, Phillip, blind. Despite Phillip's racist upbringing, he comes to rely on and trust Timothy, whose

shrewd judgement allows the pair to survive. Eventually Phillip comes to realize that racism is a product of sight, for Timothy feels "neither white nor black." Charles Dorsey, reviewing the book in *New York Times Book Review,* calls *The Cay* "a story with a high ethical purpose but no sermon." Many critics and reviewers praised the book, citing its fast-paced plot and vivid characterizations. The book also won many awards, including the Jane Addams Children's Book Award and the Lewis Carroll Shelf Award.

However, the book has also been attacked as racist, primarily for what some interpret as the stereotypical characterization of Timothy, whose dialect Taylor modeled after the West Indian sailors he knew in the Caribbean. The Interracial Council on Children's Books led the attack, and as a result the book was banned in many public libraries. Eventually the Jane Addams Book Award group asked that Taylor return the award, which he did in 1975.

Taylor denies the charges of racism leveled against his best-known book, saying in *SAAS* that "*The Cay* is *not* racist, in my firm belief, and the character of Timothy, the old black man, modeled after a real person and several composites, is 'heroic' and not a stereotype." The author told Bagnall that he can't let these criticisms affect the way he writes: "[If] I have to be worried about that kind of thing, I can't write. And the only way I can do it, is simply to forget all that stuff and do my story in the hope that as a human being I'll be fair. I try to do that."

After Taylor left the Navy, he became a press agent for a Hollywood film production company, and in turn soon became a story editor and then a producer's assistant. However, he soon departed Hollywood to make his own documentary films, and many of his experiences he converted into a book called *People Who Make Movies,* a children's book that explains the movie-making process and describes the many jobs that people perform in the movie industry. But Taylor writes for adults as well, and has published nearly as many adult books as books for children. "The change of pace is important and rejuvenating for me," he remarks in *SAAS.* T. Jefferson Parker, writing in the *Los Angeles Times Book Review,* calls Taylor's adult suspense novel *The Stalker* "a well-plotted, economical thriller," noting that "Taylor is . . . very good at moving his story along." Taylor has also tackled a study of the assassination of Senator Robert F. Kennedy and biographies of the Amazing Kreskin, the mentalist, and composer Jule Styne. The hard-working author now writes seven days a week—except during football season, when he takes weekends off—in the office of his home three blocks from the Pacific Ocean in California.

BIOGRAPHICAL/CRITICAL SOURCES:

BOOKS

Authors and Artists for Young Adults, Volume 2, Gale (Detroit), 1989, pp. 223-234.

Marquardt, Dorothy A., and Martha E. Ward, *Authors of Books for Young People,* supplement to the 2nd edition, Scarecrow (Metuchen, NJ), 1979.

Something about the Author Autobiography Series, Volume 4, Gale, 1987, pp. 303-320.

Twentieth-Century Children's Writers, 3rd edition, St. James Press (Detroit), 1989, pp. 953-54.

PERIODICALS

Christian Science Monitor, May 6, 1988; January 25, 1989, p. 13.

Growing Point, January, 1991, pp. 5447-5451.

Horn Book, October, 1974, p. 145; December, 1975, p. 596; April, 1982, p. 170; February, 1984, p. 79; January, 1990, p. 72.

Kirkus Reviews, February 25, 1991, p. 252.

Kliatt, winter, 1982, pp. 57-58.

Language Arts, January, 1980, pp. 86-91.

Los Angeles Times Book Review, June 21, 1987, pp. 3, 8.

New York Times Book Review, September 17, 1967, p. 34; November 3, 1968, p. 53; June 26, 1969, p. 26; July 11, 1971, p. 8; January 9, 1972, p. 8; October 6, 1974, p. 8; October 24, 1976, p. 43; November 15, 1981, pp. 54, 69; March 6, 1983, p. 30.

Publishers Weekly, December 14, 1990, p. 67.

Saturday Review, August 19, 1967, p. 35; June 28, 1969, p. 39; August 21, 1971, p. 27; October 16, 1971, p. 57.

School Library Journal, November, 1984, p. 139; July, 1990, p. 27; March, 1991, p. 196.

Times Educational Supplement, June 10, 1983, p. 22.

Times Literary Supplement, October 30, 1970, p. 1258.

Top of the News, November, 1971; April, 1975.

Voice of Youth Advocates, June, 1984, p. 111; February, 1985, p.

333; December, 1985, p. 336; June, 1986, p. 83; April, 1988, p. 30; June, 1990, pp. 93-94.

Washington Post, May 26, 1979.

*   *   *

TEICH, Albert H(arris) 1942-

PERSONAL: Surname is pronounced "tyke"; born December 17, 1942, in Chicago, IL; son of Maurice (a textile salesman) and Ina (Szuldiner) Teich; married Carolyn Richmond (a social scientist), June 3, 1965 (divorced, 1988); married Jill H. Pace (director of the American College of Real Estate Lawyers), January 29, 1989; children: Mitchell Craig, Kenneth David, Samantha Lynne. *Educa-*

tion: Massachusetts Institute of Technology, B.S., 1964, Ph.D., 1969.

ADDRESSES: Office—American Association for the Advancement of Science, 1333 H St. N.W., Washington, DC 20005.

CAREER: Syracuse University, Syracuse, NY, director of science and technology studies for Research Corp., 1969-73, adjunct assistant professor of political science, 1969-70; State University of New York at Binghamton, coordinator of research, and assistant professor of political science, 1973-74; State University of New York at Albany, Institute of Public Policy Alternatives, director of research, 1974-78; George Washington University, Washington, DC, associate professor of public affairs, 1976-79; American Association for the Advancement of Science, Washington, DC, manager of science policy studies, 1980-84, head of office of public sector programs, 1984-89, director of directorate for science and policy programs, 1990—. Consultant to Oak Ridge National Laboratory, U.S. Congress, National Science Foundation, National Academy of Sciences, Organization for Economic Cooperation and Development, and Syracuse Research Corp. Director of research projects. Guest lecturer in Australia, Romania, Canada, Hungary, Norway, China, Russia, and other countries.

MEMBER: American Association for the Advancement of Science (fellow; chairman of section X, 1988), Society for Social Studies of Science (member of executive council, 1979-81), American Society for Public Administration, Technology Transfer Society (vice-president, 1987-93, member of board of directors, 1993—).

AWARDS, HONORS: Grants from National Science Foundation, 1970—, U.S. Department of Energy, 1977-79, Alfred P. Sloan Foundation, 1987—, Carnegie Corporation of New York, 1991—, and National Institutes of Health, 1995—.

WRITINGS:

(With W. Henry Lambright and others) *Redeploying Big Science: A Study of Diversification at Oak Ridge National Laboratory,* Institute for Public Policy Alternatives, State University of New York, 1975.

Trends in the Organization of Academic Research: The Role of ORU's and Full-time Researchers, Graduate Program in Science, Technology, and Public Policy, George Washington University (Washington, DC), 1978.

(Senior author with wife, Jill H. Pace and others) *Science and Technology in the U.S.A.,* Longman (New York City), 1986.

EDITOR

Technology and Man's Future, St. Martin's (New York City), 1972, 6th edition published as *Technology and the Future,* 1993.

Scientists and Public Affairs, MIT Press (Cambridge, MA), 1974.

(With Ray Thornton) *Science, Technology, and the Issues of the Eighties: Policy Outlook,* Westview (Boulder, CO), 1982.

(With Morris A. Levin) *Biotechnology and the Environment: Risk and Regulation,* American Association for the Advancement of Science (Washington, DC), 1985.

(With Gilbert S. Omenn) *Biotechnology and the Environment: Research Needs,* Noyes Press (Park Ridge, NJ), 1987.

(With Stephen D. Nelson and Celia McEnaney) *AAAS Science and Technology Policy Yearbook, 1994,* AAAS Press (Washington, DC), 1994.

(With Mark S. Frankel) *The Genetic Frontier: Ethics, Law and Policy,* AAAS Press, 1994.

OTHER

Contributor to journals, including *Public Administration Review, Social Studies of Science, Technology and Culture, Technology Review,* and *Bulletin of the Atomic Scientists.* Member of editorial boards, *Science, Technology and Human Values* and *Science Communication.*

SIDELIGHTS: Albert H. Teich spent almost a year during 1966-67 traveling in Europe to collect data for his study of international scientific institutions. In collaboration with his wife, Jill Pace, he has published several travel articles in newspapers and magazines. Teich is responsible for the activities of the American Association for the Advancement of Science in science and technology policy as well as programs in science and ethics, law, and human rights. Teich personally directs a number of research projects, including a study of ethical and legal aspects of computer-mediated communication and a study of how universities enhance their research capabilities. He is also director of a project to produce a series of "trigger" videos for use in courses and seminars intended to enhance ethical behavior among scientists.

BIOGRAPHICAL/CRITICAL SOURCES:

PERIODICALS

Journal of Political Science, August, 1975.
Science Books and Films, May, 1973; November, 1986.

TERRACE, Vincent 1948-

PERSONAL: Born May 14, 1948, in Manhattan, NY; son of Vincent (a printer) and Anne (Lauro) Terrace. *Education:* New York Institute of Technology, B.F.A., 1971. *Religion:* Roman Catholic.

ADDRESSES: Home and office—1830 Delancey Pl., Bronx, NY 10462.

CAREER: Korvette's Department Store, New York, NY, salesman, 1971-75; writer, 1975—; television researcher for Baseline (an entertainment industry computer database company), 1984—.

WRITINGS:

The Complete Encyclopedia of Television Programs, 1947-1976, 2 volumes, A. S. Barnes (San Diego, CA), 1976, 2nd edition published as *The Complete Encyclopedia of Television Programs, 1947-1979,* 1979.

Radio's Golden Years, 1930-1960, A. S. Barnes, 1980.

Television 1970-1980, A. S. Barnes/Oak Tree, 1981.

Actors' TV Credits, Supplement II, 1977-81, Scarecrow (Metuchen, NJ), 1982, *Supplement III, 1982-85,* 1985.

Encyclopedia of Television: Series, Pilots and Specials, Volume I: *1937-1973,* Volume II: *1974-1984,* New York Zoetrope (New York City), 1985.

Who's Who in Television, 1937-1984, New York Zoetrope, 1985.

Fifty Years of Television, 1939-1988, Cornwall (East Brunswick, NJ), 1989.

The Complete Actors' Television Credits, 1948-1988, Scarecrow, *Volume One: Actors,* 1988, *Volume Two: Actresses,* 1989.

The Ultimate TV Trivia Book, Faber & Faber (Winchester, MA), 1992.

Television Character and Story Facts: Over 110,000 Details from 1008 Shows, 1945-1993, McFarland & Co. (Jefferson, NC), 1993.

1001 Toughest TV Trivia Questions of All Time, Citadel (Secaucus, NJ), 1994, revised edition published as *1201 Toughest TV Trivia Questions of All Time,* 1995.

Television Specials: 3201 Entertainment Spectaculars, 1939-1993, McFarland & Co., 1995.

The TV Theme Song Quiz Book, Citadel, 1996.

Experimental TV, Test Films, Pilots, and Trial Series, 1925-1995: 70 Years of What Almost Was, McFarland & Co., 1996.

Contributor to numerous books, including, James Robert Parish, *The Great Spy Pictures,* Scarecrow, 1974, *Supplement I,* 1987; Parish, *The Great Gangster Pictures,* Scarecrow, 1976, *Supplement I,* 1987; Parish, *The Great Western Pictures,* Scarecrow, 1976, *Supplement I,* 1987; Parish, *The Great Science Fiction Pictures,* Scarecrow, 1977, *Sup-*

plement I, 1987; Judy Fireman, *The Television Book,* Workman Publishing (New York City), 1977; Alvin H. Marill, *Movies Made for Television,* Arlington House (New York City), 1980; David Strauss and Fred L. Worth, *Hollywood Trivia,* Warner Books (New York City), 1981; Marill, *Movies Made for Television: The Telefeature and the Miniseries, 1964-1984,* New York Zoetrope, 1985; and Steven Eberly, *Patty Duke: A Bibliography,* Greenwood Press (Westport, CT), 1988.

WORK IN PROGRESS: Books on radio and television.

SIDELIGHTS: Vincent Terrace told *CA:* "My television books were the first of their kind and I hope to continue in the future with additional volumes that document, in the most complete detail possible, the countless programs that have and will become a part of American broadcasting history."

*   *   *

TINTNER, Adeline R. 1912-

PERSONAL: Born February 2, 1912, in New York, NY; daughter of Benjamin Abner (a clergyman) and Ray (a housewife; maiden name, Sarnoff) Tintner; married Henry D. Janowitz (a physician), October 31, 1942; children: Mary R., Anne F.. *Education:* Barnard College, B.A., 1932; Columbia University, M.A., 1933, further graduate study, 1933-36. *Politics:* None.

ADDRESSES: 180 East End Ave., New York, NY 10128.

MEMBER: Henry James Society (president, 1987-88), Modern Language Association, Edith Wharton Society.

AWARDS, HONORS: Carnegie scholar at Courtauld Institute of Art, London, 1934.

WRITINGS:

The Museum World of Henry James, UMI Research Press (Ann Arbor, MI), 1986.
The Book World of Henry James, UMI Research Press, 1987.
(With Leon Edel) *The Library of Henry James,* UMI Research Press, 1987.
The Pop World of Henry James, UMI Research Press, 1989.
The Cosmopolitan World of Henry James, Louisiana State University Press (Baton Rouge, LA), 1991.
Henry James and the Lust of the Eyes, Louisiana State University Press, 1993.
The Legacy of Henry James, Louisiana State University Press, in press.

SIDELIGHTS: Adeline R. Tintner's criticism of the work of Henry James encompasses his entire body of writings.

In the *Times Literary Supplement,* Nicola Bradbury wrote that *The Museum World of Henry James* is "the first extensive study of James's use of actual works of art in his fiction." Though the author concentrates on the influence of the Italian Renaissance on James's writing, she does not neglect the role of classical or early modern art in his work. Bradbury praised Tintner: "Her guidance is informed, interesting, and masterly." She has provided "a view of James's work which is grounded in good sense and lightened with ingenious perceptions."

BIOGRAPHICAL/CRITICAL SOURCES:

PERIODICALS

Times Literary Supplement, September 26, 1986.

*   *   *

TIPTON, James (Sherwood) 1942-

PERSONAL: Born January 18, 1942, in Ashland, OH; son of J. Robert (in business) and Ruth (Burcher) Tipton; married Lynn Ellen Johnson (a teacher), September 5, 1965 (divorced); children: Jennifer Lynn, James Daniel. *Education:* Purdue University, B.A., 1964, M.A., 1968.

ADDRESSES: Home—1742 DS Road, Glade Park, CO 81523.

CAREER: Kalamazoo College, Kalamazoo, MI, writer in residence, 1969-70; Alma College, Alma, MI, began as assistant professor, became associate professor of English, chair of department, and director of cultural affairs, 1970-83; stockbroker, 1983-94; writer and beekeeper, 1995—. Director of U.S. Department of Education project to discover and work with young Michigan writers. Guest speaker at numerous educational institutions, and for Michigan Poetry in the Schools project.

AWARDS, HONORS: Bread Loaf scholar in poetry, 1969; National Endowment for the Humanities grant, 1972, to study ritual in contemporary poetry; first prize, Festival of the Arts (Birmingham, AL), 1973, for story "Baby Jesus"; Michigan Council for the Arts grants, 1975, 1982; *The Giant Alphabet* named one of ten best poetry books of the year by *Bloomsbury Review,* 1987.

WRITINGS:

POETRY

Matters of Love, Cranium Press, 1970.
Sentences, Cranium Press, 1970.
Bittersweet, Cold Mountain Press, 1975.
The Giant Alphabet, Leaping Mountain Press, 1987.
The Wizard of Is, Bread and Butter Press, 1995.

EDITOR

(With Herbert Scott and Conrad Hilberry, and contributor) *The Third Coast: Contemporary Michigan Poetry*, Wayne State University Press (Detroit), 1976.

(With Robert Wegner) *The Third Coast: Contemporary Michigan Fiction*, Wayne State University Press (Detroit), 1982.

OTHER

Work anthologized in numerous publications, including *The Haiku Anthology*, Doubleday (New York City), 1974; *Heartland II: Poets of the Midwest*, Northern Illinois University Press (DeKalb, IL), 1975; and *The Other Voice*, Norton (New York City), 1976. Contributor of poems, stories, translations, and reviews to literary journals and magazines, including *Nation, Esquire, South Dakota Review, Carolina Quarterly, Contemporary Poetry*, and *Southern Humanities Review*.

WORK IN PROGRESS: Something at the Heart of Flesh, a poetry collection.

*   *   *

TOLLEY, A(rnold) T(revor) 1927-

PERSONAL: Born May 15, 1927, in Birmingham, England; son of Arthur William (a bank clerk) and Dorothy Letty (Freeman) Tolley; married Grace Margaret Ronaldson Swanson, December, 1952 (died, July, 1969); married Glenda Mary Patrick (a university teacher), June, 1974. *Education:* Queen's College, Oxford, B.A. (with honors), 1951. *Religion:* None.

ADDRESSES: Home—R.R.2, Williamsburg, Ontario, Canada K0C 2H0. *Office*—Department of Comparative Literature, Carleton University, Ottawa, Ontario, Canada K1S 5B6.

CAREER: National Coal Board, London, England, administrative officer, 1951-55; University of Turku, Turku, Finland, lecturer in English, 1955-61; Monash University, Melbourne, Australia, lecturer, 1961-63, senior lecturer in English, 1963-65; Carleton University, Ottawa, Ontario, assistant professor, 1965-67, associate professor, 1967-72, professor of English, 1972-90, professor of comparative literary studies, 1990—, chair of comparative literature department, 1984-90, dean of faculty of arts, 1969-74, Marston Lafrance fellow, 1978-79. President of Stormont, Dundas, and Glengarry New Democratic Party Provincial Riding Association, 1977-90; member of Provincial Executive, Ontario New Democratic Party, 1991—; councillor, Williamsburg Township, 1988-94. Chair of board of trustees of SAW Gallery, 1978-81. *Military service:*

Hospital service as the alternative service of a conscientious objector to military duty, 1946-48.

MEMBER: Montreal Vintage Music Society (president, 1984—).

AWARDS, HONORS: Award from Ontario Arts Council, 1986, for *My Proper Ground*.

WRITINGS:

The Early Published Poems of Stephen Spender: A Chronology, Carleton University Press, 1967.
The Poetry of the Thirties, Gollancz, 1975, St. Martin's (New York City), 1976.
The Poetry of the Forties, Carleton University Press, 1985.
(Editor) *John Lehmann: A Tribute*, Carleton University Press, 1987.
My Proper Ground: A Study of the Work of Philip Larken and Its Development, Carleton University Press, 1991.
(Editor) *Roy Fuller: A Tribute*, Carleton University Press, 1993.

Also author of *Larkin at Work*, 1996. Contributor to *Dictionary of Literary Biography* and *Oxford Companion to Twentieth Century Poetry in English*. Contributor to magazines, including *Southern Review, Coda, Storyville, Poetry Review, New Review*, and *Studies in Short Fiction*. Guest editor of *Aquarius*.

SIDELIGHTS: A. T. Tolley's works on poetry of the 1930s and 1940s have been described as "conscientious and encyclopedic" surveys of an era. Though the author could not hope to include every poet, an effort was made to highlight the work of poets sometimes neglected by more conventional writers. According to Bernard Bergonzi, reviewing *The Poetry of the Thirties* in *New Review:* "The thirties were a remarkable period. . . . Tolley's book shows what it was all about; he has done the job so well that it need never be done again." William Scammell, writing in the *Times Literary Supplement*, commented that Tolley's 1985 book, *The Poetry of the Forties*, contained "a sympathetic treatment of Roy Fuller . . . , and it's good to see fine poets like Bernard Spencer and Alan Ross getting their due."

Tolley told *CA:* "My interest in British poets of the 1930s and 1940s goes back to the mid-1940s, when I started reading modern poetry and when these poets were the new poets. It had always been my wish to write about these poets, just because their work has been so much a part of my life. The poets from this period whose work has meant the most to me are W. H. Auden and Louis MacNeice.

"My interest in jazz goes back even further, to 1942 when I was fifteen years old. The great music for me will always be that of the Golden Era, from 1927 to 1932. I particularly like the music of Bix Beiderbecke and Frank Teschemacher, but I also enjoy Louis Armstrong, Duke Ellington, Henry Allen, Sidney Bechet, and Johnny Dodds. Nonetheless, the music of more modern players—Charlie Parker, Bud Powell, Thelonious Monk, Miles Davis, John Coltrane, and Cecil Taylor, for example—has been tremendously important to me. I write regularly about jazz and would like to write a book-length study of certain features of jazz history and jazz historiography."

*   *   *

TSERNIANSKI, Milos
See CRNJANSKI, Milos

*   *   *

TY-CASPER, Linda   1931-

PERSONAL: Surname is pronounced "Tee-Cas-per"; born September 17, 1931, in Manila, Philippines; came to the United States in 1956; daughter of Francisco Figueroa (a civil engineer) and Catalina (an educator and writer; maiden name, Velasquez) Ty; married Leonard R. Casper (a professor and writer), July 14, 1956; children: Gretchen, Kristina. *Education:* University of the Philippines, A.A., 1951, LL.B., 1955; Harvard University, LL.M., 1957. *Politics:* Independent. *Religion:* Roman Catholic.

ADDRESSES: Home—Saxonville, MA. *Agent*—Bonnie Crown, International Literature and Arts Agency, 50 East 10th St., No. R5, New York, NY 10003.

CAREER: Conducted writers' workshop at Ateneo de Manila University, 1978, 1980; writer-in-residence at University of the Philippines, 1980, 1982.

MEMBER: Iskuwelahang Pilipino, Birthright, PEN Women (Wellesley branch), Society of Radcliffe Fellows, Boston Authors.

AWARDS, HONORS: Fellow at Silliman University, 1963, and Radcliffe Institute, 1974-75; Djerassi writing fellowship, 1984; literature award, Filipino-American Women's Network, 1985; *Awaiting Trespass* chosen as one of five fiction titles in twenty selected for 1986, Feminist Book Fortnight of Britain and Ireland; Southeast Asia WRITE Award, Bangkok, 1993; UNESCO/PEN Short Story Prize, 1993; Rockefeller/Bellagio fellowship, 1994.

WRITINGS:

The Transparent Sun and Other Stories, Peso Books (Manila, Philippines), 1963.
The Peninsulars (historical novel), Bookmark (Manila), 1964.
The Secret Runner and Other Stories, Florentino (Manila), 1974.

The Three-Cornered Sun (historical novel), New Day (Quezon City, Philippines), 1979.
Dread Empire (novella), Heinemann Asia (Hong Kong), 1980.
Hazards of Distance (novella), New Day, 1981.
Fortress in the Plaza (novella), New Day, 1985.
Awaiting Trespass (novella), Readers International (London, England), 1985.
Wings of Stone (novella), Readers International, 1986.
Ten Thousand Seeds (historical novel), Ateneo (Quezon City), 1987.
A Small Garden Party (novella), New Day, 1988.
Common Continent (short stories), New Day, 1991.

Work represented in anthologies, including *Development of Philippine Literature in English,* 1975; *Best American Short Stories of 1977,* edited by Martha Foley; *Home to Stay,* 1990; *Fiction by Filipinos in America,* 1993; *12 Filipino Women Writers,* 1994. Contributor of stories to numerous periodicals including *Antioch Review, Boston Review, Christian Science Monitor, Cuyahoga Review, Free Press, Graphic, Hawaii Pacific Review, Hawaii Review, Kenyon Review, The Literary Apprentice, Manila Review, Mr. & Ms., Nation, Philippines Free Press, Solidarity, Sunday Times Magazine, Triquarterly,* and *Windsor Review.*

WORK IN PROGRESS: The Stranded Whale, about the Philippine-American War to 1901.

SIDELIGHTS: Linda Ty-Casper told *CA:* "It was to correct misjudgments [of Philippine history] that I wrote my first historical novel, *The Peninsulars.* The positive comments of its critics encouraged me to think about writing novels set in other critical periods of Philippine history. I began research on the revolution of 1896. It took me fifteen years to research, write, rewrite (when the manuscript was lost), and revise that project.

"I write on impulse. The first lines of stories come to me in the midst of other things. I work steadily in one sitting until the story needs only to be revised. I do not work every day, for that would make writing a drudgery. Events shape each chapter of my novels. I know the event and its public outcome, but I don't know what my characters will do as they re-enact it. I research exhaustively, until I can see the place and feel the time: newspapers, songs, letters to editors, all manner of accounts, including telephone directories, are among my sources. I read novels from the period to get the rhythm of words and sentences as distinguished from the rhythm of life which the details of daily living recreate.

"I believe writing provides alternatives, by adding still other 'selves' to literature, that house of our many selves. Because a writer writes, history cannot be entirely rewritten according to the specifications of politicians."

BIOGRAPHICAL/CRITICAL SOURCES:

BOOKS

Bresnahan, Roger J., *Conversations with Filipino Writers,* New Day (Cleveland, OH), 1987.

Casper, Leonard R., *The Opposing Thumb, Decoding Literature of the Marcos Regime,* Giraffe Books, 1995.

Galdon, Joseph A., *Philippines Fiction: Essays from Philippine Studies 1953-1972,* Ateneo, 1972.

Lim, Jaime An, *Literature and Politics: The Colonial Experience in Nine Philippine Novels,* New Day, 1993.

Montenegro, David, *Points of Departure: International Writers on Writing and Politics,* Michigan State University Press (East Lansing, MI), 1991.

Schwartz, Norda Lacey, *Articles on Women Writers, 1960-1975,* American Bibliographical Center—Clio Press, 1977.

PERIODICALS

AmerAsia Journal, Volume 13, numumber 1, 1986-87.
Asiaweek, February 16, 1986; September 27, 1987.
Belles Lettres, spring, 1987.
Booklist, January, 1986.
Boston Globe, November 24, 1985; January 25, 1987.
Filipinas, fall, 1987; spring, 1988; fall, 1988; spring, 1990.
Globe and Mail (Toronto), December 6, 1986.
Heritage, July, 1967.
Hudson Review, March, 1986.
Journal of Asian Studies, August, 1981.
Kirkus Reviews, August 15, 1985; September 15, 1986.
Los Angeles Times, February 9, 1986.
Los Angeles Times Book Review, February 2, 1986.
Manila Sunday Chronicle, March 7, 1993; July 24, 1993.
New Statesman, October 18, 1985.
New York Times Book Review, October 25, 1985.
Observer (London), March 16, 1985.
Philippine Free Press, February 4, 1992.
Philippine Studies, Volume 28, 1980; Volume 30, 1982; Volume 32, 1984; Volume 34, 1986; Volume 40, 1992.
Publishers Weekly, October 10, 1985; October 10, 1986.
San Francisco Chronicle, May 25, 1986; December 4, 1986.
Solidarity, April-June, 1990.
Women's Review of Books, July, 1986.
World Literature Today, autumn, 1982; winter, 1987; spring, 1988.

U-Z

UPTON, Dell 1949-

PERSONAL: Born June 24, 1949, in Fort Monmouth, NJ; son of Wentney B. (a carpenter) and Carley (an industrial manager; maiden name, White) Upton; married Karen Kevorkian (an editor), December 21, 1982; stepchildren: Anna, Raffi, Ellina, Soseh. *Education:* Colgate University, A.B. (cum laude), 1970; Brown University, A.M., 1975, Ph.D., 1980.

ADDRESSES: Home—1910 Sacramento, Berkeley, CA 94702. *Office*—Department of Architecture, University of California, Berkeley, CA 94720.

CAREER: Virginia Historic Landmarks Commission, Richmond, architectural historian, 1974-79; University of Virginia, Charlottesville, lecturer in architectural history, 1979-80; Case Western Reserve University, Cleveland, OH, assistant professor of American studies, 1982-83; University of California, Berkeley, assistant professor, 1983-87, associate professor, 1987-92, professor of architectural history, 1992—. Assistant professorial lecturer at George Washington University, 1979-81; visiting assistant professor at Boston University, 1979 and 1981.

MEMBER: Society of Architectural Historians (member of board of directors, 1985-88), American Historical Association, Organization of American Historians, American Studies Association, Pioneer America Society (member of board of directors, 1980-83), Vernacular Architecture Forum (member of executive board, 1980-89), Virginia Folklore Society (president, 1978-80), Phi Beta Kappa.

AWARDS, HONORS: Fellow of National Endowment for the Humanities at Winterthur Museum, 1981-82; John Hope Franklin prize for best book in American studies, 1987; Alice Davis Hitchcock book award in architectural history, 1987; Abbott Lowell Cummings prize for best book in vernacular architecture, 1987; Rachal Award for best article on Virginia history, 1988; visiting senior fellow, Center for Advanced Studies in the Visual Arts, National Gallery of Art, 1988; Getty senior research grant in art history, 1990-91; Guggenheim fellowship, 1992-93.

WRITINGS:

(Contributor) Brooke Hindle, editor, *Material Culture of the Wooden Age,* Sleepy Hollow Press (Tarrytown, NY), 1981.

(Contributor) *Three Centuries of Maryland Architecture,* Maryland Historical Trust, 1982.

(Contributor) Thomas J. Schlereth, editor, *Material Culture: A Guide to Research,* University of Kansas Press, 1985.

Holy Things and Profane: Anglican Parish Churches in Colonial Virginia, MIT Press (Cambridge, MA), 1986.

(Editor with John Michael Vlach, and contributor) *Common Places: Readings in American Vernacular Architecture,* University of Georgia Press (Athens, GA), 1986.

(Editor) *America's Architectural Roots: Ethnic Groups that Built America,* Preservation Press (Walnut Creek, CA), 1986.

(Contributor) Mary C. Beaudry and Anne Yentsch, editors, *The Art and Mystery of Historical Archaeology,* CRC Press (Boca Raton, FL), 1992.

(Contributor) Zeynep Celik and others, editors, *Streets: Critical Perspectives in Urban Space,* University of California Press (Berkeley, CA), 1994.

(Contributor) Catherine E. Hutchins, editor, *Everyday Life in the Early Republic,* Winterthur Museum (Winterthur, DE), 1994.

Madaline: Love and Survival in Antebellum New Orleans, University of Georgia Press, 1995.

Contributor to *Encyclopedia of Southern Culture* and *Encyclopedia of the North American Colonies.* Contributor of articles and reviews to history and architecture journals. Founder and editor of *Vernacular Architecture Newsletter,* 1979-89; co-editor of *Folklore and Folklife: Journal of the Virginia Folklore Society,* 1978-80; member of editorial board of *American Quarterly,* 1983-86, *Material Culture,* 1983—, *Winterthur Portfolio,* 1983-93, and *Design Book Review,* 1985—.

WORK IN PROGRESS: Introduction to Architecture of the United States, for Oxford University Press; research on urban cultural landscapes in Antebellum Philadelphia and New Orleans.

*　　*　　*

WACHTEL, Albert 1939-

PERSONAL: Born December 20, 1939, in New York, NY; son of Jacob (a doll manufacturer) and Sally Rose (a homemaker; maiden name, Kaplansky) Wachtel; married Sydelle Farber Zetkin (a homemaker), 1958; children: Sally Rose, Seth Laurence, Stephanie Allyson, Synthia Laura, Jonathan Benjamin, Jessica Eden, Jacob Ethan. *Education:* Queens College (now of the City University of New York), B.A., 1960; State University of New York at Buffalo, Ph.D., 1968.

ADDRESSES: Office—Department of English, Pitzer College, Claremont, CA 91711.

CAREER: State University of New York at Buffalo, instructor in English, 1963-66, assistant to the dean, 1966-68; University of California, Santa Barbara, assistant professor of English, 1968-74; Pitzer College, Claremont, CA, associate professor, 1974-78, professor of English, 1978—.

MEMBER: Modern Language Association of America, Dramatists Guild, James Joyce Society.

AWARDS, HONORS: Fellow of NDEA, 1960-63; fellow of Creative Arts Institute, 1970; Danforth associate, 1979; fellow of National Endowment for the Humanities Summer Institute, 1986.

WRITINGS:

(Editor with Monique Chefdor and Ricardo Quinones) *Modernism: Challenges and Perspectives,* University of Illinois Press (Champaign, IL), 1986.
The Cracked Lookingglass: James Joyce and the Nightmare of History, Associated University Presses, 1992.
(Adaptor) *Henry IV* (adaptation of two plays by William Shakespeare), produced at Odyssey Theater, Los Angeles, 1995.

Contributor of articles and stories to literature journals, literary magazines, and newspapers, including *Southern Review, Midstream, Review of Contemporary Fiction, Los Angeles Times, Journal of Aesthetics and Art Criticism, Modern Fiction Studies,* and *James Joyce Quarterly.*

WORK IN PROGRESS: A novel about an immigrant to America in the 1920s; a novel about a young black man, set in the 1990s; a study of modernism in the arts, in relation to developments in the physical, biological, and social sciences.

SIDELIGHTS: Albert Wachtel told *CA:* "In my fiction I'm concerned with finding metaphors in motion, analogical actions that make up the bed of empathy and understanding without demanding occupants. As for my scholarly work, what's distinctive about *Modernism: Challenges and Perspectives* is that by allowing all the specialists represented to make their cases, it creates a general tapestry out of strikingly individual views. *The Cracked Lookingglass: James Joyce and the Nightmare of History* traces the contributions to modern literature of James Joyce, who strove to find a language that would convey the subjective objectively, whether through epiphanies, or streams of consciousness, or styles that force readers to apprehend the universe in unfamiliar ways. Joyce sought and found ways of attaining a sort of objective subjectivity, truths of feeling, perception, intention, and understanding in the universe of flesh and stone. He realized that chance, accidental occurrences can seem causal to those affected by them, producing what I call 'psychocausal' responses. The placing of him in the context of Modernism generally comes next, perhaps."

*　　*　　*

WALLACE, Ian 1950-

PERSONAL: Born March 31, 1950, in Niagara Falls, Ontario, Canada; son of Robert Amiens and Kathleen (Watts) Wallace; married Debra Wiedman. *Education:* Graduated from Ontario College of Art, 1973; graduate studies, 1973-74. *Avocational interests:* Walking, movies, travel, dining out.

ADDRESSES: Home—184 Major St., Toronto, Ontario, Canada M5S 2L3.

CAREER: Staff writer and illustrator for Kids Can Press, 1974-76; Art Gallery of Ontario, Toronto, information officer, 1976-80. Artist; exhibitions include "Chin Chiang and the Dragon's Dance," Art Gallery of Ontario, 1986; "Once upon a Time," Vancouver Art Gallery, 1988; "Canada at Bologna," Bologna Children's Book Fair, 1990.

MEMBER: Writers Union of Canada, Canadian Children's Book Centre.

AWARDS, HONORS: Runner-up for City of Toronto Book Awards, 1976, "Our Choice" Selection, Children's Book Centre, 1977-81, Canada Council grants, 1980, 1981, 1983, 1986, 1987, Imperial Order of Daughters of the Empire Book Award, 1984, Amelia Frances Howard-Gibbon Illustrator's Award, 1984, International Board on Books for Young People Honor List citation, 1986, all for *Chin Chiang and the Dragon's Dance;* Ontario Arts Council grants, 1985, 1988; American Library Association Notable Book citation, 1987, and White Raven Award, International Youth Library, 1987, both for *Very Last First Time;* Mr. Christie Award, Elizabeth Mrazik Cleaver Award, and Amelia Francis Howard Gibbon Award, all for *The Name of the Tree;* nominee from Canada for Hans Christian Anderson medal (illustration), 1994; Gibbon Medal short list, 1994, for *Hansel & Gretel.*

WRITINGS:

JUVENILE

Julie News (self-illustrated), Kids Can Press (Ontario), 1974.

(With Angela Wood) *The Sandwich,* Kids Can Press, 1975, revised edition, 1985.

The Christmas Tree House (self-illustrated), Kids Can Press, 1976.

Chin Chiang and the Dragon's Dance (self-illustrated), Atheneum (New York City), 1984.

The Sparrow's Song (self-illustrated), Viking (New York City), 1986.

Morgan the Magnificent (self-illustrated), Macmillan (New York City), 1987.

Mr. Kneebone's New Digs (self-illustrated), Groundwood, 1991.

ILLUSTRATOR

Jan Andrews, *Very Last First Time,* Atheneum, 1985, published as *Eva's Ice Adventure,* Methuen (New York City), 1986.

Tim Wynne-Jones, *The Architect of the Moon,* Groundwood, 1988, published as *Builder of the Moon,* Macmillan, 1989.

Celia Barker Lottridge, *The Name of the Tree: A Bantu Folktale,* Macmillan, 1990.

Teddy Jam, *The Year of the Fire,* Macmillan, 1993.

Bud Davidge, *The Mummer's Song,* Orchard Books, 1994.

The Brothers Grimm, *Hansel & Gretel,* Groundwood, 1994.

Contributor to periodicals, including *Canadian Books for Young People.*

SIDELIGHTS: Canadian Ian Wallace both writes and illustrates children's books. He is best known for his award-winning *Chin Chiang and the Dragon's Dance.* Wallace told *Something about the Author (SATA)* that "like most children growing up in Niagara Falls, Ontario, in the 1950s, Sunday afternoons were spent with my family driving leisurely through the countryside counting cows, cars and the many species of trees that my brothers and I could see through the back window of our father's car. This activity was far removed from the one carried out by a fair percentage of large city dwellers of the 80s, many of whom bring their children indoors on Sunday afternoons to expansive spaces we know as art galleries and museums. Free to roam those hallowed halls, children count the numbers of Renoirs and Modiglianis, or the stuffed horn-rimmed owls and the variety and colour of rare duck's eggs to be found in a single glass case.

"My first exposure to the world of art came not through pictures hung on gallery and museum walls, but through the picture books my brothers and I carted out of our local library. Contained within the covers of each book were worlds so foreign and exciting that we marvelled at the daring of the characters, thrilled to their singular and collective bravery, and were often chillingly jerked back by great waves of fear. For children growing up in small city Ontario, these books and their images carried us out of our sheltered environment to places we never imagined and only discovered within those treasured pages. Just as important, they made us keenly aware of the fact that a painter was not merely someone who, like our father, picked up a brush or roller and stroked or rolled it over the walls of our house whenever the rooms had grown tired around the edges. But rather, an artist was someone who made dreams real.

"My creative life hiccuped along, dropping in and out with unpredictable regularity, until the day at age thirteen when I gave up the notion of being a fireman and announced that I was going to be an artist. My parents' response was not surprising, since they were consistently supportive of my brothers and me, no matter what wild dreams we espoused or what strange predicament we had managed to get ourselves into. 'Of course you will,' they said.

"And that was that. The decision was made. And with it came the unconditional support of my parents, so crucial to anyone risking the possibility of living a creative life. This desire to become an artist did not diminish as my teenage years progressed, but helped to conquer those racing hormones, the battle against teenage angst and love, and the ability to put in countless hours alone in my room with only the sound of a pencil scratching over the surface of stacks of paper.

"My training has been mainly visual, but the single most important lesson I've learned is that everything creative must have a purpose and a reason for its expression. My first three books were labors of love. Writing and illustrating do not come easily to me; the challenge is in the struggle. I have had the opportunity to read to 325,000 children across Canada, the United States and Australia, and I now understand how important books are to our lives. To watch children laugh or cry at a story with you is achieving a high level of communication."

Chin Chiang and the Dragon's Dance is about a Chinese-Canadian boy who wants to take part in the New Year's Day street dance commemorating the Year of the Dragon, but suffers from stage fright. Sandra Martin comments on the book's illustrations in the *Globe and Mail,* which she says "are subtle yet brilliantly colored, particularly in the reds and blues, and for me they pass the acid test: they exist independently of the verbal story and possess enough depth and integrity to tell their own tale. . . . Wallace has painted them with such authenticity and meticulous care that they speak eloquently of centuries of Chinese heritage transplanted onto the Canadian west coast." Wallace explained in *SATA:* "The task of creating this book was not completed in the short term, but over six years. having endured that long gestation, I cannot stress enough the value of time—time to allow the right works to come forth, time to allow the drawings to formulate in the head before they appear on paper, and time to allow both to be as polished as a piece of rare jade."

"As much as I am in need of solitude when I am lost in the activity of writing or illustrating," Wallace told *SATA,* "I am also a social creature by nature, enjoying the camaraderie of friends and people in general. Writing and illustrating provide me with the former, while storytelling provides me with the latter. At times my life does appear somewhat schizophrenic, but for the most part, I love the balance of the two activities: writing and illustrating or storytelling.

"What a luxury it is to wake up each morning and know that this new day will not be the same as the one before and never the same as those that come after."

BIOGRAPHICAL/CRITICAL SOURCES:

BOOKS

Something about the Author, Volume 56, Gale, 1989, pp. 164-67.
Writers on Writing, Overlea House, 1989.

PERIODICALS

Canadian Children's Literature, number 48, 1987.
Emergency Librarian, February, 1985.

Globe and Mail (Toronto), August 4, 1984; November 1, 1986.
In Review, April, 1979.
New Advocate, spring, 1989.
Quill and Quire, February, 1985.

VIDEO

Ian Wallace, "Meet the Authors" series, Mead Educational, 1989.

*   *   *

WALLIS, Jim 1948-

PERSONAL: Born June 4, 1948, in Detroit, MI; son of James E. (in business) and Phyllis (in business) Wallis. *Education:* Michigan State University, B.S., 1970; attended Trinity Evangelical Divinity School, 1970-72.

ADDRESSES: Office—*Sojourners,* 1309 L St. N.W., Washington, DC 20005.

CAREER: Sojourners, Washington, DC, editor, 1971—. Pastor at Sojourners Fellowship, 1975—.

WRITINGS:

Agenda for Biblical People, Harper (San Francisco), 1976, 2nd edition, 1984.
The Call to Conversion, Harper, 1981, paperback edition published as *The Call to Conversion: Recovering the Gospel for These Times,* 1992.
Revive Us Again: A Sojourner's Story, Abingdon Press (Nashville), 1983.
The Soul of Politics: A Practical and Prophetic Vision for Change, Orbis Books, 1994.

EDITOR

Waging Peace: A Handbook for the Struggle to Abolish Nuclear Weapons, Harper, 1982.
Peacemakers: Christian Voices from the New Abolitionist Movement, Harper, 1983.
The Rise of Christian Conscience: The Emergence of a Dramatic Renewal Movement in the Church Today, Harper, 1987.
(With Joyce Hollyday) *Crucible of Fire: The Church Confronts Apartheid,* Orbis Books (Maryknoll, NY), 1989.
(With Hollyday) *Cloud of Witnesses,* Orbis Books, 1991.

Also contributor to periodicals.

SIDELIGHTS: Jim Wallis is a social activist and evangelical Christian minister whose written works reflect his years working among America's poor. Wallis was founder of Sojourners, an ecumenical social action group and residential community in one of the bleakest neighborhoods of Washington, D.C. As a leader of Sojourners and the editor of *Sojourners* magazine, Wallis calls American Christians to reflect on the tenets of their faith and ask themselves if they are truly living as the Bible demands. According to Richard Higgins in the *Boston Globe*, Wallis seeks to reclaim the biblical tradition of prophecy "by proposing an evangelical politics not stamped in the Moral Majority's template."

Among Wallis's many publications is the 1994 title *The Soul of Politics: A Practical and Prophetic Vision for Change*. In this work the author-minister rejects the familiar labels of "liberal" and "conservative" and offers a vision of a society that would link personal moral responsibility with a genuine concern for social justice and change. This combination, he suggests, would offer "an alternative to the limits of secular humanism and the oppressions of religious fundamentalism." One outcome of this community vision, he feels, would be a radical re-dedication to serving the needs of the poor. As Jim Naughton notes in the *Washington Post Book World*, Wallis's is "a faith based on personal sacrifice and an ongoing involvement with the downtrodden."

The Soul of Politics has been widely reviewed by those concerned about the gulf between the religious right and the humanist left. According to *Nation* essayist John Brown Childs, the book "draws from the well of spirituality to replenish social commitment and re-establish community in a society parched by individualized materialistic strivings and denuded of hope by powerful profit-driven elites." The critic adds: "Wallis hopes that a return to fundamental religious tradition will have progressive rather than conservative political consequences." *Commonweal* reviewer Stephen J. Pope notes that the work's strength lies in its "consistent call to conversion and an unmistakable commitment to the politics of compassion. Wallis effectively challenges his readers to scrutinize their own integrity as Christians and, in particular, to examine whether their concrete life decisions, from family structure to the uses of money, are consistent with professed Christian faith." Calling Wallis "an original and persuasive diagnostician of our social and spiritual woes," Naughton concludes: "Few people are in a better position to reflect critically on the successes and failures of our policies toward the poor."

BIOGRAPHICAL/CRITICAL SOURCES:

BOOKS

Wallis, Jim, *The Soul of Politics: A Practical and Prophetic Vision for Change*, Orbis Books (Maryknoll, NY), 1994.

PERIODICALS

Boston Globe, November 28, 1994, p. 31.

Commonweal, December 16, 1994, pp. 18-19.
Nation, November 7, 1994, pp. 536-42.
Washington Post Book World, January 22, 1995, p. 6.*

*   *   *

WANIEK, Marilyn Nelson 1946-

PERSONAL: Born April 26, 1946, in Cleveland, OH; daughter of Melvin M. (in U.S. Air Force) and Johnnie (a teacher; maiden name, Mitchell) Nelson; married Erdmann F. Waniek, September, 1970 (divorced); married Roger R. Wilkenfeld (a university professor), November 22, 1979; children (second marriage): Jacob, Dora. *Education:* University of California, Davis, B.A., 1968; University of Pennsylvania, M.A., 1970; University of Minnesota, Ph.D., 1979. *Politics:* "Yes." *Religion:* "Yes."

ADDRESSES: Office—Department of English, University of Connecticut, 337 Mansfield Rd., U-25, Storrs, CT 06269-1025.

CAREER: National Lutheran Campus Ministry, lay associate, 1969-70; Lane Community College, Eugene, OR, assistant professor of English, 1970-72; Norre Nissum Seminariam, Norre Nissum, Denmark, teacher of English, 1972-73; Saint Olaf College, Northfield, MN, instructor in English, 1973-78; University of Connecticut, Storrs, assistant professor, 1978-82, associate professor, 1982-88, professor of English, 1988—. Visiting assistant professor, Reed College, 1971-72, and Trinity College, 1982; visiting professor, New York University, 1988, 1994, and XT College, 1991; Elliston Professor, University of Cincinnati, 1994.

MEMBER: Society for the Study of Multi-Ethnic Literature of the United States, Society for Values in Higher Education, Associated Writing Programs.

AWARDS, HONORS: Kent fellow, 1976; National Endowment for the Arts fellow, 1981 and 1990; CT Arts award, 1990; National Book Award finalist, 1991; Annisfield-Wolf award, 1992; Fulbright teaching fellow (France), 1995.

WRITINGS:

POEMS

For the Body, Louisiana State University Press (Baton Rouge), 1978.
(With Pamela Espeland) *The Cat Walked through the Casserole and Other Poems for Children*, Carolrhoda (Minneapolis, MN), 1984.
Mama's Promises, Louisiana State University Press, 1985.
The Homeplace, Louisiana State University Press, 1990.
Magnificat, Louisiana State University Press, 1994.

OTHER

(Translator) Pil Dahlerup, *Literary Sex Roles,* Minnesota Women in Higher Education (Minneapolis), 1975.

(Translator with Espeland) Halfdan Rasmussen, *Hundreds of Hens and Other Poems for Children,* Black Willow Press (Minneapolis), 1982.

Contributor to *Gettysburg Review* and *Obsidian II.*

SIDELIGHTS: "Aframerican" poet Marilyn Nelson, who dropped the "Waniek" from her name in 1995, writes in a variety of styles about many subjects. She has also written verse for children and translated poetry from Danish and German. Kirkland C. Jones in the *Dictionary of Literary Biography* calls Waniek "one of the major voices of a younger generation of black poets."

Waniek's first collection, *For the Body,* focuses on the relationships between individuals and the larger social groupings of family, extended family, and society. Using domestic settings and memories of her own childhood, Waniek fashions poetry which "sometimes sings, sometimes narrates," as Jones describes it. In *Mama's Promises,* Waniek continues experimentation with poetic forms in poems about her childhood, her relationship with her mother and daughter, and a woman's role in marriage and society, but she utilizes stanzaic division more than in her previous work. The poems in *Mama's Promises* also seem to bear a cumulative theological weight, as the "Mama" named in each poem is revealed in the last poem to be God.

In *The Homeplace* Waniek turns her attention to the history of her own family, telling their story from the time of her great-great-grandmother to the present in a series of interconnected poems ranging in style from traditional forms to colloquial free-verse. Some critics praised the variety of poetic expression which Waniek displays. "The sheer range of Waniek's voice," Christian Wiman writes in *Shenandoah,* "is one of the book's greatest strengths, varying not only from poem to poem, but within individual poems as well." Suzanne Gardinier, reviewing the book for *Parnassus,* finds that through her poems Waniek "reaches back through generations hemmed in on all sides by slavery and its antecedents; all along the way she finds sweetness, and humor, and more complicated truth than its disguises have revealed."

In her poetry for children Waniek also writes of family situations, although in a humorous manner. Her collection *The Cat Walked through the Casserole and Other Poems for Children,* written with Pamela Espeland, contains poems about domestic problems and pleasures. The title poem, for example, tells of the family dog and cat and the trouble they cause throughout the neighborhood, leading the mother to decide that they must go. Such poems as "Grampa's Whiskers," "When I Grow Up," and "Queen of the Rainbow" also focus on family life in a light-hearted manner.

Although biblical allusions appear in even her earliest poems, only with the collection *Magnificat* does Waniek write directly of spiritual subjects. Inspired by her friendship with a Benedictine monk, Waniek tells of her religious awakening to a more profound sense of Christian devotion. Writing in *Multicultural Review,* Mary Walsh Meany finds Waniek's voice—"humorous, earthy, tender, joyous, sorrowful, contemplative, speculative, attached, detached, sometimes silent"—to be what "makes the poems wonderful." The critic for *Publishers Weekly* believes that Waniek's "passion, sincerity and self-deprecating humor will engage even the most skeptical reader."

BIOGRAPHICAL/CRITICAL SOURCES:

BOOKS

Dictionary of Literary Biography, Volume 120: *American Poets since World War II, Third Series,* Gale (Detroit), 1992.

PERIODICALS

Booklist, September 1, 1994, p. 20.
Hudson Review, summer, 1991, p. 346.
Kenyon Review, spring, 1991, p. 179.
Multicultural Review, March, 1995.
Parnassus, Volume 17, number 1, 1992, pp. 65-78.
Publishers Weekly, November 16, 1990, p. 52; August 29, 1994, p. 67.
School Library Journal, June, 1991, p. 137.
Shenandoah, winter, 1992.

*   *   *

WARK, Wesley K. 1952-

PERSONAL: Born December 31, 1952, in Edmonton, Alberta, Canada; son of Kenneth A. (a general in the Royal Canadian Air Force) and Noreen (Wellman) Wark. *Education:* Carleton University, B.A. (with honors), 1975; Cambridge University, M.A., 1977; London School of Economics and Political Science, London, Ph.D., 1984.

ADDRESSES: Office—Department of History, University of Toronto, 100 St. George St., Toronto, Canada M5S 1A1.

CAREER: McGill University, Montreal, Quebec, visiting lecturer in history, 1982; University of Calgary, Calgary, Alberta, sessional lecturer, 1983-84, assistant professor, 1984-86, associate professor of history, 1986-87; University of Toronto, Toronto, Ontario, associate professor,

1988—, director of international relations program, 1992—.

MEMBER: Royal United Services Institute, Canadian Institute of International Affairs, Canadian Association for Security and Intelligence Studies.

AWARDS, HONORS: Book Award from National Intelligence Study Center, Washington, DC, 1985, for *The Ultimate Enemy: British Intelligence and Nazi Germany, 1933-1939;* Arthur Ellis Award, 1991, for *Spy Fiction, Spy Films and Real Intelligence.*

WRITINGS:

The Ultimate Enemy: British Intelligence and Nazi Germany, 1933-1939, Cornell University Press (Ithica, NY), 1985.

EDITOR

Security and Intelligence in a Changing World, Frank Cass (London), 1991.
Spy Fiction, Spy Films and Real Intelligence, Frank Cass (London), 1991.
Espionage: Past, Present, Future?, Frank Cass (London), 1994.

OTHER

Editor of *Intelligence and National Security.*

WORK IN PROGRESS: A history of the "intelligence revolution" and international relations during the twentieth century; a study of the popular culture of espionage during the Cold War.

SIDELIGHTS: Wesley K. Wark told *CA:* "I am interested in the study of intelligence as an intriguing field of historical research and as a much misunderstood force in international relations. My first book, *The Ultimate Enemy: British Intelligence and Nazi Germany, 1933-1939,* explored the nature of British intelligence assessments of German power in the 1930s. The argument of the book is that poor intelligence contributed to the failure of appeasement policy and the outbreak of World War II. My future work in this field will concentrate on the impact of changes in the power of intelligence services on the conduct of international relations, and on popular attitudes towards espionage, as shaped by spy fiction and film.

"My research for a biography of Field Marshal Ironside stems from my interest in Ironside's career as a senior military leader in Britain in the 1930s. Access to the Ironside private papers allows me fresh insights into the role and thought of this controversial figure, who began his rise to fame as a spy in the Boer War and ended as Chief of the Imperial General Staff during the debacle in France in 1940."

BIOGRAPHICAL/CRITICAL SOURCES:

PERIODICALS

Times Literary Supplement, July 4, 1986.

*   *   *

WERTSMAN, Vladimir (F.) 1929-

PERSONAL: Born April 6, 1929, in Secureni, Romania; immigrated to the United States, 1967; naturalized U.S. citizen, 1972; son of Filip and Anna Wertsman. *Education:* University of A. I. Cuza, LL.M. (legal sciences; summa cum laude), 1953; Columbia University, M.S.L.S., 1969. *Avocational interests:* Chess, stamp-collecting, music, travel (including Europe, Asia, South America, Africa, and Central America).

ADDRESSES: Office—330 West 55th St., Apt. 3G, New York, NY 10019.

CAREER: Lawyer with practice in criminal and civil law in Romania, 1953-67; First National City Bank, New York City, stock certificates examiner, 1967-68; Brooklyn Public Library, Brooklyn, NY, reference librarian in Science and Industry Division, 1969-74, assistant branch librarian at Canarsie Branch, 1974-77, and at Greenpoint Branch, 1977-80, branch librarian at Leonard Branch, 1980-82; New York Public Library, New York City, senior librarian and Slavic and Romanian languages specialist at Foreign Language Library, Donnell Library Center, 1982-86, senior librarian at Learner's Advisory Service and Job Information Center, Mid-Manhattan Library, 1987-92.

MEMBER: International Social Science Honor Society, American Library Association, Public Library Association (chair of multilingual materials and library service committee, 1985-87, and Leonard Wertheimer multilingual award committee, 1988-90), Ethnic Materials Information Exchange Round Table (chair of publishing and multicultural materials committees, 1988—; member of multicultural award committee, 1994—), American Association for the Advancement of Slavic Studies, American Romanian Academy of Arts and Sciences, American Society of Writers, Independent Press Association, Slavic American Cultural Association (member of board of directors), Delta Tau Kappa.

AWARDS, HONORS: Distinguished Literary Achievement Award, American Society of Writers, 1977, for article "Dracula's Revenge: 500 Years of Facts, Fiction, and Mystery"; Special Merit Award, Public Library Association, 1988, for "services contributing to the continuing success of America's public libraries in serving their communities."

WRITINGS:

The Romanians in America, 1748-1974, Oceana (Dobbs Ferry, NY), 1975.

The Ukrainians in America, 1608-1975, Oceana, 1976.

The Russians in America, 1727-1970, Oceana, 1977.

The Armenians in America, 1618-1976, Oceana, 1978.

(Editor) *The Romanians in America and Canada: A Guide to Information Sources,* Gale (Detroit), 1980.

(Coauthor) *The Ukrainians in Canada and the United States,* Gale, 1981.

(With Bosiljka Stevanovic) *Free Voices in Russian Literature, 1950s-1980s,* Russica (New York, NY), 1986.

(Contributor) *Proceedings of the Second International Conference of Slavic Librarians,* Russica, 1986.

(Contributor) *The Immigrant Labor Press in North America, 1840s-1970s,* Greenwood (Westport, CT), 1987.

Librarian's Companion: A Handbook of Facts and Figures on Books, Libraries, and Librarians, Greenwood Press, 1987.

Multilingual America: Directory of Education and Employment Resources for Job Hunters with Language Skills, Scarecrow (Metuchen, NJ), 1990, enlarged second edition, 1994.

(Contributor) *Multicultural Acquisitions,* Howarth, 1993.

(Contributor) *Gale Encyclopedia of Multicultural America,* Gale, 1995.

(Editor and compiler) *Directory of Ethnic and Multicultural Publishers, Distributors and Resource Organizations,* 3rd edition, Ethnic Materials Information Exchange Round Table (New York, NY), 1995.

(Editor and compiler) *What's Cooking in Multicultural America: An Annotated Bibliographic Guide to over 400 National/Ethnic Cuisines,* Scarecrow, 1995.

Editorial consultant for *Harvard Encyclopedia of American Ethnic Groups,* Harvard University Press (Cambridge, MA), 1980. Contributor of over fifty articles and book reviews to periodicals, including *Booklist, Ethnic Forum, Law Books in Review, Topical Time,* and *What's New in Scholarly Books.* Editor, *EMIE Bulletin,* 1982-86.

WORK IN PROGRESS: A reference book devoted to memorable quotations about New York City "from over 500 American and foreign notables, covering the last five centuries. Many quotations appear for the first time in English translation."

SIDELIGHTS: Vladimir Wertsman once told *CA:* "As a book lover since early school days, I view my present professions—librarian and author—as twin brothers, two happy companions who inspire and supplement each other. Being an ethnic American and multilingual, I have devoted my writings to various ethnic American groups and languages. Multi-ethnicity (multiculture) is the spice

of America, and American history is, in essence, multi-ethnic."

Wertsman is fluent in Russian, Romanian, and Ukrainian, and has a working knowledge of all the Slavic and Romance languages.

BIOGRAPHICAL/CRITICAL SOURCES:

PERIODICALS

American Romanian Review, May, 1980.
Choice, January, 1988.
Ethnic American News, October, 1975.
Ethnic Forum, spring, 1982.
National Genealogical Inquirer, summer, 1980.
National Genealogical Society Quarterly, June, 1981.
RQ, spring, 1988.
Solia, May, 1980.
Unirea, May, 1980.

*   *   *

WHARTON, Annabel (Jane)
(Ann Wharton Epstein)

PERSONAL: Born in New Rochelle, NY; daughter of H. Jerome and Jane (Holman) Wharton; children: Nicole Alexandra Epstein, Andrea Jerry Epstein. *Education:* University of Wisconsin—Madison, B.Sc., 1966; University of Chicago, M.A., 1969; Courtauld Institute of Art, London, Ph.D., 1975.

ADDRESSES: Office—Department of Art and Art History, Box 90764, Duke University, Durham, NC 27708-0764.

CAREER: University of Birmingham, Birmingham, England, research fellow in Byzantine art at Barber Institute, 1971-75; Oberlin College, Oberlin, OH, assistant professor of medieval art, 1975-78; Duke University, Durham, NC, professor of art history, 1979—.

MEMBER: International Center for Medieval Art (past member of board of directors), Byzantine Studies Conference (past president of board of directors), College Art Association.

AWARDS, HONORS: Visiting fellow at Dumbarton Oaks, 1978-79; fellow of American Council of Learned Societies, 1981-82; fellow at National Humanities Center, 1985-86; fellow, Center for the Advanced Study of the Visual Arts, National Gallery, Washington, DC, 1992-93.

WRITINGS:

(Under name Ann Wharton Epstein; with A. P. Kazhdan) *Change in Byzantine Culture in the Eleventh and*

Twelfth Centuries, University of California Press (Berkeley, CA), 1985.

(Under name Ann Wharton Epstein) *Tokalikilise: Tenth Century Metropolitan Art in Byzantine Cappadocia,* Dumbarton Oaks (Washington, DC), 1986.

(Under name Ann Wharton Epstein) *Art of Empire: Painting and Architecture of the Byzantine Periphery,* Pennsylvania State University Press (State College, PA), 1987.

(Under name Annabel Wharton) *Refiguring the Post Classical City,* Cambridge University Press (Cambridge, England), 1995.

OTHER

Contributor to art, history, and archaeology journals. Byzantine editor of *Greek, Roman, and Byzantine Studies;* editor of *Journal of Medieval and Early Modern Studies.* Former member of editorial board, *Art Bulletin.*

SIDELIGHTS: Change in Byzantine Culture in the Eleventh and Twelfth Centuries was described by Cyril Mango in the *Times Literary Supplement* as a book which "ranges over a wide assortment of cultural manifestations set within a social context," a work in which Annabel Wharton and her co-author have given detailed consideration to the factors which contributed to significant changes in Byzantine culture in the eleventh and twelfth centuries. These include a geographical movement of the population away from urban areas toward the provinces coupled with the rise of feudal government; the emergence of intellectual and aristocratic elites; an increase in verbal opposition to authority and an increase in the popularity of vernacular, as opposed to traditional, literature; and a more widespread acceptance of foreign culture. Mango concluded in his review that Wharton and her co-author "have given us an abundance of raw material needed to construct an explanation of these phenomena."

BIOGRAPHICAL/CRITICAL SOURCES:

PERIODICALS

American Historical Review, June, 1986.
Times Literary Supplement, October 17, 1986.

*   *   *

WHEELER, Richard 1922-

PERSONAL: Born January 8, 1922, in Reading, PA; son of Clarence E. and Margaret (Wenrich) Wheeler. *Education:* Attended public school in Laureldale, PA. *Politics:* Nonpartisan.

ADDRESSES: Home—RD 1, Box 135, Pine Grove, PA 17963 (summer); 328 Pilgrim Rd., West Palm Beach, FL

33405 (winter). *Agent*—McIntosh & Otis, Inc., 310 Madison Ave., New York, NY 10017.

CAREER: Worked on a small weekly newspaper, now defunct, for several years after World War II; full-time writer, 1949—, writing light verse for magazines for about fifteen years before switching to prose. *Military service:* U.S. Marines, 1942-45; received Purple Heart for wounds received on Iwo Jima.

AWARDS, HONORS: Christopher Award, 1973, for *Voices of 1776;* Fletcher Pratt Award, 1977, for *Voices of the Civil War.*

WRITINGS:

The Bloody Battle for Suribachi, Crowell (New York City), 1965.
In Pirate Waters, Crowell, 1969.
Voices of 1776, Crowell, 1972.
Voices of the Civil War (Book-of-the-Month Club alternate selection), Crowell, 1976.
We Knew Stonewall Jackson, Crowell, 1977.
We Knew William Tecumseh Sherman, Crowell, 1977.
The Siege of Vicksburg, Crowell, 1978.
Sherman's March, Crowell, 1978.
Iwo (Military Book Club main selection), Crowell, 1980.
A Special Valor: The U.S. Marines and the Pacific War (Military Book Club main selection), Harper (New York City), 1983.
Sword over Richmond, Harper, 1986.
Witness to Gettysburg (Book-of-the-Month Club alternate selection), Harper, 1987.
Witness to Appomattox, Harper, 1989.
On Fields of Fury, Harper, 1991.
Lee's Terrible Swift Sword (Military Book Club main selection), Harper, 1992.
A Rising Thunder, Harper, 1994.

WORK IN PROGRESS: Another Civil War history.

SIDELIGHTS: "I began writing at age five in 1927," writes Richard Wheeler to *CA,* "and still have my very first manuscript, a little tale with a sylvan setting entitled, 'A Day in the Woos (sic).' All I ever wanted to do was write, and, except for time out during the war years, I have done little else. Handicapped by a lack of brilliance, I had to tackle the job wholly as a craft. It has been extremely hard work, and I am still a plodder. My best efforts net me only a page or two a day. But I have persisted and am now working on my seventeenth book. All have been concerned with presenting the human side of American military history. My rewards? The convenience of working at home; the privilege of living North in summer and South in winter; a great many letters from readers who seem to have understood what I've been trying to do; and generally happy reviews, including two cherished ones in the

New Yorker. Money? Well, it's been a living—which, considering the odds against me, I suppose is saying pretty much."

During the battle for Mount Suribachi, Wheeler's platoon lost forty-two of its original forty-six men. While recuperating in the hospital from his injuries, Wheeler wrote a long account of what actually had happened and used it for his first magazine article, "The *First* Flag Raising on Iwo Jima," which appeared in *American Heritage,* June, 1964, as well as for his book *The Bloody Battle for Suribachi.* He says of his part in the battle, "I was a very scared marine surrounded by heroes."

BIOGRAPHICAL/CRITICAL SOURCES:

PERIODICALS

New Yorker, July 26, 1976; May 12, 1980.
Saturday Review, November 6, 1965.
Time, August 30, 1976.
Washington Post Book World, December 18, 1983.

* * *

WHEELWRIGHT, Edward Lawrence 1921-

PERSONAL: Born August 19, 1921, in Sheffield, England; son of Lawrence (a steel worker) and Gladys Wheelwright; married Wendy McGregor, August 17, 1945; children: Helga, Sarah Jane. *Education:* University of St. Andrews, M.A. (with first class honors), 1949; attended Harvard University, 1958, University of Toronto, National Institute of Economic and Planning Research (London, England), National Planning Commission (New Delhi, India), and University of Djakarta. *Politics:* Socialist. *Religion:* Atheist. *Avocational interests:* "Early morning swim in the sea year-round."

ADDRESSES: Home—14 Somerset St., Mosman, Sydney, New South Wales 2088, Australia. *Office*—Department of Economics, University of Sydney, Sydney, New South Wales 2006, Australia.

CAREER: University of Bristol, Bristol, England, assistant lecturer in economics, 1949-52; University of Sydney, Sydney, Australia, lecturer, 1952-57, senior lecturer, 1957-65, associate professor of economics, 1965-86, acting head of department, 1967-68, founder and director of Transnational Corporations Research Project, 1975—. Visiting fellow at Research School of Pacific Studies, Australian National University, 1962; lecturer at University of Malaya, University of Singapore, and Catholic University of Buenos Aires; visiting professor at Di Tella Institute of Economic Research, 1965-66, Institute of Economics, Moscow, Soviet Union, 1966, Academy of Science, Peking, China, 1966-67, Institute of International Research,

University of Chile, 1970-71, and University of Alberta, Canada, 1982. Member of Committee of Enquiry Into Government Procurement Policy, 1973-74; member of committee of Enquiry Into Australian Manufacturing Industry, 1974-75; director of Commonwealth Banking Corporation, 1975-80; council member of University of New England, 1983-84. United Nations consultant to government of Malaysia. *Military service:* Royal Air Force, 1941-46; became squadron leader; received Distinguished Flying Cross.

MEMBER: Economic Society, Australian Consumer Association, Teachers Federation, Friends of the Earth.

WRITINGS:

Ownership and Control of Australian Companies, Law Book Co. of Australia, 1957.
Industrialization in Malaysia, Melbourne University Press (Melbourne, Australia), 1965.
Radical Political Economy: Collected Essays, Australia and New Zealand Book Co. (Brookvale), 1974.
Capitalism, Socialism, or Barbarism?: The Australian Predicament, Australia and New Zealand Book Co., 1978.
Oil and World Politics: From Rockefeller to the Gulf War, Left Book Club, 1991.

COAUTHOR

(With Brian Fitzpatrick) *The Highest Bidder: A Citizen's Guide to Problems of Foreign Investment in Australia,* Lansdowne Press (Willoughby, Australia), 1965.
(With Judith Miskelly) *Anatomy of Australian Manufacturing Industry,* Law Book Co. of Australia, 1967.
(With Bruce McFarlane) *The Chinese Road to Socialism,* Monthly Review Press, 1971.
(With Greg Crough) *Australia: A Client State,* Allen & Unwin (North Sydney, Australia), 1982.
(With Ken Buckley) *Capitalism and the Common People in Australia: The First 200 Years,* Oxford University Press (Melbourne), 1987.
(With Abe David) *The Third Wave: Australia and Asian Capitalism,* Left Book CLub, 1989.

EDITOR

Higher Education in Australia, F. W. Cheshire (Melbourne), 1965.
(With Buckley) *Essays in the Political Economy of Australian Capitalism,* Australia and New Zealand Book Co., Volume I, 1975, Volume II, 1978, Volume III, 1978, Volume IV, 1980, Volume V, 1982.
(With Frank J. B. Stilwell) *Readings in Political Economy,* two volumes, Australia and New Zealand Book Co., 1978.
(With Crough and Ted Wilshire) *Australia and the World Capitalism,* Penguin (Ringwood, Australia), 1980.

Consumers, Transnational Corporations, and Development, Transnational Corporations Research Project, University of Sydney, 1986.

(With Buckley) *Communications and the Media in Australia,* Allen & Unwin, 1986.

OTHER

Contributor to numerous books including *Education for International Understanding,* Australian National Advisory Committee for United Nations Educational, Scientific, and Cultural Organization, 1959; *Economics of Australian Industry,* edited by Alex Hunter, Melbourne University Press, 1963; *Sociology of Education,* edited by F. M. Katz and R. K. Browne, Melbourne University Press, 1970; *Capitalism in Australia: A Socialist Critique,* edited by John Playford, Penguin, 1972; *Unemployment: Are There Lessons from History?,* edited by Jill Roe, Hale & Ironmonger, 1985; *Looking Ahead: Can Marx Help?,* edited by Edwin Dowdy, Queensland University Press, 1986; *A Biographical Dictionary of Dissenting Economists,* edited by Philip Arestis and Malcolm Sawyer, Edward Elgar (London), 1992; *Beyond the Market,* edited by Stuart Rees, Gordon Ridley, and Frank Stilwell, Pluto Press (Sydney), 1993; and *Five Voices for Lionel,* edited by V. G. Venturini, Federation Press (Sydney), 1994. Also contributor to journals and popular magazines.

The Chinese Road to Socialism has been translated into six languages.

WORK IN PROGRESS: Writing memoirs, *Confessions of an Economic Heretic in Australia;* (with Abe David) *The Struggle for Australia.*

SIDELIGHTS: Edward Lawrence Wheelwright told *CA:* "My major interest is what makes the world tick. I decided that the main answer is to be found in the study of political economy. The economics profession is dominated by conservative 'dessicated calculating machines' who have no answer to the world's problems. I firmly believe, with John Ruskin, that 'there is no wealth but life'—hence the importance of studying how the other half lives.

"I am now concentrating on the spread of international capitalism and on the reaction to it in various parts of the world by governments, trade unions, consumer organizations, churches, and environmentalists. I see this as a prime mover in shaping the future of the world economically, politically, socially, and culturally.

"I am convinced that giant global corporations must be made more socially responsible and I shall be concentrating on how this may be achieved, especially in financial matters, and their impact on the environment. The corporation, which enjoys limited liability, is a creature of society, and must be made more responsible to it, if there is to be a stable future for the earth and its peoples.

"My . . . work is concentrating on the new form that global capitalism is taking, especially after the collapse of communism. All the contradictions of capitalism are now much freer to emerge on the world stage, increasing concentration, over-production, inequality, instability, and environmental degradation. Free market dogmas, enshrined in economic rationalism, are creating a new kind of ideological totalitarianism which must be combatted if mankind is to move forward into the 21st century, and not backwards into the 19th."*

*　　*　　*

WHITCOMB, Meg W.   1930-

PERSONAL: Born December 14, 1930, in Minneapolis, MN; daughter of Harold F. and Ruth Whittle; married Arthur Bryant Whitcomb (a publishing executive), July 28, 1957; children: Glenny Halliday, Mary Bryant, Arthur Bryant, Jr. *Education:* Attended University of Colorado, Pasadena City College, and L'Institut Britanic, University of Paris. *Religion:* Protestant.

ADDRESSES: Home—32 Ravine Rd., Pawling, NY 12564. *Office*—Murdoch Magazines, 660 White Plains Rd., Tarrytown, NY 10591; Robbins Office, 866 Second Ave., New York, NY 10017.

CAREER: Life, New York, NY, editor of "Letters to the Editor," 1954-58; *Weekly Review,* London, England, United Nations correspondent, 1962-69; Murdoch Magazines, Tarrytown, NY, weekly advice columnist for *Star* under by-line "Dear Meg," 1973—. Executive editor of *50 Plus,* 1978-84; host of *The Dear Meg Show,* on NBC's Talknet, 1985-86.

AWARDS, HONORS: ERA America Award from the White House, 1979.

WRITINGS:

Dear Meg: New Ways of Living Well in the Eighties, William Morrow (New York City), 1984.
How to Write the Ten Most Important Letters of Your Life, Warner Books (New York City), 1986.
Size 14 Is Not a Sin, Merit Press, 1994.

*　　*　　*

WHITFORD, Frank   1941-

PERSONAL: Born August 11, 1941, in Bishopstoke, England; son of Percy (a public servant) and Pat (a teacher; maiden name, Rowe) Whitford; married Cecilia Josephine Dresser (a librarian), July 18, 1972. *Education:* Wadham College, Oxford, B.A., 1963; Courtauld Institute of Art,

London, M.A., 1965; attended Free University of Berlin, 1968-69; Royal College of Art, London, Higher Doctorate, 1989. *Avocational interests:* Travel (Europe, North America, India, Australia, the Far East, including Japan).

ADDRESSES: Home—69 High St., Great Wilbraham, Cambridge CB1 5JD, England. *Agent*—Abner Stein, 10 Roland Gardens, London SW7, England.

CAREER: University of London, England, lecturer in art history, 1970-75; Cambridge University, Homerton College, Cambridge, England, lecturer in art history, 1975—. Royal College of Art, London, visiting tutor in cultural history, 1982—, and tutor, 1986-92. Sunday *Times* (London), art critic, 1991-93.

AWARDS, HONORS: Award from Yorkshire Post, 1977, for *Japanese Prints and Western Painters.*

WRITINGS:

Kandinsky, Paul Hamlyn (London), 1967.

Expressionism, Paul Hamlyn, 1970.

Japanese Prints and Western Painters, Macmillan (London), 1977.

Tokio, DuMont, 1980.

Egon Schiele, Oxford University Press (New York City), 1980.

(With Keith Hartley) *Kathe Kollwitz, 1867-1945; The Graphic Works: An Exhibition* (monograph), Kettle's Yard Gallery (Cambridge, England), 1981.

Bauhaus, Thames & Hudson (London and New York City), 1984.

(Author of introduction and notes) Grosz, George, *The Face of the Ruling Class* (monograph), Allison & Busby (New York City), 1984.

(Author of introduction and notes) Grosz, *The Day of Reckoning* (monograph), Allison & Busby, 1984.

Oskar Kokoschka: A Life, Antheneum (New York City), 1986.

Understanding Abstract Art, Dutton (New York City), 1987.

Expressionist Portraits, Abbeville Press (New York City), 1987.

Klimt, Thames & Hudson, 1990.

(Editor) *The Bauhaus: Masters and Students by Themselves,* Overlook Press (Woodstock, NY), 1993.

Contributing editor of *Studio International,* 1964-74.

SIDELIGHTS: Frank Whitford's biography *Egon Schiele,* "with its carefully selected illustrations, its sensitive analyses of individual works, and its clear presentation of an important artist's ambience and development, is sure to help its readers to understand and appreciate even where they cannot unreservedly love or admire," writes S. S. Prawer in the *Times Literary Supplement.* Prawer adds: "The texture and structure of Whitford's book are equally satisfactory. He writes in an attractively plain, jargon-free manner and has found a simple and thoroughly sensible way of ordering his abundant material."

Whitford's 1986 work, *Oskar Kokoschka: A Life,* is the biography of Kokoschka, a Viennese expressionist painter and dramatist. "Frank Whitford's 'Oskar Kokoschka: A Life' makes poignant reading as the story of an artist whose career was caught up in the turbulent European events of our self-destructive century but who kept his faith in human and humane values to the end," asserts Marc Jordan in the *New York Times Book Review.* Jordan further describes the biography as "intelligent, informative and brisk." A *Washington Post Book World* critic notes that the book "provides much new information on one of the chief architects of German Expressionism."

Whitford himself states in the acknowledgments following the text that *Oskar Kokoschka: A Life* cannot be considered the definitive biography of the Austrian artist. Joy Hakanson Colby of the *Detroit News* concedes but considers the book "intelligent and readable." John Gross of the *New York Times* comments that Whitford "writes with a clarity and mastery of detail that inspire confidence in his judgment when he comes to deal with the many confused or controversial episodes that punctuate his story." Gross concludes that the author "provides a coherent and convincing portrait of a remarkable man." Rudolf Arnheim of the *Los Angeles Times Book Review* remarks, "Whitford's descriptions of events and characters are detailed and accurate, and given the captivating wealth of the panorama, especially that of the Europe preceding the Nazi period, his book makes for fascinating reading." While Arnheim questions Whitford's descriptions of Kokoschka's work, labeling them "dry technicalities," he nonetheless finds the book "the most careful documentation yet put together on the subject."

Whitford told *CA:* "Typecasting is the bane not only of the actor's life and I'm certainly not the only writer of modest gifts and reputation who finds it difficult to get out of a narrow rut. Having been commissioned to produce a small number of books about art I am now considered by publishers only as a likely author of similar books about similarly narrow subjects and historical periods. It would be churlish to complain too loudly about this for I'm lucky to receive commissions at all, but I hope that it will eventually be possible to publish something entirely different: that thriller, for instance, set in an exotic location which we all have boiling merrily away in the pot but can't quite bring to completion because other things are always demanding our attention first.

"So far, and with the exception of a book about Tokyo, my subjects have always been aspects of the visual arts. Writing and publishing such books have their peculiar difficulties. There's the uneasy feeling that both readers and publishers regard the text as so much gray matter whose only purpose is to set off the illustrations to the best advantage. There's also the problem of finding the right tone of voice. How does one produce a text that fellow academics won't dismiss as journalism and the lay public won't regard as hopelessly specialized?

"It is not only a privilege to write and be paid for it; there are also numerous fringe benefits. The best of these for me is that travel is frequently involved. There may be something to the celebrated saying that 'travel is a substitute for real experience' but I believe travel to be the best way of learning to experience the most mundane things as thought they were freshly minted. The more different the culture and society of the country you visit are from your own, the easier it is to do this. This is why I try to travel to Japan as often as possible. The more I discover about the place the more ignorant I feel. That, too, is a salutary experience."

BIOGRAPHICAL/CRITICAL SOURCES:

PERIODICALS

Detroit News, October 12, 1986.
Los Angeles Times Book Review, June 1, 1986, p.2.
New Yorker, November 10, 1986.
New York Times, July 19, 1986.
New York Times Book Review, September 7, 1986.
Times Literary Supplement, April 3, 1981; October 3, 1986.
Village Voice, January 20, 1987.
Washington Post Book World, July 13, 1986.

*   *   *

WINNIFRITH, Thomas John   1938-

PERSONAL: Born April 5, 1938, in London, England; son of John Digby (a civil servant) and Lesbia (Cochrane) Winnifrith; married Joanna Victoria Lee Booker, July 3, 1967 (died October 1, 1976); married Helen Mary Young, March 19, 1988; children: (first marriage) Thomas, Tabitha, Naomi; (second marriage) three stepchildren. *Education:* Christ Church, Oxford, B.A., 1960, M.A., 1963; Corpus Christi College, Oxford, B.Phil., 1968; University of Liverpool, Ph.D., 1970.

ADDRESSES: Home—40 Newbold Terrace East, Leamington Spa, Warwickshire, England. *Office*—Department of English and Comparative Literary Studies, University of Warwick, Conventry, Warwickshire, England.

CAREER: Assistant master of private boys' secondary school in Eton, England, 1961-66; University of Warwick, Conventry, England, lecturer, 1970-77, senior lecturer in English and comparative literary studies, 1977-92, chair of Graduate School of Comparative Literature, 1975-79, chair of Joint School of Classics, 1982-88, chair of Department of English and Comparative Studies, 1989-92. Visiting research fellow, All Souls College, Oxford, 1984; director of European Humanities Research Centre, 1985-90.

WRITINGS:

The Brontes and Their Background: Romance and Reality, Barnes & Noble (New York City) and Macmillan (London), 1973.
The Brontes, Macmillan (London and New York City), 1977.
(With Edward Chitham) *Bronte Facts and Bronte Problems,* Humanities Press (Atlantic Highlands, NJ), 1983.
(With William V. Whitehead) *1984 and All's Well?,* Macmillan (London), 1984.
The Vlachs: The History of the Balkan People, St. Martin's Press (New York City) and Duckworth (London), 1987.
A New Life of Charlotte Bronte, St. Martin's Press (New York City) and Macmillan (London), 1988.
(With Chitham) *Charlotte and Emily Bronte: A Literary Life,* St. Martin's Press (New York City) and Macmillan (London), 1989.
Fallen Women in the Nineteenth Century Novel, St. Martin's Press (New York City) and Macmillan (London), 1994.

EDITOR

(With Penelope Murray, and author of introduction) *Greece Old and New,* Macmillan (London), 1983.
(And author of introduction) *The Poems of Patrick Branwell Bronte,* New York University Press (New York City) and Blackwell (London), 1983.
The Poems of Charlotte Bronte, Blackwell (Oxford and New York City), 1984.
(With Murray and K. W. Grandsden) *Aspects of the Epic,* St. Martin's Press (New York City) and Macmillan (London), 1984.
(With Chitham) *Selected Bronte Poems,* Blackwell (Oxford and New York City), 1985.
(With Cyril Barrett) *The Philosophy of Leisure,* St. Martin's Press (New York City) and Macmillan (London), 1989.
(With Barrett) *Leisure in Art and Literature,* Macmillan (London), 1992.
(And author of introduction) *Perspectives on Albania,* St. Martin's Press (New York City) and Macmillan (London), 1992.
Balkan Fragments, Duckworth, 1995.
Hardy of Wessex, Macmillan, in press.

OTHER

(Translator with James O'Malley) Janos Nyiri, *Streets,* Wildwood Press, 1979.

Contributor to *Dictionary of Literary Biography;* contributor to periodicals, including *Durham University Journal, Bronte Society Transactions,* and *Notes and Queries.* Editor, *Warwick Studies in the European Humanities,* 1985-90.

SIDELIGHTS: Thomas John Winnifrith once told *CA:* "I became interested in both the Brontes and the Balkans almost by chance, but have been allowed to develop both interests by a generous university and a generous family."

BIOGRAPHICAL/CRITICAL SOURCES:

BOOKS

Dictionary of Literary Biography, Volume 155: *Twentieth-Century British Literary Biographers,* Gale (Detroit), 1995.

PERIODICALS

Times Literary Supplement, July 13, 1984; August 9, 1985.

*   *   *

WOOD, Bari   1936-

PERSONAL: Born in 1936, in Illinois. *Education:* Graduated from Northwestern University.

ADDRESSES: Home—Ridgefield, CT. *Agent*—Owen Laster, William Morris, 1325 Avenue of the Americas, New York, NY 10019.

CAREER: Writer. Worked as editor and bibliographer for the American Cancer Society; former editor for *Drug Therapy* magazine, New York, NY.

AWARDS, HONORS: Putnam Prize, 1975, for *The Killing Gift.*

WRITINGS:

NOVELS

The Killing Gift, Putnam (New York City), 1975.
(With Jack Geasland) *Twins* (Literary Guild selection), Putnam, 1977.
The Tribe, New American Library (New York City), 1981.
Lightsource (Literary Guild alternate selection), New American Library, 1984.
Amy Girl, New American Library, 1987.
Doll's Eyes, Morrow (New York City), 1993.
The Basement Club, Morrow, 1995.

Also author of three screenplays.

ADAPTATIONS: Twins was adapted into a film entitled *Dead Ringers,* directed by David Cronenberg, starring Jeremy Irons.

WORK IN PROGRESS: A novel.

SIDELIGHTS: Bari Wood is the author of a number of fast-paced thrillers, many of them having to do with psychic powers and the ruthless devastation of serial murderers. A former magazine editor who also worked for the American Cancer Society, Wood became a full-time writer in the late 1970s with the publication of her first two novels, *The Killing Gift* and *Twins,* which she co-authored with Jack Geasland. Since then she has worked to create realistic female characters who strive to exert control over their lives and destinies. The author told *CA:* "I write women whose primary concern is not their love life, and who are at some level or other powerful in their own right; they don't derive their power from other souces such as their husbands or sex or even money. They are quite capable of behaving in powerful ways." She added: "I'd like to see more fiction in which it's just taken for granted that the woman has power, so I try to create that kind of character."

One such character is Jennifer List Gilbert, the heroine of Wood's *The Killing Gift.* The novel relates the story of Gilbert, a young woman possessed of psychokinetic powers—she is capable of controlling the physical world in violent ways simply by using her thoughts. A critic for *Publishers Weekly* believes that Wood "has done a fine job of plotting and sustaining suspense, providing new chills and surprises right up to the last page." *Spectator* reviewer Patrick Cosgrave calls *The Killing Gift* "one of the best crime novels for a long time."

In 1977 Wood, in collaboration with Jack Geasland, transformed the outlines of a sensational news story into fiction. The novel *Twins* closely follows the details as reported in the press of what investigators and reporters were able to piece together after finding the dead bodies of Cyril and Stewart Marcus in their garbage-strewn Manhattan apartment in 1975. The Marcuses, twin brothers who were both doctors and drug addicts, had apparently died of either an overdose of barbituates or of withdrawal from them. The main characters in *Twins* are also twin brothers practicing medicine who have grown up sharing a "mysterious bond" which gradually leads them into a homosexual incestuous relationship, to drug addiction, and finally, to death. Carol Eisen Rinzler, reviewing *Twins* in the *Washington Post Book World,* calls the book a "good read of the first order, a gripping, stunningly paced novel, a first-rate entertainment with which to while away a few hours."

Wood's 1981 novel *The Tribe* deals with the golem of Hebrew folklore, a giant creature made of clay who is brought to life through a ritual known only to a select few. When a crime is violently avenged in present-day New York, the victims covered with clay, a police detective must investigate the case and discover who is manipulating the golem. Discussing the work in *Library Journal,* Marcia R. Hoffman describes it as an "engrossing, fast-paced story . . . a tightly constructed novel that explores, behind the action, the nature of and justification for revenge."

In the 1980s Wood continued to pursue her fascination with "people [who] do things . . . with their minds," as she told *CA. Lightsource,* a thriller based in the near future, pits a self-reliant nuclear scientist named Emily Brand against a veritable army of foes, including the police and the henchmen of an oil magnate who views Emily as a threat to his company. *Amy Girl,* released in 1987, follows the adventures of a psychic child who has witnessed her mother's murder and who is persecuted by the teenaged son of the family who has adopted her. *Doll's Eyes,* described in *Publishers Weekly* as "a nerve-snapping, stomach-churning thriller," tells the story of Eve Klein, a psychic who is hunted by a serial killer after she "sees" his past criminal exploits. *Chicago Tribune Books* contributor Chris Petrakos notes that Wood "has displayed a knack for bizarre setups," but nonetheless one of her "more impressive achievements is her refusal to romanticize or stereotype the lead character's powers."

Wood told *CA* that her "larger" aim as an author is to endow her characters with the ability to alter their own and others' destinies. "The books are popular fiction; they're meant to be fun to read and entertaining and not to have a hell of a lot of deeper meaning," she concluded. "But I have tried to do a little more in this way."

BIOGRAPHICAL/CRITICAL SOURCES:

PERIODICALS

Chicago Tribune Books, July 18, 1993, p. 6.
Kirkus Reviews, February 15, 1987, pp. 257-58; May 15, 1993, p. 623.
Library Journal, April 1, 1981.
Los Angeles Times Book Review, August 19, 1984, p. 9.
New Statesman, July 1, 1977.
New York Times, June 9, 1977.
New York Times Book Review, May 1, 1977; August 19, 1984, p. 18.
Publishers Weekly, July 14, 1975; April 27, 1984, p. 74; March 20, 1987, p. 67; May 17, 1993, p. 62.
Spectator, April 17, 1976.
Washington Post Book World, April 24, 1977.

WOODS, Stockton
See FORREST, Richard (Stockton)

*   *   *

YOUNG, David P(ollock)   1936-

PERSONAL: Born December 14, 1936, in Davenport, IA; son of Cecil T. (a businessman) and Mary (Pollock) Young; married Chloe Hamilton (a museum curator), June 17, 1963 (died February, 1985); children: Newell Hamilton, Margaret Helen. *Education:* Carleton College, A.B., 1958; Yale University, M.A., 1959, Ph.D., 1965.

ADDRESSES: Home—220 Shipherd Circle, Oberlin, OH 44074. *Office*—Department of English, Rice Hall, Oberlin College, Oberlin, OH 44074.

CAREER: Oberlin College, Oberlin, OH, instructor, 1961-65, assistant professor, 1965-69, associate professor, 1969-73, professor, 1973-86, Longman Professor of English, 1986—.

MEMBER: Modern Language Association of America, American Association of University Professors, PEN.

AWARDS, HONORS: Tane Prize for poetry, *Massachusetts Review,* 1965; National Endowment for the Humanities fellow in England, 1967-68; U.S. Award, International Poetry Forum, 1968; Guggenheim fellow, 1978-79; National Endowment for the Arts fellow, 1981-82; major artist fellowship, Ohio Arts Council, 1990; Ohio State University Press/*The Journal* Award, 1994.

WRITINGS:

Something of Great Constancy: The Art of "A Midsummer Night's Dream," Yale University Press (New Haven, CT), 1966.
(Editor) *Twentieth-Century Interpretations of "Henry IV, Part 2,"* Prentice-Hall (New York City), 1968.
Sweating Out the Winter (poetry), University of Pittsburgh Press (Pittsburgh, PA), 1969.
(Contributor) *The Major Young Poets,* World Publishing, 1971.
(Contributor) *Just What the Country Needs: Another Poetry Anthology,* Wadsworth (Belmont, CA), 1971.
The Heart's Forest: Shakespeare's Pastoral Plays, Yale University Press, 1972.
Boxcars (poetry), Ecco Press (New York City), 1972.
Work Lights (prose poems), Cleveland State University Press (Cleveland, OH), 1977.
The Names of a Hare in English (poetry), University of Pittsburgh Press, 1979.
(Editor with Stuart Friebert) *A Field Guide to Contemporary Poetry and Poetics,* Longman (New York City), 1980.

(Editor with Friebert and Richard Zipser) *Contemporary East German Poetry: A Special Issue of "Field,"* Oberlin College (Oberlin, OH), 1980.

(Editor with Friebert) *The Longman Anthology of Contemporary American Poetry,* Longman, 1983.

Foraging (poetry), Wesleyan University Press (Middletown, CT), 1986.

Troubled Mirror: A Study of Yeats's "The Tower," University of Iowa Press (Iowa City, IA), 1987.

The Planet on the Desk: Selected and New Poems 1960-1990, Wesleyan University Press, 1991.

Night Thoughts and Henry Vaughan, Ohio State University Press (Columbus, OH), 1994.

Also author of *Earthshine* (poetry), Wesleyan University Press. Editor, with Keith Hollman, of *Magical Realist Fiction,* 1984.

TRANSLATOR

Rainer M. Rilke, *Duino Elegies,* Norton (New York City), 1978.

Four T'ang Poets, Field Translation Series/Oberlin College, 1980, revised edition published as *Five T'ang Poets,* 1990.

(With Friebert and Walker) *Valuable Nail: Selected Poems of Guenter Eich,* Field Translation Series/Oberlin College, 1981.

Miroslav Holub, *Interferon; or, On Theater,* Field Translation Series/Oberlin College, 1982.

Rainer M. Rilke, *Sonnets to Orpheus,* Wesleyan University Press, 1987.

Pablo Neruda, *The Heights of Macchu Picchu,* Songs before Zero Press, 1987.

Miroslav Holub, *Vanishing Lung Syndrome,* Faber & Faber (Winchester, MA), 1990.

Miroslav Holub, *The Dimension of the Present Moment* (essays), Faber & Faber, 1990.

Rainer M. Rilke, *The Book of Fresh Beginnings: Selected Poems,* Oberlin College Press, 1994.

OTHER

Contributor to *Criticism* and other periodicals. Editor, *Field: Contemporary Poetry and Poetics,* 1969—.

WORK IN PROGRESS: The Poet's Year: Essays on the Months and Seasons.

*　　　*　　　*

YOUSUF, Ahmed
　See ESSOP, Ahmed

ZAFREN, Herbert C(ecil) 1925-

PERSONAL: Born August 25, 1925, in Baltimore, MD; son of Morris (a tailor) and Sadie Mildred (Edlavitch) Zafren; married Miriam Koenigsberg (a librarian and author of short stories), February 11, 1951; children: Ken, Edie. *Education:* Johns Hopkins University, B.A., 1944, additional study, 1946-49; Baltimore Hebrew College, diploma, 1944; University of Michigan, A.M.L.S., 1950.

ADDRESSES: Home—3863 Middleton Ave., Cincinnati, OH 45220. *Office*—Library, Hebrew Union College-Jewish Institute of Religion, 3101 Clifton Ave., Cincinnati, OH 45220.

CAREER: Hebrew Union College-Jewish Institute of Religion, Cincinnati, OH, librarian, 1950-91, director of libraries, 1966-95, director emeritus, 1995—, professor of Jewish bibliography, 1968—. American Jewish Periodical Center, Cincinnati, OH, executive director, 1958-80, co-director, 1980—. *Military service:* U.S. Navy, 1944-46.

MEMBER: World Council on Jewish Archives (vice president, 1977-81), American Library Association, American Historical Association, Association for Jewish Studies, Council of Archives and Research Libraries in Jewish Studies (president, 1974-78), Association of Jewish Libraries (founder; first president, 1966-67), Jewish Libraries Association (president, 1965-66), (secretary-treasurer, 1961—), American Printing History Association, Jewish Book Council (member of executive board, 1979—), Typophiles, Grolier Club, Phi Beta Kappa.

AWARDS, HONORS: Honorary doctorate in Hebrew literature from Baltimore Hebrew College, 1969; American Philosophical Society research grant, 1974.

WRITINGS:

(Editor) *Jewish Newspapers and Periodicals on Microfilm at the American Jewish Periodical Center,* American Jewish Periodical Center, 1960, revised edition, 1984.

(Editor) *A Gathering of Broadsides,* Society of Jewish Bibliophiles, 1967.

(Editor) *Judaica: A Short Title Catalogue of the Books, Pamphlets, and Manuscripts in the Library of Ludwig Rosenberger,* Hebrew Union College Press (Cincinnati, OH), 1971.

(Compiler with Abraham J. Peck) *The Writings of Jacob Rader Marcus,* American Jewish Archives, 1978.

Also contributor to books, including *Essays in Honor of Solomon B. Freehof,* edited by W. Jacob and others, Rodef Shalom Congregation, 1964; *Studies in Jewish Bibliography, History, and Literature in Honor of I. Edward Kiev,* Ktav (New York City), 1971; *Studies in Judaica, Karaitica and Islamica Presented to Leon Nemoy,* Bar-Ilan University Press, 1982; and *Bibliotheca Rosenthaliana: Trea-*

sures of Booklore, edited by Adrik Offenberg and others, Amsterdam University Press, 1994. Founder and editor of monograph series *Bibliographica Judaica,* 1969—. Contributor to numerous periodicals, including *College and Research Libraries, Jewish Bookland, Library Quarterly, Microform Review, Quarrendo,* and *Judaica Librarianship.* Also founder and editor of *Studies in Bibliography and Booklore,* 1953—.

WORK IN PROGRESS: Research in the history of Hebrew printing.

* * *

ZIFF, Larzer 1927-

PERSONAL: Born October 2, 1927, in Holyoke, MA; son of Isadore Menden (a manufacturer) and Sara (Rosenbloom) Ziff; married Linda Geisenberger, March 21, 1951; children: Joshua, Oliver, Joel, Abigail. *Education:* Attended Middlebury College, 1945-47; University of Chicago, M.A., 1950, Ph.D., 1955.

ADDRESSES: Office—Department of English, Johns Hopkins University, Baltimore, MD 21218.

CAREER: University of Chicago, Chicago, IL, director of academic programs at University College, 1954-56; University of California, Berkeley, professor of English, 1965-73; Oxford University, Exeter College, Oxford, England, university lecturer and fellow, 1973-78; University of Pennsylvania, Philadelphia, professor of English, 1978-81; Johns Hopkins University, Baltimore, MD, Caroline Donovan Professor of English, 1981—, department chair, 1991—. Fulbright Professor at University of Copenhagen, 1959-60, University of Warsaw, 1963, and University of Sussex, 1964. Member of State of California Commission on Teachers' Professional Standards. Consultant in English to Mills College, Birmingham, AL.

MEMBER: Modern Language Association of America (chairperson of literature and society group, 1965), American Studies Association, American Academy of Arts and Sciences (fellow).

AWARDS, HONORS: Huntington Library fellow, 1958; Newberry Library fellow, 1964; American Council of Learned Societies fellow, 1964-65; National Endowment for the Humanities senior research fellow, 1968-69; Christian Gauss Award, Phi Beta Kappa, 1967, for *The American 1890s: Life and Times of a Lost Generation;* National Book Award nominee, 1974; Guggenheim fellow, 1976; Woodrow Wilson Center fellow, 1986-87.

WRITINGS:

(Editor) *Writings of Benjamin Franklin,* Rinehart (New York City), 1959.

(Editor) Henry David Thoreau, *Walden,* Holt (New York City), 1961.

The Career of John Cotton: Puritanism and the American Experience: New Culture in a New World, Princeton University Press (Princeton, NJ), 1962.

(Editor) Nathaniel Hawthorne, *The Scarlet Letter,* Bobbs-Merrill (New York City), 1963.

The American 1890s: Life and Times of a Lost Generation, Viking (New York City), 1966.

(Editor) *John Cotton on the Churches of New England,* Harvard University Press (Cambridge, MA), 1968.

Puritanism in America: New Culture in a New World, Viking, 1973.

Literary Democracy: The Declaration of Cultural Independence in America, Viking, 1981.

(Editor and author of introduction) Ralph Waldo Emerson, *Selected Essays,* Penguin (New York City), 1982.

Upon What Pretext?: The Book and Literary History, American Antiquarian Society (Worcester, MA), 1986.

Writing in the New Nation: Prose, Print, and Politics in the Early United States, Yale University Press (New Haven, CT), 1991.

Editor of *The Genius,* by Theodore Dreiser, 1967; *The Financier,* by Dreiser, 1967; *The Literature of America: Colonial Period,* 1970; and *Selected Writings of Benjamin Franklin,* Benjamin Franklin, 1979. Also editor with Robie Macauley of *America and Its Discontents,* 1971.

Contributor to *Encyclopaedia Britannica.* Also contributor of essays to *Saturday Review* and scholarly journals.

WORK IN PROGRESS: A study of cultural reconstruction in the period of political Reconstruction following the American Civil War.

SIDELIGHTS: "Larzer Ziff is one of the foremost historians of American culture, his efforts ranging in scope from early 17th-century New England Puritanism to the beginning of the 20th-century," writes Melvin H. Buxbaum in the *Nation.* In his studies of American intellectual history, Ziff has attempted to synthesize the social and literary influences on American culture by focusing on literary works within their social context.

"It is a pleasure to welcome a study in American cultural history that is at the same time a dissertation in that field and a contribution to it," writes a *Times Literary Supplement* contributor about Ziff's *The American 1890s: Life and Times of a Lost Generation.* "The old phrase about 'wearing one's learning lightly' suits . . . Ziff very well." Ziff examines the writing of several little-known but gifted writers of the last decade of the nineteenth century, including Kate Chopin, Harold Frederic, and Frank Norris, who struggled against the accepted literary standards of morality and artistic expression. According to Stanley

Kauffmann in the *New Republic,* Ziff perceives these "morally and artistically revolutionary" writers to be "truly our lost generation—as against the celebrated lost generation of the 1920's who were in fact quickly and widely received. These earlier writers arrived too soon to overcome completely the prevailing attitudes both of the literary panjandrums and of society." Kauffmann, who finds the book "exceptional" and Ziff's critical comments "perceptive," believes that "Ziff's thesis—well articulated—is that the expanding consciousness of the best writers of the 1890's was hindered, ignored, or combated." And according to Kauffmann, "Ziff's collation of his materials, including the developments in newspapers, the arty magazines of the time, and the differing forces in fiction . . . is skillful and enlightening." The *Times Literary Supplement* contributor, who refers to Ziff's style as "allusive yet flowing," observes that "this is a splendidly readable book, but rarely at the expense of critical balance."

In a *New York Times* review of *Puritanism in America: New Culture in a New World,* Alden Whitman suggests that Ziff's "brilliantly argued and elegantly written book directly challenges" the idealistic interpretation of Puritanism. "Ziff tries to recover the human ground of Puritan experience, variously qualified by status and occupation, and subject to the external and internal stresses created by trade, Indians, the French wars and changes in England's colonial policy," writes Quentin Anderson in the *New York Times Book Review.* Buxbaum indicates in the *Nation* that Ziff "has very sensibly avoided treating ideas as if they enjoyed lives independent of daily experience, rooting them instead in material contexts." Although he wishes that Ziff had made a greater use of more recent studies of Puritanism which offer a broader scope and which "could have provided him with keener insights into Puritan social structure, belief and character," Buxbaum acknowledges that "few scholars have so successfully made Puritan experience concrete. Ziff moves skillfully among various levels of economic, political, intellectual and social structure in Puritan America, showing where those elements intermeshed." Whitman thinks that Ziff "subjects the data of history to a scrutiny that is skeptical of received authority." Similarly, in the *Yale Review,* Edmund S. Morgan notes that despite Ziff's almost exclusive dependence upon literary sources, "he has nevertheless written a book that helps us to think about Puritanism. And that is quite enough."

A concern for a synthetic understanding of culture also marks *Literary Democracy: The Declaration of Cultural Independence in America,* in which Ziff examines the literature of the period from 1837 to the Civil War, when, according to Paul Zweig in the *New York Times Book Review,* a "handful of isolated masters . . . declared America's literary maturity to a country that wasn't listening."

In a *Nation* review, Jackson Lears comments: "The book focuses on the relationship between great writers and their social milieu—in this case, the link between the classic American writers (Hawthorne, Melville, Poe, Thoreau, Emerson, Whitman) and the wave of democratic nationalism that crested during the period of their greatest work, the 1840s and 1850s. Ziff wants to show that these writers were the products and articulators of a new democratic culture that was just then declaring its independence from European tradition." Ziff examines specific literary works within their cultural-historical setting. "He interweaves the analysis of texts with sweeping, often brilliant perceptions of American social reality," states Zweig, who finds that "overall, the wealth and variety of . . . Ziff's insights prevail, making a particularly fine example of literary and intellectual history." Lears considers *Literary Democracy* to be "an exciting, provocative book, the most challenging reading of our classic literature that has appeared in recent years." And the *New York Times*'s John Leonard lauds the book as a "splendid exercise in cultural history," concluding that it "deserves every prize they give."

BIOGRAPHICAL/CRITICAL SOURCES:

PERIODICALS

Book World, October 21, 1973.
Books of the Times, October 1981.
Hudson Review, winter 1981.
Los Angeles Times Book Review, September 13, 1981.
Nation, July 5, 1975; October 17, 1981.
New Republic, December 3, 1966.
New York Review of Books, May 18, 1967.
New York Times, July 14, 1981; December 29, 1973.
New York Times Book Review, September 25, 1966; December 16, 1973; August 23, 1981; September 12, 1982.
Times Literary Supplement, February 1, 1968; May 10, 1974.
Village Voice, July 22, 1981.
Virginia Quarterly Review, autumn 1966; winter 1974.
Yale Review, spring 1974.

*   *   *

ZOHN, Harry 1923-

PERSONAL: Surname is pronounced "zone"; born November 21, 1923, in Vienna, Austria; son of A. Leon (a signpainter) and Adele (Awin) Zohn; married Judith A. Gorfinkle, September 3, 1962; children: Steven David, Marjorie Eve. *Education:* Suffolk University, B.A., 1946; Clark University, M.A. in Ed., 1947; Harvard University, A.M., 1949, Ph.D., 1952. *Religion:* Jewish.

ADDRESSES: Home—48 Davis Ave., West Newton, MA 02165. *Office*—Shiffman Hall, Brandeis University, Waltham, MA 02154.

CAREER: Brandeis University, Waltham, MA, instructor, 1951-55, assistant professor, 1955-61, associate professor, 1961-67, professor of German, 1967—, chairperson of department of Germanic and Slavic languages, 1966-77 and 1987-90, chairperson of School of Humanities, 1979-80 and 1982-83, chairperson of graduate program in literary studies, 1981-84. Violist, Brandeis University Symphony, 1974-94. Member, Commonwealth of Massachusetts Advisory Committee on Foreign Languages, 1961-64; trustee, Suffolk University, 1978-81 and 1983—.

MEMBER: International Arthur Schnitzler Research Association (vice president, 1979—), International Stefan Zweig Society (vice president, 1957-86), International Franz Werfel Society (board chairperson, 1995—), PEN American Center, PEN Center of German-Speaking Writers Abroad, American Literary Translators Association, Modern Language Association of America, American Translators Association (director, 1970-71), American Association of Teachers of German (president of Massachusetts chapter, 1956-59), Austrian PEN, New England Modern Language Association (secretary-treasurer, 1960-61; director, 1962-65), New England Translators Association, Goethe Society of New England (executive director, 1963-68), Austro-American Association of Boston (board chairperson, 1965—).

AWARDS, HONORS: Officer's Cross of the Order of Merit, Federal Republic of Germany, 1960; Litt.D., Suffolk University, 1976; Cross of Honor for Science and Art, Republic of Austria, 1984; gold medal of honor from city of Vienna, Austria, 1994; a Festschrift in honor of Zohn, *Bridging the Abyss,* edited by Amy Colin, was published by Wilhelm Fink Verlag, 1994.

WRITINGS:

Karl Kraus, Twayne (Boston, MA), 1971.
"Ich bin ein Sohn der deutschen Sprache nur": Juedisches Erbe in der oesterreichischen Literatur, Amalthea Verlag, 1986.
Amerikanische "Thirty-Eighters" aus Wien, Picus Verlag, 1994.
Austriaca and Judaica: Essays and Translations, Peter Lang, 1995.

EDITOR

Liber Amicorum Friderike Maria Zweig, Dahl Publishing, 1952.
(Coeditor) *Wie sie es sehen,* Holt (New York City), 1952.
(And translator) *The World Is a Comedy: A Kurt Tucholsky Anthology,* Sci-Art, 1957.

Stefan Zweig, *Schachnovelle,* Norton (New York City), 1960.
Wiener Juden in der deutschen Literatur, Olamenu (Tel Aviv), 1964.
(And translator with Karl F. Ross) *What If—?: Satirical Writings of Tucholsky,* Funk (New York City), 1968.
(And translator with E. William Rollins) *Men of Dialogue: Martin Buber and Albrecht Goes,* Funk, 1969.
Oesterreichische Juden in der Literatur: Ein bio-bibliographisches Lexikon, Olamenu, 1969.
Der Farbenvolle Untergang, Prentice-Hall (Englewood Cliffs, NJ), 1971.
Kurt Tucholsky, *Deutschland, Deutschland, ueber alles,* University of Massachusetts Press (Amherst, MA), 1972.
(And cotranslator) Friderike Maria Zweig, *Greatness Revisited,* Branden Press (Brookline Village, MA), 1972.
(And translator) Marianne Weber, *Max Weber: A Biography,* Wiley (New York City), 1975.
(And translator) Karl Kraus, *Half-Truths and One-and-a-Half Truths,* Engendra Press, 1976, reprinted, University of Chicago Press (Chicago, IL), 1990.
(And cotranslator) Kraus, *In These Great Times: A Karl Kraus Reader,* Engendra Press, 1976, reprinted, University of Chicago Press, 1990.
(And cotranslator) Rudolf Kayser, *The Saints of Qumran,* Fairleigh Dickinson University Press (East Brunswick, NJ), 1977.
(And cotranslator) *Germany? Germany: A Kurt Tucholsky Reader,* Carcanet Press (Manchester, England), 1990.

TRANSLATOR FROM THE GERMAN

Sigmund Freud, *Delusion and Dream,* Beacon Press (Boston, MA), 1956.
Jacob Burckhardt, *Judgments on History and Historians,* Beacon Press, 1958.
Walter Toman, *A Kindly Contagion,* Bobbs-Merrill (New York City), 1959.
The Complete Diaries of Theodor Herzl, Yoseloff, 1960-61.
Walter Benjamin, *Illuminations: Essays and Reflections,* edited by Hannah Arendt, Harcourt (New York City), 1968.
Theodor Herzl, *The Jewish State,* Herzl Press (New York City), 1970.
Herzl, *Zionist Writings,* Herzl Press, Volume I, 1973, Volume II, 1975.
Benjamin, *Charles Baudelaire,* New Left Books, 1973.
Gershom Scholem, *From Berlin to Jerusalem,* Schocken (New York City), 1980.
Scholem, *Walter Benjamin: The Story of a Friendship,* Jewish Publication Society of America (Philadelphia, PA), 1982.
Josef Rattner, *Alfred Adler,* Ungar (New York City), 1983.

Ernst Ettisch, *The Hebrew Vowels and Consonants as Symbols of Ancient Astronomic Concepts,* Branden Press, 1983.

Brigitte B. Fischer, *My European Heritage: Life among Great Men of Letters,* Branden Press, 1986.

Andre Kaminski, *Kith and Kin,* Fromm International Publishing (New York City), 1988.

Alex Bein, *The Jewish Question: Biography of a World Problem,* Fairleigh Dickinson University Press, 1988.

Gerd Rueithel, *Awful America,* Maledicta Press (Waukesha, WI), 1988.

Martin Buber, *Correspondence,* Schocken, 1988.

Fritz Molden, *The Fires in the Night,* Westview Press (Boulder, CO), 1989.

Manes Sperber, *The Unheeded Warning,* Holmes & Meier (New York City), 1991.

(Cotranslator) Martin Buber, *Letters,* Schocken, 1992.

Hermann Langbein, *Against All Hope: Resistance in the Nazi Concentration Camps,* Paragon House, 1994.

Sperber, *Until My Eyes Are Closed with Shards,* Holmes & Meier, 1994.

OTHER

Member of editorial board, *Ungar's Encyclopedia of World Literature in the Twentieth Century;* general editor, "Austrian Culture Series," published by Peter Lang. Contributor to yearbooks, encyclopedias, dictionaries, and other reference works on Judaism and literature, and to periodicals. Member of editorial board, *Modern Austrian Literature* and *Cross Currents.*

WORK IN PROGRESS: Karl Kraus and the Critics, for Camden House (Columbia, SC), to be published in 1996; "a gently satiric study (in German) on the Wienerlied (the Winegarden songs of Vienna), to be published in 1997."

SIDELIGHTS: "Harry Zohn, a teacher at Brandeis University and noted intellectual historian of Central Europe, has gathered the first essential collection of [Karl] Kraus' writings in English translations," reports Peter Demetz in the *Washington Post Book World. In These Great Times: A Karl Kraus Reader* presents selected essays, lyric poems, and an excerpt from the play *The Last Days of Mankind* originally written in German by the Viennese satirist Karl Kraus, whom Zohn believes to be "the most eloquent witness of the Austrian debacle from the end of the Empire to the last years of the first Republic," and perhaps the greatest of the generation that included Rainer Maria Rilke, Franz Kafka, and Thomas Mann, notes *New York Times Book Review* contributor J. P. Stern. "Kraus was an Isaiah of *Mitteleuropa* doom, a Viennese H. L. Mencken, and a demonic Woody Allen, all rolled into one," Demetz observes. For example, he says, "The scenes from *The Last Days of Mankind* yield a taste of Kraus's total theater of our disordered universe. In his massive spectacle of 209 scenes, Kraus anticipates both the absurd and the documentary theater of our age, shows a disjointed world of brutalities and lies, and works with collages of abominable quotations from war-happy Austrian journals and official speeches." Casting himself as a professional complainer in this dramatic replication of his times, Kraus claimed to have held up its combined atrocities and banalities to permanent indictment by simply chronicling his daily observations. Demetz and Stern both commend Zohn's work as editor and translator. Stern's praise for the book suggests its historical importance: "Kraus's satire, . . . essentially untranslatable (a challenge to which Mr. Zohn and his colleagues have nevertheless proved equal), appeals to our language-conscious age, but it does more than that: like a powerful magnifying glass held at random, it reveals, in astonishing detail, snatches of our past."

"I have long considered my activities as a teacher, lecturer, writer, editor, and translator," Zohn told *CA,* "as those of a cultural mediator in the spirit of Stefan Zweig, who believed in promoting understanding and arousing enthusiasm. Other writers who have exerted a profound influence on me are the brilliant satirists Kurt Tucholsky and Karl Kraus—bridges between the Berlin of the Weimar Republic and the Vienna of my childhood. This linguistic, humanistic, and moral influence has been deepened by my altogether fortuitous and long-standing friendship with two noble ladies who shared the lives of two of these writers, Friderike Maria Zweig and Mary Gerold Tucholsky. Of my other beloved mentors and model mediators I shall mention only Ludwig Lewisohn and Sol Liptzin.

"I have attempted to put my sentimental attachment (of the *Hassliebe* variety) to my native country to positive and productive use, and I have not permitted the yahoos who cast a shadow over my childhood and soon thereafter drove me out of my native city to deprive me of my cultural birthright. Between 1984 and 1994 I have revisited Vienna ten times, lecturing and participating in symposia and other special events. Even though most of my writing has been in English, my heritage leads me to endorse this seemingly paradoxical statement made in 1943 by another admired writer, the Nobel laureate Elias Canetti, also long a resident of an English-speaking country: 'The language of my intellect will remain German because I am a Jew.'"

BIOGRAPHICAL/CRITICAL SOURCES:

PERIODICALS

New York Review of Books, May 3, 1973.
New York Times Book Review, July 14, 1985.
Washington Post Book World, March 31, 1985.